Human Rights in the Prevention and Punishment of Terrorism

Alex Conte

Human Rights in the Prevention and Punishment of Terrorism

Commonwealth Approaches:
The United Kingdom, Canada,
Australia and New Zealand

 Springer

Dr. Alex Conte

ISBN 978-3-642-11607-0   e-ISBN 978-3-642-11608-7
DOI 10.1007/978-3-642-11608-7
Springer Heidelberg Dordrecht London New York

Library of Congress Control Number: 2010921804

Cover design: WMXDesign GmbH, Heidelberg, Germany

Printed on acid-free paper

Springer is part of Springer Science+Business Media (www.springer.com)

To my mother, Dr Carol Conte

Preface

The objective of this work is to provide an analysis of the legislative approaches to counter-terrorism and human rights in Australia, Canada, New Zealand and the United Kingdom. The text is aimed at lawyers and practitioners within and outside common law nations. Although the text analyses the subject within the four jurisdictions named, many parts of the book will be of interest and relevance to those from outside those jurisdictions. Considerable weight is placed on international obligations and directions, with a unique and hopefully useful feature of the text being the inclusion and consideration of a handbook written by me on human rights compliance when countering terrorism (set out in Appendix 4 and considered in Chap. 13).

A significant part of the research undertaken for this work was as a result of my being awarded the International Research Fellowship, *Te Karahipi Rangahau a Taiao*, an annual fellowship generously funded by the New Zealand Law Foundation. The New Zealand Law Foundation is an independent trust and registered charitable entity under the Charities Act 2005 (NZ). This project would not have been possible without the Law Foundation's award, which allowed me to undertake research and associated work over reasonably lengthy periods of time in Australia, Canada, Israel, England, Austria, Switzerland and Finland. It is not just the geographical location of this work that was made possible, however. The prestige of the International Research Fellowship presented me with opportunities that, without the backing of such a fellowship, would not have come easily. It is a considerable credit to the Foundation that this award, established in 2002, has already grown to such recognition. I am most grateful for the Foundation's support and extend my thanks to its trustees and staff for their assistance during the project, particularly the Executive Director of the Foundation, Lynda Hagen.

Thanks must also be extended to various other individuals and organisations that assisted, or facilitated, the conduct of this research. The project was built on research that began in 2001 as part of my doctorate at the University of Canterbury in New Zealand, and even earlier work on the interface between human rights and security. My doctoral supervisors, Professor John Burrows QC (New Zealand's

Law Commissioner) and Professor Scott Davidson of the University of Lincoln in the United Kingdom, along with Professor Christopher Joyner of the University of Georgetown in the United States, influenced the early ruminations of a number of the issues considered this text.

Special thanks go to Professor Martin Scheinin of the European University Institute in Florence, Italy, with whom I have worked and had contact since Professor Scheinin's appointment as Special Rapporteur on the promotion and protection of human rights and fundamental freedoms while countering terrorism. I have had the great pleasure of being a member of the expert panel supporting the mandate of the UN Special Rapporteur since its establishment in 2005. My work with Professor Scheinin has included a desk-top study of Australia's counter-terrorism law and practice; participation in the country missions by him to the United States of America and Israel; and assisting in the preparation of thematic reports on the definition of terrorism and the right to a fair hearing in the fight against terrorism. I am particularly indebted to Professor Scheinin for his time, generosity, and friendship.

One of the most significant advantages of the funding provided by the International Research Fellowship was the ability it gave to work with experts in the field throughout the world. The first associated fellowship was at the Faculty of Law at the University of New South Wales at Sydney in Australia, as well as an earlier fellowship (undertaken in 2004 outside the auspices of the Law Foundation's funding) at the Centre for International and Public Law at the Australian National University at Canberra in Australia. My thanks, in that regard, to Professor Andrew Byrnes, Associate Professor Penelope Mathew, Professor George Williams, and Associate Professor Andrew Lynch. Thanks must also be provided to my Australian-based research assistant, Miss Kathryn Neal. The second Foundation-sponsored secondment took place at the Faculty of Law at the University of Alberta at Edmonton in Canada. Associate Professor Joanna Harrington acted as principal contact for this visit and was most helpful in providing resources and facilitating discussion of issues. Again, thanks are expressed to my Canadian-based research assistant, Mr Roman Kotovych.

From Canada, research moved to Israel, attending the Inter-Disciplinary Center at Herzlyia as a research fellow to the International Policy Institute on Counter-Terrorism. As an international lawyer, the author's work there was both challenging and rewarding, faced with policy rather than legal issues and working with practitioners with a practical understanding of the domestic and regional challenges of terrorism and counter-terrorism. Research was undertaken there with the former Executive Director of the Institute, Dr Boaz Ganor, leading to the establishment by the author and Dr Ganor of an early version of the Guide to Legislators, Policy-Makers and Judges on Human Rights Compliance When Countering Terrorism. The warm land of Israel during August and September 2005 was replaced by the comparatively cold climate of northern England, undertaking research at the University of Leeds School of Law working alongside prominent expert on criminal justice and terrorism, Professor Clive Walker.

The balance of the overseas component of the Fellowship programme was spent working with practitioners at the United Nations Secretariat level. November 2005 was spent undertaking thematic and project work at the Terrorism Prevent Branch of the UN Office on Drugs and Crime at Vienna in Austria. A two-month consultancy with the Office of the High Commissioner for Human Rights at Geneva in Switzerland followed, working in the Special Procedures Branch of the Office on the counter-terrorism mandate. I have been fortunate enough to undertake further consultancy work with the Office of the High Commissioner in the preparation of a Fact Sheet on human rights, terrorism, and counter-terrorism; as well as work with the Organisation for Security and Cooperation in Europe (OSCE) Office for Democratic Institutions and Human Rights, and the UN Counter-Terrorism Implementation Task Force (CTITF) Working Group on Protecting Human Rights While Countering Terrorism.

On a personal note, I need to thank my friends and family, and my fiancée Alice Priddy especially, for their patience and support. Completing this manuscript while working full-time in a non-academic position has been very difficult and has been greatly helped by all the encouragement and backing I have received from them. I would finally express my thanks for the help and courtesy of the staff at Springer-Verlag GmbH in Heidelberg, the publishers of this work, Brigitte Reschke in particular.

October 2009   Dr Alex Conte
                                               Consultant on Security and Human Rights

Contents Overview

Contents

Table of Cases

Table of Treaties and Statutory Instruments

International Treaties

Domestic Statutory Instruments

Chapter 1
Introduction

The phenomenon of terrorism and the idea of a 'war against terrorism' have been much publicised since the events of 11 September 2001. A considerable number of issues arise when considering terrorism, which can be classified in three main groups. First is the subject of the military responses to September 11, borne out through the interventions in Afghanistan and Iraq under *Operation Enduring Freedom, Operation Iraqi Freedom*: matters concerning the use of force between States. Second are those issues involved in the prosecution, arrest and extradition of the perpetrators of terrorist acts: matters concerning international and transnational criminal law. Finally, and partly linked with the second set of issues, is the question of how to suppress and deal with terrorist acts: preventive counter-terrorism. This text is focussed on the second and third set of issues, the prevention and punishment of terrorism. It examines the counter-terrorism obligations of four case study countries and the interface between those and the international human rights obligations of those countries, including the domestic instruments through which counter-terrorism and human rights obligations have been implemented. The case study countries are Australia, Canada, New Zealand and the UK. The choice of jurisdictions is based upon both the common and distinctive elements of law and practice, international obligations pertaining to, and threats of terrorism against each country.

The four case study countries are all common law jurisdictions and members of the Commonwealth and the United Nations. They are all subject to the same counter-terrorism obligations under international law (Chap. 3) and have, as common law countries, similar mechanisms for the implementation into domestic law of international counter-terrorist obligations (Chap. 4). Their geographical distribution and political histories have resulted in a differing array of terrorist threats against each country so that the level and range of counter-terrorist measures within each jurisdiction differs widely in some contexts (Chaps. 5–8). All four countries are parties to the International Covenant on Civil and Political Rights and thus have a common reference point on the question of international human rights obligations (Chap. 9) and the international framework for the limitation of rights (Chap. 10). They also have distinctive features in their domestic human rights protection

A. Conte, *Human Rights in the Prevention and Punishment of Terrorism*,
DOI 10.1007/978-3-642-11608-7_1, © Springer-Verlag Berlin Heidelberg 2010

frameworks, which present interesting points for comparison (Chap. 11). Australia has no federal human rights statute. Canada, in contrast, has a constitutionally entrenched legislative instrument for the protection of human rights, which has the ability to strike down inconsistent legislation, while New Zealand's bill of rights is neither entrenched nor supreme. The UK takes a different approach again, linking its domestic protection of human rights to the European Convention on Human Rights.

This text is divided into three parts: first, considering counter-terrorism; next, considering human rights law; and then examining the interface between the two subjects in the context of particular issues in focus. Part I of the title begins by examining the nature and definition of terrorism (Chap. 2), moving to provide an examination of the international framework for countering terrorism and the means by which those obligations have been transformed into domestic law (Chaps. 3–8, as outlined earlier). Part II looks at the international and regional human rights obligations applicable to the four case study countries and, again, how these have been received domestically (Chaps. 9–11, as outlined earlier). These first two parts make up ten of the 22 chapters in this title.

Part III of the title builds on what is established under Parts I and II by undertaking a comparative analysis of the interface between counter-terrorism and human rights. Chapters 2 and 3 look at the relationship between terrorism, counter-terrorism and human rights. Chapter 12 considers the interface between *terrorism* and relevant aspects of international law pertaining to human rights, the law of armed conflict, international criminal law, and refugee law. Chapter 13 examines the question of what is required to achieve human rights compliance when *countering* terrorism, establishing a framework for the later analysis of the discreet issues in Chaps. 14–21. The subject-specific issues studied in those subsequent chapters are approached by using thematic and case study based analyses. The aim, in doing so, is to enable a critical assessment of issues by focussing upon the treatment of thematic issues in context.

Chapter 14 takes a comparative approach to the question of the criminalisation of terrorism, paying attention to all four countries, and examining the extent to which the criminalisation of terrorism goes beyond the requirements of international law on counter-terrorism, as well as the compatibility of the domestic terrorism-related offences with the human-rights compatible approach to defining terrorism advocated in Chap. 2.

The focus of Chap. 15 is upon counter-terrorism and criminal procedure, including special investigative powers, and considers the establishment of such powers under New Zealand's Counter-Terrorism Bill 2003, i.e. special police powers of questioning, and the use of tracking devices. Briefly considered is the question of the onus proof in bail hearings for terrorism-related charges in Australia. Attention is also paid to the use of special investigative techniques outside the framework of combating terrorism, as well as the role and accountability of intelligence agencies in the prevention and investigation of terrorism. Remaining with pre-trial issues, Chap. 16 examines investigative detention and investigative hearings. Police powers of arrest in the UK, and continued detention without trial, is explained and evaluated. Comparable powers held by Australian police and intelligence services is also considered. The use in Canada of investigative hearings, and their impact on the privilege against self-incrimination and the right to a fair and open hearing, is also considered.

Moving from pre-trial issues to the broader application of the right to liberty, Chap. 17 examines the derogations by the UK from the right to liberty, first in the context of executive detention powers applying to Northern Ireland, and then to the derogation made in 2001 in conjunction with the establishment of the UK's indefinite detention regime. The implications of these and other derogations are taken into account to draw out principles regarding terrorism and the derogation from rights and freedoms. Chapter 18 follows the progression of the UK's indefinite detention regime, which was replaced in 2004 with 'non-custodial' control orders, comparing this apparatus with control orders in Australia. Also looked at in this chapter is the mechanism of preventative detention orders under Australia's Criminal Code Act 1995.

The focus of Chap. 19 is upon the designation of individuals and groups as terrorist entities, largely flowing the Security Council's regime administered by the Committee established under resolution 1267 (1999). It considers the way in which designations impact upon the freedoms of assembly and association. Using New Zealand as a case study, the chapter also examines whether such designation processes are, or a capable of being, compatible with natural justice and the right to a fair hearing. Moving to the freedom of expression, Chap. 20 looks at two issues. It first considers the way in which counter-terrorism measures might impact upon the media (New Zealand having been the only one of the four case study countries to provide for media control during and following counter-terrorist operations). The chapter then examines the incitement to terrorism offence, called upon in Security Council resolution 1624 (2005), paying attention to the enactment of this offence by the UK.

The final thematic chapter, Chap. 21, concerns measures to prevent the transboundary movement of terrorists, using Australia as a case study. It also examines the general issue of rendition in the fight against terrorism, and the more specific question of the use of diplomatic assurances by the UK. Added to the case studies mentioned, Chap. 11 (which provides an overview of the frameworks for civil liberties protection in the four countries) includes a case study on the making and status of regulations under New Zealand's United Nations Act 1946 and its interrelationship with the New Zealand Bill of Rights Act 1990.

Appended to this work are two documents and two sets of comparative tables. Chapter 23 sets out the United Nations Global Counter-Terrorism Strategy, relevant both to counter-terrorism and human rights, as well as their interface. Chapter 24 tabulates the party status of the case study countries to international treaties related to terrorism, those on human rights, and those pertaining to refugee law and humanitarian law, including international criminal law. Chapter 25 contains a complete list and description of offences, as defined within the scope of the international terrorism-related conventions and relevant Security Council resolutions, as well as all domestic law offences related to terrorism within each of the four case study jurisdictions. Chapter 26 reproduces a handbook written by the author, and published by the Center on Global Counterterrorism Cooperation, on human rights compliance while countering terrorism, bringing together various issues discussed in this title within one, easily accessible, document.

Part I

Chapter 2
The Nature and Definition of Terrorism

International terrorism is not a new phenomenon. Indeed, the origin of the word 'terrorism' dates back to the French Revolution of 1789 as the label used by the establishment to describe the conduct of revolutionaries.[1] Terrorism has likewise been a subject of concern for the United Nations since the 1960s, following a series of aircraft hijackings. Some would argue that terrorism has entered a new phase at around the time of 11 September 2001: an age where transnational activity has intensified and become easier, and where technology and the media can be taken advantage of by terrorist entities to further the impact of terrorist conduct and the delivery of messages or fear-inducing images.[2]

Despite the long-lasting presence of terrorism in domestic and international life, however, there is currently no comprehensive, concise, and universally accepted legal definition of the term. With that in mind, this chapter first considers the nature of terrorism and the problems with achieving, as well as attempts made to achieve, an internationally agreed-upon definition of the term. It then examines a human rights based approach to defining terrorism, as advocated by the UN Special Rapporteur on counter-terrorism.

2.1 The Nature of Terrorism

In its popular understanding the term 'terrorism' tends to refer to an act that is wrong, evil, illegitimate, illegal, and a crime. The term has come to be used to describe a wide range of violent, and sometimes not-so violent, conduct (especially in the hands of the media since 11 September 2001). Acts characterised as terrorist in nature can occur both in conflict and peace-time. They may constitute crimes in domestic and international law, and they are motivated by a complex matrix of

---

[1]Berg (2004) and Stephens (2004, p. 457).
[2]Ibid.

A. Conte, *Human Rights in the Prevention and Punishment of Terrorism*,
DOI 10.1007/978-3-642-11608-7_2, © Springer-Verlag Berlin Heidelberg 2010

reasons and ideals. Their characterisation can also depend upon the person or institution using the label and may even change over time. To give two striking examples, the list of most wanted terrorists kept by the United States featured, at one time, Yassir Arafat and Nelson Mandela, both of whom were subsequently awarded the Nobel Peace Prize: evidence that this is a highly political and controversial issue.[3] In the months prior to his death, Yassir Arafat was in again described as a terrorist by the United States Administration.[4]

2.1.1 Terrorism and Crime

Having regard to the complex nature of terrorism, and the political and popular conceptions held about the term and about those who perpetrate terrorist acts, care must be taken when considering and assessing situations and how they might impact upon the topic. In the context of terrorism and crime, an interesting question might be posed: why talk about terrorism at all? An act of 'terrorism' will, after all, comprise a series of acts which, in and of themselves, constitute various criminal offences. To take an example, a bombing of an Embassy will likely involve the unlawful possession of explosives, the wilful destruction of property and the wilful or reckless injury to or killing of persons. Each element is a criminal offence in most jurisdictions and, as such, is capable of being dealt with by the relevant municipal jurisdiction.

In submissions before the New Zealand Foreign Affairs, Defence and Trade Committee on the Counter-Terrorism Bill 2003, for example, Professor Matthew Palmer argued that there are no good policy grounds to justify a separate, parallel regime of counter-terrorism law.[5] Having regard to the composite nature of terrorist conduct, there might be some initial attraction to that argument. Why then add to the extant law and why adopt different standards? Some experts would answer this on the basis that the political nature of terrorist acts and the high level of threat that terrorism poses to public safety and public order demand a distinction to be made between terrorism and other criminal acts.[6] There are, furthermore, crimes that cannot be prosecuted without defining terrorist acts or membership in a terrorist organisation including, for example, the offence of financial support to a terrorist

---

[3]This list is maintained by the United States Federal Bureau of Investigation and may be accessed online: http://www.fbi.gov/wanted/terrorists/fugitives.htm.

[4]Associated Press, "Timeline: Yasser Arafat", Foxnews.com US and the World, 8 February 2005, online: http://www.foxnews.com/story/0,2933,136880,00.html.

[5]New Zealand, "Counter-Terrorism Bill. Government Bill. Commentary", as reported from the Foreign Affairs, Defence and Trade Committee (2003) 2. See also Palmer (2002); Bassiouni (1981, p. 11); Roach (2002, pp. 124–126); Roach (2005, p. 512); and the report of the Independent Reviewer Lord Carlile of Berriew QC, The Definition of Terrorism (Presented to Parliament by the Secretary of State for the Home Department, March 2007), para 22 (proposition 1).

[6]Ganor (2005, pp. 8–9).

entity, common to Australia, Canada, New Zealand and the United Kingdom, as well as many other nations (see Chap. 14). Taking a practical enforcement-based approach to the issue, and recognising the trend for many terrorist acts to be perpetrated transnationally rather than exclusively within a single territory, the creation of distinct terrorist offences with common elements throughout the international community would also assist in issues of mutual legal assistance and extradition.[7] At a further end of the scale, should terrorism instead be judged as an act of warfare and the struggle against it conducted according to the norms and rules of war? These are issues considered further in Chap. 12.

2.1.2 Terrorism and Warfare

Researchers are divided in their opinions on whether terrorism should be considered a criminal act or a political-military act. Jenkins (former head of the Terrorism Project at the Rand Institute) has observed that if one looks at terrorism as a crime, there will be a need to gather evidence, arrest perpetrators and put them on trial. This approach provokes problems of international cooperation, he argues, and is not a suitable response for acts of terrorism perpetrated by a distant organisation or a country involved in terrorism.[8] Approaching terrorism as warfare, however, one can be less concerned with the aspect of individual guilt, and an approximate assessment of guilt and intelligence are sufficient. The focus is not on a single perpetrator, but rather on proper identification of the enemy. Contrary to Jenkins, Barzilai argues that terrorists *are* criminals, and that if terrorism-related crimes are treated differently to ordinary crimes, this will result in municipal authorities employing tougher, more stringent tools to gain illegitimate political advantages.[9]

2.1.3 Features of Terrorist Conduct

Whether treated as crimes or acts of warfare, terrorist conduct is distinguishable by reason of its focus, participants, and victims. Each of those factors has parallels with warfare and crime, but terrorism is distinct by virtue of its combination of factors. First, setting aside the situation of organised crime, criminal conduct is normally focused upon a particular goal (e.g. the burglary of premises to obtain stereo equipment), with a final end-point (e.g. obtaining the desired stereo equipment).

---

[7]It must be acknowledged that, for the reasons that follow in this chapter (concerning the lack of a common definition of terrorism), this practical advantage is currently limited. On the subject of mutual legal assistance and extradition in the context of counter-terrorism, see Duffy (2005, pp. 106–115). See also the discussion on the *Lockerbie Cases* in Chap. 3, Sect. 3.2.2.1.

[8]Jenkins (1999, p. xii).

[9]Barzilai (2000).

Terrorist acts have, in contrast, shown themselves to be generally continuous, given the much longer-term motivations of terrorist organisations; developing, with individuals perhaps starting as youths throwing stones but eventually moving to sophisticated operations such as that undertaken on 11 September 2001; and sometimes escalating, such as the intensification of acts by Al-Qa'ida from the bombing of US Embassy in Nairobi in 1998, to the attack on the USS Cole in the Yemen in 2000, to the attacks on 11 September in New York, Washington DC, and Pennsylvania.

Secondly, terrorist conduct is unique by virtue of its participants. Again setting aside organised crime, most criminal enterprises are undertaken by the few and as quietly as possible. Terrorist organisations, while being secretive about impending operations and the identity of secret cells and the like, instead rely on publication of their causes and the recruitment of as many as possible to further those objectives. Finally, while criminal acts are targeted, terrorist ones are often indiscriminate.

2.1.4 The Ideological Nature of Terrorism

The most important feature of terrorism, distinguishing it from other criminal acts or conduct during armed conflict, is the motivation of terrorists and the codex against which terrorists measure their conduct. Generally speaking, those perpetrating 'normal' criminal offences do so out of some personal, hedonistic motivation – whether that be the material rewards of a burglary, the thrill and high of challenging 'the system' or using drugs, or the desperation of stealing necessities where no alternatives appear to be available. Personal gain is the common feature of criminal conduct, setting aside crimes of passion and those of the mentally insane. In contrast, the primary motivation of terrorists is altruistic, motivated by a higher cause or ideology that is greater than his or her personal impulses or gains. It should be recognised that the *individual* terrorist may not be motivated in this way, instead acting out of a sense of revenge borne out of the individual's personal or familial experience or perceptions of ill-treatment or humiliation, a matter recognised, for example, by the Israeli Security Agency and the Israeli Counter-Terrorism Bureau,[10] and also implied in the United Nations Global Counter-Terrorism Strategy (see Chap. 13).[11] It can be generally said, however, that a terrorist (or at least the entity that recruited the individual) will act for the furtherance of an external cause (whether it be a localised secessionist movement or global jihad) and for the benefit this has to both the cause and the people of it.[12] Combined with

---

[10]Report of the Special Rapporteur on the promotion and protection of human rights and fundamental freedoms while countering terrorism, Martin Scheinin, Mission to Israel, including visit to occupied Palestinian Territory, UN Doc A/HRC/6/17/Add.4 (2007), para 5.

[11]United Nations Global Counter-Terrorism Strategy, UN GAOR, 60th Sess, 99th Plen Mtg, UN Doc A/Res/60/288 (2006), Pillar I, preambular para.

[12]Ilan (2005).

the honour derived from such conduct in this life, and the rewards in the next, the motivations of a terrorist are far beyond those of an 'ordinary' criminal offender. Consider, for example, the following description of rewards attainable by the Shahid (suicide bomber) in the afterlife:[13]

> When the Shahid meets Allah, he will be forgiven from the first drop of blood. He is saved from the grave. He sees his place in heaven. He is saved from the great horror. He is given 72 dark-eyed women. And he is champion of the right for 70 members of his family. A crown is placed on his head, with a precious gem. That is better than anything that exists in this world.

Added to these distinct motivations are the standards against which terrorists measure their conduct. The fact that a terrorist act might be unlawful according to the law of the State in which the act is perpetrated, or under international law, is argued to be irrelevant to a terrorist. Terrorists measure their conduct against the codex of the ideology they are pursuing.[14] If the ideology mandates the killing of Jews or Christians,[15] then that killing is not murder but, instead, a legitimate and appropriate act. The consequence of these features is significant. Standard criminology does not apply. The notion of personal deterrence is largely irrelevant, with the language of terrorists often entirely divorced from that of the 'normal' criminal offender.

Moving from these more abstract ideologies, one can also categorise the impetus for particular terrorist acts as falling within one or more of the following four motivations: secession; insurgency; regional retribution; and the phenomenon of what has come to be known as 'the global jihad'.

2.1.4.1 Secession

It is an all-too-common assertion that one person's terrorist is another's freedom fighter.[16] For instance, would a bombing carried out by a rebel group, which is directed towards the destabilisation of dictatorial authorities perpetrating horrific crimes against the local population (the Pol Pot Regime, for example), amount to a terrorist act or an act of a legitimate liberation movement? Such propositions have been the subject of much debate.[17]

---

[13]As identified in a statement by Dr Ismail Radwan, Sheik of the Ajlin Mosque in the Gaza Strip entitled "Paradise", uncovered by intelligence agencies and aired on Israeli television in 2005.

[14]Ibid.

[15]As called for in the World Islamic Front's "Jihad Against Jews and Crusaders", 23 February 1998 (signed, amongst others, by Usama bin Laden), online: http://www.fas.org/irp/world/para/docs/980223-fatwa.htm.

[16]Such assertions were made, for example, in numerous submissions to the New Zealand Foreign Affairs, Defence and Trade Committee on the Terrorism Suppression Bill (NZ). See, amongst others, the submissions of the Socialist Party of Aotearoa, 31 November 2001, Parliamentary Library Ref TERRO/61. In the context of Al-Qa'ida, see Meltzer (2002).

[17]See, for example, Ganor (2000).

Early resolutions of the General Assembly addressing the issue of terrorism contained express affirmations of the principle of self-determination. In the very first resolution of the United Nations on the subject of terrorism, the General Assembly expressed deep concern over terrorism, urged States to solve the problem by addressing the underlying issues leading to terrorist conduct, and then stated that the General Assembly:[18]

> *Reaffirms* the inalienable right to self-determination and independence of all peoples under colonial and racist regimes and other forms of alien domination and upholds the legitimacy of their struggle, in particular the struggle of national liberation movements, in accordance with the purposes and principles of the Charter and the relevant resolutions of the organs of the United Nations;

A number of subsequent General Assembly resolutions echoed this affirmation, adding that such liberation movements should also be conducted in accordance with the Declaration on Principles of International Law Concerning Friendly Relations and Co-operation among States.[19] One of the most problematic issues in this area is distinguishing terrorists from lawful combatants in legitimate struggles for self-determination. Here, States that do not recognise a claim to self-determination will commonly claim that those using force against the State's military forces are terrorists.

The right to self-determination is the right of a people (sharing a common historical tradition, racial or ethnic identity, cultural homogeneity, linguistic unity, religious or ideological affinity, territorial connection, and or a common economic life)[20] to determine their political status and freely pursue their own economic, social and cultural development.[21] It holds a prominent position within various international documents.[22] However, the precise scope of this right, and in

---

[18]GA Res 3034 (XXVII), UN GAOR, 27th Sess, 2114th Plen Mtg, UN Doc A/Res/27/3034 (1972), para 3.

[19]The Declaration on Principles of International Law concerning Friendly Relations and Co-operation among States was adopted by the General Assembly in GA Res 2625(XXV), UN GAOR 25th Sess, 1883rd Plen Mtg, UN Doc A/Res/25/2625 (1970). The further qualification was first added by GA Res 38/130, UN GAOR, 38th Sess, 101st Mtg, UN Doc A/Res/38/130 (1983), preambular para 6, and reiterated within: GA Res 40/61, UN GAOR, 40th Sess, 108th Plen Mtg, UN Doc A/Res/40/61 (1985), preambular para 8; GA Re 42/159, UN GAOR, 42nd Sess, 94th Plen Mtg, UN Doc A/Res/42/159 (1987), preambular para 12; GA Res 44/29, UN GAOR, 44th Sess, 72nd Plen Mtg, UN Doc A/Res/44/29 (1989), preambular para 17; and GA Res 46/51, UN GAOR, 46th Sess, 67th Plen Mtg, UN DocA/Res/46/51 (1991), preambular para 14.

[20]As defined by the United Nations Educational, Scientific and Cultural Organization, Final Report and Recommendations of the International Meeting of Experts on the further Study of the Concept of the Right of People, UNESCO Archives Doc SHS-89/CONF.602/7 (1990), para 22.

[21]*Western Sahara, Advisory Opinion* (1975) ICJ Reports, 31.

[22]Including: the International Covenant on Economic, Social and Cultural Rights, opened for signature 16 December 1966, 993 UNTS 3 (entered into force 3 January 1976) and the International Covenant on Civil and Political Rights, opened for signature 16 December 1966, 999 UNTS 171 (entered into force 23 March 1976), common article 1; the Charter of the United Nations 1945, articles 1(2), 55 and 56, and chapter IX; the Declaration on Principles of International Law

particular whether it includes a right to use armed force and engage in wars of national liberation, has always been a point of contention.[23] This controversy, as recognised by the Special Rapporteur to the former Sub-Commission on the Promotion of Human Rights, has been the major obstacle to the development of a comprehensive definition of the term 'terrorism', and of the completion of work towards the Comprehensive Convention on International Terrorism.[24] The Comprehensive Convention is to be considered further later in this chapter, and also in Chap. 3 (Sect. 3.1.2), while the interface between terrorism and international humanitarian law is considered in Chap. 12 (Sect. 12.2.2/1). What can be said at this point is that, since its adoption of the 1994 Declaration on Measures to Eliminate International Terrorism, the General Assembly has made it clear that self-determination does not legitimate the use of terrorism by those seeking to achieve self-determination.[25] This is a point reiterated by the Special Rapporteur on the promotion and protection of human rights and fundamental freedoms while countering terrorism, in the context of the terrorist organisation ETA (Euskadi Ta Askatasuna) in Spain, whose proclaimed political goal is self-determination for the Basque Country.[26]

2.1.4.2 Insurgency and Regional Retribution

The second and third motivations for terrorist acts are those arising out of the occupation of a territory by foreign military forces, either in the form of insurgency occurring within the occupied territory or acts directed towards occupying forces but occurring outside the territory. Insurgency and regional retribution have been portrayed by many as the prime motivations for terrorist events linked to the occupations in Afghanistan and Iraq during these early years of the twenty-first century. Examples include the attack on United Nations headquarters in Baghdad

---

Concerning Friendly Relations and Cooperation among States in Accordance with the Charter of the United Nations (n 19); the Declaration on the Granting of Independence to Colonial Countries and Peoples, adopted under GA Res 1514(XV), UN GAOR, 15th Sess, 847th Plen Mtg, UN Doc A/Res/15/1514 (1960); and the Principles which should guide members in determining whether or not an obligation exists to transmit the information called for under article 73e of the Charter adopted under GA Res 1541(XV), UN GAOR, 15th Sess, 948th Plen Mtg, UN Doc A/Res/15/1541 (1960).

[23]Report of the Sub-Commission Special Rapporteur on terrorism and human rights, Specific Human Rights Issues: New priorities, in particular terrorism and counter-terrorism, UN Doc E/CN.4/Sub.2/2004/40 (2004), para 30. See also the Rapporteur's 1997 report, UN Doc E/CN.4/Sub.2/1997/28.

[24]Sub-Commission Special Rapporteur 2004 report (ibid) para 28.

[25]Declaration on Measures to Eliminate International Terrorism, adopted under GA Res 49/60, UN GAOR, 49th Sess, 84th Plen Mtg, UN Doc A/Res/49/60 (1994), para 1.

[26]Special Rapporteur on the promotion and protection of human rights and fundamental freedoms while countering terrorism, Mission to Spain, UN Doc A/HRC/10/3/Add.2 (2008), paras 3, 46 and 47. See also Scheinin (2006).

on 19 August 2003, which claimed the lives of the Special Representative of the Secretary-General, Sergio Vieira de Mello, and 21 other men and women. Following the commencement of the multi-national Operation Enduring Freedom in Afghanistan, a manifesto issued by Salem Almakhi and first aired on Aljazeera in October 2002, announced a warning to Christians and members of the alliance waging war against Afghanistan and Al-Qa'ida.[27] A further example can be seen in a video statement of Noordin Mohamad Top directed to various nations, including Australia and the United Kingdom, and identifying senior members of the Australian Government:[28]

> As long as you keep your troops in Iraq and Afghanistan and intimidate Muslim people, you will feel our intimidation... You will be the target of our next attack... Our enemy is America, Australia, England and Italy... We especially remind Australia that you, Downer and Howard, are killing Australia, leading it into darkness and misfortune and mujahedeen terror...

2.1.4.3 Islam and 'the Global Jihad'

Finally, closely linked to the ideological nature of terrorism, is the question of Islam and terrorism. An all-too-common and unfortunate expression is that not all Muslims are terrorists, but all international terrorists are Muslim. While that is not entirely correct, and certainly not advocated by the author,[29] it is true that the modern phenomenon of international terrorism (in the form of what has come to be known as 'the Global Jihad') is perpetrated by radical Muslims. The adoption of terrorism by radical Islamic movements as their modus operandi stems, in part, from the historical development and subsequent manipulation of the Islamic faith.[30]

Islam began as a faith of a small community of believers during the seventh century in what is now Saudi Arabia.[31] It is based upon the belief that Muhammad, a respected businessman in Mecca in around 600 AD, received revelations from

---

[27]Salem Almakhi, "Mending the Hearts of the Believers", online: http://www.jihadonline.brave-pages.com/mending.htm. Salem Almakhi is said to be one of Usama bin Laden's supporters and admirers, and personally knowledgeable of Al-Qa'ida operations: see Fighel and Kehati (2002, un-numbered para 23).

[28]Peter Gelling, "Indonesia Television Airs Terror Warning" (International Herald Tribune, 17 November 2005), online: http://www.iht.com/articles/2005/11/17/news/indo.php.

[29]Secessionist-motivated terrorist organisations, for example, are local to a particular State and often bear the racial and religious characteristics of that State. Such organisations are capable of undertaking, and have undertaken, transnational acts of terrorism.

[30]See Palbir Punj, "Root of Islamic Radicalism" (The Pioneer, 31 August 2005), online: http://dailypioneer.com/columnist1.asp?main_variable=Columnist&file_name=punj%2Fpunj66.txt&writer=punj. See also; Juergensmeyer (2003); Khan (2006); Rosand (2007, pp. 4–5); Saggerman (2004); and Shay (2002). Contrast with Rehman (2005).

[31]Following Mohammad's flight from Mecca, where his teachings had been rejected, he settled in Medina (the second most holy site for Muslims, after Mecca and before Jerusalem) where Islam was accepted by the community and from where it grew.

Allah (God) that were later written down in the Qur'an.[32] A period of divisions followed the death of the prophet Muhammad, leading to the characterisation of two Muslim loyalties today: the Sunni (representing the vast majority of Muslims today under the Sunnah Islamic faith); and the Shi'ite (who treat Muhammad's son-in-law Ali as their caliph and subsequently elevated him to the status of prophet).[33] Within what is now the main-stream Sunnah faith, four 'schools' of interpretation of the complex text of the Qur'an came to be accepted as legitimate (from liberal to radical): the Hanafi, Maliki, Shafi'i, and Hanbali.[34] The greater majority of Muslims advocate and practice the more moderate interpretations of the Sunnah revelations of the Qur'an. For such Muslims, their faith advocates tolerance of others and their religious choices and customs. On the subject of those that are not Muslim, for example, the Qur'an instructs:[35]

4. And I shall not worship that which you are worshipping.
5. Nor will you worship that which I worship.
6. To you be your religion, and to me my religion.

The core of Islamic life for all Sunnah is said to be the 'five pillars of Islam': publicly bearing witness to the basic affirmation of faith; saying prescribed prayers five times a day; fasting during the month of Ramadan; giving a tithe or alms for support of the poor; and making a pilgrimage to Mecca at least once during the believer's lifetime, if this is possible.[36]

Calls for the killing of Jews and Christians by the likes of Usama bin Laden and Al-Qa'ida is based upon a radical reading of the already conservative school of Sunnah interpretation (Hanbali). The motivation of Al-Qa'ida, for example, is the spreading of the Muslim faith and the elimination of what such groups see as the evil of modernity.[37] The advancement of religious beliefs is not, in and of itself, problematic and is in fact a common tenet of almost all religions. Viewing modernity (democracy, capitalism, Statehood) as an evil that must be eliminated at all cost is, however, an extreme view and one that poses a threat to all western nations. The World Islamic Front Statement of 1998, entitled "Jihad Against Jews

---

[32]See Wuthnow (1998, pp. 383–393). See also Abu-Rabi (1995).

[33]Ali was a cousin of Muhammad who was an early convert to Islam at the age of 10, and became the husband of Muhammad's daughter Fatimah. Sunni Muslims consider Ali to be a companion of Muhammad only and therefore consider Shi'ite Muslims to be following a false prophet.

[34]These schools were named after their four founders Abu Hanifa, Abu Abdullah, Mohammad bin Idris, Ahmad bin Hanbal respectively.

[35]Surah (chapter) 110, "Al-Kafirun" (The Disbelievers), Ayat (verses) 4–6: *The Noble Qur'an in the English Language* (Saudi Arabia, Darussalam, 1996) 788.

[36]Wuthnow (1998, pp. 383–393).

[37]The International Policy Institute for Counter-Terrorism has written much on this subject. See, for example (available online: http://www.ict.org.il): Fighel and Shahar (2002), Shahar (2002), Kahati (2003), and Kahati and Fighel (2003).

and Crusaders",[38] purports to be a fatwa (religious ruling) requiring the killing of Americans, and claims to base itself upon a call by Allah to "slay the pagans wherever ye find them, seize them, beleaguer them, and lie in wait for them in every stratagem (of war)".[39] The 1998 Statement concludes with the following direction:[40]

> We – with Allah's help – call on every Muslim who believes in Allah and wishes to be rewarded to comply with Allah's order to kill the Americans and plunder their money wherever and whenever they find it. We also call on Muslim ulema, leaders, youths, and soldiers to launch the raid on Satan's US troops and the devil's supporters allying with them, and to displace those who are behind them so that they may learn a lesson.

While this fatwa is particularly directed towards Americans, due to the purported occupation and plundering of the Arabian Peninsula by the United States during the 1991 and 1998 Gulf wars,[41] the sentiment of the jihad is one that is opposed to modernity in general. Its desire is to eliminate modernity and return to the era when Islam formed a prosperous ummah (community of Islamic believers) in the Middle East and beyond, without restriction by State borders: an era in which modernity was absent in the region.

Following the commencement of the multi-national Operation Enduring Freedom in Afghanistan a further manifesto, issued by Salem Almakhi, announced a warning to Christians and members of the alliance waging war against Afghanistan and Al-Qa'ida.[42] This most palpably applies to States participating in Operation Enduring Freedom, but is also of much broader application. It conceivably attaches to all members of the United Nations taking action against Usama bin Laden, the Taliban and Al-Qa'ida pursuant to various Security Council resolutions and the directions of the Council's 1267 Sanctions Committee.[43] The manifesto finally instructs:[44]

> Anyone who possesses an arrow in his quiver, make haste and [shoot] it for the sake of Allah, and aim it at the enemies of religion – the Jews and the Christians [. . .].

Along the same lines, an audio tape aired by Aljazeera in 2003, a senior aide to Usama bin Laden, Ayman Zawahri, exhorted his audience with the following words:[45]

---

[38]World Islamic Front, Jihad Against Jews and Crusaders (published in the Arabic Newspaper *Al-Quds al-Arabi* [London, 23 February 1998], p. 3), un-numbered para 1. An English translation of the statement can be found online at http://www.fas.org/irp/world/para/docs/980223-fatwa.htm.

[39]The quoted phrase is taken from *The Holy Qura'an* (n 35) 9:5.

[40]Jihad Against Jews and Crusaders (n 38) un-numbered para 8.

[41]Ibid, un-numbered para 3.

[42]Ibid, un-numbered para 23.

[43]Concerning the Security Council resolution 1267 (1999) Sanctions Committee see Chap. 3, Sect. 3.2.4.2.

[44]Salem Almakhi (n 27) penultimate paragraph.

[45]Aljazeera, "New Al-Qaeda Tape Calls for Attacks" (Aljazeera.net, 21 May 2003), online: http://english.aljazeera.net/archive/2003/05/200849135715154191.html.

Oh Muslims! Carry out attacks against the embassies, companies, interests and officials of
the US, Britain, Australia and Norway. Burn the ground under their feet.

Opposed to this, writers such as Al-Muhajabah condemn the use of terrorism and
point to the following Qur'anic versus as restricting the circumstances in which
recourse to acts of aggression may be had:[46]

Permission to fight (against disbelievers) is given to those (believers) *who are fought
against, because they have been wronged* [emphasis added].[47]
   And what is wrong with you that you fight not in the Cause of Allah, and *for those weak,
ill-treated and oppressed* among men, women and children [emphasis added].[48]
   Allah does not forbid that you to deal justly and kindly with those who fought not
against you on account of religion nor drove you out from your homes. Verily, Allah loves
those who deal with equity. . . It is only as regards *those who fought against you on account
of your religion, and have driven you out of your homes, and helped to drive you out*, that
Allah forbids you to befriend them [emphasis added].[49]

So it is that the one text of a relatively young religion has given rise to two Muslim
loyalties, with four schools of thought arising from the more widely-practised
Sunnah devotion of Islam. Of those four schools, the minority conservative school
of Hanbali[50] has been adopted and distorted by some to advocate jihad, through
terrorist means, against modernity.[51]

2.1.5   Rationalising a Distinct Approach to Terrorism

The need for a distinct approach to the criminalisation and suppression of terrorism
should be apparent from the discussion of the nature of terrorism to this point.
Approaching terrorism as a phenomenon justifying a distinct regime of counter-
terrorism law is not just supported by those features of terrorist conduct discussed.
Such an approach is also driven by most States. The desire of States to take a special
approach to the suppression of terrorism appears to be rooted in a combination of
factors, not all of which are unique to terrorism, but which may cumulatively have

---

[46]Al-Muhajabah, "Some Quranic Versus on Jihad", online: http://www.muhajabah.com/quran-
jihad.htm.

[47]Surah (chapter) 22, "Al-Hajj" (The Pilgrimage), Ayat (verse) 39: *The Qur'an* (n 34) 426.

[48]Surah 4, "An-Nisa" (The Women), Ayat 75: *The Qur'an* (ibid) 124.

[49]Surah 60, "Al-Mumtahinah" (The Woman to be Examined), Ayat 8–9: *The Qur'an* (ibid) 700.

[50]Contrary to the more moderate schools of Islam, the *Hanbali* school of Sunni Islam prohibits all
forms of public religious expression other than that of those who follow the *Hanbali* school. The
government of Saudi Arabia vigorously enforces this school of Islam, for example, and allows
judges to discount the testimony of people who are not practicing Muslims or who do not have the
correct faith: see GlobalSecurity.org, "Hanbali Islam", online: http://www.globalsecurity.org/
military/intro/islam-hanbali.htm.

[51]Interview with Yoni Fighel, Researcher at the International Policy Institute for Counter-
Terrorism, 31 August 2005, Herzlyia, Israel.

been treated by States as calling for a different approach. The common thread in each factor, or at least in the way each factor can be perceived, is not unique: the political interests of States.

The most apparent reason for States taking distinct action against terrorism is the fear-inducing nature of terrorist conduct and the attention this brings to terrorist events through the media and public alike. This in turn adversely affects the credibility of national executive administrations in the eyes of the national public, and also the credibility of the United Nations as an institution established to maintain international peace and security in the eyes of the international community. The more severe the terrorist act, the greater the terror induced, to the extent that the public may in fact be paralysed in a real sense, affecting their freedom of movement and association, and enjoyment of life.[52] That again serves to adversely impact upon national and international 'executive' credibility. As will be seen through the discussion of international documents on terrorism that follows, terrorism is therefore viewed as being a crime of 'international concern' (using the wording of the Rome Statute on the International Criminal Court) and contrary to the principles of the Charter of the United Nations.[53] Terrorism was, in that regard, proposed to be included within the jurisdiction of the International Criminal Court, to stand beside genocide, war crimes and crimes against humanity.

A further issue of concern to States is the transnational nature of terrorist offending. Whether through Embassy bombings on foreign soil or direct attacks within the territory of a State (such as the 2001 attacks in the United States and those in 2005 in London), national interest and national security are often affected. Through an international framework on counter-terrorism, those interests can be arguably better protected through the ability to secure mutual legal assistance and the extradition of perpetrators of such attacks, and cut off the means by which terrorist organisations operate.

A final and individual self-interest of States is that of combating revolutionary and secessionist terrorism, that is, terrorism occurring solely within a State and aimed at destabilising or overthrowing the established government of the State, or conduct aimed at 'breaking away' from the State.[54] The established government has, in those circumstances, a very real and pressing desire to eradicate terrorism.[55] The international community, in seeking to maintain the integrity of statehood and the stability of regions, also has a vested interest. Examples include the Basque

---

[52]As explicitly recognised within various resolutions of the United Nations General Assembly, including GA Res 54/164, UN GAOR, 54th Sess, 83rd Plen Mtg, UN Doc A/Res/54/164 (1999). On the impact of terrorism upon the rule of law and human rights see Chap. 13.

[53]See, for example, the Report of the Secretary-General's High-level Panel on Threats, Challenges and Change, A More Secure World: Our Shared Responsibility, UN Doc A/59/565 (2004), para 145.

[54]For more discussion on this point, see Ganor (2000).

[55]By way of example, India's Prevention of Terrorism Act 2002 describes a terrorist act as one including conduct by a person "with intent to threaten the unity, integrity, security or sovereignty of India" (section 3(1)(a) of the Act).

Fatherland and Liberty movement in Spain,[56] the Kurdistan Workers' Party in Turkey[57] and the Liberation Tigers of Tamil Eelam in Sri Lanka.[58]

2.2 Reaching Consensus on a Legal Definition of Terrorism

The foregoing discussion has considered various popular and political aspects involved in characterising terrorism. These are complex and open to differing, and strongly held, views. It is therefore of little surprise that the international community has been unable to reach consensus on a concise and comprehensive legal definition of the term 'terrorism', not even within the UN Global Counter-Terrorism Strategy.[59] Confirming many of the issues identified earlier in this chapter, the United Nations Terrorism Prevention Branch has described terrorism as a unique form of crime, often containing elements of warfare, politics and propaganda, and:[60]

> For security reasons and due to lack of popular support, terrorist organisations are usually small, making detection and infiltration difficult. Although the goals of terrorists are sometimes shared by wider constituencies, their methods are generally abhorred.

The failure of the international community to achieve consensus on a global definition of terrorism has been criticised by many. The founding Executive Director of the International Policy Institute for Counter-Terrorism, Boaz Ganor, has proposed that UN Security Council resolutions can only have an effective impact once all States agree upon what types of conduct constitute terrorist acts.[61] Thirteen universal conventions related to terrorism have been adopted since the 1970s (see Chap. 3, Sect. 3.1.1). The conventions, however, deal with specific forms of terrorist conduct and are thereby precise in nature and not of general application. Furthermore, they are not a solution in themselves, since treaties are only binding upon States parties.[62] Nor does the United Nations Charter contain a definition of the term. Likewise, the Rome Statute of the International

---

[56]See Appendix A "Background Information on Designated Foreign Terrorist Organizations" in Howard and Sawyer (2003, p. 507).

[57]Ibid, 514.

[58]Ibid, 516.

[59]Adopted by the United Nations General Assembly under GA Res 60/288, UN GAOR, 60th Sess, 99th Plen Mtg, UN Doc A/Res/60/288 (2006).

[60]United Nations Office on Drugs and Crime, "UN Action Against Terrorism", online: http://www.odccp.org/terrorism.html (as accessed 19 June 2002; copy on file with the author).

[61]Ganor (1999).

[62]By application of the legal principle *pacta tertii nec nocent nec prosunt* (treaties are not binding upon States unless their consent to be bound has been signified) – as reflected within article 34 of the Vienna Convention on the Law of Treaties, opened for signature 23 May 1969, 1155 UNTS 331 (entered into force 27 January 1980).

Criminal Court does not include terrorism as one of the international crimes within the Court's jurisdiction.[63] The Court has within its jurisdiction the "most serious international crimes", according to its preamble. It was proposed, within the draft Statute, to include terrorism within the Court's jurisdiction, but the failure of States to agree upon a definition of the term resulted in the crime being removed from the scope of the Court's jurisdiction and subject matter of the constitutive treaty.[64] Perhaps most surprising is the fact that Security Council resolution 1373 (2001), which imposes various obligations concerning counter-terrorism upon member States of the United Nations, does not define the term.[65]

2.2.1 Attempts to Define Terrorism

Attempts to define terrorism have been made since before the establishment of the United Nations.[66] The Draft League of Nations Convention for the Prevention and Punishment of Terrorism was to provide that terrorism comprised:[67]

> All criminal acts directed against a State and intended or calculated to create a state of terror in the minds of particular persons or a group of persons or the general public.

This Draft Convention never came into force as not enough States ratified it, due mainly to dissent over definition of the term.[68]

There have been suggestions that terrorism be defined as the peacetime equivalent of war crimes. In a report to the United Nations Office on Drugs and Crime (UNODC), Alex Schmidt proposed taking the already agreed upon definition of war crimes (comprising deliberate attacks on civilians, hostage-taking and the killing of prisoners)

---

[63]Rome Statute of the International Criminal Court, opened for signature 17 July 1998, 2187 UNTS 90 (entered into force 1 July 2002).

[64]There are arguments, however, that terrorist acts fall within the jurisdiction of the Court as constituting crimes against humanity (crimes under article 7 of the Rome Statute).

[65]Having said this, the lack of definition was most likely due to the fact (as will be seen through subsequent discussions) that there is a lack of consensus on just what amounts to terrorism. In a desire to issue a forceful, and at the same time early, resolution in the wake of September 11 it is likely that the Council saw use of the term, without definition, as the only viable option in the short term. The problem with this approach is that it has left the question of defining the term with individual member States, leading to inconsistent definitions and, arguably, a weak rather than forceful resolution.

[66]For an overview, see Golder and Williams (2004, pp. 273–275). See also Saul (2006).

[67]As recorded by the United Nations Office on Drugs and Crime on its website, "Definitions of Terrorism", online: http://www.odccp.org/terrorism_definitions.html (as accessed 19 June 2002; copy on file with the author).

[68]Geneva Convention for the Prevention and Punishment of Terrorism 1937 (Draft). See discussion on this point within the website of the United Nations Office on Drugs and Crime, "Definitions of Terrorism" (ibid). See also Andreu-Guzmán (2002, p. 185).

and extending it to peacetime.[69] Terrorism would then be defined as the "peacetime equivalents of war crimes". It does not appear, however, that this has gained any popular acceptance. Schmidt's earlier and more complex definition of terrorism is, on the other hand, cited by UNODC as representing "academic consensus":[70]

> An anxiety-inspiring method of repeated violent action, employed by a (semi-) clandestine individual, group or state actors, for idiosyncratic, criminal or political reasons, whereby – in contrast to assassination – the direct targets of violence are not the main targets. The immediate human victims of violence are generally chosen randomly (targets of opportunity) or selectively (representative or symbolic targets) from a target population, and serve as message generators. Threat and violence-based communication processes between terrorist (organisation), (imperilled) victims, and main targets are used to manipulate the main target (audience(s)), turning it into a target of terror, a target of demands, or a target of attention, depending on what the intimidation, coercion, or propaganda is primarily sought.

At the European Union level, the crime of terrorism has been defined by the Parliamentary Assembly of the Union as:[71]

> Any offence committed by individuals or groups resorting to violence or threatening to use violence against a country, its institutions, its population in general or specific individuals which, being motivated by separatist aspirations, extremist ideological conceptions, fanaticism or irrational and subjective factors, is intended to create a climate of terrors among official authorities, certain individuals or groups in society, or the general public.

Three practical distinctions between terrorist and criminal conduct have been made earlier in this chapter, concerning the focus, participants in, and victims of terrorism. The two definitions of terrorism just cited contain three further common threads: firstly, that the victims or 'physical' target(s) of a terrorist act (a building, or people) are not the 'primary' target of the act (the target against whom a message is being sent, usually a government or international organisation); next, the purpose of the threat or violence is to intimidate and create a situation of fear or terror (hence the term terrorism) or to persuade or dissuade the primary target to do or abstain from doing something; and, finally, that this is done to advance an ideological, political, or religious cause.

2.2.2 Objective Versus Subjective Definitions of the Term

The sticking point in achieving international consensus on a definition of the term is not so much with the technical wording of what physical conduct amounts to a

---

[69]This definition was put to the United Nations Crime Branch by Schmidt in 1992 (ibid). See also Schmid (2004).

[70]This definition comes from an earlier text by Schmidt and Jongman (1988, p. 5).

[71]Recommendation 1426 (1999) of the Parliamentary Assembly of the European Union, "European Democracies Facing up to Terrorism", 23 September 1999, para 5. See also the much more precise definition within article 3(1) of the European Council Common Position of 27 December 2001.

terrorist act. The problem lies more with what the *purpose* of the conduct is. This, as discussed earlier, is particularly controversial in the context of secession and the boundaries of permissible conduct by a peoples in pursuit of their self-determination. A number of States argue that a subjective analysis and definition of such conduct (by considering its purpose) should therefore be made. The UN Office on Drugs and Crime reports that Arab States such as Libya, Syria and Iran have all campaigned for a definition that excludes acts of 'freedom fighters' from the international definition of terrorism by employing the argument that a justified goal may be pursued by any available means.[72]

While these positions are firmly held by a small number of States, the majority of States adhere to an objective definition of terrorism (one which does not take into account the motives of the conduct). In 1994, the UN General Assembly adopted the Declaration on Measures to Eliminate International Terrorism.[73] The Declaration was based on the notion of peace and security and the principle of refraining from the threat or use of force in international relations.[74] It pronounced that terrorism constitutes a grave violation of the purpose and principles of the United Nations.[75] While it did not purport to define terrorism, it did say that criminal acts intended or calculated to provoke a state of terror in the general public for political purposes are in any circumstances unjustifiable:[76]

> The States Members of the United Nations solemnly reaffirm their unequivocal condemnation of *all* acts, methods and practices of terrorism, as criminal and unjustifiable, *wherever and by whomever committed*, including those which jeopardise the friendly relations among States and peoples and threaten the territorial integrity and security of States. [emphasis added]

In reaffirming the Declaration in 1995,[77] the General Assembly was even more precise on this point:[78]

---

[72]United Nations Office on Drugs and Crime, "Definitions of Terrorism" (n 67).

[73]GA Res 49/60 (n 25).

[74]Ibid, as is evident through its preamble.

[75]Ibid, para 2.

[76]Ibid, para 1.

[77]GA Res 50/53, UN GAOR, 50th Sess, 87th Plen Mtg, UN Doc A/Res/50/53 (1995), para 3.

[78]Ibid, para 2. See also common para 2 of the following resolutions of the General Assembly: GA Res 51/210, 51st Sess, 88th Plen Mtg, UN Doc A/Res/51/210 (1996); GA Res 52/165, UN GAOR, 52nd Sess, 72nd Plen Mtg, UN Doc A/Res/52/165 (1997); GA Res 54/110, UN GAOR, 54th Sess, 76th Plen Mtg, UN Doc A/Res/54/110 (1999); GA Res 55/158, UN GAOR, 55th Sess, 84th Plen Mtg, UN Doc A/Res/55/158 (2000); GA Res 56/88, UN GAOR, 56th Sess, 85th Plen Mtg, UN Doc A/Res/56/88 (2001); GA Res 57/27, UN GAOR, 57th Sess, 52nd Plen Mtg, UN Doc A/Res/57/27 (2002); GA Res 58/81, UN GAOR, 58th Sess, 72nd Plen Mtg, UN Doc A/Res/58/81 (2003); and GA Res 59/46, UN GAOR, 59th Sess, 65th Plen Mtg, UN Doc A/Res/59/46 (2004). See further: GA Res 61/40, UN GAOR, 61st Sess, 64th Plen Mtg, UN Doc A/Res/61/40 (2007), preambular para 19, and operative para 4; GA Res 61/171, UN GAOR, 61st Sess, 81st Plen Mtg, UN Doc A/Res/61/171 (2007), preambular para 12; GA Res 62/71, UN GAOR, 62nd Sess, 62nd Plen Mtg, UN Doc A/Res/62/71 (2008), preambular para 19, and operative para 4; and GA Res 62/159, UN GAOR, 62nd Sess, 76th Plen Mtg, UN Doc A/Res/62/159 (2008), preambular para 11.

Reiterates that criminal acts intended or calculated to provoke a state of terror in the general public, a group of persons or particular persons are in any circumstances unjustifiable, *whatever the considerations of a political, philosophical, ideological, racial, ethnic, religious or any other nature that may be invoked to justify them*; [emphasis added]

Of even greater value in this respect, according to the Executive Director of the International Policy Institute for Counter-Terrorism, is the Security Council's resolution 1269 (1999).[79] While the resolution also fails to define terrorism, it clearly takes an objective approach to the question of terrorist conduct, stating that the Security Council:[80]

Unequivocally condemns all acts, methods and practices of terrorism as criminal and unjustifiable, *regardless of their motivation*, in all their forms and manifestations, wherever and by whomever committed, in particular those which would threaten international peace and security; [emphasis added]

Resolution 1373 (2001) also points to an objective approach, paragraph 3(g) of the resolution calling upon States to ensure that "claims of political motivation are not recognized as grounds for refusing requests for the extradition of alleged terrorists".[81] Security Council resolution 1566 (2004) further provides as follows:[82]

Recalls that criminal acts, including against civilians, committed with the intent to cause death or serious bodily injury, or taking of hostages, with the purpose to provoke a state of terror in the general public or in a group of persons or particular persons, intimidate a population or compel a government or an international organization to do or to abstain from doing any act, which constitute offences within the scope of and as defined in the international conventions and protocols relating to terrorism, *are under no circumstances justifiable by considerations of a political, philosophical, ideological, racial, ethnic, religious or other similar nature*, and *calls upon* all States to prevent such acts and, if not prevented, to ensure that such acts are punished by penalties consistent with their grave nature; [emphasis added].

---

[79]Ganor (2000).

[80]SC Res 1269, UN SCOR, 4053rd Mtg, UN Doc S/Res/1269 (1999). See also Roach (2007) and Saul (2007).

[81]SC Res 1373, UN SCOR, 5385th Mtg, UN Doc S/Res/1373 (2001).

[82]SC Res 1566, UN SCOR, 5053rd Mtg, UN Doc S/Res/1566 (2004), para 3. See also the United Nations Office on Drugs and Crime, Handbook on Criminal Justice Responses to Terrorism (United Nations, New York, 2009), p. 40, as well as the following resolutions of the Security Council: SC Res 1617, UN SCOR, 5244th Mtg, UN Doc S/Res/1617 (2005), preambular para 2; SC Res 1735, UN SCOR, 5609th Mtg, UN Doc S/Res/1735 (2006), preambular para 2; SC Res 1787, UN SCOR 5795th Mtg, UN Doc S/Res/1787 (2007), preambular para 2; SC Res 1805, UN SCOR, 5856th Mtg, UN Doc 1805 (2008), preambular para 1; SC Res 1617, UN SCOR, 5244th Mtg, UN Doc S/Res/1617 (2005), preambular para 2; and SC Res 1822, UN SCOR, 5928th Mtg, UN Doc S/Res/1822 (2008), preambular para 2.

2.2.3 *International Conventions Relating to Terrorism*

Chapter 3 will consider in more detail the 13 universal terrorism-related conventions, all of which have entered into force (see Sect. 3.1.1). The number and scope of these conventions might, at first instance, seem impressive and comprehensive. They have, however, various limitations. To begin with, they only apply to States parties to the conventions. Beyond this, the conventions are of limited application because of the very precise subject matter of each treaty. The conventions are not of general application but, rather, relate to specific situations in which terrorist acts might have effect, whether on board aircraft, in airports or on maritime platforms.

The only treaty with the potential to impact a wider audience and scope of activity is the International Convention for the Suppression of the Financing of Terrorism (the Suppression of Financing Convention).[83] This is said for two reasons. Firstly, the Convention mirrors much of the suppression of financing obligations contained in Security Council resolution 1373 (2001). As a resolution binding upon all members of the United Nations,[84] this has had a significant impact upon the status of the Convention. Prior to 11 September 2001, there were just four States parties to the Convention and, accordingly, the Convention was not in force. Due at least in part to resolution 1373 (2001) and the work of the Counter-Terrorism Committee, there are now 160 States parties to the Convention.[85]

The Suppression of Financing Convention is also of greater relevance because of the wording of article 2(1)(b) of the Convention. Although this provision does not purport to define the term 'terrorism', it explains (for the purpose of prohibiting the financing of terrorist entities or operations) what type of acts may not be financed:

> Any other act intended to cause death or serious bodily injury to a civilian, or to any other person not taking an active part in the hostilities in a situation of armed conflict, when the purpose of such act, by its nature or context, is to intimidate a population, or to compel a government or an international organization to do or to abstain from doing any act.

The Convention does therefore have some potentially wider application and is useful for States in determining the type of conduct they are to prohibit.

---

[83]International Convention for the Suppression of the Financing of Terrorism, opened for signature 10 January 2000, 2179 UNTS 232 (entered into force 10 April 1992).

[84]By application of article 25 of the Charter of the United Nations.

[85]Counter-Terrorism Committee, "International Law and Terrorism", online: http://www.un.org/sc/ctc/law.shtml (as accessed on 22 August 2008).

2.2.4 The Draft Comprehensive Convention on International Terrorism

Also considered in Chap. 3 is the work undertaken since 2000 towards establishing a comprehensive convention against terrorism (see Sect. 3.1.2). One of the expected sticking points in the progress of this work has been that of definitions, not just in terms of defining what amounts to a terrorist act (draft article 2), but also with regard to the wording of draft article 18, which concerns exemptions. In particular, the definition and/or inclusion of acts of "armed forces" or "parties" to a conflict (this being relevant to the proposed limited exemptions from jurisdiction and/or liability under the Convention); whether "foreign occupation" should be included within that category of exemptions; and whether the activities of military forces should be "governed" or "in conformity" with international law. Draft article 18 has been described by the Chairman of the Committee as the crux of the Convention.[86] Hinging upon these matters has been a lack of consensus on a preamble. The Draft Convention definition of terrorist acts is as follows:

Article 2
1. Any person commits an offence within the meaning of this Convention if that person, by any means, unlawfully and intentionally, causes:
   (a) Death or serious bodily injury to any person; or
   (b) Serious damage to public or private property, including a place of public use, a State or government facility, a public transportation system, an infrastructure facility or the environment; or
   (c) Damage to property, places, facilities, or systems referred to in paragraph 1 (b) of this article, resulting or likely to result in major economic loss,
   when the purpose of the conduct, by its nature or context, is to intimidate a population, or to compel a Government or an international organization to do or abstain from doing any act.
2. Any person also commits an offence if that person makes a credible and serious threat to commit an offence as set forth in paragraph 1 of this article.
3. Any person also commits an offence if that person attempts to commit an offence as set forth in paragraph 1 of this article.
4. Any person also commits an offence if that person:
   (a) Participates as an accomplice in an offence as set forth in paragraph 1, 2 or 3 of this article;
   (b) Organizes or directs others to commit an offence as set forth in paragraph 1, 2 or 3 of this article; or
   (c) Contributes to the commission of one or more offences as set forth in paragraph 1, 2 or 3 of this article by a group of persons acting with a common purpose. Such contribution shall be intentional and shall either:
      (i) Be made with the aim of furthering the criminal activity or criminal purpose of the group, where such activity or purpose involves the commission of an offence as set forth in paragraph 1 of this article; or

---

[86]Ad Hoc Committee Established by General Assembly Resolution 51/210, UN Press Release L/2993.

(ii) Be made in the knowledge of the intention of the group to commit an offence as set forth in paragraph 1 of this article.

The very real advantage of the definition proposed is that it is comprehensive in nature, rather than operational and limited to addressing particular types of terrorist acts, or potential targets, or potential means of furthering terrorist activities. It is therefore a great pity that scepticism surrounds the realisation of the Draft Convention.

2.2.5   *United Nations High-Level Panel Definition of Terrorism*

Albeit non-binding, mention should be made of the 2004 report of the Secretary-General's High-level Panel on Threats, Challenges and Change in which terrorism was described as:[87]

> ...any action, *in addition to* actions already specified by the existing conventions on aspects of terrorism, the Geneva Conventions and Security Council resolution 1566 (2004), that is intended to cause death or serious bodily harm to *civilians or non-combatants*, when the purpose of such an act, by its nature and context, is to intimidate a population, or to compel a Government or an international organization to do or to abstain from doing any act [emphasis added].

There are two problems with this definition, corresponding to each of the emphasised sections of text in the quotation. Firstly, the definition does not confine itself to the extant terrorism-related conventions. That is, it goes further than the description within Security Council resolution 1566 (2004), discussed next, of acts to be suppressed in the fight against terrorism by expressing itself to be "in addition to" actions already specified within that resolution. The UN Special Rapporteur on counter-terrorism has expressed dissatisfaction with this approach, instead advocating for precision by restricting 'terrorism' to the cumulative characteristics set out within resolution 1566 (2004).[88] This is a matter to be considered in Sect. 2.3 below.

Furthermore, the definition within the High-Level Panel's report is potentially confusing because of its imprecise reference to "civilians or non-combatants". By doing so, the definition immediately invokes war-time terminology which has

---

[87]High-level Panel on Threats, Challenges and Change, A More Secure World: Our Shared Responsibility, UN Doc A/59/565 (2004), para 164(d).

[88]Report of the UN Special Rapporteur on the promotion and protection of human rights while countering terrorism, Martin Scheinin, The Protection and Promotion of Human Rights While Countering Terrorism, UN Doc E/CN.4/2006/098 (2005), para 36.

significant implications and consequences under international humanitarian law, whereas it has already been observed in this chapter that acts of terrorism predominantly occur during peacetime.

2.2.6   United Nations Resolutions on Terrorism

Chapter 3 explains the development of General Assembly and Security Council resolutions on the subject of terrorism and counter-terrorism (see Sect. 3.2 therein). What is relevant, for the purposes of this chapter, is to recognise the absence of an express definition of the term 'terrorism' within any of those resolutions. This includes resolutions 1269 (1999) and 1373 (2001) of the Security Council, resolutions through which important obligations upon member States of the United Nations were established.

There is one resolution of the Security Council, however, which is of considerable value. Although it does not express itself as establishing a universally accepted definition of the term terrorism, Security Council resolution 1566 (2004) called on all States to cooperate fully in the fight against terrorism and, in doing so, to prevent and punish acts that have three cumulative characteristics.[89] The United Nations Special Rapporteur on the promotion and protection of human rights and counter-terrorism has expressed support for this approach.[90] This is the subject of consideration next.

2.3   A Comprehensive, Concise, and Human Rights-Based Approach to Defining Terrorism

As concluded to this point, none of the 13 conventions on anti-terrorism contain a comprehensive definition of the term 'terrorism', but are instead confined to specific subjects, whether air safety, maritime navigation and platforms, the protection of persons, or the suppression of the means by which terrorist acts may be perpetrated or supported. Neither do resolutions of the various United Nations bodies adopt a definition, save that the General Assembly and Security Council have expressed that all acts of terrorism are unjustifiable regardless of their motivation. In the first substantive report of the Special Rapporteur on counter-terrorism under his mandate, reflections and recommendations were made concerning the proper characterisation of 'terrorism' and the consequent definitional requirements of proscribing terrorist conduct.

---

[89]SC Res 1566 (n 82), para 3.
[90]Report of the UN Special Rapporteur on Counter-Terrorism (n 88), para 38.

2.3.1 Links to Existing Operational Definitions ('Trigger Offences')

The first observation to be made is that four relatively recent documents utilise a very useful trigger in determining what conduct, in the absence of a comprehensive definition, should be characterised as 'terrorist' by linking the term to existing conventions on terrorism. The first of these documents is the Council of Europe Convention on the Prevention of Terrorism, adopted in May 2005, which defines a "terrorist offence" as any of the offences within 10 of the 12 anti-terrorism conventions in force (excluding the Tokyo Convention on Offences and Certain Other Acts Committed on Board Aircraft and the Convention on the Marking of Plastic Explosives for the Purpose of Detection).[91] All of the offences within the COE Convention are thus linked to the offences created by and definitions within the universal conventions on countering terrorism that are currently in force. Next, in proscribing the financing of certain conduct, article 2(1)(a) of the Convention for the Suppression of the Financing of Terrorism takes a similar approach, linking itself to 9 of the 11 other terrorism conventions in force at that time. Finally, Security Council resolution 1566 (2004), as well as the Report of the Secretary-General's High-level Panel on Threats, Challenges and Change, also make reference to conduct prohibited under the existing conventions on aspects of terrorism.[92]

The use of the counter-terrorism conventions as a trigger for determining what conduct is to be proscribed in the fight against terrorism is, in the absence of a universal and comprehensive definition of 'terrorism', advocated by the UN Special Rapporteur as the proper starting point.[93] Although subject-specific, the conventions are universal in nature, so that the use of offences described in them can be treated as broadly representative of international consensus. This approach must be qualified in one respect, to note that this linkage is not applicable in the case of the Convention on the Marking of Plastic Explosives. Because that Convention does not actually proscribe any conduct, but instead places obligations upon States relating to the marking of explosives, it cannot be used as a 'trigger offence' treaty.[94]

By itself, however, the use of trigger offences is not sufficient to determine what conduct is truly 'terrorist' in nature. To that extent, the expression of the link to existing conventions within the High-Level Panel report is not fully satisfactory.

---

[91]Council of Europe Convention on the Prevention of Terrorism, opened for signature 16 May 2005, 16 CETS 196 (entered into force 1 June 2007). The list of conventions mirrors the list contained within the International Convention for the Suppression of the Financing of Terrorism, but also includes the latter Convention.

[92]SC Res 1566 (n 82) para 3; and Report of the Secretary-General's High-level Panel on Threats, Challenges and Change (n 87) para 164(d).

[93]As advocated in his report (n 88) para 33.

[94]Convention on the Marking of Plastic Explosives for the Purpose of Detection, opened for signature 1 March 1991, ICAO Doc 9571 (entered into force 21 June 1998), articles 2 and 3(1).

The point can be illustrated with reference to the Tokyo Convention on Offences and Certain Other Acts Committed on Board Aircraft. The Convention calls on States to establish jurisdiction over acts that may or do jeopardise the safety of a civil aircraft, or of persons or property therein, or which jeopardise good order and discipline on board.[95] While this would certainly capture conduct of a terrorist nature, the description of acts over which States must establish jurisdiction is very broad and likely also to include conduct with no bearing at all to terrorism. Thus, the High-Level Panel formulation of "any action, *in addition to* actions already specified by the existing conventions on aspects of terrorism" is problematic, since not all acts caught under these conventions (the Tokyo Convention being a prime example) will be of a terrorist nature. It is notable in that regard that neither the European Convention on the Prevention of Terrorism, nor the International Convention on the Suppression of the Financing of Terrorism, link themselves to the Tokyo Convention.

2.3.2   Cumulative Characteristics of Conduct to Be Suppressed

The solution to the problem just identified can be drawn from Security Council resolution 1566 (2004). As explained earlier, the resolution calls on all States to cooperate fully in the fight against terrorism and, in doing so, to prevent and punish acts that have three cumulative characteristics, which are as follows:[96]

- Acts, including against civilians, committed with the intention of causing death or serious bodily injury, or the taking of hostages; and
- Irrespective of whether motivated by considerations of a political, philosophical, ideological, racial, ethnic, religious or other similar nature, also committed for the purpose of provoking a state of terror in the general public or in a group of persons or particular persons, intimidating a population, or compelling a government or an international organization to do or to abstain from doing any act; and
- Such acts constituting offences within the scope of and as defined in the international conventions and protocols relating to terrorism.

The third criterion represents the 'trigger-offence' approach already identified. The important feature of the resolution is the cumulative nature of its characterisation of terrorism, requiring the trigger-offence to be accompanied with: the intention of causing death or serious bodily injury (or the taking of hostages); for the purpose of provoking terror, intimidating a population, or compelling a government or an international organization to do or to abstain from doing any act. This cumulative

---

[95]Convention on Offences and Certain Other Acts Committed on Board Aircraft, opened for signature 14 September 1963, 704 UNTS 219 (entered into force 4 December 1969), articles 1(1) and (4), and 3(2).
[96]SC Res 1566 (n 82) para 3.

approach acts as a safety threshold to ensure that it is only conduct of a *terrorist nature* that is identified as terrorist conduct. As properly stated by the UN Special Rapporteur, not all acts that are crimes under national or even international law, are acts of terrorism, nor should be defined as such.[97]

By way of further example, there are clear parallels between acts of terrorism and other international crimes, including crimes against humanity (whether in the terms set out in the Statute of the International Criminal Court, or the proscription of such crimes under general international law). The Security Council, General Assembly, and Commission on Human Rights have also identified terrorism as something that: endangers or takes innocent lives; has links with transnational organised crime, drug trafficking, money-laundering, and trafficking in arms as well as illegal transfers of nuclear, chemical and biological materials; and is also linked to the consequent commission of serious crimes such as murder, extortion, kidnapping, assault, the taking of hostages and robbery.[98] Notwithstanding such linkages, counter-terrorism must be limited to the countering of offences within the scope of, and as defined in, the international conventions and protocols relating to terrorism, or the countering of associated conduct called for within resolutions of the Security Council, when combined with the intention and purpose elements identified in Security Council resolution 1566 (2004). That an act is criminal does not, by itself, make it a terrorist act.

A cumulative approach is, in fact, the one taken in defining prohibited conduct under the International Convention against the Taking of Hostages. Hostage-taking is defined as the seizure or detention of a person (a hostage) accompanied by a threat to kill, injure or continue to detain the hostage, in order to compel a third party to do or to abstain from doing any act. To that extent, hostage-taking (as described) encapsulates all three characteristics identified within Security

---

[97] Special Rapporteur report (n 88) para 38.

[98] See: SC Res 1269 (n 80) preambular para 1; SC Res 1373 (n 81) para 4; SC Res 1377, UN SCOR, 4413rd Mtg, UN Doc S/Res/1377 (2001) para 6; SC Res 1456, UN SCOR, 4688th Mtg, UN Doc S/Res/1456 (2003) preambular paras 3 and 6; SC Res 1540, UN SCOR, 4956th Mtg, UN Doc S/Res/1540 (2004) preambular para 8; GA Res 3034 (XXVII), UN GAOR, 27th Sess, 2114th Plen Mtg, UN Doc A/Res/27/3034 (1972) para 1; GA Res 31/102, UN GAOR, 31st Sess, 99th Plen Mtg, UN Doc A/Res/31/102 (1976) para 1; GA Res 32/147, UN GAOR, 32nd Sess, 105th Plen Mtg, UN Doc A/Res/32/147 (1977) para 1; GA Res 34/145, UN GAOR, 34th Sess, 105th Plen Mtg, UN Doc A/Res/34/145 (1979) para 1; GA Res 36/109, UN GAOR, 36th Sess, UN Doc A/Res/36/109 (1981) para 1; GA Res 48/122, UN GAOR, 48th Sess, 85th Plen Mtg, UN Doc A/Res/48/122 (1993) preambular para 7; GA Res 49/185, UN GAOR, 49th Sess, 94th Plen Mtg, UN Doc A/Res49/185 (1994) preambular para 9; GA Res 50/186, UN GAOR, 50th Sess, 99th Plen Mtg, UN Doc A/Res/50/186 (1995) preambular para 12; GA Res 52/133, UN GAOR, 52nd Sess, 70th Plen Mtg, UN Doc A/Res/52/133 (1997) preambular para 11; GA Res 54/164 54/164, UN GAOR, 54th Sess, 83rd Plen Mtg, UN Doc A/Res/54/164 (1999) preambular para 13; GA Res 56/160, UN GAOR, 56th Sess, 88th Plen Mtg, UN Doc A/Res/56/160 (2001) preambular para 18; GA Res 58/136, UN GAOR, 58th Sess, 77th Plen Mtg, UN Doc A/Res/58/136 (2004) preambular para 8; GA Res 58/174, UN GAOR, 58th Sess, 77th Plen Mtg, UN Doc A/Res/ 58/174 (2003) preambular para 12; CHR Res 2001/37, UN Doc E/CN.4/Res/2001/37, preambular para 16 and operative para 2; and UNCHR Res 2004/44, UN Doc E/CN.4/Res/2004/44, preambular para7.

Council resolution 1566, except that it does not expressly state that the motivations of such conduct cannot render it justifiable.

It should be noted that the International Convention for the Suppression of Acts of Nuclear Terrorism, is at odds with the cumulative approach described. The Convention requires States parties to prohibit the possession or use of nuclear material or devices with the intent: (1) to cause death or serious bodily injury; *or* (2) to cause serious property damage or damage to the environment; *or* (3) to compel a person, organisation or State to do or abstain from doing any act.[99] The wording of article 2(1) does not fit with Security Council resolution 1566 (2004), treating the resolution's first two characteristics (intent to cause death or injury or the taking of hostages; for the purpose of influencing conduct) as alternatives, rather than cumulative requirements. The UN Special Rapporteur has expressed concern that, just as in the case of the Tokyo Convention already discussed, this may capture conduct that does not meet the general criteria for defining what acts are terrorist in nature.[100]

By way of summary, it is essential to ensure that the term 'terrorism' is confined in its use to conduct that is of a genuinely terrorist nature. The three-step characterisation of conduct to be prevented, and if not prevented punished, in the fight against terrorism in Security Council resolution 1566 (2004) takes advantage of the currently agreed upon offences concerning aspects of terrorism by using these as 'trigger-offences' and goes on to establish an appropriate threshold by requiring that such offences are also committed with the intention of causing death or serious bodily injury, or the taking of hostages *and* for the purpose of provoking a state of terror, intimidating a population, or compelling a government or international organization to do or abstain from doing any act.

2.3.3 Dealing with Threats of Terrorist Acts Outside the Scope of 'Trigger Offences'

A question that arises to this point is how a comprehensive, concise, and human rights-based approach to defining terrorism is able to deal with potentially unique threats of terrorism that are real and specific to a country, but fall outside the offences defined in the international conventions and protocols relating to terrorism. The question goes to the heart of the problem: how can this be accomplished without opening the door for the classification as terrorism of any undesired, but

---

[99]International Convention for the Suppression of Acts of Nuclear Terrorism, adopted by the General Assembly and opened for signature on 15 April 2005 under GA Res 59/290, UN GAOR, 59th Sess, 91st Plen Mtg, UN Doc A/Res/59/290 (2005) and entered into force 7 July 2007, article 2(1). See also paras (2) to (4) of article 2, which set out party and associated offences.

[100]Special Rapporteur report (n 88) 41.

'normal', criminal conduct. How can this be accommodated whilst retaining the objective of dealing with conduct which is truly terrorist in nature?

The approach of the Special Rapporteur on counter-terrorism has been to suggest replacing the third cumulative characteristic (terrorism trigger offences) with the requirement that the defined conduct is one that corresponds "to all elements of a serious crime as defined by the law".[101] In other words, if the conduct in question amounts to a serious offence in domestic law *and* is intended to cause serious bodily injury or death *and* is undertaken for the purpose of invoking a state of terror or compelling a government or international organisation to do or abstain from doing something, then this is sufficient to amount to 'terrorism' even if the conduct does not fall within the scope of the offences defined within the international terrorism-related conventions. This approach is a sensible one. It retains the classic features of terrorism of intending to cause death or serious bodily injury for the purpose of invoking terror or influencing a government or international organisation. Although it expands upon the third cumulative characteristic identified by the Security Council, it restricts this expanded approach to serious offences prescribed by law.

The only level of uncertainty that this approach creates is the question of what amounts to a 'serious' offence in domestic law. Nevertheless, this is not an impossible task, and it is one that allows for States to take into account serious threats to them that are not encompassed within the existing terrorism-related conventions.

2.3.4 Conduct in Support of Terrorist Offences

The approach just described is not inconsistent with a number of directions by, and recommendations of, the Security Council concerning conduct *in support* of terrorist offences. By way of example, and although not phrased in mandatory language, Security Council resolution 1624 calls on States to prohibit and prevent the *incitement* to commit a terrorist act or acts.[102] Again, the resolution does not define what terrorist acts are. The answer lies in making reference back to the three-step cumulative methodology of resolution 1566 (2004). Only the incitement of conduct (which itself meets the three characteristics) should be treated as the "incitement to terrorism". While the incitement of *other* criminal conduct might be unlawful, and making it punishable may in some cases even be required under article 20(2) of the International Covenant on Civil and Political Rights (ICCPR) or article 4 of the

---

[101]Special Rapporteur's report on his Mission to Spain (n 26) para 6.

[102]SC Res 1624, UN SCOR, 5261st mtg, UN Doc S/Res/1624 (2005) para 1(a) and (b). See also SC Res 1373 (n 81) para 5(3), which: "*Declares* that acts, methods, and practices of terrorism are contrary to the purposes and principles of the United Nations and that knowingly financing, planning and inciting terrorist acts are also contrary to the purposes and principles of the United Nations".

International Convention for the Elimination of Racial Discrimination (CERD), such incitement should not be characterised as "incitement to terrorism".

This confinement of 'conduct in support' type offences and State obligations by reference back to the three-step cumulative methodology of resolution 1566 (2004) is equally applicable to the Security Council's calls upon States to themselves refrain from providing any form of support to those involved in terrorist acts;[103] prevent the commission of terrorist acts;[104] bring to justice any person who supports, facilitates, participates, or attempts to participate in the financing, planning, preparation or commission of terrorist acts or provides safe haven to terrorists;[105] prevent the movement of terrorists;[106] ensure, prior to the granting of refugee status, that the person claiming asylum has not planned, facilitated or participated in terrorist acts;[107] and prevent and suppress all active and passive support to terrorism.[108]

2.3.5 Further Definitional Requirements of Criminal Proscriptions

In addition to the question of what type of conduct should be characterised as 'terrorist' in nature for the purpose of establishing criminal offences, human rights law and the rule of law impose certain requirements. The UN Office on Drugs and Crime explains that, in the definition of terrorist acts or terrorism-related crimes, States must observe the rule of law and the basic human rights principle of legality.[109] Rather than being an obstacle, these requirements help in countering the negative consequences of the lack of an agreed definition of terrorism. Article 15(1) of the ICCPR, which is an absolute and non-derogable right and enshrines the principle of legality, is particularly instructive, providing that:

> No one shall be held guilty of any criminal offence on account of any act or omission which did not constitute a criminal offence, under national or international law, at the time when it was committed. Nor shall a heavier penalty be imposed than the one that was applicable at the time when the criminal offence was committed. If, subsequent to the commission of the offence, provision is made by law for the imposition of the lighter penalty, the offender shall benefit thereby.

---

[103]SC Res 1373 (ibid) para 2(a).

[104]Ibid para 2(b).

[105]Ibid para 2(c) (d) and (e). See also SC Res 1566 (n 82) para 2, and SC Res 1456 (n 98) para 3.

[106]SC Res 1373 (n 81) para 3(f) and (g).

[107]SC Res 1373 (ibid) para 2(h).

[108]SC Res 1456 (n 98) para 1.

[109]Handbook on Criminal Justice Responses to Terrorism (n 82) p. 36. See also Duffy (2005, pp. 95–96); and the Report of the United Nations High Commissioner for Human Rights on the protection of human rights and fundamental freedoms while countering terrorism, UN Doc A/HRC/8/13 (2008), para 21.

The first requirement of article 15(1) is that the prohibition of terrorist conduct must be undertaken by national or international 'prescriptions of law'. The demands of this expression are considered later in this book (see Chap. 10, Sect. 10.2.2) but, in short, require that the law is adequately accessible and written with precision.[110] Terrorism offences should therefore plainly set out what elements of the crime make it a *terrorist* crime. Similarly, where any offences are linked to "terrorist acts", there must be a clear definition of what constitutes such acts.[111] Arising from the need for precision, and to avoid use of the fight against terrorism as an excuse to unnecessarily extend the reach of criminal law, it is essential that offences created under counter-terrorist legislation, along with any associated powers of investigation or prosecution, be limited to countering terrorism.

The final element of article 15 of the ICCPR concerns non-retroactivity. Any provision defining a crime must not criminalise conduct that occurred prior to its entry into force as applicable law. Likewise, any penalties are to be limited to those applicable at the time that any offence was committed and, if the law has subsequently provided for the imposition of a lighter penalty, the offender must be given the benefit of the lighter penalty.[112]

2.3.6 Summary

The foregoing discussion presents an approach to defining terrorism in a concise, comprehensive and human rights-compatible way, drawn from approaches taken by the UN Special Rapporteur on counter-terrorism, existing international and regional terrorism-related conventions, the UN High-Level Panel on Threats, Challenges and Change, and the Security Council. It is not impossible, nor in fact difficult, for States to achieve the goal of defining terrorism in a way that is restricted to acts of a truly terrorist nature. The advantage of doing so is not only that such an approach is compatible with the human rights obligations of States, but that it also lends considerably greater credibility to special counter-terrorist measures adopted by States if it can be shown that these measures are restricted to terrorism and are not being used as an excuse to abuse or unjustifiably expand upon executive powers.

The approach advocated can be summarised as follows:

1. The starting point is that terrorist acts are restricted to the three cumulative characteristics identified by the Security Council in its resolution 1566 (2004), namely:

---

[110]Ibid.

[111]Special Rapporteur report (n 88) para 46. See also the limited distribution resolution of the Human Rights Council during its 7th Session, UN Doc A/HRC/7/L.20 (2008), para 15; and also its resolution 7/7, UN Doc A/HRC/Res/7/7 (2008), para 16.

[112]Special Rapporteur report (n 88) para 49; UN Doc A/HRC/7/L.20 (ibid) para 15; and HRC Res 7/7 (ibid) para 16.

- The taking of hostages, or acts committed with the intention of causing death or serious bodily injury;
- Where such conduct is undertaken for the purpose of either (i) provoking a state of terror, or (ii) compelling a government or international organisation to do or abstain from doing something;
- And where the conduct falls within the scope of the trigger offences defined in the international terrorism-related conventions.

2. Conduct falling outside the scope of the trigger offences might still be classified as terrorist if it possesses the first two characteristics identified in resolution 1566 (2004) and corresponds to all elements of a serious crime as defined by law.
3. The approaches identified in items 1 and 2 above are applicable to the treatment of conduct in support of terrorist offences.
4. Finally, the definition of terrorist conduct (i) must not be retroactive, and (ii) must be adequately accessible and written with precision so as to amount to a prescription of law.

2.4 Conclusions

The nature of terrorism is complex. A range of acts might fall within the ambit of a 'terrorist act', depending on how that term is defined and perhaps even upon the entity using the term. Terrorism will almost invariably involve criminal acts. It may also be perpetrated during armed conflict. Terrorism can, however, be distinguished from 'normal' criminal conduct by various means. The focus of terrorist acts tends to be continuous, developing and even escalating, rather than based upon quite precise short-term goals. Terrorist organisations operate in a prepared and secure way, while at the same time relying upon wide dissemination of their conduct and ideology, and upon the recruitment of as many followers as possible. While criminal acts are targeted, terrorist ones are often indiscriminate. Relating also to targets, terrorism employs differential targeting whereby the physical targets of an act are used as tools to manipulate and put pressure upon an entity against whom the action is ultimately being taken, i.e. a government or international organisation. Inherent to the term 'terrorism', such acts are undertaken with the aim of intimidation or creating a situation of fear. Finally, terrorist acts are motivated by certain ideological, political or religious causes.

Ideological motivations are seen by most as the primary distinguishing feature of terrorist conduct from ordinary criminal offending. This affects the views of the perpetrator of terrorist acts as to the value of and culpability for such acts. On a more precise level, terrorist conduct tends to be motivated by secession, insurgency, regional retribution, and/or the 'global jihad'. While the particular individual terrorist may be driven by more personal goals, the motivations described are those of the person or entity by whom the individual actor is recruited and directed to act.

These various features support a distinct approach to the criminalisation of terrorist conduct. The political interests of most States tend to favour a distinctive approach too. Despite this, there remains no concise, comprehensive and universal legal definition of the term 'terrorism'. The only commonly held view is that any definition must be objective, such that terrorist conduct is unjustifiable whatever the considerations that may be invoked to justify them. Despite the lack of a universal definition, this chapter has presented a definitional approach which draws from existing conventions, resolutions, and commentary; is not difficult in its application; and is restricted to acts of a truly terrorist nature.

References

Abu-Rabi, Ibrahim. 1995. *Intellectual Origins of Islamic Resurgence in the Modern Arab World.* New York: New York Press.

Andreu-Guzmán, 2002. *Terrorism and Human Rights.* Geneva: International Commission of Jurists.

Barzilai, Gad. 2000. Center vs Periphery: Rules for 'Preventing Terrorism' as Politics. 8 *Criminal Cases (Pelilim)* 247.

Bassiouni, Cherif. 1981. Terrorism, Law Enforcement, and the Mass Media: Perspectives, Problems, Proposals. 72(1) *The Journal of Criminal Law and Criminology* 1.

Berg. 2004. Terrorism: The New International Challenge (paper presented at the public workshop, *How Should Fiji Respond to the Threat of Terrorism?*, Citizens' Constitutional Forum and the Fiji Human Rights Commission, 17 July 2004, Suva, Fiji).

Duffy, Helen. 2005. *The 'War on Terror' and the Framework of International Law.* Cambridge: Cambridge University Press.

Fighel, Yoni, and Shahar, Yael. 2002. The Al-Qaida-Hizballah Connection. Papers of the International Policy Institute on Counter-Terrorism, online: http://www.ict.org.il.

Fighel, Yoni, and Kehati, Yoram. 2002. Analysis of Recent Al-Qa'ida Documents, Part 1. Paper of the International Policy Institute on Counter-Terrorism, online: http://212.150.54.123/articles/articledet.cfm?articleid=453.

Ganor, Boaz. 1999. Security Council Resolution 1269: What it Leaves Out. Papers of the International Policy Institute on Counter-Terrorism, online: http://www.ict.org.il.

Ganor, Boaz. 2000. Defining Terrorism: Is One Man's Terrorist Another Man's Freedom Fighter? Online publications of the International Policy Institute for Counter-Terrorism, online: http://www.ict.org.il/Portals/0/Articles/17070-Def%20Terrorism%20by%20Dr.%20Boaz%20Ganor.pdf.

Ganor, Boaz. 2005. *The Counter-Terrorism Puzzle. A Guide for Decision Makers.* New Brunswick: Transaction Publishers.

Golder, Ben, and Williams, George. 2004. What is 'Terrorism'? Problems of Legal Definition. 27 (2) *University of New South Wales Law Journal* 270.

Howard, RD, and Sawyer, RL, (eds). 2003. *Terrorism and Counterterrorism. Understanding the New Security Environment (Revised and Updated).* Guilford, CT: The McGraw-Hill Companies.

Ilan, Ehud. 2005. Intelligence Challenges in Counter-Terrorism (paper presented at the *Terrorism's Global Impact Conference*, Interdisciplinary Center Herzlyia, 13 September 2005, Herzlyia, Israel).

Jenkins, Brian. 1999. Foreword. In Lesser, Ian, and Hoffman, Bruce, et al. *Countering the New Terrorism.* Washington: RAND Project Air Force.

Juergensmeyer, Mark. 2003. *Terror in the Mind of God. The Global Rise of Religious Violence*. Los Angeles: University of California Press.

Kahati, Yoram. 2003. The Continuing Al-Qaida Threat. Papers of the International Policy Institute on Counter-Terrorism, online: http://www.ict.org.il.

Kahati, Yoram and Fighel, Yoni. 2003. Osama bin Ladin as the New Prophet of Islam. Papers of the International Policy Institute on Counter-Terrorism, online: http://www.ict.org.il.

Khan, Ali. 2006. *A Theory of International Terrorism. Understanding Islamic Militancy*. Leiden: Martinus Nijhoff Publishers.

Meltzer, David. 2002. Al Qa'ida: terrorists or irregulars? In Strawson, John (ed). *Law after Ground Zero*. London: GlassHouse Press.

Palmer, Matthew. 2002. Counter-Terrorism Law. *New Zealand Law Journal* 456.

Rehman, Javaid. 2005. *Islamic State Practices, International Law and the Threat from Terrorism. A Critique of the 'Clash of Civilisations' in the New World Order*. Oxford: Hart Publishing.

Roach, Kent. 2002. Canada's New Anti-Terrorism Law. *Singapore Journal of Legal Studies* 122.

Roach, Kent. 2005. Canada's response to terrorism. In Ramraj, Victor, Hor, Michael, and Roach, Kent (Eds). *Global Anti-Terrorism Law and Policy*. Cambridge: Cambridge University Press.

Roach, Kent. 2007. The Case for Defining Terrorism With Restraint and Without Reference to Political or Religious Motive. In Lynch, Andrew, MacDonald, Edwina, and Williams, George (Eds). *Law and Liberty in the War on Terror*. Sydney: The Federation Press.

Rosand, Eric. 2007. Global Terrorism: Multilateral Responses to an Extraordnary Threat. *Coping with Crisis Working Paper Series* (International Peace Academy).

Saggerman, Marc. 2004. Jihadi Networks of Terror. In von Knopp, Katherina, Neisser, Heinrich, and van Creveld, Martin (Eds). *Countering Modern Terrorism. History, Current Issues and Future Threats*. Bielefeld: W. Bertelsmann Verlag.

Saul, Ben. 2006. The Legal Response of the League of Nations to Terrorism. 4 *Journal of International Criminal Justice* 78.

Saul, Ben. 2007. The Curious Element of Motive in Definitions of Terrorism: Essential Ingredient or Crimialising Thought? In Lynch, Andrew, MacDonald, Edwina, and Williams, George (Eds). *Law and Liberty in the War on Terror*. Sydney: The Federation Press.

Scheinin, Martin. 2006. (Il)legalità internazionale. 1 *Intelligence* 28.

Schmid, Alex. 2004. Terrorism – The Definitional Problem. 36 *Case Western Reserve Journal of International Law* 375.

Schmidt, Ale, and Jongman, AI, et al. 1988. *Political Terrorism*. Amsterdam: Transaction Books.

Shahar, Yael. 2002. Al-Qaida's Asian Web. Papers of the International Policy Institute on Counter-Terrorism, online: http://www.ict.org.il.

Shay, Shaul. 2002. *The Endless Jihad... The Mujahadin, the Taliban and Bin Laden*. Herzlyia: The International Policy Institute for Counter-Terrorism.

Stephens, Tim. 2004. International Criminal Law and the Response to International Terrorism. 27 (2) *University of New South Wales Law Journal* 454.

Wuthnow, Robert (ed). 1998. *Encyclopedia of Politics and Religion*. Washington: Congressional Quarterly Inc.

Chapter 3
The International Framework for Countering Terrorism

Chapter 2 considered the phenomenon of terrorism, having regard to popular and political perceptions of terrorist conduct, and the challenges facing the adoption by the international community of a universal, concise and comprehensive legal definition of the term. This chapter moves on to explore the international framework for the suppression of terrorism. The two principal sources of public international law are international conventions (treaties) and customary international law.[1] The legal framework in the fight against international terrorism is almost entirely limited to international treaties and the binding and non-binding mechanisms that flow from these, including United Nations action under the Charter of the United Nations.[2] There is some, albeit limited, overlap between treaty and customary law on the subject. The question of regional and other multilateral initiatives for countering terrorism is also considered briefly within this chapter.

3.1 International Conventions Relating to Terrorism

Following the September 11 attacks, the United Nations was quick to defend its position on counter-terrorism, stating that it has long been active in the fight against international terrorism.[3] This is correct, since the organisation has, from as early as 1963, been a catalyst for the creation of a number of agreements providing the basic legal means to counter international terrorism, from the seizure of aircraft to the financing of terrorism.

The phenomenon of terrorism became an international concern in the 1960s when a series of aircraft hijackings hit the headlines. When the 1972 Munich Olympic Games were later disrupted by the kidnapping of Israeli athletes by

---

[1] Statute of the International Court of Justice 1948, article 38(1)(a) and (b).
[2] Charter of the United Nations 1945.
[3] UN Press Release, 19 September 2001.

A. Conte, *Human Rights in the Prevention and Punishment of Terrorism*,
DOI 10.1007/978-3-642-11608-7_3, © Springer-Verlag Berlin Heidelberg 2010

a Palestinian group, the then UN Secretary-General, Kurt Waldheim, asked that the issue be placed on the General Assembly's agenda. In the heated debate that followed, the Assembly assigned the issue to its Sixth (Legal) Committee, which subsequently proposed several conventions on terrorism.

There are now 13 conventions and protocols related to terrorism, all of which have entered into force. Those conventions and protocols are identified by the United Nations Counter-Terrorism Committee and Terrorism Prevention Branch as the principal international counter-terrorist treaties. If one were to take a more comprehensive approach, a considerably greater list of international treaties would be listed.[4] In its first report to the Security Council Counter-Terrorism Committee, for example, New Zealand referred to other treaties as relevant to its fight against international terrorism, including the United Nations Convention against Transnational Organized Crime and its two Protocols against the Smuggling of Migrants and Trafficking in Persons.[5] For the purpose of this text, however, consideration will be confined to the 13 universal instruments identified by the Terrorism Prevention Branch, these being commonly identified as the principal terrorism-related conventions which are open to ratification or accession by all States.[6]

---

[4]Including, by way of illustration, the Convention on the Safety of United Nations and Associated Personnel (opened for signature 9 December 1994, 2051 UNTS 391, entered into force 15 January 1999), the Convention for the Reciprocal Recognition of Proof Marks on Small Arms (opened for signature 1 July 1969, 795 UNTS 248, entered into force 3 July 1971), the Convention on the Prohibition of the Development, Production and Stockpiling of Bacteriological (Biological) and Toxin Weapons and on their Destruction (opened for signature 10 April 1972, 1015 UNTS 168, entered into force 26 March 1975), Convention on the Non-Proliferation of Nuclear Weapons (opened for signature 1 July 1968, 729 UNTS 169, entered into force 5 March 1970), and the Convention on the Prohibition of the Development, Production, Stockpiling and Use of Chemical Weapons and on Their Destruction (opened for signature 13 January 1993, CD/CW/WP.400/Rev.1, entered into force 29 April 1997). The Terrorism Prevention Branch had itself identified a list of factors that require action in the elimination of terrorism. The list of factors alone ran to seven pages, as once available online: "Classification of Counter-Terrorism Measures", online: http://www.odccp.org/terrorism_measures.html (as accessed 2 June 2002; copy on file with author). The United Nations' publication, International Instruments related to the Prevention and Suppression of International Terrorism (New York, 2001) also lists the four Geneva Conventions of 1949 and its two Additional Protocols of 1977: pp. iv–v.

[5]Report to the Counter-Terrorism Committee pursuant to paragraph 6 of Security Council resolution 1373 (2001) of 28 September 2001, New Zealand, UN Doc S/2001/1269, 4.

[6]See the United Nations list of "International Instruments to Counter Terrorism", online: http://untreaty.un.org/English/Terrorism.asp. Note also that the Security Council's Counter-Terrorism Committee (see Sect. 3.2.4.1) now speaks of 16 conventions relating to terrorism, being the 13 conventions identified at Sect. 3.1.1 herein, plus three amending documents: Amendments to the Convention on the Physical Protection of Nuclear Material, opened for signature 8 July 2005 (subject to ratification and not yet entered into force); Protocol to the Convention for the Suppression of Unlawful Acts against the Safety of Maritime Navigation, opened for signature 14 October 2005 (subject to ratification and not yet entered into force); and Protocol to the Protocol for the Suppression of Unlawful Acts against the Safety of Fixed Platforms Located on the Continental Shelf, opened for signature 14 October 2005 (subject to ratification and not yet entered into force). See also Greenwood (2002, p. 301).

3.1.1 Extant Conventions Related to Terrorism

The current terrorism-related conventions are directed at the protection of potential terrorist targets, or concern themselves with the means through which terrorist organisations operate. They do three main things: they require States parties to criminalise certain conduct; they provide for the prosecution or extradition of perpetrators of such acts; and they impose obligations upon States to suppress the conduct in question.[7] Three potential target groups are identified within the 13 conventions: civil aviation (the Tokyo, Hague and Montreal Conventions and the Montreal Protocol); operations at sea (the Rome Convention and Rome Protocol); and persons (the Protected Persons Convention and the Hostages Convention). Four means through which terrorist acts might be executed or facilitated are the subject matter of the remaining conventions: the Plastic Explosives and Nuclear Materials Conventions, and the Suppression of Bombing, Suppression of Financing, and Suppression of Nuclear Acts of Terrorism Conventions.

3.1.1.1 Protection of Potential Targets: Conventions Relating to Civil Aviation

The first universal terrorism-related convention, adopted in 1963, was the Convention on Offences and Certain Other Acts Committed on Board Aircraft (the Tokyo Convention).[8] The Tokyo Convention applies to acts affecting in-flight safety. It authorises an aircraft commander to impose reasonable measures, including restraint, on any person he or she believes has committed or is about to commit an act affecting in-flight safety, when necessary to protect the safety of the aircraft. It also requires contracting States to take custody of offenders and to return control of the aircraft to the lawful commander.

The Tokyo Convention was shortly followed by two further conventions concerned with air safety. The Convention for the Suppression of Unlawful Seizure of Aircraft (the Hague Convention)[9] makes it an offence for any person on board an aircraft in flight to "unlawfully, by force or threat thereof, or any other form of intimidation, seize or exercise control of that aircraft" or to attempt to do so. Parties to the Hague Convention are required to make hijackings punishable by severe

---

[7]Contrast this with the requirements of the Convention on the Marking of Plastic Explosives, discussed further within this part of the chapter.

[8]Convention on Offences and Certain Other Acts Committed on Board Aircraft, opened for signature 14 September 1963, 704 UNTS 219 (entered into force 4 December 1969). There are currently 185 States parties to the Convention, online: http://www.un.org/sc/ctc/law.shtml (as accessed on 1 October 2009).

[9]Convention for the Suppression of Unlawful Seizure of Aircraft, opened for signature 16 December 1970, 860 UNTS 105 (entered into force 14 October 1971). There are currently 184 States parties to the Convention, online: http://www.un.org/sc/ctc/law.shtml (as accessed on 1 October 2009).

penalties. The Convention also requires parties that have custody of offenders to either extradite the offender or submit the case for prosecution, as well as to assist each other in connection with criminal proceedings brought under the Convention. The Convention for the Suppression of Unlawful Acts Against the Safety of Civil Aviation (the Montreal Convention)[10] makes it an offence for any person unlawfully and intentionally to perform an act of violence against a person on board an aircraft in flight, if that act is likely to endanger the safety of that aircraft; to place an explosive device on an aircraft; and to attempt such acts or be an accomplice of a person who performs or attempts to perform such acts. As with the Hague Convention, the Montreal Convention requires parties to make offences punishable by severe penalties and again requires parties that have custody of offenders to either extradite the offender or submit the case for prosecution.

The Protocol on the Suppression of Unlawful Acts of Violence at Airports Serving International Civil Aviation (the Montreal Protocol), adopted in 1988, was a further addition to air-safety-related counter-terrorist conventions.[11] The Protocol extends the provisions of the Montreal Convention of 1971 to encompass terrorist acts at airports servicing international civil aviation.

3.1.1.2 Protection of Potential Targets: Conventions Relating to Operations at Sea

The Convention for the Suppression of Unlawful Acts against the Safety of Maritime Navigation (the Rome Convention) was adopted in 1988.[12] The Rome Convention establishes a legal regime applicable to international maritime navigation that is similar to the regimes established concerning international aviation. More specifically, it makes it an offence for a person unlawfully and intentionally to seize or exercise control over a ship by force, threat, or intimidation; to perform an act of violence against a person on board a ship if that act is likely to endanger the safe navigation of the ship; to place a destructive device or substance aboard a ship; and other acts against the safety of ships. As an optional protocol to the latter

---

[10]Convention for the Suppression of Unlawful Acts Against the Safety of Civil Aviation, opened for signature 23 September 1971, 974 UNTS 177 (entered into force 26 January 1973). There are currently 187 States parties to the Convention, online: http://www.un.org/sc/ctc/law.shtml (as accessed on 1 October 2009).

[11]Protocol on the Suppression of Unlawful Acts of Violence at Airports Serving International Civil Aviation, opened for signature 24 February 1988, ICAO Doc 9518 (entered into force 6 August 1989). There are currently 168 States parties to the Protocol, online: http://www.un.org/sc/ctc/law.shtml (as accessed on 1 October 2009).

[12]Convention for the Suppression of Unlawful Acts against the Safety of Maritime Navigation, opened for signature 10 March 1988, 1678 UNTS 221 (entered into force 1 March 1992). There are currently 154 States parties to the Convention, online: http://www.un.org/sc/ctc/law.shtml (as accessed on 1 October 2009).

Convention, the Protocol for the Suppression of Unlawful Acts against the Safety of Fixed Platforms Located on the Continental Shelf (the Rome Protocol) was also adopted in 1988,[13] at the same time as its parent Convention. Again by way of extension, the Protocol establishes a legal regime applicable to fixed platforms on the continental shelf (similar to the regimes established with regard to international airports).

3.1.1.3 Protection of Potential Targets: Conventions Relating to the Safety of Persons

Continuing with conventions relating to the protection of potential targets, the second set of treaties relate – broadly speaking – to the safety of persons. In 1973, the Convention on the Prevention and Punishment of Crimes against International Protected Persons, including Diplomatic Agents (the Protected Persons Convention) was adopted.[14] Internationally protected persons are defined as a Head of State, a Minister for Foreign Affairs, and representatives or officials of a State or of an international organisation who are entitled to special protection from attack under international law (these people being popular terrorist targets). The Convention requires each State party to criminalise and make punishable by appropriate penalties which take into account their grave nature, the intentional murder, kidnapping, or other attack upon the person or liberty of an internationally protected person; a violent attack upon the official premises, the private accommodations, or the means of transport of such person; a threat or attempt to commit such an attack; and an act constituting participation as an accomplice.

Also within the theme of protecting persons, the International Convention against the Taking of Hostages (the Hostages Convention)[15] states that "any person who seizes or detains and threatens to kill, to injure, or to continue to detain another person in order to compel a. . . State, an international intergovernmental organisation, a natural or juridical person, or a group of persons, to do or abstain from doing any act as an explicit or implicit condition for the release of the hostage" commits the offence of taking of hostage within the meaning of this Convention.

---

[13]Protocol for the Suppression of Unlawful Acts against the Safety of Fixed Platforms Located on the Continental Shelf, opened for signature 10 March 1988, 1678 UNTS 304 (entered into force 1 March 1992). There are currently 143 States parties to the Protocol, online: http://www.un.org/sc/ctc/law.shtml (as accessed on 1 October 2009).

[14]Convention on the Prevention and Punishment of Crimes against International Protected Persons, including Diplomatic Agents, opened for signature 14 December 1973, 1035 UNTS 167 (entered into force 20 February 1977). There are currently 172 States parties to the Convention, online: http://www.un.org/sc/ctc/law.shtml (as accessed on 1 October 2009).

[15]International Convention against the Taking of Hostages, opened for signature 18 December 1979, 1316 UNTS 205 (entered into force 3 June 1983). There are currently 167 States parties to the Convention, online: http://www.un.org/sc/ctc/law.shtml (as accessed on 1 October 2009).

3.1.1.4 Conventions Relating to the Suppression of the Means by Which Terrorist Acts Might Be Perpetrated or Facilitated

The remaining five treaties concerning the suppression of international terrorism relate to four particular means by which terrorist acts might be perpetrated or facilitated: nuclear materials, plastic explosives, bombings, and the financing of terrorism.

Relevant to the suppression of nuclear terrorism are two conventions. The first is the Convention on the Physical Protection of Nuclear Material (the Nuclear Materials Convention).[16] This criminalises the unlawful possession, use or transfer of nuclear material, the theft of nuclear material, and threats to use nuclear material (to cause death or serious injury to any person or substantial property damage). Adding to the Nuclear Materials Convention is the International Convention for the Suppression of Acts of Nuclear Terrorism (the Nuclear Terrorism Convention), which is the most recent of the 13 conventions and entered into force in July 2007.[17] The Nuclear Terrorism Convention prohibits the possession or use of nuclear materials or devices for the intention of death, injury or substantial damage to property or the environment for the purpose of compelling a person, State or organisation to do or abstain from doing any thing. It sets out obligations of States parties concerning the seizure of materials and devices and the prosecution or extradition of persons acting in breach of the offences established by the Convention. Relevant to the suppression of acts of nuclear terrorism, and of the means by which weapons of mass destruction might be accessed by terrorists, is the Proliferation Security Initiative (see Sect. 3.4.2 below).

Within the jurisdiction of the Secretary-General of the International Civil Aviation Organisation, is the Convention on the Marking of Plastic Explosives for the Purpose of Detection (the Plastic Explosives Convention).[18] This is designed to control and limit the use of unmarked and undetectable plastic explosives (negotiated in the aftermath of the 1988 Pan Am 103 bombing). Parties are obligated in their respective territories to ensure effective control over "unmarked" plastic explosives, i.e. those that do not contain one of the detection agents

---

[16]Convention on the Physical Protection of Nuclear Material, opened for signature 3 March 1980, 1456 UNTS 124 (entered into force 8 February 1987). There are currently 141 States parties to the Convention, online: http://www.un.org/sc/ctc/law.shtml (as accessed on 1 October 2009).

[17]International Convention for the Suppression of Acts of Nuclear Terrorism, adopted by the General Assembly and opened for signature on 15 April 2005 under GA Res 59/290, UN GAOR, 59th Sess, 91st Plen Mtg, UN Doc A/Res/59/290 (2005) and entered into force 7 July 2007. There are currently 54 States parties to the Convention, online: http://www.un.org/sc/ctc/law.shtml (as accessed on 1 October 2009).

[18]Convention on the Marking of Plastic Explosives for the Purpose of Detection, opened for signature 1 March 1991, ICAO Doc 9571 (entered into force 21 June 1998). There are currently 141 States parties to the Convention, online: http://www.un.org/sc/ctc/law.shtml (as accessed on 1 October 2009).

described in the Technical Annex to the treaty. Each party must, among other things: take necessary and effective measures to prohibit and prevent the manufacture of unmarked plastic explosives; prevent the movement of unmarked plastic explosives into or out of its territory; ensure that all stocks of such unmarked explosives not held by the military or police are destroyed or consumed, marked, or rendered permanently ineffective within three years; take necessary measures to ensure that unmarked plastic explosives held by the military or police are destroyed or consumed, marked, or rendered permanently ineffective within 15 years; and ensure the destruction, as soon as possible, of any unmarked explosives manufactured after the date of entry into force of the Convention for that State. The Plastic Explosives Convention differs from the other 12 terrorism-related conventions to the extent that it places these obligations upon States parties, without requiring the creation of offences, or setting out corresponding extradition, prosecution, or legal assistance responsibilities.

More recent in time is the International Convention for the Suppression of Terrorist Bombing (the Suppression of Bombing Convention).[19] As the name suggests, this creates a regime of universal jurisdiction over the unlawful and intentional use of explosives and other lethal devices in, into, or against various public places with intent to kill or cause serious bodily injury, or with intent to cause extensive destruction in a public place.

Finally, there is the International Convention for the Suppression of the Financing of Terrorism (the Suppression of Financing Convention).[20] Of the 13 conventions, this is possibly the most important, and controversial. It requires parties to take steps to prevent and counteract the financing of terrorists, whether direct or indirect, through groups claiming to have charitable, social or cultural goals or which also engage in such illicit activities as drug trafficking or gun running. It commits States to hold those who finance terrorism criminally, civilly or administratively liable for such acts and provides for the identification, freezing and seizure of funds allocated for terrorist activities, as well as for the sharing of the forfeited funds with other States on a case-by-case basis. Bank secrecy is no longer a justification for refusing to cooperate under the treaty.

The suppression of terrorist financing is a key feature of international counter-terrorism, and is a vital part of the work of the UN Counter-Terrorism Committee and Al-Qa'ida Sanctions Committee (see Sect. 3.2.4 below). It is a matter of concern within much of the Security Council's resolution 1373 (2001), and of the

---

[19]International Convention for the Suppression of Terrorist Bombing, opened for signature 12 January 1998, 2149 UNTS 286 (entered into force 23 May 2001). There are currently 162 States parties to the Convention, online: http://www.un.org/sc/ctc/law.shtml (as accessed on 1 October 2009).

[20]International Convention for the Suppression of the Financing of Terrorism, opened for signature 10 January 2000, 2179 UNTS 232 (entered into force 10 April 1992). There are currently 169 States parties to the Convention, online: http://www.un.org/sc/ctc/law.shtml (as accessed on 1 October 2009).

Financial Action Task Force's Special Recommendations on Terrorist Financing, as is considered below in Sect. 3.4.1.[21]

3.1.1.5 Offences Under the Universal Terrorism-Related Conventions

The terrorism-related conventions identified require the establishment of a number of offences, each of which are set out in Appendix 3, Table 1. The creation of these offences within each of the Commonwealth cases study countries is considered in Chaps. 5–8 (which provide an overview of the counter-terrorism laws of each country), and Chap. 14 (which looks at the question of the criminalisation of terrorism, having regard to rule of law and human rights standards).

3.1.2 Draft Comprehensive Convention on International Terrorism

Almost one year prior to the September 11 attacks, India had proposed that there be a comprehensive convention against terrorism, and there is much merit in this. Former UN Secretary-General, Kofi Annan, had called for an extensive coalition to combat terrorism and had predicted that such a campaign would be a long one and must involve all countries. Shortly after September 11, he followed in the steps of the Indian proposal and indicated that the General Assembly would take steps to complete a comprehensive anti-terrorism treaty encompassing all current conventions.[22]

As will be considered below (Sect. 3.2.1), the UN General Assembly adopted the Declaration on Measures to Eliminate International Terrorism in 1994.[23] At the end of 1996, it established an Ad Hoc Committee, known as the Ad Hoc Committee Established by General Assembly resolution 51/210 (1996).[24] The Committee was primarily tasked with work on conventions for the suppression of terrorist bombings and financing of terrorist operations and, thereafter, to address means of developing a comprehensive legal framework dealing with international

---

[21]Financial Action Task Force, FATF Special Recommendations on Terrorist Financing, 22 October 2004, online: http://www.oecd.org/dataoecd/8/17/34849466.pdf. See further: Radicati di Brozolo and Megliani (2004) and Pieth et al. (2009).

[22]United Nations Secretary-General's Report to the United Nations General Assembly, 56th General Assembly Meeting, GA/9914, 24 September 2001. For a more detailed discussion of the Draft Comprehensive Convention, see Andreu-Guzmán (2002, pp. 202–210).

[23]Declaration on Measures to Eliminate International Terrorism, adopted under GA Res 49/60, UN GAOR, 49th Sess, 84th Plen Mtg, UN Doc A/Res/49/60 (1994).

[24]Established under GA Res 51/210, UN GAOR, 51st Sess, 88th Plen Mtg, UN Doc A/Res/51/210 (1996).

terrorism.[25] India's Draft Comprehensive Convention on International Terrorism was subsequently referred to the Ad Hoc Committee. As yet, the Convention has not been finalised and is likely to be some time away, if it is ever to become a reality. Due to the lack of unanimity on key issues, the Committee has concluded that finalising a comprehensive international treaty on terrorism will depend primarily on agreement as to who would be entitled to exclusion from the treaty's scope, and on what grounds.[26] Otherwise, the majority of the 27 articles of the Draft Convention have been preliminarily agreed upon by the Committee. The General Assembly nonetheless continues to press for completion of work on the Comprehensive Convention.[27]

3.2 United Nations Action

Beyond the work of the Sixth (Legal) Committee of the UN General Assembly in working towards the various counter-terrorism conventions discussed, the General Assembly, Security Council and UN Secretariat have been working in concert on the issue of counter-terrorism. UN action on counter-terrorism arises as a functional aspect of the operation of the Charter of the United Nations. There are a number of agencies involved in the UN's programme of work on terrorism-related matters, with sometimes overlapping mandates. The problems associated with such a system mainly concern coordination, which is a matter sought to be addressed by the UN Counter-Terrorism Implementation Task Force (CTITF, see Sect. 3.2.5 below). The CTITF has compiled a useful Online Handbook that contains information on the counter-terrorism activities of its member entities and also provides information on and access to counter-terrorism resources available through the UN system.[28]

3.2.1 Resolutions of the General Assembly

The General Assembly has adopted a series of resolutions concerning terrorism since December 1972, following the kidnapping of Israeli athletes during the Munich Olympic Games. These resolutions take two forms: those relating to measures to eliminate international terrorism; and those, beginning in 1993, concerning the relationship between terrorism, counter-terrorism and human rights.

---

[25]Ibid, para 9.

[26]Draft Comprehensive Convention, article 18. See further (infra) at Sect. 3.2.4.

[27]See: GA Res 61/40, UN GAOR, 61st Sess, 64th Plen Mtg, UN Doc A/Res/61/40 (2007), para 22; GA Res 62/71, UN GAOR, 62nd Sess, 62nd Plen Mtg, UN Doc A/Res/62/71 (2008), para 21; and GA Res 63/129, UN GAOR, 63rd Sess, 61st Plen Mtg, UN Doc A/Res/63/129 (2009), paras 21–22.

[28]UN Counter-Terrorism Online Handbook, online: http://www.un.org/terrorism/cthandbook.

The latter set of resolutions will be considered within Chaps. 12 and 13, which address the interface between terrorism, counter-terrorism and human rights. What follows here is consideration of General Assembly resolutions concerning the suppression of terrorism.

The first resolution of the General Assembly concerning itself solely with the issue of terrorism, resolution 3034 (XXVII), was adopted on 18 December 1972.[29] Its title illustrates the early opinion that terrorism is a matter affecting security as well as the enjoyment of human rights: "Measures to prevent international terrorism which endangers or takes innocent lives or jeopardises fundamental freedoms, and study of the underlying causes of those forms of terrorism and acts of violence which lie in misery, frustration, grievance and despair and which cause some people to sacrifice lives, including their own, in an attempt to effect radical changes". The same title was used to name eight subsequent resolutions of the General Assembly, from 1976 to 1989.[30]

The last decade and a half has seen the Assembly adopt and affirm the Declaration on Measures to Eliminate International Terrorism, first adopted in early December 1994 under its resolution 49/60 (1994).[31] The Declaration was reaffirmed in the following two years, with a Declaration to Supplement the 1994 Declaration on Measures to Eliminate International Terrorism adopted in 1996.[32] Except for silence on the issue during the General Assembly's 53rd session in 1998, the Declaration and Supplement have since been reaffirmed on an annual basis.[33]

---

[29]GA Res 3034 (XXVII), UN GAOR, 27th Sess, 2114th Plen Mtg, UN Doc A/Res/XXVII/3034 (1972).

[30]GA Res 31/102, UN GAOR, 31st Sess, 99th Plen Mtg, UN Doc A/Res/31/102 (1976); GA Res 32/147, UN GAOR, 32nd Sess, 105th Plen Mtg, UN Doc A/Res/32/147 (1977); GA Res 34/145, UN GAOR, 34th Sess, 105th Plen Mtg, UN Doc A/Res/34/145 (1979); GA Res 36/109, UN GAOR, 36th Sess, 92nd Plen Mtg, UN Doc A/Res/36/109 (1981); GA Res 38/130, UN GAOR, 38th Sess, 101st Plen Mtg, UN Doc A/Res/38/130(1983); GA Res 40/61, UN GAOR, 40th Sess, 108th Plen Mtg, UN Doc A/Res/40/61 (1985); GA Res 42/159, UN GAOR, 42nd Sess, 94th Plen Mtg, UN Doc A/Res/42/159 (1987); and GA Res 44/29, UN GAOR, 44th Sess, 72nd Plen Mtg, UN Doc A/Res/44/29 (1989).

[31]Declaration on Measures to Eliminate International Terrorism (n 23).

[32]GA Res 51/210, UN GAOR, 51st Sess, 88th Plen Mtg, UN Doc A/Res/51/210 (1996) Annex.

[33]GA Res 52/165, UN GAOR, 52nd Sess, 72nd Plen Mtg, UN Doc A/Res/52/165 (1997) para 7; GA Res 54/110, UN GAOR, 54th Sess, 75th Plen Mtg, UN Doc A/Res/54/110 (1999) para 8; GA Res 55/158, UN GAOR, 55th Sess, 84th Plen Mtg, UN Doc A/Res/55/158 (2000) para 9; GA Res 56/88, UN GAOR, 56th Sess, 85th Plen Mtg, UN Doc A/Res/56/88 (2001) para 10; GA Res 57/27, UN GAOR, 57th Sess, 52nd Plen Mtg, UN Doc A/Res/57/27 (2002) para 10; GA Res 58/81, UN GAOR, 58th Sess, 72nd Plen Mtg, UN Doc A/Res/58/81 (2003) para 10; GA Res 59/46, UN GAOR, 59th Sess, 65th Plen Mtg, UN Doc A/Res/59/46 (2004) para 12; GA Res 60/43, UN GAOR, 60th Sess, 61st Plen Mtg, UN Doc A/Res/60/43 (2005) para 13; GA Res 60/288, UN GAOR, 60th Sess, 99th Plen Mtg, UN Doc A/Res/60/288 (2006), preambular para 3; GA Res 61/40 (n 27) para 15; GA Res 62/71 (n 27) para 15; and GA Res 63/129 (n 27), para 15.

The 1994 Declaration was based on the notion of peace and security and the principle of refraining from the threat or use of force in international relations.[34] It pronounces that terrorism constitutes a grave violation of the purpose and principles of the United Nations.[35] While it does not purport to define terrorism, it does say that criminal acts intended or calculated to provoke a state of terror in the general public for political purposes are unjustifiable in any circumstances.[36] The Declaration urged all States to consider, as a matter of priority, becoming party to the conventions on terrorism adopted up to that time.[37]

The Declaration calls on States to refrain from organising, instigating, assisting or participating in terrorist acts, and from acquiescing in or encouraging activities within their territories directed towards the commission of such acts.[38] It directs that, in order to do so, States must refrain from facilitating terrorist activities. Paragraph 5(a) of the 1994 Declaration appears to indicate that a State must be proactive in doing so, urging States to take appropriate practical measures to ensure that their territory is not used for terrorist installations or training camps, or for the preparation or organisation of terrorist acts. Paragraph 5(b) then refers to the need to apprehend and prosecute or extradite perpetrators of terrorist acts.

The practical observation to make at this point is that, although compelling and strongly worded, this is a declaration adopted and reaffirmed under resolutions of the General Assembly and therefore does not have the same weight as a convention, nor does it have signatories that are bound by its content. Indeed, article 10 of the UN Charter specifically provides that resolutions and declarations of the United Nations General Assembly are recommendatory only:

> Article 10
> The General Assembly may discuss any questions or any matters within the scope of the present Charter or relating to the powers and functions of any organs provided for in the present Charter, and, except as provided in Article 12, may make recommendations to the Members of the United Nations or to the Security Council or to both on any such questions or matters.

It is clear through reading minutes of General Assembly meetings immediately following September 11 that there were calls for the United Nations to engage its full potential to identify and attempt to eradicate the roots of terrorism.[39] India's representative pointed out that integral to the efforts to end terrorism and prevent armed conflict is the need to deny to the perpetrators of such conduct access to arms

---

[34]Declaration on Measures to Eliminate International Terrorism (n 23), as is evident through its preamble.

[35]Ibid, para 2.

[36]Ibid, para 1.

[37]Ibid, para 6.

[38]Ibid, para 4.

[39]See, for example, Report of the Ad Hoc Committee Established by General Assembly Resolution 51/210 on a Draft Comprehensive Convention on International Terrorism, UN Doc A/AC.252/2002/CPR.1 and Add.1 (2002).

and ammunition.[40] Amongst various steps towards is the Programme of Action by the United Nations Conference on the Illicit Trade in Small Arms. Likewise, the General Assembly has given specific consideration to the issue of counter-terrorism within its very lengthy resolution on General and Complete Disarmament.[41] The General Assembly has urged all States to become parties to the Suppression of Financing Convention, as well as to the Nuclear Terrorism Convention.[42] An issue gaining increased international attention is that of preventing the acquisition by terrorists of radioactive materials and sources, leading to resolutions on the subject,[43] as well as multilateral cooperation outside the UN framework (the latter of which is discussed below in Sect. 3.4).

The General Assembly has also issued resolutions in 2003 and 2008 concerned with strengthening international cooperation and technical assistance in promoting the implementation of the terrorism conventions and protocols within the framework of the activities of the UN Office on Drugs and Crime.[44] The most significant of the General Assembly's recent action on counter-terrorism, however, is its adoption in September 2006 of the United Nations Global Counter-Terrorism Strategy, discussed in Sect. 3.2.5 below

3.2.2   Resolutions of the Security Council

Just as the General Assembly has been long-acting in its consideration of and work against international terrorism, the UN Security Council (UNSC) has also considered the issue for some time. The spate of aircraft hijackings during the 1960s in fact saw the Council be the first UN body to take action in response to terrorist

---

[40]United Nations Press Release, "Poverty Reduction, Terrorism, Disarmament, Humanitarian Relief Discussed as General Assembly Continues Review of Secretary-General Report", from the 56th General Assembly Plenary Meeting, 25 September 2001, statement of Kamalesh Sharma, United Nations General Assembly representative for India.

[41]General and Complete Disarmament, GA Res 56/24, UN GAOR, 56th Sess, 68th Plen Mtg, UN Doc A/Res/56/24 (2001) – see Part T "Multilateral Cooperation in the Area of Disarmament and Non-Proliferation and Global Efforts Against Terrorism".

[42]Concerning the Financing of Terrorism Convention, see GA Res 54/109, UN GAOR, 54th Sess, 76th Plen Mtg, UN Doc A/Res/54/109 (1999). Concerning the Nuclear Terrorism Convention, see GA Res 60/78, UN GAOR, 60th Sess, 61st Plen Mtg, UN Doc A/Res/60/78 (2005), para 2; GA Res 61/86, UN GAOR 61st Sess, 67th Plen Mtg, UN Doc A/Res/61/86 (2006), para 2; GA Res 62/33, UN GAOR, 62nd Sess, 61st Plen Mtg, UN Doc A/Res/62/33 (2007), para 2; and GA Res 62/46, UN GAOR, 62nd Sess, 61st Plen Mtg, UN Doc A/Res/62/46 (2007), para 4.

[43]GA Res 62/46 (ibid).

[44]Strengthening international cooperation and technical assistance in promoting the implementation of the universal conventions and protocols related to terrorism within the framework of the activities of the Centre for International Crime Prevention, adopted under GA Res 58/136, UN GAOR, 58th Sess, 77th Plen Mtg, UN Doc A/Res/58/136 (2003). See also GA Res 62/172, UN GAOR, 62nd Sess, 77th Plen Mtg, UN Doc A/Res/62/172 (2007).

conduct, calling on States to take all possible measures to prevent further hijackings or interference with international civil air travel.[45] The crash of Pan Am 103 in 1988, following its in-flight bombing, subsequently led to contentious resolutions by the UNSC. The tragic events of 11 September 2001 resulted in resolutions which are now central to international counter-terrorist efforts, but which are also controversial.

3.2.2.1 Resolutions Concerning Pan Am 103

On 21 December 1988, Pan Am flight 103 from London to New York was destroyed over Lockerbie, Scotland. In November 1991, the Lord Advocate for Scotland brought charges against two Libyan nationals suspected of having caused a bomb to be placed on board the aircraft, the explosion of which caused the aircraft to crash. Relying on the Montreal Convention discussed above (Sect. 3.1.1.1), a number of States whose nationals had been killed in the incident requested that Libya surrender the suspects for prosecution. Invoking the *aud dedere aut judicare* principle (contained in article 7 of the Montreal Convention), the Libyan Arab Jamahiriya refused to extradite its nationals, claiming that it had investigated the allegation and that its authorities had determined that there was no case to answer. Libya thus took the position that it had complied with article 7 of the Montreal Convention.

The Security Council subsequently issued resolutions 731 (1992), 748 (1992) and 883 (1993), in which it demanded that the Libyan Government surrender the suspects or render a full and effective response to the requests for extradition, and issued non-military sanctions against Libya.[46] In two identical claims before the International Court of Justice, one against the United Kingdom and the other against the United States, Libya argued that the Montreal Convention was applicable to the dispute and that, having fully complied with its obligations under the Convention, Libya was not bound by the Security Council resolutions in question since they sought to reverse the legal effect of the Convention.[47] In these *Lockerbie Cases*, the US and UK objected to the Court's jurisdiction, contending (in part) that Security Council resolutions 748 and 883 (which had been adopted after Libya issued proceedings before the ICJ) created legal obligations upon Libya that rendered Libya's claim redundant, so that the ICJ could not proceed to a judgment on the merits. Their argument was based on the premise that: (1) Libya was obligated to comply with the resolutions by virtue of article 25 of the UN Charter;

---

[45]See, for example, SC Res 286, UN SCOR, 1552nd Mtg, UN Doc S/Res/286 (1970).

[46]SC Res 731, UN SCOR, 3033rd Mtg, UN Doc S/Res/731 (1992), para 3; SC Res 748, UN SCOR, 3063rd Mtg, UN Doc S/Res/748 (1992), para 1; and SC Res 883, UN SCOR, 3312nd Mtg, UN Doc S/Res/883 (1993), para 1.

[47]*Case Concerning Questions of Interpretation and Application of the 1971 Montreal Convention Arising from the Aerial Incident at Lockerbie (Libyan Arab Jamahiriya v United Kingdom and Libyan Arab Jamahiriya v United States of America), Jurisdiction* (1998) ICJ Rep.

and (2) in assessing any conflict between Libya's article 25 Charter obligations and the Montreal Convention, article 103 of the Charter dictated that the Charter obligations were to prevail:[48]

> Article 25
> The Members of the United Nations agree to accept and carry out the decisions of the Security Council in accordance with the present Charter.
>
> Article 103
> In the event of a conflict between the obligations of the Members of the United Nations under the present Charter and their obligations under any other international agreement, their obligations under the present Charter shall prevail.

By twelve votes to four, the Court rejected the objection to admissibility. Ultimately, however, the *Lockerbie Cases* were removed from the Court's list at the joint request of the parties and a decision on the merits has therefore not been made.[49] The cases raise important issues about the status and role of Security Council resolutions, discussed further below (Sect. 3.2.3).

3.2.2.2   Resolution 1267 (1999)

Strongly condemning the use of Afghan territory by the Taliban for the sheltering and training of terrorists and planning of terrorist acts, the Security Council imposed a number of sanctions against the Taliban under resolution 1267 (1999).[50] The Security Council was particularly critical of the Taliban's continued provision of "safe haven to Usama bin Laden and to allow him and others associated with him to operate a network of terrorist training camps from Taliban-controlled territory and to use Afghanistan as a base from which to sponsor international terrorist operations".[51] Security Council resolution 1267 demanded that the Taliban cease providing sanctuary to terrorists and take measures to ensure that the territory under its control would not be used for such purposes (para 1), and turn over Usama bin Laden to authorities in response to the indictment against him concerning the 1998 bombings of US embassies in Nairobi, Kenya, and Dar es Salaam, Tanzania and for conspiracy to kill American nationals outside the United States (para 2).

Resolution 1267 established the Al-Qa'ida and Taliban Sanctions Committee (1267 Committee – see Sect. 3.2.4.2).[52] It required members of the United Nations to impose a travel ban on aircraft owned, leased or operated by or on behalf of the Taliban (para 4(a)) and to freeze funds and other financial resources controlled by

---

[48]Ibid, paras 37 and 41.

[49]International Court of Justice, "Cases Removed from the Court's List at the Joint Request of the Parties", Press Release 2003/29 (10 September 2003).

[50]SC Res 1267, UN SCOR, 4051st Mtg, UN Doc S/Res/1267 (1999).

[51]Ibid, preambular paras 6–7.

[52]Ibid, para 6.

or on behalf of the Taliban or any other individuals of entities designated by the 1267 Committee (para 4(b)). The resolution also required States to bring proceedings against persons within their jurisdiction who violated the sanctions under paragraph 4 (see Appendix 3, Table 1(E)).

3.2.2.3 Resolution 1373 (2001)

On the day after the September 11 attacks, the Security Council adopted resolution 1368 (2001), through which it unequivocally condemned the terrorist attacks and expressed that it regarded them as a threat to international peace and security.[53] It called on all States to urgently work together to bring to justice the perpetrators, organisers and sponsors of the terrorist attacks.[54] Security Council resolution 1373 (2001) was adopted later that month, through which the SC determined that all States were to prevent and suppress the financing of terrorist acts, including the criminalisation of such financing and the freezing of funds and financial assets.[55] Described as one of the most strongly worded resolutions in the history of the Security Council,[56] it also requires countries to cooperate on extradition matters and the sharing of information about terrorist networks.[57]

Interestingly, the only resolution of the Security Council prior to September 11 dealing with terrorism in the international context, rather than relating to and restricted to specific events, is its resolution 1189 of 1998. Although that resolution was adopted in response to the 1998 bombings in Nairobi, Kenya and Tanzania, it called upon all States "to adopt, in accordance with international law and as a matter of priority, effective and practical measures for security cooperation, for the prevention of such acts of terrorism, and for the prosecution and punishment of their perpetrators".[58]

Resolution 1373 (2001) does two main things. The resolution sets out a number of specific counter-terrorism obligations and recommendations. It also establishes a Counter-Terrorism Committee, with a regime by which States report to the Committee on steps taken to implement the resolution (discussed below, at Sect. 3.2.4.1). In the context of the counter-terrorism measures identified in resolution 1373, these comprise binding obligations under paragraphs 1 and 2, and recommendations (albeit strongly worded ones) under paragraph 3:

---

[53]SC Res 1368, UN SCOR, 4370th Mtg, UN Doc S/Res/1368 (2001).

[54]Ibid, para 3.

[55]SC Res 1373, UN SCOR, 4385th Mtg, UN Doc S/Res/1373 (2001).

[56]Rowe (2002). Richard Rowe at that time worked in the International Organisations and Legal Division of the Australian Department of Foreign Affairs and Trade. He was the Australian representative and Vice-Chairman of the Ad Hoc Committee Established by General Assembly Resolution 51/210 during its Sixth Session, which followed the September 11 attacks.

[57]SC Res 1373 (n 55) para 3.

[58]SC Res 1189, UN SCOR, 3915th Mtg, UN Doc S/Res/1189 (1998), para 5.

Acting under Chapter VII of the Charter of the United Nations,

1. *Decides* that all States shall:

    (a) Prevent and suppress the financing of terrorist acts;
    (b) Criminalize the wilful provision or collection, by any means, directly or indirectly, of funds by their nationals or in their territories with the intention that the funds should be used, or in the knowledge that they are to be used, in order to carry out terrorist acts;
    (c) Freeze without delay funds and other financial assets or economic resources of persons who commit, or attempt to commit, terrorist acts or participate in or facilitate the commission of terrorist acts; of entities owned or controlled directly or indirectly by such persons; and of persons and entities acting on behalf of, or at the direction of such persons and entities, including funds derived or generated from property owned or controlled directly or indirectly by such persons and associated persons and entities;
    (d) Prohibit their nationals or any persons and entities within their territories from making any funds, financial assets or economic resources or financial or other related services available, directly or indirectly, for the benefit of persons who commit or attempt to commit or facilitate or participate in the commission of terrorist acts, of entities owned or controlled, directly or indirectly, by such persons and of persons and entities acting on behalf of or at the direction of such persons;

2. *Decides also* that all States shall:

    (a) Refrain from providing any form of support, active or passive, to entities or persons involved in terrorist acts, including by suppressing recruitment of members of terrorist groups and eliminating the supply of weapons to terrorists;
    (b) Take the necessary steps to prevent the commission of terrorist acts, including by provision of early warning to other States by exchange of information;
    (c) Deny safe haven to those who finance, plan, support, or commit terrorist acts, or provide safe havens;
    (d) Prevent those who finance, plan, facilitate or commit terrorist acts from using their respective territories for those purposes against other States or their citizens;
    (e) Ensure that any person who participates in the financing, planning, preparation or perpetration of terrorist acts or in supporting terrorist acts is brought to justice and ensure that, in addition to any other measures against them, such terrorist acts are established as serious criminal offences in domestic laws and regulations and that the punishment duly reflects the seriousness of such terrorist acts;
    (f) Afford one another the greatest measure of assistance in connection with criminal investigations or criminal proceedings relating to the financing or support of terrorist acts, including assistance in obtaining evidence in their possession necessary for the proceedings;
    (g) Prevent the movement of terrorists or terrorist groups by effective border controls and controls on issuance of identity papers and travel documents, and through measures for preventing counterfeiting, forgery or fraudulent use of identity papers and travel documents;

3. *Calls* upon all States to:

    (a) Find ways of intensifying and accelerating the exchange of operational information, especially regarding actions or movements of terrorist persons or networks; forged or falsified travel documents; traffic in arms, explosives or sensitive materials; use of communications technologies by terrorist groups; and the threat posed by the possession of weapons of mass destruction by terrorist groups;

(b) Exchange information in accordance with international and domestic law and cooperate on administrative and judicial matters to prevent the commission of terrorist acts;

(c) Cooperate, particularly through bilateral and multilateral arrangements and agreements, to prevent and suppress terrorist attacks and take action against perpetrators of such acts;

(d) Become parties as soon as possible to the relevant international conventions and protocols relating to terrorism, including the International Convention for the Suppression of the Financing of Terrorism of 9 December 1999;

(e) Increase cooperation and fully implement the relevant international conventions and protocols relating to terrorism and Security Council resolutions 1269 (1999) and 1368 (2001);

(f) Take appropriate measures in conformity with the relevant provisions of national and international law, including international standards of human rights, before granting refugee status, for the purpose of ensuring that the asylum-seeker has not planned, facilitated or participated in the commission of terrorist acts;

(g) Ensure, in conformity with international law, that refugee status is not abused by the perpetrators, organizers or facilitators of terrorist acts, and that claims of political motivation are not recognized as grounds for refusing requests for the extradition of alleged terrorists;

This set of measures expands upon and significantly strengthens the Council's earlier resolution 1269 (1999).[59] While resolution 1269 considered steps to be taken by States to suppress terrorism, deny safe haven to terrorists and cooperate with others in the bringing to justice of perpetrators of terrorist conduct, this earlier resolution is much weaker than resolution 1373 (2001). First, the measures in paragraphs 1 and 2 of resolution 1373 are binding, whereas the earlier resolution used less forceful language *calling upon* States to take *appropriate steps* to achieve the stated objectives. As discussed below (Sect. 3.2.3), this difference in language is important since the content of Security resolutions, even those adopted under Chapter VII of the UN Charter, is not always binding. Furthermore, resolution 1373 transforms and expands upon two of the non-binding directions in resolution 1269. The first of those relates to the prevention and suppression of the financing of terrorism,[60] which became the subject of detailed attention within paragraphs 1 and 2 of resolution 1373 (2001). The second concerns the apprehension, prosecution or extradition of those who plan, finance or commit terrorist acts,[61] becoming the subject of attention within paragraph 2 of resolution 1373 (2001). Resolution 1373 (2001) thus takes a considerable step forward in the imposition of counter-terrorism obligations upon members of the United Nations, as well as setting out complementary recommendations.

It might be observed that, from a practical perspective, the use of mandatory language is problematic when one considers some of the specific instructions within paragraphs 1 and 2. Indeed, some instructions may not be possible to comply with, at least not in absolute terms. One might contrast, for example, paragraphs 2(d) and

---

[59] SC Res 1269, UN SCOR, 4053rd Mtg, UN Doc S/Res/1269 (1999).

[60] SC Res 1269 (n 59) para 4 (second unnumbered subparagraph).

[61] SC Res 1269 (n 59) para 4 (third unnumbered subparagraph).

2(f). Paragraph 2(f) requires UN member States to "afford one another the greatest measure of assistance" in the criminal investigation and prosecution of terrorists, while paragraph 2(d) requires States to "*prevent* those who finance, plan, facilitate or commit terrorist acts" from using their territories for those purposes (emphasis added). Measuring compliance with paragraph 2(f) is possible since this is a reactive activity (activity following a terrorist incident) and thus capable of being evaluated. This cannot be said in the case of compliance with paragraph 2(d), *prevention* of the financing, planning and commission of terrorist acts. All that can be done by a State is to undertake all reasonable or practicable steps to prevent such conduct, but a member State cannot ever truly guarantee that their territory *will not* be used for those purposes.

On the subject of compliance with resolution 1373 (2001), this is something monitored by the Security Council's Counter-Terrorism Committee. In June 2008, the Counter-Terrorism Committee reported to the Council and provided an assessment of the implementation of resolution 1373 in regions and sub-regions, drawing conclusions about progress in the implementation of the resolution in key thematic areas. The Committee, and its report, are considered below (Sect. 3.2.4.1). Its report, as it applies to the four case study countries, is considered in chapter 4 (Sect. 4.3).

3.2.2.4   Resolutions 1373 (2001) and 1456 (2003)

One further issue arises from the Security Council's resolution 1373 (2001) and its later resolution 1456 (2003).[62] Adopted in January 2003, resolution 1456 (2003) calls upon the Counter-Terrorism Committee to intensify its efforts to promote the implementation of resolution 1373 (2001).[63] It also contains the following provisions:

The Security Council therefore calls for the following steps to be taken:

1. All States must take urgent action to prevent and suppress all active and passive support to terrorism, and in particular comply fully with all relevant resolutions of the Security Council, in particular resolutions 1373 (2001), 1390 (2002) and 1455 (2003);
2. The Security Council calls upon States to:

    (a) become a party, as a matter of urgency, to all relevant international conventions and protocols relating to terrorism, in particular the 1999 international convention for the suppression of the financing of terrorism and to support all international initiatives taken to that aim, and to make full use of the sources of assistance and guidance which are now becoming available;
    (b) assist each other, to the maximum extent possible, in the prevention, investigation, prosecution and punishment of acts of terrorism, wherever they occur;
    (c) cooperate closely to implement fully the sanctions against terrorists and their associates, in particular Al-Qaeda and the Taliban and their associates, as reflected

---

[62]SC Res 1456, UN SCOR, 4688th Mtg, UN Doc S/Res/1456 (2003).

[63]Ibid, para 4.

in resolutions 1267 (1999), 1390 (2002) and 1455 (2003), to take urgent actions to deny them access to the financial resources they need to carry out their actions, and to cooperate fully with the Monitoring Group established pursuant to resolution 1363 (2001);

The content of paragraph 1 and paragraphs 2(b) and 2(c), by themselves, do not cause any particular concern. Indeed, they are entirely consistent with earlier resolutions of the Security Council. It is paragraph 2(a), building upon paragraph 3(d) of resolution 1373 (2001), that raises some issues about the proper role of the Security Council. By calling upon States to become party to all counter-terrorist conventions and protocols, the question to consider is whether the Security Council is over-stepping its function and impinging upon State sovereignty.

This is an interesting constitutional question that warrants at least some consideration within this chapter. On the one hand, member States of the United Nations have to some degree surrendered their sovereignty by becoming a party to the United Nations Charter, to the extent that they have agreed to be bound by decisions of the Security Council (considered below at Sect. 3.2.3). At the same time, however, it could hardly have been intended by those becoming party to the Charter to grant the Security Council the authority to direct members in their treaty-making decision processes. A considerable number of States have complex rules concerning the executive's treaty-making power, some of which must be complied with as a matter of constitutional law before a State can ratify or accede to a treaty (in the case of the Commonwealth case study countries, see Chap. 4, Sect. 4.2.2). The inherent basis of these rules is the protection of the balance of power within democratic States, and safeguarding against excesses by the executive branch. Is the Security Council, by issuing the directions contained in paragraph 3(d) of resolution 1373 (2001) and paragraph 2(a) of resolution 1456 (2003), able to override such domestic constitutional safeguards?

Much has been made of this issue, the answer to which appears to lie in one further enquiry: whether these provisions are binding within the terms of article 25 of the UN Charter.[64] There appear to be two bases upon which this second question can be answered. The first is to consider whether the resolution has been made within the mandate of the Security Council, since the various powers given to the Council, conferred under article 24 of the Charter, are conferred for the purpose of discharging its duties for the maintenance of international peace and security and for no other reason. Thus, if a resolution is not made for that purpose, the resolution would be made outside the authority of the Security Council and, arguably, could not then be binding upon member States. In the context of the resolutions at hand, the subject matter concerns the suppression of terrorism which, as repeatedly stated by both the Security Council and General Assembly, is seen as one of the most serious threats to peace and security. Also relevant is the fact that the principle of non-intervention by the UN and its organs in the sovereign affairs of its members does not apply, under article 2(7), to resolutions of the Security Council adopted

---

[64]See, for example, Szasz (2002, p. 901).

under Chapter VII of the Charter. Resolutions 1373 (2001) and 1456 (2003) were made, it is therefore concluded, within the proper authority of the Security Council.

The nature and consequence of the provisions at hand ultimately rests upon whether they are "decisions" within the meaning of article 25 of the Charter. In light of the discussion which follows concerning the status of Security Council decisions (Sect. 3.2.3), and given the fact that the chapeau to the paragraphs in question "calls upon" States to do what is then listed, the paragraphs do not represent "decisions" of the Security Council. They are therefore only recommendatory in nature.[65] Even so, it is worth noting the Security Council's preparedness, at least in the context of counter-terrorism, to adopt provisions affecting matters which might traditionally have been considered to be outside its purview.

The practical implications of this position are unclear when considering the Commonwealth case studies at hand. In the case of New Zealand, for example, it was (prior to 9/11) party to eight of the now 13 terrorism-related conventions, excluding the International Convention for the Suppression of Terrorist Bombing and the International Convention for the Suppression of the Financing of Terrorism.[66] New Zealand is now party to all 12 conventions and protocols which were open for signature and ratification at that time. Whether New Zealand would have ratified all outstanding conventions, even absent the provisions of resolutions 1373 (2001) and 1456 (2003), is moot – although its first report to the Counter-Terrorism Committee indicated that it had already intended to do so.[67]

3.2.2.5 Resolution 1624 (2005)

The next major Security Council resolution following resolution 1456 (2003) is a resolution dealing mainly with the prevention of incitement to terrorism, Security Council resolution 1624 (2005).[68] Resolution 1624 (2005) requires UN member States to report to the Counter-Terrorism Committee on steps taken by them to implement the resolution (see Sect. 3.2.4.1 below).[69] As well as addressing the incitement to terrorism, the Security Council called on States to address issues concerning the denial of safe haven, cooperation for the strengthening of

---

[65]Note that these paragraphs are also reflected within resolutions of the General Assembly, although such resolutions are *expressly* not binding by virtue of article 10 of the Charter of the United Nations. See GA Res 56/88 (n 33) para 7; GA Res 57/27 (n 33) para 7; GA Res 58/81 (n 33) para 7; and GA Res 59/46 (n 33) para 9.

[66]For a tabulated break-down of the party status of each of the Commonwealth case study countries, see Appendix 2 herein.

[67]Report to the Counter-Terrorism Committee pursuant to paragraph 6 of Security Council resolution 1373 (2001) of 28 September 2001, New Zealand, 2 January 2002, S/2001/1269, 16. This report predates United Nations Security Council Resolution 1456 by approximately 12 months.

[68]SC Res 1624, UN SCOR, 5261st Mtg, UN Doc S/Res/1624 (2005).

[69]Ibid, para 5.

international borders, and enhancing the dialogue and understanding amongst States. The relevant provisions of the resolution provide:

1. *Calls upon* all States to adopt such measures as may be necessary and appropriate and in accordance with their obligations under international law to:

   (a) Prohibit by law incitement to commit a terrorist act or acts;
   (b) Prevent such conduct;
   (c) Deny safe haven to any persons with respect to whom there is credible and relevant information giving serious reasons for considering that they have been guilty of such conduct;

2. *Calls upon* all States to cooperate, inter alia, to strengthen the security of their international borders, including by combating fraudulent travel documents and, to the extent attainable, by enhancing terrorist screening and passenger security procedures with a view to preventing those guilty of the conduct in paragraph 1 (a) from entering their territory;

3. *Calls upon* all States to continue international efforts to enhance dialogue and broaden understanding among civilizations, in an effort to prevent the indiscriminate targeting of different religions and cultures, and to take all measures as may be necessary and appropriate and in accordance with their obligations under international law to counter incitement of terrorist acts motivated by extremism and intolerance and to prevent the subversion of educational, cultural, and religious institutions by terrorists and their supporters;

The language of the resolution is exhortatory, which means that its provisions do not constitute binding decisions within the terms of article 25 of the UN Charter (see next at Sect. 3.2.3). However, the question of incitement to terrorism has become a pressing issue (see Chap. 20, Sect. 20.2), and paragraphs 1(c) and 2 complement the binding decisions of the Security Council in resolution 1373 (2001) concerning measures to prevent the transboundary movement of terrorists (see Chap. 21, Sects. 21.1 and 21.2).[70]

3.2.3   The Status of Security Council Resolutions

Not all resolutions of the Security Council result in binding duties, nor do all parts of potentially binding resolutions impose legal obligations. The starting point is to look at article 25 of the UN Charter:

> The Members of the United Nations agree to accept and carry out the decisions of the Security Council in accordance with the present Charter.

In considering the application of article 25, it is all too often stated by international lawyers that only resolutions of the Security Council which are made under chapter VII of the UN Charter (those concerned with the maintenance of international peace and security) are capable of having a binding effect. The Security Council has

---

[70]See further the report of the Counter-Terrorism Committee to the Security Council on the implementation of resolution 1624 (2005), UN Doc S/2006/737 (2006).

powers under Chapters VI, VII, VIII, and XII of the Charter. The powers under chapter VII (articles 41 and 42) permit the Council to require action to be undertaken, or to itself take action. Other powers appear to be recommendatory in nature, such as allowing the UNSC to "call upon" States to act in a certain way (as in the case of article 33(2)), or to "recommend" or "encourage" certain action (as in the case of articles 36(1) and 52(3) of the Charter).

Despite the logic behind this approach, a position argued in the *Namibia Advisory Opinion*, the International Court of Justice has instead focussed on the specific wording or article 25 of the Charter and said that there is no reason why article 25 should be limited to chapter VII resolutions.[71] The World Court instead held that a resolution (or part of it) which is couched in exhortatory rather than mandatory language should not be taken as imposing a legal duty upon States.[72] A single resolution can therefore contain both binding provisions and recommendatory ones. In the case of resolution 1373 (discussed at Sect. 3.2.2.3 above), the chapeau to paragraphs 1 and 2 provides that all States "shall" do what is listed in the body of those paragraphs, whereas paragraph 3 begins by stating that it "calls upon States" to do what is listed therein. A practical observation is that, although the ICJ held that article 25 is not in principle restricted to Chapter VII resolutions, the very nature of those resolutions means that they are far more likely to contain mandatory language.

Considered below (Sect. 3.2.4.2) is the obligation upon members of the UN to list entities and individuals designated as being terrorists by the Security Council Al-Qa'ida and Taliban Sanctions Committee, or of persons or groups associated with them. As a mandatory obligation under article 25 of the Charter, this obligation presents important challenges as a result of potential conflicts between this responsibility and a State's other obligations (such as international and domestic human rights law, and rule of law requirements). These challenges are considered further within various parts of this title: Chap. 4 (concerning the constitutional mechanisms of the case study countries for compliance with Security Council resolutions); Chap. 13 (human rights compliance while countering terrorism); Chap. 19 (terrorist designations and the freedoms of assembly and association, and the rights to justice and fair trial).

3.2.4 Security Council Committees

Specialised Committees and Working Groups of the Security Council have been established over the past decade under resolutions 1267 (1999), 1373 (2001), 1540 (2004) and 1566 (2004). The Security Council describes the mandate and the

---

[71]*Legal Consequences for States of the Continued Presence of South Africa in Namibia (South-West Africa) notwithstanding Security Council Resolution 276, Advisory Opinion* (1971) ICJ Rep 16.
[72]Ibid, 53.

activities of these Committees as different but complementary. The bodies oversee the implementation of specific measures decided upon by the Security Council, but do so from different perspectives. In its recent resolutions pertaining to three of these bodies (the Al-Qa'ida and Taliban Sanctions Committee, the Counter-Terrorism Committee (CTC) and the 1540 Committee), the Security Council has called for enhancement of the ongoing cooperation between the three Committees, mostly through their expert groups.[73]

3.2.4.1 Counter-Terrorism Committee

Under paragraph 6 of Security Council resolution 1373 (2001), the Counter-Terrorism Committee (CTC) was established for the purpose of monitoring the implementation by UN member States of the resolution. The mandate of the CTC has been expanded through subsequent resolutions, to be discussed, and comprises three primary functions: monitoring of States' compliance with resolutions 1373 (2001) and 1624 (2005); the provision by the Committee of technical assistance to those member States who request such assistance; and consultation on best practices in the fight against international terrorism.

The Counter-Terrorism Committee was initially assisted by a group of 10 experts. In a revitalisation of the CTC in 2004, the Security Council subsequently established two main organs of the Committee.[74] The first, the Plenary, is composed of Security Council member States and acts to monitor the second part of the Committee and provide it with policy guidance. The functional part of the Committee is the Bureau composed of the Chair and Vice-Chairs of the Security Council and a Counter-Terrorism Committee Executive Directorate (CTED).[75] Of significance to the interface between counter-terrorism and human rights, the Executive Directorate has an officer dedicated to the subject of the promotion and protection of human rights while countering terrorism.[76]

---

[73]SC Res 1735, UN SCOR, 5609th Mtg, UN Doc S/Res/1735 (2006); SC Res 1805, UN SCOR, 5856th Mtg, UN Doc S/Res/1805 (2008); and SC Res 1810, UN SCOR, 5877th Mtg, UN Doc S/Res/1810 (2008). See also Joint intervention on the cooperation between the Al-Qa'ida and Taliban Sanctions Committee, the Counter-Terrorism Committee (CTC) and the Committee established pursuant to resolution 1540 (2004) (6 May 2008, copy on file with author). For a general overview of the role of the Security Council's committees, see Mammen (2005).

[74]SC Res 1535, UN SCOR, 4936th Mtg, UN Doc S/Res/1535 (2004), para 2.

[75]A very useful web site has been established by the Counter-Terrorism Committee, explaining the mandate, practices and assistance programme of the Committee and containing State reports to the Committee and other useful documents and papers, online: http://www.un.org/sc/ctc.

[76]On the question of the role of human rights in the review by the Security Council Counter-Terrorism Committee of State reports, see the report of the UN Special Rapporteur on the promotion and protection of human rights while countering terrorism, Martin Scheinin, The Protection and Promotion of Human Rights While Countering Terrorism, UN Doc E/CN.4/2006/098 (2005), Chapter IV. See also GA Res 62/272, UN GAOR, 62nd Sess, 120th Plen Mtg, UN Doc A/Res/62/272 (2008), para 7, which calls on UN entities involved in supporting counter-

As to the first of the CTC's main functions, paragraph 6 of Security Council resolution 1373 (2001) established what might be described as a reporting and monitoring dialogue between States and the CTC:

> 6. *Decides* to establish, in accordance with rule 28 of its provisional rules of procedure, a Committee of the Security Council, consisting of all the members of the Council, to monitor implementation of this resolution, with the assistance of appropriate expertise, and *calls upon* all States to report to the Committee, no later than 90 days from the date of adoption of this resolution and thereafter according to a timetable to be proposed by the Committee, on the steps they have taken to implement this resolution;

Security Council resolution 1455 (2003) subsequently called on UN member States to submit updated reports, and the dialogue process has been continuing since that time.[77] Resolution 1624 (2005) added to the CTC reporting regime, on the subject of steps taken by States towards the suppression of the incitement to terrorism, and other matters raised under that resolution.[78] Of note, and despite the non-binding nature of these reporting regimes, which only *call upon* States to report to the CTC (see the above discussion concerning the status of Security Council resolutions, at Sect. 3.2.3), there has been an overwhelmingly high response by States, including those which are not members of the United Nations.

In the case of the four Commonwealth countries being considered in this title: Australia has submitted six reports in total, the most recent of which (in 2005) acted as a report under both resolutions 1373 (2001) and 1624 (2005);[79] Canada has reported five times, most recently in 2006, the latest report again standing as one submitted under resolutions 1373 and 1624;[80] New Zealand has submitted five

---

terrorism efforts to facilitate the promotion and protection of human rights and fundamental freedoms while countering terrorism.

[77]See SC Res 1452, UN SCOR, 4678th Mtg, UN Doc S/Res/1452 (2002), and SC Res 1455, UN SCOR, 4686th Mtg, UN Doc S/Res/1455 (2003). The latter resolution also concerns itself with further reporting by States to the Counter-Terrorism Committee. For an overview of this function, see Rosand (2003, pp. 335–336).

[78]SC Res 1624 (n 68), UN SCOR, 5261st Mtg, UN Doc S/Res/1624 (2005), para 5.

[79]Report of Australia to the Counter-Terrorism Committee pursuant to paragraph 6 of Security Council resolution 1373 (2001) of 28 September 2001, UN Doc S/2001/1247 (2002); Supplement to first report of Australia to the Counter-Terrorism Committee pursuant to paragraph 6 of Security Council resolution 1373 (2001) of 28 September 2001, UN Doc S/2002/776 (2002); Supplement to second report of Australia to the Counter-Terrorism Committee pursuant to paragraph 6 of Security Council resolution 1373 (2001) of 28 September 2001, UN Doc S/2003/513 (2003); Fourth Report to the UN Counter-Terrorism Committee, Australia, UN Doc S/2003/1204 (2003); Fifth Report to the Counter-Terrorism Committee, Australia, UN Doc S/2005/90 (2005); and Sixth Report to the Counter-Terrorism Committee, Australia, UN Doc S/2005/671 (2005).

[80]Report of the Government of Canada to the Counter-Terrorism Committee of the United Nations Security Council on measures taken to implement resolution 1373 (2001), UN Doc S/2001/1209 (2001); Report of the Government of Canada to the Counter-Terrorism Committee of the Security Council in response to the letter of the Chairman of the Committee dated 7 March 2002, UN Doc S/2002/667 (2002); Letter dated 18 February 2003 from the Permanent Representative of Canada to the United Nations addressed to the Chairman of the Security Council Committee established pursuant to resolution 1373 (2001) concerning counter-terrorism, UN Doc S/2003/403 (2003);

reports to the Committee, the most recent comprising reports under both resolutions;[81] and the United Kingdom has reported five times under resolution 1373 (2001) and once under resolution 1624 (2005).[82] These reports are considered further in Chaps. 4–8 when discussing steps taken by the case study countries in the implementation of counter-terrorism measures.

In response to Security Council resolution 1805 (2008), the CTC prepared a report on a survey undertaken by experts of the CTED on the implementation of resolution 1373 (2001).[83] The survey focuses on the major thematic areas addressed by resolution 1373 and provides an assessment of its implementation by regions and sub-regions, as well as drawing some conclusions on global progress in implementation of the areas considered in the report.[84] The four Commonwealth case study countries are assessed under the regional label "Western European and other States".[85] This part of the CTC's report is considered further in Chap. 4 (see Sect. 4.3).

Implementation of United Nations Security Council Resolution 1373 Canada's Fourth Report to the United Nations Counter-Terrorism Committee, UN Doc S/2004/132 (2004); and Enclosure to Note Verbale dated 20 March 2006 from the Permanent Mission of Canada to the United Nations addressed to the Chairman of the Counter-Terrorism Committee, UN Doc S/2006/185 (2006).

[81]Report to the Counter-Terrorism Committee pursuant to paragraph 6 of Security Council resolution 1373 (2001) of 28 September 2001, New Zealand, UN Doc S/2001/1269 (2002); Supplementary report providing additional information on the measures taken by New Zealand to implement the provisions of Security Council resolution 1373 (2001), UN Doc S/2002/795 (2002); New Zealand response to the questions and comments of the Security Council Counter-Terrorism Committee contained in the Chairman's letter of 30 May 2003, UN Doc S/2003/860 (2003); New Zealand response to the United Nations Security Council Counter-Terrorism Committee questions for response by 30 April 2004, UN Doc S/2004/359 (2004); and New Zealand national report to the United Nations Security Council Counter-Terrorism Committee, UN Doc S/2006/384 (2006).

[82]The United Kingdom of Great Britain and Northern Ireland Report to the Counter-Terrorism Committee pursuant to paragraph 6 of Security Council resolution 1373 (2001) of 28 September 2001, UN Doc S/2001/1232 (2001); The United Kingdom of Great Britain and Northern Ireland: second report to the Counter-Terrorism Committee pursuant to paragraph 6 of Security Council resolution 1373 (2001) of 28 September 2001, UN Doc S/2002/787 (2002); Third report of the United Kingdom of Great Britain and Northern Ireland to the Counter-Terrorism Committee pursuant to paragraph 6 of Security Council resolution 1373 (2001) of 28 September 2001, UN Doc S/2003/264 (2003); Fourth report of the United Kingdom of Great Britain and Northern Ireland to the Counter-Terrorism Committee pursuant to paragraph 6 of Security Council resolution 1373 (2001) of 28 September 2001, UN Doc S/2004/157 (2004); Letter dated 7 September 2005 from the Permanent Representative of the United Kingdom of Great Britain and Northern Ireland to the United Nations addressed to the Chairman of the Counter-Terrorism Committee, UN Doc S/2005/583 (2005); and Implementation of Security Council resolution 1624 (2005): report of the United Kingdom in response to the Counter-Terrorism Committee's questions, UN Doc S/2006/398 (2006).

[83]SC Res 1805 (n 73), para 8.

[84]Survey of the implementation of Security Council resolution 1373 (2001): Report of the Counter-Terrorism Committee, UN Doc S/2008/379 (2008).

[85]Ibid, paras 133–139.

Recognising the considerable burden upon States in the domestic implementation process following their party status to the international terrorism-related conventions, and in complying with resolution 1373 (2001), the Security Council has also tasked the Counter-Terrorism Committee with exploring ways in which States can be assisted.[86] The Committee has to that end (amongst other initiatives) set up a database of available expertise and technical assistance as a resource for States, and a Technical Assistance Matrix.[87]

In a number of resolutions subsequent to 9/11, the Security Council has made reference to best practices in the fight against terrorism, as well as codes and standards as tools that can assist States in their implementation of resolution 1373 (2001). In its resolution 1377 (2001), the Security Council invited the CTC to explore ways in which States could be assisted, and in particular to explore with international, regional and sub-regional organisations the promotion of best practices in the areas covered by resolution 1373 (2001), including the preparation of model laws as appropriate.[88] The CTC has thereby established an online Directory of International Best Practices, Codes and Standards on counter-terrorism.[89] The UNODC Terrorism Prevention Branch is in the process of establishing a document on Model Legislative Provisions against Terrorism (see Sect. 3.2.6 below).

3.2.4.2   Al-Qa'ida and Taliban Sanctions Committee

As opposed to the broad mandate of the CTC, the Al-Qa'ida and Taliban Sanctions Committee was established in 1999 for the specific purpose of listing and de-listing certain entities and individuals. The Committee was established under resolution 1267 (1999), through which sanctions were imposed by the Security Council on the then Taliban-controlled Afghanistan in response to the Taliban's support of Usama bin Laden and Al-Qa'ida.[90] The sanctions regime has been modified and strengthened through a number of subsequent resolutions of the Security Council.[91] Following the events of 9/11, the work of the Committee is no longer limited to the

---

[86]SC Res 1377, UN SCOR, 4413rd Mtg, UN Doc S/Res/1377 (2001).

[87]United Nations CTED Technical Assistance Matrix, online: http://www.un.org/sc/ctc/htdocs/index.html.

[88]See also SC Res 1456, UN SCOR, 4688th Mtg, UN Doc S/Res/1456 (2003), para 4(iii).

[89]United Nations Security Council Resolution 1373 (2001) Directory of International Best Practices, Codes and Standards, online: http://www.un.org/sc/ctc/bestpractices/best_prac.html.

[90]SC Res 1267 (n 50).

[91]Including: SC Res 1333, UN SCOR, 4251st Mtg, UN Doc S/Res/4251 (2000); SC res 1390, UN SCOR, 4452nd Mtg, UN Doc S/Res/1390 (2002); SC Res 1455 (n 77); 1526, UN SCOR, 4908th Mtg, UN Doc S/Res/1526 (2004); SC Res 1617, UN SCOR, 5244th Mtg, UN Doc S/Res/1617 (2005); and SC Res 1735 (n 73).

territory of Afghanistan but now applies to any individuals or entities designated on the Committee's Consolidated List, wherever they may be.[92]

There has been much criticism over the way in which the Committee undertakes its listing and de-listing functions, as well as concerns about potential conflicts between that process and the human rights and rule of law obligations of UN member States. As mentioned in Sect. 3.2.3 above, the challenges posed by these issues are considered further within various parts of this title (see mainly Chap. 19).

3.2.4.3   Resolution 1540 Committee

In 2004, the Security Council established a further Committee of the Security Council, tasked with monitoring compliance with its resolution 1540, which calls on States to prevent non-State actors (including terrorist groups) from accessing weapons of mass destruction.[93] The mandate of the Committee was most recently extended under resolution 1810 (2008), which called for the Committee to intensify its work. Similar to the CTC, the Committee receives reports from members States on their implementation of resolution 1540 (2004). It cooperates with international, regional, and sub-regional organisations, and has submitted two reports up to July 2008 on States' compliance with the resolution.[94] It has also established an open database of legislation used to implement resolution 1540 (2004).[95]

3.2.4.4   Resolution 1566 Working Group

In 2004, the Security Council adopted resolution 1566 which called on UN member States to take action against groups and organisations engaged in terrorist activities that were not subject to the 1267 Committee's review (considered earlier). Resolution 1566 (2004) established the 1566 Working Group to recommend practical measures against such individuals and groups, as well as to explore the possibility of setting up a compensation fund for victims of terrorism.[96]

The Working Group has held meetings with interested members States and relevant UN agencies to hear their views on the issues involved, and has agreed

---

[92]See The Consolidated List established and maintained by the 1267 Committee with respect to Al-Qa'ida, Usama bin Laden, and the Taliban and other individuals, groups, undertakings and entities associated with them, online: http://www.un.org/sc/committees/1267/consolist.shtml.

[93]SC Res 1540, UN SCOR, 4956th Mtg, UN Doc S/Res/1540 (2004).

[94]Report of the Committee established pursuant to resolution 1540 (2004), UN Doc S/2006/257 (2006); and Report of the Committee established pursuant to resolution 1540 (2004), UN Doc S/2008/493 (2008).

[95]Security Council committee established pursuant to resolution 1540 (2004), List of legislative documents by submitting UN Member States, online: http://www.un.org/sc/1540/legisdocuments.shtml.

[96]SC Res 1566, UN SCOR, 5053rd Mtg, UN Doc S/Res/1566 (2004), paras 9 and 10.

that members and non-members could submit written proposals and ideas on how to achieve its mandate.[97] The Working Group has reported just once, in December 2005, noting that attention should be paid to a number of practical measures: freezing of financial assets; preventing movement; preventing the supply of arms; strengthening prosecution and extradition; curtailing recruitment and training; preventing public provocation; and use of the internet.[98]

On the issue of victims, members of the Working Group agreed to discuss the support for victims and the possible establishment of a compensation fund for them.[99] In the area of the scope of the application of the measures against terrorist individuals, groups and entities other than those designated by the Al-Qa'ida and Taliban Sanctions Committee, it agreed to discuss the question of establishing effective means to identify those individuals, groups and entities, including the possibility of establishing a new Security Council list that would identify such individuals, groups and entities. Agreement was not reached on this issue and thus remains open.[100]

The current status of the Working Group and its mandate remains unclear. Although, technically, it remains an established Working Group of the Security Council, it has not reported since December 2005 and the scope of issues just identified are now captured within the mandate of the Counter-Terrorism Implementation Task Force (CTITF), which was institutionalised under General Assembly resolution 62/272 (2008).[101] It should be noted that the CTITF held a symposium in September 2008 on the victims of terrorism and that, as a result, there may be renewed interest in the notion of establishing an international victims' fund. As a matter under the mandate of the Working Group under paragraph 10 of resolution 1566 (2004), this might therefore see a reactivation of the Group's work. The CTITF and its mandate are considered further in the section that follows.

3.2.5   UN Global Counter-Terrorism Strategy

In 2005, the UN Secretary-General established a Counter-Terrorism Implementation Task Force, comprised of representatives from various offices and agencies within the United Nations system and making up subject-specific Working Groups. The CTITF was established with the aim of ensuring a coordinated and coherent

---

[97]Report of the Security Council working group established pursuant to resolution 1566 (2004), UN Doc S/2005/789 (2005), paras 5, 7 and 9.

[98]Ibid, paras11, and 16–30.

[99]Ibid, paras11, 31 and 32.

[100]Ibid, paras 11, 33 and 34.

[101]GA Res 62/272 (n 76), para 11.

effort across the United Nations system to counter international terrorism.[102] It has compiled an Online Handbook that explains the activities of the Task Force and also provides information on and access to existing counter-terrorism resources available through the UN system.[103]

There are currently nine Working Groups of the CTITF, tasked with consideration of: preventing and resolving conflicts; addressing radicalisation and extremism that lead to terrorism; supporting and highlighting victims of terrorism; preventing and responding to attacks using weapons of mass destruction; tackling the financing of terrorism; countering the use of the internet for terrorist purposes; strengthening the protection of vulnerable targets; protecting human rights while countering terrorism; and facilitating the integrated implementation of the United Nations Global Counter-Terrorism Strategy.[104]

A key prelude to the UN Global Counter-Terrorism Strategy (see Appendix 1 herein) was the former UN Secretary-General's report, Uniting Against Terrorism.[105] Flowing from that report, the Global Counter-Terrorism Strategy was adopted by the General Assembly in September 2006, reaffirming the principles and purposes of the international framework for countering terrorism, already discussed in this chapter.[106] Reading more like a plan of action, rather than a "strategy" in the pure sense of the word, the Strategy identified four pillars of action:

I. Measures to address the conditions conducive to the spread of terrorism.
II. Measures to prevent and combat terrorism.
III. Measures to build States' capacity to prevent and combat terrorism and to strengthen the role of the United Nations system in that regard.
IV. Measures to ensure respect for human rights for all and the rule of law as the fundamental basis for the fight against terrorism.

The final pillar of the Strategy is considered in further detail in Chap. 12. The second and third pillars bring together the various aspects of the international framework for countering terrorism, reflecting the work of both the General Assembly and Security Council. Cooperation amongst States, between States and the UN, and between the UN and other international and regional agencies, is a theme repeated throughout these pillars. Capacity-building through technical

---

[102]For further information on the Counter-Terrorism Implementation Task Force, see UN Action to Counter Terrorism, "Coordinating counter-terrorism actions within and beyond the UN system", online: http://www.un.org/terrorism/cttaskforce.shtml.

[103]UN Counter-Terrorism Online handbook, online: http://www.un.org/terrorism/cthandbook.

[104]Report of the Secretary-General, United Nations Global Counter-Terrorism Strategy: activities of the United Nations system in implementing the Strategy, UN Doc A/62/898 (2008), Annex.

[105]Report of the Secretary-General, Uniting Against Terrorism: Recommendations for a Global Counter-terrorism Strategy, UN Doc A/60/825 (2006), para 5. See also Part VI of the Report.

[106]United Nations Global Counter-Terrorism Strategy, GA Res 60/288 (n 33), preambular paragraphs. See Chap. 23 herein. The Global Strategy has been reaffirmed in GA Res 61/40 (n 27) preambular para 2; and GA Res 62/71 (n 27) preambular para 2.

assistance programmes is identified as a core requirement in Pillar III, as is the enhancement of institutions who deal with various aspects of the international framework on counter-terrorism.

The first pillar of the UN Counter-Terrorism Strategy (measures to address the conditions conducive to the spread of terrorism) is a new feature in the work and language of the international community on the subject of countering terrorism. Whereas States had previously been very reluctant to acknowledge the "root causes" of terrorism, in the fear that this might be seen as somehow condoning the motivations of terrorist actors, the first pillar of the Strategy represents the first global attempt to deal with such issues in an official document of the UN. While the second preambular paragraph of the Strategy reiterates the General Assembly's strong condemnation of terrorism, irrespective of its motivations, Pillar I recognises that any long-term strategy to counter international terrorism must address "the conditions conducive to the spread of terrorism", which are identified as including:[107]

> . . .prolonged unresolved conflicts, dehumanization of victims of terrorism in all its forms and manifestations, lack of the rule of law and violations of human rights, ethnic, national and religious discrimination, political exclusion, socio-economic marginalization and lack of good governance. . .

A further feature of the Global Counter-Terrorism Strategy is its express reference to civil society. The General Assembly has undertaken to encourage non-governmental organisations and civil society to engage, as appropriate, on how to enhance efforts to implement the Strategy.[108] Pillar I speaks of fostering the involvement of civil society in a global campaign against terrorism, and for its condemnation.[109] Pillar II recognises the importance of the proposal in the Secretary-General's report on Uniting Against Terrorism to bring together the major biotechnology stakeholders, including industry, the scientific community, civil society and Governments, into a common programme aimed at ensuring that biotechnology advances are not used for terrorist or other criminal purposes but for the public good.[110] As identified by the Center on Global Counterterrorism Cooperation, civil society has played, and will continue to play, a critical role in encouraging governments and the United Nations to calibrate their response to terrorism by working to be effective against those who mean harm without eroding human rights and the rule of law.[111]

In adopting the Global Strategy, the General Assembly agreed to undertake its review during the Assembly's 62nd Session in September 2008.[112] Following a

---

[107]Ibid, preamble to Pillar I.

[108]Ibid, substantive para 3(e).

[109]Ibid, Pillar I, para 8.

[110]Ibid, Pillar II, para 11.

[111]Center on Global Counterterrorism Cooperation, *Civil Society and the UN Global Counter-Terrorism Strategy: Opportunities and Challenges* (September 2008), online: http://www.globalct.org/images/content/pdf/reports/civil_society.pdf, p. 3.

[112]GA Res 60/288 (n 33), para 3(b).

report of the Secretary-General on the activities of the UN system in implementing the Strategy, the General Assembly agreed to reaffirm the Global Counter-Terrorism Strategy.[113] The Assembly at that time also recognised the need to formally institutionalise the CTITF within the Secretariat of the United Nations.[114] A further review of the implementation of the Global Strategy is scheduled to occur during the 64th Session of the General Assembly in September 2010.[115]

3.2.6 Capacity-Building and Technical Assistance by the UNODC Terrorism Prevention Branch

Identified in the foregoing section was the need to build the capacity of States to adopt and implement measures for the effective fight against international terrorism. Following the train bombing in Madrid on 11 March 2004, in which nearly 200 people were killed, Spain's Ambassador to the United Nations (who then chaired the Security Council Counter-Terrorism Committee) criticised unnamed nations for a "lack of effort" in countering terrorism.[116] The A point later made by the former US Ambassador to the United Nations, John Danworth, was as follows:[117]

> [The Counter-Terrorism Committee] must never forget that so long as a few states are not acting quickly enough to raise their capacity to fight terrorism or are not meeting their international counterterrorism obligations, all of us remain vulnerable.

While this point is well-made (and further discussed in Chap. 4, Sect. 4.1), the fact remains that some countries have struggled to act quickly and comprehensively not through a lack of desire, but as a result of inexperience or lack of resources. Technical assistance and capacity-building is a task of the UN Office on Drugs and Crime (UNODC) Terrorism Prevention Branch, as part of its global project on strengthening the legal regime against terrorism.[118] As a matter falling directly

---

[113]UN Secretary-General 2008 report (n 104). The Strategy was reaffirmed in GA Res 62/272 (n 76), preambular para 1, and substantive para 2.

[114]GA Res 62/272 (n 76), preambular para 8, and substantive para 11.

[115]Ibid, paras 13 and 14.

[116]United Nations Foundation, "Spanish Diplomat Blames Nations for 'Lack of Effort' on Terrorism", UN Wire, 12 March 2004, previously available online: http://www.unwire.org/UNWire (copy held on file by author).

[117]United Nations Foundation, "Counterterrorism Cooperation Improving, Security Council Told", UN Wire, 20 July 2004, previously available online: http://www.unwire.org/UNWire (copy held on file by author).

[118]On the subject of the increased role of the Terrorism Prevention Branch since September 11, see the report of the UN Secretary-General, Strengthening the Terrorism Prevention Branch of the Secretariat, UN Doc A/57/152/Add.1 (2002).

under the scope of Pillar III to the Global Counter-Terrorism Strategy, the Secretary-General reported as follows on the work of the TPB's global project:[119]

> The work of the global project has contributed to increasing the number of States becoming parties to the international legal counter-terrorism instruments and the elaboration of new or revised counter-terrorism legislation. An estimated 120 ratifications or accessions were undertaken between 8 September 2006 and 31 May 2008, and an estimated 47 new or revised counter-terrorism laws were drafted by assisted countries. These gains must be reinforced, as less than 100 countries have ratified all first 12 universal legal instruments against terrorism. Overall, since its launch in January 2003, the global project has assisted more than 150 countries, trained more than 6,700 national criminal justice officials and developed a dozen technical assistance tools, including legislative databases and model legislative provisions against terrorism.

Alongside a number of technical assistance tools created by the Terrorism Prevention Branch, is its Guide for the Legislative Incorporation and Implementation of the Universal Anti-Terrorism Instruments.[120] The TPB is now in the process of developing an updated Model Legislative Provisions against Terrorism. Its aim is to present a uniform and harmonised model of how the universal legal framework against terrorism can be "translated" into concretely applicable domestic legal provisions. This updated version will address various additional issues, including an expanded section on offences to cover the criminalisation requirements contained in recently adopted instruments; a new part dealing with some procedural aspects of counter-terrorism (including freezing and confiscation of funds, and the procedural rights of the accused), and new provisions dealing with the Al Qaida and Taliban sanctions regime.

3.3 Customary International Law Relating to Counter-Terrorism

Moving from treaties, and mechanisms established under them including UN action, the relevance of customary international law should be acknowledged. Customary law is relevant to the fight against terrorism in two principal contexts: first, concerning the customary law reflections of the Geneva Conventions; and, secondly, concerning the practice of States in response to resolutions of the Security Council and General Assembly, often reflecting the statements and restatements of the General Assembly's Declaration on Measures to Eliminate International Terrorism.

---

[119]This work is also called upon by the General Assembly, including in: GA Res 61/40 (n 27) para 18; and GA Res 62/71 (n 27) para 18. See also GA Res 62/172, UN GAOR, 62nd Sess, 77th Plen Mtg, UN Doc A/Res/62/172 (2008), preambular para 6, and operative para 1.

[120]Available online: http://www.unodc.org/pdf/terrorism/TATs/en/2LIGen.pdf.

As to the Geneva Conventions, it is well accepted that the vast majority of provisions within the Conventions have now come to reflect equivalent norms of customary international law. The Geneva Conventions prohibit violence to life, in particular murder, mutilation, cruel treatment and torture, and the taking of hostages (on the relationship between the Geneva Conventions and terrorism, see Chap. 12, Sect. 12.2.2.1).[121] Of more specific relevance, article 13(2) of the First Optional Protocol states that:[122]

> The civilian population as such, as well as individual civilians, shall not be the object of attack. Acts or threats of violence the primary purpose of which is to spread terror among the civilian population are prohibited.

Turning to the Declaration on Measures to Eliminate International Terrorism, it has already been discussed in this chapter that the Declaration was adopted by the General Assembly in 1994, added to by a Supplement in 1996, and continually restated and confirmed by the General Assembly on an annual basis. As also discussed, however, although these resolutions are compelling and strongly worded (despite their lack of a definition of the term "terrorism") they are not, in and of themselves, binding upon members of the United Nations. Article 10 of the UN Charter specifically dictates that resolutions of the General Assembly are recommendatory only.

At first instance, then, the utility and relevance of the Declarations may seem lacking, particularly from a domestic law perspective. There is, however, a means through which the *contents* of the Declarations might influence or inform municipal courts. Although resolutions of the Assembly are not, by virtue of article 10, binding upon members of the UN, they might nevertheless constitute prima facie evidence of customary international law. If the Declarations do indeed reflect the content of customary international law, they may be consequently binding in domestic law (see further the discussion in Chap. 4, Sect. 4.2.1).

In brief terms, customary international law comprises two elements: a *corpus* (a custom or practice that has evolved over time) and an *animus* (a sense on the part of the participants in the custom that they act in they way they do because they are legally bound to – *opinio juris sive necessitatis*).[123] Custom takes the form of State conduct. It must be uniform and consistent to such a degree that the core of

---

[121]Geneva Convention for the Amelioration of the Condition of the Wounded and Sick in Armed Forces in the Field, opened for signature 12 August 1949, 75 UNTS 32 (entered into force 21 October 1950); Geneva Convention for the Amelioration of the Condition of the Wounded, Sick and Shipwrecked Members of Armed Forces at Sea, opened for signature 12 August 1949, 75 UNTS 85 (entered into force 21 October 1950); Geneva Convention Relative to the Treatment of Prisoners of War, opened for signature 12 August 1949, 75 UNTS 136 (entered into force 21 October 1950); and the Geneva Convention Relative to the Protection of Civilian Persons in Time of War, opened for signature 12 August 1949, 75 UNTS 288 (entered into force 21 October 1950).

[122]Protocol Additional to the Geneva Conventions of 12 August 1949 and Relating to the Protection of Victims of International Armed Conflicts, opened for signature 8 June 1977, 1125 UNTS 4 (entered into force 7 December 1978).

[123]Brownlie (2003, pp. 6–9).

the State practice exhibits these characteristics.[124] The practice must have a sufficient number of participating States so that it can be said to be generally applied.[125] It must normally also have existed for a period of time so that it may indeed be called a 'custom'.[126] Most importantly, it must be exercised through a sense of legal obligation, rather than merely for convenience of political expedience.[127]

Whether or not the General Assembly Declarations are reflective of customary law is therefore dependent on whether they mirror actual State practice, and if such practice is undertaken through a sense of legal obligation. If one considers the various State reports lodged with the Security Council Counter-Terrorism Committee, assuming that those reports mirror *actual* conduct, one can see that there has been a reasonable level of consistency between State conduct and the various principles enumerated in the Declarations.[128] Furthermore, the repeated adoption of the principles tends to point towards a practice of duration, from 1994 to the present, albeit that this is reasonably brief in the normal life of the emergence of customary law. In terms of generality, however, although all members of the United Nations have reported to the Committee, they have not all adopted counter-terrorist measures within the terms recommended by the Declarations.[129] In determining whether the elements of generality and *opinio juris* are satisfied, therefore, one would need to undertake a very close and careful analysis of the State reports and the actual status and use of counter-terrorist legislation within each reporting State.

This is not an issue that will be taken any further in this chapter for two reasons. First, such an examination would need to be extensive to produce any determinative findings. Second, the value of such findings would add little to the thesis of this title, concerning the interface between human rights and the counter-terrorism laws and practices of the Commonwealth case study countries. In general terms, the principles within the Declarations are mirrored within the Security Council resolutions

---

[124]See, for example, the judgment of the International Court of Justice in the *Asylum Case (Colombia v Peru)* (1950) ICJ Reports 266, 276–277.

[125]See, for example, the judgment of the International Court of Justice in the *Fisheries Jurisdiction Case (United Kingdom v Iceland)* (1974) ICJ Reports 3, 23–26.

[126]Although it should be said that if the other two aspects of consistency and generality are found in strong measure, the requirement for duration is not as important: see *North Sea Continental Shelf Cases (Federal Republic of Germany v Denmark; Federal Republic of Germany v The Netherlands)* (1969) ICJ Reports 3, para 74.

[127]See, for example, the *Lotus Case*, Permanent Court of International Justice, Ser. A, no. 10, 28, and the *North Sea Continental Shelf Cases* (ibid) para 71.

[128]See the Counter-Terrorism Committee's survey of the implementation of Security Council resolution 1373 (n 84). State reports to the Committee are available online: http://www.un.org/sc/ctc/countryreports.shtml.

[129]Take for example, Fiji, who reported to the Committee in 2002 and 2003, but only announced in 2004 that it was preparing counter-terrorism legislation: see Report of the Government of Fiji pursuant to paragraph 6 of Security Council resolution 1373 (2001) of 28 September 2001, 4 June 2002, S/2002/616, and Fiji's second round of responses based on the letter dated 8 August 2002, 25 April 2003, S/2003/481; and compare with Shameem (2004).

discussed and within the international conventions relating to terrorism, to which the case study countries are party. Through incorporating legislation, those obligations have become part of municipal law. The Declarations therefore add little value, in practical terms, to the manner in which domestic law on counter-terrorism is to be applied by the judiciary in those countries.

3.4 Regional and Multilateral Action Related to Countering Terrorism

This chapter has so far looked at the various sources of international counter-terrorism obligations. The chapters that follow in this first part of the text will consider the means by which those obligations can be and have been implemented into domestic law by the four Commonwealth countries being examined. Before doing so, it is relevant to also acknowledge the importance of regional and other multilateral action.

3.4.1 Regional Action

A very wide range of instruments, organisations, and less formal initiatives work to implement and supplement the international framework on counter-terrorism.[130] The Financial Action Task Force (FATF), associated with but not strictly part of the Organisation for Economic Cooperation and Development (OECD), is an inter-governmental body whose purpose is to adopt and implement measures designed to counter the use of financial systems by criminals. Its primary focus is money-laundering and, in October 2001, it adopted the Special Recommendations on Terrorist Financing.[131] The Special Recommendations are important to the suppression of terrorist financing (see Sects. 3.1.1.4 and 3.2.2.3 above) and thus also impact upon the work of the Al-Qa'ida and Taliban Sanctions Committee (Sect. 3.2.4.2 above). The Council of Europe Committee of Experts on the Evaluation of Anti-Money Laundering Measures and the Financing of Terrorism (MONEYVAL) does the same work on a European level, for European countries which are not members of the FATF.

Also at the European level, both the European Union (EU) and the Council of Europe (COE) have extensive programmes related to countering terrorism. The Justice and Home Affairs Council of the EU adopted, in December 2005, the

---

[130]See, for example, the discussion by Graham (2005, pp. 49–52).

[131]Financial Action Task Force on Money Laundering, *Special Recommendations on Terrorist Financing*, online: http://www.oecd.org/dataoecd/8/17/34849466.pdf.

European Union Counter-Terrorism Strategy.[132] In response to Security Council resolution 1373 (2001) (see Sect. 3.2.2.3 above), the EU established its own mechanism for the listing and delisting of terrorist and associated entities to allow for the freezing of funds and financial assets, thus overlapping significantly with the mandate of the Al-Qa'ida and Taliban Sanctions Committee (Sect. 3.2.4.2 above). The Council of Europe has a Committee of Experts on Terrorism (CODEX-TER), which coordinates the implementation of the COE's action against terrorism. Three terrorism-related conventions have been established under the auspices of the Council of Europe: the Convention on the Suppression of Terrorism; the Convention on the Prevention of Terrorism; and the Convention on Laundering, Search, Seizure and Confiscation of the Proceeds from Crime and on the Financing of Terrorism.[133]

The Organisation for Security and Cooperation in Europe (OSCE) established an Action against Terrorism Unit in the wake of the 9/11 attacks, which undertakes various tasks directed towards countering terrorism.[134] The OSCE comprises 56 States from Europe, Central Asia and North America, including Canada and the United Kingdom. The OSCE Office for Democratic Institutions and Human Rights

---

[132]Council of the European Union, *The European Union Counter-Terrorism Strategy*, EU Doc 14469/4/05 REV4 (2005). For further information on the work of the European Union in this area, including the role of institutions and bodies within the EU, see site of the EU Justice and Home Affairs Council http://ec.europa.eu/justice_home/fsj/terrorism/fsj_terrorism_intro_en.htm.

[133]Council of Europe Convention on the Prevention of Terrorism, opened for signature 16 May 2005, CETS No 196 (entered into force 1 June 2007); European Convention on the Suppression of Terrorism, opened for signature 27 January 1977, CETS No 090 (entered into force 4 August 1978). Work is currently being undertaken to update and modify this treaty, under the Protocol amending the European Convention on the Suppression of Terrorism, opened for signature 15 May 2003, CETS No 190 (not yet in force); and Council of Europe Convention on Laundering, Search, Seizure and Confiscation of the Proceeds from Crime and on the Financing of Terrorism, opened for signature 16 May 2005, CETS No 198 (entered into force 1 May 2008). For a full list of European instruments and standards on combating terrorism, see Council of Europe, *The Fight Against Terrorism. Council of Europe standards*, (Strasbourg: Council of Europe Publishing, 3rd edition, 2005). The United Nations' publication, International Instruments related to the Prevention and Suppression of International Terrorism (New York, 2001) lists the following additional regional instruments: Organisation of American States (OAS) Convention to Prevent and Punish the Acts of Terrorism Taking the Form of Crimes Against Persons and Related Extortion that are of International Significance, opened for signature 2 February 1971, 1428 UNTS (entered into force 16 October 1973); States of the South Asian Association for Regional Cooperation (SAARC) Regional Convention on Suppression of Terrorism, opened for signature 4 November 1987 (entered into force 22 August 1988); Arab Convention on the Suppression of Terrorism, opened for signature 22 April 1998 (entered into force 7 May 1999); Treaty on Cooperation among the States Members of the Commonwealth of Independent States in Combating Terrorism, opened for signature 4 June 1999 (entered into force 4 June 1999, in accordance with article 22); Convention of the Organisation of the Islamic Conference on Combating International Terrorism, opened for signature 1 July 1999 (not yet entered into force); and Organisation of African Unity (OUA) Convention on the Prevention and Combating of Terrorism, opened for signature 14 July 1999 (entered into force 6 December 2002).

[134]OSCE Secretariat – Action against Terrorism unite, online: http://www.osce.org/atu/13054.html.

also undertakes important work in the area, including the publication in November 2007 of a manual on countering terrorism and protecting human rights.[135] Canada and the United Kingdom are members of the North Atlantic Treaty Organization (NATO), under which the fight against terrorism is identified as a permanent agenda item and priority.[136] Canada is also a party to the Inter-American Convention against Terrorism.[137]

Relevant to Australia and New Zealand are the Pacific Islands Forum and the Asia-Pacific Economic Cooperation (APEC). Forum Leaders adopted the Nasonini Declaration on Regional Security the 33rd Pacific Islands Forum in Fiji.[138] The Declaration underlined the commitment of Forum Leaders to the implementation of internationally agreed anti-terrorism measures, with express reference to Resolution 1373, and tasked the Forum Regional Security Committee to review the regional implementation of the Resolution.[139] Although APEC is predominantly concerned with trade and economic issues, its leaders adopted the Shanghai Counter-Terrorism Statement on 21 October 2001.[140] Leaders characterised terrorism as a direct challenge to APEC's vision of free, open and prosperous economies, and identified various practical measures through which Member Economies could cooperate to enhance counter-terrorism.[141]

APEC's 2002 Statement on Fighting Terrorism was particularly detailed in setting out ways through which secure trade could be achieved, with attention paid to protecting cargo, ships, international aviation, people in transit, and upon cyber security and halting terrorist financing. It established a Counter-Terrorism Task Force, with the mandate to implement and assist with achieving the measures identified (labelled 'STAR', Secure Trade in the APEC Region). By requiring Member Economies to each submit a Counter-Terrorism Action Plan, working with various international organizations, and expanding APEC's extant Finance Ministers' Process to include a focus on the suppression of terrorist financing, the

---

[135]OSCE Office for Democratic Institutions and Human Rights, *Countering Terrorism, Protecting Human Rights: A Manual* (Warsaw, 2007), available online: http://www.osce.org/publications/odihr/2007/11/28294_980_en.pdf.

[136]NATO and the fight against terrorism, 21 August 2008 online: http://www.nato.int/issues/terrorism/index.html.

[137]Inter-American Convention against Terrorism, opened for signature 6 March 2002, OAS Treaty A-66 (entered into force 7 October 2003).

[138]Thirty-Third Pacific Islands Forum, Suva, Fiji Islands, 15–17 August 2002, Forum Communiqué, Annex 1, Nasonini Declaration on Regional Security. See, more generally, the report of the Center on Global Counterterrorism Cooperation, *Implementing the United Nations General Assembly's Global Counter-Terrorism Strategy in the Asia-Pacific* (New York: 2005).

[139]Ibid, paras 5 and 9.

[140]Asia-Pacific Economic Cooperation, APEC Leaders' Statement on Counter-Terrorism, Shanghai, People's Republic of China, 21 October 2001.

[141]Ibid, paras 1, 2 and 6.

Task Force has reported that Member Economies have significantly strengthened counter-terrorist measures.[142]

3.4.2   Proliferation Security Initiative

An issue gaining increased international attention is that of preventing the acquisition by terrorists of radioactive materials and sources and, thereby, preventing the risk of nuclear acts of terrorism (see Sect. 3.1.1.4 above).[143] Linked to this is the Proliferation Security Initiative (PSI), launched by the US Bush Administration in March 2003 and now including more than 70 participating States, including all four Commonwealth case study countries. The stated purpose of the PSI is to counter the trafficking of weapons of mass destruction and, more particularly, denying terrorists, "rogue States", and their supplier networks access to WMD-related materials and delivery systems by interdicting cargo carrying these materials, whether transported by land, air, or sea. It should be noted that the PSI is not an organisation, but an *activity* of participating States, and is governed by what have become known as the six PSI "interdiction principles":[144]

   (a) Not to transport or assist in the transport of any such cargoes to or from states or non-state actors of proliferation concern, and not to allow any persons subject to their jurisdiction to do so.
   (b) At their own initiative, or at the request and good cause shown by another state, to take action to board and search any vessel flying their flag in their internal waters or territorial seas, or areas beyond the territorial seas of any other state, that is reasonably suspected of transporting such cargoes to or from states or non-state actors of proliferation concerns, and to seize such cargoes that are identified.
   (c) To seriously consider providing consent under the appropriate circumstances to the boarding and searching of its own flag vessels by other states, and to the seizure of such WMD-related cargoes in such vessels that may be identified by such states.

---

[142]APEC Counter Terrorism Task Force, "Counter Terrorism", online: http://www.apec.org/apec/apec_groups/som_special_task_groups/counter_terrorism.html.

[143]For recent UN resolutions on the subject, see: GA Res 61/74, UN GAOR, 61st Sess, 67th Plen Mtg, UN Doc A/Res/61/74 (2007); GA Res 61/83, UN GAOR, 61st Sess, 67th Plen Mtg, UN Doc A/Res/61/83 (2007); GA Res 61/86, UN GAOR, 61st Sess, 67th Plen Mtg, UN Doc A/Res/61/86 (2007); GA Res 62/24, UN GAOR, 62nd Sess, 61st Plen Mtg, UN Doc A/Res/62/24 (2008); GA Res 62/33, UN GAOR, 62nd Sess, 61st Plen Mtg, UN Doc A/Res/62/33 (2008); GA Res 62/37, UN GAOR, 62nd Sess, 61st Plen Mtg, UN Doc A/Res/62/37 (2008); GA Res 62/39, UN GAOR, 62nd Sess, 61st Plen Mtg, UN Doc 62/39 (2008); GA Res 62/46, UN GAOR, 62nd Sess, 61st Plen Mtg, UN Doc A/Res/62/46 (2008); GA Res 62/51, UN GAOR, 62nd Sess, 61st Plen Mtg, UN Doc A/Res/62/51 (2008); GA Res 63/60, UN GAOR, 63rd Sess, 61st Plen Mtg, UN Doc A/Res/63/60 (2009); SC Res 1673 (2006), UN SCOR, 5429th Mtg, UN Doc S/Res/1673 (2006); SC Res 1810, UN SCOR, 5877th Mtg, UN Doc S/Res/1810 (2008); and SC Res 1887 (2009), UN SCOR, 6191st Mtg, UN Doc S/Res/1887 (2009).

[144]Proliferation Security Initiative: Statement of Interdiction Principles, Adopted in Paris, 4 September 2003 (para 4), online: http://www.proliferationsecurity.info/principles.html.

(d) To take appropriate actions to (1) stop and/or search in their internal waters, territorial seas, or contiguous zones (when declared) vessels that are reasonably suspected of carrying such cargoes to or from states or non-state actors of proliferation concern and to seize such cargoes that are identified; and (2) enforce conditions on vessels entering or leaving their ports, internal waters, or territorial seas that are reasonably suspected of carrying such cargoes, such as requiring that such vessels be subject to boarding, search, and seizure of such cargoes prior to entry.

(e) At their own initiative or upon the request and good cause shown by another state, to (a) require aircraft that are reasonably suspected of carrying such cargoes to or from states or non-state actors of proliferation concern and that are transiting their airspace to land for inspection and seize any such cargoes that are identified; and/or (b) deny aircraft reasonably suspected of carrying such cargoes transit rights through their airspace in advance of such flights.

(f) If their ports, airfields, or other facilities are used as transshipment points for shipment of such cargoes to or from states or non-state actors of proliferation concern, to inspect vessels, aircraft, or other modes of transport reasonably suspected of carrying such cargoes, and to seize such cargoes that are identified.

The precursor to the PSI was an incident on 10 December 2002, where Spanish forces acting in concert with the United States seized a North Korean ship, the *So San*, which had been on the high seas in the Indian Ocean. Beneath the deck and 40,000 sacks of cement, naval inspectors found 15 scud missiles and 15 conventional warheads. Following a declaration by Yemeni officials that they had purchased the missiles, the US allowed the *So San* and its cargo to continue to its destination the next day. This was consistent with the seriousness with which the freedom of the high seas is treated, but exposed a problem of how to deal with countries such as North Korea which are known to regularly facilitate the sale and transport of missile technology to various States including to those known to harbour, or take no action against, terrorist organisations. The Initiative attempts to address this problem by establishing a voluntary, cooperative basis for the interdiction of vessels which might carry such materials.

The PSI is also promoted as a practical tool for the implementation of Security Council resolutions 1540 (2004) and 1673 (2006),[145] which are principally directed towards adopting national measures to combat the proliferation of nuclear, chemical and biological weapons and their means of delivery, but which also call upon UN members to undertake multilateral cooperation to this end.[146] It should be noted, however, that the PSI predates the resolutions in question and that neither resolution endorses, or mentions, the Initiative. Furthermore, when talking of multilateral cooperation, the resolutions speak of cooperation with the International Atomic Energy Agency (IAEA), and the Organisation for the Prohibition of Chemical Weapons (OPCW).

While this text does not purport to undertake a comprehensive legal analysis of the PSI, it is worthwhile considering some of the challenges to the Initiative posed

---

[145]SC Res 1540 (2004) (n 93), para 8(c), and SC Res 1673 (2006), UN SCOR, 5429th Mtg, UN Doc S/Res/1673 (2006).

[146]See the Proliferation Security Initiative website, hosted by the Government of Canada: http://www.proliferationsecurity.info/introduction.html.

by the legal regime pertaining to maritime navigation, the legality of which has not yet been tested by an international judicial body.[147] The starting point is to consider the UN Convention on the Law of the Sea (UNCLOS), which codifies the principle of the freedom of the high seas, while at the same time recognising two reasons for which a vessel on the high seas might be stopped.[148] Article 92 of UNCLOS permits the flag State of a vessel to stop the vessel on the high seas. Where a vessel is flying no flag on the high seas, as was the case in the *So San* incident, any State may interdict. Article 92 is reflected within principles 4(b) and (c) of the PSI Interdiction Principles, expanding upon the exception by calling upon flag States which partici- pate in the PSI to allow (on a case by case basis) the interdiction and search of a flag-bearing vessel at the request of another participating State where good cause is shown for doing so; and to assist in the interdiction of a vessel if called upon to do so. These principles are not problematic from a legal perspective, since they are consent-based, although they rely heavily on the cooperation of the flag State.

The next point is that, although the interdiction of the *San So* was lawful under UNCLOS, the cargo could not be seized as illicit cargo since North Korea was not a party to the Missile Technology Control Regime. Cargo can become subject to inspection and seizure, however, where a vessel docks in port and where the cargo violates the law of the port State. This feature is reflected within principles 4(d)(2) and (f) of the PSI Interdiction Principles. Although this is useful, the concern is that vessels may use navigation routes by which they can avoid inspection in "unfriendly" ports.

The way in which the PSI attempts to overcome the latter problem is by establishing agreement between participating States to permit interdiction of ves- sels that transit the territory of participating States. Interdiction principle 4(d)(1) calls on participating States to stop and search in their internal waters, territorial seas, or contiguous zones vessels that are suspected of carrying WMDs to or from States or non-State actors of proliferation concern, and to seize such cargoes if found. The principle is again consent-based, and thus raises questions of effective- ness and enforceability, but the principal objection to it is the right of innocent passage. Broadly speaking, territorial waters fall within the normal jurisdiction of a State so that States are able to prescribe law applicable to their territorial waters. A State may therefore establish rules about what constitutes lawful cargo, and when vessels may be boarded and searched.

This position is restricted, however, by the long-standing principle of customary international law of allowing ships an innocent passage through one's territorial waters (codified under article 19 of UNCLOS). The same right of innocent passage applies to passage through narrow straights controlled by States. Passage is inno- cent under article 19 where it is not prejudicial to the peace, good order, or security

---

[147]For further analysis of the Initiative, see: Byers (2004, p. 526); Shulman (2006, p. 771); Valencia (2005, p. 66); and von Heinegg (2002). For further background information, see also Allison (2004, p. 64).

[148]United Nations Convention on the Law of the Sea, opened for signature 10 December 1982, 1833 UNTS 3 (entered into force 16 November 1994).

of the coastal State. Article 19(2) sets out an exhaustive list of what constitutes prejudicial conduct for the purpose of that provision, the content of which is difficult to reconcile with Interdiction Principle 4(d)(1). Furthermore, article 23 of UNCLOS expressly extends the right of innocent passage to nuclear-powered vessels, or vessels carrying nuclear substances.

In summary, the Proliferation Security Initiative is a useful activity of participating States attempting to circumvent the sale and transport of WMD technology to States and non-State actors of "proliferation concern", but is not without its practical and legal difficulties. While almost all of the Interdiction Principles of the PSI comply with UNCLOS, Principle 4(d)(1) appears incompatible with articles 19 and 23 of the Convention. The balance of the Principles rely heavily on consent, particularly from the flag State of a vessel in respect of which interdiction might be contemplated. The availability of those Principles is also severely limited by the application of the freedom of the high seas. While these limitations and challenges might be capable of resolution, by application of arguments relying upon changing custom or the application of anticipatory self-defence for example, it is far from clear that such contentions would find favour.[149]

3.5 Conclusions

International law on counter-terrorism is principally based upon treaty law and the action of various agencies of the United Nations. Thirteen quite specific conventions exist and apply with the aim of protecting potential targets of terrorist conduct, or suppressing access to the means by which terrorist acts are perpetrated or funded. They do not, however, have general application and are limited in their binding nature to States parties. Having said this, the Suppression of Financing Convention does have potentially wider application in its description of conduct that may not be financed. Both the General Assembly and Security Council have issued numerous resolutions on the topic of counter-terrorism, culminating in the adoption by the General Assembly in September 2006 of the UN Global Counter-Terrorism Strategy. Although resolutions of the General Assembly are not binding, the General Assembly has built on various guiding principles and expectations in its declarations on measures to eliminate international terrorism. The Security Council has established a number of subsidiary bodies to deal with particular aspects of the fight against international terrorism, including creation of the Counter-Terrorism Committee very soon after the terrorist attacks of September 11, 2001. The Security Council has imposed various specific obligations upon States under resolutions 1373 (2001) and 1456 (2003).

The challenges faced by the international framework for countering terrorism are many, and are not limited to the inherently difficult nature of "terrorism",

---

[149]It is beyond the contemplation of this chapter to examine these arguments, but see further Byers (2004) and Shulman (2006).

discussed in Chap. 2. The application and enforceability of international treaties, as opposed to the more general application (but limited scope) of customary international law and obligations under Security Council resolutions, combine to create a complex web of intersecting law and principles. The multitude of organisations involved in various aspect of the fight against terrorism, coupled with the vast amount of legal instruments that States are required to implement and report upon, result in the need to take careful, coordinated action which takes capacity-building and technical assistance into account.

References

Allison, Graham. 2004. How to Stop Nuclear Terror. 83 *Foreign Affairs* 64.

Andreu-Guzmán. 2002. *Terrorism and Human Rights*. Geneva: International Commission of Jurists.

Brownlie, Ian. 2003. *Principles of Public International Law*. Oxford: 6th edition, Oxford University Press.

Byers, Michael. 2004. Policing the High Seas: The Proliferation Security Initiative. 98(3) *The American Journal of International Law* 526.

Graham, Kennedy. 2005. The Security Council and Counterterrorism: Global and Regional Approaches to an Elusive Public Good. 17 *Terrorism and Political Violence* 37.

Greenwood, Christopher. 2002. International Law and the 'War Against Terrorism'. 78(2) *International Affairs* 301.

Mammen, Lars. 2005. The Role of the Security Council and its Sanction Committees in Combating International Terrorism. In von Knopp, Katharina, Neisser, Heinrich, Salnikov, Alexey, and Ganor, Boad (Eds). *Security, Terrorism and Privacy in Information Society*. Bielefeld: W. Bertelsmann Verlag.

Pieth, Mark, Thelesklaf, Daniel, and Ivory, Radha (Editors). 2009. *Countering Terrorist Financing. A practitioner's point of view*. Bern: Barns & Noble.

Radicati di Brozolo, Luca, and Megliani, Mauro. 2004. Freezing the Assets of International Terrorist Organisations. In Bianchi, Andrea (Ed). *Enforcing International Law Norms Against Terrorism*. Oxford: Hart Publishing.

Rosand, Eric. 2003. Security Council Resolution 1373, the Counter-Terrorism Committee, and the Fight Against Terrorism. 97(2) *American Journal of International Law* 333.

Rowe, Richard. 2002. Key Developments: Year of International Law in Review (paper presented at the 10th Annual Meeting of the Australian & New Zealand Society of International Law, *New Challenges and New States: What Role for International Law?*, 15 June 2002, Australian National University, Canberra).

Shameem, Shaista. 2004 Tension Between Anti-Terrorism Laws and Human Rights (paper presented at the Citizens' Constitutional Forum and the Fiji Human Rights Commission conference, *How Should Fiji Respond to the Threat of Terrorism?*, 17 July 2004, Suva, Fiji).

Shulman, Mark. 2006. The Proliferation Security Initiative and the Evolution of the Law on the Use of Force. 28 *Houston Journal of International Law* 771.

Szasz, Paul. 2002. The Security Council Starts Legislating. 96(4) *American Journal of International Law* 901.

Valencia, Mark. 2005. The Proliferation Security Initiative: Making Waves in Asia. *The International Institute for Security Studies* 66.

Von Heinegg, Heintschel. 2002. The Legality of Maritime Interception Operations within the Framework of Operation Enduring Freedom. In Heere, Wybo (Ed). *Terrorism and the Military. International Legal Applications*. The Hague: TMC Asser Press.

Chapter 4
Counter-Terrorism in the Commonwealth

Chapters 5 through 8 of this title provide an overview of the counter-terrorism laws in Australia, Canada, New Zealand and the United Kingdom. They consider measures adopted both in response to international counter-terrorism obligations, and those motivated by domestic or regional perspectives and priorities. For the purpose of better understanding the types of measures adopted, this chapter addresses three issues. First, it considers the question of whether counter-terrorism is relevant for all States, taking the approach that this is indeed relevant for all four case study countries and explaining the reasons for this. Next, this chapter explains the means by which the four Commonwealth countries incorporate into law and apply their international obligations, whether these obligations arise as a result of treaties, customary international law, or resolutions of the UN Security Council. The chapter finishes with an overview of outstanding issues in the implementation by each country of international counter-terrorism obligations, including the identification by international bodies of areas requiring further attention.

4.1 Is Counter-Terrorism Relevant for All States?

For those countries which have experienced terrorist acts within their own territories, or against their nationals, the relevance of counter-terrorism is apparent. The United Kingdom has had a long history of dealing with terrorist acts within its borders, including the 1972 "Bloody Friday" bombing in Belfast, Northern Ireland;[1] the destruction of Pan American Airlines Flight 103 over Lockerbie, Scotland, in which 40 UK passengers and 1 British crew member were killed, as

---

[1] On Bloody Friday, 21 July 1972, an Irish Republican Army (IRA) bomb attack killed 11 people and injure 130 in Belfast, Northern Ireland. Ten days later, three IRA car bomb attacks in the village of Claudy left six dead.

A. Conte, *Human Rights in the Prevention and Punishment of Terrorism*,
DOI 10.1007/978-3-642-11608-7_4, © Springer-Verlag Berlin Heidelberg 2010

well as 11 residents of Lockerbie;[2] the 1996 and 1998 IRA bombings in London and
Northern Ireland;[3] the BBC Studios bombing in 2001;[4] and the more recent London
bombings of July 2005.[5] Australian and British leaders have been the subject of
terrorist threats, including by senior aide to Usama bin Laden, Ayman Zawahri, in
2003, and Malaysian terrorist Noordin Mohamad Top in 2005.[6] Three Australian
missionaries were kidnapped in August 1996 by Sudan People's Liberation Army
(SPLA) rebels;[7] and Australian nationals have been killed in terrorist attacks in
nearby Bali and Jakarta in 2002 and 2003.[8] There have been numerous prosecutions
in Australia of terrorism offences committed within the territory of Australia
(see Chap. 5, Sect. 5.1.1.6). Terrorist acts have also been carried out in Canada,
the most notable being the 1985 bombing of Air India Flight 182 in which 329
passengers were killed, including 279 Canadians.[9] In October 2008, the Ontario
Superior Court of Justice convicted Mohammad Momin Khawaja, as the first
person charged and convicted under Canada's terrorism provisions, for participating in a plot to bomb targets in Britain.[10]

---

[2]See Chap. 3, Sect. 3.2.2.1.

[3]On 9 February 1996, an IRA bomb detonated in London, killing two people and wounding more
than 100 others. On 1 August 1998, a 500-pound car bomb planted by the Real IRA exploded
outside a shoe store in Banbridge, North Ireland, injuring 35 people and damaging at least 200
homes. Two weeks later, another 500-pound car bomb planted by the Real IRA exploded outside a
local courthouse in the central shopping district of Omagh, Northern Ireland, killing 29 and
injuring over 330.

[4]At midnight, on 4 March 2001, a car bomb exploded outside the British Broadcasting Corporation's main production studios in London. One person was injured. British authorities suspected
the Real IRA had planted the bomb.

[5]See the consequent Security Council resolution, SC Res 1611, UN SCOR, 5223rd Mtg, UN Doc
S/Res/1611 (2005).

[6]See Chap. 14, Sect. 14.3.1.

[7]Later, on 1 November 1996, a breakaway group of the Sudanese People's Liberation Army
kidnapped three International Committee of the Red Cross workers, including one Australian
national.

[8]On 12 October 2002, car bomb exploded outside the Sari Club Discotheque in Denpasar, Bali,
Indonesia, killing 202 people and wounding 300 more. Most of the casualties, including 88 of the
dead, were Australian tourists. See the consequent Security Council resolution, SC Res 1438, UN
SCOR, 4624th Mtg, UN Doc S/Res/1438 (2002). On 5 August 2003, a car bomb exploded outside
the Marriott Hotel in Jakarta, Indonesia, killing 10 and wounding 150.

[9]Canada's Integrated Threat Assessment Centre also makes note of: the assassination in 1982 of
Turkish military attaché, Colonel Attila Altikat, in Ottawa; the detonation of a van outside Litton
Industries' Toronto plant in 1982; the capture of, and hostage taking in, the Turkish Embassy in
Ottawa by three members of the Armenian Revolutionary Army in 1985; and the arrest in 1995 of
Ahmed Ressam by US Customs officials while he was carrying timing devices and 130 pounds of
explosives from Victoria, British Columbia to Port Angeles, Washington. See Integrated Threat
Assessment Centre, "Terrorism in Canada", online: http://www.itac-ciem.gc.ca/thrt/cnd-eng.asp.

[10]Queen v Khawaja (Unreported, Ontario Superior Court of Justice, File No 04-G30282, 20
October 2008). On the relevance of the terrorist threat to Canada more generally, see Jenkins
(2003); Gabor (2004, pp. 12–15); and Roach (2005, pp. 511–512).

This is not to say that the risk of terrorism is ever-present for the United Kingdom, Australia and Canada. Indeed, the particular level of such a risk is something that should be continually assessed and reviewed. The point to make is that it is understandable that these countries, having experienced and been the targets of terrorist attacks, take the view that counter-terrorism is an important objective for their national security. In contrast, there has been a much stronger debate within New Zealand as to whether there has been a need for counter-terrorism legislation and measures to be adopted. A view often repeated in submissions to the New Zealand Foreign Affairs, Defence and Trade Committee on the Terrorism Suppression Bill 2002 (NZ) was that there was no need for New Zealand to adopt counter-terrorist legislation. From a regional perspective, Pacific Island States have not been subject to, or had to deal directly with, international terrorism – other than the unique event of the bombing by French military agents of the *Rainbow Warrior* in New Zealand in 1985 (see Sect. 4.1.2.2 below).

This position is simplistic at best, however, and there are various reasons why all four case study countries should and must adhere and contribute to the international framework for countering terrorism. The discussion below considers the four most vital factors, those being:

- International and regional counter-terrorism obligations
- The threat of terrorism
- Supporting an international framework on counter-terrorism
- Other related national interests

4.1.1 International and Regional Obligations

The most simple reason for the relevance of, and need for, counter-terrorist action is that such action is an obligation at international law. The conventions, protocols and resolutions discussed in Chap. 3 form the basis of obligations at international law and directions by international agencies which must be acted upon by all four Commonwealth case study countries. As members of the United Nations, they are bound by decisions of the Security Council on counter-terrorism (see Chap. 3, Sects. 3.2.2 and 3.2.3) and are also committed to the UN's Global Counter-Terrorism Strategy and related General Assembly resolutions (see Chap. 3, Sects. 3.2.1 and 3.2.5). The four countries are parties to 12 of the 13 international terrorism-related conventions and have all signed, but not yet ratified (other than the United Kingdom), the most recent convention on the suppression of acts of nuclear terrorism.[11]

---

[11]See Appendix 2, Table 1, for a breakdown of the party status of each country to the international terrorism-related conventions.

Concerning New Zealand and Australia, it is notable that, at the 33rd Pacific Island Forum in Fiji, Forum Leaders adopted the Nasonini Declaration on Regional Security.[12] The Declaration underlined the commitment of Forum Leaders to the implementation of internationally agreed anti-terrorism measures, with express reference to resolution 1373 (2001), and tasked the Forum Regional Security Committee to review the regional implementation of the resolution.[13] Similar commitments exist for the United Kingdom under the European Union Counter-Terrorism Strategy and as a result of membership in the Organisation for Security and Cooperation in Europe (see Chap. 3, Sect. 3.4.1). Canada is also a member of the Organisation for Security and Cooperation in Europe.

4.1.2 The Threat of Terrorism

Terrorist acts have been perpetrated against the State and nationals of Australia, Canada and the United Kingdom, or by those operating within those countries. Discussed below is the question of assessing the threat of terrorism. Consideration is then given to the question of terrorism in the South Pacific.

4.1.2.1 Assessing the Threat of Terrorism

Assessing the threat of terrorism is an imprecise science. If it was not so, countering terrorism would not be as great a concern as it is to the international community. Two things need to be taken into account: the actual threat of immediate acts of terrorism against the State; and the potential threat of such acts.[14]

The *actual* threat of terrorist acts against the State is a natural starting point for determining the threat of terrorism to it and the importance of the objective of countering terrorism. Albeit the obvious place to begin, however, evidence of actual threats is not so obvious. Establishing their existence normally relies upon intelligence which, while very important, has its own set of complications.[15] Intelligence is not always available, said to be the case in the Bali bombings of October 2002 and 2005, and the London bombings in July 2005.[16] It is not always reliable, as was

---

[12]Thirty-Third Pacific Islands Forum, Suva, Fiji Islands, 15–17 August 2002, Forum Communiqué, Annex 1, "Nasonini Declaration on Regional Security".

[13]Ibid, paras 5 and 9.

[14]See Conte and Ganor (2005, p. 31). See also Ganor (2005 Chap. 1); and Sinai (2005).

[15]As acknowledged by John Lewis, Deputy Director of the United States Federal Bureau of Investigation Counter-Terrorism Division, "intelligence is an imperfect business at best": see Lewis (2005).

[16]Concerning the 2002 Bali Bombings, see Mark Forbes, 'No Warning of Bali Bombing' (The Age, 11 December 2002), online: http://www.theage.com.au/articles/2002/12/10/1039379835160.html (as last accessed 21 August 2005, copy on file with author). Compare this with assertions that

the case with the intelligence failures concerning the presence of weapons of mass destruction in Iraq in the lead-up to the 2003 invasion of Iraq.[17] Furthermore, intelligence information may not always be properly assessed, as is alleged to have been the case prior to the 11 September 2001 attacks in the United States of America, and the 2008 attacks in Mumbai, India.[18] Further complicating matters, an absence of intelligence does not mean an absence of threat.

Assessing the *potential* threat of terrorist acts against the State, which is to be measured against both the probability of that potential being actualised and the likely consequences of such acts, also relies upon intelligence, but to a lesser extent.[19] Potential threats are to be assessed by having regard to the motivation and operational capacity of terrorist networks. Operational capacity refers to the ability of terrorist networks to gain access to the territory or facilities of the State and perpetrate terrorist acts therein. While border security is a matter that almost all States have paid increased attention to in the new millennium, it must be acknowledged that transboundary activity and the relatively simple and inexpensive means of perpetrating terrorist acts[20] means that the operational capacity of most terrorist entities should be viewed as being reasonably high.

Concerning the second factor in assessing the potential threat of terrorism, motivation refers, in simple terms, to the question of whether the State is a likely or possible target of terrorist networks. As discussed in Chap. 2, for example, the motivation of Al-Qa'ida and many Islamic radicals is not only the spreading of the Muslim faith, but also the elimination of what such groups see as the evil of

---

intelligence agencies did indeed have information pointing to such an event: see, for example, Laura Tiernan, 'Australian Intelligence Inquiry into Bali Warnings "a Whitewash"' (World Socialist Web Site, 7 January 2003), online: http://www.wsws.org/articles/2003/jan2003/igis-j07.shtml. Concerning the London Bombings on 7 July 2005, compare: Wikipedia, '7 July 2005 London Bombings', online: http://en.wikipedia.org/wiki/7_July_2005_London_bombings with Wikinews, 'Coordinated Terrorist Attack Hits London' (7 July 2005), online: http://en.wiki-news.org/wiki/Explosions,_'serious_incidents'_occuring_across_London.

[17]See, for example, CNN.com, 'Report: Iraq intelligence "dead wrong"' (1 April 2005), online: http://www.cnn.com/2005/POLITICS/03/31/intel.report.

[18]Subcommittee on Terrorism and Homeland Security, House Permanent Select Committee on Intelligence, *Counterterrorism Intelligence Capabilities and Performance Prior to 9–11*, July 2002, online: http://www.fas.org/irp/congress/2002_rpt/hpsci_ths0702.html. Concerning the 2008 attacks in Mumbai, compare ABC News, 'U.S. Warned India in October of Potential Terror Attack', 1 December 2008, online: http://abcnews.go.com/print?id=6368013, with CNN.com, 'Mumbai police chief: No warning given of impending attack', 2 December 2008, online: http://edition.cnn.com/2008/WORLD/asiapcf/12/02/mumbai.warning/index.html.

[19]On the issue of assessing potential threats of terrorism see, for example: University of Arizona, Eller College of Management, and Artificial Intelligence Lab, *Terrorism Knowledge Discovery Project. A Knowledge Discovery Project to Addressing the Threats of Terrorism* (September 2004).

[20]See, for example, Marc Nicholson, 'An Essay on Terrorism', 2003 *AmericanDiplomacy.org*, online: http://www.unc.edu/depts/diplomat/archives_roll/2003_0709/nicholson_terr/nicholson_terr.html (as accessed 10 August 2005, copy on file with author).

modernity (see Sect. 3.1.4). To such groups, all modern, non-Muslim, States are a potential target.

4.1.2.2 Terrorism in the South Pacific

As discussed in the introduction to this part of the chapter, there has been a particularly strong sentiment expressed in New Zealand that there was no need for New Zealand to adopt counter-terrorism legislation, including because there was no threat of terrorism against it. Having said that the *Rainbow Warrior* bombing was the only incident of international terrorism within the South Pacific, it should be recognised that this statement is dependent on what definition of terrorism is adopted. Certainly, it is the only *international* terrorist act occurring within the South Pacific. On 10 July 1985, French military agents Mafart and Prier bombed and sank the Greenpeace flag-ship the *Rainbow Warrior* in the Auckland harbour port, resulting in the death of a Greenpeace activist on board the vessel. The bombing took place just days before the *Rainbow Warrior* was to undertake a protest voyage to the French nuclear test site at Moruroa Atoll.[21]

In addition, Simpson points to various *national* acts of terrorism within the Pacific.[22] In New Caledonia in the 1980s, the Kanak Socialist National Liberation Front (FLNKS) was denounced as a separatist terrorist movement.[23] It subsequently formed part of the coalition government in 2001.[24] The Fiji coups of 1987 and 2000 have likewise been classified as terrorist events,[25] although they might more properly be categorised as internal civil conflicts. The "civil conflict" in the Solomon Islands during 2000, in contrast, has been said to include terrorist conduct on the part of both main factions, the Malaita Eagles Force and the Isatabu Freedom Movement.[26]

There appears to be a commonly held view that the likelihood of terrorist acts being perpetrated within the South Pacific is remote, such that counter-terrorism

---

[21]Greenpeace, 'The Bombing of the Warrior', online: http://archive.greenpeace.org/comms/rw/pkbomb.html. Mention might also be made to other incidents (which may, or may not, be considered to amount to terrorist acts, depending on the definition adopted) within New Zealand. For example, on 18 November 1982, Neil Roberts carried and exploded a gelignite bomb in the entrance to the Wanganui police computer, said to have been perpetrated to advance his anarchist beliefs: see http://cw178.tripod.com/neil1.htm (as accessed on 6 July 2005 – copy on file with author). Two years later, there was a bomb attack at the Wellington Trade Union Centre, in which one person was killed: see Submissions of the Socialist Workers' Organisation to the Foreign Affairs, Defence and Trade Committee on the Terrorism Suppression Bill, online: http://www.converge.org.nz (as accessed on 6 July 2005 – copy on file with author).

[22]Simpson (2004).

[23]Ibid.

[24]Electionworld.org, "Elections in New Caledonia", online: http://www.electionworld.org/newcaledonia.htm (as accessed on 16 September 2004 – copy on file with author).

[25]Simpson (2004).

[26]Ibid.

should remain at the low-end of priorities for the region. While this risk assessment might be correct, there are various factors that count in favour of a more proactive approach, from even a purely self-serving perspective. As evident from the foregoing discussion, the South Pacific has been subject to terrorist incidents in the past, however defined. Regard should also be had to the possibility and consequences of a direct attack. Of particular relevance to a number of Pacific Island States, as States reliant upon the export of commodities such as dairy, meat and fruit,[27] is the bio security of those States. This is a matter dealt with primarily under the domestic legislation of each State including, for example, the Biosecurity Act 1993 in New Zealand. New Zealand took steps in 2003 towards including bioterrorism as an offence under its domestic law.[28]

Of even greater relevance, the reality of the contemporary world is that globalisation has dissolved distances that may have once protected New Zealand and the Pacific Islands, despite their geographical isolation. Transport and communications systems, access to the internet, and more efficient means of moving people and money, mean that it is easier for the world to interact with the South Pacific.[29] Individuals thought to be connected with Al-Qa'ida have been reported to have been present in New Zealand, Australia and Fiji.[30] Former Pacific Forum Secretary General, Greg Urwin, has stated that while terrorists may not seek to attack citizens and institutions of South Pacific countries, the region might prove to be a tempting target, either for an attack like the one in Bali in October 2002 (see Sect. 4.1 above), or as a base or staging point from which terrorist cells might undertake planning for an attack elsewhere.[31] The New Zealand Security Intelligence Service (NZSIS) reported in 2004, for example, that Islamic extremists with links to international terrorist organisations were thought likely to be operating in New Zealand:[32]

---

[27]By way of example, Statistics New Zealand identifies exports for the years ended June 2001, 2002 and 2003 to be as follows: milk powder, butter and cheese at $(million) 5,790 (2001), 5,891 (2002) and 4,679 (2003); meat and edible offal at $(million) 4,182 (2001), 4,429 (2002) and 4,112 (2003); logs, wood and wood article at $(million) 2,192 (2001), 2,378 (2002) and 2,386 (2003); fish, crustaceans and molluscs at $(million) 1,374 (2001), 1,402 (2002) and 1,032 (2003); and fruit at $(million) 1,045 (2001), 1,159 (2002) and 1,032 (2003): see Statistics New Zealand online information "Quick Facts – Economy", online: http://www.stats.govt.nz/domino/external/web/nzstories.nsf/htmldocs/Quick+Facts+Economy (as accessed on 17 September 2004 – copy on file with author).

[28]The Crimes Act 1961 was amended to include new sections 298A and 298B, making it an offence to contaminate food, crops, water or other products. See further Chap. 14, Sect. 14.2.3.2.

[29]Urwin (2004, para 8).

[30]Ibid, para 9. Anecdotal reports are that one of the September 11 hijackers spent a considerable time living in Fiji up until six months prior to the World Trade Centre attacks.

[31]Ibid, para 10.

[32]New Zealand Security Intelligence Service, Report to the House of Representatives for the year ended 30 June 2004, presented to the House of Representatives pursuant to section 4J of the New Zealand Security Intelligence Service Act 1969, p. 11.

> From the Service's own investigations we assess that there are individuals in or from
> New Zealand who support Islamic extremist causes. The Service views these develop-
> ments, most of which have come to attention within 2003/04, with considerable concern.
> They indicate attempts to use New Zealand as a safe haven from which activities of security
> concern elsewhere can be facilitated and/or the involvement of people from New Zealand
> in such activities.

This assessment should be compared with that for the 12 months up to June 2006, in which the NZSIS stated that: "The Service is not aware of any specific terrorist threat to New Zealand" and consequently judged the threat of a terrorist attack as being low.[33] The earlier point made by the NZSIS and the Pacific Forum Secretary-General nevertheless remains: even if a country is not at a high risk of being a direct target of terrorism, it might still be used as a platform from which terrorists might operate, train, launder money, or otherwise facilitate international terrorism.

4.1.3 Supporting an International Framework on Counter-Terrorism

Drawing from the latter discussion, one of the most important points to make is a relatively simple one, although the consequences of it are wide-ranging. The international conventions and protocols, reinforced by customary law and resolu-tions of the General Assembly, and added to by Security Council resolutions, create an *international framework* for countering terrorism. A considerable measure of their effectiveness lies in the universal adoption and implementation of the obliga-tions under that framework in order to prevent any State being either targeted by terrorists or used by them as a base of operations.

Following the train bombing in Madrid on 11 March 2004, in which nearly 200 people were killed, Spain's Ambassador to the United Nations (who then chaired the Security Council Counter-Terrorism Committee) reflected this sentiment, criti-cising unnamed nations for a "lack of effort" in countering terrorism.[34] The point later made by the former US Ambassador to the United Nations, John Danworth, was as follows:[35]

> [The Counter-Terrorism Committee] must never forget that so long as a few states are not
> acting quickly enough to raise their capacity to fight terrorism or are not meeting their
> international counterterrorism obligations, all of us remain vulnerable.

---

[33]New Zealand Security Intelligence Service, Report to the House of Representatives for the year ended 30 June 2006, presented to the House of Representatives pursuant to section 4J of the New Zealand Security Intelligence Service Act 1969, p. 12.

[34]United Nations Foundation, "Spanish Diplomat Blames Nations for 'Lack of Effort' on Terror-ism", UN Wire, 12 March 2004, previously available online: http://www.unwire.org/UNWire (copy on file with author).

[35]United Nations Foundation, "Counterterrorism Cooperation Improving, Security Council Told", UN Wire, 20 July 2004, previously available online: http://www.unwire.org/UNWire (copy on file with author).

The question is thus no longer one of domestic security in order to prevent attacks from occurring within a State's own borders and, in doing so, assessing the risks of such attacks and the appropriate measures in response. Although those assessments and corresponding national security interests remain, effective counter-terrorism requires – to achieve international security and in light of the manner in which terrorists and terrorist organisations operate – that *all* States prevent and preclude terrorist conduct and preparations. A high level of threat posed to a State might cause that State to impose measures above those required by the international framework, but the reverse does not apply. Even if it is accepted, for example, that New Zealand does not bear any substantial risk of being the subject of a terrorist attack, its role in combating international terrorism through the implementation of the obligations set out in Chap. 3 are equal to all other States.

All of these various points are reiterated on the website of the New Zealand Security Intelligence Service:[36]

> The terrorist threat to New Zealand is low, but it cannot be discounted. The country learned at the time of the Rainbow Warrior bombing that relative geographic isolation, in itself, is no guarantee of immunity. The events in the United States on 11 September 2001 confirmed that terrorism is an international phenomenon and terrorists consider the world their stage when they look for a way to advance their cause.
>
> There are individuals and groups in New Zealand with links to overseas organisations that are committed to acts of terrorism, violence and intimidation. Some have developed local structures that are dedicated to the support of their overseas parent bodies. There are also isolated extremists in New Zealand who advocate using violence to impress on others their own political, ethnic or religious viewpoint.
>
> But the threat of terrorism could come equally from beyond New Zealand. Modern transport and communication have effectively made the world a smaller place. Events such as a visit by and overseas dignitary, or a major international gathering may be seen by off-shore terrorists as providing the opportunity to do something spectacular to capture world wide publicity, or to otherwise further their cause.
>
> There is also the risk that individuals or groups may use New Zealand as a safe haven from which to plan or facilitate terrorist acts elsewhere.

Similarly, Canada's National Security Policy defines three principal national security interests, all of which correspond to the idea, in the context of combating terrorism, of supporting the international framework on counter-terrorism: protecting Canada and the safety and security of Canadians at home and abroad; ensuring that Canada is not a base for threats to its allies; and contributing to international security.[37] As succinctly put by Canada's Department of Foreign Affairs and

---

[36]New Zealand Security Intelligence Service website, Protecting New Zealand from Terrorism, online: http://www.nzsis.govt.nz/work/work.html (as accessed on 16 November 2004 – copy on file with author). For the Service's current description of the treat of terrorist acts to New Zealand, see http://www.nzsis.govt.nz/work/terrorism.aspx.

[37]Public Safety Canada, Securing an Open Society: Canada's National Security Policy 2004, online: http://www.publicsafety.gc.ca/pol/ns/secpol04-eng.aspx.

International Trade: "Canada's security is inextricably linked to that of other States".[38]

4.1.4   Other Related National Interests

Measures to counter international terrorism are also capable of contributing to the furtherance of national interests. It is safe to assume, for example, that it will be in the national interest of responsible international actors to contribute to the international framework on counter-terrorism and thereby contribute to the maintenance of a peaceful, secure, and free-functioning international society. On a more specific level, border security, for example, is not just relevant to international counter-terrorism, but also to the maintenance of import and export trades, the thwarting of drug-trafficking, and illegal migration. Anti-money laundering practices contribute to the suppression of organised crime of all types, not just the financing of terrorism. The protection of nuclear material is relevant not only to preventing terrorist organisations from gaining access to and using nuclear weapons as tools of terrorism, but also to the objective of disarmament and non-proliferation.

4.2   Mechanisms for the Implementation of International Obligations by the Case Study Countries

The counter-terrorism obligations of Australia, Canada, New Zealand and the United Kingdom exist through various sources of international law: through customary international law; as a States parties to the international conventions related to terrorism; and through membership in the United Nations (and the treaty obligations that flow from such membership). Each source of law displays different means of implementation and obligation. In turn, those different means of implementation bear upon the way in which domestic courts can deal with the application of the law.

It is useful to briefly note, at this stage, the divergent views on the status of international law norms in domestic law. As explained by Brownlie, there are two theories on the relationship between municipal and international law.[39] The dualist theory posits that international and domestic laws operate in entirely separate systems, and is largely based upon the notion of State sovereignty: the principle that a State has the right to perform governmental actions to the exclusion of all

---

[38]Department of Foreign Affairs and International Trade Canada, International Crime and Terrorism, online: http://www.dfait-maeci.gc.ca/foreign_policy/internationalcrime-old/terrorism-en.asp.

[39]Brownlie (2003, pp. 31–53).

others within its territory.[40] Dualists distinguish international law from municipal law by three principal means. First, the subjects of international law are sovereign States, while in municipal law both individuals and the State enjoy legal personality. Next, the sources of international law are founded on the notion of the equality of its subjects (States), whereas domestic law is derived from the parliamentary authority of the State giving rise to the domestic constitutional notion of parliamentary sovereignty. Finally, the inter-State structure of international law is different from the intra-State implementation and enforcement of domestic law. On those bases, dualist exponents such as Triepel and Strupp hold that international law is an inferior source of law and therefore does not apply at the national level unless there has been some act on the part of the State transforming the international norm into a domestic one.[41]

In contrast to the dualist theory, the monist theory on the reception of international obligations holds that there is one, all-embracing legal order, comprising both international and domestic law. Lauterpacht, one of the more forceful and practical proponents of monism, argues that it is impossible for two norms with separate bases to be valid at the same time in the same territory.[42] Indeed, he effectively turns the dualist approach on its head and proposes that international law employs domestic law to govern human affairs. That is, the idea that the State is purely a vehicle used by individuals to represent their interests in the international community (by extension of the idea of the social contract by which the State is empowered to govern its people)[43] so that when the State does something at the international level, including the making of international law, it is acting under the authority given to it by those individuals. Under the monist view there is no need to transform an international law rule into a domestic one.

Turning from theory to practice, different domestic courts adopt alternative approaches, depending upon the particular source of the international law obligation. The Commonwealth case study countries are no different, and the approach of each country to the different sources of law is examined next.

Before doing so, an important distinction should be made. What is being discussed in this part of the chapter is the *reception* of international law by the domestic courts, i.e. whether and how the courts will apply an international law rule in any matter before them, such as a terrorism prosecution, or the review of a determination to designate and freeze the assets of a person under counter-terrorism legislation. This does not impact upon the *jurisprudential weight* of the international obligation,

---

[40]As defined by Arbitrator Huber in the *Island of Palmas Case*, United Nations 2 Reports of International Arbitral Awards 829, 858–859.

[41]Triepel, *Völkerrecht und Landesrecht* (1899), and Strupp, *Eléments* (2nd edition, 1930), as cited by Brownlie (2003, p. 31 note 2).

[42]See, by way of example, Lauterpacht (1950).

[43]See, for example, Locke (1960) (see the section on Consent, Political Obligation, and the Ends of Government in Chap. 5), and Russeau (1968).

i.e. whether or not the rule is binding upon the State. Indeed, as made clear by article 27 of the Vienna Convention on the Law of Treaties, a party to a treaty cannot invoke the provisions of its internal (domestic) law as justification for its failure to perform a treaty.[44] This codifies a pre-existing customary rule to this effect, as first set out in *Alabama Claims Arbitration*, where the arbitral tribunal concluded that States could not plead their municipal law as a means of avoiding their international obligations.[45] This applies not just to legislation, but also to common law. In principle, therefore, a domestic court might refuse to receive an international law obligation and thus render the State in breach of its international obligation, or might receive the rule in such a way which is likewise in violation of international law.

4.2.1   *The Reception of Customary International Law Obligations*

Most Commonwealth States adopt what can be described, overall, as a monist approach to the reception of customary international law rules. The viewpoint of courts in Australia, Canada, New Zealand and the United Kingdom is that customary international law will form part of the common law, albeit that this might be subject to a level of "judicial recognition". Thus, when a court is satisfied that a given proposition amounts to a rule of customary law, and thereby judicially recognises the rule, it will apply it and thereby transform it into common law.

Development of this approach can be seen in English case law. A monist approach, rendering customary international law automatically applicable, was taken until the 1970s, as evident in the House of Lords decision in *Zoernsch v Wadlock* where it was said that "international law... forms part of the law of England administered by the Courts".[46] In *ex parte Thakrar*, Lord Denning later stated that "the rules of international law only become part of our law insofar as they are accepted by us".[47] The UK Court of Appeal clarified, in *Thai-Europe Tapioca Service Ltd v Government of Pakistan*, that it was "important to realise that a rule of international law is incorporated into our municipal law by a decision of a competent Court... and the rule of stare decisis".[48] Technically, therefore, the judicial recognition of a rule of customary international law transforms the rule into common law, and thereby incorporates the rule into domestic law.

---

[44]Vienna Convention on the Law of Treaties, opened for signature 23 May 1969, 1155 UNTS 331 (entered into force 27 January 1980).

[45]*Alabama Claims Arbitration* (1872) in Moore, International Arbitrations (New York, 1988) 653.

[46]*Zoernsch v Wadlock* [1964] 2 All ER 256, 265.

[47]*R v Secretary of State for the Home Department, ex parte Thakrar* [1974] QB 694, 671.

[48]*Thai-Europe Tapioca Service Ltd v Government of Pakistan* [1975] 3 All ER 961, 969.

The same approach is taken by Canada[49] and New Zealand.[50] A subtle point to make is that, as a consequence of this approach, the incorporation of customary international law does not mean that such rules, by themselves, bind courts in these jurisdictions. Rather, they bind courts at least to the same extent as the common law in general binds them.[51] The implications of this observation come to bear when one considers the approach of courts to the interpretation of statutory rules, or in the case of direct conflict between a customary rule and an Act of Parliament. To the extent possible, courts will interpret domestic legislation consistently with customary international law. In *Worth v Worth*, for example, the New Zealand Court of Appeal stated that "if the enactment is ambiguous and is capable of two constructions, one of which would, and the other would not, conflict with the rules of international law, the latter construction should prevail".[52] This stems from the basic constitutional presumption that parliament does not intend to legislate in a manner contrary to the State's international obligations. This presumption was first enunciated nearly 200 years ago in the English case of *Le Louis*.[53]

Case law concerning the constitutional presumption in favour of conformity, which also applies to the reception of treaties, identifies two reasons for this approach. The first is that Parliament should be presumed to have legislated in a way which conforms with international law, unless it makes a clear expression to the contrary. Lord Escher, in *Colquhoun v Brooks* explained that "the English parliament cannot be supposed merely by reason of its having used general words to be intending to do that which is against the comity of nations".[54] Common law courts have also tended to take the view that it is a *duty* of the judiciary to achieve conformity between domestic legislation and international rules, wherever possible. Lord Denning described it as "the duty of [the] courts to construe our legislation so as to be in conformity with international law".[55] In Canada, Chief Justice Dickson

---

[49]See, for example: *The Ship "North" v The King* (1906) 37 SCR 385; *Re Foreign Legations* [1943] SCR 209 (see, especially, the judgment of Duff CJ); *Saint John v Fraser-Brace Overseas* [1958] SCR 263; *Re Regina and Palacios* (1984) 45 OR (2d) 269 (Ont CA); and *Bouzari v Iran* [2002] OJ No 1624 (HCJ) (QL).

[50]As evidenced through a long line of authority in New Zealand courts concerning the doctrine of sovereign immunity. See *Marine Steel v Government of the Marshall Island* [1981] 2 NZLR 1, 9–10, in which Barker J recognised, in an obiter statement, the relevance of the customary international law rule of sovereign immunity and that no special act of transformation was required in the application of such rules by New Zealand courts. In *Reef Shipping v The Ship "Fua Kavenga"* [1987] 1 NZLR 550, 569 Smellie J applied the doctrine in New Zealand. The New Zealand Court of Appeal also applied the doctrine in *Governor of Pitcairn and Associated Islands v Sutton* [1995] 1 NZLR 426, Cooke P referring to the doctrine as part of "common law, reflecting international law" (428).

[51]Van Ert (2004).

[52]*Worth v Worth* [1931] NZLR 1109. See also: *Van Gorkam v Attorney General* [1977] 1 NZLR 535, 542; and *Yan v Minister of Internal Affairs* [1997] 3 NZLR 450, 460.

[53]*Le Louis* [1817] 165 ER 1465.

[54]*Colquhoun v Brooks* (1888) 21 QBD 52, 57–88.

[55]*Corocraft v Pan American Airways* [1968] 3 WLR 1273, 1281.

called it "the duty of the Court" to construe legislation so as to give it "a fair and liberal interpretation with a view to fulfilling Canada's international obligations".[56]

In the case of an irreconcilable conflict between customary law and a statutory provision, however, the courts will defer to Parliament and apply the domestic statutory provision. This was held to be the rule by the Privy Council in *Chung Cheung v The King*.[57] The New Zealand Court of Appeal has emphasised, in *Governor of Pitcairn v Sutton*, that this will only be the case where the conflict is irreconcilable, i.e. where there is no way in which, without misconstruing the statutory provision or rending its interpretation absurd, there is no way to adopt an interpretation which is in harmony with the customary law rule.[58]

The position concerning the reception of customary international law by domestic courts in Australia is more complex. Although the High Court of Australia has in the past accepted that customary international law forms part of Australian law,[59] Australian courts do not now support a strictly automatic incorporation. As explained by Justice Wilcox in the 1999 decision of the High Court in *Nulyarimma v Thompson*, which considered whether the customary international law prohibition against genocide formed part of Australian law:

> [I]t is one things to say Australia has an international legal obligation to prosecute or extradite a genocide suspect found within its territory, and that the Commonwealth Parliament may legislate to ensure that obligation is fulfilled; it is another thing to say that, without legislation to that effect, such a person may be put on trial for genocide before an Australian court. If this were the position, it would lead to the curious result that an international obligation incurred pursuant to customary law has greater domestic consequences than an obligation incurred, expressly and voluntarily, by Australia signing and ratifying an international convention.

It has to be said that the case law in which this issue is considered has been primarily concerned with the question of evidence, i.e. proof of the existence of the rule of customary law. This is natural, given the complexity of customary international law and the elements required to establish the existence of binding principles.[60] As concluded by Anton, Mathew and Morgan, it appears that the view now holding sway in Australia is that a rule of customary international law is to be adopted by the judiciary, rather than by parliamentary incorporation into a statute, upon finding that the rule is not inconsistent with legislation or public policy.[61] While this is perhaps a little broader than the judicial recognition approach in the other three jurisdictions considered, it is nevertheless more akin to a monist approach than a dualist one.

[56]*R v Zingre* [1981] 2 SCR 392, 409–410.

[57]*Chung Cheung v The King* [1939] AC 160.

[58]*Governor of Pitcairn v Sutton* (n 50) 438.

[59]See, for example, *Potter v Broken Hill Co Ltd* (1906) 3 CLR 479, 495, 506–507, and 510.

[60]See the discussion on the elements of customary international law in Chap. 3 herein, Sect. 3.3.

[61]Anton et al. (2005, pp. 407–412, particularly p. 410).

4.2.2 The Reception of Treaty Obligations

Unlike customary international law, treaties require incorporation to become part of domestic law. Here, the Commonwealth case study countries adopt a common dualist approach. In the often cited decision of the House of Lords in *Attorney-General for Canada v Attorney-General for Ontario*, Lord Atkin drew a distinction between the formation of a treaty on the one hand and the performance of the obligations under the treaty on the other.[62] He observed that the formation of a treaty is a matter for the executive, while performance lay within the purview of the legislature, by enactment into statute of the responsibilities undertaken through an international treaty.

4.2.2.1 Treaty Action by the Executive

The power to make treaties is a prerogative power vested in the Crown. This applies to all treaty action which impacts upon international treaty obligations of Australia, Canada, New Zealand or the United Kingdom (ratification, accession, the confirmatory exchange of letters, or the modification or withdrawal from treaties to which those countries are parties). While this remains the case today, all four countries have developed mechanisms to allow for a greater level of parliamentary scrutiny of treaty action in order to achieve greater levels of transparency, and to avoid a situation where the executive binds its country to treaty obligations but parliament refuses to 'perform' those obligations by incorporating them into domestic law.

4.2.2.2 Parliament's Role

As explained by Lord Atkin in *Attorney-General for Canada v Attorney-General for Ontario*, it is for the legislature to 'perform' a treaty by enacting into statute the responsibilities undertaken through a treaty.[63] This lies at the heart of the dualist approach to the reception of treaty obligations.

Added to this, as mentioned earlier, is the development in the case study countries of an increased role for legislatures in the treaty-making process. The oldest, but least developed (in terms of parliamentary oversight), of these mechanisms exists in the United Kingdom under the Ponsonby Rule. Since 1924, the text of all treaties must be laid before parliament for at least 21 sitting days before any treaty action can take place. This is done by means of a 'Command Paper' and,

---

[62]*Attorney-General for Canada v Attorney-General for Ontario* [1937] AC 326, 347–348. See also *JH Rayner (Mincing Lane) Ltd v Department of Trade and Industry* [1990] 2 AC 418. The principle was reaffirmed by the Supreme Court of Canada in *Francis v The Queen* [1956] SCR 618, 621.

[63]*Attorney-General for Canada v Attorney-General for Ontario* (ibid).

since 1997, treaties have been laid before parliament together with an Explanatory Memorandum.[64] An Explanatory Memorandum describes the subject matter of the treaty and why it is proposed that the United Kingdom should take the treaty action concerned. It highlights the benefits for the UK from participation in the treaty as well as any burdens which would result.[65] Since November 2000, when a Command Paper is laid under the Ponsonby Rule it is also sent, with its accompanying Explanatory Memorandum, to the relevant Department Select Committee in the House of Commons.

Canada's policy and practice on treaty-making is very similar to that in the United Kingdom.[66] The Minister of Foreign Affairs tables all agreements before the House of Commons for at least 21 sitting days before taking any treaty action.[67] Tabling is accompanied by an Explanatory Memorandum, the purpose of which is the same as Explanatory Memoranda in the United Kingdom, although Canada has adopted guidelines calling for various points to be covered in a Memorandum, including the national interest in the treaty action, the policy considerations involved, and the implications for provincial jurisdictions.[68]

In Australia, the executive branch of government has an exclusive and unlimited power to enter into treaties, although the content of treaties must again be incorporated into domestic law by parliament before the courts are able to apply them.[69] Despite this, the Australian Constitution does not give parliament any formal role in the treaty-making process. Following a report of the Senate Legal and Constitutional Reference Committee, the treaty-making and implementation process in Australia was reformed in 1996 and further reviewed in 1999.[70] Once the government has decided to take treaty action, the treaty-making process is undertaken in two stages:[71]

---

[64]Foreign and Commonwealth Office, *The Ponsonby Rule*, online: http://www.fco.gov.uk/resources/en/pdf/pdf2/fco_nopdf_ponsonbyrule.

[65]Foreign and Commonwealth Office, *Treaties and MOUs. Guidance on Practice and Procedures* (2nd edition, revised May 2004), online: http://www.fco.gov.uk/resources/en/pdf/3706546/treatiesmousguidance, pp. 9–16.

[66]See, generally, Currie (2001, Chap. 6).

[67]Department of Foreign Affairs and International Trade (Treaty Section), The Treaty-Making Process: Departmental Guidelines, Annex A in Canada Treaty Information, *Policy on Tabling of Treaties in Parliament*, online: http://www.treaty-accord.gc.ca/procedure.asp, section 6.

[68]Department of Foreign Affairs and International Trade, Procedures for the Tabling of Treaties in the House of Commons, Annex B in Canada Treaty Information, *Policy on Tabling of Treaties in Parliament*, online: http://www.treaty-accord.gc.ca/procedure.asp.

[69]On the authority of the executive, see *Commonwealth v Tasmania* (1983) 158 CLR 1, 303. See also Anton et al. (2005, pp. 426–427).

[70]Senate Legal and Constitutional Reference Committee, *Trick or Treaty? Commonwealth Power to Make and Implement Treaties* (Canberra, November 1995). See also the online publication of the Australian Department of Foreign Affairs and Trade, *Australia and International Treaty Making Information Kit*, at URL http://www.austlii.edu.au/au/other/dfat/infokit.html.

[71]See Charlesworth et al. (2003, pp. 441–444).

- All treaties (and related action, including amendments to or withdrawal from treaties) must now be tabled in the federal parliament for at least 15 sitting days before the government can take binding action such as ratification, accession, or an exchange of letters. The one exception to this rule concerns treaties certified by the Minister for Foreign Affairs as being particularly urgent or sensitive, involving significant commercial, strategic or foreign policy interests. When tabled, each treaty must be accompanied by a National Interest Analysis (NIA), which notes the reasons why Australia should become a party to the treaty. Where relevant, this includes a discussion of the foreseeable economic, environmental, social and cultural effects of the treaty action; the obligations imposed by the treaty; its direct financial costs to Australia; how the treaty will be implemented domestically; what consultation has occurred in relation to the treaty action and whether the treaty provides for withdrawal or denunciation.[72]
- The treaty and its accompanying NIA, are then considered by the Joint Standing Committee on Treaties (JSCOT), established under the 1996 reforms, whose role it is to review and report on all treaty actions proposed by government before action is taken which would bind Australia to the terms of a treaty. The Committee normally advertises its reviews in the national press and on its website, and routinely takes evidence at public hearings from government agencies, and may also invite people who have made written submissions to appear.[73] At the completion of its inquiries, the Committee presents a report to parliament containing advice on whether Australia should take binding treaty action and on other related issues that have emerged during the review.

New Zealand provides for legislative oversight in a similar way to Australia, although it goes further by expressly linking this mechanism to the enactment of incorporating legislation. In response to a report of the New Zealand Law Commission in 1997,[74] procedures for the making of treaties and the incorporation of their provisions are now governed by the Standing Orders of the House of Representative and the Cabinet Manual.[75] The treaty-making process in New Zealand is undertaken in four principal stages:[76]

- The first involves steps to be taken when a treaty is first adopted and signed, or where the executive is contemplating acceding to a treaty. In that event, Standing Order 387 requires all multilateral treaties and "significant" bilateral treaties to

---

[72]Australian Department of Foreign Affairs and Trade, Treaties, *The Constitution and the National Interest*, online: http://www.dfat.gov.au/treaties/making/making2.html.

[73]Parliament of Australia, Joint Standing Committee on Treaties, *Committee establishment, role and history*, online: http://www.aph.gov.au/house/committee/jsct/ppgrole.htm.

[74]New Zealand Law Commission, *The Treaty Making Process: Reform and the Role of Parliament*, Report No 45 (Wellington, 1997).

[75]Standing Orders of the House of Representatives (with effect 12 August 2005), Parliamentary Standing Orders 387 to 390; Cabinet Manual (Department of the Prime Minister and Cabinet, 2001), paragraphs 5.83–5.91.

[76]For a more detailed explanation of this process, see Conte (2006, pp. 77–80).

be presented to the House with a National Interest Assessment (NIA). Standing Order 388(1) sets out the various issues that must be address within a NIA, including the reasons for becoming a party to the treaty, the advantages and disadvantages of this, the costs of compliance and the steps that need to be taken to implement the obligations under the treaty.

- The treaty, with the accompanying NIA, must then be considered by Parliament's Foreign Affairs, Defence and Trade Committee for it to prepare a report to the House. In undertaking this second step, the Committee is required to determine whether the treaty should be brought to the attention of the House for consideration of any matters covered by the NIA or "for any other reason".[77] The Select Committee may seek public submissions at this stage, although it is not obliged to do so.[78]
- The next step is to introduce legislation through which the treaty obligations are to be incorporated into domestic law. This will be accompanied by the Committee's report, to which the National Interest Assessment must be appended.[79] Unlike in Australia, the Standing Orders thereby establish an express link between the review by parliament of the government's proposed treaty action, and the consequent enactment of incorporating legislation.
- Only once the incorporating legislation has been passed as an Act of Parliament will the executive be free to take the final step of ratifying the treaty, thereby making its provisions (as translated by an enactment) binding at international law upon New Zealand once the treaty enters into force.

4.2.2.3   Reception of Treaty Obligations by the Judiciary

The direct consequence of the dualist approach to the reception of treaty obligations is that the provisions of a treaty cannot be relied upon in judicial proceedings unless first incorporated into domestic law. Relying on the House of Lords decision in *Attorney-General for Canada v Attorney-General for Ontario*, for example, the New Zealand Court of Appeal concerned itself with a police warrant to recover the black boxes of an Ansett aircraft in *New Zealand Air Line Pilot's Association Incorporated v Attorney-General and Others*.[80] Although certain provisions of the Chicago Convention on International Civil Aviation seemed to preclude the recovery of black boxes, the particular provisions had not been implemented into New Zealand law by legislation and the warrants were thus allowed to stand.[81]

---

[77]Standing Orders 389 and 390.

[78]Cabinet Manual (n 75) para 5.88.

[79]Standing Order 390; and Cabinet Manual para 5.91.

[80]*New Zealand Air Line Pilot's Association Incorporated v Attorney-General and Others* [1997] 3 NZLR 269, 280–285.

[81]Chicago Convention on International Civil Aviation, opened for signature 7 December 1944, 15 UNTS 295 (entered into force 4 April 1947).

Similarly, in considering the status of the Treaty of Waitangi in *Te Heuheu Tukino v Aotea District Maori Land Board*, Chief Justice Myers had earlier held that:[82]

> A treaty only becomes enforceable as part of the municipal law if and when it is made so by legislative authority.

The position in Australia is the same. The provisions of a treaty which engage international obligations for Australia have no direct effect unless they are transformed directly into operative statutory provisions.[83]

Although treaties have no direct legal effect without implementing legislation, they may have a degree of indirect legal effect by means of the interpretive presumption that legislation is intended to conform with international law. The presumption was first enunciated nearly 200 years ago in English case of *Le Louis* (discussed at Sect. 4.2.1 above). In the more recent 1976 case of *The Jade*, Lord Diplock said that:[84]

> ...as the Act was passed to enable Her Majesty's government to give effect to the obligations in international law which it would assume on ratifying the convention to which it was a signatory, the rule of statutory construction laid down in *Salomon v Customs and Excise Commissioners* [1966] 3 All ER 871 and *Post Office v Estuary Radio Ltd* [1967] 3 All ER 633 is applicable. If there be any difference between the language of the statutory provision and that of the corresponding provision of the convention, the statutory language should be construed in the same sense as that of the convention if the words of the statute are reasonably capable of bearing that meaning.

The majority of the Supreme Court of Canada observed, in *Ordon Estate v Grail*, that: "Although international law is not binding upon Parliament or the provincial legislatures, a court must presume that legislation is intended to comply with Canada's obligations under international instruments...".[85] The same approach is taken in Australia, where the High Court of Australia has recognised that "the courts should, in case of ambiguity, favour a construction of a Commonwealth statute which accords with the obligations of Australia under an international

---

[82]*Te Heuheu Tukino v Aotea District Maori Land Board* [1939] NZLR 107, 120. See also the judgment of Cooke J in *Ashby v Minister of Immigration* [1981] 1 NZLR 222, 224, where he said, referring to the Convention on the Elimination of All Forms of Racial Discrimination, that: "the Convention has not been incorporated into New Zealand law by any Act of Parliament. It is elementary that international treaty obligations are not binding in domestic law until they have become incorporated in that way".

[83]*Chow Hung Ching v The King* (1949) 77 CLR 449. See also McGinley 1990.

[84]*The Jade* [1976] 1 All ER 920, 924. This decision was cited favourably by the High Court of New Zealand in *Mewes v Attorney-General* [1979] 1 NZLR 648, 666.

[85]*Ordon Estate v Grail* [1998] 3 SCR 437, para 137. Recent judgments of the Court have cited *Ordon Estate* as authority for the presumption of conformity. See, for example: *Quebec (Commission des droits de la personne et des droits de la jeunesse) v Maksteel Québec Inc* [2003] SCC 68, para 73; and *Canadian Foundation for Children, Youth and the Law v Canada (Attorney General)* [2004] SCC 4. para 31. See also: *Canadian Foundation for Children, Youth and the Law v Canada (Attorney General)* 2004 SCC 4, paras 31–33; and van Ert (2002, pp. 214–219).

treaty".[86] In the case of New Zealand, the principle of conformity was recognised by the High Court of New Zealand in *Mewes v Attorney-General*, where it referred favourably to the statement of Lord Diplock in *The Jade*.[87] It should be noted, however, that if the terms of the domestic legislation are clear and unambiguous and irreconcilably conflict with a treaty, it will be the statute which will be given effect to by domestic courts.[88]

The principle of interpreting domestic legislation consistently with treaty law extends to the manner in which any statutory discretion is applied. See, for example, *Ashby v Minister of Immigration* where compliance with international obligations was treated as a relevant consideration in the exercise of a Ministerial discretion.[89] This approach can also apply during the hiatus between signature and ratification. Once a State has signed a treaty text subject to ratification, acceptance or approval, it is obliged to refrain from acts which would defeat the "object and purpose of the treaty" until it has made its intention clear not to become a party to the treaty.[90] This principle was applied by the Environment Court at Auckland, New Zealand, in *Environmental Defence Society v Auckland Regional Council* where the Court took the view that New Zealand, as a signatory to the Kyoto Protocol, was required to refrain from acts which would defeat the object and purpose of the protocol even before it had ratified the instrument.[91] Although the Framework Convention had not been specifically enacted into New Zealand law, and New Zealand had not yet ratified the Kyoto Protocol, both instruments were treated as relevant considerations to be taken into account under section 104(1)(i) of the Resource Management Act 1991.

4.2.3 Implementation of Security Council Resolutions

Security Council resolutions may impose obligations upon members of the United Nations, or call upon those members to undertake (i.e. recommend) certain action (see Chap. 3, Sect. 3.2.3). Depending upon the nature of those obligations or recommendations, member States may chose to take action by various means, including by statute, regulations, or policy statements or guidelines.

---

[86]*Chu Kheung Lim v Minister of Immigration, Local Government and Ethnic Affairs* [1992] HCA 64. By amendments introduced in 1984, Australia's Acts Interpretation Act 1901 allows courts to refer to treaties in the interpretation of federal statutes where it is clear from extrinsic materials, such as parliamentary debates, that it was the intention of Parliament to give effect to a treaty – see Shearer (1997, pp. 34 and 53).

[87]*Mewes v Attorney-General* [1979] 1 NZLR 648, 666. See also *R v Bain, application by Television New Zealand* (unreported judgment of 22 July 1996, CA 255/95); and *Attorney General v E* [2000] 3 NZLR 257, 259–260 and 262–264.

[88]See, for example, *Ashby v Minister of Immigration* (n 82), 229.

[89]*Ashby v Minister of Immigration* (ibid), 224. See also Cranwell (2001).

[90]Vienna Convention on the Law of Treaties (n 44), article 18.

[91]*Environmental Defence Society (Inc) v Auckland Regional Council* [2002] NZRMA 492.

Where binding action is required in response to a Security Council resolution, the United Kingdom provides for steps to be taken by way of Orders in Council, rather than the lengthy process of enacting legislation. Section 1 of the United Nations Act 1946 (UK) allows for Orders in Council to be made where the Security Council calls on the UK to take action under article 41 of the United Nations Charter. Article 41 of the Charter allows the Security Council to adopt resolutions which impose non-military sanctions and require members of the UN to implement and comply with those sanctions. An example, in the context of counter-terrorism, are the sanctions imposed against the Taliban under Security Council resolution 1267 (1999), which are considered further in Chap. 19.[92] Since 1999, Orders in Council made under the United Nations Act must be laid before parliament for its information as soon as they are made (section 1(4)).

The position in Canada and New Zealand is very similar to that in the United Kingdom. The implementation of sanctions under article 41 of the UN Charter can be given effect to through Orders in Council, which must be tabled before parliament as soon as they are made.[93] The implementation of Security Council sanctions in Australia is achieved through a range of administrative and legislative measures.[94] In the case of financial sanctions, including those adopted by the Security Council for the purpose of countering terrorism, these are implemented under the Charter of the United Nations Act 1945 (Australia) and regulations made and promulgated under it. It is useful, at this point, to note some distinctive features between the legislation in the four case study countries:

- Unlike the United Nations Act in the UK, the equivalent legislation in Australia, Canada and NZ establishes offences. Under common section 3(1) of the United Nations Act 1985 (Canada) and the United Nations Act 1946 (NZ), any person who contravenes an order or regulation made under the legislation is guilty of an offence. Australia's Charter of the United Nations Act contains a similar offence in section 27, and various more specific offences relating to terrorism and dealing with proscribed assets in Part 4 of the Act.
- Unique to Canada, the United Nations Act expressly provides for the annulment of regulations made under it by agreement of both the Senate and House of Commons (section 4(2)). The effect of this is to protect the sovereign status of the legislative branch against undue interference by the Crown.
- Unique to Australia and New Zealand, regulations made under the Charter of the United Nations Act (Australia) or the United Nations Act (NZ) are capable of

---

[92]SC Res 1267, UN SCOR, 4051st Mtg, UN Doc S/Res/1267 (1999).

[93]See: United Nations Act 1985 (Canada), section 2 (authorising the making of Orders in Council) and section 4(1) (requiring the Order in Council to be laid before parliament); and United Nations Act 1946 (New Zealand), section 2(1) (setting out the authorisation) and 2(3) (requiring tabling).

[94]For example: civil aviation restrictions are implemented by amendments to the Air Navigation Regulations 1947; and arms embargoes are implemented by promulgating regulations under the Charter of the United Nations Act 1945, amending the Customs (Prohibited Exports) Regulations 1958 and under Regulation 13E the Customs (Prohibited Exports) Regulations 1958.

overriding inconsistent primary legislation. Sections 9 (Australia) and 2 (New Zealand) thus fall within the category of what are known as 'Henry VIII clauses'. This feature, and its inter-relationship with the New Zealand Bill of Rights Act 1990, is a matter examined in Chap. 11 (see Sect. 11.6).

4.3   Implementation of International Counter-Terrorism Obligations by the Case Study Countries

The Commonwealth Statement on Terrorism committed Commonwealth members to implementing UN Security Council resolution 1373 (2001), in keeping with the fundamental values of the association. Within this context, Heads of Government agreed that any member State that aided, supported, instigated, financed or harboured terrorists, or permitted such activities within its jurisdiction, violated the fundamental values of the Commonwealth and should have no place in it.[95] Of relevance to this, and in response to Security Council resolution 1805 (2008), the UN Counter-Terrorism Committee (CTC – see Chap. 3, Sect. 3.2.4.1) prepared a report on a survey undertaken by experts of the Committee's Executive Directorate on the implementation of resolution 1373 (2001).[96] The 2008 survey focuses on the major thematic areas addressed by resolution 1373 and provides an assessment of its implementation by regions and sub-regions, as well as drawing some conclusions on global progress in implementation of the areas considered in the report. Also of relevance is an earlier report of the Security Council Working Group established pursuant to resolution 1566 (2004) – see Chap. 3, Sect. 3.2.4.4 – which submitted recommendations to the Security Council on practical measures to be addressed in the fight against terrorism.[97] Useful too is the report of the Center on Global Counterterrorism Cooperation on best practices in the implementation of Security Council mandates.[98]

Chapters 5–8 in this title end with a summary and conclusion of the compliance by each of the case study countries with the international framework for countering terrorism. The four countries are included in the 2008 report of the CTC under the regional label "Western European and other States".[99] The report assesses the areas

---

[95]Report of the Commonwealth Committee on Terrorism (CCT): Commonwealth Plan of Action, online: http://www.thecommonwealth.org/Templates/Internal.asp?NodeID=35145, para 2.

[96]Report of the Counter-Terrorism Committee, Survey of the implementation of Security Council resolution 1373 (2001), UN Doc S/2008/379 (2008).

[97]Report of the Security Council Working Group established pursuant to resolution 1566 (2004), UN Doc S/2005/789 (2005).

[98]Center on Global Counterterrorism Cooperation, Report on Standards and Best Practices for Improving States' Implementation of UN Security Council Counter-Terrorism Mandates (New York, 2006).

[99]Survey of the implementation of Security Council resolution 1373 (2001): Report of the Counter-Terrorism Committee, UN Doc S/2008/379 (2008), paras 133–139.

of legislation, countering the financing of terrorism, border control, institutional structures and mechanisms on domestic security and law enforcement, and international cooperation. The resolution 1566 Working Group emphasised the importance of each of those areas, and added that practical measures should be taken for curtailing recruitment and training, preventing public provocation, concerning the use of the internet, and relating to victims of terrorist acts.

4.3.1   Legislation

In order to implement Security Council resolution 1373 (2001), it is essential for each country to establish a comprehensive and coherent legal framework on counter-terrorism.[100] The Counter-Terrorism Committee noted that States have taken significant steps towards the development of such a framework, but concluded that progress has been more limited in certain regions, including in South-East Asia, although it did not specifically identify Australia or New Zealand as falling within this category.[101] An overview of the legal frameworks for the countering of terrorism in Australia, Canada, New Zealand and the United Kingdom is provided in Chaps. 5–8.

4.3.1.1   Terrorism-Related Offences

The Committee recommended that legal frameworks include all relevant terrorist offences and define the scope of terrorist acts. Appendix 3 in this text sets out terrorism-related offences under international law, and those under the national law of the four case study countries. These are considered and commented upon in Chap. 14.

4.3.1.2   Curtailing Recruitment and Training

Paragraph 2(c) of Security Council resolution 1373 (2001) obliges States to deny safe haven to those who finance, plan, support, or commit terrorist acts. Paragraph 2(a) of the resolution adds that States must suppress recruitment of members of terrorist groups, although it does not expressly require criminalisation of the recruitment and training of terrorists. Such criminalisation has, however, been subsequently recommended by the resolution 1566 Working Group.[102] Canada and New Zealand have taken steps to expressly criminalise the recruitment of

---

[100]Ibid, para 140.

[101]Ibid, para 142.

[102]Resolution 1566 Working Group Report (n 97), para 28.

terrorists and participation in terrorist groups.[103] Although Australia and the United Kingdom also have offences concerning participation and recruitment, these are limited to participation in and recruitment to "terrorist organisations" as defined by section 102.1(1) of the Criminal Code Act 1995 (Australia) or "proscribed organisations" (as listed in Schedule 2 of the Terrorism Act 2000 (UK)), which is more narrow than the offences in New Zealand and Canada (see further Chap. 14, Sect. 14.2.2).[104]

4.3.1.3 Preventing Public Provocation

Public provocation to commit acts of terrorism was described by the resolution 1566 Working Group as "an insidious activity contributing to the spread of the scourge of terrorism".[105] Although the Security Council has, under paragraph 1(a) of resolution 1624 (2005), called on States to suppress incitement to commit terrorism, the laws in New Zealand and Canada are deficient in several respects in adequately criminalising such incitement (see Chap. 14, Sects. 14.3.3 and 14.3.4). The resolution 1566 Working Group has also identified as a threat to peace and security the use of the internet by individuals and groups involved in or associated with terrorist activities to spread hate and to incite violence.[106] The UN Counter-Terrorism Implementation Task Force has established a Working Group on the subject (see Chap. 3, Sect. 3.2.5). This is an issue that can be assisted by the effective criminalisation of the suppression to incite terrorism.

4.3.2 Countering the Financing of Terrorism

The adequacy of the criminalisation of terrorist financing by Western European and other States received a mixed assessment by the Counter-Terrorism Committee. Of the 30 countries included in the group, the Committee commented as follows:[107]

> A total of 11 States have adequately criminalized terrorist financing, and a further 16 have some legal provisions to address the issue. Anti-money-laundering laws are in place in all 30 States. Similarly, all States have set up financial intelligence units. The implementation of measures to regulate financial transfers through informal remittance systems is uneven. Only 7 States have adopted a range of measures to regulate financial transfers through informal remittance systems; 14 others have set up some mechanisms to address the issue; 2 have no mechanisms in place; while for the remaining 7, there is insufficient information.

---

[103]See: section 83.18 of the Criminal Code 1985 (Canada) [Chap. 6, Sect. 6.1.4.3]; section 12 of the Terrorism Suppression Act 2002 (New Zealand) [Chap. 7, Sect. 7.1.4.3].

[104]See section 102.4 of the Criminal Code Act 1995 (Australia) [Chap. 5, Sect. 5.1.1.4].

[105]Resolution 1566 Working Group Report (n 97), para 29.

[106]Resolution 1566 Working Group Report (n 97), para 30.

[107]Ibid, para 134.

> Almost all States have the capacity to freeze without delay funds and assets linked to terrorism, with a few of them having reached a high level of implementation... Only 3 States implement adequate measures to protect non-profit organizations from terrorist financing, although 21 States have some measures in place.

While the CTC's report does not specify to whom these statistics apply, this text provides an overview of the legislation in the four case study countries relating to the countering of the financing of terrorism. Chapters 5–8 include an overview of relevant offences, the designation of terrorist entities, the forfeiture of terrorist property and financial transactions reporting.[108] Each of those chapters also considers the overall state of implementation of Security Council resolution 1373, paragraph 1 of which relates to the suppression of terrorist financing.[109] Chapter 19 considers the human rights implications of the designation regimes, using the regime in New Zealand as a case study.

On this subject, both the Counter-Terrorism Committee and the resolution 1566 Working Group have recommended that States should promote the implementation of new initiatives for preventing terrorist financing in predominately cash-based economies.[110] While this might not pertain directly to the four case study countries, it may have implications for their external relations with neighbouring countries or dependent territories, such as the Cook Islands in the case of New Zealand.

4.3.3 Border Control

The Counter-Terrorism Committee reported a generally good level of implementation of border control requirements, including measures for issuing and controlling identity and travel documents, implementation of international standards on aviation and maritime security, and the regulation and control of the importing and exporting of arms and explosives.[111] The screening of travellers was assessed by the CTC as being effective in 24 of the 30 States in the regional sub-group, and controls over asylum processes to prevent abuse by persons who have committed terrorist acts effective by 25 States in the group.[112] The individual reports to the CTC from the four case study countries do not indicate problems by those countries in the implementation of border control measures.[113] The Committee noted, however, that

---

[108]For Australia, see Chap. 5, Sects. 5.1.1.4, 5.1.6 and 5.2.2; for Canada, see Chap. 6, Sect. 6.1.4; for New Zealand, see Chap. 7, Sect. 7.1.4; and for the United Kingdom, see Chap. 8, Sect. 8.1.5.

[109]For Australia, see Chap. 5, Sect. 5.3.3; for Canada, see Chap. 6, Sect. 6.3.3; for New Zealand, see Chap. 7, Sect. 7.5.3; and for the United Kingdom, see Chap. 8, Sect. 8.3.3.

[110]CTC Survey (n 96), paras 146 and 147(c); and Resolution 1566 Working Group Report (n 97), para 19.

[111]CTC Survey (n 96), para 135.

[112]Ibid.

[113]For Australia, see Chap. 5, Sect. 5.3.3; for Canada, see Chap. 6, Sect. 6.3.3; for New Zealand, see Chap. 7, Sect. 7.5.3; and for the United Kingdom, see Chap. 8, Sect. 8.3.3.

it has been impeded in undertaking a full and proper assessment of such measures in some countries due to a lack of detailed reporting by many States, including those in the Pacific islands region, which may again be of relevance to New Zealand, and Australia, concerning their external relations and development assistance.[114]

Prevention of the movement of terrorists is, according to the CTC and the resolution 1566 Working Group, an essential measure in the fight against terrorism requiring careful implementation.[115] Amongst the priority recommendations of the Counter-Terrorism Committee were the enhancement of coordination among police and border control agencies, and gaining and providing better access to international counter-terrorism and criminal databases in order to enhance detection and exclusion of persons involved in terrorism.[116] Measures to prevent the transboundary movement of terrorists are considered in Chap. 21 (see Sect. 21.1 concerning border security).

4.3.4 Domestic Security, Law Enforcement and International Cooperation

The CTC's survey commented favourably on the mechanisms and institutional structures in place in the regional sub-group, including their level of internal and external cooperation, as well as the adoption of policies and measures to effectively monitor, regulate and control the production, sale and transfer of arms and explosives.[117] Of note, are the non-military sanctions mandated under Security Council resolution 1267 (1999), requiring members of the United Nations to impose a travel ban and an arms embargo on the Taliban and Al-Qa'ida. These sanctions appear to have been adequately implemented by the four case study countries.[118]

The resolution 1566 Working Group echoed the fact that a principal obligation under resolution 1373 (2001) is to bring terrorists to justice. Law enforcement techniques involved in the detection and investigation of terrorist acts or preparatory conduct are examined in Chaps. 15 and 16 of this title. The Working Group also recommended to the Security Council that it continue to urge States to become parties to all international terrorism-related conventions.[119] It might be noted, in the latter regard, that the United Kingdom is the only one of the four case study countries to have ratified the Nuclear Terrorism Convention.[120] Nor has New Zealand ratified

---

[114]CTC Survey (n 96), para 149.

[115]CTC Survey (n 96), para 148; and Resolution 1566 Working Group Report (n 97), para 21.

[116]CTC Survey (n 96), para 152(c) and (d).

[117]CTC Survey (n 96), paras 136–137.

[118]For Australia, see Chap. 5, Sect. 5.2.3; for Canada, see Chap. 6, Sect. 6.2; for New Zealand, see Chap. 7, Sect. 7.5; and for the United Kingdom, see Chap. 8, Sect. 8.2.

[119]Resolution 1566 Working Group Report (n 97), para 25.

[120]As at 1 October 2009.

the Firearms Protocol to the UN Convention against Transnational Organized Crime, and it does not appear to have fully implemented the Plastic Explosives Convention by putting in place an adequate reporting and registration regime to control existing stocks of unmarked plastic explosives.[121]

4.3.5   Emerging Trends in Legislative Responses to Terrorism

Chapters 5–8 that follow will provide an overview of the legislative framework of each country for the combating of terrorism. This chapter has, in part, summarised the assessments in Chaps. 5–8 of the compliance of those frameworks with international law on counter-terrorism. Part 3 of this title will examine the human rights compliance of discreet issues arising from those frameworks. In aiming to provide a comprehensive analysis of the legislative responses of the four case study countries to counter-terrorism and human rights, some further comments and observations should be made about the overall legislative processes utilised by the countries in this area, and some of the trends that have emerged.

4.3.5.1   The Speed with Which Counter-Terrorist Legislation Has Been Enacted

The speed with which counter-terrorist legislation has been passed in the case study countries has been raised as a matter of concern by many, especially when considering the volume of these legislative texts. It should be acknowledged that this is a criticism made of many States and is particularly relevant in the case of legislation that soon followed September 11,[122] although Walker observes that counter-terrorism legislation in the United Kingdom "is replete with examples of bills which received an expedited passage through Parliament".[123] The Prevention of Terrorism (Temporary Provisions) Act 1974 (UK) was passed in the space of three days after the Provisional IRA bombing at Birmingham. Following the 1998 Omagh bombing

---

[121]See: New Zealand Ministry of Foreign Affairs and Trade, National Interest Analysis, Convention on the Marking of Plastic Explosives for the Purpose of Detection, para 14; and Chap. 7, Sects. 7.5.2 and 7.5.3 (item 5).

[122]See, for example, the Report of the Eminent Jurists Panel on Terrorism, Counter-terrorism and Human Rights, Assessing Damage, Urging Action (Geneva: International Commission of Jurists, 2009), p. 124.

[123]Clive Walker, Submissions to the House of Lords Constitution Committee: Emergency Legislation, February 2009, para 3. See also Walker 2009, p. 25, concerning the "curtailed" debates on the Anti-terrorism, Crime and Security Act 2001 (UK).

by the Real IRA, the Criminal Justice (Terrorism and Conspiracy) Act 1998 (UK) was passed in just two days. More recently, the Terrorism Act 2006 has been described as a "hurried" piece of legislation in direct response to the London bombings in July 2005, although others point to a period of about seven months between inception and enactment as representing "a commendable reflective period given the backdrop of July 2005".[124]

In the case of the Anti-Terrorism Act (No 2) 2005 in Australia, it appears that the federal Government had not intended to release the Bill for public consultation prior to its introduction to Parliament. The Bill was instead leaked by the Chief Minister of the Australian Capital Territory.[125] The initial timetable set by the Government had forecast that the Bill would be introduced into Parliament, debated, and passed in a short period of time. This schedule was adjusted so that the Bill was referred to the Senate Legal and Constitutional Legislation Committee on 3 November 2005 for inquiry and report by 28 November 2005. The Committee advertised the inquiry in the *Australian* newspaper on Saturday 5 November 2005 and submissions were called for by Friday 11 November 2005.[126] The Committee held three public hearings, in Sydney only, on 14, 17 and 18 November 2005. Civil society complained that this was a highly truncated period for public consultation, although the Committee received 294 submissions. The Bill was introduced as an urgent amendment because the Government of Australia had received specific intelligence and police information which it reported gave cause for serious concern about a potential terrorist threat. This information was provided to the Leader of the Opposition and the shadow Minister for Homeland Security. In his study on Australia's legislative framework to combat terrorism, the UN Special Rapporteur on counter-terrorism identified concerns with various aspects of law enacted under the Anti-Terrorism Act (No 2) 2005.[127] He therefore expressed regret that a more thorough level of public consultation was not undertaken, particularly since Australia has no federal human rights legislation capable of guarding against undue limits being placed upon the rights and freedoms of individuals, observing that:[128]

> States should endeavour to consult widely when enacting counter-terrorism legislation that may limit the rights and freedoms of those within its territory. Because of the potentially profound impact of counter-terrorism legislation on human rights and fundamental freedoms, it is particularly important that Governments seek to secure the broadest possible political and popular support for such legislation.

---

[124]Walker (2009, p. 30). Contrast with Jones et al. (2006, p. v).

[125]'Howard on attack over draft bill release', Sydney Morning Herald (15 October 2005).

[126]Commonwealth of Australia, Department of the Senate, Legal and Constitutional Legislation Committee, Provisions of the Anti-Terrorism Bill (No. 2) 2005 (Canberra: Senate Printing Unit 2005), p. 1.

[127]Special Rapporteur on the promotion and protection of human rights and fundamental freedoms while countering terrorism, Australia: Study on Human Rights Compliance While Countering Terrorism, UN Doc A/HRC/4/26/Add.3.

[128]Special Rapporteur report (ibid), paras 8 and 65.

Criticism has also been directed at the retarded level of consultation when terrorism offences were introduced into Australia's Criminal Code Act 1995 under the Security Legislation Amendment (Terrorism) Act 2002. Whereas there was a careful drafting and consultative process for the establishment of the Criminal Code, the terrorism, espionage and treason offences under Chap. 6 of the Code were inserted as a result of a compressed timeframe, which McSherry assesses as rendering "impossible a thorough analysis of how these new crimes reflected the general [criminal law] principles enshrined in ch 2 of the existing Criminal Code".[129]

As recognised by the UN Special Rapporteur, the position in Australia is particularly significant in the absence of a national human rights instrument capable of rectifying any deficiencies in legislation. The supreme and entrenched nature of Canada's human rights legislation might act to temper a speedy legislative process (see Chap. 11, Sect. 11.1.2). It might also be argued that the civil liberties framework in New Zealand and the United Kingdom offers a similar tempering effect through the required review of legislative proposals to determine whether such proposals are compatible with human rights. As is discussed in Chap. 11, however, this does not necessarily prevent the enactment of legislation which is inconsistent with human rights (see Sect. 11.3.1). Nor does it answer the question of whether certain measures are necessary and appropriate, irrespective of their compliance with discreet provisions of civil liberties legislation. A rushed legislative agenda decreases the exchange of considered analyses of legislative proposals and significantly increases the chance that the end product will be flawed, both from a counter-terrorism and human rights perspective.

Canada's main legislative response to September 11 was the Anti-terrorism Act 2001. The Bill, consisting of over 180 pages of legislative text, was introduced on 15 October 2001 (less than a month after the adoption by the Security Council of resolution 1373 (2001)) and assented to on 18 December 2001. Although the Bill was subject to extensive debate in Canada, partly due to the organisation of an academic conference on the subject,[130] the legislature could hardly be said to have been afforded an opportunity to reflect in a manner consistent with the adoption of major and wide-impacting legislation. Paccioco also argues that, if exceptional measures to combat terrorism are indeed required and established in a proportional way, they should be contained in separate counter-terrorism legislation rather than by amendment of, or addition to, 'normal' laws. Canada's Anti-terrorism Act 2001, for example, is not a stand-alone piece of legislation but instead amends various items of legislation, including the Criminal Code 1985, the Official Secrets Act 1985, the Canada Evidence Act 1985, and the Proceeds of Crime (Money Laundering) Act 2000 (see Chap. 6, Sect. 6.1.4). Arguing in favour of a single self-contained

---

[129]McSherry (2004, pp. 355–357). See also Hocking (2004) concerning amendments in 2003 to the powers of Australia's Security Intelligence Organisation, at pp. 327–328.

[130]The Security of Freedom, a two-day conference held at the Faculty of Law, University of Toronto, 9–10 November 2001. The conference led to the publication of the text by Daniels et al. (2002).

enactment on combating terrorism, Paccioco observes that: "Then we would have know it was an unfortunate and unique aberration from our customary legal restraint, wrought only by unspeakable acts".[131] Also commenting on the dangers of not isolating counter-terrorism law, Roach states:[132]

> The criminal law has a tendency to replicate itself and language and law designed to deal with terrorism has been applied to street gangs and street gang legislation applied to terrorism... We can expect that the incursions on fundamental values in Bill C-36 [Canada's Anti-terrorism Bill] will be a model the next time another menace becomes pressing...

Walker proposes that the United Kingdom has "partially learned... the importance of devising a rational legal code and not panic legislation" to combat terrorism.[133] He points, in particular, to institutional features such as the use of joint parliamentary committees with cross-party support for the scrutiny of proposed legislation, and the post-facto use of independent reviewers.[134] This brings the current discussion to the next issue at hand: that of sunset clauses and review mechanisms.

4.3.5.2 Sunset Clauses and Review Mechanisms

The review of counter-terrorism legislation in the four cases study countries has shown that, by enlarge, sunset clauses and legislative reviews do not result in a change in law. One might argue that this has been so because there has been a considered view taken at select committee and parliamentary levels that such legislation should continue. The experience in New Zealand does not support this, however. As discussed in Chap. 7, the select committee charged with the review of the Terrorism Suppression Act 2002 (NZ) was forced to speedily consider issues and note them within just eight substantive pages, without proper debate and commentary (see Sect. 7.1.4.7). This heightens the need to be concerned about the speedy enactment of legislation on combating terrorism since, once enacted, its provisions are likely to stay. As observed by Justice Binnie of the Supreme Court of Canada:[135]

> In these circumstances we can take limited comfort from the declared intention of the government that the *Antiterrorist Act* is a temporary measure. While its continued existence will depend on Parliament's appreciation of developments in the "war on terrorism", such temporary measures may well slide into a state of *de facto* permanence.

---

[131]Paccioco (2002, p. 190).

[132]Roach (2002, p. 137). See also Dyzenhaus (2002); Stuart (2002); and Clarke, Hon John QC. *Report of the Inquiry into the Case of Dr Mohamed Haneef* (Australia: Commonwealth of Australia, 2008), pp. 253–524.

[133]Walker (2007, p. 187).

[134]Walker (2007, pp. 187–189).

[135]*Re Application under section 83.28 of the Criminal Code* [2004] 2 SCR 248, para 115.

Walker also warns that legislation enacted in a speedy response to acts of terrorism, or other situations categorised as creating an emergency, can become permanent, despite the existence of sunset or review clauses:[136]

> The circumstances may be depicted as an 'emergency', and the legislation may be entitled 'emergency provisions' or 'temporary provisions' and may even contain a sunset or renewal clause. But the lesson of experience is that such legislation may endure. The Prevention of Terrorism Acts [which began in 1974] continued until 2001, when the Terrorism Act 2000 came into force. Of course, that current legislation reproduces much of the earlier legislation.

A further mechanism for review is that of independent review, such as that in place in the United Kingdom (see Chap. 8, Sect. 8.1.10). Although Walker identifies independent review as worthwhile, he suggests that the role of the Independent Reviewer in the United Kingdom could be improved in three ways: by having statutory terms of appointment, with the authority to investigate and staff to assist; by establishing a panel of multiple reviewers in order to build a spread of expertise; and through the establishment of explicit links to a parliamentary select committee rather than needing to wait for a government to set the terms of any consequent debate.[137]

4.3.5.3 The Extension of State Powers Through Counter-Terrorism Laws

Experience has also shown that governments have used counter-terrorism, and other emergency laws, to extend State powers beyond what is strictly required in the exigencies of the situation, and/or that governments have seized upon such situations as an opportunity to justify the enactment of powers which have been long-sought but would not have been favourably received if proposed in a 'normal' situation.[138] On the latter point, Walker warns that the appearance of legislation being drawn up in emergency circumstances is highly misleading. Although legislation might be revealed and passed in emergency circumstances, it will have "almost certainly been drafted in non-emergency circumstances".[139] Referring to the Prevention of Terrorism (Temporary Provisions) Act 1974 (UK), which was introduced following the Birmingham bombing and subsequently enacted in just three days, Walker records:[140]

> ...the 1974 Act should not be viewed solely as a response to the Birmingham bombings, since numerous terrorist attacks had previously occurred. Repeated bombings had been carried out in England by the IRA since February 1972. In the first ten months of 1974, there were 99 further incidents, producing 17 deaths and 145 other casualties. Indeed, in November 1974 alone, there had already been 11 attacks with 4 dead and 35 injured. With

---

[136]Walker submissions to the House of Lords Constitution Committee (n 123) para 6.

[137]Walker (2007, p. 189).

[138]See the Report of the Eminent Jurists Panel on Terrorism (n 122) p. 124.

[139]Walker submissions to the House of Lords Constitution Committee (n 123) para 7.

[140]Walker submissions to the House of Lords Constitution Committee (n 123) para 8.

this background in mind, the Home Office has since admitted that it drew up contingency plans during 1973, including a draft Bill to proscribe the IRA, exclude suspects and restrict movement from Ireland. Indeed, the Government would rightly have been condemned if it had ignored the continuing mayhem and had not considered counter-measures. What was objectionable was not this stage of preparedness but the secrecy in which it was undertaken and the cynicism with which it was revealed only when the vigilance of Parliament was at its lowest ebb.

A further worrying trend is that special powers for combating terrorism are either included within ordinary legislation, increasing the risk of the 'normalisation' of such powers, and/or enacted in terms which are not restricted to the countering of terrorism. The latter point is explored in some detail in a case study in Chap. 15 concerning the introduction of tracking devices and special powers of police questioning under the Counter-Terrorism Bill 2003 (NZ), powers which are not restricted in their application to counter-terrorism, but are instead available in the investigation of any offence under New Zealand law for which the penalty is greater than three months (see Sect. 15.4). One might also point, here, to the inappropriate use by the United Kingdom of its anti-terror laws in 2008 to categorise Icelandic banks as terrorist organisations in order to freeze their assets.[141]

4.4 Conclusions

The type and level of actual and potential terrorist threats faced by the Commonwealth case study countries varies significantly, as do the experiences of those countries in dealing with terrorist threats, their immediate aftermath and their longer-term consequences. The countering of terrorism is nevertheless relevant to all four countries, whether as a result of their international legal obligations or their commitments to and support for an international framework on counter-terrorism. Measures to counter international terrorism are also capable of contributing to national interests, such as border security, aviation and external trade.

The sources of obligations related to the countering of international terrorism are various, although they generally fall within one or more of three categories: international treaties, customary international law, and binding decisions of the UN Security Council. The mechanisms for the implementation of those obligations by the case study countries are much the same. Rules under international treaties must be incorporated into domestic law by parliament before they can have direct legal effect, or made the subject of prosecution or the like, albeit that each country adopts a slightly different approach to the way in which treaty incorporation takes place. In contrast, rules of customary international law need not be incorporated by parliament before they may be relied upon in judicial proceedings, although they are in a sense 'incorporated' by the act of judicial recognition of such rules and their consequent transformation into common law.

---

[141]BBC News, 'Icelandic anger at UK terror move', 24 October 2008, online: http://news.bbc.co.uk/2/hi/uk_news/politics/7688560.stm.

In the case of obligations imposed by the Security Council concerning non-military sanctions, the case study countries normally respond to these by making regulations. In the case of regulations made under the United Nations incorporating legislation in Australia, Canada and New Zealand, a failure to comply with those regulations will amount to an offence. While Canada expressly allows for its legislative branch to annul such regulations, those made in Australia and Canada are able to override inconsistent primary legislation.

An overview of the legislative responses to terrorism by the four case study countries exposes a number of trends which, in combination, show cause for concern. Legislative packages on counter-terrorism have, more often than not, involved lengthy texts which have received an expedited passage through Parliament, thus reducing the ability of legislators to give careful consideration and debate to provisions which might represent a shift from customary legal restraint. The speedy passage of such laws has also been to the detriment of allowing adequate public consultation. Of relevance here is the observation that the appearance of legislation being drawn up in emergency circumstances is misleading. Taking the example of the UK's Prevention of Terrorism (Temporary Provisions) Act 1974, introduced following the Birmingham bombing and passed in just three days, the Home Office has subsequently admitted that the Act was drawn from a Bill drafted in 1973 but not introduced until after the bombing. These factors combined increase the risk of the enactment of anti-terrorism laws which run counter to the establishment under those laws of human rights limitations which are strictly necessary and proportionate. This is particularly problematic for jurisdictions such as Australia, which has no national bill of rights (see Chap. 11, Sect. 11.1.1), and New Zealand and the United Kingdom, which can at best declare provisions incompatible with human rights and then leave the matter for consideration by the executive and parliament (see Chap. 11, Sect. 11.2.3).

It should also be noted that counter-terrorism laws are in some cases not enacted as items of stand-alone legislation, instead establishing special and unusual powers within ordinary Acts, and thereby contributing to the risk of the normalisation of such powers and/or their eventual 'creepage' for use in traditional law enforcement. Of even greater concern is the practice of establishing special powers in terms such that they are not restricted to the countering of terrorism, but are instead applicable to the investigation of ordinary crimes. Cause for concern is in theory alleviated through the inclusion in counter-terrorism legislation of mechanisms such as sunset clauses, parliamentary review mechanisms, or the provision for independent review of the legislation. Once laws are in place, however, practice shows that sunset clauses rarely result in a repeal or amendment of legislation, such laws instead often sliding into a state of de facto permanence. Parliamentary review can be an effective tool, but may be thwarted by timetabling issues, or an indifferent treatment of the subject at select committee level. The utility of independent reviews depends upon the terms of appointment of, and resources available to, the Independent Reviewer, not to mention whether reports of the Reviewer are linked to a parliamentary select committee capable of triggering debate in parliament.

References

Anton, Donald, Mathew, Penelope, and Morgan, Wayne. 2005. *International Law: Cases and Materials*. Melbourne: Oxford University Press.

Brownlie, Ian. 2003. *Principles of Public International Law*. Oxford: 6th edition, Oxford University Press.

Charlesworth, Hilary, Chiam, Madelaine, Hovell, Devika, and Williams, George. 2003. Deep Anxieties: Australia and the International Legal Order. 25 *Sydney Law Review* 423.

Conte, Alex. 2006. *An Introduction to International Law*. Wellington: LexisNexis.

Conte, Alex, and Ganor, Boaz. 2005. *Legal and Policy Issues in Establishing an International Framework for Human Rights Compliance When Countering Terrorism*. Herzilyia, Israel: International Policy Institute on Counter-Terrorism.

Cranwell, Glen. 2001. Treaties and Australian Law: Administrative Discretions, Statutes and the Common Law. 1 *Queensland University of Technology Law and Justice Journal* 49.

Currie, John. 2001. *Public International Law*. Ottawa: Urwin Law.

Daniels, Ronald, Macklem, Patrick, and Roach, Kent (Eds). 2002. *Essays on Canada's Anti-Terrorism Bill*. Toronto: University of Toronto Press.

Dyzenhaus, David. 2002. The Permanence of the Temporary: Can Emergency Powers be Normalized?. In Daniels, Ronald, Macklem, Patrick, and Roach, Kent (Eds). *Essays on Canada's Anti-Terrorism Bill*. Toronto: University of Toronto Press.

Gabor, Thomas. 2004. *The Views of Canadian Scholars on the Impact of the* Anti-terrorism Act. Ottawa: University of Ottawa Research and Statistics Division.

Ganor, Boaz. 2005. *The Counter-Terrorism Puzzle. A Guide for Decision Makers*. Herzilya: The International Policy Institute for Counter-Terrorism.

Hocking, Jenny. 2004. Protecting Democracy by Preserving Justice: 'Even for the Feared and the Hated'. 27(2) *The University of New South Wales Law Journal* 354.

Jenkins, David. 2003. In Support of Canada's Anti-Terrorism Act: A Comparison of Canadian, British, and American Anti-Terrorism Law. 66 *Saskatchewan Law Review* 419.

Jones, Alun, Bowers, Rupert, and Lodge, Hugo. 2006. *Blackstone's Guide to the Terrorism Act 2006*. Oxford: Oxford University Press.

Lauterpacht, Hersch, 1950. *International Law and Human Rights*. London: Stevens.

Lewis, John. 2005. Intelligence Challenges in Counter-Terrorism (paper presented at the conference *Terrorism's Global Impact Conference*, Interdisciplinary Center Herzlyia, 13 September 2005).

Locke, John. 1960. *Two Treaties of Government*. Cambridge: Cambridge University Press.

McGinley, G P J. 1990. The Status of Treaties in Australian Municipal Law: The principle of *Walker v Baird* reconsidered. 12 *Adelaide Law Review* 367.

McSherry, Bernadette. 2004. Terrorism Offences in the Criminal Code: Broadening the Boundeeries of Australian Criminal Laws. 27(2) *The University of New South Wales Law Journal* 354.

Paccioco, David. 2002. Constitutional Casualties of September 11: Limiting the Legacy of the *Anti-terrorism Act*. 16 *Supreme Court Law Review* (2d) 185.

Roach, Kent. 2002. The Dangers of a Charter-Proof and Crime-Based Response to Terrorism. In Daniels, Ronald, Macklem, Patrick, and Roach, Kent (Eds). 2002. *Essays on Canada's Anti-Terrorism Bill*. Toronto: University of Toronto Press.

Roach, Kent. 2005. Canada's response to terrorism. In Ramraj, Victor, Hor, Michael, and Roach, Kent (Eds). *Global Anti-Terrorism Law and Policy*. Cambridge: Cambridge University Press.

Russeau, Jean-Jacques. 1968. *The Social Contract*. London: Penguin Classics.

Shearer, Ian. 1997. The Relationship between International Law and Domestic Law. In Opeskin and Rothwell (eds). *International Law and Australian Federalism*. Melbourne: Melbourne University Press.

Simpson, S. 2004. A Brief History of Terrorism in the South Pacific (paper presented at the Citizens' Constitutional Forum and the Fiji Human Rights Commission conference, *How Should Fiji Respond to the Threat of Terrorism?*, 17 July 2004, Suva, Fiji).

Sinai, Joshua. 2005. Terrorism Assessment, Forecasting and Preemptive Response Model. In Ganor, Boaz (Ed). *Post Modern Terrorism*. Herzilya: The International Policy Institute on Counter-Terrorism.

Stuart, Don. 2002. The Dangers of Quick Fix Legislation in the Criminal Law: The Anti-Terrorism Bill C-36 should be Withdrawn. In Daniels, Ronald, Macklem, Patrick, and Roach, Kent (Eds). *Essays on Canada's Anti-Terrorism Bill*. Toronto: University of Toronto Press.

Urwin, Greg. 2004. The Need for Anti-Terrorism Legislation in Fiji (paper presented at the Citizens' Constitutional Forum and the Fiji Human Rights Commission conference, *How Should Fiji Respond to the Threat of Terrorism?*, 17 July 2004, Suva, Fiji).

Van Ert, Gib. 2002. *Using International Law in Canadian Courts*. The Hague: Kluwer Law International.

Van Ert, Gib. 2004. International Law Does Bind Canadian Courts. 30(1) *Canadian Council on International Law Bulletin*.

Walker, Clive. 2007. The United Kingdom's Anti-terrorism Laws: Lessons for Australia. In Lynch, Andrew, MacDonald, Edwina, and Williams, George (Eds). *Law and Liberty in the War on Terror*. Sydney: The Federation Press.

Walker, Clive. 2009. *Blackstone's Guide to The Anti-Terrorism Legislation*. Oxford: 2nd Edition, Oxford University Press.

Chapter 5
Counter-Terrorism Law in Australia

Building on the account in Chap. 4 of the means by which international counter-terrorist obligations may be implemented by the four case study countries, this chapter sets out the first country-specific overview of counter-terrorism law, focussing in this case on Australia. An overview and explanation of legislation is provided, as these relate to counter-terrorism in Australia. The full list of enactments passed and regulations made by Australia in this area is reasonably extensive, rather than being limited to a few key instruments (as in the case of Canada and New Zealand for example). As with all other countries, it should be noted that there are numerous further pieces of domestic legislation that might be seen as contributing to the countering of terrorism. This chapter restricts itself to the items of legislation identified by Australia in its reports to the Counter-Terrorism Committee as being part of its counter-terrorist legislative regime.

This chapter, and the following three chapters, are broken down into three main parts: first, looking at legislation through which the universal terrorism-related conventions have been implemented by each country; next, examining any further specific legislation applicable to action required by decisions of the Security Council concerning the fight against terrorism; and, finally, setting out a summary and set of conclusions on each country's compliance with the international framework on counter-terrorism. Some general observations will also be made concerning Australia's human rights compliance while countering terrorism, due to the fact that Australia's counter-terrorism framework was made the subject of a report by the UN Special Rapporteur on the promotion and protection of human rights and fundamental freedoms while countering terrorism.

The overview provided in this chapter includes identification of offences established under Australia's legislation, a full list of which is set out in Appendix 3, Table 2 (the criminalisation of terrorism is considered further in Chap. 14). It looks at the definition of "terrorist act", and the listing of "terrorist organisations" under the Criminal Code Act 1995. This chapter also provides an overview of the legislative reviews of 2006 and 2008, and the proposal for the establishment of a permanent and independent reviewer of Australia's terrorism laws.

A. Conte, *Human Rights in the Prevention and Punishment of Terrorism*,
DOI 10.1007/978-3-642-11608-7_5, © Springer-Verlag Berlin Heidelberg 2010

Before considering each of the three main parts of this chapter it is relevant to note that, in 2006, the UN Special Rapporteur on the promotion and protection of human rights and fundamental freedoms while countering terrorism undertook a desk-top study on Australia's counter-terrorism framework and the human rights compliance of that framework.[1] The study was based on an interactive written process as part of the Rapporteur's mandate to undertake a series of comprehensive thematic and country/region-specific studies.[2] Those aspects of the report which comment on specific features of Australia's counter-terrorism law are considered within the framework of Chaps. 14–21 (the Special Rapporteur's comments and recommendations concerning the definition of terrorism, for example, are looked at in Chap. 14, Sect. 14.1.1). For present purposes, reference is made to a number of general aspects of the report.

The report noted that, in May 2005, the Australian Government announced a regional counter-terrorism assistance package totalling $40.3 million AUD over four years aimed at the development of counter-terrorism legal frameworks and measures to improve border-control and maritime security. The Special Rapporteur applauded Australia's initiative and leadership in the region and placed weight on the Government's advice that these initiatives were being adopted in a way that would not reduce Australia's development assistance budget. On that subject, he took the opportunity to note that counter-terrorism assistance should not replace, but rather supplement, development assistance.[3] This is important since the United Nations Global Counter-Terrorism Strategy welcomes initiatives to eradicate poverty and promote sustained economic growth, to reinforce development, to reduce marginalisation and to promote the rule of law, human rights and good governance.[4] In contrast to this approach, however, Australia's development assistance programme, AusAID, published a report in 2003 on Counter-Terrorism and Australian Aid, in which terrorism was treated only as a threat to development and where much focus was paid to building counter-terrorism capacity.[5] In the same year, the then Minister for Foreign Affairs, Alexander Downer, stated that "the Australian aid programme is helping to build the capacity of developing countries

---

[1]Special Rapporteur on the promotion and protection of human rights and fundamental freedoms while countering terrorism, Australia: Study on Human Rights Compliance While Countering Terrorism, UN Doc A/HRC/4/26/Add.3.

[2]Special Rapporteur report (ibid), paras 1–2. See also the mandate of the Special Rapporteur in Commission on Human Rights resolution 2005/80, UN ESCOR, 61st Sess, 60th Mtg, UN Doc E/CN.4/Res/2005/80 (2005), para 14(a) and (c).

[3]Special Rapporteur report (n 1), para 6. See also para 64, where the Special Rapporteur urged Australia to ensure that its programmes of assistance in the area of counter-terrorism does not occur at the expense of development assistance.

[4]United Nations Global Counter-Terrorism Strategy, adopted under GA Res 60/288, UN GAOR, 60th Sess, 99th Plen Mtg, UN Doc A/Res/60/288 (2006), final preambular para.

[5]Australian Government, AusAID, Counter-Terrorism and Australian Aid, Commonwealth of Australia, 2003.

in the region to respond effectively to potential terrorist threats, including through strengthening police, banking and customs authorities, drafting and enacting new legislation, and improving law and justice systems".[6]

As with many other countries, including Canada and New Zealand, civil society within Australia has questioned the need for legislative reform since 11 September 2001.[7] In the case of Australia, the public questioned the need for *further* legislation. Australia had itself reported to the Counter-Terrorism Committee that "extensive and effective legislation" was already in place before 2001.[8] The Special Rapporteur accepted, however, that legislative reform was at least necessary to bring Australia into compliance with Security Council resolution 1373 (2001) and with the work of the Al-Qa'ida and Taliban Sanctions Committee.[9] Australia's Security Legislation Review Committee also reported in 2006 that it was satisfied that separate security legislation, in addition to general criminal law, was necessary in Australia.[10] The Special Rapporteur was critical, however, of the speed with which some of Australia's legislation, the Anti-Terrorism Act (No 2) 2005 for example, had been enacted and the lack of effective public consultation in this process.[11] Chapter 4 has commented on the overall legislative processes utilised by the four case study countries in this area, including in the case of Australia's Anti-Terrorism Act (No 2) 2005 (see Sect. 4.3.5.1).

The final, general, aspect of the report to be noted is the commentary on Australia's lack of federal human rights legislation capable of guarding against undue limits being placed upon the rights and freedoms of individuals. Although the Special Rapporteur noted with encouragement that certain states within Australia had moved towards the adoption of such legislation (see further Chap. 11, Sect. 11.1.1), he reiterated that the defence of human rights is essential to the fulfilment of all aspects of a global counter-terrorism strategy (see further Chap. 13), concluding:[12]

> Although the Government of Australia points to a robust constitutional structure and framework of legislation capable of protecting human rights and prohibiting discrimination, this is an outstanding matter that has been previously raised by the Human Rights

---

[6]Alexander Downer, MP, speech of 13 May 2003.

[7]See, for example: Head (2002); Burnside (2005); and Eminent Jurists Panel on Terrorism, Counter-Terrorism and Human Rights, Press Release: Eminent Jurists Panel Concludes Australia Hearing on Counter-Terrorism Law, Practices and Policies (17 March 2006). Contrast with Ruddock (2004) and Downer (2005).

[8]Fourth Report to the Counter-Terrorism Committee, UN Doc S/2003/1204 (2003), p. 3.

[9]Special Rapporteur report (n 1), para 7.

[10]Report of the Security Legislation Review Committee, June 2006 (Canberra: Australian Parliament, Parliamentary Paper 137 (2006)), pp. 3 and 9, available online at: http://www.ag.gov.au/slrc.

[11]Special Rapporteur report (n 1), para 8.

[12]Special Rapporteur report (n 1), paras 9–10 and 65.

Committee in its observations on Australia's reports under the International Covenant on Civil and Political Rights (ICCPR). The Special Rapporteur identifies in this report a number of areas in which the rights and freedoms of those in Australia have been, or may be, limited in the pursuit of countering terrorism. It is therefore essential that there be means of dealing with potential excesses, and the Special Rapporteur urges Australia to move towards enacting federal legislation implementing the Covenant and providing remedial mechanisms for the protection of rights and freedoms.

5.1 Implementation by Australia of the Universal Terrorism-Related Treaties

Australia is a party to 12 of the existing 13 terrorism-related conventions (see Appendix 3, Table 1). It was an original signatory to the International Convention for the Suppression of Acts of Nuclear Terrorism (Nuclear Terrorism Convention), but has not yet deposited its instrument of ratification.[13] Australia has implemented its obligations under the treaties to which it is party under various items of legislation (on the reception of treaty law in Australia, see Chap. 4, Sect. 4.2.2). The bulk of these obligations have been implemented by Australia under the Criminal Code Act 1995. Also relevant are the Crimes (Aviation) Act 1991; the Crimes (Ships and Fixed Platforms) Act 1992; legislation concerning hostage-taking and internationally protected persons; the Nuclear Non-Proliferation (Safeguards) Act 1987; the Financial Transactions Reports Act 1998; the Law and Justice Legislation Amendment (Marking of Plastic Explosives) Act 2006; the Anti-Money-Laundering and Counter-Terrorism Financing Act 2006; and legislation concerning the Australian Security Intelligence Organisation.

5.1.1 Crimes Act 1914 and Criminal Code Act 1995

Since much of the international framework for combating terrorism involves undertakings to criminalise terrorism-related conduct (see Chap. 3, Sect. 3.1), a good deal of its implementation by Australia is through the establishment of offences in Australia's domestic law. This has been effected through legislation amending the Crimes Act 1914 and the Criminal Code Act 1995 for the purposes of strengthening powers of law enforcement authorities, establishing terrorism offences,

---

[13]International Convention for the Suppression of Acts of Nuclear Terrorism, adopted by the General Assembly and opened for signature on 15 April 2005 under GA Res 59/290, UN GAOR, 59th Sess, 91st Plen Mtg, UN Doc A/Res/59/290 (2005) and entered into force 7 July 2007.

addressing issues of bail and parole with respect to those offences, and establishing procedures for preventative detention and control orders (i.e. under the Anti-Terrorism Act 2004, the Anti-Terrorism Act (No. 2) 2004, the Anti-Terrorism Act (No. 3) 2004, the Anti-Terrorism Act (No. 2) 2005, the Charter of the United Nations (Terrorism and Dealings with Assets) Regulations 2002, the Crimes Amendment Act 2002, the Crimes Amendment Act 2005, the Criminal Code Amendment (Anti-Hoax and Other Measures) Act 2002, the Criminal Code Amendment (Espionage and Related Matters) Act 2002, the Criminal Code Amendment (Offences Against Australians) Act 2002, the Criminal Code Regulations 2002, the Security Legislation Amendment (Terrorism) Act 2002, the Surveillance Devices Act 2004, and the Telecommunications Interception Legislation Amendment Act 2002).

The bulk of the terrorism-related provisions in the Criminal Code are found in Chapter 5.3 of the Criminal Code Act, dealing with: definitions; most of the Act's terrorism-related offences; the listing of "terrorist organisations"; the financing of terrorism; control orders; and preventative detention. Chapter 4 of the Act also contains a division concerning international terrorist acts using explosive and lethal devices.

5.1.1.1 Treaty Implementation

The Criminal Code Act 1995 implements Australia's treaty obligations under the International Convention for the Suppression of the Financing of Terrorism (the Financing Convention) and the International Convention for the Suppression of Terrorist Bombing (the Bombing Convention).[14]

5.1.1.2 Definition of "Terrorist Act"

Although the term "terrorism" is not defined in Australian law, Chapter 5.3 of the Criminal Code Act 1995 instead sets out a range of offences related to a "terrorist act" (as defined by section 100.1(1) of the Act). The Act makes it an offence to engage in a terrorist act; provide or receive training connected with terrorist acts; possess things connected with terrorist acts; collect or make documents likely to facilitate terrorist acts; and other acts done in preparation for, or planning, terrorist acts (see below). An organisation engaged in a terrorist act can be listed

---

[14]International Convention for the Suppression of the Financing of Terrorism, opened for signature 10 January 2000, 2179 UNTS 232 (entered into force 10 April 1992); and International Convention for the Suppression of Terrorist Bombing, opened for signature 12 January 1998, 2149 UNTS 286 (entered into force 23 May 2001).

by the Attorney-General as a terrorist organisation, with a further range of offences linked to such organisations (also see below). Section 100.1(1) of the Criminal Code defines a "terrorist act" as involving the following cumulative elements:

- An act which is done, or a threat which is made, with the intention of advancing a political, religious, or ideological cause (see the definition of terrorist act in section 100.1(1), subparagraph (b)); and
- Where the act is done, or threat is made, with the intention of either: (i) coercing, or influencing by intimidation, the government of Australia (or the government of an Australian State or Territory) or that of a foreign country; or (ii) intimidating the public or a section of the public (see the definition of terrorist act in section 100.1(1), subparagraph (c)); and
- The action falls within subsection (2) of section 100.1, namely action which:

  (a) causes serious harm that is physical harm to a person; or
  (b) causes serious damage to property; or
  (c) causes a person's death; or
  (d) endangers a person's life, other than the life of the person taking the action; or
  (e) creates a serious risk to the health or safety of the public or a section of the public; or
  (f) seriously interferes with, seriously disrupts, or destroys, an electronic system including, but not limited to:
      (i) an information system; or
      (ii) a telecommunications system; or
      (iii) a financial system; or
      (iv) a system used for the delivery of essential government services; or
      (v) a system used for, or by, an essential public utility; or
      (vi) a system used for, or by, a transport system.

Subsection 100.1(2) does not include action which involves advocacy, protest, dissent or industrial action which is not intended to cause harm, death, the endangerment of the life of a person, or a serious risk to the health or safety of the public (see section 100.1(1)(a) and (3)). Despite this safeguard, the UN Special Rapporteur on the promotion and protection of human rights and fundamental freedoms while countering terrorism has criticised Australia's definition as going beyond the Security Council's categorisation of acts which must be suppressed in the fight against terrorism (see Chap. 14, Sect. 14.1.1).[15]

The significance of the term "terrorist act" is that it is linked to various terrorism offences under the Criminal Code, including engaging in a terrorist act, and providing support to a terrorist organisation where this would help it to engage in, prepare, plan, assist in or foster the doing of a "terrorist act" (see section 102.7). It is also linked to the definition and listing of "terrorist organisations" under Division 102 of the Code.

---

[15]Special Rapporteur report (n 1), paras 12–17.

5.1.1.3 Listing of "Terrorist Organisations"

Additional to the listing process of the Al-Qa'ida and Taliban Sanctions Committee, which is dealt with by Australia under Part 4 of the Charter of the United Nations Act 1945 and the Charter of the United Nations (Terrorism and Dealings with Assets) Regulations 2008 (see Sect. 5.2.2 below), Australia has taken steps to allow it to deal with "terrorist organisations". Although separate from the Sanctions Committee process, all 19 organisations listed in Australian law as a "terrorist organisation" are also listed by the Committee. A "terrorist organisation" is defined by section 102.1(1) of the Criminal Code Act as:

- An organisation that is directly or indirectly engaged in, preparing, planning, assisting in or fostering the doing of a terrorist act (whether or not a terrorist act occurs); or
- An organisation that is specified to be so by the terrorist organisation regulations (i.e. listed under the Criminal Code Regulations 2002).

The listing of a "terrorist organisation" may therefore occur as a result of a judicial finding to that effect consequent to a prosecution of a person or entity for a terrorist offence. However, all currently listed terrorist organisations, have been listed under the authority of section 102.1(2) of the Criminal Code Act, which allows the Attorney-General to list an organisation if satisfied on reasonable grounds that the organisation (i) is directly or indirectly engaged in, preparing, planning, assisting in or fostering the doing of a terrorist act, or (ii) advocates the doing of a terrorist act. This test is one of an ordinary, rather than criminal, standard of proof. This listing process is subject to various political safeguards, including giving notice to the Leader of the Opposition, the ability for a listed organisation to seek de-listing, and review of listings by a Parliamentary Joint Committee (section 102.1A). A listed organisation can apply in writing to be delisted (section 102.1(17)).

The effect of a listing under this process is more significant than a designation based upon a Sanctions Committee listing. Whereas the listing of a person or entity under the Charter of the United Nations (Terrorism and Dealings with Assets) Regulations 2008 is not itself an offence (see Sect. 5.2.2 below), it is an offence to be a member of, or associate with, a "terrorist organisation" listed under Division 102 of the Criminal Code Act 1995 (see sections 102.3 and 102.8). It is also an offence to direct the activities of, recruit persons into, receive training from or provide training to, receive funds from or make funds available to, or provide support or resources to a terrorist organisation (see sections 102.2, 102.4, 102.5, 102.6 and 102.7 respectively). Penalties for these offences can be up to 25 years imprisonment. In his report on Australia's counter-terrorism laws, the UN Special Rapporteur expressed concern with the fact that an organisation can be listed based upon an ordinary, rather than criminal, standard of proof, with severe criminal penalties flowing from such a listing.[16]

---

[16]Special Rapporteur report (n 1), para 23.

5.1.1.4   Offences Under the Criminal Code Act 1995

Various parts of the Criminal Code Act 1995 establish terrorism-related offences (see Appendix 3, Table 2(A)). As explained earlier, the bulk of these offences are to be found in Chapter 5.3 of the Act (Divisions 101 to 105). Division 101 relates to terrorist acts and terrorism generally and includes the following offences:

- *Engaging in a terrorist act* (section 101.1(1)), making it unlawful to engage in a "terrorist act" (as defined), an offence which is punishable by imprisonment for life.[17]
- *Providing or receiving training connected with terrorist acts* (section 101.2), prohibiting persons from providing or receiving training, knowing that (or being reckless as to whether) this is connected with preparation for, the engagement of a person in, or assistance in a terrorist act.[18] Acting with knowledge renders a person liable to 25 years imprisonment. Recklessness as to the fact invokes a maximum penalty of 15 years imprisonment. An offence under section 101.2 will occur even if a terrorist act does not result, and if the training is not actually connected with preparation for, the engagement of a person in, or assistance in a specific terrorist act (subsection (3)).
- *Possessing things connected with terrorist acts* (section 101.4), making it an offence to posses any thing, knowing that (or being reckless as to whether) it is connected with preparation for, the engagement of a person in, or assistance in a terrorist act.[19] Doing so with full knowledge invokes a maximum penalty of 15 years imprisonment, while recklessness is limited to 10 years imprisonment. It is irrelevant whether or not a terrorist act occurs as a result, or whether the thing is connected with a specific terrorist act (subsection (3)).
- *Collecting or making documents likely to facilitate terrorist acts* (section 101.5), prohibiting the making or collection of a document, knowing that (or being reckless as to whether) it is connected with preparation for, the engagement of a person in, or assistance in a terrorist act.[20] Knowledge or recklessness render a person liable to 15 or 10 years imprisonment respectively. An offence under section 101.5 is complete even if a terrorist act does not result, or if the document is not connected with a specific terrorist act (subsection (3)).
- *Other acts done in preparation for, or planning, terrorist acts* (section 101.6), making it an offence to act in any way which amounts to preparation for, or planning, a terrorist act,[21] and rendering a person liable to life imprisonment. It is again irrelevant that a terrorist act does not result, nor that the act is connected with a specific terrorist act (subsection (2)).

---

[17]Corresponding to para 2(d) of SC Res 1373, UN SCOR, 4385th Mtg, UN Doc S/Res/1373 (2001).

[18]Corresponding to para 2(a) and (d) of SC Res 1373 (ibid).

[19]Corresponding to para 2(d) of SC Res 1373 (n 17).

[20]Corresponding to para 2(d) of SC Res 1373 (n 17).

[21]Corresponding to para 2(d) of SC Res 1373 (n 17).

As discussed earlier, Division 102 of the Criminal Code Act allows for the listing of "terrorist organisations", in respect of which there are the following offences:

- *Directing the activities of a terrorist organisation* (section 102.2), making it an offence to intentionally direct the activities of a terrorist organisation, knowing that (or being reckless as to whether) the organisation is a terrorist organisation. Acting in such a way with knowledge that the organisation is a terrorist organisation renders a person liable to 25 years imprisonment. Recklessness as to the fact invokes a maximum penalty of 15 years imprisonment.
- *Membership in a terrorist organisation* (section 102.3), prohibiting membership in a terrorist organisation where the person knows that the organisation is a terrorist organisation. It is a defence to a charge under section 102.3 if the person took all reasonable steps to cease to be a member of the organisation as soon as practicable after he or she became aware that the organisation was a terrorist organisation. Conviction renders a person liable to imprisonment up to 10 years.
- *Recruiting for a terrorist organisation* (section 102.4), criminalising the recruitment of persons to join, or participate in the activities of, a terrorist organisation knowing that (or being reckless as to whether) the organisation is a terrorist organisation. Acting with full knowledge renders a person liable to 25 years imprisonment. Recklessness as to the fact invokes a maximum penalty of 15 years imprisonment.
- *Training a terrorist organisation or receiving training from a terrorist organisation* (section 102.5), prohibiting the provision of training to a terrorist organisation (or receipt of training from such an organisation) where either: the person is reckless as to whether the organisation is a terrorist organisation (subsection (1)); or the organisation is listed under the Criminal Code Regulations 2002 (subsection (2)). Conviction renders a person liable for imprisonment up to 25 years. It is a defence to a charge under section 102.5(2) to have been reckless as to the fact of listing.
- *Getting funds to, from, or for a terrorist organisation* (section 102.6), making it an offence to intentionally receive funds from, make funds available to, collect funds for or on behalf of a terrorist organisation, knowing that (or being reckless as to whether) the organisation is a terrorist organisation. Acting in such a way with knowledge that the organisation is a terrorist organisation renders a person liable to 25 years imprisonment. Recklessness as to the fact invokes a maximum penalty of 15 years imprisonment. "Funds" include property and assets of any kind, and related legal documents and instruments.[22]

---

[22]The term "funds" is defined under section 100.1(1) of the Criminal Code Act 1995 as "(a) property and assets of every kind, whether tangible or intangible, movable or immovable, however acquired; and (b) legal documents or instruments in any form, including electronic or digital, evidencing title to, or interest in, such property or assets, including, but not limited to, bank credits, travellers cheques, bank cheques, money orders, shares, securities, bonds, debt instruments, drafts and letters of credit".

- *Providing support to a terrorist organisation* (section 102.7), making it an offence to intentionally provide a terrorist organisation with support or resources that would help it to engage in, prepare, plan, assist in or foster the doing of a terrorist act, knowing that (or being reckless as to whether) the organisation is a terrorist organisation. Acting with full knowledge renders a person liable to 25 years imprisonment. Recklessness as to the fact invokes a maximum penalty of 15 years imprisonment.
- *Associating with terrorist organisations* (section 102.8), which creates two types of offences. The first is where a person, on two or more occasions, associates with a member of a terrorist organisation listed under the Criminal Code Regulations 2002 (or a person who promotes or directs its activities) to provide support for the purpose of assisting the organisation to expand or to continue to exist (section 102.8(1)). Where a person has already been convicted of an offence under section 102.8(1), a further offence will be committed if that person again associates with a member of a listed organisation (or a person who promotes or directs its activities) to provide support for the purpose of assisting the organisation to expand or to continue to exist (section 102.8(2)). Both offences carry a maximum penalty of 3 years imprisonment. Certain defences exist under subsection (4), including if the association is with a close family member and relates only to a matter that could reasonably be regarded (taking into account the person's cultural background) as a matter of family or domestic concern.

Division 103 of the Criminal Code sets out offences intended to deal with the suppression of the financing of terrorist activities, including the following offences:

- *Financing terrorism* (section 103.1), prohibiting the provision or collection of funds (as defined by section 100.1(1) – see above) where a person is reckless as to whether the funds will be used to facilitate or engage in a "terrorist act".[23] It is irrelevant that terrorist the act is not actually perpetrated, as is the actual use of the funds, i.e. it is sufficient that the funds may be used to facilitate the commission of a terrorist act. Conviction renders a person liable to life imprisonment.
- *Financing a terrorist* (section 103.2), prohibiting the provision or collection of funds to another person (directly or indirectly) being reckless as to whether the other person will use the funds to facilitate or engage in a terrorist act.[24] It is again irrelevant whether the terrorist act occurs or whether the funds are actually used for facilitating a terrorist act. The offence carries a maximum penalty of life imprisonment.

Division 104 of the Criminal Code Act 1995 sets out mechanisms for the issuing, variation and lapse of control orders (see below on control orders). A further regime

---

[23]Corresponding to article 2(1) of the Financing Convention (n 14); and para 1(b) of SC Res 1373 (n 17).

[24]Corresponding to article 2(1) of the Financing Convention (n 14); and para 1(b) of SC Res 1373 (n 17).

discussed below is that of preventive detention, governed by Division 105 of the Code. Offences related to control orders and preventive detention are as follows:

- *Contravening a control order* (section 104.27), making it an offence, imprisonable by up to 5 years, for a person subject to a control order to contravene the order.
- *Disclosure offences related to preventative detention* (section 105.41), prohibiting the disclosure of certain information by a person subject to preventive detention, as well as others involved in the process including his or her lawyer, and parents or guardians of a minor who is made subject to a preventative detention order. Commission of an offence under section 105.41 renders a person liable to imprisonment of up to 5 years. A person subject to a preventive detention order (i.e. the detained person) commits an offence if, during the period of preventive detention, he or she discloses to any person either: (i) the fact that a preventative detention order has been made in relation to them; or (ii) that they are being detained; or (iii) the period for which they are being detained (see section 105.41(1)). The only exceptions relate to the communication of such information to the Commonwealth Ombudsman or to the detained person's lawyer (see sections 105.36 and 105.37). Special contact rules apply to minors made the subject to a preventive detention order (section 105.39).

A lawyer contacted by a person detained under a preventative detention order (under the authority of section 105.36) is also prohibited from disclosing certain information (section 105.41(2)). During the period of detention, the lawyer cannot disclose to anyone (other than for the purposes of proceedings for a remedy relating to the order or the treatment of the detainee, or to make a complaint to the Ombudsman, or other purposes specified under section 105.41(2)(d)) the following: (i) the fact that a preventative detention order has been made in relation to the detainee; or (ii) the fact that the detainee is being detained; or (iii) the period for which the detainee is being detained; or (iv) any information that the detainee gives the lawyer in the course of the contact. Similar restrictions apply to a police officer or an interpreter assisting in monitoring contact with a detainee or between the detainee and his or her lawyer (section 105.41(5) and (7)), and to a parent or guardian of a minor who is made subject to a preventative detention order (section 105.41(3) and (4A)) and to whom information has been provided under section 105.39. Section 105.41(4) clarifies that a parent or guardian a person does not commit an offence by letting another person know that the minor is safe but is not able to be contacted for the time being. A person who has received information which cannot be disclosed becomes subject to an obligation, the breach of which is also an offence, not to further disclose the information (section 105.41(6)).

Additional to the offences found in Chapter 5.3 of the Criminal Code Act 1995, Division 72 in Chapter 4 of the Act also includes offences related to international terrorist activities using explosive and lethal devices. As expressed in sections 72.1 and 72.11, this part of the Criminal Code Act is expressed to be for the purpose of giving effect to the Bombing Convention and the Convention on the Marking of Plastic Explosives for the Purpose of Detection (the Plastic Explosives Convention),[25] and includes the following offences:

- *Terrorist bombing* (section 72.3), prohibiting persons from intentionally delivering, placing, discharging or detonating an explosive or other lethal device (being reckless as to that fact) in a place of public use, a government facility, a public transportation system, or an infrastructure facility. It is an offence for a person to do so with the intent to cause death or serious harm (subsection (1)).[26] It is an offence for a person to do so with the intent to cause extensive destruction and be reckless as to whether that would result or be likely to result in major economic loss (subsection (2)).[27] Both offences are punishable by life imprisonment. An explosive device is defined by section 72.36 to include a bomb, a grenade, a mine, a missile, a perforator, a projectile, a rocket, a shaped charge, or a shell.
- *Trafficking in unmarked plastic explosives* (section 72.12), making it an offence to traffic in plastic explosives where the explosives are not properly marked and the trafficking is not authorised. Conviction renders a person liable to a maximum of 10 years imprisonment. On marking requirements, see section 72.33.
- *Importing or exporting unmarked plastic explosives* (section 72.13), criminalising the import or export of plastic explosives that are not properly marked where such export or import has not been authorised. The offence carries a penalty of up to 10 years imprisonment.
- *Manufacturing unmarked plastic explosives* (section 72.14), prohibiting the manufacture (or the exercise of control or direction over the manufacture) of plastic explosives where this is in breach of marking requirements and the manufacture is not authorised. Such manufacture is punishable by imprisonment of up to 10 years.
- *Possessing unmarked plastic explosives* (section 72.15), making it an offence, punishable by up to 2 years imprisonment, to possess an unmarked plastic explosive without authorisation.
- *Packaging requirements for plastic explosives* (section 72.17), requiring persons who manufacture plastic explosives to pack and wrap the explosives with a notice of its date of manufacture, its type, the presence of any detection agents and the words "Plastic Explosive" in upper-case lettering within 24 hours of its manufacture. Failure to do so renders a manufacturer liable to 2 years imprisonment.

---

[25]Convention on the Marking of Plastic Explosives for the Purpose of Detection, opened for signature 1 March 1991, ICAO Doc 9571 (entered into force 21 June 1998).

[26]Corresponding to article 2(1)(a) of the Bombing Convention (n 14).

[27]Corresponding to article 2(1)(b) of the Bombing Convention (n 14).

5.1.1.5 Special Measures: Control Orders and Preventive Detention

As discussed earlier in this part of the chapter, when looking at offences under the Criminal Code Act 1995, Division 104 of the Act sets out mechanisms for the issuing, variation and lapse of control orders. A further regime governed by Division 105 of the Code provides for preventive detention. Offences related to control orders and preventive detention are identified above (see also Appendix 3, Table 2(A)). The human rights implications of control orders and preventive detention is discussed in Chap. 18 (Sect. 18.1). For the purposes of this chapter, a brief description of each mechanism is provided.

A control order is one that imposes obligations on a person, under section 104.1, for the purpose of protecting the public from a terrorist act (including, for example, house arrest, the attachment to a person of an electronic tracking device, and various limitations upon where a person may go and whom he or she may meet). The range of conditions that may be imposed are set out in section 104.5. It is a criminal offence to contravene the terms of a control order, rendering the person liable to imprisonment for up to 5 years (section 104.27). Control orders can be no longer than 12 months, but can be renewed for subsequent periods of up to 12 months, with no limit on the number of renewals (section 104.5(1)(f) and (2)). Division 104 of the Criminal Code is subject to a sunset clause of 10 years (section 104.32) and is accompanied by a requirement for the Attorney General to report annually on the use of control orders in Australia (section 104.29).

In his report on Australia's counter-terrorism law, the Special Rapporteur welcomed the adoption by Australia of measures capable of protecting the public which fall short of actual detention. At the same time, however, he urged Australia to ensure that the imposition of obligations upon the subject of a control order are proportionate, and are only imposed for as long as strictly necessary, particularly having regard to the fact that control orders are issued based upon the non-criminal standard of proof on the balance of probabilities.[28] He raised further issues about the use of control orders, which are examined in Chap. 18.

The Anti-Terrorism Act (No 2) 2005 established "preventative detention orders" under a new Division 105 to the Criminal Code Act 1995. Preventative detention orders may be issued in two situations. The first is where there are reasonable grounds to suspect that a person will commit an imminent terrorist act (or is in possession of materials for that purpose, or has done something in pursuit of that purpose) *and* the person's detention would substantially assist in preventing a terrorist act from occurring *and* detaining the person is reasonably necessary for the latter purpose (section 105.4(4) and (5)). A person may also be made subject to a preventative detention order if a terrorist act has occurred within the last 28 days *and* the person's detention is necessary to preserve relevant evidence *and* detaining the person is reasonably necessary for the latter purpose (section 105.4(6)).

---

[28]Report of the Special Rapporteur (n 1), para 37.

The normal period that a person may be detained under such orders is no more than 24 hours, and only one order can be issued against any person relating to any one event (sections 105.8(5), 105.6 and 105.10(5)). In limited circumstances, a "continued preventative detention order" can see a person detained for up to 48 hours, upon extension by a judicial officer (section 105.12). A preventative detention order can be accompanied by a "prohibited contact order", on terms issued by the court, although the right to contact one's lawyer is specifically preserved (see sections 105.15 to 105.17, and 105.34). The question of orders under Division 105 of the Criminal Code is considered further in Chap. 18 (Sect. 18.4).

5.1.1.6   Prosecutions Under the Criminal Code Act[29]

Zeky Mallah was the first person to be charged with a terrorism offence in Australia. After receiving an adverse security assessment from the Australian Intelligence Security Organisation (ASIO), resulting in a refusal to renew Mallah's Australian passport, he recorded a video message in which he set out a plan to kill officials of ASIO and the Department of Foreign Affairs and Trade. This message was sold to an undercover officer, posing as a journalist.[30] Jihadi material and a gun were also found in Mallah's house and he was charged in December 2003 with two counts of doing an act in preparation for a terrorist act (section 101.6(1) of the Criminal Code), related to his possession of a gun and his recording of a threatening video message. Mallah was also charged with a non-terrorism offence under section 147.2 of the Act of making a threat to seriously harm an officer of the Commonwealth. Mallah pleaded guilty to the non-terrorism charge and was acquitted of the terrorism charges.[31]

Since that time, the following further prosecutions have been undertaken in Australia:

- Izhar Ul-Haque was charged in April 2004 with one count of intentionally receiving training from a terrorist organisation, Lashkar-e-Taiba in Pakistan (section 102.5 of the Criminal Code). Following his return to Australia from Pakistan, Ul-Haque was allegedly subjected to a series of oppressive interviews with the Australian Federal Police and ASIO in which he is said to have admitted

---

[29]The information that follows is drawn from the stocktaking exercise undertaken by the Gilbert & Tobin Centre of Public Law at the University of New South Wales, see online: http://www. gtcentre.unsw.edu.au/resources/terrorism-and-law/stocktake-of-terrorism-prosecutions.asp.

[30]In a pre-trial motion, the Court rejected a submission that the undercover police officer had engaged in unlawful and/or improper conduct and therefore ruled that the evidence gathered by him (including the videotape) was inadmissible: see *R v Mallah* [2005] NSWSC 358.

[31]Mallah was sentenced to 2 years and 6 months imprisonment: see *R v Mallah* [2005] NSWSC 317.

his involved with Lashkar-e-Taiba.[32] Charges against Ul-Haque were dropped in November 2007.

- Faheem Lodhi was convicted in June 2006 of possessing a thing (a document about how to make bombs) connected with preparation for a terrorist act (section 101.4(1) of the Criminal Code); collecting documents (maps of the Sydney electrical supply system) connected with preparation for a terrorist act (section 101.5(1)); and doing an act (seeking information about the availability of materials used to make bombs) in preparation for a terrorist act (section 101.6).[33] He was sentenced to concurrent terms of imprisonment of 10 years for the first two convictions, and 20 years on the final count.[34]

- Belal Khazaal was convicted in September 2008 of intentionally making a document in connection with preparation for a terrorist act (section 101.5(1) of the Criminal Code), i.e. a 102-page book entitled "Provision on the Rules of Jihad", subsequently published on the internet and said to be a do-it-yourself guide to Jihad, setting out targets for and methods of assassination. He was sentenced to 12 years in prison, with a non-parole period of 9 years. Khazaal had also been charged with attempting to incite others to commit the offence of engaging in a terrorist act (sections 11.1, 11.4 and 101.1 of the Criminal Code), but was acquitted by jury.

- Joseph Thomas (nicknamed 'Jihad Jack' by the media) was convicted in February 2006 of intentionally receiving funds from a terrorist organisation, Al Qa'ida (section 102.6(1) of the Criminal Code), and acquitted of two counts of intentionally providing support to a terrorist organisation (section 102.7(1)) relating to allegations that he had trained with Al Qa'ida in Afghanistan. His conviction was overturned by the Court of Appeal of the Supreme Court of Victoria on the basis that admissions he made in Pakistan in March 2003 had not been voluntary.[35] In February 2006, Thomas gave an interview with the Australian Broadcasting Association's 'Four Corners' program in which he discussed his involvement with the Taliban and Al Qa'ida and, in December 2006, the Court of Appeal directed that he be retried.[36] Although Thomas was convicted of possessing a falsified passport, he was acquitted by jury in October 2008 of receiving funds from a terrorist organisation. In late August 2006, Thomas became the first person to be subjected to a control order. A constitutional challenge to the control order regime was rejected by the High Court of Australia, a matter discussed further in Chap. 18 (see Sect. 18.1).[37]

---

[32]See University of New South Wales, Gilbert & Tobin Centre of Public Law, "Stocktake of Terrorism Prosecutions in Australia", online: http://www.gtcentre.unsw.edu.au/resources/terrorism-and-law/stocktake-of-terrorism-prosecutions.asp.

[33]Lodhi's appeal against conviction and sentence were dismissed by the New South Wales Court of Criminal Appeal in December 2007: see *Faheem Khalid Lodhi v Regina* [2007] NSWCCA 360.

[34]*Regina v Lodhi* [2006] NSWSC 691.

[35]*R v Thomas* [2006] VSCA 165.

[36]*R v Thomas (No 3)* [2006] VSCA 300.

[37]See *Thomas v Mowbray* [2007] HCA 33.

- In November 2005, a joint operation of the New South Wales, Victorian and Federal police culminated in raids of houses in Melbourne and Sydney (Operation Pendennis). Thirteen men were arrested in the Melbourne raids and were alleged to be part of a Melbourne-based terrorist group that planned to wage holy jihad against the Australian government with the intention of coercing it to withdraw from Iraq. Of this group, Izzydeen Atik pleaded guilty to one charge of being a member of a terrorist organisation (section 102.3(1) of the Criminal Code), and one further charge of proving resources (himself) to a terrorist organisation (section 102.7(1)).[38]

  The remaining 12 men arrested in the 2005 Operation Pendennis raids were charged with a range of terrorism-related offences including membership, preparation for a terrorist act, and providing funds to a terrorist organisation (Abdul Nacer Benbrika, Amer Haddara, Aimen Joud, Shane Kent, Abdullah Merhi, Ahmed Raad, Ezzit Raad, Fadal Sayadi, Hany Taha, Shoue Hammoud, Majed Raad and Bassam Raad). All 12 men were charged with intentionally being a member of a terrorist organisation (section 102.3 of the Criminal Code), seven of whom were found guilty by jury in September 2008. Three of those seven were also found guilty of providing resources to a terrorist organisation (section 102.7 (1)), two of which, with one other, were also found guilty of attempting to intentionally make funds available to a terrorist organisation (sections 11.1 and 102.6). Abdul Benbrika, who was alleged to be the spiritual leader of the group, was charged and convicted of directing the activities of a terrorist organisation (section 102.2(1)). He and one other were also convicted of two counts of possessing a compact disk connected with preparation for a terrorist act (section 101.4(1)). Benbrika was sentenced to five, seven, and 15 years imprisonment to be served cumulatively with a non-parole period of 12 years.[39] The seven convicted men have all lodges appeals against their convictions and sentences. Benbrika, Joud, Sayadi and Kent are to be retried and/or tried for additional offences relating to their alleged involvement in making an internet video advocating terrorism and/or placing an order for laboratory equipment to be used in the making of an explosive.
- Nine men (Mohamed Elomar, Abdul Hasan, Khaled Cheikho, Moustafa Cheikho and Mohammed Jamal) were charged in November 2005 of conspiracy to do an act in preparation for a terrorist act (sections 11.5 and 101.6(1) of the Criminal Code). The charges are based on circumstantial evidence including material (such as guns, hexamine fuel and bomb-making guides) found in their homes, the purchase of these materials using false names, communication

---

[38]On each count, Atik was sentenced to 5 years imprisonment (to commence on 23 August 2007) and 5 years imprisonment (to commence on 23 February 2008). A minimum non-parole period set at 4 years, 1 month and 14 days (with 652 days already having been served whilst on remand): see *R v Atik* [2007] VSC 299.

[39]For a break-down of convictions and sentences, see University of New South Wales, Gilbert & Tobin Centre of Public Law, "Stocktake of Terrorism Prosecutions in Australia", online: http://www.gtcentre.unsw.edu.au/resources/terrorism-and-law/benbrika-and-11-others.asp.

between them using code words, meetings between the men and Abdul Nacer Benbrika (referred to above), and allegations that the men undertook paramilitary training. Pre-trial arguments took more than 100 days, during which the trial judge delivered 65 written judgments. The trial, which commenced in November 2008, is on-going.

- In May 2006, John Amunsden was charged with making a thing (an explosive device) connected with preparation for a terrorist act (section 101.4 of the Criminal Code). He was also charged with a range of offences under Queensland law, including buying explosives dishonestly, using a carriage service to make a threat to kill, possessing a false passport, and counterfeiting Australian banknotes. The charges related to allegations that Amundsen had made threats to Queensland police to expect an Al Qa'ida-style attack in Brisbane. He was found in possession for 53 kilograms of the explosive Powergel, as well as four homemade bombs, 10 detonators, and a book about Osama Bin Laden. After subsequently admitting that his plan was to detonate bombs outside his girlfriend's house to win back her love, the terrorism charge was dropped and Amunsden pleaded guilty to the remaining charges under Queensland law.

- Charges were brought against Aruran Vinayagomoorthy, Sivarajah Yathavan and Arumugan Rajeevan in May 2007 alleging the involvement of the three men with the Liberation Tamil Tigers of Eelam (LTTE) by using the Melbourne-based Tamil Co-ordination Committee to raise $1.9 million AUD to support the terrorist activities of the LTTE. Three counts were brought, but then subsequently dropped, under the Criminal Code: being a member of a terrorist organisation (section 102.3(1)); making funds available to a terrorist organisation (section 102.6(1)); and providing support or resources to a terrorist organisation (section 102.7(1)). The accused are now charged only with making assets available to a prescribed entity (contrary to section 21 of the Charter of the United Nations Act 1945 – see Sect. 5.2.2 below).

- Mohamed Haneef was arrested in July 2007 and detained for 12 days before being charged with providing resources to a terrorist organisation, being reckless as to whether the organisation was a terrorist organisation (section 102.7(2) of the Criminal Code) due to him giving his mobile phone SIM card to his second cousin in England. His second cousins were believed to be involved in the attempted terrorist attack at Glasgow International Airport in June 2007. Haneef was granted bail but immediately afterwards the Minister for Immigration cancelled his visa on character grounds under section 502 of the Migration Act 1958. The decision to cancel Haneef's visa was set aside by the Federal Court of Australia on the basis that the Minister applied the wrong test.[40] In March 2008, the Commonwealth commissioned an inquiry into the case of Haneef (chaired by the Hon John Clarke QC).[41] Aspects of the inquiry report will be considered

---

[40]See: *Haneef v Minister for Immigration and Citizenship* [2007] FCA 1273; and *Minister for Immigration & Citizenship v Haneef* [2007] FCAFC 203.

[41]Clarke (2008).

below in this chapter (concerning the recommendation to establish an independent reviewer of counter-terrorism legislation), Chap. 14 (concerning a recommendation relating to section 102.7 of the Criminal Code), and Chap. 21 (concerning visa waivers). The case of Dr Haneef's detention is considered further in Chap. 16, Sect. 16.2.1.

- In early August 2009, four men were arrested in connection with a suspected suicide plot to storm a military base in Sydney.[42] The men are said to have ties to the Al-Qa'ida-linked Somali Islamist group al-Shabaab.[43]

5.1.2   Crimes (Aviation) Act 1991

The Crimes (Aviation) Act 1991 implements Australia's obligations under the Convention on Offences and Certain Other Acts Committed on Board Aircraft (the Tokyo Convention), the Convention for the Suppression of Unlawful Seizure of Aircraft (the Hague Convention), the Convention for the Suppression of Unlawful Acts against the Safety of Civil Aviation (the Montreal Convention), and the Protocol on the Suppression of Unlawful Acts of Violence at Airports Serving International Civil Aviation (the Montreal Protocol).[44] The Crimes (Aviation) Act contains the following offences relating to civil aviation (see Appendix 3, Table 2(B)):[45]

- *Aircraft hijacking* (sections 13 and 16) Section 13 makes it an indictable offence punishable by life imprisonment to hijack an aircraft in flight (as proscribed by

---

[42]Channel Asia News, 'Australia foils suicide attack on army base, 4 arrested', online: http://www.channelnewsasia.com/stories/afp_asiapacific/view/446687/1/.html.

[43]As at the date of completing this manuscript, no further information was available on the status of any charges against the men.

[44]Convention on Offences and Certain Other Acts Committed on Board Aircraft, opened for signature 14 September 1963, 704 UNTS 219 (entered into force 4 December 1969), articles 1 and 2; Convention for the Suppression of Unlawful Seizure of Aircraft, opened for signature 16 December 1970, 860 UNTS 105 (entered into force 14 October 1971); Convention for the Suppression of Unlawful Acts Against the Safety of Civil Aviation, opened for signature 23 September 1971, 974 UNTS 177 (entered into force 26 January 1973); and Protocol on the Suppression of Unlawful Acts of Violence at Airports Serving International Civil Aviation, opened for signature 24 February 1988, ICAO Doc 9518 (entered into force 6 August 1989).

[45]A number of the provisions in question relate to what is referred to in the Act as "Division 3 aircraft", defined by section 3 of the Act as a "Division 3 aircraft" means: "(a) an Australian aircraft (other than a Commonwealth aircraft or a defence aircraft) that is mainly used for the purpose of any of the following flights, or is engaged, or is intended or likely to be engaged, in such a flight: (i) a prescribed flight; (ii) a flight between a part of Australia and a place outside Australia; (iii) a flight wholly outside Australia; or (b) a Commonwealth aircraft; or (c) a defence aircraft; or (d) a foreign aircraft that is in Australia; or (e) a foreign aircraft that is outside Australia while engaged in a flight that started in Australia or that was, when the flight started, intended to end in Australia".

article 1(a) of the Hague Convention).[46] Section 9 of the Act defines hijacking as the seizure, or exercise of control of, an aircraft by force or threat of force, or by any other form of intimidation, by any person while on board the aircraft. The hijacking offence in section 13 is supplemented by three further offences under section 16 of the Act. At the lowest end of the scale, section 16(1) makes it an offence, punishable by up to 7 years imprisonment, to take or exercise control of an empty aircraft (an aircraft on which there is only the offender and any accomplice). Section 16(2) criminalises the taking or exercise of control over an aircraft on which other people are also present, punishable by imprisonment for 14 years. The third offence, under section 16(3), which is punishable by imprisonment of up to 20 years, involves taking or exercising control of an aircraft by force or threat of force (or by any trick or false pretence) while others are on board the aircraft.

- *Other acts of violence on an aircraft in flight* (sections 14, 21 and 25).[47] Section 14 extends the application of criminal law offences under the law of Australia's Jervis Bay Territory to the commission of an act of violence by a person on board an aircraft in flight against passengers or crew. The applicable penalty for such conduct is the same as that provided for under the law of Australia's Jervis Bay Territory (section 14(2)). It is also an offence to assault, threaten with violence, or otherwise intimidate, a member of the crew of an aircraft (section 21(1)), punishable by up to 14 years imprisonment. By combination of sections 10(1)(a) and 25(1), it is an offence to commit an act of violence against anyone on board an aircraft in flight if that act is likely to endanger the safety of the aircraft, punishable by up to 14 years imprisonment.

- *Destruction of an aircraft* (sections 17, 18 and 25).[48] It is an offence under section 17(1), punishable by up to 14 years imprisonment, to intentionally destroy an aircraft. Destruction of an aircraft with the intention of causing death, or reckless as to the safety of anyone's life, is an indictable offence punishable by imprisonment for life (section 18(1)). Destruction of an aircraft in service, or causing damage to such an aircraft, is an offence punishable by up to 14 years imprisonment if this renders the aircraft incapable of flight or is likely to endanger its safety in flight (sections 10(1)(b) and 25(1)). Sections 10(2)(a), 10(2)(b) and 25(2) make it an offence to place, or cause to be placed, on an aircraft in service a substance or thing that is likely to destroy the aircraft, or likely to cause damage to the aircraft which either renders it incapable of flight or is likely to endanger its safety. The latter offence is punishable by imprisonment of up to 7 years.

---

[46]Corresponding to article 1(a) of the Hague Convention (ibid).

[47]Corresponding to article 1(1)(a) of the Montreal Convention (n 44) and article 4 of the Hague Convention (n 44).

[48]Corresponding to article 1(1)(b) of the Montreal Convention (n 44).

- *Prejudicing the safe operation of an aircraft* (sections 19, 20, 22 and 23).[49] Any act capable of prejudicing the safe operation of an aircraft, with the intention of prejudicing its safe operation, is an offence under section 19(1), punishable upon conviction by 14 years imprisonment. Doing so with the intention of causing death, or reckless as to the safety of anyone's life, is an offence punishable by life imprisonment (section 20(1)). It is also an offence to do anything being reckless as to whether this will endanger the safety of an aircraft (section 22(1)), carrying a maximum penalty of 7 years imprisonment. Carrying or placing dangerous goods on an aircraft is an offence under section 23(1) of the Act, punishable by up to 7 years imprisonment.
- *Destruction to, or damage of, air navigation facilities* (sections 10(2)(c) and 25(2)), making it an offence to destroy or damage any navigation facilities, or interfere with their operation, where this is likely to endanger the safety of an aircraft in flight.[50] Conviction renders a person liable to imprisonment up to 7 years.
- *Threats and false statements* (sections 24 and 25). Subsection 24(1) makes it an offence to threaten to destroy, damage or endanger the safety of an aircraft, or to threaten to kill or injure anyone on board an aircraft. It is an offence under subsection (2) to communicate false information, knowing it to be false, and from which it can be reasonably inferred that there is an intention or plan to hijack an aircraft, destroy or damage an aircraft so as to endanger its safety, or to threaten to kill or injure someone on board an aircraft.[51] Offences under section 24 are punishable by 2 years imprisonment. It is also an offence under sections 10(2)(d) and 25(2) to communicate false information which thereby endangers the safety of an aircraft in flight. The latter offence is punishable by up to 7 years imprisonment.
- *Acts of violence at airports* (section 26), making it an offence to perform acts of violence against any person (subsection (1)), or causing any damage to airport facilities (subsection (2)), where this is likely to endanger safety at that airport.[52] Conviction under section 26(1) renders a person liable to imprisonment for 15 years. An offence under section 26(2) carries a maximum penalty of 10 years imprisonment.

Added to the offences under the Crimes (Aviation) Act are two sets of offences established under the Aviation Transport Security Act 2004 (see Appendix 3, Table 2(C)):

- *Possession of weapons at an airport* (sections 46 and 47), making it an offence to pass through a security screening point with a weapon, or otherwise be in possession of a weapon in an airside area of an airport, or a landside security

---

[49]Corresponding to articles 1(1)(b) and 1(1)(c) of the Montreal Convention (n 44) and article 1(1) (b) of the Tokyo Convention (n 44).

[50]Corresponding to article 1(1)(d) of the Montreal Convention (n 44).

[51]Corresponding to article 1(1)(e) of the Montreal Convention (n 44).

[52]Corresponding to article 1(1bis) of the Montreal Convention (n 44).

area of an airport, without appropriate authorisation. The offences are punishable by up to 7 years imprisonment.

- *Possession of weapons in an aircraft* (sections 48 and 49), making it an offence to be in possession of a weapon on an aircraft without appropriate authorisation.

5.1.3   Crimes (Ships and Fixed Platforms) Act 1992

The Convention for the Suppression of Unlawful Acts against the Safety of Maritime Navigation (the Rome Convention) and its Protocol (the Rome Protocol) have been implemented by Australia under the Crimes (Ships and Fixed Platforms) Act 1992.[53] The Act contains the following offences relating to operations at sea (see Appendix 3, Table 2(D)):

- *Seizing a ship* (section 8), making it an offence punishable by life imprisonment to take possession or control of a private ship by threat of use of force, or by any other kind of intimidation.[54] A "private ship" is defined by section 3 of the Act as a ship that is not a warship or other ship operated for naval, military, customs or law enforcement purposes by Australia or another State.[55]
- *Violence on a ship* (section 9), criminalising acts of violence against persons on board a ship knowing that this is likely to endanger the safe navigation of the ship.[56] Conviction renders a person liable to 15 years imprisonment.
- *Destroying or damaging a ship* (section 10), making it an offence to destroy a ship (subsection (1)), or to cause damage to a ship or its cargo, knowing that this is likely to endanger the safe navigation of the ship (subsection (2)).[57] Both offences are punishable by life imprisonment.
- *Placing destructive devices on a ship* (section 11), making it an offence to place or cause to be placed on a ship, by any means, a device or substance which is likely to destroy that ship (subsection (1)), or to cause damage to it or its cargo knowing that this is likely to endanger the safe navigation of the ship (subsection (2)).[58] The offences under section 11 are punishable by up to 15 years imprisonment.

---

[53]Convention for the Suppression of Unlawful Acts against the Safety of Maritime Navigation, opened for signature 10 March 1988, 1678 UNTS 221 (entered into force 1 March 1992); and the Protocol for the Suppression of Unlawful Acts against the Safety of Fixed Platforms Located on the Continental Shelf, opened for signature 10 March 1988, 1678 UNTS 304 (entered into force 1 March 1992).

[54]Corresponding to article 3(1)(a) of the Rome Convention (ibid).

[55]"Ship" is in turn defined as a vessel of any type not permanently attached to the sea-bed, and includes any dynamically supported craft, submersible, or any other floating craft, other than a vessel that has been withdrawn from navigation or is laid up.

[56]Corresponding to article 3(1)(b) of the Rome Convention (n 53).

[57]Corresponding to article 3(1)(c) of the Rome Convention (n 53).

[58]Corresponding to article 3(1)(d) of the Rome Convention (n 53).

- *Destroying or damaging navigational facilities* (section 12), criminalising the destruction of or serious damage to maritime navigational facilities, or serious interference with the operation of such facilities, if this would be likely to endanger the safe navigation of a ship.[59] The maximum penalty upon conviction is 15 years imprisonment.
- *Communicating false information* (section 13), making it an offence to communication false information knowing that this will endanger the safe navigation of a private ship, and rendering a person liable to 15 years imprisonment on conviction.[60]
- *Causing injury or death* (sections 14 to 16), establishing offences of causing death (section 14), causing grievous bodily harm (section 15), or causing injury (section 16) in connection with the commission or attempted commission of an offence against sections 8 to 13 of the Act.[61] The maximum applicable penalties for each offence is life imprisonment, 15 years imprisonment, and 10 years imprisonment respectively.
- *Threats to commit offences under the Convention* (section 17), making it an offence to threaten to do an act that would constitute an offence against sections 9, 10 or 12 (violence on a ship, destroying or damaging a ship, or destroying or damaging navigational facilities) with the intention to compel a person to do or refrain from doing an act, if that threat is likely to endanger the safe navigation of the ship concerned.[62] The making of such threats renders a person liable to imprisonment for up to 2 years.
- *Seizing control of a fixed platform* (section 21), criminalising the taking of possession, or exercise of control over, a fixed platform by the threat or use of force or by any other kind of intimidation.[63] A person convicted of an offence against section 21 of the Act is liable to life imprisonment.
- *Violence on a fixed platform* (section 22), prohibiting acts of violence against a person on board a fixed platform knowing that the act is likely to endanger the safety of the platform, and rendering a person liable to 15 years imprisonment upon conviction.[64]
- *Destroying or damaging a fixed platform* (section 23), criminalising conduct that causes the destruction of, or damage to, a fixed platform knowing that the destruction or damage is likely to endanger its safety.[65] Conviction exposes a person to a maximum penalty of life imprisonment.

---

[59]Corresponding to article 3(1)(e) of the Rome Convention (n 53).
[60]Corresponding to article 3(1)(f) of the Rome Convention (n 53).
[61]Corresponding to article 3(1)(g) of the Rome Convention (n 53).
[62]Corresponding to article 3(2)(c) of the Rome Convention (n 53).
[63]Corresponding to article 2(1)(a) of the Rome Protocol (n 53).
[64]Corresponding to article 2(1)(b) of the Rome Protocol (n 53).
[65]Corresponding to article 2(1)(c) of the Rome Protocol (n 53).

- *Placing destructive devices on a fixed platform* (section 24), making it an offence to place or cause to be placed on a fixed platform, by any means, a device or substance knowing that it is likely to destroy the fixed platform or endanger its safety.[66] An offence against this section is punishable by up to 15 years imprisonment.
- *Causing injury or death* (sections 25 to 27), establishing offences of causing death (section 25), causing grievous bodily harm (section 26), or causing injury (section 27) in connection with the commission or attempted commission of an offence against sections 21 to 24 of the Act.[67] The maximum applicable penalties for each offence is life imprisonment, 15 years imprisonment, and 10 years imprisonment respectively.
- *Threats to commit offences under the Protocol* (section 28), making it an offence to threaten to do an act that would constitute an offence against section 22 or 23 (violence on a fixed platform, or destroying or damaging a fixed platform) with the intention to compel a person to do or refrain from doing an act, if that threat is likely to endanger the safety of the fixed platform concerned.[68] The making of such threats renders a person liable to imprisonment for up to 2 years.

5.1.4 Legislation Concerning Hostage-Taking and Internationally Protected Persons

The preamble to the Crimes (Hostages) Act 1989 describes the Act as one "to give effect to the International Convention Against the Taking of Hostages, and for related purposes" (see Appendix 3, Table 2(E)).[69] To that end, section 8(1) makes it an offence to commit an act of "hostage-taking", with section 7 defining this expression as seizing or detaining a person (a hostage) accompanied by a threat to kill, injure, or continue to detain the hostage with the intention of compelling Australia, an international organisation, or any other person to do, or abstain from doing, any act as an explicit or implicit condition for the release of the hostage.[70] The offence under section 8(1) is punishable by life imprisonment.

Similarly, the preamble to the Crimes (Internationally Protected Persons) Act 1976 refers to this Act as being the vehicle through which Australia has given effect to the Convention on the Prevention and Punishment of Crimes against Internationally Protected Persons, including Diplomatic Agents (the Protected

---

[66]Corresponding to article 2(1)(d) of the Rome Protocol (n 53).

[67]Corresponding to article 2(1)(e) of the Rome Protocol (n 53).

[68]Corresponding to article 2(2)(c) of the Rome Protocol (n 53).

[69]International Convention against the Taking of Hostages, opened for signature 18 December 1979, 1316 UNTS 205 (entered into force 3 June 1983).

[70]Corresponding to article 1 of the Hostages Convention (ibid).

Persons Convention).[71] The Act uses an extended definition of "internationally protected persons" (IPP), to include the Governor-General of Australia and certain prescribed officials and agents (section 3A). Section 8 of the Act establishes the following offences (see Appendix 3, Table 2(F)):

- *Attacks against the person or liberty of an internationally protected person.*[72] Section 8(1) makes it an offence punishable by life imprisonment to murder or kidnap an internationally protected person.[73] The consequences of any other attack on the person or liberty of an IPP (including assault, or administration of a poison, drug or other destructive or noxious substance or thing)[74] depends upon the consequences of such an attack, ranging from life imprisonment to 10 years imprisonment.[75]
- *Attacks against the premises of an internationally protected person.*[76] Section 8 (3) and its amendments sets out a range of offences involving the intentional destruction or damage of official premises, private accommodation or means or transport, of an IPP, or any other premises or property in which an IPP is present or likely to be present. Where this is intended to endanger the like of a protected person, such conduct is punishable by imprisonment of up to 20 years (section 8 (3A)). Where the attack uses fire or explosives, the maximum penalty is 15 years imprisonment (section 8(3B)), or up to 25 years if this is intended to endanger the like of the protected person (section 8(3C)). In all other cases, such attacks are punishable by up to 10 years imprisonment (section 8(3)).
- *Threats to commit offences* (section 8(4)), making it an offence to threaten to do anything that would constitute one of the previously-mentioned offences under the Act, punishable by up to 7 years imprisonment.

---

[71]Convention on the Prevention and Punishment of Crimes against International Protected Persons, including Diplomatic Agents, opened for signature 14 December 1973, 1035 UNTS 167 (entered into force 20 February 1977).

[72]Corresponding to article 2(1)(a) of the Protected Persons Convention (ibid).

[73]For the purpose of section 8 of the Act, kidnapping a person "consists of leading, taking or enticing the person away, or detaining the person, with intent to hold the person for ransom or as a hostage or otherwise for the purpose of inducing compliance with any demand or obtaining any advantage" (section 8(7)(a)). Murdering a person "consists of causing the death of that person in circumstances in which the person causing the death would be guilty of murder according to the law in force in the Australian Capital Territory at the time of the conduct causing the death, whether or not the conduct took place in that Territory" (section 8(7)(b)).

[74]For the purpose of section 8 of the Act, a reference to an attack upon the person of an internationally protected person "shall be read as including a reference to assaulting an internationally protected person or to administering or applying to an internationally protected person, or causing an internationally protected person to take, a poison, drug or other destructive or noxious substance or thing" (section 8(7)(c)).

[75]See section 8(2) of the Act, which provides for the following consequences: (a) where the attack causes death – by imprisonment for life; (b) where the attack causes grievous bodily harm – by imprisonment for a period not exceeding 20 years; or (c) in any other case – by imprisonment for a period not exceeding 10 years.

[76]Corresponding to article 2(1)(b) of the Protected Persons Convention (n 71).

5.1.5 Nuclear Non-proliferation (Safeguards) Act 1987

For the purpose of implementing aspects of the Convention on the Physical Protection of Nuclear Material (the Nuclear Material Convention)[77] and the Nuclear Terrorism Convention, Division 2 of the Nuclear Non-Proliferation (Safeguards) Act 1987 contains the following offences relating to nuclear material and nuclear facilities (see Appendix 3, Table 2(G)):

- *Stealing nuclear material* (section 33), making it an offence to steal, fraudulently misappropriate or convert to one's own use, or obtain by false pretences any nuclear material.[78] "Nuclear material" is given the same meaning as in article 1(a) of the Nuclear Material Convention (see section 33 of the Act). The offence under section 33 is punishable by up to 10 years imprisonment.
- *Demanding nuclear material by threats* (section 34), criminalising the making of demands for nuclear material where this is by force or threat of force or by any form of intimidation.[79] The applicable penalty is 10 years imprisonment.
- *Carrying, sending or moving nuclear material* (section 34A), prohibiting a person from unlawfully carrying, sending or moving nuclear material into or out of Australia or a foreign country, the penalty for which is also 10 years imprisonment.
- *Use of nuclear material causing death or injury to persons or damage to property or the environment* (section 35), making it an offence punishable by up to 20 years imprisonment to use nuclear material to cause either: (a) the death of, or serious injury to, any person; or (b) substantial damage to property or to the environment.[80]
- *Acts against nuclear facilities* (section 35A), making it an offence to interfere with the operation of a nuclear facility intending to cause, or knowing that it will likely cause, the death of, or serious injury to, any person, or substantial damage to property or to the environment by exposure to radiation or by the release of radioactive substances.[81] Commission of an offence under section 35A renders a person liable to imprisonment of up to 20 years.
- *Threat to use nuclear material* (section 36), criminalising threats to use nuclear material to cause death or injury, or damage to property of the environment.[82] It is also an offence to threaten to use nuclear material in order to interfere with the operation of a nuclear facility in a way which would amount to an

---

[77]Convention on the Physical Protection of Nuclear Material, opened for signature 3 March 1980, 1456 UNTS 124 (entered into force 8 February 1987).

[78]Corresponding to article 7(1)(b) and (c) of the Nuclear Material Convention (ibid).

[79]Corresponding to article 7(1)(d) of the Nuclear Material Convention (n 77).

[80]Corresponding to article 7(1)(a) of the Nuclear Material Convention (n 77).

[81]Corresponding to article 2(1)(b) of the Nuclear Terrorism Convention (n 13).

[82]Corresponding to article 7(1)(e)(i) of the Nuclear Material Convention (n 77).

offence under section 35A.[83] Conviction carries a maximum penalty of 10 years imprisonment.

- *Threat to commit certain offences* (section 37), making it an offence to threaten to commit an offence under section 33 (stealing nuclear material) or section 35A (interfering with the operation of a nuclear facility) in order to compel a person, an international organisation or a State to do or refrain from doing any act.[84] The maximum penalty for such an offence is 10 years imprisonment.

5.1.6 Financial Transactions Reports Act 1998

The Financial Transactions Reports Act 1998 was amended under Schedule 2 of the Suppression of the Financing of Terrorism Act 2002. Financial institutions, insurers, and other "cash dealers" within the meaning of the Financial Transactions Reports Act (see section 3(1)) have reporting obligations which have been extended to the suppression of the financing of terrorism. Section 16(1A) of the Act now demands that, where a cash dealer has reasonable grounds to suspect that a transaction is preparatory to the commission of a financing of terrorism offence, or may be relevant to the investigation or prosecution of such an offence, a report of the transaction must be prepared and communicated. A "financing of terrorism offence" is defined as (see section 16(6)) an offence under section 102.6 of the Criminal Code (getting funds to, from, or for a terrorist organisation – see Sect. 5.1.1.4 above); an offence under Division 103 of the Criminal Code (financing terrorism or financing a terrorist – see Sect. 5.1.1.4 above); or section 20 or 21 of the Charter of the United Nations Act 1945 (dealing with assets of, or making assets available to persons of entities on the Consolidated List of Entities – see Sect. 5.2.2 below).

In addition, the Director of the Australian Transaction Reports and Analysis Centre (AUSTRAC, Australia's financial intelligence unit), the Australian Federal Police Commissioner and the Director-General of Security have been empowered to disclose financial transaction reports information directly to foreign countries, foreign law enforcement agencies and foreign intelligence agencies, subject to appropriate undertakings to protect the confidentiality of the information, control the use of the information and ensure that the information is used only for the purpose for which it was communicated.[85]

---

[83]Corresponding to article 2(2)(a) of the Nuclear Terrorism Convention (n 13).

[84]Corresponding to article 7(1)(e)(ii) of the Nuclear Material Convention (n 77); and article 2(2)(a) of the Nuclear Terrorism Convention (n 13).

[85]Supplement to First Report of Australia to the Counter-Terrorism Committee pursuant to paragraph 6 of Security Council resolution 1373 (2001) of 28 September 2001, UN Doc S/2002/ 776 (2002), para 10.

5.1.7   Law and Justice Legislation Amendment (Marking of Plastic Explosives) Act 2006

The Law and Justice Legislation Amendment (Marking of Plastic Explosives) Act 2006 was the vehicle through which Australia implemented aspects of the Plastic Explosives Convention, which was subsequently acceded to by Australia on 26 June 2007.[86] Related offences are dealt with under Division 72 of the Criminal Code Act 1995 (see Sect. 5.1.1.4 above and Appendix 3, Table 2(A)).

5.1.8   Anti-Money Laundering and Counter-Terrorism Financing Act 2006

Following the release of an exposure Bill in December 2005, Australia enacted the Anti-Money Laundering and Counter-Terrorism Financing Act 2006 for the purpose of implementing key aspects of the Revised Financial Action Task Force (FAFT) 40 Recommendations (adoption of which was urged by the Security Council in its resolution 1617 (2005)).[87] On the implementation of the FATF Revised Recommendations, see Australia's fifth and sixth reports to the Counter-Terrorism Committee.[88]

5.1.9   Legislation Concerning the Australian Security Intelligence Organisation

For the purpose of setting out, and extending, the jurisdiction and powers of the Australian Security Intelligence Organisation (ASIO), and to provide for the protection of national security information, Australia enacted the Anti-Terrorism Act (No. 3) 2004, the Australian Security Intelligence Organisation Act 1979, the Australian Security Intelligence Organisation Legislation Amendment (Terrorism) Act 2003, the Australian Security Intelligence Organisation Legislation Amendment Act 2006, the National Security Information (Criminal and Civil Proceedings) Act 2004, and the National Security Information Legislation Amendment Act 2005.

In 2003, the powers of ASIO were enhanced through the addition of a (then) new Division III to Part III of the ASIO Act. As a consequence of the passage of the Australian Security Intelligence Organisation Legislation Amendment Act 2006, these powers were extended for a further 10 years. Under the amendments, the definition of politically motivated violence, which falls within the investigative

---

[86]Plastic Explosives Convention (n 25).

[87]SC Res 1617, UN SCOR, 5244th Mtg, UN Doc S/Res/1617 (2005), para 7.

[88]Fifth Report to the Counter-Terrorism Committee, UN Doc S/2005/90 (2005), pp. 3–5; and Sixth Report to the Counter-Terrorism Committee, UN Doc S/2005/671 (2005).

jurisdiction of ASIO, was expanded to include terrorism offences (section 4 of the principal Act). ASIO, which is responsible for the gathering of intelligence about terrorist threats to Australia, was given the power to detain and question terrorist suspects, and non-suspects, who may have information on terrorist activities. The Act requires a person to provide information and answer questions where a warrant for questioning is issued (sections 34D and 34G). Since this overrides the internationally recognised privilege against self-incrimination, the Special Rapporteur was encouraged to see that measures are in place so that the use of information provided at ASIO hearings is restricted to the gathering of intelligence.[89] Such information is accordingly subject to "use immunity", which means that the information may not be used in criminal proceedings against the person (section 34(G)(9)). The Special Rapporteur did note concerns, however, about the potential "derivative use" of such information.

ASIO's power to detain extends to 168 hours (7 days) continuously (section 34SC). Before questioning and detention can take place, the Director-General of ASIO must obtain the consent of the Attorney-General to seek a warrant for questioning and detention, and an "issuing authority" must be satisfied that there are reasonable grounds for believing that such questioning and detention will substantially assist the collection of intelligence that is important in relation to a terrorism offence (see sections 34D, 34E, 34F and 34G). Upon execution of the warrant, a person taken into custody must be brought before a "prescribed authority" for the questioning to be conducted (section 34H). An "issuing authority" is a federal magistrate or judge appointed by the Minister of Justice as an issuing authority. A "prescribed authority" is a person, also appointed by the Minister, who has served as a judge in one or more superior courts for a period of 5 years and no longer holds a commission as a judge of a superior court (sect. 34B (1)). Although a detained person may make a complaint at any time to the Inspector-General of Security Intelligence, a detained person has no right to seek a judicial review of the validity, or terms, of an issuing authority's warrant. Nor does a detained person have the right to be brought before any judicial body other than a prescribed authority. The absence of these rights was noted as being of grave concern to the UN Special Rapporteur, causing him to conclude that this offends the right to a fair hearing and the right to have the legality of one's detention determined by an independent and competent authority (see further Chap. 16, Sect. 16.2.2).

5.1.10 Review of Australia's Counter-Terrorism Legislation

Section 4 of the Security Legislation Amendment (Terrorism) Act 2002 set out a requirement for review of the provisions of the Security Legislation Amendment (Terrorism) Act 2002, Suppression of the Financing of Terrorism Act 2002, Border Security Legislation Amendment Act 2002 and the Criminal Code Amendment (Suppression of Terrorist Bombings) Act 2002. This provision required a review to

---

[89]Special Rapporteur report (n 1), para 31.

be undertaken as soon as practicable after the third anniversary of the commencement of the amendments (i.e., as soon as practicable after 6 July 2005). To that end, the Attorney-General of Australia established the Security Legislation Review Committee, chaired by retired judge The Hon. Simon Sheller, which completed its report in June 2006 after hearing from major stakeholders.[90] The Sheller report was then forwarded to the Parliamentary Joint Committee on Security and Intelligence.[91] After taking into account the Sheller report and hearing further submissions, the Joint Committee reported to Parliament in December 2006.[92] The reviews led to 26 recommendations in the Parliamentary Joint Committee report. Amongst those recommendations, the following subjects were included as matters of concern:[93]

- The need for a defence to the offences of terrorist financing under Division 103 of the Criminal Code Act 1995.
- Review mechanisms for the listing of prescribed entities under the Charter of the United Nations Act 1945.

The Parliamentary Joint Committee also recommended that the Australian government support or sponsor a study into the causes of violent radicalisation in Australia, and that the Attorney-General's department raise awareness about the legislative regime on counter-terrorism, including by making such information available in different languages.[94] A matter also taken up by the Clarke Inquiry (see Sect. 5.1.1.6 above concerning the detention and visa revocation of Dr Mohamed Haneef)[95] and the 2008 report of the Law Council of Australia (considered immediately below), the Joint Committee recommended that:

(a) The Government appoint an independent person of high standing as an Independent Reviewer of terrorism law in Australia.
(b) The Independent Reviewer be free to set his or her own priorities and have access to all necessary information.
(c) The Independent Reviewer report annually to Parliament.
(d) The Intelligence Services Act 2001 be amended to require the PJCIS to examine the reports of the Independent Reviewer tabled in Parliament.

Also of relevance is the 2008 report of the Law Council of Australia, which brings together a wide range of past Law Council advocacy, including submissions to

---

[90]Report of the Security Legislation Committee, tabled before Parliament on 15 June 2006 (Commonwealth of Australia), online: http://www.ag.gov.au/www/agd/agd.nsf/Page/National_securityReviewsSecurity_Legislation_Review_Committee.

[91]Second report of Australia to the Counter-Terrorism Committee (n 85), para 15.

[92]Parliamentary Joint Committee on Security and Intelligence, Review of Security and Counter Terrorism Legislation, December 2006 (Commonwealth of Australia), online: http://www.aph.gov.au/house/committee/pjcis/securityleg/report.htm.

[93]Parliamentary Joint Committee report (ibid), recommendations 17 and 22 respectively.

[94]Parliamentary Joint Committee report (ibid), recommendations 1 and 4.

[95]Clarke (2008, p. xii).

Parliamentary Inquiries, the Australian Law Reform Commission, and other national and international bodies.[96] The analyses and recommendations of the Law Council will be considered in Part 3 of this book where appropriate. Of note, for the purpose of this chapter, the Law Council's report also reiterated the importance of continued review of Australia's counter-terrorism legislation. Quoting the observation of New South Wales Chief Justice Spigelman in *Lodhi v R* (see Sect. 5.1.1.6 above) that "the particular nature of terrorism has resulted in a special, and in many ways unique, legislative regime",[97] the Law Council itself said:[98]

> For many years, the Law Council has submitted that the exceptional nature of Australia's anti-terrorism measures – and the often disproportionate impact they have on the enjoyment of individual rights – should not become normalised within the Australian criminal justice system and must be subject to regular and comprehensive review. As noted by the PJCIS [Parliamentary Joint Committee on Security and Intelligence], without such review 'there is a real risk that the terrorism law regime may, over time, influence legal policy more generally with potentially detrimental impacts on the rule of law'.

The Law Council of Australia accordingly also recommended that a mechanism for ensuring regular, comprehensive, independent review of Australia's terrorism laws should be created.[99] The calls by the Law Council, the Clarke Inquiry, and the Parliamentary Joint Committee for the establishment of an Independent Reviewer of Australia's terrorism laws is drawn directly from the existence of such an office in the United Kingdom (see Chap. 8, Sect. 8.1.10). The National Security Legislation Monitor Bill 2009 and is currently on the legislative agenda of the Australian Senate.[100]

Added to the Law Council, Joint Committee and Haneef Inquiry recommendations, the Anti-Terrorism Laws Reform Bill 2009 was introduced by the Australian Greens party, aiming to "restore core democratic principles into Australian laws dealing with terrorism offences".[101] The Bill was referred to the Senate Legislation Committee on Legal and Constitutional Affairs in June 2009, for inquiry and report. The Bill seeks to amend the Criminal Code Act 1995, the Crimes Act 1914, and the Australian Security Intelligence Organisation Act 1979, and to repeal the National Security Information (Criminal and Civil Proceedings) Act 2004. The Bill aims to bring about amendments relating to the definition of terrorism offences, provisions relating to the proscription of terrorist organisations as well as interaction with them, and offences related to reckless possession of a thing potentially relating to the commission of a terrorist offence, and to repealing the offence of sedition. The

---

[96]Law Council of Australia, Anti-Terrorism Reform Project: A consolidation of the Law Council of Australia's advocacy in relation to Australia's anti-terrorism measures, November 2008, online: http://www.lawcouncil.asn.au/initiatives/anti-terrorism_reform.cfm.

[97]*Lodhi v R* [2006] NSWCCA 121, para 66 (see Sect. 5.1.1.6 above for a description of the case).

[98]Law Council report (n 96), p. 16.

[99]Law Council report (n 96), p. 17.

[100]See Parliament of Australia, Senate, National Security Legislation Monitor Bill, online: http://www.aph.gov.au/Senate/committee/fapa_ctte/national_security_leg/report/index.htm.

[101]Anti-Terrorism Laws Reform Bill 2009, Explanatory Note, p. 2.

Committee reported on the Bill in October 2009, just after completion of this manuscript.[102] Its content, and the legislative process that followed, is therefore not addressed further in this chapter.

5.2 Implementation by Australia of Security Council Decisions

As considered in Chap. 4, there are numerous resolutions of the Security Council dealing with the subjects of terrorism and counter-terrorism. Three principal resolutions govern the action required by, or recommended to, members of the United Nations (on the resolutions of the Security Council identified below, see Chap. 3, Sect. 3.2.2):

- Security Council resolution 1267 (1999), which required members of the United Nations to impose a travel ban and an arms embargo on the Taliban and Al-Qa'ida, and to freeze funds and other financial resources controlled by or on behalf of the Taliban or any other individuals of entities designated by the Al-Qa'ida and Taliban Sanctions Committee.[103]
- Security Council resolution 1373 (2001), which imposed various obligations upon States, mainly focussed upon suppressing the financing of terrorism, and recommended further action.[104]
- Security Council resolution 1624 (2005), which called on States to adopt measures to prohibit the incitement to commit terrorist acts, and to prevent such conduct.[105]

Resolutions 1267 (1999) and 1373 (2001) have been partly implemented by Australia through the Charter of the United Nations Act 1945 and regulations made under it (on the implementation of Security Council resolutions by Australia, see Chap. 4, Sect. 4.2.3). Various aspects of resolution 1373 (2001) have been implemented under the legislation identified at Sect. 5.1 above. For a full summary of the status of implementation, see Sect. 5.3 below.

5.2.1 Criminal Code Act 1995 on Incitement and Sedition

Amongst other things, the Anti-Terrorism Act (No 2) 2005 provided for the proscription of sedition under a new section 80.2 of the Criminal Code Act,

---

[102]Senate Legislation Committee on Legal and Constitutional Affairs, Anti-Terrorism Laws Reform Bill 2009 (report of October 2009).

[103]SC Res 1267, UN SCOR, 4051st Mtg, UN Doc S/Res/1267 (1999).

[104]SC Res 1373 (n 17).

[105]SC Res 1624, UN SCOR, 5261st Mtg, UN Doc S/Res/1624 (2005).

which had previously been dealt with under sections 24A to 24F of the Crimes Act 1914. The Criminal Code now includes offences of incitement and assisting the enemy or those engaged in armed hostilities (see Appendix 3, Table 2(A)):

- *Incitement* (section 80.2(5)), making it an offence to urge a group or groups to use force or violence against another group or groups if this would threaten the peace, order and good government of Australia. The offence carries a maximum penalty of 7 years imprisonment.
- *Assisting the enemy or those engaged in armed hostilities* (section 80.2(7) and (8)), prohibiting persons from urging another person to in conduct that is intended to assist an organisation or country which is at war with Australia, or engaged in hostilities against the Australian Defence Force. Conviction renders a person liable to imprisonment of up to 7 years.

Although section 80.2(5) will capture some aspects of the incitement to terrorism, it will not encompass incitement by individuals, of individuals, nor will it capture the incitement of terrorist acts against individuals or organisations, or of transboundary acts of terrorism.[106] Notwithstanding this, and the absence of an express offence of incitement to terrorism, section 11 of the Criminal Code (which sets out the inchoate offence of incitement, applicable to all Commonwealth offences) is sufficient to capture the incitement to terrorism offences under the Code (see Chap. 14, Sect. 14.3.4).

Concerning the sedition offences under section 80.2(7) and (8) of the Criminal Code, the UN Special Rapporteur has noted that, although it may not have been the intention of the legislative amendment under the Anti-Terrorism Act (No 2) 2005, the extraterritorial application of these "Category D" offences (see section 15.4 of the Criminal Code) means that commanders of enemy forces overseas who order their troops to attack Australian forces may be liable for prosecution for sedition under Australian law. He pointed out, however, that under international humanitarian law combatants lawfully participating in armed conflict are entitled to immunity and prisoner-of-war status upon capture. Although Australia reported that there was no intention for these provisions to interfere with international humanitarian law, the possibility exists, and the Special Rapporteur therefore urged Australia to bring these laws in compliance with international humanitarian law.[107]

5.2.2   Charter of the United Nations (Terrorism and Dealings with Assets) Regulations 2008

Australia has implemented its obligations to freeze the assets of entities listed by the Security Council's resolution 1267 Sanctions Committee under Part 4 of the

---

[106]As concluded in the Special Rapporteur's report on Australia (n 1), paras 25–27 and 67.

[107]Special Rapporteur report (n 1), paras 29 and 67.

Charter of the United Nations Act 1945 and the Charter of the United Nations (Terrorism and Dealings with Assets) Regulations 2008.[108] Section 18 of the Act operates so that where the Sanctions Committee lists a person or entity under its procedures, that person or entity is automatically proscribed under Australian law and added to a Consolidated List maintained by Australia's Department of Foreign Affairs and Trade (DFAT).

The listing of an individual or entity does not itself establish a criminal offence (i.e. it is not an offence to be on the list). Certain acts done in relation to such entities are criminalised however. Once an individual or entity is listed on the DFAT Consolidated List, it becomes a criminal offence under the Charter of the United Nations Act 1945 to either deal with their assets (section 20) or to make available assets, directly or indirectly, to them (section 21).[109] Conviction for either offence renders a person liable to a maximum term of 10 years imprisonment. This has the effect of freezing property belonging to listed entities. Safeguards exist so that holders of assets are not liable for actions done in good faith and without negligence (section 24 – see also Chapter 5 of the 2008 Regulations), with compensation is available for persons wrongly affected (section 25). The responsible Minister has the authority, under section 22 of the Act, to allow a person to use or deal with a terrorist asset in a specified way (see also Part 4 of the 2008 Regulations).

Once listed, a person or entity can apply to the responsible Minister to have the listing revoked, although he or she is not required to consider the application if the application is made within 12 months of the listing (section 17). The Minister can remove a person or entity from the DFAT Consolidated List if satisfied that the listing is no longer necessary to give effect to a Security Council decision (section 16).

5.2.3 Charter of the United Nations (Sanctions – Al-Qaida and the Taliban) Regulations 2008

The travel ban and arms embargo on the Taliban and Al-Qa'ida, as well as listing and asset freezing obligations applying to them, were initially implemented by Australia under the Charter of the United Nations (Sanctions – Afghanistan) Regulations 2001. The listing and freezing obligations were subsequently taken up under Part 4 of the Charter of the United Nations Act 1945 and the Charter of the United Nations (Terrorism and Dealings with Assets) Regulations 2008

---

[108]The Charter of the United Nations (Terrorism and Dealings with Assets) Regulations 2008 repealed and replaced the Charter of the United Nations (Terrorism and Dealings with Assets) Regulations 2002 (see regulation 3 of the 2008 Regulations).

[109]Corresponding to: article 2(1) of Financing Convention (n 14); para 4(b) of SC Res 1267 (n 103); and para 1(b) and (c) of SC Res 1373 (n 17).

(see Sect. 5.2.1 above). Following the repeal of the 2001 Regulations, the travel ban and arms embargo were dealt with under the Charter of the United Nations (Sanctions – Al-Qaida and the Taliban) Regulations 2008. All names from the UN's Consolidated List of terrorist entities that meet minimum data requirements (full name and at least year of birth), are included on the Movement Alert List of the Department of Immigration and Multicultural and Indigenous Affairs.[110]

Arms and related materials are classified as "export sanctioned goods" under the 2008 Regulations (regulations 4 and 5), the supply of which is prohibited by regulation 8(3). Under section 2B of the United Nations Act 1945, a provision of Australia's federal law can be specified to be a "UN sanction enforcement law". Regulation 8 has been specified as UN sanction enforcement laws under the Charter of the United Nations (UN Sanction Enforcement Law) Declaration 2008. The consequence of this is that it is an offence, under section 27 of the Act, to contravene such a law, an offence which is punishable by up to 10 years imprisonment.

The Charter of the United Nations (Sanctions – Al-Qaida and the Taliban) Regulations 2008 also make it an offence to provide technical advice, assistance or training related to military activities to the Taliban or Al-Qa'ida (regulations 4, 7 and 9(3)).

5.3   Summary and Conclusions on Australia's Compliance with the International Framework for Countering Terrorism

As for other members of the United Nations, Australia's compliance with international counter-terrorism obligations and recommendations has been subject to reporting to and review by the Security Council Counter-Terrorism Committee (CTC) and the SC Resolution 1267 Al-Qa'ida and Taliban Sanctions Committee (1267 Committee) – on these Committees, see Chap. 3, Sect. 3.2.4. Australia submitted one report in 2003 to the 1267 Committee and six reports to the CTC between 2001 and 2006.[111] Australia's compliance is summarised under the following three heads, as is also done in the case of the three other case study countries.

---

[110]Report of Australia pursuant to Security Council resolution 1455 (2003) to the Security Council Committee established under Security Council resolution 1267 (1999), UN Doc S/AC.37/2003/ (1455)/13 (2003), paras 49–53.

[111]Report of Australia pursuant to SC Res 1455 (2003), ibid; (first) Report of Australia to the Counter-Terrorism Committee of the United Nations Security Council pursuant to paragraph 6 of Security Council resolution 1373 (2001) of 28 September 2001, UN Doc S/2001/1247 (2001); second report to the Counter-Terrorism Committee (n 85); (third report) Supplement to Second Report of Australia to the Counter-Terrorism Committee pursuant to paragraph 6 of Security Council resolution 1373 (2001) of 28 September 2001, UN Doc S/2003/513 (2003); fourth report to the Counter-Terrorism Committee (n 8); fifth report to the Counter-Terrorism Committee (n 88); and sixth report to the Counter-Terrorism Committee (n 88).

5.3.1 Terrorism-Related Offences

Chapter 14 in this title undertakes an analysis of the criminalisation of terrorism by the four case study countries, including a comparison between the offences required under the universal terrorism-related conventions and Security Council resolutions (Appendix 3, Table 1) and the terrorism-related offences under Australia law (Appendix 3, Table 2).

5.3.2 Treaty Action and Implementation

At the time of the September 11 attacks and adoption of Security Council resolution 1373 (2001), Australia was a party to nine of the universal terrorism-related conventions. Those conventions had been implemented under the Crimes (Aviation) Act 1991 (see Sect. 5.1.2 above); the Crimes (Ships and Fixed Platforms) Act 1992 (see Sect. 5.1.3 above); the Crimes (Hostages) Act 1989 (see Sect. 5.1.4 above); the Crimes (Internationally Protected Persons) Act 1976 (see Sect. 5.1.4 above); and the Nuclear Non-Proliferation (Safeguards) Act 1987 (see Sect. 5.1.5 above). Since the time of resolution 1373 (2001):

- Australia acceded to the Terrorist Bombing Convention on 9 August 2002, incorporating its obligations under the Convention into domestic law under Division 72 in Chapter 4 of the Criminal Code Act 1995 (see Sect. 5.1.1.4 above).
- It ratified the Suppression of Terrorist Financing Convention on 26 September 2002, incorporating those obligations under Division 103 of the Criminal Code (see Sect. 5.1.1.4 above).
- Australia acceded to the Marking of Plastic Explosives Convention on 26 June 2007, following its enactment of the Law and Justice Legislation Amendment (Marking of Plastic Explosives) Act 2006 (see Sect. 5.1.7 above).
- Australia became an original signatory to the Nuclear Terrorism Convention, but has not yet ratified the Convention, nor implemented the obligations under the Convention into domestic law.[112]

A large part of the implementation of the universal terrorism-related conventions involves the criminalisation of conduct identified under those treaties. This aspect of the conventions to which Australia is party has been almost fully implemented by Australia.

5.3.3 Implementation of Security Council Resolutions

Consideration has already been given above, under Sect. 5.3.1, to Security Council resolution 1624 (2005), which called upon States to adopt measures to prohibit and

---

[112]As at 1 October 2009.

prevent the incitement to commit terrorist acts. The travel ban and arms embargo against the Taliban and Al-Qa'ida under resolution 1267 (1999) were initially implemented by Australia under the Charter of the United Nations (Sanctions – Afghanistan) Regulations 2001 and then subsequently taken up under Part 4 of the Charter of the United Nations (Sanctions – Al-Qaida and Taliban) Regulations 2008 (see Sect. 5.2.3 above). Those aspects of the same resolution concerning the freezing of funds and other financial resources controlled by or on their behalf of the Taliban or any other individuals of entities designated by the Committee are linked to paragraphs 1(c) and (d) of Security Council resolution 1373 (2001), which are identified below. Security Council resolution 1373 (2001) contains 11 binding directions under paragraphs 1 and 2 of the resolution (see Chap. 3, Sect. 3.2.2.3), which have been implemented by Australia as follows:

1. Prevention and suppression of the financing of terrorist acts (para 1(a))
   Paragraph 1(a), which requires the prevention and suppression of the financing of terrorist acts, is a general provision, expanded upon by the subparagraphs that follow it. In its first report to the Counter-Terrorism Committee on measures taken to implement resolution 1373 (2001), Australia noted that it had established a working group on financial controls on terrorists and sponsors of terrorism and that AUSTRAC, Australia's financial intelligence unit, had issued interim notifications to all cash dealers.[113]

2. Criminalising the provision of funds for terrorist acts (para 1(b))
   In compliance with this provision of resolution 1373 (2001), Division 103 of the Criminal Code Act 1995 establishes offences of financing terrorism and financing a terrorist (sections 103.1 and 103.2 – see Sect. 5.1.1.4 above, and Appendix 3, Table 2(A)). Australia has also established a regime concerning "terrorist organisations" beyond that required by the Security Council resolution 1267 (1999) Sanctions Committee, in respect of which it is unlawful under section 102.6 of the Act to provide funds to, or obtain funds from (see Sect. 5.1.1.3 above concerning the listing of "terrorist organisations"). The offences under sections 102.6, 103.1 and 103.2 are classified as "financing of terrorism offences" under the Financial Transactions Reports Act 1998, with the result that cash dealers must report any suspicion that a transaction is preparatory to such an offence (see Sect. 5.1.6 above). Section 21 of the Charter of the United Nations Act 1945 also prohibits the giving of any assets to a proscribed person or entity (see Sect. 5.2.2 above).[114]

3. Freezing of funds and assets of terrorist entities (para 1(c))
   The freezing of terrorist assets was given effect to by Australia through section 20 of the Charter of the United Nations Act, which makes it an offence to hold, deal with, or allow terrorist assets to be dealt with (see

---

[113]First report of Australia to the Counter-Terrorism Committee (n 111), paras 1 and 3.

[114]Concerning the potential abuse of charitable foundations, see Australia's second and third reports to the Counter-Terrorism Committee (n 85 and n 111) paras 12–15, and p. 4 respectively.

Sect. 5.2.2 above). While Canada and New Zealand have enacted provisions to specifically deal with the forfeiture of terrorist assets (see Chap. 6, Sect. 6.1.4.6, and Chap. 7, Sect. 7.6.5), Australia relies on its normal criminal forfeiture provisions.

4. Prohibiting the provision of financial or related services to terrorist entities (para 1(d))

    Responding to paragraph 1(d) of the resolution, it is an offence under section 102.7 of the Criminal Code to provide support or resources to a terrorist organisation (see Sect. 5.1.1.4 above).

5. Suppression of support to terrorists and elimination of the supply of weapons (para 2(a))

    The provision of the Criminal Code just mentioned also goes towards compliance with paragraph 2(a) of resolution 1373 (2001). Australia has reported that it imposes strict controls on the import and possession of firearms, and the export of defence and dual-use good from Australia, which would have the effect of preventing such goods being supplied to terrorists.[115] Arms and related materials are classified as export sanctioned goods under the Charter of the United Nations (Sanctions – Al-Qaida and the Taliban) Regulations 2008, the supply of which is prohibited by regulation 8(3) (see Sect. 5.2.3 above). Division 72 of the Criminal Code also prohibits the possession, manufacture, import and export, and trafficking of unmarked plastic explosives (see Sect. 5.1.1.4 above).

6. Preventing the commission of terrorist acts (para 2(b))

    As discussed in Chap. 3, measuring a State's compliance with this direction is technically impossible, since all that can be done by a State is to undertake *all reasonable and practical steps* to prevent the commission of terrorist acts (see Sect. 3.2.2.3). Additional to the measures in response to items 1–5 above, Australia has pointed to increased powers of detention and questioning by the Australian Security Intelligence Organisation (see Sect. 5.1.9 above), and the amendment of the Telecommunications (Interception) Act 1979 to include terrorism offences in the definition of "class 1 offences" for the purposes of telecommunications interception warrants.[116]

7. Denial of safe haven (para 2(c))

    Australia has strict immigration clearance procedures, and its Migration Act 1958 allows refusal of entry into Australia, and removal from Australia, of persons who do not meet the Act's test of "good character".[117]

8. Preventing the use of State territory by terrorists (para 2(d))

    Relevant in this regard are various offences under the Criminal Code Act 1995, including: engaging in a terrorist act (section 101.1(1)); providing or receiving

---

[115]First report of Australia to the Counter-Terrorism Committee (n 111), paras 14–16.

[116]First report of Australia to the Counter-Terrorism Committee (n 111), para 18.

[117]First report of Australia to the Counter-Terrorism Committee (n 111), paras 23–26 and 60–63.

training connected with terrorist acts (section 101.2); possessing things connected with a terrorist act (section 101.4); collecting or making documents likely to facilitate a terrorist act (section 101.5); acts done in preparation for, or planning, terrorist acts (section 101.6(1)); directing the activities of a terrorist organisation (section 102.2); membership in, or recruiting for, a terrorist organisations (sections 102.3(1) and 102.4); training a terrorist organisation, or receiving training from such an organisation (section 102.5); providing support to a terrorist organisation (section 102.7); and associating with a terrorist organisation (section 102.8) – see Sect. 5.1.1.4 above and Appendix 3, Table 2(A). Also relevant is the prohibition against providing technical advice, assistance or training related to military activities to a proscribed entity under regulation 9(3) of the Charter of the United Nations (Sanctions – Al-Qaida and the Taliban) Regulations 2008 (see Sect. 5.2.3 above and Appendix 3, Table 2(H)).

9. Ensuring the prosecution and severe punishment of terrorists (para 2(e))
   The extraterritorial nature of the offences under the Criminal Code, together with general provisions of Australia's criminal law dealing with criminal conspiracy and other inchoate offences, means that Australia is better placed to exercise jurisdiction over persons who perpetrate or plan terrorist acts partly within and partly outside Australia.[118] As identified earlier in this chapter, the various offences under the Criminal Code and other enactments in Australia carry severe penalties (see Sect. 5.1 above). Unlike Canada and New Zealand, however, there has been no change to sentencing laws expressly requiring the commission of terrorism offences to be treated as an aggravating feature (see, for example, Chap. 6, Sect. 6.1.4.3).

10. Assisting in criminal investigations and prosecutions (para 2(f))
    Australia has reported that current law permits it to comply with paragraph 2(f) of resolution 1373 (2001), referring to the Mutual Assistance in Criminal Matters Act 1987 and the Extradition Act 1988.[119]

11. Establishing and maintaining effective border controls to prevent the movement of terrorists (para 2(g))
    For the purpose of improving border security and preventing the use of Australia's territory as a base of operations for terrorists and terrorist networks, the Passports Act 1938 was amended by the Anti-Terrorism Act (No. 3) 2004 and the Border Security Legislation Amendment Act 2002.[120] Measures to prevent the transboundary movement of terrorists are considered in Chap. 21.

---

[118]Second report of Australia to the Counter-Terrorism Committee (n 85), paras 16–19.

[119]First report of Australia to the Counter-Terrorism Committee (n 111), paras 45–52.

[120]See further the first report of Australia to the Counter-Terrorism Committee (n 111), paras 55–67; and the fourth report of Australia to the Counter-Terrorism Committee (n 8), pp. 8–9.

References

Burnside, Julian QC. 2005. What price 'freedom'? The legacy of 9/11. 68 *Precedent* 4.

Clarke, Hon John QC. 2008. *Report of the Inquiry into the Case of Dr Mohamed Haneef*. Australia: Commonwealth of Australia, online: http://www.haneefcaseinquiry.gov.au

Downer, Hon Alexander MP. 2005. Securing Australia's Interests – Australian foreign policy priorities. 59(1) *Australian Journal of International Affairs* 7.

Head, Michael. 2002. "Counter-Terrorism" Laws: A Threat to Political Freedom, Civil Liberties and Constitutional Rights. 26 *Melbourne University Law Review* 666.

Ruddock, Hon Philip MP. 2004. Australia's Legislative Response to the Ongoing Threat of Terrorism. 27(2) *University of New South Wales Law Journal* 254.

Chapter 6
Counter-Terrorism Law in Canada

This chapter examines the legislation through which obligations under the international framework for combating terrorism have been implemented in Canada. An overview and explanation of the following items of legislation is provided, as these relate to counter-terrorism in Canada: the Aeronautics Act 1985; the Anti-terrorism Act 2001; the Canada Evidence Act 1985; the Charities Registration (Security Information) Act 2001; the Criminal Code 1985; the Explosives Act 1985; the Immigration and Refugee Protection Act 2001; the Income Tax Act 1985; the Proceeds of Crime (Money Laundering) and Terrorist Financing Act 2000; the Security of Information Act 1985; the United Nations Act 1985. It should be noted that there are numerous other pieces of domestic legislation that might be seen as contributing to the countering of terrorism. This chapter restricts itself to the items of legislation just mentioned, those having been identified by Canada in its reports to the Counter-Terrorism Committee as being part of its counter-terrorist legislative regime.

As for the other country-specific chapters on counter-terrorism law, this chapter is broken down into three main parts: first, looking at legislation through which the universal terrorism-related conventions have been implemented by Canada; next, examining any further specific legislation applicable to action required by decisions of the Security Council; and, finally, setting out a summary and set of conclusions on Canada's compliance with the international framework on counter-terrorism. The overview provided includes identification of offences established under the legislation, a full list of which is set out in Appendix 3, Table 4 (the criminalisation of terrorism is considered in Chap. 14). It looks at the definitions of "terrorist activity", "terrorist group" and "terrorism offence" under the Criminal Code, and the term "terrorism" under the Immigration and Refugee Protection Act 2001. This chapter also provides an overview of the recommendations to Canada's legislature following the 2007 reviews of the Anti-terrorism Act by the Senate Special Committee on the Anti-terrorism Act and the House of Commons Public Safety and National Security sub-committee of the Standing Committee on Justice, Human Rights, Public Safety and Emergency Preparedness.

A. Conte, *Human Rights in the Prevention and Punishment of Terrorism*,
DOI 10.1007/978-3-642-11608-7_6, © Springer-Verlag Berlin Heidelberg 2010

6.1 Implementation by Canada of the Universal Terrorism-Related Treaties

Canada is a party to 12 of the existing 13 terrorism-related conventions (see Appendix 2, Table 1). It was an original signatory to the International Convention for the Suppression of Acts of Nuclear Terrorism, but has not yet deposited its instrument of ratification.[1] Canada has implemented its obligations under the treaties to which it is party under various items of legislation (as listed in the introduction to this chapter), each of which will be considered in chronological order (on the reception of treaty law in Canada, see Chap. 4, Sect. 4.2.2).

6.1.1 Aeronautics Act 1985

The Aeronautics Act 1985 includes a number of offences relating to aeronautics, one of which corresponds to the requirements of the Convention on Offences and Certain Other Acts Committed on Board Aircraft (the Tokyo Convention).[2] Section 7.41 of the Aeronautics Act establishes the offence of endangering the safety or security of an aircraft in flight, which prohibits behaviour that would endanger the safety or security of an aircraft in flight or of persons on board an aircraft in flight by intentionally acting in certain ways (see Appendix 3, Table 3 (A)). If convicted on indictment, the maximum available penalty is 5 years imprisonment. Consistent with article 5(2) of the Tokyo Convention, section 7.41(3) deems an aircraft to be "in flight" from the time when all external doors are closed following embarkation until the time at which any external door is opened for the purpose of disembarkation.

6.1.2 Criminal Code 1985

The Criminal Code 1985 sets out almost all of the terrorism-related offences under Canadian law and, by doing so, is one of the principal items of legislation through which Canada has implemented its obligations under the terrorism-related treaties

---

[1]International Convention for the Suppression of Acts of Nuclear Terrorism, adopted by the General Assembly and opened for signature on 15 April 2005 under GA Res 59/290, UN GAOR, 59th Sess, 91st Plen Mtg, UN Doc A/Res/59/290 (2005) and entered into force 7 July 2007.

[2]Convention on Offences and Certain Other Acts Committed on Board Aircraft, opened for signature 14 September 1963, 704 UNTS 219 (entered into force 4 December 1969), articles 1 and 2.

to which it is party. This part of the chapter focuses on those aspects of the Criminal Code relating to counter-terrorism that existed prior to its amendment under to the Anti-Terrorism Act 2001. The offences listed below implemented into domestic law the offences defined in the Convention on the Physical Protection of Nuclear Material (the Nuclear Material Convention), the Convention for the Suppression of Unlawful Seizure of Aircraft (the Hague Convention), the Convention for the Suppression of Unlawful Acts against the Safety of Civil Aviation (the Montreal Convention) and its Protocol (the Montreal Protocol), the Convention for the Suppression of Unlawful Acts against the Safety of Maritime Navigation (the Rome Convention) and its Protocol (the Rome Protocol), the International Convention against the Taking of Hostages (the Hostages Convention), and the Convention on the Prevention and Punishment of Crimes against Internationally Protected Persons, including Diplomatic Agents (the Protected Persons Convention).[3]

The following terrorism-related offences were in place under the Criminal Code prior to its 2001 amendment (see Appendix 3 herein, Table 3(B)):

- *Offences in respect of nuclear material* (section 7(3.2) and (3.4) and associated provisions). The effect of section 7(3.2)(a) of the Criminal Code is to extend extraterrestrial jurisdiction over persons who receive, posses, use, transfer, send or deliver transport, alter, dispose of, disperse or abandon "nuclear material" (as defined by section 7(3.6)) where this is likely to cause death or serious injury to any person, or substantial damage to property.[4] Section 7(3.4) links various other offences under the Criminal Code to nuclear material, i.e. its theft or robbery (sections 334 and 344), fraudulent obtaining (sections 341, 362(1)(a), and 380), demand by threat or use of force (section 423), or threat to use (section 264.1(1) (a) and (b)).[5]

---

[3]Convention on the Physical Protection of Nuclear Material, opened for signature 3 March 1980, 1456 UNTS 124 (entered into force 8 February 1987); Convention for the Suppression of Unlawful Seizure of Aircraft, opened for signature 16 December 1970, 860 UNTS 105 (entered into force 14 October 1971); the Convention for the Suppression of Unlawful Acts Against the Safety of Civil Aviation, opened for signature 23 September 1971, 974 UNTS 177 (entered into force 26 January 1973); the Protocol on the Suppression of Unlawful Acts of Violence at Airports Serving International Civil Aviation (the Montreal Protocol), opened for signature 24 February 1988, ICAO Doc 9518 (entered into force 6 August 1989); the Convention for the Suppression of Unlawful Acts against the Safety of Maritime Navigation, opened for signature 10 March 1988, 1678 UNTS 221 (entered into force 1 March 1992); the Protocol for the Suppression of Unlawful Acts against the Safety of Fixed Platforms Located on the Continental Shelf, opened for signature 10 March 1988, 1678 UNTS 304 (entered into force 1 March 1992); the International Convention against the Taking of Hostages, opened for signature 18 December 1979, 1316 UNTS 205 (entered into force 3 June 1983); and the Convention on the Prevention and Punishment of Crimes against International Protected Persons, including Diplomatic Agents, opened for signature 14 December 1973, 1035 UNTS 167 (entered into force 20 February 1977).

[4]Corresponding to article 7(1)(a) of the Nuclear Material Convention (ibid).

[5]Corresponding to article 7(1)(b) to (e) of the Nuclear Material Convention (n 3).

- *Hijacking* (section 76), prohibiting the unlawful seizure or exercise of control of an aircraft by force, or threat of force, or by any other form of intimidation, rendering a person liable to life imprisonment.[6]
- *Endangering the safety of an aircraft or airport* (section 77), which prohibits various conduct which endangers, or is likely to endanger, the safety of an aircraft in flight, or safety at an airport servicing international civil aviation.[7] The commission of such acts will render a person guilty of an indictable offence under section 77, punishable by life imprisonment.

   As in the case of the offence of endangering the safety or security of an aircraft in flight under section 7.41 of the Aeronautics Act (see Sect. 6.1.1 above), the term "in flight" is defined under the Criminal Code as being from the time when all external doors are closed following embarkation until the time at which any external door is opened for the purpose of disembarkation (section 7 (8)). Section 7(9) of the Criminal Code deems an aircraft to be "in service" from the time when pre-flight preparation of the aircraft by ground personnel or the crew begins for a specific flight until either: (a) the flight is cancelled before the aircraft is in flight; (b) twenty-four hours after the aircraft, having commenced the flight, lands, or (c) the aircraft, having commenced the flight, ceases to be in flight; whichever is the latest. This is consistent with the definitions of the terms under both the Tokyo Convention and the Montreal Convention.
- *Seizing control of a ship or fixed platform* (section 78.1(1)), making it an offence punishable by life imprisonment to seize or exercise control over a ship or fixed platform (as defined by section 78.1(5)) by force or threat of force or by any other form of intimidation.[8]
- *Endangering safety of ship or fixed platform* (section 78.1(2)), which prohibits various conduct which endangers, or is likely to endanger, the safety of a ship or a fixed platform.[9] Conviction renders a person liable to imprisonment for life.
- *False communication* (section 78.1(3)), prohibiting the communication of false information that endangers the safe navigation of a ship, punishable by up to life imprisonment.[10]
- *Threats to cause death or injury* (section 78.1(4)), making it an offence punishable by life imprisonment to threaten to either: (a) commit an act of violence against a person on board a ship or fixed platform; (b) destroy or cause damage to a ship or its cargo or to a fixed platform; or (c) destroy or cause serious damage to or interferes with the operation of any maritime navigational facility; in order to compel a person to do or refrain from doing any act, and

---

[6]Corresponding to article 1(a) of the Hague Convention (n 3).

[7]Corresponding to articles 1(1) and 1(1*bis*) of the Montreal Convention (n 3).

[8]Corresponding to: article 3(1)(a) of the Rome Convention (n 3); and article 2(1)(a) of the Rome Protocol (n 3).

[9]Corresponding to articles 3(1)(b) to (f) of the Rome Convention (ibid), and articles 2(1)(b) to (e) of the Rome Protocol (ibid).

[10]Corresponding to article 3(1)(f) of the Rome Convention (ibid).

where the threat is likely to endanger the safe navigation of a ship or the safety of a fixed platform.[11]

- *Hostage-taking* (section 279.1), criminalising the taking of a hostage with intent to induce any person (other than the hostage), or any group of persons or a State or international organization, to do or abstain from doing anything as a condition for the release of the hostage.[12] Depending upon the particular circumstances of the hostage-taking, a convicted person may be liable to 5 years imprisonment, or up to life imprisonment (section 279.1(2)).

- *Threats against an internationally protected person* (section 424), making it an offence to threaten to commit certain Criminal Code offences,[13] where this related to an internationally protected person.[14] An "internationally protected person" is defined by section 2 of the Criminal Code. Conviction will render a person liable to imprisonment for a term not exceeding 5 years.

- *Attack on premises, residence or transport of an internationally protected person* (section 431), prohibiting a violent attack on the official premises, private accommodation or means of transport of an internationally protected person where this is likely to endanger the life or liberty of the protected person.[15]

6.1.3 Explosives Act 1985

In line with the Convention on the Marking of Plastic Explosives for the Purpose of Detection (the Plastic Explosives Convention),[16] the Explosives Act 1985 prohibits the manufacture, possession, transport, importation and export of unmarked plastic explosives. It is an offence under the Act to acquire, possess, sell, store, use, make, transport, import or export any explosives or restricted components, except as authorised by the Explosives Act (section 21), punishable by up to 5 years imprisonment on indictment, or 2 years imprisonment on summary conviction (see Appendix 3 herein, Table 3(C)).

---

[11]Corresponding to article 3(2)(c) of the Rome Convention (ibid) and article 2(2)(c) of the Rome Protocol (ibid).

[12]Corresponding to article 1(1) of the Hostages Convention (n 3).

[13]The offences referred to in section 424 are offences under sections 235 (murder), 236 (manslaughter), 266 (assault), 267 (assault with a weapon or causing bodily harm), 268 (aggravated assault), 269 (unlawfully causing bodily harm), 269.1 (torture), 271 (sexual assault), 272 (sexual assault with a weapon), 273 (aggravated sexual assault), 279 (kidnapping), 279.1 (hostage taking) and 431 (attack on premises, residence or transport of an internationally protected person) of the Criminal Code.

[14]Corresponding to article 2(1)(c) of the Protected Persons Convention (n 3).

[15]Corresponding to article 2(1)(b) of the Protected Persons Convention (ibid).

[16]Convention on the Marking of Plastic Explosives for the Purpose of Detection, opened for signature 1 March 1991, ICAO Doc 9571 (entered into force 21 June 1998).

6.1.4 Anti-terrorism Act 2001

In its first report to the UN Counter-Terrorism Committee, Canada described itself as having substantial anti-terrorism measures in place, a position supported by the discussion in this chapter up to this point.[17] The Canadian government recognised, however, that further legislation was needed to deal more effectively with the global threat of terrorism. The result was the introduction by the Canadian government of the Anti-terrorism Bill C-36 on 15 October 2001.[18] In a background paper on the Bill, the Department of Justice described its proposed measures as adopting a three-tier approach intending to identify, prosecute, convict and punish terrorists; grant more investigative powers to both law enforcement and national security agencies; and attach terrorism at its foundations by strengthening provisions related to hate crimes and the dissemination of hate propaganda.[19]

Bill C-36 was assented to on 18 December 2001, but does not stand as a self-contained piece of legislation on counter-terrorism. The Act instead brought about the amendment of various items of legislation, including the Criminal Code 1985, the Official Secrets Act 1985, the Canada Evidence Act 1985, and the Proceeds of Crime (Money Laundering) Act 2000. The first part of the Anti-terrorism Act amended the Criminal Code to include a new Part II.1 on terrorism, dealing under section 83 of the Code with definitions; the financing of terrorism; the listing of terrorist entities; the freezing, seizure and forfeiture of property; offences and penalties; and special powers such as the convening of investigative hearings. It also provides for the deletion of hate propaganda from public websites under new section 320.1 of the Criminal Code (on incitement to racial or religious hatred, see Chap. 20, Sect. 20.2.1). Part 2 of the Act amended the Official Secrets Act 1985 (which thereafter became the Security of Information Act 1985) for the purpose of addressing national security concerns, including "threats of espionage by ... terrorist groups".[20] This second part of the Anti-terrorism Act also introduced new offences to counter intelligence-gathering activities by foreign powers and terrorist groups, as well as other offences, including the unauthorised communication of special operational information.

Part 3 of the Anti-terrorism Act amended the Canada Evidence Act 1985 to protect the disclosure of information in legal proceedings which would encroach upon a public interest or be injurious to international relations or national defence or

---

[17]Report of the Government of Canada to the Counter-Terrorism Committee of the United Nations Security Council on measures taken to implement resolution 1373 (2001), UN Doc S/2001/1209 (2001), p. 3.

[18]On the Bill, which was 175 pages in length, see Daniels (2002, pp. 3–5).

[19]Department of Justice Backgrounder, 'Highlights of *Anti-terrorism Act*' (15 October 2001), online: http://canada.justice.gc.ca/en/news/nr/2001/doc_27787.html (as accessed on 1 June 2002). See further Jenkins (2003, pp. 422–424); and Gabor (2004, p. 11).

[20]Statutes of Canada 2001, Chapter 41, Summary, un-numbered p. 2 (also available online at http://www2.parl.gc.ca/HousePublications/Publication.aspx?pub=bill&doc=C-36&parl=37&ses=1&language=E&File=11).

security. The amendments to sections 37 and 38 of the Evidence Act give the Attorney General the power to prohibit the disclosure of information in connection with a proceeding for the purpose of protecting international relations or national defence or security. This adds to Part VI of the Criminal Code, which allows for electronic surveillance to investigate criminal offences listed in the Act, including the terrorism-related offences mentioned in this chapter. These features are considered in more detail in Chap. 18 (Sect. 18.2). Part 4 of the Anti-terrorism Act amended the Proceeds of Crime (Money Laundering) Act (which thereafter became the Proceeds of Crime (Money Laundering) and Terrorist Financing Act). Part 5 makes a number of consequential and other reasonably minor amendments.[21] The final part of the Anti-terrorism Act, Part 6, enacted the Charities Registration (Security Information) Act 2001 and amended the Income Tax Act 1985 to prevent those who support terrorist or related activities from enjoying the tax privileges granted to registered charities. The Charities Registration (Security Information) Act provides an administrative mechanism to prevent the registration of an organisation as a charity, and to revoke the registration of a charity, if there are reasonable grounds to believe that the organisation makes or will make resources available directly or indirectly to an organisation engaged in terrorist activities.[22]

6.1.4.1 Treaty Implementation

As well as seeking to strengthen Canada's capacity to suppress, investigate and incapacitate terrorist activity,[23] one of the purposes of the Anti-terrorism Act was to implement, and thereafter allow ratification of, the International Convention for the Suppression of the Financing of Terrorism (the Financing Convention), and the International Convention for the Suppression of Terrorist Bombing (the Bombing Convention).[24] The Ministry of Justice explains that the Anti-terrorism Act also enabled Canada to implement and ratify the Convention on the Safety of United Nations and Associated Personnel.[25]

---

[21] On the application of the Proceeds of Crime (Money Laundering) and Terrorist Financing Act to the seizure and forfeiture of funds, see *Sellathurai v Canada (Public Safety and Emergency Preparedness)* [2007] FC 208.

[22] See, for example, *Canadian Magen David Adom for Israel v Minister of National Revenue* [2002] FCA 323.

[23] See the preamble to the Anti-terrorism Act 2001, para 4.

[24] International Convention for the Suppression of the Financing of Terrorism, opened for signature 10 January 2000, 2179 UNTS 232 (entered into force 10 April 1992); and International Convention for the Suppression of Terrorist Bombing, opened for signature 12 January 1998, 2149 UNTS 286 (entered into force 23 May 2001).

[25] Convention on the Safety of United Nations and Associated Personnel, opened for signature 9 December 1994, 2051 UNTS 363 (entered into force 15 January 1999): see Department of Justice, "International Dimensions of the *Anti-terrorism Act*", online: http://www.justice.gc.ca/eng/antiter/sheet-fiche/INTERNAT.HTML.

6.1.4.2 Definition of "Terrorist Activity" and "Terrorist Group"

For the first time in Canadian law, the Anti-terrorism Act introduced a definition of a "terrorist activity" under section 83.01(1) of the Criminal Code. The definition describes three types of terrorist activities:

- The first is the commission of offences, whether committed in or outside Canada, under ten of the extant universal terrorism-related treaties, i.e. the Hague Convention, the Montreal Convention and its Protocol, the Protected Persons Convention, the Hostages Convention, the Nuclear Material Convention, the Rome Convention and its Protocol, as well as the Bombings Convention and the Financing Convention.
- The second type of terrorist activity defined by the Act involves an act or omission, in or outside Canada, which is committed for the following purposes and intention:
  - in whole or in part for a political, religious or ideological purpose, objective or cause;
  - *and* in whole or in part with the intention of intimidating the public, or a segment of the public, with regard to its security, including its economic security, or compelling a person, a government or a domestic or an international organisation to do or to refrain from doing any act, whether the public or the person, government or organisation is inside or outside Canada;
  - *and* which intentionally:
    - (a) causes death or serious bodily harm to a person by the use of violence,
    - (b) endangers a person's life,
    - (c) causes a serious risk to the health or safety of the public or any segment of the public,
    - (d) causes substantial property damage, whether to public or private property, if causing such damage is likely to result in the conduct or harm referred to in paragraphs (a) to (c), or
    - (e) causes serious interference with or serious disruption of an essential service, facility or system, whether public or private, other than as a result of advocacy, protest, dissent or stoppage of work that is not intended to result in the conduct or harm referred to in any of paragraphs (a) to (c).

- Terrorist activity also expressly includes a conspiracy, attempt or threat to commit any of the two types of activity already described, or being an accessory after the fact or counselling in relation to such activity. It does not, however include an act or omission that is committed during an armed conflict and that, at the time and in the place of its commission, is in accordance with customary international law or conventional international law applicable to the conflict. Nor does it include activities undertaken by military forces of a State in the exercise of their official duties, to the extent that those activities are governed by other rules of international law.

The Anti-terrorism Act also introduced the concept of a "terrorist group", which is defined by section 83.01(1) as either:

- An entity that has as one of its purposes or activities facilitating or carrying out any terrorist activity; or
- An entity listed under section 83.05 of the Criminal Code (see below on the listing process).

The definition of a terrorist group includes an association of such entities. The significance of this expression is that it is linked to certain offences under the Criminal Code 1985, such as the provision of property, or financial or related services, for the benefit of a terrorist group – section 83.03 of the Code.

As well as being linked to almost all of the offences under Part II.1 of the Criminal Code (see below), the term "terrorist activity" (as defined under the Criminal Code) is also liked to the use of that term in the Security of Information Act 1985 (section 2(1)) and the Proceeds of Crime (Money Laundering) and Terrorist Financing Act 2000 (section 2). The term "terrorist group" is similarly linked to use of the term in the Security of Information Act 1985 (section 2(1)). The first implication of this linkage is that, as a result of the Anti-terrorism Act 2001, the meaning of a purpose which is "prejudicial to the safety or interests of the State" was extended to include situations where a person (see section 3(1)(a) and (b) of the Security of Information Act 1985):

- Commits an offence that is punishable by a maximum term of imprisonment of 2 years or more in order to advance a political, religious or ideological purpose, objective or cause or to benefit a foreign entity or terrorist group; or
- Commits a terrorist activity, whether inside or outside Canada.

The meaning of "harm to Canadian interests" was also extended to include anything done under section 3(1) of the Security of Information Act by a terrorist group (section 3(2)). The term "special operational information" was expanded to include information or intelligence that is in relation to, or received from, a foreign entity or terrorist group (section 8(1)).

6.1.4.3   Offences Established by the Anti-terrorism Act

Sometimes referred to as an act of prevention, the Anti-terrorism Act 2001 introduced the following new terrorism offences under section 83 of the Criminal Code 1985 (see Appendix 3, Table 3(B)), many of which criminalise conduct which would precede a terrorist act:

- *Providing or collecting property for certain activities* (section 83.02), prohibiting the wilful provision or collection of property (directly or indirectly), intending (or knowing) that those funds are to be used for one of the following purposes, without lawful justification or excuse:[26]

- To carry out a "terrorist activity", as defined by section 83.01(1) (see above); or
- To carry out "any other act or omission intended to cause death or serious bodily harm to a civilian or to any other person not taking an active part in the hostilities in a situation of armed conflict, if the purpose of that act or omission, by its nature or context, is to intimidate the public, or to compel a government or an international organization to do or refrain from doing any act".

Conviction renders an offender liable to imprisonment for a term not exceeding 10 years. The term "property" is defined by section 2 of the Criminal Code to include almost anything of value.[27]

- *Providing or making available property or services for terrorist purposes* (section 83.03), prohibiting the provision (direct or indirect) of any property, or any financial or related services, either: (a) for the benefit of a "terrorist group" (as defined by section 83.01, see above); or (b) accompanied by an intention (or knowing) that these be used to facilitate a terrorist activity (or benefiting a person who is facilitating or carrying out such an activity).[28] A person found guilty of such an offence is liable to up to 10 years imprisonment.
- *Using or possessing property for terrorist purposes* (section 83.04), which focuses not on the provision of property for terrorist activities, but instead on the possession or use itself of property for such purposes.[29] Conviction for this offence also renders a person liable to 10 years imprisonment.
- *Dealing with terrorist property* (sections 83.08(1) and 83.12(1)), prohibiting any person in Canada, or any Canadian abroad, to knowingly: deal (directly or indirectly) in any property that is owned or controlled by or on behalf of a "terrorist group" (as defined above); enter into or facilitate (directly or indirectly) any transaction in respect of such property; or provide any financial or

---

[26]Corresponding to article 2(1) of the Financing Convention (ibid); and para 1(b) of SC Res 1373, UN SCOR, 4385th Mtg, UN Doc S/Res/1373 (2001).

[27]Section 2 of the Criminal Code 1985 provides that "property" includes (a) real and personal property of every description and deeds and instruments relating to or evidencing the title or right to property, or giving a right to recover or receive money or goods, (b) property originally in the possession or under the control of any person, and any property into or for which it has been converted or exchanged and anything acquired at any time by the conversion or exchange, and (c) any postal card, postage stamp or other stamp issued or prepared for issue under the authority of Parliament or the legislature of a province for the payment to the Crown or a corporate body of any fee, rate or duty, whether or not it is in the possession of the Crown or of any person.

[28]Corresponding to articles 2(1) and 2(5)(c) of the Financing Convention (n 24); and para 1(b) and (d) of SC Res 1373 (n 26).

[29]Corresponding to article 2(1) of the Financing Convention (n 24); and para 1(c) of SC Res 1373 (n 26).

other related services in respect of such property.[30] In the case of any failure to comply with these prohibitions, liability can be avoided if the person took all reasonable steps to satisfy him or herself that the property in question was not owned or controlled by or on behalf of a terrorist group (section 83.08(2)). Summary conviction renders a person liable to a fine of not more than $100,000 CAD and/or to imprisonment for up to 1 year, while a conviction on indictment can lead to a term of imprisonment of up to 10 years.

- *Participating in or contributing to activities of a terrorist group* (section 83.18 (1)), which prohibits direct or indirect participation in, or contribution to, any activity of a terrorist group for the purpose of enhancing the ability of any terrorist group to facilitate or carry out a terrorist activity.[31] Section 83.18 sets out a non-exhaustive list of factors which might point to such participation or contribution,[32] and identifies certain means by which participation and contribution can occur for the purpose of the offence (section 83.18(3)), namely:
  - providing, receiving or recruiting a person to receive training;
  - providing or offering to provide a skill or an expertise for the benefit of, at the direction of or in association with a terrorist group;
  - recruiting a person in order to facilitate or commit a "terrorism offence" (as defined by section 2 – see below), or an act or omission outside Canada that, if committed in Canada, would be a terrorism offence;
  - entering or remaining in any country for the benefit of, at the direction of or in association with a terrorist group; and
  - making oneself, in response to instructions from any of the persons who constitute a terrorist group, available to facilitate or commit a terrorism offence, or an act or omission outside Canada that, if committed in Canada, would be a terrorism offence.
- *Facilitating terrorist activity* (section 83.19), prohibiting persons from knowingly facilitating a terrorist activity, the maximum penalty for which is 14 years' imprisonment.[33]
- *Commission of an offence for a terrorist group* (section 83.2), which prohibits the commission of any indictable offence under the Criminal Code, or any other Act of Parliament, where this is done for the benefit of, at the direction of, or in association with a terrorist group.[34] This is itself an indictable offence, punishable by life imprisonment.

---

[30]Corresponding to para 1(c) of SC Res 1373 (n 26).

[31]Corresponding to para 2(d) of SC Res 1373 (n 26).

[32]Section 83.18(4) identifies such factors as: using a name, word, symbol or other representation that identifies, or is associated with, the terrorist group; frequently associating with any of the persons who constitute the terrorist group; receiving any benefit from the terrorist group; or repeatedly engaging in activities at the instruction of any of the persons who constitute the terrorist group.

[33]Corresponding to para 2(d) of SC Res 1373 (n 26).

[34]Corresponding to para 2(d) of SC Res 1373 (n 26).

- *Instructing to carry out activities for a terrorist group* (section 83.21), prohibiting persons from knowingly instructing, directly or indirectly, any person to carry out any activity for the benefit of, at the direction of or in association with a terrorist group, for the purpose of enhancing the ability of any terrorist group to facilitate or carry out a terrorist activity.[35] The maximum penalty, upon conviction, is life imprisonment.
- *Instructing to carry out a terrorist activity* (section 83.22), prohibiting persons from knowingly instructing, directly or indirectly, any person to carry out a terrorist activity, the maximum penalty for which is life imprisonment.[36]
- *Harbouring or concealing terrorists* (section 83.23), making a person liable to an indictable offence punishable by up to 10 years imprisonment if he or she knowingly harbours or conceals any person whom he or she knows to be a person who has carried out, or is likely to carry out, a terrorist activity, for the purpose of enabling that person to facilitate or carry out any terrorist activity.[37]
- *Use of explosive or other lethal device* (section 431.2(2)), establishing the offence of using an explosive or other lethal device in a public place, a government facility, an infrastructure system, or a public transportation system with the intent to either: (a) cause death or serious bodily injury; or (b) cause extensive damage that results, or is likely to result, in major economic loss.[38] Subsection 431.2(1) defines the terms "infrastructure facility", "place of public use", and "public transportation system". It also explains that an explosive or other lethal device is either: an explosive or incendiary weapon or device that is designed to cause, or is capable of causing, death, serious bodily injury or substantial material damage; or a weapon or device that is designed to cause, or is capable of causing, death, serious bodily injury or substantial material damage through the release, dissemination or impact of toxic chemicals, biological agents or toxins or similar substances, or radiation or radioactive material.

Although not strictly speaking a "terrorist" offence, section 83.231 of the Criminal Code also makes it an offence for any person to make a hoax regarding a terrorist activity where this is without lawful excuse and with the intent to cause any person to fear death, bodily harm, substantial damage to property or serious interference with the lawful use or operation of property. If, as a result of such a hoax, bodily injury or death is caused to any person, the person committing the hoax will be liable to be imprisoned for up to 5 years in the first case, or life imprisonment in the case of causing death.

---

[35]Corresponding to para 2(a) of SC Res 1373 (n 26).

[36]Corresponding to para 2(a) of SC Res 1373 (n 26).

[37]Corresponding to para 2(c) of SC Res 1373 (n 26).

[38]Corresponding to article 2(1) of the International Convention for the Suppression of Terrorist Bombing, opened for signature 12 January 1998, 2149 UNTS 286 (entered into force 23 May 2001).

Under its general interpretative provision in section 2, the Criminal Code also defines the expression "terrorism offence" as:

- An offence under any of sections 83.02–83.04 or 83.18–83.23;
- An indictable offence under this or any other Act of Parliament committed for the benefit of, at the direction of or in association with a terrorist group (as defined above);
- An indictable offence under this or any other Act of Parliament where the act or omission constituting the offence also constitutes a terrorist activity (as defined above); or
- A conspiracy or an attempt to commit, or being an accessory after the fact in relation to, or any counselling in relation to, any of the latter offences.

This definition expressly covers almost all of the offences listed above, expect that of dealing with terrorist property (section 83.08(1)). Depending upon the circumstances of such dealings, however, dealing with terrorist property might also amount to a "terrorism offence", e.g. if such dealing was for the benefit of a terrorist group. The term is itself linked to the commission of certain offences including, for example, the recruitment of a person to commit a terrorism offence (section 83.18 (1) and (3)(c)). Any prosecution of a terrorism offence, or an offence under section 83.12 (dealing with terrorist property), must be commenced with the consent of the Attorney General (section 83.24). A terrorism offence, or an offence under section 83.12, also invokes extra-territorial jurisdiction under section 83.25 of the Criminal Code.

In terms of sentencing, the fact that an offence is a terrorism offence must be treated as an aggravating feature in the sentencing of a convicted person (section 718.2(a)(v)). Section 83.26 of the Criminal Code also requires that any sentences imposed in respect of terrorism offences, even if arising out of the same event or series of events, must be served consecutively (except in the case of terms of life imprisonment). Where a person is convicted of an indictable offence which also constitutes a "terrorist activity", the person will become liable to imprisonment for life (section 83.27). Furthermore, if the killing of a person is caused while committing or attempting to commit an indictable offence which constitutes a terrorist activity, section 231(6.01) deems the killing to be first degree murder irrespective of whether the murder is planned and deliberate.

As well as these significant additions to Canada's criminal law, the Anti-terrorism Act also amended the Security of Information Act 1985. The amendments affected the following offences which had previously been restricted to action by or for foreign entities (see Appendix 3, Table 3(D)):

- *Approaching and entering a prohibited place* (section 6), which makes it an offence to approach, inspect, pass over, be in the neighbourhood of, or enter a prohibited place where this is done: (a) at the direction of, for the benefit of or in association with a foreign entity or a terrorist group; and (b) for any purpose prejudicial to the safety or interests of the State (which includes, as discussed above, the commission of a terrorist activity, in our outside Canada). A "prohibited place" is defined by section 2(1) of the Act and includes, for example, armed forces establishments or stations.

- *Communications with foreign entities or terrorist groups* (sections 16–18), which prohibits the communication to a foreign entity or a terrorist group of safeguarded information or special security information (the latter of which includes information or intelligence that is in relation to, or received from, a terrorist group – see above).
- *Terrorist-influenced threats or violence* (section 20), prohibiting any person from making violence or a threat of violence where this is at the direction of or for the benefit of or in association with a foreign entity or a terrorist group; and this is done for the purpose of increasing the capacity of such entities to harm Canadian interests, or is reasonably likely to do so.

6.1.4.4   Prosecutions Under the Anti-terrorism Act

Mohammad Momin Khawaja was the first person charged and convicted of terrorism offences established under the Anti-terrorism Act 2001. In October 2008, he was convicted of offences under section 83.03 (providing and inviting others to provide property and financial services to various persons with the intent or knowledge that they would be used to carry our of facilitate a terrorist activity or for the benefit of a terrorist group); two counts under section 83.18 (participating in activities of a terrorist group (Omar Kyam) by receiving training, and participating in meetings regarding the development of an explosives device intended to endanger life or cause serious damage to property); section 83.10 (facilitating a terrorist activity); and section 83.21 (instructing a person to open a bank account and conduct financial transactions on his behalf for the benefit of the same group).[39] Mohammad Khawaja was sentenced to ten and a half years imprisonment. It should be noted that the proceedings involved an application by the Attorney-General for non-disclosure of information on the basis that such disclosure would be injurious to national security or international relations (considered in Chap. 18, Sect. 18.2).[40]

The Anti-terrorism Act was also used in 2006 to bring charges against the so-called "Toronto 18" (four youths and 14 men) connected to an alleged conspiracy to bomb high-profile targets in Ontario and behead the Prime Minister.[41] Lorne Matthew Lapolean was also convicted in 2007 under section 83.231(2) of the Criminal Code for making a hoax regarding a terrorist activity with the intent to cause fear.[42]

---

[39]*Queen v Khawaja* (29 October 2008) Ontario Superior Court of Justice 04-G30282 (available online at http://multimedia.thestar.com/acrobat/c1/ab/bf9c99dc4b87b854428bc30574d8.pdf).

[40]See *Canada (Attorney General) v Khawaja* [2007] FC 490.

[41]This case remains in progress. See Joanna Smith, 'Khawaja guilty of terrorism', Thestar.com (30 October 2008), available at http://www.thestar.com/News/Canada/article/527222.

[42]*R v Lapoleon* [2007] BCPC 309.

Although not a prosecution under the Anti-terrorism Act, mention should also be made of the trials concerning the 1985 bombing of Air India Flight 182 in which 329 passengers were killed, including 279 Canadians. In 2003, Inderjit Singh Reyat was convicted after pleading guilty to being involved in the bombing. Ripudaman Singh Malik and Ajaib Singh Bagri were later tried. Finding that the evidence had fallen "markedly short" of proof beyond reasonable doubt, Malik and Bagri were found not guilty on all counts.[43] During the course of the trial, the wife of Inderjit Reyat, who had been convicted in 2003, was made the subject of an investigative hearing order under section 83.28 of the Criminal Code. Investigative hearings were introduced under the Anti-terrorism Act and the investigative hearing order against Reyat's wife is considered in Chap. 16 (Sect. 16.3).

6.1.4.5 Entities Involved in or Facilitating Terrorist Activities

As discussed above, the Anti-terrorism Act introduced the concept of a "terrorist group", which is defined by section 83.01(1) as including an entity listed under section 83.05 of the Criminal Code. On the recommendation of the Minister of Public Safety and Emergency Preparedness, the Governor in Council is able to establish (and add to) a list of entities if the Governor is satisfied that there are reasonable grounds to believe that (a) the entity has knowingly carried out, attempted to carry out, participated in or facilitated a "terrorist activity" (as defined above); or (b) the entity is knowingly acting on behalf of, at the direction of or in association with such an entity (section 83.05(1)). The Governor in Council has, as a result, established and updated the 2002 Regulations Establishing a List of Entities which, under regulation 1, includes Al Qaida. These are supplemented by the United Nations Al-Qaida and Taliban Regulations 1999, which were made to implement Security Council resolution 1267 (1999), and later amended following Security Council resolution 1373 (2001) (see Sect. 6.2 below).

The Regulations Establishing a List of Entities comprise two regulations only. The first is the list of entities, under regulation 1. Regulation 2 provides for the entry into force of the Regulations. The procedural aspects pertaining to the making and maintenance of the List of Entities are exclusively dealt with under section 83.05–83.07 of the Criminal Code. Once an individual or entity is listed, it may be de-listed as a result of the following courses of action:

- Every two years, the Minister of Public Safety and Emergency Preparedness is required to review the List of Entities to determine whether there are still reasonable grounds for an entity to be a listed entity, i.e. reasonable grounds to believe that the entity has knowingly carried out, attempted to carry out, participated in or facilitated a terrorist activity, or is knowingly acting on behalf of, at the direction of, or in association with such an entity. Based on that review, the Minister must make a recommendation to the Governor in Council as to

---

[43] *R v Malik and Bagri* (2005) BCSC 350.

whether the listed entities should remain a listed (section 83.05(9)). Two reviews of the List of Entities have taken place so far.[44]

- The individual or entity concerned can apply in writing to the Minister, who will determine whether there are reasonable grounds to recommend to the Governor in Council that the applicant no longer be a listed entity (section 83.05(2)). If such a recommendation is not made within 60 days after the application is received, the Minister will be deemed to have recommended that the applicant remain a listed entity (section 83.05(3)). The Minister is required to give notice without delay to the applicant of any decision taken or deemed to have been taken (section 83.04(4)). Within 60 days after the receipt of the notice, the applicant can apply for judicial review of the Minister's decision (section 83.05(5)). The rules applicable to the judicial review of such a decision, including the potential for protection of classified information, are considered in more detail in Chaps. 18 and 19 (Sects. 18.2 and 19.3.2.4). The applicant cannot make a further application to the Minister unless there has been a material change in its circumstances since the time of the last application (section 83.05(8)). A fresh application can also be made following a review of the List of Entities under section 83.05(9) by the Minister of Public Safety and Emergency Preparedness (section 83.05(8)).
- Where an individual or entity claims to be the victim of mistaken identity, section 83.07 provides for a fast-track application to the Minister. In such cases, the Minister must, within 15 days after receiving the application, issue a certificate if he or she is satisfied that the applicant is not in fact a listed entity (section 83.07(2)).

6.1.4.6 Freezing and Forfeiture of Property

Any property that is owned or controlled by or on behalf of a terrorist group is frozen by virtue of the prohibition under section 83.04, 83.08 and 83.12 against dealing with such property (see above). As in other jurisdictions, the freezing of property in Canada is subject to certain exceptions. The Minister of Public Safety and Emergency Preparedness, or his or her delegate, can authorise a specific activity or transaction that would otherwise be prohibited under section 83.09, and can make this authorisation subject to any terms and conditions (section 83.09 (2) and (3)). Section 83.09(4) provides for any secured and unsecured rights and interests in the property to be maintained.

Following the seizure and restraint of terrorist property under section 83.13, the Attorney General can apply to the Federal Court for an order of forfeiture to the Crown in respect of property owned or controlled by or on behalf of a terrorist group; or property that has been or will be used, in whole or in part, to facilitate or carry out a terrorist activity (section 83.14). Any proceeds from the disposal of such

---

[44]Correct as at 1 April 2008: see Department of Justice. Human Rights Safeguards in the *Anti-terrorism Act*, online: http://www.justice.gc.ca/eng/antiter/sheet-fiche/SAFE-SUR.HTML.

property can be used to compensate victims of terrorist activities, and to fund anti-terrorist initiatives (section 83.14(5.1)).[45] Of the four case study countries, this feature appears to be unique to Canada, albeit that it derives at least partly from article 9(4) of the Financing of Terrorism Convention, to which all four countries are parties.

6.1.4.7 Financial Transactions and Other Reporting

Financial, insurance and securities institutions are, on a continuing basis, required to determine whether they are in possession or control of property owned or controlled by or on behalf of a listed entity (section 83.11(1)), and must report on a monthly basis accordingly (section 83.11(2)). As well as these more traditional reporting obligations upon financial institutions, which are well-used in anti-money laundering measures, certain reporting obligations also apply to any other person in Canada (or Canadian outside Canada). Section 83.1(1)(a) of the Criminal Code requires immediate disclose to the Commissioner of the Royal Canadian Mounted Police and to the Director of the Canadian Security Intelligence Service of the existence of property in their possession or control that they know is owned or controlled by or on behalf of a terrorist group. Information about a transaction or proposed transaction in respect of such property must also be disclosed (section 83.1(1)(b)).

As a result of Part 4 of the Anti-terrorism Act 2001, reporting obligations now also exist concerning terrorist financing. Every financial and other institution to whom the Proceeds of Crime (Money Laundering) and Terrorist Financing Act 2000 applies (see section 5 of that Act) is obliged to report every financial transaction in respect of which there are reasonable grounds to suspect that the transaction is related to a terrorist activity financing offence. Amendments to the Proceeds of Crime (Money Laundering) and Terrorist Financing Act also expanded the mandate of Canada's financial intelligence unit (the Financial Transactions and Reports Analysis Centre of Canada – FINTRAC) to include the analysis of these reports, and the ability to share information related to terrorist financing with its international counterparts.[46]

The classification of "terrorist activity financing offences" was also a creation of the Anti-terrorism Act, which is defined as an offence under the following sections of the Criminal Code (see above): 83.02 (providing or collecting property for certain activities), 83.03 (providing or making available property or services for terrorist purposes), 83.04 (using or possessing property for terrorist purposes), or 83.08 and 83.12 combined (dealing with terrorist property).

---

[45]Note, however, that forfeiture under section 83.14(5) can be made only to the extent that the property is not required to satisfy the operation of any other provision of this or any other Act of Parliament respecting restitution to, or compensation of, persons affected by the commission of offences: see section 83.17(2) of the Criminal Code 1985.

[46]First report of Canada to the Security Council Counter-Terrorism Committee (n 17), p. 4.

6.1.4.8 Special Powers

The Anti-terrorism Act 2001 also introduced special investigative and associated powers. Where the Attorney-General is able to apply for forfeiture of terrorist property (see above), he or she may also apply to have that property seized or restrained under section 83.13 of the Criminal Code. More controversial, and the subject of constitutional consideration by the Supreme Court of Canada, sections 83.28 and 83.29 establishes a regime for judicial investigative hearings. Also controversial are the provisions of sections 83.3–83.33 authorising recognizance. Investigative hearings are considered in Chap. 16 (see Sect. 16.3).

6.1.4.9 Review Mechanism and Sunset Clause

Evident from the foregoing discussion in this part of the chapter, the Anti-terrorism Act 2001 does not stand as a self-contained piece of legislation on counter-terrorism. In fact, the only provision of substance which remains isolated to the Anti-terrorism Act itself is section 145 of the Act, which provides for a review and reporting mechanism. The section required that, within three years after the Act receives royal assent, a comprehensive review of the provisions and operation of the Act would be undertaken by a committee of the Senate, or of the House of Commons, or of both Houses. It further provided that within a year of the review, or any further authorised period, the committee would report on its review to parliament, including a statement of any recommended changes.

In December 2004, both the House of Commons and the Senate adopted motions authorising committees to undertake a review of the Anti-terrorism Act, rather than establishing a single, joint, committee. The House of Commons review was undertaken by the Public Safety and National Security sub-committee of the Standing Committee on Justice, Human Rights, Public Safety and Emergency Preparedness. In the Senate, a Special Committee was established for this purpose. The two Committees reported to Parliament in February and March 2007.[47]

Unlike the review of the Terrorism Suppression Act in New Zealand (see Chap. 7, Sect. 7.1.4.7), but more like the review of counter-terrorism legislation in Australia (see Chap. 5, Sect. 5.1.10), the reviews undertaken under Canada's review mechanism were substantive and resulted in a number of constructive recommendations – 40 recommendations in the case of the Senate Special Committee and 60 in the case of the House of Commons Committee (on the use of review mechanisms for counter-terrorist legislation, see Chap. 4, Sect. 4.5).

---

[47]Special Senate Committee on the Anti-terrorism Act, Fundamental Justice in Extraordinary Times, February 2007, online: http://www.parl.gc.ca/39/1/parlbus/commbus/senate/com-e/anti-e/rep-e/rep02feb07-e.pdf; and House of Commons Standing Committee on Public Safety and National Security: A Comprehensive Review of the Anti-terrorism Act and Related Issues, March 2007, online: http://www2.parl.gc.ca/content/hoc/Committee/391/STER/Reports/RP2798915/sterrp07/sterrp07-e.pdf.

Amongst those recommendations, the following subjects were of concern to the Committees:

- The definition of "terrorism", "terrorist activity", and "threats to the security of Canada" (considered further in Chap. 14, Sect. 14.1.2);[48]
- The incitement and glorification of terrorism (Chap. 14, Sect. 14.3);[49]
- The use of, and procedures for, investigative hearings (see Chap. 16, Sect. 16.3);[50]
- The interception of private communications;[51]
- The process for the listing and de-listing of entities, including measures for non-disclosure of information (see Chap. 19, Sect. 19.3.2); and[52]
- The adoption of clear policies on racial profiling along with associated training (see Chap. 21, Sect. 21.1.3).[53]

The Special Senate Committee on the Anti-terrorism Act also recommended that a standing committee of the Senate, with dedicated staff and resources, be established to monitor, examine and periodically report on matters relating to Canada's anti-terrorism legislation and national security framework on an ongoing basis.[54] It further recommended that similar comprehensive reviews of the Anti-terrorism Act be undertaken every five years.[55]

It should also be noted that, in its examination of the Anti-terrorism Bill, the Special Committee of the Senate recommended the additional step of including a 5-year expiration, or 'sunset', clause to the provisions of the Bill. In this way, said the Committee: "the government would be required to return to Parliament to justify the continuance of the powers granted, assuring Canadians that the tools are sufficient, yet not exorbitant and that they continue to be justifiable and necessary in the battle against terrorism".[56] The "section 83" series of amendments to the Criminal Code included, in section 83.23, such a provision, whereby certain provisions within that series of amendments would cease to apply at the end of the 15th sitting day of Parliament after 31 December 2006 unless the application of

---

[48]Senate report (ibid), recommendations 1–3; House of Commons report (ibid), recommendations 1 and 6–8.

[49]House of Commons report (n 47), recommendation 2.

[50]Senate report (n 47), recommendations 16–17; House of Commons report (n 47), recommendations 44–45.

[51]Senate report (n 47), recommendations 18–20.

[52]Senate report (n 47), recommendations 7–15; House of Commons report (n 47), recommendations 23–26, and 42.

[53]Senate report (n 47), recommendations 4–6.

[54]Senate report (n 47), recommendation 39.

[55]Senate report (n 47), recommendation 40. See also recommendations 59–60 of the House of Commons report (n 47).

[56]Parliament of Canada, The Special Senate Committee on the Subject Matter of Bill C-36, First Report, 1 November 2001, p. 3.

those sections was extended by a resolution passed by both Houses of Parliament. The sunset clause applied to investigative hearings (sections 83.28 and 83.29) and recognizance conditions (section 83.3). Following its review of the Anti-terrorism Act, Parliament passed a resolution to extend the application of those provisions by a further three years (on sunset clauses, see Chap. 4, Sect. 4.3.5.2).[57]

6.1.5 Immigration and Refugee Protection Act 2001

Although the Canadian government has relied heavily on the Anti-terrorism Act 2001 as the vehicle through which it has implemented its international obligations to combat terrorism, Roach (amongst others) observes that immigration laws have in reality been the focus of Canada's anti-terrorism efforts. It has been immigration laws under the Immigration and Refugee Protection Act 2001 that have been most frequently used against terrorist suspects.[58]

Assented to just one month prior to the Anti-terrorism Act, the Immigration and Refugee Protection Act replaced and expanded upon the former Immigration Act 1985. Although those aspects of the Immigration and Refugee Protection Act relevant to counter-terrorism will be considered in Chap. 21, it is useful to note at this point that section 34 of the Act makes a foreign national or a permanent resident inadmissible to Canada on security grounds for "engaging in terrorism". This expression is a continuation of that used in section 19 of the former 1985 Immigration Act, in respect of which there has been a long line of judicial decisions. The most well-known of those decisions is the 2002 judgment of the Supreme Court of Canada in Suresh v Canada (Minister of Citizenship and Immigration).[59] One of the questions before the Court in that case was whether the term "terrorism" in the section 19 deportation provisions of the Immigration Act 1985 were unconstitutionally vague for the purposes of section 7 of the Canadian Charter of Rights and Freedoms. Although the Court recognised that there is disagreement on the definition of the term, it held that the term provided a sufficient basis for adjudication and was thus not unconstitutionally vague (see further Chap. 14, Sect. 14.1.2).[60]

---

[57]Order Establishing the Text of a Resolution Providing for the Extension of the Application of Sections 83.28, 83.29 and 83.3 of the Criminal Code, SOR/2007-25.

[58]Roach (2005, pp. 521–528). See also Harrington (2003).

[59]Suresh v Canada (Minister of Citizenship and Immigration) [2002] SCC 1. See also: Ali v Canada (Minister of Citizenship and Immigration) [2004] FC 1174; Fuentes v Canada (Minister of Citizenship and Immigration) [2003] FCT 379; and Khan v. Canada (Minister of Citizenship and Immigration) [2005] FC 1053.

[60]Suresh v Canada (ibid), paras 93–98.

6.2 Implementation by Canada of Security Council Decisions

Three principal resolutions govern the action required by, or recommended to, members of the United Nations, namely: Security Council resolution 1267 (1999), imposing a travel ban and arms embargo against the Taliban and Al-Qa'ida, and an obligation to freeze funds and other financial resources controlled by or on their behalf of the Taliban or any other individuals of entities designated by the Committee; resolution 1373 (2001), which imposed various obligations upon States, and recommended further action; and Security Council resolution 1624 (2005), which called on States to adopt measures to prohibit and prevent the incitement to commit terrorist acts (on the resolutions of the Security Council identified below, see Chap. 3, Sect. 3.2.2).[61] These resolutions have been implemented by Canada (on the implementation of Security Council resolutions by Canada, see Chap. 4, Sect. 4.2.3) through the Anti-terrorism Act 2001 (Sect. 6.1.4 above) and three sets of statutory regulations. The first relates to the travel ban and arms embargo against the Taliban under Security Council resolution 1267 (1999).[62] The second relates to terrorist entities listed pursuant to section 83.05 of the Criminal Code 1985. The other relates to the temporary measures adopted by Canada in response to Security Council resolution 1373 (2001).[63]

6.2.1 United Nations Al-Qaida and Taliban Regulations 1999

The United Nations Al-Qaida and Taliban Regulations 1999 were made by Canada for the purpose of implementing Security Council resolution 1267 (1999), although the listing and suppression of financing aspects of these Regulations were, following Security Council resolution 1373 (2001), made the subject of more specific legislation (under the Anti-terrorism Act 2001, see Sect. 6.1.4 above, and the Regulations Establishing a List of Entities 2002, see Sect. 6.2.2 below). Regulations 4.2–4.4 implement the embargos under resolution 1269 (1999) – see Appendix 3, Table 3(E). Failure to comply with the Regulations renders a person liable to imprisonment for up to 10 years (in the case of a charge laid indictably), or a fine up to $100,000 CAD or imprisonment up to 1 year (on summary conviction) – as provided for under section 3 of the United Nations Act 1985.

Complementing this, the travel ban imposed under paragraphs 2(b) of Security Council resolution 1390 (2002) is enforced by through section 34 and 35 of the Immigration and Refugee Protection Act and corresponding immigration controls.

---

[61]SC Res 1267, UN SCOR, 4051st Mtg, UN Doc S/Res/1267 (1999); SC Res 1373, UN SCOR, 4385th Mtg, UN Doc S/Res/1373 (2001); and SC Res 1624, UN SCOR, 5261st Mtg, UN Doc S/Res/1624 (2005).

[62]SC Res 1267, UN SCOR, 4051st Mtg, UN Doc S/Res/1267 (1999).

[63]SC Res 1373, UN SCOR, 4385th Mtg, UN Doc S/Res/1373 (2001).

Section 34(1)(c) and (f) of the Act render permanent residents or foreign nationals inadmissible to Canada on several security grounds including terrorism. Members of al Qaida and persons associated with Osama bin Laden's regime are inadmissible under these provisions.[64]

6.2.2   Regulations Establishing a List of Entities 2002

As discussed at Sect. 6.1.4.2 above, the Anti-terrorism Act introduced the concept of a "terrorist group", which is defined by section 83.01(1) of the Criminal Code as including an entity listed under section 83.05 of the Criminal Code. Pursuant to this provision, the Governor in Council has established and updated the 2002 Regulations Establishing a List of Entities. The Regulations comprise two regulations only, the first of which sets out the list of entities itself. Regulation 2 provides for the entry into force of the Regulations. The procedural aspects concerning the making and maintenance of the List of Entities are exclusively dealt with under section 83.05–83.07 of the Criminal Code (see Sect. 6.1.4.5 above).

6.2.3   Regulations Implementing the United Nations Resolutions on the Suppression of Terrorism 2001

The 2001 Regulations Implementing the United Nations Resolutions on the Suppression of Terrorism were made by way of interim measure in response to Security Council resolution 1373 (2001), pending amendments to Criminal Code 1985 under the Anti-terrorism Act 2001 and the subsequent establishment of the Regulations Establishing a List of Entities 2002.[65] The Regulations made it an offence for any person in Canada, or any Canadian outside Canada, to knowingly provide or collect funds with the intention or knowledge that they be used by a listed person, or to deal in any property of a listed person, and prohibit the making available of funds and financial or other related services to a listed person (regulations 3, 4 and 6). They also established a temporary list of terrorist entities, which was later subsumed under the 2002 Regulations Establishing a List of Entities.

---

[64]See further Report of Canada to the Security Council Committee established under Security Council resolution 1267 (1999), UN Doc S/AC.37/2003/(1455)/20 (2003), pp. 8–9.

[65]First report of Canada to the Security Council Counter-Terrorism Committee (n 17), p. 4.

6.3   Summary and Conclusions on Canada's Compliance with the International Framework for Countering Terrorism

Canada's compliance with international counter-terrorism obligations and recommendations has been subject to reporting to and review by the Security Council Counter-Terrorism Committee (CTC) and the SC Resolution 1267 Al-Qa'ida and Taliban Sanctions Committee (1267 Committee) – on these Committees, see Chap. 3, at Sect. 3.2.4.2. Canada submitted one report in 2003 to the 1267 Committee and five reports to the CTC between 2001 and 2006.[66] Canada's compliance is summarised under the following three heads.

6.3.1   Terrorism-Related Offences

Chapter 14 in this title undertakes an analysis of the criminalisation of terrorism by the four case study countries, including a comparison between the offences required under the universal terrorism-related conventions and Security Council resolutions (Appendix 3, Table 1) and the terrorism-related offences under Canadian law (Appendix 3, Table 3). Other than in respect of the offence of incitement to terrorism, Chap. 14 concludes that Canada's law adequately criminalises all of the conduct listed in Appendix 3, Table 1. In the case of incitement to terrorism, Security Council resolution 1624 (2005) called upon States (i.e. recommended – see Chap. 3, Sect. 3.2.3) to prevent and criminalise incitement to commit a terrorist act or acts.[67] Chapter 14 concludes that Canada's law is deficient in this respect (see Sect. 14.3.4.1).

6.3.2   Treaty Action and Implementation

At the time of the September 11 attacks and adoption of Security Council resolution 1373 (2001), Canada was a party to ten of the universal terrorism-related conventions.

---

[66]Report of Canada to the Security Council Committee established under Security Council resolution 1267 (n 64); first report (n 17); (second) Report of the Government of Canada to the Counter-Terrorism Committee of the Security Council in response to the letter of the Chairman of the Committee dated 7 March 2002, UN Doc S/2002/667 (2002); (third report) Letter dated 18 February 2003 from the Permanent Representative of Canada to the United Nations addressed to the Chairman of the Security Council Committee established pursuant to resolution 1373 (2001) concerning counter-terrorism, UN Doc S/2003/403 (2003); (fourth report) Implementation of United Nations Security Council Resolution 1373; Canada's Fourth Report to the Counter-Terrorism Committee, UN Doc S/2004/132 (2004); and Fifth Report of the Government of Canada on the implementation of Security Council resolution 1373 (2001), UN Doc S/2006/185 (2006).
[67]SC Res 1624, UN SCOR, 5261st Mtg, UN Doc S/Res/1624 (2005), para 1(a).

Those conventions had been implemented under the Aeronautics Act 1985, the Criminal Code 1985, and the Explosives Act 1985 (see Sects. 6.1.1, 6.1.2 and 6.1.3 above). Since the time of resolution 1373 (2001):

- Canada ratified the Financing Convention on 19 February 2002 and the Bombing Convention on 3 April 2002, incorporating these instruments into domestic law under the Anti-terrorism Act 2001 (Sect. 6.1.4.1 above).
- Canada became an original signatory to the Nuclear Terrorism Convention, but has not yet ratified the Convention,[68] nor implemented the obligations under the Convention into domestic law.

A large part of the implementation of the universal terrorism-related conventions involves the criminalisation of conduct identified under those treaties. This aspect of the conventions to which Canada is party has been implemented in full by Canada.

6.3.3   Implementation of Security Council Resolutions

Consideration has already been given above, under Sect. 6.3.1, to Security Council resolution 1624 (2005), which called upon States to adopt measures to prohibit and prevent the incitement to commit terrorist acts. The travel ban and arms embargo against the Taliban and Al-Qa'ida under resolution 1267 (1999) were implemented by Canada under the United Nations Al-Qaida and Taliban Regulations 1999 (see Sect. 6.2.1 above). Those aspects of the same resolution concerning the freezing of funds and other financial resources controlled by or on their behalf of the Taliban or any other individuals of entities designated by the Committee are linked to paragraphs 1(c) and (d) of Security Council resolution 1373 (2001), which are identified below. Security Council resolution 1373 (2001) contains 11 binding directions under paragraphs 1 and 2 of the resolution (see Chap. 3, Sect. 3.2.2.3), which have been implemented by Canada as follows:

1. Prevention and suppression of the financing of terrorist acts (para 1(a))
   Paragraph 1(a), which requires the prevention and suppression of the financing of terrorist acts, is a general provision, expanded upon by the subparagraphs that follow it. In its first report to the Counter-Terrorism Committee on measures taken to implement resolution 1373 (2001), Canada noted that it had made the Regulations Implementing the United Nations Resolutions on the Suppression of Terrorism 2001 (see Sect. 6.2.3 above), and that it had introduced the Anti-terrorism Bill for the purpose of establishing terrorist financing offences under the Criminal Code 1985.[69]
2. Criminalising the provision of funds for terrorist acts (para 1(b))

---

[68] As at 1 October 2009.

[69] First report of Canada to the Security Council Counter-Terrorism Committee (n 17), p. 4.

In compliance with this provision of resolution 1373 (2001), the Anti-terrorism Act created the offences of providing or collecting property for certain activities, and providing or making available property or services for terrorist purposes under sections 83.02 and 83.03 of the Criminal Code 1985 (see Sect. 6.1.4.3 above and Appendix 3, Table 3(B)).

3. Freezing of funds and assets of terrorist entities (para 1(c))

The freezing of terrorist assets was given effect to by Canada through various provisions of the Anti-terrorism Act.[70] Its amendment of the Criminal Code provides for the listing of terrorist entities (see Sects. 6.1.4.5 and 6.2.2 above) and prohibits using or possessing property for terrorist purposes, and dealing with terrorist property (sections 83.04, and 83.08 and 83.12 of the Criminal Code – see Sect. 6.1.4.3 above and Appendix 3, Table 3(B)). Obligations are imposed on financial institutions and others to report suspicions of the holding or control of property belonging to or controlled by listed entities (see Sect. Sect. 6.1.4.7 above). Section 83.14 of the Criminal Code contains procedures through which terrorist assets can be forfeited (see Sect. 6.1.4.6 above).

4. Prohibiting the provision of financial or related services to terrorist entities (para 1(d))

Responding to paragraph 1(d) of the resolution, section 83.03 of the Criminal Code makes it an offence to make financial or related services available for terrorist purposes (see Sect. 6.1.4.3 above and Appendix 3, Table 3(B)). Canada has also pointed to compliance with this part of resolution 1373 (2001) by referring to Part 6 of the Anti-terrorism Act, which enacted the Charities Registration (Security Information) Act 2001 and amended the Income Tax Act 1985 to prevent those who support terrorist or related activities from enjoying the tax privileges granted to registered charities, and to prevent the use of registered charities to provide funds to support terrorist activities.[71]

5. Suppression of support to terrorists and elimination of the supply of weapons (para 2(a))

In compliance with paragraph 2(a) of resolution 1373 (2001), the Criminal Code prohibits persons from instructing anyone to carry out terrorist activities, or activities on behalf of a terrorist group (sections 83.21 and 83.22) – see Sect. 6.1.4.3 above and Appendix 3, Table 3(B). Canada has reported that its legislation has established a system of strict control over the import, export and internal possession of firearms and military weapons and explosives, as well as controls over other sensitive goods and technologies that could be used in the design, development and production of weapons of mass destruction (see Sect. 6.1.3 above).[72] Canada also enacted, in 2004, the Biological and Toxin Weapons Convention Implementation Act, which includes measures to give

---

[70]First report of Canada to the Security Council Counter-Terrorism Committee (n 17), p. 4.

[71]First report of Canada to the Security Council Counter-Terrorism Committee (n 17), p. 5.

[72]First report of Canada to the Security Council Counter-Terrorism Committee (n 17), p. 6.

the government of Canada the power to tighten internal controls on and regulate the export of civilian explosives.

6. Preventing the commission of terrorist acts (para 2(b))

   As discussed in Chap. 3, measuring a State's compliance with this direction is technically impossible, since all that can be done by a State is to undertake *all reasonable and practical steps* to prevent the commission of terrorist acts (see Sect. 3.2.2.3).

   Additional to the measures in response to items 1–5 above, Canada has pointed to the early warning function of the Canadian Security Intelligence Service, the primary responsibility of which is to collect information, forewarn and advise the government of Canada regarding activities that may constitute a threat to the security of Canada including terrorist threats.[73] It also pointed to provisions under the Anti-terrorism Bill concerning the use of electronic surveillance (see Sect. 6.1.4.8 above), and the ability of FINTRAC to share certain information with foreign counterparts.[74]

7. Denial of safe haven (para 2(c))

   Canada's Immigration and Refugee Protection Act 2001 prohibits the entry into Canada, and provides for the removal from Canada, of persons in respect of whom there are reasonable grounds to believe have engaged, are engaged or will engage in acts of terrorism or are members of an organisation involved in terrorism (see Sect. 6.1.4 above). Section 83.23 of the Criminal Code makes it an offence to harbour or conceal terrorists (see Sect. 6.1.4.3 above and Appendix 3, Table 3(B)).

8. Preventing the use of State territory by terrorists (para 2(d))

   The extraterritorial nature of the offences under the Criminal Code, together with general provisions of Canada's criminal law dealing with criminal conspiracy and other inchoate offences, have been identified by Canada as assisting in preventing terrorists acting from Canada against citizens of other States.[75] Also relevant are various offences under the Criminal Code, including: sections 83.18 and 83.2 which criminalise participation in activities of a terrorist group, and the commission of an offence for a terrorist group; section 83.19, outlawing the facilitation of terrorist activities; and section 83.23 which prohibits a person from harbouring or concealing a terrorist (see Sect. 6.1.4.3 above and Appendix 3, Table 3(B)).

9. Ensuring the prosecution and severe punishment of terrorists (para 2(e))

   As identified earlier in this chapter, the various offences under the Criminal Code carry severe penalties (see Sects. 6.1.2 and 6.1.4.3 above). The amendments to the Code pursuant to the Anti-terrorism Act also categorised certain offences as "terrorism offences", in respect of which a sentencing judge must

---

[73]First report of Canada to the Security Council Counter-Terrorism Committee (n 17), p. 6.

[74]First report of Canada to the Security Council Counter-Terrorism Committee (n 17), p. 7. See also pp. 13–14 of the same report and pp. 3–4 of Canada's fourth report to the Committee (n 66).

[75]First report of Canada to the Security Council Counter-Terrorism Committee (n 17), pp. 6–8.

treat this as an aggravating feature, and for which sentences must be served consecutively (see further Sect. 6.1.4.3 above).

10. Assisting in criminal investigations and prosecutions (para 2(f))

    Canada has reported that current law permits it to comply with paragraph 2(f) of resolution 1373 (2001), referring to the Mutual Legal Assistance in Criminal Matters Act 1985.[76]

11. Establishing and maintaining effective border controls to prevent the movement of terrorists (para 2(g))

    The Aeronautics Act 1985, the Canadian Passport Order 1986, and the Immigration and Refugee Protection Act 2001 have been identified by Canada as means through which compliance with paragraph 2(g) of the resolution can be achieved.[77] Measures to prevent the transboundary movement of terrorists are considered in Chap. 21.

References

Daniels, Ronald. 2002. Introduction. In Daniels, Ronald, Macklem, Patrick, and Roach, Kent (Eds). *Essays on Canada's Anti-Terrorism Bill*. Toronto: University of Toronto Press.

Gabor, Thomas. 2004. *The Views of Canadian Scholars on the Impact of the* Anti-terrorism Act. Ottawa: University of Ottawa Research and Statistics Division.

Harrington, Joanna. 2003. Punting Terrorists, Assassins and Other Undesirables: Canada, the Human Rights Committee, and Requests for Interim Measures of Protection. 48 *McGill Law Journal* 55.

Jenkins, David. 2003. In Support of Canada's Anti-Terrorism Act: A Comparison of Canadian, British, and American Anti-Terrorism Law. 66 *Saskatchewan Law Review* 419.

Roach, Kent. 2005. Canada's response to terrorism. In Ramraj, Victor, Hor, Michael, and Roach, Kent (Eds). *Global Anti-Terrorism Law and Policy*. Cambridge: Cambridge University Press.

---

[76]First report of Canada to the Security Council Counter-Terrorism Committee (n 17), p. 8.

[77]First report of Canada to the Security Council Counter-Terrorism Committee (n 17), pp. 9–10. See also Canada's fifth report to the Counter-Terrorism Committee (n 66), pp. 10–12.

Chapter 7
Counter-Terrorism Law in New Zealand

This chapter examines the legislation through which obligations under the international framework for combating terrorism have been implemented by New Zealand, as well as one item of legislation that exists outside the scope of those obligations. An overview and explanation of the following items of legislation is provided: the Aviation Crimes Act 1972; the Crimes (Internationally Protected Persons, United Nations and Associated Personnel, and Hostages) Act 1980; the International Terrorism (Emergency Powers) Act 1987; Maritime Crimes Act 1999; regulations responding to United Nations sanctions; the Terrorism Suppression Act 2002; the Counter-Terrorism Bill 2003; and the Anti-Money Laundering and Countering of Financing of Terrorism Bill 2008. It should be noted that there are numerous other pieces of domestic legislation that might be seen as contributing to the countering of terrorism. This chapter restricts itself to the items of legislation just mentioned, those having been identified by New Zealand in its reports to the Counter-Terrorism Committee as being part of its counter-terrorist legislative regime.

Similar to the other country-specific chapters on counter-terrorism law, this chapter is broken down into four main parts: first, looking at legislation through which the universal terrorism-related conventions have been implemented by New Zealand; next, examining any further specific legislation applicable to action required by decisions of the Security Council; then, turning to other items of legislation applicable to counter-terrorism in New Zealand; and, finally, setting out a summary and set of conclusions on New Zealand's compliance with the international framework on counter-terrorism. The overview provided includes identification of offences established under the legislation, a full list of which is set out in Appendix 3, Table 4 (the criminalisation of terrorism is considered in Chap. 14). It looks at the definition of "terrorist acts" under the Terrorism Suppression Act, and the expression "international terrorist emergency" in the International Terrorism (Emergency Powers) Act 1987. This chapter also considers some of the more negative aspects of the legislative processes in this area since September 11, including the review of the Terrorism Suppression Act, and the use of the Counter-Terrorism Bill to introduce law which applies not just to the countering of terrorism.

A. Conte, *Human Rights in the Prevention and Punishment of Terrorism*,
DOI 10.1007/978-3-642-11608-7_7, © Springer-Verlag Berlin Heidelberg 2010

7.1 Implementation by New Zealand of the Universal Terrorism-Related Treaties

New Zealand is a party to 12 of the existing 13 terrorism-related conventions (see Appendix 2, Table 1). It was an original signatory to the International Convention for the Suppression of Acts of Nuclear Terrorism, but has not yet deposited its instrument of ratification.[1] New Zealand has implemented its obligations under the treaties to which it is party under the following items of legislation, each of which will be considered in turn (on the reception of treaty law in New Zealand, see Chap. 4, Sect. 4.2.2):

- The Aviation Crimes Act 1972;
- The Crimes (International Protected Persons, United Nations and Associated Personnel, and Hostages) Act 1980;
- The Maritime Crimes Act 1999;
- The Terrorism Suppression Act 2002 (as amended); and
- The legislative amendments to New Zealand law made under the Counter-Terrorism Bill 2003.

7.1.1 Aviation Crimes Act 1972

The Aviation Crimes Act 1972 was the vehicle through which New Zealand transformed its obligations under the four conventions concerning the safety of aviation (see Chap. 3, Sect. 3.2.1), it preamble stating that it is:

> An Act to give effect to the provisions of the Hague Convention for the Suppression of Unlawful Seizure of Aircraft, the Montreal Convention for the Suppression of Unlawful Acts against the Safety of Civil Aviation, the Montreal Protocol for the Suppression of Unlawful Acts of Violence at Airports Serving International Civil Aviation, and the Tokyo Convention on Offences and Certain Other Acts Committed on Board Aircraft, and for matters incidental thereto.

The Act contains 21 sections and establishes the following offences relating to aircraft and international airports (see Appendix 3, Table 4(A)):

- *Hijacking* (section 3),[2] being the unlawful seizure of, or exercise of control over, an aircraft (while on board an aircraft "in flight",[3] which is from the time when

---

[1]International Convention for the Suppression of Acts of Nuclear Terrorism, adopted by the General Assembly and opened for signature on 15 April 2005 under GA Res 59/290, UN GAOR, 59th Sess, 91st Plen Mtg, UN Doc A/Res/59/290 (2005) and entered into force 7 July 2007.

[2]Corresponding to article 1(a) of the Convention for the Suppression of Unlawful Seizure of Aircraft (the Hague Convention), opened for signature 16 December 1970, 860 UNTS 105 (entered into force 14 October 1971).

[3]The term "in flight" is defined by section 2(2) of the Act.

all the aircraft's external doors are closed after embarkation until any external door is opened for disembarkation) by force, intimidation or threat of force, whether in or outside New Zealand. Conviction on indictment renders a person liable to life imprisonment.

- *Crimes in connection with hijacking* (section 4),[4] which includes any act or omission that is an offence under New Zealand law *and* occurs while on board an aircraft in flight and "in connection with the crime of hijacking". Section 4(2) deems such a connection to exist when the conduct facilitates a hijacking or is intended to avoid the detection or arrest of any person connected with the hijacking.
- *Crimes relating to aircraft* (section 5),[5] being a list of offences relating to conduct affecting an aircraft in flight or "in service" (as defined by section 2 (3)). The offences relate to conduct that might damage an aircraft or otherwise put it at risk.
- *Crimes relating to international airports* (section 5A),[6] which again sets out a list of offences, this time concerning the use of any "device, substance or weapon" which endangers the safety of an international airport through violence, damage of facilities or aircraft not in service, or disruption of services.

The commission of any of these offences renders a person liable to prosecution under New Zealand law or, in the alternative, liable to extradition in accordance with the procedures under the Extradition Act 1999 (sections 7 and 7A). The Aviation Crimes Act also makes it an offence to take firearms, dangerous or offensive weapons or instruments, ammunition, or any explosive substance or device onto an aircraft without lawful authority or reasonable excuse (section 11, punishable by up to 5 years imprisonment).

In terms of compliance with obligations, the Tokyo Convention requires contracting States to take measures necessary to establish jurisdiction over offences committed on board aircraft registered in their State (article 3(2)). The more specific obligations imposed under the Tokyo Convention appear to have been fully implemented through sections 5 (offences), 15–17 inclusive (powers of the aircraft commander) and 19 (exemption of military, customs or police services) of the Aviation Crimes Act. The Hague Convention, concerning the hijacking of aircraft, requires States parties to make hijacking an offence punishable by severe penalties (article 2). Again, the requirements of the Convention appear to have been

---

[4]Corresponding to article 1(b) of the Hague Convention.

[5]Corresponding to article 1(1) and (2) of the Convention on Offences and Certain Other Acts Committed on Board Aircraft (the Tokyo Convention), opened for signature 14 September 1963, 704 UNTS 219 (entered into force 4 December 1969); and article 1 of the Convention for the Suppression of Unlawful Acts against the Safety of Civil Aviation (the Montreal Convention), opened for signature 23 September 1971, 974 UNTS 177 (entered into force 26 January 1973).

[6]Corresponding to article 2(1) of the Protocol on the Suppression of Unlawful Acts of Violence at Airports Serving International Civil Aviation (the Montreal Protocol), opened for signature 24 February 1988, ICAO Doc 9518 (entered into force 6 August 1989).

implemented in this regard. The position is also true of the Montreal Convention and its Protocol.

Sections 12 and 13 of the Act set out powers of search of passengers, baggage and cargo. Security of the person is also a matter impacted upon by the Aviation Crimes Act, an aircraft commander holding powers of search and restraint under sections 15 and 17. Related to the powers of restraint are the provisions of articles 6–10 and 13–15 inclusive of the Tokyo Convention, and article 6 of the Hague Convention.

7.1.2 The Crimes (International Protected Persons, United Nations and Associated Personnel, and Hostages) Act 1980

The Crimes (Internationally Protected Persons, United Nations and Associated Personnel, and Hostages) Act 1980 incorporates the two treaties on terrorism concerning the safety of persons, as well as the Convention on the Safety of United Nations and Associated Personnel.[7] Its preamble reads:

> An Act to give effect to–
> The Convention on the Prevention and Punishment of Crimes Against Internationally Protected Persons, including Diplomatic Agents 1973; and
> The Convention Against the Taking of Hostages 1979; and
> The Convention on the Safety of United Nations and Associated Personnel 1994;–
> and for matters incidental to the implementation of those Conventions.

The discussion that follows focuses on the first two conventions, the Protected Persons and Hostages Conventions, these having been identified by the Terrorism Prevention Branch as terrorism-related conventions. The Act establishes three related categories of offending (see Appendix 3, Table 4(B)):

- *Hostage-taking* (section 8(1)),[8] defined as the unlawful seizure or detention of any person, whether in or outside New Zealand, with intent to compel the government of any country or any international intergovernmental organisation to do or abstain from doing something. Section 8(2) excludes conduct that would essentially amount to the domestic-based offence of kidnapping.

---

[7]The Convention on the Prevention and Punishment of Crimes against Internationally Protected Persons, including Diplomatic Agents (the Protected Persons Convention), opened for signature 14 December 1973, 1035 UNTS 167 (entered into force 20 February 1977); the International Convention against the Taking of Hostages (the Hostages Convention), opened for signature 18 December 1979, 1316 UNTS 205 (entered into force 3 June 1983); and the Convention on the Safety of United Nations and Associated Personnel, opened for signature 9 December 1994, 2051 UNTS 363 (entered into force 15 January 1999).

[8]Corresponding to article 1(1) of the Hostages Convention.

- *Crimes against persons protected by a convention* (sections 3 and 5),[9] which includes conduct in or outside New Zealand in relation to a person who is known to be a protected person that would amount to certain crimes listed in the First Schedule to the Act (section 3), or threats of such conduct (section 5). The listed crimes include homicide, violent offending, sexual offending and kidnapping.
- *Crimes against premises or vehicles of persons protected by a convention* (sections 4 and 6),[10] again including conduct within or outside New Zealand this time in relation to the official premises of, or vehicles used by, protected persons that would amount to certain crimes listed in the Second Schedule to the Act (section 4), or threats of such conduct (section 6). The Second Schedule includes the offences of arson, attempted arson, intentional damage and endangering transport.

As for the Aviation Crimes Act, any offence against the Crimes (Internationally Protected Persons, United Nations and Associated Personnel, and Hostages) Act renders an offender liable to prosecution in New Zealand or, in the alternative, to extradition. To that end, the international obligations under the two conventions identified appear to have been fully implemented into national law.

7.1.3 The Maritime Crimes Act 1999

The two maritime safety conventions relating to terrorism (the Rome Convention and Protocol)[11] were incorporated into New Zealand law through the final piece of pre-September 11 legislation, the Maritime Crimes Act 1999, described in its preamble as an Act:

> ...to give effect to the provisions of the Rome Convention for the Suppression of Unlawful Acts Against the Safety of Maritime Navigation and the Rome Protocol for the Suppression of Unlawful Acts Against the Safety of Fixed Platforms Located on the Continental Shelf.

Similar in nature to the Aviation Crimes Act 1972, the Maritime Crimes Act establishes offences mandated by the Rome Convention and Protocol and aimed at securing the safety of ships (other than warships, customs or police vessels: see section 3) and maritime platforms (see Appendix 3, Table 4(D)):

- *Crimes relating to ships* (section 4),[12] prohibiting the unlawful seizure of ships and acts that damage ships or place their safe navigation in danger. It also

---

[9]Corresponding to article 2(1)(a) and (c) of the Protected Persons Convention.

[10]Corresponding to article 2(1)(b) and (c) of the Protected Persons Convention.

[11]The Convention for the Suppression of Unlawful Acts against the Safety of Maritime Navigation (the Rome Convention), opened for signature 10 March 1988, 1678 UNTS 221 (entered into force 1 March 1992); and the Protocol for the Suppression of Unlawful Acts against the Safety of Fixed Platforms Located on the Continental Shelf (the Rome Protocol), opened for signature 10 March 1988, 1678 UNTS 304 (entered into force 1 March 1992).

[12]Corresponding to article 3 of the Rome Convention.

renders a person liable to prosecution if, in the commission of the latter acts, s/he injures or causes death to any person (section 4(2)).

- *Crimes relating to fixed platforms* (section 5),[13] prohibiting the same conduct, but relating to fixed platforms (any artificial island, installation or structure permanently attached to the seabed for the purpose of exploration or resources exploitation, as defined by section 2).

Such conduct, whether within or outside New Zealand (sections 8 and 9), renders a person liable to prosecution within New Zealand or arrest and surrender to a State party to the Rome Convention or Protocol (sections 13–16). The Act provides the master of a ship with powers of detention and surrender, as well as search and seizure, of any person on board a ship, incorporating the obligations under article 8 of the Rome Convention (sections 11 and 12). The Convention and Protocol are, in all respects, implemented into New Zealand law.

7.1.4 Terrorism Suppression Act 2002

The Terrorism Suppression Act 2002 was enacted to achieve two purposes: first to allow New Zealand to become party to a number of terrorism-related conventions; and also to give effect to obligations upon New Zealand under Security Council resolution 1373 (2001).[14] Because of the timing of New Zealand's decision to pursue each objective, the intervening attacks of September 11, and the adoption by the UN General Assembly of the Nuclear Terrorism Convention,[15] the process from Bill to Act was a rather unusual one. First, the Bill was introduced as incorporating legislation for the bombings and financing conventions. Next, the Bill was significantly amended to incorporate obligations under Security Council Resolution 1373. A further set of substantive provisions were added to the Act through the Counter-Terrorism Bill 2003 (which created the Terrorism Suppression Amendment Act 2003). Further minor amendments took place under the Terrorism Suppression Amendment Bill (No 2), which was introduced in December 2004. More recent changes were made under the Terrorism Suppression Amendment Act 2007.

---

[13]Corresponding to article 2 of the Rome Protocol.

[14]Discussed below. See also Gobbi (2004). Note that the Act does not contain any preambular statement setting out the purpose of the legislation, but that the purpose of the legislation is addressed within section 3 of the Act.

[15]International Convention for the Suppression of Acts of Nuclear Terrorism (the Nuclear Terrorism Convention), adopted and opened for signature on 15 April 2005 under General Assembly resolution 58/290 (2005), UN GAOR, 58th Sess, 91st Plen Mtg, UN Doc A/Res/58/290 (2005).

7.1.4.1 Treaty Implementation and the Process from Bill to the Current Act

The Terrorism Suppression Act 2002 began its life as the Terrorism (Bombings and Financing) Bill, introduced in early 2001 following the Executive's decision to become party to the International Convention for the Suppression of Terrorist Bombings and the International Convention for the Suppression of the Financing of Terrorism.[16] National Interest Analyses were prepared, with the Foreign Affairs, Defence and Trade Committee subsequently lodging treaty examination reports with the House on 1 December 2000 (on this domestic process, see Chap. 4, Sect. 4.2.2.2). The reports did not bring any matters to the attention of the House, but the Analyses each noted that domestic implementing legislation would be needed to create new criminal offences, establish extra-territorial jurisdiction and facilitate the prosecution or extradition of alleged offenders.[17]

The most recent addition to the international legal framework on counter-terrorism is the International Convention for the Suppression of Acts of Nuclear Terrorism. New Zealand is an original signatory State to the Nuclear Terrorism Convention, which was adopted in April 2005. At the same time as the negotiation of the Convention, work was being undertaken by the International Atomic Energy Agency towards adopting amendments to the Convention on the Physical Protection of Nuclear Material.[18] One of the purposes of the Terrorism Suppression Amendment Act 2007 was to allow New Zealand to implement obligations under, and take treaty action in respect of, both the Nuclear Terrorism and Nuclear Materials Conventions.[19] Despite this stated objective, New Zealand has still not ratified the Nuclear Terrorism Convention (see Appendix 2, Table 1).

After the preparation of the National Interest Analyses and the presentation of reports required by Parliamentary Standing Orders, the horrific events of 11 September 2001, transpired. The Security Council subsequently adopted resolution 1373 (2001),[20] imposing both binding and non-binding obligations upon New Zealand. The Resolution was adopted when the Terrorism (Bombings and Financing) Bill was in its final stages of the select committee process.[21] Compliance

---

[16]The International Convention for the Suppression of Terrorist Bombing (the Bombing Convention), opened for signature 12 January 1998, 2149 UNTS 286 (entered into force 23 May 2001); and the International Convention for the Suppression of the Financing of Terrorism (the Financing Convention), opened for signature 10 January 2000, 2179 UNTS 232 (entered into force 10 April 1992).

[17]New Zealand Ministry of Foreign Affairs and Trade, National Interest Analysis, International Convention for the Suppression of Terrorist Bombings, para 9, and National Interest Analysis, International Convention for the Suppression of the Financing of Terrorism, para 12.

[18]Convention on the Physical Protection of Nuclear Material (the Nuclear Material Convention), opened for signature 3 March 1980, 1456 UNTS 124 (entered into force 8 February 1987).

[19]New Zealand Parliamentary Library, Bills Digest. Terrorism Suppression Amendment Bill 2007 (Bills Digest 1498, 21 March 2007), 2.

[20]SC Res 1373, UN SCOR, 4385th Mtg, UN Doc S/Res/1373 (2001).

[21]Report to the Counter-Terrorism Committee pursuant to paragraph 6 of Security Council resolution 1373 (2001) of 28 September 2001, New Zealand, UN Doc S/2001/1269 (2002), p. 3.

with the obligations under the resolution thus became the second aim of the 2001
Bill, as amended. To achieve that objective, the reasonably unusual step was
taken of adding a considerable number of new substantive provisions to the Bill,
seeing the Bill almost double in size.[22] Due to these circumstances, the Foreign
Affairs Defence and Trade Committee presented to the House an interim report on
the Bill, drawing to its attention the new provisions in the Bill, with explanatory
notes.[23] The Committee also called for public submissions on the draft amendments
and received 143 submissions from interest groups and individuals.[24] The Committee had received no submissions on the original Terrorism (Bombings and
Financing) Bill.[25]

The next stage in the development of the Terrorism Suppression Act came
through amendments to the legislation enacted under the Counter-Terrorism Bill
2003. The latter legislation is discussed in more detail below, concerning the
purpose of the legislation and the nature of legislative amendments achieved
under it. What should be noted at this stage is that Part 2 of the Counter-Terrorism
Bill was directed towards amendment of the Terrorism Suppression Act. The
primary purpose of these amendments was to incorporate obligations under the
Convention on the Physical Protection of Nuclear Material and the Convention on
the Marking of Plastic Explosives for the Purpose of Detection.[26] The amendments
also added substantive provisions concerning the search and seizure, and related
issues, by the Customs Service of goods owned or controlled by designated terrorist
entities.[27]

On 14 December 2004, further amending legislation was introduced to the
House: the Terrorism Suppression Amendment Bill (No 2). The amendments to
the principal Act under this Bill achieved two things: the creation of a new offence
of providing financial support to terrorist organisations (including those that might
not yet be formally designated under the Act); and extend the length of time that
designations remain in force without further extension by High Court order (from 3
to 5 years). These features of the Terrorism Suppression Act are considered in
Chap. 19 (Sect. 19.2).

---

[22]As noted in New Zealand's first report to the Counter-Terrorism Committee, ibid. See Dunworth
(2002).

[23]Foreign Affairs, Defence and Trade Committee, Interim Report on the Terrorism (Bombings and
Financing) Bill, 8 November 2001.

[24]Ibid, cover page; and Foreign Affairs, Defence and Trade Committee, Final Report on the
Terrorism <(Bombings and Financing)> Suppression Bill, 22 March 2002, 2.

[25]See the Committee's interim report (n 23) p. 2.

[26]The Convention on the Marking of Plastic Explosives for the Purpose of Detection (the Plastic
Explosives Convention), opened for signature 1 March 1991, ICAO Doc 9571 (entered into force
21 June 1998); and the Convention on the Physical Protection of Nuclear Material (the Nuclear
Materials Convention), opened for signature 3 March 1980, 1456 UNTS 124 (entered into force
8 February 1987). See clauses 10 to 14 and 16 to 23 of the Counter-Terrorism Bill 2003.

[27]Clause 15 of the Counter-Terrorism Bill 2003.

The Terrorism Suppression Amendment Act 2007 made further changes to the principal Act for the three main purposes:

- The Act facilitates New Zealand's ratification of the Nuclear Terrorism Convention, and treaty action in respect of amendments to the Nuclear Materials Convention. As a consequence of the obligations under this treaty action, the Act created new offences concerning the use of radioactive material and radioactive devices, and amended existing offences concerning the physical protection of nuclear material.
- The next set of amendments concern the regime under the principal Act for the designation of terrorist entities. These amendments are considered in Chap. 19.
- The final set of amendments concern reasonably minor changes to existing offences, relating to 'avoidance of doubt' provisions and the offence of participating in a terrorist group. The Act also introduced a new offence of committing a "terrorist act". These amendments are considered in Chap. 14.

It should finally be noted that the New Zealand Bill of Rights Act 1990 requires the Attorney-General, under section 7, to advise the House of any inconsistency between any provision of a Bill before the House and the Bill of Rights (see Chap. 11, Sect. 11.3.1.3). In practical terms, this in turn relies on advice given to the Attorney-General by the New Zealand Crown Law Office. In the case of the Terrorism (Bombings and Financing) Bill, the Solicitor-General (who is the head of the Crown Law Office) examined the Bill and concluded that it was consistent with the Bill of Rights Act.[28] The proposed changes to the principal Act under the 2007 Amendment Act were also, based on advice from the Crown Law Office to the Attorney-General, assessed as "not inconsistent" with the NZ Bill of Rights.[29]

7.1.4.2 Definition of "Terrorist Act"

There has been no overwhelming consensus within the international community on a definition of terrorism, resulting in the lack of a definition within relevant Security Council and General Assembly resolutions (see Chap. 2, Sect. 2.2). The result is that individual States have been required to formulate their own definitions of the term. In the New Zealand context, this is addressed within sections 4 and 5 of the Terrorism Suppression Act.

---

[28]Letter from the Solicitor-General to the Attorney-General, "re Terrorism Suppression Bill: Slip Amendments – PCO 3814B/11 Our Ref: ATT114/1048 (15)", 9 November 2001. It should be noted, as pointed out by the Solicitor-General in his letter, that his office was only provided with the Slip Amendments (which amended the original form of the Bill to incorporate the Resolution 1373 obligations) on the previous day, 8 November 2001.

[29]Letter from the Crown Law Office to the Attorney-General, "Legal Advice. Consistency with the New Zealand Bill of Rights Act 1990: Terrorism Suppression Amendment Bill. Our Ref: ATT395/24", 4 December 2006, online: http://www.justice.govt.nz/bill-of-rights/bill-list-2006/t-bill/terrorism-suppression-amend-bill.html.

Section 5 of the Act, combined with definitions contained within section 4(1) and the conventions listed in Schedule 3, provides for three distinct types of "terrorist acts". The term is significant for three main reasons.[30] First, it is linked to offences such as the financing of terrorist acts (section 8). It also plays a role in the designation of terrorist entities, which include those entities that have perpetrated terrorist acts. Finally, the 2007 Amendment Act created a new offence, under section 6A(1), of engaging in a terrorist act (as defined in section 5(1) of the principal Act), publishable by a maximum of life imprisonment. The 2007 Act did not make any changes to the definition of terrorist acts.

The first type of terrorist act defined reflects the international obligations assumed by New Zealand under the various international terrorism-related conventions. Sections 4(1) and 5(1)(b) prohibit acts that constitute an offence under one of the ten terrorism conventions listed in Schedule 3 to the Act.[31] Schedule 3 does not list the Convention for the Suppression of the Financing of Terrorism, the Convention on the Marking of Plastic Explosives for the Purpose of Detection, nor the Convention on Offences and Certain Other Acts Committed On Board Aircraft. In submissions to the Foreign Affairs, Defence and Trade Committee on the Counter-Terrorism Bill, the author of this text notified the Committee of this omission.[32] Clause 22 of the Counter-Terrorism Bill proposed to amend Schedule 3 to the Terrorism Suppression Act by including in the list of treaties the Convention on the Physical Protection of Nuclear Material. The author submitted to the Committee that this was not sufficient since, upon the enactment of the Counter-Terrorism Bill, New Zealand was to become party to all of the international conventions on counter-terrorism. The Terrorism Suppression Act should therefore include in its definition of a "terrorist act", it was submitted, any act against *any* of those terrorism-related conventions to which New Zealand is party.[33] The Committee did not, however, recommend amendment of clause 22, nor did it report on the reasons for this.

The second type of terrorist act defined is that of terrorist acts in armed conflict, established under sections 5(1)(c) and 4(1) as conduct:

(a) that occurs in a situation of armed conflict; and
(b) the purpose of which, by its nature or context, is to intimidate a population, or to compel a government or an international organisation to do or abstain from doing any act; and
(c) that is intended to cause death or serious bodily injury to a civilian or other person not taking an active part in the hostilities in that situation; and
(d) that is not excluded from the application of the Financing Convention by article 3 of that Convention.

---

[30] As highlighted in the Interim Report on the Bill (n 23) p. 5.

[31] Through its definition of "act against a specified terrorism convention" and "specified terrorism convention", and through the associated list of conventions contained in Schedule 3 to the Act.

[32] Alex Conte, Submissions to the Foreign Affairs, Defence and Trade Committee on the Counter-Terrorism Bill (27-1, 2003), 12 May 2003, part IIIA.

[33] Ibid, paras 23 and 24.

Finally, a more general (albeit complex) definition is provided within the balance of section 5. A terrorist act is:

- conduct intended to advance an ideological, political, or religious cause (section 5(2)),
- *and* with the following intention (section 5(2)(a) and (b)):
  (a) to induce terror in a civilian population; or
  (b) to unduly compel or to force a government or an international organisation to do or abstain from doing any act,
- *and* with the intention to cause (section 5(3)):
  (a) the death of, or other serious bodily injury to, 1 or more persons (other than a person carrying out the act):
  (b) a serious risk to the health or safety of a population:
  (c) destruction of, or serious damage to, property of great value or importance, or major economic loss, or major environmental damage, if likely to result in 1 or more outcomes specified in paragraphs (a), (b), and (d):
  (d) serious interference with, or serious disruption to, an infrastructure facility, if likely to endanger human life:
  (e) introduction or release of a disease-bearing organism, if likely to devastate the national economy of a country.

This general definition of terrorist acts is examined in Chap. 14 (Sect. 14.1), where it is tested against the approach advocated by the UN Special Rapporteur on the promotion and protection of human rights while countering terrorism (discussed earlier in Chap. 2, Sect. 2.3).

7.1.4.3 Offences Under the Terrorism Suppression Act

The Terrorism Suppression Act 2002 establishes the following offences (see Appendix 3, Table 4(D)):

- *Terrorist bombing* (section 5(2)), prohibiting the intentional and unlawful delivery, placement, discharge or detonation of an explosive or other lethal device with the intention to cause death (or serious injury) or extensive destruction.[34] Conviction renders an offender liable to imprisonment for life.
- *Financing of terrorism* (section 8), prohibiting the wilful provision or collection of funds (directly or indirectly), intending (or knowing) that those funds are to be used to carry out a "terrorist act" (as defined, see above), without lawful justification or reasonable excuse. The maximum penalty, upon conviction, is 14 years imprisonment.[35]

---

[34]Corresponding to article 2(1) of the Bombing Convention.

[35]Corresponding to article 2(1) of the Financing Convention (n 16), and para 1(a) and (b) of SC Res 1373 (n 20).

This offence was added to by the Terrorism Suppression Amendment Bill (No 2) 2004. The explanatory notes to that Bill referred to doubt that the offence, as just described, was enough to prohibit general financial support to an organisation involved in terrorism (whether designated or not), such as the payment of routine expenses (e.g., rent).[36] It should also be noted that the 2007 Amendment Act repealed the 'avoidance of doubt' provisions in the terrorist financing offences.

- *Dealing with terrorist property* (section 9), making it an offence to deal with property known to be owned, controlled or derived by a designated terrorist entity, without lawful justification or reasonable excuse. This effectively freezes such property by prohibiting anyone from dealing with it, and thus preventing a designated terrorist entity from accessing it.[37] Conviction renders a person liable to a maximum of 7 years imprisonment. To "deal with" terrorist property:[38]

  (a) means to use or deal with the property, in any way and by any means (for example, to acquire possession of, or a legal or equitable interest in, transfer, pay for, sell, assign or dispose of (including by way of gift) the property); and

  (b) includes allowing the property to be used or dealt with, or facilitating the use of it of dealing with it.

- *Making property, or financial or related services, available* (section 10), prohibiting the provision (direct or indirect) of any property, or any financial or related services, to (or for the benefit of) a designated terrorist entity, without lawful justification or reasonable excuse. Section 11 limits the operation of this prohibition, where the Prime Minister permits, by notice in writing, any particular dealing. Otherwise, the offence renders a convicted person liable to up to 7 years imprisonment. The terms "make available" and "property" are defined within the Act (sections 10(6) and 4(1) respectively), but the phrase "financial or related services" is not. As with the offences under section 9, the Terrorism Suppression Amendment Act 2007 removed the 'avoidance of doubt' provision which had existed under section 10(2) of the Act.

- *Recruiting members of terrorist groups* (section 12), making it an offence to recruit another person into an organisation or group, knowing that the organisation or group is either a "terrorist entity" or participates in "terrorist acts". This is much broader in its scope than the previous three offences, since it goes beyond conduct relating to a "terrorist entity" as designated under the Act by also prohibiting conduct relating to entities that participate in "terrorist acts". As seen already, there are three categories and definitions of terrorist acts under the combination of sections 4 and 5, the more general of which is reasonably complex.

---

[36]New Zealand Ministry of Justice, Terrorism Suppression Amendment Bill (No 2), Government Bill, 242-1, Explanatory Note, presented to the House 14 December 2005, 1. Clause 4 of the Bill proposes to create this offence through a new section 8(2A) of the Terrorism Suppression Act 2002.

[37]Corresponding to SC Res 1267, UN SCOR, 4051st Mtg, UN Doc S/Res/1267 (1999) para 8; and SC Res 1373 (n 20) para 1(c).

[38]This term had been defined under section 9(5) of the 2002 Act. The Terrorism Suppression Amendment Act 2007 removed the definition from section 9 to the general definitions provision of section 4.

- *Participating in terrorist groups* (section 13), prohibiting participation in an organisation or group, knowing that the organisation or group is either a "terrorist entity" or participates in "terrorist acts" and for the purpose of enhancing the ability of the group to carry out terrorist acts. The maximum penalty is 14 years imprisonment.
- *Harbouring or concealing terrorists* (section 13A), making the intended assistance of a person to avoid arrest, escape custody, or avoid conviction an offence where it is known (or ought to be known) that the person has carried out, or intends to commit, a "terrorist act". Seven years imprisonment can result from conviction. This offence was added to the Terrorism Suppression Act by section 12 of the Counter-Terrorism Bill 2003. The Terrorism Suppression Amendment Act 2007 further amended the offence by including the element of recklessness (see section 11(1) of the 2007 Act).
- *Using or moving unmarked plastic explosives* (section 13B), prohibiting the possession, use, manufacture, importation or export of unmarked plastic explosives, except as allowed by the Hazardous Substances and New Organisms Act 1996 or by the Environmental Risk Management Authority. The maximum penalties are a fine of $500,000 or imprisonment of no more than 10 years. This offence was added to the Terrorism Suppression Act by section 12 of the Counter-Terrorism Bill 2003.
- *Offences involving nuclear material* (section 13C and 13D), prohibiting a range of conduct relating to nuclear material, including its importation and its use to intimidate. These offences were also added to the Terrorism Suppression Act by section 12 of the Counter-Terrorism Bill 2003.

The following further offences were added to the Terrorism Suppression Act under the 2007 Amendment Act:

- *Terrorist acts* (section 6A), making a person criminally responsible for engaging in a "terrorist act" as defined by the Act (see above). Conviction on indictment renders a person liable to imprisonment for life, or a lesser term (section 6A(2)). The broad nature of this offence is considered in Chap. 14 (see Sect. 14.2.3.1).
- *Offences involving radioactive material and radioactive devices* (section 13E), prohibiting a range of conduct relating to radioactive material and devices, including its possession and its use to intimidate. These offences were added as a result of changes adopted by the International Atomic Energy Agency to the Nuclear Materials Convention and, according to the Explanatory Note to the Bill, to enable ratification by New Zealand of the Nuclear Terrorism Convention.[39] A person convicted on indictment is subject to imprisonment up to 10 years, and/or a fine not exceeding $500,000 NZD.

---

[39]Explanatory Note (n 36) p. 4.

7.1.4.4 Designation of Terrorist Entities

As seen from the foregoing discussion, a number of offences under the Terrorism Suppression Act concern conduct in support of or related to a terrorist entity. The Act establishes a regime by which organisations, groups, or even individuals may be designated as such. The designation process, governed by sections 20–42 inclusive, empowers the Prime Minister to designate terrorist entities based on "any relevant information, including classified security information" (section 30).

The Prime Minister may make an interim designation, after consulting with the Attorney-General and the Minister of Foreign Affairs and Trade, if s/he has good cause to believe that the entity has in the past undertaken one or more "terrorist acts" or is knowingly facilitating such acts (section 20). An interim designation automatically expires after 30 days, during which time certain notice must be given about the designation (sections 21, and 26–29). The Act contemplates that a final designation, if appropriate, will be made prior to the expiry of the interim designation (section 22). Again, steps are required to notify and, in addition, publish the designation (sections 21, and 26–29).

A final designation currently expires after three years, unless the High Court extends the designation (section 35). The period of final designation was extended under the Terrorism Suppression Amendment Bill (No 2) 2004 to allow consideration of the Select Committee's review of the Terrorism Suppression Act (as required under section 70 of the Act), part of which was to address the designation process, current designations are to continue for two years after presentation of the Committee's report to the House.[40] Minister of Justice Phil Goff explained:[41]

> At the time that the original form of the Terrorism Suppression Bill was first introduced, there was uncertainty as to the nature and extent of the terrorism phenomenon. An assumption that some designations might be short-lived has since proved false.

The Minister continued:

> Provisions in the existing Act mean that New Zealand's designations of terrorist organisations – including the 318 organisations listed by the United Nations Security Council – expire after three years unless renewed by order of the High Court.
>
> Drafting of that provision created the unintended need for each designation to be renewed individually, meaning it will be impossible to renewal all the 318 UNSC-listed designations before they expire next October. That would put New Zealand in breach of Security Council Resolution 1373 – which was passed unanimously by the UN in the wake of September 11 – and related resolutions.

Both the interim and final designation processes are open to judicial review (section 33). A designated entity may at any time apply to the Prime Minister to revoke the designation (sections 34 and 42).

---

[40] The review report was due on 1 December 2005, under section 70(3) of the Terrorism Suppression Act 2002.

[41] See also the Explanatory Note to the Bill (n 36) p. 2.

New Zealand has so far only designated as terrorist entities those identified by the UN Security Council 1267 Committee (see Chap. 3, Sect. 3.2.4.2) in its most recent consolidated list.[42] The lack of use by New Zealand of this procedure for the designation of non-UN listed terrorist entities has been criticised as a failure by New Zealand to "add its considerable moral and symbolic voice to the international chorus against terrorist violence".[43]

The Terrorism Suppression Amendment Act 2007 made three main changes to the regime just described:

- First, the listing of entities by the Security Council 1267 Sanctions Committee were subject to subsequent designation by the Prime Minister before they were prohibited entities under New Zealand law. The 2007 Amendment Act removed the designation process, as it applies to entities listed by the 1267 Sanctions Committee, instead applying the provisions of the Act automatically to those that are listed by the Committee. Section 31 of the 2002 Act, which relates to United Nations Security Council information, was repealed. Security Council listed entities are now automatically designated.[44]
- The next set of changes relate to the extension of designations made by the Prime Minister. Final designations originally expired after three years, unless extended by the High Court. The Terrorism Suppression Amendment Act 2007 shifted the role of making extensions from the High Court to the Prime Minister and limits the extension procedure to non-UN-designated entities (sections 35–37 of the 2002 Act were repealed and substituted with a new section 35).
- The final change made under the 2007 Amendment Act concerns the protection of classified security information. The 2002 Act previously set out two procedures by which such information could be protected, whereas there is now a single procedure under new section 38.

The designation process, including the changes made under the 2007 Amendment Act, is considered in further detail in Chap. 19 (Sect. 19.2).

7.1.4.5   Freezing and Forfeiture of Terrorist Property

Any property that is owned or controlled by or on behalf of a designated terrorist entity is frozen by virtue of the prohibition under section 9 against dealing with such property (see above). As in other jurisdictions, the freezing of property in New

---

[42]See New Zealand response to the questions and comments of the Security Council Counter-Terrorism Committee contained in the Chairman's letter of 30 May 2003, UN Doc S/2003/860 (2003), p. 4. The consolidated list is available at URL http://www.un.org/Docs/sc/committees/1267/tablelist.htm. See also Response of New Zealand to the Security Council Committee under Security Council resolution 1455 (2003), UN Doc S/AC.37/2003/(1455)21 (2003), pp. 2–4, especially para 4.

[43]Smith (2003, p. 3).

[44]Bills Digest (n 19) p. 1; and Explanatory Note (n 36) p. 5.

Zealand is subject to certain exceptions. The Prime Minister can permit by notice in writing, under section 11, any particular dealing. The Prime Minister can also direct the Official Assignee to take custody and control of any such property in New Zealand (section 48), in respect of which a person with an interest in the property can apply to the High Court for relief (section 54).

The power of forfeiture is one vested in the High Court under section 55 of the Terrorism Suppression Act, allowing the Attorney-General to apply for an order for forfeiture in respect of property owned by an entity in respect of which a final designation has been made and where the mere prohibition against dealing with such property is not enough, by itself (section 55(2)(b)).

7.1.4.6   Financial Transactions Reporting

Section 43 of the Terrorism Suppression Act requires financial institutions and other persons in possession or control of suspected terrorist property to report that suspicion to the police. The provision was enacted, explained the Select Committee, to ensure that the mere *holding* of terrorist property, without necessarily dealing in it, is detected and made unlawful.[45] The process for reporting suspicious property is aligned with the process for reporting suspicious transactions in the Financial Transactions Reporting Act 1996, which is limited to reporting for the purposes of money laundering offences or for proceeds of crime action.[46] "Double-reporting" is avoided by deeming a report under the Terrorism Suppression Act to be notice under section 15 of the Financial Transactions Reporting Act.[47]

The provision applies to property directly, or indirectly, owned or controlled by any entity that has been designated a terrorist entity. "Property" is defined within the Act in such a way as to include any form or real or personal property or interest therein. Section 43 of the Act applies to such property within the ownership or control of a "terrorist" entity, as designated, such designation resulting in public notification of both interim and permanent designations in the Gazette.[48] There is, from that perspective, a small level of certainty for financial and other institutions in knowing the extent to which the reporting procedures apply: institutions need not bother themselves with the question of whether any particular organisation

---

[45]See the final report on the 2002 Bill (n 24) p. 13.

[46]Reporting under the Terrorism Suppression Act operates, however, independently of section 15 of the Financial Transactions Reporting Act – the latter Act being limited to reporting for the purposes of the investigation or prosecution of money laundering offences or for Proceeds of Crime Act action.

[47]See sections 44(4) and 77 of the Terrorism Suppression Act 2002 and the (amended) section 15 (1) of the Financial Transactions Reporting Act 1996.

[48]See sections 21(a), pertaining to interim designations, and 23(e) as to permanent designations. Upon permanent designation, such designation remains in force for a period of 3 years, unless earlier revoked or later extended by Court order: see section 35. Notification of revocation, expiry or invalidity is also subject to notification through the Gazette: see section 42.

or person is a terrorist.[49] They will be informed of this through the Gazetted designation.

The reporting procedures described apply not only to property within the ownership or control of a designated terrorist entity (section 43(1)(a)), but also to any property derived or generated from any such property (section 43(1)(b)). It will be interesting to see the extent to which the Government reviews, or even requires, compliance with these reporting provisions given their potentially wide application. If one was to apply the provisions to their full extent, such compliance would involve a level of financial regulation and investigation that is not commonly seen within New Zealand's deregulated environment.[50]

Once these preliminary issues are dealt with, it is then a question of what obligations are in fact imposed upon financial institutions. Having just made the criticism that proper compliance would be burdensome, this is countered by what is in the author's view a low threshold. The test for determining whether an institution is obliged to report to the Commissioner of Police is that of "suspicion, on reasonable grounds" that the institution is in possession or control of "property" within the jurisdiction of section 43 (see section 43(2)). Where such suspicion exists, a report is to be made as soon as practicable in accordance with section 44 and Schedule 5 to the Act. Failure to report constitutes an offence under section 43 (4) of the Act, punishable by up to 1 year's imprisonment.[51]

7.1.4.7 Review Mechanism

Following receipt of public submissions on the November 2001 version of the Terrorism (Bombings and Financing) Bill, the Foreign Affairs, Defence and Trade Committee recommended inclusion of a review mechanism pertaining to provisions

---

[49]It has to be said, however, that the New Zealand Bankers' Association had in fact asked for an even greater level of notice to financial institutions when the Bill was being considered before the Select Committee. The Association requested that its members receive automatic direct notice of interim and final designations, thereby achieving a more effective reporting regime and ensuring that members did not unwittingly assist in the financing of terrorism through ignorance. See Submissions by the New Zealand Bankers' Association to the Foreign Affairs, Defence and Trade Committee on the Terrorism <Bombings and Finance> Suppression Bill, TERRO/133, Parliamentary Library, para 2.2. By way of compromise, the Act contains a provision whereby the Prime Minister can direct that notice of designations be made to any persons or bodies that the Prime Minster thinks fit (see section 28(2)). No such directions have yet been made.

[50]On that point, a high-level official within the New Zealand Ministry of Foreign Affairs and Trade advised the author of their view that New Zealand could, for that very reason, find itself receiving harsh criticism from the Organisation for Economic Co-operation & Development (OECD) Financial Action Task Force (which is in the process of consulting with member States on the suppression of terrorist financing).

[51]Note that section 43(2) does not require a lawyer to disclose any "privileged communication" (although the term is restricted somewhat by statutory definition in section 45). For a more detailed examination of the reporting provisions of the Terrorism Suppression Act, see Conte (2003).

through which Resolution 1373 was implemented.[52] Section 70 of the Terrorism Suppression Act was the result, requiring a select committee to consider the operation of those provisions and whether they should be retained or amended (section 70 (2)). The review was to take place as soon as practicable after 1 December 2004, with the committee required to report to the House by no later than 1 December 2005 (section 70(2) and (3)). Due again to the timing of elections and the consequent uncertainty as to membership in the Foreign Affairs, Defence and Trade Committee, the Committee was unable to undertake a comprehensive review of the Act, the Committee recording in the opening section of its report that:[53]

> ...We have had limited opportunity to consider the evidence and advice that has been received on the review.
> ...We have not made specific recommendations on how the legislation might be amended. In the time available to us we have focussed on recording those issues that we consider warrant further scrutiny.

This is a most unfortunate result and undermines the integrity of legislative review mechanisms such as this. The intention of review mechanisms is to allow Parliamentary committees, made up of elected representatives, to review the operation of legislation based on public submissions and advice from relevant government departments. What instead happened was that the Committee was forced to speedily consider issues and note them within just eight substantive pages, without proper debate and commentary. Albeit that the Committee had an opportunity to examine the issues again in its consideration of the Terrorism Suppression Amendment Bill 2007, the reality is that the amendments under that Bill had been drawn up entirely by government officials without input from the Committee, whereas a proper review process would have seen the opposite occur. Rather than leaving the Committee with the limited time it was given, section 70 of the Act should instead have been amended to allow the Committee to undertake a proper review of the legislation.

Of interest, section 70 does not identify which provisions of the Terrorism Suppression Act are "provisions of this Act that are to implement New Zealand's obligations under the Anti-terrorism Resolution" (section 70(1)). This can, however, be gleaned through close examination of New Zealand's reports to the Counter-Terrorism Committee in which New Zealand has had to report on how it has given effect to the provisions of resolutions 1373 (2001):

- Offences created under sections 8, 9, 10, 12, 13, 13A, 13B, 13C and 13D;
- The definition of the term "terrorist act", through the combination of sections 4 (1) and 5;
- The authority of the Prime Minister under section 11 to allow financial or related services to be provided to terrorist entities;

---

[52]See the Committee's Interim Report (n 23) 16.

[53]Foreign Affairs, Defence and Trade Select Committee, Review of the Terrorism Suppression Act 2002 (48th Parliament, November 2005), p. 1.

- The designation process under sections 20–42 inclusive;
- The financial reporting obligations under sections 43–47; and
- The terrorist property forfeiture provisions within sections 55–61 inclusive.

New Zealand's first report to the Counter-Terrorism Committee identifies compliance with paragraph 2(b) of resolution 1373 as being achieved through legislation other than the Terrorism Suppression Act. This was achieved through amendments to the Crimes Act 1961 and Summary Proceedings Act 1957 (under the Counter-Terrorism Bill 2003), which created the authority to obtain interception warrants, warrants to attach tracking devices to persons or things, deterrence through more severe penalties, and requiring a computer owner or user to provide information to access data subject to security codes and the like. Under section 70 of the Terrorism Suppression Act, however, those provisions would not have been the subject of review, since section 70 only required the review of "provisions *of this Act* [the Terrorism Suppression Act] that are to implement New Zealand's obligations under the Anti-Terrorism Resolution" [emphasis added].

7.1.5 Counter-Terrorism Bill 2003

As for the Terrorism Suppression Act 2002, the Counter-Terrorism Bill 2003 was also a multi-purpose piece of legislation: primarily enacted to allow New Zealand to become party to the Plastic Explosives and Nuclear Materials Conventions;[54] to implement the remaining obligations under Security Council resolution 1373 (2001);[55] and to establish supplementary powers and investigative measures "designed to combat terrorism and address problems encountered by agencies in the investigation and enforcement of [terrorism-related] offences".[56]

It is notable that the Bill was subject to scrutiny by the New Zealand Crown Law Office, inherent in the execution of the Attorney-General's function under section 7 of the Bill of Rights Act. Again, the Attorney-General was advised that there appeared to be no inconsistency between the Bill and the NZ Bill of Rights Act.[57] It should also be noted that this item of legislation does not exist as an Act of Parliament with its own life. As introduced, the Bill was to become a stand-alone

---

[54]See the Foreign Affairs, Defence and Trade Committee, Report on the Counter-Terrorism Bill, A Government Bill, 27-2, Commentary, presented to the House 8 August 2003, p. 1.

[55]Ibid.

[56]Foreign Affairs, Defence and Trade Committee, Counter-Terrorism Bill, A Government Bill, 27-1, Explanatory Note, presented to the House 2 April 2003, p. 1. See also the report of the Foreign Affairs, Defence and Trade Committee (n 54) p. 2; and Gobbi (2004, pp. 265–266).

[57]Letter from Crown Counsel to the Attorney General, "re: Counter-Terrorism Bill PCO 4663/14 Our Ref: ATT114/1124 (15)", 10 December 2002.

Act. Following submissions during the select committee process, however, its provisions were instead incorporated into other extant legislation, namely:

- The Crimes Act 1961, under Part 1 of the Counter-Terrorism Bill;
- The Terrorism Suppression Act 2002, including consequential amendments to the Mutual Assistance in Criminal Matters Act 1992, under Part 2 of the Counter-Terrorism Bill; and
- The Misuse of Drugs Amendments Act 1978, the New Zealand Security Intelligence Service Act 1969, the Sentencing Act 2002, and the Summary Proceedings Act 1957, under Part 3 of the Counter-Terrorism Bill.

7.1.5.1 Treaty Implementation

Within the scope of the Bill's first objective, to allow treaty accession, National Interest Analyses were presented to the House on 22 February 2002 with the accompanying reports of the Foreign Affairs, Defence and Trade Committee. The Analyses noted that implementing legislation would need to create new criminal offences prohibiting the movement or use of unmarked plastic explosives and nuclear materials.[58] The Counter-Terrorism Bill achieved this through introduction into the Terrorism Suppression Act of sections 13B (use and movement of plastic explosives), 13C (physical protection of nuclear material) and 13D (importation and acquisition of radioactive material) of that Act (see above).[59]

The National Interest Analyses also considered the question of reporting, registration and monitoring obligations under the relevant treaties. It was noted that the transport safety standards within the Nuclear Materials Convention would not require implementation, since New Zealand had already incorporated International Atomic Energy Agency regulations, which contain more stringent requirements than those under the Nuclear Materials Convention.[60] The Analysis on the Plastic Explosives Convention reported:[61]

> A reporting and registration regime needs to be put in place adequately to control the existing stock of unmarked plastic explosives in New Zealand. This administrative function is already carried out in relation to other explosives under the Hazardous Substances and New Organisms Act 1996. Slight modifications to the operational procedures under that

---

[58]New Zealand Ministry of Foreign Affairs and Trade, National Interest Analysis, Convention on the Marking of Plastic Explosives for the Purpose of Detection, para 13, and National Interest Analysis, Convention on the Physical Protection of Nuclear Materials, para 21.

[59]Note that the unlawful possession of nuclear material and nuclear explosive devices was already prohibited under New Zealand law under the Hazardous Substances and New Zealand Organisms Act 1996 and the New Zealand Nuclear Free Zone, Disarmament, and Arms Control Act 1987.

[60]New Zealand Ministry of Foreign Affairs and Trade, National Interest Analysis, Convention on the Physical Protection of Nuclear Materials, para 20. Incorporation was effected through the Radiation Protection Act 1965.

[61]New Zealand Ministry of Foreign Affairs and Trade, National Interest Analysis, Convention on the Marking of Plastic Explosives for the Purpose of Detection, para 14.

Act would be required to facilitate plastic explosives of the type covered by the Convention being captured by the tracking and reporting mechanisms of the HSNO Act.

The Counter-Terrorism Bill did not, however, address this issue. To that extent, the plastic explosives reporting and registration regime has not been fully implemented into New Zealand law.

7.1.5.2 Resolution 1373 Obligations and Investigative/Supplementary Powers

The Explanatory Notes to the Counter-Terrorism Bill identify two further objectives of implementing the remaining obligations under Security Council resolution 1373 (2001) and establishing investigative powers to assist in the detection of terrorists, terrorist acts and terrorist entities. Within New Zealand's reports to the Counter-Terrorism Committee, New Zealand similarly identified the various new investigative powers as furthering New Zealand's compliance with resolution 1373. The following provisions of the Counter-Terrorism Bill are relevant in this regard:

- Clauses 4, 5, 33 and 34 (pertaining to interception warrants, tracking devices and computer access – each discussed further below) were identified by New Zealand as adding to its compliance with paragraph 2(b) of the resolution;
- Creation of the offence of harbouring or concealing terrorists under clause 12 of the Bill was said to add to New Zealand's compliance with resolution 1373, paragraph 2(d); and
- Sentencing directions under clauses 30 and 31 (discussed below) were said to be in furtherance of the requirements of paragraph 2(e) of resolution 1373.

7.1.5.3 Offences, and Supplementary Powers, Under the Counter-Terrorism Bill

Reflecting the second and third stated purposes of the Counter-Terrorism Bill (to further implement resolution 1373 (2001) and to establish supplementary powers and investigative measures), Parts 1 and 3 of the Bill amended various items of legislation to achieve six main things (as these pertain to terrorism-related offences, see Appendix 3, Table 4(F)):

- First, new terrorism-related offences were created under the Crimes Act 1961. New sections 298A, 298B and 307A make it an offence to cause disease or sickness in animals; contaminate food, crops, water or other products; or make threats of harm to people or property to achieve terrorist ends.[62] These offences are considered further in Chap. 14 (see Sect. 14.2.3.2). Associated provisions

---

[62]Clauses 6 and 7 of the Counter-Terrorism Bill 2003.

provide extraterritorial jurisdiction over these offences and restrict the ability to prosecute by requiring the consent of the Attorney-General.[63]

- The second feature of Parts 1 and 3 was to extend the ability of police to obtain warrants to intercept private communications relating to terrorist offences, by amending section 312 of the Crimes Act 1961 and section 26 of the Misuse of Drugs Act 1978.[64]

- Next, a new section 198B was inserted into the Summary Proceedings Act 1957, allowing police to demand assistance to access computer data by providing police with any data protection codes necessary to effect access to that data.[65] This is also considered in Chap. 15 (see Sect. 15.1).

- Fourth, the Summary Proceedings Act was further amended to authorise police or customs officers to obtain a warrant to attach a tracking device to any property or person where it is suspected that an offence has been, is being, or will be committed. The power, and restrictions thereon, was enacted through new sections 200A to 200O of the Summary Proceedings Act.[66] Notably, the suspected offence need not be limited to terrorism-related offences.[67] This is considered in Chap. 15 (see Sect. 15.2).

- The fifth feature involved a minor amendment of the New Zealand Security Intelligence Service Act 1969, but with major potential effect.[68] The amendment concerns the definition of the term "security" within the Act. Terrorism was already a matter within the ambit of the Act, but not in as wide terms as it is now. Prior to the Counter-Terrorism Bill, "security" included the protection of New Zealand from acts of terrorism.[69] The term now includes "the prevention of any terrorist act and of any activity relating to the carrying out or facilitating of any terrorist act".[70] Interception and seizure warrants may be authorised for the purpose of detecting activities prejudicial to "security" or for the purpose of gathering foreign intelligence information essential to "security".[71] The impact of these types of amendments on the blurring between intelligence-gathering on the one hand and criminal investigations on the other is considered in Chap. 15 (see Sect. 15.5).

- Finally, the Sentencing Act 2002 was amended so that offending that forms part of, or involves, a terrorist act is to be treated as an aggravating feature under

---

[63]Clauses 4 and 5 of the Counter-Terrorism Bill 2003.

[64]Clauses 7B, 8 and 26 of the Counter-Terrorism Bill 2003.

[65]Clause 33 of the Counter-Terrorism Bill 2003.

[66]Amendments effected under clause 34 of the Counter-Terrorism Bill 2003.

[67]See section 200B(2) of the Summary Proceedings Act 1957.

[68]Clause 27 of the Counter-Terrorism Bill 2003.

[69]This was a matter included within the definition from 16 November 1977 through section 2(2)(b) of the New Zealand Security Intelligence Service Amendment Act 1977.

[70]Section 2 of the New Zealand Security Intelligence Service Act 1969.

[71]Section 4 of the New Zealand Security Intelligence Service Act 1969.

section 9 of that Act.[72] Where murder is committed as part of a terrorist act, section 104 of the Sentencing Act has been amended to provide for a minimum period of 17 years imprisonment for such offending.[73] The question of sentencing for terrorism offences is considered in Chap. 14 (see Sect. 14.2.4).

7.2 Implementation by New Zealand of Security Council Decisions

Three principal resolutions govern the action required by, or recommended to, members of the United Nations, namely: Security Council resolution 1267 (1999), imposing a travel ban and arms embargo against the Taliban and Al-Qa'ida, and an obligation to freeze funds and other financial resources controlled by or on their behalf of the Taliban or any other individuals of entities designated by the Committee; resolution 1373 (2001), which imposed various obligations upon States, and recommended further action; and Security Council resolution 1624 (2005), which called on States to adopt measures to prohibit and prevent the incitement to commit terrorist acts (on the resolutions of the Security Council identified below, see Chap. 3, Sect. 3.2.2).[74] These resolutions have been implemented by New Zealand (on the implementation of Security Council resolutions by New Zealand, see Chap. 3, Sect. 3.2.3) through the Terrorism Suppression Act 2002 and the Counter-Terrorism Bill 2003 (Sects. 7.1.4 and 7.1.5 above) and two sets of statutory regulations. The first relates to the travel ban and arms embargo against the Taliban and Al-Qa'ida under Security Council resolution 1267 (1999).[75] The second relates to the temporary measures adopted in response to Security Council resolution 1373 (2001).[76]

7.2.1 United Nations Sanctions (Al-Qaida and Taliban) Regulations 2007

The requirements imposed on New Zealand as a member of the United Nations, under Security Council resolution 1267 (2001), had been implemented by

---

[72]Clause 30 of the Counter-Terrorism Bill 2003.

[73]Clause 31 of the Counter-Terrorism Bill 2003.

[74]SC Res 1267, UN SCOR, 4051st Mtg, UN Doc S/Res/1267 (1999); SC Res 1373 (n 20); and SC Res 1624, UN SCOR, 5261st Mtg, UN Doc S/Res/1624 (2005).

[75]SC Res 1267, UN SCOR, 4051st Mtg, UN Doc S/Res/1267 (1999).

[76]SC Res 1373 (n 20).

New Zealand by the United Nations Sanctions (Afghanistan) Regulations 2001.[77] Regulation 12A prohibited the entry into NZ of persons designated by the 1267 Committee (see Chap. 3, Sect. 3.2.4.2), except in accordance with the exception in paragraph 2(b) of Security Council resolution 1390 (2002).[78] Regulations 7–12 implemented the arms embargo. The 2001 regulations were updated under and replaced by the United Nations Sanctions (Al-Qaida and Taliban) Regulations 2007. Failure to comply with the 2007 Regulations renders a person liable to imprisonment of up to 12 months or a fine not exceeding $10,000 NZD or, in the case of a company or other corporation, to a fine not exceeding $100,000 NZD (see Appendix 3, Table 4(G)).

7.2.2   United Nations Sanctions (Terrorism Suppression and Afghanistan Measures) Regulations 2001 and Amending Regulations

The obligations imposed by the Security Council upon New Zealand under its resolution 1373 (2001) were, by way of interim measure, incorporated into domestic law under the United Nations Sanctions (Terrorism Suppression and Afghanistan Measures) Regulations 2001 and Amending Regulations of 2002 – the Terrorism Regulations. The Terrorism Regulations were made pursuant to the empowering provision of the United Nations Act 1946, that enactment established to permit the New Zealand Government to implement directions of the Security Council by a domestic Order in Council.

The Terrorism Regulations did four things.[79] First, they prohibited certain conduct relating to the financing of terrorist activities: the provision of funds to specified entities, the dealing with property of such entities and the making of services and property available to entities (Regulations 6, 7 and 9). The Regulations also imposed duties upon any person in possession or control of property suspected to be owned or controlled by a specified entity to report this to the police (Regulation 8). Regulation 8(2) excluded, from application of this duty, any "privileged communication" with a lawyer, as defined under the Financial Transactions Reporting Act 1996.

Third, the Regulations prohibited the recruitment of any person as a member of a specified entity, or the participation by any person in such an entity (Regulations 11 and 12). Finally, the Regulations identified Al-Qa'ida, the Taliban and Usama bin Laden as "specified entities" under the Regulations.[80] On the operation of the

---

[77]See New Zealand's 2003 report to the United Nations 1267 Committee (n 42), paras 15–23.

[78]SC Res 1390, UN SCOR, 4452nd Mtg, UN Doc S/Res/1390 (2002).

[79]Gobbi (2004).

[80]Regulation 4(1) and 5 and the Schedule to the United Nations Sanctions (Terrorism Suppression and Afghanistan Measures) Regulations 2001, and Regulation 3 of the United Nations Sanctions (Afghanistan) Amendment Regulations 2001.

Security Council's Al-Qa'ida and Taliban Sanctions Committee, see Sect. 4.2.4. The prohibitions potentially impact upon the freedom of association, discussed within Chap. 19 (Sect. 19.3.1).

7.3 International Terrorism (Emergency Powers) Act 1987

The International Terrorism (Emergency Powers) Act 1987 is an Act adopted by New Zealand in reaction to the Rainbow Warrior bombing of 10 July 1985 (Chap. 4, Sect. 4.1.2.2), rather than in response to international counter-terrorist obligations. In the Parliamentary debates concerning the Bill, the then Minister of Justice Geoffrey Palmer said:[81]

> Sadly, it can no longer be assumed that New Zealand will remain immune from acts of international terrorism.

7.3.1 Declaration of a State of Emergency

The Act establishes emergency powers, which can be authorised by a meeting of at least three Ministers of the Crown if they reasonably believe (based on advice to the Prime Minister from the Commissioner of Police) that an international terrorist emergency is occurring and that the exercise of emergency powers is necessary to deal with that emergency (sections 5 and 6). This authority must be given by way of a notice in writing (within the terms specified under section 6(3)) and tabled before the House of Representatives with reasons for giving the notice (section 7).[82] The House then has the authority to either revoke the notice or, if necessary, to extend it at any time and for any reason (sections 7(2) and 8). The emergency authority otherwise remains valid for 7 days, unless extended by a resolution of Parliament under section 7(2) of the Act – each resolution only enabling an extension of a maximum of 7 days.

---

[81]New Zealand, New Zealand Parliamentary Debates, No 482, 10115, 30 June 1987. It should be recognised that not all agreed at the time that this was the case and that specific anti-terrorism legislation was necessary: see, for example, New Zealand Human Rights Commission, Report on the International Terrorism (Emergency Powers) Bill 1987.

[82]The notice must be tabled immediately if the House is at that time sitting, or otherwise at the earliest practicable opportunity – section 7(1) of the Act.

7.3.2 Definition of a Terrorist Emergency

An international terrorist emergency is defined under the Act as:

Section 2 Interpretation
"International terrorist emergency" means a situation in which any person is threatening, causing, or attempting to cause—

(a) The death of, or serious injury or serious harm to, any person or persons; or
(b) The destruction of, or serious damage or serious injury to,—
    (i) Any premises, building, erection, structure, installation, or road; or
    (ii) Any aircraft, hovercraft, ship or ferry or other vessel, train, or vehicle; or
    (iii) Any natural feature which is of such beauty, uniqueness, or scientific, economic, or cultural importance that its preservation from destruction, damage or injury is in the national interest; or
    (iv) Any chattel of any kind which is of significant historical, archaeological, scientific, cultural, literary, or artistic value or importance; or
    (v) Any animal—
    in order to coerce, deter, or intimidate—
(c) The Government of New Zealand, or any agency of the Government of New Zealand; or
(d) The Government of any other country, or any agency of the Government of any other country; or
(e) Any body or group of persons, whether inside or outside New Zealand,—
for the purpose of furthering, outside New Zealand, any political aim.

There are two main things to note about this definition. Although it appears to be detailed, it is in fact relatively broad. A wide range of criminal conduct, accompanied by coercive or intimidatory elements, will satisfy the definition and might thereby invoke the powers discussed. The second aspect of the definition to note is the final sentence, which requires that the conduct in question be done for the purpose of furthering any political aim outside New Zealand. In other words, if a bombing (or other criminal act) was committed with the aim of changing the New Zealand Government's policy and/or conduct within New Zealand, this would not give rise to an "international terrorist emergency".

7.3.3 Emergency Powers and Associated Offences

Where an international terrorist emergency is declared, certain emergency powers are vested in the police under section 10 of the Act, also exercisable by members of the armed forces acting as an aid to the civil power and where requested to act by a member of the police (section 12). Subsections (2) and (3) of section 10 set out these powers as follows:

(2) Subject to this Act, any member of the Police may, for the purpose of dealing with any emergency to which this section applies, or of preserving life or property threatened by that emergency—

(a) Require the evacuation of any premises or place (including any public place), or the exclusion of persons or vehicles from any premises or place (including any public place), within the area in which the emergency is occurring:

(b) Enter, and if necessary break into, any premises or place, or any aircraft, hovercraft, ship or ferry or other vessel, train, or vehicle, within the area in which the emergency is occurring:

(c) Totally or partially prohibit or restrict public access, with or without vehicles, on any road or public place within the area in which the emergency is occurring:

(d) Remove from any road or public place within the area in which the emergency is occurring any aircraft, hovercraft, ship or ferry or other vessel, train, or vehicle impeding measures to deal with that emergency; and, where reasonably necessary for that purpose, may use force or may break into any such aircraft, hovercraft, ship or ferry or other vessel, train, or vehicle:

(e) Destroy any property which is within the area in which the emergency is occurring and which that member of the Police believes, on reasonable grounds, constitutes a danger to any person:

(f) Require the owner or person for the time being in control of any land, building, vehicle, boat, apparatus, implement, or equipment (in this paragraph referred to as requisitioned property) that is within the area in which the emergency is occurring forthwith to place that requisitioned property under the direction and control of that member of the Police, or of any other member of the Police:

(g) Totally or partially prohibit or restrict land, air, or water traffic within the area in which the emergency is occurring.

(3) Notwithstanding anything in any other Act, but subject to this Act, any member of the Police may, for the purpose of preserving life threatened by any emergency to which this section applies—

(a) Connect any additional apparatus to, or otherwise interfere with the operation of, any part of the telecommunications system; and

(b) Intercept private communications—

in the area in which the emergency is occurring.

The power of interception under section 12(3) is exercisable by police only (see section 10(4)). The Act also provides an emergency power to requisition any property, with compensation later payable to the owner of the property (sections 11 and 13).

Most controversial is section 14 of the Act which allows the Prime Minister to restrict or prohibit the publication or broadcasting of the identity (or any information capable of identifying) of any person involved in dealing with an international terrorist emergency, as well as restricting or prohibiting information about any piece of equipment used to deal with the emergency that could prejudice measures used to resolve an international terrorist emergency. These powers are capable of being used for a ban on all media for up to 21 days. Criticisms that the censorship provisions amounted to an unjustified encroachment on the right to freedom of expression[83] led the New Zealand Law Commission to recommend that the Act be

---

[83]Discussed in the report of the Advisory Council of Jurists, *Reference on the Rule of Law in Combating Terrorism*, Final Report to the Asia Pacific Forum of National Human Rights Institutions, May 2004, p. 116.

repealed.[84] The Act remains in force without amendment. This feature of the Act is examined in Chap. 20, concerning counter-terrorism and media control.

The Act creates offences for failure to comply with directions issued by police or military under the powers under section 10, or for breach of a section 14 media gag (see section 21(1)(a) and (b), qualified by the defences under subsection (4)).

7.4 Other Legislation

As already indicated, there are numerous other pieces of legislation that add, to greater or lesser extents, to the body of what might be described as New Zealand's terrorism-related legislation. When referring to the Maritime Security Bill,[85] by way of example, Customs Minister Rick Barker said:[86]

[This] is part of a whole-of-government approach toward strengthening New Zealand's national security in the post-September 11 environment.

While such legislation does indeed act to strengthen national security and impacts upon counter-terrorism, this chapter has restricted itself to consideration of the legislation identified. Those enactments and regulations are specifically targeted to New Zealand's compliance with international anti-terrorism obligations and counter-terrorism within New Zealand.

It should be noted that New Zealand's Ministry of Justice has been tasked with restructuring the legal regime on anti-money laundering and countering the financing of terrorism, driven principally in response to its obligations as a member of the Financial Action Task Force (see Chap. 3, Sect. 3.4.1). The Ministry released a draft Anti-Money Laundering and Countering Financing of Terrorism Bill for public consultation at the end of 2008, with the aim of formally introducing the Bill to parliament in April 2009.[87] The Bill reflects the following Cabinet decisions on the new regulatory framework:[88]

- To implement the new framework over two phases: the first extending to financial institutions and casinos; the second to certain categories of non-financial businesses and professions;
- To be supervised by existing agencies, being those with responsibilities for the sectors concerned;

---

[84]New Zealand Law Commission, *Final Report on Emergencies*, NZLC Report 22 (Wellington, 1991), section 7.139.

[85]Now the Maritime Security Act 2004, assented to on 5 April 2004.

[86]New Zealand Government Press Release, 'Minister of Customs introduces Border Security Bill', 18 June 2003. On New Zealand's 'whole of government' approach to countering terrorism, see Higgie (2005).

[87]For the Ministry of Justice's webpage on the topic, see http://www.justice.govt.nz/fatf.

[88]Ibid.

- To include new civil and criminal offences; and
- To include a set of core requirements relating to customer due diligence, reporting, and policies for anti-money laundering and the countering of terrorist financing.

7.5 Summary and Conclusions on New Zealand's Compliance with the International Framework for Countering Terrorism

New Zealand's compliance with international counter-terrorism obligations and recommendations has been subject to reporting to and review by the Security Council Counter-Terrorism Committee (CTC) and the SC Resolution 1267 Al-Qa'ida and Taliban Sanctions Committee (1267 Committee) – on these Committees, see Chap. 3, Sect. 3.2.4.2. New Zealand has submitted one report in 2003 to the 1267 Committee and five reports to the CTC between 2001 and 2006.[89] For the purpose of this chapter, New Zealand's compliance is summarised under the following three heads.

7.5.1 Terrorism-Related Offences

Chapter 14 in this title undertakes an analysis of the criminalisation of terrorism by the four case study countries, including a comparison between the offences required under the universal terrorism-related conventions and Security Council resolutions (Appendix 3, Table 1) and the terrorism-related offences under New Zealand law (Appendix 3, Table 4). Other than in respect of the offence of incitement to terrorism, Chap. 14 concludes that New Zealand's law adequately criminalises all of the conduct listed in Appendix 3, Table 1. In the case of incitement to terrorism, Security Council resolution 1624 (2005) called upon States (i.e. recommended – see Chap. 3, Sect. 3.2.3) to prevent and criminalise incitement to commit a terrorist act or acts.[90] Chapter 14 concludes that New Zealand's law is deficient in this respect in a number of ways (see Sect. 14.3).

---

[89]Report to the 1267 Committee (n 42); first report of 2001 to the Counter-Terrorism Committee (n 21); (second report to the CTC) Supplementary report providing additional information on the measures taken by New Zealand to implement the provisions of Security Council resolution 1373 (2001), UN Doc S/2002/795 (2002); (third report to the CTC) New Zealand Response to the Questions and Comments of the Security Council Counter-Terrorism Committee Contained in the Chairman's Letter of 30 May 2003, UN Doc S/2003/860 (2003); (fourth report to the CTC) New Zealand Response to the United Nations Security Council Counter-Terrorism Committee: Questions for Response by 30 April 2004, UN Doc S/2004/359 (2004); and (fifth report to the CTC) New Zealand National Report to the United Nations Security Council Counter-Terrorism Committee, UN Doc S/2006/384 (2006).

[90]SC Res 1624, UN SCOR, 5261st Mtg, UN Doc S/Res/1624 (2005), para 1(a).

7.5.2 Treaty Action and Implementation

At the time of the September 11 attacks and adoption of Security Council resolution 1373 (2001), New Zealand was a party to eight of the universal terrorism-related conventions. Those conventions had been implemented under the Aviation Crimes Act 1972 (Sect. 7.1.1 above), the Crimes (Internationally Protected Persons, United Nations and Associated personnel, and Hostages) Act 1980 (Sect. 7.1.2 above) and the Maritime Crimes Act 1999 (Sect. 7.1.3 above). Since resolution 1373 (2001):

- New Zealand acceded to the Bombing Convention and ratified the Financing Convention on 4 November 2002. The conventions were incorporated under the Terrorism Suppression Act 2002 (Sect. 7.1.4 above).
- New Zealand acceded to the Nuclear Material and Plastic Explosives conventions on 19 December 2003, which were incorporated in part under the Terrorism Suppression Act through amendments to the Act introduced under the Counter-Terrorism Bill 2003 (Sects. 7.1.4 and 7.1.5 above). It might be noted that the National Interest Analyses accompanying this treaty action recorded that New Zealand neither manufactures explosives domestically, nor engages in the transportation of nuclear material (see Chap. 4, Sect. 4.2.2.2 concerning the function of National Interest Analyses).[91] Notwithstanding this, the Analyses noted the change in the post-September 11 international context and the call by the Security Council for UN members to become party to all anti-terrorism conventions[92] as sound bases for New Zealand becoming a party to the conventions.[93]

  The National Interest Analysis pertaining to the Plastic Explosives Convention noted that steps would need to be taken to put in place a reporting and registration regime to control existing stocks of unmarked plastic explosives in New Zealand (see Sect. 7.1.5 above).[94] The Counter-Terrorism Bill did not, however, address this issue and the Convention thus remains not fully implemented in New Zealand.

- New Zealand was an original signatory to the Nuclear Terrorism Convention and implemented those obligations, in part, under the Terrorism Suppression Amendment Act 2007. New Zealand has not ratified this most recent of the terrorism-related conventions.[95]

---

[91]New Zealand Ministry of Foreign Affairs and Trade, National Interest Analysis, Convention on the Marking of Plastic Explosives for the Purpose of Detection, para 2, and National Interest Analysis, Convention on the Physical Protection of Nuclear Materials, para 4.

[92]SC Res 1373 (n 20) para 3(d).

[93]New Zealand Ministry of Foreign Affairs and Trade, National Interest Analysis, Convention on the Marking of Plastic Explosives for the Purpose of Detection, para 2, and National Interest Analysis, Convention on the Physical Protection of Nuclear Materials, paras 5 and 7.

[94]Ibid.

[95]As at 1 October 2009.

A large part of the implementation of the universal terrorism-related conventions involves the criminalisation of conduct identified under those treaties.

7.5.3 Implementation of Security Council Resolutions

Consideration has already been given above, at Sect. 7.5.1, to Security Council resolution 1624 (2005), which called upon States to adopt measures to prohibit and prevent the incitement to commit terrorist acts. The travel ban and arms embargo against the Taliban and Al-Qa'ida under resolution 1267 (1999) are implemented by New Zealand under the United Nations Sanctions (Al-Qaida and Taliban) Regulations 2007 (see Sect. 7.2.1 above). Those aspects of the same resolution concerning the freezing of funds and other financial resources controlled by or on their behalf of the Taliban or any other individuals of entities designated by the Committee are linked to paragraphs 1(c) and (d) of Security Council resolution 1373 (2001), which are identified below. Security Council resolution 1373 (2001) contains 11 binding directions under paragraphs 1 and 2 of the resolution (see Chap. 3, Sect. 3.2.2.3), which have been implemented by New Zealand as follows:

1. Prevention and suppression of the financing of terrorist acts (para 1(a))
   Paragraph 1(a), which requires the prevention and suppression of the financing of terrorist acts, is a general provision, expanded upon by the subparagraphs that follow it. In addition to those more specific requirements, New Zealand identified the fact that the Reserve Bank of New Zealand took steps to notify financial institutions of these requirements and prohibitions.[96] Funding for security and counter-terrorism was also boosted, with the Minister for Foreign Affairs and Trade identifying the post-September 11 environment as requiring this.[97]

2. Criminalising the provision of funds for terrorist acts (para 1(b))
   In compliance with this provision of resolution 1373 (2001), the Terrorism Suppression Act 2002 created the offence of the financing of terrorism (see Sect. 7.1.4.3 above and Appendix 3, Table 4(E)).

3. Freezing of funds and assets of terrorist entities (para 1(c))
   The freezing of terrorist assets is given effect through various provisions of the Terrorism Suppression Act.[98] The Act provides for the designation of terrorist entities and prohibits under section 9 any dealing with terrorist property (see Sect. 7.1.4.3 above and Appendix 3, Table 4(E)). Obligations are imposed on financial institutions to report suspicions of the holding or control of property

---

[96]See New Zealand's first report to the Counter-Terrorism Committee (n 21) p. 6.

[97]The Budget 2003 provided an additional $5.9 million for 2004 and $1.9 million in future years: Hon Phil Goff, 'Funding boost for security, counter-terrorism and emergency responses', Beehive Press Release 12 May 2003, online: http://www.behive.govt.nz/PrintDocumentcfm?DocumentID=16723 (as accessed on 17 May 2003 – copy on file with author).

[98]See New Zealand's first report to the Counter-Terrorism Committee (n 21) pp. 7–9.

belonging to or controlled by designated entities. Sections 55–61 of the Act establish procedures through which terrorist assets can be forfeited.

4. Prohibiting the provision of financial or related services to terrorist entities (para 1(d))

Responding to paragraph 1(d) of the resolution, section 10 of the Terrorism Suppression Act makes it unlawful to make property, or financial or related services available to designated terrorist entities (see Sect. 7.1.4.3 above and Appendix 3, Table 4(E)).

5. Suppression of support to terrorists and elimination of the supply of weapons (para 2(a))

In compliance with paragraph 2(a) of resolution 1373 (2001), the Terrorism Suppression Act prohibits the recruitment of persons into terrorist groups (section 12) and participation in terrorist groups (section 13) – see Sect. 7.1.4.3 above and Appendix 3, Table 4(E). New Zealand has reported that existing law would see New Zealand comply with the requirement to work towards the elimination of the supply of weapons to terrorists, pointing to the Customs Prohibition Order 1996,[99] the Arms Act 1983, the Crimes Act 1961 (prohibiting the unlawful possession of an offensive weapon), the New Zealand Nuclear Weapons Free Zone, Disarmament and Arms Control Act 1987, and the Chemical Weapons (Prohibition) Act 1966.[100] Relevant to this part of resolution 1373 (2001), New Zealand has become party to the Plastic Explosives and Nuclear Material Conventions. In its first report to the CTC in 2002, New Zealand also indicated that it intended to ratify the Firearms Protocol to the United Nations Convention against Transnational Organized Crime, although it has not yet done so.[101]

6. Preventing the commission of terrorist acts (para 2(b))

As discussed in Chap. 3, measuring a State's compliance with this direction is technically impossible, since all that can be done by a State is to undertake *all reasonable and practical steps* to prevent the commission of terrorist acts (see Sect. 3.2.2.3).

Additional to the measures in response to items 1–5 above, New Zealand identified the investigative and supplementary powers introduced under the Counter-Terrorism Bill 2003, i.e. the authority to obtain interception warrants, warrants to attach tracking devices to persons or things, deterrence through more severe penalties, and requiring a computer owner or user to provide the information required for accessing any data which is subject to security codes and the like (see Chap. 15, Sect. 15.1).

---

[99] Made under the Customs and Excise Act 1996.

[100] See New Zealand's second report to the Counter-Terrorism Committee (n 89) p. 6.

[101] Protocol against the Illicit Manufacturing of and Trafficking in Firearms, Their Parts and Components and Ammunition, supplementing the United Nations Convention against Transnational Organized Crime, opened for signature 2 July 2001, UN Doc A/55/383/Add.2 (entered into force 3 July 2005). See New Zealand's first report to the Counter-Terrorism Committee (n 21) p. 11. See also New Zealand's report to the United Nations 1267 Committee (n 42) pp. 8–9.

7. Denial of safe haven (para 2(c))

   Sections 7, 73 and 75 of the Immigration Act 1987 (already extant at the time of the adoption of resolution 1373) have been identified by New Zealand as satisfying the requirement to deny safe haven to terrorists.[102]

8. Preventing the use of State territory by terrorists (para 2(d))

   The extraterritorial nature of the offences created under the Terrorism Suppression Act, together with extant party liability provisions under the Crimes Act 1961, were identified as further measures to prevent terrorists acting from New Zealand territory against citizens of other States.[103] New Zealand also relied upon the creation by it of offences of harbouring or concealing terrorists under the Terrorism Suppression Act (see Sect. 7.1.4.3 above and Appendix 3, Table 4(E)).

9. Ensuring the prosecution and severe punishment of terrorists (para 2(e))

   As identified earlier in this chapter, the various offences created under the Terrorism Suppression Act carry severe penalties (see Sect. 7.1.4.3 above).[104] Furthermore, the Counter-Terrorism Bill 2003 amended the Sentencing Act 2002 so that offending that forms part of, or involves, a terrorist act is to be treated as an aggravating feature in the sentencing of a convicted person.

10. Assisting in criminal investigations and prosecutions (para 2(f))

    New Zealand has reported that current law permits New Zealand to comply with paragraph 2(f) of resolution 1373 (2001), referring to the Mutual Assistance in Criminal Matters Act 1992 and the Extradition Act 1999.[105]

11. Establishing and maintaining effective border controls to prevent the movement of terrorists (para 2(g))

    The Passports Act 1992 and Immigration Act 1987 have been identified by New Zealand as means through which compliance with paragraph 2(g) of the resolution can be achieved.[106] Measures to prevent the transboundary movement of terrorists are considered in Chap. 21.

References

Conte, Alex. 2003. New Challenges for Financial Regulation: The Suppression of the Financing of Terrorism. In Hawes, Cynthia, and Rowe, David (Eds). *Essays in Commercial Law. A New Zealand Collection*. Christchurch: Centre for Commercial & Corporate Law Inc.

Dunworth, Treasa. 2002. Public International Law. *New Zealand Law Review* 255.

Gobbi, Mark. 2004. Treaty Action and Implementation. *New Zealand Yearbook of International Law* 277.

---

[102]See New Zealand's first report to the Counter-Terrorism Committee (n 21) pp. 11–12.

[103]Ibid, p. 12.

[104]Ibid, pp. 13–14.

[105]Ibid, p. 14.

[106]Ibid, pp. 14–15.

Higgie, Dell. 2005. A Whole-of-Government Approach and New Zealand's Contribution to Combating International Terrorism. In Veitch, James (Ed). *International Terrorism. New Zealand Perspectives*. Wellington: Victoria University of Wellington Institute of Policy Studies.

Smith, John. 2003. *New Zealand's Anti-Terrorism Campaign: Balancing Civil Liberties, National Security, and International Responsibilities*. Wellington: Report on the Ian Axford New Zealand Fellowship in Public Policy.

Chapter 8
Counter-Terrorism Law in the United Kingdom

This chapter contains the last country-specific overview of counter-terrorism law, focussing in this case on the law in the United Kingdom. Of the four case study countries, the United Kingdom has had the longest history of dealing with terrorism. Unlike many jurisdictions, where no serious attention was paid to combating terrorism until the events of 9/11, Walker reminds us that "the United Kingdom has regularly experienced and legally responded to terrorism during three centuries or more".[1] Until the latter part of the twentieth century, responses were through use of the ordinary criminal law including, for example, the Explosive Substances Act 1883 (which continues to form part of the UK's legislative package on counter-terrorism).[2] Walker speaks of three phases of legislative action by the United Kingdom in responding to terrorism. The first reflects experiences of terrorist conduct in colonial conflicts, including during the British Mandate over Palestine for example.[3] The second responded to the campaigns of the Irish Republicans and their Loyalist opponents, reaching back to the military conquest of Ireland by England in 1168.[4] The third phase emerged in response to the international community's attention to transnational/international terrorism.[5] In the latter regard, the United Kingdom adopted in 2003 and most recently updated in 2009 what the Home Office describes as a comprehensive strategy to counter the threat to the UK, and to its interests overseas, from international terrorism, known as "CONTEST".[6]

---

[1]Walker (2007, p. 181). See also Trivizas and Smith (1997).

[2]Brandon (2004).

[3]See the Defence (Emergency) Regulations 1945, which remain in force in Israel today.

[4]See Schabas and Olivier (2003, p. 211), where he explains that, following the conquest of Ireland in 1168, the independent Republic of Ireland was established in 1922, but that six counties (known now as Northern Ireland) remained attached to the United Kingdom.

[5]See, for example, the report of the House of Commons Foreign Affairs Committee, Foreign Policy Aspects of the War Against Terrorism, Fourth Report of Session 2005–2006, p. 3.

[6]HM Government, Pursue Prevent Protect Prepare, The United Kingdom's Strategy for Countering International Terrorism, Cm 7547 (March 2009).

A. Conte, *Human Rights in the Prevention and Punishment of Terrorism*,
DOI 10.1007/978-3-642-11608-7_8, © Springer-Verlag Berlin Heidelberg 2010

Until relatively recent years, Britain's legislative responses to acts or threats of terrorism have been by way of temporary and fragmented measures.[7] In 1939, for example, the UK Parliament enacted the Prevention of Violence (Temporary Provisions) Act to deal with a campaign of the Irish Republican Army.[8] Although the 1939 legislation was allowed to expire, there followed in Britain a number of laws responding to escalating violence in Northern Ireland, including the Northern Ireland (Emergency Provisions) Acts 1973–1998,[9] the Criminal Justice (Terrorism and Conspiracy) Act 1998, and the Prevention of Terrorism (Temporary Provisions) Acts which were in continuous use between 1974 and 2001.[10]

The counter-terrorism laws of the United Kingdom were reviewed by a judicial inquiry under Lord Lloyd and Sir Michael Kerr that reported in 1996, and eventually resulted in the enactment of the Terrorism Act 2000.[11] Rather than treating terrorism laws as temporary responses to particular situations, the Terrorism Act of 2000 has been described as an important turning point in the UK's legislative framework on counter-terrorism, representing a more unified and permanent approach and reacting also to the paramilitary ceasefires in Northern Ireland.[12] Despite this more streamlined approach, there are still several items of legislation making up the United Kingdom's counter-terrorism legal framework. Described as one of the most draconian in Western democracies,[13] this legislative package comprises the: Explosive Substances Act 1883; Biological Weapons Act 1974; Internationally Protected Persons Act 1978; Chemical Weapons Act 1996; Civil Aviation Act 1982; Aviation Security Act 1982; Taking of Hostages Act 1982; Nuclear Material (Offences) Act 1983; Aircraft and Maritime Security Act 1990; Chemical Weapons Act 1996; Terrorism Act 2000; Anti-Terrorism, Crime and Security Act 2001; Prevention of Terrorism Act 2005; Terrorism Act 2006; and Counter-Terrorism Act 2008.

8.1 Implementation by the United Kingdom of the Universal Terrorism-Related Treaties

The United Kingdom is a party to all of the existing 13 terrorism-related conventions (see Appendix 2, Table 1). It recently ratified the International Convention for the Suppression of Acts of Nuclear Terrorism, and is the only one of the four case

---

[7]Kirby (2005, p. 8).

[8]Walker (2004).

[9]Based largely upon a review of Britain's pre-existing legislation by Lord Diplock in 1972: Report of the Commission to Consider Legal Procedures to Deal with Terrorist Activities in Northern Ireland.

[10]See: Kirby (2005. p. 16) and Walker (1983).

[11]Home Office, Inquiry into the Legislation on Terrorism, Cm, 3420, London 1996.

[12]Walker (2007, pp. 181–182).

[13]Schabas and Olivier (2003, p. 218).

study countries to have done so (as at 1 October 2009).[14] The UK has implemented its obligations under the treaties to which it is party under various items of legislation (as listed in the introduction to this chapter), each of which will be considered in roughly chronological order (on the reception of treaty law in the United Kingdom, see Chap. 4, Sect. 4.2.2).

8.1.1   Legislation to Deal with Terrorist Bombings

The International Convention for the Suppression of Terrorist Bombing (the Bombing Convention) requires States parties to criminalise the unlawful and intentional use of explosives and other lethal devices in, into, or against various public places with intent to kill or cause serious bodily injury, or with intent to cause extensive destruction in a public place.[15] Pre-dating this are three items of legislation in the United Kingdom dealing with different types of explosive and lethal devices which, when combined with the provisions of the Terrorism Act 2000 concerning extraterritorial jurisdiction, contain offences which correspond to those under the Convention.

8.1.1.1   Explosive Substances Act 1883

The Explosive Substances Act 1883 is the oldest enactment relating to the suppression of terrorist acts which remains in force in the United Kingdom.[16] Although the Act predates the Bombing Convention by more than a century, the offences under the Act partly implement the requirements of the Bombing Convention when combined with the extraterritorial jurisdiction over the offences, established under section 62 of the Terrorism Act 2000 (see Sect. 8.1.5.3 below).[17] The following offences are of relevance in this regard (see Appendix 3 herein, Table 5(A)):

- *Causing an explosion likely to endanger life or property* (section 2), making it an offence to unlawfully and maliciously cause an explosion of a nature likely to endanger life or to cause serious injury to property.[18] Conviction on indictment makes a person liable to imprisonment for life.

---

[14]International Convention for the Suppression of Acts of Nuclear Terrorism, adopted by the General Assembly and opened for signature on 15 April 2005 under GA Res 59/290, UN GAOR, 59th Sess, 91st Plen Mtg, UN Doc A/Res/59/290 (2005) and entered into force 7 July 2007.

[15]International Convention for the Suppression of Terrorist Bombing, opened for signature 12 January 1998, 2149 UNTS 286 (entered into force 23 May 2001).

[16]Walker (2002, p. 11).

[17]Walker (2002, p. 177).

[18]Corresponding to article 2(1) of the Bombing Convention (n 15).

- *Attempts and conspiracies* (sections 3 and 5). An attempt to cause explosion, or making or keeping explosive with intent to endanger life or property, is an offence under section 3(1) of the Act, punishable by life imprisonment.[19] An accessory is liable to conviction under section 5, and to the same maximum penalty as a principal offender.

8.1.1.2   Biological Weapons Act 1974

Section 1 of the Biological Weapons Act 1974 prohibits the development, production, stockpiling, acquisition, retention or transfer of biological weapons (see Appendix. 3, Table 5(B)). Conviction under section 1 renders a person liable to life imprisonment. Together with the jurisdictional provision in section 62 of the Terrorism Act 2000 (see Sect. 8.1.5.3 below), this corresponds to the party offences under article 2(3) of the Bombing Convention.

8.1.1.3   Chemical Weapons Act 1996

Section 2(1) of the Chemical Weapons Act 1996 makes it an offence to use, develop or produce, possess, or transfer a chemical weapon (see Appendix 3, Table 5(C)). Conviction renders a person liable to imprisonment for life. By virtue, again, of the extraterritorial jurisdiction provided under section 62 of the Terrorism Act 200 (see Sect. 8.1.5.3 below), this offence corresponds to the offences under article 2 of the Bombing Convention.

8.1.2   Legislation to Deal with Aviation and Maritime Security

As well as the legislation concerning terrorist bombings, six other Acts of Parliament have continued to remain free-standing despite the consolidation of counter-terrorism law at the beginning of this century under the Terrorism Act 2000. Of those, the Civil Aviation Act 1982, the Aviation Security Act 1982, and the Aircraft and Maritime Security Act 1990 are the domestic instruments through which the United Kingdom has implemented its obligations under the Convention on Offences and Certain Other Acts Committed on Board Aircraft (the Tokyo Convention);[20] the Convention for the Suppression of Unlawful Seizure of Aircraft

---

[19]Corresponding to article 2(2) of the Bombing Convention (n 15).

[20]Convention on Offences and Certain Other Acts Committed on Board Aircraft, opened for signature 14 September 1963, 704 UNTS 219 (entered into force 4 December 1969).

(the Hague Convention);[21] the Convention for the Suppression of Unlawful Acts Against the Safety of Civil Aviation (the Montreal Convention);[22] the Protocol on the Suppression of Unlawful Acts of Violence at Airports Serving International Civil Aviation (the Montreal Protocol);[23] the Convention for the Suppression of Unlawful Acts against the Safety of Maritime Navigation (the Rome Convention);[24] and the Protocol to the Convention for the Suppression of Unlawful Acts against the Safety of Maritime Navigation (the Rome Protocol).[25]

8.1.2.1 Civil Aviation Act 1982

Section 92 of the Civil Aviation Act 1982 (as supplemented by the Civil Aviation (Amendment) Act 1996) replaced the Tokyo Convention Act 1967 to establish extraterritorial jurisdiction over *any* offence which if committed in the UK would be a criminal offence (see Appendix 3, Table 5(D)). It thus transports the criminal law of the United Kingdom, in almost all respects, to aircraft which are under British control (section 92(1)) or which are next scheduled to land in the United Kingdom (section 92(1A)). Section 92 is thus wide enough to include acts which may or do jeopardise the safety of the aircraft or of persons or property therein, or which jeopardise good order and discipline on board an aircraft (article 1(1)(b) of the Tokyo Convention). Section 94 of the Act gives an aircraft commander certain powers of restraint and forced disembarkation in respect of such conduct.

8.1.2.2 Aviation Security Act 1982

The Aviation Security Act 1982 is the instrument through which the UK implements the Hague Convention (replacing, in this regard, the earlier Hijacking Act 1971), and (in part) the Montreal Convention (replacing the earlier Protection of

---

[21]Convention for the Suppression of Unlawful Seizure of Aircraft, opened for signature 16 December 1970, 860 UNTS 105 (entered into force 14 October 1971).

[22]Convention for the Suppression of Unlawful Acts Against the Safety of Civil Aviation, opened for signature 23 September 1971, 974 UNTS 177 (entered into force 26 January 1973).

[23]Protocol on the Suppression of Unlawful Acts of Violence at Airports Serving International Civil Aviation (the Montreal Protocol), opened for signature 24 February 1988, ICAO Doc 9518 (entered into force 6 August 1989).

[24]Convention for the Suppression of Unlawful Acts against the Safety of Maritime Navigation, opened for signature 10 March 1988, 1678 UNTS 221 (entered into force 1 March 1992).

[25]Protocol for the Suppression of Unlawful Acts against the Safety of Fixed Platforms Located on the Continental Shelf, opened for signature 10 March 1988, 1678 UNTS 304 (entered into force 1 March 1992).

Aircraft Act 1973). The Aviation Security Act contains the following offences to implement the obligations in those Conventions (see Appendix 3, Table 5(E)):

- *Hijacking* (section 1), making it an offence punishable by life imprisonment for a person on board an aircraft in flight to unlawfully, by the use of force or by threats of any kind, seize the aircraft or exercise control of it.[26]
- *Destroying, damaging or endangering safety of aircraft* (section 2), establishing a number of criminal offences concerning the safety of aircraft, all of which are punishable on indictment by up to imprisonment for life. Section 2(1) criminalises: (a) the unlawful and intentional destruction of an aircraft in service or so to damage such an aircraft as to render it incapable of flight or as to be likely to endanger its safety in flight;[27] and (b) the unlawful and intentional commission of any act of violence which is likely to endanger the safety of the aircraft.[28] Section 2(2) makes it an offence to unlawfully and intentionally place, or cause to be placed, on an aircraft in service any device or substance which is likely to destroy the aircraft, or is likely so to damage it as to render it incapable of flight or as to be likely to endanger its safety in flight.[29]
- *Other acts endangering or likely to endanger safety of aircraft* (section 3), establishing two further offences, also punishable by life imprisonment. It is an offence under section 3(1) for any person unlawfully and intentionally to destroy or damage any property used for the provision of air navigation facilities, or to interfere with the operation of any such property, where this is likely to endanger the safety of aircraft in flight.[30] It is an offence under section 3(3) for any person to intentionally communicate any information which is false, misleading or deceptive in a material particular, where the communication of the information endangers the safety of an aircraft in flight or is likely to endanger the safety of aircraft in flight.[31]

8.1.2.3 Aviation and Maritime Security Act 1990

The Aviation and Maritime Security Act 1990 implemented the balance of offences required under the Montreal Convention (as supplement by its Protocol), as well as obligations under the Rome Convention and the Rome Protocol. The Act contains the following offences (see Appendix 3, Table 5(F)):

- *Endangering safety at aerodromes* (section 1), which establishes two offences concerning the safety of international airports. It is an offence under section 1(1) for any person by means of any device, substance or weapon to intentionally

---

[26]Corresponding to article 1(a) of the Hague Convention (n 21).

[27]Corresponding to article 1(1)(b) of the Montreal Convention (n 22).

[28]Corresponding to article 1(1)(a) of the Montreal Convention (n 22).

[29]Corresponding to article 1(1)(c) of the Montreal Convention (n 22).

[30]Corresponding to article 1(1)(d) of the Montreal Convention (n 22).

[31]Corresponding to article 1(1)(e) of the Montreal Convention (n 22).

commit any act of violence at an aerodrome serving international civil aviation which causes or is likely to cause death or serious personal injury, *and* endangers or is likely to endanger the safe operation of the airport or the safety of persons at the airport.[32] Section 1(2) makes it an offence for any person by means of any device, substance or weapon to unlawfully and intentionally (a) destroy or seriously damage property used for the provision of any facilities at an international airport, or any aircraft which is at such an airport but is not in service; or (b) disrupt the services of an international airport; in such a way as to endanger or be likely to endanger the safe operation of the airport or the safety of persons at the airport.[33]

- *Hijacking of ships* (section 9), making it an offence punishable by life imprisonment to unlawfully, by the use of force or by threats of any kind, seize a ship or exercise control of it.[34]
- *Seizing or exercising control of fixed platforms* (section 10(1)), criminalising the unlawful seizure or exercise of control of a fixed platform, by the use of force or by threats of any kind.[35] Conviction on indictment renders a person liable to imprisonment for life.
- *Destroying ships or fixed platforms or endangering their safety* (section 11), establishing a number of offences concerning the safety of ships and fixed platforms, all of which are punishable by life imprisonment. Section 11(1)(a) and (b) create offences of unlawfully and intentionally destroying or damaging a ship, its cargo, or a fixed platform so as to endanger, or to be likely to endanger, the safe navigation of the ship, or the safety of the platform.[36] It is an offence under section 11(1)(c) to commit on board a ship or on a fixed platform an act of violence which is likely to endanger the safe navigation of a ship, or the safety of a fixed platform.[37] Section 11(2) criminalises the unlawful and intentional placing, or causing to be placed, on a ship or fixed platform any device or substance which: (a) in the case of a ship, is likely to destroy the ship or is likely so to damage it or its cargo as to endanger its safe navigation;[38] or (b) in the case of a fixed platform, is likely to destroy the fixed platform or so to damage it as to endanger its safety.[39]
- *Acts endangering or likely to endanger safe navigation* (section 12), establishing two offences relating to maritime navigation, punishable following a conviction

---

[32]Corresponding to article 1(1*bis*)(a) of the Montreal Convention (n 22).

[33]Corresponding to article 1(1*bis*)(b) of the Montreal Convention (n 22).

[34]Corresponding to article 3(1)(a) of the Rome Convention (n 24).

[35]Corresponding to article 2(1)(a) of the Rome Protocol (n 25).

[36]Corresponding to article 3(1)(c)of the Rome Convention (n 24) and article 2(1)(c) of the Rome Protocol (n 25).

[37]Corresponding to article 3(1)(b)of the Rome Convention (n 24) and article 2(1)(b) of the Rome Protocol (n 25).

[38]Corresponding to article 3(1)(d) of the Rome Convention (n 24).

[39]Corresponding to article 2(1)(d) of the Rome Protocol (n 25).

on indictment by life imprisonment. Section 12(1) makes it an offence for any person to unlawfully and intentionally destroy or damage any property used for the provision of maritime navigation facilities, or seriously interfere with the operation of such property, where its destruction, damage or interference is likely to endanger the safe navigation of any ship.[40] It is an offence under section 12(3) to intentionally communicate any false information, where this endangers the safe navigation of any ship.[41]

- *Offences involving threats* (section 13(1)), making it an offence to threaten to do an act in relation to any ship or fixed platform which is an offence under section 11(1) (destruction or damage of a ship, its cargo, or a fixed platform) where this is done: (a) in order to compel a person to do or abstain from doing any act; and (b) this is likely to endanger the safe navigation of the ship or the safety of the fixed platform.[42] A person guilty of an offence section 13 is liable on conviction on indictment to imprisonment for life.
- *Offences involving injury or death* (section 14), making it an aggravated offence to commit murder, attempted murder, manslaughter, culpable homicide or assault if done in connection with an offence under section 9, 10, 11 or 12 of the Act.[43] Commission of such an aggravated offence, even in the case of assault, carries a maximum penalty of life imprisonment.

8.1.3   Legislation to Deal with the Protection of Persons

Falling under the ambit of legislation to deal with the protection of persons are two items of legislation: the Internationally Protected Persons Act 1978; and the Taking of Hostages Act 1982.

8.1.3.1   Internationally Protected Persons Act 1978

The Internationally Protected Persons Act 1978 was enacted to implement the Convention on the Prevention and Punishment of Crimes against Internationally Protected Persons adopted by the United Nations General Assembly in 1973 (the Protected Persons Convention).[44] Section 1 of the Act establishes the following

---

[40]Corresponding to article 3(1)(e) of the Rome Convention (n 24).

[41]Corresponding to article 3(1)(f) of the Rome Convention (n 24).

[42]Corresponding to article 3(2)(c)of the Rome Convention (n 24) and article 2(2)(c) of the Rome Protocol (n 25).

[43]Corresponding to article 3(1)(g)of the Rome Convention (n 24) and article 2(1)(e) of the Rome Protocol (n 25).

[44]Convention on the Prevention and Punishment of Crimes against International Protected Persons, including Diplomatic Agents, opened for signature 14 December 1973, 1035 UNTS 167 (entered into force 20 February 1977).

offences concerning attacks and threats of attacks on protected persons, irrespective of whether the person committing the offence knows that the person in question is a protected person[45] (see Appendix 3, Table 5(G)):

- *Attacks against a protected person* (section 1(1)(a)),[46] establishing universal jurisdiction (i.e. jurisdiction over a person, whether a citizen of the United Kingdom or not, who acts outside the United Kingdom) over a person who does anything to or in relation to a protected person (within the terms of the Protected Persons Convention) which, if it had been done in the United Kingdom, would have constituted the offence of certain violent offences against the person.[47]
- *Attacks against the property or vehicle of a protected person* (section 1(1)(b)),[48] establishing universal jurisdiction over a person who, in connection with an attack on the premises or vehicle used by a protected person (in which the protected person is on or in), commits any act which, if it had been done in the United Kingdom, would constitute certain property offences.[49]
- *Party offences* (section 1(2)), criminalising the attempted commission of the offences under section 1(1)(a) and (b), or aiding, abetting, counselling or procuring the commission of such offences.[50]
- *Threats to attack a protected person or their property or vehicle* (section 1(3)), making it an offence to make a threat to do an act which would constitute an attempted commission of an offence under section 1(1), or attempts, aids, abets, counsels or procures the making of such a threat, with the intention that the other person will fear that the threat will be carried out. Conviction for an offence under section 1(3) carries a maximum penalty of 10 years (so long as this does not exceed the maximum term of imprisonment to which a person would be liable for the act threatened).

8.1.3.2   Taking of Hostages Act 1982

The Taking of Hostages Act 1982 was the means by which the United Kingdom implemented its obligations under the International Convention against the

---

[45]See section 1(4) of the Act.

[46]Corresponding to article 2(1)(a) of the Protected Persons Convention (n 44).

[47]That is, murder, manslaughter, culpable homicide, rape, assault occasioning actual bodily harm or causing injury, kidnapping, abduction, false imprisonment or plagium or an offence under section 18, 20, 21, 22, 23, 24, 28, 29, 30 or 56 of the Offences against the Person Act 1861 or section 2 of the Explosive Substances Act 1883.

[48]Corresponding to article 2(1)(b) of the Protected Persons Convention (n 44).

[49]That is, an offence under section 2 of the Explosive Substances Act 1883, section 1 of the Criminal Damage Act 1971 or article 3 of the Criminal Damage (Northern Ireland) Order 1977 or the offence of wilful fire-raising.

[50]Corresponding to article 2(1)(d) and (e) of the Protected Persons Convention (n 44).

Taking of Hostages (the Hostages Convention).[51] Section 1 of the Act establishes the offence of hostage-taking, making it an offence punishable by life imprisonment to detain any person ("the hostage") and to threatens to kill, injure or continue to detain the hostage in order to compel a State, international governmental organisation or person to do or abstain from doing any act (see Appendix 3, Table 5(H)).[52]

8.1.4   Nuclear Material (Offences) Act 1983

The final item of legislation to remain 'free-standing' following the consolidation of counter-terrorism laws under the Terrorism Act 2000 is the Nuclear Material (Offences) Act 1983. The Act was enacted for the specific purpose of implementing the Convention on the Physical Protection of Nuclear Material (the Nuclear Material Convention).[53] It contains two provisions concerning terrorism-related offences (see Appendix 3, Table 5(I)):

- *Extended application of existing offences* (section 1), which extends extraterritorially the application of certain offences (including murder, theft, embezzlement, fraud and extortion) if the offences are committed "by means of nuclear material".[54]
- *Offences involving preparatory acts and threats* (section 2), establishing three further offences, all punishable by up to life imprisonment.[55] It is an offence under section 2(2) to receive, hold or deal with nuclear material intending, or for the purpose of enabling another person, to do by means of nuclear material an act which is an offence listed in section 1(1)(a) or (b), or being reckless as to whether another person would so do such an act.[56] Section 2(3) makes it an offence to threaten to do such an act, intending that the person to whom the threat is made will fear that it will be carried out.[57] It is an offence under section 2(4) to threaten to unlawfully obtain nuclear material in order to compel a State, international governmental organisation or person to do, or abstain from doing, any act.[58]

---

[51]International Convention against the Taking of Hostages, opened for signature 18 December 1979, 1316 UNTS 205 (entered into force 3 June 1983).

[52]Corresponding to article 1(1) of the Hostages Convention (ibid).

[53]Convention on the Physical Protection of Nuclear Material, opened for signature 3 March 1980, 1456 UNTS 124 (entered into force 8 February 1987).

[54]Corresponding to article 7(1)(b), (c) and (d) of the Nuclear Material Convention (ibid).

[55]The maximum sentence for offences under section 2 were increased from 14 years to life imprisonment under section 14(1) of the Terrorism Act 2006.

[56]Corresponding to article 7(1)(a) of the Nuclear Material Convention (n 53).

[57]Corresponding to article 7(1)(e)(i) of the Nuclear Material Convention (n 53).

[58]Corresponding to article 7(1)(e)(ii) of the Nuclear Material Convention (n 53).

8.1.5 Terrorism Act 2000

Following the Lloyd and Kerr judicial inquiry of 1996 to review the United Kingdom's counter-terrorism laws, the Terrorism Act 2000 was enacted to establish permanent measures to combat terrorism.[59] The Terrorism Act 2000 is divided into eight parts, six of these dealing with the substantive themes of the Act: proscribed organisations; terrorist property; investigations; special powers; and offences. It is the vehicle through which much of the UK's pre-existing counter-terrorism laws were consolidated.[60] It is also the means by which the United Kingdom incorporated its obligations under the International Convention for the Suppression of the Financing of Terrorism (the Financing Convention) and Security Council resolutions 1373 (2001) and 1624 (2005).[61]

8.1.5.1 Definition of "Terrorism"

The Terrorism Act 2000 begins with a new definition of the term "terrorism", which contains three cumulative elements:

- The use or threat of action, whether within or outside the United Kingdom, which (see section 1(1)(a) and 1(2)):

  (a) involves serious violence against a person; or
  (b) involves serious damage to property; or
  (c) endangers a person's life, other than that of the person committing the action; or
  (d) created a serious risk to the health or safety of the public or a section of the public; or
  (e) is designed seriously to interfere with or seriously to disrupt an electronic system.

- Where the act or threat is designed to influence the government or to intimidate the public or a section of the public (section 1(1)(b)); and
- The act or threat is made for the purpose of advancing a political, religious, racial or ideological cause (section 1(1)(c)).[62]

---

[59]Inquiry into the Legislation on Terrorism (n 11).

[60]For commentary on the overall successes and failures of such consolidation, see Walker (2009, pp. 23–25).

[61]International Convention for the Suppression of the Financing of Terrorism, opened for signature 10 January 2000, 2179 UNTS 232 (entered into force 10 April 1992); SC Res 1373, UN SCOR, 4385th Mtg, UN Doc S/Res/1373 (2001); and SC Res 1624 (2005), UN SCOR, 5261st Mtg, UN Doc S/Res/1624 (2005).

[62]As amended by section 75 of the Counter-Terrorism Act 2008.

If the use or threat of action falling within section 1(2) involves the use of firearms or explosives, it is not necessary that the conduct be designed to influence the government or to intimidate the public or a section of the public (section 1(3)). A further extension of the definition exists pursuant to subsection (5), which explains that "action taken for the purposes of terrorism" includes action taken for the benefit of a proscribed organisation (as defined by section 3 of the Act, see next). The definition is linked to offences under this and other legislation (see below and also Sect. 8.1.8.1), the definition of "terrorist property" (see below), and the definition of "proscribed organisations" (see next).

8.1.5.2   Definition of "Proscribed Organisations"

The Terrorism Act 2000 defines "proscribed organisations" as those which are listed in Schedule 2 of the Act by the Secretary of State (section 3(1)). Listing will occur where the Secretary of State believes that the organisation is "concerned in terrorism" (section 3(4)). This expression is said to apply if the organisation commits or participates in acts of terrorism; prepares for terrorism; or promotes or encourages terrorism (section 3(5)(a)(c)); or if it "is otherwise concerned in terrorism" (section 3(5)(d)). The latter catch-all is not defined further and thus provides the Secretary of State with a wide authority to list proscribed organisations.

An organisation listed in Schedule 2 of the Terrorism Act 2000, or any person affected by an organisation's proscribed status, can apply to the Secretary of State to have the organisation removed from Schedule 2 (section 4). Where the Secretary of State rejects such an application an appeal may be made to the Proscribed Organisations Appeal Commission, which is empowered to require removal of the organisation from Schedule 2 if it considers that the Secretary of State's decision "was flawed when considered in the light of the principles applicable on an application for judicial review" (section 5). Further rights of appeal exist on questions of law (section 6).

The proscription of organisations is linked to two features of the Terrorism Act 2000. First, a number of offences are linked to "proscribed organisations" including, for example, membership in a proscribed organisation (section 11 – see below). In addition, as identified earlier, "action taken for the benefit of a proscribed organisation" falls within the definition of "terrorism" under section 1 of the Act without the need to establish that the action was designed to influence the British government or to intimidate the public (see section 1(3)).

From a practical perspective, this feature of the Terrorism Act 2000 had not originally been used as the vehicle through which the United Kingdom proscribed individuals or entities listed by the Security Council resolution 1267 (1999) Sanctions Committee (on the Sanctions Committee, see Chap. 3, Sect. 3.2.4.2). It was instead used to proscribe organisations such as The Irish Republican Army, the Ulster Freedom Fighters, the Loyalist Volunteer Force and the Orange Volunteers. Since 2001, however, the organisations listed in Schedule 2 of the Act include organisations within the Consolidated List maintained by the United Nations including, for example, Jemaah Islamiyah and the Islamic Jihad Union.

8.1.5.3   Offences Under the Terrorism Act 2000

The Act contains a number of offences relating to proscribed organisations, the suppression of the financing of terrorism, and other terrorist-related activities (see Appendix 3, Table 4(J)). Three offences exist concerning proscribed organisations:

- *Membership in a proscribed organisation* (section 11), making it an offence to belong, or profess to belong, to an organisation listed in Schedule 2 of the Act.[63] On indictment, a convicted person will be liable to imprisonment for up to 10 years (section 11(3)).
- *Support for a proscribed organisation* (section 12), prohibiting persons from inviting support for a proscribed organisation. The offence provisions under section 12 are restricted to non-financial support of a proscribed organisation, relating to managing, or assisting in arranging, a meeting to support a proscribed organisation, to further its activities, or to be addressed by a person who belongs or professes to belong to a proscribed organisation (subsection (2)), or addressing a meeting if the purpose of the address is to encourage support for such an organisation (subsection (3)).[64] Conviction on indictment renders a person liable to a maximum of 10 years imprisonment (section 12(6)).
- *Wearing a uniform or emblem of a proscribed organisation* (section 13(1)), making it an offence to ear an item of clothing, or carry or display something, in such a way and in such circumstances as to arouse reasonable suspicion that the person is a member or supporter of a proscribed organisation.[65] A person found guilty of an offence under section 13(1) is liable to imprisonment on summary conviction to a term not exceeding 6 months. There is some overlap between this offence and section 1 of the Public Order Act 1936 which has, for example, been invoked against leaders of the Provisional Sinn Fein protest march against internment in Northern Ireland.[66]

"Terrorist property" is defined by section 14 of the Act as: money or other property "which is likely to be used for the purposes of terrorism" (including any resources of a proscribed organisation);[67] proceeds of the commission of acts

---

[63]Not required by, but relevant to, SC Res 1373 (n 61), para 2(a) and (d).

[64]Not required by, but relevant to, SC Res 1373 (n 61), para 2(a) and (d).

[65]Not required by, but relevant to, SC Res 1373 (n 61), para 2(a) and (d).

[66]See *Whelan v DPP* [1975] QB 864. See also Fenwick (2002, pp. 520–521).

[67]Section 14(2)(b) explains that reference to an organisation's resources includes a reference to any money or other property which is applied or made available, or is to be applied or made available, for use by the organisation.

of terrorism; and proceeds of acts carried out for the purposes of terrorism.[68] Where a person suspects that a person has committed any of the terrorist property offences under the Act, he or she has a duty to report this to the police (see sections 19–21). The following offences are established under the Terrorism Act relating to terrorist property, in respect of which a conviction on indictment will render a person liable to 14 years imprisonment, also allowing the sentencing court to make a forfeiture order in respect of such property (sections 22 and 23):

- *Fund-raising for terrorist purposes* (section 15), criminalising the raising of funds for terrorist purposes, made up of three types of offences: the solicitation of funds or property for terrorism (subsection (1)); the receipt of money or property for terrorism (subsection (2)); or the provision itself of money or property knowing, or having reasonable cause to suspect, that this may be used for the purposes of terrorism (subsection (3)).[69]
- *Use or possession of money for terrorist purposes* (section 16), making it an offence to use money or other property for the purposes of terrorism (subsection (1)), or possess money or property intending that it should be used, or has reasonable grounds to suspect that it may be used, for the purposes of terrorism (subsection (2)).[70]
- *Funding terrorism* (section 17), making it an offence to be involved in an arrangement to provide money or property to another person knowing, or having reasonable cause to suspect, that this will be used for the purposes of terrorism.[71]
- *Money laundering for terrorist purposes* (section 18(1)), prohibiting the concealment, removal from jurisdiction, transfer, or other form of action which facilitates the retention or control of terrorist property (as defined).[72]

Part 6 of the Act sets out various further offences:

- *Weapons training* (section 54),[73] making it an offence to provide (subsection (1)), receive (subsection (2)), or invite another to receive (subsection (3)) information or training in the making or use of firearms, explosives, or chemical,

---

[68]Section 14(2)(a) explains that reference to proceeds of an act includes a reference to any property which wholly or partly, and directly or indirectly, represents the proceeds of the act (including payments or other rewards in connection with its commission).

[69]Corresponding to article 2(1) of the Financing Convention (n 61), and paras 1(b) and 1(d) of SC Res 1373 (n 61).

[70]Not required by, but relevant to, article 2(1) of the Financing Convention (n 61), and paras 1(b) and 1(d) of SC Res 1373 (n 61).

[71]Corresponding to article 2(1) of the Financing Convention (n 61), and paras 1(b) and 1(d) of SC Res 1373 (n 61).

[72]Not required by, but relevant to, article 2(1) of the Financing Convention (n 61), and paras 1(b) and 1(d) of SC Res 1373 (n 61).

[73]Relevant to SC Res 1373 (n 61) para 2(d).

biological or nuclear weapons.[74] A conviction on indictment renders a person liable to imprisonment for a term of up to 10 years.

- *Directing a terrorist organisation* (section 56(1)), prohibiting the direction (at any level) of the activities of an organisation which is concerned in the commission of acts of terrorism.[75] A person found guilty of directing a terrorist organisation is liable on indictment to life imprisonment.
- *Possessing an article for terrorist purposes* (section 57(1)), making it an offence to posses any physical thing in circumstances which give rise to a reasonable suspicion that this "is for a purpose connected with the commission, preparation or instigation of an act of terrorism".[76] Upon conviction on indictment, a person guilty of such an offence may be imprisoned for up to 15 years.[77]
- *Collection of information for terrorist purposes* (section 58(1)), criminalising the collection, recording or possession of information which is likely to be useful to a person committing or preparing an act of terrorism, punishable on indictment by up to 10 years imprisonment.[78]
- *Eliciting, publishing or communicating information about members of armed forces* (section 58A),[79] making it an offence to (a) elicit, or attempt to elicit information about an individual who is or has been a member of the armed forces, police, or of any of the intelligence services, where that information is of a kind likely to be useful to a person committing or preparing an act of terrorism; or (b) to publish or communicate any such information.
- *Inciting terrorism* (sections 59–61), prohibiting the incitement of an act of terrorism within or outside the United Kingdom.[80] Each section deals with the incitement of acts which would constitute offences in the different territories within the United Kingdom, i.e. incitement in England and Wales (section 59),[81] Northern Ireland (section 60),[82] or Scotland (section 61).[83] Incitement carries with it the penalties applicable to the principal offence which is incited.
- *Terrorist bombings* (section 62). Rather than creating an offence of terrorist bombings, section 62 of the Terrorism Act 2000 establishes extraterritorial

---

[74]"Chemical", "biological" and "nuclear" weapons are defined by section 54 of the Terrorism Act 2000.

[75]Relevant to SC Res 1373 (n 61) para 2(a) and (d).

[76]Relevant to SC Res 1373 (n 61) para 2(d).

[77]The maximum sentence for this offence was increased from 10 years to 15 years under section 13 (1) of the Terrorism Act 2006.

[78]Relevant to SC Res 1373 (n 61) para 2(d).

[79]Inserted by section 76 of the Counter-Terrorism Act 2008.

[80]Relevant to SC Res 1624 (n 61) para 1(a).

[81]Where the offence incited is murder, wounding with intent, poisoning, explosions, or endangering life by damaging property: see section 59(2).

[82]Where the offence incited is murder, wounding with intent, poisoning, explosions, or endangering life by damaging property: see section 60(2).

[83]Where the offence incited is murder, assault to severe injury, or reckless conduct which causes actual injury: see section 61(2).

jurisdiction over certain offences under the Explosive Substances Act 1883, the
Biological Weapons Act 1974 and the Chemical Weapons Act 1996 *if* this is
done as an act of terrorism within the definition of the Terrorism Act.[84]

• *Terrorist financing* (section 63), which, similar to section 62, establishes extraterritorial jurisdiction over the terrorist financing offences under sections 15–18
of the Act.[85]

8.1.5.4 Freezing, Seizure and Forfeiture of Terrorist Property

The offences under sections 15–18 of the Terrorism Act do not have the effect of
freezing terrorist property, since bona fide innocent agents will remain able to deal
with such property, i.e. the offences are limited require the existence of knowledge,
or reasonable suspicion, that the property will be used for terrorist purposes. Such
property is, however, subject to forfeiture. This had been deal with under sections 23–31 of the Act, but has since been updated and replaced by Schedule 1 of
the Anti-terrorism, Crime and Security Act 2001 (see Sect. 8.1.6.2 below).

8.1.5.5 Investigative Powers

Part 4 of the Terrorism Act 2000 deals with terrorist investigations, associated
cordons, information and evidence. A "terrorist investigation" is widely defined by
section 32 as an investigation of:

• The commission, preparation or instigation of acts of terrorism;
• An act which appears to have been done for the purpose of terrorism;
• The resources of a proscribed organisation;
• The possibility of making an order for the inclusion of an organisation in the list
of proscribed organisations in Schedule 2 of the Act; or
• The commission, preparation or instigation of any offence under the Terrorism
Act 2000.

Special powers are established pertaining to the establishment and maintenance
of cordons (sections 33–37). A constable can obtain a warrant to enter and search
premises for the purpose of a terrorist investigation, and to seize any material found
on the property or on a person found in the property (Schedule 5 to the Act,
paragraph 1). In a case of "great emergency" where immediate action is required,
a superintendent of police (or higher rank) can issue such a warrant in the place of a
justice of the peace (Schedule 5, paragraph 15). This is subject to oversight by the
Secretary of State (Schedule 5, paragraph 15(3)), but not by judicial authorities.
Police may obtain customer information from a financial institution for the purpose

---

[84]Corresponding to article 2(1) of the Bombing Convention (n 15).

[85]Corresponding to article 2(1) of the Financing Convention (n 61) and para 1(b) and (d) of SC Res
1373 (n 61).

of a terrorist investigation (Schedule 6). Disclosing information which is likely to prejudice a terrorist investigation, or interfering with material likely to be relevant to such an investigation, is an offence under section 39 of the Act.

8.1.5.6   Counter-Terrorist Powers

Part 5 of the Terrorism Act establishes a limited set of powers concerning the stop, arrest and search of a suspected terrorist. A "terrorist" is defined by section 40 of the Act as a person who is "concerned in the commission, preparation of instigation of acts of terrorism", or who has committed one of the offences under sections 11, 12, 15–18, 54, and 56–63 of the Terrorism Act 2000 (see above). Such a person can be arrested without warrant if the police reasonably suspect s/he is a terrorist (section 41). Schedule 8 governs the subsequent powers of police to detain a terrorist suspect. The question of pre-charge investigative detention in the United Kingdom is considered in Chap. 16 (Sect. 16.1). The premises or person of a "terrorist" may be searched (sections 42 and 43).

8.1.5.7   Special Measures for Northern Ireland

As indicated, the Terrorism Act 2000 took the step of bringing together counter-terrorism law in Great Britain and Northern Ireland.[86] This is with one exception. Part 7 of the Act retained 'temporary' (i.e. subject to annual renewal) specific measures applied in Northern Ireland. These measures find their origin in the Northern Ireland (Emergency Provisions) Act 1973, which established special powers of arrest and detention (see Chap. 17, Sect. 17.2), as well as special courts (known as "Diplock courts") for the purpose of dealing with terrorist cases, with modified pre-trial procedures. Diplock courts remain today and have jurisdiction over the offences listed in Schedule 9 of the Terrorism Act 2000. Trials were, under the 1973 Emergency Powers Act and Part 7 of the Terrorism Act, conducted before a single judge sitting without a jury, and the burden of proof is in some cases reversed. These, and other features of Diplock courts, have been criticised by the Human Rights Committee, lawyers and academics, and non-governmental organisations.[87]

---

[86]For a review of the operation in 2000 of counter-terrorism law in Northern Ireland, see the report of John Rowe QC, Review of the Operation in 2000 of the Prevention of Terrorism (Temporary Provisions) Act 1989 and the Northern Ireland (Emergency Provisions) Act 1996 (Home Office, London, 2001).

[87]Human Rights Committee, Concluding Observations: United Kingdom of Great Britain and Northern Ireland, UN Doc CCPR/CO/73/UK (2001), paras 18–19. See also Livingstone (1994); Schabas and Olivier (2003, pp. 213–214 and 218); and the report of the Special Rapporteur on the promotion and protection of human rights and fundamental freedoms while countering terrorism, Protection of human rights and fundamental freedoms while countering terrorism, UN Doc A/63/223 (2008), paras 25–27.

Although Part 7 of the Act was repealed under the Terrorism (Northern Ireland) Act 2006, some features of the special measures have been continued under the Justice and Security (Northern Ireland) Act 2007.[88] In the most recent Concluding Observations of the Human Rights Committee on the sixth periodic report of the United Kingdom, the Committee expressed concern that this was the position, despite the improvements of the security situation in Northern Ireland. It noted that, under the Justice and Security (Northern Ireland) Act, persons whose cases are certified by the Director of Public Prosecutions for Northern Ireland are tried in the absence of a jury and that there remains no right of appeal against such a decision. The Committee recalled its interpretation of the International Covenant on Civil and Political Rights as requiring that objective and reasonable grounds be provided by the appropriate prosecution authorities to justify the application of different rules of criminal procedure in particular cases and recommended that the UK:[89]

> ...should carefully monitor, on an ongoing basis, whether the exigencies of the situation in Northern Ireland continue to justify any such distinctions with a view to abolishing them. In particular, it should ensure that, for each case that is certified by the Director of Public Prosecutions for Northern Ireland as requiring a non-jury trial, objective and reasonable grounds are provided and that there is a right to challenge these grounds.

The need for continued review is important. As noted by the Independent Reviewer of terrorism laws, however, there remains justification for continual vigilance in Northern Ireland, despite what he describes as "recent and remarkable progress", pointing to the existence of small, dissident and active paramilitary groups who do not accept the political settlement achieved in Northern Ireland.[90]

8.1.6   Anti-terrorism, Crime and Security Act 2001

The Anti-terrorism, Crime and Security Act 2001 (ATCS Act) represents the UK's response to the events of 9/11 and adds significantly to the legislative regime under the Terrorism Act 2000. It deals with the forfeiture and seizure of terrorist property and cash, thus also responding to decisions of the Security Council under resolution 1373 (2001). The Act also deals with dangerous substances (including nuclear weapons, and pathogens and toxins – see Parts 6–8), and the security of aviation facilities (Part 9).

---

[88]See Walker (2009, pp. 30–31).

[89]Human Rights Committee, Concluding Observations: United Kingdom of Great Britain and Northern Ireland, UN Doc CCPR/C/GBR/CO/6 (2008), para 18.

[90]Report by the Independent Reviewer Lord Carlile of Berriew QC, Report on the Operation in 2007 of the Terrorism Act 2000 and of Part I of the Terrorism Act 2006 (Presented to Parliament pursuant to section 26 of the Terrorism Act 2006, June 2008), para 13. See also the 22nd Report of the Independent Monitoring Commission, Presented to the Houses of Parliament by the Secretary of State for Northern Ireland in accordance with the Northern Ireland (Monitoring Commission, etc.) Act 2003, 4 November 2009.

8.1.6.1 The Now Repealed Part 4 on Immigration and Asylum Matters

The most controversial part of the Anti-terrorism, Crime and Security Act is Part 4, which addressed immigration and asylum matters. Despite strong objection to this part of the Act at the time of its enactment, the detention without trial regime under this part of the legislation was implemented and accompanied by a derogation from article 5(1)(f) of the European Convention on Human Rights.[91] It was only on this basis that a statement of compatibility with the Human Rights Act 1998 could be issued, under section 19 of the Human Rights Act (see Chap. 11, Sects. 11.1.4 and 11.3.1.4, concerning derogations and statements of compatibility under the Act).[92] This continued until an adverse decision of the House of Lords led to a repeal of Part 4 of the Act and the introduction of a control orders regime under the Prevention of Terrorism Act 2005 (see Sect. 8.1.7 below, and Chap. 18, Sect. 18.1.1).[93]

8.1.6.2 Dealing with Terrorist Cash and Property

Section 1 of the ATCS Act brings into effect Schedule 1 of the Act, enabling the forfeiture of cash which is: intended to be used for the purposes of terrorism; or consists of resources of a proscribed organisation; or is obtained through terrorism. Schedule 1 updated and replaced sections 24–31 of the Terrorism Act 2000 and vests reasonably wide powers of seizure in the police, customs, and immigration services in respect of cash.[94] Schedules 2 and of the ATCS Act also amended the Terrorism Act 2000 concerning account monitoring and freezing orders.[95]

8.1.6.3 Offences Under the ATCS Act

The Crime and Disorder Act 1998 had included assault, criminal damage, public order offences, and harassment to be aggravated offences if they were motivated by the race of the victim (see sections 29, 30, 31 and 32). Part 5 of the ATCS Act amends those provisions to also include the religious denomination of the victim of such offences to constitute an aggravated offence. Part 5 also increases the penalties

---

[91]Convention for the Protection of Human Rights and Fundamental Freedoms, opened for signature 4 November 1950, 213 UNTS 222 (entered into force 3 September 1953).

[92]Walker (2009, p. 26).

[93]See further Walker (2007, p. 182).

[94]Paragraph 1 of Schedule 1 defines "cash" as coins and notes in any currency, postal orders, travellers' cheques, bankers' drafts, and such other kinds of monetary instruments as the Secretary of State may specify by order.

[95]For a more detailed account of the operation of seizure and forfeiture under the Terrorism Act 2000, as amended, see Walker (2009, pp. 76–85).

for racial hatred and fear offences (under the Public Order Act 1986 and the Public Order (Northern Ireland) Order 1987) to be increased from 2 years to 7 years.

The ACTS Act also amended the Biological Weapons Act 1974 to criminalise the transfer of any biological agent or toxin to another person, or to enter into an agreement to do so (section 1A of the Biological Weapons Act – see Sect. 8.1.1.2 above). It established the following offences concerning the use or transfer of weapons of mass destruction (Appendix 3, Table 5(K)):

- *Use of nuclear weapons* (section 47), making it an offence to cause a nuclear explosion; develop, produce or participate in the development or production of a nuclear weapon (defined under section 47(6) as including a nuclear explosive device which is not intended for use as a weapon); or possess or participate in the transfer of such weapons. A person guilty of an offence section 47 is liable on conviction on indictment to imprisonment for life.
- *Party offences* (section 50), making it an offence punishable by life imprisonment, to aid, abet, incite, counsel or procure a person who falls outside the criminal jurisdiction of the United Kingdom to undertake offences outside the UK relating to biological, chemical or nuclear weapons.

8.1.7 Prevention of Terrorism Act 2005

The sole purpose of the enactment of the Prevention of Terrorism Act 2005 was to replace the regime of detention without trial under Part 4 of the Anti-terrorism, Crime and Security Act 2001 (see Sect. 8.1.6.1 above) by repealing sections 21–32 of the latter Act (see section 16(2)(a) of the Prevention of Terrorism Act 2005). The 2005 Act replaced that regime with one of control orders, described in the Act as orders imposing obligations on persons for "purposes connected with protecting members of the public from a risk of terrorism" (section 1(1)).[96] Two types of control orders are permissible: (1) non-derogating control orders (which represents the class of control orders issued so far under the legislation); and (2) derogating control orders (which would be ones that are deemed to interfere with liberty rights to such an extent that a derogation from article 5 of the European Convention on Human Rights would be required – see section 4). Control orders are the subject of examination in Chap. 18 (Sect. 18.1). For present purposes, the offences connected with the control order regime in the United Kingdom are identified (see Appendix 3, Table 5(L)):

- *Contravention of a control order* (section 9(1)), criminalising any failure to comply with an obligation imposed on him or her by a control order. Conviction on indictment carries a maximum penalty of 5 years imprisonment (section 9(4)).

---

[96]Walker (2009, p. 29).

A sentencing court may not conditionally discharge the person, nor make a probation order (section 9(6)).

- *Leaving and re-entering the United Kingdom without notification* (section 9(2)). A complex offence is also established by section 9(2) of the Act concerning the exit from and re-entry into the United Kingdom. If a control order does not prohibit a person from leaving the United Kingdom, it will be likely that a condition of the order will require the person, whenever he or she re-enters the United Kingdom, to report to a specified person that he or she is or has been the subject of a control order. Where this is the case, and if the control order has expired since the person left the United Kingdom, it will be an offence for the person to fail to report to the specified person notwithstanding the expiry of the control order. As for the offence under section 9(1), conviction on indictment carries a maximum penalty of 5 years imprisonment (section 9(4)). Again, a sentencing court may not conditionally discharge the person, nor make a probation order (section 9(6)).
- *Obstructing the service of a control order* (section 9(3)), making it an offence to intentionally obstruct the service of a control order (as governed by section 7(9)).

8.1.8 Terrorism Act 2006

One of the main purposes of the Terrorism Act 2006, which was a direct response to the London bombings in July 2005, was to create offences and penalise conduct which was thought to fall outside existing statutes and the common law.[97] The Act also supplemented and amended the Terrorism Act 2000 (see Sect. 8.1.5 above), including the extension of the period for which terrorist suspects can be detained without charge for questioning by the police (see Chap. 16, Sect. 16.1.1.2). The 2006 Terrorism Act was also the vehicle through which the United Kingdom incorporated into domestic law some of the obligations under the 2005 Council of Europe Convention on the Prevention of Terrorism, albeit that the Convention has not yet been ratified by the United Kingdom,[98] as well as obligations under the International Convention for the Suppression of Acts of Nuclear Terrorism (the Nuclear Terrorism Convention).[99]

---

[97]Jones et al. (2006, p. 1).

[98]Council of Europe Convention on the Prevention of Terrorism, opened for signature 16 May 2005, CETS 196 (entered into force 1 July 2007). The Convention was signed by the United Kingdom on 16 May 2005.

[99]Above n 14.

8.1.8.1 Offences Under the Terrorism Act 2006

The Terrorism Act 2006 includes extraterritorial jurisdiction over the offences created under it (section 17). The Act establishes the following offences (see Appendix 3, Table 5(M)):

- *Encouragement of terrorism* (section 1), comprising three elements (considered in further detail in Chap. 20, Sect. 20.2.3.1).[100] First, there must be an act of publishing a statement (or causing another to do so on the person's behalf). Next, the published statement must be likely to be understood by members of the public to whom it is published as a direct or indirect encouragement or other inducement to them to the commission, preparation or instigation of acts of terrorism. The final element of the offence requires that the person publishing such a statement must intend (at the time of publication) that the statement be understood in the way just described, or be reckless as to whether or not it is likely to be so understood. Conviction on indictment renders a person liable to imprisonment for up to 7 years.
- *Dissemination of terrorist publications* (section 2), prohibiting the dissemination of any article capable of storing data, or any record (permanent or otherwise) containing matter to be read, looked at, or listened to where: (1) the information is likely to be understood by members of the public to whom it is published as a direct or indirect encouragement or other inducement to them to the commission, preparation or instigation of acts of terrorism; or (2) the information is likely to be useful in the commission or preparation of terrorist acts and to be understood, by some or all recipients, as having been made available wholly or mainly for the purpose of being useful in this way. This offence is considered in further detail in Chap. 20, Sect. 20.2.3.2. Conviction on indictment carries a maximum penalty of 7 years imprisonment.
- *Preparation of terrorist acts* (section 5), making it an offence punishable by life imprisonment to engage in any conduct in preparation to give effect to an intention to commit an act of terrorism (as defined in the Terrorism Act 2000), or assist another to do so.[101]
- *Training for terrorism* (section 6), making it an offence to provide or receive training in certain skills.[102] The provision of such training is an offence under section 6(1) if the person at that time knows that the person receiving it intends

---

[100]Corresponding to article 5 of the Council of Europe Convention on the Prevention of Terrorism (n 98), and para 1(a) of SC Res 1624 (n 61). On the related offences of hate speech and stirring up racial hatred, see Fenwick (2002, pp. 327–329).

[101]Corresponding to SC Res 1373 (n 61) para 2(d).

[102]Corresponding to SC Res 1373 (n 61) para 2(d). The skills in question are listed under section 6 (3) as: (a) the making, handling or use of a noxious substance, or of substances of a description of such substances; (b) the use of any method or technique for doing anything else that is capable of being done for the purposes of terrorism, in connection with the commission or preparation of an act of terrorism or Convention offence or in connection with assisting the commission or preparation by another of such an act or offence; and (c) the design or adaptation for the purposes

to use the skills either: (1) for or in connection with the commission or preparation of acts of terrorism or Convention offences;[103] or (2) for assisting the commission or preparation by others of such acts or offences. It is an offence under section 6(2) to receive such training for such purposes. Both offences are punishable by imprisonment for up to 10 years.

- *Attendance at a place used for terrorist training* (section 8), making it an offence to attend a place (anywhere in the world) where training (within the term prohibited under section 6) or weapons training (prohibited under section 54 (1) of the Terrorism Act 2000 – see Sect. 8.1.5.3 above) is being provided wholly or partly for purposes connected with the commission or preparation of acts of terrorism or Convention offences where either: (1) the person knows or believes that the instruction or training is being provided wholly or partly for those purposes; or (2) the person could not reasonably have failed to understand that that the instruction or training was being provided wholly or partly for those purposes.[104] Attendance at such a place of training is enough to constitute an offence under section 8 (within the parameters just mentioned), even if the person does not him or herself receive training. Conviction on indictment carries a maximum penalty of 10 years imprisonment.
- *Making and possession of radioactive devices or materials* (section 9(1)), making it an offence punishable by life imprisonment to make or possess a radioactive device,[105] or posses radioactive material,[106] with the intention of using the device or material in the course of or in connection with the commission or preparation of an act of terrorism or for the purposes of terrorism, or of making it available to be used for those purposes.[107]
- *Misuse of radioactive devices or material and misuse and damage of nuclear facilities* (section 10), establishing two separate offences, both punishable by life imprisonment.[108] It is an offence under section 10(1) to use a radioactive device, or radioactive material, in the course of or in connection with the commission of an act of terrorism or for the purposes of terrorism. Section 10(2) establishes a

---

of terrorism, or in connection with the commission or preparation of an act of terrorism or Convention offence, of any method or technique for doing anything.

[103]Convention offences are listed in Schedule 1 of the Terrorism Act 2006.

[104]Corresponding to SC Res 1373 (n 61) para 2(d).

[105]As defined by section 9(4), a "radioactive device" is: (a) a nuclear weapon or other nuclear explosive device; (b) a radioactive material dispersal device; or (c) a radiation-emitting device.

[106]As defined by section 9(4), "radioactive material" means nuclear material or any other radioactive substance which: (a) contains nuclides that undergo spontaneous disintegration in a process accompanied by the emission of one or more types of ionising radiation, such as alpha radiation, beta radiation, neutron particles or gamma rays; and (b) is capable, owing to its radiological or fissile properties, of (1) causing serious bodily injury to a person; (2) causing serious damage to property; (3) endangering a person's life; or (4) creating a serious risk to the health or safety of the public.

[107]Corresponding to article 2(1)(a) of the Nuclear Terrorism Convention (n 14).

[108]Corresponding to article 2(1)(b) of the Nuclear Terrorism Convention (n 14).

further offence of using or damaging a nuclear facility, in the course of or in connection with the commission of an act of terrorism or for the purposes of terrorism, where this causes a release of radioactive material, or creates or increases a risk that such material will be released.

- *Terrorist threats relating to devices, materials or facilities* (section 11), establishing two offences relating to threats concerning radioactive devices and materials and nuclear facilities, also punishable by life imprisonment. The first offence, under section 11(1), prohibits the making of a demand for radioactive devices or materials, or for access to a nuclear facility, by threat that the person, or another, will take action and in circumstances such that it is reasonable to assume that there is real risk that the threat will be carried out if the demand is not met.[109] It is an offence under section 11(2) to threaten to use radioactive devices or materials, or a nuclear facility in a manner which would or could release radioactive material, in the course of or in connection with the commission of an act of terrorism or for the purposes of terrorism, and in circumstances such that it is reasonable to assume that there is real risk that the threat will be carried out, or would be carried out if demands made are not met.[110]

8.1.8.2 Sentencing

The Terrorism Act 2006 increases the maximum sentences for certain offences under section 54 of the Terrorism Act 2000 and section 2 of the Nuclear Material (Offences) Act 1983. It also increases the maximum penalty applicable to non-terrorism related offences under section 53 of the Regulation of Investigatory Powers Act 2000.

8.1.9 *Counter-Terrorism Act 2008*

The most recent legislation on the combating of terrorism in the United Kingdom is the Counter-Terrorism Act 2008. The Act "deepens and widens" existing legal measures on counter-terrorism,[111] including enhanced powers to gather and share information (Part 1). It also further addressed the question of sentencing, making it an aggravating feature for the purpose of sentencing if an offence "has or may have a terrorist connection" (section 30).

---

[109]Corresponding to article 2(2)(b) of the Nuclear Terrorism Convention (n 14).
[110]Corresponding to article 2(2)(a) of the Nuclear Terrorism Convention (n 14).
[111]Walker (2009, p. 31).

8.1.10   Operation of the UK's Counter-Terrorism Laws

Before leaving the current overview of the United Kingdom's counter-terrorism laws, and the implementation by the UK of the universal terrorism-related conventions, it is relevant to consider two features of the operation of those laws: their review; and investigations and prosecutions under those laws.

8.1.10.1   Review of Terrorism Legislation

As a form of consolidating legislation, the Terrorism Act 2000 is a permanent piece of legislation, as opposed to the annually renewable Prevention of Terrorism (Temporary Provisions) Acts of 1974–2001. Section 126 of the 2000 Act requires the Home Secretary to present a report to both Houses of Parliament on an annual basis on the working of the legislation. This is a retrospective report, rather than one requiring Parliament to consider whether or not to continue with the measures under the Act, and thus does away with the annual Parliamentary debates on the subject.[112] While such debates had not, according to Walker, presented any serious chance that the UK's prior counter-terrorism measures would be struck down or seriously analysed, Walker notes that it is regrettable that Parliament did not include any provision in the Terrorism Act 2000 to keep the legislation under systematic scrutiny.[113]

Notwithstanding this position, in the latter part of 2001, Lord Carlile of Berriew QC was appointed as Independent Reviewer of the Terrorism Act 2000. Lord Carlile's reports took the form of two reports each year, the first looking at the operation of Part 7 of the Terrorism Act 2000 (relating to continuing measures in Northern Ireland – see Sect. 8.1.5.7 above), and the second looking at the operation of the balance of the Terrorism Act 2000. This continued until his role as Independent Reviewer was statutorily formalised under section 36 of the Prevention of Terrorism Act 2005, since which time he produced two further reports on the operation of the Terrorism Act 2000 as a whole, and continues to report annually on the operation of the Prevention of Terrorism Act (which essentially focus on the operation of the control orders regime under the 2005 Act – see Chap. 18, Sect. 18.1). Lord Carlile was also appointed reviewer of the detention provisions in Part 4 of the Anti-terrorism, Crime and Security Act 2001, until its repeal under the 2005 Prevention of Terrorism Act. He has also produced two thematic reports. The first was in response to an invitation by the Government for Lord Carlile to comment on the draft Terrorism Bill 2005.[114] The second was a report in 2007 on

---

[112]Walker (2009, p. 25).

[113]Walker (2009, p. 25).

[114]Report by the Independent Reviewer Lord Carlile of Berriew QC, Proposals by Her Majesty's Government for Changes to the Laws against Terrorism (Home Office, London, 2006).

the definition of terrorism in the United Kingdom, a matter considered further in Chap. 14 (Sect. 14.1).[115]

Lord Carlile has observed a shift of emphasis towards international terrorism as the process of 'normalisation' in Northern Ireland has become more evident in the evolution of the Good Friday Agreement and the St Andrews Agreement. As noted earlier, however, he has warned that there remains justification for continual vigilance in Northern Ireland (Sect. 8.1.5.7 above). On the question of control orders, Lord Carlile has noted that there has been a reduction in the number of control orders in operation in recent years, observing that this may be due, at least in part, to the establishment of the offence of preparation of terrorist acts under section 5 of the Terrorism Act 2006.[116]

8.1.10.2 Investigations and Prosecutions in the UK

Given the long history of terrorism in the United Kingdom, it is not possible within the aims and constraints of this chapter to trace the full extent of terrorist acts in the UK and the investigations and prosecutions that followed them. An illustrative selection of some of the most notable and recent terrorist events is set out below. It is worth noting, first, that the Home Office published in 2009 a statistical report for the period 11 September 2001 to 31 March 2008 on terrorism arrests and outcomes in Great Britain.[117] The main points of that report, and other notable arrests and trials,[118] are as follows:

- There were 1,471 terrorism arrests during the period covered in the Home Office report, not counting 38 arrests made between the introduction of the Terrorism Act 2000 in February 2001 and 11 September 2001 and 119 stops at Scottish ports under Schedule 7 of the Terrorism Act 2000 in that same period.[119] In 2007/8 there were 231 terrorism arrests compared with an annual average of 227 since 1 April 2002. Thirty-five per cent of terrorism arrests (521) resulted in a charge, of which 340 (65%) were considered terrorism related. The proportion of those arrested (35%) who were charged is noted as being similar to that for other criminal offences.[120] For a further 9% of terrorism arrests, the Home Office

---

[115]Report by the Independent Reviewer Lord Carlile of Berriew QC, The Definition of Terrorism (Presented to Parliament by the Secretary of State for the Home Department, March 2007).

[116]Report on the Operation in 2007 of the Terrorism Act 2000 and of Part I of the Terrorism Act 2006 (ibid) para 36.

[117]Home Office Statistical Bulletin, Statistics on Terrorism Arrests and Outcomes in Great Britain (Home Office, London, May 2009).

[118]See the website of the MI5 Security Service, 'Criminal Cases', at http://www.mi5.gov.uk/output/news-criminal-cases.html.

[119]Statistics on Terrorism Arrests and Outcomes (n 117) p. 1.

[120]Statistics on Terrorism Arrests and Outcomes (n 117) para 5.

report states that some alternative action was taken, such as the transfer of those persons to the immigration authorities.[121]

- The main offences for which suspects were charged under terrorism legislation in the UK were possession of an article for terrorist purposes (section 57 of the Terrorism Act 2000), membership of a proscribed organisation (section 11 of the Terrorism Act 2000), and fundraising for terrorist purposes (section 15 of the Terrorism Act 2000). The main offences for which suspects were charged under what the Home Office described as non-terrorist legislation, but considered as terrorism related, were conspiracy to murder and offences under the Explosive Substances Act 1883.[122]

- On 7 July 2005 Shehzad Tanweer, Mohammad Sidique Khan, Hasib Hussain and Jermaine Lindsay, described by the Metropolitan Police Authority as "four home-grown British citizens", killed 52 people and themselves in suicide bomb attacks on the transport system in London. No-one has been charged in connection with this.[123]

- Just two weeks later, on 21 July 2005, would-be suicide bombers sought but failed to kill many more people on London's transport system. Muktar Ibrahim, Manfo Asiedu, Hussein Osman, Yassin Omar, Ramzi Mohammed and Adel Yahya were charged with their alleged involvement in this attempted attack. Four of the men were convicted in July 2007 for their parts in the bomb plot and sentenced to life imprisonment, with a minimum term of 40 years.[124] The fifth, Manfo Asiedu, was found guilty of conspiracy to cause explosions likely to endanger life in November 2007 and sentenced to 33 years' imprisonment. In February 2008, five further men (Siraj Yassin Abdullah Ali, Ismail Abdurahman, Abdul Waxid Sherif, Wahbi Mohamed and Muhedin Ali) were sentenced to a total of 56 years imprisonment for assisting the would-be London suicide bombers of 21 July 2005. The men, who were all close associates or relatives of the failed bombers, were convicted of offences including assisting an offender and not disclosing information about acts of terrorism.[125]

- In February 2006, Abu Hamza, a former imam at the North London Central Mosque in Finsbury Park, was jailed for 7 years after being found guilty of encouraging his followers to murder non-Muslims. Hamza was also found guilty of possessing a document likely to be useful to a terrorist, the "Encyclopaedia of Afghani Jihad", which contained sections on explosives, handguns and

---

[121]Statistics on Terrorism Arrests and Outcomes (n 117) p. 1.

[122]Ibid.

[123]Metropolitan Police Authority, Counter-Terrorism: The London Debate (March 2007), p. 16.

[124]Metropolitan Police Authority, Bomb plotters jailed, online: http://cms.met.police.uk/news/convictions/bomb_plotters_jailed.

[125]Metropolitan Police Authority, Five jailed for assisting terrorists, online: http://cms.met.police.uk/news/convictions/five_jailed_for_assisting_terrorists.

intelligence gathering. The document also provided information on carrying out assassinations and forming terrorist units, plus recipes for poisons and instructions on methods of killing.

- After pleading guilty to charges of conspiracy to murder, Dhiren Barot was jailed for life in November 2006. Barot had planned to blow up targets in the United Kingdom and United States through a series of attacks on trains, financial institutions and other targets in London, New York and Washington. He was arrested in August 2004 before he could carry out his plans.

- In late April 2007, five men (Omar Khyam, Waheed Mahmood, Jawad Akbar, Anthony Garciaand Salahuddin Amin) were convicted for terrorist offences, including conspiracy to cause explosions in the United Kingdom.[126] The plotters acquired a large amount of ammonium nitrate fertiliser from which they planned to make explosives with the aim of causing mass casualties. The trial, which took a year, followed arrests in March 2004 after a joint investigation involving the police and the Security Service. The investigation into the 'fertiliser bomb plotters' arose as a result of investigations following the 7 July 2005 terrorist attacks in London, which revealed a number of connections between the fertiliser bomb plotters and two of the 7 July bombers, who appeared on the periphery of the fertiliser bomb plot. The men were sentenced to life imprisonment and were unsuccessful in their appeals against conviction and sentencing.

- Two months later, seven terrorists (Qaisar Shaffi, Abdul Aziz Jalil, Nadeem Tarmohamed, Junade Feroze, Mohammed Naveed Bhatti, Zia Ul Haq and Omar Abdur Rehman) were sentenced to a total of 136 years' imprisonment following a joint investigation in 2004 by the police and Security Service, Operation Rhyme.[127] The seven, who were associates of the convicted Al Qa'ida terrorist Dhiren Barot (see above), pleaded guilty to or were found guilty of charges including conspiracy to murder and conspiracy to cause explosions with intent to endanger life. The plotters were successfully stopped before they could carry out planned attacks on both sides of the Atlantic.

- In July 2007, five students were sentenced to a total of 13 years' detention and imprisonment after being convicted on charges of possessing material for terrorist purposes.[128] The students (Irfan Raja, aged 19, Aitzaz Zafar, 19, Usman Malik, 20, Awaab Iqbal, 20, and Akber Butt, 20) had downloaded material from the internet, which included ideological propaganda as well as communications

---

[126]MI5 Security Service, Terrorist trial convictions, online: http://www.mi5.gov.uk/output/news/terrorist-trial-convictions.html.

[127]Metropolitan Police Authority, Operation Rhyme terror convictions, online: http://cms.met.police.uk/news/convictions/terrorism/operation_rhyme_terror_convictions.

[128]Metropolitan Police Authority, Five men sentenced for possessing extremist material, online: http://cms.met.police.uk/news/convictions/five_men_sentenced_for_possessing_extremist_material.

between the appellants and others which the prosecution alleged showed a settled plan under which the appellants would travel to Pakistan to receive training and thereafter commit a terrorist act or acts in Afghanistan. On appeal, all five convictions were quashed.[129]

- Samina Malik became the first woman to be convicted of a terrorism offense in Britain in November 2007 when she was convicted of possessing information of a kind likely to be useful to a person committing or preparing an act of terrorism (section 58 of the Terrorism Act 2000). Malik was found to be in possession of a number of documents downloaded from the internet, including "The Terrorist's Handbook", "The Mujahideen Poisons Handbook", and manuals for various firearms. On appeal, Malik's conviction was quashed based on the decision in *R v K* that a document only falls within the scope of section 58 of the Terrorism Act 2000 "if it is of a kind that is likely to provide practical assistance to a person committing or preparing an act of terrorism".[130] In light of the decision in *R v K*, the Court of Appeal determined that Malik's conviction was unsafe, from the perspective of justice, because there was a very real danger that the jury became confused.[131]

- Abu Izzadeen was amongst six men arrested in 2007 and convicted in April 2008 of inciting terrorism overseas. He was found guilty of inciting worshippers at a London mosque to join the mujahedeen to fight British and American forces in Iraq.[132] He was sentenced to four and a half years imprisonment, but released in May 2009 following a reduction in his sentence on appeal.[133]

- In the first prosecutions for providing training for terrorism and attending a place for the purpose of terrorism training (sections 6 and 8 of the Terrorism Act 2006), seven men were convicted in February 2008 for seeking to radicalise young men in London and encourage them to murder non-Muslims.[134]

- In September 2008, Hammaad Munshi was convicted along with Aabid Khan and Sultan Muhammad of possessing terror-related documents, including instructions for making napalm, other high explosives, detonators and grenades. Munishi was 16 when arrested and is the youngest convicted terrorist in Britain, jailed for 2 years in a young offenders institution.[135]

---

[129]*Zafar & Ors v R* [2008] EWCA Crim 184.

[130]*R v K* [2008] EWCA Crim 185.

[131]*R v Malik* [2008] EWCA Crim 1450. See further Middleton (2008).

[132]BBC News, 'Six guilty of terrorism support', 17 April 2008, online: http://news.bbc.co.uk/2/hi/uk_news/7352969.stm.

[133]BBC News, 'Radical preacher released early', 6 May 2009, online: http://news.bbc.co.uk/2/hi/uk_news/8035827.stm.

[134]MI5 Security Service, Terrorist recruiters convicted, online: http://www.mi5.gov.uk/output/news/terrorist-recruiters-convicted.html.

[135]Sky News, 'UK's Teen Terrorist Sent to Jail', 19 September 2008, online: http://news.sky.com/skynews/Home/UK-News/UKs-Youngest-Terrorist-Hammaad-Munshi-Sentenced/Article/200809315102833?f=rss.

- Bilal Abdulla, a 29-year-old Iraqi citizen who worked as a doctor in Scotland, was convicted on 16 November 2008 of conspiracy to murder and cause explosions in central London and Glasgow Airport.[136] He was sentenced to life with a minimum of 32 years' imprisonment.
- Two men were convicted on 18 December 2008 for Al-Qa'ida-related terrorist offences. Habib Ahmed and Rangzieb Ahmed were convicted for membership of Al-Qa'ida and possession of articles connected with terrorism. Rangzieb Ahmed was also convicted for directing a terrorist organisation, the first such conviction in the UK under section 56 of the Terrorism Act 2000.[137]
- In September 2009, three years after their arrest, verdicts were handed down on eight men accused of planning to detonate home-made bombs on passenger flights, disguised as soft drinks.[138] Abdulla Ahmed Ali, Assad Sarwar, and Tanvir Hussain were found guilty of the 'airline plot'. Three others were found not guilty and the remaining two, while found not guilty of the airline plot, were convicted of conspiracy to murder.

8.2 Implementation by the United Kingdom of Security Council Decisions

Three principal resolutions govern the action required by, or recommended to, members of the United Nations, namely: Security Council resolution 1267 (1999), imposing a travel ban and arms embargo against the Taliban and Al-Qa'ida, and an obligation to freeze funds and other financial resources controlled by or on their behalf of the Taliban or any other individuals of entities designated by the Committee; resolution 1373 (2001), which imposed various obligations upon States, and recommended further action; and Security Council resolution 1624 (2005), which called on States to adopt measures to prohibit and prevent the incitement to commit terrorist acts (on the resolutions of the Security Council identified below, see Chap. 3, Sect. 3.2.2).[139] These resolutions have been primarily implemented by the United Kingdom (on the implementation of Security Council resolutions by the UK, see Chap. 4, Sect. 4.2.3) through the Terrorism Acts 2000 and 2006, the Al-Qa'ida and Taliban (United Nations Measures) Order 2002, and the Terrorism (United Nations Measures) Order 2001.

---

[136]Metropolitan Police Authority, Man found guilty of car bomb attacks, online: http://cms.met. police.uk/news/convictions/man_found_guilty_of_car_bomb_attacks.

[137]The Crown Prosecution Service, First conviction for directing terrorism as a member of al-Qaeda, online: http://www.cps.gov.uk/news/press_releases/187_08/index.html.

[138]BBC News, Profiles: Airline plot accused, 7 September 2009, online: http://news.bbc.co.uk/2/hi/uk_news/7604808.stm.

[139]SC Res 1267, UN SCOR, 4051st Mtg, UN Doc S/Res/1267 (1999); SC Res 1373 (n 61); and SC Res 1624 (n 61).

8.2.1 Terrorism Act 2000

The first element of the UK's framework for compliance with the requirement to take action in respect of persons in the UN Consolidated List (see Chap. 19, Sect. 19.1) is the Terrorism Act 2000 (see Sect. 8.1.5.2 above).[140] The Act allows the Secretary of State to list "proscribed organisations" in Schedule 2 of the Act, being those organisation which the Secretary of State believes that the organisation is "concerned in terrorism" (section 3(4)). Although not originally used as the vehicle through which the UK proscribed individuals or entities listed by the Security Council resolution 1267 Sanctions Committee, the organisations listed in Schedule 2 of the Act now list organisations within the Consolidated List including, for example, Jemaah Islamiyah and the Islamic Jihad Union.

8.2.2 The Al-Qa'ida and Taliban (United Nations Measures) Order 2002

The second element for compliance with the UN Consolidated List, and with other resolutions of the Security Council, is the Al-Qa'ida and Taliban (United Nations Measures) Order 2002. The Order defines "listed persons" as including Usama bin Laden and any person designated by the Sanctions Committee and listed in the Consolidated List (article 2). It establishes the following offences concerning dealings with listed persons (see Appendix 3, Table 5(N)):

- *Supply of restricted goods* (article 3), making it an offence to supply, deliver, agree to supply or deliver, or do anything calculated to the supply or delivery, "restricted goods", defined under article 2 as goods listed in Schedule 1 of the Export of Goods, Transfer of Technology and Provision of Technical Assistance (Control) Order 2003 (including, for example, military software, technology and arms).
- *Provision of certain technical assistance or training* (article 5), criminalising the provision to a listed person of any technical assistance or training related to military activities or the supply, delivery, manufacture, maintenance or use of any restricted goods.
- *Use of ships, aircraft and vehicles: restricted goods, technical assistance and training* (article 6(3)), making it an offence to use a UK ship, aircraft or vehicle (as defined in article 6(2)) for the carriage of restricted goods to a listed person.
- *Making funds available to Usama bin Laden and associates* (article 7), prohibiting the provision of any funds to or for the benefit of a listed person or any person acting on behalf of a listed person.

---

[140]Report to the 1267 Committee, Report of the United Kingdom pursuant to paragraphs 6 and 12 of resolution 1455 (2003), UN Doc S/AC.37/2003/(1455)/19 (2003), para 8.

- *Contravention of a freezing order* (article 8(9)), making it an offence to contravene a direction made by the Treasury under article 8(1) that certain funds are not to be made available to listed persons.
- *Facilitation of activities prohibited under article 7 or 8(9)* (article 9), prohibiting any person from knowingly and intentionally engaging in any activities the object or effect of which is to enable or facilitate the commission of an offence under article 7 or 8(9).
- *Failure to disclose knowledge or suspicion of measures offences* (article 10(1)), making institutions (including banks, for example) guilty of an offence if they know or suspect that a person who is a customer of the institution, or is a person with whom the institution has had dealings in the course of its business since that time, is a listed person or acting on behalf of a listed person, or has committed an offence under article 7, 8(9) or 12(2); and they fail to disclose this information to the Treasury as soon as is reasonably practicable after that information or other matters comes to their attention.

8.2.3   The Terrorism (United Nations Measures) Order 2001

The Terrorism (United Nations Measures) Order 2001 is a further means by which the United Kingdom implemented Security Council resolution 1373 (2001) – the resolution was also implemented through the Terrorism Act 2000 (Sect. 8.1.5 above) and the Anti-terrorism, Crime and Security Act 2001 (Sect. 8.1.6 above). The 2001 Order mirrors a number of the provisions within the Terrorism Act 2000, and also overlaps with some offences under the Al-Qa'ida and Taliban (United Nations Measures) Order 2002. The principal difference between the 2002 and 2001 Orders is that the 2002 Order is specific to persons listed in the UN Consolidated List, whereas the 2001 Order is more broadly applicable to persons who commit, attempt to commit, facilitate or participate in the commission of acts of terrorism. By way of example, the Terrorism (United Nations Measures) Order 2001 establishes the following offences (see Appendix 3, Table 5(O)):

- *Making funds available* (article 3), creating an offence for any person to make funds or financial or related services available to or for the benefit of a person who commits, attempts to commit, facilitates or participates in the commission of acts of terrorism (or persons controlled or owned directly or indirectly by such a person, or a person acting on their behalf, or at their direction).
- *Contravention of a freezing order* (article 4(9)), making it an offence to contravene a direction made by the Treasury under article 4(1) that certain funds are not to be made available to a person who commits, attempts to commit, facilitates or participates in the commission of acts of terrorism (or persons controlled or owned directly or indirectly by such a person, or a person acting on their behalf, or at their direction).

8.2.4 Terrorism Act 2006

Walker identifies two main motivations for the Terrorism Act 2006, which was enacted on the heels of London bombings of July 2005: implementation of the Council of Europe Convention on the Prevention of Terrorism;[141] and addressing the radicalisation of young British Muslim men.[142] The Terrorism Act 2006 is also relied on by the United Kingdom as the vehicle through which it has implemented the call upon member States of the United Nations to suppress the incitement to terrorism.[143] As identified above (at Sect. 8.1.8.1), the Act establishes offences of encouragement of terrorism and dissemination of terrorist publications (sections 1 and 2). The compatibility of these offences with the freedom of expression, and with human rights more generally, is considered in Chap. 20 (Sect. 20.2.3).

8.3 Summary and Conclusions on the Compliance of the United Kingdom with the International Framework for Countering Terrorism

The compliance of the United Kingdom with international counter-terrorism obligations and recommendations has been subject to reporting to and review by the Security Council Counter-Terrorism Committee (CTC) and the SC Resolution 1267 Al-Qa'ida and Taliban Sanctions Committee (1267 Committee) – on these Committees, see Chap. 3, Sect. 3.2.4.2. The United Kingdom submitted one report in 2003 to the 1267 Committee and six reports to the CTC between 2001 and 2006.[144] For the purpose of this chapter, the UK's compliance is summarised under the following three heads.

---

[141]Council of Europe Convention on the Prevention of Terrorism, opened for signature 16 May 2006, CETS 196 (entered into force 1 June 2007).

[142]Walker (2007, p. 183).

[143]Implementation of Security Council resolution 1624 (2005): report of the United Kingdom in response to the Counter-Terrorism Committee's questions, UN Doc S/2006/398 (2006), p. 3.

[144]Report to the 1267 Committee (n 140); (first report to the CTC) The United Kingdom of Great Britain and Northern Ireland Report to the Counter-Terrorism Committee pursuant to paragraph 6 of Security Council resolution 1373 (2001) of 28 September 2001, UN Doc S/2001/1232 (2001); The United Kingdom of Great Britain and Northern Ireland: second report to the Counter-Terrorism Committee pursuant to paragraph 6 of Security Council resolution 1373 (2001) of 28 September 2001, UN Doc S/2002/787 (2002); Third report of the United Kingdom of Great Britain and Northern Ireland to the Counter-Terrorism Committee pursuant to paragraph 6 of Security Council resolution 1373 (2001) of 28 September 2001, UN Doc S/2003/264 (2003); Fourth report of the United Kingdom of Great Britain and Northern Ireland to the Counter-Terrorism Committee pursuant to paragraph 6 of Security Council resolution 1373 (2001) of 28 September 2001, UN Doc S/2004/157 (2004); (fifth report to the CTC) Letter dated 7 September 2005 from the Permanent Representative of the United Kingdom of Great Britain and Northern Ireland to the United Nations addressed to the Chairman of the Counter-Terrorism Committee, UN Doc S/2005/583 (2005); and Implementation of Security Council resolution 1624 (2005): report of the United Kingdom (n 143).

8.3.1   Terrorism-Related Offences

Chapter 14 in this title undertakes an analysis of the criminalisation of terrorism by
the four case study countries, including a comparison between the offences required
under the universal terrorism-related conventions and Security Council resolutions
(Appendix 3, Table 1) and the terrorism-related offences under the law of the
United Kingdom (Appendix 3, Table 5). Chapter 14 concludes that the United
Kingdom's law adequately criminalises all of the conduct listed in Appendix 3,
Table 1.

8.3.2   Treaty Action and Implementation

At the time of the September 11 attacks and adoption of Security Council resolution
1373 (2001), the United Kingdom was a party to all of the universal terrorism-
related conventions adopted by that time. Those conventions had been implemented
under the Explosive Substances Act 1883 (see Sect. 8.1.1.1 above); the Biological
Weapons Act 1974 (Sect. 8.1.1.2 above); the Internationally Protected Persons Act
1978 (Sect. 8.1.3.1 above); the Chemical Weapons Act 1996 (Sect. 8.1.1.3 above);
the Civil Aviation Act 1982 (Sect. 8.1.2.1 above); the Aviation Security Act 1982
(Sect. 8.1.2.2 above); the Taking of Hostages Act 1982 (Sect. 8.1.3.2 above); the
Nuclear Material (Offences) Act 1983 (Sect. 8.1.4 above); the Aircraft and Maritime Security Act 1990 (Sect. 8.1.2.3 above); and the Terrorism Act 2000
(Sect. 8.1.5 above). Since the time of resolution 1373 (2001), the United Kingdom
became an original signatory of, and ratified, the Nuclear Terrorism Convention
and implemented those obligations under the Terrorism Act 2006 (Sect. 8.1.8
above). A large part of the implementation of the universal terrorism-related
conventions involves the criminalisation of conduct identified under those treaties.
This aspect of the conventions has been implemented in full.

8.3.3   Implementation of Security Council Resolutions

Consideration has already been given above, at Sect. 8.2.4, to the implementation
by the United Kingdom of Security Council resolution 1624 (2005), which called
upon States to adopt measures to prohibit and prevent the incitement to commit
terrorist acts.[145] The travel ban and arms embargo against the Taliban and Al-
Qa'ida under resolution 1267 (1999) are implemented by the United Kingdom
under the Terrorism (United Nations Measures) Order 2001 and the Al-Qa'ida

---

[145]See the United Kingdom's report on Implementation of Security Council resolution 1624
(n 143).

and Taliban (United Nations Measures) Order 2002 (see Sects. 8.2.2 and 8.2.3 above). Those aspects of the same resolution concerning the freezing of funds and other financial resources controlled by or on their behalf of the Taliban or any other individuals of entities designated by the Committee are linked to paragraphs 1(c) and (d) of Security Council resolution 1373 (2001), which are identified below.

Security Council resolution 1373 (2001) contains 11 binding directions under paragraphs 1 and 2 of the resolution (see Chap. 3, Sect. 3.2.2.3), which have been implemented by the United Kingdom as follows:

1. Prevention and suppression of the financing of terrorist acts (para 1(a))
   Paragraph 1(a), which requires the prevention and suppression of the financing of terrorist acts, is a general provision, expanded upon by the subparagraphs that follow it. Additional to the points made under the following items, the United Kingdom has pointed to: the training of law enforcement officers in techniques for the investigation of terrorist financing;[146] the use of multi-agency co-ordination in this field;[147] and suspicious transactions reporting under the UK's anti-money laundering legislation.[148]

2. Criminalising the provision of funds for terrorist acts (para 1(b))
   In compliance with this provision of resolution 1373 (2001), sections 15–18 and 63 of the Terrorism Act 2000 (Sect. 8.1.5.3 above), supplemented by the Terrorism (United Nations Measures) Order 2001 and articles 7–10 of the Al-Qa'ida and Taliban (United Nations Measures) Order 2002 (see Sects. 8.2.2 and 8.2.3 above), contain offences pertaining to the financing of terrorism.[149]

3. Freezing of funds and assets of terrorist entities (para 1(c))
   The freezing of terrorist assets is given effect through various provisions of the UK's law, including especially the Terrorism Act 2000 (Sect. 8.1.5.4 above), supplemented by article 4 of the Terrorism (United Nations Measures) Order 2001 and article 8 of the Al-Qa'ida and Taliban (United Nations Measures) Order 2002 (see Sects. 8.2.2 and 8.2.3 above).[150] Obligations are imposed on financial institutions to report suspicions of the holding or control of property belonging to or controlled by listed persons or persons concerned with terrorism (Sects. 8.1.5 and 8.2.2 above).

4. Prohibiting the provision of financial or related services to terrorist entities (para 1(d))
   Responding to paragraph 1(d) of the resolution, article 3 of the Terrorism (United Nations Measures) Order 2001 sets out an offence for any person to make funds or financial or related services available to or for the benefit of a

---

[146]See the United Kingdom's fourth report to the CTC (n 144) pp. 3–4.

[147]See the United Kingdom's fourth report to the CTC (n 144) pp. 4–5.

[148]See the United Kingdom's fourth report to the CTC (n 144) p. 7.

[149]See the United Kingdom's first report to the CTC (n 144) p. 6.

[150]See the United Kingdom's report to the 1267 Committee (n 140) pp. 3–4; its first report to the CTC (n 144) p. 6; its second report to the CTC (n 144) p. 3; and its fourth report to the CTC (n 144) pp. 8–11.

person who commits, attempts to commit, facilitates or participates in the commission of acts of terrorism (or persons controlled or owned directly or indirectly by such a person, or a person acting on their behalf, or at their direction) – see Sect. 8.2.3 above and Appendix 3, Table 5(O).[151]

5. Suppression of support to terrorists and elimination of the supply of weapons (para 2(a))

   In compliance with paragraph 2(a) of resolution 1373 (2001), the Terrorism Act 2000 criminalises membership in proscribed organisations (section 11), support for or wearing the uniform of such organisations (sections 12 and 13), the provision of weapons training (section 54), directing a terrorist organisation (section 56), and possessing an article or collecting information for terrorist purposes (sections 57 and 58) – see Sect. 8.1.5.3 above and Appendix 3, Table 5 (J).[152] Concerning the requirement to prohibit recruitment to terrorist groups, there is no specific offence to that effect in UK law, although the United Kingdom has pointed to compliance with this requirement through the criminalisation of membership in proscribed organisations (as just mentioned) and the offence in section 54(3) of the Terrorism Act 2000 to invite another to receive information or training in the making or use of firearms, explosives, or chemical, biological or nuclear weapons.[153]

6. Preventing the commission of terrorist acts (para 2(b))

   As discussed in Chap. 3, measuring a State's compliance with this direction is technically impossible, since all that can be done by a State is to undertake *all reasonable and practical steps* to prevent the commission of terrorist acts (see Sect. 3.2.2.3). Additional to the measures in response to items 1–5 above, the United Kingdom has identified its active role in promoting international co-operation on terrorism bilaterally and in multinational fora (the EU, UN and G8) and its commitment to enhance practical and effective co-operation with other countries to deny terrorists a safe haven and bring them to justice.[154]

7. Denial of safe haven (para 2(c))

   As well as its commitment to enhance co-operation with other countries to deny terrorists a safe haven, the United Kingdom has referred to its immigration control mechanisms, including under the Immigration Act 1971.[155]

8. Preventing the use of State territory by terrorists (para 2(d))

---

[151]See the United Kingdom's first report to the CTC (n 144) p. 7. See also the United Kingdom's second report to the CTC (n 144) pp. 3–4. Concerning the potential use and abuse of charitable organisations, see the United Kingdom's fourth report to the CTC (n 144) pp. 7–8.

[152]See the United Kingdom's first report to the CTC (n 144) pp. 7–8. See also the United Kingdom's second report to the CTC (n 144) pp. 4–5.

[153]See the United Kingdom's first report to the CTC (n 144) p. 7.

[154]See the United Kingdom's first report to the CTC (n 144) p. 9. See also the United Kingdom's fourth report to the CTC (n 144) pp. 12–17.

[155]See the United Kingdom's first report to the CTC (n 144) p. 9. See also the United Kingdom's fourth report to the CTC (n 144) pp. 18–20; and its report on Implementation of Security Council resolution 1624 (n 143) pp. 3–4.

The offences under the Terrorism Act 2000, referred to under item 5 above, contribute to the implementation of paragraph 2(d) of resolution 1373 (2001).[156] The Terrorism Act 2006 has added further relevant offences, including preparation of terrorist acts (section 5), training for terrorism (section 6), and attendance at a place for terrorist training (section 8) – see Sect. 8.1.8.1 above and Appendix 3, Table 5(M). The provision of certain types of technical assistance and training is also prohibited under article 5 of the Al-Qa'ida and Taliban (United Nations Measures) Order 2000 – see Sect. 8.2.2 above and Appendix 3, Table 5(N).

9. Ensuring the prosecution and severe punishment of terrorists (para 2(e))

   As identified earlier in this chapter, the various offences under the United Kingdom's counter-terrorism legislation carry severe penalties (see Sect. 8.1 above).[157] The question of sentencing is addressed in both the Terrorism Act 2006 and the Counter-Terrorism Act 2008 (see Sects. 8.1.8.2 and 8.1.9 above). The 2006 Act increased maximum sentences for certain offences under section 54 of the Terrorism Act 2000 and section 2 of the Nuclear Material (Offences) Act 1983. The Counter-Terrorism Act 2008 further addressed the question of sentencing, making it an aggravating feature for the purpose of sentencing if an offence "has or may have a terrorist connection" (section 30).

10. Assisting in criminal investigations and prosecutions (para 2(f))

    The United Kingdom has reported that it plays an active role in promoting international co-operation on terrorism bilaterally and in multinational for a, including its support for the extension of Europol's remit to include counter-terrorism activity.[158] It has pointed to the Criminal Justice (International Co-operation) Act 1990 as providing the general framework for provision of mutual legal assistance by the UK.[159]

11. Establishing and maintaining effective border controls to prevent the movement of terrorists (para 2(g))

    The United Kingdom concentrates most of its immigration control at sea and airports, using visa regimes and examination on arrival, backed by intelligence,

---

[156]See the United Kingdom's first report to the CTC (n 144) p. 9.

[157]See the United Kingdom's first report to the CTC (n 144) p. 10. See also the United Kingdom's second report to the CTC (n 144) p. 6. Compare this with the Home Office report on Statistics on Terrorism Arrests and Outcomes (n 117), para 20, which states: "In 2007/8, based upon year of conviction and principal offence, there were 31 convictions under terrorism legislation and 25 convictions under non-terrorism legislation which were considered significant. Shorter sentences were given under terrorism legislation with the majority (76%) under 10 years. The more serious nature of offences dealt with under non-terrorism legislation has meant that only 1 custodial sentence was under 4 years with 19 (84%) over 10 years, including 9 life sentences and a single Indeterminate sentence for Public Protection (IPP)."

[158]See the United Kingdom's first report to the CTC (n 144) p. 10.

[159]See the United Kingdom's second report to the CTC (n 144) p. 6. See also the United Kingdom's third report to the CTC (n 144) pp. 3–9; and the United Kingdom's fourth report to the CTC (n 144) pp. 17–18.

to prevent the movement of terrorists.[160] For further consideration of immigration and border control issues, and the use by the United Kingdom of diplomatic assurances, see Chap. 21 (Sect. 21.3.3).[161]

References

Brandon, Ben. 2004. Terrorism, Human Rights and the Rule of Law: 120 Years of the UK's Legal Response to Terrorism. *Criminal Law Review* 969.

Fenwick, Helen. 2002. *Civil Liberties and Human Rights*. London: 3rd Edition, Cavendish Publishing.

Kirby, The Hon Justice Michael. 2005. Terrorism and the Democratic Response: A Tribute to the European Court of Human Rights. *University of New South Wales Law Journal* 10.

Jones, Alun, Bowers, Rupert, and Lodge, Hugo. 2006. *Blackstone's Guide to the Terrorism Act 2006*. Oxford: Oxford University Press.

Middleton, Ben. 2008. Jury directions: interpreting s. 57 and s. 58 of the Terrorism Act 2000. 72(5) *The Journal of Criminal Law* 349.

Livingstone, Stephen. 1994. The House of Lords and the Northern Ireland Conflict. 57(3) *The Modern Law Review* 333.

Schabas, William, and Olivier, Clémentine. 2003. United Kingdom Anti-Terrorist Legislation. In Doucet, Ghislaine (Ed). *Terrorism, Victims, and International Criminal Responsibility*. Paris: SOS Attentats.

Trivizas, Eugene, and Smith, Philip. 1997. The Deterrent Effect of Terrorist Incidents on the Rates of Luggage Theft in Railway and Underground Station. 37(1) *British Journal of Criminology* 63.

Walker, Clive. 1983. The Jellicoe Report on the Prevention of Terrorism (Temporary Provisions) Act 1976. 46(4) *The Modern Law Review* 484.

Walker, Clive. 2002. *Blackstone's Guide to The Anti-Terrorism Legislation*. Oxford: Oxford University Press.

Walker, Clive. 2004. 50th Anniversary Article: Terrorism and Criminal Justice – Past, Present and Future. *Criminal Law Review* 311.

Walker, Clive. 2007. The United Kingdom's Anti-terrorism Laws: Lessons for Australia. In Lynch, Andrew, MacDonald, Edwina, and Williams, George (Eds). *Law and Liberty in the War on Terror*. Sydney: The Federation Press.

Walker, Clive. 2009. *Blackstone's Guide to The Anti-Terrorism Legislation*. Oxford: 2nd Edition, Oxford University Press.

---

[160]See the United Kingdom's first report to the CTC (n 144) p. 10.

[161]See also the United Kingdom's second report to the CTC (n 144) p. 7; the United Kingdom's fourth report to the CTC (n 144) pp. 14–16; and its report on Implementation of Security Council resolution 1624 (n 143) p. 4.

Part II

Chapter 9
International and Regional Human Rights Law

Broadly speaking, human rights comprise rights and freedoms said to inherently belong to humans by virtue of their being human. The full spectrum of human rights and freedoms involve the respect for, and protection and fulfilment of, civil, cultural, economic, political and social rights, as well as the right to development. Although the historical development of human rights has led to the categorisation by some of rights into first, second and third generation rights,[1] it is recognised that human rights are universal, which means that they belong inherently to all human beings, as well as being inter-dependent and indivisible.[2]

This chapter provides an introduction to international human rights law and the obligations of States under this body of law. Due to the nature of the rights which tend to be most affected by counter-terrorism, particular attention is paid to the International Covenant on Civil and Political Rights and the European Convention on Human Rights. Consideration is also given to the extraterritorial application of human rights obligations, and the interaction between human rights and international humanitarian law.

---

[1] In 1979 Karel Vasak, the then head of the UN Educational, Scientific and Cultural Organization (UNESCO), categorised human rights as falling into three categories: (1) first generation (civil and political) rights, which broadly speaking prevent the State from interfering with the day-to-day lives of its citizens (e.g. right to a fair trial and the freedom of expression); (2) second generation (economic, social and cultural) rights, which require the State to ensure that goods and services are evenly distributed throughout all levels of society (e.g. the rights to education and employment); and (3) third generation rights, said to require States to cooperate in order to achieve the progressive improvement of the lives of their entire populations (e.g. development and emergency assistance).

[2] See, for example: World Conference on Human Rights, Vienna Declaration and Programme of Action, UN Doc A/CONF.157/23 (1993); the Universal Declaration on Human Rights, adopted under General Assembly resolution 217(III) (1948), article 2; and the Charter of the United Nations, article 55(c).

A. Conte, *Human Rights in the Prevention and Punishment of Terrorism*,
DOI 10.1007/978-3-642-11608-7_9, © Springer-Verlag Berlin Heidelberg 2010

9.1 International Human Rights Law

Modern international human rights law is made up of what is known as the 'International Bill of Human Rights', together with a number of further subject-specific human rights treaties, as well as customary international law.[3] The International Bill of Human Rights is not a treaty itself, but refers to five documents: the Universal Declaration on Human Rights (adopted under a resolution of the General Assembly),[4] the International Covenant on Economic, Social and Cultural Rights, the International Covenant on Civil and Political Rights, and its two Optional Protocols.[5] Added to these are several core universal human rights treaties: the Convention on the Elimination of All Forms of Racial Discrimination; the Convention on the Elimination of All Forms of Discrimination against Women; the Convention against Torture and other Cruel, Inhuman or Degrading Treatment or Punishment; the Convention on the Rights of the Child; the International Convention on the Protection of the Rights of All Migrant Workers and Members of Their Families.[6] Recently adopted are the International Convention for the Protection of All Persons from Enforced Disappearance, and the International Convention on the

---

[3]See the list of treaties set out in the website of the Office of the High Commissioner for Human Rights, "The Core International Human Rights Instruments and their Monitoring Bodies", online: http://www2.ohchr.org/english/law/index.htm#core. For a useful summary of the development of human rights law at the international level, including its various sources, see Office of the High Commissioner for Human Rights in cooperation with the International Bar Association, *Human Rights in the Administration of Justice: A Manual on Human Rights for Judges, Prosecutors and Lawyers* (New York: United Nations, 2003), pp. 2–12.

[4]Universal Declaration on Human Rights, GA Res 217(III), UN GAOR, 3rd sess, 183rd plen mtg, UN Doc A/Res/3/217 (1948).

[5]International Covenant on Economic, Social and Cultural Rights, opened for signature 16 December 1966, 993 UNTS 3 (entered into force 3 January 1976); International Covenant on Civil and Political Rights, opened for signature 16 December 1966, 999 UNTS 171 (entered into force 23 March 1976); Optional Protocol to the International Covenant on Civil and Political Rights, opened for signature 16 December 1966, 999 UNTS 302 (entered into force 23 March 1976); and Second Optional Protocol to the International Covenant on Civil and Political Rights, opened for signature 15 December 1989, 1642 UNTS 414 (entered into force 11 July 1991). See Office of the High Commissioner for Human Rights, Fact Sheet No 2 (Rev 1), "The International Bill of Human Rights", online: http://www.ohchr.org/Documents/Publications/FactSheet2Rev. 1en.pdf.

[6]Convention on the Elimination of All Forms of Racial Discrimination, opened for signature 7 March 1966, 9464 UNTS 211 (entered into force 4 January 1969); the Convention on the Elimination of All Forms of Discrimination Against Women, opened for signature 18 December 1979, 1249 UNTS 13 (entered into force 3 September 1981); the Convention Against Torture and other Cruel, Inhuman or Degrading Treatment or Punishment, opened for signature 10 December 1984, 1465 UNTS 112 (entered into force 26 June 1987); and the Convention on the Rights of the Child, opened for signature 20 November 1989, 1577 UNTS 43 (entered into force 2 September 1990).

Protection and Promotion of the Rights and Dignity of Persons with Disabilities.[7] There is a growing body of subject-specific treaties and protocols, as well as various regional treaties on the protection of human rights and fundamental freedoms.[8]

It should be noted that international human rights law is not limited to the enumeration of rights within treaties, but also includes rights and freedoms that have become part of customary international law. Many of the rights set out within the Universal Declaration on Human Rights are said to hold this character. The Human Rights Committee, established under the International Covenant on Civil and Political Rights, has similarly observed that some rights within the International Covenant reflect norms of customary international law.[9] Furthermore, some rights are recognised as having a special status as norms of *jus cogens* (peremptory norms of customary international law), which means that there are no circumstances in which derogation of those rights is permissible. The prohibitions of torture, slavery, genocide, racial discrimination, crimes against humanity, and the right to self-determination are widely recognised as peremptory norms, as reflected in the International Law Commission's Articles on State Responsibility.[10] The Committee on the Elimination of Racial Discrimination has said that the principle of non-discrimination has also become a norm of *jus cogens*.[11]

[7]International Convention for the Protection of All Persons from Enforced Disappearance, adopted on 13 November 2006 by the Third Committee of the General Assembly; and International Convention on the Protection and Promotion of the Rights and Dignity of Persons with Disabilities, adopted on 5 December 2006 by the Ad Hoc Committee of the General Assembly on a Comprehensive and Integral International Convention on the Protection and Promotion of the Rights and Dignity of Persons with Disabilities.

[8]Including, for example, the (European) Convention for the Protection of Human Rights and Fundamental Freedoms, opened for signature 4 November 1950, 213 UNTS 222 (entered into force 3 September 1953); the American Convention on Human Rights, 1144 UNTS 123 (entered into force 18 July 1978); the Charter of the Organization of American States, opened for signature in 1948, 119 UNTS 3 (entered into force 13 December 1951); the African Charter on Human and Peoples' Rights, opened for signature 27 June 1981, OAU Doc CAB/LEG/67/3 rev 5, (1982) 21 ILM 58 (entered into force 21 October 1986); and the Arab Charter on Human Rights, adopted by the Arab League Council and opened for signature 15 September 1994 (the Charter remains unratified; its unofficial English translation can be found in the ICJ Review 56/1996).

[9]Human Rights Committee, General Comment 24: General comment on issues relating to reservations made upon ratification or accession to the Covenant or the Optional Protocols thereto, or in relation to declarations under article 41 of the Covenant, UN Doc CCPR/C/21/Rev.1/Add.6 (1994), para 8; and Human Rights Committee, General Comment 29: States of Emergency (Article 4), UN Doc CCPR/C/21/Rev.1/Add.11 (2001), para 13.

[10]International Law Commission, Draft Articles on Responsibility of States for Internationally Wrongful Acts with commentaries, 2001 (United Nations, 2005) 281 (n 675). See also *Prosecutor v Furundzija* Case IT-95-17/1 (judgment of 10 December 1998).

[11]Committee on the Elimination of Racial Discrimination, "Statement on Racial Discrimination and Measures to Combat Terrorism", in Report of the Committee on the Elimination of Racial Discrimination, UN Doc A/57/18, para 107.

Those human rights that are part of customary international law are applicable to all States.[12] In the case of human rights treaties, those States that are party to a particular treaty have obligations under that treaty.[13] Added to this, and particularly relevant to a number of human rights challenges in countering terrorism, all members of the United Nations are obliged to take joint and separate action in co-operation with the United Nations for the achievement of the purposes set out in article 55 of the UN Charter, including the universal respect for, and observance of, human rights and fundamental freedoms for all without distinction as to race, sex, language, or religion.[14]

9.2   The International Covenant on Civil and Political Rights and the European Convention on Human Rights

Following the foundation of the Council of Europe in May 1949, its membership drafted the (European) Convention for the Protection of Human Rights and Fundamental Freedoms (ECHR), which was adopted in November 1950 and entered into force 3 September 1953.[15] The European Convention has been added to and amended under 14 Additional Protocols, not all of which remain in force.[16] The International Covenant on Civil and Political Rights (ICCPR) was adopted by the United Nations General Assembly in December 1966 and entered into force on 23 March 1976, three months after it had received its 35th ratification.[17] Since the Covenant is of potentially worldwide application it is occasionally referred to as one of the United Nations' 'universal' instruments. At the time of writing this chapter, the ICCPR has 162 parties, with eight further States who are currently signatories only, representing adherence to the Covenant by a substantial majority of the world's States and self-governing territories.[18] This includes all four case study countries. The ECHR has 47 States parties, including the United Kingdom.

---

[12]*Military and Paramilitary Activities in and against Nicaragua (Nicaragua v United States of America), Merits* (1986) ICJ Reports, paras 172–201.

[13]See the Vienna Convention on the Law of Treaties, opened for signature 23 May 1969, 1155 UNTS 331 (entered into force 27 January 1980), article 34.

[14]Charter of the United Nations, articles 55(c) and 56.

[15]Convention for the Protection of Human Rights and Fundamental Freedoms, opened for signature 4 November 1950, 213 UNTS 222 (entered into force 3 September 1953), article 59(2).

[16]For a list of signatures and ratifications to the Convention and its Additional Protocols, see http://conventions.coe.int/Treaty/Commun/ListeTableauCourt.asp?MA=3&CM=16&CL=ENG.

[17]International Covenant on Civil and Political Rights, opened for signature 16 December 1966, 999 UNTS 171 (entered into force 23 March 1976), article 49.

[18]Office of the United Nations High Commissioner for Human Rights 'Status of Ratifications of the Principal International Human Rights Treaties'. For a breakdown of party status to the ICCPR and its Optional Protocol, see Conte and Burchill (2009, Appendix 4).

9.2.1 The General Nature of Human Rights Obligations Under the ICCPR and ECHR

Article 1 of the European Convention provides that its parties "shall secure to everyone within their jurisdiction the rights and freedoms defined in Section I of this Convention". Article 2(1) of the International Covenant similarly provides that States parties assume the following obligation:[19]

> Each State Party to the present Covenant undertakes to respect and to ensure to all individuals within its territory and subject to its jurisdiction the rights recognised in the present Covenant, without distinction of any kind, such as race, colour, sex, language religion, political or other opinion, national or social origin, property, birth or other status.

The limits of the obligations under article 1 and article 2(1) have not been greatly analysed by the Human Rights Committee or the European Court of Human Rights, but a number of preliminary points might be made about their content.

9.2.1.1 Obligations Owed to Individuals

The obligation to respect and ensure rights under the International Covenant and European Convention is owed to *individuals* within a State's territory and subject to its jurisdiction. The two instruments are concerned with the individual person and not collectives of individuals (despite the wording of article 1 of the ICCPR, which guarantees the right of peoples to self-determination) or artificial legal persons such as corporations, charitable organisations or other similar legal foundations.[20] There are certain rights which appear to be collective in nature, such as the right of individuals to belong ethnic, linguistic or religious minorities, but it is the right of the individual in question to belong to these pre-existing minorities which is of significance.[21]

9.2.1.2 Temporal Scope of Obligations

It is a rule of international law that a State is not bound by the terms of a treaty in respect of any dispute if the events in question occurred before the treaty entered into force or if the subject matter of the treaty ceased to exist before it entered into force for the State in question.[22] This is the position also with

---

[19]On the nature and effect of this obligation see Nowak (2005, pp. 27–34 and 37–45); and Harris (1995, pp. 3–4).

[20]This has now become a well established part of the Committee's jurisprudence, see *Länsman et al v Finland*, Communication 1023/2001, UN Doc CCPR/C/83/D/1023/2001 (2005), para 6.1.

[21]See Conte and Burchill (2009, Chap. 10).

[22]Vienna Convention on the Law of Treaties (n 13), article 28.

respect to the application of the International Covenant and the European Convention.[23] There is an exception to this rule, however, where the effects of a violation of a treaty provision continue after the entry into force of the treaty for the State. These were the circumstances which occurred in *Massera v Uruguay*, the first case dealt with by the Human Rights Committee under the First Optional Protocol to the ICCPR. Here, the Committee held that part of the communication was inadmissible in so far as it dealt with events which had allegedly occurred before the entry into force of the ICCPR. In the case of one of the victims, who was allegedly still being detained, the Committee found that the continuing effects of the detention permitted the admissibility of the communication.[24] The European Court of Human Rights has taken the same approach to the temporal application of the ECHR.[25]

Where a party to the ECHR denounces the Convention under article 58, denunciation does not have immediate effect. Denunciation is only possible five years after a State has become party to the ECHR, and it will not release the State from its obligations for a period of six months after the notice of denunciation is given. Although the International Covenant does not expressly provide for denunciation, article 56 of the Vienna Convention on the Law of Treaties provides for certain grounds for withdrawal and termination from international treaties. In these circumstances, a State party must give at least 12 months' notice of its intention to withdraw from the treaty.[26]

9.2.1.3   Jurisdictional Scope of Obligations

The obligations under the ICCPR and ECHR are owed in respect of individuals that are within the State's *territory or subject to its jurisdiction*, although article 1 of the ECHR speaks only of securing rights to those within the jurisdiction of States parties. This does not mean that all individuals are treated exactly the same for the purposes of the attribution of various rights, since there are inevitably certain limitations on the rights of aliens and those who are not lawfully present within the territory of the State.[27] In other respects, however, all individuals, be they citizens or non-citizens, are on an equal footing as far as they are the

---

[23]See, for example, the statement of the European Commission on Human Rights in *Nielsen v Denmark* (1959–1960) 2 *Yearbook* 412, p. 454.

[24]*Massera v Uruguay*, Communication 5/1977, UN Doc CCPR/C/7/D/5/1977 (1979). See also Nowak (2005, pp. 855–856) and *A et al v S*, Communication 1/1976, UN Doc CCPR/C/OP/1 at 3 (1984), para (d).

[25]*De Becker v Belgium* (1959–1960) 2 *Yearbook* 214.

[26]Vienna Convention on the Law of Treaties (n 13), article 56(2).

[27]See, for example, article 25 of the ICCPR, the application of which is limited to citizens of the State.

subjects of the relevant civil and political right guaranteed by the ICCPR and ECHR.[28]

It is also possible that individuals who are not within a State's territory might be subject to its jurisdiction. As a number of communications have demonstrated, the personal relationship between a State based on ties of nationality may operate to impose responsibility on a State where it has violated the rights of one of its citizens, even though that citizen may be situated abroad (see Sect. 9.3.1 below).

9.2.1.4 Vertical and Horizontal Obligations

There is little doubt, according to the wording of article 1 of the ECHR and article 2(1) of the ICCPR, that the primary obligation for ensuring the protection of rights is imposed upon the State. In most circumstances there will be a more or less clear relationship between the organs of the State and the violation of human rights which imposes responsibility upon it for that violation.[29] This can be described as a vertical relationship between the State and the citizen.

Article 1 of the ECHR and article 2(1) of the ICCPR also raise the question of whether the State has a legal responsibility to ensure that the rights of its citizens are not violated by other private citizens. This may be called the enforcement of a horizontal relationship or, as it is known in German, *Drittwirkung*, or the protection by a State of third party rights. The Human Rights Committee has explained that article 2(1) does not create any direct horizontal effects but that:[30]

> ...the positive obligations on States Parties to ensure Covenant rights will only be fully discharged if individuals are protected by the State, not just against violations of Covenant rights by its agents, but also against acts committed by private persons or entities that would impair the enjoyment of Covenant rights in so far as they are amenable to application between private persons or entities.

Certainly, there are particular rights espoused in the ICCPR which seem to imply the right of protection by the State from third parties. Article 6(1), for example, requires the right to life to be protected by law. This would suggest that a State which failed to criminalise the homicidal behaviour of 'private' death squads would fail in its obligation to protect the right to life. Article 23 of the ICCPR, concerning family rights, recognises that the exercise of family rights is subject to protection from both the State and society, the latter of which would include private parties. The Human Rights Committee has referred to article 17 (right to privacy) and

---

[28]See McGoldrick (1990, pp. 20–21) and Lillich (1984, p. 145). General Comment 15 states that: "the general rule is that each one of the rights of the Covenant must be guaranteed without discrimination between citizens and aliens" – see General Comment 15: The position of aliens under the Covenant, UN Doc CCPR General Comment 15 (1986).

[29]Nowak (2005, pp. 38–39).

[30]General Comment 31: Nature of the General Legal Obligations Imposed on States Parties to the Covenant UN Doc CCPR/C/21/Rev.1/Add.13 (2004), para 8.

article 7 (freedom from torture) as particular areas of rights protection where the State will need to ensure that the actions of private persons or parties impair the ability of individuals to enjoy their rights under the Covenant.[31] The European Court has similarly stated that article 8 of the ECHR imposes a positive duty to protect the essential features of family and private life, and that article 3 requires not only that the State protects against torture and inhuman and degrading treatment or punishment but that it also carry out a thorough and effective investigation of alleged incidents of torture.[32]

9.2.1.5 Obligations Applicable Without Distinction

The final part of article 2(1) of the ICCPR requires the rights recognised to be protected "without distinction of any kind, such as race, colour, sex, language religion, political or other opinion, national or social origin, property, birth or other status". This is a broad non-discrimination provision which forbids all types of non-justifiable differentiation of individuals in the protection of their rights.[33] This broad prohibition is supported by the more specific prohibition of discrimination between men and women in the enjoyment of all civil and political rights set out in article 3 of the ICCPR. Furthermore, article 26 of the International Covenant provides an autonomous prohibition on discrimination before the law which has been used in a creative, and not altogether universally approved, manner by the Human Rights Committee. Although article 1 of the ECHR does not express that Convention rights are to be secured without distinction, non-discrimination is guaranteed under article 14. On the issue of non-discrimination generally, and as it applies to the derogation from rights, see Chap. 10, Sect. 10.2.5.

9.2.1.6 Incorporation of Obligations

As noted by Ovey and White, there have been differing views on whether article 1 of the European Convention imposes an obligation to incorporate the actual text of the Convention into domestic law, or at least of the declaration of rights in Section I.[34] Article 2(2) of the International Covenant provides more certainty on the matter, stating that:

> Where not already provided for by existing legislative or other measures, each State Party to the present Covenant undertakes to take the necessary steps, in accordance with its constitutional processes and with the provisions of the present Covenant, to adopt such legislative or other measures as may be necessary to give effect to the rights recognized in the present Covenant.

---

[31]General Comment 31 (ibid) para 8.
[32]See *Marckx v Belgium* (1979–1980) 2 EHRR 330, and *Aksoy v Turkey* (1997) 23 EHRR 553.
[33]Nowak (2005, pp. 45–57).
[34]Ovey and White (2002, pp. 14–15).

It has been suggested by one former member of the Human Rights Committee, Elizabeth Evatt, that the preference of the Committee is for the rights protected by the Covenant to be constitutionally entrenched in domestic law rather than simply protected by the ordinary law of the land.[35] This, of course, raises some constitutional difficulties in States such as the United Kingdom and New Zealand where the concept of constitutional entrenchment is, in a formal sense, unknown (see Chap. 11, Sect. 11.1.3.1). As observed by Ovey and White, "the question by what means the rights are implemented may in the end be a matter of legal technique, though certainly some techniques may be more effective than others".[36] The European Court has succinctly captured the essence of the issue by emphasising that States are obliged, by appropriate means, "to ensure that their domestic legislation is compatible with the Convention and, if need be, to make any necessary adjustments to this end".[37]

9.2.2 Rights Guaranteed by the ICCPR and ECHR

9.2.2.1 Rights Under the International Covenant

The full catalogue of individual rights contained in Part III of the International Covenant on Civil and Political Rights are: the right to life; the prohibition of torture or cruel, inhuman or degrading treatment or punishment; the prohibition of slavery, the slave trade, forced or compulsory labour; the right liberty and security of the person and freedom from arbitrary arrest or detention; humane treatment of prisoners; no imprisonment for failure to fulfil a contractual obligation; freedom of movement; freedom to choose a place of residence and freedom to leave a country; limitations upon the expulsion of aliens lawfully resident in a state; equality before all courts and tribunals and for due process guarantees in criminal and civil proceedings; prohibition on retroactive criminal laws; the right to recognition as a person; freedom from arbitrary or unlawful interference with privacy, family home or correspondence and of unlawful attacks upon a person's honour or reputation; freedom of thought conscience and religion; freedom of opinion and expression; prohibition of propaganda for war and of advocacy of national, racial or religious hatred that constitutes and incitement to discrimination, hostility or violence; the right of peaceful assembly; freedom of association; the right to marry and found a family; measures of protection for children; the right of every citizen to participate in the conduct of public affairs, to have the right to vote and be elected and to have equal access to public service in one's own country; equality of all persons before the law; and the protection of ethnic, religious or linguistic minorities.[38]

---

[35]See Evatt (2002, p. 283).

[36]Ovey and White (2002, p. 16).

[37]*De Becker v Belgium* (n 25), p. 234.

[38]Part I of the ICCPR guarantees the right of all peoples to self-determination.

9.2.2.2   Rights Under the European Convention

For the most part, the same rights are guaranteed under the European Convention on Human Rights and its Additional Protocols 4, 7 and 12, albeit that differences in the expression of rights between the ICCPR and ECHR can impact upon their interpretation and application. The ECHR and its Additional Protocols do not expressly prohibit propaganda for war or the advocacy of national, racial or religious hatred, as article 20(2) of the ICCPR does.[39] Nor does the European Convention expressly provide for the protection of minorities.[40] Unique to the ECHR is the protection of the right to education.[41]

9.2.2.3   The Death Penalty

Although the ICCPR implicitly recognises that the death penalty is, in itself, not contrary to the right to life, nonetheless, the Second Optional Protocol to the ICCPR requires States not to execute anyone within their territories and to take necessary measures to abolish the death penalty.[42] The only reservation which may be made is to reserve the death penalty during times of war pursuant to a conviction for a most serious crime of a military nature.[43] Additional Protocol 6 to the ECHR similarly abolishes the death penalty under article 1, providing an express exception to this during times of war under article 2.[44]

---

[39]Interference with the freedom of expression, where such expression amounts to hate speech or speech which incites violence, is nevertheless capable of justification under article 10(2) of the European Convention. See, for example, *Jersild v Denmark* (1994) 19 EHRR 1. See also Ovey and White (2002, pp. 280–282).

[40]The only specific reference to minorities in the European Convention on Human Rights is in article 14, which guarantees that the enjoyment of rights and freedoms in the Convention must be secured without discrimination on grounds including national or social origin, or association with a national minority. Although it contains no complaints mechanism for individuals or groups, the Council of Europe's 1995 Framework Convention for the Protection of National Minorities should also be noted.

[41]First Protocol to the European Convention on Human Rights, article 2. The right to education is guaranteed under article 13 of the International Covenant on Economic, Social and Cultural Rights (n 5).

[42]Second Optional Protocol to the International Covenant on Civil and Political Rights (n 5), article 1.

[43]Ibid, article 2(1).

[44]Compare this to Additional Protocol 13 to the European Convention on Human Rights, which abolishes the death penalty without exception and without the possibility of reservations or derogations.

9.2.2.4   Reservations and Derogations

Article 57 of the European Convention expressly permits reservations to be made at the time of ratification of the Convention, provided that the reservation is not of a general nature but is instead made in respect of a particular provision of the Convention and to the extent that any law at that time in force for the reserving State is inconsistent with the provision. The United Kingdom maintains a single reservation, applicable to the right to education under the First Additional Protocol to the ECHR.

Although the ICCPR does not mention reservations, the effect of article 19(c) of the Vienna Convention on the Law of Treaties is that reservations to the ICCPR can be lodged so long as they are compatible with the object and purpose of the International Covenant.[45] The Human Rights Committee has defined the object and purpose of the ICCPR to be:[46]

> . . .to create legally binding standards for human rights by defining certain civil and political rights and placing them in a framework of obligations which are legally binding for those States which ratify; and to provide an efficacious supervisory machinery for the obligations undertaken.

Of the four case study countries, Australia is the only party to the ICCPR which maintains reservations to the ICCPR. These pertain to articles 10(2) (segregation of detained persons), 14(6) (compensation for miscarriage of justice) and 20 (propaganda and incitement), although the third of these 'reservations' would be more accurately described as an expression of Australia's understanding of the inter-relationship between articles 19 to 22 of the Covenant:

- Article 10:
  "In relation to paragraph 2 (a) the principle of segregation is accepted as an objective to be achieved progressively. In relation to paragraph 2 (b) and 3 (second sentence) the obligation to segregate is accepted only to the extent that such segregation is considered by the responsible authorities to be beneficial to the juveniles or adults concerned."
- Article 14:
  "Australia makes the reservation that the provision of compensation for miscarriage of justice in the circumstances contemplated in paragraph 6 of article 14 may be by administrative procedures rather than pursuant to specific legal provision."
- Article 20:
  "Australia interprets the rights provided for by articles 19, 21 and 22 as consistent with article 20; accordingly, the Common wealth and the constituent States, having legislated with respect to the subject matter of the article in matters of

---

[45] As confirmed by the Human Rights Committee in its General Comment 24 (n 9), para 6.
[46] Ibid, para 7.

practical concern in the interest of public order (*ordre public*), the right is reserved not to introduce any further legislative provision on these matters."

Both the ICCPR and ECHR allow States parties to temporarily suspend the application of certain rights during a state of emergency which threatens the life of the nation. The general nature and procedural conditions of the derogation provisions in article 4 of the International Covenant and article 15 of the European Convention are considered in Chap. 10, Sect. 10.4. Chapter 17 examines the application of the substantive requirements of those articles to the derogations by the United Kingdom from the right to liberty.

9.2.3 The Human Rights Committee and the European Court of Human Rights

Article 28 of the ICCPR establishes the Human Rights Committee (HRC) to supervise States parties' compliance with the obligations under the Covenant. Article 1 of the Optional Protocol confers jurisdiction upon the Committee to consider individual communications. The Committee consists of 18 members who must be nationals of the States parties to the ICCPR. They must also be "persons of high moral character and recognised competence in the field of human rights".[47] Members of the Committee are elected for a 4 year term and serve in their personal capacity, not as government representatives.[48] Although it was envisaged that the HRC should not simply be a 'legal' body in the sense of being composed entirely by lawyers, the majority of Committee members have been, and continue to be, lawyers of some distinction, although some past and present members have also come from diplomatic or governmental, rather than legal, backgrounds.

While there has been some discussion of the precise nature of the HRC, it now seems that there is a more or less general consensus of opinion that it is neither a judicial nor a quasi-judicial institution, even when acting in its capacity as the final agency for determining authoritatively whether or not there has been a violation of an individual's rights under the Optional Protocol procedure.[49] This view has been propounded by former member and authoritative commentator upon the ICCPR, Tomuschat, and former member and chair, Ando.[50] The Committee has itself declared that it is neither a court nor a quasi-judicial institution.[51] This view was endorsed by the European Court of Justice in *Grant v South-West*

---

[47]ICCPR, article 28(2).

[48]ICCPR, articles 32(1) and 28(3).

[49]See, for example, Nowak (2005, p. 75).

[50]See Tomuschat (1980) and Ando (1991).

[51]See *Selected decisions of the Human Rights Committee under the Optional Protocol. Volume 2*, UN Doc CCPR/C/OP/2 (1990), pp. 1–2, where the Committee stated: ". . .the Committee is neither

Trains Ltd in which it said that the HRC "is not a judicial institution" and that its findings "have no binding force in law".[52] These comments leave open the question of the precise status of the HRC. It is tempting to suggest that the Committee is an institution *sui generis*, but this advances the issue little. What can be said with a high degree of certainty is that the Human Rights Committee is the sole body which is permitted to make authoritative interpretations of the ICCPR, thus when the Committee pronounces upon the content or the meaning of a right contained in the Covenant it does so with undeniable authority. Whether this makes its final 'views', the term used for the conclusion of the process of individual communication, either directly or indirectly binding is a matter of controversy.[53] It also has implications for the concept of precedent or, perhaps more accurately for an institution this nature, the development of a *jurisprudence constante*.

In contrast to the ICCPR, the European Convention on Human Rights establishes, as a judicial body, the European Court of Human Rights "to ensure observance of the engagements undertaken by the High Contracting Parties in the Convention and the Protocols thereto".[54] The total number of judges serving at the Court in Strasbourg is equal to the number of States parties to the Convention, each of whom sits in a personal capacity and must be of high moral character (as in the case of the HRC), and must also possess the qualifications required for appointment to high judicial office, or be *jurisconsults* of recognised competence.[55] States parties to the Convention undertake, under article 46(1), to abide by the final judgment of the Court in any case to which they are party.

The Human Rights Committee is charged with four supervisory functions under the ICCPR and the Optional Protocol: the consideration of periodic reports by States parties; the making of General Comments; management of the inter-State complaints procedure; and management of the individual communication procedure. The jurisdiction of the European Court of Human Rights extends to all matters concerning the interpretation and application of the ECHR and its Protocols as this arises through: inter-State cases; individual applications; and requests of the Committee of Ministers for an advisory opinion.

9.2.3.1 Interpretation of the ICCPR and ECHR

The interpretation of the International Covenant and the European Convention is governed in large part by the principles of interpretation contained in articles 31

---

a court nor a body with a quasi-judicial mandate. . .". For Further observations on the status of the Human Rights Committee, see: McGoldrick (1990, pp. 53–54).

[52]*Grant v South-West Trains Ltd* [1998] ICR 449, ECJ case C-249/96, para 46.

[53]See further Conte and Burchill (2009, Chap. 2).

[54]ECHR, article 19.

[55]ECHR, article 20.

and 32 of the Vienna Convention on the Law of Treaties (VCLT).[56] Article 31 of
the VCLT requires a treaty to be interpreted in good faith in accordance with
the ordinary meaning to be given to the terms of the treaty in their context and in
the light of the treaty's object and purpose.[57] Relying upon article 32 of the Vienna
Convention, the HRC and European Court have also referred to *travaux préparatoires* in elucidating and elaborating upon the meaning of the rights protected by
the ICCPR and ECHR.[58]

Despite the fact that both the Human Rights Committee and the European Court
apply the interpretative principles under the VCLT, there is a significant difference
in the approach of the two bodies to the interpretation of rights and the application
of their parent instruments. While the European Court has extensively developed a
'margin of appreciation' doctrine, encompassing the idea that each society is
entitled to a certain latitude in resolving the inherent conflicts between individual
rights and national interests or among different moral convictions,[59] the doctrine
has been rejected by the Human Rights Committee (see Chap. 10, Sect. 10.2.1).

It should additionally be noted that, under article 40(4) of the ICCPR, the Human
Rights Committee is empowered to issue such general comments as it considers
appropriate on the interpretation and application of the provisions of the ICCPR.[60]
Through its use of general comments, the HRC is able to develop its interpretation
of the Covenant and thereby further assist States in the fulfilment of their obligations under it. The Committee has issued General Comments relating to a number of
provisions of the Covenant including those relating to the right to life, torture,
freedom of expression, treatment of detainees, war propaganda, the administration
of justice, privacy, the rights of children and their families, sexual equality and
public emergencies. Some of these General Comments, including the most recent
on the right to a fair trial, are quite detailed, while others are exiguous and opaque.[61]

It should also be noted that, at the request of the Committee of Ministers, the
European Court has jurisdiction to give advisory opinions on legal questions
concerning the interpretation of the Convention and its Additional Protocols.[62]
Consideration of such requests must be by the 17-judge Grand Chamber.[63] The

---

[56]As this applies to the ICCPR, see, for example, *JB v Canada*, Communication 118/1982, UN
Doc CCPR/C/28/D/118/1982 (1986). As it applies to the ECHR, see *Golder v United Kingdom*
(1979–1980) 1 ECHRR 524, para 29.

[57]On treaty interpretation in general see Sinclair 1984. As this applies to the ICCPR, see Conte and
Burchill (2009, pp. 13–18). As it applies to the ECHR, see Ovey and White (2002, pp. 31–35).

[58]As this applies to the ICCPR, see, for example, *JB v Canada* (n 56). As it applies to the ECHR,
see Ovey and White (2002, pp. 29–30).

[59]See Steiner and Alston (2000, pp. 854–857).

[60]ICCPR, article 40(4). On the evolution of the practice of issuing General Comments see
McGoldrick (1990, pp. 89–96).

[61]All of the Committee's General Comments may be found at http://www2.ohchr.org/english/
bodies/hrc/comments.htm.

[62]ECHR, article 47.

[63]ECHR, article 31(b).

ability of the Committee of Ministers to request an advisory opinion is severely limited, however, by article 47(2) of the ECHR, which has mean that this procedure has never been used to date. Article 47(2) states:

> Such opinions shall not deal with any question relating to the content or scope of the rights or freedoms defined in Section I of the Convention and the protocols thereto, or with any other question which the Court or the Committee of Ministers might have to consider in consequence of any such proceedings as could be instituted in accordance with the Convention.

9.2.3.2 Individual Applications to the HRC and the European Court

Article 34 of the ECHR allows any person, non-governmental organisation or group of persons claiming to be the victim of a violation by a State party of the rights guaranteed by the Convention and its Protocols. The European Court handles both the admissibility and merits phases of applications before it.[64] Applications are initially considered by a three-judge committee which will determine whether the application meets the Convention's admissibility criteria under article 35, although the Committee of judges can only rule an application to be inadmissible if it is unanimous.[65] The combination of articles 34 and 35 of the Convention require consideration of the following nine questions to determine whether an application is admissible:[66]

1. Can the applicant claim to be a victim?
2. Is the defendant State a party to the Convention?
3. Have domestic remedies been exhausted?
4. Is the application filed within six-months from the date on which the final decision on the matter was taken?
5. Is the application signed?
6. Has the application been brought before?
7. Is the application compatible with the Convention?
8. Is the application manifestly ill-founded?
9. Is there an abuse of the right of petition?

Applications which are not ruled inadmissible progress to a hearing before a seven-judge Chamber of the Court, which will consider the written arguments of the parties, investigate contentious material facts, and hear oral arguments, for the purpose of deciding whether the complaint is admissible. The admissibility phase of the hearing is followed by consideration of the merits, although the two phases

---

[64]This became the case since 1 November 1998 with the entry into force of Additional Protocol 11 to the European Convention on Human Rights. See Ovey and White (2002, pp. 6–9).

[65]ECHR, article 28.

[66]See Ovey and White (2002, pp. 8–9), who state that around one in four to one in seven applications have been declared admissible in recent years.

can be joined in some cases since it is at times impossible to separate the question of the merits of an application from that of admissibility. Where a case raises a serious question affecting the interpretation of the Convention and its Protocols, the chamber can relinquish its jurisdiction and refer the matter to the 17-judge Grand Chamber, unless one of the parties objects.[67] Following a judgment of the Chamber of the Court, parties to the case can request the case to be referred to the Grand Chamber within three months of the judgment of the Chamber.[68] A panel of five judges of the Grand Chamber will then determine whether to accept the request, i.e. whether the case raises a serious question affecting the interpretation or application of the Convention and its Protocols, or a serious issue of general importance.[69]

The position of individuals affected by the conduct of States parties to the ICCPR is much more precarious than under the ECHR. Individual communications can only be received by the Human Rights Committee if the State in question has become a party to the First Optional Protocol to the ICCPR.[70] When the HRC receives a communication from an individual subject to the jurisdiction of one of the States parties, it then deals with the communication in two stages, much as is done by the European Court: first, it must determine whether or not the communication is admissible, i.e. whether it satisfies the formal requirements set out in the Protocol, these being that:[71]

1. The communication must be brought by an individual human being.
2. The individual must be a victim of a violation by a State party to the ICCPR and the First Optional Protocol.
3. The communication must be admissible *ratione materiae*, i.e. it must allege violation of one or more of the rights protected by the ICCPR.
4. The communication must not be anonymous and cannot be an abuse of process.
5. The communication must be admissible *ratione temporis*, i.e. the State in question must, at the time of the violation, have been a party to both the ICCPR and the Optional Protocol.
6. The communication must be admissible *ratione loci*, i.e. the violation must have occurred within the territory or subject to the jurisdiction of the allegedly delinquent State.
7. The subject matter of the communication cannot be, or have been, examined under another procedure of international investigation or settlement.
8. The individual must have exhausted all available domestic remedies.

If the Committee determines that the communication is admissible, it then proceeds to the second stage of determining whether or not there has been a substantive

---

[67]ECHR, articles 30, 31 and 43.

[68]ECHR, articles 43(1) and 44(2).

[69]ECHR, article 43(2).

[70]First Optional Protocol to the ICCPR, article 1.

[71]Optional Protocol, articles 2, 3 and 5. See Conte and Burchill (2009, Chap. 2).

violation of any of the rights protected in the ICCPR.[72] In some circumstances the two stages are dealt with simultaneously, for the same reasons that the European Court might do so. This is particularly the case where there is some doubt about whether the ICCPR applies *ratione materiae* (see Sect. 9.2.3.2 above). Furthermore, while the process is a two-stage procedure, the Human Rights Committee usually deals with the questions of admissibility and the merits of communications at the same sitting.[73] All proceedings before the Human Rights Committee take place on the written evidence before it.[74] The normal procedure is for an applicant to lodge a complaint.[75] The State party concerned will then be asked for its response, which it must make within six months.[76] The applicant is given the opportunity to comment on the State's response. This process might be extended to further replies and responses until the Committee is satisfied that it has the information it requires. The entire process is concluded when the Committee issues its final views.[77]

9.2.3.3 Inter-State Complaints

The inter-State complaint machinery enables any State party to complain to the Human Rights Committee or the European Court that another party is failing to give effect to the provisions of the Covenant or Convention.[78] An important difference exists between the machinery under the ICCPR and ECHR. While parties to the ECHR enjoy this right without exception, the inter-State complaint machinery under the ICCPR is optional and depends upon reciprocal acceptance of the right of complaint by States.[79] State A may thus only bring a complaint against State B if both have accepted the optional procedure. Despite acceptance of this procedure by a number of States parties to the ICCPR, it has never been resorted to by its parties, in contrast to a reasonable level of such complaints brought before the European Court.

9.2.3.4 Consideration of Periodic Reports by the Human Rights Committee

Unlike the European Convention on Human Rights, the International Covenant on Civil and Political Rights requires States parties to submit periodic reports

---

[72]Optional Protocol, article 1.

[73]Rule 91, Rules of Procedure of the Human Rights Committee.

[74]Optional Protocol, articles 2 and 5.

[75]There is a model complaint form by which this might be done, but it is not necessary to use this as long as the requisite information is made available to the HRC.

[76]Optional Protocol, article 4(2).

[77]Optional Protocol, article 5(4).

[78]ICCPR, article 41; ECHR article 33.

[79]ICCPR, article 41.

concerning the implementation and enjoyment of Covenant rights within their territory.[80] Such reports must be submitted by each State within one year of becoming party to the Covenant and at regular periods thereafter (normally about 5 years), as determined by the HRC.[81] These periodic reports are examined in public in the presence of a State party's representative. The Committee may request further details from a State party and may put questions to its representatives. The Committee normally holds three sessions of three weeks each year, and reports annually to the General Assembly. While the HRC is supposed to undertake all of its work during this short period of time, including consideration of individual communications, the majority of the time is taken up by consideration of periodic reports. The principal objective of the Committee in considering periodic reports under the Covenant is not to treat States as if they were defendants in a criminal trial, but to develop a constructive dialogue with them.[82] The rationale is that such a dialogue will be more effective in promoting State party compliance with Covenant obligations. On completion of the reporting process, the Committee issues concluding statements which reflect the main areas of discussion. Here, the Committee may note its concerns regarding aspects of a State's implementation of obligations, or it may make suggestions and recommendations indicating ways in which the State's obligations might be fulfilled more effectively.

9.2.4 Remedies

In almost identical terms to article 2(3)(a) of the ICCPR, States parties to the ECHR undertake, under article 13 of the European Convention, to ensure that:

> Everyone whose rights and freedoms as set forth in this Convention are violated shall have an effective remedy before a national authority notwithstanding that the violation has been committed by persons acting in an official capacity.

As well as requiring States parties to themselves provide effective remedies for human rights violations, the European Convention on Human Rights empowers the European Court to award remedies by way of 'just satisfaction' under article 41. The Court has spoken of three heads of satisfaction: pecuniary loss (involving financial loss suffered as a result of a rights violation); non-pecuniary loss (including, for example, damages arising from pain, suffering and physical or mental injury);[83] and costs and expenses (awarded if they were actually and necessarily incurred in order to prevent, or obtain redress for, the breach of the Convention, and

---

[80]ICCPR, article 40.

[81]ICCPR, article 40(1)(a) and (b).

[82]On this practice see Nowak (2005, pp. 730–733).

[83]Non-pecuniary damages are often described as being awarded on an 'equitable basis', taking into account of what is fair in the circumstances, as was the case in *Caballero v United Kingdom*, Case 32819/96 judgment of 08/02/2000.

were reasonable as to quantum).[84] Monetary compensation is discretionary and will only be awarded if necessary, which is decided on the circumstances as a whole. For example, the court at Strasbourg commonly refuses applications for damages on the basis that a declaration of unlawful conduct is a sufficient remedy for an applicant. It will also take into account the nature and conduct of the applicant to assess whether the applicant is deserving, declining damages in the case of terrorist suspects claiming damages in the 1995 case of *McCann v United Kingdom*, where the Court concluded that "having regard to the fact that the three terrorist suspects who were killed had been intending to plant a bomb in Gibraltar, the Court does not consider it appropriate to make an award under this head".[85] The European Court has also held that there must be a causal link between the compensation sought and the breach of the applicant's Convention rights. Compensation is applied on the basis of the principle of *restitutio in integrum*, the aim of which is to put the applicant back into the position he or she would have been in had the violation not occurred, as far as this is possible.[86] This means that exemplary or punitive damages will not be awarded.

Neither the ICCPR nor its First Optional Protocol expressly provides the Human Rights Committee with the jurisdiction to award remedies. Nonetheless, where a State is found in breach of its obligations, it is normally required by the HRC to undertake remedial action, which may include: modifying its domestic law; commuting a criminal sentence and/or releasing a detained person; returning a victim's passport to enable movement; reconsidering a victim's application for registration of an association (or re-registering the association); reconsidering a victim's request for pension without discrimination on grounds of sex or sexual orientation; prompt resolution of on-going proceedings; allowing a review of a victim's conviction and sentence by a higher domestic tribunal; undertaking a thorough and effective investigation into the disappearance and death of a victim and providing the victim's family with appropriate information on the outcome of its investigation, as well as prosecuting, trying and punishing the culprits; protecting a victim from threats and/or intimidation from members of security forces; or providing restitution or compensation to victims.[87] The Committee often also reminds the State

---

[84]For a useful summary of the general principles utilised by the European Court of Human Rights when determining awards under article 41, see *R v Secretary of State for Home Department ex parte N* [2003] EWHC 207.

[85]*McCann v United Kingdom* (1995) 21 EHRR 97, para 219.

[86]*Kingsley v United Kingdom* (2002) 35 EHRR 10.

[87]See, for example: *Zvozskov et al v Belarus*, Communication 1039/2001, UN Doc CCPR/C/88/D/1039/2001 (2006); *El Dernawi v Libyan Arab Jamahiriya*, Communication 1143/2002, UN Doc CCPR/C/89/D/1043/2002 (2007); *Kornetov v Uzbekistan*, Communication 1057/2002, UN Doc CCPR/C/88/D/1057/2002 (2006); *Korneenko et al v Belarus*, UN Doc 1274/2004, UN Doc CCPR/C/88/D/1274/2004 (2006); *El Awani v Libyan Arab Jamahiriya*, Communication 1295/2004, UN Doc CCPR/C/90/D/1295/2004 (2007); *Pimentel et al v the Philippines*, Communication 1320/2004, UN Doc CCPR/C/89/D/1320/2004 (2007); *Shafiq v Australia*, Communication 1324/2004, UN Doc CCPR/C/88/D/1324/2004 (2006); *Conde v Spain*, Communication 1325/2004, UN Doc CCPR/C/88/D/1325/2004 (2006); *Grioua v Algeria*, Communication 1327/2004, UN Doc CCPR/

party of its obligation to prevent similar violations in the future. When pronouncing a remedy, the Committee observes that:[88]

> Bearing in mind that, by becoming a party to the Optional Protocol, the State party has recognized the competence of the Committee to determine whether there has been a violation of the Covenant or not and that, pursuant to article 2 of the Covenant, the State party has undertaken to ensure to all individuals within its territory and subject to its jurisdiction the rights recognized in the Covenant and to provide an effective and enforceable remedy in case a violation has been established, the Committee wishes to receive from the State party, within 90 days, information about the measures taken to give effect to the Committee's Views.

In order to ensure compliance with its final views, the Committee has developed a follow-up procedure in which a *rapporteur* is appointed to investigate the measures which delinquent States have taken to remedy their breaches of the ICCPR.[89] While this procedure is, like most of the Committee's activities, heavily underfunded, it has proved to be a useful measure of supervision. Another useful mode of supervision is the requirement that States, when making their periodic reports, indicate the measures which they have adopted to give effect to the HRC's final views in applicable communications.

9.3 Extraterritoriality and the Application of Human Rights in Armed Conflict

Important to the understanding of international human rights law and the extent to which it provides protection are the questions of how and when this body of law can apply outside the territory of a State, and how it overlaps with and complements international humanitarian law.

9.3.1 The Extraterritorial Application of Human Rights Law

Discussed above was the principle that the obligations under the ECHR are owed to individuals within the "territory" of States parties or, in the case of the ICCPR, within the State's "territory or subject to its jurisdiction" (see Sect. 9.2.1.3). At a minimum, this means that a State is responsible for acts of foreign officials

---

C/90/D/1328/2004 (2007); *Afuson v Cameroon*, Communication 1353/2005, UN Doc CCPR/C/89/D/1353/2005 (2007); and *X v Colombia*, Communication 1361/2005, UN Doc CCPR/C/89/D/1361/2005 (2007).

[88]This is the common formulation used by the Committee, as explained in its annual reports to the UN General Assembly. See, for example, the Report of the Human Rights Committee, UN Doc A/62/40 (2007), Volume I, para 186.

[89]Rule 95, Rules of Procedure.

exercising acts of sovereign authority on its territory, if such acts are performed with the consent or acquiescence of the State, even if those foreign officials are exercising acts of their own sovereign authority.[90] As mentioned at Sect. 9.2.1.3 above, it is also possible that individuals who are not within a State's territory might be subject to its jurisdiction for the purpose of triggering the State's obligations under the ICCPR and ECHR.

In the context of the International Covenant the Human Rights Committee has confirmed, in its General Comment 31, that the article 2 obligation upon States to ensure Covenant rights to all persons within their territory and subject to their jurisdiction means that a State party must ensure such rights to anyone within its power or effective control, even if not situated within the territory of the State party. This means that human rights obligations under the ICCPR have extra-territorial application, an issue which has arisen in a number of cases before the Human Rights Committee. In *López Burgos v Uruguay* and *Celiberti v Uruguay*, for example, Uruguayan citizens who had fled abroad were kidnapped by State agents and returned to Uruguay where they were subjected to serious human rights abuses. The HRC noted that neither article 2(1) ICCPR nor article 1 of the Optional Protocol was a bar to admissibility:[91]

> Article 2(1) of the Covenant places an obligation upon a State party to respect and ensure rights 'to all individuals within its territory and subject to its jurisdiction', but it does not imply that the State party concerned cannot be held accountable for violations of rights under the Covenant which its agents commit upon the territory of another State, whether with the acquiescence of the Government for that State or in opposition to it.

This holding, which relies on the doctrine of imputability, is consistent with general principles of international law in which the acts of a State's agents are taken to be the acts of the State itself. The Committee has explained this notion further in its General Comment 31:[92]

> States Parties are required by article 2, paragraph 1, to respect and to ensure the Covenant rights to all persons who may be within their territory and to all persons subject to their jurisdiction. This means that a State party must respect and ensure the rights laid down in the Covenant to anyone within the power or effective control of that State Party, even if not situated within the territory of the State Party. As indicated in General Comment 15 adopted at the 27th session (1986), the enjoyment of Covenant rights is not limited to citizens of States Parties but must also be available to all individuals, regardless of nationality or statelessness, such as asylum seekers, refugees, migrant workers and other persons, who may find themselves in the territory or subject to the jurisdiction of the State Party. This principle also applies to those within the power or effective control of the forces of a State Party acting outside its territory, regardless of the circumstances in which such power or effective control was obtained, such as forces constituting a national contingent of a State Party assigned to an international peace-keeping or peace-enforcement operation.

---

[90]See *Agiza v Sweden*, CAT/C/233/2003 (2005); *Alzery v Sweden*, CCPR/C/88/D/1416/2005 (2006).

[91]*Celiberti v Uruguay*, Communication 56/1979, UN Doc CCPR/C/13/D/56/1979 (1981), para 10.3; and *Burgos v Uruguay*, Communication 52/1979, UN Doc CCPR/C/13/D/52/1979 (1981).

[92]General Comment 31 (n 30), para 10.

The International Court of Justice took the same approach concerning the extra-territorial application of the ICCPR and the Covenant on Economic, Social and Cultural Rights in its 2004 Advisory Opinion concerning the construction of the barrier in the occupied Palestinian territory, stating that "the International Covenant on Civil and Political Rights is applicable in respect of acts done by a State in the exercise of its jurisdiction outside its own territory".[93] The International Court reached the same conclusion with regard to the applicability of the Convention on the Rights of the Child.[94]

Turning to the European Convention, article 1 provides that the parties to the ECHR "shall ensure to everyone within their jurisdiction the rights and freedoms defined in Section I of this Convention". Taking a similar approach as the International Court of Justice concerning the application of the ICCPR and ECHR, the European Court of Human Rights has taken the position that the concept of jurisdiction is not restricted to the national territory of a State party. Reiterating its position in *Loizidou v Turkey*, the Court stated:[95]

> Bearing in mind the object and purpose of the Convention, the responsibility of a Contracting Party may also arise when as a consequence of military action – whether lawful or unlawful – it exercises effective control of an area outside its national territory. The obligation to secure, in such an area, the rights and freedoms set out in the Convention derives from the fact of such control whether it be exercised directly, through its armed forces, or through a subordinate local administration.

9.3.2   Human Rights and International Humanitarian Law

International humanitarian law (also known as the law of armed conflict) and human rights law were traditionally regarded as separate areas of international law. It is now a well-established principle, however, that regardless of issues of classification, international human rights law continues to apply in armed conflict (see Chap. 12, Sect. 12.2.2.2).

---

[93]*Legal Consequences of the Construction of a Wall in the Occupied Palestinian Territories*, Advisory Opinion (2004) ICJ Reports, para 111. See also the Concluding Observations of the Human Rights Committee on Israel's 1998 periodic report, UN Doc CCPR/C/79/Add.93 (1998), para 10.

[94]Ibid, para 113.

[95]*Loizidou v Turkey (Preliminary Objections)* [1995] 20 EHRR 99, para 62, confirmed in *Cyprus v Turkey* [2001] ECHR 331. On the extraterritorial application of the Human Rights Act 1998 (UK), the instrument through which the United Kingdom incorporated the ECHR, see *Al-Skeini and others v Secretary of State for Defence* [2007] UKHL 26.

9.4 Conclusions

International human rights law obliges States to do certain things and prevents them from doing others. States have a duty to respect, protect and fulfil human rights. Respect for human rights involves not interfering with their enjoyment and also taking steps to ensure that others do not interfere with the enjoyment of rights. To ensure the fulfilment of human rights, States must adopt appropriate measures, including legislative, judicial, administrative or educative measures, in order to fulfil their legal obligations. A State party may be found equally responsible for attacks by private persons or entities upon the enjoyment of human rights. Human rights law also places a certain responsibility upon States to provide effective remedies in the event of violations. It is important to recall that human rights have extraterritorial effect, requiring States to ensure rights and freedoms to anyone within their power or effective control, even if not situated within the territory of the State party. International human rights law also continues to apply in armed conflict.

The International Covenant on Civil and Political Rights and the European Convention on Human Rights guarantee a broad scope of civil and political rights. Reservations to both instruments are permissible, as are derogations from certain rights during a state of emergency threatening the life of a nation. Although the bodies established under each document, the Human Rights Committee and the European Court of Human Rights, differ in their status and as to the effect of their decisions, they have similar functions. Both undertake an important role in interpreting the scope of each instrument, albeit that they take different approaches to the application of any margin of appreciation. The Committee may also issue general comments on the meaning or application of the International Covenant, while the European Court may be asked to provide an advisory opinion on the same. The Committee and Court serve to hear applications concerning alleged violations of rights and freedoms, whether initiated by an individual victim or by way of inter-State complaint. Both institutions will, upon finding a violation of rights, award remedies. The HRC has the additional function of considering and commenting upon periodic reports of States parties to the ICCPR.

References

Ando, Nisuke. 1991. The Future of Monitoring Bodies – Limitations and Possibilities of the Human Rights Committee. *Canadian Human Rights Yearbook* 169.

Conte, Alex, and Burchill, Richard. 2009. *Defining Civil and Political Rights: The Jurisprudence of the UN Human Rights Committee*. Dartmouth: 2nd edition, Ashgate Publishing Limited.

Evatt, Elizabeth. 2002. The Impact of International Human Rights on Domestic Law. In Huscroft, Grant, and Rishworth, Paul. *Litigating Rights: Perspectives from Domestic and International Law*. Oxford and Portland, Oregon: Hart Publishing Limited.

Harris, David. 1995. The International Covenant on Civil and Political Rights and the United Kingdom: An Introduction. In Harris, David, and Joseph, Sarah (editors), *The International Covenant on Civil and Political Rights and United Kingdom Law*. Oxford: Clarendon Press.

Lillich, Richard. 1984. *The Human Rights of Aliens in Contemporary International Law*. Manchester: Manchester University Press.

McGoldrick, Dominic. 1990. *The Human Rights Committee: Its Role in the Development of the International Covenant on Civil and Political Rights*. Oxford: Clarendon Press.

Nowak, Manfred. 2005. *UN Covenant on Civil and Political Rights*. Kehl, Germany: 2nd revised edition, NP Engel.

Ovey, Clare, and White, Robin. 2002. *The European Convention on Human Rights*. Oxford: 3rd ed, Oxford University Press.

Sinclair, Ian. 1984. *The Vienna Convention on the Law of Treaties*. Manchester: 2nd ed, Manchester University Press.

Steiner, Henry, and Alston, Philip. 2000. *International Human Rights in Context*. Oxford: 2nd ed, Oxford University Press.

Tomuschat, Christian. 1980. Evolving Procedural Rules: The United Nations Human Rights Committee's First Two Years of Dealing with Individual Communications. 1 *Human Rights Law Journal* 249.

Chapter 10
Limiting Rights Under International Law

The nature of international human rights law is such that, other than in the case of a limited number of absolute rights, the guarantee of rights and freedoms incorporates a level of flexibility. This allows States to give effect to those rights and freedoms, while at the same time pursue important democratic objectives designed to protect society (such as national security) and to maintain a balance between conflicting rights (such as freedom of expression, balanced against privacy or the right to a fair hearing). In the context of the International Covenant on Civil and Political Rights (ICCPR),[1] and the European Convention on Human Rights (ECHR) to which the United Kingdom is also party,[2] this accommodation is effected through two means. Limitations are permitted by virtue of the particular expression of the right or freedom within the ICCPR and ECHR. There is also the capacity, under article 4 of the ICCPR or article 15 of the ECHR, to temporarily suspend the application of certain rights during a state of emergency which threatens the life of a nation.

Two documents are of particular relevance to this chapter. The first is General Comment 29 of the Human Rights Committee which, while its primary focus is upon states of emergency under the ICCPR, sets out principles of relevance to the entirety of this chapter.[3] This document is particularly instructive since none of the States parties to the ICCPR have lodged any objection to General Comment 29 under art 40(5) of the Covenant. One might argue that the document has thereby gained the status of representing subsequent practice in the application of the Covenant which establishes the agreement of the parties regarding its interpretation.[4] Also worthy of consideration are the *Siracusa Principles on the Limitation*

---

[1]International Covenant on Civil and Political Rights, opened for signature 16 December 1966, 999 UNTS 171 (entered into force 23 March 1976).

[2]Convention for the Protection of Human Rights and Fundamental Freedoms, opened for signature 4 November 1950, 213 UNTS 222 (entered into force 3 September 1953).

[3]General Comment 29: States of Emergency (Article 4), UN Doc CCPR/C/21/Rev.1/Add.11 (2001).

[4]See Vienna Convention on the Law of Treaties, opened for signature 23 May 1969, 1155 UNTS 331 (entered into force 27 January 1980), article 31(3).

A. Conte, *Human Rights in the Prevention and Punishment of Terrorism*,
DOI 10.1007/978-3-642-11608-7_10, © Springer-Verlag Berlin Heidelberg 2010

and Derogation Provisions in the International Covenant on Civil and Political Rights, which includes short but useful standards adopted by the United Nations Economic and Social Council in 1985.[5]

10.1 Absolute and Non-derogable Rights

Before considering the means by which rights might be limited or suspended, it is important to note that certain rights are either expressed in a way which permits no limitation, or fall outside the derogations regime under article 4 of the ICCPR and article 15 of the ECHR.

10.1.1 Absolute Rights

Certain rights within the ICCPR and ECHR are expressed in such a way that they do not allow for any limitation. Articles 7 of the ICCPR and 3 of the ECHR provide a good example of this, both stating that: "No one shall be subjected to torture or to cruel, inhuman or degrading treatment or punishment". The prohibition is expressed in plain language which makes clear that no exception to it is permitted. The prohibitions against slavery and servitude are similarly expressed in clear, absolute terms (article 8(1) and (2) of the ICCPR and article 4(1) and (2) of the ECHR).

The guarantee under article 10(1) of the ICCPR that all persons deprived of their liberty are to be treated with humanity and with respect for the inherent dignity of the human person is also expressed in plain language which makes clear that no limitation is permitted. One's right to hold opinions is guaranteed under article 19(1) of the ICCPR 'without interference' and without any wording which either expressly or impliedly allows any limitation upon the exercise of the right. Also expressed in absolute terms are: the prohibition against imprisonment for failure to perform a contractual obligation (articles 11 of the ICCPR and 1 of the Fourth Protocol to the ECHR); the principle of no punishment without law (article 15 of the ICCPR and article 7 of the ECHR); the right to be recognised before the law (article 16 of the ICCPR);[6] and the prohibition in article 20 of the ICCPR against propaganda and incitement to discrimination, hostility or violence.

---

[5]Siracusa Principles on the Limitation and Derogation Provisions in the International Covenant on Civil and Political Rights, UN Doc E/CN.4/1985/4 (1985), Annex.

[6]Although the European Convention on Human Rights does not contain a provision equivalent to article 16 of the ICCPR, it should be noted that the principle is recognised as a "fundamental principle" in the preamble of Protocol 12 to the ECHR.

10.1.2   Non-derogable Rights

10.1.2.1   The List of Non-derogable Rights

Article 4 of the ICCPR allows temporary derogation from some rights during a state of emergency and, in establishing this regime, lists certain rights within paragraph 2 as being non-derogable. Article 4(2) identifies non-derogable rights as those under articles: 6 (life); 7 (torture, or cruel, inhuman or degrading treatment); 8(1) and (2) (slavery and servitude); 11 (imprisonment for failure to perform a contractual obligation); 15 (no punishment without the law); 16 (recognition before the law); and 18 (manifestation of religious belief). The European Convention does the same thing through article 15(2), listing the rights under the following articles as non-derogable: 2 (life, except in respect of deaths resulting from lawful acts of war); 3 (torture); 4(1) (slavery and servitude); and 7 (no punishment without the law). What can be noted at this point is that the lists in article 4(2) of the ICCPR and article 15(2) of the ECHR do not coincide precisely.[7]

   In the context of the ICCPR, the Human Rights Committee has commented that the list of non-derogable rights in article 4(2) of the Covenant is not an exhaustive one. The Committee has made the point that provisions of the ICCPR relating to procedural safeguards, which often correspond to judicial guarantees, can never be made subject to measures if this would circumvent the protection of the non-derogable rights within article 4(2).[8] Thus, for example, any trial leading to the imposition of the death penalty must conform to all the procedural requirements of article 14 of the ICCPR. Indeed, even when derogation from article 14 is permissible, the Committee has explained that the extent of any such derogation is limited.[9]

   The Committee has also noted that the full complement of 'non-derogable rights' includes rights applicable as part of obligations under international human rights law, international humanitarian law, and international criminal law since article 4(1) requires that no measure derogating from the provisions of the ICCPR may be inconsistent with the State party's other obligations under international law.[10] Expanding upon this position, the Committee has identified certain rights under customary international law (applicable to all States) as being non-derogable. These include: the right of all persons deprived of their liberty to be treated with humanity and with respect for the inherent dignity of the human person (reflected within article 10 of the ICCPR); the prohibition against taking of hostages, abductions, or unacknowledged detention (also prohibited under article 9 of the

---

[7]The ECHR does not list as non-derogable: the prohibition against imprisonment for failure to perform a contractual obligation; the principle of recognition before the law; and the right to manifest religious belief.

[8]General Comment 29 (n 3) para 15.

[9]General Comment 29 (n 3) para 16. See also Chap. 5 herein, and the Siracusa Principles (n 5) para 67.

[10]General Comment 29 (n 3) paras 9–13.

Covenant); the international protection of the rights of persons belonging to minorities (corresponding to article 27); the deportation or forcible transfer of a population without grounds permitted under international law; and the prohibition against propaganda for war or in advocacy of national, racial, or religious hatred that would constitute incitement to discrimination, hostility, or violence (article 20 of the ICCPR).[11] Thus, for example, no declaration of a state of emergency under article 4 may be invoked as justification for a State party to engage itself in propaganda for war.[12] Nor could derogation from article 12 (freedom of movement) justify measures involving the forcible transfer of a population without grounds permitted under international law.[13]

10.1.2.2 'Absolute' Versus 'Non-derogable' Rights

Not all of the rights identified as being 'absolute' (see Sect. 10.1.1) were also identified in the preceding section as being 'non-derogable', and vice versa. This raises fine but important distinctions between the notions of absolute versus non-derogable rights. The first is that most, but not all, absolute rights are also non-derogable. Of the rights identified as being absolute, those under articles 6, 7, 8, 11, 15 and 16 of the ICCPR, these are also identified within article 4(2) of the Covenant as non-derogable, even during a state of emergency. The Human Rights Committee has furthermore recognised the rights under articles 10 and 20 of the International Covenant as reflecting norms of customary international law, thus also not capable of being derogated from in a state of emergency. The prohibitions under articles 7 and 8 reflect peremptory norms of customary international law (*jus cogens*).[14] This means that the rights set out within these eight articles (6, 7, 8, 10, 11, 15, 16 and 20) are both *expressed* in absolute terms, so that they cannot be interpreted in a way which permits any limitation upon them, *and* are also not capable of being suspended, even temporarily during a state of emergency. The same analysis applies to the rights and freedoms under articles 2, 3 4(1) and 7 of the European Convention on Human Rights.

The only right under the ICCPR which is expressed in absolute language but is not either expressly or impliedly included in the list of non-derogable rights is article 19(1), concerning the right to hold opinions without interference. While this seems illogical at face value, it should be noted that the right to hold opinions is given effective protection during states of emergency since the freedom of thought (protected under article 18(1) of the ICCPR) *is* non-derogable under article 4(2) of the Covenant. The ECHR also contains a discrepancy between absolute and non-derogable rights, although this exists as a result of the Fourth Protocol to the

---

[11]General Comment 29 (n 3) para 13.

[12]General Comment 29 (n 3) para 13(e).

[13]General Comment 29 (n 3) para 13(D).

[14]International Law Commission (1966). See also General Comment 29 (n 3) para 11.

Convention, i.e. the prohibition against imprisonment for failure to perform a contractual obligation, which is set out in article 1 of the Fourth Protocol, is not included in the list of non-derogable rights under article 15(2) of the Convention.

The second distinction to be made between absolute and non-derogable rights concerns the ability of some non-derogable rights to be made subject to limitations, whether under the ICCPR or the ECHR. As explained by the Human Rights Committee in its General Comment 29, the status of a substantive right as non-derogable does not mean that limitations or restrictions upon such a right cannot be justified.[15] The Committee gives the example of the freedom to manifest one's religion or beliefs (article 18 of the ICCPR).[16] Article 18 is listed within article 4(2) and cannot therefore be derogated from under the article 4 procedure. This listing does not, however, remove the permissible limitations upon the right expressed within article 18(3) itself, i.e. limitations as are prescribed by law that are necessary to protect public safety, order, health or morals, or the fundamental rights and freedoms of others. The same can be said about the right to life under article 2 of the European Convention. Although listed as a non-derogable right under article 15(2) of the ECHR, the right under article 2 is subject to an express limitation concerning death resulting from the use of force which is, for example, necessary for the defence of any person from unlawful violence and proportionate to that end (article 2(2)(a)). Thus, whereas an absolute right may not be the subject of any limitation at all, a non-derogable treaty right may be capable of limitation depending upon its particular expression.

10.2 Features Common to the Limitation or Suspension of Rights

As noted earlier, there are two principal means through which the ICCPR and ECHR accommodate the limitation of, or temporary suspension from, the unrestricted enjoyment of rights and freedoms. The first, discussed at Sect. 10.3 below, is through limitations which are permitted as a result of the particular expression of the right or freedom. The second involves the capacity under article 4 of the ICCPR or article 15 of the ECHR to temporarily suspend the application of certain rights during a state of emergency which threatens the life of a nation (see Sect. 10.4). Relevant to both mechanisms are four matters to be discussed here: the doctrine of the margin of appreciation; the requirement that limitations be 'prescribed by law'; the principles of necessity and proportionality; and the principle of non-discrimination.

---

[15]General Comment 29 (n 3) paras 4 and 7.

[16]Ibid, paras 7 and 11.

10.2.1   Margin of Appreciation

The doctrine of the margin of appreciation has been developed extensively by the European Court of Human Rights, and involves the idea that each society is entitled to certain latitude in resolving the inherent conflicts between individual rights and national interests or among different moral convictions.[17] Macdonald asserts that the margin of appreciation lies "at the heart of virtually all major cases that come before the Court, whether the judgments refer to it expressly or not".[18] It should be noted here that the notion of a margin of appreciation is capable of applying in two contexts: first, in determining the means of application of rights within the jurisdiction of one State party as opposed to another (i.e. in the interpretation of rights); and, secondly, in the degree of leniency, if any, to be accorded to a State party in the determination of the existence of a state of emergency for the purpose of applying article 4 of the International Covenant or article 15 of the European Convention.

10.2.1.1   Margin of Appreciation in the Application of Substantive Rights

In the context of the application of substantive rights, the margin of appreciation doctrine posits that States have a certain amount of discretion in the conduct of their legislative, judicial or administrative action in so far as these impinge upon the enjoyment of human rights by those within its territory and jurisdiction.[19] While this is subject to oversight by the European Court to ensure objective compliance with the protected rights, it is designed primarily to allow States to take account of local conditions and sensibilities in their implementation of rights. It is a principle which may therefore impact upon the interpretation of words or provisions that are capable of justifying limits upon the exercise of rights and freedoms.

The Human Rights Committee has flirted with the concept of a margin of appreciation in *Hertzberg v Finland*, where it was required to give consideration to the notion of 'public morals' under article 19(3), stating that: "[i]t has to be noted, first, that public morals differ widely. There is no universally applicable common standard. Consequently, in this respect, a certain margin of discretion must be accorded to the responsible national authorities".[20] The Committee soon after pointed out, however, that each international treaty, including the ICCPR, has a life of its own and must be interpreted in a fair and just manner *by the body* entrusted with the monitoring of its provisions, rather than national authorities.[21]

---

[17]See Benvenisti (1999), Arai-Takahashi (2002), and Steiner and Alston (2000, pp. 854–857).

[18]Macdonald (1987, p. 208).

[19]Harris et al. (1995, pp. 12–15).

[20]*Hertzberg et al v Finland*, Communication 61/1979, UN Doc CCPR/C/15/D/61/1979 (1982), para 10.3.

[21]*JB and others v Canada*, Communication 118/1982, UN Doc CCPR/C/28/D/118/1982 (1986), para 6.2.

Even in the difficult context of 'morals', it took a much more robust approach in *Toonen v Australia* (some years after its views in *Hertzberg*):[22]

> The Committee cannot accept either that for the purposes of article 17 of the Covenant, moral issues are exclusively a matter of domestic concern, as this would open the door to withdrawing from the Committee's scrutiny a potentially large number of statutes interfering with privacy. It further notes that with the exception of Tasmania, all laws criminalizing homosexuality have been repealed throughout Australia and that, even in Tasmania, it is apparent that there is no consensus as to whether Sections 122 and 123 should not also be repealed. Considering further that these provisions are not currently enforced, which implies that they are not deemed essential to the protection of morals in Tasmania, the Committee concludes that the provisions do not meet the 'reasonableness' test in the circumstances of the case, and that they arbitrarily interfere with Mr Toonen's right under article 17, paragraph 1.

Ghandhi has reported that former Committee member Judge Higgins has gone as far as suggesting that the Human Rights Committee does not apply a margin of appreciation doctrine.[23] Schmidt, on the other hand, has identified incipient elements of the doctrine in some of the Committee's jurisprudence, but most especially in the separate opinions relating to article 26 of the Covenant.[24] However, while it is apparent in cases involving article 26 that the Committee is prepared to excuse discrimination which is objectively justifiable, reasonable and proportionate, this cannot be regarded as being the same as the fully fledged margin of appreciation doctrine in the European system.

The contrast between the approaches of the European Court of Human Rights and the Human Rights Committee is most apparent in the context of national security. While the European Court has said that States are to be given a very wide margin of appreciation when the protection of national security is in issue, the Committee has taken the view that it is for it, not States parties, to determine whether any measures taken are in fact necessary for the protection of national security.[25]

10.2.1.2 Margin of Appreciation in Declaring a State of Emergency

Common to the International Covenant and the European Convention is the facility for States parties to derogate from certain rights during a state of emergency threatening the life of the nation. It is notable that here too the approaches of the European Court and the Human Rights Committee differ. Taking the approach that a wide margin of appreciation must be afforded to States in determining whether a

---

[22]*Toonen v Australia*, Communication 488/1992, UN Doc CCPR/C/50/D/488/1992 (1994), para 8.6.

[23]Ghandhi (1998, p. 14).

[24]Schmidt (1995, p. 629).

[25]Contrast *Hadjianastassiou v Greece* (1993) 16 EHRR 219 with *Park v Republic of Korea*, Communication 628/1995, UN Doc CCPR/C/64/D/628/1995 (1998).

state of emergency exists, and that it should do no more than proclaim whether a government's decision is 'on the margin' of the powers conferred by a derogating provision, the European Court has said:[26]

> By reason of their direct and continuous contact with the pressing needs of the moment, the national authorities are in principle in a better position than the international judge to decide both on the presence of such an emergency and on the nature and scope of derogations necessary to avert it.

In contrast, the Human Rights Committee has taken the view that compliance with all aspects of article 4 of the ICCPR, including the determination of whether a state of emergency exists, is a matter in respect of which it has final say.

This mechanism for allowing the temporary derogation from rights, including the application of it to the margin of appreciation, is discussed in more detail below (Sect. 10.4) and in the case study concerning the United Kingdom's derogations from the right to liberty (Chap. 17).

10.2.2   Limitations 'Prescribed by Law'

Common to all mechanisms authorising the limitation of rights, any measure seeking to limit a right or freedom must be prescribed by law.[27] Inherent to the principle of legality codified in article 15 of the ICCPR and article 7 of the ECHR, the expression 'prescribed by law' has been subject to careful examination by the European Court of Human Rights, with commentary on the expression within the *Siracusa Principles* also.

10.2.2.1   Establishing a Legal Basis for the Interference

The European Court has established a threefold test for determining whether a limitation is prescribed by law, requiring that the interference has some basis in national law, is accessible, and is precise. There is no requirement that the law be statutory, the European Court having accepted the prescription of limitations under the common law.[28] As to the second and third requirements, the European Court in the *Sunday Times* case concluded that the law must:[29]

---

[26]*Ireland v United Kingdom* [1978] ECHR 1, para 207. See Marks (1995).

[27]Siracusa Principles (n 5) para 5.

[28]*Sunday Times v United Kingdom* (1978) 58 ILR 491. The Court also validated the authority of the Veterinary Surgeon's Council to make professional rules as amounting to legal prescriptions in *Barthold v Germany* [1984] 7 EHRR 383.

[29]*Sunday Times* (ibid), 524–527 (reaffirmed by the European Court in *Silver v UK* [1983] 5 EHRR 347). The principles of 'clarity' and 'accessibility' are contained within the Siracusa Principles also (n 5) para 17. See also Ovey and White (2002, pp. 199–204).

- Be adequately accessible so that the citizen has an adequate indication of how the law limits his or her rights.
- Formulated with sufficient precision so that the citizen can regulate his or her conduct.

In the particular context of derogations, General Comment 29 reaffirms that derogations must be based upon the principles of legality and the rule of law, said to be inherent in the ICCPR as a whole.[30]

10.2.2.2 Discretionary Powers

It should be noted that limiting measures may, even if they are prescribed by law, involve the conferral of a discretionary power. This may be a practical requirement of the implementation of limiting measures and there is, in principle, no prohibition against the conferral of discretions. The *Siracusa Principles* provide, however, that limitations must not be arbitrary or unreasonable (terms which have been considered and defined by the Human Rights Committee and the European Court of Human Rights, as discussed below at Sect. 10.3.1).[31] The *Principles* also state that adequate safeguards must exist to protect against the illegal or abusive imposition or application of limitations on human rights, and that limitations must be subject to the possibility of challenge to and remedy against abusive application.[32] Translating these principles into practical requirements applicable to the conferral and exercise of discretionary powers which might restrict the enjoyment of rights and freedoms, one can say that:

- Any law authorising a restriction upon rights and freedoms must not confer an *unfettered* discretion on those charged with its execution.
- Any discretion must not be *arbitrarily or unreasonably* applied.

Both requirements call for the imposition of adequate safeguards to ensure that discretionary powers are capable of being checked, with appropriate mechanisms to deal with any abuse or arbitrary application of the discretion.

10.2.3 Necessity

Necessity and proportionality are elements common to derogation and limitation powers.[33] While these principles are inherent to the exercise of such powers, they

---

[30]General Comment 29 (n 3) para 17.

[31]Siracusa Principles (n 5) para 16.

[32]Siracusa Principles (n 5) paras 8 and18.

[33]General Comment 29 (n 3) para 4.

may also be activated by the particular words used to express a right or freedom. As discussed below, for example, the requirement of 'reasonableness' implies that any interference with a right must be proportional to the end sought and necessary in the circumstances of any given case. The Human Rights Committee has observed that the words 'necessary' and 'proportionate' are interlinked, stating in *de Morais v Angola*, for example, that the requirement of necessity itself implies an element of proportionality.[34] There are, nevertheless, some distinct features attaching to each term (see Sect. 10.2.4 on proportionality).

In the context of derogations, the principle of necessity permits States parties to derogate from certain rights under the Covenant only "to the extent strictly required by the exigencies of the situation" (article 4(1) of the ICCPR and article 15(1) of the ECHR).[35] This feature is considered in further detail below (Sect. 10.4.2). Necessity is also a key feature of express limitations, commonly calling on two requirements, each considered next.

10.2.3.1   Express Limitations Rationally Linked to the Pursuit of Legitimate Aims

Firstly, reliance upon an express limitation will always require a State to establish that the limiting measure is in pursuit of an objective which is permitted by the expression of the right concerned.[36] There must exist a rational link between the limiting measure and the objective being pursued.[37] Limitation clauses include various express objectives, including the protection of national security or public morals. The nature and meaning of these legitimate objectives is considered further below (Sect. 10.3.2).

10.2.3.2   Express Limitations Necessary in a Democratic Society

Once a rational link is established between the objective of the limiting measure and one of the objectives listed in the rights-specific limitation clause, necessity will commonly require the establishment of a link between the objective of the measure and the notion of a free and democratic society.[38] By way of example:

---

[34]See: *Faurisson v France*, Communication 550/1993, UN Doc CCPR/C/58/D/550/1993(1996), para 8; and *de Morais v Angola*, Communication 1128/2002, UN Doc CCPR/C/83/D/1128/2002 (2005), para 6.8. See also the Siracusa Principles (n 5) para 10(d). See also Ovey and White (2002, p. 209), as this link applies to the European Convention.

[35]General Comment 29 (n 3) paras 3–5; and the Siracusa Principles (n 5) para 51.

[36]Siracusa Principles (n 5) paras 6 and 10(a). In the context of the European Convention, see also Ovey and White (2002, p. 204).

[37]Siracusa Principles (n 5) para 10(b) and 10(c).

[38]On this point, see paras 19–21 of the Siracusa Principles (n 5).

- Article 14(1) of the ICCPR which states that "[t]he press and the public may be excluded from all or part of a trial for reasons of morals, public order (ordre public) or national security *in a democratic society*" (emphasis added).
- Article 21 of the ICCPR similarly prohibits restrictions on the right of peaceful assembly, other than those imposed in conformity with the law and which are "necessary in a democratic society in the interests of national security. . ." and the like.
- Article 8(2), 9(2), 10(2) and 11(2) of the European Convention also all refer to the requirement that the limitations permitted therein must be necessary in a democratic society.

The Committee has stated that reference to 'democratic society' indicates, in these contexts, that the existence and operation of the particular right is a cornerstone of a democratic society.[39] In considering such a qualification upon limits to the freedom of association with others, for example, the Committee stated in *Lee v Republic of Korea* that that the existence and functioning of a plurality of associations, including those which peacefully promote ideas not favourably received by the government or the majority of the population, is one of the foundations of a democratic society.[40] The European Court of Human Rights has explained that the expression means that, to be compatible with the European Convention, the interference must correspond to a 'pressing social need'.[41] The needs of a democratic society in the context of censorship is discussed further below at Sect. 10.3.2.6.

10.2.4 Proportionality

Establishing the *need* for any limit upon rights, or derogation therefrom, will normally involve a reasonably mechanical exercise whereby a State will point to permitted objectives and draw links between the limiting measure and those objectives. Critically, however, the establishment of such a relationship does not provide the State with the ability to limit the right or freedom to whatever extent it wishes. The limiting measure must also be shown to be proportionate, such that the State may not use more restrictive means than are required to achieve the purpose of the limitation.[42] Proportionality calls into question not only the validity of the

---

[39]In the context of the right to freedom of association with others under article 22(2), see, for example, *Zvozskov et al v Belarus*, Communication 1039/2001, UN Doc CCPR/C/88/D/1039/2001 (2006), para 7.2.

[40]*Lee v Republic of Korea*, Communication 1119/2002, UN Doc CCPR/C/84/D/1119/2002 (2005), para 7.2.

[41]*Silver v United Kingdom* (n 29), para 97(c).

[42]Siracusa Principles (n 5) para 11. Concerning the European Convention, see *Silver v United Kingdom* (ibid).

measure as a prescription by law (e.g. whether or not the criminalisation of certain conduct is proportional to the need to dissuade the conduct in question), but also the way in which it is applied to each particular case (e.g. whether a sentence imposed upon conviction is proportional to the severity of the conduct). Proportionality assessments must be based on a full consideration of all relevant issues,[43] although there are two common factors which are brought to bear in the evaluation of whether limiting measures are proportional, namely: the negative impact of the limiting measure upon the enjoyment of the right; and the ameliorating effects of the limiting measure.

The negative impact of limiting measures upon the enjoyment of the particular right or freedom is the obvious starting point in determining whether the measure is proportional. In the context of criminal defamation acting as a limit upon the freedom of expression, for example, the Human Rights Committee has considered the severity of the sanction imposed as relevant to the proportionality of the limit upon expression.[44] It will be important in this regard to consider the importance of the right and the 'value' that might be ascribed prescribed to it. While all rights are said to be equal and indivisible, it has already been mentioned that some rights and freedoms, such as the freedom of association with others, have been recognised by the Committee as part of the 'foundations of a democratic society'. Limitations imposed upon such rights will therefore be carefully scrutinised by the Committee.

In evaluating the negative impact of a limiting measure, it will also be important to establish that the limitation is not so severe or so broad in its application so as to destroy the very essence of the right in question.[45] This has been treated as especially important to justifying any distinctions between individuals in the protection of their rights.[46] It is notable in this regard that the Committee has expressed the view that restrictions on Covenant rights, even where permissible under a rights-specific limitation provision, must be interpreted narrowly and with careful scrutiny of the reasons advanced by way of justification.[47] The *Siracusa Principles* add that "[a]ll limitation clauses shall be interpreted strictly and in favour of the rights at issue".[48]

---

[43]See, for example, *Burgess v Australia*, Communication 1012/2001, UN Doc CCPR/C/85/D/1012/2001 (2005), para 4.13.

[44]See, for example: *Pietraroia v Uruguay*, Communication 44/1979, UN Doc CCPR/C/OP/1 at 65 (1984), para 16; *Jong-Cheol v Republic of Korea*, Communication 968/2001, UN Doc CCPR/C/84/D/968/2001 (2005), para 8.3; and *de Morais v Angola* (n 34) para 6.8.

[45]Siracusa Principles (n 5) para 2.

[46]See, for example: *Jacobs v Belgium*, Communication 943/2000, UN Doc CCPR/C/81/D/943/2000 (2004), para 9.5; *Althammer et al v Austria*, Communication 998/2001, UN Doc CCPR/C/78/D/998/2001 (2003), para 10.2; and *Haraldsson and Sveinsson v Iceland*, Communication 1306/2004, UN Doc CCPR/C/91/D/1306/2004 (2007), para 8.10.

[47]See, for example, *Sisters of the Holy Cross of the Third Order of Saint Francis in Menzingen of Sri Lanka v Sri Lanka*, Communication 1249/2004, UN Doc CCPR/C/85/D/1249/2004 (2005), para 7.2.

[48]Siracusa Principles (n 5) para 3.

Also central to proportionality will be the importance of the objective being pursued and the extent to which the limiting measure contributes to that objective, i.e. it's ameliorating effects. The Committee has thus said that the scope of any restriction imposed on a right or freedom must be proportional to the value which the restriction serves to protect.[49] When examining the reliance by States parties upon limitation provisions, the Committee has taken into account the importance of the limitation to the enjoyment of other rights under the Covenant, as well as to other democratic principles. In the context of limits upon the right to freedom of expression, for example, the Committee has taken into account the importance of public debate in a democratic society, especially in the media, including that concerning figures in the political domain.[50]

10.2.5 Non-discrimination

Measures limiting the exercise of rights and freedoms must be non-discriminatory in nature.[51] This is brought to bear through a combination of often overlapping features of international human rights law.

10.2.5.1 Non-discrimination in the Derogation from Rights

Non-discrimination is a specific condition upon the ability to derogate from certain rights under article 4 of the International Covenant, paragraph 1 expressly providing that any derogating measure must not involve discrimination solely on the ground of race, colour, sex, language, religion or social origin. When resorting to measures that derogate from the Covenant, the Committee has emphasised that this aspect of article 4 must be complied with if any distinctions are made between persons under the derogating measures.[52] This list is more limited than the prohibited grounds of discrimination contained in article 2(1) of the ICCPR, since it may be permissible, during war or national emergency, to discriminate against enemy aliens and their property.[53]

In contrast to article 4 of the ICCPR, article 15 of the European Convention does not make specific mention to the need for derogating measures to be non-discriminatory. Despite this, article 14 of the ECHR contains a general prohibition

---

[49]See, for example, *de Morais v Angola* (n 34) para 6.8.

[50]See, for example, *Bodrožić v Serbia and Montenegro*, Communication 1180/2003, UN Doc CCPR/C/85/D/1180/2003 (2006), para 7.2. See also, in the context of South Africa's blanket ban on the use of cannabis, *Prince v South Africa*, Communication 1474/2006, UN Doc CCPR/C/91/D/1474/2006 (2007), para 4.6.

[51]Siracusa Principles (n 5) para 9.

[52]General Comment 29 (n 3) para 8.

[53]Nowak (2005, pp. 99–100).

against discrimination. Of more relevance is the fact that any derogating measure under article 15 must comply with other obligations under international law (see Sect. 10.4.2), including the international law principle of non-discrimination under customary international law and as codified in article 26 of the ICCPR. Adopting this approach to the question of the United Kingdom's derogation from liberty rights (see Chap. 17, Sect. 17.3.2.2), the House of Lords stated in *A and Ors v Secretary of State for the Home Department* that:[54]

> What cannot be justified here is the decision to detain one group of suspected international terrorists, defined by nationality or immigration status, and not another. To do so was a violation of article 14. It was also a violation of article 26 of the ICCPR and so inconsistent with the United Kingdom's other obligations under international law within the meaning of article 15 of the European Convention.

10.2.5.2 Non-discrimination in the Application of Rights More Generally

Outside the context of derogations under the ICCPR and the ECHR, the principle of non-discrimination becomes involved in the limitation of rights through concepts such as arbitrariness and proportionality. The Human Rights Committee has explained that the concept of arbitrariness is intended to guarantee that even reasonable conduct which is provided for by law should be in accordance with the provisions, aims and objectives of the ICCPR, including non-discrimination.[55] In determining whether the different treatment of persons is compatible with article 14 of the ECHR the European Court of Human Rights has required that there must be a "reasonable relationship of proportionality" between the means and effect of the different treatment and the aims sought to be realised thereby.[56]

10.3   Limitations Permitted by the Expression of Rights and Freedoms

The principal way in which the ICCPR and ECHR facilitate the needs of States to accommodate competing rights or interests is through the *expression* of individual rights and freedoms, as articulated within each article and paragraph of the Covenant and Convention. This can in turn be broken down into two means by which the expression of rights can allow for limitations: either through the particular words

---

[54]*A and Ors v Secretary of State for the Home Department* [2004] UKHL 56, per Lord Bingham at para 68.

[55]See, for example, General Comment 16: The right to respect of privacy, family, home and correspondence, and protection of honour and reputation (Art 17), UN Doc CCPR General Comment 16 (1988), para 4. See also the Siracusa Principles (n 5) para 5.

[56]*Lithgow and others v United Kingdom* [1986] 8 EHRR 329.

used to define the right (limitations by interpretation); or through an accompanying sentence or paragraph which sets out permissible objectives, the pursuit of which can justify limitation (rights-specific limitation provisions, also referred to as 'express limitations').[57]

10.3.1 Limitations by Interpretation

Limitations by interpretation are ones that rely upon the meaning of the words contained within the expression of the right itself. The ICCPR and ECHR incorporate concepts such as 'fair' trial (article 14(1); and article 6(1)), 'reasonableness' (articles 9(3) and 25; and articles 5(1)(c), 5(3) and 6(1)), 'arbitrariness' (relating to various rights); the need to take 'prompt' action in the context of persons deprived of their liberty or subject to criminal proceedings (articles 9 and 14; and articles 5 and 6), and the provision of 'adequate' time and facilities for the preparation of one's defence (article 14(3)(b); and article 6(3)(b)). Common to all limitations by interpretation is the inherent flexibility involved in the need to interpret the particular term, a feature which can be equally negative through lack of certainty. Considered next in this chapter are the interpretative approaches taken to the terms 'fair', 'reasonable', and 'arbitrary'. The expressions 'prompt' and 'adequate' are not considered here since they are interpreted in terms which are very specific to the exercise of the particular rights under 9 and 14 of the ICCPR and articles 5 and 6 of the ECHR.[58]

10.3.1.1 Fair and Reasonable

The existence of a 'fair trial' for the purpose of article 14(1) is one which incorporates a number of elements, including equality of arms between parties, attendance at hearings, the ability to hear from and examine witnesses, and the prompt disposal of proceedings. It is based upon the idea that parties should not be prejudiced or otherwise disadvantaged in being able to put their case to a tribunal, and entails the absence of any direct or indirect influence, pressure or intimidation, or intrusion from whatever side and for whatever motive.[59] These notions of equality and lack of prejudice appear to lie at the heart of the term 'fair', and the use of that term enables an assessment of each case on its own merits, something

---

[57]Ovey and White (2002, pp. 5, and 198–201).

[58]Concerning the interpretation of these terms under the ICCPR, see Conte and Burchill (2009), Chaps. 20 (concerning non-disclosure of classified information), 21 (concerning investigative detention and control orders), and 23 (concerning fair trial and natural justice rights in the context of terrorist designations).

[59]See further Conte and Burchill (2009, Chap. 5).

that both the Human Rights Committee and European Court have stressed to be important to the evaluation of fairness.[60]

Reasonableness is a concept seen within article 9(3) of the ICCPR and article 5(3) of the ECHR, guaranteeing an entitlement to trial within a reasonable time after arrest or detention. It is also a condition of article 25 of the ICCPR, which recognises and protects the right of every citizen to take part in the conduct of public affairs, vote and be elected, and participate in the public administration of one's country 'without unreasonable restrictions'. As with the notion of fairness, the Committee and Court have taken a case-by-case approach to assessing reasonableness, based upon the particular circumstances of each case.[61] In the context of determining what might or might not constitute 'reasonable restrictions' under article 25, the Committee has commented that it will be important that any restriction is based on *objective* criteria.[62] It may, for example, be reasonable to require a higher age for election or appointment to particular offices, or that established mental incapacity may be a ground for denying a person the right to vote or to hold office.[63] In *Toonen v Australia*, concerning interference with one's private life, the Committee interpreted the requirement of reasonableness "to imply that any interference with privacy must be proportional to the end sought and be necessary in the circumstances of any given case".[64] This link between reasonableness on the one hand, and necessity and proportionality on the other, is important, although it should be remembered that necessity and proportionality are essential elements in the limitation of all rights and freedoms, by whatever mechanism.

10.3.1.2   Arbitrary Conduct

Although not a feature of the European Convention on Human Rights, a number of provisions within the International Covenant guarantee that certain rights are to be enjoyed in the absence of arbitrary interference, namely: the right not to be arbitrarily deprived of life (article 6(1)); the prohibition against arbitrary arrest or detention (article 9(1)); the exclusion of arbitrary deprivation of the right to enter one's own country (article 12(4)); and the right to be free from arbitrary or unlawful interference with one's privacy (article 17(1)). Added to these express prohibitions against the arbitrary limitation of rights, the *Siracusa Principles* provide that no

---

[60]See, for example: *de Polay v Peru*, Communication 575/1994, UN Doc CCPR/C/53/D/575 (1995), para 8.8; and *Kostoviski v The Netherlands* [1990] 12 EHRR 434.

[61]See, for example, *van Alphen v The Netherlands*, 305/1988, UN Doc CCPR/C/39/D/305/1988 (1990).

[62]General Comment 25: The right to participate in public affairs, voting rights and the right of equal access to public service (Art 25), UN Doc CCPR/C/21/Rev.1/Add.7 (1996), para 4. See also *Sohn v Republic of Korea*, Communication 518/1992, UN Doc CCPR/C/54/D/518/1992 (1995), para 10.4.

[63]General Comment 25 (ibid) para 4. See further Conte and Burchill (2009, Chap. 4).

[64]*Toonen v Australia* (n 22) para 8.3.

limitation at all may be applied in an arbitrary manner.[65] Common to the interpretation of the term 'arbitrary' are three features. The first is that arbitrary conduct may, but need not, involve an act or omission which is against the law. As an adjective, one of the ordinary meanings of the word 'arbitrary' is that the associated conduct is dependent on will or pleasure, rather than law.[66] The approach of the Human Rights Committee has been that arbitrariness is more, however, than just illegal conduct. It is interesting to note, in this regard, that article 17(1) prohibits 'arbitrary *or unlawful*' interference with privacy, which may represent recognition by the drafters of the ICCPR that illegality is not the defining feature or arbitrariness.

Drawn from this is the second common feature involved in defining or ascertaining the existence of arbitrary conduct: a link between arbitrariness and reasonableness, such that the Committee has treated arbitrary conduct as including elements of unreasonableness. In the context of the arbitrary deprivation of liberty, for example, the Committee has said that to be deemed arbitrary, the detention of a person must include elements of inappropriateness, injustice, lack of predictability, and lack of due process of law.[67] In the context of the ICCPR, the final feature of arbitrariness is rather novel and appears to be based on a desire by the Human Rights Committee to uphold the entirety of the Covenant. The Committee has considered that the concept of arbitrariness is intended to guarantee that even reasonable conduct which is provided for by law (the first two factors just identified) should be in accordance with the provisions, aims and objectives of the ICCPR.[68] The *Siracusa Principles* state rather more broadly that it is implicit that *any* restrictions upon rights recognised in the Covenant must be consistent with other rights within it.[69] As indicated earlier, this has been key to the rule that all measures which limit the enjoyment of rights must be in accordance with the principle of non-discrimination.

10.3.2 Express Limitations

The mechanism most commonly relied upon to impose restrictions upon rights and freedoms is through rights-specific limitation provisions. Express limitations are those that are authorised by a sentence or words, or a stand-alone paragraph, found within the article of the International Covenant or European Convention which enumerates the particular right in question. The provision explains the

---

[65]Siracusa Principles (n 5) para 7.

[66]*Shorter Oxford English Dictionary* (Oxford: Oxford University press, 5th ed, 2002) 109.

[67]See, for example: *Mukong v Cameroon*, Communication 458/1991, UN Doc CCPR/C/51/D/458/1991 (1994), para 9.8; and *de Morais v Angola* (n 34) para 6.1.

[68]See: General Comment 16 (n 55) para 4; and *García v Colombia*, Communication 687/1996, UN Doc CCPR/C/71/D/687/1996 (2001).

[69]Siracusa Principles (n 5) para 13.

circumstances in which the right may be limited. In the context of the right to a fair and open hearing, for example, the first two sentences of article 14(1) of the ICCPR express the substance of the right. The next sentence then sets out the circumstances in which it is permissible to limit the right to an 'open' hearing, allowing the exclusion of the press for reasons of morals, public order, or national security. The third sentence of article 14(1) provides that: "[t]he press and the public may be excluded from all or part of a trial for reasons of morals, public order (*ordre public*) or national security in a democratic society, or when the interest of the private lives of the parties so requires, or to the extent strictly necessary in the opinion of the court in special circumstances where publicity would prejudice the interests of justice". Using the same mechanism, article 5(1) of the European Convention first states the guarantee of the right to liberty and security of the person and then sets out, in sub-paragraphs (1)(a) to (f), a full list of the circumstances under which a person might be deprived of their liberty.

It is notable that the drafters of the ICCPR and ECHR took the approach of including express limitations, rather than adopting a general limitations clause applicable to all rights. The latter approach, in contrast, is the one taken under the Universal Declaration of Human Rights:[70]

Article 29
1. Everyone has duties to the community in which alone the full and free development of his personality is possible.
2. In the exercise of his rights and freedoms, everyone shall be subject only to such limitations as are determined by law solely for the purpose of securing due recognition and respect for the rights and freedoms of others and of meeting the just requirements of morality, public order and the general welfare in a democratic society.
3. These rights and freedoms may in no case be exercised contrary to the purposes and principles of the United Nations.

10.3.2.1 Limited Rights

Express limitations can be further broken down into limitations applicable to 'limited' and 'qualified' rights. Limited rights are those which explain the precise and limited extent to which the right or freedom may be restricted. A particularly good example of such a right is contained in article 5(1) of the European Convention on Human Rights, which contains an exhaustive list of the circumstances in which a person's liberty may be deprived including, for example, the lawful detention of a person after conviction by a competent court (article 5(1)(a)).[71] The ICCPR contains only one limited right, within the second sentence of article 7, which guarantees the right to be free from medical or scientific experimentation

---

[70]Universal Declaration of Human Rights, adopted under General Assembly Resolution 217(III), UN GAOR, 3rd Session, 183rd Plenary Meeting (1948).

[71]See also article 2(2) of the European Convention, concerning the deprivation of life resulting from the use of force.

except in the case where a person gives his or her 'free consent' to such experimentation. The advantage of limited rights is that they are precise in nature and do not call for any further consideration to be had. Thus, if a person gives their free consent to medical treatment, there is no need to consider the 'necessity' or 'proportionality' of the treatment involved, albeit that the Committee has the ability to have regard to just what amounts to 'free' consent under article 7. Special protection is necessary in this regard, the Committee has said, in the case of persons not capable of giving their consent.[72]

10.3.2.2 Qualified Rights

Qualified rights are those where the right is asserted as a general principle, but then qualified by stating that it is lawful to interfere with the right if it is necessary to achieve certain objectives. This involves a more detailed assessment of the legitimacy of the interference, requiring that the limit is: (1) prescribed by law; (2) in pursuit of one of the listed objectives; (3) necessary and proportional to that end; and (4) non-discriminatory. Rights-specific limitation provisions affecting qualified rights affect rights and freedoms under the ICCPR and ECHR, namely the liberty of movement (article 12(3); and article 2(3)), the expulsion of aliens (article 13; and article 1(2) of Protocol 7 to the ECHR), the right to a fair and public hearing (article 14(1); and article 6(1)), the freedom of thought, conscience and religion (article 18 (3); and article 9(2)), the freedom of expression (article 19(3); and article 10(2)), the freedom of association and right to peaceful assembly (articles 21 and 22(2); and article 11(2)), and privacy under the ECHR (article 8(2)).

Each provision lists specific objectives, the pursuit of which may legitimise limitations upon the right or freedom if the limit is also prescribed by law, necessary and proportionate, and non-discriminatory (see Sect. 10.2 above). The full complement of permissible objectives found in the articles mentioned includes the protection of national security; public order (*ordre public*), referred to in the European Convention as the prevention of disorder or crime; public safety; public health; public morals; or the rights and freedoms of others. Linked to national security, the European Convention also refers to the interests of territorial integrity. Unique to the European Convention, certain provisions therein also permit the limitation of rights for the purpose of maintaining the authority and impartiality of the judiciary (article 10(2), as a justifiable objective in the limitation of the freedom of expression); or for the prevention of the disclosure of information received in confidence (also applicable to article 10(2)); or in the interests of the economic well-being of a country (article 8(2), concerning the interference by public authorities in private and family life).

---

[72]General Comment 7: Article 7, UN Doc HR\GEN\1\Rev.1 at 7 (1994), para 3. General Comment 7 was replaced by General Comment 20: Prohibition of torture and cruel treatment or punishment (Art 7), UN Doc CCPR General Comment 20 (1992).

10.3.2.3 National Security and the Interests of Territorial Integrity

The Human Rights Committee has spoken of limitations for the protection of national security as ones which must be necessary to avert a real, and not only hypothetical, danger to the national security or democratic order of the State.[73] The *Siracusa Principles* similarly speak of national security being capable of being invoked to justify the limitation of rights only where taken to protect the existence of the nation or its territorial integrity or political independence against force or threat of force.[74] The *Principles* add that national security cannot be invoked to prevent merely local or relatively isolated threats to law and order.[75]

Despite these restrictive approaches, the majority of the Committee took a wider view in *Peltonen v Finland*, where it considered that it was a reasonable legislative requirement to refuse to issue a passport to a person who had avoided military service.[76] This decision might, however, be treated as unique in light of the fact that the *travaux préparatoires* to the freedom of movement under article 12(3) reveal that it was agreed that the right to leave one's country could not be claimed in order to avoid national service.[77] The Committee has normally taken a very robust approach to the determination of whether a situation is linked to the objective of protecting national security, rejecting any margin of discretion on the part of national authorities.[78] In the context of summaries of information used in judicial proceedings and redacted for security concerns, for example, the Committee has treated such summaries as compatible with article 14 only in circumstances where compensatory mechanisms are adopted to ensure that this does not prejudice the overall right of a litigant to a fair trial.[79]

The approach of the Committee is to be contrasted with that of the European Court, which applies a margin of appreciation and does so in a relatively liberal way in the context of national security. This approach is particularly evident in the context of derogating measures which are based upon national security grounds (see Chap. 17, Sect. 17.1.2). In the application of national security as an objective justifying the limitation of qualified rights, the Court has found various measures permissible including: interference with the freedom of expression in the context of statements made concerning the security situation in South-East Turkey;[80] secret

---

[73]*Lee v Republic of Korea* (n 40) para 7.2. See also *Belyatsky et al v Belarus*, Communication 1296/2004, UN Doc CCPR/C/90/D/1296/2004 (2007), para 7.3.

[74]Siracusa Principles (n 5) para 29.

[75]Siracusa Principles (n 5) para 30.

[76]*Peltonen v Finland*, Communication 492/1992, UN Doc CCPR/C/51/D/492/1992 (1994), para 8.4. Contrast with the individual dissenting opinion of Committee Member Bertil Wennergren.

[77]As noted in *Peltonen v Finland* (ibid) para 8.3.

[78]As in the case of *Park v Republic of Korea* (n 25), discussed above.

[79]*Ahani v Canada*, Communication 1051/2002, UN Doc CCPR/C/80/D/1051/2002 (2004), para 10.4.

[80]*Zana v Turkey* [1997] ECHR 94.

surveillance undertaken to counter espionage and terrorism;[81] and a ban on political activities and party affiliations by police officers and members of the armed forces and security services aimed at depoliticising those services during a period when Hungary was being transformed from a totalitarian regime to a pluralistic democracy.[82] The margin of leniency afforded to States by the Court is particularly apparent in its 1993 decision of *Hadjianastassiou v Greece*, where Hadjianastassiou had been convicted and sentenced for having disclosed military secrets. He argued that this was a disproportionate interference with his freedom of expression because the information he had leaked was of very minor importance. The European Court agreed with Greece that any disclosure of State secrets was capable of compromising national security and thus found no violation of the Convention.[83]

As noted in the introduction to qualified rights above, the European Convention refers not only to 'national security' but also to 'the interests of territorial integrity'. While the interests of territorial integrity are not expressly mentioned within the ICCPR, the link between national security and territorial integrity seems implicit. This was the approach taken by the UN Economic and Social Council in the preparation of the *Siracusa Principles*.[84] It is notable, also, that the European Court has treated territorial integrity as linked or closely related to national security.[85] Ovey and White conclude that this approach seems to require the existence of some threat of violence or disorder before resort can be made to the ground of preserving the interests of territorial integrity.[86]

10.3.2.4 Public Order

The protection of public order, or the 'prevention of disorder or crime' under the ECHR, is an objective which may justify the limitation of a number of qualified rights and is frequently raised before the Human Rights Committee and the European Court. The Committee has again taken a generally strict approach to the application of this ground of limitation, careful to ensure that limits are both necessary for and proportional to the risk posed to public order by any given situation. The arrest of the author in *Joana v Madagascar* was found to be in violation of the ICCPR, for example, in circumstances where it was claimed that his public denunciation of elections as fraudulent endangered public order and security.[87]

---

[81]*Klass and others v Germany* [1978] 2 EHRR 214.

[82]*Rekvényi v Hungary* [1999] ECHR 31.

[83]*Hadjianastassiou v Greece* (1993) 16 EHRR.

[84]Siracusa Principles (n 5) para 29.

[85]As in *Zana v Turkey* (n 80).

[86]Ovey and White (2002, p. 205).

[87]*Joana v Madagascar*, Communication 132/1982, UN Doc CCPR/C/24/D/132/1982 (1985), para 14.

While the meaning of 'public order' is one which, according to the *Siracusa Principles*, should be interpreted in the context of the purpose of the particular human right which is being limited, there are two principal features the protection of which fall under the umbrella of 'public order':[88]

- Rules which ensure the functioning of society or the set of fundamental principles on which society is founded; and
- Respect for human rights.

Falling within the first category is the case of *Gauthier v Canada* where, although certain restrictions on the freedom of expression were ultimately found to be disproportionate, the Committee agreed that the protection of Parliamentary procedure could be seen as a legitimate goal of public order.[89] As for the second feature of public order, a controversial case which raised questions about the relationship between objective justifications for differential treatment, issues of human dignity, and limitations upon one's private life was *Wackenheim v France*. The author, who suffered from dwarfism, complained about a law which prohibited dwarf tossing, alleging that this prevented him from working and was thus an affront to his human dignity. The Committee accepted France's argument that the ban was necessary to protect public order and due respect for the human dignity of the individual concerned.[90]

10.3.2.5   Public Health and Safety

The objectives of protecting 'public health' and 'public safety' are sometimes interlinked in nature. In *Malakhovsky and Pikul v Belarus*, for example, the Human Rights Committee determined that it was necessary for public safety, and proportionate to this end, for the registration of a religious association to be conditional upon the use by it of premises which satisfied health and fire safety standards.[91] In *Buckley v United Kingdom*, the European Court was concerned with the refusal of planning permission to a gypsy family for caravans to be used as homes, alleged to be in contravention of the right to family life under article 8 of the Convention. The United Kingdom argued that the refusal of planning permission was aimed at furthering highway safety, the preservation of the environment, and public health. The Court accepted that these aims came within the exceptions relating to public safety, and the protection of public health.[92]

---

[88]Siracusa Principles (n 5) paras 22–23.

[89]*Gauthier v Canada*, Communication 633/1995, UN Doc CCPR/C/65/D/633/1995 (1999), para 13.5.

[90]*Wackenheim v France*, Communication 854/1999, UN Doc CCPR/C/75/D/854/1999 (2002), para 7.4 (discussed further in Conte and Burchill 2009, Chaps. 7 and 11 herein).

[91]*Malakhovsky and Pikul v Belarus*, Communication 1207/2003, UN Doc CCPR/C/84/D/1207/2003 (2005), para 7.4.

[92]*Buckley v United Kingdom* (1997) 23 EHRR 101.

The objectives of 'public health' and 'public safety' do, however, have some distinctive characteristics. Public safety is understood to refer to the protection against danger to the safety of persons, to their life or physical integrity, or serious damage to their property.[93] Public health is much narrower in its scope, said to be capable of being invoked as a ground of limitation only in order to allow a State to take measures dealing with a serious threat to the health of the population or individual members of the population. Such measures must be specifically aimed at preventing disease or injury or providing care for the sick and injured.[94] There have as yet been no claims before the Committee or Court in which the objective of public safety has been relied on alone. It is conceivable, however, that public safety might by itself justify interference with the freedom of expression in order to prohibit misleading publications on health-threatening substances (such as medicines, illicit drugs, or poisons) or practices (such as those relating to safe sexual conduct), or to restrict advertising for tobacco, alcohol and other similar substances.

10.3.2.6 Public Morals

The issue of public morals has already been referred to in the context of the margin of appreciation (Sect. 10.2.1.1 above), where the Committee initially referred in *Hertzberg v Finland* to this ground as one calling for a margin of discretion to be applied, but later took a much more robust approach in *Toonen v Australia*. The *Siracusa Principles*, adopted by the Economic and Social Council in 1985, reflect the Committee's earlier position in *Hertzberg* and are somewhat out of step with the Committee's 1994 views in *Toonen*, stating at paragraph 27 that:[95]

> Since public morality varies over time and from one culture to another, a state which invokes public morality as a ground for restricting human rights, while enjoying a certain margin of discretion, shall demonstrate that the limitation in question is essential to the maintenance of respect for fundamental values of the community.

The European Court has given more detailed consideration to the objective of protecting public morals in the context of censorship. In the leading case of *Handyside v United Kingdom*, the Court noted that because there was no uniform European concept of 'morality', States would be entitled to enjoy a wide margin of appreciation in assessing whether censorship measures were required to protect moral standards.[96] This approach was followed in *Müller and Others v Switzerland* concerning a contemporary art exhibition, which included three paintings depicting sexual acts. The paintings were seized by authorities on the grounds that they were obscene, and seizure of the paintings was found to be lawful by the Swiss courts for the same reason. The European Court found that it was not unreasonable for the

---

[93]Siracusa Principles (n 5) para 33.
[94]Siracusa Principles (n 5) para 25.
[95]Siracusa Principles (n 5) para 27. See also para 28.
[96]*Handyside v United Kingdom* (1976) 1 EHRR 737.

Swiss courts to have found the paintings liable to offend the sense of sexual propriety of persons of ordinary sensitivity.[97]

Wingrove v United Kingdom concerned a video portraying a woman dressed as a nun and described in the credits as Saint Teresa, having an erotic fantasy involving the crucified figure of Christ. The British Board of Film Classification refused to grant the movie a certificate for distribution because it considered that its public distribution would outrage and insult the feelings of believing Christians. The Court concluded that there was not enough common ground within Europe for it to be able to say whether laws prohibiting blasphemy were incompatible with the Convention.[98] Almost 10 years on since that decision, the case of *Klein v Slovakia* might indicate a shift in approach by the Court. The case concerned a poster advertising the movie The People v Larry Flint, in which the main character had a US flag around his hips and was depicted as crucified on a woman's pubic area dressed in a bikini. The Common Declaration of Ecumenical Council of Churches and of the Slovak Bishops' Conference protested against the display of the poster on the basis that it was a profanation of God. Klein, in response, published an article criticizing one of the Bishops. He was subsequently convicted of blasphemy. In Strasbourg, the European Court found that the application of the law of blasphemy amounted, in the circumstances, to an interference with that freedom of expression that was not 'necessary in a democratic society' (see Sect. 10.2.3.2 for a discussion of the latter expression).[99]

10.3.2.7   Rights and Freedoms of Others

The balancing of one person's right against another is a difficult matter, but one based on the principle that membership in society involves not only rights but also special duties and responsibilities to others. Preambular paragraph 5 to the ICCPR recognises that each person has responsibilities and duties "to other individuals and to the community to which he belongs".[100] The preamble to the European Convention does not reflect this sentiment, but article 17 of the Convention mirrors article 5(1) of the ICCPR, which provides:[101]

> Nothing in the present Covenant may be interpreted as implying for any State, group or person any right to engage in any activity or perform any act aimed at the destruction of any of the rights and freedoms recognized herein or at their limitation to a greater extent than is provided for in the present Covenant.

In the context of the express limitations under article 19(3) of the ICCPR and article 10(2) of the ECHR, it is there specifically mentioned that the exercise of the freedom of expression carries with it special duties and responsibilities. This is a matter

---

[97]*Müller and Others v Switzerland* (1991) 13 EHRR 212.

[98]*Wingrove v United Kingdom* (1997) 24 EHRR 1.

[99]*Klein v Slovakia* [2006] ECHR 909.

[100]See also the Universal Declaration of Human Rights (n 70) article 29(1).

[101]See also the Universal Declaration of Human Rights (n 70) article 29(3).

which has been subject to much consideration before the European Court of Human Rights in the context of the responsibilities of the media,[102] although not in communications before the Human Rights Committee (due to the fact that such communications may only be brought by individuals).[103] Also relating to limits on the freedom of expression, the European Court was required to consider the Austrian Penal Code in *Otto-Preminger Institut v Germany*, which allowed for the seizure of a film considered to offence the religious sensibilities of Roman Catholics as a matter of 'justified indignation' (as provided for in the Code). The Court accepted that the seizure of the film was in pursuit of the protection of the rights and freedoms of others, as a legitimate aim under article 10(2) of the Convention.[104]

The rights and freedoms of others has also been accepted as a valid ground for limiting family rights, where the rights of the child have been readily accepted as justifying the placement of children in social care.[105] A more controversial decision of the European Court concerns the use of this ground to uphold Germany's Unfair Competition Act.[106] It should also be noted that limitations based on the protection of the reputation of others (article 17(2) of the ICCPR and article 8(2) of the ECHR) cannot be used to protect the State and its officials from public opinion or criticism.[107]

10.3.2.8 Maintaining the Authority and Impartiality of the Judiciary

A difference in approach concerning the maintenance of the authority and impartiality of the judiciary can be seen between the International Covenant and the European Convention, albeit with the same effect. The ECHR treats this objective as an express objective permitting the limitation of the freedom of expression under article 10(2). The same cannot be said of the ICCPR, thus requiring the Human Rights Committee to rely on the more general objective of pursuing public order (in particular, the protection of rules which ensure the functioning of society or the set of fundamental principles on which society is founded).[108] European jurisprudence has treated the objective of maintaining the authority and impartiality of the judiciary as including two elements:

- Protecting against unjustified judicial criticism; and
- Protecting the fair conduct of proceedings.

As to the first objective, the Court has had no trouble with accepting the validity of interfering with expression in circumstances where there is a personal and

---

[102]See, for example, *De Haes and Gijsels v Belgium* [1997] ECHR 7.

[103]See Conte and Burchill (2009, Chap. 2).

[104]*Otto-Preminger Institut v Germany* [1994] ECHR 26.

[105]See, for example, *Buckley v New Zealand*, Communication 858/1999, UN Doc CCPR/C/70/D/858/1999 (2000), and *Johansen v Norway* [1996] ECHR 31.

[106]*Jacubowski v Germany* [1994] ECHR 21.

[107]Siracusa Principles (n 5) para 37, and European Convention (n 2) article 17.

[108]Siracusa Principles (n 5) para 22.

destructive attack upon a judge, rather than criticism of a judgment issued.[109] Personal attacks might otherwise be dealt with on the basis of protecting the rights and freedoms of the judge concerned (whether under the ICCPR or the ECHR). Where, however, a criticism relates to the substance of a decision, or forms part of a reasonable public debate on the functioning of the judiciary, interference with such expressions will be difficult to justify. Thus, in *De Haes and Gijsels v Belgium*, defamation convictions following the publication of articles written by the applicants which strongly criticised a judge's decision were held to amount to a violation of the Convention in circumstances where the majority of the Court accepted that the articles has been well researched and formed part of a public debate in Belgium on incest, child abuse, and judicial reactions to these problems.[110]

10.3.2.9   Prevention of the Disclosure of Information Received in Confidence

Different approaches between the ICCPR and ECHR can again be seen concerning limitations upon the freedom of expression. While article 10(2) of the European Covenant expressly permits a limitation on expression for the prevention of the disclosure of information received in confidence, the Human Rights Committee would need to be satisfied that such a limitation was necessary for the protection of public order, national security, or the rights or freedoms of others. The objective was successfully relied upon by the United Kingdom in the *Spycatcher* cases before the European Court, concerned with material received in confidence by a former officer of Britain's MI5 security service.[111]

10.3.2.10   Economic Well-being

Article 8(2) of the European Convention permits the interference by a public authority in the private and family life of a person in the interests of the economic well-being of a country. This objective was successfully relied upon by France in two cases brought against it before the European Court. The cases involved the exercise of search and seizure powers, on one occasion by customs authorities, and the other concerning enquiries into financial dealings with foreign countries contrary to French law.[112] The Court did not attempt to explain what 'the economic well-being' of a country means, instead preferring to deal with each case on its particular merits.

---

[109]*Barfod v Denmark* (1991) 13 EHRR 493. See also *Schöpfer v Switzerland* [1998] ECHR 40, and contrast with *Wille v Liechtenstein* [1999] ECHR 107.

[110]*De Haes and Gijsels v Belgium* (1997) ECHR 7.

[111]*Observer and Guardian v United Kingdom* [1992] 14 EHRR 153; and *Sunday Times v United Kingdom (No 2)* [1992] 14 EHRR 299.

[112]*Miailhe v France* [1993] 16 EHRR 332; and *Funke v France* [1993] 16 EHRR 297.

10.4 Rights Derogable During States of Emergency

The second mechanism under the International Covenant and European Convention allowing for restrictions upon the enjoyment of rights and freedoms involves the capacity under article 4 and article 15 to temporarily suspend the application of certain rights during a state of emergency which threatens the life of a nation. Paragraph (1) of each article sets out the essence of this exceptional measure, in almost identical terms to each other. Article 4(1) of the ICCPR provides:

> In time of public emergency which threatens the life of the nation and the existence of which is officially proclaimed, the States Parties to the present Covenant may take measures derogating from their obligations under the present Covenant to the extent strictly required by the exigencies of the situation, provided that such measures are not inconsistent with their other obligations under international law and do not involve discrimination solely on the ground of race, colour, sex, language, religion or social origin.

There are some differences in the text used in the European Convention, which can be summarised as follows:

- The ICCPR begins by iterating that the application of the measure is available in time of "public emergency", whereas the European Convention speaks of times of *"war or other* public emergency" (emphasis added; see further Sect. 10.4.2 below).
- As indicated earlier in this chapter (see Sect. 10.2.5), article 15(2) does not make express mention of the principle of non-discrimination, which is included in the final part of article 4(1) of the Covenant (see further Sect. 10.4.2 below).
- Mention is made in article 4(1) of the ICCPR of the need to make an official proclamation of a public emergency. Although this is not mentioned in article 15 (1) of the ECHR, it is included in article 15(3) of the Convention.

Unlike express limitations (see Sect. 10.3.2 above), which might be semi-permanent in nature, derogations involve: a suspension in the application of certain rights within the territory and jurisdiction of the State party; for a limited period (i.e. during a state of emergency threatening the life of the nation). In more technical terms, articles 4 and 15 allow a State to suspend the application to it of obligations under certain articles of the International Covenant and European Convention. For a derogation to be valid, two procedural conditions and four substantive conditions must be satisfied.

10.4.1 Procedural Conditions

10.4.1.1 Non-derogable Rights

The ICCPR and ECHR explain that certain rights may not be derogated from, even during a state of emergency. This is a matter considered earlier in this chapter (see

Sect. 10.1). Bringing together that analysis in a practical way, the result is that, when examining the possibility of temporarily suspending the application of rights under article 4 of the ICCPR or article 15 of the ECHR, consideration must be had to six 'types' of rights and freedoms:

1. Those that are *expressly non-derogable* under article 4(2) of the ICCPR or article 15(2) of the ECHR (e.g. the right to life).
2. Those that are not expressly included under article 4(2) or 15(2), but which are *non-derogable by implication* as a result of their status as absolute rights under customary international law, compliance with which is mandated by both articles 4(1) and 15(1) (e.g. the right of all persons deprived of their liberty to be treated with humanity and with respect for the inherent dignity of the human person).
3. Those that are not expressly included under article 4(2) or 15(2), but which are *not capable of limitation if this would circumvent the protection of non-derogable rights*, whether expressly or impliedly non-derogable (e.g. the right to a fair trial in proceedings leading to the imposition of the death penalty).
4. Those rights that are not identified as 'non-derogable' but in respect of which *no limitation may be imposed due to their absolute nature* (e.g. the right to hold opinions without interference and, in the case of the ECHR, the prohibition against imprisonment for failure to perform a contractual obligation).
5. Rights and freedoms which are *non-derogable but nevertheless capable of limitation* due to the manner in which they are expressed (e.g. the freedom to manifest one's religion or beliefs, capable of limitation under article 18(3) of the ICCPR if prescribed by law and necessary to protect public safety, order, health or morals, or the fundamental rights and freedoms of others).
6. Rights and freedoms which are *derogable and also capable of limitation* due to the manner in which they are expressed (e.g. the right to privacy), in which case the State must pursue such limitation before making recourse to the derogations regime.

The procedure under articles 4 and 15 cannot be engaged with respect to non-derogable rights, although this has not prevented States from claiming to do so. The Human Rights Committee has on several occasions expressed its concern about non-derogable rights being either derogated from or under a risk of derogation owing to inadequacies in the legal regime of a State party.[113]

---

[113]General Comment 29 (n 3) para 7. See, for example, the Concluding Observations of the Committee concerning: Armenia, UN Doc CCPR/C/79/Add.100 (1998), para 7; Colombia, UN Doc CCPR/C/79/Add.76 (1997), para 25; the Dominican Republic, UN Doc CCPR/C/79/Add.18 (1993), para 4; Gabon, UN Doc CCPR/C/79/Add.71 (1996), para 10; Israel, UN Doc CCPR/C/79/Add.93 (1998), para 11; Iraq, UN Doc CCPR/C/79/Add.84 (1997), para 9; Jordan, UN Doc CCPR/C/79/Add.35 (1994), para 6; Kyrgyzstan, UN Doc CCPR/CO/69/KGZ (2000), para 12; Mongolia, UN Doc CCPR/C/79/Add.120 (2000), para 14; Nepal UN Doc CCPR/C/79/Add.42 (1994), para 9; Russian Federation, UN Doc CCPR/C/79/Add.54 (1995), para 27; Uruguay, UN Doc CCPR/C/79/Add.90 (1998), para 8; and Zambia, UN Doc CCPR/C/79/Add.62 (1996), para 11.

10.4.1.2 Notice of Derogation

The second procedural condition is found in paragraph 3 of both articles, which requires that a State party must officially proclaim the existence within its territory of a public emergency that threatens the life of the nation. Through the intermediary of the UN Secretary-General, of the Secretary-General of the Council of Europe in the case of the ECHR, a derogating State must immediately inform other States parties of the provisions from which it has derogated and the reasons for which it has done so. The Human Rights Committee has emphasised that notification should include full information about the measures taken and a clear explanation of the reasons for them, with full documentation attached concerning the relevant law.[114] The *Siracusa Principles* are even more detailed in setting out the requirements of a notification of derogation, stating that such notification must contain:[115]

- The provisions of the Covenant from which the State has derogated;
- A copy of the proclamation of emergency, together with the constitutional provisions, legislation, or decrees governing the state of emergency in order to assist the States parties to appreciate the scope of the derogation;
- The effective date of the imposition of the state of emergency and the period for which it has been proclaimed;
- An explanation of the reasons which actuated the government's decision to derogate, including a brief description of the factual circumstances leading up to the proclamation of the state of emergency; and
- A brief description of the anticipated effect of the derogation measures on the rights recognised by the Covenant, including copies of decrees derogating from these rights issued prior to the notification.

Explaining the rationale behind the need for detailed proclamations, the Committee has stated that this:[116]

> ...is essential for the maintenance of the principles of legality and rule of law at times when they are most needed. When proclaiming a state of emergency with consequences that could entail derogation from any provision of the Covenant, States must act within their constitutional and other provisions of law that govern such proclamation and the exercise of emergency powers.

The European Court has taken an approach which is less prescriptive than the list of obligations contained in the *Siracusa Principles*. In *Lawless v Ireland*, it took the approach that, so long as the notification was sufficient to enable the Secretary-General to understand the nature and reasons for the derogation, the derogation will not be invalidated by virtue only of a lack of compliance with additional technical

---

[114]General Comment 29 (n 3) paras 5, 16, and 17. See, for example, *de Montejo v Colombia*, Communication 64/179, UN Doc CCPR/C/64/179 (1982) para 10.3.

[115]Siracusa Principles (n 5) para 45.

[116]General Comment 29 (n 3) para 2. See also the Siracusa Principles (n 2) para 43.

requirements.[117] This is a pragmatic approach, although it can be observed that adherence to the *Siracusa* list would ensure that such an understanding is achieved.

Articles 4(3) and 15(3) require a further communication on the date on which a State terminates such derogation.

10.4.2   Substantive Conditions

Article 4, paragraph 1, contains four substantive requirements applicable to the adoption by a State party of measures which derogate from the ICCPR:

- The measures must be ones that are adopted during a "time of public emergency which threatens the life of the nation";
- The derogating measures must be limited to those "strictly required by the exigencies of the situation";
- The measures must not be "inconsistent with [the State's] other obligations under international law"; and
- Such measures must not "involve discrimination solely on the ground of race, colour, sex, language, religion or social origin".

The nature and application of these requirements is considered in Chap. 17, which examines derogations by the United Kingdom from the right to liberty.

10.5   Conclusions

The human rights treaties to which the four case study countries are party allow for the limitation of certain rights. Although the foregoing analysis discloses that the framework for the accommodation of limitations is complex, the International Covenant and European Convention are nonetheless capable of meeting the pursuit of democratic objectives and maintaining a balance between individual interests. At the outset, though, it must be recognised that certain rights are not capable of limitation in any circumstance, including a state of emergency, whether expressed in absolute terms or as a result of their absolute status as norms of *jus cogens* under customary international law. These include the prohibitions against torture and slavery and the principle of no punishment without law.

Interference with the unrestricted enjoyment of rights is allowed through two principal means under the Covenant and Convention. Certain rights and freedoms may be temporarily suspended during a state of emergency. Most others are capable of limitation as a result of the means by which they are expressed in the substantive provisions of the ICCPR and ECHR. In the latter case, limitations can arise as a

---

[117]*Lawless v Ireland (No 3)* [1961] ECHR 2.

result of the interpretation of terms such as 'fair', 'reasonable' or 'arbitrary', or by application of express limitations provided for within the text.

Express limitations can be either very specific (setting out the precise or limited extent to which a right or freedom may be restricted, resulting in a 'limited right') or more general (explaining that the pursuit of certain objectives can justify interference, creating a 'qualified right'). The full list of objectives capable of justifying the limitation of qualified rights, although not applicable to all qualified rights, includes: national security and the interests of territorial integrity; public order (referred to in the European Convention as the prevention of disorder or crime); public health and safety; public morals; the protection of the rights and freedoms of others; maintaining the authority and impartiality of the judiciary; preventing the disclosure of information received in confidence; or the economic well-being of the country. The last two objectives are contained in the European Convention only.

Any measure seeking to limit rights and freedoms, by whatever mechanism, must conform to three requirements. First, it must be prescribed by national law, requiring the prescription to be accessible and precise. Secondly, limiting measures must be necessary and proportionate. Although linked to each other, distinctive features are attached to the terms 'necessary' and 'proportionate'. Necessity requires any derogation to be limited "to the extent strictly required by the exigencies of the situation". In the context of qualified rights, necessity demands the existence of a rational link between the limitation and the pursuit of one of the permissible objectives allowing for limitation of the right and often also requires that the limitation is "necessary in a democratic society". Proportionality lies at the heart of any limitation upon rights and freedoms, such that the limiting measure may be no more restrictive than required to achieve the purpose of the limitation. Although proportionality requires a full evaluation of all relevant issues, regard will at least be had to the negative impact of the limiting measure upon the enjoyment of the right and the ameliorating effects of the limiting measure. Finally, any measure impacting upon the unrestricted enjoyment of rights and freedoms must be non-discriminatory in nature.

In the application and interpretation of rights, an important difference exists between the approach of the Human Rights Committee and the European Court of Human Rights. While the European Court has developed a margin of appreciation doctrine, allowing States a certain level of latitude, the Committee has steered clear of this approach, insisting that it be the final arbiter of the meaning of rights under the ICCPR and whether compliance with Covenant obligations has been met. The same tension exists in the approaches of the Committee and Court to the application of the derogations regimes under article 4 of the ICCPR and article 15 of the ECHR.

When considering recourse to the derogations regimes under article 4 of the ICCPR or article 15 of the ECHR, regard must first be had to whether the right or freedom is capable of temporary suspension. Certain rights are expressly or impliedly non-derogable, or not capable of limitation due to their absolute nature. On the other hand, some non-derogable rights are capable of limitation due to the manner in which they are expressed. In the case of rights that are both derogable and capable of limitation (by interpretation of the substantive provision or by application of an express limitations clause), the State must pursue such limitation before making recourse to the derogations regime. Where recourse to the temporary suspension of a right is available, notice of the derogation must be given to the Secretary-General of the United Nations (or of the Council of Europe in the case of the ECHR) in terms that are at the very least sufficient for the Secretary-General to understand the nature and reasons for the derogation. Considered further in Chap. 17 are the substantive conditions of derogating measures, namely that the derogating measure(s): are adopted during a time of public emergency which threatens the life of the nation; are limited to those strictly required by the exigencies of the situation; are consistent with the State's other obligations under international law; and do not involve discrimination solely on the ground of race, colour, sex, language, religion or social origin.

References

Arai-Takahashi, Yutaka. 2002. *The Margin of Appreciation Doctrine and the Principle of Proportionality in the Jurisprudence of the ECHR*. Antwerp: Intersentia.

Benvenisti, Eyal. 1999. Margin of Appreciation, Consensus, and Universal Standards. 31 *International Law and Politics* 843.

Conte, Alex, and Burchill, Richard. 2009. *Defining Civil and Political Rights: The Jurisprudence of the United Nations Human Rights* Committee. Aldershot: 2nd ed, Ashgate Publishing Ltd.

Ghandhi, PR. 1998. *The Human Rights Committee and the Right of Individual Communication: Law and Practice*. Aldershot: Ashgate Publishing Ltd.

Harris, David, O'Boyle, Michael, and Warbrick, Colin. 1995. *Law of the European Convention on Human Rights*. London: Butterworths.

International Law Commission. 1966. Commentary on the Vienna Convention on the Law of Treaties. 2 *Yearbook of the International Law Commission* 248.

Macdonald, R. 1987. The Margin of Appreciation in the Jurisprudence of the European Court of Human Rights. In Giaffré, A (ed). *International Law at the Time of its Codification: Essays in Honor or Roberto Ago*. Milan: Vol. 3, Academy of European Law.

Marks, Susan. 1995. Civil Liberties at the Margin: The UK Derogation and the European Court of Human Rights. 15(1) *Oxford Journal of Legal Studies* 69.

Nowak, Manfred. 2005. *UN Covenant on Civil and Political Rights*. Kehl, Germany: 2nd revised ed, NP Engel.

Ovey, Clare, and White, Robin. 2002. *The European Convention on Human Rights*. Oxford: 3rd ed, Oxford University Press.

Schmidt, Markus. 1995. The Complementarity of the Covenant and the European Convention on Human Rights – Recent Developments. In Harris, David, and Joseph, Sarah (eds). *The International Covenant on Civil and Political Rights and United Kingdom Law*. Oxford: Clarendon Press.

Steiner, Henry, and Alston, Philip. 2000. *International Human Rights in Context*. Oxford: 2nd ed, Oxford University Press.

Chapter 11
Human Rights in the Commonwealth

The full spectrum of human rights and freedoms involve the respect for, and protection and fulfilment of, civil, cultural, economic, political and social rights, as well as the right to development. When one comes to consider human rights in the domestic sphere, the term usually employed to encompass this is the protection of 'civil liberties'. Although this term, at least technically speaking, refers to first generation civil and political rights (see the introduction to Chap. 9 concerning the notion that rights developed over three generations), the reality is that civil liberties are understood to capture a broader set of rights, including education and property rights for example. The aim of this chapter is to provide an overview of the civil liberties protection frameworks within each of the Commonwealth case study countries. The chapter is divided into four parts, considering first the approach of each country to civil liberties protection and the application of the legislative human rights instruments in Canada, New Zealand and the United Kingdom. The chapter then moves on to consider issues relating to the role of civil liberties in statutory interpretation, including the question of declarations of incompatibility. The role of civil liberties in the law-making process is then considered, as well as the provision of remedies for violations of rights and freedoms. Given the importance attached to the limitation of rights within proper boundaries when countering terrorism, the final part of this chapter looks at the available means in each country to this end.

11.1 Frameworks for Human Rights Protection in the Case Study Countries

Other than Australia, each of the case study countries has a legislative framework for the domestic protection of human rights. It should be recalled, however, that civil liberties are also to be found in the common law. Rights discourse has, in reality, been largely developed under the common law and this is particularly important to the protection of civil liberties in Australia, which has no federal human rights

A. Conte, *Human Rights in the Prevention and Punishment of Terrorism*,
DOI 10.1007/978-3-642-11608-7_11, © Springer-Verlag Berlin Heidelberg 2010

statute. Common law rights, and the application of presumptions on statutory interpretation, instead lie at the heart of civil liberties protection in Australia. Generally speaking, the judiciary has guarded against the erosion of common law rights. Lord Goff recalled in *Attorney-General v Guardian Newspapers* that "everybody is free to do anything, subject only to the provisions of the law".[1] As will be seen in the discussion that follows on the protection frameworks within each case study country, the status of common law rights is treated with a degree of reverence by the statutory frameworks in Canada, New Zealand and the United Kingdom.

11.1.1   Human Rights Protection in Australia

Australia has no national legislation capable of guarding against undue limits being placed upon rights and freedoms and is alone amongst western nations in not having a bill of rights.[2] Hanks describes this position as a product of the philosophical and historical context in which Australia's constitutional documents were drafted, products of the mid-to-late nineteenth century and thus after the period of Enlightenment but before the post-World War II movement to codify and provide greater protection for rights and freedoms.[3] Australia's Constitution of 1901 makes express reference to relatively few civil and political rights, limited to voting and property rights, the freedom of religion, the right to trial by jury, and the prohibition against discrimination between residents of different states within Australia.[4] Certain rights have been found to be implied in the Constitution by the High Court of Australia.[5] However, efforts to include further rights protection in the Constitution have been repeatedly rejected, as have proposals to enact comprehensive national human rights legislation (as occurred with the Australian Bill of Rights Bill 1985).[6]

Although the Australian government points to a 'robust' constitutional structure and legislative framework capable of protecting human rights and prohibiting discrimination, the Human Rights Committee has expressed concern about the absence of a constitutional bill of rights, or a constitutional provision giving effect to the International Covenant on Civil and Political Rights (ICCPR), noting that there remain lacunae in the protection of Covenant rights in the Australian legal

---

[1]*Attorney-General v Guardian Newspapers Ltd (No 2)* [1990] 1 AC 109, as noted with approval by Lord Steyn in *Reynolds v Times Newspapers Ltd* [1999] 4 All ER 609.

[2]Williams (2003). Note, however, that Australia's new Labor government Attorney-General announced, in December 2008, the establishment of a panel for a national consultation on human rights: see McClelland (2008).

[3]Hanks (1996, p. 495).

[4]Flynn (2003, p. 277) and Hanks (1996, Chap. 14).

[5]Flynn (2003, pp. 277–278) and Hanks (1996, pp. 497–498).

[6]Kildea (2003).

system.[7] While there has been some movement within Australia's non-federal legislatures to enact human rights legislation, this does not protect against the limitation of rights by federal legislation.[8] The position is further complicated by the mixture of English and American influences upon the legal and political system in Australia, summarised by Gaze and Jones as follows:[9]

> Australia has nine separate legal jurisdictions: the federal level, the six States, and the two mainland Territories, each with its own courts and Parliament. The sources of law in each jurisdiction include judicial decisions, Acts of Parliament, and written constitutions. The High Court, at the apex of the Australian legal system, not only hears matters under federal laws, but has to resolve problems concerning the interaction of all these laws and, in some cases, to act as a final court of appeal from the States or Territories. The process of ascertaining the law on any particular area of concern to civil liberties is often complex. Different rules can exist in each jurisdiction, whether by judicial decision or by statute.

Cooray argues that the absence of a national bill of rights in Australia does not necessarily mean disrespect for human rights, pointing to the important role of the common law in the protection of rights and freedoms, a source of law which can be drawn from jurisdictions outside Australia.[10] While he is correct, this overlooks the precarious position of rights and freedoms which rely solely upon the common law, namely their ability to be 'trumped' by inconsistent legislation by virtue of Parliamentary sovereignty. Nor does it take into account the generally legalistic, positive law, approach of the High Court of Australia.[11] This vulnerability is particularly relevant in the context of Australia's legislation on counter-terrorism. In his study on counter-terrorism law in Australia, the Special Rapporteur on the promotion and protection of human rights and fundamental freedoms while countering terrorism concluded:[12]

> Given that this study identifies a number of actual and potential human rights violations within Australia's counter-terrorism regime, the Special Rapporteur urges Australia to move towards enacting federal legislation implementing the International Covenant on

---

[7]Human Rights Committee: Concluding Observations on Australia, UN Doc CCPR/A/38/40 (1983), para 140; and Human Rights Committee: Concluding Observations on Australia, UN Doc CCPR/CO/69/AUS (2000), para 13.

[8]The Australian Capital Territory enacted a Human Rights Act in 2004. The State of Victoria has enacted the Charter of Human Rights and Responsibilities Act 2006. Consideration is being given in the Northern Territory, and the States of Western Australia and Tasmania, for the adoption of human rights legislation.

[9]Gaze and Jones (1990, p. 25).

[10]Cooray (1985, Chap. 3, Sect. 3.1).

[11]See, for example, *McInnis v The Queen* (1979) 143 CLR 575.

[12]Special Rapporteur on the promotion and protection of human rights and fundamental freedoms while countering terrorism, Australia: Study on Human Rights Compliance While Countering Terrorism, UN Doc A/HRC/4/26/Add.3 (2006), para 65. See similar comments, in the context of human rights protections pertaining to control orders, by the Parliament of Australia Department of Library Services, Research Paper: Anti-terrorism control orders in Australia and the United Kingdom: a comparison (2008), pp. 18–19.

Civil and Political Rights and providing remedial mechanisms for the protection of rights
and freedoms.

11.1.2   Human Rights Protection in Canada

Canada has enjoyed a reasonably streamlined progression in its constitutional law,
which may partly explain the establishment in 1982 of what some consider to be a
model framework for civil liberties protection. British North America had been
made up of three British colonies, which were united to become the Dominion of
Canada under the British North America Act 1867 (Constitution Act 1867), remaining a part of the British Empire. The Act established the rules of federalism in the
Dominion of Canada, but did not contain any guarantee of rights and freedoms.
Dedicated human rights legislation did not appear in Canada until the enactment of
the Canadian Bill of Rights 1960. The 1960 Bill of Rights continues to apply today,
although there remain two significant deficiencies with it. The first is that it was
enacted as an ordinary statute, thus subject to implied and express repeal. Furthermore, the document applies to federal laws only. The United Kingdom's legislative
control over Canada was terminated under the Constitution Act 1982. Part I of the
Act, which is applicable to provincial as well as federal levels of government,
contains the Canadian Charter of Rights and Freedoms.[13] The Charter is both
supreme and entrenched.

11.1.2.1   Entrenched Status of the Charter

Resulting also as a consequence that it forms part of the Constitution Act, the
Charter of Rights and Freedoms can only be altered by a constitutional amendment,
known as the 'Seven-Fifty Procedure'. Sections 38 and 52(3) of the Constitution
Act require any amendment of the Act to be made consequent to the concurrence of
the Federal Parliament along with the Legislatures of two-thirds of the provinces
(amounting to 'seven' legislative bodies), those bodies representing at least 50% of
the population of all the provinces (hence 'fifty' in the Seven-Fifty Procedure). The
Charter therefore has a level of entrenchment that makes it more difficult to amend
than other comparable instruments.

11.1.2.2   Supreme Status of the Charter

As part of the Constitution Act 1982, the Charter of Rights and Freedoms expressly
overrides inconsistent statutes, making it part of supreme law rather than having the

---

[13]On the application of the Constitution Act 1982 to all levels of government, see section 32(1).

status of an ordinary statute. This occurs by virtue of the supremacy clause in section 52(1) of the Constitution Act, which provides:

> The Constitution of Canada is the supreme law of Canada, and any law inconsistent with the provisions of the Constitution is, to the extent of the inconsistency, of no force or effect.

Determining whether any law is 'inconsistent' with the provisions of the Constitution, including the Charter, is a matter for the judiciary and section 52 thus provides an explicit basis for judicial review of Canadian legislation.[14] Where such an inconsistency is found, the plain wording of section 52(1) suggests that the inconsistent law will be found to be "of no force or effect". The Supreme Court of Canada has developed a more pragmatic approach, however, identifying six options for dealing with inconsistent legislation:

1. Nullification: where, as evident from the words of section 52(1), the court will declare invalid and strike down the enactment which is inconsistent with the Charter, or other provisions of the Constitution.[15]
2. Temporary validity: striking down the whole of the inconsistent statute, but temporarily suspending the coming into force of the declaration of invalidity, thus enabling the executive to take measures in order to avoid a vacuum in the law.[16]
3. Severance: holding that only part of the statute is inconsistent, striking down that part, and severing it from the valid remainder of the statute, so long as this does not render the legislation incapable of application (i.e. the part of the statute being severed is not a key operative provision of the legislation).[17]
4. Reading in: adding words to an inconsistent statute in order to make it consistent with the Constitution Act, so long as such reading in does not amount to a strained or absurd interpretation of the provision.[18]
5. Reading down: adopting an interpretation of the statute, where more than one is available, that is consistent with the Constitution.[19]

---

[14]Although it should be noted that the Canadian courts had already assumed that role before the enactment of the 1982 Constitution.

[15]If the accompanying litigation is a criminal prosecution, the person charged under the invalid law will be entitled to be acquitted. In the case of civil litigation, the party relying on the invalid law will lose the legal basis for their claim. See Hogg (2004, Chap. 37, Sect. 37.1(c)).

[16]See, for example, *Re Manitoba Language Rights* [1985] 1 SCR 721 where the failure of the Manitoba Legislature to enact laws in French as well as English invalidated the entire Manitoba statute book.

[17]Severance occurs in most Charter cases. See, for example, *Hunter v Southam* [1984] 2 SCR 145, and *R v Valliancourt* [1987] 2 SCR 636.

[18]See, for example, *Schachter v Canada* [1992] 2 SCR 679, where the Supreme Court concerned itself with the federal Unemployment Insurance Act and the child care benefits conferred only on adoptive parents. Finding that the unequal treatment of natural parents was in violation of section 15 of the Charter, the Supreme Court read in the class of natural parents to the statutory provision benefiting adoptive parents.

[19]See Hogg (2004, Chap. 15, Sect. 15.7).

6. The final option indicated by the Supreme Court, by way of obiter, has been the possibility of treating the inconsistency as a constitutional exemption.[20]

11.1.2.3   The Charter and the Common Law

The expression of certain rights and freedoms within the Charter of Rights does not negate the existence or application of other rights and freedoms in Canada, including common law civil liberties. This is reflected within two provisions of the Charter. First, section 1 restricts its guarantee of rights to those "set out in" the Charter, implying that the Charter leaves untouched those rights and freedoms not contained in the document. More expressly on point, section 26 provides that:

> The guarantee in this Charter of certain rights and freedoms shall not be construed as denying the existence of any other rights or freedoms that exist in Canada.

This means that if a right exists in the common law that is not set out in the Charter, those in Canada are still entitled to rely on the common law right. A question considered in *Dolphin Delivery* was that of a potential conflict between a common law right and one within the Charter, and which of those should prevail should the conflict be irreconcilable.[21] In that case, the Retail, Wholesale and Department Store Union was the subject of an injunction preventing it from picketing the premises of Dolphin Delivery because of a common law rule that secondary picketing amounts to a tort of inducing a breach of contract.[22] The Union sought to have the injunction set aside on the basis that the common law rule was inconsistent with the Charter freedom of expression. The Supreme Court unanimously held, however, that the Charter does not apply to the common law and that the injunction therefore remained valid, despite its limitation upon the freedom of expression.

This position should be contrasted with that in which a common law rule is codified, thus creating a conflict between the Charter and legislation. This is the case, for example, in the Canadian province of British Columbia, where the prohibition against secondary picketing has been enacted within its Labour Code. Despite the fact that the prohibition is the same in substance, although not in form, Hogg concludes that the Canadian Charter would act to override British Columbia's Labour Code prohibition against secondary picketing.[23] The rationale behind this difference in approach is to be found in section 32(1) of the Charter of Rights and Freedoms, which states that the Charter applies to the legislative and executive

---

[20]See, for example, *R v Big M Drug Mart* [1985] 1 SCR 295, 315; and *R v Edwards Books and Art* [1986] 2 SCR 713, 783.

[21]*Retail, Wholesale and Department Store Union v Dolphin Delivery* [1986] 2 SCR 537.

[22]Secondary picketing involves the picketing of the premises of a business that is not a party to an employment dispute. Here, the Union was representing the employees of another courier company and, in an effort to have other courier companies put pressure on their own employer, began picketing other courier companies.

[23]Hogg (2004, Chap. 34, Sect. 34.2(g)).

branches of Canada and its provinces, i.e. to public conduct and legislation rather than private conduct. Since the common law is created by judges and is mostly, and especially in the context of common law civil liberties, the result of actions brought by private individuals, the Charter can act to override statutes but not the common law.

11.1.3 Human Rights Protection in New Zealand

New Zealand became part of the British Empire in 1840 through the signing of the Treaty of Waitangi between the British Crown and the Maori indigenous peoples of New Zealand. New Zealand became an independent colony, albeit retaining the Privy Council and Queen of New Zealand, under the New Zealand Constitution Act 1852 (UK). Its constitutional structure is a Westminster one, rather than federal, except that it only has a uni-cameral Parliament, with no upper house, and it recently abolished the Privy Council and established, in its place, a Supreme Court of New Zealand. Although New Zealand did not enact a comprehensive legislative framework for human rights protection until 1990, it had provided for certain levels of protection under the Race Relations Act 1971 and the Human Rights Commission Act 1977.[24]

In 1985, a White Paper on a Bill of Rights for New Zealand was presented to Parliament. The White Paper identified several reasons for adoption by New Zealand of a single Bill of Rights, including the implementation of the country's international human rights obligations. In his introduction to the White Paper, the then Minister of Justice, Sir Geoffrey Palmer, stated:[25]

> A Bill of Rights for New Zealand is based on the idea that New Zealand's system of government is in need of improvement. We have no second House of Parliament. And we have a small Parliament. We are lacking in most of the safeguards which many other countries take for granted. A Bill of Rights will provide greater protection for the fundamental rights and freedoms vital to the survival of New Zealand's democratic and multicultural society.

11.1.3.1 Scope and Status of the Bill of Rights

The White paper for the Bill of Rights intended that the document be entrenched, requiring any amendment to be subject to a 75% majority in Parliament or a simple majority by referendum. The Bill of Rights Act was also to have a higher standing than ordinary legislation, similar in that regard to the Canadian Charter of

---

[24]The two Acts were consolidated in 1993 under the Human Rights Act 1993.

[25]New Zealand Department of Justice, *A Bill of Rights for New Zealand – White Paper* (Wellington: Government Printer, 1985), p. 5. Contrast with Elkind (1990, p. 101).

Rights and Freedoms. It was also to include explicit reference to the Treaty of
Waitangi, and the ability to make reference to New Zealand's Waitangi Tribunal for
reports and opinions on the interpretation and application of rights. Ultimately,
though, the Bill of Rights was enacted without reference to the Treaty and without
any entrenchment provision. As a result of concerns by the House of Representatives
that a supreme Bill of Rights would unduly fetter Parliamentary sovereignty, this
feature was also removed with a provision in section 4 inserted which effectively
makes the NZ Bill of Rights Act subordinate to ordinary legislation (discussed
next).

Despite the idea in the White Paper for a Bill of Rights to establish a single Bill
of Rights for New Zealand, this feature has also failed to come to fruition.
Notwithstanding the fact that the preamble to the New Zealand Bill of Rights Act
1990 asserts itself as being an Act "To affirm New Zealand's commitment to the
International Covenant on Civil and Political Rights", a large part of the rights
under the International Covenant are not contained within the Bill or Rights and
have not, until relatively recently, been reflected in domestic legislation. Privacy,
race relations, and non-discrimination fall under the scope of the Privacy Act 1993
and the Human Rights Act 1993.[26] The New Zealand government has pointed
to further items of legislation through which civil liberties are protected in
New Zealand.[27] In its first set of comments on NZ following the enactment of the
NZBORA, the Human Rights Committee observed as follows:[28]

> The Committee regrets that the provisions of the Covenant have not been fully incorporated
> into domestic law and given an overriding status in the legal system. Article 2, paragraph 2,
> of the Covenant requires States parties to take such legislative or other measures which may
> be necessary to give effect to the rights recognized in the Covenant. In this regard the
> Committee regrets that certain rights guaranteed under the Covenant are not reflected in the
> Bill of Rights, and that it does not repeal earlier inconsistent legislation, and has no higher
> status than ordinary legislation.

11.1.3.2   Application of the Bill of Rights

The Bill of Rights applies only to acts done by the legislative, executive, or judicial
branches of government, or to acts by any person or body in the performance of a
public function, power, or duty (section 3).[29] The express application of the Bill of

---

[26]For further consideration of the Privacy Act 1993 and the Human Rights Act 1993, see Conte
(2007, pp. 186–188).

[27]In its fourth periodic report to the Human Rights Commission in 2001, New Zealand referred to
the Ombudsman Act 1975, the Official Information Act 1982, the Police Complaints Authority Act
1988, the Children, Young Persons and Their Families Act 1989, and the Health and Disability
Commissioner Act 1994.

[28]Concluding Observations of the Human Rights Committee: New Zealand, UN Doc CCPR/CO/
75/NZL (2002), para 11.

[29]See further Rishworth et al. (2003, pp. 70–115).

Rights to the judiciary is to be contrasted with the approach in section 32(1) of the Canadian Charter. Although untested, this is likely to avoid the situation which exists in Canada concerning the ability of common law rights to take precedence over statutory ones (discussed above). The application of the Bill of Rights to the judiciary has also had an impact on the development of remedies in New Zealand (see Sect. 11.2.4 below).

The operative provisions of the Bill of Rights (sections 4, 5 and 6) have been described as an 'unholy trinity' due to doubts early on concerning the interaction of those provisions, largely due to the late introduction during the enactment of the legislation of section 4 as a means of protecting Parliamentary sovereignty, accompanied by making section 5 "subject to" section 4. The operative provisions read as follows:

4. Other enactments not affected
   No court shall, in relation to any enactment (whether passed or made before or after the commencement of this Bill of Rights),–
   (a) Hold any provision of the enactment to be impliedly repealed or revoked, or to be in any way invalid or ineffective; or
   (b) Decline to apply any provision of the enactment –
   by reason only that the provision is inconsistent with any provision of this Bill of Rights.
5. Justified limitations
   Subject to section 4 of this Bill of Rights, the rights and freedoms contained in this Bill of Rights may be subject only to such reasonable limits prescribed by law as can be demonstrably justified in a free and democratic society.
6. Interpretation consistent with Bill of Rights to be preferred
   Wherever an enactment can be given a meaning that is consistent with the rights and freedoms contained in this Bill of Rights, that meaning shall be preferred to any other meaning.

In an early decision of the New Zealand Court of Appeal following the enactment of the Bill of Rights, *Noort v MOT; Curran v Police*, two diverging approaches were taken on the application of the operative provisions.[30] The President of the Court took the view that, due to the protection given to other legislation through section 4, the primary focus should be placed upon that section by determining whether there is an "irreconcilable conflict" between a potentially inconsistent legislative provision and the Bill of Rights. If the conflict is reconcilable, section 6 would demand adoption of an interpretation which is most favourable to the Bill of Rights. If irreconcilable, section 4 would demand that the legislation prevail over the Bill of Rights. The contrasting approach of Justices Richardson and McKay was to place emphasis on section 5, which played little if any role in the President's methodology, by first asking whether or not any limitation under the provision or practice in question could be justified. This is, arguably, a more practical approach since, if the

---

[30]*Noort v MOT; Curran v Police* [1992] 3 NZLR 260.

provision or practice could be found justifiable under section 5, there would be no need to apply sections 4 and 6.

The same court, eight years later in *Moonen v Film and Literature Board of Review*, delivered a unanimous judgment in which it set out a guide to the practical application of sections 4, 5 and 6.[31] Drawing from this, and noting that the final 'step' in *Moonen* simply announces the result of the preceding step, Rishworth has advocated a useful four-step approach to the application of the operative provisions of the Bill of Rights when examining a potentially inconsistent legislative provision (for an example of the application of this approach to special powers of questioning, see Chap. 15, Sect. 15.1.4):[32]

1. Does the enactment establish a limit on a right?

   It is for the party seeking to invoke the Bill of Rights to firstly define the right being invoked and demonstrate that it applies to the circumstances being complained of. If the party is unable to do so, then the Bill of Rights is neither applicable nor relevant.[33]

2. Is the advocated meaning 'inconsistent' with the right?

   An enactment is 'consistent' with the Bill of Rights, explains Rishworth, if it either (a) effects no limitation on a right or freedom at all, or (b) limits a right or freedom to the extent permitted by section 5.[34] This second step therefore calls

---

[31]*Moonen v Film and Literature Board of Review* [2000] 2 NZLR 9, 17. The five-step process outlined by Justice Tipping was described as follows: (1) Identify the different interpretations of the words contained in the enactment being examined: if only one interpretation is open: that meaning should be adopted (section 4); if more than one meaning is open, proceed to the next step. (2) Identify the meaning which constitutes the least possible limitation on the right or freedom in question and adopt that meaning (section 6). (3) Having adopted the appropriate meaning (through either steps one or two), identify the extent – if any – to which that meaning limits the relevant right or freedom. (4) Consider whether that limitation (if found) can be demonstrably justified in a free and democratic society (section 5): if it can, then that is the end of the matter; if it cannot, proceed to the next step. (5) Although a particular meaning to the enactment will have been adopted by this stage (section 4 or 6), if that meaning "fails" the section 5 test, then it is a limitation that is *not* justifiable in a free and democratic society. Step 5 accordingly requires the Court to issue a declaration to that effect (termed a declaration of inconsistency or incompatibility). It is notable that this methodology was later expressed by the Court of Appeal as not intended to be prescriptive and that other approaches were open to application of the operative provisions of the Bill of Rights Act: see *Moonen v Film and Literature Board of Review (No 2)* [2002] 2 NZLR 754, 760 (para 15). See also *Hopkinson v Police* [2004] 3 NZLR 704, 709 (para 28), in which Justice France observed that the five-step process outlined in *Moonen (No 2)* was not a prescriptive one and other approaches were available in Bill of Rights cases.

[32]Rishworth et al. (2003, pp. 135–157). As explained by Rishworth, the second and third steps in *Moonen (No 1)* are reversed in order to make the exercise more efficient by considering consistency before ambiguity.

[33]See, for example, *Palmer v Superintendent Auckland Maximum Security Prison* [1991] 3 NZLR 315 (where it was held that section 4 of the Criminal Justice Act 1985 had no application to the right of a prisoner to be credited with time spent on remand in determining eligibility for parole), and *Hart v Parole Board* [1999] 3 NZLR 97 (where it was held that recall from parole was part of the punishment for the original offending and did not therefore amount to a double punishment).

[34]Rishworth et al. (2003, p. 138).

for careful consideration of whether the enactment *does* limit a right or freedom and, if it does, whether (by application of section 5) such a limit is justified. This is analogous to the methodology adopted under the Canadian Charter. There are three potential outcomes. Firstly, the enactment does not effect a limitation upon the advocated right, in which case the right is fully protected and there is no need for further enquiries to be made. Secondly, if the enactment does effect a limitation, it might be concluded that the limitation is demonstrably justified in a free and democratic society (see Sect. 11.3 below on the application of section 5). In that event, the enactment is not 'inconsistent' with the Bill of Rights and this again brings consideration of the Bill of Rights to a close. It is only in the third potential outcome that the matter must proceed to steps 3 and 4: where the enactment does effect a limitation upon a right or freedom and the limitation cannot be justified under section 5.

3. Is an alternative meaning possible?

   The third step is to establish whether an alternative interpretation of the enactment (one that *is* consistent with the right invoked) is possible. The important feature here is that any alternative meaning must not be as a result of a strained interpretation of the enactment, contrary to its ordinary meaning or to Parliament's intent.[35] Butler adds that, since consideration of section 5 needs to precede the determination of a binding interpretation of an enactment, section 6 can only demand that the courts apply a meaning which least reasonably limits the NZBORA.[36]

4. Adopt the consistent meaning, if properly available

   The previous investigations all lead to the application of the directions under sections 4 and 6 of the Bill of Rights Act. If there is an alternative meaning properly available in the interpretation of the enactment, then section 6 directs that this must be adopted. If there is no alternative meaning, then the enactment is in an irreconcilable conflict with the Bill of Rights and must, by application of section 4, prevail. The resultant vulnerability of human rights in New Zealand is seen in the examination of judicial review proceedings under the Terrorism Suppression Act 2002 (NZ) in the context of the right to a fair hearing and the protection afforded to classified security information (see Chap. 19, Sect. 19.3.2).

---

[35]Rishworth et al. (2003, pp. 143–147). See, in particular, *R v Clarke* [1985] 2 NZLR 212, 214, where the Court of Appeal criticised an earlier obiter approach in *Flickenger v Crown Colony of Hong Kong* [1991] 1 NZLR 439, in which the Court has discounted the statutory context and history of section 66 of the Judicature Act 1908 in favour of a literal meaning of the provision. The meaning adopted must be 'reasonably available': see, for example: *R v Phillips* [1991] 3 NZLR 175, 176–177; *Noort v MOT; Curran v Police* (n 30) 272; and *Simpson v Attorney-General (Baigent's Case)* [1994] 3 NZLR 667, 674.

[36]Butler (2002, p. 577). Compare this to the approach under section 3(1) of the Human Rights Act 1998 (UK), where the UK Parliament rejected the New Zealand model of requiring a reasonable interpretation: see discussion on this point by the House of Lords in *Ghaidan v Mendoza* [2004] 3 All ER 411, 426.

11.1.3.3   The Bill of Rights and the Common Law

One of the stated aims of the Bill of Rights, reflected in the preamble to the Act and within section 2, is to 'affirm' human rights and fundamental freedoms in New Zealand. Commenting on the significance of this, and the nature of the Bill of Rights as a document which codified (rather than created) rights, Justice Thomas of the New Zealand Court of Appeal stated in *Dunlea v AG*:[37]

> In enacting the New Zealand Bill of Rights Act 1990, Parliament deliberately affirmed the fundamental rights and freedoms of New Zealand citizens. Those rights, for the most part, had already existed at common law, but they were now given a constitutional significance.

The NZ Bill of Rights also makes it clear that the act of codifying rights within it did not limit other rights and freedoms. Section 28 provides that "An existing right or freedom shall not be held to be abrogated or restricted by reason only that the right or freedom is not included in this Bill of Rights or is included only in part".

11.1.4   Human Rights Protection in the United Kingdom

The territory of the United Kingdom (UK) encompasses Great Britain (England, Wales and Scotland) and Northern Ireland. Strictly speaking, three legal systems operate within the United Kingdom, although laws enacted by the UK Parliament normally apply to all territories within the UK.[38] The UK Human Rights Act 1998, which was enacted as an Act incorporating the (European) Convention for the Protection of Human Rights and Fundamental Freedoms (ECHR) and its Protocols, applies to Great Britain and Northern Ireland.

Fenwick identifies four means by which civil liberties were protected in the United Kingdom prior to the enactment of the Human Rights Act:[39]

- She first points to the Union's long democratic history, through which civil liberties have been protected by virtue of the fact that Parliament is made up elected representatives, thereby reflecting the will of the population to retain their individual liberties. While a desire for governments to be re-elected and therefore guard against interference with voters' rights and freedoms is relevant, coupled with the role of the judiciary in the review of executive action and statutory powers, the 'majority-rules' nature of democracy does not by itself guarantee the rights of minorities.

---

[37]*Dunlea v AG* [2000] 3 NZLR 136.

[38]Laws passed by Parliament can, if specified, apply to different areas of uniformity: see Shabas and Olivier (2003, p. 211).

[39]Fenwick (2002, pp. 94–117).

- Fenwick next notes that, in addition to administrative law, the judiciary plays an important role in human rights protection through its interpretation of legislation and the development of the common law in a manner that protects fundamental freedoms. One of the more famous judicial decisions to that effect can be found in the judgment of Chief Justice Lord Camden in *Entick v Carrington*, where the Court held that the issuing and execution of a search warrant was, in the circumstances, illegal and void.[40] The common law, however, is subject to ebbs and flows depending upon the active or passive roles that judicial bodies may take from time to time, and is capable of being overridden by statute (see, however, the discussion below at Sect. 11.2.1).
- The influence of the European Convention on Human Rights, even prior to the enactment of incorporating legislation, is also noted. Parties to the Convention are obliged, under article 1, to secure the rights and freedoms contained within the Convention (see Chap. 9, Sect. 9.2.1). Parties are, however free to decide how this will be done, a position confirmed by the Supreme Court of Ireland in *Lawless v O'Sullivan and the Minister for Justice*.[41] Although the British government has argued, since its ratification of the Convention in 1951, that it was not necessary to incorporate the Convention into domestic law because the UK's unwritten constitution was in conformity with it, a person in Britain was not able to rely upon Convention rights in judicial proceedings. Despite this fact, the content of the Convention and decisions of the European Court of Human Rights did have an impact on civil liberties protection in the United Kingdom. It was a principle of statutory construction even before 2000 that, where possible, statutes should be interpreted in a manner consistent with the European Convention (see Sect. 11.2.1 below). Of less impact, but still worth mention, was the political desire of the British government not to be seen acting inconsistently with decisions of the European Court of Human Rights, nor with the substance of the rights contained within the ECHR.
- The influence of European Union law is a matter also worth noting. Although EU law is concerned more with social and economic matters, rather than civil rights, the influence of the European Convention on Human Rights upon EU law has become increasingly important. The European Court of Justice has established that respect for fundamental rights should be ensured within the context of the European Union.[42] This principle is now set out within the Treaty on European Union, article F(2)(6)(2).

Despite this analysis, the absence of a constitutional bill of rights in the United Kingdom was subject to much criticism, including by the Human Rights Committee in its concluding observations on the UK's fourth periodic report under the ICCPR

---

[40]*Entick v Carrington* [1765] All ER 41.

[41]*Lawless v O'Sullivan and the Minister for Justice* (1958–1959) Yearbook of the Convention on Human Rights 608.

[42]See *Nold v Commission* [1974] ECR 481, and *Amministrazione delle Finanze dello Stato v Simmenthal* [1978] ECR 629.

in 1995.[43] The United Kingdom enacted the Human Rights Act 1998, which came into force on 2 October 2000 (almost 50 years after the UK's ratification of the ECHR), and thereby expressly incorporated into domestic law the substantive rights guaranteed under the European Convention. While this is a positive step, the UN Committee has noted that this step does not equate to full incorporation of the ICCPR, since several Covenant rights are not included among the provisions of the European Convention.[44]

11.1.4.1 Convention Rights

Unlike the Canadian Charter or the New Zealand Bill of Rights, which codify and spell-out the rights and freedoms guaranteed by them, the UK Human Rights Act refers back to the European Convention on Human Rights. Its provisions centred around "Convention rights", defined by section 1(1) of the Human Rights Act as the rights and fundamental freedoms set out in articles 2-12 and 14 of the ECHR, articles 1-3 of the First Protocol to the ECHR, and articles 1 and 2 of the ECHR's Sixth Protocol.

An important qualification to the definition of Convention rights is to be found within section 1(2), which provides that those rights "are to have effect for the purposes of this Act subject to any designated derogation or reservation". Section 14 of the Human Rights Act allows the UK Secretary of State to make an order by which the United Kingdom derogates from one of the Convention rights (as permitted by article 15 of the Convention, considered further in Chap. 17). A derogation order can be made in anticipation of the lodging of a notice of derogation from the European Convention. Designated derogations only last for five years and, if they are to continue, they must be renewed by the government (section 16). Since the repeal of the Anti-terrorism, Crime and Security Act 2001 in April 2005, the United Kingdom has no current derogations to the ECHR.

The United Kingdom maintains a reservation to article 2 of the First Protocol to the European Convention on Human Rights, stating that it guarantees the right to education "only so far as it is compatible with the provision of efficient instruction and training, and the avoidance of unreasonable expenditure".

---

[43]Concluding Observations of the Human Rights Committee: United Kingdom of Great Britain and Northern Ireland, UN Doc CCPR/C/79/Add.55 (1995), para 9.

[44]Concluding Observations of the Human Rights Committee: United Kingdom of Great Britain and Northern Ireland, UN Doc CCPR/C/GBR/CO6 (2008), para 6.

11.1.4.2 Application of the Human Rights Act

The Human Rights Act is applicable to private as well as public action.[45] Although it does not apply to events that existed prior to the entry into force of the Act, the House of Lords has indicated that it might in some instances apply to pre-Act events such as the conduct of post-Act criminal trials in respect of pre-Act happenings.[46]

Section 6 of the Human Rights Act 1998 makes it unlawful for any public authority in the United Kingdom to act in a manner which is incompatible with a Convention right. A public authority includes the executive, any person whose functions include functions of a public nature, and courts and tribunals (including the House of Lords in its judicial capacity). It does not include an act of either of the houses of parliament (section 6(3)), thus allowing parliament to enact legislation that is inconsistent with the Convention. Nor does it include a failure by a Minister of the Crown to introduce any legislation or make any order (section 6(6)).

Although section 6 requires that judicial conduct must not be inconsistent with the Convention rights (section 6(3)(a)), the ability to bring proceedings against a judicial officer is restricted by section 9. Proceedings can only be brought in the form of an appeal against, or review of, a decision of a court or tribunal. This does not, however, give rise to a right of review where such review is expressly excluded in any particular case. Section 6 further provides that, so long as the judicial officer has acted in good faith, damages cannot be awarded except to the extent required by article 5(5) of the European Convention, i.e. a situation where a person has been arrested or detained contrary to the provisions of article 5. Where such damages are awarded, the order for damages will lie against the Crown, not against the individual judicial officer.

11.2 Human Rights and Statutory Interpretation

The role of human rights in the interpretation of primary and secondary legislation is significant. The following considers the use of international human rights treaties in the interpretation of domestic law, and the role of domestically recognised rights in the interpretation of legislation. The ability of British courts to make declarations of incompatibility under the Human Rights Act is outlined, together with the same feature developed by the judiciary in New Zealand. The position of subordinate legislation is also considered.

---

[45]See, for example, *Wilson v First County Trust Ltd (No 2)* [2001] EWCA Civ 633.
[46]*Wilson & Ors v Secretary of State for Trade and Industry* [2003] UKHL 40.

11.2.1   The Use of International Law in the Application and Interpretation of Civil Liberties

The four case study countries adopt a dualist approach to the reception of international treaties (see Chap. 4, Sect. 4.2.2). This means that, to become part of domestic law and capable of being relied upon in judicial proceedings, the substance of those treaties must be incorporated, normally achieved through an implementing Act of Parliament. The same is true of international and regional human rights treaties. In the New Zealand case of *Ashby v Minister of Immigration*, for example, Justice Cooke said, in referring to the Convention on the Elimination of All Forms of Racial Discrimination, that: "The Convention has not been incorporated into New Zealand law by any Act of Parliament. It is elementary that international treaty obligations are not binding in domestic law until they have become incorporated in that way".[47] In the same case, Justice Richardson was even more firm:[48]

> ... if the terms of the domestic legislation are clear and unambiguous they must be given effect in our courts whether or not they carry out New Zealand's international obligations.

The courts do, however, tend to take an approach which is less legalistic when it comes to using human rights treaties to apply or interpret the content and scope of human rights on a domestic level, attempting to reconcile the meaning of a statute so as to give effect to the State's treaty obligations. This is consistent with the interpretative presumption that legislation is intended to conform with international law (see Chap. 4, Sect. 4.2.2.3), generally applied in a pro-civil liberties way when considering human rights treaties. In interpreting human rights provisions of the Bermudan Constitution in *Minister of Home Affairs v Fisher*, Lord Wilberforce said that the court was entitled to apply ". . . a generous interpretation avoiding what has been called 'the austerity of tabulated legalism', suitable to give individuals the full measure of the fundamental rights and freedoms referred to".[49] Describing Lord Wilberforce's statement as "destined for judicial immortality", President Cooke of the New Zealand Court of Appeal observed as follows about the relationship between the NZ Bill of Rights and the ICCPR, Cooke observed that:[50]

---

[47]*Ashby v Minister of Immigration* [1981] 1 NZLR 222, 224.

[48]Ibid.

[49]*Minister of Home Affairs v Fisher* [1980] AC 319.

[50]*Ministry of Transport v Noort; Police v Curran* (n 30) 268 and 270. A generous approach to the interpretation of legislation incorporating international human rights instruments is also seen in the case of other international human rights instruments. See, for example, *H v Y* [2005] NZFLR 152, 169–173, where the New Zealand Court of Appeal made generous reference to the UN Convention on Rights of the Child in determining the construction of New Zealand legislation. See also *Zaoui v Attorney-General* [2004] 2 NZLR 339, 376–381, and *Zaoui v Attorney-General (No 2)* [2005] 1 NZLR 690, 720–726, where the High Court and Court of Appeal made reference to numerous international instruments in the interpretation of the Immigration Act 1987. Compare this approach, however, with *Wellington District Legal Services Committee v Tangiora* [1998] 1 NZLR 129, 137–139, where the Court of Appeal held that the Legal Services Act 1991 should

The long title shows that, in affirming the rights and freedoms contained in the Bill of Rights, the Act requires development of the law where necessary. Such a measure is not to be approached as if it did no more than preserve the status quo. That it envisaged change is implicit in the allowance of a 28-day interval before it came into force. In approaching the Bill of Rights Act it must be of cardinal importance to bear in mind the antecedents. The International Covenant on Civil and Political Rights speaks of inalienable rights derived from the inherent dignity of the human person. Internationally there is now general recognition that some human rights are fundamental and anterior to any municipal law, although municipal law may fall short of giving effect to them.

The same approach is taken in Canada, despite the fact that the Charter of Rights and Freedoms is not, in a formal sense, an instrument through which the ICCPR was incorporated into Canada's domestic law. The Charter nevertheless covers much of the same ground as the International Covenant, and where the Covenant is more detailed in its expression of the content of particular rights than the Charter is, the terms of the ICCPR may be used to interpret the Charter.[51] Although Australian courts have tended to take a more legalistic approach to the use of international treaties in the interpretation of domestic law, there have been some instances where reference to international human rights law has been used to justify a rights-based approach to interpretation.[52]

In the context of the European Convention on Human Rights, it became a general principle of construction in the United Kingdom, even before the enactment of the Human Rights Act 1998, that statutes would be interpreted in a manner consistent with the ECHR wherever possible.[53] Section 2(1) of the Act now requires British courts and tribunals to take into account the following when determining the scope of 'Convention rights' or otherwise applying the Human Rights Act: any decision, declaration, or advisory opinion of the European Court of Human Rights; any opinion of the European Commission of Human Rights adopted in a report of the European Court under article 31 of the Convention; any decision of the Commission concerning procedural matters dealt with by articles 26 and 27 of the Convention; and any decision of the Committee of Ministers made under article 46 concerning the execution of a judgment of the European Court of Human Rights.

---

not be interpreted expansively beyond ensuring that it was interpreted in so far as was possible consistently with international obligations.

[51]Hogg (2004, Chap. 33, Sect. 33.8(c)).

[52]See, for example: *Mabo v Queensland (No 2)* (1992) 175 CLR 1, concerning native title rights; *Dietrich v R* (1992) 177 CLR 292, concerning the right to a fair trial; and *Minister of State for Immigration and Ethnic Affairs v Ah Hin Teoh* (1995) 183 CLR 273 concerning the implications of Australia's ratification of the UN Convention on Rights of the Child upon the exercise of Ministerial discretions.

[53]See, for example, *Re M and H (Minors)* [1988] 3 WLR 485, 498.

11.2.2   The Use of Human Rights in the Interpretation
of Legislation

The tension between human rights and the ability of a sovereign Parliament to
legislate as it wishes is a matter directly affected by the status of the statutory
framework for human rights protection. The contrast between Canada's 'supreme'
Charter of Rights and New Zealand's 'subordinate' Bill of Rights serves as an ideal
illustration of this point. While Canada's Supreme Court is able to nullify inconsistent legislation, New Zealand courts must apply legislation in preference to the
Bill of Rights where there is an irreconcilable conflict between the two (see
Sect. 11.1.1 above). The consequence for New Zealand was aptly described by
Justice McGechan of the New Zealand Court of Appeal:[54]

> ... provided Parliament proceeds according to mandatory law governing the procedure for
> enacting legislation... Parliament is sovereign and can pass any legislation it sees fit... It is
> not for the unelected Courts to frustrate that legislative ability. If content of legislation
> offends, the remedies are political and ultimately electoral. The fact those alternatives seem
> monumentally difficult, indeed unreal, to particular persons, or to those espousing unpopu-
> lar causes, is no more than a dark side of democracy.

As pointed out by Canadian constitutional lawyer Peter Hogg, however, only a bill
of rights that is immune from ordinary legislative change is able to guarantee civil
liberties from legislative encroachment.[55] The position of civil liberties under the
common law is even more precarious, since common law rules are normally
capable of modification or annulment by the superior status of Acts of Parliament.[56]
As discussed by Joseph, however, the courts take a guarded approach when a
legislature has attempted to restrict the role of the judiciary or take away the rights
of citizens.[57] In the New Zealand Court of Appeal, Cooke posited that "some
common law rights may go so deep that even Parliament cannot be accepted by
the Courts to have destroyed them".[58] The vulnerable position of common law
rights is improved by various factors, including the principle of legality, the
presumption that legislation is intended to conform with international law, including international human rights (see Chap. 4, Sect. 4.2.2.3), and any applicable
provision concerning the interpretation of enactments in a manner consistent with
human rights. The following features applicable to each case study country should
be noted:

---

[54]*Westco Lagan Ltd v Attorney-General* [2001] 1 NZLR 40, 63.

[55]Hogg (2004, Chap. 33).

[56]As recognised in the statement of Lord Goff in *Attorney-General v Guardian Newspapers Ltd*
(n 1), discussed in Sect. 11.1.1 above.

[57]Joseph (2001, pp. 485–495).

[58]*Fraser v State Services Commission* [1984] 1 NZLR 116 (CA), 121. See also *Taylor v New
Zealand Poultry Board* [1984] 1 NZLR 394, 398.

11.2.2.1 Australia

Civil liberties protection in Australia relies heavily upon rights developed under the common law, or upon common law principles on statutory construction. Criticising the adequacy of reliance in Australia upon common law presumptions concerning statutory interpretation, Gaze and Jones identify three problems with this:[59]

> ... first, their content is not adequate to meet demands for protection of individual rights in the modern world; secondly, judges have often been unwilling to apply them, or too ready to interpret legislation to override them, so that even within the areas they cover, their full potential has not been realised; and thirdly, they cannot prevail where the clear words of a statute override them.

11.2.2.2 Canada

Section 52(1) of the Canadian Constitution has been utilised not just to invalidate legislation which is inconsistent with the Charter of Rights and Freedoms, but also to adopt an interpretation of legislation which is consistent with the Charter by either 'reading down' the statute in a consistent manner, or 'reading in' words which will render it compatible with the Charter (see Sect. 11.1.2.2 above).

11.2.2.3 New Zealand

New Zealand's Bill of Rights Act contains a provision dealing specifically with the interpretation of enactments. Section 6 of the Act demands that, where an enactment can be given a meaning that is consistent with the rights and freedoms in the Bill of Rights, that meaning must be preferred to any other meaning. The interaction of section 6 with the remaining operation provisions in sections 4 and 5 is considered in Sect. 11.1.3.2 above.

The influence of human rights upon presumptions on statutory interpretation can be illustrated through the way in which the Bill of Rights has strengthened two such principles:

- The first is the presumption regarding ouster, or 'privative', clauses (provisions within an enactment that purport to exclude a person's right to seek judicial review of a decision by an executive decision-maker). The presumption is that such clauses should be read in as narrow a context as possible, thereby protecting the right of those affected by such decisions to retain access to the courts. The Courts have been particularly unwilling to hold that a statute which establishes a tribunal, or creates an executive discretion, takes away the right to have any

---

[59]Gaze and Jones (1990, p. 32).

consequent decision reviewed by the judiciary.[60] This presumption is strengthened by the section 27(2) of the Bill of Rights, which guarantees one's right to
justice and, with section 6, requires enactments (ouster clauses included) to be
read in a manner that least impinges upon the Bill of Rights.

- Concerning the presumption against retrospectivity, it is notable that, until
  relatively recently, New Zealand and English common law did not find fault
  with a statute that increased the penalty for an existing offence applying to the
  commission of offences prior to the coming into force of that statutory provision.[61] Section 4(1) of the Criminal Justice Act 1985 now expressly prohibits the
  retrospective application of penalties, albeit in very cumbersome language. The
  presumption is reflected within sections 25(g) and 26(1) of the Bill of Rights.[62]
  This has now come to be further reflected in section 7 of the Interpretation
  Act 1999.

11.2.2.4   United Kingdom

In *R v Secretary of State for the Home Department, ex parte Simms*, the House of
Lords was faced with a conflict between the freedom of expression and provisions
of the UK's Prison Standing Orders.[63] Simms and another were serving life
sentences on convictions for murder and claimed that they had been the victims
of a miscarriage of justice. To try to have their cases re-opened, they wanted to
participate in oral interviews with journalists that had taken an interest in the case.
The prison authorities would only allow this if the journalists signed an undertaking
not to publish any part of the interview, relying on Prison Standing Order 5A, paras
37 and 37A. Relying on the freedom of the press, the journalists refused to sign such
an undertaking. They were consequently refused access to the prisoners. The
question before the House of Lords was whether the ban was lawful. The Lords
decided it was not. Applying the principle of legality, they came to the conclusion
that the Standing Order was not specific enough to override the freedom of speech,
Lord Steyn stating that: "Applying this principle I would hold that paras 37 and 37A
leave untouched the fundamental and basic rights asserted by the prisoners in the
present case."

With the advent of the Human Rights Act 1998, this principle is now codified
in section 3(1). Section 3 applies to legislation enacted prior to and since the entry
into force of the Human Rights Act. Subsection (2), however, protects Parliamentary sovereignty and is similar in its effect to section 4 of the NZ Bill of Rights,

---

[60]Burrows (1999, p. 206). See, for example: *New Zealand Waterside Workers Federation Industrial Association of Workers v Frazer* [1924] NZLR 689; and *Bulk Gas Users Group v Attorney-
General* [1983] NZLR 129.

[61]See *Director of Public Prosecutions v Lamb* [1941] 2 KB 89; and *Campbell v Robins* [1959]
NZLR 474.

[62]See *R v Pora* [2001] 2 NZLR 37.

[63]*R v Secretary of State for the Home Department, ex p Simms* [2000] 2 AC 115.

providing that section 3 does not affect the validity, continuing operation or enforcement of any incompatible primary legislation (see section 3(2)(b)); and that it does not affect the validity, continuing operation or enforcement of any incompatible subordinate legislation if the primary legislation under which it is made prevents removal of the incompatibility (section 3(2)(c)). The latter provision is considered further below (see Sect. 11.2.4). The difference between the UK Human Rights Act and the NZ Bill of Rights Act is that British courts have an express authority to make a declaration of incompatibility, a subject considered next.

11.2.3   Declarations of Incompatibility

Where an irreconcilable conflict is identified between an enactment and the rights and freedoms guaranteed under a bill of rights instrument, the result varies markedly between Canada's Charter, New Zealand's Bill of Rights, and the UK's Human Rights Act. Subject to the ability to achieve a consistent interpretation (as developed under section 52(1) of the Charter, and as provided for in section 6 of the NZ Bill of Rights and section 3(1) of the UK Human Rights Act), Canada's courts are able to nullify or sever the offending provision, while the courts those in NZ and Britain are unable to invalidate the provision. In New Zealand and the United Kingdom, the principle of Parliamentary sovereignty thus prevails. As a compromise, however, the NZ courts have developed the judicial 'remedy' of declarations of incompatibility, while the British Parliament chose to expressly provide for such declarations within the Human Rights Act. Following the lead of the United Kingdom, Australia's Human Rights Act 2004 (of the Australian Capital Territory) and Charter of Human Rights and Responsibilities Act 2006 (of the State of Victoria) also provide express mechanisms for such recourse.[64]

11.2.3.1   Declarations of Incompatibility Under the UK Human Rights Act

Although section 3(2) of the Human Rights Act 1998 means that the judiciary in the United Kingdom is unable to invalidate any legislation which is inconsistent with Convention rights, section 4 of the Act provides authority to issue a declaration of incompatibility. This occurred in the context of control orders under the Prevention of Terrorism Act 2006 (see Chap. 18, Sect. 18.1), for example, which were held to be incompatible with liberty rights and the right to fair trial.[65] Declarations of

---

[64]See: Human Rights Act 2004 (ACT), section 32; and Charter of Human Rights and Responsibilities Act 2006 (Victoria), section 36.

[65]See *Re MB* [2006] EWHC 1000, and *Secretary of State for the Home Department v JJ and Ors* [2006] EWCA Civ 1141.

incompatibility can also be made in respect of subordinate legislation, the effect of which will depend upon the empowering provision under which the regulations were made (see Sect. 11.2.4 below). The making of a declaration of incompatibility under the Human Rights Act is meant to stand as an exceptional measure, to be avoided unless a conflict between the Act and another enactment is irreconcilable, and thus strengthening the interpretative presumption in section 3 of the Act.[66]

Where a declaration of incompatibility is issued, Parliament has the option of modifying the offending provision under section 10 of the Human Rights Act. Where there are "compelling reasons", a Minister of the Crown can make a remedial order amending the legislation to the extent necessary to remove the incompatibility (section 10(2)). The remedial order must be tabled before both Houses in draft form and approved by a resolution of each House within 60 days (see Schedule 2 of the Act). Remedial orders can also be made by a Minister of the Crown where, after the entry into force of the Human Rights Act, the European Court of Human Rights has determined that a provision of UK legislation is incompatible with an obligation of the United Kingdom under the European Convention (section 10(1)(b)). Remedial orders have been made on a number of occasions since the entry into force of the Human Rights Act.[67]

Where a court is considering whether or not to issue a declaration of incompatibility, the Crown must be notified of this and has the right to be joined to the proceedings (section 5). In practical terms, this means that the Crown will be able to make submissions to the court on the question of whether or not the legislation being examined is compatible with Convention rights.

11.2.3.2 The Development of Declarations of Incompatibility in New Zealand

Unlike the UK Human Rights Act, New Zealand's Bill of Rights is silent on the question of declarations of incompatibility. Nonetheless, the potential for the judiciary to issue a declaration upon finding an inconsistency between the Bill of Rights and another piece of legislation was indicated as being available as early

---

[66] See *R v A (No 2)* [2001] UKHL 25, judgment of Lord Steyn at para 44. See further Stone (2008, pp. 59–63).

[67] See, for example, *R (on the application of H) v Mental Health Review Tribunal and the Secretary of State for Health* [2001] EWCA Civ 415, concerning the admission to hospital of H pursuant to section 3 of the Mental Health Act 1983. H sought to be discharged from hospital on the basis that it could not be shown that he was suffering from a mental disorder that warranted detention. He was refused a discharge order by the Mental Health Review Tribunal, relying on sections 72 and 73 of the Mental Health Act which did not require the Tribunal to discharge a patient even if it could not be shown that he was suffering from a mental disorder that warranted detention. The Court of Appeal declared that sections 72 and 73 were incompatible with the right to liberty under article 5 (1) of the European Convention and the right under article 5(4) to take proceedings to determine the lawfulness of one's detention. As a result of that declaration (issued in March 2001), the Mental Health Act 1983 was amended by the Mental Health Act 1983 (Remedial) Order 2001.

as 1992.[68] It was not until the 2000 decision in *Moonen v Film and Literature Review Board*, however, that the judiciary in New Zealand took up this approach. In summary, the Court of Appeal set out the circumstances in which a declaration might be made, namely where there is a provision in an enactment which; conflicts with the Bill of Rights; cannot be interpreted consistently with it; and cannot be justified as a reasonable limit in a free and democratic society; thus requiring it to take precedence over the Bill of Rights (see Sect. 11.1.3.2 above). In such a situation, the Court suggested that it was open to the judiciary to issue a declaration advising that, although the enactment must be given effect, it is inconsistent with the rights and freedoms contained in the Bill of Rights.[69] While the implications of this approach are weighty, the courts in New Zealand have not issued a declaration of incompatibility to date, despite cases in which such action could have been taken.[70]

11.2.4   Subordinate Legislation

The treatment of subordinate legislation merits consideration in two contexts: the making of declarations of incompatibility under the UK Human Rights Act; and the meaning of the term "enactments" under section 4 of the NZ Bill of Rights.

11.2.4.1   UK Human Rights Act

The consequences of a declaration of incompatibility under the Human Rights Act made in respect of subordinate legislation depend upon the empowering provision under which the regulations were made. The first is where the enabling provision of the primary legislation is such that it prevents removal of the incompatibility (i.e. the enabling provision in fact *requires* the subordinate legislation to be made in a manner which is inconsistent with Convention rights). In such cases, the subordinate legislation cannot be invalidated (section 3(2)(c)), although the courts can issue a declaration of incompatibility concerning both the regulations (section 4(3) and (4)) and the enabling Act (section 4(1) and (2)). Again, remedial action under section 10 of the Human Rights Act is available (section 10(3)).

In the case of subordinate legislation where the enabling provision of the primary legislation does not require the subordinate legislation to be incompatible with Convention rights, the courts are this time able to declare the subordinate legislation invalid. This is a direct consequence of section 3(1) of the Human Rights

---

[68]Brookfield (1992, p. 239).

[69]*Moonen v Film and Literature Board of Review* (n 31), 17.

[70]See *R v Poumako* [2000] 2 NZLR 695, and *R v Pora* (n 62). For further discussion on declarations of incompatibility in New Zealand, see: Butler (2000), Joseph (2000) and Conte and Wynn-Williams (2003).

Act which, in the circumstances, requires the enabling provision to be interpreted in a manner consistent with Convention rights (i.e. the enabling provision cannot be interpreted as allowing the making of regulations that are incompatible with Convention rights). The regulations thereby become ultra vires the enabling provision, through an interpretation of the enabling provision under section 3(1). The invalidation of the subordinate legislation will mean that the relevant law no longer applies, which may result in a situation of urgency. To cater for such urgent situations, the Human Rights Act allows a Minister of the Crown to make a remedial order without first tabling this before parliament (section 10(4) and Schedule 2, para 2(b)). Where this is done, the Minister must subsequently table the order and then substitute the urgent remedial order with an amended remedial order if required to do so by parliament (Schedule 2, para 4).

11.2.4.2   NZ Bill of Rights Act

Section 4 of the New Zealand Bill of Rights Act protects any "enactment" from invalidity in the case of any irreconcilable conflict with the Act (see Sect. 11.1.3.2 above). An issue of importance is how far this protection extends, i.e. whether the protection afforded to "enactments" is limited to Acts of Parliament or includes subordinate legislation. The Interpretation Act 1999 defines the term as including both primary and subordinate legislation. Burrows also points to the language of section 4, which refers to enactments "passed" or "made". Since Acts of Parliament are passed by Parliament, and subordinate legislation made by delegates, the logical conclusion to be drawn is that Parliament must have intended enactments to include both primary and subordinate legislation. Section 4(a) similarly speaks of provisions impliedly "repealed" or "revoked" (terms associated with primary and subordinate legislation respectively).[71] In the absence of good reasons to the contrary, the Court of Appeal has also referred to the term as a convenient and succinct one embracing any Act or rules or regulations made thereunder and any provision thereof.[72]

The latter analysis might suggest that section 4 is thus capable of protecting subordinate legislation which is incompatible with the Bill of Rights. Instead, however, the approach in New Zealand is similar to that under the UK Human Rights Act. Dealing with the ability of authorities to refuse permission for an inmate to be represented by a lawyer in prison disciplinary hearings (under regulation 144 of the Penal Institutions Regulations 1999), the Court of Appeal in *Drew* concluded that the regulation was an "enactment" but that it was not protected by section 4 of the Bill of Rights. The Court instead focussed on whether the empowering provision in section 45(1) of the Penal Institutions Act 1954 had been applied in a manner consist with the Bill of Rights, and concluded that it should be

---

[71]Burrows (1999, p. 337).
[72]*Black v Fulcher* [1988] 1 NZLR 417.

interpreted so to exclude the possibility of making regulations in conflict with the Bill of Rights.[73]

11.3 Law-Making, and Remedies

Before proceeding to a discussion of the means by which rights and freedoms may be limited, two further matters warrant brief consideration: the role of human rights in the enactment of primary legislation or the making of regulations; and the means by which the violation of civil liberties may be remedies at the domestic level.

11.3.1 The Role of Human Rights in Law-Making

Reflecting the important role of human rights in democratic societies, all of the legislative mechanisms described earlier provide a role for human rights in the preparation and enactment of legislation. The idea is to ensure a continued level of compliance with human rights and, where rights are to be limited, the adoption of such limitations in a transparent and deliberate way.

11.3.1.1 Australia

Commenting on the 1985 proposal for an Australian Bill of Rights, the Senate Standing Committee on Constitutional and Legal Affairs stated:[74]

> The Committee considers that Parliaments in Australia have performed unevenly and their traditions of debate ad examination of government action and proposed legislation could well be more vigorously undertaken. Human rights seldom enjoy a high priority in legislative programs.

Despite this observation made more than 20 years ago, there remains no formal mechanism through which proposed legislation at the federal level is scrutinised for consistency with human rights. In the Australian Capital Territory (ACT), however, the Attorney General is obliged to prepare a written 'compatibility statement' on whether or not any bill before the Legislative Assembly is compatible with the rights set out in the ACT Human Rights Act 2004. The relevant legislative standing committee must also report to the Assembly on any human rights issues raised by a bill, although a failure to comply with this duty, or that of the Attorney General, will

---

[73]*Drew v Attorney-General* [2002] 1 NZLR 58, 73.

[74]Senate Standing Committee on Constitutional and Legal Affairs, *A Bill of Rights for Australia? An Exposure Report for the Consideration of Senators* (Canberra, 1985), para 2.84.

not invalidate any enacted legislation.[75] Similar mechanisms exist under the State of Victoria's Charter of Human Rights and Responsibilities Act 2006.[76]

11.3.1.2 Canada

The scrutiny of legislation for consistency with the Canadian Charter is not a matter provided for within the Charter itself. Instead, the federal Minister of Justice has a statutory obligation under section 4.1 of the Department of Justice Act 1985 to review all proposed statutes and regulations for compliance with the Charter, and to report instances of non-compliance to the House of Commons. Similar duties exist for the Ministers of Justice or Attorneys-General in the provinces, although there is not always a positive duty to report.

This does not mean, however, that the Charter does away with Parliamentary sovereignty, including the notion that Parliament cannot bind its successors. Special provision is made under section 33(1) of the Charter to allow the federal Parliament, or a provincial Legislature, to enact law in a manner inconsistent with the Charter, albeit only temporarily, if this is the express intention of Parliament:

> Parliament or the legislature of a province may expressly declare in an Act of Parliament or of the legislature, as the case may be, that the Act or a provision thereof shall operate notwithstanding a provision included in section 2 or sections 7 to 15 of this Charter.

Known as the 'notwithstanding clause', section 33(1) retains the ability of elected representatives to make law that is inconsistent with the Charter, so long as they make a specific decision to that effect and indicate this by use of the notwithstanding clause. This means that the process is both intentional and transparent and leaves no room for the implied repeal of rights and freedoms in the Charter. There is, however, a time limitation on such clauses, since they cease to have effect five years after they come into force (section 33(3)–(4)), thus forcing the legislature to consider the matter again if it wants an inconsistent provision to continue by re-enacting it. It should be noted that the notwithstanding clause is that section 33 does not apply to all rights and freedoms. Some rights under the Charter cannot be overridden, even by invocation of the clause, since the provision only applies to the rights contained in section 2 or sections 7 to15 of the Charter. The result is that there is a hierarchy of sorts in the list of rights contained within the Charter. All democratic rights (sections 3 to 6 inclusive) and all official language, minority language, enforcement, gender, and aboriginal rights (sections 16 to 31 inclusive) may not be subject to the mechanism under section 33. The final point to make is that, although section 33 contains safety mechanisms in its compromise between parliamentary sovereignty and rights protection, it might still be criticised it as insufficient. Section 33 can be used to comfort opposing parliamentarians at the

---

[75]Human Rights Act 2004 (ACT), sections 37–39.

[76]Charter of Human Rights and Responsibilities Act 2006 (Victoria), sections 28–30.

time of enacting inconsistent legislation. Although the notwithstanding clause requires renewal after five years, it is arguable that parliament will be more inclined to keep the status quo than to do away with the law in question.

11.3.1.3 New Zealand

In response to the criticism of the Human Rights Committee that the NZ Bill of Rights does not repeal earlier inconsistent legislation and has no higher status than ordinary legislation (see Sect. 11.1.3.1 above), New Zealand's fourth periodic report to the Committee stated:[77]

> Section 7 constitutes a safeguard designed to alert Members of Parliament to legislation which may give rise to an inconsistency with the Bill of Rights Act and, accordingly, to enable them to debate the proposals on that basis (see *Mangawaro Enterprises Ltd. v. Attorney-General* [1994] 2 NZLR 451, 457). The role of scrutinizing bills for consistency with the Bill of Rights Act and providing advice to the Attorney-General on the exercise of his or her duties under Section 7 is performed by the Ministry of Justice (in the case of legislation being promoted by a Minister other than the Minister of Justice), and by the Crown Law Office (in the case of legislation being promoted by the Minister of Justice).

The role of Attorney General under section 7 was not something that had been provided for under the White Paper version of the Bill of Rights, but was introduced as a compromise to the removal of the entrenched status of the Act and the introduction of the section 4 'sovereignty' clause.[78] Analogous to section 4.1 of Canada's Department of Justice Act 1985, the purpose of the provision is to promote compliance with the Bill of Rights' substantive rights and freedoms, prompting Parliament to turn its mind to the passing of any legislation that would abrogate one of those substantive rights.[79] Given the subordinate status of the Bill of Rights under section 4, however, the following comparisons should be made between the position in Canada (including the notwithstanding clause under section 33 of the Charter) and the operation of the Bill of Rights:

- Section 33 of the Charter will only enable a legislative interference with Charter rights to co-exist with the Charter if Parliament expresses its intent to do so, thus forcing it to make a conscious decision to that effect. This is also the rationale behind section 7 of the Bill of Rights.[80] The obligation to report to the House

---

[77]New Zealand's Fourth Periodic Report to the Human Rights Committee, UN Doc CCPR/C/NZL/2001/4 (2001), para 27.

[78]*White Paper* (n 25).

[79]Rishworth et al. (2003, pp. 195–196).

[80]For an example of the operation of section 7 to this effect, see *Living Word Distributors Ltd v Human Rights Action Group Inc* [2000] 3 NZLR 570. Prior to the enactment of section 131(3) of New Zealand's Films, Videos, and Publication Classifications Act 1993 (which removed a defence for an accused who had no knowledge or reasonable cause to believe that a publication which the accused possessed was objectionable), the Attorney-General had expressed the opinion that imposing liability without such a defence could not be justified under section 5 of the Bill of

under section 7 only arises, however, when any Bill is 'introduced', or as soon as possible thereafter. There is no duty to review and report on any amendments to a Bill made or recommended as a result of the select committee review process.[81] The Courts in New Zealand have considered themselves powerless to interfere with the consequences of this anomaly.[82]

- Secondly, while Canada's section 33 provides for a temporary (five-year) legislative departure from full compliance with the Charter, there is no such safeguard within New Zealand's legislation.
- The final matter of importance is the relevance of section 5 to the Attorney General's function under section 7 of the Bill of Rights. Section 5 sets out a 'justified limitations' provision (see Sect. 11.3 below) and, according to Crown Law officer Andrew Butler, "almost all advices prepared by the Ministry of Justice and the Crown Law Office for the Attorney General as part of the section 7 NZBORA vetting process rely to some extent on section 5".[83] The Attorney General's office in New Zealand thereby wields considerable influence in the determination of whether limits on rights are justifiable. The same is presumably true in Canada as a result of the Minister of Justice's reporting function under section 4.1 of the Department of Justice Act 1985. The consequences of that influence are quite different in New Zealand, though, due to the protection afforded to legislation under section 4 of the Bill of Rights Act.

Rights. Parliament nevertheless chose to enact s 131(3) of the Act which, while capable of being criticised, was at least consciously done by Parliament.

[81]See, for example, *R v Poumako* (2000) 17 CRNZ 530, where Justice Thomas (at para 96 of the judgment) that the Criminal Justice Act had not been scrutinised under section 7. This had occurred because the Attorney-General's report is only required when a Government Bill is introduced or "as soon as practicable" after the introduction of a Bill. Because of its wording, section 7 does not apply to amendments introduced by way of a supplementary order paper during the committee stage or second reading of a Bill, meaning that such amendments do not receive the scrutiny considered necessary by Parliament when a Bill is first introduced.

[82]See *Westco Lagan Ltd v A-G* [2001] 1 NZLR 40, 63, where Justice McGechan stated: "There is no supreme law in New Zealand which inhibits those powers. In particular, Parliament can pass laws which are directly contrary to provisions of the BOR. Section 3, referring to the legislative branch, does not enact otherwise. The safeguard, following upon decision to not enact the BOR as supreme law, is provision for the Attorney-General to give s 7 notification to the House. The House must know this is occurring, and give proper consideration to proposed legislation in that light. It is not for the unelected Courts to frustrate that legislative ability. If content of legislation offends, the remedies are political and ultimately electoral. The fact those alternatives seem monumentally difficult, indeed unreal, to particular persons, or to those espousing unpopular causes, is no more than a dark side of democracy."

[83]Butler (2002, p. 538). See, for example, *Living Word Distributors Ltd v Human Rights Action Group Inc* (n 80).

11.3.1.4   United Kingdom

Prior to the second reading of a bill, in either House, the Minister in charge of the bill must make a statement of compatibility, a matter required by section 19 of the Human Rights Act 1998. The statement must explain their either the provisions of the bill are, in the Minister's view, compatible with Convention rights; or that, although the Minister is "unable to make a statement of compatibility", the government nevertheless wishes the bill to proceed. This is similar in nature to the operation of section 7 of the NZ Bill of Rights, except that the statement must be made before the second reading of a bill instead of at the time of, or immediately following, its introduction. While this has the potential to better reflect any amendments suggested by a select committee, the actual timing of the Minister's statement may make a difference to whether or not parliament is made aware of any potential incompatibility. Unlike the mechanism under section 33 of the Canadian Charter, there is no provision made within the Human Rights Act for a review of, or required extension to, any limiting measure enacted.

11.3.2   Remedies

The provision of remedies for violations of civil liberties varies greatly according to the nature and context of the violation. Evidence obtained in breach of privacy rights, or more explicit guarantees against unreasonable search and seizure, may be excluded from admissibility in proceedings. Coerced statements, or those made in the absence of legal representation, may be excluded. Prosecutions are capable of being stayed for unreasonable delays in trying an accused.

The provision of remedies in Australia depends, due to the lack of a national bill of rights, upon the particular right (including whether it is a common law right, or one expressly or impliedly included under the Constitution) and the jurisdiction within which the violation occurred. Civil liberties legislation in Canada and the United Kingdom include express remedial provisions. While New Zealand's Bill of Rights does not include a remedies clause, the courts have provided for remedies, including civil damages.

11.3.2.1   Remedies Under the Canadian Charter

In addition to the supremacy clause in section 52 of the Constitution, the Charter of Rights contains its own broad remedies provision in section 24. Subsection (2) provides a specific power to exclude evidence obtained in breach of the Charter. Section 24(1) contains a more broad remedial power as follows:

> 24. Enforcement of guaranteed rights and freedoms
> (1) Anyone whose rights or freedoms, as guaranteed by this Charter, have been infringed or denied may apply to a court of competent jurisdiction to obtain such remedy as the court considers appropriate and just in the circumstances.

The following distinctions can be made between section 52 (discussed at Sect. 11.1.2.2 above) and section 24:

- As to the application of each provision, section 24(1) only applies to breaches of the Charter, whereas section 52(1) pertains to the entirety of the Constitution Act 1982.
- As to the standing of a person to rely on the provisions, section 24(1) is only available to those whose Charter rights have been infringed (thus limited to victims of civil liberties infringements), while section 52(1) is available in some circumstances to a person whose rights have not been infringed. Section 24(1) thus imposes stricter requirements of standing than are applicable to many remedies under the general law.[84]
- As to the availability of the provisions, section 52(1) is available to any court or tribunal which has the power to decide questions of law, whereas remedies under section 24 can only be granted by a "court of competent jurisdiction". Generally speaking, a court of competent jurisdiction is: a superior court; a trial court concerning matters related to the conduct of the trial); or an administrative tribunal if its constituent statute gives it power over the parties to the dispute, the subject matter of the dispute, and the Charter remedy that is being sought.
- As to the type of remedy, section 24(1) authorises a competent court to award a wide range of potential remedies, as considered "appropriate and just in the circumstances", whereas section 52(1) only authorises a holding of invalidity of legislation. This observation must be reconciled with the interpretative approaches adopted by the Supreme Court of Canada on the application of section 52(1) (see Sect. 11.1.2.2 above).

11.3.2.2 Remedies Under the United Kingdom Human Rights Act

Section 8 of the Human Rights Act sets out a general power relating to any act or omission by a public authority in breach of an individual's civil liberties, allowing a court to "grant such relief or remedy, or make such order, within its powers as it considers just and appropriate". There are again a number of features to note about availability and nature of remedies under this provision:

- First, section 8(2) allows the courts to make an award of damages under the Act only if the court itself has the jurisdiction to award compensation as a remedy and restricts such awards to civil proceedings.

---

[84]See, for example, *R v Edwards* [1996] 1 SCR 128, where the applicant complained about the search of his girlfriend's apartment by police which resulted in the discovery of drugs, later relied on by the Crown in a prosecution against the applicant. Because the applicant had no reasonable expectation of privacy in someone else's home, the search was not a breach of his right under section 8 of the Charter to be secure against unreasonable search and seizure and no remedy was available to him.

- Secondly, damages are to be awarded only where they are necessary to afford 'just satisfaction' to the victim, taking into account all of the circumstances of the case including the availability or granting of any other relief or remedy (section 8(3)).
- Finally, section 8(4) directs British courts to take into account the principles applied by the European Court in the award of compensation under article 41 of the European Convention on Human Rights (see Chap. 9, Sect. 9.2.4).

11.3.2.3 Remedies Under the New Zealand Bill of Rights Act

In its White Paper form, the Bill of Rights was to contain a remedies clause, providing for "such remedy as the Court considers appropriate and just in the circumstances", in similar terms to section 24(1) of the Canadian Charter.[85] As enacted, however, the Bill of Rights is silent on the issue of remedies. In early case law involving the Bill of Rights, the Crown therefore argued that the courts were powerless to grant remedies even in the case of a proven violation of rights.[86] The Court of Appeal has instead taken the approach that the absence of a remedies clause meant that Parliament "has chosen to leave [the ability to award remedies] unconstrained".[87] The rationale for this approach stems from the long title to the Bill of Rights Act, stating in paragraph (a) that it is an Act to "affirm, protect, and promote human rights and fundamental freedoms in New Zealand". In this respect, Justice McKay stated in *Simpson v Attorney-General (Baigent's Case)*:[88]

> One cannot see how rights can be protected and promoted if they are merely affirmed, but there is no remedy for their breach, and no other legal consequence.

In the same case, emphasis was also placed on paragraph (b) of the long title to the Bill of Rights Act, which affirms New Zealand's commitment to the International Covenant on Civil and Political Rights. The Court found article 2(3)(a) of the Covenant to be of particular relevance in this regard, that article obliging States parties to ensure that any person whose rights or freedoms under the ICCPR are violated must be given an "effective remedy" (see Chap. 9, Sect. 9.2.4). Concluding that this obligation extends to the judiciary in New Zealand, President Cooke of the Court of Appeal stated in *Baigent's Case*:[89]

> Section 3 of the New Zealand Act makes it clear that the Act binds the Crown in respect of functions of the executive government and its agencies. It "otherwise specially provides" within the meaning of s 5(k) of the Acts Interpretation Act 1924. Section 3 also makes

---

[85]White Paper (n 25), p. 114.

[86]See *Noort v MOT; Curran v Police* (n 30), 266.

[87]Per Justice Gault in *R v Butcher* [1992] 2 NZLR 257, 269.

[88]*Simpson v Attorney-General (Baigent's Case)* [1994] 3 NZLR 667, 677.

[89]Ibid, 676. See also *Auckland Unemployed Workers' Rights Centre Inc v Attorney-General* [1994] 3 NZLR 720.

it clear that the Bill of Rights applies to acts done by the Courts. The Act is binding on us, and we would fail in our duty if we did not give an effective remedy to a person whose legislatively affirmed rights have been infringed. In a case such as the present the only effective remedy is compensation. A mere declaration would be toothless. In other cases a mandatory remedy such as an injunction or an order for return of property might be appropriate.

11.4   The Limitation of Rights

Considered in Chap. 10 was the notion that human rights law incorporates a level of flexibility, allowing States to give effect to rights and freedoms, while at the same time pursue important democratic objectives designed to protect society and to maintain a balance between conflicting rights. The focus of that chapter was upon the limitation of rights at international law, focussing upon the International Covenant on Civil and Political Rights and the European Convention on Human Rights. In the case of Australia and the United Kingdom, the frameworks under those instruments for limiting rights are of direct relevance. Since there is no national bill or rights in Australia, assessing human rights compliance by Australia while countering terrorism (undertaken in the chapters that follow) will be measured against the international standards considered in Chap. 10. Due to the linkage between the UK's Human Rights Act and the European Convention on Human Rights, assessing Britain's compliance will also require reference to external factors.

For the reasons just explained, the question of justifying rights limitations in Australia and the United Kingdom will rely heavily on the framework for limiting rights under international law. Consideration must be had to limitations by interpretation (based upon the use of terms such a 'fair' and 'reasonable' – see Chap. 10, Sect. 10.3.1) and express limitations applying to limited or qualified rights (Chap. 10, Sect. 10.3.2). The UK Human Rights Act also includes direct reference to the temporary measure of derogations from rights and freedoms under the European Convention (see Sect. 11.1.4.2 above).

The Canadian Charter and NZ Bill of Rights will also call for the use of limitations by interpretation. In setting out the rights and freedoms assured by them, both instruments guarantee, for example, the right to a 'fair' trial (section 11 (d) of the Charter and section 25(a) of the Bill of Rights), the right to be secure against 'unreasonable' search and seizure (sections 8 and 21 respectively), and the prohibition against 'arbitrary' detention (sections 9 and 22 respectively). Relevant too is section 7 of the Charter, which guarantees the right not to be deprived of life, liberty and security of the person except in accordance with "the principles of fundamental justice". Section 7, and its relationship with the Charter's general limitations clause in section 1, is discussed below (Sect. 11.5.3). The Charter also contains an example of a limited right, i.e. one which explains the precise and limited extent to which the right or freedom may be restricted (see Chap. 11,

Sect. 11.3.2), section 6 guaranteeing mobility rights and then, in subsections (3) and (4), setting out permissible limitations thereon. Added to this are two provisions which allow for the limitation of rights and freedoms in Canada. The first is to be found in the section 33 notwithstanding clause (see Sect. 11.3.1.2 above). The other is the general limitations provision under section 1 of the Charter, discussed next.

11.5 Human Rights Limitations Justifiable in a Free and Democratic Society

Added to the means of limitation just described, there is one further, generally applicable, mechanism for the limitation of rights which is relevant to the case study countries. The Canadian Charter and NZ Bill of Rights provide for the rights and freedoms set out within them to be subject to "such reasonable limits prescribed by law as can be demonstrably justified in a free and democratic society" (section 1 of the Charter and section 5 of the Bill of Rights).[90] The non-federal human rights legislation of Australia's Capital Territory and State of Victoria contain similar provisions.[91] The focus of this part of the chapter, however, will be upon the mechanisms under the Canadian Charter and the NZ Bill of Rights.

11.5.1 Preliminary Observations on the Application of Sections 1 and 5

The jurisprudence in Canada and New Zealand has developed a substantive test for the application of sections 1 and 5, discussed below. Some preliminary observations should first be made:

11.5.1.1 Burden of Proof

From a procedural perspective, it should be noted that once the complainant of a Charter or Bill of Rights breach has established the existence of a prima facie rights violation, the onus of proving that the breach is justified is placed on the party

---

[90]Section 5 of the Bill of Rights was modelled on section 1 of the Canadian Charter, although it is made "subject to" the section 4 supremacy clause (see Sect. 11.1.3 above). On the link between the Charter of Rights and Freedoms and international law on the limitation of human rights, see Ross (1984).

[91]Human Rights Act 2004 (ACT), section 28(1); and Charter of Human Rights and Responsibilities Act 2006 (Victoria), section 7.

seeking to rely on section 1 or 5, which will in most cases be the Crown.[92] It is for that party, in other words, to 'demonstrate' that the limitation falls within the scope of those provisions.

11.5.1.2   Standard of Proof

The New Zealand High Court has added that discharging this onus must be to the civil standard of the balance of probabilities, and that this must be applied rigorously, consistent with the requirement that the restriction be demonstrably justified.[93] The position regarding the standard of proof is not as clear in Canada. In *KIS Films Inc v Vancouver*, the court spoke about the possibility, in some cases, of applying a standard of proof somewhere between the civil and criminal standards because of the importance of ensuring that rights limitations are necessary.[94]

11.5.1.3   Limits Versus Exceptions or Denials

Sections 1 and 5 both refer to reasonable "limits". Canadian case law has drawn a distinction, in this regard, between "limits" and "exceptions" or "denials". The rule on non-justifiability was set out by the Supreme Court in *Attorney General of Quebec v Quebec Association of Protestant School Boards*.[95] In that case, section 72 of the Charter of the French Language limited admission to English-language schools to children of persons who themselves had been educated in English in Quebec. The Supreme Court held that this restriction amounted to an "exception" to section 23(1)(b) of the Charter of Rights. The Court explained that a prescription of law cannot create an exception to a provision of the Charter, nor can it purport to amend any provision thereof. It held that if a prescription collides directly with a provision of the Charter so as to negate it in whole, that prescription is not a "limit" capable of justification. Hogg criticises this distinction on the basis that there is no legal standard by which Charter infringements can be sorted into the two categories.

The latter case was considered in *Ford v Quebec (Attorney General)*, where the Supreme Court examined the distinction in more detail. The Court began by describing the *Quebec Association of Protestant School Boards* case as a "rare case of a truly complete denial of a guaranteed right or freedom" and, in doing so, recognised that most if not all legislative qualifications of a right or freedom will

---

[92]See *Re Southam (No 1)* [1983] 41 OR (2d) 113, 124. This approach was confirmed in New Zealand in *Ministry of Transport v Noort; Police v Curran* (n 30), 271 and 283, and *Solicitor-General v Radio New Zealand Ltd* [1994] 1 NZLR 48.

[93]*Solicitor-General v Radio New Zealand Ltd* (ibid).

[94]*KIS Films Inc v Vancouver* (1992) CRR (2d) 98, 113–114.

[95]*Attorney General of Quebec v Quebec Association of Protestant School Boards* [1984] 2 SCR 66, 87

amount to a denial of the right or freedom to that limited extent.[96] On the other hand, it said, a limit that permits no exercise of a guaranteed right or freedom in a limited area of its potential exercise is not justifiable. The same observation was made by UN Economic and Social Council in its *Siracusa Principles on the Limitation and Derogation Provisions in the International Covenant on Civil and Political Rights.*[97]

11.5.1.4 Limits Prescribed by Law

The wording of both provisions also requires that any limitation must be "prescribed by law". This is a common feature in all mechanisms authorising the limitation of rights and is supported by the principle of legality. The requirements of the expression (accessibility and precision), as set out in the *Sunday Times Case*, are discussed in Chap. 10 (Sect. 10.2.2). These requirements were first accepted and applied in New Zealand by the Indecent Publications Tribunal in *Re "Penthouse (US)" Vol 19 No 5 and others.*[98] Putting this test into a practical perspective, Justice Le Dain of the Supreme Court of Canada said that this included common law rules, statutes and regulations.[99] Two further points should be noted:

- In both Canada and New Zealand it has been held that the "operating requirements" of a statute may also amount to a prescription by law. The term refers to those limits on rights which are not expressed in a statute, nor implied, but which arise as a result of the practical operation of the enactment in the manner in which it was designed to operate. In *R v Therens*, a case concerning blood/breath alcohol legislation, it was held that the operating requirements of the statute meant that full opportunity to consult and instruct a lawyer was not possible, and that telephone access within a reasonable time could be permitted.[100] The Supreme Court concluded:

  The requirement that the limit be prescribed by law is chiefly concerned with the distinction between a limit imposed by law and one that is arbitrary. The limit will be prescribed by law within the meaning of s. 1 if it is expressly provided for by statute or regulation, or results by necessary implication from the terms of a statute or regulation or from its operating requirements.

---

[96]*Ford v Quebec (Attorney General)* [1988] 2 SCR 712, 773–774.

[97]Siracusa Principles on the Limitation and Derogation Provisions in the International Covenant on Civil and Political Rights, UN Doc E/CN.4/1985/4 (1985), Annex, para 2.

[98]*Re "Penthouse (US)" Vol 19 No 5 and others* 1 NZBORR 429.

[99]*R v Thomsen* (1988) 63 CR (3d) 1, 10. This consideration of the expression was approved by the New Zealand Court of Appeal in *MOT v Noort; Police v Curran* (n 30).

[100]*R v Therens* [1985] 1 SCR 613.

The New Zealand Court of Appeal adopted the same approach in *MOT v Noort; Police v Curran* concerning the operating requirements of New Zealand's Land Transport Act 1962.[101]

- The second point to note concerns discretionary powers. The international law approach to this issue is summarised in Chap. 10 as requiring that: any law authorising a restriction upon rights and freedoms must not confer an *unfettered* discretion on those charged with its execution; and any discretion must not be *arbitrarily or unreasonably* applied (see Sect. 10.2.2.2). In the Ontario Court of Appeal, the *Sunday Times Case* requirement of precision was applied to find that a statute authorising film censorship failed to meet the requirements of a limitation "prescribed by law" because the censor board was given an unfettered discretion to ban or cut film.[102] The Supreme Court of Canada, in *R v Nova Scotia Pharmaceutical Society*, similarly found that a vague statutory provision offended the requirement that limitations upon rights must be precise.[103]

The Supreme Court of Canada has subsequently drawn a distinction between two types of statutory conferrals of discretion.[104] First, are those that either expressly, or by necessary implication, authorise decisions that would limit a Charter right. In this case, the conferring statute will be incompatible with the Charter, unless the limitation required by the statute is justifiable. The second type of conferral is one that is broad enough to allow the decision-maker to act in a manner that may or may not infringe a Charter right. Here, the focus will be on the particular decision made under the conferring statute. If the decision imposes no limitation on a Charter right, the matter need not be taken any further. If, however, the decision does impose a limitation on a Charter right two possibilities exist: the limitation imposed by the decision is not justifiable under section 1 and will thus be deemed *ultra vires*; or the limitation imposed by the decision is justifiable under section 1, in which case it is rendered compatible with the Charter.

Although this point has not been considered in New Zealand, one would expect the same approach to be adopted under the Bill of Rights. The application of the Bill of Rights to subordinate legislation relies there on the interpretation of the enabling provision and the question of whether the subordinate legislation is *ultra vires*. This bears much resemblance with the approach of the Supreme Court to discretionary powers and its reliance upon the statutory provision conferring the discretion.

11.5.1.5 Democratic Society

The final point to make before discussing the substantive test under sections 1 and 5 is that both provisions refer to limitations which can be justified in a "free and

---

[101]*MOT v Noort; Police v Curran* (n 30).

[102]*Re Ontario Film and Video Appreciation Society* (1984) 45 OR (2d) 80.

[103]*R v Nova Scotia Pharmaceutical Society* [1992] 2 SCR 606.

[104]*Slaight Communications Inc v Davidson* [1989] 1 SCR 1038, 1077–1080.

democratic society". Reference to 'democratic society' is made within a number of express limitation provisions under the International Covenant and European Convention. The Human Rights Committee has stated that this indicates that the existence and operation of the qualified right in question is at the cornerstone of democratic society (see Chap. 10, Sect. 10.2.3.2). This approach is justifiable in the context of qualified rights under the ICCPR and ECHR since reference to "democratic society" is made to some but not all qualified rights, i.e. where the expression is attached to a qualified right, then it is proper to treat is as one at the cornerstone of democratic society. This approach should be distinguished, however, from that to be taken in the application of section 1 of the Charter and section 5 of the Bill of Rights, since those provisions set out a general limitations clause applicable to all rights.

The significance of the expression in the context of the Canadian Charter and the NZ Bill of Rights falls more squarely under the understanding of the European Court of Human Rights set out in *Silver v United Kingdom*, i.e. that reference to 'democratic society' means that an interference with rights and freedoms must correspond to a 'pressing social need'.[105] This corresponds directly with the first part of the substantive test under sections 1 and 5.

11.5.2   Substantive Test Under Sections 1 and 5

To determine what is justifiable in a free and democratic society, Canadian and New Zealand courts have developed almost identical principles. The Supreme Court of Canada first formulated the substantive test under section 1 of the Charter in *R v Oakes*, stating that a limit will be reasonable and demonstrably justified in a free and democratic society if it satisfies the following elements:[106]

1. The objective sought to be achieved by the limitation at hand must relate to concerns which are pressing and substantial in a free and democratic society; and
2. The means utilised must be proportional or appropriate to the objective. In this connection there are three aspects:
   (a) the limiting measures must be carefully designed or rationally connected to the objective;
   (b) they must impair the right or freedom as little as possible;
   (c) their effects must not so severely trench on individual or group rights that the objective of the limitation, albeit important, is nevertheless outweighed by the restriction of the right or freedom concerned.

---

[105]*Silver v UK* [1983] 5 EHRR 347, para 97(a).

[106]*R v Oakes* (1986) 26 DLR (4th) 200.

The combined effect of the test is to address the requirement that limitations on rights and freedoms are necessary and proportional (see Chap. 10, Sects. 10.2.3 and 11.2.4). The decision in *Oakes* was affirmed in subsequent jurisprudence of the Supreme Court of Canada.[107] It was referred to with approval by the New Zealand Court of Appeal in *MOT v Noort; Police v Curran*, and restated slightly by the High Court of New Zealand in *Solicitor-General v Radio New Zealand Ltd* (see below).[108]

11.5.2.1 Pressing and Substantial Objective in a Free and Democratic Society

The *Oakes* test will first require identification of the objective of the limiting provision and whether that objective relates to "concerns which are pressing and substantial in a free and democratic society". This is analogous to the observation of the European Court of Human Rights that an interference with rights and freedoms must correspond to a 'pressing social need'.[109]

The application of this part of the *Oakes* test will depend upon the particular provision being examined. By way of example, the following objectives of limiting provisions have been treated as being sufficiently important:

- The censorship of indecent publications, as a limitation upon the freedom of expression;[110]
- Roadside testing for breath-alcohol levels, with accompanying limits placed on the ability to consult a lawyer of choice in person;[111]
- The suppression of trafficking in narcotics, concerning the impact of a reverse onus clause on the presumption of innocence;[112]
- Measures to protect abuse of tax-credit schemes, in the context of requirements under the Canada Elections Act for political parties to qualify for benefits, and the impact of this upon democratic rights;[113] and
- The implementation of a separate code of discipline for members of the armed forces, concerning the various limitations this can impose on criminal process rights.[114]

---

[107]See, for example: *Re A Reference re Public Service Employee Relations Act* [1987] 1 SCR 313, 373–374; and *Irwin Toy Ltd v Quebec (Attorney-General)* (1989) 58 DLR (4th) 577.

[108]*MOT v Noort; Police v Curran* (n 30); and *Solicitor-General v Radio New Zealand Ltd* (n 92).

[109]*Silver v UK* (n 105).

[110]See, for example, *Re "Penthouse (US)" Vol 19 No 5 and others* (n 98).

[111]See, for example: *R v Therens* (n 100); and *MOT v Noort; Police v Curran* (n 30).

[112]*R v Oakes* (n 106).

[113]*Figueroa v Canada (AG)* [2003] 1 SCR 912.

[114]*MacKay v Rippon* [1978] 1 FC 233, 235–236; and *Genereux v R* [1992] 1 SCR 259, 293.

11.5.2.2 Rational Connection

The second limb of the *Oakes* test demands that the means utilised to achieve the objective (i.e. the nature of the rights limitation) are proportional and appropriate to the objective. This is in turn broken down into three aspects, the first of which calls for the limiting measure to be carefully designed or rationally connected to the objective. The need for a rational link is also reflected in the *Siracusa Principles*.[115] As explained by the Supreme Court of Canada in *Lavigne*, this requires is that the measures logically further the objective:[116]

> The *Oakes* inquiry into 'rational connection' between objectives and means to attain them requires nothing more than a showing that the legitimate and important goals of the legislature are logically furthered by the means the government has chosen to adopt.

Specific evidence of a rational connection might be necessary, however, where such a link is not plainly evident. The Supreme Court in *Figueroa v Canada (AG)* was critical, for example, of aspects of the Canada Elections Act concerning the registration of political parties and the tax benefits that flow from such registration.[117] The Act required that a political party nominate candidates in at least 50 electoral districts to qualify for registration. While the Court was satisfied that it was a pressing objective to ensure that the tax credit scheme was cost-efficient, it found that there was no rational connection between that objective and the 50-candidate threshold. For the majority, Justice Iacobucci was particularly critical of the fact that the government had provided no evidence that the threshold actually improved the cost-efficiency of the tax credit scheme.

The Supreme Court of Canada has nonetheless seldom found that legislation fails this first part of the second limb to the *Oakes* test, although there are instances where this has occurred. In *Oakes* itself, for example, the Court concerned itself with section 8 of the Narcotic Control Act, which contained a statutory presumption that possession of even small amounts of narcotics meant that the offender was deemed to be trafficking in narcotics.[118] There was no rational connection, said the Court, between the possession of small amounts of narcotics and the countering of trafficking.

11.5.2.3 Minimal Impairment

The test set out in *R v Oakes* spoke of the requirement that the means utilised to achieve a pressing objective must impair the right or freedom "as little as possible". Soon after *Oakes*, however, the Supreme Court restated the test to ask whether the

---

[115]Siracusa Principles on the Limitation and Derogation Provisions in the International Covenant on Civil and Political Rights (n 97), para 10(b) and (c).

[116]*Lavigne v Ontario Public Service Employees Union* [1991] 2 SCR 211, 219.

[117]*Figueroa v Canada (AG)* (n 113).

[118]*R v Oakes* (n 106).

provision being examined infringed a protected right or freedom "as little as *reasonably* possible" (emphasis added).[119] This involves an element of proportionality (see Chap. 10, Sect. 10.2.4) and also reflects the idea that section 1 of the Charter is capable of justifying limitations upon rights and freedoms, but not exclusions or denials (see Sect. 11.5.1.3 above).

There is a slight departure here in the jurisprudence in New Zealand, although it is not clear that this was intentional. In providing an overview of Canada's approach to section 1 of the Charter, the High Court of New Zealand restated this element of the test to say that "the measures or the law should impair as little as possible the right or freedom".[120] The Court chose to ignore, or overlooked, the Supreme Court's qualification that an impairment upon rights should be as little as *reasonably* possible, although this is not apparent from the judgment. Despite this difference, it is possible that the interaction of sections 5 and of the Bill of Rights achieve the same result as in Canada. When speaking of the interaction of the two provisions, Butler takes the view that section 6 does not demand an interpretation of enactments that favours rights in their absolute form:[121]

> Because section 5 NZBORA is a step in the process which needs must *precede* the determination of a binding interpretation of the other enactment, section 6 can only demand the courts to interpret statutes subject to *reasonable limits*, not subject to the least possible limit that is linguistically available. (emphasis added)

In the actual application of the minimal impairment element of *Oakes*, the Supreme Court initially displayed a degree of deference, reluctant to consider the availability of alternative means of achieving an objective where the impairment upon the right was not serious. In *R v Schwartz*, for example, it was suggested that the statutory provision (which provided for a presumption that a person did not have a firearms licence if she or he failed to produce one upon request) unnecessarily infringed the presumption of innocence. Counsel for Schwartz argued that police could simply check their computerised records to ascertain whether a licence had indeed been obtained. Rejecting this argument, Justice McIntyre stated:[122]

> Even if there is merit in the suggestion... Parliament has made a reasonable choice in the matter and, in my view, it is not for the Court, in circumstances where the impugned provision clearly involves, at most, minimal – or even trivial – interference with the right guaranteed in the Charter, to postulate some alternative which in its view would offer a better solution to the problem.

This approach has been subsequently rejected on the basis that it would pre-empt the final stage of the proportionality analysis.[123]

---

[119]*R v Edwards Books & Art Limited* [1986] 2 SCR 713, 772.

[120]*Solicitor-General v Radio New Zealand Ltd* (n 92).

[121]Butler (2002).

[122]*R v Schwartz* [1988] 2 SCR 443, 494–493.

[123]*RJR-MacDonald Inc v Canada (AG)* [1995] 3 SCR 199, 200.

11.5.2.4 Proportionality

The final part of the test under sections 1 and 5 requires that the effects of the limiting measure "must not so severely trench on individual or group rights that the objective of the limitation, albeit important, is nevertheless outweighed by the restriction of the right or freedom concerned".[124] It incorporates the proportionality principle and is the most difficult part of the test to apply. Much will depend on the particular wording of the limiting provision and the way in which this has been, or might be, applied. As discussed in Chap. 10, there are two there are two common factors which are brought to bear in the evaluation of whether limiting measures are proportional (see Sect. 10.2.4), namely the negative impact of the limiting measure upon the enjoyment of the right and the ameliorating effects of the limiting measure:

- In evaluating the negative impact of a limiting measure, it will be important to establish that the limitation is not so severe or so broad in its application so as to destroy the very essence of the right in question. This is a matter recognised by the Supreme Court of Canada and in the *Siracusa Principles*.[125] It will be also important to have regard to the importance of the right and the 'value' that might be ascribed to it.[126]
- The ameliorating effects of the limiting measure must also be considered so that, in the words of Chief Justice Lamer in *Dagenais v Canadian Broadcasting Corp*, "there must be a proportionality between the deleterious and the salutary effects of the measures".[127]

11.5.3 Principles of Fundamental Justice and Section 1 of the Canadian Charter

Section 7 of the Canadian Charter of Rights and Freedoms guarantees the right not to be deprived of life, liberty and security of the person except in accordance with "the principles of fundamental justice". The relevance of section 7 to the application of section 1 is significant, since consideration of section 1 is unlikely to occur where a legislative limitation upon life, liberty and security of the person is found not to infringe section 7 because it was compatible with the principles of fundamental justice.

In the 2004 case of *Re Application under s. 83.28 of the Criminal Code*, the Supreme Court considered the ability of a judge to issue an order for the purposes of an investigation of a terrorism offence requiring a person to attend a judicial

---

[124]*R v Oakes* (n 106).

[125]*R v Oakes* (n 106); and Siracusa Principles on the Limitation and Derogation Provisions in the International Covenant on Civil and Political Rights (n 97), paras 2 and 3.

[126]*R v Lucas* [1998] 1 SCR 439.

[127]*Dagenais v Canadian Broadcasting Corp* [1994] 3 SCR 835.

examination.[128] The applicable provisions of the Criminal Code, and the substance of the Court's decision, are examined in Chap. 16 (see Sect. 16.3). The point to make at this juncture is that the Court concluded that section 83.28 established a regime through which a person could be detained in accordance with the principles of fundamental justice and was thus compatible with section 7 of the Charter. The Court did not find it necessary to then consider section 1 of the Charter.

In examining the parameters of section 7, the Supreme Court reaffirmed its earlier jurisprudence that a "principle of fundamental justice" must fulfil three criteria: first, the principle must be a basic tenet of the legal system, and not just a matter of policy; second, there must be sufficient consensus that the alleged principle is "vital or fundamental to our societal notion of justice"; and, third, the principle must be capable of being identified with precision and applied to situations in a manner that yields predictable results.[129] It is evident, then, that there are a good number of similarities between the application of section 1 of the Charter and the manner in which an analysis under section 7 is conducted.[130] The only conceivable problem is that the factors do not expressly form part of the section 7 test, compared with the reasonably mechanical, step-by-step approach mandated by *Oakes* under section 1.

11.6   Case Study: New Zealand's United Nations Act 1946

Discussed in Chap. 4 were the means of implementing international obligations, including those relating to non-military sanctions as a consequence of Security Council resolutions (see Sect. 4.2.3). In such cases, it was identified that the common law countries being studied normally respond by making regulations. Unique to Australia and New Zealand, regulations made under the Charter of the United Nations Act 1945 (Australia) or the United Nations Act 1946 (New Zealand) are capable of overriding inconsistent primary legislation by way of what are known as 'Henry VIII clauses'. This feature, and its inter-relationship with the New Zealand Bill of Rights Act, forms the basis of the current case study. The case study examines the constitutional issues relating to the making of regulations in New Zealand. Against that background, it considers how the United Nations Act should interact with the Bill of Rights Act, and makes recommendations on that question. Section 2(2) of the United Nations Act (NZ) provides:

> No regulation made under this Act shall be deemed to be invalid because it deals with any matter already provided for by an Act, or because of any repugnancy to any Act.

---

[128]*Re Application under s. 83.28 of the Criminal Code* [2004] 2 SCR 248.

[129]Ibid, para 68. In saying so, the Court affirmed the approach to this affect in *R v Malmo-Levine* [2003] 3 SCR 571 and *Canadian Foundation for Children, Youth and the Law v Canada (AG)* [2004] 1 SCR 76, para 8. See also *R v Malmo-Levine* [2003] 3 SCR 571, para 113; *Re BC Motor Vehicle Act* [1985] 2 SCR 486, 503; and *Rodriguez v British Columbia (AG)* [1993] 3 SCR 519, 590.

[130]As recognised in *Godbout v Longueuil (City)* [1997] 3 SCR 844, paras 77–92.

11.6.1   Regulation-Making Powers in New Zealand

In March 2002, the Regulations Review Committee of New Zealand's 46th Parliament presented a report entitled on regulation-making powers that authorise international treaties to override provisions of New Zealand enactments.[131] The report was concerned with regulations that authorise international *treaties* to override an Act of Parliament, the view of the Committee being that, in principle, only Acts should be able to amend other Acts. While this focus on international treaties is due to the particular terms of reference of the Committee inquiry, it is unfortunate that the Committee did not concern itself in any detail with regulation-making powers that might authorise obligations under the United Nations Charter to override any Act of Parliament. The Committee took a peculiar approach to the issue of section 2 of the United Nations Act. On the one hand, it noted concern with the breadth of these regulation-making powers. It nevertheless dismissed the need to review those powers, stating without any further explanation:[132]

> We do not seek review of section 2(2) of the United Nations Act 1946, as this provision falls within the exceptional circumstances in which regulation-making powers authorising overriding treaty regulations are justifiable...

Notwithstanding the lack of direct consideration of the United Nations Act, there are various matters discussed within the report, and recommendations made, that are of relevance to the regulation-making power under the Act. The Committee was critical of Henry VIII Clauses, the overriding message being that regulation-making powers should enable the derogation of an Act of Parliament only in exceptional circumstances.[133] It accordingly recommended that the House consider limiting such powers in a number of ways, with the following suggestions having some bearing on section 2 of the United Nations Act:

- Limiting enabling provisions to override the principal Act only;[134]
- Expressing the particular primary legislative provisions that may be overridden by such regulations;[135]

---

[131]Report of the Regulations Review Committee, *Inquiry into Regulation-Making Powers that Authorise International Treaties to Override any Provisions of New Zealand Enactments*, NZAJHR (2002) I. 16H.

[132]Ibid, p. 29.

[133]Ibid, Recommendation 1, p. 17. See also the Regulation Review Committee's discussion of Henry VIII Clauses at page 15 and an earlier report of the Committee concerning such clauses: *Inquiry into the Resource Management (Transitional) Regulations 1994 and the Principles that Should Apply to the Use of Empowering Provisions Allowing Regulations to Override Primary Legislation During a Transitional Period*, NZAJHR (1995) I. 16C.

[134]Ibid, Recommendation 3(2), p. 4 (discussed within pp. 21–22 of the report).

[135]Ibid, Recommendations 3(3) and 4, p. 4 (discussed within pp. 21–23 of the report).

- Limiting such operation to matters of a technical nature or emergency measures;[136]
- Providing for additional parliamentary scrutiny of any such regulations;[137] and
- Prohibiting the derogation of the common law and the New Zealand Bill of Rights Act 1990.[138]

As well as enabling the making of regulations, the United Nations Act provides for liability for breach of any regulations made under the Act and application of the Act in the Cook Islands. That is, however, the extent of the Act. The first recommendation listed therefore has little application to the UN Act, the sole purpose of which is to establish a mechanism by which the New Zealand Government can comply with decisions of the Security Council.

The second recommendation listed, pertaining to explicit reference within an empowering provision to statutory provisions that may be overridden by such regulations, is self-explanatory and does not need any further consideration. This will effectively be a question for parliament to answer. The remaining suggestions do, however, raise some interesting issues for United Nations regulations, particularly in the context of the protection of civil liberties, and might assist in deciding the level to which regulations can and should override primary legislation.

11.6.1.1   Limiting Enabling Provisions to Emergency Measures

Although the Committee recognised that there may be a need to make regulations which, in a situation of emergency, require enactments to be superseded, it was very cautious in doing so. It noted, for example, that mechanisms already exist for the rapid adoption of legislation through the House by way of urgency.[139] All the same, it considered that in exceptional circumstances, citing the example of the need for the government to respond to Security Council resolutions when parliament is not sitting, regulations may be made.[140]

While not given further consideration, it therefore seems that the Committee was willing to recognise that regulations made under the United Nations Act can be appropriately used to override an Act of Parliament. What seems clear, however, is that this should be limited to exceptional circumstances, and possibly also limited in circumstances where a Security Council resolution requires immediate action and parliament is not sitting.

It is notable that a similarly restrictive view is adopted under the International Covenant on Civil and Political Rights. Article 4 of the Covenant permits

---

[136]Ibid, Recommendation 2, p. 4 (discussed within pp. 19–20 of the report).

[137]Ibid, Recommendation 5, p. 4 (discussed within pp. 23–26 of the report).

[138]Ibid, Recommendation 3(4), p. 4 (discussed within pp. 16 and 22 of the report).

[139]The practical observation, however, is that this does not occur very frequently: discussion between the author and Professor John Burrows, University of Canterbury, 10 March 2005.

[140]Committee Report (n 131) p. 20.

derogations from rights and freedoms when a public emergency which threatens the life of a nation arises (see Chap. 10, Sect. 10.4). A State party cannot, however, derogate from certain rights and may not do so in a discriminatory way. States are also under an obligation to inform other States parties immediately, through the UN Secretary-General, of the derogations it has made including the reasons for such derogations. The Human Rights Committee signalled in its general comment on the application of article 4 that this is limited to states of emergency, as provided for within municipal legislation setting out grounds upon which a state of emergency may be declared.[141] It also expressed the view that measures taken under article 4 are of an exceptional and temporary nature and can only last as long as the life of the nation concerned is threatened.

11.6.1.2 Providing Additional Parliamentary Scrutiny

Greater scrutiny by parliament of Henry VIII regulations was recommended by the Committee. Under current procedures in New Zealand, the Regulations (Disallowance) Act 1989 provides for what is known as a 'negative' procedure of parliamentary approval.[142] Under this procedure, regulations remain in force unless specifically disallowed by parliament. As this relates to the United Nations Act, the affect of the Regulations (Disallowance) Act is to allow parliament to disallow regulations made under the UN Act.[143] The alternative 'positive' procedure would provide that regulations do not come into force until first allowed by parliament.[144] As well as positive and negative approval procedures, a third method is used in England, the 'super affirmative procedure'. This procedure is intended for scrutiny of regulations of an important or sensitive nature so that parliament should consider, through a specialised parliamentary committee, the regulations in their draft form rather than waiting for them to be made and subsequently disallowing them.[145]

---

[141]General Comment 29: States of Emergency (Article 4), UN Doc CCPR/C/21/Rev.1/Add.11 (2001), para 2.

[142]See section 6 of the Regulations (Disallowance) Act 1989, and Standing Order 387 of New Zealand Standing Orders of the House of Representatives.

[143]Compare with the situation in Canada, under section 4(2) of the United Nations Act 1985 (Canada), which expressly allows for the annulment of regulations made under it by agreement of the Senate and House of Commons.

[144]For further discussion on positive approval procedures, see Thornton (1996, p. 337). The only positive procedures in New Zealand are contained within: the enabling provision of section 4(1) of the Misuse of Drugs Act 1975, which requires a resolution of the House approving any regulations made under that Act before they can come into force; and section 78B of the Dog Control Act 1996 (inserted by section 46 of the Dog Control Amendment Act 2003).

[145]For further discussion on the process, see Tudor (2000).

11.6.1.3 Regulations Abrogating Rights and Freedoms

In its submissions to the Regulations Review Committee, the Ministry of Foreign Affairs and Trade made the valid point that there are significant benefits to be gained from the use of overriding treaty regulations.[146] It pointed to the fact that this allows the executive to ensure compliance with treaty obligations and avoid wasted time by parliament in considering technical, rather than policy, matters.

A similar approach might be adopted to the situation of international obligations under the United Nations Charter, although an important difference needs to be noted. The submissions of the Ministry made a broad distinction between matters of policy and technical matters and equated bilateral treaties as being technical, versus multilateral treaties as often involving policy issues.[147] The former, according to the Ministry's formulation, may properly override primary legislation. Where, however, do obligations imposed by the UN Security Council fall within that scale? There is no absolute answer. From one perspective, resolutions of the Security Council are adopted as an exercise by the Security Council of its mandate under the United Nations Charter (a multilateral treaty) and are likewise binding upon States through the Charter.[148] Adopting the Ministry's broad categorisation, such resolutions might therefore be considered as involving matters of policy. The reality, however, is that obligations imposed under resolutions of the Security Council are quite often very specific and technical, particularly when calling for the imposition of trade sanctions and the like.

The question must be addressed having regard to the substance of each particular resolution and its effect. If, for example, certain UN regulations impact upon the enjoyment of human rights, this is clearly a matter of policy rather than mere technicalities. Adopting the philosophy behind the Ministry's own submissions, such matters should therefore fall within the influence of parliament. Where human rights are to be affected, the ability of parliament to carry out its role as "guardian of the public interest" (in the words of the Review Committee) must be protected.[149] Central to this role is the protection of rights and freedoms.[150]

This is not to suggest that non-compliance with Security Council resolutions is acceptable. Indeed, this would be contrary to New Zealand's obligations as a member of the United Nations, which would entitle the Security Council to issue sanctions against New Zealand for its failure to comply.[151] The issue being addressed here concerns the manner in which such obligations are implemented

---

[146]Submissions by the Ministry of Foreign Affairs and Trade to the Regulations Review Committee in its Inquiry into Regulation-Making Powers that Authorise International Treaties to Override any Provisions of New Zealand Enactments, Parliamentary Library, Wellington.

[147]Ibid.

[148]Charter of the United Nation 1945, articles 24 and 25.

[149]Committee Report (n 131), p. 16.

[150]As recognised by the Committee (ibid) p. 17.

[151]See Chapter VII of the Charter of the United Nations, articles 41 and 42 in particular.

by New Zealand, by whom they are implemented (the executive alone, parliament alone, or the executive with parliamentary scrutiny), having regard to the consequences of the implementing regulations (potentially abrogating or limiting human rights).

11.6.2 How Should the United Nations Act and Bill of Rights Act Interact?

The operative provisions of the Bill of Rights direct how it is to be applied to other legislation and, thereby, how the Bill of Rights is to be used as a tool of statutory interpretation (see Sect. 11.1.3.2 above). Given that regulations made under the United Nations Act are made under a 'Henry VIII' empowering provision, the question is how the operative sections of the Bill of Rights apply to such regulations. Two questions arise. First, does section 6 of the Bill of Rights require the regulations to be made consistently with the Bill of Rights Act? Secondly, does section 4 of the Bill of Rights, combined with section 2(2) of the United Nations Act, provide United Nations regulations with special protection?

11.6.2.1 Applying Section 6 of the Bill of Rights

By application of the general principles of statutory interpretation, it is arguable that section 6 of the Bill of Rights requires any item of subordinate legislation (including those made under the United Nations Act) to be made in a manner that is consistent with the Bill of Rights Act, to avoid those regulations being ultra vires the empowering Act. This was the approach taken by the New Zealand Court of Appeal in *Drew v Attorney-General*, where the Court was faced with the question of whether regulations preventing legal representation were ultra vires the empowering section of the Penal Institutions Act 1954 by reason of inconsistency with the New Zealand Bill of Rights Act 1990 (see Sect. 11.2.4 above). Adopting this approach, the preliminary conclusion is that the United Nations Act empowering provision must be construed consistently with the Bill of Rights so that it does not confer a power to make subordinate legislation which infringes the Bill of Rights Act.

11.6.2.2 Applying Section 4 of the Bill of Rights to Section 2(2) of the United Nations Act

The next question to consider is whether section 4 of the Bill of Rights, combined with section 2(2) of the United Nations Act, provides United Nations regulations with special protection. The effect of section 4 is that no provision of an enactment can be treated as invalid or ineffective if that provision is irreconcilably in conflict with the Bill of Rights. Does section 4 thus protect the Henry VIII status of regulations made under the United Nations Act? To answer this, a further question needs to be considered: is section 2(2) of the United Nations Act irreconcilably in conflict with the Bill of Rights?

Nowhere in the United Nations Act is there an authority to regulate in a manner inconsistent with the Bill of Rights, although this is natural given that the UN Act preceded the Bill of Rights by almost 45 years. One possible interpretation is that since such authority is not contained within the Act itself, regulations made under the UN Act cannot be repugnant to the provisions of the Bill of Rights. On the other hand, it might be argued that the words of section 2(2) do not avail themselves of such an interpretation, since they clearly provide validity to regulations despite "*any* repugnancy to *any* Act" (emphasis added).

By arriving at this neutral position, or at least one that is arguable either way, it is difficult to draw a positive conclusion. What the analysis illustrates, however, is the potential dichotomy between the maintenance of peace and security and that of human rights standards. Within the recommendations that follow, it will be proposed that this dichotomy is such that it places itself squarely within the realm of policy considerations that should remain within the purview of parliament and not the government alone.

11.6.2.3 Recommendations

In the absence of a specific and comprehensive review and report by the Regulations Review Committee on the subject, the following recommendations are made regarding the regulation-making power under the United Nations Act 1946:

- The issues raised within the preceding discussion are such that a review by the New Zealand parliament of the empowering provision under section 2 of the Act is warranted. Such review should take place within the framework of the recommendations that follow.
- Closely in line with the Committee's Recommendation 3(3) pertaining to international treaties, parliament should consider expressing the particular primary legislation provisions that may be overridden by United Nations regulations. Alternatively, the empowering provision might be amended to at least prohibit the overriding of any provision within the New Zealand Bill of Rights Act, and possibly any provision of the Privacy Act 1993 and Human Rights Act 1993.
- The regulation-making power and process under the United Nations Act should be limited to the following extents:
  - Empowering the making of regulations only *if* the Security Council resolution in question requires immediate action *and* Parliament is not sitting; and/or
  - Empowering the making of regulations only *if* the Security Council resolution in question concerns a matter which threatens the life of New Zealand *and then* only by way of temporary measures; and/or
  - Introducing a 'super affirmative' parliamentary approval procedure for the making of United Nations regulations, through which a specialised

parliamentary committee would consider the regulations in their draft form and, in doing so, reflect upon the question of what limitations those regulations might place upon the rights and freedoms guaranteed under the Bill of Rights and, if any such limitations are exposed, whether these are justifiable in a free and democratic society.

By adopting the latter restrictions, parliament would retain control over the policy aspects involved in weighing any conflict between New Zealand's obligations under the UN Charter versus those under the ICCPR and thereby preserve its role and the 'protector of the public interest'.

11.7 Conclusions

The protection of civil liberties in the four Commonwealth case study countries is varied and multi-layered, impacted upon by constitutional and political factors, the existence or status of human rights legislation, the impact and role of the common law and statutory presumptions, and the mechanisms applicable to law-making, the provision of remedies and the limitation of rights.

Although Australia's Capital Territory and State of Victoria have enacted human rights legislation, there is no national human rights instrument in Australia. The protection of civil liberties is dependent largely upon the common law, as well as a limited range of expressly recognised rights under the Commonwealth Constitution, and those implied from it. There are no federal mechanisms in Australia dealing specifically with the role of human rights in the enactment of laws, nor is there a generally-applicable right to remedies for violations of human rights. This, combined with a generally legalistic approach to the reception of international human rights law by the judiciary, leaves human rights in a vulnerable position in Australia. In the absence of clear rules pertaining to the permissible extent to which rights may be limited in Australia, the examination of this issue in the context of counter-terrorism (see Part III herein) will be measured against the rights-limitation mechanisms under the International Covenant on Civil and Political Rights.

In contrast to Australia, Canada has a supreme and entrenched bill of rights under the Canadian Charter of Rights and Freedoms. Canada's Supreme Court is able to invalidate inconsistent legislation, and has developed mechanisms to allow for the interpretation of ordinary law consistent with Charter rights. Federal and provincial mechanisms call for the scrutiny of new legislation to determine their compatibility with the Charter of Rights. While the federal parliament retains its sovereign ability to enact statutes that restrict rights and freedoms, it must do so by express reference to the notwithstanding clause in the Charter and can only effect such restrictions by five-year, renewable, periods. The Charter provides for a broad remedial power and guarantees that the rights and freedoms set out within it may be subject only to reasonable limits prescribed by law as can be demonstrably justified in a free and democratic society.

New Zealand's Bill of Rights Act is modelled on the Canadian Charter but is weaker than the Charter in three main respects. The Bill of Rights is not entrenched, nor does it include a remedies clause. It is also an ordinary statute and, by virtue of the sovereignty clause in section 4 of the Act, the rights contained in it are capable of limitation or exclusion when in an irreconcilable conflict with another enactment. The judiciary has nevertheless taken a rights-based approach to the application of the Act, developing remedies for the violation of rights, identifying the possibility of making declarations of incompatibility, and requiring provisions which allow for the making of subordinate legislation to be interpreted in a manner consistent with the Bill of Rights where possible. Although deficient in some respects, section 7 of the Act calls for the Attorney General to scrutinise proposed legislation for consistency with the Bill of Rights. Like Canada's Charter, the Bill of Rights includes a mechanism for the limitation of human rights where demonstrably justified in a free and democratic society.

The Human Rights Act in the United Kingdom is a non-autonomous instrument, incorporating the rights in the European Convention on Human Rights by reference rather than setting out those rights within the Act. As in New Zealand, the judiciary is unable to invalidate legislation where there is an irreconcilable conflict between it and the Human Rights Act. The judiciary has the express power, however, to make declarations of incompatibility. Remedial orders allow for the subsequent modification of the offending provision to bring it into compliance with Convention rights. The government has a role in the scrutiny of proposed legislation, in a manner similar to Canada and New Zealand. The provision of remedies for the violation of human rights is again linked to the European Convention, as is any question of justifying limitations upon the unrestricted enjoyment of rights in the United Kingdom.

The case study in Sect. 11.6 above considered how the balance of power between the executive and legislature is to be achieved in the situation of subordinate legislation made under the United Nations Act 1946 (NZ). While there has been little direct consideration of the issue within New Zealand, the potential dangers that exist with the regulation-making power under the Act have been identified. The UN Act allows the executive to make regulations that are not subject to scrutiny. Those regulations have superior status over Acts of Parliament, and may be used to limit human rights with no power of recourse to the judiciary. The case study therefore makes recommendations to achieve a balance between national and international security, with the aim of also maintaining and protecting civil liberties and preserving the checking function under the separation of powers doctrine.

References

Brookfield, F. 1992. Constitutional Law. *New Zealand Recent Law Review* 231.
Burrows, John. 1999. *Statute Law in New Zealand*. Wellington: 2nd edition, Butterworths.
Butler Andrew. 2000. Judicial Indications of Inconsistency – A New Weapon in the Bill of Rights Armoury? *New Zealand Law Review* 43.

Butler, Andrew. 2002. Limiting Rights. 33 *Victoria University of Wellington Law Review* 537.

Conte, Alex. 2007. *Counter-Terrorism and Human Rights in New Zealand*. Christchurch: New Zealand Law Foundation (also available online at http://www.lawfoundation.org.nz/ publications).

Conte, Alex, and Wynn-Williams, Sarah. 2003. Declarations of Inconsistency under the Bill of Rights. Part I: Judicial Jurisdiction, Discretion or Obligation? 6 *Human Rights Law and Practice* 243.

Cooray, Mark. 1985. *Human Rights in Australia* (online publication: http://mywebsite.bigpond. com/smartboard/rights).

Elkind, Jerome. 1990. The Optional Protocol: A Bill of Rights for New Zealand. *New Zealand Law Review* 96.

Fenwick, Helen. 2002. *Civil Liberties and Human Rights*. London: 3rd edition, Cavendish Publishing Limited.

Flynn, Martin. 2003. *Human Rights in Australia. Treaties, Statutes and Cases*. Sydney: Lexis-Nexis Butterworths.

Gaze, Beth, and Jones, Melinda. 1990. *Law, Liberty and Australian Democracy*. Sydney: The Law Book Company Limited.

Hanks, Peter. 1996. *Constitutional Law in Australia*. Sydney: 2nd edition, LexisNexis Butterworths.

Hogg, Peter. 2004. *Constitutional Law of Canada*. Ontario: Thomson Carswell.

Joseph, Philip. 2000. Constitutional Law. *New Zealand Law Review* 301.

Joseph, Philip. 2001. *Constitutional and Administrative Law in New Zealand* (Wellington: 2nd ed, Brookers).

Kildea, Paul. 2003. The Bill of Rights debate in Australian Political Culture. *Australian Journal of Human Rights* 7.

McClelland, Robert. 2008. Speech given by Attorney-General for Australia, The Hon Robert McClelland MP (presented at the United Nations Association of Australia Conference *60th Anniversary of the Signing of the Universal Declaration of Human Rights*, 10 December 2008, Sydney, Australia).

Rishworth, Paul, Huscroft, Grant, Optican, Scott, and Mahoney, Richard. 2003. *The New Zealand Bill of Rights*. Oxford: Oxford University Press.

Ross, June. 1984. Limitations on Human Rights in International Law: Their Relevance to the Canadian Charter of Rights and Freedoms. 6(2) *Human Rights Quarterly* 180.

Shabas, William, and Olivier, Clémentine. 2003. United Kingdom Anti-Terrorist Legislation. In Doucet, Ghislaine (Ed). *Terrorism, Victims, and International Criminal Responsibility*. Paris: SOS Attentats.

Stone, Richard. 2008. *Textbook on Civil Liberties and Human Rights*. Oxford: 7th edition, Oxford University Press.

Thornton, GC. 1996. *Legislative Drafting*. Gateshead: 4th ed, Butterworths.

Tudor, P. 2000. Secondary Legislation: Second Class or Crucial? 21(3) *Statute Law Review* 149.

Williams, George. 2003. National Security, Terrorism and Bills of Rights. *Australian Journal of Human Rights* 13.

Part III

Chapter 12
Terrorism, Counter-Terrorism and International Law

The first and second parts of this text focussed upon terrorism and counter-terrorism, and then considered the subject of human rights law. The nature of terrorism and the associated problems with arriving at an internationally agree-upon definition of the term, which is both concise and comprehensive, have been considered. Part I of the text outlined the international framework for countering terrorism, the means by which those international obligations are received into the domestic law of the four case study countries, and provided a synopsis of the corresponding domestic law on counter-terrorism in those countries. Part II of the text looked at international and regional human rights law, including the means by which rights might be limited to accommodate important objectives such as the countering of terrorism. The current chapter is the first in Part III of the text, which considers the relationship of terrorism and counter-terrorism with human rights. This chapter examines, in the main, the relationship between *terrorism* and international law, including human rights law.

Properly defined, a terrorist act will correspond to proscribed conduct under one of the universal terrorism-related conventions, or a serious crime under national law (accompanied by the cumulative characteristics in Security Council resolution 1566 (2004) – see Chap. 2, Sect. 2.3.6). Such conduct attacks the values that lie at the heart of the Charter of the United Nations: respect for human rights; the rule of law; rules of war that protect civilians; tolerance among people and nations; and the peaceful resolution of conflict.[1] Since States have a duty to protect their societies and to contribute to the maintenance of international peace and security, terrorism is something that must therefore be suppressed and countered by all members of the international community.[2]

---

[1] As identified, for example, in the Report of the High-level Panel on Threats, Challenges and Change, "A More Secure World: Our Shared Responsibility", UN Doc A/59/565 (2004), para 145.

[2] The latter obligation is set out, for example, within the purposes and principles of the Charter of the United Nations, articles 1 and 2.

A. Conte, *Human Rights in the Prevention and Punishment of Terrorism*,
DOI 10.1007/978-3-642-11608-7_12, © Springer-Verlag Berlin Heidelberg 2010

Depending on the particular circumstances surrounding any given terrorist act, terrorism not only impacts upon human rights and the rule of law but may also amount to an act of aggression or use of force within the meaning of article 39 of the UN Charter; an act committed during the course of an armed conflict; an international criminal law offence; and/or an act which has the result of precluding the actor's protection under international refugee law. Recognising this dynamic interplay between terrorism and international legal norms, this chapter considers the relationship between terrorism and human rights, armed conflict, international criminal and humanitarian law, and international refugee law. By doing so, Chap. 13 can focus on the more specific question of the interface between *counter*-terrorism and human rights, and the chapters that follow it can take into account the question of other international law issues where appropriate.

12.1   Terrorism, Human Rights, and International Peace and Security

As considered in Chap. 9, human rights are universal legal guarantees which protect individuals and groups against actions and omissions that interfere with fundamental freedoms, entitlements and human dignity. As the executive head of the United Nations, the Secretary-General has commented upon *counter-terrorism* and human rights within various documents, press releases and meetings. Prominent is one of the reports of former Secretary-General Kofi Anan entitled Uniting Against Terrorism, in which he identified the defence of human rights as having a central role in the fulfilment of all aspects of a counter-terrorism strategy.[3] This is a matter considered in more detail within Chap. 13.

The focus of this section is on the impact of *terrorism* upon human rights and the rule of law. Terrorism has a direct impact on the enjoyment of a number of human rights, in particular on human life, liberty, and physical integrity. Terrorist acts can destabilise governments, undermine civil society, jeopardise peace and security, threaten social and economic development and may negatively affect certain groups. All of these have a direct impact on the enjoyment of fundamental human rights, something recognised in a long line of General Assembly resolutions beginning in 1993 and entitled "Terrorism and Human Rights". Echoing many of the expressions of concern contained in the General Assembly's Declarations on Measures to Eliminate International Terrorism (considered in Chap. 3, Sect. 3.2.1), the preamble to the first of these resolutions spoke of the serious concern of the General Assembly at the gross violations of human rights perpetrated by terrorist groups.[4] Resolutions since 1995 did the same, adding that terrorism creates an

---

[3]Report of the Secretary-General, Uniting Against Terrorism: Recommendations for a Global Counter-terrorism Strategy, UN Doc A/60/825 (2006), para 5. See also Part VI of the Report.
[4]GA Res 48/122, UN GAOR, 48th Sess, 85th Plen Mtg, UN Doc A/Res/48/122 (1993).

environment that destroys the right of people to live in freedom from fear.[5] The preamble to the Assembly's resolution 56/160 (2001) added:[6]

> *Noting* the growing consciousness within the international community of the negative effects of terrorism in all its forms and manifestations on the full enjoyment of human rights and fundamental freedoms and on the establishment of the rule of law and domestic freedoms as enshrined in the Charter of the United Nations and the International Covenants on Human Rights.

The destructive impact of terrorism upon human rights and security has been recognised by the Security Council, the General Assembly and the predecessor to the Human Rights Council, the Commission on Human Rights. Member States have identified terrorism as something which:

- Has links with transnational organised crime, drug trafficking, money-laundering, and trafficking in arms as well as the illegal transfer of nuclear, chemical and biological materials;[7]
- Is linked to the consequent commission of serious crimes such as murder, extortion, kidnapping, assault, the taking of hostages, and robbery;[8]

---

[5]GA Res 50/186, UN GAOR, 50th Sess, 99th Plen Mtg, UN Doc A/Res/50/186 (1995) preambular paras 3, 4, 5 and 11, and operative para 2; GA Res 52/133, UN GAOR, 52nd Sess, 70th Plen Mtg, UN Doc A/Res/52/133 (1997) preambular paras 6, 7, 8 and 10, and operative para 3; GA Res 54/164, UN GAOR, 54th Sess, 83rd Plen Mtg, UN Doc A/Res/54/164 (1999) preambular paras 7, 8, 9 and 12, and operative para 3; GA Res 56/160, UN GAOR, 56th Sess, 88th Plen Mtg, UN Doc A/Res/56/160 (2001) preambular paras 11, 12 and 13; GA Res 58/174, UN GAOR, 58th Sess, 77th Plen Mtg, UN Doc A/Res/58/174 (2003) preambular paras 12, 13 and 14; and GA Res 59/195, UN GAOR, 59th Sess, 74th Plen Mtg, UN Doc A/Res/59/195 (2004) preambular paras 12 and 13.

[6]GA Res 56/160 (ibid). See further Koufa (2005, pp. 53–57).

[7]For resolutions of the Security Council, see: SC Res 1373, UN SCOR, 4385th Mtg, UN Doc S/Res/1373 (2001), para 4; SC Res 1456, UN SCOR, 4706th Mtg, UN Doc S/Res/1456 (2003), preambular paras 3 and 6; and SC Res 1540, UN SCOR, 4956th Mtg, UN Doc S/Res/1540 (2004), preambular para 8. By the General Assembly, see: GA Res 58/136, UN GAOR, 58th Sess, 77th Plen Mtg, UN Doc A/Res/58/136 (2004), preambular para 8; GA Res 61/86, UN GAOR, 61st Sess, 67th Plen Mtg, UN Doc A/Res/61/86 (2006), preambulara para 2; GA Res 62/33, UN GAOR, 62nd Sess, 61st Plen Mtg, UN Doc A/Res/62/33 (2008), preambular para 3; and GA Res 62/46, UN GAOR, 62nd Sess, 61st Plen Mtg, UN Doc A/Res/62/46 (2008), preambular para 3. For resolutions of the Commission on Human Rights, see: CHR Res 2001/37, UN Doc E/CN.4/Res/2001/37, preambular para 16; and CHR Res 2004/44, UN Doc E/CN.4/Res/2004/44, preambular para 7. See also the report of the Sub-Commission Special Rapporteur, Kalliope Koufa, Progress Report on Terrorism and Human Rights, UN Doc E/CN.4/Sub.2/2001/31, paras 104 and 105.

[8]For resolutions of the General Assembly, see: GA Res 48/122 (n 4) preambular para 7; GA Res 49/185, UN GAOR, 49th Sess, 94th Plen Mtg, UN Doc A/Res49/185 (1994), preambular para 9; GA Res 50/186 (n 5) preambular para 12 and operative para 2; GA Res 52/133 (n 5) preambular para 11; GA Res 54/164 (n 5) preambular para 13; GA Res 56/160 (n 5) preambular para 18; and GA Res 58/174 (n 5) para 12. For resolutions of the Commission on Human Rights, see: CHR Res 2001/37 (ibid) preambular para 16; and CHR Res 2004/44 (ibid) preambular para 7. See also Sub-Commission Special Rapporteur (ibid) paras 104 and 105.

- Endangers or takes innocent lives;[9]
- Creates an environment that destroys the freedom from fear of the people;[10]
- Threatens the dignity and security of human beings everywhere;[11]
- Has an adverse effect upon the establishment and maintenance of the rule of law;[12]
- Jeopardises fundamental freedoms;[13]
- Aims at the destruction of human rights;[14]

---

[9]For resolutions of the Security Council, see: SC Res 1269, UN SCOR, 54th Sess, 4053rd Mtg, UN Doc S/Res/1269 (1999), preambular para 1; and SC Res 1377, UN SCOR, 55th Sess, 4413rd Mtg, UN Doc S/Res/1377 (2001), Annex (Declaration), para 6. See also the first operative paragraphs of the following General Assembly resolutions: GA Res 3034 (XXVII), UN GAOR, 27th Sess, 2114th Plen Mtg, UN Doc A/Res/27/3034 (1972); GA Res 31/102, UN GAOR, 31st Sess, 99th Plen Mtg, UN Doc A/Res/31/102 (1976); GA Res 32/147, UN GAOR, 32nd Sess, 105th Plen Mtg, UN Doc A/Res/32/147 (1977); GA Res 34/145, UN GAOR, 34th Sess, 105th Plen Mtg, UN Doc A/Res/34/145 (1979); GA Res 36/109, UN GAOR, 36th Sess, UN Doc A/Res/36/109 (1981); GA Res 61/40, UN GAOR, 61st Sess, 64th Plen Mtg, UN Doc A/Res/61/40 (2007), preambular para 10; and GA Res 62/71, UN GAOR, 62nd Sess, 62nd Plen Mtg, UN Doc A/Res/62/71 (2008), preambular para 10. For resolutions of the Commission on Human Rights, see: CHR Res 2001/37 (n 7) para 2; and CHR Res 2004/44 (n 7) preambular para 7. See also Sub-Commission Special Rapporteur (n 7) para 109.

[10]For resolutions of the General Assembly, see: GA Res 50/186 (n 5) preambular para 5; GA Res 52/133 (n 5) preambular para 8; GA Res 54/164 (n 5) preambular para 9; and GA Res 61/40 (ibid) para 4. For resolutions of the Commission on Human Rights, see: CHR Res 2001/37 (n 7) preambular para 12, and operative para 2; and CHR Res 2004/44 (n 7) preambular para 12. See also Sub-Commission on Human Rights Resolution 2001/18, UN Doc E/CN.4/Sub.2/Res/2001/18, preambular para 8.

[11]See SC Res 1377 (n 9) Annex (Declaration), para 6. See also CHR Res 2001/37 (n 7) para 2; and Sub-Commission Special Rapporteur (n 7) para 107.

[12]See GA Res 56/160 (n 5) preambular para 24. For resolutions of the Commission on Human Rights, see: CHR Res 2001/37 (n 7) preambular para 13, and operative para 1; and CHR Res 2004/44 (n 7) preambular para 13. See also Sub-Commission on Human Rights Resolution 2001/18 (n 10) preambular para 9.

[13]See the following resolutions of the General Assembly: GA Res 48/122 (n 4) para 1; GA Res 49/185 (n 8) para 1; GA Res 50/186 (n 5) para 2; GA Res 52/133 (n 5) para 3; GA Res 56/160 (n 5) preambular para 24 and para 3; GA Res 58/174 (n 5) para 1; GA Res 61/171, UN GAOR, 61st Sess, 81st Plen Mtg, UN Doc A/Res/61/171 (2007), preambular para 11; and GA Res 62/159, UN GAOR, 62nd Sess, 76th Plen Mtg, UN Doc A/Res/62/159 (2008), preambular para 9. For resolutions of the Commission on Human Rights, see: CHR Res 2001/37 (n 7) preambular para 23, and operative para 1; and CHR Res 2004/44 (n 7) preambular para 12, and operative para 1.

[14]As recognised in the first-stated Declaration on Measures to Eliminate International Terrorism, adopted under GA Res 49/60, UN GAOR, 49th Sess, 84th Plen Mtg, UN Doc A/Res/49/60 (1994), operative para 2. For resolutions of the General Assembly, see also: GA Res 48/122 (n 4) para 1; GA Res 49/185 (n 8) para 1; GA Res 50/186 (n 5) para 2; GA Res 52/133 (n 5) para 3; GA Res 56/160 (n 5) preambular para 24 and operative para 3; GA Res 58/174 (n 5) para 1; GA Res 61/171 (ibid) preambular para 11; and GA Res 62/159 (ibid) preambular para 9. For resolutions of the Commission on Human Rights, see: CHR Res 2001/37 (n 7) preambular para 23, and operative para 1; and CHR Res 2004/44 (n 7) preambular para 12 and 23, and operative para 1. See also Report of the High-level Panel on Threats, Challenges and Change (n 1) para 145.

- Undermines pluralistic civil society;[15]
- Aims at the destruction of the democratic bases of society;[16]
- Destabilises legitimately constituted governments;[17]
- Has adverse consequences upon the economic and social development of States;[18]
- Constitutes a grave violation of the purpose and principles of the United Nations;[19]
- Jeopardises friendly relations among States;[20]
- Has a pernicious impact upon relations of co-operation among States, including co-operation for development;[21]

---

[15]As recognised in the first-stated Declaration on Measures to Eliminate International Terrorism (ibid) operative para 2. For resolutions of the General Assembly, see also: GA Res 48/122 (n 4) para 1; GA Res 49/185 (n 8) para 1; GA Res 50/186 (n 5) para 2; GA Res 52/133 (n 5) para 3; GA Res 56/160 (n 5) preambular para 24 and operative para 3; and GA Res 58/174 (n 5) para 1. For resolutions of the Commission on Human Rights, see: CHR Res 2001/37 (n 7) para 1; and CHR Res 2004/44 (n 7) para 1. See also Report of the High-Level Panel (n 1) para 145.

[16]As recognised in the first-stated Declaration on Measures to Eliminate International Terrorism (n 14) operative para 2. For resolutions of the General Assembly, see also: GA Res 48/122 (n 4) para 1; GA Res 49/185 (n 8) para 1; GA Res 50/186 (n 5) para 2; GA Res 52/133 (n 5) para 3; GA Res 56/160 (n 5) para 3; GA Res 58/174 (n 5) para 1; GA Res 61/171 (n 13) preambulara para 11; and GA Res 62/159 (n 13) preambular para 9. For resolutions of the Commission on Human Rights, see: CHR Res 2001/37 (n 7) preambular para 13; and CHR Res 2004/44 (n 7) preambular para 13, and operative para 1. See also Sub-Commission on Human Rights Resolution 2001/18 (n 10) preambular para 9.

[17]For resolutions of the General Assembly, see: GA Res 48/122 (n 4) para 1; GA Res 49/185 (n 8) para 1; GA Res 50/186 (n 5) para 2; GA Res 52/133 (n 5) para 3; GA Res 56/160 (n 5) para 3; GA Res 58/174 (n 5) para 1; GA Res 61/171 (n 13) preambulara para 11; and GA Res 62/159 (n 13) preambular para 9. For resolutions of the Commission on Human Rights, see also: CHR Res 2001/37 (n 7) para 1; and CHR Res 2004/44 (n 7) para 1.

[18]See SC Res 1377 (n 9) Annex (Declaration), para 6. For resolutions of the General Assembly, see: GA Res 48/122 (n 4) para 1; GA Res 49/185 (n 8) para 1; GA Res 50/186 (n 5) para 2; GA Res 52/133 (n 5) para 3; GA Res 56/160 (n 5) para 3; and GA Res 58/174 (n 5) para 1. For resolutions of the Commission on Human Rights, see: CHR Res 2001/37 (n 7) para 1; and CHR Res 2004/44 (n 7) para 1.

[19]For resolutions of the Security Council, see: SC Res 1189, UN SCOR, 3915th Mtg, UN Doc S/Res/1189 (1998), preambular para 2; SC Res 1373 (n 7) para 5; and SC Res 1377 (n 9) Annex (Declaration), para 5. See also GA Res 51/210, UN GAOR, 51st Sess, 88th Plen Mtg, UN Doc 51/210 (1996), para 2. See also Report of the High-level Panel on Threats (n 1) para 145.

[20]See the first operative paras of the following resolutions of the General Assembly: GA Res 38/130, UN GAOR, 38th Sess, 101st Plen Mtg, UN Doc A/Res/38/130 (1983); GA Res 40/61, UN GAOR, 40th Sess, 108th Plen Mtg, UN Doc A/Res/40/61 (1985); GA Res 42/159, UN GAOR, 42nd Sess, 94th Plen Mtg, UN Doc A/Res/42/159 (1987); GA Res 44/29, UN GAOR, 44th Sess, 72nd Plen Mtg, UN Doc A/Res/44/29 (1989); and GA Res 51/210 (ibid). See also Report of the High-level Panel on Threats (n 1) para 145.

[21]See GA Res 38/130 (ibid) para 1. See also the third operative paras of the following resolutions of the General Assembly: GA Res 40/61 (ibid); GA Res 42/159 (ibid); and GA Res 44/29 (ibid).

- Threatens the territorial integrity and security of States;[22]
- Is a threat to international peace and security; and[23]
- Must be suppressed for the maintenance of international peace and security.[24]

12.2   Terrorism and Armed Conflict

The relationship between terrorism and armed conflict, and the applicable norms of international law, is one of the most challenging issues facing international law compliance today. It is first relevant to recognise that, as well as conduct by non-State actors, States can themselves perpetrate or be responsible for acts of terrorism, either within their own territory, against other States, or within the territory of other States.[25] In considering terrorism and armed conflict, it is necessary to distinguish between two categories of international legal rules: those rules governing the use of force between States (*jus ad bellum*); and those governing the actual conduct of hostilities (*jus in bello*, also known as international humanitarian law).

---

[22]For resolutions of the Security Council, see: SC Res 1189 (n 19) preambular para 2; and SC Res 1377 (n 9) Annex (Declaration), para 3. See also the first-stated Declaration on Measures to Eliminate International Terrorism (n 14) preambular para 3 and operative para 1. For resolutions of the General Assembly, see also: GA Res 48/122 (n 4) para 1; GA Res 49/185 (n 8) para 1; GA Res 61/171 (n 13) preambulara para 11; and GA Res 62/159 (n 13) preambular para 9. For resolutions of the Commission on Human Rights, see: CHR Res 2001/37 (n 7) para 1; and CHR Res 2004/44 (n 7) para 1.

[23]See: SC Res 1189 (n 19); preambular para 2; SC Res 1368, UN SCOR, 4370th Mtg, UN Doc S/Res/1368 (2001) preambular para 1; SC Res 1373 (n 7) preambular para 3; SC Res 1377 (n 9) preambular para 2; SC Res 1390, UN SCOR, 4452nd Mtg, UN Doc S/Res/1390 (2001), preambular para 9; SC Res 1438, UN SCOR, 4624th Mtg, UN Doc S/Res/1438 (2002), preambular para 2; SC Res 1440, UN SCOR, 4632nd Mtg, UN Doc S/Res/1440 (2002), preambular para 2; SC Res 1450, UN SCOR, 4667th Mtg, UN Doc S/Res/1450 (2002), preambular para 4; SC Res 1455, UN SCOR, 4686th Mtg, UN Doc S/Res/1455 (2003), preambular para 7; SC Res 1456, UN SCOR, 4688th Mtg, UN Doc S/Res/1456 (2003), preambular para 1; SC Res 1526, UN SCOR, 4908th Mtg, UN Doc S/Res/1526 (2004), preambular para 3; SC Res 1530, UN SCOR, 4923rd Mtg, UN Doc S/Res/1530 (2004), preambular para 2; SC Res 1535, UN SCOR, 4936th Mtg, S/Res/1535 (2004), preambular para 2; SC Res 1566, UN SCOR, 5053rd Mtg, UN Doc S/Res/1566 (2004), preambular para 7; SC Res 1611, UN SCOR, 5233rd, UN Doc S/Res/1611 (2005), preambular para 2; SC Res 1617, UN SCOR, 5244th Mtg, UN Doc S/Res/1617 (2005), preambular para 2; SC Res 1618, UN SCOR, 5246th Mtg, UN Doc S/Res/1618 (2005), preambular para 4; SC Res 1735, UN SCOR, 5609th Mtg, UN Doc S/Res/1735 (2006), preambular para 2; SC Res 1787, UN SCOR 5795th Mtg, UN Doc S/Res/1787 (2007), preambular para 2; SC Res 1805, UN SCOR, 5856th Mtg, UN Doc 1805 (2008), preambular para 1; and SC Res 1822, UN SCOR, 5928th Mtg, UN Doc 1822 (2008), preambular para 2.

[24]For resolutions of the Security Council, see: SC Res 1189 (n 19) preambular para 3; and SC Res 1269 (n 9) preambular para 8.

[25]As in the case of the bombing of the Rainbow Warrior in Auckland harbour in New Zealand by French agents: see Chap. 4, Sect. 4.1.3.

12.2.1 The Use of Force Between States (Jus Ad Bellum)

The Charter of the United Nations contains a general prohibition under article 2(4) against the use of force, or threat of the use of force, between States. This prohibition is recognised by many as representing a peremptory norm of international law, meaning that force between States is only ever permitted within the limited exceptions contained within the Charter.[26] The UN Charter provides for two exceptions to the general prohibition against the use of force between States:

- The first is where the Security Council authorises the use of military action under Chapter VII of the Charter. Where the Security Council determines that a situation amounts to a threat to the peace, breach of the peace, or act of aggression, it must decide what measures are to be taken under articles 41 and 42 to maintain or restore international peace and security. Article 41 of the Charter allows the Security Council to impose non-military sanctions, such a trade or arms embargos. Following the indictment of Usama bin Laden and Al-Qa'ida for the 1998 bombings of the US embassies in Kenya and Tanzania, and the request by the United States to the Taliban to surrender them for trial, for example, Security Council resolution 1267 (1999) imposed a travel ban and arms embargo against the Taliban and Al-Qa'ida, and obliged States to freeze funds and other financial resources controlled by or on their behalf of the Taliban.[27] Where non-military sanctions fail to achieve the desired result, however, the Security Council is able to authorise the use of military force under article 42 of the Charter.[28]
- The second exception to the prohibition against the use of force is the codified and expanded right of inherent and collective self defence, as set out in article 51 of the Charter. Article 51 retains the inherent right of a State to act in defence of itself, and extends the principle to one of 'collective self-defence', whereby members of the United Nations are also permitted to use force in the defence of a State seeking the assistance of others to defend itself.[29] The military intervention in Afghanistan in 2002, following the September 11 terrorist attacks in the United States, for example, was undertaken in reliance upon article 51.[30]

---

[26]See, for example, the judgment of Sir Ivor Jennings in *Case Concerning Military and Paramilitary Activities in and Against Nicaragua (Nicaragua v United States), Merits Phase* [1986] ICJ Reports 4, 518–524; and Henkin et al (1980, p. 910).

[27]SC Res 1267, UN SCOR, 4051st Mtg, UN Doc S/Res/1267 (1999).

[28]For example, following the unsuccessful result of the trade sanctions issued against Iraq following its invasion of Kuwait in 1990, the Security Council gave Iraq a final opportunity to withdraw from Kuwait by 15 January 1991, failing which military intervention was authorised: SC Res 678, UN SCOR, 2963rd Mtg, UN Doc S/Res/678 (1990).

[29]This relationship with, and extension of, customary international law at the time of the adoption of the United Nations Charter is discussed by the International Court of Justice in the *Nicaragua v United States* (n 26) pp. 534–536.

[30]For an analysis of this intervention and the issues arising from it Conte (2005, Chap. 6).

The significance of these rules in the context of terrorism is important. Because terrorism has been identified by the Security Council as a threat to international peace and security (see Sect. 12.1 above), the commission of acts of international terrorism by States is prohibited.[31] Included within this prohibition is the support by a State of such conduct by a non-State actor, where that level of support would incur international responsibility.[32] The further consequence of the accepted rules on the use of force is that any military action by a State in response to an act of terrorism must either be consequent to an express authorisation by the Security Council, or in response to a terrorist act which is attributable to a State and constitutes an armed attack within the terms of article 51. These were critical issues in the 11 September 2001, attacks against the United States by Al-Qa'ida and the subsequent military intervention against Afghanistan in 2002.[33]

Contrasting positions are held on the question of whether the pre-Charter right to anticipatory self-defence continues to exist as an exception to the prohibition against the use of force between States.[34] Following the events of 9/11, anticipatory self-defence was used as the primary basis, for example, upon which the USA Bush Administration adopted its policy of pre-emptive strikes against States harbouring or supporting terrorists.[35] The problems with that policy are numerous. Even if the doctrine of anticipatory self-defence did survive the Charter, for example, it requires a State to demonstrate necessity and proportionality. While proportionality cannot be prospectively assessed, it can be said that the Bush doctrine falls outside the requirement of necessity, the Security Council having rejected (at the very least) the concept of *pre-emptive* as opposed to *preventive* action.[36] Britain was required to justify its conduct, in the *Caroline Case*, by showing that it acted out of "necessity of self-defence, instant, overwhelming, leaving no choice of means, and no moment for deliberation".[37] In contrast, the US National Security Strategy claims a right to pre-emptive self-defence where there is "uncertainty" about the time or place of an attack and therefore takes a step beyond the already controversial concept of anticipatory self-defence.[38]

In the context of inter-state conflicts throughout the twentieth century, it is interesting to note the General Comments of the Human Rights Committee

---

[31]See further Charney (2001); Dinstein (2002); and Franck (2001).

[32]See the Articles on the Responsibility of States for Internationally Wrongful Acts, adopted under GA Res 56/83, UN GAOR, 56th Sess, 85th Plen Mtg, UN Doc A/Res/56/83 (2001).

[33]See Cassese (1989); Conte (2005, pp. 41–51); Greenwood (2002); and Gill (2002).

[34]See, for example: Arend (2003); and Brownlie (1963, p. 275).

[35]See the National Security Strategy of the United States of America (2002).

[36]United Nations, Repertory of Practice of United Nations Organs Supplement No 6, Volume III (1979–1984) Article 51, para 33.

[37]*Caroline Case*, 29 British Forces and State Papers (BFSP) 1137–1138; 30 BFSP 195–196. The *Caroline Case* was later confirmed by the International Military Tribunal at Nuremberg, where it had been argued that the German invasion of Norway in 1940 was an act of self-defence in the face of an imminent Allied landing there. The Tribunal said that preventive action in foreign territory is justified only in the circumstances cited by Mr Webster in the *Caroline Case*: (1947) 41 *American Journal of International Law* 204. See also Jennings 1938.

[38]For consideration of the policy and its legality, see Conte (2005, Chap. 5).

(established under the International Covenant on Civil and Political Rights – see Chap. 9, Sect. 9.2.3) pertaining to the use of force between states. In its General Comment No 6, the Committee described war and other acts of mass violence as a scourge of humanity that takes the lives of thousands of innocent human beings every year.[39] It emphasised the fact that, under the Charter of the United Nations, the threat or use of force by any State against another, except in exercise of the inherent right of self-defence, is prohibited. The Committee considered that States therefore have a "supreme duty" to prevent wars, acts of genocide and other acts of mass violence causing arbitrary loss of life. Every effort they make to avert the danger of war, especially thermonuclear war, and to strengthen international peace and security would constitute the most important condition and guarantee for the safeguarding of the right to life, the Committee said in its General Comment 6.

12.2.2 International Humanitarian Law (Jus In Bello)

International humanitarian law is described by the UN Office of the High Commissioner for Human Rights as a body of principles and norms intended to limit human suffering in times of armed conflict and to prevent atrocities.[40] It comprises international treaty and customary law and seeks to achieve two main purposes: first, to protect persons who are not, or are no longer, taking part in the hostilities (i.e. sick, wounded or shipwrecked combatants, prisoners of war and civilians); and also to restrict the method and means of warfare between parties to a conflict. Following the Second World War, and building upon the 1899 and 1907 Hague Conventions, duties on States and individuals in this regard were codified under the four Geneva Conventions of 1949, latter added to under their two Additional Protocols of 1977, as well as a number of other international instruments aimed at reducing human suffering in armed conflict.[41] Many provisions of these treaties

---

[39]Human Rights Committee, General Comment 6: Article 6, UN Doc HR\GEN\1\Rev.1 at 6 (1994), para 2.

[40]Office of the High Commissioner for Human Rights, *Human Rights. A Basic Handbook for UN Staff*, p. 6.

[41]Geneva Convention for the Amelioration of the Condition of the Wounded and Sick in Armed Forces in the Field (First Geneva Convention), opened for signature 12 August 1949, 75 UNTS 32 (entered into force 21 October 1950); Geneva Convention for the Amelioration of the Condition of the Wounded, Sick and Shipwrecked Members of Armed Forces at Sea (Second Geneva Convention), opened for signature 12 August 1949, 75 UNTS 85 (entered into force 21 October 1950); Geneva Convention Relative to the Treatment of Prisoners of War (Third Geneva Convention), opened for signature 12 August 1949, 75 UNTS 136 (entered into force 21 October 1950); Geneva Convention Relative to the Protection of Civilian Persons in Time of War (Fourth Geneva Convention), opened for signature 12 August 1949, 75 UNTS 288 (entered into force 21 October 1950); and Protocol Additional to the Geneva Conventions of 12 August 1949 and Relating to the Protection of Victims of International Armed Conflicts (First Protocol), opened for signature 8 June 1977, 1125 UNTS 4 (entered into force 7 December 1978); and Protocol Additional to the Geneva Conventions of 12 August 1949 and Relating to the Protection of Victims of Non-International Armed Conflicts (Second Protocol), opened for signature 8 June 1977, 1125 UNTS 610 (entered into force 7 December 1978).

are now recognised as forming part of customary international law.[42] The Geneva Conventions and *Nuremberg List* of war crimes have been subsequently used as the basis for the crimes set out in the Rome Statute of the International Criminal Court.[43]

12.2.2.1 International Humanitarian Law and Terrorism

There is no explicit definition of 'terrorism' in international humanitarian law. However, international humanitarian law prohibits many acts committed in armed conflict which would be considered terrorist acts if they were committed in times of peace.[44] For example, deliberate acts of violence against civilians and civilian objects constitute war crimes under international law for which, according to the principle of universal jurisdiction, individuals may be prosecuted by all States. This rule derives from a fundamental principle of international humanitarian law related to the protection of civilians in armed conflict, the principle of distinction. According to this principle, all parties to a conflict must at all times distinguish between civilians and combatants. In essence, this means that attacks may be directed only at military objectives – those objects which by their nature, location, purpose or use make an effective contribution to military action and whose total or partial destruction, capture or neutralisation, in the circumstances ruling at the time, offers a definite military advantage.

Civilians may only be targeted for such time as they participate directly in the hostilities. Article 27 of the Fourth Geneva Convention otherwise demands that civilians be "humanely treated, and protected especially against all acts of violence or threats thereof and against insults and public curiosity". Indiscriminate attacks are strictly prohibited under international humanitarian law. This includes attacks which are not directed at a specific military objective, employ a method or means of combat which cannot be directed at a specific military objective, or employ a method or means of combat the effects of which cannot be limited as required by international humanitarian law, and consequently are of a nature to strike military objectives and civilians or civilian objects without distinction.

---

[42]The International Court of Justice has referred to the Conventions as representing "general principles of humanitarian law", i.e. customary international law on the subject of *jus in bello*: see *Nicaragua v United States of America* (n 26) paras 125–220. See also Henckaerts and Doswald-Beck (2004).

[43]Rome Statute of the International Criminal Court, opened for signature 17 July 1998, 2187 UNTS 90 (entered into force 1 July 2002).

[44]See International Committee of the Red Cross, "International humanitarian law and terrorism: questions and answers", online: http://www.icrc.org/Web/Eng/siteeng0.nsf/html/5YNLEV. See also Bos (2002) and Roberts (2002).

International humanitarian law also specifically prohibits "measures of terrorism" or "acts of terrorism". These prohibitions aim to highlight the individual criminal accountability and protect against collective punishment and "all measures of intimidation or of terrorism".[45] More specifically, "acts or threats of violence the primary purpose of which is to spread terror among the civilian population" are strictly prohibited under international humanitarian law (see Chap. 3, Sect. 3.3).[46] According to the International Committee of the Red Cross, while even a lawful attack on a military objective may spread fear among civilians, these provisions seek to prohibit attacks that specifically aim to terrorise civilians, for example campaigns of shelling or sniping of civilians in urban areas.[47]

Article 34 of the Fourth Geneva Convention prohibits the taking of hostages, hostage-taking being one of the well-recognised discreet terrorist offences under the universal terrorism-related conventions (see Chap. 3, Sect. 3.1.1.3).[48] Also, although Common Article 3 of the Geneva Conventions does not use the word "terrorism", it prohibits comparable conduct against persons taking no active part in hostilities, i.e. violence to life and person, in particular murder of all kinds, mutilation, cruel treatment and torture, taking of hostages, and outrages upon personal dignity, in particular humiliating and degrading treatment.

As concluded by Veuthey, these various prohibitions are all the more significant since they apply to both State and non-State actors.[49] In its 1986 *Nicaragua* judgment, the International Court of Justice held that these general principles apply to all conflict situations.[50] The principal difficulty, however, is not in determining which rules are of relevance to terrorism and counter-terrorism, but when and to what extent those rules apply. As observed by Bos:[51]

> ...the law of war is not the only body of law potentially relevant to the consideration of terrorist actions. Acts committed by terrorists would indeed be violations of the laws of war, if they were conducted in the course of an international or internal armed conflict... However, acts of terrorism frequently occur in what is widely viewed as peacetime. The illegality of such acts has to be established first and foremost by reference to the national laws of States, international treaties on terrorism and related measures and other

---

[45]Geneva Convention Relative to the Protection of Civilian Persons in Time of War (n 41) article 33.

[46]First Protocol (n 41) article 13(2). See also common article 51(2) of both Additional Protocols.

[47]See International Committee of the Red Cross, "International humanitarian law and terrorism: questions and answers" (n 44).

[48]International Convention against the Taking of Hostages, opened for signature 18 December 1979, 1316 UNTS 205 (entered into force 3 June 1983), article 1.

[49]Veuthey (2003, p. 371).

[50]*Nicaragua v United States of America* (n 26).

[51]Bos (2002 p. 205).

relevant parts of international law that apply in peacetime as well as in wartime. For example, the rules relating to genocide, crimes against humanity and certain rules relating to human rights.

It is notable, also, that the Security Council has directed that all States members of the United Nations combat terrorism in compliance with international law, including international humanitarian law.[52]

12.2.2.2 International Humanitarian Law and Human Rights

International humanitarian law and human rights law were traditionally regarded as separate areas of international law.[53] It is now a well-established principle, however, that regardless of issues of classification, international human rights law continues to apply in armed conflict, subject only to certain permissible limitations in accordance with the strict requirements contained in international human rights treaties.[54] In the 1993 Vienna Declaration and Programme of Action, for example, the World Conference on Human Rights expressed deep concern about violations of human rights during armed conflicts, affecting the civilian population, especially women, children, the elderly and the disabled and stated:[55]

> The Conference therefore calls upon States and all parties to armed conflicts strictly to observe international humanitarian law, as set forth in the Geneva Conventions of 1949 and other rules and principles of international law, as well as minimum standards for protection of human rights, as laid down in international conventions.

In essence, the difference between the two bodies of law is that whilst human rights law protects the individual at all times, international humanitarian law is the *lex specialis* which applies only in situations of armed conflict. In affirming that the

---

[52]See, for example, SC Res 1624, UN SCOR, 5261st Mtg, UN Doc S/Res/1624 (2005), para 4. This is a point reiterated by the Special Rapporteur on the promotion and protection of human rights and fundamental freedoms while countering terrorism in his report, Mission to Israel, Including visit to occupied Palestinian territory, UN Doc A/HRC/6/17/Add.4 (2007), para 5.

[53]Office of the High Commissioner for Human Rights, *Human Rights. A Basic Handbook for UN Staff*, p. 7.

[54]As reiterated by the UN Special Rapporteur on human rights and counter-terrorism in his mission report on Israel (n 52), paras 8–9; and in his further report, Mission to the United States of America, UN Doc A/HRC/6/17/Add.3 (2007), para 7. See also Office of the High Commissioner for Human Rights, International Humanitarian Law and Human Rights, Fact Sheet No 13 (New York and Geneva: United Nations, 1991, available online at http://www.ohchr.org/Documents/Publications/FactSheet13en.pdf), p. 1.

[55]World Conference on Human Rights, Vienna Declaration and Programme of Action, UN Doc A/CONF.157/23 (1993), para 29. See also: Office of the High Commissioner for Human Rights in cooperation with the International Bar Association, *Human Rights in the Administration of Justice: A Manual on Human Rights for Judges, Prosecutors and Lawyers* (New York: United Nations, 2003), pp. 12–13; and Inter-American Commission on Human Rights, Recommendations of the Inter-American Commission on Human Rights for the Protection by OAS Member States of Human Rights in the Fight Against Terrorism (Washington, 8 May 2006), paras 6–7.

International Covenant on Civil and Political Rights (ICCPR) is applicable during armed conflicts, for example, the International Court of Justice stated that:[56]

> The right not arbitrarily to be deprived of one's life applies also in hostilities. The test of what constitutes an arbitrary deprivation of life, however, then must be determined by the applicable *lex specialis*, namely, the law applicable in armed conflict.

The 1993 World Conference on Human Rights reaffirmed, for example, that under human rights law and international humanitarian law, freedom from torture is a right which must be protected under all circumstances, including in times of internal or international disturbance or armed conflicts.[57] This is also a point made clear by the Human Rights Committee in its General Comment 31, where it referred to the continuous application of human rights, even during armed conflict, and stated that "while, in respect of certain Covenant rights, more specific rules of international humanitarian law may be specially relevant for the purposes of the interpretation of Covenant rights, both spheres of law are complementary, not mutually exclusive".[58] Noting the mutually reinforcing character of human rights and humanitarian law, the General Assembly called upon States in 2008 to:[59]

> ...cooperate fully, through constructive dialogue, to ensure the promotion and protection of all human rights for all and in promoting peaceful solutions to international problems of a humanitarian character and, in their actions towards that purpose, to comply strictly with the principles and norms of international law, inter alia, by fully respecting international human rights law and international humanitarian law.

This is a position confirmed by the International Court of Justice. The Court observed, in its advisory opinions on the *Legality of the Threat or Use of Nuclear Weapons*, and the *Legal Consequences of the Construction of a Wall in the Occupied Palestinian Territories*, that the protection of the ICCPR does not cease in times of war, except by operation of article 4 whereby certain provisions may be derogated from in a time of national emergency (see Chap. 10, Sect. 10.4).[60] The International Court more recently applied both human rights law and international humanitarian law to the armed conflict between the Congo and Uganda.[61] The conduct of States involved in armed conflict must therefore comply not only with international humanitarian law, but also with applicable international human rights law.

---

[56]*Military and Paramilitary Activities Case* (n 26) para 25.

[57]Vienna Declaration and Programme of Action (n 55) para 56.

[58]General Comment 31: Nature of the General Legal Obligations Imposed on States Parties to the Covenant UN Doc CCPR/C/21/Rev.1/Add.13 (2004), para 11.

[59]GA Res 62/166, UN GAOR, 62nd Sess, 76th Plen Mtg, UN Doc A/Res/62/166 (2008), para 6.

[60]*Legality of the Threat or Use of Nuclear Weapons, Advisory Opinion* (1996) ICJ Reports 226, at 240, para 25; and *Legal Consequences of the Construction of a Wall in the Occupied Palestinian Territories, Advisory Opinion* (2004) ICJ Reports, para 106. See also Human Rights Committee, General Comment 29: States of Emergency (Article 4), UN Doc CCPR/C/21/Rev.1/Add.11 (2001), para 3.

[61]*Armed Activities on the Territory of the Congo (Democratic Republic of the Congo v Uganda)*, Merits [2005] ICJ Reports, paras 216–220 and 345(3).

It should be noted that the Office of the High Commissioner for Human Rights is in the process of producing a handbook on international human rights law and international humanitarian law. The handbook will provide an overview of the sources of both bodies of law, as well as the 'fundamental standards of humanity'. It will reiterate the principles of dual applicability and *lex specialis* (as already discussed). The handbook will also look at the question of accountability and the rights of victims, as well as identifying dual protections applicable to certain rights including, for example, the right to personal security and the prohibition against torture.

12.3   Terrorism and International Criminal Law

International instruments and law concerning crimes at the international level can be thought of on two levels. At a more general level, international criminal law establishes obligations upon States to prosecute and punish certain conduct. International criminal law also requires States to take legislative action to establish offences or mechanisms for international cooperation. The international community has developed 13 conventions relating to the prevention and suppression of terrorism (see Chap. 3, Sect. 3.1). These instruments illustrate both features of international criminal law. They require States to criminalise specific conduct, ranging from the unlawful seizure of aircraft and the taking of hostages, to the financial support of terrorist and associated entities. The conventions also facilitate international cooperation by requiring States parties to establish certain jurisdictional criteria, including the principle *aut dedere aut judicare* (the 'extradite or prosecute' principle), and provide a legal basis for cooperation in the areas of extradition and mutual legal assistance.[62]

Depending upon the context in which a terrorist act occurs, acts of terrorism may also constitute offences under other instruments or norms of international criminal law. During the elaboration of the Rome Statute of the International Criminal Court, several delegations argued for the inclusion of a separate crime of terrorism in the jurisdiction of the International Criminal Court.[63] The majority of States disagreed, however, precisely because of the issue of the definition. The Final Act of the Diplomatic Conference of Plenipotentiaries on the Establishment of the ICC, adopted in Rome on 17 July 1998, recommended that a Review Conference, which may take place seven years following the entry into force of the Statute, in 2009, should consider the inclusion of several crimes within the jurisdiction of the Court, including terrorism, with a view to arriving at an acceptable definition.[64]

---

[62]On the importance of international legal cooperation to the countering of terrorist conduct, see Maged (2002).

[63]Rome Statute of the International Criminal Court, opened for signature 17 July 1998, 2187 UNTS 90 (entered into force 1 July 2002).

[64]Reflected within the Rome Statute (ibid) article 123(1).

Although the Rome Statute does not include the crime of terrorism as a separate crime, it does contain various offences which may include terrorist conduct, depending on the particular facts and circumstances of each case. A terrorist act might constitute a crime against humanity, an offence defined under article 7 of the Statute to include certain acts committed as part of a widespread or systematic attack directed against any civilian population, with knowledge of the attack.[65] War crimes, as defined under article 8 of the Rome Statute, may also be applicable including, for example, the deliberate or indiscriminate killing of (or causing great suffering or serious bodily injury to) a person protected under the Geneva Conventions.

The international criminal law provisions against terrorism have also been addressed in practice by international tribunals. In 2003, the International Criminal Tribunal for the Former Yugoslavia convicted, for the first time, an individual for his responsibility for the war crime of terror against the civilian population in Sarajevo, under article 3 of its Statute.[66] The Court concluded that the crime of terror against the civilian population is constituted of elements common to other war crimes. Drawing from the International Convention for the Suppression of the Financing of Terrorism,[67] the Court added the following three requirements:[68]

1. Acts of violence directed against the civilian population or individual civilians not taking direct part in hostilities causing death or serious injury to body or health within the civilian population.
2. The offender wilfully made the civilian population or individual civilians not taking direct part in hostilities the object of those acts of violence.
3. The above offence was committed with the primary purpose of spreading terror among the civilian population.

12.4 Terrorism and International Refugee Law

International refugee law is the body of law which provides a legal framework for the protection of refugees by defining the term 'refugee', setting out States' obligations to them, and establishing standards for their treatment. Aspects of international refugee law also relate to persons seeking asylum. The 1951

---

[65]Greenwood (2002, p. 305) (n 15). In 2001, the then UN High Commissioner for Human Rights described the terrorist attacks which occurred in the United States on 11 September 2001 as a crime against humanity. See also Duffy (2005, pp. 73–95).

[66]See the Statute of the International Criminal Tribunal for the Former Yugoslavia, as initially adopted by the Security Council under SC Res 827, UN SCOR, 3217th Mtg, UN Doc S/Res/827 (1993).

[67]International Convention for the Suppression of the Financing of Terrorism, opened for signature 10 January 2000, 2179 UNTS 232 (entered into force 10 April 1992).

[68]*Prosecutor v Galic*, Case No IT-98-29-T (Judgment of the Trial Chamber, 5 December 2003), para 133.

Convention relating to the Status of Refugees and its 1967 Protocol are the two universal instruments in the field of international refugee law.[69] The Convention and its Protocol incorporate a system of checks and balances that are able of taking account of the security interests of States and host communities while protecting the rights of persons who, unlike other categories of foreigners, no longer enjoy the protection of their country of origin.

It has already been mentioned that the Security Council has obliged States, under its resolution 1373 (2001) to take a number of measures to prevent terrorist activities and to criminalise various forms of terrorist conduct (see Chap. 3, Sect. 3.2.2.3). The resolution touches upon a number of issues related to immigration and refugee status. States are required, for example, to prevent the movement of terrorists by implementing effective border controls and take measures to secure the integrity of identity papers and travel documents (para 2(g)). States are also called upon to take measures to ensure that refugee status is not granted to asylum-seekers that have planned, facilitated or participated in the commission of terrorist acts (para 3(f)), and to ensure that refugee status is not abused by perpetrators, organisers or facilitators of terrorist acts (para 3(g)).

It should be noted that resolution 1373 (2001) did not introduce new obligations into international refugee law. The 1951 Convention, when properly implemented, ensures that international refugee protection is not extended to those who have induced, facilitated or perpetrated terrorist acts. The UN High Commissioner for Refugees (UNHCR) has endorsed the position that those responsible for committing terrorist acts must not be permitted to manipulate refugee mechanisms in order to find safe haven or achieve impunity.[70] The framework of international refugee law contains a number of provisions aimed at guarding against abuse and is thus able to respond to possible exploitation of refugee mechanisms by those responsible for terrorist acts.

First, refugee status may only be granted to those who fulfill the criteria of the refugee definition contained in article 1A of the Convention; that is, those who have a "well-founded fear of being persecuted for reasons of race, religion, nationality, membership of a particular social group or political opinion". In many cases, persons responsible for terrorist acts may not fear persecution for a Convention reason, but rather may be fleeing legitimate prosecution for criminal acts they have committed.

Secondly, according to article 1F of the Convention, persons who would otherwise meet the refugee criteria of article 1A are to be excluded from international refugee protection if there are serious reasons for considering that they have

---

[69]Convention relating to the Status of Refugees, opened for signature 28 July 1951, 189 UNTS 150 (entered into force 21 April 1954); and Protocol relating to the Status of Refugees, opened for signature 31 January 1967, 606 UNTS 267 (entered into force 4 October 1967).

[70]See, for example, the following reports of the UN High Commissioner for Refugees: "Ten Refugee Protection Concerns in the Aftermath of September 11" (October 2001); and "Addressing Security Concerns with Undermining Refugee Protection – UNHCR's perspective" (November 2001).

committed a war crime, a crime against humanity, a serious non-political crime outside the country of refuge prior to admission to that country as a refugee, or have been guilty of acts contrary to the purposes and principles of the United Nations. Particularly relevant is article 1F(b), which relates to the commission of a serious non-political crime by an asylum-seeker prior to the person's admission to the country of refuge. Acts which bear the characteristics of terrorism (see Chap. 2, Sect. 2.3) will almost invariably amount to serious non-political crimes. The UNHCR has issued guidelines on the application of exclusion clauses under the Convention noting, in particular, their exceptional nature and the need for their scrupulous application.[71]

While indications of an asylum-seeker's involvement in acts of terrorism would make it necessary to examine the applicability of article 1F, international refugee law requires an assessment of the context and circumstances of the individual case in a fair and efficient procedure before any decision is taken. Any summary rejection of asylum-seekers, including at borders or points of entry, may amount to *refoulement*, which is prohibited by international refugee and human rights law. All persons have the right to seek asylum.[72]

Thirdly, persons who have been recognised as refugees, as well as asylum-seekers who are awaiting a determination of their claims, are bound to conform to the laws and regulations of their host country, as reflected within article 2 of the Convention. If they do not do so, they may be prosecuted to the full extent of the law.

In addition, it is also relevant that exceptions to the principle of *non-refoulement* exist under article 33(2). Denial of protection from refoulement and return to the country of origin is foreseen in cases where there are reasonable grounds for regarding a refugee as a danger to the security of the country in which the person is, or, if having been convicted of a particularly serious crime, constitutes a danger to the community of the host State. Finally, the Convention provides for the possibility of expulsion to a third country on national security grounds under article 32. Implementation of either of these articles may only be carried out following a decision taken by a competent authority in accordance with due process of law, including the right to be heard and the right of appeal. The application of either article 32 or 33(2) is also subject to the various other human rights obligations of the State.

In cases where a person has already been granted refugee status, such status may be cancelled where there are grounds for considering that a person should not have been granted refugee status. This is the case where there are indications that, at the time of the initial decision, the applicant did not meet the inclusion criteria of the

---

[71]See: UN High Commissioner for Refugees, "Guidelines on International Protection: Application of the Exclusion Clauses: Article 1F of the 1951 Convention relating to the Status of Refugees", UN Doc HCR/GIP/03/05 (2003); and "Background Note on the Application of the Exclusion Clauses: Article 1F of the 1951 Convention relating to the Status of Refugees" (2003).

[72]See the Universal Declaration of Human Rights, adopted under General Assembly Resolution 217(III), UN GAOR, 3rd Session, 183rd Plenary Meeting (1948), article 14.

Convention, or that an exclusion clause of that Convention should have been applied to him or her. This might include evidence that the person committed terrorist acts.[73] Cancellation of refugee status is in keeping with the object and purpose of the Convention if it is established, by proper procedures, that person did not fall within the refugee definition at time of recognition.

12.5   Conclusions

Properly defined, a terrorist act will correspond to proscribed conduct under one of the universal terrorism-related conventions, or a serious crime under national law. Depending on the particular circumstances surrounding any given terrorist act, terrorism also impacts upon human rights and the rule of law and may in addition amount to: an act of aggression or use of force within the meaning of article 39 of the UN Charter; an act committed during the course of an armed conflict, and thus impacted upon by international humanitarian law; an international criminal law offence, whether under the universal terrorism-related conventions or the Statute of the International Criminal Court; and/or an act which has the result of precluding the actor's protection under international refugee law. There is therefore a dynamic interaction between terrorism and different, and sometimes overlapping, sets of international law norms.

What is clear is that terrorism attacks the values that lie at the heart of the Charter of the United Nations: respect for human rights; the rule of law; rules of war that protect civilians; tolerance among people and nations; and the peaceful resolution of conflict. The Security Council has itself pronounced that terrorism is (or, at least, may be) a threat to international peace and security and must therefore be suppressed for the maintenance of international peace and security. Since States have a duty to protect their societies and to contribute to the maintenance of international peace and security, terrorism is something that must therefore be suppressed and countered by all members of the international community.

Also clear is that terrorism does not create an additional justification for the use of force between States, but can instead be dealt with under the existing international law framework concerning *jus ad bellum*. While States are bound by the *jus cogens* prohibition against the use of force, the UN Charter allows for two exceptions to this. The first involves military action authorised by the Security Council where the Council determines that a particular act of terrorism amounts to a threat to the peace, breach of the peace, or act of aggression. The second is where a victim State, or group of States asked by the victim State for assistance,

---

[73]See UN High Commissioner for Refugees, Note on the Cancellation of Refugee Status, 22 November 2004.

act under the right of individual or collective self-defence, provided that the particular act (which will most likely be perpetrated by a non-State actor) can be attributed to the State against whom the self-defence action is taken. Less clear is the ability of States to take anticipatory self-defence action in the face of suspected terrorist conduct, at the very least not unless there is a necessity of self-defence, which is instant and overwhelming, leaving no choice of means, and no moment for deliberation.

Terrorist acts might amount to a crime against humanity or a war crime under the Rome Statute, depending upon the particular facts and circumstances involved. An act of terrorism might also involve the application of international humanitarian law, if committed during an armed conflict, since that body of law prohibits conduct which could easily include acts of terrorism. If that is the case, it is now a well-established principle that, regardless of issues of classification, international human rights law continues to apply in armed conflict, subject only to certain permissible limitations in accordance with the strict requirements contained in international human rights treaties.

References

Arend, Anthony. 2003. International Law and the Preemptive Use of Military Force. 26(2) *The Washington Quarterly* 89.

Bos, Adrianne. 2002. Ius in Bello – Conlusions. In Heere, Wybo (Ed). *Terrorism and the Military. International Legal Applications.* The Hague: TMC Asser Press.

Brownlie, Ian. 1963. *International Law and the Use of Force by States.* Oxford: Clarendon Press.

Cassese, Antonio. 1989. The International Community's "Legal" Response to Terrorism. 38(3) *The International Comparative Law Quarterly* 589.

Charney, Johnathan. 2001. The Use of Force against Terrorism and International Law. 95(4) *The American Journal of International Law* 835.

Conte, Alex. 2005. *Security in the 21st Century: The United Nations, Afghanistan and Iraq.* London: Ashgate Publishing Limited.

Dinstein, Yoram. 2002. Ius ad Bellum Aspects of the 'War on Terrorism'. In Heere, Wybo (Ed). *Terrorism and the Military. International Legal Applications.* The Hague: TMC Asser Press.

Duffy, Helen. 2005. *The 'War on Terror' and the Framework of International Law.* Cambridge: Cambridge University Press.

Franck, Thomas. 2001. Terrorism and the Right of Self-Defense. 95(4) *The American Journal of International Law* 839.

Gill, Terry. 2002. The Eleventh of September and the Right of Self-Defense. In Heere, Wybo (Ed). *Terrorism and the Military. International Legal Applications.* The Hague: TMC Asser Press.

Greenwood, Christopher. 2002. International Law and the 'War against Terrorism'. 78(2) *International Affairs* 301.

Henckaerts, Jean-Marie, and Doswald-Beck, Louise (eds). 2004. *Customary International Humanitarian Law, 3 Vols.* Cambridge: Cambridge University Press.

Henkin, Louis, Pugh, Richard, Schachter, Oscar, and Smit, Hans. 1980. *International Law Cases and Materials.* St Paul: West Publishing.

Jennings, Robert. 1938. The Caroline and McLeod Cases. 32(1) *American Journal of International Law* 82.

Koufa, Kalliopi. 2005. The UN, Human Rights and Counter-terrorism. In Nesi, Giuseppe (Ed). *International Cooperation in Counter-terrorism. The United Nations and Regional Organizations in the Fight Against Terrorism.* Aldershot: Ashgate Publishing.

Maged, Adel. 2002. International Legal Cooperation: An Essential Tool in the War Against Terrorism. In Heere, Wybo (Ed). *Terrorism and the Military. International Legal Applications.* The Hague: TMC Asser Press.

Roberts, Adam. 2002. The Laws of War in the War on Terror. In Heere, Wybo (Ed). *Terrorism and the Military. International Legal Applications.* The Hague: TMC Asser Press.

Veuthey, Michel. 2003. International Humanitarian Law and the War on Terrorism. In Doucet, Ghislaine (Ed). *Terrorism, Victims, and International Criminal Responsibility.* Paris: SOS Attentats.

Chapter 13
Human Rights Compliance in the Fight Against Terrorism

The relationship between terrorism and human rights is a matter that has been reflected upon well before the events of 11 September 2001. Since 9/11, with events such as the establishment of the detention camp at Guantánamo Bay and the proliferation of security and counter-terrorist legislation throughout the world, more attention has been paid to the issue of the extent to which counter-terrorism impacts upon human rights. As noted by the UN Office of the High Commissioner for Human Rights:[1]

> Some States have engaged in torture and other ill-treatment to counter terrorism, while the legal and practical safeguards available to prevent torture, such as regular and independent monitoring of detention centres, have often been disregarded. Other States have returned persons suspected of engaging in terrorist activities to countries where they face a real risk of torture or other serious human rights abuse, thereby violating the international legal obligation of non-refoulement. The independence of the judiciary has been undermined, in some places, while the use of exceptional courts to try civilians has had an impact on the effectiveness of regular court systems. Repressive measures have been used to stifle the voices of human rights defenders, journalists, minorities, indigenous groups and civil society. Resources normally allocated to social programmes and development assistance have been diverted to the security sector, affecting the economic, social and cultural rights of many.

In September 2006, the General Assembly adopted the United Nations Global Counter-Terrorism Strategy, as recommended by Kofi Annan in his report entitled

---

[1] Office of the High Commissioner for Human Rights, Human Rights, Terrorism and Counter-terrorism, Fact Sheet No 32 (New York and Geneva: United Nations, 2008), available online at http://www.ohchr.org/Documents/Publications/Factsheet32EN.pdf, p. 1. See also: Almqvist (2005), and Human Rights Watch, In the Name of Counter-Terrorism: Human Rights Abuses Worldwide (Human Rights Watch Briefing Paper for the 59th Session of the United Nations Commission on Human Rights, 25 March 2003), available online at http://www.hrw.org/sites/default/files/reports/counter-terrorism-bck_0.pdf; and International Council on Human Rights Policy, Human Rights After September 11 (Versoix, 2002).

A. Conte, *Human Rights in the Prevention and Punishment of Terrorism,*
DOI 10.1007/978-3-642-11608-7_13, © Springer-Verlag Berlin Heidelberg 2010

Uniting Against Terrorism (see also Chap. 3, Sect. 3.2.5).[2] In his report, the former Secretary-General emphasised that effective counter-terrorism measures and the protection of human rights are not conflicting goals, but complementary and mutually reinforcing ones.[3] He identified the defence of human rights as essential to the fulfilment of all aspects of an effective counter-terrorism strategy and identified human rights as having a central role in every substantive section of his report. The Secretary-General identified that: "Only by honouring and strengthening the human rights of all can the international community succeed in its efforts to fight this scourge".[4]

These sentiments are reflected within the Global Counter-Terrorism Strategy in three ways. First, respect for human rights for all and the rule of law forms one of the four pillars of the Strategy. It is also identified as 'the fundamental basis of the fight against terrorism', thus applicable to all four pillars of the Strategy. Finally, the Strategy's recognition of the importance of respect for human rights while countering terrorism is significantly strengthened through the express identification that a lack of the rule of law and violations of human rights amount to conditions conducive to the spread of terrorism.[5] While these are very positive steps, however, the language of the Global Strategy is very broad and it does not deal with the question of whether Chapter VII resolutions of the Security Council, including those on counter-terrorism, are capable of modifying or somehow suspending human rights obligations. It is therefore necessary to further consider the question of human rights obligations in the context of countering terrorism.

Not only are counter-terrorism and human rights protection interlinked and mutually reinforcing, but compliance with human rights has practical advantages in bringing the perpetrators of terrorist acts to justice. On a national level, the obtaining of evidence by means which are found to be in violation of human rights may be inadmissible in a prosecution. At an international level, such violations may impact upon the ability of other States to rely on such evidence through mutual

---

[2]The United Nations Global Counter-Terrorism Strategy, GA Res 60/288, UN GAOR, 60th sess, 99th plen mtg, UN Doc A/Res/60/288 (8 September 2006). The UN General Assembly reaffirmed the UN Global Counter-Terrorism Strategy in September 2008: see GA Res 62/272, UN GAOR, 62nd sess, 120th plen mtg, UN Doc A/Res/62/272 (2008).

[3]Report of the Secretary-General, Uniting Against Terrorism: Recommendations for a Global Counter-terrorism Strategy, UN Doc A/60/825 (27 April 2006), para 5. See also Part VI thereof. See also the 2008 Report of the United Nations High Commissioner for Human Rights on the protection of human rights and fundamental freedoms while countering terrorism, UN Doc A/HRC/8/13 (2008), p. 2.

[4]Ibid, para 118.

[5]Global Counter-Terrorism Strategy (n 2), Pillar I, preambular para. See also Walker (2007, p. 186), where he states that: "'Preventing' terrorism is achieved by tackling the radicalisation of individuals through tackling disadvantage and supporting reform, including in the reduction of inequalities and discrimination. . .". For further elaboration on the concept of conditions conducive to the spread of terrorism, see the report of the United Nations High Commissioner for Human Rights on the protection of human rights and fundamental freedoms while countering terrorism, UN Doc A/HRC/12/22 (2009), paras 43–46.

legal assistance.[6] It should also be observed that fighting terrorism in a non-human-rights-compliant way can lead to a decline in a State's own moral and human rights standards and/or a progressive decline in the effectiveness of checks and balances on agencies involved in fighting terrorism. As Neitzsche wrote in 1886, "He who fights monsters should be careful lest he thereby becomes a monster. And if thou gaze long into the abyss, the abyss will also gaze into thee".[7] The Supreme Court of Canada has similarly observed that it would be a "Pyrrhic victory" if terrorism was defeated at the cost of sacrificing liberty, the rule of law, and the principles of fundamental justice.[8]

This chapter first considers the general obligation upon States to comply with human rights when countering terrorism, pointing to relevant international and regional documents on the subject. It then moves to explain the practicalities for achieving human rights compliance while countering terrorism by setting out an explaining the author's stand-along handbook on human rights compliance while countering terrorism (which is reproduced as Appendix 4 hereto).

13.1 States' Duty to Comply with Human Rights While Countering Terrorism

Added to the obligation of States to protect those within their jurisdiction from acts of terrorism, a feature of human rights law itself vis a vis the duty of States to act against violence in order to safeguard the right to life of those within its jurisdiction,[9] an obvious point should be made about the nature of international law obligations. Not only are human rights essential to the countering of terrorism, as recognised in the UN Counter-Terrorism Strategy, but States are obliged by law to comply with their international human rights obligations when countering terrorism. This is due to the fact that States have human rights obligations under customary

---

[6]Hampson (2006).

[7]Neitzsche (1973, Chap. IV "Apophthegms and Interludes", Sect. 146). See also Ignatieff (2004).

[8]*Suresh v Canada (Minister of Citizenship and Immigration)* [2002] SCC 1, 13. See also the judgment of Lord Hoffman in *A v Secretary of State for the Home Department* [2005] 2 AC 68, p. 132, where (with reference to the detention without charge regime under Part 4 of the Anti-terrorism, Crime and Security Act 2001) he stated: "The real threat to the life of the nation, in the sense of a people living in accordance with its traditional laws and political values, comes not from terrorism but from laws such as these". United States President Obama recently criticised the Bush Administration's counter-terrorism strategy as including decisions based on fear and rooted in an "anything goes" attitude toward traditional restraints on the chief executive. This, he suggested, unnecessarily sacrificed American ideals, alienated allies and produced more terrorists, not fewer. See USA Today, 'A course correction, not a retreat, on fighting terrorism', 26 May 2009, p. 7A (copy on file with author).

[9]See the International Covenant on Civil and Political Rights, opened for signature 16 December 1966, 999 UNTS 171 (entered into force 23 March 1976), article 6 (right to life).

international law (applicable to all States)[10] and international treaties (applicable to States parties to such treaties).[11] Compliance with human rights is not something requiring States to do something extra, or something special. In commenting on human rights in the fight against terrorism, Judge Myjer of the European Court of Human Rights succinctly stated: "Just do what you have promised to do".[12]

This principle is based not only upon a State's international obligations, but also upon directions of the UN Security Council, General Assembly, Commission on Human Rights, and Human Rights Council. It was a clear message of the 2005 World Summit Outcome on the question of respect for human rights while countering terrorism, the General Assembly concluding that:[13]

> ...international cooperation to fight terrorism must be conducted in conformity with international law, including the Charter and relevant international conventions and protocols. States must ensure that any measures taken to combat terrorism comply with their obligations under international law, in particular human rights law, refugee law and international humanitarian law.

Before considering applicable documents of the United Nations and others, it should be noted that the universal treaties on counter-terrorism expressly require compliance with various aspects of human rights law. In the context of the International Convention for the Suppression of the Financing of Terrorism, for example, this is illustrated in article 15 (expressly permitting States to refuse extradition or legal assistance if there are substantial grounds for believing that the requesting State intends to prosecute or punish a person on prohibited grounds of discrimination); article 17 (requiring the "fair treatment" of any person taken into custody, including enjoyment of all rights and guarantees under applicable international human rights law); and article 21 (a catch-all provision making it clear that the Convention does not affect the other rights, obligations and responsibilities of States).[14]

---

[10] *Military and Paramilitary Activities in and against Nicaragua (Nicaragua v United States of America), Merits* [1986] ICJ Reports, paras 172–201.

[11] See the Vienna Convention on the Law of Treaties (opened for signature 23 May 1969, entered into force 27 January 1980) 1155 UNTS 331, article 34.

[12] Myjer (2009, p. 1).

[13] 2005 World Summit Outcome, GA Res 60/1, UN GAOR, 69th Sess, 8th Plen Mtg, UN Doc A/Res/60/1 (2005), para 85. See also the G8 Declaration on Counter-Terrorism (2009), which states at p. 2: "... while we stress the fundamental importance of disrupting and prosecuting terrorists, we are convinced that in the long term the most effective response to their criminal strategy remains the promotion of democracy, human rights, the rule of law and equitable social conditions".

[14] International Convention for the Suppression of the Financing of Terrorism, opened for signature 10 January 2000, 2179 UNTS 232 (entered into force 10 April 1992).

13.1.1 UN General Assembly

Mention has already been made in Chap. 3 of the adoption by the UN General Assembly of a series of resolutions concerning terrorism since 1972, initially taking the form of resolutions concerning measures to eliminate international terrorism, and then addressing more directly the topic of terrorism, counter-terrorism and human rights (see Sect. 3.2.1). This second series of General Assembly resolutions began in December 1993, with the adoption of resolution 48/122, entitled "Terrorism and Human Rights".[15] Some analysis of those resolutions has already been provided in Chap. 12 (see Sect. 12.1). Of importance to this chapter, both sets of resolutions contain various statements about the need, when implementing counter-terrorist measures, to comply with international human rights standards. A common phrasing of this idea is seen in General Assembly resolution 50/186 (1995):[16]

> *Mindful* of the need to protect human rights of and guarantees for the individual in accordance with the relevant international human rights principles and instruments, particularly the right to life, [...]
> *Reaffirming* that all measures to counter terrorism must be in strict conformity with international human rights standards, [...]
> 3. *Calls upon* States to take all necessary and effective measures in accordance with international standards of human rights to prevent, combat and eliminate all acts of terrorism wherever and by whomever committed; [...].

A slightly less robust expression of these ideas was seen in General Assembly resolution 56/88 (2001) following the events of September 11, although still requiring measures to be taken consistently with human rights standards.[17] That should not, however, be taken as a signal that the General Assembly was minded to turn a blind eye to adverse impacts of counter-terrorism upon human rights. To the

---

[15]GA Res 48/122, UN GAOR, 48th Sess, 85th Plen Mtg, UN Doc A/Res/48/122 (1993).

[16]See also GA Res 50/186, UN GAOR, 50th Sess, 99th Plen Mtg, UN Doc A/Res/50/186 (1995), preambular paras 13 and 14, and operative para 3; GA Res 52/133, UN GAOR, 52nd Sess, 70th Plen Mtg, UN Doc A/Res/52/133 (1997), preambular paras 12 and 13, and operative para 4; GA Res 54/164, UN GAOR, 54th Sess, 83rd Plen Mtg, UN Doc A/Res/54/164 (1999), preambular paras 15 and 16, and operative para 4; GA Res 56/160, UN GAOR, 56th Sess, 88th Plen Mtg, UN Doc A/Res/56/160 (2001), preambular paras 22 and 23, and operative paras 5 and 6; and GA Res 58/174, UN GAOR, 58th Sess, 77th Plen Mtg, UN Doc A/Res/58/174 (2003), preambular paras 20 and 21, and operative para 7.

[17]GA Res 56/88, UN GAOR, 56th Sess, 85th Plen Mtg, UN Doc A/Res/56/88 (2001), preambular para 9 and operative para 3. The preambular paragraph returned to the language of combating terrorism "in accordance with the principles of the Charter", and operative paragraph 4 talked of combating terrorism in accordance with international law "including international standards of human rights". See also similar statements within GA Res 57/27, UN GAOR, 57th Sess, 52nd Plen Mtg, UN Doc A/Res/57/27 (2002), preambular para 8 and operative para 6; GA Res 58/81, UN GAOR, 58th Sess, 72nd Plen Mtg, UN Doc A/Res/58/81 (2003), preambular para 9 and operative para 6; GA Res 58/136, UN GAOR, 58th Sess, 77th Plen Mtg, UN Doc A/Res 58/136 (2003), preambular para 10 and operative para 5; and GA Res 59/46, UN GAOR, 59th Sess, 65th Plen Mtg, UN Doc A/Res/59/46 (2004), preambular para 10 and operative para 3.

contrary, the issue became the subject of annual resolutions on that subject alone, entitled "Protection of Human Rights and Fundamental Freedoms While Countering Terrorism".[18] The first operative paragraphs of these resolutions affirm that:

> States must ensure that any measure taken to combat terrorism complies with their obligations under international law, in particular international human rights, refugee and humanitarian law.

These directions on the part of the General Assembly are reasonably strong in the language they use. It must be recalled, however, that resolutions of the General Assembly do not hold the same weight as international conventions, or binding resolutions of the Security Council. Indeed, Article 10 of the Charter of the United Nations specifically provides that resolutions and declarations of the General Assembly are recommendatory only (see Chap. 3, Sect. 3.2.1). This principle is equally applicable to resolutions of the Commission on Human Rights, as a subsidiary organ of the Economic and Social Council (which is only empowered to make recommendations),[19] and those of the new Human Rights Council (a subsidiary organ of the General Assembly). Thus, the resolutions just discussed, and those of the Commission and Human Rights Council to be discussed, represent guiding principles and non-binding recommendations (what might be termed 'soft law'), rather than binding resolutions, treaty provisions or norms of customary international law ('hard law'). Notwithstanding this, having regard to their repeated and consistent approach, these resolutions are very influential and, importantly, representative of international comity. It is also relevant to recall that resolutions may constitute evidence of customary international law, if supported by State conduct that is consistent with the content of the resolutions and with the accompanying *opinio juris* required to prove the existence of customary law.[20]

---

[18]GA Res 57/219, UN GAOR, 57th Sess, 77th Plen Mtg, UN Doc A/Res/57/219 (2002); GA Res 58/187, UN GAOR, 58th Sess, 77th Plen Mtg, UN Doc A/Res/8/187 (2003); and GA Res 59/191, UN GAOR, 59th Sess, 74th Plen Mtg, UN Doc A/Res/59/191 (2004). See also: GA Res 59/46, UN GAOR, 59th Sess, 65th Plen Mtg, UN Doc A/Res/59/46 (2004), preambular para 10 and operative para 3; GA Res 59/153, UN GAOR, 59th Sess, 74th Plen Mtg, UN Doc A/Res/59/153 (2004), preambular paras 11 and 12; GA Res 59/195, UN GAOR, 59th Sess, 74th Plen Mtg, UN Doc A/Res/59/195 (2004), preambular paras 5, 23 and 24 and operative paras 8 and 10; GA Res 60/158, UN GAOR, 60th Sess, 64th Plen Mtg, UN Doc A/Res/60/158 (2005), preambular paras 2, 3 and 7, and operative para 1; GA Res 61/40, UN GAOR, 61st Sess, 64th Plen Mtg, UN Doc A/Res/61/40 (2007), preambular para 12 and 20, and operative para 5; GA Res 61/171, UN GAOR, 61st Sess, 81st Plen Mtg, UN Doc A/Res/61/171 (2006), preambular paras 3 and 5 and operative para 1; GA Res 62/71, UN GAOR, 62nd Sess, 62nd Plen Mtg, UN Doc A/Res/62/71 (2008), preambular para 12 and 20, and operative para 5; GA Res 62/159, UN GAOR, 62nd Sess, 76th Plen Mtg, UN Doc A/Res/62/159 (2007), preambular paras 3, 4 and 9 and operative para 1; and GA Res 63/185, UN GAOR, 63rd Sess, 70th Plen Mtg, UN Doc A/Res/63/185 (2008), preambular paras 3, 5, and 10 and operative para 1.

[19]Charter of the United Nations, article 62(2).

[20]An example of the use of resolutions of the General Assembly to determine the content of customary rules can be seen in *Military and Paramilitary Activities in and against Nicaragua (Nicaragua v United States of America), Merits* (1986) ICJ Rep, 76 ILR 349, where the

13.1.2 UN Security Council

In general terms, Security Council resolutions concerning terrorism have confined their attention upon the threat of terrorism to international peace and security, reflecting the role of the Council as the organ of the United Nations charged with the maintenance of peace and security.[21] That role is reflected in the language and scope of Security Council resolutions on terrorism which, compared with General Assembly resolutions on the subject, are much narrower in focus. In general terms, the Security Council's resolutions concern themselves with the adverse impacts of terrorism upon the security of States and the maintenance of peaceful relations, while the General Assembly, Human Rights Council and former Commission on Human Rights have taken a much broader approach to the subject in light of their plenary roles and mandates.

Apart from two notable exceptions, the main inference that can be taken from Security Council resolutions about counter-terrorism measures and their need to comply with human rights arises from general statements that counter-terrorism is an aim that should be achieved in accordance with the Charter of the United Nations and international law.[22] This means that such measures must themselves be compliant with the principles of the Charter (which, inter alia, seeks to promote and maintain human rights) and international human rights law (as a specialised subset

---

International Court of Justice gave consideration to two resolutions of the Assembly as evidence of the content of the principle of non-intervention: those being the Declaration on the Inadmissibility of Intervention in the Domestic Affairs of States, UNGA Res 213 (XX) (1965) GAOR (20th Sess, 1408th Plen Mtg) UN Doc A/Res/2131; and the Declaration on Principles of International Law Concerning Friendly Relations and Co-Operation Among States, UNGA Res 2625 (XXV) (1970) GAOR (25th Sess, 1883rd Plen Mtg) UN Doc A/Res/2625.

[21] Under Article 24 of the Charter of the United Nations, the Security Council is charged with the maintenance of international peace and security, paragraph 1 providing that: "In order to ensure prompt and effective action by the United Nations, its Members confer on the Security Council primary responsibility for the maintenance of international peace and security, and agree that in carrying out its duties under this responsibility the Security Council acts on their behalf".

[22] See, for example, SC Res 1373, UN SCOR, 4385th Mtg, UN Doc S/Res/1373 (2001), preambular para 5; SC Res 1438, UN SCOR, 4624th Mtg, UN Doc S/Res/1438 (2002), preambular para 2; SC Res 1440, UN SCOR, 4632nd Mtg, UN Doc S/Res/1440 (2002), preambular para 2; SC Res 1450, UN SCOR, 4667th Mtg, UN Doc S/Res/1450 (2002), preambular para 4; SC Res 1455, UN SCOR, 4686th Mtg, UN Doc S/Res/1455 (2003), preambular para 3; SC Res 1456, UN SCOR, 4668th Mtg, UN Doc S/Res/1456 (2004), preambular para 8; SC Res 1535, UN SCOR, 4936th Mtg, UN Doc S/Res/1535 (2004), preambular para 4; SC Res 1540, UN SCOR, 4956th Mtg, UN Doc S/Res/1540 (2004), preambular para 14; SC Res 1566, UN SCOR, 5053rd Mtg, UN Doc S/Res/1566 (2004), preambular paras 3 and 6; SC Res 1611, UN SCOR, 5223rd Mtg, UN Doc S/Res/1611 (2005), preambular para 2; SC Res 1617, UN SCOR, 5244th Mtg, UN Doc S/Res/1617 (2005), preambular para 4; SC Res 1618, UN SCOR, 5246th Mtg, UN Doc S/Res/1618 (2005), preambular para 4; SC Res 1624, UN SCOR, 5261st Mtg, UN Doc A/Res/1624 (2005), preambular para 2 and operative paras 1 and 4; SC Res 1735, UN SCOR, 5609th Mtg, UN Doc S/Res/1735 (2006), preambular para 4; SC Res 1787, UN SCOR 5795th Mtg, UN Doc S/Res/1787 (2007), preambular para 4; SC Res 1805, UN SCOR, 5856th Mtg, UN Doc 1805 (2008), preambular para 8; and SC Res 1822, UN SCOR, 5928th Mtg, UN Doc 1822 (2008), preambular para 3.

of international law). Notable is the fact that members of the United Nations have undertaken, under Article 55(c) and through the preamble to the UN Charter, to observe human rights and fundamental freedoms for all without distinction as to race, language or religion.

The first more express exception mentioned is contained in the 2003 Declaration of the Security Council meeting with Ministers of Foreign Affairs, adopted under resolution 1456.[23] The Resolution directs its attention to the question of compliance with human rights and, in paragraph 6 of the Declaration, provides that:

> States must ensure that any measure [sic] taken to combat terrorism comply with all their obligations under international law, and should adopt such measures in accordance with international law, in particular international human rights, refugee, and humanitarian law;

While persuasive in its wording in this regard, the status of the Declaration should be noted. Security Council resolutions, when couched in mandatory language, are binding upon members of the United Nations.[24] In the context of the Declaration adopted under resolution 1456 (2003), the text of the Declaration (including the mentioned paragraph 6) is preceded by the sentence: "The Security Council therefore *calls for* the following steps to be taken" [emphasis added]. Such an expression, although influential, is exhortatory and therefore not a binding "decision" within the contemplation of Article 25 of the Charter (see further Chap. 3, Sect. 3.2.3).

The second resolution to be considered is, however, both direct and binding in its terms. Security Council resolution 1624 of 2005 provides, after setting out the obligations of States to counter various aspects of terrorism, that:[25]

> ...States must ensure that any measures taken to implement paragraphs 1, 2 and 3 of this resolution comply with all of their obligations under international law, in particular international human rights law, refugee law, and humanitarian law.

The latter provision is not preceded by exhortatory language, but instead constitutes a clearly binding decision of the Security Council.

13.1.3   UN Human Rights Council and the Former Commission on Human Rights

Not surprisingly, the United Nations Commission on Human Rights has paid considerable attention to the issue of the adverse consequences that counter-terrorism can have upon the maintenance and promotion of human rights. It did so even

---

[23]Ibid.

[24]Member States of the United Nations have agreed to be bound by "decisions" of the Security Council: see Charter of the United Nations, article 25.

[25]SC Res 1624 (n 22) para 4.

before the flurry of anti-terrorist legislation that followed Security Council resolution 1373 (2001). In the pre-9/11 resolutions of the Commission, and its Sub-Commission on the Protection and Promotion of Human Rights, it was affirmed that all States have an obligation to promote and protect human rights and fundamental freedoms, and that all measures to counter terrorism must be in strict conformity with international law, "including international human rights standards".[26] Post-September 11, resolutions of the Commission became more strongly worded. Two resolutions on the subject were adopted in 2004 alone. First, the issue was addressed within the Commission's annual resolution on human rights and terrorism.[27] In a resolution later that month, the Commission again reaffirmed that States must comply with international human rights obligations when countering terrorism.[28] The Commission's resolution 2005/80, pursuant to which it appointed a Special Rapporteur on the promotion and protection of human rights while countering terrorism, stated at paragraphs 1 and 6 that it:[29]

> *Reaffirms* that States must ensure that any measure taken to combat terrorism complies with their obligations under international law, in particular international human rights, refugee and humanitarian law;
> *Reaffirms* that it is imperative that all States work to uphold and protect the dignity of individuals and their fundamental freedoms, as well as democratic practices and the rule of law, while countering terrorism [. . .].

In the year 2006, the Human Rights Council was established by the UN General Assembly under its resolution 60/251 as a subsidiary body of the General Assembly and for the purpose of replacing and enhancing the former Commission on Human Rights.[30] The first years of the Council's operation have been plagued, however, by procedural issues and it was not until March 2008 that the new Human Rights Council adopted a substantive resolution on the question of human rights compliance while countering terrorism. Resolution 7/7 (2008), and its 2009 restatement, do not add anything particularly new to the existing statements of the General Assembly and Commission on Human Rights, although they assist by reaffirming

---

[26]CHR Res 2001/37, UN ESCOR, 57th Sess, 72nd Mtg, UN Doc E/CN.4/Res/2001/37 (2001), preambular paras 18 and 19 and operative paras 7 and 8. Preambular para 19 was later reflected in UN Sub-Commission on Human Rights Res 2001/18, UN ESCOR, 53rd Sess, 26th Mtg, UN Doc E/CN.4/Sub.2/2001/18 (2001), preambular para 13.

[27]CHR Res 2004/44, UN ESCOR, 60th Sess, 55th Mtg, UN Doc E/CN.4/Res/2004/44 (2004), preambular para 24 and operative paras 10, 11 and 12.

[28]CHR Res 2004/87, UN ESCOR, 60th Sess, 58th Mtg, UN Doc E/CN.4/Res/2004/87 (2004), paras 1 and 2.

[29]CHR Res 2005/80, UN ESCOR, 61st Sess, 60th Mtg, UN Doc E/CN.4/Res/2005/80 (2005).

[30]GA Res 60/251, UN GAOR, 60th Sess, 72nd Plen Mtg, UN Doc A/Res/60/251 (2006). The resolution establishing the Human Rights Council was adopted by a vote of 170 in favour to four against (voting against the resolution were Israel, the Marshall Islands, Palau and the United States), with three abstentions (abstaining were Belarus, Iran and Venezuela).

the principle that any measure taken to counter terrorism must comply with international human rights law.[31]

13.2   UN and Other Action Reinforcing and Assisting States' Duty to Comply with Human Rights

The various statements referred to in the previous part of this chapter do not stand as mere lip service to human rights advocates. The United Nations has acted upon these statements in a consistent way, including in the production of guidelines for achieving human rights compliance while combating terrorism. International and regional bodies, both governmental and non-governmental, have done the same.

13.2.1   The Security Council's Counter-Terrorism Committee

The Counter-Terrorism Committee (CTC), which was established under Security Council resolution 1373 of 2001, is charged with receiving reports from UN member States on their compliance with the counter-terrorist obligations specified within that resolution (see Chap. 3, Sect. 3.2.4.1). In her report and follow-up to the 2001 World Conference on Human Rights, the then United Nations High Commissioner for Human Rights, Mary Robinson, prepared guidelines for the use of the Counter-Terrorism Committee (discussed below at Sect. 13.2.1). The Commissioner sought to have the CTC issue these guidelines to States, so that they might be directed in specific and useful terms on how to counter-terrorism in a manner consistent with human rights. The Committee ultimately declined to issue the Commissioner's Guidelines, something anticipated from the remarks of the then Chair of the Counter-Terrorism Committee in his briefing of the Security Council in January 2002:[32]

> The Counter-Terrorism Committee is mandated to monitor the implementation of resolution 1373 (2001). Monitoring performance against other international conventions, including human rights law, is outside the scope of the Counter-Terrorism Committee's mandate. But we will remain aware of the interaction with human rights concerns, and we will keep ourselves briefed as appropriate. It is, of course, open to other organizations to study States' reports and take up their content in other forums.

In his 2005 report to the Commission on Human Rights, the Special Rapporteur on the promotion and protection of human rights and fundamental freedoms while

---

[31]HRC Res 7/7, UN Doc A/HRC/Res/7/7 (2008), para 1; and HRC Res 10/L.31. UN Doc A/HRC/Res/10/L.31 (2009), para 1.

[32]Sir Jeremy Greenstock, *Threats to International Peace and Security Posed by Terrorism*, 18 January 2002, UN Doc S/PV.4453, 5.

countering terrorism expressed concern that States were not receiving a clear enough message from the Counter-Terrorism Committee concerning their duty to respect human rights while combating terrorism.[33] Since that time, however, there has been a gradual and significant shift in the approach of the Counter-Terrorism Committee to the role of human rights in its work.[34] Shortly after the Special Rapporteur's meetings with the Counter-Terrorism Committee in New York, the Committee stated in its comprehensive review report of 16 December 2005 that States must ensure that any measure taken to combat terrorism should comply with all their obligations under international law and that they should adopt such measures in accordance with international law, in particular human rights law, refugee law and humanitarian law.[35] It also stressed that the Counter-Terrorism Committee Executive Directorate should take this into account in the course of its activities.

The same approach is found in statements contained in the CTC's 2008 survey of the implementation of Security Council resolution 1373 (2001) where the Committee stated, for example, that domestic legal frameworks on counter-terrorism should ensure due process of law in the prosecution of terrorists, and protect human rights while countering terrorism as effectively as possible.[36] It is an approach also reflected in the Committee's questions under the reporting dialogue between the CTC and UN member States. In response to New Zealand's fourth report to the CTC, for instance, the Committee asked "What is New Zealand doing to ensure that any measures taken to implement paragraphs 1, 2 and 3 of resolution 1624 (2005)

---

[33]Report of the Special Rapporteur on the promotion and protection of human rights and fundamental freedoms while countering terrorism, Promotion and Protection of Human Rights, ESCOR (62nd Sess) UN Doc E/CN.4/2006/98 (2005), chapter IV, and para 73.

[34]Recognised by the UN Secretary-General in his report entitled United Nations Global Counter-Terrorism Strategy: Activities of the United Nations system in implementing the Strategy, UN Doc A/62/898 (2008), para 42. The Committee's website now includes a page dedicated to the subject of human rights, online at http://www.un.org/sc/ctc/rights.html. See also Koufa (2005, pp. 58–60).

[35]Counter-Terrorism Committee, Report of the Counter-Terrorism Committee to the Security Council for its consideration as part of its comprehensive review of the Counter-Terrorism Committee Executive Directorate, UN Doc S/2005/800 (2005). See also the recent briefing to the Security Council by the Acting Chairman of the Counter-Terrorism Committee on 26 May 2009, where he stated: "In its dialogue with Member States, the Committee continued reminding them that they must ensure that any measures taken to combat terrorism comply with all their obligations under international law, in particular international human rights, refugee and humanitarian law. The senior human rights officer in CTED regularly contributes relevant information for inclusion in the PIAs, provides briefings for CTED country visits and has participated in two of them, as well as promotes consistent approach to human rights issues in CTED's activities". See also the Joint Statement issued at the outcome of the Fifth Special Meeting of the Counter-Terrorism Committee with international, regional and sub-regional organizations, "Prevention of Terrorism Movement and Effective Border Security", 29–31 October 2007, Nairobi, Kenya, preambular para 12, and para 8, online at http://www.un.org/sc/ctc/pdf/Nairobi_joint_statement.pdf.

[36]Survey of the implementation of Security Council resolution 1373 (2001): Report of the Counter-Terrorism Committee, UN Doc S/2008/379 (2008), paras 141 and 143(a).

comply with all of its obligations under international law, in particular international human rights law, refugee law and humanitarian law?".[37] The Committee similarly preceded a question asked of Canada in response to Canada's fourth report: "The committee is aware of the need to bring terrorists to justice while preserving defendants' rights to due process of law...".[38]

13.2.2   UNODC Terrorism Prevention Branch

Paragraph 4 in the fourth (human rights) pillar of the Global Counter-Terrorism Strategy encourages States to make use of technical assistance delivered by, inter alia, the United Nations Office on Drugs and Crime. The General Assembly's reaffirmation of the Strategy in 2008 added a call for all UN agencies involved in supporting counter-terrorism efforts to continue to facilitate the promotion and protection of human rights and fundamental freedoms while countering terrorism.[39] This must be taken to include the technical assistance work of the UNODC Terrorism Prevention Branch. The Secretary-General's 2008 report on the work of the UN in implementing the Global Strategy states that the UNODC's legal and related capacity-building work underlines that an effective and holistic response to terrorism "should be based on a strong criminal justice-based approach, guided by the normative framework provided by the universal legal regime against terrorism and embedded in respect for the rule of law and human rights".[40]

13.2.3   UN Office of the High Commissioner for Human Rights

Past and present UN High Commissioners for Human Rights have been vocal in their criticism of counter-terrorism measures that have restricted the enjoyment of rights in an unnecessary or disproportionate way. Mention has already been made of the guidelines prepared by former High Commissioner Mary Robinson, annexed to

---

[37]New Zealand National Report to the United Nations Security Council Counter-Terrorism Committee, UN Doc S/2006/384 (2006), item 2.6. See also item 2.4 on the report, which reflects the Committee's question: "What international efforts is New Zealand participating in or considering participating in/initiating in order to enhance dialogue and broaden understanding among civilisations in an effort to prevent the indiscriminate targeting of different religions and cultures?".

[38]Recorded in the (fifth) Report of the Government of Canada on the implementation of Security Council resolution 1373 (2001), UN Doc S/2006/185 (2006), question 1.5.

[39]GA Res 62/272 (n 2), para 7.

[40]UN Secretary-General's 2008 report (n 34), para 81. See further Schmid (2004); and Rosand et al. (2008, pp. 9–10).

her 2002 report (the Commissioner's Guidelines).[41] Commissioner Robinson's report begins with an introduction in which she states:

> An effective international strategy to counter terrorism should use human rights as its unifying framework. The suggestion that human rights violations are permissible in certain circumstances is wrong. The essence of human rights is that human life and dignity must not be compromised and that certain acts, whether carried out by State or non-State actors, are never justified no matter what the ends. International human rights and humanitarian law define the boundaries of permissible political and military conduct. A reckless approach towards human life and liberty undermines counter-terrorism measures.

The Commissioner's Guidelines begin by making statements that go to answering an important ideological question: are the objectives of countering terrorism and maintaining human rights compatible? The Guidelines recognise the counter-terrorist obligations imposed upon States by the Security Council and reaffirms that such action must be in compliance with human rights principles contained in international law.[42] They confirm the notion that human rights law allows for a balance to be truck between the unlimited enjoyment of rights and freedoms and legitimate concerns for national security through the limitation of some rights in specific and defined circumstances.[43] Paragraphs 3 and 4 of the Guidelines then set out some instructions on how to formulate counter-terrorist measures that might seek to limit human rights:

3. Where this is permitted, the laws authorizing restrictions:
   (a) Should use precise criteria;
   (b) May not confer an unfettered discretion on those charged with their execution.
4. For limitations of rights to be lawful they must:
   (a) Be prescribed by law;
   (b) Be necessary for public safety and public order, i.e. the protection of public health or morals and for the protection of the rights and freedoms of others, and serve a legitimate purpose;
   (c) Not impair the essence of the right;
   (d) Be interpreted strictly in favour of the rights at issue;
   (e) Be necessary in a democratic society;
   (f) Conform to the principle of proportionality;
   (g) Be appropriate to achieve their protective function, and be the least intrusive instrument amongst those which might achieve that protective function;
   (h) Be compatible with the object and purposes of human rights treaties;
   (i) Respect the principle of non-discrimination;
   (j) Not be arbitrarily applied.

In explaining the author's Handbook on Human Rights Compliance While Countering Terrorism, the Commissioner's Guidelines will be revisited later (see

---

[41]Report of the United Nations High Commissioner for Human Rights and Follow-up to the World Conference on Human Rights, Human Rights: A Uniting Framework, ESCOR (58th Sess) UN Doc E/CN.4/2002/18 (2002), Annex entitled Proposals for "further guidance" for the submission of reports pursuant to paragraph 6 of Security Council resolution 1373 (2001).

[42]Ibid para 1.

[43]Ibid para 2.

Sect. 13.3 below). Also of relevance, a digest of jurisprudence on the protection of human rights while countering terrorism was prepared by the UN Office of the High Commissioner for Human Rights in September 2003.[44] Its declared aim was to assist policy makers and other concerned parties to develop counter-terrorist strategies that respect human rights, introducing itself by stating:[45]

> No one doubts that States have legitimate and urgent reasons to take all due measures to eliminate terrorism. Acts and strategies of terrorism aim at the destruction of human rights, democracy, and the rule of law. They destabilize governments and undermine civil society. Governments therefore have not only the right, but also the duty, to protect their nationals and others against terrorist attacks and to bring the perpetrators of such acts to justice. The manner in which counter-terrorism efforts are conducted, however, can have a far-reaching effect on overall respect for human rights.

The Digest considers decisions of UN treaty-monitoring bodies, such as the Human Rights Committee, and those of other regional bodies, including the European Court of Human Rights and the Inter-American Court of Human Rights. It looks at general considerations, states of emergency and specific rights. On the subject of general considerations, two types of jurisprudence are relevant here. The first is that which emphasises the duty of States to protect those within their territories from terrorism.[46] The second is the identification of jurisprudence observing that the lawfulness of counter-terrorism measures depends upon their conformity with international human rights law.[47]

13.2.4   Special Rapporteurs

Under the auspices of the former Commission on Human Rights, the Sub-Commission on the Promotion and Protection of Human Rights had established a Working Group to elaborate detailed principles and guidelines, with relevant commentary, concerning the promotion and protection of human rights when combating terrorism. The Working Group was chaired by Special Rapporteur Kalliopi Koufa who produced, in 2005, a report setting out a Preliminary Framework Draft of Principles and Guidelines Concerning Human Rights and Terrorism.[48] Although the original

---

[44]Digest of Jurisprudence of the UN and Regional Organizations on the Protection of Human Rights While Countering Terrorism (United Nations Office of the High Commissioner for Human Rights, September 2003). The Office of the High Commissioner is currently working on an updated edition of the Digest.

[45]Ibid 3.

[46]Ibid 11–12. See, for example, *Delgado Paez v Colombia*, Human Rights Committee communication 195/1985, views adopted 12 July 1990, para 5.5.

[47]Ibid 13–15.

[48]Sub-Commission Special Rapporteur on terrorism and human rights, Kalliopi Koufa, Specific Human Rights Issues: New Priorities, in Particular Terrorism and Counter-Terrorism. A Preliminary Framework Draft of Principles and Guidelines Concerning Human Rights and Terrorism, UN

mandate of the Special Rapporteur was to consider the impact of terrorism on human rights,[49] she commented in her 2004 report that a State's over-reaction to terrorism can itself also impact upon human rights. The Sub-Commission Rapporteur's mandate was therefore extended to develop a set of draft principles and guidelines concerning human rights and terrorism (which are to be discussed further in this part of the paper). Of note at this point, the first-stated principle under the heading "Duties of States Regarding Terrorist Acts and Human Rights" reads:[50]

> All States have a duty to promote and protect human rights of all persons under their political or military control in accordance with all human rights and humanitarian law norms.

The report of the Special Rapporteur on terrorism and human rights includes a reasonably basic analysis of issues relating to the protection of human rights while countering terrorism. On the question of permissible limitations, the document adopts a more absolute approach than do the other guidelines, paragraph 34 providing that:

> Any exceptions or derogations in human rights law in the context of counter-terrorism measures must be in strict conformity with the rules set out in the applicable international or regional instruments. A State may not institute exceptions or derogations unless that State has been subjected to terrorist acts that would justify such measures. States shall not invoke derogation clauses to justify taking hostages or to impose collective punishments.
>
> (a) Great care should be taken to ensure that exceptions and derogations that might have been justified because of an act of terrorism meet strict time limits and do not become perpetual features of national law or action.
> (b) Great care should be taken to ensure that measures taken are necessary to apprehend actual members of terrorist groups or perpetrators of terrorist acts in a way that does not unduly encroach on the lives and liberties of ordinary persons or on procedural rights of persons charged with non-terrorist crimes.
> (c) Exceptions and derogations undertaken following a terrorist incident should be carefully reviewed and monitored. Such measures should be subject to effective legal challenge in the State imposing exceptions or derogations.

In 2004, Dr Robert Goldman of the American University was appointed as an independent expert and produced a very useful report to the Commission on Human Rights.[51] His report adopts a rights-based approach, and emphasises the need to

---

Doc E/CN.4/Sub.2/2005/39 (2005). In 2006, the Special Rapporteur issued a further version of the Preliminary Framework Draft of Principles and Guidelines, this time under the auspices of the Human Rights Council, UN Doc A/HRC/Sub.1/58/30 (2006).

[49]This mandate was consequent to the request of the General Assembly for the Commission to do so (see GA Res 49/185, UN GAOR, 49th Sess, 94th Plen Mtg, UN Doc A/Res/49/185 (1994), para 6) and through the Commission's own decision to consider the issue: see CHR Res 1994/46, UN ESCOR, 50th Sess, 56th Mtg, UN Doc E/CN.4/Res/1994/46 (1994).

[50]Sub-Commission Special Rapporteur (n 48) para 25.

[51]Independent Expert on the protection of human rights and fundamental freedoms while countering terrorism, Robert Goldman, Protection of Human Rights and Fundamental Freedoms While Countering Terrorism ESCOR (61st Sess) UN Doc E/CN.4/2005/103. Dr Goldman was appointed under UNCHR Res 2004/87 (2004) ESCOR (60th Sess) UN Doc E/CN.4/Res/2004/87.

uphold the rule of law while confronting terrorism, Goldman stating that: "Properly viewed, the struggle against terrorism and the protection of human rights are not antithetical, but complementary responsibilities of States".[52]

Consequent to this report, the Commission on Human Rights established a mandate for a Special Rapporteur on the promotion and protection of human rights and fundamental freedoms while countering terrorism.[53] This mandate, which was most recently renewed by the Human Rights Council in December 2007, has been held by Professor Martin Scheinin of the European University Institute.[54] In September 2005, the Special Rapporteur presented his first preliminary report to the General Assembly, setting out the conceptual framework for his work.[55] His first substantive report to the Commission on Human Rights included consideration of the issue of the human rights implications of the definition of terrorism, a matter considered in Chap. 2 (see Sect. 2.3).[56] He has subsequently undertaken country reports on Australia, Israel, South Africa, Spain, Turkey, and the United States; and thematic studies on the designation of terrorists, profiling, suicide attacks, immigration and refugee status, the right to a fair trial, and the role of intelligence agencies and their oversight in the fight against terrorism.[57] The Special Rapporteur also addresses allegations of human rights violations in the course of countering terrorism, and has engaged in correspondence with more than 40 countries about their law and practice.[58]

13.2.5   Counter-Terrorism Implementation Task Force

In 2005, the UN Secretary-General established a Counter-Terrorism Implementation Task Force (CTITF), comprised of representatives from various offices and agencies within the United Nations system and making up nine subject-specific working groups (see further Chap. 3, Sect. 3.2.5).[59] Of those working groups, the Working Group on Protecting Human Rights while Countering Terrorism is

---

[52]Ibid para 7.

[53]UNCHR Res 2005/80 (n 29).

[54]HRC Res 6/28, UN Doc A/HRC/Res/6/28 (2007), para 2.

[55]Report of the Special Rapporteur on the promotion and protection of human rights and fundamental freedoms while countering terrorism, Promotion and Protection of Human Rights, GAOR (60th Sess) UN Doc A/60/370 (2005).

[56]Report of the Special Rapporteur on the promotion and protection of human rights and fundamental freedoms while countering terrorism (n 33).

[57]To access all of the Special Rapporteur's reports, see the website of the Office of the High Commissioner for Human Rights, http://www2.ohchr.org/english/issues/terrorism/rapporteur/reports.htm.

[58]Fact Sheet No 32 (n 1), p. 45.

[59]For a full list of agencies represented in the Counter-Terrorism Implementation Task Force, see the UN Secretary-General's 2008 report (n 34), Annex.

facilitating information exchange between UN Member States, civil society, and human rights groups on priority human rights concerns and good practices.[60] Also relevant are the working groups on supporting and highlighting victims of terrorism; and countering the use of the internet for terrorist purposes.

The Working Group on Protecting Human Rights while Countering Terrorism is supported in its work by the Office of the High Commissioner for Human Rights. It is currently preparing a set of practical tools to assist States in protecting human rights while countering terrorism, including on the subjects of conformity of national counter-terrorism legislation with international human rights standards; the proscription of organisations; the stopping and searching of persons; and security infrastructures.[61] The tools will be part of the Working Group's Basic Technical Reference Guide Series, which is meant to offer to all stakeholders in counter-terrorism law and policy (policy makers, government officials, the legislature, judges, law enforcement officers, and civil society at large) easy and reliable guidance on how to enact and implement counter-terrorism measures consistent with international human rights law standards. It aims to support States' efforts to adopt and review their legislation, policy and practice adopted to counter-terrorism by providing them with clear guidance based on international standards.[62]

13.2.6 International Guidelines and Documents

Numerous international guidelines and reports on the relationship between human rights and counter-terrorism have been issued since the advent of September 11 and the proliferation of counter-terrorist legislative action that followed. Unlike Security Council decisions, such guidelines and reports are clearly not binding. Nor do they hold the same status as resolutions of the General Assembly, Commission on Human Rights, of Human Rights Council, which have been adopted by a consensus of State representatives. Notwithstanding this, the consistent approach of these guidelines is telling.

---

[60]UN Secretary-General's 2008 report (n 34), para 86. The current Special Rapporteur on the promotion and protection of human rights and fundamental freedoms while countering terrorism, who is a member of the Working Group, plans to complete his mandate in 2010 with a report to the General Assembly or the Human Rights Council on best practices in protecting human rights while countering terrorism.

[61]The Basic Technical Reference Guide Series is likely to also include guides on detention, formulation of criminal charges, sanctions against individuals or entities, interception of communications, demolition of housing or other personal property, and the use of firearms, particularly in the context of suicide bombing.

[62]UN Office at Geneva, Terms of Reference for consultancy to Alex Conte on development of a Basic Technical Reference Guide on Designing Security Infrastructure, p. 1.

As part of its series of occasional papers, the International Commission of Jurists (ICJ) commissioned a paper on terrorism and human rights in 2002.[63] The paper concluded with a list of minimum criteria that States must observe in the administration of justice when countering terrorism, including: the observance of the primacy of the rule of law and of international human rights obligations; and maintaining and guaranteeing at all times rights and freedoms that are non-derogable.[64] At the its biennial conference in August 2004, the ICJ was also instrumental in the adoption of the Berlin Declaration on Upholding Human Rights and the Rule of Law in Combating Terrorism.[65] The Berlin Declaration recognises the need to combat terrorism and the duty of States to protect those within their jurisdiction.[66] It also expresses that contemporary human rights law allows States a reasonably wide margin of flexibility to combat terrorism without contravening the essence of rights.[67]

The ICJ also established an Eminent Jurists Panel on Terrorism, Counter-terrorism and Human Rights, which was composed of eight distinguished jurists from throughout the world. The Panel undertook 16 hearings in Argentina, Australia, Belgium, Canada, Colombia, Egypt, India, Indonesia, Israel, Kenya, Morocco, Northern Ireland, Pakistan, the Russian Federation, the United Kingdom, and the United States of America. In early 2009 it released its report Assessing Damage, Urging Action, which draws from its hearings and considers the role of intelligence in counter-terrorism and preventive measures such as control orders.[68]

In July 2002, the Committee of Ministers to the Council of Europe also adopted guidelines on human rights and the fight against terrorism.[69] In the preface to its guidelines, Secretary General Walter Schwimmer warned that although the suppression of terrorism is an important objective, States must not use indiscriminate measures to achieve that objective.[70] For a State to react in such a way, he said, would be to fall into the trap set by terrorists for democracy and the rule of law. He urged that situations of crisis, such as those brought about by terrorism, called for even greater vigilance in ensuring respect for human rights. Drawing from the

---

[63]International Commission of Jurists, *Terrorism and Human Rights*, (International Commission of Jurists, 2002).

[64]Ibid 248–251.

[65]International Commission of Jurists, Berlin Declaration on Upholding Human Rights and the Rule of Law in Combating Terrorism, adopted 28 August 2004, available online: http://www.icj. org/IMG/pdf/Berlin_Declaration.pdf (last accessed 27 July 2005).

[66]Ibid preambular para 2 and operative para 1.

[67]Ibid preambular para 5.

[68]Report of the Eminent Jurists Panel on Terrorism, Counter-terrorism and Human Rights, Assessing Damage, Urging Action (Geneva: International Commission of Jurists, 2009).

[69]Council of Europe, Guidelines on Human Rights and the Fight Against Terrorism (Council of Europe Publishing, 2002).

[70]Ibid 5.

jurisprudence of the European Court of Human Rights,[71] and the UN Human Rights Committee, the Council's guidelines set out general rules on the interaction between counter-terrorism and human rights, as well as addressing specific rights and freedoms, with commentary on each stated guideline. Five of the more specific guidelines warrant mention. The first reflects the idea that counter-terrorism is an important objective in a free and democratic society. Guideline I accordingly talks of a positive obligation upon States to protect individuals within their territory from the scourges of terrorism, pointing to decisions of the European Court in which it recognised this duty and the particular problems associated with the prevention and suppression of terrorism.[72] In *Klass v Germany*, for example, the Court agreed with the European Commission that: "some compromise between the requirements for defending democratic society and individual rights is inherent in the system of the Convention".[73]

The second and third Guidelines of the Council are directly relevant to the question of compliance with human rights. Guideline II prohibits the arbitrary limitation of rights,[74] and Guideline III requires limiting measures to be lawful, precise, necessary and proportional:[75]

Guideline II
All measures taken by States to fight terrorism must respect human rights and the principle of the rule of law, while excluding any form of arbitrariness, as well as any discriminatory or racist treatment, and must be subject to appropriate supervision.
Guideline III

1. All measures taken by States to combat terrorism must be lawful.
2. When a measure restricts human rights, restrictions must be defined as precisely as possible and be necessary and proportionate to the aim pursued.

Further guidance on possible derogations is found in Guideline XV, concerning derogations during situations of war or states of emergency threatening the life of a nation. Finally, Guideline XVI underlines that States may never act in breach of peremptory norms of international law.

Next in the list of significant documents and guidelines is the 2007 manual of the Organisation for Security and Cooperation in Europe (OSCE) Office for Democratic Institutions and Human Rights, entitled Countering Terrorism, Protecting

---

[71]Which has compulsory jurisdiction over States parties to the (European) Convention for the Protection of Human Rights and Fundamental Freedoms, opened for signature 4 November 1950, 213 UNTS 222 (entered into force 3 September 1953), article 46.

[72]See, for example, *Ireland v the United Kingdom*, ECHR, 18 January 1978, para 11; *Askoy v Turkey*, ECHR, 18 December 1996, paras 70 and 84; *Zana v Turkey*, ECHR, 25 November 1997, paras 59 and 60; *Incal v Turkey,* ECHR, 9 June 1998, para 58; *United Communist Party of Turkey and Others v Turkey,* ECHR, 20 November 1998, para 59; and *Brogan and Others v the United Kingdom*, ECHR, 29 November 1999, para 48.

[73]*Klass and Others v Germany*, ECHR, 6 September 1978, para 59

[74]Compare Article II with paras 3 and 4(i) and (j) of the Commissioner's Guidelines (n 41).

[75]Compare Article III with para 4(a), (b), (e), (f), and (g) of the Commissioner's Guidelines (n 41).

Human Rights.[76] The Manual provides an overview of the international human rights framework and discusses the application of specific human rights in countering terrorism (the right to life, the prohibition against torture and cruel, inhuman and degrading treatment, detention, the right to a fair trial, the collection of evidence, and the freedoms of expression and association).

A report of the Inter-American Commission on Human Rights (IACHR) on terrorism and human rights was issued in late 2002, shortly after the adoption of the Inter-American Convention Against Terrorism.[77] Article 15 of the Convention specifically requires all States parties to comply with human rights standards:[78]

> The measures carried out by the states parties under this Convention shall take place with full respect for the rule of law, human rights, and fundamental freedoms.

The IACHR report undertakes a right-based approach, focussing upon the scope and potential limitation of particular rights.[79] It also emphasises the general need for any limitation to comply with the doctrines of necessity, proportionality and non-discrimination.[80] As one of its annexes, the report recalls resolution 1906 (2002) of the Organization of American States General Assembly, the first operative paragraphs resolving:[81]

1. To reiterate that the fight against terrorism must be waged with full respect for the law, human rights, and democratic institutions, so as to preserve the rule of law, freedoms, and democratic values in the Hemisphere.
2. To reaffirm the duty of the member states to ensure that all measures taken to combat terrorism are in keeping with obligations under international law.

The Inter-American Commission adopted recommendations, in May 2006, for the protection by OAS member States of human rights in the fight against terrorism. The recommendations reiterate the position of other that: "The struggle against terrorism and the protection of human rights are complementary, not

---

[76]Countering Terrorism, Protecting Human Rights. A Manual (Warsaw: Organisation for Security and Cooperation in Europe Office for Democratic Institutions and Human Rights, 2007).

[77]Inter-American Commission on Human Rights, Report on Terrorism and Human Rights, Doc OEA/Ser.L/V/II.116 (22 October 2002), online: http://www.cidh.org/Terrorism/Eng/toc.htm (last accessed 6 September 2005).

[78]Inter-American Convention against Terrorism, opened for signature 3 June 2002, OAS Treaty A-66 (2003) 42 ILM 19, Article 15.

[79]The report considers the right to life (part III.A), the right to personal liberty and security (part III.B), the right to humane treatment (part III.C), rights to due process and a fair trial (part III.D), the freedom of expression (part III.E), non-discrimination (part III.F), refugee and asylum rights (part III.H), and other civil rights (part III.G): Inter-American Commission on Human Rights report (n 77).

[80]Ibid paras 51 and 55.

[81]OAS General Assembly Resolution 1906, Human Rights and Terrorism, 4th Plen Sess, 4 June 2002, OAS Doc AG/Res 1906 (XXXII-O/02).

antithetical, responsibilities of member states, and respect for fundamental human rights constitutes an essential component of a successful campaign against terrorism".[82]

Although outside the scope of guidelines on the specific subject of counter-terrorism and human rights, attention should be paid to two generally-applicable and very useful documents on the subject of human rights limitations: the Siracusa Principles on the Limitation and Derogation of Provisions in the International Covenant on Civil and Political Rights;[83] and General Comment 29 of the Human Rights Committee.[84] These documents have been referred to earlier in this book, when considering the subject of limiting rights under international law (Chap. 10). Reference is also made below to the Ottawa Principles of 2007, developed by individual experts on human rights and terrorism.[85] Although these documents focus primarily on civil and political rights, and as noted by the UN High Commissioner for Human Rights in her 2009 report on the protection of human rights and fundamental freedoms while countering terrorism, the principles concerning human rights compliance include the need for States to respect, protect and fulfil their obligations regarding economic, social and cultural rights.[86]

13.3 Handbook on Human Rights Compliance While Countering Terrorism

Stating that counter-terrorism measures must comply with human rights is one thing. Achieving human rights compliance is another, much more complex, matter. Appendix 4 in this title includes the text of a Handbook on Human Rights Compliance While Countering Terrorism, published by the Center on Global Counter-terrorism Cooperation in January 2008.[87] The Handbook was first developed by this author as part of the New Zealand Law Foundation International Research Fellowship in a project undertaken at the International Policy Institute on Counter-

---

[82]Inter-American Commission on Human Rights, Recommendations of the Inter-American Commission on Human Rights for the Protection by OAS Member States of Human Rights in the Fight Against Terrorism (Washington, 8 May 2006), para 3.

[83]United Nations Economic and Social Council Sub-Commission on Prevention of Discrimination and Protection of Minorities, Siracusa Principles on the Limitation and Derogation of Provisions in the International Covenant on Civil and Political Rights, UN Doc E/CN.4/1985/4 (1985).

[84]Human Rights Committee, General Comment 29: States of Emergency (Article 4), UN Doc CCPR/C/21/Rev.1/Add.11 (2001).

[85]Ottawa Principles on Anti-terrorism and Human Rights, available online at: http://www.unhcr.org/refworld/type,THEMGUIDE,,,470e0e642,0.html.

[86]Report of the United Nations High Commissioner for Human Rights (n 5), para 3. See also the report of the Special Rapporteur on the promotion and protection of human rights and fundamental freedoms while countering terrorism, UN Doc A/HRC/6/17 (2007).

[87]Conte (2008).

Terrorism in Israel, with the assistance of the founder of the Institute, Dr Boaz Ganor.[88] The Handbook has developed since its initial inception, in response to feedback and experience gained in presenting the document to governmental and non-governmental organisations and agencies. It seeks to address the issue of what human rights compliance means and how it is to be achieved in the context of counter-terrorism law and practice. Particular emphasis is placed upon the development of a test to determine the balance between counter-terrorism and human rights claims and the identification of relevant factors to be considered in the application of that test.

The preparation of the Handbook was motivated by a recognition that legislators and policy-makers are faced with difficult choices in determining the proper boundary between the two pressing public objectives of countering terrorism and maintaining human rights. At the international level, States are told that they must do both and, domestically, the public demands no less. Decision-makers will be easily criticised for adopting legislative or other action that fails to find a proportional balance between the two aspirations. When called upon to rule upon the legality of counter-terrorist measures, judges are similarly placed in a position of balancing due deference to national interest decisions and considerations of the State against their role to uphold constitutionally protected rights and applicable standards of international human rights.

An important point about language should be noted. Deliberate reference is made to the balancing of counter-terrorism with the 'unlimited enjoyment of human rights' (or with 'human rights claims'), rather than of a balance between counter-terrorism and human rights. The distinction might seem semantic but its consequences are significant. To speak of a 'balance between counter-terrorism and human rights' might be seen to imply that there is still room for balancing after an all-things-considered human rights analysis.[89] This is not the intention of the Handbook. As a whole, it is based upon the fact that the balancing of objectives is *part* of a human rights analysis, rather than something consequent to it. Counter-terrorism objectives are fully taken into account in this process. The result can therefore be described as an all-things-considered human rights assessment, which leaves no room for any further 'balancing'.

The desired benefits of the Guide are two-fold. First, to provide practical and functional assistance to decision-makers on the subject. Second, to do so in a manner that is able to give proper account to a State's international human rights obligations, while at the same time recognising the duty of States to protect their societies and to contribute to the maintenance of international peace and security, and to ensure that an accurate and balanced account is taken of the imperatives of, and difficulties in, countering terrorism.

The step-by-step process advocated in the Handbook on Human Rights Compliance can be summarised below. The Handbook includes commentary on each of the

---

[88]Conte and Ganor (2005).

[89]As implied in the approach of Keijzer (2002, p. 129).

steps outlined above and explains and rationalises each element. Some commentaries are reasonably brief, for the sake of achieving an easy-to-use document. Wherever possible, the summary below does not replicate those commentaries, but instead includes footnote references to features of international human rights law already discussed in Chaps. 9 and 10, or to the documents and guidelines identified at Sect. 13.1.

Condition 1: Counter-Terrorist Law and Practice Must Comply with Human Rights Law

1.1 **The Duty to Comply with Human Rights**
    States must ensure that any measures taken to counter terrorism comply with all of their obligations under international law, in particular international human rights law, refugee law, and humanitarian law.[90]
1.2 **Applicable Human Rights Law**
    States are bound by international human rights treaties to which they are party, as well as by human rights norms reflected within customary international law.[91] These obligations have extraterritorial application and continue to apply during armed conflict.[92]

Condition 2: The Right or Freedom to Be Restricted by a Counter-Terrorism Measure Must Allow for Limitation

In determining the availability of any measure taken to counter terrorism that seeks to limit a right or freedom, it must be determined whether the right in question is capable of limitation.[93]

2.1 **Peremptory Rights at Customary International Law (*Jus Cogens* Rights)**
    Counter-terrorist measures may not impose any limitations upon rights or freedoms that are peremptory norms of customary international law.[94]

---

[90]See Sect. 13.1 above.

[91]See Chap. 9.

[92]See Chap. 9, Sect. 9.3. See also the 2006 Recommendations of the Inter-American Commission on Human Rights (n 82), paras 6–7; Becker (2006, pp. 66–82); and, more generally, Borelli (2004).

[93]See Chap. 10, Sect. 10.1.

[94]See Chap. 10, Sect. 10.1. See also the guidelines of the Council of Europe (n 69), Guideline XVI.

2.2 **Non-derogable Rights under Human Rights Treaties**

Where a counter-terrorist measure seeks to limit a right that is non-derogable under an applicable human rights treaty, this will normally mean that the measure cannot be adopted, although this will depend upon the particular expression of the right.[95]

2.3 **Rights Derogable Only in States of Emergency**

Where a counter-terrorist measure seeks to limit a right that is only derogable during a state of emergency threatening the life of the nation, the State must determine whether such an emergency exists and invoke the applicable derogation mechanisms.[96]

2.4 **Other Rights**

Where a counter-terrorist measure seeks to limit a right that is not a peremptory norm of international law, the limitation upon the right must be within the permissible range of limits provided within the applicable treaty or customary definition of the right.[97]

Condition 3: Counter-Terrorism Law and Practice Must Be Established by Due Process

A number of procedural requirements are applicable to ensure that counter-terrorist measures are established and undertaken by proper means.[98]

3.1 **Establishing Counter-Terrorism Measures through Legal Prescriptions**

Counter-terrorist measures seeking to impose limitations upon rights and freedoms must be prescribed by law, requiring such prescriptions to be adequately accessible and formulated with sufficient precision so that citizens may regulate their conduct.[99]

---

[95]See Chap. 10, Sects. 10.1 and 10.3. See also Golder and Williams (2006).

[96]See Chap. 10, Sect. 10.4. See also the guidelines of the Council of Europe (n 70), Guideline XV; the OSCE Manual (n 76), pp. 87–91; the 2006 Recommendations of the Inter-American Commission on Human Rights (n 82), para 8; and the Ottawa Principles (n 85), principle 2.4.

[97]See Chap. 10, Sect. 10.3.

[98]See Chap. 10, Sect. 10.2.

[99]See Chap. 10, Sect. 10.2.2. See also the Commissioner's Guidelines (n 41), paras 3(a) and 4(a); the guidelines of the Council of Europe (n 69), Guideline III; the report of the Inter-American Commission on Human Rights (n 77), para 53; the 2006 Recommendations of the Inter-American Commission on Human Rights (n 82), para 8; and the Ottawa Principles (n 85), principle 2.1.1.

3.2 Respect for the Principles of Non-discrimination and Equality Before the Law

Counter-terrorist measures must respect the principles of non-discrimination and equality before the law.[100]

3.3 Discretionary Powers must not be Unfettered

Counter-terrorist law must not confer an unfettered discretion, it must not be arbitrarily applied, and it must be implemented by means that establish adequate checks and balances against the potential misuse or arbitrary application of counter-terrorist powers.[101]

3.4 Confining Measures to the Objective of Countering Terrorism

Counter-terrorist measures must be confined to the countering of terrorism.

A commentary on condition 3.4 is necessary, since this is a matter which has not been identified earlier in this chapter, or within Chaps. 9 and 10. The objective of countering terrorism must not be used as an excuse by the State to broaden its powers in such a way that those powers are applicable to other matters. This is an important issue expressly dealt with by the Special Rapporteur on the promotion and protection of human rights and fundamental freedoms while countering terrorism, and by the former Sub-Commission Special Rapporteur on terrorism and human rights.[102] It is also reflected within the guidelines adopted by the Committee of Ministers to the Council of Europe and the Inter-American Commission on Human Rights. These guidelines require that those measures seeking to limit or restrict rights or freedoms for the purposes of counter-terrorism must be defined as precisely as possible and be confined to the sole objective of countering terrorism.[103] This principle is relevant to both the creation and application of counter-terrorism measures. Although seemingly unproblematic in theory, this issue poses some difficulties in practice due to the lack of a universally agreed-upon definition of "terrorism", although this book has advocated an approach to the definition of terrorism

---

[100]See Chap. 10, Sect. 10.2.5. See also the Commissioner's Guidelines (n 41), para 4(i); the guidelines of the Council of Europe (n 69), Guideline II; GA Res 59/191 (n 18), preambular para 12; GA Res 61/171 (n 18) preambular para 13; GA Res 62/159 (n 18), preambular para 12; CHR Res 2005/80 (n 29), preambular para 15; Committee on the Elimination of Racial Discrimination, "Statement on Racial Discrimination and Measures to Combat Terrorism" in Report of the Committee on the Elimination of Racial Discrimination, UN Doc A/57/18 (2002), p. 107; the OSCE Manual (n 76), pp. 80–81; the 2006 Recommendations of the Inter-American Commission on Human Rights (n 82), para 8; the Ottawa Principles (n 85), principle 1.1; and Duffy (2005, pp. 348–350).

[101]See Chap. 10, Sect. 10.2.2.2. See also the Commissioner's Guidelines (n 41), paras 3(b) and 3 (j); the guidelines of the Council of Europe (n 69), Guideline II; and the Ottawa Principles (n 85), principles 2.1.1 and 2.1.2.

[102]See Report of the Special Rapporteur to the General Assembly (n 55) para 47; and the Sub-Commission Special Rapporteur's 2005 report (n 48), para 33.

[103]See Council of Europe's Guidelines (n 69), Guideline III(2); and the report of the Inter-American Commission on Human Rights (n 77), paras 51 and 55.

which is comprehensive, concise, and human-rights compliant (see Chap. 2, Sect. 2.3).

Condition 4: Counter-Terrorist Measures Seeking to Limit Rights Must Be Necessary

Where a counter-terrorist measure seeks to limit a right, this limitation must be necessary to pursue a pressing objective and rationally connected to the achievement of that objective.[104]

4.1 The Pursuit of Permissible Objectives

Where a counter-terrorist measure seeks to limit a right, this limitation must be in furtherance of the permissible objectives identified in the expression of the right.[105]

As noted in the Handbook, the permissible objectives most relevant to counter-terrorism include the protection of national security, territorial integrity, public order and safety, or the rights and freedoms of others.[106]

4.2 Pressing and Substantial Concerns in a Free and Democratic Society

In principle, the objective of countering terrorism is one that is pressing and substantial in a free and democratic society and one that may therefore justify the limitation of human rights falling outside the category of peremptory norms.[107] Notwithstanding the importance of counter-terrorism per se, however, it is the objective of the particular legislative provision or counter-terrorist policy/measure that must be assessed.

A commentary on condition 4.2 is also necessary, since this is a matter which has not been identified earlier in this chapter, or within Chaps. 9 and 10. Condition 4.2 stems from the principle of necessity. In this regard, the State has an undeniable duty to protect its nationals; and it cannot be doubted that counter-terrorism is a sufficiently important objective in a free and democratic society to warrant, in principle, measures to be taken that might place limits upon rights and freedoms. The fear-inducing nature of terrorist acts has far-reaching consequences. Likewise, the means through which terrorist activities are facilitated have links to other negative conduct and impacts upon individuals, societies, and international security. This is clearly recognised within the international guidelines mentioned and within a multitude of resolutions of

---

[104]See Chap. 10, Sects. 10.2.3 and 10.3.2.

[105]See Chap. 10, Sect. 10.3.2.

[106]Ibid. See also the Commissioner's Guidelines (n 41), paras 4(b) and 4(e); the guidelines of the Council of Europe (n 69), Guideline II(2); and the 2006 Recommendations of the Inter-American Commission on Human Rights (n 82), para 8.

[107]See, for example, the judgment of the Supreme Court of Canada to this effect in *Suresh v Canada* (n 8), 19.

the Security Council, General Assembly, Commission on Human Rights, and Human Rights Council.

There is a clear recognition that terrorism impacts both individuals and society as a whole so that the countering of those adverse effects must constitute an important objective in and of itself. Care should be taken, however, not to oversimplify this position. Regard must be had to the objectives of the particular counter-terrorist measure being examined. Paragraph 4 of the Commissioner's Guidelines advocates that limits must be necessary for public safety and public order (limiting this to the protection of public health or morals and for the protection of the rights and freedoms of others); must serve a legitimate purpose; and must be necessary in a democratic society. It will be instructive in this regard to consider the objectives of and reasons for counter-terrorism law and practice, discussed in Chap. 4 (see Sect. 4.1).

4.3 Rational Connection

For a counter-terrorism measure to "necessarily" limit a right or freedom, it must be rationally connected to the achievement of the objective being pursued by the measure in question.[108]

Condition 5: Counter-Terrorist Measures Seeking to Limit Rights Must Be Proportional

As well as being necessary, any limitation upon the enjoyment of rights imposed by a counter-terrorist measure must be proportional.[109]

5.1 Limitation, Rather than Exclusion, of Rights

To achieve proportionality, the counter-terrorism measure or legislative provision must effect a "limitation" upon rights, rather than an exclusion of them or such a severe limitation that would impair the "very essence" of the right or freedom being affected.[110]

5.2 Assessing the Human Rights Impact of the Counter-terrorist Measure

Assessing the human rights impact of the counter-terrorist measure requires identification of the importance of or the degree of protection provided by the right or freedom affected and the effects (impact) of the limiting provision or practice upon the right or freedom.[111]

5.3 Assessing the Value of the Counter-terrorist Measure

Assessing the 'value' of the counter-terrorist measure requires identification of the importance of the objective being pursued by the counter-terrorist provision

---

[108]See Chap. 10, Sect. 10.2.3.1.

[109]See Chap. 10, Sect. 10.2.4. See also the Commissioner's Guidelines (n 41), para 4(f).

[110]See Chap. 10, Sect. 10.2.4. See also the Commissioner's Guidelines (n 41), paras 4(c), (d), (g) and (h); and Michaelson (2008).

[111]See Chap. 10, Sect. 10.2.4.

or measure and the effectiveness of that provision or measure in achieving its objective (its ameliorating effect).

The value or importance of the counter-terrorist objective being pursued must also be assessed, as well as the efficacy of it, recognising that different counter-terrorist measures will not just impact upon rights in a different way but will have different levels of effectiveness. The importance of the counter-terrorist measure will have already been assessed when determining whether the measure is necessary (Condition 4). Equally crucial, an analysis must be undertaken whether the measure limiting or restricting the right in question will be effective.[112] It is beyond question that it can be notoriously difficult to make fair estimates on the effectiveness of counter-terrorism measures. Yet, the difficulty of the task cannot be an excuse for the lack of thorough analysis and sound decision-making. An in-depth analysis may include an examination of the experiences from previous terrorism crises and comparable campaigns, such as the so-called war on drugs.

5.4 Assessing the Proportionality of the Counter-terrorist Measure

Having regard to the importance of the right or freedom [Condition 5.2], is the effect of the measure or provision upon the right [Condition 5.2] proportional to the importance of the objective and the effectiveness of the legislative provision or measure [Condition 5.3]?

A further proportionality requirement of international and national human rights law is that measures of limitation or restriction must impair rights and freedoms as little as reasonably possible. If the particular human rights limitation is trivial, then the availability of alternatives that might lessen that impact have tended to be seen as falling within the appropriate exercise of legislative choice, rather than one demanding intervention by the judiciary.[113] Other than this understandable and reasonably minor degree of deference, this requirement fits with paragraph 4(g) of the Commissioner's Guidelines (being the least intrusive means of achieving the protective function of the limitation). In doing so, this also appears to fit with the reasonably broad requirement in paragraph 4(h) that any limitation must be compatible with the objects and purposes of human rights treaties. Arising from the latter requirements but expressly stated within paragraph 4(d) of the Commissioner's Guidelines is the

---

[112]See, for example, Commissioner's Guidelines (n 41), paras 4(b) and 4(e)–(g).

[113]In *R v Schwartz*, for example, it was suggested that the statutory provision, which provided for a presumption that a person did not have a firearms license if he or she failed to produce one upon request, unnecessarily infringed the presumption of innocence. Counsel for Schwartz argued that police could simply check their computerized records to ascertain whether a license had indeed been obtained. McIntyre J of the Supreme Court of Canada stated that "[e]ven if there is merit in the suggestion... Parliament has made a reasonable choice in the matter and, in my view, it is not for the Court, in circumstances where the impugned provision clearly involves, at most, minimal – or even trivial – interference with the right guaranteed in the Charter, to postulate some alternative which in its view would offer a better solution to the problem": *R v Schwartz* [1988] 2 SCR 443, 492–493.

important point that any counter-terrorist provisions be interpreted and applied in favour of rights.

The issues raised by the question formulated in condition 5.4 will not normally be black and white, and its consideration is likely to require debate and the complex interaction of value judgments. Dispute remains over the peremptory versus qualified status of some human rights. Cultural ideals and political persuasions will likewise result in different values being attached to certain rights, a matter that is inherently recognised in the margin of appreciation jurisprudence of the European Court of Human Rights (see Chap. 10, Sect. 10.2.1.1). What the Handbook on Human Rights Compliance seeks to ensure is that such debate reflects upon all relevant factors germane to both countering terrorism and complying with international human rights obligations.

13.4 Discrete Issues Concerning the Interface Between Counter-Terrorism and Human Rights

The balance of this title undertakes a series of detailed case studies concerning the issue of human rights compliance while countering terrorism. Chapter 14 takes a comparative approach to the question of the criminalisation of terrorism, paying equal attention to all four countries, and examining the extent to which the criminalisation of terrorism goes beyond the requirements of international law on counter-terrorism, as well as the compatibility of the domestic terrorism-related offences with the human-rights compatible approach to defining terrorism advocated in Chap. 2. The focus of Chap. 15 is upon counter-terrorism and criminal procedure, including special investigative powers, and considers the establishment of such powers under New Zealand's Counter-Terrorism Bill 2003, i.e. special police powers of questioning, and the use of tracking devices. Briefly considered is the question of the onus proof in bail hearings for terrorism-related charges in Australia. Attention is also paid to the use of special investigative techniques outside the framework of combating terrorism, as well as the role and accountability of intelligence agencies in the prevention and investigation of terrorism. Remaining with pre-trial issues, Chap. 16 examines investigative detention and investigative hearings. Police powers of arrest in the United Kingdom, and continued detention without trial, is explained and evaluated. Comparable powers held by Australian police and intelligence services is also considered. The use in Canada of investigative hearings, and their impact on the privilege against self-incrimination and the right to a fair and open hearing, is also considered.

Moving from pre-trial issues to the broader application of the right to liberty, Chap. 17 examines the derogations by the United Kingdom from the right to liberty, first in the context of executive detention powers applying to Northern Ireland, and then to the derogation made in 2001 in conjunction with the establishment of the

UK's indefinite detention regime. The implications of these, and other, derogations is taken into account to draw out principles regarding terrorism and the derogation from rights and freedoms. Chapter 18 follows the progression of the United Kingdom's indefinite detention regime, which was replaced in 2004 with 'non-custodial' control orders, comparing this apparatus with control orders in Australia. Also looked at in this chapter is the mechanism of preventative control orders under Australia's Criminal Code Act 1995.

The focus of Chap. 19 is upon the domestic designation of persons and entities as terrorists, largely flowing the Security Council's regime administered by the Committee established under resolution 1267 (1999). It considers the way in which designations impact upon the freedoms of assembly and association. Using New Zealand as a case study, the chapter also examines whether such designation processes are, or a capable of being, compatible with natural justice and the right to a fair hearing. Moving to the freedom of expression, Chap. 20 looks at two issues. It first considers the way in which counter-terrorism measures might impact upon the media (New Zealand having been the only one of the four case study countries to provide for media control during and following counter-terrorist operations). The chapter then examines the incitement to terrorism offence, called upon in Security Council resolution 1624 (2005). The final thematic chapter, Chap. 21, concerns the impact of measures to prevent the transboundary movement of terrorists upon human rights, including some aspects of immigration and refugee law, using Australia and the United Kingdom as case studies.

It must be acknowledged that this title does not, nor could it, seek to assess the interface between all forms of counter-terrorism measures and the enjoyment of rights and freedoms. Attention is not paid, for example, to the detention of persons at Guantanamo Bay, the construction of the barrier by Israel, the 'extraordinary rendition' program of the United States' Central Intelligence Agency and associated places of secret detention, or the targeted killing of terrorists.[114]

13.5 Conclusions

Rather than being opposed to each other, the aims of countering terrorism and maintaining human rights are complementary and mutually reinforcing. At the very least, this is the case if one is pursuing a long-term, or even medium-term, goal of countering terrorism. The UN Global Counter-Terrorism Strategy identifies respect for human rights and the rule of law as the fundamental basis of the fight against

---

[114]On those subjects, see: Report of the Special Rapporteur on the promotion and protection of human rights and fundamental freedoms while countering terrorism, Mission to the United States of America, UN Doc A/HRCA/6/17/Add.3 (2007), chapters II, III and IV; Report of the Special Rapporteur on the promotion and protection of human rights and fundamental freedoms while countering terrorism, Mission to Israel, including visit to occupied Palestinian territory, UN Doc A/HRCA/6/17/Add.4 (2007), chapters IV and VI.

terrorism. It dedicates its attention to that subject in one of its four pillars, and it expressly recognises that a lack of the rule of law, and violations of human rights, amount to conditions conducive to the spread of terrorism. Human rights compliance also has practical law-enforcement implications, and avoids a descent into a moral vacuum where checks and balances against government agencies become ineffective such that those agencies threaten the very society they were designed to protect.

States have international human rights obligations under customary international law, applicable to all States, and international treaties to which they are parties. Human rights compliance is also mandated by the universal terrorism-related conventions. States are directed, in both mandatory and recommendatory terms, to comply with human rights while countering terrorism by the Security Council, the General Assembly, the Human Rights Council (HRC), and the HRC's predecessor the Commission on Human Rights. At an institutional level, the General Assembly's reaffirmation in 2008 of the Global Counter-Terrorism Strategy confirms that UN agencies involved in supporting counter-terrorism should continue to facilitate the promotion and protection of human rights while countering terrorism. The Secretary-General has confirmed that this should be the basis of the technical assistance work of the UN Office on Drugs and Crime Terrorism Prevention Branch. The Security Council Counter-Terrorism Committee (CTC) has itself stated that any measure taken to combat terrorism must comply with human rights, an approach which is reflected in the CTC's reporting dialogue with UN member States.

Notwithstanding the clear position that measures to combat terrorism must comply with human rights, legislators, policy-makers, and judges are faced with difficult choices in determining the proper boundary between the unlimited enjoyment of human rights and the adoption and implementation of effective counter-terrorism strategies and action. Numerous guidelines, reports and recommendations on the relationship between human rights and counter-terrorism have been adopted since the proliferation of counter-terrorism legislation that followed the shocking events of September 11. Drawing from those documents, and more specific guidance and decisions on particular aspects of international human rights law, this author has produced a Handbook on Human Rights Compliance while Countering Terrorism.

The Handbook advocates a step-by-step process aimed at guiding decision-makers through all relevant considerations on the subject, enabling him or her to progressively examine the validity of existing or proposed counter-terrorism law and practice. It identifies five cumulative conditions applicable to human rights compliance while countering terrorism. Condition 1 begins with the established notion that counter-terrorism law and practice must comply with applicable human rights law. Condition 2 draws from the flexibility of international human rights law to explain that, in determining the availability of any measure to combat terrorism which would limit a right or freedom, it must be determined whether the right in question in capable of limitation. Drawing from the discussion in Chap. 10, Condition 2 explains the nature of rights, including absolute and non-derogable rights, and the permissible framework for rights limitations. Condition 3 focuses on the due process and rule of law aspects of permissible rights limitations, namely the requirement that any limitation be prescribed by law; that it respects the principles of non-discrimination and equality before the law; that discretionary powers be subject to appropriate checks and balances; and that counter-terrorism measure be confined to the countering of 'terrorism'. Condition 4 concentrates on the principle of necessity, explaining that limitations imposed by measures to combat terrorism must be necessary to pursue a pressing and permissible objective, and that there must be a rational connection between that objective and the limitation imposed. The final condition, Condition 5, explains the important principle of proportionality, formulating the test that "having regard to the importance of the right or freedom. . . , is the effect of the measure or provision upon the right. . . proportional to the importance of the objective and the effectiveness of the legislative provision or measure. . .?".

References

Almqvist, Jessica. 2005. Rethinking Security and Human Rights in the Struggle against Terrorism (paper presented at the European Society of International Law *Forum on International Law: Contemporary Issues*, 26–28 May 2005, Geneva, Switzerland).

Becker, Tal. 2006. *Terrorism and the State. Rethinking the Rules of State Responsibility*. Oxford: Hart Publishing.

Borelli, Silvia. 2004. The Treatment of Terrorist Suspects Captured Abroad: Human Rights and Humanitarian Law. In Bianchi, Andrea (Ed) Enforcing International Law Norms Against Terrorism. Oxford: Hart Publishing.

Conte, Alex. 2008. *Handbook on Human Rights Compliance While Countering Terrorism*. New York: Center on Global Counterterrorism Cooperation (available online at http://www.globalct. org/images/content/pdf/reports/human_rights_handbook.pdf).

Conte, Alex, and Ganor, Boaz. 2005. Legal and Policy Issues in Establishing an International Framework for Human Rights Compliance When Countering Terrorism. Herzelia: International Policy Institute on Counter-Terrorism.

Duffy, Helen. 2005. *The 'War on Terror' and the Framework of International Law*. Cambridge: Cambridge University Press.

Golder, Ben, and Williams, George. 2006. Balancing National Security and Human Rights: Assessing the Legal Response of Common Law Nations to the Threat of Terrorism. 8(1) *Journal of Comparative Policy Analysis* 43.

Hampson, Françoise. 2006. Human Lights Law and Judicial Co-operation in the Field of Counter-Terrorist Activities (paper presented at the *Expert Workshop on Human Rights and International Co-operation in Counter-Terrorism*, 15–17 November 2006, Triesenberg, Liechtenstein).

Ignatieff, Michael. 2004. *The Lesser Evil. Political Ethics in the Age of Terror*. Princeton: Princeton University Press.

Keijzer, Nico. 2002. Terrorism as a Crime. In Heere, Wybo (Ed). *Terrorism and the Military. International Legal Applications*. The Hague: TMC Asser Press.

Koufa, Kalliopi. 2005. The UN, Human Rights and Counter-terrorism. In Nesi, Giuseppe (Ed). *International Cooperation in Counter-terrorism. The United Nations and Regional Organizations in the Fight Against Terrorism*. Aldershot: Ashgate Publishing.

Michaelson, Christopher. 2008. The Proportionality Principle in the Context of Anti-Terrorism Laws: An Inquiry into the Boundaries between Human Rights Law and Public Policy. In Gani,

Miriam, and Mathew, Penelope (Eds). *Fresh Perspectives on the 'War on Terror'*. Canberra: ANU E-Press.

Myjer, Egbert. 2009. Human Rights and the Fight Against Terrorism – Case-law of the Strasbourg Court (paper presented at the Round Table *Fight against Terrorism: Challenges for the Judiciary*, 18–19 September 2009, Fiesole, Italy).

Neitzsche, Frederich. 1973. *Beyond Good and Evil*. London: Penguin Classics.

Rosand, Eric, Millar, Alistair, and Ipe, Jason. 2008. *Human Rights and the Implementation of the UN Global Counter-Terrorism Strategy. Hopes and Challenges*. New York: Center on Global Counterterrorism Cooperation.

Schmid, Alex. 2004. United Nations Measures against Terrorism and the Work of the Terrorism Prevention Branch: The Rule of Law, Human Rights and Terrorism. In Benedek, Wolfgang, and Yotopoulos-Marangopoulos (Eds). *Anti-Terrorism Measures and Human Rights*. Leiden: Martinus Nijhoff Publishers.

Walker, Clive. 2007. The United Kingdom's Anti-terrorism Laws: Lessons for Australia. In Lynch, Andrew, MacDonald, Edwina, and Williams, George (Eds). *Law and Liberty in the War on Terror*. Sydney: The Federation Press.

Chapter 14
The Domestic Criminalisation of Terrorism, and Its Definition

The international framework for the combating of terrorism calls for steps to be taken to hold accountable those who commit terrorist acts, and to adopt measures for the prevention of such acts. All but one of the 13 universal terrorism-related conventions require States parties to take steps to criminalise conduct specified under each of those conventions.[1] Under article 2 of the Hague Convention, for example, States undertake to make the offences defined in article 1 of the treaty (concerning the hijacking of aircraft) punishable by severe penalties.[2] The Security Council has also required, or in some cases called up, member States of the United Nations to prohibit certain conduct (concerning the distinction between recommendations and binding decisions of the Security Council, see Chap. 3, Sect. 3.2.3). Security Council resolution 1373 (2001) requires States to prevent and suppress the financing of terrorist acts, including by criminalising the provision or collection of funds for use in order to carry out terrorist acts.[3] It also demands that States:[4]

> Ensure that any person who participates in the financing, planning, preparation or perpetration of terrorist acts or in supporting terrorist acts is brought to justice and ensure that, in addition to any other measures against them, such terrorist acts are established as serious criminal offences in domestic laws and regulations and that the punishment duly reflects the seriousness of such terrorist acts;

---

[1] The Convention on the Marking of Plastic Explosives for the Purpose of Detection, opened for signature 1 March 1991, ICAO Doc 9571 (entered into force 21 June 1998) is the exception to this. The Convention does not require States parties to proscribe any conduct, but instead places obligations upon States relating to the marking of explosives: see articles 2 and 3(1).

[2] Convention for the Suppression of Unlawful Seizure of Aircraft, opened for signature 16 December 1970, 860 UNTS 105 (entered into force 14 October 1971).

[3] SC Res 1373, UN SCOR, 4385th Mtg, UN Doc S/Res/1373 (2001), para 1(a) and (b).

[4] SC Res 1373 (ibid) para 2(e).

A. Conte, *Human Rights in the Prevention and Punishment of Terrorism*,
DOI 10.1007/978-3-642-11608-7_14, © Springer-Verlag Berlin Heidelberg 2010

The Security Council has also called on States to prohibit by law incitement to commit a terrorist act or acts.[5] Added to these requirements, States have adopted other terrorism-related offences, either due to particular threats posed within their territories (such as those in Northern Ireland, for example) or as an enforcement mechanism for preventive measures (such as offences linked to the freezing of terrorist funds, or those relating to compliance with control orders).

The focus of this chapter is on three broad subjects. The question of domestic definitions of terrorism within the four case study countries is first evaluated, these being linked to many of the terrorism-related offences in those countries, as well as to other preventive mechanisms. Consideration is then given to the domestic terrorism-related offences in those countries, with special focus on the offence of incitement to terrorism. Brief reference is also made to the matter of sentencing.

14.1 Definitions of Terrorism

A large portion of the terrorism-related offences in the four case study countries relate to one of two features. Many are linked to domestic definitions of "terrorism" (as in the United Kingdom – see Chap. 8, Sect. 8.15), a "terrorist act" (as in Australia and New Zealand – see Chap. 5, Sect. 5.1.1.2 and Chap. 7, Sect. 7.1.4.2) or "terrorist activity" (as in Canada – see Chap. 6, Sect. 6.1.4.2). It is an offence in Canada, for example, to provide or collect property intending (or knowing) that this is to be used to carry out a "terrorist activity" (section 83.02 of the Criminal Code). Publishing a statement intended indirectly to encourage acts of "terrorism" is an offence under the UK's Terrorism Act 2006 (section 1). Other offences are linked to proscribed organisations, the description of which is likewise linked to definitions of terrorism. In Australia, for example, an organisation engaged in a "terrorist act" can be listed by the Attorney-General as a terrorist organisation, with a further range of offences linked to such organisations (see Chap. 5, Sect. 5.1.1.3). The seizure and the forfeiture of property belonging to or controlled by such entities is thus also linked to the definition of these terms (see Chap. 5, Sect. 5.3.3, Chap. 6, Sect. 6.1.4.6, Chapter 7, Sect. 7.1.4.5, and Chap. 8, Sect. 8.1.5.4). As well as having these important associations with criminal offences, the definitions of terrorism in Australia, Canada, New Zealand and the United Kingdom are also linked to special investigative powers, the cordoning of areas, and powers of detention and of stop and search (see, for example, the special powers of arrest without charge in the United Kingdom under section 41 of the Terrorism Act 2000 – Chap. 16, Sect. 16.1.1.2).

The domestic definitions of terrorism adopted by the four case study countries therefore have wide implications for criminal law offences and investigative powers in those countries. It is for that reason troubling that, in all four countries,

---

[5]SC Res 1624, UN SCOR, 5261st mtg, UN Doc S/Res/1456 (2005), para 1(a).

the domestic definitions of terrorism go beyond that advocated by the UN Special Rapportuer on counter-terrorism and expounded upon in Chap. 2.[6] One of the problems here is that, as discussed in Chap. 2, there is no overwhelming consensus within the international community on a definition of terrorism, so that individual States have been required to formulate their own definitions of the term. However, as also discussed in Chap. 2, a comprehensive, concise and human rights-compliant approach to defining terrorism, drawn from approaches taken by the UN Special Rapporteur on counter-terrorism, existing international and regional terrorism-related conventions, the UN High-Level Panel on Threats, Challenges and Change, and the Security Council, is achievable (see Chap. 2, Sect. 2.3). This approach is summarised as follows:

1. Terrorist acts should be restricted to the three cumulative characteristics identified by the Security Council in its resolution 1566 (2004), namely:[7]

   • The taking of hostages, or acts committed with the intention of causing death or serious bodily injury;
   • Where such conduct is undertaken for the purpose of either (a) provoking a state of terror, or (b) compelling a government or international organisation to do or abstain from doing something;
   • And where the conduct falls within the scope of the trigger offences defined in the international terrorism-related conventions.

2. Conduct falling outside the scope of the trigger offences might still be classified as terrorist if it possesses the first two characteristics identified in resolution 1566 (2004) and corresponds to all elements of a serious crime as defined by law.
3. The approaches identified in items 1 and 2 above are applicable to the treatment of conduct in support of terrorist offences.
4. The definition of terrorist conduct must also not be retroactive, and must be adequately accessible and written with precision so as to amount to a prescription of law.

Before considering the compatibility with these principles of the domestic definitions of terrorism in the case study countries, it is worth reflecting on aspects of a report prepared in 2007 by the Independent Reviewer of terrorism laws in the United Kingdom, Lord Carlile. In summarising the principal submissions and

---

[6]Report of the UN Special Rapporteur on the promotion and protection of human rights while countering terrorism, Martin Scheinin, The Protection and Promotion of Human Rights While Countering Terrorism, UN Doc E/CN.4/2006/098 (2005), chapter 3. This has been reported to be the case in many other countries also – see, for example: the Report of the United Nations High Commissioner for Human Rights on the protection of human rights and fundamental freedoms while countering terrorism, UN Doc A/HRC/8/13 (2008), para 20; and the Report of the Eminent Jurists Panel on Terrorism, Counter-terrorism and Human Rights, Assessing Damage, Urging Action (Geneva: International Commission of Jurists, 2009), p. 124.

[7]See SC Res 1566, UN SCOR, 5053rd Mtg, UN Doc S/Res/1566 (2004), para 3.

arguments presented to him for the purpose of his report, Lord Carlile categorised those representations as falling into four propositions.[8] The substance of the first two propositions has already been considered in Chap. 2. They propose that no definition of terrorism is necessary, or that a definition is useful but that no "terrorism" offences are required, reasoned to be so because ordinary criminal law and procedure is sufficient. It has already been argued in this book, however, that there are various good reasons to justify a distinct approach to combating terrorism and establishing terrorism-related offences (Chap. 2, Sect. 2.1.3). These propositions are therefore not considered further. The two propositions which remain are as follows:

- That a definition is needed, including special procedures and offences, drawn broadly enough to enable it to anticipate estimates of future terrorism activity. This proposition is, according to Lord Carlile, based on pragmatic problem-solving in the face of a threat, but runs the risk of the dilution of rights and freedoms.[9]
- That a definition is needed, including special procedures and offences, but that a 'tighter' definition is required than under section 1 of the Terrorism Act 2000 (UK). The Independent Reviewer describes this proposition as being close to the current UK legislative position.[10] It would, one would assume, also correspond to the approach advocated by the Special Rapporteur and identified immediately above. Lord Carlile concludes, however, that the definition in the Terrorism Act 2000 is "consistent with international comparators and treaties, and is useful and broadly fit for purpose, subject to some alteration".[11] Conversely, the conclusion drawn in this chapter is that the definition requires a number of important alterations and that it is currently not consistent with international standards (see Sects. 14.1.3 and 14.1.4 below).

Reference is also made in Lord Carlile's report to an earlier definition of terrorism in the UK under the Prevention of Terrorism (Temporary Provisions) Act 1989, which referred to the use of violence for political ends, including "... any use of violence for the purpose of putting the public or any section of the public in fear...". The Independent Reviewer described this definition as having major drawbacks because it did not establish a threshold for the violent acts concerned.[12] This is an important observation, consistent with the inclusion by the Security Council of its first cumulative characteristic, i.e. that the conduct should not just be violent, but should either involve the taking of hostages (a serious offence in

---

[8]Report by the Independent Reviewer Lord Carlile of Berriew QC, The Definition of Terrorism (Presented to Parliament by the Secretary of State for the Home Department, March 2007), para 22. See also Walker (2007, pp. 190–191).

[9]Report on The Definition of Terrorism (ibid) para 23.

[10]Report on The Definition of Terrorism (ibid) para 22 (proposition 3).

[11]Report on The Definition of Terrorism (ibid) para 86(4).

[12]Report on The Definition of Terrorism (ibid) para 8.

itself) or should be committed with the intention of causing death or serious bodily injury.

The other two cumulative requirements identified in item 1 above restrict the characterisation of terrorism to coercive intimidation and to the existing range of offences under the universal terrorism-related conventions. As noted by the Special Rapporteur, however, conduct falling outside the scope of the latter 'trigger' offences might still be classified as terrorist in nature. This will be so if the prohibited conduct coincides with the first two characteristics in resolution 1566 (2004) – coercive intimidation, and intention to hijack or to cause death or injury – if it also corresponds to elements of a serious crime under national law.[13]

14.1.1 Special Rapporteur Evaluation of Australia's Definition of a "Terrorist Act"

The UN Special Rapporteur on counter-terrorism has taken the view that Australia's definition of a "terrorist act" goes beyond the Security Council's characterisation of conduct to be suppressed in the fight against terrorism.[14] In response to Australia's fifth periodic report under the International Covenant on Civil and Political Rights (ICCPR), the Human Rights Committee has also criticised Australia's definition as being overly broad.[15] The definition of a terrorist act in section 100.1 of the Criminal Code of Australia captures acts which: (1) are done or threatened with the intention of advancing a political, religious, or ideological cause; (2) with the intention of intimidating the public or coercing the Australian government, or a foreign government; and (3) where the action falls within the scope of conduct described in section 100.1(2). The first element is not listed in Security Council resolution 1566 (2004), although it is a common characteristic of terrorism (see Chap. 2, Sect. 2.1.4). This element is not problematic, since it constitutes a restrictive feature of the definition, thus narrowing the scope of its application. Furthermore, as recognised by Jenkins, the incorporation of an ideological element to the description of terrorism and terrorist offences recognises the unique phenomenon being addressed.[16] The second element of the

---

[13]Special Rapporteur on the promotion and protection of human rights and fundamental freedoms while countering terrorism, Mission to Spain, UN Doc A/HRC/10/3/Add.2 (2008), para 6.

[14]Special Rapporteur on the promotion and protection of human rights and fundamental freedoms while countering terrorism, Martin Scheinin, Australia: Study on Human Rights Compliance While Countering Terrorism, UN Doc A/HRC/4/26/Add.3 (2006), para 15.

[15]Human Rights Committee, Concluding Observations: Australia, UN Doc CCPR/C/AUS/CO/5 (2009), para 11. See also the criticisms of the Law Council of Australia, which largely mirror those of the UN Special Rapporteur: Anti-Terrorism Reform Project: A consolidation of the Law Council of Australia's advocacy in relation to Australia's anti-terrorism measures (November 2008), pp. 20–22.

[16]Jenkins (2003, p. 431). Contrast with McSherry (2004, pp. 360–364).

definition of a terrorist act corresponds to the second cumulative characteristic in resolution 1566 (2004), i.e. conduct undertaken for the purpose of provoking a state of terror or for compelling a government to do or abstain from doing something.

Where an act meets the first and second elements of section 100.1 of the Criminal Code, it will amount to a "terrorist act" if it falls within the types of conduct listed in section 100.1(2), i.e. action which:

(a) causes serious harm that is physical harm to a person; or
(b) causes serious damage to property; or
(c) causes a person's death; or
(d) endangers a person's life, other than the life of the person taking the action; or
(e) creates a serious risk to the health or safety of the public or a section of the public; or
(f) seriously interferes with, seriously disrupts, or destroys, an electronic system including, but not limited to:
  (i)   an information system; or
  (ii) a telecommunications system; or
  (iii) a financial syst em; or
  (iv) a system used for the delivery of essential government services; or
  (v)   a system used for, or by, an essential public utility; or
  (vi) a system used for, or by, a transport system.

It is this third element of the definition in section 101.1 that is problematic, because some of the conduct listed in section 100.1(2) goes beyond the first cumulative characteristic of Security Council resolution 1566. In this respect, the first element of paragraph 3 of resolution 1566 (2004) restricts itself to the taking of hostages, or acts committed with the intention of causing death or serious bodily injury. While none of the action listed in section 100.1(2) corresponds to hostage-taking, the action listed in subparagraphs (a) (causing physical harm to a person) and (c) (causing death) clearly do fall within the intended scope of element 1 of paragraph 3 of resolution 1566 (2004). The other types of conduct, however, relate not to acts committed with the intention of causing death or serious bodily injury, but instead to acts causing damage to property (subsection (b)), creating a risk to health or safety (subsection (e) – without any accompanying threshold), or interfering with certain types of electronic systems (subsection (f)). The UN Special Rapporteur therefore concluded that Australia's definition of a "terrorist act" includes acts the commission of which go beyond the first cumulative characteristic identified in Security Council resolution 1566 (2004).[17] He also noted that the conduct listed is not defined in the international conventions and protocols relating to terrorism, thus also falling outside the scope of the third cumulative characteristic in the resolution. This over-reaching definition is not cured by the qualification (above) that conduct falling outside the scope of the trigger offences in para 3 (element 3) of resolution 1566 might still be classified as terrorist, since this will only be the case if the conduct also possesses the first two characteristics identified in resolution 1566

---

[17]Special Rapporteur on the promotion and protection of human rights and fundamental freedoms while countering terrorism, Australia: Study on Human Rights Compliance While Countering Terrorism, UN Doc A/HRC/4/26/Add.3, para 15.

(2004) and corresponds to all elements of a serious crime as defined by law. As just discussed, the subparagraphs in question do not possess the first characteristic in paragraph 3 of resolution 1566 and thus cannot be categorised as a properly constrained domestic definition of terrorism under item 2 of the Special Rapporteur's approach above.

It is important to once again clarify a point already made in Chap. 2, which was acknowledged in the Special Rapporteur's criticism of Australia's definition of a terrorist act. That an act is criminal does not, by itself, make it a terrorist act. Nor does a concise human-rights based approach to defining terrorism preclude criminal culpability. As concluded by the Special Rapporteur in the case of Australia:[18]

> The latter aspects of Australia's definition of "terrorist acts" clearly include criminal activity, such as the interference with an information system with the intent to create a serious risk to the safety of the public (through the combination of sections 100.1(2)(f)(1) and 100.1(3)(b)(iv)). The Special Rapporteur takes the view, however, that although it is permissible to criminalize such conduct it should not be brought within a framework of legislation intended to counter international terrorism unless that conduct is accompanied by an intention to cause death or serious bodily injury. The Government of Australia reports that Australia has been identified by jihadist groups as a terrorist target and that authorities consider that a terrorist attack within Australia could well occur, possibly without notice, thus assessing the level of alert as "medium" (a terrorist act could occur). To go beyond the cumulative restrictions of resolution 1566 (2004), however, there must be a rational link between threats faced by Australia and the types of conduct proscribed in its legislation that go beyond proscriptions within the universal terrorism-related conventions. Australia must clearly distinguish terrorist conduct from ordinary criminal conduct.

14.1.2 Definitions in Canada and New Zealand

The position in New Zealand and Canada is similar to that in Australia. The definitions of "terrorist act" (in New Zealand) and "terrorist activity" (in Canada) go beyond the cumulative characteristics in paragraph 3 of Security Council resolution 1566 (2004). As for Australia, the Human Rights Committee has also criticised Canada's definition as being overly broad.[19] Two principal types of terrorist activity are defined under section 83.01(1) of Canada's Criminal Code. The first is the commission of offences, either within or outside Canada, under

---

[18]Special Rapporteur report on Australia (ibid) para 16.

[19]Human Rights Committee, Concluding Observations: Canada, UN Doc CCPR/C/CAN/CO/5 (2006), para 12. At the time of the consideration by the Human Rights Committee of New Zealand's most recent periodic report (during its session in July 2002), New Zealand had not enacted the Terrorism Suppression Act 2002 and the definition under the Act was thus not considered by the Committee. The Committee did, however, urge New Zealand to ensure that its definition would be in conformity with the ICCPR and would not lead to abuse – see Human Rights Committee, Concluding Observations: New Zealand, UN Doc CCPR/CO/75/NZL (2002), para 11.

certain of the universal terrorism-related conventions (see Chap. 6, Sect. 6.1.4.3). The same approach is taken in New Zealand, where one of the definitions of a "terrorist act" under sections 4(1) and 5(1)(b) of the Terrorism Suppression Act 2002 includes acts that constitute an offence under the universal conventions listed in Schedule 3 of the Act (see Chap. 7, Sect. 7.1.4.2). This methodology corresponds to the third cumulative, 'trigger offence', characteristic in resolution 1566, but is not linked with the intention to take hostages or cause death or serious injury, nor with the intention to provoke terror or compel a government or international organisation to do or abstain from doing something.

The second type of terrorist activity under Canadian law involves an act or omission, in or outside Canada, which is committed: (1) in whole or in part for a political, religious or ideological purpose, objective or cause; (2) with the intention of intimidating the public, or compelling a person, a government or a domestic or an international organisation to do or to refrain from doing any act; and (3) which intentionally:

(a) causes death or serious bodily harm to a person by the use of violence,
(b) endangers a person's life,
(c) causes a serious risk to the health or safety of the public or any segment of the public,
(d) causes substantial property damage, whether to public or private property, if causing such damage is likely to result in the conduct or harm referred to in paragraphs (a) to (c), or
(e) causes serious interference with or serious disruption of an essential service, facility or system, whether public or private, other than as a result of advocacy, protest, dissent or stoppage of work that is not intended to result in the conduct or harm referred to in any of paragraphs (a) to (c).

This second definition matches up quite closely to the definition in Australia's Criminal Code Act 1995. While aspects of the definition correspond to the first cumulative requirement in resolution 1566 (2004), such as causing death, others include property damage or include conduct such as the disruption of services where this is *not* intended to cause death or serious bodily injury. The same can be said of the 'catch all' definition of a terrorist act under section 5 of NZ's Terrorism Suppression Act 2002, which includes conduct intended to cause damage to property, major economic loss, major environmental damage, or serious interference with or disruption of infrastructure (see Chap. 7, Sect. 7.1.4.2). Also problematic is that the definitions just described are not linked with the 'trigger offences' identified by the Security Council.

In the Canadian context, it should be noted that shortly after the enactment of the Anti-terrorism Act 2001, the Supreme Court of Canada delivered a judgment concerning section 19(1) of the now repealed Canadian Immigration Act 1985, which provided that persons involved in terrorism or in terrorist organisations were to be refused entry into Canada. Because the term terrorism was not defined in the Act, the Supreme Court was called upon to define the word. Although the Court recognised that there is disagreement on the definition of the term, it held that the term provided a sufficient basis for adjudication and was thus not unconstitutionally vague. Notably, the Supreme Court relied on the definition of conduct the financing of which is to be prohibited under the Convention for the Suppression of the

Financing of Terrorism.[20] This definition restricts itself to conduct "intended to cause death or serious bodily injury" (and also thus corresponding to the first element of paragraph 3 in Security Council resolution 1566 (2004)).

14.1.3   The Definition of "Terrorism" in the United Kingdom

In the case of the definition of "terrorism" under section 1 of the Terrorism Act 2000 (UK), not only does this definition suffer from the faults identified in the Australian, Canadian and NZ definitions, but it also includes an exemption from application of all elements of the definition in certain circumstances. Section 1 defines "terrorism" as containing, three cumulative elements, and has been described by the House of Lords as a "far-reaching definition of terrorism":[21]

- The use or threat of action, whether within or outside the United Kingdom, which (see section 1(1)(a) and 1(2)):

  (a) involves serious violence against a person; or
  (b) involves serious damage to property; or
  (c) endangers a person's life, other than that of the person committing the action; or
  (d) created a serious risk to the health or safety of the public or a section of the public; or
  (e) is designed seriously to interfere with or seriously to disrupt an electronic system.

- Where the act or threat is designed to influence the government or to intimidate the public or a section of the public (section 1(1)(b)); and
- The act or threat is made for the purpose of advancing a political, religious, racial or ideological cause (section 1(1)(c)).

Considering each of the Security Council's characteristic in turn, it is again notable that certain parts of the definition go beyond "acts committed with the intention of causing death or serious bodily injury, or the taking of hostages". Section 1(2)(d) relates to acts creating a serious risk to the health or safety of the public or a section of the public. Section 1(2)(e) concerns acts designed to seriously interfere with or disrupt an electronic system. While such acts are no doubt criminal in nature, they are not within the cumulative characteristics of terrorism identified.

---

[20]*Suresh v Canada (Minister of Citizenship and Immigration)* [2002] SCC 1, para 98. See also Golder and Williams (2004, pp. 280–281).

[21]*Gillan and Another v Commissioner of Police for the Metropolis and Another* [2006] UKHL 12, para 4 (Lord Bingham).

Concerning the second cumulative element of the definition under section 1 of the Terrorism Act 2000, it should be noted that it was unsuccessfully argued in the Court of Appeal that the motivation of such acts to influence a "government" should be limited to influencing a government in a country which is governed by what may be broadly described as democratic and representative principles and, as a consequence, that acts perpetrated against dictatorial or tyrannical regimes should not qualify as being "terrorist" in nature.[22] It was argued that this approach was mandated by section 3 of the Human Rights Act 1998 (UK), i.e. that section 1 of the Terrorism Act had to be interpreted in a manner consistent with rights under the European Convention on Human Rights, namely the principles of democracy enshrined within the Convention.[23] Consistent with the international position that no act of terrorism is justifiable, regardless of its motivations (see Chap. 2, Sect. 2.2.2), the UK Court of Appeal rejected this argument and stated that: "There is no exemption from criminal liability for terrorist activities which are motivated or said to be morally justified by the alleged nobility of the terrorist cause".[24]

Also concerning the second cumulative element in section 1 of the Act, section 1 (3) of the Act goes beyond the requirement in Security Council resolution 1566 that the conduct is "for the purpose of provoking a state of terror, intimidating a population, or compelling a Government or international organization to do or abstain from doing any act". It does so by waving the requirement that a terrorist act be designed to influence the government or intimidate the public (normally a requirement under section 1(1)(b) of the Terrorism Act 2000) where the conduct involves the use of firearms or explosives. The likely intention of the provision was to act as a deeming provision. Namely, that where an act under section 1(2) is perpetrated (one involving serious violence and the like) for the purpose of advancing a cause *which involves the use of explosives or firearms*, then the latter aspect of such an act is deemed to satisfy subsection (1)(b) by in fact intimidating the pubic or a section of the public. This, however, is a generous interpretation since not all acts involving the use of explosives or firearms need come to the knowledge of the public and, if they do not, they cannot therefore be said to intimidate the public.

Finally, the Terrorism Act 2000 definition fails to meet the Special Rapporteur's and the Security Council's cumulative characteristics by not restricting itself to acts that constitute offences within the scope of and as defined in the international conventions and protocols relating to terrorism.

---

[22]*R v F* [2007] EWCA Crim 243.

[23]Ibid, paras 22–23.

[24]Ibid, para 32. Leave to appeal to the House of Lords was rejected.

14.1.4 Evaluative Summary

Two principal approaches to the definition of terrorism emerge in the four case study countries. The first is to equate conduct prohibited under the universal terrorism-related conventions as amounting to terrorism, in and of itself without any further element of intention (such as an intention to provoke terror or to influence a government or international organisation). This approach is taken by New Zealand and Canada in their definitions of a "terrorist act" and "terrorist activity" (Sect. 14.1.2 above). While this might seem logical, the problem with this definitional approach is that it is able to capture conduct which does not pass a certain threshold of seriousness, in terms of either intention or effect. This was a criticism of early definitions of terrorism in the United Kingdom. Nor is there a link in these definitions to one of the most commonly understood attributes of terrorist conduct: that it be perpetrated for the purpose of provoking a state of terror, or compelling a government or international organisation to do or abstain from doing something. When compared to Australia and the United Kingdom, New Zealand and Canada are therefore out of step in this approach, not to mention that this fails to correspond to the cumulative requirements in Security Council resolution 1566 (2004).

The second definitional approach, which is common to all four countries, is to use definitions which comprise the following three elements:

- The first is that the conduct be undertaken for political, religious or ideological purposes.[25] The definition in the United Kingdom also includes conduct undertaken to advance a racial cause.[26] As indicated earlier, this first element is not included in the Security Council's characterisation of conduct to be suppressed in the fight against terrorism, although it is a commonly understood feature of terrorism. Nor is this problematic, since it constitutes a restrictive feature of the definition of terrorism, thus narrowing its potential scope of application.
- The second element common to definitions in Australia, Canada, NZ and the UK is that the conduct have a coercive or intimidatory character, i.e. undertaken for the purpose of either (1) provoking a state of terror, or (2) compelling a government or international organisation to do or abstain from doing something.[27] This corresponds to the characteristic of terrorism identified in paragraph 3 (element 2) of Security Council resolution 1566 (2004).

---

[25]In Australia, see section 100.1(1) of the Criminal Code Act 1995 (paragraph (b) of the definition of "terrorist act"). In Canada, see section 83.01(1) of the Criminal Code 1985 (paragraph (b)(i)(A) of the definition of "terrorist activity"). In New Zealand, see section 5(2) of the Terrorism Suppression Act 2002. In the United Kingdom, see section 1(1)(c) of the Terrorism Act 2000.

[26]This followed the amendment of section 1 of the Terrorism Act 2000 under section 75 of the Counter-Terrorism Act 2008.

[27]In Australia, see section 100.1(1) of the Criminal Code Act 1995 (paragraph (c) of the definition of "terrorist act"). In Canada, see section 83.01(1) of the Criminal Code 1985 (paragraph (b)(i)(B) of the definition of "terrorist activity"). In New Zealand, see section 5(2)(a) and (b) of the

- The final common element is the one most problematic for consistency of the definitions with paragraph 3 (element 1) of Security Council resolution 1566 (2004) and with the meaning of terrorism advocated by the Special Rapporteur on the promotion and protection of human rights and fundamental freedoms while countering terrorism. The definitions adopted by the case study countries require that the conduct must fall within one of a list of acts, including action which causes, or is intended to cause, death or serious bodily injury.[28] While the example just given corresponds to paragraph 3 of resolution 1566 (2004), the list of acts included in the domestic definitions of terrorism go beyond this.

Common to all four countries, the list includes conduct which causes a serious risk to the health or safety of the public.[29] As currently expressed, this is overly broad and may capture effects of conduct which, while appropriate to be suppressed and criminalised, is not truly 'terrorist' in nature, i.e. is not intended to cause death or serious bodily injury. This could be easily rectified, however, by amending this part of the list to refer to "conduct which causes a serious risk to the health or safety of the public *and is likely to cause death or serious bodily injury*" (emphasis added). This would capture acts, or threats, of biological, chemical, or radiological warfare. It would retain the objective of protecting the public from acts of terrorism which target the health or safety of the public, while at the same time complying with the Special Rapporteur's recommendation that offences falling outside the scope of the 'trigger offences' in the universal terrorism-related conventions (identified in the third element of paragraph 3 of resolution 1566) might still be classified as terrorist in nature if they coincide with the first two characteristics in resolution 1566 and if they correspond to elements of a serious crime under national law.

Also listed in all four countries is conduct which constitutes a serious interference, disruption, or destruction of infrastructure or electronic systems. In Australia this includes, but is not limited to, information systems, telecommunications, financial systems, and systems for an essential public utility, transport, or the delivery of "essential government services".[30] Canada applies a broad description, that of a serious interference with or serious disruption of "an essential service,

---

Terrorism Suppression Act 2002. In the United Kingdom, see section 1(1)(b) of the Terrorism Act 2000.

[28]In Australia, see section 100.1(2) of the Criminal Code Act 1995. In Canada, see section 83.01(1) of the Criminal Code 1985 (paragraph (b)(ii) of the definition of "terrorist activity"). In New Zealand, see section 5(3) of the Terrorism Suppression Act 2002. In the United Kingdom, see section 1(1)(a) and (2) of the Terrorism Act 2000.

[29]In Australia, see section 100.1(2)(e) of the Criminal Code Act 1995. In Canada, see section 83.01 (1) of the Criminal Code 1985 (paragraph (b)(ii)(C) of the definition of "terrorist activity"). In New Zealand, see section 5(3)(b) of the Terrorism Suppression Act 2002. In the United Kingdom, see section 1(2)(d) of the Terrorism Act 2000.

[30]Section 100.1(2)(f) of the Criminal Code Act 1995.

facility or system, whether public or private".[31] The United Kingdom's definition includes action "designed seriously to interfere with or seriously disrupt an electronic system".[32] Attention to infrastructure and electronic systems can be understood from a policy perspective. The potential for terrorist acts to impact upon the operation of critical infrastructure, including communications, transportation, energy, banking and finance, and government services, has been identified by government agencies as an important consideration.[33] As well as the flow-on effects of a terrorist act upon infrastructure, these services have also been identified as potential direct targets of terrorist acts.[34] This is undoubtedly correct, and it is reasonable to assume that such attacks may place lives in danger, although this will depend on the nature and level of the attack as well as the nature and bearing of the particular infrastructure attacked or threatened. An attack intended to kill or cause injury, or likely to do so, will be of a terrorist nature if accompanied by coercive or intimidatory intent and corresponding either to an offence under the terrorism-related conventions or a serious crime under national law. An attack which does not fall within the scope of such crimes, such as an electronic disruption to ATM banking machines for example, would be inconvenient and might cause financial loss, and might also be criminalised, but should not be categorised as a terrorist act. Such an act would, however, currently amount to terrorism under the definitions in Australia, Canada and the UK, despite the fact that it would not fall within the parameters of paragraph 3 of Security Council resolution 1566 (2004), nor within the Rapporteur's advocated approach. The approach in New Zealand is, in comparison, consistent with the approach advocated. Section 5(3)(d) of the Terrorism Suppression Act 2002 (NZ) restricts itself to "serious interference with, or serious disruption to, an infrastructure facility *if this is likely to endanger human life*" (emphasis added).

The final type of conduct listed by all four countries is conduct which causes substantial property damage (restricted under New Zealand's definition to destruction of damage of property "of great value or importance").[35] Again, while it is appropriate for such conduct to be criminalised, this also falls beyond the scope of

---

[31]Section 83.01(1) of the Criminal Code 1985 (paragraph (b)(ii)(E) of the definition of "terrorist activity").

[32]Section 1(2)(e) of the Terrorism Act 2000.

[33]See, for example, Government of Canada Office of Critical Infrastructure Protection and Emergency Preparedness, The September 11, 2001 Terrorist Attacks – Critical Infrastructure Protection Lessons Learned (Incident Analysis IA02-001, 27 September 2002).

[34]See, for example: Lord Carlile's report on The Definition of Terrorism (n 8) p. 31; Baev 2006; Coleman (2006); Australian Government Department of Foreign Affairs and Trade, Transnational Terrorism: The Threat to Australia (Commonwealth of Australia 2004), pp. 13–14; and Contingency Today, 'UK infrastructure protection needs a rethink', 10 February 2009, online: http://www.contingencytoday.com/online_article/UK-infrastructure-protection-needs-a-rethink-/1740.

[35]In Australia, see section 100.1(2)(b) of the Criminal Code Act 1995. In Canada, see section 83.01 (1) of the Criminal Code 1985 (paragraph (b)(ii)(D) of the definition of "terrorist activity"). In New Zealand, see section 5(3)(c) of the Terrorism Suppression Act 2002. In the United Kingdom, see section 1(2)(b) of the Terrorism Act 2000.

conduct to be suppressed in the fight against terrorism. The Independent Reviewer of terrorism laws in the United Kingdom would disagree, however. Lord Carlile has stated that: "So far as offences against property are concerned, I have no doubt that these and threats to damage property should be included in any definition. Damage to property can induce a real sense of terror for the future".[36] It should be noted that, in the case of Canada's identification of conduct which causes property damage, paragraph (b)(ii)(C) of the definition of "terrorist activity" in section 83.01(1) of the Criminal Code requires that such property damage is likely to cause death or serious bodily injury (a qualification which makes this item compatible with the advocated definition of terrorism), or property damage which is likely to cause a serious risk to the health or safety of the public (a qualification which, if also linked to the likelihood of causing death or injury, would be compatible). New Zealand similarly qualifies its identification of causing property damage to situations where such damage is likely to cause death or serious bodily injury (compatible with the advocated definition for the reasons just mentioned), a serious risk to health or safety (compatible if also linked with the likelihood of causing death or injury), or "serious interference with, or serious disruption to, an infrastructure facility, if likely to endanger human life" (also compatible with paragraph 3 (element 1) of resolution 1566).

Unique to New Zealand, the list of conduct which would constitute a terrorist act (if accompanied by ideological motives and coercive or intimidatory intent) includes conduct intended to cause "... major economic loss, or major environmental damage..." if this is also: (1) likely to endanger human life or cause death or serious bodily injury, which is not problematic since it is linked to consequences which match those in element 1 of paragraph 3 of resolution 1566; or (2) likely to cause a serious risk to the health or safety of a population, which (as discussed earlier) is overly broad but could be rectified by restricting itself to such risks which are also likely to cause death or serious bodily injury (section 5(3)(d) of the Terrorism Act 2002). Also unique to New Zealand's list of qualifying conduct is that which is intended to cause the "introduction or release of a disease-bearing organism, if likely to devastate the national economy of a country" (section 5(3)(e)). This approach again goes further than that envisaged by Security Council resolution 1566 (2004). Including elements of economic and environmental damage and the prospect of the release of disease-bearing organisms is perhaps not surprising for a country like New Zealand which relies so heavily on agricultural exports.[37] International

---

[36]Report on The Definition of Terrorism (n 8) para 50.

[37]By way of example, Statistics New Zealand identifies exports for the years ended June 2001, 2002 and 2003 to be as follows: milk powder, butter and cheese at $(million) 5,790 (2001), 5,891 (2002) and 4,679 (2003); meat and edible offal at $(million) 4,182 (2001), 4,429 (2002) and 4,112 (2003); logs, wood and wood article at $(million) 2,192 (2001), 2,378 (2002) and 2,386 (2003); fish, crustaceans and molluscs at $(million) 1,374 (2001), 1,402 (2002) and 1,032 (2003); and fruit at $(million) 1,045 (2001), 1,159 (2002) and 1,032 (2003): see Statistics New Zealand online information "Quick Facts – Economy", online: http://www.stats.govt.nz/domino/external/web/nzstories.nsf/htmldocs/Quick+Facts+Economy (as accessed on 17 September 2004 – copy on file with author).

terrorism-related treaties do not currently include 'bio-terrorism' offences, however. Nor do the approaches of the Security Council and the Special Rapporteur on counter-terrorism contemplate coverage of acts which impact on the economy or environment without an accompanying intention to cause death or injury. While it is easy to sympathise with the policy objectives behind these parts of NZ's definition of terrorism, these are matters which can, and should, be dealt with as separate offences.

Regrettably, therefore, the domestic definitions of terrorism adopted by all four case study countries, which have wide implications for criminal law offences as well as investigative and intelligence powers, go beyond the characteristics of terrorism identified by the Security Council and the definition of terrorism advocated by the UN Special Rapporteur on counter-terrorism.

14.2 Terrorism Offences in the Case Study Countries

The implementation by the case study countries of their international counter-terrorism obligations entails, in part, the criminalisation of certain terrorist and terrorism-related conduct. Criminalisation is not only a legal obligation for States parties to the various terrorism-related treaties, and in response to Security Council decisions, but it is also a prerequisite for effective international cooperation.[38] Appendix 3 in this text sets out the offences under the universal terrorism-related conventions, as well as conduct to be suppressed under relevant Security Council resolutions (see Table 1). The corresponding offences in the domestic law of the case study countries is explained in Chaps. 5–8, and reproduced in Tables 2–5 in Appendix 3. As can be seen from these chapters, and Appendix 3, a wide range of conduct is criminalised under counter-terrorism laws in Australia, Canada, New Zealand and the United Kingdom. Many of these offences relate directly to the implementation by those countries of their international counter-terrorism obligations. Others relate to particular threats posed within their territories, such as Northern Ireland in the case of the United Kingdom. Offences also act as mechanisms to enforce the execution of preventive measures such as control orders and the freezing of terrorist assets.

14.2.1 Principal, Inchoate, and Party Offences

One of the common features of the universal terrorism-related conventions is that they not only call for a principal offender to be prosecuted and severely punished, but they also require States parties to criminalise the conduct of those who assist

---

[38]United Nations Office on Drugs and Crime, Handbook on Criminal Justice Responses to Terrorism (United Nations, New York, 2009), p. 37.

principal offenders, and those who attempt to commit the principal offence. By way of example, the International Convention against the Taking of Hostages requires States parties to criminalise hostage-taking, as defined by article 1(1) of the Convention. It also requires parties to hold accountable those who attempt to commit an act of hostage-taking (article 1(2)(a)) and those who participate as an accomplice of a person who commits or attempts to commit an act of hostage-taking (article 1(2)(b)). The Convention thereby includes the principal offence of hostage-taking, the inchoate offence of attempted hostage-taking, and the party offence of acting as an accomplice to a hostage-taker.

In most cases, the case study countries have only expressly criminalised the principal offences in the universal conventions, although there are some exceptions to this. Section 7(3.4) of Canada's Criminal Code 1985, for example, explicitly covers a conspiracy or attempt to commit an offence of demanding nuclear material, or being an accessory after the fact in relation to that offence (see Appendix 3, Table 3(B)). Generally, however, inchoate and party offences are left to be dealt with under general criminal law provisions. In Australia, for example, attempts, complicity and common purpose, incitement, and conspiracy to commit any Commonwealth offence are provided for under Division 11 of the Criminal Code Act 1995.

Beyond inchoate and party offences, Walker observes that counter-terrorism offences have begun to include 'precursor' offences as principal offences in themselves. His observation relates to offences which do not rely on the *actus reus* of a traditional offence, such as harm to a person or damage to property, but instead criminalise conduct at an earlier preparatory stage on the grounds that to wait for the commission of a terrorism offence is too dangerous.[39] This is seen in the legislation of all four case study countries including, for example, the offence of possession of materials useful to terrorism, and the crime of possessing information useful to terrorism.[40] In this regard, the UN Office on Drugs and Crime and the Special Rapporteur on counter-terrorism have acknowledged that preparatory offences constitute a necessary preventive element to a successful counter-terrorism strategy, the Rapporteur stating that:[41]

> As such, terrorist groups, organizations or entities which are involved in the planning or preparation of terrorist acts must be prevented from carrying them out and should be sanctioned even if a planned terrorist act is not committed or attempted. This implies that it is permissible to take measures such as criminalizing preparatory acts of terror planned by groups, which in turn implies the need to take measures that interfere with the freedom of peaceful assembly and the freedom of association.

---

[39]Walker (2007, p. 190).

[40]See, for example, sections 57 and 58 of the Terrorism Act 2000 (UK) [Appendix 3, Table 4(J)]. For commentary on comparable offences in Australia, see McSherry (2004, pp. 366–367).

[41]Special Rapporteur on the promotion and protection of human rights and fundamental freedoms while countering terrorism, Protection of human rights and fundamental freedoms while countering terrorism, UN Doc A/61/267, para 11. See also the Handbook on Criminal Justice Responses to Terrorism (n 38) p. 37.

He and others have also warned, however, that the definition of terrorism and corresponding offences (including offences relating to conduct in support of terrorism), must be precise and must correspond to the cumulative requirements of Security Council resolution 1566 (2004), as discussed earlier (Sect. 14.1 above).[42]

Precursor and inchoate offences can also be problematic due to the tension between the need for such offences to be very precise in their terms in order to avoid ambiguity, compared to the fact that overly precise terms may exclude the practical enforcement of the offence through obstacles to the prosecution of the offence. This point can be illustrated having regard to the offence in Australia of providing support to a terrorist organisation, an offence defined as follows under section 102.7(2) of the Criminal Code Act 1995:

A person commits an offence if:
(a) the person intentionally provides to an organisation support or resources that would help the organisation engage in an activity described in paragraph (a) of the definition of terrorist organisation in this Division; and
(b) the organisation is a terrorist organisation; and
(c) the person is reckless as to whether the organisation is a terrorist organisation.

In his Inquiry report on the case of Dr Mohamed Haneef, Clarke considers the accompanying fault elements in Division 5 of the Criminal Code and deduces that two alternative interpretations of this offence are available. The first is that the offence consists of two physical elements (that of providing support, plus the consequence of helping the organisation). The alternative interpretation is that there is only one physical element, i.e. the provision of support. Combined with the accompanying *mens rea* elements of intent and recklessness, Clarke contemplates how a trial judge might need to sum up. Assuming that the offence consists of two physical elements, and that recklessness is the fault element of the second physical element (helping the organisation), he concludes that a judge would need to instruct a jury that it must be satisfied of the following in order to convict:[43]

- The defendant intentionally provided a resource – for example, a can of petrol – to an organisation.
- The defendant was reckless as to whether the can of petrol would help the organisation in preparing, planning, assisting in or fostering the commission of a terrorist act.
- To be satisfied as to recklessness, the jury must further be satisfied that the defendant was aware of a substantial risk that the can of petrol would help the organisation engage in, for example, fostering the commission of a terrorist act

---

[42]Report of the UN Special Rapporteur on the promotion and protection of human rights while countering terrorism, Martin Scheinin, The Protection and Promotion of Human Rights While Countering Terrorism, UN Doc E/CN.4/2006/098 (2005), chapter III, especially para 44. See also the report of the UN High Commissioner for Human Rights (n 6) para 23; and the Law Council of Australia's Anti-Terrorism Reform Project (n 15) pp. 24–27.

[43]Clarke, Hon John QC. Report of the Inquiry into the Case of Dr Mohamed Haneef (Australia: Commonwealth of Australia, 2008), p. 260.

and that, having regard to circumstances known to the defendant, it was unjustifiable for the defendant to take that risk.

• The organisation was a terrorist organisation.
• The defendant was aware that there was a substantial risk that the organisation
  was a terrorist organisation or was to become one, and it was unjustifiable for the
  defendant to take that risk.

Clarke opines that such a summing up is confusing and tautologous. He concluded
that, particularly because of the risk of judicial error, the wording of the offence
under section 102.7(2) should be reconsidered.[44] The danger of such uncertainties
is not isolated to terrorism offences, but appears to be particularly relevant in the
area due to the increasing use of inchoate and precursor offences in counter-
terrorism law.

14.2.2   Recruitment and Training Offences

Paragraph 2(c) of Security Council resolution 1373 (2001) obliges States to deny
safe haven to those who finance, plan, support, or commit terrorist acts. Paragraph 2
(a) of the resolution adds that States must suppress recruitment of members of
terrorist groups, although it does not expressly require criminalisation of the
recruitment and training of terrorists. Such criminalisation has, however, been
subsequently recommended by the Security Council Working Group established
pursuant to resolution 1566 (2004).[45] Canada and New Zealand and have taken
steps to expressly criminalise the recruitment of terrorists and participation in
terrorist groups. Section 83.18 of Canada's Criminal Code Act 1985 prohibits the
direct or indirect participation in, or contribution to, any activity of a terrorist group
for the purpose of enhancing the ability of any terrorist group to facilitate or carry
out a terrorist activity (see Chap. 6, Sect. 6.1.4.3 and Appendix 3, Table 3(B)).
Section 83.18 sets out a non-exhaustive list of factors which might point to such
participation or contribution and identifies certain means by which participation and
contribution can occur for the purpose of the offence (section 83.18(3)), including
recruiting a person in order to facilitate or commit a terrorism offence. The
Terrorism Suppression Act 2002 (NZ) is even more explicit, stating that a person
commits an offence against section 12 of the Act if he or she "recruits another
person as a member of a group or organisation, knowing that the group or organisation is (a) a designated terrorist entity; or (b) an entity that carries out, or participates in the carrying out of, 1 or more terrorist acts" (Chap. 7, Sect. 7.1.4.3, and
Appendix 3, Table 4(E)).

---

[44]Haneef Inquiry Report (Ibid) p. 260. See also the Law Council of Australia's Anti-Terrorism
Reform Project (n 15) pp. 25–27.

[45]Report of the Security Council Working Group established pursuant to resolution 1566 (2004),
UN Doc S/2005/789 (2005), para 28.

Although Australia also has offences concerning participation and recruitment, these are limited to participation in and recruitment for "terrorist organisations" as defined by section 102.1(1) of the Criminal Code Act 1995 (Australia), which is more narrow than the offences in New Zealand and Canada. Whereas the offences in the latter countries contemplate recruitment for terrorist activity or acts more generally, the offence in Australia is restricted to the recruitment of specifically defined organisations. There is also no specific recruitment offence in the United Kingdom, although the UK has pointed to compliance with this requirement through the criminalisation of membership in proscribed organisations (section 11 of the Terrorism Act 2000 (UK)) and the offence in section 54(3) of the Terrorism Act 2000 to invite another to receive information or training in the making or use of firearms, explosives, or chemical, biological or nuclear weapons (Chap. 8, Sect. 8.1.5.3, and Appendix 3, Table 5(J)).[46] This does not mean a lack of compliance with Paragraphs 2(a) and (c) of Security Council resolution 1373 (2001), or with the resolution of the 1566 Working Group. In light of the concerns expressed earlier relating to the broad nature of the definitions of terrorism, this may in fact be seen as a positive feature of the recruitment-related offences in Australia and the United Kingdom.

14.2.3 Offences Beyond the Scope of Terrorism-Related Conventions

As indicated in the introduction to this part of the chapter, most but not all of the terrorism-related offences in the case study countries are directly linked to the universal terrorism-related conventions. These further offences can be categorised as falling within one of the following categories:

- Some offences are not expressly required of the terrorism treaties or Security Council resolutions, but are in furtherance to their implementation. Thus, for example, whereas the Convention on the Marking of Plastic Explosives for the Purpose of Detection does not require States parties to criminalise any particular conduct,[47] Australia has chosen to make it an offence to traffic in unmarked plastic explosives (section 72.12(1) of the Criminal Code Act 1995 – see

---

[46]The United Kingdom of Great Britain and Northern Ireland Report to the Counter-Terrorism Committee pursuant to paragraph 6 of Security Council resolution 1373 (2001) of 28 September 2001, UN Doc S/2001/1232 (2001), p. 7.

[47]The Convention on the Marking of Plastic Explosives for the Purpose of Detection, opened for signature 1 March 1991, ICAO Doc 9571 (entered into force 21 June 1998) does not require States parties to proscribe any conduct, but instead places obligations upon States relating to the marking of explosives: see articles 2 and 3(1) – see also Chap. 3, Sect. 3.1.1.4.

Appendix 3, Table 2(A)).[48] The way in which these offences have been framed does not appear to be problematic.

- Other offences act as mechanisms for the enforcement of preventive measures such as control orders and the freezing of assets. Contravention of a control order is an offence under section 104.27 of Australia's Criminal Code Act 1995 and section 9(1) of the UK's Terrorism Prevention Act 2005 (see Appendix 3, Tables 2(A) and 5(L)).[49] Australia also provides offences concerning disclosure of information related to preventative detention (section 105.41 of the Criminal Code Act – Appendix 3, Table 2(A)). Subject to the proper administration and making of control orders and preventative detention orders (see Chap. 18), enforcement mechanisms of this kind are reasonable in principle. Their application in practice, however, must be carefully monitored to ensure that their impact is not disproportionate, particularly relevant in the case of the enforcement of preventative detention.

- Some offences can be described as constituting preventive measures in themselves. For example, it is an offence under section 20 of Canada's Security of Information Act 1985 (as amended by the Anti-terrorism Act 2001) for any person to make a threat of violence where this is at the direction of or for the benefit of or in association with a terrorist group, and this is done for the purpose of increasing the capacity of the terrorist group to harm Canadian interests (see Appendix 3, Table 3(D)).[50] Again, such preventive measures appear reasonable in principle, but depend upon a proper definition of terrorism (discussed above at Sect. 14.1).

- A small category of offences can be described as reactive in nature, aimed at enabling authorities to cope with an emergency situation caused by a terrorist act. Most countries have emergency legislation which is capable of being activated to deal with such circumstances. In New Zealand, certain emergency powers were introduced under the International Terrorism (Emergency Powers) Act 1987 (see Chap. 7, Sect. 7.3). The Act makes it an offence to fail or refuse to comply with directions or requirements imposed under the Act (section 21 – see Appendix 3, Table 4(C)).

- Finally, and problematically, various offences introduced under counter-terrorism legislation in Australia, Canada, New Zealand and the United Kingdom are linked to features that go beyond the cumulative characteristics in Security Council Resolution 1566 (2004). These are identified and discussed next.

---

[48] See also: section 72.13 of the Criminal Code Act 1995 (Australia), in Appendix 3, Table 2(A); sections 46–49 of the Aviation Transport Security Act 2004 (Australia), in Appendix 3, Table 2 (C); section 78 of the Criminal Code 1985 (Canada), in Appendix 3, Table 3(B); section 13B of the Terrorism Suppression Act 2002 (NZ); and section 2 of the Terrorism Act 2006 (UK), in Appendix 3, Table 5(M), discussed in Chap. 20, Sect. 20.2.3.2.

[49] See also section 9(2) and (3) of the Terrorism Prevention Act 2005 (UK), in Appendix 3, Table 5(L).

[50] See also sections 6 and 16–18 of the Security of Information Act 1985 (Canada).

14.2.3.1 The Offence of Committing a Terrorist Act

Section 101.1 of Australia's Criminal Code Act 1995 provides that a person commits an offence, punishable by life imprisonment, if the person engages in a "terrorist act". The same offence, also punishable by life imprisonment, is seen in section 6A of the Terrorism Suppression Act 2002 (NZ). These offences can be argued to be in furtherance of the requirement on UN member States, under paragraph 2(d) of Security Council resolution 1373 (2001), to prevent those who commit terrorist acts from using their territory for that purpose. They can also be said to respond to the requirement in paragraph 2(e) of the same resolution to ensure the prosecution and severe punishment of terrorists. What is problematic, however, is that both offences are linked directly to the definitions of a "terrorist act" under section 100.1 of Australia's Criminal Code and sections 4 and 5 of NZ's Terrorism Suppression Act, both of which have been concluded to go beyond the character-istics of terrorism (see Sect. 14.1 above).

14.2.3.2 'Bioterrorism' Offences in New Zealand

New Zealand's Counter-Terrorism Bill 2003 led to the creation of two 'bioterrorism' offences under the Crimes Act 1961. New sections 298A and 298B of the Crimes Act make it an offence to cause disease or sickness in animals, or contaminate food, crops, water or other products (see Chap. 7, Sect. 7.1.5.3 and Appendix 3, Table 4 (F)). The offence under section 298A is linked to the causing of a serious risk to the health or safety of the animal population, or the likelihood of causing major damage to the economy of New Zealand. Section 298B also links itself to economic damage, or to an intention to harm a person. The offences under sections 298A and 298B are punishable by imprisonment of up to 10 years.

As discussed earlier, one can understand the policy reasons for introducing such offences in a country which relies heavily on agricultural exports. Indeed, in 2005, New Zealand's Ministry of Agriculture and Forestry was faced with a claimed deliberate release of foot and mouth virus on Waiheke Island.[51] Although this turned out to be a hoax, had the incident led to the actual release of foot and mouth on the Island, this would have constituted a terrorism-related offence of causing disease or sickness in animals (section 298A of the Crimes Act) and, depending on the person's intention,[52] an offence of contaminating food (section 298B). It is proper for such conduct to be prohibited and, if committed, to be prosecuted and treated seriously.

---

[51]For further details, see Ministry of Agriculture and Forestry, 'Operation Waiheke Island', online: http://www.maf.govt.nz/mafnet/press/operation-waiheke.

[52]Section 298B of the Crimes Act 1961 requires the actus reus to be accompanied by: (a) an intention to harm a person, or recklessness as to whether any person is harmed; or (b) an intention to cause major economic loss to a person, or recklessness in that regard; or (c) and intention to cause major economic damage to the national economy of New Zealand, or recklessness in that regard.

Since neither offence under section 298A nor 298B correspond to the cumulative characteristics in resolution 1566 (2004), however, they should not have been introduced into law under counter-terrorism legislation.

14.2.3.3 Other Offences Going Beyond the Cumulative Characteristics in Security Council Resolution 1566 (2004)

A missing element in a number of terrorism offences in the case study countries is the inclusion of the cumulative characteristics in Security Council resolution 1566 (2004). By way of example, section 5(2) of the Terrorism Suppression Act 2002 (NZ) prohibits the intentional and unlawful delivery, placement, discharge or detonation of an explosive or other lethal device with the intention to cause death (or serious injury) or extensive destruction.[53] The provision does not specify that such conduct be aimed at inducing fear or influencing an organisation or government, nor does it specify that this be for the advancement of any particular cause. It thus only holds two of the cumulative characteristics of terrorism identified by the Security Council in its resolution 1566 (2004).[54] Thus, if one considers the definition of the offence closely, it is not one of "terrorist" bombing, but one of "bombing" where death or serious injury results, or where extensive damage to public facilities results.

Some offences in the UK's Terrorism Act 2000 also lack a proper link to terrorism. Section 54 of the Act makes weapons training an offence, punishable by up to 10 years imprisonment. Such training need not, however, be linked to terrorism (see the expression of the offence – Appendix 3, Table 5(J)). Although the offence has some bearing on the countering of terrorism, it is capable of applying in other contexts.[55] Such a broadly-applicable offence of this kind should not therefore have been introduced under counter-terrorism legislation. Doing so further illustrates the emerging trend of countries to use counter-terrorism legislation as an opportunity to extend State powers, or to introduce provisions under counter-terrorism law which should in fact be included in more broadly applicable laws (see Chap. 4, Sect. 4.3.5.3).

---

[53]Corresponding to article 2(1) of the International Convention for the Suppression of Terrorist Bombing, opened for signature 12 January 1998, 2149 UNTS 286 (entered into force 23 May 2001).

[54]See also the offence of threats to people or property under section 307A of the Crimes Act 1961 (NZ), introduced under the Counter-Terrorism Bill 2003, which has no link with any of the characteristics under Security Council resolution 1566 (2004) – see Appendix 3, Table 4(F). Consider also the weapons training offence under section 54 of the Terrorism Act 2000 (UK) which is not linked to terrorism – see Appendix 3, Table 5(J).

[55]See also: section 58A of the Terrorism Act 2008 (UK), in Appendix 3, Table 5(J); sections 47 and 50 of the Anti-terrorism, Crime and Security Act 2001 (UK), in Appendix 3, Table 5(K).

14.2.3.4 Sedition Offences in Australia

As a final point, mention should be made of section 80.2(7) and (8) of Australia's Criminal Code Act 1995, which establish offences of urging a person to assist the enemy, and urging a person to assist those engaged in armed hostilities (see Chap. 5, Sect. 5.2.1 and Appendix 3, Table 2(A)). These offences were added to the Criminal Code as a result of the Anti-Terrorism Act (No 2) 2005, although they were previously offences under sections 24A–24F of the Crimes Act 1914. Although it may not have been the intention of the legislative amendment under the Anti-Terrorism Act (No 2) 2005, the extraterritorial application of these "Category D" offences (see section 15.4 of the Criminal Code) means that commanders of enemy forces overseas who order their troops to attack Australian forces may be liable for prosecution for sedition under Australian law. In his study of Australia's counter-terrorism laws, the UN Special Rapporteur on counter-terrorism pointed out that, under international humanitarian law, combatants lawfully participating in armed conflict are entitled to immunity and prisoner-of-war status upon capture. Although Australia reported that there was no intention for these provisions to interfere with international humanitarian law, the possibility exists, and the Special Rapporteur therefore urged Australia to bring these laws in compliance with international humanitarian law.[56]

14.2.4 Sentencing for Terrorism Offences

The universal instruments related to terrorism specify that the penalties for terrorism offences must be serious, and in conformity with the principle of proportionality as between the gravity of the sanction and the gravity of the act. The Hague Convention, for example, requires States parties to impose "severe penalties" in the event of the hijacking of an aircraft, and the Convention for the Suppression of the Financing of Terrorism calls on States parties to adopt measures necessary to "make those offences punishable by appropriate penalties which take into account the grave nature of the offences".[57] Furthermore, Security Council resolution 1373

---

[56]Special Rapporteur report on Australia (n 17), paras 29 and 67.

[57]Convention for the Suppression of Unlawful Seizure of Aircraft (n 2) article 2; International Convention for the Suppression of the Financing of Terrorism, opened for signature 10 January 2000, 2179 UNTS 232 (entered into force 10 April 1992), article 4. See also the Convention on the Prevention and Punishment of Crimes against International Protected Persons, including Diplomatic Agents, opened for signature 14 December 1973, 1035 UNTS 167 (entered into force 20 February 1977), which requires each State Party to penalise and to impose "appropriate penalties which take into account their grave nature" (article 2(2)); the International Convention against the Taking of Hostages, opened for signature 18 December 1979, 1316 UNTS 205 (entered into force 3 June 1983), which indicates that each State shall punish the offences set forth "by appropriate penalties which take into account the grave nature of those offences" (article 2); the same applies to the Convention for the Suppression of Unlawful Acts against the Safety of

(2001) requires States to ensure that punishments imposed for those who participate in the financing, planning, preparation or perpetration of terrorist acts, or in supporting terrorist acts, duly reflect the seriousness of such terrorist acts.[58]

While acknowledging that determining the level of sanctions is a matter for each member of the United Nations (recognising the sovereign independence of each State), the UN Office on Drugs and Crime (UNODC) Guide for the Legislative Incorporation and Implementation of the Universal Instruments Against Terrorism advocates that: "The system of penalties must be especially dissuasive and heavy sentences need to be laid down for perpetrators of such acts".[59]

14.2.4.1   Maximum Penalties for Terrorism Offences

A review of the domestic terrorism offences in Australia, Canada, NZ and the UK shows maximum levels of sentencing which generally accord with this guidance. Offences such as hostage-taking, hijacking, engaging in a terrorist act, and committing a terrorist bombing can carry maximum terms of life imprisonment.[60] Other offences such as the possession of things connected with terrorist acts or facilitating such acts, and membership in or recruitment for a terrorist organisation, are punishable by maximum terms of imprisonment of 10 years or more.[61] Australia provides

---

Maritime Navigation, opened for signature 10 March 1988, 1678 UNTS 221 (entered into force 1 March 1992), article 5, and the International Convention for the Suppression of Terrorist Bombing, opened for signature 12 January 1998, 2149 UNTS 286 (entered into force 23 May 2001), article 4(b).

[58]SC Res 1373 (n 3) para 2(e).

[59]United Nations Office on Drugs and Crime, Guide for the Legislative Incorporation and Implementation of the Universal Anti-Terrorism Instruments (United Nations, New York, 2006), para 245.

[60]See, in Australia, offences under sections 17, 18 and 25 of the Crimes (Aviation) Act 1991; section 8(1) of the Crimes (Hostages) Act 1989; sections 8, 10, 21, and 23 of the Crimes (Ships and Fixed Platforms) Act 1992; and sections 72.3 and 101.1 of the Criminal Code Act 1995. In Canada, see sections 7(3.2), 76–78, 83.2, 83.21, 83.22 and 279.1 of the Criminal Code 1985. In New Zealand, see section 3 of the Aviation Crimes Act 1972; and sections 5 and 6A(1) of the Terrorism Suppression Act 2002. In the United Kingdom, see sections 47 and 50 of the Antiterrorism, Crime and Security Act 2001; sections 9–14 of the Aviation and Maritime Security Act 1990; sections 1–3 of the Aviation Security Act 1982; section 1 of the Biological Weapons Act 1974; section 2 of the Chemical Weapons Act 1996; sections 2, 3 and 5 of the Explosive Substances Act 1883; section 2 of the Nuclear Material (Offences) Act 1983; section 1 of the Taking of Hostages Act 1982; section 56 of the Terrorism Act 2000; and sections 5 and 9–11 of the Terrorism Act 2006.

[61]See, in Australia, sections 20, 21 and 27 of the Charter of the United Nations Act 1945; sections 14, 16, 19–23 and 25–26 of the Crimes (Aviation) Act 1991; section 8(3) and (4) of the Crimes (Hostages) Act 1989; sections 9, 11–16, 22, and 25–27 of the Crimes (Ships and Fixed Platforms) Act 1992; sections 72.12, 72.13, 72.14, 101.4, 101.5, 102.4 and 102.5 of the Criminal Code Act 1995; and sections 33–37 of the Nuclear Non-Proliferation (Safeguards) Act 1987. In Canada, see sections 83.02-83.04, 83.08, 83.12, 83.19, 83.23 of the Criminal Code 1985; section 3 of the United Nations Act 1985. In New Zealand, see sections 8, 13, 13B, and 13E of the Terrorism Suppression Act 2002. In the United Kingdom, see section 1 of the Internationally Protected

for certain offences, including the provision or receipt of training or funding connected with terrorist acts, or the direction of the activities of a terrorist organisation, to be punishable by up to 25 years imprisonment.[62] By way of general observation, the maximum penalties for terrorism offences is often higher in the United Kingdom and Australia than in Canada and New Zealand. Having said this, there are some offences in Australia which carry much lower maximum penalties than for most other terrorism offences.[63]

14.2.4.2 Sentencing Directions

As well as providing for high maximum penalties for terrorism offences, Canada, NZ and the UK have also taken legislative steps to direct courts on the question of sentencing such offences. Section 718.2(a)(v) of Canada's Criminal Code 1985 requires that where there is evidence that an offence is a terrorism offence, this must be treated by a sentencing court as an aggravating feature. Section 83.26 of the Criminal Code also requires that any sentences imposed in respect of terrorism offences, even if arising out of the same event or series of events, must be served consecutively (except in the case of terms of life imprisonment). Furthermore, where a person is convicted of an indictable offence which also constitutes a "terrorist activity", the person will become liable to imprisonment for life (section 83.27). If the killing of a person is caused while committing or attempting to commit an indictable offence which constitutes a terrorist activity, section 231 (6.01) deems the killing to be first degree murder irrespective of whether the murder is planned and deliberate.

In New Zealand, the Sentencing Act 2002 was amended so that offending that forms part of, or involves, a terrorist act is to be treated as an aggravating feature under section 9 of that Act (as amended by the Counter-Terrorism Bill 2003). Where murder is committed as part of a terrorist act, section 104 of the Sentencing Act provides for a minimum period of 17 years imprisonment for such offending. The question of sentencing directions in the United Kingdom is addressed in the Counter-Terrorism Act 2008, making it an aggravating feature for the purpose of sentencing if an offence "has or may have a terrorist connection" (section 30).

Persons Act 1978; sections 11–12, 15–18, 54, 57 and 58 of the Terrorism Act 2000; and sections 6 and 8 of the Terrorism Act 2006.

[62]See sections 101.2, 102.2 and 102.6 of the Criminal Code Act 1995. The same level of maximum penalty is also provided for the offence of providing support to a terrorist organisation under section 102.7 of the Criminal Code.

[63]Including, for example, the offences of associating with terrorist organisations (section 102.8 of the Criminal Code Act 1995 – three years), making threats and false statements affecting aviation security (sections 24 and 25 of the Crimes (Aviation) Act 1991 – two years), possessing unmarked plastic explosives (section 72.15 of the Criminal Code – two years), breaching packaging requirements for plastic explosives (section 72.17 of the Criminal Code – two years), and threats to commit offences under the Convention for the Suppression of Unlawful Acts against the Safety of Maritime Navigation (section 17 of the Crimes (Ships and Fixed Platforms) Act 1992 – two years).

The principle of treating terrorism as an aggravating feature is not problematic in itself. It is not unusual for certain types of offending, or accompanying character-istics such as home invasion or sexual misconduct, to be designated as aggravating features for the purpose of sentencing. What is problematic in the directions just identified, however, is the use of terms which have already been identified as overly broad and reaching beyond what is truly terrorist in nature, i.e. linking the aggravating features to the terms "terrorist activity", "terrorist act" and "terrorist connection" which all go beyond the characterisation of conduct to be suppressed in the fight against terrorism (see Sect. 14.1 above).

14.3   The Incitement to Terrorism

Public provocation to commit acts of terrorism is described by the Security Council Working Group established pursuant to resolution 1566 (2004) as "an insidious activity contributing to the spread of the scourge of terrorism".[64] The Security Council has declared that knowingly inciting terrorist acts is contrary to the purposes and principles of the United Nations,[65] and has called on States, under paragraph 1(a) of its resolution 1624 (2005), to prohibit by law incitement to commit a terrorist act or acts.[66] The current part of this chapter considers the incidence of incitement to terrorism over recent years, the means by which this type of conduct can and/or should be criminalised, and then evaluates the compli-ance by each country, using New Zealand as a case study, with paragraph 1(a) of Security Council resolution 1624 (2005).

14.3.1   The Phenomenon of the Incitement to Terrorism

There have been numerous instances of incitement to, and glorification of, terrorism, some of which have been noted in Chap. 2 (see Sect. 2.1.4). The now well-known World Islamic Front Statement of 1998, the 'Jihad Against Jews and Crusaders', which purports to be a fatwa (a religious ruling) is a good example.[67] It calls for the killing of Americans, claiming to base itself upon a call by Allah to "slay the pagans wherever ye find them, seize them, beleaguer them, and lie in wait for them in every stratagem (of war)".[68] The document concludes with the direction that:[69]

---

[64]Report of the Security Council Working Group established pursuant to resolution 1566 (2004), UN Doc S/2005/789 (2005), para 29.

[65]SC Res 1373 (n 3) para 5(3).

[66]SC Res 1624 (n 5).

[67]World Islamic Front, Jihad Against Jews and Crusaders, 23 February 1998 (signed, amongst others, by Usama bin Laden), online: http://www.fas.org/irp/world/para/docs/980223-fatwa.htm.

[68]Ibid, un-numbered para 1. The phrase is taken from *The Holy Qura'an*, 9:5.

[69]Ibid, un-numbered para 8.

> We – with Allah's help – call on every Muslim who believes in Allah and wishes to be rewarded to comply with Allah's order to kill the Americans and plunder their money wherever and whenever they find it. We also call on Muslim ulema, leaders, youths, and soldiers to launch the raid on Satan's US troops and the devil's supporters allying with them, and to displace those who are behind them so that they may learn a lesson.

While this fatwa is particularly directed towards Americans, due to the purported occupation and plundering by the United States of the Arabian Peninsula during its presence there during Operation Desert Storm in 1990 and Operation Desert Fox in 1998,[70] the sentiment of the jihad is one that is opposed to modernity in general. Its desire is to eliminate modernity and return to the era when Islam formed a prosperous ummah (a community of Islamic believers) in the Middle East (and possibly beyond) without restriction by State borders – an era in which modernity was absent in the region.[71] It is a particularly common tool of global jihadists.[72]

Following the commencement of the multi-national Operation Enduring Freedom in Afghanistan a further manifesto, issued by Salem Almakhi and first aired on Aljazeera in October 2002,[73] announced a warning to Christians and members of the alliance waging war against Afghanistan and Al-Qa'ida.[74] This most palpably applies to States participating in Operation Enduring Freedom, and might therefore be characterised as incitement of an insurgent nature, but it is also of much broader application. By identifying those acting against Al-Qa'ida, the warning conceivably also attaches to all those taking action against Usama bin Laden, the Taliban and Al-Qa'ida. Since all members of the United Nations are required to take action against those entities pursuant to various resolutions of the Security Council, and directions of the Al-Qa'ida and Taliban Sanctions Committee, the warning is at least in principle applicable to all 191 members of the United Nations (on the Al-Qa'ida and Taliban Sanctions Committee, see Chap. 19, Sect. 19.1.1). The Sanctions Committee, which describes itself as "a key instrument in the fight against terrorism",[75] maintains a list of individuals and entities that are part of, or associated with, the Taliban, Al-Qa'ida and Usama bin Laden. UN member States

---

[70]Ibid, un-numbered para 3.

[71]See further Conte and Ganor (2005), parts II(D)(3) and II(D)(4).

[72]The International Policy Institute for Counter-Terrorism has written much on this subject. See, for example (all available online, at http://www.ict.org.il): Fighel and Shahar (2002); Shahar (2002); Kahati (2003); and Kahati and Fighel (2003).

[73]Salem Almakhi, Mending the Hearts of the Believers, online: http://www.jihadonline. bravepages.com/mending.htm. Salem Almakhi is said to be one of Usama bin Laden's supporters and admirers, and personally knowledgeable of Al-Qa'ida operations: see Fighel and Kehati (2002).

[74]Almakhi (ibid) un-numbered para 23.

[75]Security Council Committee Established Pursuant to Resolution 1267 (1999), Guidance for Reports Required of all States pursuant to paragraphs 6 and 12 of Resolution 1455 (2003), online: http://www.un.org/Docs/sc/committees/1267/guidanc_en.pdf, un-numbered para 1.

are required to freeze funds and other financial resources, and ensure that their nationals do not make funds or financial resources available to such listed entities. The manifesto finally instructs:[76]

> Anyone who possesses an arrow in his quiver, make haste and [shoot] it for the sake of Allah, and aim it at the enemies of religion – the Jews and the Christians. . .

In an audio tape aired by Aljazeera in 2003, a senior aide to Usama bin Laden, Ayman Zawahri, exhorted his audience with the following words:[77]

> Oh Muslims! Carry out attacks against the embassies, companies, interests and officials of the US, Britain, Australia and Norway. Burn the ground under their feet.

A video found in 2005 in the hideout of Malaysian terrorist Noordin Mohamad Top contained the following threats:[78]

> As long as you keep your troops in Iraq and Afghanistan and intimidate Muslim people, you will feel our intimidation. . . You will be the target of our next attack. . . Our enemy is America, Australia, England and Italy. . . We especially remind Australia that you, Downer and Howard, are killing Australia, leading it into darkness and misfortune and mujahedeen terror. . .

The United Kingdom has arrested and successfully prosecuted persons for inciting terrorism and murder (see Chap. 8, Sect. 8.1.10). In February 2006, Abu Hamza, a former imam at the North London Central Mosque in Finsbury Park, was jailed for 7 years after being found guilty of encouraging his followers to murder non-Muslims. Abu Izzadeen was amongst six men arrested in 2007 and convicted in April 2008 of inciting terrorism overseas. He was found guilty of inciting worshippers at a London mosque to join the mujahedeen to fight British and American forces in Iraq. He was sentenced to four and a half years imprisonment, but released in May 2009 following a reduction in his sentence on appeal.

These are just some of the few statement inciting terrorism in the years leading up to and following the events of 9/11.

14.3.2 Criminalising the Incitement to Terrorism

There are two general means by which the incitement to terrorism may be criminalised. The first is by reactive means, where a person who has incited or glorified terrorism may be prosecuted as a party to a principal terrorist act. Many

---

[76]Almakhi (n 73) penultimate para.

[77]Aljazeera, 'New Al-Qaeda Tape Calls for Attacks' (Aljazeera.net, 21 May 2003), online: http://english.aljazeera.net/NR/exeres/293D19D4-CBB9-4296-B158-D54246F6259E.htm (as accessed 22 November 2005 – copy on file with author).

[78]Associated Press, 'Indonesia Video Warning on Terror' (CNN.com International, 17 November 2005), online: http://edition.cnn.com/2005/WORLD/asiapcf/11/16/indonesia.terror.ap/ (as accessed 22 November 2005 – copy on file with author).

jurisdictions have such party offences, where the conduct of anyone who incites, counsels, or procures any person to commit an offence is also guilty of the offence. This is the case in all four case study countries. The second, proactive, means of criminalisation is one that seeks to create liability without needing to wait for a terrorist act to occur. A 'proactive' offence criminalises the act of incitement itself as a primary, rather than secondary, offence.

The UNODC Terrorism Prevention Branch takes the view that the general obligation of States to abstain from tolerating terrorist activities implies that they must adopt active measures in order to prevent those acts.[79] The adoption by States of a proactive approach in countering terrorism is also encouraged within resolutions of the General Assembly and Security Council.[80] Security Council resolution 1373 (2001) in fact requires States to take proactive measures, paragraph 2(b) stating that member States shall: "Take the necessary steps to prevent the commission of terrorist acts...".[81] One should also note that the prohibition against the incitement to offending, in the international criminal law context, is not unique. Article 3(1)(c)(iii) of the Convention Against the Illicit Traffic in Narcotic Drugs and Psychotropic Substances requires States parties to establish as a criminal offence the intentional public incitement or inducement of others to commit any of the article 3 offences, or to use narcotic drugs or psychotropic substances illicitly.[82] The 1998 Statute of the International Criminal Court also contemplates criminal responsibility in the case of any person who: "In respect of the crime of genocide, directly and publicly incites others to commit genocide".[83] Similarly, article 20(2) of the International Covenant on Civil and Political Rights (ICCPR) requires States to prohibit the advocacy of national, racial or religious hatred that constitutes incitement to discrimination, hostility or violence.[84]

There is currently no common obligation upon States to proscribe the incitement to terrorism. The matter is not addressed within any of the extant universal

---

[79]United Nations Office on Drugs and Crime, Guide for the Legislative Incorporation and Implementation of the Universal Instruments Against Terrorism (Division of Treaty Affairs, Terrorism Prevention Branch, 2006), para 250.

[80]See, for example: GA Res 58/136, UN GAOR, 58th sess, 77th plen mtg, UN Doc A/Res/58/136 (2003), paras 1 and 5; GA Res 58/140, UN GAOR; 58th sess, 77th plen mtg, UN Doc A/Res/58/140 (2003), para 2; GA Res 59/46, UN GAOR, 59th sess, 65th plen mtg, UN Doc A/Res/59/46 (2004), paras 13 and 15; GA Res 59/80, UN GAOR, 59th sess, 66th plen mtg, UN Doc A/Res/59/80 (2004), paras 1 and 2 (see also newly adopted GA resolutions 60/43, 60/73 and 60/78); SC Res 1456, UN SCOR, 4668th mtg, UN Doc S/Res/1456 (2003), para 5; SC Res 1566, UN SCOR, 5053rd mtg, UN Doc S/Res/1566 (2004), para 2; SC Res 1618, UN SCOR, 5246th mtg, UN Doc S/Res/1618 (2005), para 6; and SC Res 1624 (n 5) paras 1, 2 and 3.

[81]SC Res 1373 (n 3) para 2(b).

[82]Convention Against the Illicit Traffic in Narcotic Drugs and Psychotropic Substances, opened for signature 14 December 1984, 28 ILM 493 (entered into force 11 November 1990).

[83]Statute of the International Criminal Court, opened for signature 17 July 1988, 2187 UNTS 90, entered into force 1 July 2002), article 25(3)(e).

[84]International Covenant on Civil and Political Rights, opened for signature 16 December 1966, 999 UNTS 171 (entered into force 23 March 1976).

terrorism-related conventions. It is, however, required of States parties to the 2005 Council of Europe Convention on the Prevention of Terrorism, which entered into force in July 2007 but in respect of which the United Kingdom has not yet deposited an instrument of ratification.[85] Within the United Nations framework, the subject is addressed in resolutions of the UN General Assembly and Security Council.

14.3.2.1   Suppressing the Incitement to Terrorism

Turning first to the resolutions of the United Nations, General Assembly resolution 40/61 (1985) calls on UN member States to refrain from organising, instigating, assisting or participating in terrorist acts in other States, or "in acquiescing in activities within their territory directed towards the commission of such acts".[86] Similarly, the Declaration on Measures to Eliminate International Terrorism, adopted by the General Assembly in 1994 and subsequently reaffirmed on an almost annual basis, calls for States:[87]

> To refrain from organizing, instigating, facilitating, financing, encouraging *or tolerating terrorist activities* and to take appropriate practical measures *to ensure that their respective territories are not used for* terrorist installations or training camps, or for the preparation or *organization of terrorist acts* intended to be *committed against other States or their citizens*; (emphasis added).

The emphasised portions of the extract can be taken to support a proactive approach in countering terrorism, and emphasise the need to suppress terrorism against other States. Any criminalisation of the incitement to terrorism needs, therefore, to be both applicable within the territory of the State and also outwardly looking. Added to this, General Assembly resolution 59/195 (2004): "condemns the incitement ethnic hatred, violence and terrorism".[88] While resolutions of the General Assembly are recommendatory only,[89] it might be argued, given the consistent pattern of reaffirming the Declaration on Measures to Eliminate International Terrorism for a decade now (see Chap. 3, Sect. 3.2.1), that the calls for action within the Declaration form part of customary international law. Such an assertion, however, would need to be treated carefully.[90] Suffice it to say, for the purposes of this chapter, that

---

[85]Council of Europe Convention on the Prevention of Terrorism, opened for signature 16 May 2005, CETS 196 (entered into force 1 July 2007). The Convention was signed by the United Kingdom on 16 May 2005.

[86]GA Res 40/61, UN GAOR, 40th Sess, 108th Plen Mtg, UN Doc A/Res/40/61 (1985), para 6.

[87]Declaration on Measures to Eliminate International Terrorism, adopted under GA Res 49/60, UN GAOR, 49th Sess, 84th Plen Mtg, UN Doc A/Res/49/60 (1994), para 5(a).

[88]GA Res 59/195, UN GAOR, 59th Sess, 74th Plen Mtg, UN Doc A/Res/59/195 (2004), para 12.

[89]See article 10 of the Charter of the United Nations 1945.

[90]For that to be the case, it would need to be shown that the relevant provision(s) of the declaration represent the conduct of States, such conduct being undertaken out of a sense of legal obligation (*opinio juris*): see the Statute of the International Court of Justice, opened for signature 26 June 1945 (entered into force 24 October 1945), article 38(1)(b).

there have been repeated calls for States to be proactive in their countering of terrorism, including the incitement thereof.

As far as the Security Council is concerned, two of its resolutions address the issue of incitement to terrorism. The first is resolution 1373 (2001), in which paragraph 5(3) declares:[91]

> ...that acts, methods, and practices of terrorism are contrary to the purposes and principles of the United Nations and that knowingly financing, planning and *inciting* terrorist acts are also contrary to the purposes and principles of the United Nations; (emphasis added).

Paragraph 1 of resolution 1624 (2005), which was made by the Security Council a few months after the adoption of the Council of Europe Convention on the Prevention of Terrorism, is even more direct, providing that the Security Council:[92]

> *Calls upon* all States to adopt such measures as may be necessary and appropriate and in accordance with their obligations under international law to
>
> (a) Prohibit by law incitement to commit a terrorist act or acts;
> (b) Prevent such conduct;

It should be noted that, although article 25 of the Charter of the United Nations directs Member States to comply with decisions of the Security Council, the particular wording of the latter provisions are not couched in mandatory language and do not, therefore, have binding effect (on this issue, see further Chap. 3, Sect. 3.2.3). As statements emanating from the body of the United Nations responsible for the maintenance of international peace and security, however, they should be treated as highly persuasive.

14.3.2.2 The Council of Europe Convention on the Prevention of Terrorism

The Council of Europe Convention on the Prevention of Terrorism, adopted on 16 May 2005, requires States parties to criminalise the unlawful and intentional "public provocation to commit a terrorist offence", defining that phrase in Article 5(1) as:[93]

> ... the distribution, or otherwise making available, of a message to the public, with the intent to incite the commission of a terrorist offence, where such conduct, whether or not directly advocating terrorist offences, causes a danger that one or more such offences may be committed.

The Special Rapporteur on the promotion and protection of human rights and fundamental freedoms while countering terrorism has expressed the view that this provision represents a best practice in defining the proscription of the incitement to

---

[91]SC Res 1373 (n 3).

[92]SC Res 1624 (n 5).

[93]Council of Europe Convention on the Prevention of Terrorism (n 85) article 5.

terrorism.[94] Although the Convention is a regional instrument, the proscription in article 5 was the result of careful negotiation. In defining what amounts to a "public provocation to commit a terrorist offence", article 5 contains three elements. There must first be an act of communication ("the distribution, or otherwise making available, of a message to the public ..."). Secondly, there must be a *subjective* intention on the part of the person to incite terrorism ("...with the intent to incite the commission of a terrorist offence... whether or not directly advocating terrorist offences ..."). Finally, there must be an additional *objective* danger that the person's conduct will incite terrorism ("...where such conduct ... causes danger that one or more such offences may be committed"). The latter objective requirement separates the incitement to terrorism from an act of glorification of terrorism. The requirement of intention in article 5(2) reaffirms the subjective element within the definition of public provocation to commit a terrorist offence and requires the act of communication to be intentional also.

Of note, article 8 of the Convention clarifies that a terrorist offence need not actually be committed for the provocation of such offending to amount to conduct proscribed under article 5. The offence is thus proactive in nature. Of note also, the term "terrorist offence" is defined under article 1 as any of the offences within 10 of the anti-terrorism conventions in force at the time the Convention was adopted (excluding the Tokyo Convention and the Convention on the Marking of Plastic Explosives). The latter convention is properly omitted as a 'trigger offence' treaty, since it does not proscribe any conduct, but instead places obligations upon States relating to the marking of explosives (see further Chap. 2, Sect. 2.3.1). The Tokyo Convention was omitted due to the broad nature of the conduct proscribed under the treaty which, while criminalising terrorist conduct, also captures conduct with no bearing at all to terrorism (for example, conduct which may jeopardise good order on an aircraft).[95]

14.3.3   Incitement Under New Zealand Law

New Zealand does not have a specific offence dealing with the incitement to terrorist, instead relying on general provisions of law, and provisions within the Human Rights Act 1993 and the Crimes Act 1961.

---

[94]Special Rapporteur on Australia (n 17) paras 26–27.

[95]See further on this point the report of the Special Rapporteur on the promotion and protection of human rights and fundamental freedoms while countering terrorism, Promotion and Protection of Human Rights, UN Doc E/CN.4/2006/98 (2006), paras 32–36.

14.3.3.1 General Proscription Against Incitement

New Zealand's Human Rights Act 1993 prohibits threatening, abusive or insulting publications or speech likely "to excite hostility against or bring into contempt" any group of persons on the grounds of discrimination (sections 61 and 63). It is, in that regard, similar to the prohibition in article 20(2) of the ICCPR but is more limited in its potential application to the incitement of terrorism. The first limitation concerns a jurisdictional restriction. The prohibition only applies to such conduct that excites hostility against persons in New Zealand (or who may be coming to New Zealand): section 61(1). Jurisdictional limitations such as this fail to address the need for States to prohibit the incitement to terrorism (and to hostility or violence more generally) both within their own borders and those of other States.

The second limitation is that the prohibition is restricted to the incitement of discrimination and hostility. It does not prohibit incitement to violence, although it should be acknowledged that 'violence' is conceivably captured within the scope of 'hostility'. The prohibited conduct under the Human Rights Act is that which, inter alia, is: "likely to excite hostility against or bring into contempt any group of persons in or who may be coming to New Zealand on the ground of the colour, race, or ethnic or national origins of that group of persons". Furthermore, the maximum penalty for the offence of incitement under the Human Rights Act is a term of imprisonment not exceeding 3 months, or a fine not exceeding $7,000 (section 131(1)). This maximum sentence does not meet with the call for heavy sentences against those involved in terrorism (see Sect. 14.2.4 above).

14.3.3.2 Party Offences

Party offences are created under section 66(1)(d) of the Crimes Act 1961 (NZ), such that the conduct of anyone who "incites, counsels, or procures any person to commit an offence" is also guilty of the principal offence. Thus, a person who has incited the commission of any of the terrorism offences under New Zealand law, as identified, would be liable for prosecution. The point to be made is that this is a 'reactive' form of criminalisation, rather than the proactive criminalisation of the incitement to terrorism called for. To be guilty of an offence under section 66(1) (d), case law has confirmed that the principal offence (including an act of terrorism) must have actually been committed.[96]

14.3.3.3 Procuring the Commission of Offences

Section 311 of the Crimes Act is the corollary to party offences under section 66(1) (d). Whereas party offences can only be committed where the principal offence has

---

[96]See *R v Bowern* [1915] 34 NZLR 696.

been carried out, section 311(2) prohibits the incitement, counselling, or attempt to procure any person to commit any offence, "when that offence is not in fact committed". This would clearly capture the incitement of terrorist offences under New Zealand law.

However, in the way that section 311(1) can relate to terrorism-specific offences (none of which carry a sentence of life imprisonment), a person who incites, counsels, or attempts to procure the commission of such offences is liable to not more than half of the maximum punishment one would be liable for had the offence been committed. This form of secondary liability is likely grounded in the fact that section 311 applies only where the principal offence has not been committed, with the consequence that there is no victim (unlike the commission of party offences under section 66). As discussed, the UNODC ultimately takes the view that determining the precise level of sanctions is a matter for each State having regard to proportionality between the gravity of the act and the sanction imposed. Notwithstanding this, an observation to make is that incitement to terrorism (as referred to in the resolutions of the General Assembly and the Security Council) and incitement to hostility or violence (under article 20(2) of the ICCPR) are treated as primary offences. It is thus questionable whether the reduced form of secondary liability provided for in section 311(1) is appropriate to deal with the procuring of terrorism offences.

14.3.3.4   Seditious Offences

Again relevant to the incitement to terrorism, section 81 of the Crimes Act 1961 defines a seditious intention as an intention: to incite, procure, or encourage violence, lawlessness, or disorder (section 81(1)(c)); or to incite, procure, or encourage the commission of any offence that is prejudicial to the public safety or to the maintenance of public order (section 81(1)(d)). An offence of 'seditious conspiracy' is then created through the combination of sections 81(3) and 82, such that an agreement between two or more persons to carry into execution any seditious intention makes a person liable to imprisonment for a term not exceeding 2 years. Two limitations are identified. The maximum penalty for an offence of sedition is 2 years' imprisonment, which probably fails to meet the call for heavy sentences. Also, an intention to incite those things identified in section 81(1)(c) and (d) only becomes an offence of sedition if two or more people agree to do so. Section 81 of the Crimes Act would thus fail to capture a person acting alone to incite terrorism (as has occurred in the examples cited earlier, at Sect. 14.3.1).

14.3.3.5   Making Threats of Harm

Amendment of the Crimes Act in 2003 saw the introduction of section 307A, which criminalises certain threats of harm to people or property. The making of such threats is again limited in its relevance to the incitement to terrorism. The threats must be ones that significantly disrupt matters relating to New Zealand (subsection (2)), thus failing to address the need for States to prohibit the incitement to terrorism both within their own borders and those of other States. Furthermore, the threats must have resulted in certain outcomes (subsection (3)), thus adopting a reactive rather than proactive approach. Most importantly, the prohibition relates to the making of threats, rather than the incitement of others to hostility, violence or terrorism and thus only criminalises acts of incitement that themselves contain threats falling within the jurisdiction of section 307A.

14.3.3.6 Jurisdictional Issues in New Zealand's Applicable Law

The various offences described fall into one of the following four categories.

- First are those offences committed entirely within the territory of New Zealand. In such circumstances, by application of the offence provisions alone, there are no jurisdictional issues of concern.
- Next would be offences commenced (or completed) within the territory of New Zealand. By application of section 7 of the Crimes Act 1961, such offences are deemed to have been committed in New Zealand, whether or not the person charged with the offence was in New Zealand at the time of the relevant act, omission, or event.
- Finally are those offences that amount to a "terrorist act" (as defined by section 5 (1) of the Terrorism Suppression Act 2002), and occur wholly outside New Zealand. By application of section 7A of the Crimes Act 1961, proceedings may be brought in respect of such acts if: (1) the person is a New Zealander or in New Zealand (section 7A(1)(a)); (2) any part of the offence occurs on any place in respect of which New Zealand has jurisdiction abroad (section 7A(1)(b)); or (3) the offence is perpetrated against a New Zealander (section 7A(1)(c)).
- Added to this, the offences described are capable of dealing with the following persons or events overseas: (1) conduct falling within one of the defined terrorism offences relating to activities outside New Zealand (e.g. the prohibition against dealing with property owned or controlled by a designated terrorist entity, those entities all being outside New Zealand, as the position currently stands); or (2) being a party to the latter offences, procuring the commission of the latter offences, or undertaking a seditious conspiracy relating to the latter offences.

Notwithstanding this framework of jurisdiction, none of the offences described in this part of this paper are able to deal with the situation where a person incites others to commit terrorist acts abroad.

14.3.3.7 Summary and Evaluation of New Zealand's Law on Incitement

Having regard to the practical relevance of the incitement to terrorism to New Zealand and the Pacific region, and to the international obligations and recommendations on the prohibition of the incitement to hostility, violence and terrorism, New Zealand's criminal law appears deficient in a number of ways. The incitement offence under the Human Rights Act 1993 is limited in its jurisdictional application, by the fact that it does not expressly apply to the incitement of violence, and in the low level of maximum penalty upon conviction. Party offences under section 66(1)(d) of the Crimes Act 1961 are reactive, requiring an actual act of hostility, violence or terrorism to occur before proceedings can commence. Procuring offences under section 311 of the Crimes Act 1961 limit the maximum penalty upon conviction to not more than half of the relevant principal offence. Sedition offences under sections 81 and 82 of the Crimes Act 1961 have a maximum penalty of 2 years' imprisonment upon conviction and do not capture a person acting alone to incite terrorism. The 'threat of harm' offence under section 307A of the Crimes Act 1961 is limited in its jurisdictional application, by the reactive approach of the offence, and the fact that it only criminalises acts of incitement that themselves contain threats falling within the jurisdiction of section 307A. Furthermore, despite New Zealand's reasonably robust jurisdictional framework, none of the offences described are able to deal with the situation where a person incites others to commit terrorist acts abroad.

14.3.4   *Incitement Under Australian, Canadian and UK Law*

The United Kingdom is the only one of the four case study countries which has a specific offence of incitement to terrorism. As described in Chap. 8, section 1 of the Terrorism Act 2006 (UK) establishes the offence of encouragement to terrorism, comprising three elements (see Sect. 8.1.8.1). First, there must be an act of publishing a statement (or causing another to do so on the person's behalf). Next, the published statement must be likely to be understood by members of the public to whom it is published as a direct or indirect encouragement or other inducement to them to the commission, preparation or instigation of acts of terrorism. The final element of the offence requires that the person publishing such a statement must intend (at the time of publication) that the statement be understood in the way just described, or be reckless as to whether or not it is likely to be so understood. Conviction on indictment renders a person liable to imprisonment for up to 7 years. The human rights compliance of this offence is considered in Chap. 20 (Sect. 20.2.3.1).

14.3.4.1   Canada

Part 8 of Canada's Criminal Code 1985 includes a section dedicated to hate propaganda, which establishes the offences of advocating genocide (section 318) and public incitement of hatred (section 319). Section 320 of the Code allows for the issue of warrants of seizure of hate propaganda. New section 320.1 of the Code, inserted as a result of the Anti-terrorism Act 2001, provides for the deletion of hate propaganda from public web sites. Section 319 of the Criminal Code includes two offences concerning the incitement of hatred (see Appendix 3, Table 3(B)). The first, under section 319(1), prohibits the communication of statements in any public place which incite hatred against any identifiable group where such incitement is likely to lead to a breach of the peace (punishable, upon indictment, by imprisonment for a term not exceeding 2 years). Section 319(2) establishes the offence of wilful promotion of hatred, i.e. the communication of statements in public which wilfully promotes hatred against any identifiable group, also punishable by up to 2 years imprisonment. The distinction between the two offences is that the former must be likely to lead to a breach of the peace, but need not include a wilful promotion of hatred, whereas the latter must wilfully promote hatred, but need not be likely to lead to a breach of the peace.

Like New Zealand, Canada does not otherwise have a specific, separate, offence of incitement to terrorism. It instead relies on the general sections of the Criminal Code making a person liable for furthering the commission of any of the specific crimes in the Code (i.e. secondary liability), as is also the case in New Zealand.[97] What might at first blush distinguish the position in Canada from that in New Zealand is that Canada's definition of "terrorist activity" includes "a conspiracy, attempt or threat to commit any such act or omission, or being an accessory after the fact or counselling in relation to any such act or omission...". Thus, in its fifth report to the Counter-Terrorism Committee, Canada explained that counselling an act or omission that falls within the definition of "terrorist activity" is itself caught by the definition of "terrorist activity".[98] Counselling, under section 22(3) of the Criminal Code, includes inciting. Hence, someone who incites another to commit an act or omission that constitutes "terrorist activity" him or herself engages in "terrorist activity". The problem with this, however, is that there is no offence in Canada of engaging in terrorist activity, although there are offences such as participation in, or contribution to, any activity of a terrorist group for the purpose of enhancing the ability of the group to facilitate or carry out a terrorist activity (section 83.18(1) of the Criminal Code), and the more general prohibition in section 83.10 of facilitating a terrorist activity. These offences do not amount, however, to one comparable to a proactive offence of incitement to terrorism, as exists in the United Kingdom.

---

[97]Ribbelink (2006, p. 197).

[98]Fifth Report of the Government of Canada on the implementation of Security Council resolution 1373 (2001), UN Doc S/2006/185 (2006), pp. 14–15.

14.3.4.2 Australia

It is an offence under section 80.2 of Australia's Criminal Code Act 1995 for a person to urge a group(s) to use force or violence against another group(s) (see Chap. 5, Sect. 5.2.1, and Appendix 3, Table 2(A)). Although extended geographical jurisdiction applies for offences under division 80 of the Criminal Code, the conduct just described is only an offence if it would threaten the peace, order and good government of Australia (contrast section 80.4 with section 80.2(5)(b)). Therefore, although section 80.2 will capture some aspects of the incitement to terrorism, it will not encompass incitement by individuals, of individuals, nor will it capture the incitement of terrorist acts against individuals or organisations, or of transboundary acts of terrorism. Indeed, the Government of Australia has reported that these provisions were not intended to cover incitement to terrorist acts.[99] The Special Rapporteur on the promotion and protection of human rights and fundamental freedoms while countering terrorism has therefore reminded Australia, in his desk-top study of Australia's counter-terrorism laws, that the Security Council has called on States to suppress the incitement to terrorism and that article 20(2) of the ICCPR requires States to proscribe any advocacy of national, racial or religious hatred that constitutes incitement to hostility or violence.[100]

Despite this observation and reminder to Australia, the Special Rapporteur has noted that legislative reforms in Australia have captured some elements of the Security Council's call for the suppression of the incitement to terrorism. Advocating the commission of a terrorist act (whether or not it has occurred or will occur) is one of the grounds upon which the Attorney-General may list a "terrorist organisation" (see Chap. 5, Sect. 5.1.1.3). What is perhaps surprising is that Australia's comments on the draft report of the Special Rapporteur made no mention of the application of inchoate offences and, in particular, of the application of section 11.4 of the Criminal Code. In an article published since the Rapporteur's study, MacDonald and Williams note that incitement under section 11.4 applies to all Commonwealth crimes and is capable of punishing a person where the substantive offence is not completed and no harm is caused, punishable by the same maximum penalty as the offence incited.[101] Incitement to the terrorism offences in the Criminal Code is thus a proactive offence, compared to New Zealand's reactive approach. It should therefore be concluded that, although there is no specific offence of incitement to terrorism in Australia, its law is capable of complying with paragraph 1(a) of Security Council resolution 1624 (2005).

---

[99]Special Rapporteur report on Australia (n 17) para 25.

[100]Special Rapporteur report on Australia (n 17) para 26.

[101]MacDonald and Williams (2007, p. 31).

14.4 Conclusions

A large portion of the terrorism-related offences in the four case study countries relate to one of two features. Many are linked to domestic definitions of "terrorism", a "terrorist act" or "terrorist activity". Other offences are linked to proscribed organisations, the description of which is likewise linked to definitions of terrorism. As well as having these important associations with criminal offences, the definitions of terrorism in Australia, Canada, New Zealand and the United Kingdom are also linked to special investigative powers, the cordoning of areas, and powers of detention and of stop and search. The domestic definitions adopted therefore have wide implications for criminal law offences and investigative powers in those countries.

Two principal approaches to the definition of terrorism emerge in the four case study countries. The first is to equate conduct prohibited under the universal terrorism-related conventions as amounting to terrorism, in and of itself without any further element of intention (such as an intention to provoke terror or to influence a government or international organisation) or without any threshold of seriousness. This approach is taken by New Zealand and Canada in their definitions of a "terrorist act" and "terrorist activity". The second definitional approach, which is common to all four countries, is to use definitions which comprise the following three elements: (1) that the conduct be undertaken for political, religious or ideological purposes; (2) that the conduct have a coercive or intimidatory character, i.e. undertaken for the purpose of either provoking a state of terror, or compelling a government or international organisation to do or abstain from doing something; and (3) that the conduct fall within one of a list of acts.

Concerning the first element, although this is not included in the Security Council's characterisation of conduct to be suppressed in the fight against terrorism, it is a commonly understood feature of terrorism and is not problematic, since it constitutes a restrictive feature of the definition of terrorism. The second element common to definitions in Australia, Canada, NZ and the UK corresponds to the characteristic of terrorism identified in paragraph 3(b) of Security Council resolution 1566 (2004). The final common element is the one most problematic for consistency of the definitions with paragraph 3(a) of Security Council resolution 1566 (2004) and with the meaning of terrorism advocated by the Special Rapporteur on counter-terrorism. The lists of conduct include acts which go beyond the Security Council's characterisation of terrorism, including conduct which causes a serious risk to the health or safety of the public; conduct which constitutes a serious interference, disruption, or destruction of infrastructure or electronic systems; and conduct which causes substantial property damage. As currently expressed, these lists are overly broad and may capture effects of conduct which are not truly 'terrorist' in nature, i.e. are not restricted to hijacking, or conduct intended to cause death or serious bodily injury. It has also been noted that, unique to New Zealand, the list of conduct which would constitute a terrorist act (if accompanied by ideological motives and coercive or intimidatory intent) includes conduct intended to cause economic and environmental damage and the prospect of the release of disease-bearing organisms. While this is perhaps not surprising for a country like New Zealand, which relies so heavily on agricultural exports, these are matters which can, and should, be dealt with as separate offences.

The implementation by the case study countries of their international counter-terrorism obligations entails, in part, the criminalisation of certain terrorist and terrorism-related conduct. Criminalisation is not only a legal obligation for States parties to the various terrorism-related treaties, and in response to Security Council decisions, but it is also a prerequisite for effective international cooperation. One of the common features of the universal terrorism-related conventions is that they not only call for a principal offender to be prosecuted and severely punished, but they also require States parties to criminalise the conduct of those who assist principal offenders, and those who attempt to commit the principal offence. It has been noted that counter-terrorism offences have begun to include 'precursor' offences, such as offences of possession of materials useful to terrorism, or possession of information useful to terrorism. In this regard, the UN Office on Drugs and Crime and the Special Rapporteur on counter-terrorism have acknowledged that preparatory offences constitute a necessary preventive element to a successful counter-terrorism strategy. The Special Rapporteur and others have also warned, however, that the definition of terrorism and corresponding offences (including offences relating to preparatory conduct or conduct in support of terrorism), must be precise and must correspond to the cumulative requirements of Security Council resolution 1566 (2004).

Most, but not all, of the terrorism-related offences in the case study countries are directly linked to the universal terrorism-related conventions. These further offences can be categorised as falling within one of the following categories: (1) those which are not expressly required by terrorism treaties or Security Council resolutions, but are in furtherance of them; (2) offences that act as mechanisms for the enforcement of preventive measures, such as control orders; (3) some offences which are preventive in nature by their own right; (4) a small category of offences that react to emergencies caused by a terrorist act and seek to ensure the effective operation of measures implemented in such emergencies; and (5) offences that do not fall within one of the former categories and that were introduced under counter-terrorism legislation, but go beyond the cumulative characterises of terrorism identified in Security Council resolution 1566 (2004). Falling within the latter category are the offences in Australia and New Zealand of committing a terrorist act, problematic because they are directly linked to the overly-broad definitions of terrorism in those countries. While important, bioterrorism offences introduced under New Zealand's Counter-Terrorism Bill 2003 also fail to correspond to the characteristics of terrorism. Some offences in the UK's Terrorism Act 2000 lack any direct link to terrorism, but are instead applicable in many other contexts.

Public provocation to commit acts of terrorism is described by the Security Council Working Group established pursuant to resolution 1566 (2004) as an insidious activity contributing to the spread of the scourge of terrorism. The Security Council has declared that knowingly inciting terrorist acts is contrary to the purposes and principles of the United Nations, and has called on States, under paragraph 1(a) of its resolution 1624 (2005), to prohibit by law incitement to commit a terrorist act or acts. There are two general means by which the incitement to terrorism may be criminalised. The first is by reactive means, where a person who has incited or glorified terrorism may be prosecuted as a party to a principal terrorist act. Many jurisdictions have such party offences, where the conduct of anyone who incites, counsels, or procures any person to commit an offence is also guilty of the offence. This is the case in all four case study countries. The second, proactive, means of criminalisation is one that seeks to create liability without needing to wait for a terrorist act to occur. A 'proactive' offence criminalises the act of incitement itself as a primary, rather than secondary, offence.

The UN Terrorism Prevention Branch has taken the view that the general obligation of States to abstain from tolerating terrorist activities implies that they must adopt active measures in order to prevent those acts. This is also encouraged within resolutions of the General Assembly and Security Council. Furthermore, article 20(2) of the International Covenant on Civil and Political Rights requires States to prohibit the advocacy of national, racial or religious hatred that constitutes incitement to discrimination, hostility or violence. Despite this, the United Kingdom is the only one of the four case study countries which has a specific offence of incitement to terrorism. The other countries instead rely on general provisions of law. In New Zealand's case, it has been concluded that these provisions are deficient in a number of ways. The incitement offence under the Human Rights Act 1993 (NZ) is limited in its jurisdictional application, by the fact that it does not expressly apply to the incitement of violence, and in the low level of maximum penalty upon conviction. Party offences under section 66(1)(d) of the Crimes Act 1961 (NZ) are reactive, requiring an actual act of hostility, violence or terrorism to occur before proceedings can commence. Procuring offences under section 311 of the Crimes Act limit the maximum penalty upon conviction to not more than half of the relevant principal offence. Sedition offences under sections 81 and 82 of the Crimes Act have a maximum penalty of 2 years' imprisonment upon conviction and do not capture a person acting alone to incite terrorism. The 'threat of harm' offence under section 307A of the Crimes Act 1961 is limited in its jurisdictional application, by the reactive approach of the offence, and the fact that it only criminalises acts of incitement that themselves contain threats falling within the jurisdiction of section 307A. Furthermore, despite New Zealand's reasonably robust jurisdictional framework, none of the offences described are able to deal with the situation where a person incites others to commit terrorist acts abroad.

The universal instruments related to terrorism specify that the penalties for terrorism offences must be serious, and in conformity with the principle of proportionality as between the gravity of the sanction and the gravity of the act. The UN Office on Drugs and Crime therefore advocates that the system of penalties for terrorism offence must be especially dissuasive and that heavy sentences need to be imposed for perpetrators of such acts. This is reflected in the range of maximum sanctions applicable to terrorism offences in Australia, Canada, New Zealand and the United Kingdom. The latter three countries have also taken the legislative step of directing judges to treat offences involving terrorism as an aggravating feature in the determination of the length of sentence to be imposed. Such directions are not problematic in principle, except that the directions use terms ("terrorist activity", "terrorist act" and "terrorist connection") which have been identified in this chapter as being overly broad and not restricted to the characteristics identified in Security Council resolution 1566 (2004).

References

Baev, Pavel. 2006. Reevaluating the Risks of Terrorist Attacks Against Energy Infrastructure in Eurasia. 4(2) *China and Eurasia Forum Quarterly* 33.

Coleman, Kevin. 2006. Critical Infrastructure Protection. Directions Magazine (23 Mat 2006), online: http://www.directionsmag.com/article.php?article_id=2184.

Conte, Alex, and Ganor, Boaz. 2005. Legal and Policy Issues in Establishing an International Framework for Human Rights Compliance When Countering Terrorism. Herzelia: International Policy Institute on Counter-Terrorism.

Fighel, Yoni, and Kehati, Yoram. 2002. Analysis of Recent Al-Qaida Documents, Part 1. Paper of the International Policy Institute on Counter-Terrorism, online: http://212.150.54.123/articles/articledet.cfm?articleid=453.

Fighel, Yoni, and Shahar, Yael. 2002. The Al-Qaida-Hizballah Connection. Papers of the International Policy Institute on Counter-Terrorism, online: http://www.ict.org.il.

Golder, Ben, and Williams, George. 2004. What is 'Terrorism'? Problems of Legal Definition. 27(2) *University of New South Wales Law Journal* 270.

Jenkins, David. 2003. In Support of Canada's Anti-Terrorism Act: A Comparison of Canadian, British, and American Anti-Terrorism Law. 66 *Saskatchewan Law Review* 419.

Kahati, Yoram. 2003. The Continuing Al-Qaida Threat. Papers of the International Policy Institute on Counter-Terrorism, online: http://www.ict.org.il.

Kahati, Yoram and Fighel, Yoni. 2003. Osama bin Ladin as the New Prophet of Islam. Papers of the International Policy Institute on Counter-Terrorism, online: http://www.ict.org.il.

MacDonald, Edwina, and Williams, George. 2007. Combating terrorism: Australia's Criminal Code Since September 11, 2001. 16(1) *Griffiths Law Review* 27.

McSherry, Bernadette. 2004. Terrorism Offences in the Criminal Code: Broadening the Boundaries of Australian Criminal Laws. 27(2) *The University of New South Wales Law Journal* 354.

Ribbelink, Olivier. 2006. Analytical Report. In Council of Europe. *"Apologie du terrorisme"* and "incitement to terrorism". Strasbourg: Council of Europe Publishing.

Shahar, Yael. 2002. Al-Qaida's Asian Web. Papers of the International Policy Institute on Counter-Terrorism, online: http://www.ict.org.il.

Walker, Clive. 2007. The United Kingdom's Anti-terrorism Laws: Lessons for Australia. In Lynch, Andrew, MacDonald, Edwina, and Williams, George (Eds). *Law and Liberty in the War on Terror*. Sydney: The Federation Press.

Chapter 15
Special Investigative Techniques and Rules of Criminal Procedure

Numerous special investigative techniques and procedures have been adopted in counter-terrorism legislation in Australia, Canada, New Zealand and the United Kingdom. Amongst those are powers of investigative detention and investigative hearings, considered in Chap. 16. Rules of criminal procedure have also been impacted on. Canada, for example, has amended its Evidence Act 1985 under Part 3 of the Anti-terrorism Act 2001 to allow for the protection of information which would encroach upon a public interest or be injurious to international relations or national defence or security (see Chap. 18, Sect. 18.2.2). Various other special techniques and rules have already been identified in this title, or will be considered as discrete matters in the chapters that follow. It is not possible to examine each and every issue arising. The aim of the current chapter is to examine some isolated issues concerning special investigative techniques and rules of procedure introduced under counter-terrorism legislation, including exploration of rights not otherwise considered (the right to privacy, for example).

The use of 'special' powers in countering terrorism is often justified by the special nature and difficulties in combating this insidious form of conduct.[1] While this is correct, one must take great care when establishing special techniques and rules to ensure that adequate checks and balances are in place. As observed by Fenwick and Phillipson, the experience of the use of special powers in Northern Ireland has not been a happy one: "there is substantial evidence of the use of powers in an oppressive manner, of their use against persons later turning out to be innocent, and of more oppressive practices being carried out in secret".[2]

The first case study considered in this chapter looks at special powers of questioning vested in police under New Zealand's Counter-Terrorism Bill 2003, its impact on the right not to incriminate oneself, and the common law and statutory protections of that right in New Zealand. Interception warrants and tracking devices are examined next, followed by a brief study of the onus for granting bail in

---

[1] Walker (2005, p. 387).
[2] Fenwick and Phillipson (2005, p. 456). See also Schabas and Olivier (2003, p. 87).

A. Conte, *Human Rights in the Prevention and Punishment of Terrorism*,
DOI 10.1007/978-3-642-11608-7_15, © Springer-Verlag Berlin Heidelberg 2010

terrorism-related cases. The final parts of the chapter look at two more widely-impacting subjects: the role of security intelligence services in the prevention and investigation of terrorism; and the operation outside the framework of combating terrorism of special investigative techniques introduced under counter-terrorism legislation.

15.1   Special Powers of Questioning in New Zealand

As explained in Chap. 7, a number of legislative amendments were made in New Zealand under the Counter-Terrorism Bill 2003, which was ultimately enacted as a series of separate Amendment Acts, rather than as one stand-alone Act of Parliament (see Sect. 7.1.5). The purpose of the Bill was to allow New Zealand to accede to the Convention on the Physical Protection of Nuclear Material, and the Convention on the Marking of Plastic Explosives for the Purpose of Detection.[3] The Explanatory Notes to the Counter-Terrorism Bill identify two further objectives: implementing the remaining obligations under Security Council resolution 1373 (2001); and establishing investigative powers to assist in the detection of terrorists, terrorist acts and terrorist or associated entities.[4] The significance of these stated reasons becomes particularly important when examining the investigative tools incorporated within the Summary Proceedings Act 1957 (NZ).

Under the Counter-Terrorism Bill, section 198B was inserted into the Summary Proceedings Act 1957 to allow police to demand assistance to access computer data by providing police with any data protection codes or other information necessary to access that data. In evidence before the Foreign Affairs, Defence and Trade Committee, it had been submitted that this provision (under clause 33 of the Counter-Terrorism Bill) offended the privilege against self-incrimination. By compelling a person to provide assistance to police (who may be investigating an offence against that person or who might, as a result of gaining access to the computer data, be provided with information that would incriminate that person) it was submitted to the Committee that the provision would offend the privilege against self-incrimination.[5] Two principal issues arise. The first concerns the

---

[3]Convention on the Physical Protection of Nuclear Material, opened for signature 3 March 1980, 1456 UNTS 124 (entered into force 8 February 1987); and the Convention on the Marking of Plastic Explosives for the Purpose of Detection, opened for signature 1 March 1991, ICAO Doc 9571 (entered into force 21 June 1998).

[4]Foreign Affairs, Defence and Trade Committee, Counter-Terrorism Bill, A Government Bill, 27-1, Explanatory Note, presented to the House 2 April 2003, 1. In reality, the latter objective (investigative powers) supports the first objective (Security Council resolution 1373 (2001) obligations).

[5]Alex Conte, Submissions to the Foreign Affairs, Defence and Trade Committee on the Counter-Terrorism Bill (27-1, 2003), Parliamentary Library 12 May 2003, paras 29–58.

impact of section 198B of the Summary Proceedings Act upon the right not to incriminate oneself. The second involves the operation of this investigative tool outside the context of combating terrorism (see Sect. 15.4 below).

Although the special powers of questioning under the Summary Proceedings Act do not signify a particularly startling deviation from human rights law, some time is spent on this issue for various reasons. The examination that follows illustrates the vulnerability of reliance on common law rights when faced with inconsistent legislative provisions in counter-terrorism law. Although this examination looks at the position in New Zealand, this vulnerability is particularly relevant to the protection and promotion of human rights in Australia, which are based to a very large extent upon the common law (see Chap. 11, Sect. 11.1.1). It also provides an opportunity to illustrate, in practical terms, how the complex interface between sections 4, 5 and 6 of the New Zealand Bill of Rights Act 1990 (NZBORA) applies. It furthermore discloses a disturbing trend, common throughout, of using the pretext of combating terrorism to extend executive powers beyond counter-terrorism.

15.1.1 Special Powers of Questioning

In apparent response to submissions made to NZ's Foreign Affairs, Defence and Trade Committee, clause 33 of the Counter-Terrorism Bill was amended, with the Select Committee reporting to the House that this was to explicitly preserve the right against self-incrimination. The Committee stated that:[6]

> Whether a broadly worded statutory provision requiring the supply of information, and making no reference to the privilege against self-incrimination, overrides this privilege is a question of its construction. A Court must be satisfied that a statutory power of questioning was meant to exclude the privilege. We are advised that this conclusion is unlikely to be reached unless it is either explicitly provided for, or is a necessary implication of the provision. Our recommended amendments make it clear that a person is required to provide information that is reasonable and necessary to allow the police to access data held in, or accessible from, a computer in particular circumstances, but that does not itself tend to incriminate the person. We note that there are several other instances of statutory obligations on citizens to assist police or other agents.

As enacted, section 198B of the Summary Proceedings Act retains the original form of subsections (1) and (2), which set out the rule requiring the provision of assistance and to whom that rule applies. The final form of the section includes new subsections (3), (4) and (5), with subsection (6) retaining the penalty for failure

---

[6]Foreign Affairs, Defence and Trade Committee, Report on the Counter-Terrorism Bill, A Government Bill, 27-2, Commentary, presented to the House 8 August 2003, p. 10.

to comply with a request to provide information or assist police (as had been provided for in the first draft of the Bill). The entirety of the provision now reads as follows:

198B Person with knowledge of computer or computer network to assist access–

(1) A constable executing a search warrant may require a specified person to provide information or assistance that is reasonable and necessary to allow the constable to access data held in, or accessible from, a computer that is on premises named in the warrant.

(2) A specified person is a person who–
   (a) is the owner or lessee of the computer, or is in the possession or control of the computer, or is an employee of any of the above; and
   (b) has relevant knowledge of–
       (i) the computer or a computer network of which the computer forms a part; or
       (ii) measures applied to protect data held in, or accessible from, the computer.

(3) A person may not be required under subsection (1) to give any information tending to incriminate the person.

(4) Subsection (3) does not prevent a constable from requiring a person to provide information that–
   (a) is reasonable and necessary to allow the constable to access data held in, or accessible from, a computer that–
       (i) is on premises named in the warrant concerned; and
       (ii) contains or may contain information tending to incriminate the person; but
   (b) does not itself tend to incriminate the person.

(5) Subsection (3) does not prevent a constable from requiring a person to provide assistance that is reasonable and necessary to allow the constable to access data held in, or accessible from, a computer that–
   (a) is on premises named in the warrant concerned; and
   (b) contains or may contain information tending to incriminate the person.

(6) Every person commits an offence and is liable on summary conviction to a term of imprisonment not exceeding 3 months or a fine not exceeding $2,000 who fails to assist a constable when requested to do so under subsection (1).

An issue that becomes apparent at the outset is that of interpretation. What exactly do subsections (3), (4) and (5) mean and how do they inter-relate? In its original form, the meaning of the proposed provision was quite clear. Clause 33 was to enable a police constable executing a search warrant to require assistance or information to be given in order to access data in a computer within the premises being searched. Subclause (1) – which remains identical to section 198B(1) – set out the authority by which a constable could make such a request. Subclause (2) – again remaining the same – specified who may be the subject of such a request. Subclause (3) – which became section 198B(6) of the Summary Proceedings Act – created an offence where a person refuses to comply with the constable's request, punishable by a maximum of 3 months' imprisonment or a fine of up to $2,000.

The new subsections (3), (4) and (5), however, require a close reading. Subsection (3) appears to protect the privilege against self-incrimination, stating that "a person may not be required under subsection (1) to give any information tending to incriminate the person". Certainly, the Select Committee reported that the protection of the privilege against self-incrimination was the intention of this added provision.[7] It is doubtful, however, that this is in fact the effect of subsection (3) when read in the entirety of section 198B.

The first point to note is that subsection (3) only prevents a constable (*acting under subsection (1)*) from requiring a person to give information that might incriminate them. The reality is that subsection (1) only authorises a constable to require information to be provided for the purpose of allowing the constable to access data within a computer. That information will take the form of either a password, or information about the location within a computer of certain data. That in itself cannot be incriminating information, since it only informs a constable on how to access data. In other words, subsection (3) does nothing. Even without the additional subsection (3), section 198B(1) can only ever permit a constable to request information on how to access data. It does not authorise a constable to require any further information and the purported restriction upon section 198B(1) created by subsection (3) is therefore redundant. It is what flows from that preliminary information that is important to the privilege against self-incrimination.

Next, it appears that subsections (4) and (5) in fact expressly override the privilege against self-incrimination. The two provisions are almost identical in nature, except that subsection (4) relates to the provision of *information* necessary to access data (e.g. a password), and subsection (5) relates to the provision of *assistance* necessary to access such data (e.g. the physical operation of a computer). However, the two provisions specifically envisage that data accessed as a result of such information or assistance "contains or may contain information tending to incriminate the person" (section 198B(4)(a)(ii) and (5)(b)). Subsection 4(b) certainly limits a constable from using section 198B by ensuring that he or she may only obtain information that "does not *itself* incriminate the person" (emphasis added). The point, however, is that the information in question (a password or other information required to access data) is not likely to *itself* incriminate a person. Moreover, both subsections envisage (and do not prohibit) that the information or assistance provided may then *result* in the person incriminating him or herself. For those reasons, not even a liberal, rights-based, interpretation of section 198B could be adopted in favour of reading the provision consistently with the privilege against self-incrimination. Although subsection (3), when first read, appears to preserve the privilege against self-incrimination, the overall amendment of section 198B does the opposite. Nor does section 198B provide for use immunity (see further Chap. 16, Sect. 16.3.1).

This represents a significant extension to existing police powers and a departure from common law and statutory rights. Two questions arise: (1) what is the extent, and effect, of the common law privilege against self-incrimination and right to be presumed innocent; and (2) how does section 198B interact with the codified rights to silence and legal advice, and the presumption of innocence, under the NZBORA and the International Covenant on Civil and Political Rights (ICCPR)?

---

[7]Ibid.

15.1.2   Sources of the Right Not to Incrimination Oneself

The right to be presumed innocent until proven guilty is exercised through the burden upon the Crown throughout all stages of the criminal process, from investigation to conviction, and is guaranteed under article 14(2) of the ICCPR, article 6 (2) of the European Convention on Human Rights (ECHR), section 11(d) of the Canadian Charter of Rights, and section 25(c) of New Zealand's Bill of Rights Act.[8] Associated with this is the right to silence. For example, an accused person has no obligation to give evidence at trial, nor to disprove any allegation against him or her. This has been held to be so even where the only person in possession of information relevant to the elements of an offence is the accused.[9]

Although intimately linked with the presumption of innocence,[10] the right not to incriminate oneself is not expressly reflected in the ICCPR or the ECHR. The jurisprudence of the Human Rights Committee has not sought to infer such a right in its application or consideration of article 14(2) of the ICCPR. In *Saunders v United Kingdom*, however, the European Court of Human Rights stated:[11]

> Although not mentioned in Article 6 of the Convention, the right to silence and the right not to incriminate oneself, are generally recognised international standards which lie at the heart of the notion of a fair procedure under Article 6.

The right not to incriminate oneself is reflected in section 11(c) of the Canadian Charter (applicable once a person is charged with a criminal offence) and section 23 (4) of the NZ Bill of Rights (applicable upon arrest or detention). It should be noted, however, that those provisions (as well as articles 14(2) and 6(2) of the ICCPR and ECHR) are applicable only where a person is arrested or charged with a criminal offence.[12] The scheme of investigative hearings under section 83.28 of Canada's Criminal Code does not, however, involve a charge being brought against the

---

[8]International Covenant on Civil and Political Rights, opened for signature 16 December 1966, 999 UNTS 171 (entered into force 23 March 1976); Convention for the Protection of Human Rights and Fundamental Freedoms, opened for signature 4 November 1950, 213 UNTS 222 (entered into force 3 September 1953); Constitution Act 1982 (Canada), Part I, Charter of Rights and Freedoms; and New Zealand Bill of Rights Act 1990.

[9]See *Attygale v R* [1936] 2 All ER 116. Here, the accused was charged in respect of an illegal operation performed on a woman while she was under chloroform. The defence case was that no operation took place. The trial judge directed the jury that, the facts being specifically within the knowledge of the accused, the burden of proving the absence of any operation was upon the accused. On appeal, the Privy Council held that the direction was an incorrect statement of the law, and that the onus of proof to establish that there had been an operation remained with the prosecution.

[10]Fenwick (2002, p. 840).

[11]*Saunders v United Kingdom* [1997] 23 EHRR 313, para 74. See also *Funke v France* [1993] ECHR 7, para 44; and *Murray v United Kingdom* (1996) 22 EHRR 29, para 45.

[12]The Supreme Court of Canada has held, however, that the privilege against self-incrimination is a "principle of fundamental justice", guaranteed under section 7 of the Canadian Charter: see *Re Application under section 83.28 of the Criminal Code* [2004] 2 SCR 248 paras 70–71.

subject of an investigative hearing order. It instead aims to compel a person to attend a judicial hearing for the purpose of investigating a terrorism offence which has either been committed, or which authorities believe will be committed.

More broadly applicable in the four case study countries is the common law privilege against self-incrimination. Under the common law, no person may be compelled to say or do anything that might incriminate him or her.[13] This is not limited to testimony and discovery in judicial proceedings. The New Zealand Court of Appeal has held, for example, that the right not to incriminate oneself is capable of applying outside court proceedings when the obligation to answer questions, or give information, or to provide or disclose documents, is imposed by statute.[14] As indicated by this conclusion, however, the common law privilege is capable of being overridden by statute, by virtue of the fact that parliaments are sovereign.

The normal interaction between the common law and statute law is that Acts of Parliament prevail over rules developed under the common law. As summarised Joseph, "Parliament's words can be neither judicially invalidated nor controlled by earlier enactment".[15] Prima facie, then, the common law privilege against self-incrimination may be overridden by statute. As Joseph himself discusses, however, the courts have taken a guarded approach when parliament has attempted to restrict the role of the judiciary or take away the rights of citizens.[16] In the NZ Court of Appeal case of *New Zealand Drivers' Association v New Zealand Road Carriers*, for example, Justices Cooke, McMullin and Ongley expressed reservations as to the extent to which even an Act of Parliament could take away the right to resort to ordinary courts of law for the determination of their rights.[17] More strongly worded, Justice Cooke later posited that "some common law rights may go so deep that even Parliament cannot be accepted by the Courts to have destroyed them".[18] Despite the apparent strength of those statements, however, no New Zealand court has invalidated or refused to apply a statutory provision on the basis that it encroaches upon common law rights.

As a common law right, the privilege against self-incrimination (outside the situation where a person is arrested or charged with a criminal offence, where the right is guaranteed in Canada and NZ by their bills or rights) may therefore be subject to limitation by statute. The question is the extent to which this is possible. The European Court of Human Rights has taken the approach that, if a statute does impose an obligation to answer questions, the privilege against self-incrimination

---

[13]See *Rice v Connolly* [1966] 2 All ER 649, applied in New Zealand in *Waaka v Police* [1987] 1 NZLR 754. See also Langbein (1994) and Inbau (1999).

[14]*Taylor v New Zealand Poultry Board* [1984] 1 NZLR 394, p. 401.

[15]Joseph (2001, p. 461).

[16]Ibid, pp. 485–495.

[17]*New Zealand Drivers' Association v New Zealand Road Carriers* [1982] 1 NZLR 374, p. 390.

[18]*Fraser v State Services Commission* [1984] 1 NZLR 116, p. 121. See also *Taylor v New Zealand Poultry Board* (n 14) p. 398.

demands that those answers cannot later be used as evidence against the person concerned, stating in *Saunders v United Kingdom*:[19]

> The public interest cannot be invoked to justify the use of answers compulsorily obtained in a *non-judicial investigation* to incriminate the accused during the trial proceedings (emphasis added).

15.1.3   Application of the Common Law Privilege to the Summary Proceedings Act

The question of the application of the privilege against self-incrimination in judicial investigation hearings is a matter considered in Chap. 16 (Sect. 16.3). As it affects the Summary Proceedings Act, further discussion of *Taylor v New Zealand Poultry Board* is called for at this point, the case having similarities with the issue at hand.[20] *Taylor* concerned the operation of regulation 57(3) of the Poultry Board Regulations which, like section 198B of the Summary Proceedings Act, required a person to provide information to prescribed officers.[21] Taylor was a poultry farmer who refused to answer questions properly asked under regulation 57(3) and he was subsequently convicted on three charges under regulation 57(4).[22] Notwithstanding the fact that the Court of Appeal held that the privilege against self-incrimination was capable of applying outside court proceedings, it qualified this decision by stating that the scope of the privilege must be determined in the context of the particular statute being examined. As acknowledged by the Select Committee when reporting on the Counter-Terrorism Bill, the privilege against self-incrimination is a question of its construction.[23] For the Court of Appeal, Cooke J stated:[24]

> The common law favours the liberty of the citizen, and, *if a Court is not satisfied that a statutory power of questioning was meant to exclude the privilege*, it is in accordance with the spirit of the common to allow the privilege (emphasis added).

In a recent case concerning legal professional privilege in New Zealand, the Privy Council considered the question of statutory provisions overriding or excluding the privilege. The question before it was whether the Law Practitioners Act 1982 excluded legal professional privilege either expressly or "by necessary

---

[19]*Saunders v United Kingdom* (n 11) para 74.

[20]*Taylor v New Zealand Poultry Board* (n 14).

[21]The Poultry Board Regulations 1980 were made pursuant to an empowering provision in the Poultry Board Act 1980 (section 24(1)).

[22]Regulation 57(4) of the Poultry Board Regulations 1980 made it an offence to refuse to answer any enquiries made under regulation 57(3).

[23]Foreign Affairs, Defence and Trade Committee report (n 6) 10.

[24]*Taylor v New Zealand Poultry Board* (n 14) p. 402.

implication".[25] The Privy Council held that a necessary implication was one which the express language of the statute clearly showed must have been included.[26] In considering the issue, reference was made to Lord Hobhouse's explanation in *R (Morgan Grenfell & Co Ltd) v Special Commissioner of Income Tax:*[27]

> A necessary implication is not the same as a reasonable implication... A *necessary* [original emphasis] implication is one which necessarily follows from the express provisions of the statute construed in their context. It distinguishes between what it would have been sensible or reasonable for Parliament to have included or what Parliament would, if it had thought about it, probably have included and what it is clear that the express language of the statute shows that the statute must have included. A necessary implication is a matter of express language and logic not interpretation.

In the context of section 198B of the Summary Proceedings Act, it is concluded that the necessary implication of the structure of the provision is to exclude the privilege against self-incrimination. The common law must therefore give way. The wording of subsections (4) and (5) clearly preserves the power of questioning under subsection (1). New Zealand court will have no option but to take the statutory power as intending to exclude the privilege and could not interpret the provision as allowing the common law privilege to operate. This constitutes a major shift away from a fundamental privilege that has been developed and affirmed over a long period of time.

15.1.4 Application of the NZ Bill of Rights to the Summary Proceedings Act

As indicated above (Sect. 15.1.2), the right to silence in New Zealand relies not only on the common law privilege against self-incrimination, but is also found in section 23(4) of the Bill of Rights Act. The weakness of this is that the right is only triggered where a person is arrested or detained. The right not to answer police questions concerning access to computer data would thus only be triggered in limited circumstances. The second limitation is that one would here be faced with a conflict between a provision of the Bill of Rights Act, and one in a statute, this being problematic because of section 4 of the NZBORA which effectively protects from invalidation any enactments which are in an irreconcilable conflict with the Bill of Rights.

Considered in Chap. 11 was the means by which the NZBORA applies, advocating the four-step approach proposed by Rishworth (see Sect. 11.1.3.2). Applying this to section 198B of the Summary Proceedings Act, the following emerges:

---

[25] *B & Ors v Auckland District Law Society (New Zealand)* [2003] UKPC 38.

[26] *B v Auckland District Law Society* (ibid) para 58.

[27] *B v Auckland District Law Society* (ibid) para 58. See *R (Morgan Grenfell & Co Ltd) v Special Commissioner of Income Tax* [2002] WLR 1299, para 45.

1. Does section 198B appear to establish a limit on a right?

When applied in the context of someone arrested or detained (with the consequent right to silence under section 23(4) of the NZBORA), section 198B establishes a limitation on the right to silence by requiring information and assistance to be provided to police, the failure to do so amounting to an offence.

2. Is section 198B 'inconsistent' with the right to silence?

An enactment is 'consistent' with the Bill of Rights if it either effects no limitation on a right or freedom at all, which is not the case here, or it limits a right or freedom to the extent permitted by section 5.[28] This second step therefore calls for careful consideration of whether the limitation under section 198B the enactment *does* limit a right or freedom and, if it does, whether by application of section 5 such a limit is justified. The first question, then, is how far does the right to silence stretch? Consider the following situation:

> A (a New Zealand citizen) has made a donation to B (an organisation in Auckland, which has been made the subject of a final designation as being associated to a terrorist entity). Police arrive at A's property and formally arrest her, charging A with an offence under section 10(1) of the Terrorism Suppression Act 2002 (making money available to B, knowing that B was designated under the Act as an associated terrorist entity). A is properly cautioned under section 23(1)(b) and (4) of the NZBORA. Police have a warrant to search A's premises, suspecting that she may have funded other proscribed entities. They locate a computer in her study and request A to provide the password to the computer (under section 198B (1) of the Summary Proceedings Act). Having been told upon arrest that she has the right to silence, A refuses to provide the police with the computer password.

The right to silence extends – at least in principle – to this situation. Section 198B(1) thus purports to limit the right to silence by requiring A to provide information to the police enabling them to access data on her computer. That being the case, the next question is whether this limitation is 'consistent' with the Bill of Rights by application of section 5 of the NZBORA (on the application of section 5, see Chap. 11 at Sect. 11.5). Addressing the preliminary issues in the application of section 5, the first point is that the onus would be upon the Crown to establish that section 198B is a justified limitation in any challenge against its validity or operation. Next, it must be established that section 198B only effects a 'limitation' upon the right to silence, rather than an exclusion of the right. By being limited in its operation to the situations identified in subsections (1) and (2), section 198B satisfies this requirement. Finally, section 198B is clearly a prescription by law (being a statutory provision).

The substance of section 5 then requires the enactment to pursue a sufficiently important objective, by proportional means. There is considerable jurisprudence on this substantive test, particularly in Canada through the application of section 1 of the Canadian Charter of Rights and Freedoms 1982 (upon which section 5 of the NZBORA was based). This is a matter considered in detail in Chap. 11

---

[28]Rishworth et al. (2003, p. 138).

(Sect. 11.5.2). On the question of identifying a "pressing and substantial objective in a free and democratic society", the difficulty is that section 198B has no clear, or single, objective other than to assist general law enforcement through the investigation of offences. Although the provision was introduced under the Counter-Terrorism Bill, it is a provision of the Summary Proceedings Act and is not restricted in its application to the pursuit of counter-terrorism. Section 198B has the potential to apply to *any* situation in which the police are executing a search warrant. Taking this general objective, the first question in the application of section 5 is whether the objective (assisting law enforcement through the investigation of offences) relates to concerns which are pressing and substantial in a free and democratic society. Law enforcement is certainly an important societal concern and, for the sake of continuing with this enquiry, it will be assumed that a court would take this limb of the section 5 test to be satisfied.

Turning to the second limb of section 5, three questions must be considered. First, is the legislative provision (section 198B) rationally connected to the achievement of its objective? It is sufficient, here, to show that the provision logically furthers the objective and this question is normally answered in the affirmative without too much trouble, unless the connection is not plainly obvious. Section 198B provides police with the means to access computer data, which clearly furthers the objective of assisting law enforcement through the investigation of offences. The second proportionality question asks whether the legislative provision impairs the right to a minimal extent (as little as reasonably possible). It is reasonably difficult to consider this second factor separately from the third, proportionality, factor. Combined, there is considerable difficulty in satisfying the justified limitations test in the current examination, because of the broad nature of section 198B (applying to the execution of *any* search warrant).

Application of the final part of the proportionality test, achieving a balance between the importance of the objective and the effect of the limiting provision, requires careful consideration of the effects of the limitation, the importance of the objective, and the importance of the right being affected. The right to silence when charged with an offence, and the underlying privilege against self-incrimination, are two important rights in the criminal process. As discussed earlier, the European Court of Human Rights has described the right to silence and the accompanying privilege as "generally recognised in international standards which lie at the heart of the notion of a fair [criminal] procedure".[29] Rishworth describes the rights as "fundamental in New Zealand's criminal procedure".[30] As already discussed, they are rights that the common law has long-recognised too.

As to the level of importance of the objective of the provision, the difficulty in answering this question lies in the fact that section 198B applies to the execution of any search warrant. It must therefore be concluded that the importance of the objective depends upon the particular circumstances surrounding the issuing of the

---

[29]*Saunders v United Kingdom* (n 11) para 44, and *Murray v United Kingdom* (n 11) para 45.
[30]Rishworth et al. (2003, p. 646).

warrant (that is, the reasons for the warrant being issued, and the type of criminal conduct to which the evidence sought to be obtained through the warrant relates). In the factual scenario set out earlier, for example, the warrant to search A's premises is based upon the suspicion that A has funded terrorist entities, contrary to section 10 (1) of the Terrorism Suppression Act. This is an important objective. However, it should be noted that a search warrant can be issued for the purpose of finding evidence relating to any offence punishable by imprisonment (see section 198) including, for example, indecent exposure under the Summary Offences Act 1981 (making a person liable to imprisonment for a term not exceeding 3 months).[31] While the exposure of one's genitals in public is not something that the public should be expected to tolerate, the objective of countering such activity is clearly not as important as countering the financing of terrorist organisations. That conclusion is supported by the fact that an offence against section 10(1) of the Terrorism Suppression Act makes a person liable to imprisonment for a term of up to 7 years (as opposed to a maximum of 3 months for indecent exposure). Thus, the currently broad scope of section 198B has the very undesirable effect that the importance of its objective relies upon the particular context in which the provision is applied.

Returning to the application of Rishworth's steps in the application of the NZBORA, his second step cannot therefore be answered outside the specific application of section 198B. The most that can be said is that section 198B *might* be consistent with the Bill of Rights, depending on the nature and circumstances surrounding the issuing of the search warrant. Where this results in a finding that the operation of section 198B is justified under section 5 of the NZBORA, this means that its operation is 'consistent' with the Bill of Rights, bringing consideration of the Bill of Rights to an end. Where the operation of section 198B fails the proportionality test, however, one must proceed to Rishworth's third step.

3. Is an alternative meaning possible?

The third step is to establish whether an alternative interpretation of the enactment (one that *is* consistent with the right invoked) is possible. If it is, then section 6 of the NZBORA will demand that the courts apply this alternative interpretation. Such an alternative interpretation of section 198B is not open, however, having regard to subsections (4) and (5) of that provision. As already concluded, these subsections envisage (and do not prohibit) the provision of information and assistance which will *result* in the person incriminating him or herself.

4. Adopt the consistent meaning, if properly available

'Step four' thus results in a finding that section 198B will (in the absence of satisfying the proportionality test) be in an 'irreconcilable conflict' with the Bill

---

[31] Section 27(1) of the Summary Offences Act 1981 provides that "Every person is liable to imprisonment for a term not exceeding 3 months or a fine not exceeding $2,000 who, in or within view of any public place, intentionally and obscenely exposes any part of his or her genitals". The relevance of this to section 198B is that computer data might, for example, include electronic photographs of such an event.

of Rights. As such, section 4 of the NZBORA will demand that section 198B must prevail over the right to silence.

15.1.5 Reform

The analysis of section 198B of the Summary Proceedings Act has thus far revealed various matters. The report of the Select Committee to the House of Representatives advised that its proposed amendment to clause 33 of the Counter-Terrorism Bill would explicitly preserve the privilege against self-incrimination. In actual fact, however, the words of the provision (as enacted) show that the it actually envisages, rather than prohibit, the compelling of a person to give information and assistance which might result in the police gaining access to incriminating evidence. This is contrary to the long-held common law right to silence and privilege against self-incrimination. Due to the express terms of section 198B and the primacy of legislation over the common law, however, New Zealand courts will not be in a position to interpret section 198B as allowing these common law rights to operate.

It has also been concluded that the relationship of section 198B with section 23 of the Bill of Rights is more complex. Where section 198B is activated following an arrest or detention, there are numerous difficulties in justifying the limitation imposed by section 198B upon the right to silence. Although section 4 of the Bill of Rights ultimately acts to save section 198B from invalidation, there are significant weaknesses in finding that the provision is not a justified limitation (in the operation of the provision, for example, to the investigation of minor offences). Furthermore, section 198B is not limited in its application to the countering of terrorism.

All these factors point to the need for reform to restrict the operation of section 198B to the investigation of terrorist offences, the suppression of which can be justified as a pressing and substantial concern proportional to the important status of the right to silence. Section 198B could be restricted by inclusion of the following subsection:

A constable may require assistance under subsection (1) if–

  (a) the premises named in the warrant are owned, leased or occupied by an entity for the time being designated under the Terrorism Suppression Act 2002 as a terrorist entity or as an associated entity; or

  (b) the computer at the premises named in the warrant is owned, leased or used by an entity for the time being designated under the Terrorism Suppression Act 2002 as a terrorist entity or as an associated entity; or

  (c) the constable believes, on reasonable grounds, that the computer holds data relating to the preparation or commission of a terrorist act, as defined by section 5 of the Terrorism Suppression Act 2002.

These restrictions address the weaknesses identified in the justification of section 198B under section 5 of the Bill of Rights. The advocated reform would contain the application of section 198B to counter-terrorism by linking it to the two principal features of New Zealand's counter-terrorist legislation (the designation process and the definition of terrorist acts). As an aside, the restrictions might also be expanded to include other pressing and substantial concerns, such as the suppression of child pornography for example.

15.2   Tracking Devices and Interception Warrants

In New Zealand, authorisations to intercept communications and attach tracking devices to people or property are to be found under both the Crimes Act 1961 and Summary Proceedings Act 1957 following the legislative amendments under the Counter-Terrorism Bill 2003. The ability of police to obtain warrants for the purpose of intercepting private communications was extended to the investigation of terrorist offences (through amendment of section 312 of the Crimes Act). A new regime, introduced under new sections 200A–200O of the Summary Proceedings Act, authorises police and customs officers to obtain a warrant to attach a tracking device to any property or person where it is suspected that an offence has been, is being, or will be committed. As with the amendment of the Summary Proceedings Act 1957 (see Sect. 15.1.1 above), these provisions apply to the investigation of any offence, not just those that are related to terrorism. Other than a potential for the attachment of a tracking device to a person to constitute an assault, these provisions affect the right to privacy.

It might be noted at this point that the right to privacy will also be engaged in the interception of telecommunications.[32] Indeed, privacy rights will be occupied by a host of modern technologies allowing information to be recorded through satellite, aerial, or video surveillance, including by closed-circuit television (CCTV); the interception and recording of communications, whether by telephone or otherwise; and other monitoring tools including electro-optical and radar sensors and facial recognition software. At security checkpoints or border controls, authorities might require a person to provide fingerprints, or to have photographs or retinal scans taken. Machine Readable Travel Documents, such as biometric passports and some forms of national identity cards, have embedded integrated circuits which can process and store data. Widely used commercial technology, such as 'cookies', 'web bugs', and other advertising-supported software that monitor computer and

---

[32]For example, Australia's Telecommunications (Interception) Act 1979 was amended under counter-terrorism legislative packages to include terrorism offences in the definition of "class 1 offences" for the purposes of telecommunications interception warrants (see Chap. 5, Sect. 5.3.3). New Zealand's Counter-Terrorism Bill 2003 also extended the ability of police to obtain warrants to intercept private communications relating to terrorist offences, by amending section 312 of the Crimes Act 1961 and section 26 of the Misuse of Drugs Act 1978. See also Implementation of United Nations Security Council Resolution 1373; Canada's Fourth Report to the Counter-Terrorism Committee, UN Doc S/2004/132 (2004), pp. 21–23.

online activities, are also now being used in security strategies. These various examples of security infrastructure technologies involve the recording, collection, and storing of information, all of which must be consistent with the right to privacy, within the scope of permissible limitations.[33]

Although the right to privacy may be subject to temporary derogation during genuine emergency situations threatening the life of a nation, surveillance, interception of communications, wire-tapping, and recording of conversations should normally be prohibited.[34] However, it might be permissible to intercept communications if this has been authorised by an independent, preferably judicial, authority for specific and lawful purposes, with safeguards in place for the safe storage and limited use of the information.[35] This should be limited to circumstances where there are reasonable grounds to believe that a serious crime has been committed or prepared, or is being prepared, and where other less intrusive means of investigation are inadequate.[36] Secret surveillance can, in very exceptional circumstances, be justifiable, although this should be specifically authorised by legislation, and the authorising legislation should be accessible and precise.[37]

15.2.1 The Right to Privacy

The right to privacy is a matter addressed within the International Covenant on Civil and Political Rights, but is outside the ambit of the New Zealand Bill of Rights. In New Zealand, it instead finds protection under the Privacy Act 1993. Privacy, says Gross, is a deeply rooted value in human culture comprising the right of the individual to be left alone, the right of the individual to have control over the dissemination of information about him or her and the access to his or her person and home, and the right to be protected against the unwanted access of the public to

---

[33]See, for example, Talbot (2002, pp. 124–126).

[34]Human Rights Committee General Comment 16: The right to respect of privacy, family, home and correspondence, and protection of honour and reputation (Art 17), UN Doc CCPR General Comment 16 (1988), para 8.

[35]See, for example: Report of the Independent Expert on the protection of human rights and fundamental freedoms while countering terrorism, UN Doc E/CN.4/2005/103, paras 68 and 69; and *Klass and others v Germany* [1978] ECHR 4, paras 48–49.

[36]See, for example, Recommendation (2005)10 of the Committee of Ministers of the Council of Europe on "special investigation techniques" in relation to serious crimes including acts of terrorism (20 April 2005), paras 4 and 6. See also: Council of Europe, Protecting the Right to Privacy in the Fight against Terrorism, COE Doc CommDH/IssuePaper(2008)3; and Countering Terrorism, Protecting Human Rights. A Manual (Warsaw: Organisation for Security and Cooperation in Europe Office for Democratic Institutions and Human Rights, 2007), pp. 200–204.

[37]See, for example, Report of the Special Rapporteur on the promotion and protection of human rights and fundamental freedoms while countering terrorism, UN Doc A/HRC/6/17/Add.3 (2007), paras 49–50; and *Malone v United Kingdom* [1984] ECHR 10, paras 67–68.

the individual.[38] Notwithstanding the importance of the right to privacy Gross argues that, from both a legal and moral perspective, interference with privacy in pursuit of national security (which must include counter-terrorism) is permissible:[39]

> Contrary to privacy, absolute security is the utopian idea, and therefore "national security" as a whole is worthy of legal protection in the sense that the state has the duty and the right to protect itself and the persons who are located within its borders against security threats.

Under the ICCPR, privacy is a matter addressed in article 17, which provides:

1. No one shall be subjected to arbitrary or unlawful interference with his privacy, family, home or correspondence, nor to unlawful attacks on his honour and reputation.
2. Everyone has the right to the protection of the law against such interference or attacks.

As far as the ICCPR is concerned, then, the State is obliged to both *desist* from interfering with privacy, as well as to legislate in a way that *protects* the right to privacy (from both State authorities and natural persons).[40] The protection of privacy is, however, a necessarily relative matter as a result of the fact that all persons live in a society.[41] According to the Human Rights Committee, legislation authorising interference with privacy must specify the precise circumstances in which interference is permitted and must designate an authority to determine, on case-by-case bases, such authorisations.[42] Those that are involved in designing and implementing security infrastructure that involves the collection, storing, or sharing of information about individuals, must therefore ensure that this is done pursuant to a legal authority to do so. The Committee has pointed out that the term "unlawful" within paragraph 1 of article 17 means that an authorisation to interfere with privacy must be established by law, so long as this does not establish an arbitrary authority.[43] Any limitation upon rights must also be reasonable and proportional (see Chap. 10, Sects. 10.2.4 and 10.3.1).

In contrast to the International Covenant, the Privacy Act is weaker in its protection of the privacy of New Zealanders. Section 6 of the Privacy Act establishes 12 Information Privacy Principles, which are concerned with the collection, storage, use and disclosure of personal information. Personal information is defined, under section 2 of the Act, as "information about an identifiable individual". However, application of general principles of statutory interpretation renders the impact of the Act limited to governing the collection of "personal information" where this occurs outside a statutory authority to do so. Where a statute specifically authorises the collection (or interception) of personal information, then the rules of 'reconciliation', 'implied repeal', and *generalia specialibus non derogant* mean

---

[38]Gross (2004, p. 31).

[39]Ibid, p. 35.

[40]General Comment 16 (n 34) paras 1 and 9.

[41]General Comment 16 (n 34) para 7.

[42]General Comment 16 (n 34) paras 3 and 8.

[43]Ibid, para 3. See, for discussion, Conte and Burchill (2009, pp. 203–204).

that (unless the statute can be interpreted in a manner that is consistent with the Privacy Act) the statutory provision remains unaffected by the Privacy Act.[44]

Under NZ's domestic law, then, interference with privacy is only permissible to the extent that such interference either complies with the information privacy principles (section 6 of the Privacy Act), or is expressly authorised under an enactment which prevails by application of the principles of *implied repeal* and *generalia specialibus non derogant*. In contrast, to comply with the ICCPR and the international standards on counter-terrorism and human rights, however, legislative authorisations to interfere with privacy must: (1) not permit arbitrary interference; (2) protect the individual against arbitrary or unlawful interference; and (3) be reasonable and proportional (Chap. 10, Sects. 10.2 and 10.3).

15.2.2 Interception Warrants Under the Crimes Act 1961

As a result of the Counter-Terrorism Bill, section 312N of the Crimes Act 1961 was amended to make interception warrants available for the investigation of terrorism-related offences (defined as any offence against sections 7–13 of the Terrorism Suppression Act 2002), or conspiracy to commit such offences. Interestingly, this does not include the bioterrorism offences incorporated under the sections 298A, 298B and 307A of the Crimes Act (see Chap. 14, Sect. 14.2.3.2). By implied repeal, the issuing of such warrants is unaffected by the Privacy Act. Furthermore, article 17 of the ICCPR is satisfied by the fact that section 312N is a statutory authority which does not thereby authorise 'arbitrary' interception.

On the question of reasonableness and proportionality, this extension appears both reasonable and proportional. In its report to Parliament, the Foreign Affairs, Defence and Trade Committee pointed to the fact that there is no express international requirement to intercept communications pertaining to terrorist offences, but argued that such a power is necessary to provide for the effective investigation of such offences.[45] The interception of private communications, it explained, might be necessary "to prove certain elements of terrorist offences, such as knowledge that an entity was designated".[46] This position makes perfect sense. Counter-terrorism (including New Zealand's contribution to achieving an effective international framework on counter-terrorism) is a pressing and substantial objective justifying proportional limitations upon rights in furtherance of that objective.

---

[44]Reconciliation reflects the aim of the courts to find a construction of two conflicting statutory provisions that reconciles that inconsistency and allows the provisions to stand together. Implied repeal results in a statute later in time impliedly repealing an earlier and totally inconsistent statute. *Generalis specialibus non derogant* means that an earlier, more specific, statutory provision prevails over a later, general statutory provision. See Burrows (2003, pp. 308–317).

[45]Foreign Affairs, Defence and Trade Committee report (n 6) p. 8.

[46]Foreign Affairs, Defence and Trade Committee report (n 6) p. 8.

Sections 200A–200O of the Summary Proceedings Act introduced a regime by which tracking devices may be used by the police and customs. A tracking device is defined under the Act as a device that, when installed in or on anything, can be used to ascertain the location of a thing or person, or whether something has been opened, tampered with or in some way dealt with (section 200A). Despite the number of provisions involved, their effect is relatively simple. Section 200B of the Summary Proceedings Act allows an authorised officer to apply to the District or High Court for a tracking device warrant. The Counter-Terrorism Bill was initially to allow any "authorised public officer" to do so, allowing any officer of a government agency to apply for a warrant.[47] Agreeing with submissions that this would give an important power to too wide a range of government officers, the Select Committee successfully recommended that the authority be limited to "authorised officers", defining that term to include only the police and customs.[48]

To issue a tracking device warrant, the judge hearing the application must be satisfied: (a) that there are reasonable grounds to suspect that an offence [*any* offence] has been, is being, or will be committed; (b) that information that is relevant to the commission of the offence (whether or not including the where-abouts of any person) can be obtained through the use of a tracking device; and (c) that it is in the public interest to issue a warrant, taking into account the seriousness of the offence, the degree to which privacy or property rights are likely to be intruded upon, the usefulness of the information likely to be obtained, and whether it is reasonably practicable for the information to be obtained in another way. Once a warrant is issued (upon terms directed by the Court), the authorised officer can install, remove, maintain and monitor the tracking device and is permitted to take certain steps, including entry into premises, to do so (section 200D).

More controversial is the ability for a police or customs officer to use a tracking device without a warrant. This authority exists where the officer believes on reasonable grounds that a court would issue a warrant (that is, that a judge would be satisfied of the grounds already identified) and that, in all the circumstances, it is not reasonably practicable to obtain a warrant (section 200G). The officer concerned, within 72 hours of installing a tracking device, must either remove it, cease monitoring it, or apply for a warrant to continue use of it (section 200G(6)).

A number of public submissions proposed that this authority was excessive and unnecessary, although the Select Committee disagreed, pointing to the occasional and inevitable need to react to emergencies.[49] In what may have been as an attempt to placate criticisms of the power, the Committee succeeded in introducing a requirement that, whenever a tracking device is used without an accompanying warrant, the authorising officer must lodge a written report with the District or High

---

[47]Counter-Terrorism Bill 2003, clause 34.

[48]Summary Proceedings Act 1957, section 200A. See the report of the Foreign Affairs, Defence and Trade Committee (n 6) p. 11.

[49]See the report of the Foreign Affairs, Defence and Trade Committee (n 6) pp. 11–12.

Court on matters concerning the installation of the device and the circumstances in which it came to be installed (section 200H(2)).

15.2.2.1 Checks and Balances

The issue of checks and balances in the use of tracking devices was a matter of particular concern to the New Zealand Privacy Commissioner in his evidence before the Select Committee.[50] The response of the Foreign Affairs, Defence and Trade Committee was to point to the involvement of the courts (in determining whether or not a warrant should be, or should have been, issued) as an adequate safeguard against abuse of the process.[51] In the case of tracking devices used without a warrant, the checking mechanisms exist through sections 200G and 200H. Firstly, section 200G(8) provides civil and criminal immunity to an officer acting under the authority of section 200G, *unless* the officer "acts in bad faith or without reasonable care". Secondly, the requirement to report to the court was pointed to by the Committee as a further judicial safeguard. Reports under section 200H are to be considered by a judge of the District or High Court, with that judge having the ability to refer a copy of the report, with any comments or recommendations, to the chief executive of the New Zealand Police or Customs, or to the responsible Minister (section 200H(4) and (5)).

Concerning the use of tracking devices, both with and without a warrant, the Privacy Commissioner submitted to the Select Committee that an offence provision was an essential component of the scheme if it was to fully protect privacy:[52]

> I support the scheme proposed in this bill for the authorisation of the use of tracking devices for law enforcement purposes. However, that scheme is incomplete without the accompaniment of an offence provision. Without an offence provision the law is silent in respect of the covert use of tracking devices by citizens against other citizens, notwithstanding the effect on privacy. The law does not explain what happens if an official fails to obtain a warrant or otherwise disregards or breaches the statutory scheme... An offence provision would also mean that public officials, whether authorised or not, could not use tracking devices for purposes not contemplated by this scheme (such as investigating behaviour which does not constitute an offence).

Despite the fact that section 216(3) of the Crimes Act 1961 contains an analogous offence provision for the misuse of interception warrants, the majority of the Committee disagreed that such a provision was necessary in the case of tracking devices. The Committee commented in a rather dismissive way that "at this time, there is no evidence that the illegitimate use of tracking devices is a problem in

---

[50]See the Report by the Privacy Commissioner to the Minister of Justice in relation to the Counter-Terrorism Bill, 7 February 2003, online: http://www.privacy.org.nz/people/countter. html (as accessed 10 March 2005).

[51]Foreign Affairs, Defence and Trade Committee report (n 6) p. 12.

[52]Privacy Commissioner Report (n 50) part 3.8.

New Zealand".[53] That view seems short-sighted and does not respond to the concerns of the Privacy Commissioner, although the Select Committee did urge the Government to consider the recommendation of the Privacy Commissioner in the near future. Despite the fact that an offence provision in the nature of that recommended by the Commissioner was not enacted, it is notable that the Select Committee did recommend limiting an officer's immunity from civil or criminal liability where acting in bad faith or without reasonable care.[54]

Still, the question remains as to whether the use of tracking devices is adequately balanced. In the discussion that follows, it is concluded that the safeguards under the Summary Proceedings Act are not sufficient.

15.2.2.2 Checks on the Use of Tracking Devices Under a Warrant

The role of a judge in issuing a warrant provides a check on whether a warrant should be issued in the first place, and it permits the issuing judge to make directions on the terms upon which a tracking device may be used. A judge is required to determine whether the statutory criteria are met to allow for the use of tracking devices. The judge is also in a position to make whatever directions he or she deems appropriate for the proper use of the device, including the administration of justice and the maintenance of the right to privacy.

What is of concern is what may occur after the issuing of a warrant. The terms of sections 200A–200P of the Act do not guarantee that the use of a tracking device under a warrant will be undertaken in compliance with any directions accompanying the warrant. There is no mechanism within the Act to either censure or otherwise deal with an officer using a tracking device outside the terms directed, or to provide any redress to a person subjected to the use of a tracking device in breach of directed terms. Ultimately, the courts may be able to provide a remedy by excluding evidence obtained in breach of directions under a warrant. The courts appear powerless, however, to grant any remedy for the interference with a person's privacy outside directed terms where there are no subsequent proceedings relying upon evidence obtained as a result of the use of a tracking device. In an extreme case, for example, an officer could obtain a warrant for one purpose, use the tracking device for an entirely different purpose, with no consequences upon the officer or the State.

This is considerably problematic, since article 17(2) of the ICCPR requires States parties to ensure that the law protects individuals against arbitrary or unlawful interference with their privacy. In the absence of mechanisms to enforce compliance and authorise remedial action, the regime for the use of tracking devices under a warrant is in breach of the International Covenant.

---

[53]Foreign Affairs, Defence and Trade Committee report (n 6) p. 12.

[54]Foreign Affairs, Defence and Trade Committee report (n 6) p. 35.

15.2.2.3 Checks on the Use of Tracking Devices Without a Warrant

Arguing in favour of adequate checks in the use of tracking devices without a warrant (under section 200G), one would point to the fact that a police officer must – if the warrant is not extended beyond 72 hours by a judicial warrant – file a written report with the District or High Court giving reasons for using the device and outlining its installation and use (section 200H(2)). One could also contend that the ability to use devices without warrant is a necessary reflection of the exigencies of law enforcement operations where there is no adequate opportunity to obtain a warrant, and point to the fact that a judge reviewing an officer's report can make recommendations (including any adverse comments if appropriate) to the chief executive of the police or customs, or to the responsible Minister.

These do not, however, act as adequate checks upon the use of devices without warrant since they have little weight behind them. Section 200G(8) permits civil and criminal liability to follow where the use of tracking devices by an officer has been undertaken *in bad faith* or *without reasonable care*. This is a limited level of liability. Of particular concern is the fact that the Crown is not required to act upon any recommendations made by a judge following a review of an officer's report. Again, this does not appear to provide adequate protection of individuals' freedom from arbitrary or unlawful interference with their privacy, contrary to the requirement of article 17 of the ICCPR.

15.2.2.4 Crown Law Office Advice to the Attorney-General

In her role under section 7 of the New Zealand Bill of Rights Act, the Attorney-General sought advice from the Crown Law Office concerning any potential inconsistency between the Counter-Terrorism Bill and the Bill of Rights Act (on this role, see Chap. 11, Sect. 11.3.1.3). In the two letters of advice from the Solicitor-General's office to the Attorney-General, the use of tracking devices was the only matter identified as having an impact upon the NZBORA.[55] The advice of the office was that the tracking device scheme to be created under the Bill:[56]

> ...establishes a reasonable accommodation of law enforcement needs and reasonable expectations of privacy. The warrant regime is tightly circumscribed and while s 200G creates a warrantless tracking device power, that too is limited in scope and clearly available only in exigent-type situations.

That conclusion was arrived at by undertaking a similar analysis to that within this chapter. The critical difference, however, is that Crown Counsel did not give consideration to the question of checks and balances upon the potential abuse of

---

[55]Letters from Crown Counsel to the Attorney-General, 'Counter-Terrorism Bill PCO4663/14 Our Ref: nATT114/1124(15)', 10 December 2002 and 11 February 2003 (on file with the author).
[56]Ibid, para 7.

the provisions by an officer. This, as suggested, is where the tracking device regime fails to satisfy the need to provide an adequate protection to privacy.

15.3   Reversal of Burden for the Granting of Bail

An issue to be touched on only briefly is that of the onus for the granting of bail. In his study of Australia's counter-terrorism laws, the Special Rapporteur on the promotion and protection of human rights and fundamental freedoms while countering terrorism noted that, up to the end of April 2006, 26 persons were charged with various terrorism offences (3 had pleaded guilty or been convicted, 4 had been committed for trial, and 19 were awaiting committal for trial).[57] Of those persons, only four had been granted bail. This appeared to be a reflection of the operation of a new section 15AA of the Crimes Act 1914 (Australia), which prevents a bail authority from granting bail to a person charged with, or convicted of, certain terrorism and other offences unless the bail authority is satisfied that exceptional circumstances exist to justify bail. This not only reverses the burden of establishing the need for detention, but places the very high threshold of requiring an accused or convicted person to establish "exceptional circumstances". The Special Rapporteur noted that article 9(3) of the ICCPR provides, in part, that: "It shall not be the general rule that persons awaiting trial shall be detained in custody." The burden should instead be upon the State to establish the need for the detention of an accused person to continue. Where there are essential reasons, such as the suppression of evidence or the commission of further offences, bail may be refused and a person remanded in custody. The Special Rapporteur took the view, however, that the classification of an act as a terrorist offence in domestic law should not result in automatic denial of bail, nor in the reversal of onus.[58] Each case must be assessed on its merits, with the burden upon the State for establishing reasons for detention.

15.4   Operation of Special Techniques and Rules Outside the Framework of Combating Terrorism

A final matter requiring discussion is the use of counter-terrorism as a potential tool of manipulation by States as a means of legitimising unnecessarily broad State powers. This has been a common criticism of States throughout the world since

---

[57]Special Rapporteur on the promotion and protection of human rights and fundamental freedoms while countering terrorism, Australia: Study on Human Rights Compliance While Countering Terrorism, UN Doc A/HRC/4/26/Add.3, para 34. See also Human Rights Committee, Concluding Observations: Australia, UN Doc CCPR/C/AUS/CO/5 (2009), para 11.

[58]Ibid, para 34.

9/11. Regrettably, as evident through the examination of tracking devices and powers of questioning incorporated within the Summary Proceedings Act, New Zealand is no different. In introducing the Counter-Terrorism Bill in 2003, it was said that the Bill "reflects the need for New Zealand to ensure we have a comprehensive legislative framework in place that reflects the new, more dangerous era of international terrorism that we live in".[59] As mentioned, the Explanatory Notes to the Counter-Terrorism Bill identified the objectives the Bill as including the establishment of investigative powers to assist in the detection of terrorists, terrorist acts and terrorist or associated entities.[60] Apparent from the foregoing discussions at Sect. 15.1, however, the tracking device regime under sections 200A–200O of the Summary Proceedings Act is not restricted in its application to the investigation and combating of terrorism. Tracking devices may be used in the investigation of any offence. The powers of questioning under section 198B of the Summary Proceedings Act are similarly not restricted in their application to the investigation and combating of terrorism, in fact applying to the investigation of any offence carrying a maximum penalty of more than 3 months' imprisonment.

The establishment of broad legislative provisions like these within the umbrella of a 'Counter-Terrorism' Bill was a matter of regular criticism in submissions to, and evidence before, the Foreign Affairs, Defence and Trade Committee in New Zealand.[61] It was also a criticism from within the Select Committee, Keith Locke MP describing the Bill as "fraudulent", on the basis that a number of its legislative amendments had nothing to do with terrorism.[62] Similar concerns were expressed during the Select Committee hearing process by Committee Member Wayne Mapp MP.[63] In attempting to justify the inclusion of non-terrorism specific provisions within the Counter-Terrorism Bill, the Select Committee reported to the House that, after consulting with the Minister of Justice, the majority of the Committee agreed that the non-terrorism specific provisions should remain within the Bill. The report stated that:[64]

> The Minister told us that it is accepted that there are strong links between terrorist activity and other organised crime, such as arms smuggling and drug importation. However, these activities are not always associated with terrorism and terrorist acts are essentially the same

---

[59]Phil Goff MP, 'Counter-Terrorism Bill – Introduction', Parliamentary Speech, 1 April 2003, summarised online: http://www.beehive.govt.nz/ViewDocument.cfm?DocumentID=16392 (as accessed on 4 March 2005).

[60]Explanatory Note (n 4) p. 1.

[61]Including submissions and evidence by the author, the Privacy Commission and the New Zealand Law Society: see Submissions to the Foreign Affairs, Defence and Trade Committee on the Counter-Terrorism Bill 2003, Parliamentary Library, Wellington.

[62]Keith Locke MP, 'Counter-Terrorism Bill – First Reading', Parliamentary Speech, 2 April 2003, copy online: http://www.greens.org.nz/node/16049. See also the Foreign Affairs, Defence and Trade Committee report on the Counter-Terrorism Bill (n 6) 13.

[63]Foreign Affairs, Defence and Trade Committee Hearing on the Counter-Terrorism Bill, Old Parliament House (Room G.003), Wellington, 15 May 2003.

[64]Foreign Affairs, Defence and Trade Committee report (n 6) p. 3.

as ordinary criminal offences committed with a different motive. The investigative powers contained in the bill are critical to allowing police to identify terrorist activity effectively. Therefore, we do not believe it is possible to make this distinction in legislating for investigation of these activities.

The analysis within this chapter does not support this position. The provisions in question apply to the investigation of any offences punishable by imprisonment, the greater majority of which will fall outside any link between terrorism or organised crime. Significantly, the upshot of this concern is not limited to matters of domestic politics and internal wranglings to extend State powers. New Zealand's enactment of generally applicable provisions under the vehicle of the Counter-Terrorism Bill is also contrary to the international guidelines on counter-terrorism discussed in Chap. 13 (see Sect. 13.2.6 and, especially, Sect. 13.3 regarding condition 3.4 of the Handbook on Human Rights Compliance – Appendix 4 in this title). Although these guidelines can be characterised as 'soft law' recommendations, they are nevertheless highly influential given the consistency between the various sources of the guidelines. They represent the standards generally accepted by international society as being applicable to the countering of terrorism in democratic States.

The guidelines advocated by the Committee of Ministers to the Council of Europe direct that where measures taken by States to combat terrorism restrict human rights, those restrictions must be defined as precisely as possible and be necessary to the objective of countering terrorism.[65] Guidelines of the former High Commissioner for Human Rights provide that, to be lawful, limitations imposed by counter-terrorist legislation must be necessary for public safety and public order, and for the protection of the rights and freedoms of others.[66] Finally, the latest Draft Principles and Guidelines within the report of the UN Sub-Commission Rapporteur on terrorism and human rights provided that:[67]

Counter-terrorism measures should directly relate to terrorism and terrorist acts, not actions undertaken in armed conflict situations *or acts that are ordinary crimes* (emphasis added).

The investigative tools examined within this chapter under the Summary Proceedings Act 1957 (NZ) and the Crimes Act 1961 (NZ) (see Sects. 14.1 and 14.2) fail to comply with these guidelines.

---

[65]Council of Europe, Guidelines on Human Rights and the Fight Against Terrorism (Council of Europe Publishing, 2002), Guideline III(2).

[66]Report of the United Nations High Commissioner for Human Rights and Follow-up to the World Conference on Human Rights, Human Rights: A Uniting Framework, ESCOR (58th Sess) UN Doc E/CN.4/2002/18 (2002), Annex entitled Proposals for "further guidance" for the submission of reports pursuant to paragraph 6 of Security Council resolution 1373 (2001), para 4(b).

[67]Sub-Commission Special Rapporteur on terrorism and human rights, Kalliopi Koufa, Specific Human Rights Issues: New Priorities, in Particular Terrorism and Counter-Terrorism. A Preliminary Framework Draft of Principles and Guidelines Concerning Human Rights and Terrorism, UN Doc E/CN.4/Sub.2/2005/39 (2005), para 33. See also Report of the Special Rapporteur on the promotion and protection of human rights and fundamental freedoms while countering terrorism, Promotion and Protection of Human Rights, GAOR, 60th Sess, UN Doc A/60/370 (2005), para 47.

15.5 The Role of Security Intelligence Services

Following the 2003 terrorist attacks in Madrid, the Council of Europe expressed its intention to step up the fight against all forms of terrorism and emphasised the importance of efficient cooperation in intelligence matters, inviting member States to promote efficient and systematic cooperation between the police and intelligence services.[68] Although some had predicted that such cooperation would be difficult,[69] the actual involvement of intelligence services and information generated by them in counter-terrorism proceedings has been frequent (see, for example, Chap. 16 at Sect. 16.2.2, and Chap. 18 at Sects. 18.2.2 and 18.2.3). What has in fact been seen is a blurring of the lines between the gathering of evidence for criminal prosecutions and intelligence-gathering for national security.[70] In the United Kingdom, for example, the relationship between police and intelligence services has been formalised through the establishment of the Police International Counter-Terror Unit, based within both the police and the MI5 National Counter-Terrorism Security Office.[71] As noted by the UN Special Rapporteur in a thematic report on the role of intelligence agencies and their oversight in the fight against terrorism:[72]

> ...some Governments insisted that clear distinctions between intelligence and law enforcement powers were no longer tenable, arguing that the extraordinary character of the contemporary terrorist threat demands that intelligence agencies acquire new powers to interrogate, arrest and detain people. Giving powers of arrest, detention and interrogation to intelligence agencies is not as such a violation of international law, provided these agencies comply with all relevant human rights standards regarding arrest and detention and with domestic constitutional and other provisions prescribed for ordinary law enforcement agencies. However, the Special Rapporteur is concerned that in several countries the power shift from law enforcement agencies to intelligence agencies for countering and preventing terrorist threats was accomplished precisely to circumvent such necessary safeguards in a democratic society, abusing thereby the usually legitimate secrecy of intelligence operations. This shift can ultimately endanger the rule of law, as the collection of intelligence and the collection of evidence about criminal acts becomes more and more blurred.

The question of the role and functioning of intelligence agencies has become increasingly important in light of their growing involvement in the investigative aspects of counter-terrorism, as well as their continuing and often expanded role in prevention. As concluded in a publication of the Council of Europe on special

---

[68]Council of Europe, Terrorism: Special Investigative Techniques (Council of Europe Publishing, 2005), p. 39.

[69]See, for example, Treverton (2003).

[70]See, for example, Palmer (2004).

[71]Walker (2005, p. 387). On the functioning of the Security Intelligence Service in the United Kingdom, Canada and Australia in the field of counter-terrorism, see Chalk and Rosenau (2004, Chaps. 2, 4 and 6).

[72]Report of the Special Rapporteur on the promotion and protection of human rights and fundamental freedoms while countering terrorism, UN Doc A/HRC/10/3 (2009). See also Vervaele (2005).

investigative techniques: "It will be necessary to ensure that the legal framework for the activities of the intelligence services is such that cooperation between the judicial services, the police and the intelligence services fully respects... the right to a fair trial without impeding the lawful action of the security services".[73] Walker speaks of four modes through which, in the anti-terrorism field, intelligence arises or is used: (1) through the making of strategic assessment of the sources, nature and level of terrorist threats, linked to the question of resources and security measures; (2) through intelligence operations aimed at preventing or disrupting terrorist acts, including surveillance and interrogation; (3) through the provision of intelligence to law enforcement authorities, leading to the use of intelligence in criminal and other proceedings; and (4) through operations which restrain individuals by overt executive-directed measures.[74]

From this, three points should be made. The first is that there should always be a comprehensive legislative framework defining the mandate of intelligence services and the special powers afforded to them. The Special Rapporteur has expressed the view that, without such a framework, States are likely *not* to meet their obligation under human rights treaties to respect and ensure the effective enjoyment of human rights.[75] As an example of best practice, he has pointed to the very detailed provisions governing each investigative technique that Dutch intelligence may use under the Intelligence and Security Services Act 2002 (Netherlands). It is crucial, in this regard, that legislation clarifies the threshold criteria which might trigger intrusive actions by intelligence services.[76]

The second point to make concerns the use of information gathered or analysed by intelligence services. In this regard, it has been noted that the line between 'strategic intelligence' (information obtained by intelligence agencies for the purposes of policymaking) and probative evidence in criminal proceedings has become blurred.[77] This demands that care must be taken by investigation, prosecution and judicial authorities when seeking to rely on information obtained from intelligence agencies, paying particular regard to the sources and nature of such information.[78] It also calls for the prior judicial approval for the use of special investigative techniques in order to make permissible the fruits of such techniques as evidence in court.[79]

Finally, the ex-ante and post-facto oversight and accountability of intelligence services is crucial to ensure that the activities of intelligence agencies in the

---

[73]Council of Europe report on Special Investigate Techniques (n 68) p. 40.

[74]Walker (2005, p. 389).

[75]Special Rapporteur report on intelligence agencies (n 72) para 27. See also, analogously, *Rotaru v Romania* [2000] ECHR 192; and Cameron (2009, pp. 11–12).

[76]Special Rapporteur report on intelligence agencies (n 72) para 31, and chapter II(A)(2) more generally.

[77]Special Rapporteur report on intelligence agencies (n 72) para 29.

[78]Walker (2005, pp. 409–410).

[79]Special Rapporteur report on intelligence agencies (n 72) para 29.

prevention and criminalisation of terrorism is conducted in a manner which is compatible with States' duty to comply with human rights. Cameron speaks of the need for independent oversight bodies which are capable of overseeing the operation of intelligence agencies, vis-à-vis ethical standards, actual practices, and policies, whether official, developing, or de facto.[80] A lack of oversight and political and legal accountability has been noted by the Special Rapporteur as contributing, and even facilitating, illegal activities by the intelligence community.[81] Several States have devised independent permanent offices, such as inspectors-general, judicial commissioners or auditors, through statutes or administrative arrangements which review whether intelligence agencies comply with their duties.[82] The Special Rapportuer has suggested that a specific oversight role also falls upon parliament, which in the sphere of intelligence should play its traditional function of holding the executive branch and its agencies accountable to the general public.[83] Parliamentary committees exercising this role should be independent. In the United Kingdom, for example, although the Intelligence Security Committee is composed of sitting parliamentarians, it is appointed by and answerable to the Prime Minister.[84]

Ex post facto accountability is equally important. States should create mechanisms through which independent investigations can be conducted into alleged human rights violations by intelligence services. The adoption of indemnity or immunity provisions for intelligence agents has been noted with concern by the Rapportuer, who concludes that such provisions can bar effective access to court and violate the right to an effective remedy (on the right to an effective remedy, see Chap. 9, Sect. 9.2.4).[85]

15.6 Conclusions

The use of special investigative techniques and rules of criminal procedure in countering terrorism is most often justified by the special nature and difficulties in combating terrorist conduct. Notwithstanding this, experiences have shown that special powers may be used in an oppressive manner which impacts upon

---

[80]Cameron (2009), interventions. See also the report of the Council of Europe Venice Commission on The Democratic Oversight of the Security Services, COE Doc CDL-AD(2007)016 (2007).

[81]Special Rapporteur report on intelligence agencies (n 72) para 25. See also McCulloch and Tham (2005), especially pp. 406–407.

[82]Special Rapporteur report on intelligence agencies (n 72) para 44.

[83]Special Rapporteur report on intelligence agencies (n 72) para 44. As an example of the operation of such a mechanism, see the report of the House of Representative Parliamentary Joint Committee on ASIO, ASIS and DSD, Parliament of the Commonwealth of Australia, November 2005.

[84]Chalk and Rosenau (2004, p. 53).

[85]Special Rapporteur report on intelligence agencies (n 72) para 58.

innocent persons. The implementation of proper checks and balances, compatible with operational needs, is thus essential. This is all the more important due to the tendency of States, including New Zealand as it has been shown in this chapter, to introduce special powers, under the guise of counter-terrorism legislation, which are in fact applicable beyond the framework of combating terrorism. The need for checks and balances is further accentuated by the frequent involvement of security intelligence services in the conduct and instigation of criminal investigations. Intelligence services play a vital contributing role to the prevention and investigation of terrorism, but the nature of information from intelligence sources calls for care to be taken. There should always be a comprehensive legislative framework defining the mandate of intelligence services and the special powers afforded to them, including a clear and precise clarification of threshold criteria which might trigger intrusive actions by intelligence services. The use of information gathered or analysed by intelligence services must pay particular regard to the sources and nature of such information., and calls for the prior judicial approval for the use of special investigative techniques in order to make permissible the fruits of such techniques as evidence in court. The ex-ante and post-facto oversight and accountability of intelligence services is furthermore crucial to ensure that the activities of intelligence agencies in the prevention and criminalisation of terrorism is conducted in a manner which is compatible with States' duty to comply with human rights.

Of the case studies examined in this chapter, two have concerned special powers introduced in New Zealand under the Counter-Terrorism Bill 2003. The first involved the inclusion of a new section 198B of the Summary Proceedings Act 1957 (NZ) to introduce special powers of questioning by the police, compelling a person to provide assistance to access computer data, or any other information required to access computer data. Section 198B does not limit itself to the investigation of terrorism, but is instead applicable to the investigation of any offence under NZ law which carries a maximum penalty greater than 3 months imprisonment. The provision does not preserve the right, under either the common law or the NZ Bill of Rights Act, not to incriminate oneself. Nor does it limit the interference with this right by providing for use immunity. For these reasons, reform of section 198B is required to restrict its operation to the investigation of terrorist offences, or other serious crimes. This would at lease see the scope of the powers of questioning restricted to a proportionate level.

Also introduced in New Zealand under the Counter-Terrorism Bill 2003 were provisions now included in the Crimes Act 1961 for attaching tracking devices to people or property. These special powers are again applicable to all offences, not just those related to terrorism. Due to the subordinate protection given to privacy rights in New Zealand, they also suffer from a lack of adequate safeguards to sufficiently protect individuals from arbitrary or disproportionate interference with their privacy. Other than in the case of the exclusion of evidence which is obtained through tracking devices outside the directed terms of a warrant, courts have little power to grant to grant a remedy where there are no subsequent proceedings relying on such evidence. Action is limited, for example, where a tracking device is obtained for one purpose, and then subsequently used for a completely different purpose which does not lead to criminal proceedings but nevertheless involves an undue interference with privacy. The civil and criminal liability of police will only follow if the use of a tracking device has been undertaken in bath faith or without reasonable care.

The latter aspects of investigative law reform in New Zealand since 9/11 have gone beyond that required for the purpose of counter-terrorism and are, to that extent, in conflict with international guidelines on the interface between counter-terrorism and human rights. Also problematic, in the case of Australia, is the introduction of a new section 15AA of the Crimes Act 1914, which prevents a bail authority from granting bail to a person charged with, or convicted of, certain terrorism and other offences unless the bail authority is satisfied that exceptional circumstances exist to justify bail. This not only reverses the burden of establishing the need for detention, but places the very high threshold of requiring an accused or convicted person to establish "exceptional circumstances". This has been criticised by the UN Special Rapporteur, who took the view that the classification of an act as a terrorist offence in domestic law should not result in automatic denial of bail, nor in the reversal of onus. Each case must be assessed on its merits, with the burden upon the State for establishing reasons for detention.

References

Burrows, John. 2003. *Statute Law in New Zealand*. Wellington: 3rd edition, LexisNexis.

Cameron, Iain. 2009. Fair Trial in Terrorism Cases and Problems and Potential in Evaluation States' Laws and Practices Relating to Fair Trial (paper presented at the Round Table *Fight against Terrorism: Challenges for the Judiciary*, 18-19 September 2009, Fiesole, Italy).

Chalk, Peter, and Rosenau, William. 2004. *Confronting the "Enemy Within"*. Santa Monica: RAND Corporation.

Conte, Alex. 2007. *Counter-Terrorism and Human Rights in New Zealand*. Christchurch: New Zealand Law Foundation (available online: http://www.alexconte.com/docs/CT%20and%20HR%20in%20New%20Zealand.pdf).

Conte, Alex, and Burchill, Richard. 2009. *Defining Civil and Political Rights: The Jurisprudence of the United Nations Human Rights* Committee. Aldershot: 2nd ed, Ashgate Publishing Ltd.

Fenwick, Helen. 2002. *Civil Liberties and Human Rights*. London: 3rd edition, Cavendish Publishing Limited.

Fenwick, Helen, and Phillipson, Gavin. 2005. Legislative over-breadth, democratic failure and the judicial response: fundamental rights and the UK's anti-terrorist legal policy. In Ramraj, Victor, Hor, Michael, and Roach, Kent (Eds). *Global Anti-Terrorism Law and Policy*. Cambridge: Cambridge University Press.

Gross, Emanuel. 2004. The Struggle of a Democracy Against Terrorism. Protection of Human Rights: The Right to Privacy Versus the National Interest – the Proper Balance. 37(1) *Cornell International Law Journal* 27.

Inbau, Fred. 1999. Self-Incrimination: What Can an Accused Person Be Compelled to Do? 89(4) *The Journal of Criminal Law and Criminology* 1329.

Joseph, Philip. 2001. *Constitutional and Administrative Law in New Zealand* (Wellington: 2nd ed, Brookers).

Langbein, John. 1994. The Historical Origins of the Privilege against Self-Incrimination at Common Law. 92(5) *Michigan Law Review* 1047.

McCulloch, Jude, and Tham, Joo-Cheong. 2005. Secret State, Transparent Subject: The Australian Security Intelligence Organisation in the Age of Terror. 38(3) *The Australian and New Zealand Journal of Criminology* 400.

Palmer, Andrew. 2004 Investigating and Prosecuting Terrorism: The Counter-Terrorism Legislation and the Law of Evidence. 27(2) *The University of New South Wales Law Journal* 373.

Rishworth, Paul, Huscroft, Grant, Optican, Scott, and Mahoney, Richard. 2003. *The New Zealand Bill of Rights*. Oxford: Oxford University Press.

Schabas, William, and Olivier, Clémentine. 2003. What Criminal Procedure Should Govern Terrorist Offenses: Ordinary or Special Rules? In Doucet, Ghislaine (Ed). *Terrorism, Victims, and International Criminal Responsibility*. Paris: SOS Attentats.

Talbot, Rhiannon. 2002. The balancing act: counter-terrorism and civil liberties in British anti-terrorism law. In Strawson, John (ed). *Law after Ground Zero*. London: GlassHouse Press.

Treverton, Gregory. 2003. Reshaping Intelligence to Share with "Ourselves". Commentary 82: Canadian Security Intelligence Service, online: http://www.csis-scrs.gc.ca/pblctns/cmmntr/cm82-eng.asp

Vervaele, John. 2005. Terrorism and Information Sharing Between the Intelligence and Law Enforcement Communities in the US and the Netherlands: Emergency criminal law? 1(1) *Utrecht Law Review* 1.

Walker, Clive. 2005. Intelligence and Anti-Terrorism Legislation in the United Kingdom. 44 *Crime, Law and Social Change* 387.

Chapter 16
Arrest and Detention, and Investigative Hearings

The current chapter continues with the theme addressed in Chap. 15 of special measures to combat terrorism. Its focus is on two mechanisms: investigative detention, i.e. detention without charge for the purpose of questioning a suspect in the pre-charge process of police investigations; and investigative hearings, i.e. judicial hearings conducted for the purpose of investigating terrorist events where persons are compelled to attend and provide information. The matter of the arrest and pre-charge detention of persons is most well developed in the United Kingdom. The Police and Criminal Evidence Act 1984 allows for the detention without charge for up to 4 days of persons suspected of committing indictable offences, which includes various terrorism-related offences. The Terrorism Act 2000, as amended by the Criminal Justice Act 2003 and the Terrorism Act 2006, permits a series of police- and judge-authorised extensions of investigative detention up to a total period of 28 days. Investigative detention is also a tool used in Australia, both under the Crimes Act 1914 and the Australian Security Intelligence Organisation Act 1974. Detention of this kind engages various rights, most especially the right to be brought promptly before a judicial authority following one's arrest. It may also, as it does in the United Kingdom, impact upon the right of a detainee to consult with legal counsel.

In Canada, the Anti-terrorism Act 2001 introduced a mechanism through which persons may be compelled to attend a judicial hearing on the investigation of terrorist acts. Two central issues are involved. First is the question of the use to which compelled testimony can be made, particularly in the context of any proceedings brought against the person compelled to give evidence at an investigative hearing. The second is the issue of the role of judicial officers in such hearing, and whether their involvement in investigative matters crosses the line between the traditional separation of powers held by the judiciary and the executive. A further issue which has arisen in the particular application of the regime in Canada is that of the open administration of justice.

A. Conte, *Human Rights in the Prevention and Punishment of Terrorism*,
DOI 10.1007/978-3-642-11608-7_16, © Springer-Verlag Berlin Heidelberg 2010

16.1 Arrest and Detention in the United Kingdom

Most powers of arrest in the United Kingdom are contained within the Police and Criminal Evidence Act 1984 (PACE), although there is a common law power of arrest in respect of breaches of the peace, which allows a constable to arrest a person who is causing a breach of the peace, or who is behaving in such a way as to lead the constable reasonably to apprehend an imminent breach of the peace.[1] Arrest can be affected under warrant, where a constable obtains a warrant to arrest from a justice of the peace. Section 1 of the Magistrates Courts Act 1980 allows such warrants to be issued in respect of any person who has, or is suspected of having, committed an indictable offence. The reality, however, is that police powers of arrest under PACE and other statutes are so broad that a constable rarely needs to obtain an arrest warrant.

It is worth mentioning at this point that, as stated in section 114 of the PACE Act, a constable may, if necessary, use reasonable force for the purpose of exercising a power conferred on him or her under the Act. This, as well as the common law authority to prevent crimes and to act in self-defence have been commonly invoked in counter-terrorist operations and, as observed by Walker, their application in the UK has proven contentious.[2] There has been a long history of shootings in Northern Ireland, as well as a more recent dispute concerning the circumstances of the shooting of Jean Charles de Menzies in 2005.[3] While this is not an issue considered further within this text, it is worth noting that these are matters raised in the most recent Concluding Observations of the Human Rights Committee on the sixth periodic report of the United Kingdom.[4]

16.1.1 Powers of Arrest and Detention

16.1.1.1 Arrest and Detention Under the Police and Criminal Evidence Act 1984

There are two powers of arrest under PACE. The first is under section 24 of the Act, relating to "arrestable offences" listed in Schedule 1A. Section 24 allows a constable in the United Kingdom to arrest anyone who: is, or is reasonably suspected to be, about to commit such an offence; is, or is reasonably suspected to be, in the act of committing such an offence; or is guilty of having committed such an offence, or reasonably suspected of being guilty. Section 25 then deals with the general arrest

---

[1]*R v Howell* [1982] QB 416. See further Stone (2008, at 3.5.1). On powers of arrest, and search and seizure, in New Zealand, see Conte (2007, Chap. 19).

[2]Walker (2009, p. 134).

[3]See Kennison and Loumansky (2007).

[4]Human Rights Committee, Concluding Observations: United Kingdom of Great Britain and Northern Ireland, UN Doc CCPR/C/GBR/CO/6 (2008), paras 9 and 10.

conditions applicable when a constable witnesses the commission of an offence which is not listed in Schedule 1A, or to which no other statutory power of arrest attaches. In such cases, which relate to less serious offences, a person does not need to be arrested but can instead be proceeded against by way of summons. Other statutory powers of arrest exist in the United Kingdom, including under the Terrorism Act 2000 (see below).

Upon arrest, a person must be brought to a police station under the responsibility of a custody officer (section 36). Certain information, set out in Code C of the Police Codes of Practice, must be given to the arrested person, including confirmation of the arrest and the reasons for it, the right to consult a layer, and the right to consult the Codes of Practice. The maximum period for which a person may be detained without charge is normally 24 hours (section 41(7)), unless either (1) a superintendent approves a further 12 hour period of detention (applicable in relation to any arrestable offence); or (2) the person is arrested in respect of an indictable offence, in which case the suspect may be detained for up to 96 hours (4 days) subject to special procedures (section 42); or (3) under certain provisions of the Terrorism Act 2000 (see below). Before the amendment of PACE under the Criminal Justice Act 2003, no detention was possible beyond 24 hours except in respect of a "serious arrestable offence".[5] Once released, a person cannot be re-arrested for the same offence without a warrant.

16.1.1.2 Arrest and Detention Under the Terrorism Act 2000

Special powers of arrest to deal with terrorism were introduced in the United Kingdom under the Prevention of Terrorism (Temporary Provisions) Acts, first enacted in 1974 relating to the troubles in Northern Ireland. Common sections 12 of the Acts gave police the power to arrest and detain without charge for up to 48 hours any person suspected of involvement in acts of terrorism, and gave the Home Secretary the authority to extend detention for a further 5 days (see Chap. 17, Sect. 17.2). In *Brogan and others v United Kingdom*, the European Court of Human Rights found that the detention of a suspect under section 12 for a period of 4 days and 6 hours violated the right to be brought promptly before a judge, contrary to article 5(3) of the European Convention on Human Rights.[6] The Government subsequently derogated from article 5 of the Convention, a matter discussed in Chap. 17 (Sect. 17.2). This remained the position until the consolidation of the UK's counter-terrorism laws under the Terrorism Act 2000.

Section 41 of the Terrorism Act 2000 empowers a constable to arrest, without warrant, a person "whom he reasonably suspects to be a terrorist" (section 41(1)). The term "terrorist" is defined in section 40 as a person who has committed one of

---

[5]This is a category of particularly serious offences defined under section 166 and Schedule 5 of the Police and Criminal Evidence Act, including, for example, treason, murder and rape.

[6]*Brogan and others v United Kingdom* [1988] ECHR 24.

the terrorism-related offences under the Act (section 40(1)(a)); or a person who "is or has been concerned in the commission, preparation or instigation of acts of terrorism" (section 40(1)(b)). "Terrorism" is in turn linked to the definition of the term in section 1 of the Act (section 40(2) – see Chap. 8, Sect. 8.1.5.1). Stone identifies problems with the definition of a suspected terrorist under section 40(1) (b).[7] First, it means that a constable does not have to have a particular offence in mind when exercising the power of arrest under section 41. While this is required within the definition of a suspected terrorist under section 40(1)(a), section 40(1)(b) only demands that a constable reasonably suspects the person of involvement in "acts of terrorism". This criticism is somewhat alleviated by section 27 of the Counter-Terrorism Act 2008, which extends the meaning of "terrorism offence" to also include the specific offences under section 113 of the Anti-Terrorism, Crime and Security Act 2001 (use of noxious substances or things); and offences under sections 1, 2, 5–6, and 8–11 of the Terrorism Act 2006 (encouragement of terrorism; preparation and training for terrorism; and offences relating to radioactive devices and material and nuclear facilities).

Linked to this is the fact that the level of involvement need only require that the person is or has been "concerned" in the commission, preparation or instigation of such acts. Being concerned in prohibited conduct is much broader than being a principal or a party to an offence. This opens the door, it is feared, for the police to arrest persons based upon intelligence information, thus further contributing to the concerns already expressed in this title about the blurring line between security intelligence services and law enforcement authorities (see Chap. 15, Sect. 15.5). It also involves a less strict requirement for establishing reasonable suspicion, said to be necessary in relation to terrorist crimes due to the need to act speedily to avert terrorist violence, and the need to keep intelligence sources secret.[8] Furthermore, the definition in section 40(1)(b) of a suspected terrorism is linked to the overly broad definition of terrorism under section 1 of the Terrorism Act 2000 (see Chap. 14, Sect. 14.1).

Not only is the threshold for arrest without warrant under the Terrorism Act lower than would be the case for other offences in the United Kingdom, but this low threshold can precipitate the detention of a person without charge for up to 14 days. In 2009, the Home Office published a statistical report for the period 11 September 2001 to 31 March 2008 on terrorism arrests and outcomes in Great Britain. The report notes that 46% of those arrested under section 41 of the Terrorism Act 2000 were held in pre-charge detention for under 1 day and 66% for under 2 days, after which they were charged, released or further alternative action was taken. Since the maximum period of pre-charge detention was increased to 28 days with effect from

---

[7]Stone (2008, p. 233).

[8]*Fox, Campbell and Hartley v United Kingdom* [1990] A.182, para 32. See Cameron (2009, p. 2).

25 July 2006, the report records that six persons were detained for the full period, of which three were charged and three were released without charge.[9]

16.1.2 Investigative Detention Without Charge Beyond 36 Hours

In the investigation of terrorism-related offences, there are several possibilities for continuing the detention of a suspect, without charge, beyond of 36 hours (i.e. the normal 24 hour period, plus an extension of 12 hours by a superintendent).[10] This will, naturally, engage liberty rights protected under the International Covenant on Civil and Political Rights (ICCPR) and the European Convention on Human Rights (ECHR), the latter of which has been incorporated into UK domestic law under the Human Rights Act 1998 (see Chap. 11, Sect. 11.1.4).[11] The ICCPR and ECHR take slightly different approaches to the question of liberty rights. Article 9(1) of the International Covenant provides that:

> Everyone has the right to liberty and security of person. No one shall be subjected to arbitrary arrest or detention. No one shall be deprived of his liberty except on such grounds and in accordance with such procedure as are established by law.

Paragraphs (2) to (5) of article 9, as well as article 10, then set out rights triggered by a person's arrest or detention. The affect of article 9(1) of the ICCPR is to establish a general prohibition against interference with a person's right to liberty (first sentence) and against arbitrary arrest or detention (second sentence). It provides for two forms of limitation: (1) by interpretation of the term 'arbitrary' (see Chap. 10, Sect. 10.3.1.2); or (2) by the qualification that no deprivation of liberty may occur except on grounds and procedures established by law (a 'qualified right' – see Chap. 10, Sect. 10.3.2.2). Article 5(1) of the ECHR instead represents an example of a 'limited right', i.e. one which explains the precise and limited extent to which the right may be limited (see Chap. 10, Sect. 10.3.2.1):

> Everyone has the right to liberty and security of person. No one shall be deprived of his liberty save in the following cases and in accordance with a procedure prescribed by law:
> a. the lawful detention of a person after conviction by a competent court;
> b. the lawful arrest or detention of a person for non-compliance with the lawful order of a court or in order to secure the fulfilment of any obligation prescribed by law;

---

[9]Home Office Statistical Bulletin, Statistics on Terrorism Arrests and Outcomes in Great Britain (Home Office, London, May 2009), paras 11–13.

[10]Consequent to the amendment of the Police and Criminal Evidence Act under the Criminal Justice Act 2003.

[11]International Covenant on Civil and Political Rights, opened for signature 16 December 1966, 999 UNTS 171 (entered into force 23 March 1976); Convention for the Protection of Human Rights and Fundamental Freedoms, opened for signature 4 November 1950, 213 UNTS 222 (entered into force 3 September 1953).

c. the lawful arrest or detention of a person effected for the purpose of bringing him before the competent legal authority on reasonable suspicion of having committed an offence or when it is reasonably considered necessary to prevent his committing an offence or fleeing after having done so;

d. the detention of a minor by lawful order for the purpose of educational supervision or his lawful detention for the purpose of bringing him before the competent legal authority;

e. the lawful detention of persons for the prevention of the spreading of infectious diseases, of persons of unsound mind, alcoholics or drug addicts or vagrants;

f. the lawful arrest or detention of a person to prevent his effecting an unauthorised entry into the country or of a person against whom action is being taken with a view to deportation or extradition.

The implications of article 5(1)(f) of the ECHR to the United Kingdom's indefinite detention of foreign terrorist suspects under Part 4 of the Anti-terrorism, Crime and Security Act 2001 is a matter considered in Chap. 17 (Sect. 17.3). After expressing the limited right to liberty in paragraph (1), article 5(2) to (5) sets out the rights triggered upon arrest or detention.

16.1.2.1   The Right to be Brought Promptly Before a Judge Following Arrest or Detention

Article 5(3) of the ECHR expressly guarantees the right of any person who is arrested or detained to be brought 'promptly' before a judge or other officer authorised by law to exercise judicial power. The same guarantee is found in article 9(3) of the ICCPR and is a matter which is also considered in Chap. 17, in the context of the derogation by the United Kingdom from article 5(3) of the ECHR for the purpose of maintaining its special powers of detention in Northern Ireland under the Prevention of Terrorism (Temporary Provisions) Acts 1974–2001 (see Sect. 17.2). For the purposes of this chapter, a brief account of the facts leading up to this derogation will be made.

Common sections 12 of the Prevention of Terrorism (Temporary Provisions) Acts gave police the power to arrest and detain without charge for up to 48 hours any person suspected of involvement in acts of terrorism (as defined by common sections 1, 9 and 10 of the Acts). Common sections 12 gave the Home Secretary the authority to extend detention for a further 5 days. Suspects could thereby be held without charge for a total of 7 days without the need for them to be brought before a judge. The powers in question were only applied in Northern Ireland and the UK's subsequent derogation from the right to liberty was limited to that territory. Until 1988, this format of 'seven-day executive detention', as it came to be known, was enacted and renewed without the United Kingdom seeking to derogate from the right to liberty.

Extended periods of police detention (*détention en garde à vue*), without bringing a suspect before a judge, has been a long-standing issue of concern in several countries, for instance in France, Russia, Northern Africa and South-East Asia.[12]

---

[12]Concerning France, the Human Rights Committee has expressed concern that Act No. 2006/64 of 23 January 2006 permits the initial detention of persons suspected of terrorism for 4 days, with

In *Brogan and others v United Kingdom*, the European Court was called on to determine whether the detention of four men under section 12 of the Prevention of Terrorism (Temporary Provisions) Act violated the right to be brought promptly before a judge. The four men had been detained for periods ranging from 4 days and 6 hours to 6 days and 16.5 hours. The Court did not state what the maximum period could be for a person to be held without charge before article 5(3) was violated.[13] It did, however, rule that the least of the periods of detention in that case (4 days and 6 hours) was too long.[14] The UN Special Rapporteur has emphasised, in this regard, that a court must always be empowered to review the merits of the decision to detain and to decide, by reference to legal criteria, whether detention is justified, and, if not, to order release.[15]

16.1.2.2 Detention in Respect of Indictable Terrorism-Related Offences

As indicated already, section 42 of the Police and Criminal Evidence Act 1984 authorises the detention of a person beyond 36 hours if suspected of an indictable

---

extensions up to 6 days, in police custody (*garde à vue*), before they are brought before a judge to be placed under judicial investigation or released without charge, and that terrorism suspects in police custody are guaranteed access to a lawyer only after 72 hours, and access to counsel can be further delayed till the fifth day when custody is extended by a judge: see Human Rights Committee, Concluding Observations: France, UN Doc CCPR/C/FRA/CO/4 (2008), para 14. In the Russian Federation, the Law on Operative-Search Activity, as well as the federal Law No. 18-FZ of 22 April 2004, amending article 99 of the Code of Criminal Procedure, allows the detainment of suspects of "terrorism" for up to 30 days without being charged: see Committee against Torture, Concluding Observations: Russian Federation, UN Doc CAT/C/RUS/CO/4 (2007). See also: International Commission of Jurists, Eminent Jurists Conclude Subregional Hearing on Terrorism and Human Rights in the Maghreb, press release dated 7 July 2006; and International Commission of Jurists, International Panel Ends Hearing In South-East Asia, press release dated 6 December 2006.

[13] The European Court similarly avoided this question in *Koster v Netherlands* [1991] ECHR 53, where a period of 5 days was held to be too long.

[14] *Brogan and others v United Kingdom* [1988] ECHR 24, para 62. See also the 2005 decisions of the European Court where it held that detention of more than 6 days in custody without being brought before a judge was a breach of article 5(3) of the ECHR, "notwithstanding ... the special features and difficulties of investigating terrorist offences": *Tanrikulu and others v Turkey*, Apps 29918/96, 29919/96 and 30169/96 (6 October 2005), para 41; and *Bazancir and others v Turkey* Apps 56002/00 and 7059/02 (11 October 2005). On the application of article 9(3) of the ICCPR see, for example: *Kennedy v Trinidad and Tobago*, Human Rights Committee Communication 845/1998, UN Doc CCPR/C/74/D/845/1998 (2002), para 7.6; *Borisenko v Hungary*, Communication 852/1999, UN Doc CCPR/C/76/D/852/1999 (2002), para 7.4; and *Kurbanov v Tajikistan*, Communication 1096/2002, UN Doc CCPR/C/79/D/1096/2002 (2003), para 7.2. See also: Conte and Burchill (2009, pp. 121–122); and General Comment 8: Right to liberty and security of persons (Art 9), UN Doc CCPR General Comment 8 (1982), para 2.

[15] Report of the Special Rapporteur on the promotion and protection of human rights and fundamental freedoms while counter-terrorism terrorism, Protection of human rights and fundamental freedoms while countering terrorism, UN Doc A/63/223 (2008), para 20.

offence (Sect. 16.1.1.1 above). Beyond the offences under the Terrorism Act 2000, this includes terrorism-related offences under: section 2 of the Explosive Substances Act 1883 (causing explosion likely to endanger life or property); section 1 of the Taking of Hostages Act 1982 (hostage-taking); section 1 of the Aviation Security Act 1982 (aircraft hijacking); sections 1, 9 and 10 of the Aviation and Maritime Security Act 1990 (endangering safety at an aerodrome, hijacking of ships, and seizing or exercising control of fixed platforms); and sections 14 and 15 of the Channel Tunnel (Security) Order 1994 (hijacking of Channel Tunnel trains, and seizing or exercising control of the tunnel system – see Appendix 3, Table 5).

Where a person has been arrested for an indictable offence, the maximum period of detention can be extended to 96 hours (4 days). Such extensions are subject to special procedures and will always require the approval of a magistrate's court. Stone concludes that this judicial involvement is likely to satisfy the requirements of article 5(3) of the ECHR.[16] This seems correct, since the European Court held in *Brogan v United Kingdom* that the detention of a person for 4 days and 6 hours without being brought before a judge was not prompt enough. Detention without charge for up to 4 days (under section 42 of PACE) *with* judicial involvement would therefore appear unproblematic.

16.1.2.3   Investigative Detention Under the Terrorism Act 2000

Section 41 of the Terrorism Act 2000 enables a constable to arrest, without warrant, a person whom the constable reasonably suspects to be a terrorist (within the meaning of section 40 of the Act – see above at Sect. 16.1.1.2). An initial period of 48 hours' detention without charge is permitted on the authority of the police alone, without the need for judicial approval or intervention (section 41(3)). When first enacted, the Terrorism Act allowed, subject to special procedures, the maximum period of detention to be extended to 7 days. Following its amendment under section 306 of the Criminal Justice Act 2003, a further period of 7 days was allowed, increasing the total maximum period of detention without charge under section 41 to be 14 days. Schedule 8 of the Terrorism Act 2000 was further amended by section 23 of the Terrorism Act 2006, which now allows investigative detention without charge for up to a maximum of 28 days.

The interaction of section 41 and Schedule 8 of the Terrorism Act 2000 establish the following procedures for extended detention beyond 24 hours and up to 28 days (section 41(2)):

• Under the authority of a 'review officer' (who is a senior member of the police who is not directly involved in the investigation at hand), the detention of a

---

[16]Stone (2008, p. 125).

person arrested under section 41 must be reviewed every 12 hours.[17] On certain grounds specified under paragraph 23 of Schedule 8, 12-hour extensions of the person's detention (up to a maximum of 48 hours) can be authorised by the review officer.[18]

- Extensions beyond 48 hours are also subject to special procedures, under Part III of Schedule 8, and will always require the approval of a magistrate's court. The court is empowered to issue a warrant for further detention, up to a total of 7 days from the time of the person's arrest (paragraph 29(3)), if a judge is

---

[17]See Part II of Schedule 8 of the Terrorism Act 2000, the salient parts of which provide for the following:

- Paragraph 21 of Schedule 8 requires the detention of a person arrested under section 41 to be periodically reviewed by a review officer. The first such review must take place as soon as reasonably practicable after the person's arrest (paragraph 21(2)). Subsequent reviews must be carried out at intervals of no more than 12 hours (paragraph 21(3)).
- A review under paragraph 21 of Schedule 8 can be delayed if the person is at the time being questioned, or if no review officer is available at the time, or if review is "not practicable for any other reason" (paragraph 22(1)).

[18]The continued detention of a person arrested under section 41 can be authorised by a review officer if, and only if, the review officer is satisfied that this is necessary (paragraph 23):

  (a) to obtain relevant evidence whether by questioning the detained person or otherwise (this must relate to an investigation in connection with which the person is detailed – paragraph 23(2));
  (b) to preserve relevant evidence (this must also relate to an investigation in connection with which the person is detailed);
  (ba) pending the result of an examination or analysis of any relevant evidence or of anything the examination or analysis of which is to be or is being carried out with a view to obtaining relevant evidence;
  (c) pending a decision whether to apply to the Secretary of State for a deportation notice to be served on the detained person (the review officer must here be satisfied that the process is being conducted diligently and expeditiously – paragraph 23(3));
  (d) pending the making of an application to the Secretary of State for a deportation notice to be served on the detained person (so long as this is being conducted diligently and expeditiously);
  (e) pending consideration by the Secretary of State whether to serve a deportation notice on the detained person (so long as this is being conducted diligently and expeditiously); or
  (f) pending a decision whether the detained person should be charged with an offence (so long as this is being conducted diligently and expeditiously).

For the purpose of the first two justifications listed, "relevant evidence" refers to evidence which relates to the commission by the detained person of an offence listed in section 40(1)(a), or evidence which indicates that the person is a "terrorist" within the meaning of section 40(1)(b) (see Sect. 16.1.1.2 above). Before determining whether or not to authorise continued detention, the detained person (or his or her solicitor) has the right to make representations, either orally or in writing (paragraph 26).

satisfied that: (a) there are reasonable grounds for believing that this is necessary to obtain evidence relevant to section 40(1) of the Act (whether by questioning the detainee or to preserve relevant evidence); and (b) the investigation in connection with which the person is detained is being conducted "diligently and expeditiously" (paragraph 32).

- A magistrate can extend a warrant for further detention for an additional 7 days, on the same grounds, thus allowing a total period of 14 days' detention without charge (paragraph 36).
- Beyond 14 days' detention, and up to 28 days, any further extension must be authorised by the High Court and must be limited to a maximum extension of 7 days at a time (as a result of the amendment under section 23 of the Terrorism Act 2006).

16.1.2.4 Necessity and Proportionality of Investigative Detention in the UK

The Terrorism Act 2000, as amended by the Criminal Justice Act 2003 and the Terrorism Act 2006, allows for the detention of a terrorist suspect for up to 28 days without charge. This is, by itself, a significant deviation from the normal period of investigative detention (36 hours) under the Police and Criminal Evidence Act 1984. The Terrorism Bill 2005, which became the Terrorism Act 2006, had proposed allowing for the investigative detention of terrorist suspects for up to 90 days, but this failed to gain the support of the House of Commons. The Counter-Terrorism Bill 2008 had then proposed to extend investigative detention to 42 days, but this proposition again failed.[19] One of the questions is whether, notwithstanding the judicial involvement in granting warrants for extended detention and further extensions of detention, the possibility of being detained for up to 28 days without charge violates the right to liberty.

In its concluding observations of July 2008, the Human Rights Committee expressed its concern over both the current and the proposed law, emphasising that any terrorist suspect arrested should be promptly informed of any charge against him or her and tried within a reasonable time or released.[20] Noting that much of the justification for extending the period of pre-charge detention was premised on the situation where the reasonable suspicion for arrest is based on

---

[19]See the Joint Committee on Human Rights report, Counter-Terrorism Policy and Human Rights (Thirteenth Report): Counter-Terrorism Bill 2008, 30th report of the 2007–2008 Session. See also the criticisms of the Parliamentary Assembly of the Council of Europe in its resolution 1634 (2008).

[20]Human Rights Committee, 2008 Concluding Observations (n 4) para 15. Compare with the judgment of the European Court of Human Rights in *Chraidi v Germany* [2006] ECHR 899, where it stated that in exceptional (terrorist) cases a longer period of custody may be justified.

evidence that is inadmissible at trial, e.g. intercept evidence, it has been argued that the solution to this problem is not an extension to investigative detention, but instead a lifting of the ban against the admissibility of intercept evidence.[21] This conclusion had in fact been supported by the Privy Council's Newton Committee in 2003.[22] As Stated by Law Lord Lloyd of Berwick during the parliamentary debate on the Regulation of Investigatory Powers Bill in 2000:[23]

> We have here a valuable source of evidence to convict criminals. It is especially valuable for convicting terrorist offenders because in cases involving terrorist crime it is very difficult to get any other evidence which can be adduced in court, for reasons with which we are all familiar. We know who the terrorists are, but we exclude the only evidence which has any chance of getting them convicted; and we are the only country in the world to do so.

Metclafe notes that lifting the ban on admitting intercept evidence would bring UK criminal procedure into line with that of the great majority of common law jurisdictions, including Canada, Australia, and New Zealand.[24] This brings into question the necessity of the investigative detention regime in the United Kingdom, although this remains a matter untested before the House of Lords or the European Court of Human Rights.

It should also be noted that Code C to the Police and Criminal Evidence Act requires a detainee to be charged as soon as sufficient evidence has been obtained to provide a realistic prospect of the detainee's conviction. This will prompt charges to be brought before the court, where the continued detention of the person becomes an issue of *pre-trial* detention rather than *investigative* detention (i.e. a matter to be considered by the court in the normal course of considering an application for bail). The Terrorism Act, however, is silent about the timing of any charge. The Act simply authorises detention for the purpose of obtaining evidence without limiting this to the necessity of finding evidence in order to bring a charge.

16.1.2.5 The Right to Consult Counsel

Another area in which there is a striking difference between investigative detention under PACE versus that under the Terrorism Act 2000 concerns access to legal advice. Although the right to communicate with counsel of choosing is only

---

[21]See, for example: JUSTICE, Under Surveillance: Covert Policing and Human Rights Standards (1998), p. 76; and Terrorism Bill: JUSTICE Briefing for House of Lords Report Stage (2006), para 24.

[22]Privy Counsellors Review Committee, Anti-Terrorism Crime and Security Act 2001 Review: Report (HC100: 18 December 2003), para 208. See further Fenwick and Phillipson (2005, pp. 479–488).

[23]See Hansard, HL Debates, 19 June 2000, Col 109–110. See also Lord Lloyd's earlier review of counter-terrorism legislation in the United Kingdom: Inquiry into Legislation against Terrorism, 30 October 1996 (Cm 3420) Vol 1, p. 35.

[24]JUSTICE report on the Terrorism Bill (n 21) para 25.

activated under the ICCPR and ECHR following arrest *and* charge, the position is different under the common law. As codified in the New Zealand Bill of Rights Act and the Canadian Charter of Rights and Freedoms, the right to retain and instruct counsel without delay, and to be informed of that right, is triggered upon arrest or detention (see sections 23(1)(b) and 11(b) respectively). This is reflected within the Police Codes of Practice under the UK's Police and Criminal Evidence Act 1984.

Schedule 8 of the Terrorism Act 2000 impacts upon this right in two ways, the first of which is to permit the police to delay the right to consult with counsel. When arrested under section 41 of the Act, a superintendent may authorise the delay of consultation with counsel for up to 48 hours if he or she has reasonable grounds for believing that consultation with counsel will have any one of the following consequences (see Schedule 8, paragraph 8(3) and (4)):

(a) Interference with or harm to evidence of a serious arrestable offence
(b) Interference with or physical injury to any person
(c) The alerting of persons who are suspected of having committed a serious arrestable offence but who have not been arrested for it
(d) The hindering of the recovery of property obtained as a result of a serious arrestable offence or in respect of which a forfeiture order could be made under section 23 of the Act
(e) Interference with the gathering of information about the commission, preparation or instigation of acts of terrorism
(f) The alerting of a person and thereby making it more difficult to prevent an act of terrorism
(g) The alerting of a person and thereby making it more difficult to secure a person's apprehension, prosecution or conviction in connection with the commission, preparation or instigation of an act of terrorism

Although this amounts to an interference with the right to consult with counsel without delay, the grounds listed are likely to satisfy the *need* for such interference, and the limit of a 48 hour delay following arrest acts to assist in ensuring that the interference appears *proportional*. In its Concluding Observations to the United Kingdom's sixth periodic report under the ICCPR, however, the Human Rights Committee disagreed with the conclusion just offered:[25]

> The Committee notes with concern that, under Schedule 8 to the Terrorism Act 2000, access to a lawyer can be delayed for up to 48 hours if the police conclude that such access would lead, for instance, to interference with evidence or alerting another suspect. The Committee considers that the State party has failed to justify this power, particularly having regard to the fact that these powers have apparently been used very rarely in England and Wales and in Northern Ireland in recent years. Considering that the right to have access to a lawyer during the period immediately following arrest constitutes a fundamental safeguard

---

[25]Concluding Observations: United Kingdom (n 4) para 19. See also the criticisms of the Parliamentary Assembly of the Council of Europe in its resolution 1634 (2008), para 3.2.

against ill-treatment, the Committee considers that such a right should be granted to anyone arrested or detained on a terrorism charge (arts. 9 and 14).

The second feature of Schedule 8 pertains to the supervision of consultations with counsel, this time impacting upon the right to consult with counsel of choosing *in private*. The Terrorism Act qualifies the right to private consultation such that the consultation must take place within the sight and hearing of a police officer if there are reasonable grounds for believing that, unless such a restriction is imposed, one of the consequences listed earlier would follow (Schedule 8, paragraph 9). The officer within hearing must have no connection with the detained person's case and anything overheard cannot be used in evidence. While the latter safeguards are good in principle, the fear is that information heard or recorded could be communicated to investigating officers. A more cynical view could even envisage the situation where, following a communication of information to investigating officers (which would be in breach of Schedule 8), investigating officers might attempt to assert that the information was given by the detainee to them directly after a video-taped interview, e.g. on the way from the interview room to the detainee's cell, or the like.

The Special Rapporteur on the promotion and protection of human rights and fundamental freedoms while countering terrorism has noted that limitations upon representation by counsel of choice are sometimes being imposed out of fear that legal counsel may be used as a vehicle for the flow of improper information between counsel's client and a terrorist organisation. He has noted, in this regard, the provisions in paragraphs 8 and 9 of Schedule 8 to the Terrorism Act 2000, and observed that:[26]

> Where measures are taken to monitor the conduct of consultations between legal counsel and client, strict procedures must be established to ensure that there can be no deliberate or inadvertent use of information subject to legal professional privilege. Due to the importance of the role of counsel in a fair hearing, and of the chilling effect upon the solicitor-client relationship that could follow the monitoring of conversations, such monitoring should be used rarely and only when exceptional circumstances justify this in a specific case. The decision to prosecute someone for a terrorist crime should never on its own have the consequence of excluding or limiting confidential communication with counsel. If restrictions are justified in a specific case, communication between lawyer and client should be in sight but not in hearing of the authorities.

While Schedule 8 protects against the deliberate passing on and use of information subject to legal professional privilege, it does not guard against the inadvertent or bad faith passing on or use of such information. Monitoring should therefore be rare indeed and, as suggested by the Special Rapporteur, should not occur within hearing of police authorities.

---

[26]Special Rapporteur report on fair hearing (n 15) paras 38–39. See also *Erdem v Germany* [2001] ECHR 434, para 65; and General Comment 32: Article 14: Right to equality before courts and tribunals and to a fair trial, UN Doc CCPR/C/GC/32 (2007), para 34.

16.2   Investigative Detention in Australia

16.2.1   Detention Under the Crimes Act 1914

The general rules on arrest and detention for Commonwealth offences in Australia is set out within Part 1C of the Crimes Act 1914. Where a person is arrested for a Commonwealth offence (i.e. Federal offence), they may be detained for a reasonable period (but no more than 4 hours) for the purpose of investigating whether the person committed that or any other Commonwealth offence, having regard to the number and complexity of matters being investigated and discounting time for things such as transportation, consultation with counsel, the receipt of medical attention, or for the reasonable time involved in making and disposing of an application to extend the investigation period (section 23(C)(2), (4), (6) and (7)). Where a person is arrested for a serious Commonwealth offence (punishable by imprisonment exceeding 12 months) an application for an extension of the investigation period may be made to a judicial officer who may then extend the investigation on prescribed grounds, but for no more than a total period of 8 hours from the time of arrest (section 23(D)(1), (2), (5) and (6)).

The latter provisions were amended by the Anti-Terrorism Act 2004 in respect of terrorism offences (terrorist activities using explosives or lethal devices, or involving "terrorist acts"). In respect of all such offences, a judicial officer may extend pre-charge investigative detention for up to a total of 24 hours (section 23D (7) of the Crimes Act 1914). Given the maximum period of detention without charge and the fact that this involves judicial intervention, and in light of the earlier discussions of European Court jurisprudence concerning the right to be brought 'promptly' before a judicial officer (Sect. 16.1.2.1), this appears unproblematic at face value. As pointed out by the Australian Human Rights Commission, however, the broad scope of 'discounted' time for things such as consultation with counsel, meal breaks, times when the person is sleeping, and the like, means that it can be difficult to predict how long a person may be detained.[27]

This concern is borne out by the facts surrounding the arrest and detention of Dr Mohamed Haneef in 2007. Mohamed Haneef was arrested on 2 July 2007 as he was about to board an international flight leaving Australia and, despite the restrictions on the length of detention under the Crimes Act, he was ultimately detained for a total of 12 days before being charged with providing resources to a terrorist organisation, and being reckless as to whether the organisation was a terrorist organisation (section 102.7(2) of the Criminal Code Act 1995) due to him giving his mobile phone SIM card to his second cousin in England. His second cousins were believed to be involved in the attempted terrorist attack at Glasgow

---

[27]Australian Human Rights Commission, A Human Rights Guide to Australia's Counter-Terrorism Laws, 2008, online: http://www.hreoc.gov.au/legal/publications/counter_terrorism_laws.html, p. 13.

International Airport in June 2007. On 27 July 2007, the criminal charges against Dr Haneef were dropped due to lack of evidence. In March 2008, the Commonwealth commissioned an inquiry into the case of Dr Haneef (chaired by the Hon John Clarke QC).[28]

At the time of Dr Haneef's arrest, the police were in possession of information that a group responsible for the attempted terrorist attack in Glasgow had been using a mobile phone that was subscribed or registered in Dr Haneef's name and that Dr Haneef had sent to the United Kingdom money that had been linked to that group. Police also took into account information that Dr Haneef had been in recent contact with one of the members of the group and that Dr Haneef was associated with a person who had attracted the suspicions of the Australian Customs Service when he was on a recent visit to Australia, although those suspicions were not directly linked to the UK incidents or, indeed, to any terrorist activities. The Clarke Inquiry took the view that it was at least arguable that there existed reasonable grounds for a belief that Dr Haneef had committed an offence against section 102.7(1) or section 102.7(2) of the Criminal Code at the time the arrest was made.[29] Notwithstanding this, Clarke describes the subsequent extensions of detention without charge to be based on fairly limited material, ultimately asserting that an extension of the investigation period was necessary "because the limit on the investigation period was about to be reached and the terrorism offence for which Dr Haneef had been arrested was 'still being investigated'".[30] Concerning the discounting of 'dead time' from the period during which Hannef was detained, the Clarke Inquiry recommended that the provisions of Part 1C of the Crimes Act 1914 be reviewed, commenting within the report that:[31]

> ...the specification of a period under s. 23CB is not of itself sufficient to ensure that the period is disregarded for the purposes of ascertaining the investigation period. To establish that the time was covered by s. 23CA(8)(m), the prosecution must also show that the time was a 'reasonable' time during which the questioning of the arrested person was 'reasonably' suspended or delayed. Although the fact that a magistrate or other issuing official specified a period under s. 23CB might assist in showing reasonableness, there could be circumstances within a specified period where it is no longer reasonable to suspend or delay questioning or to disregard the time when ascertaining the investigation period – for example, if the outstanding inquiries or investigative activities are completed sooner than was anticipated when the period was specified.

In December 2008, the Government agreed that the relevant provisions of the Crimes Act should be reviewed, but no legislative amendments have yet been

---

[28]Hon John Clarke QC. Report of the Inquiry into the Case of Dr Mohamed Haneef. Australia: Commonwealth of Australia, 2008 online: http://www.haneefcaseinquiry.gov.au.

[29]Clarke Inquiry (ibid) pp. 53–54.

[30]Clarke Inquiry (ibid) p. 66.

[31]Clarke Inquiry (ibid) pp. 78–79 (and Recommendation 3). See also Law Council of Australia, Anti-Terrorism Reform Project: A consolidation of the Law Council of Australia's advocacy in relation to Australia's anti-terrorism measures, November 2008, online: http://www.lawcouncil. asn.au/initiatives/anti-terrorism_reform.cfm, pp. 61–64.

made.[32] The case clearly illustrated the dangers of allowing 'dead time' deductions from authorised periods of detention without charge, rather than looking at the overall period for which a person is detained (as is the case in the United Kingdom).

16.2.2 Detention by the Australian Security Intelligence Organisation

The Australian Security Intelligence Organisation (ASIO), which is responsible for the gathering of intelligence about terrorist threats to Australia, was – under the Australian Security Intelligence Organisation Legislation Amendment Act 2006 – given the power to detain and question terrorist suspects, and non-suspects, who may have information on terrorist activities. The principal Act of 1979 now requires a person to provide information and answer questions where a warrant for questioning is issued (sections 34D and 34G). Since this overrides the internationally recognised privilege against self-incrimination, the Special Rapporteur was encouraged, in his review of Australia's counter-terrorism laws, to see that measures are in place so that the use of information provided at ASIO hearings is restricted to the gathering of intelligence (on the privilege against self-incrimination, see below at Sect. 16.3.1).[33] Such information is accordingly subject to "use immunity", which means that the information may not be used in criminal proceedings against the person (section 34(G)(9)).

The Special Rapporteur did note concerns, however, about the potential "derivative use" of such information. His concerns related to the possibility that information provided at an ASIO hearing might steer police officers who are present at the hearing towards a particular line of inquiry that would not otherwise have been pursued, and that evidence obtained through that line of inquiry might be used in criminal proceedings against the person giving the information. The Federal Court of Australia ruled, in *A v Boulton*, that there is no derivative use immunity in respect of compulsory hearings before the Australian Crime Commission,[34] and it therefore appears that members of the police present during ASIO hearings will be in a position to use information provided during those hearings in order to further their own investigations. The Special Rapporteur therefore took the view that police officers should not be present at ASIO hearings or, in the alternative, that derivative use immunity should be provided for within the ASIO Act. A clear demarcation

---

[32]Australian Government response to Clarke Inquiry into the Case of Dr Mohamed Haneef – December 2008, online: http://www.ag.gov.au/www/agd/agd.nsf/Page/Publications_Australian GovernmentresponsetoClarkeInquiryintotheCaseofDrMohamedHaneef-December2008.

[33]Special Rapporteur on the promotion and protection of human rights and fundamental freedoms while countering terrorism, Australia: Study on Human Rights Compliance While Countering Terrorism, UN Doc A/HRC/4/26/Add.3, para 31. See also Carne (2004), Joseph (2004, pp. 440–446), and Palmer (2004, pp. 374–387).

[34]*A v Boulton* (2004) 136 FCR 420.

should exist and be maintained, he said, between intelligence gathering and criminal investigations.

As to the detention scheme itself, ASIO's power to detain extends to 168 hours (7 days) continuously (section 34SC). Before questioning and detention can take place, the Director-General of ASIO must obtain the consent of the Attorney-General to seek a warrant for questioning and detention, and an "issuing authority" (a federal magistrate or judge appointed by the Minister of Justice as an issuing authority) must be satisfied that there are reasonable grounds for believing that such questioning and detention will substantially assist the collection of intelligence that is important in relation to a terrorism offence (see sections 34D, 34E, 34F and 34G). Upon execution of the warrant, a person taken into custody must be brought before a "prescribed authority" (a person, also appointed by the Minister, who has served as a judge in one or more superior courts for a period of 5 years and no longer holds a commission as a judge of a superior court) for the questioning to be conducted (section 34H). This system of investigation bears similarities to that under Canada's Criminal Code 1985 (discussed next, at Sect. 16.3).

Although a detained person may make a complaint at any time to the Inspector-General of Security Intelligence, a detained person has no right to seek a judicial review of the validity, or terms, of an issuing authority's warrant. Nor does a detained person have the right to be brought before any judicial body other than a prescribed authority. The absence of these rights was noted as being of grave concern to the UN Special Rapporteur, causing him to conclude that this offends the right to a fair hearing and the right to have the legality of one's detention determined by an independent and competent authority.[35]

16.3 Investigative Hearings

Canada's Anti-terrorism Act 2001 amended the Criminal Code of 1985 in various respects, including the introduction of section 83.28 of the Code to allow for orders requiring a person to attend a judicial hearing on the investigation of terrorist acts. The provisions under section 83.28 allow a provincial court judge in Canada (or a judge of a superior court of criminal jurisdiction) to issue an order for the purposes of an investigation of a terrorism offence requiring a person to attend (on oath or not) an examination before that (or an alternatively designated) judge. Such an order may be made on the application of a peace officer, with the consent of the Attorney General on grounds set out within section 83.28(4) of the Criminal Code, namely:

- that there are reasonable grounds to believe that:
    (i) a terrorism offence has been committed, and

---

[35]Special Rapporteur report on Australia (n 33) para 47.

(ii) information concerning the offence, or information that may reveal the whereabouts of a person suspected by the peace officer of having committed the offence, is likely to be obtained as a result of the order; *or*

- that:
    (i) there are reasonable grounds to believe that a terrorism offence will be committed,
    (ii) there are reasonable grounds to believe that a person has direct and material information that relates to a terrorism offence referred to in subparagraph (i), or that may reveal the whereabouts of an individual who the peace officer suspects may commit a terrorism offence referred to in that subparagraph, and
    (iii) reasonable attempts have been made to obtain the information referred to in subparagraph (ii) from the person referred to in that subparagraph.

The alternative grounds in section 83.28(4) thus look to compel a person to attend a judicial hearing for the purpose of investigating a terrorism offence that either *has* been committed (section 83.28(4)(a)) or one which authorities believe *will* be committed (section 83.28(4)(b)). Under section 83.29 of the Criminal Code, an individual against whom an order is made may be imprisoned for evasion of service, or failure to attend or remain at the examination.

A challenge to the constitutionality of the scheme under section 83.28 was brought before the Supreme Court of Canada in *Re Application under section 83.28 of the Criminal Code*.[36] The case arose during the course of the trial of Ripudaman Malik and Ajaib Bagri for the 1985 bombing of Air India Flight 182, in which 329 passengers were killed, including 279 Canadians. In 2003, Inderjit Singh Reyat had been convicted for his involvement in the bombing, after pleading guilty. During the course of the trial against Malik and Bagri, the wife of Inderjit Reyat was made the subject of an investigative hearing order under section 83.28 of the Criminal Code. In the Supreme Court, two main issues arose: whether requiring a person to attend a judicial investigation hearing violated that person's privilege against self-incrimination; and whether the involvement of the judiciary in the investigation of terrorism offences infringed the principles of judicial independence and impartiality.

The investigative hearing order which was the subject of litigation in *Re Application under section 83.28* was also challenged before the Supreme Court in *Re Vancouver Sun*.[37] The case arose after a reporter from British Colombia's newspaper Vancouver Sun recognised lawyers from the Air India trial entering a closed court room and was denied access to the proceedings. The Vancouver Sun filed a notice of motion seeking an order that the court proceedings be open to the public and that its counsel and a member of its editorial board, upon filing an

---

[36]*Re Application under section 83.28 of the Criminal Code* [2004] 2 SCR 248. See the earlier commentary on investigative hearings by Paccioco (2002).

[37]*Re Vancouver Sun* [2004] 2 SCR 332.

undertaking of confidentiality, be provided with access to the pleadings and all materials from the proceedings. The motion was dismissed and the Vancouver Sun was granted leave to appeal to the Supreme Court.

16.3.1 Privilege Against Self-Incrimination

As discussed in Chap. 15 (Sect. 15.1.2), the right not to incriminate oneself is not expressly reflected within the International Covenant on Civil and Political Rights or the European Convention on Human Rights. Intimately linked to this, however, both instruments guarantee the right to be presumed innocent until proven guilty (article 14(2) of the ICCPR and article 6(2) of the ECHR). Although the jurisprudence of the Human Rights Committee has not sought to infer a right not to incriminate oneself from article 14(2), the European Court of Human Rights has recognised that the right to silence and the right not to incriminate oneself are generally recognised international standards which lie at the heart of the notion of a fair trial.[38]

In the Canadian context, the right not to incriminate oneself is reflected in section 11(c) of the Canadian Charter of Rights and Freedoms 1982, applicable once a person is charged with a criminal offence. However, article 11(c) of the Charter, as well as articles 14(2) and 6(2) of the ICCPR and ECHR, is applicable only where a person is arrested or charged with a criminal offence. The scheme of investigative hearings under section 83.28 of Canada's Criminal Code does not involve a charge being brought against the subject of an investigative hearing order. It instead aims to compel a person to attend a judicial hearing for the purpose of investigating a terrorism offence which has either been committed, or which authorities believe will be committed.

On appeal from the British Columbia Supreme Court, the majority of the Supreme Court of Canada concluded that, under section 7 of the Canadian Charter, orders under section 83.28 of the Criminal Code, and the subsequent conduct of investigative hearings, did not infringe the right to silence and the privilege against self-incrimination.[39] Section 7 of the Charter operates to protect the rights to life, liberty, and security of the person, and it demands that these rights may only be deprived if this is in accordance with the principles of 'fundamental justice'. The Court reaffirmed its earlier jurisprudence that a principle of fundamental justice must fulfil three criteria. First, the principle must be a basic tenet of the legal system, and not just a matter of policy. Second, there must be sufficient consensus

---

[38]*Saunders v United Kingdom* [1997] 23 EHRR 313, para 74. See also *Funke v France* [1993] ECHR 7, para 44; and *Murray v United Kingdom* (1996) 22 EHRR 29, para 45.

[39]*Re Application under section 83.28* (n 36) para 106.

that the alleged principle is "vital or fundamental to our societal notion of justice". And, third, the principle must be capable of being identified with precision and applied to situations in a manner that yields predictable results.[40] The Court accepted that privilege against self-incrimination was a principle of fundamental justice.[41]

The Supreme Court concluded, however, that section 83.28(10) provides both use immunity and an absolute derivative use immunity to the individual named in an order for the gathering of information, since they demand that no answer given or thing produced at a hearing can be used or received against any criminal proceedings against that person, save prosecution for perjury or giving contradictory evidence.[42] Section 83.28(10)(a) of the Criminal Code provides that no answer given or thing produced shall be used or received against any criminal proceedings against that person, save prosecution for perjury or giving contradictory evidence. Absolute derivative use immunity is provided for in section 83.28(10)(b), such that evidence derived from the evidence provided at a judicial investigative hearing may not be presented in evidence against the witness in another prosecution even if the Crown is able to establish, on a balance of probabilities, that it would have inevitably discovered the same evidence through alternative means. In essence, the Court took the view that although section 83.28 of the Criminal Code engaged section 7 of the Charter, it did not limit the privilege against self-incrimination.

The Court noted, however, that section 83.28(10) provides for such safeguards only in the context of "any criminal proceedings". Compelled testimony obtained pursuant in an investigative hearing under section 83.28 may potentially be used against individuals in extradition hearings, and subsequently passed on to foreign authorities for use in prosecution abroad.[43] Such testimony may also be used against non-citizens in deportation hearings under section 34 of the Immigration and Refugee Protection Act 2001, such that the Minister's "reasonable belief" that an individual has engaged in terrorism may be based on the testimony of that individual at a judicial investigative hearing. In order to meet the requirements of section 7 of the Charter, the Court observed that the procedural safeguards found must be extended to extradition and deportation proceedings:[44]

> As in many other areas of law, a balance must be struck between the principle against self-incrimination and the state's interest in investigating offences. We believe such a balance is struck by extending the procedural safeguards of s. 83.28 to extradition and deportation hearings. As mentioned earlier, s. 83.28(5)(e) permits the inclusion of other terms and

---

[40]Ibid. para 68. The Court affirmed that approach, as stated in *R v Malmo-Levine* [2003] 3 SCR 571 and *Canadian Foundation for Children, Youth and the Law v Canada (AG)* [2004] 1 SCR 76, para 8. See also *R v Malmo-Levine* [2003] 3 SCR 571, para 113; *Re BC Motor Vehicle Act* [1985] 2 SCR 486, p. 503; and *Rodriguez v British Columbia (AG)* [1993] 3 SCR 519, p. 590.

[41]*Re Application under section 83.28* (n 36) paras 70–71.

[42]*Re Application under section 83.28* (n 36) para 72. In the context of other, non-criminal proceedings, see the Court's discussion at paras 73–79.

[43]*Re Application under section 83.28* (n 36) para 74. See also Millard (2002, p. 81).

[44]*Re Application under section 83.28* (n 36) paras 78–79.

conditions, including those required for the protection of the witness. Moreover, under s. 83.28(7), the terms and conditions of the order may be varied to provide as much. This point was conceded by the Crown in oral argument.

16.3.2   Judicial Independence and Impartiality

In its General Comment 32, concerning article 14 of the ICCPR, the Human Rights Committee has spoken of the independence of the judiciary as requiring that judges be protected from any form of political influence in their decision-making through laws establishing clear procedures and objective criteria for the appointment, remuneration, tenure, promotion, suspension and dismissal of the members of the judiciary and disciplinary sanctions taken against them.[45] As well as this traditional understanding of independence, the Committee also stated that it is necessary to protect judges against conflicts of interest.[46]

The Supreme Court of Canada has spoken of judicial independence as the "lifeblood of constitutionalism in democratic societies".[47] This principle exists in Canadian law in a number of forms. In the Constitution, it is explicitly referred to in sections 96–100 of the Constitution Act 1867 and in section 11(d) of the Charter of Rights. However, the application of these provisions is limited. The former applies to judges of superior courts, and the latter to courts and tribunals charged with trying the guilt of persons charged with criminal offences.[48] Judicial independence has also been implicitly recognised as a residual right protected under section 7 of the Charter, i.e. a principle of fundamental justice.[49]

The twin aspects of judicial independence and impartiality require that the judiciary function independently from the executive and legislative branches of government;[50] and that judicial independence is necessary to uphold public confidence in the administration of justice.[51] In *Thomas v Mowbray*, the High Court of Australia had regard to the institutional separation of the judiciary from executive and parliamentary powers, seen as vital to assisting the public

---

[45]General Comment 32 (n 26) para 19.

[46]Ibid. See also: Consultative Council of European Judges, The Role of Judges in the Protection of the Rule of Law and Human Rights in the Context of Terrorism, COE Doc CCJE (2006) 3, para 15; Office of the High Commissioner for Human Rights, Human Rights in the Administration of Justice: A Manual on Human Rights for Judges, Prosecutors and Lawyers (New York and Geneva, 2003), pp. 117–146; and Countering Terrorism, Protecting Human Rights. A Manual (Warsaw: Organisation for Security and Cooperation in Europe Office for Democratic Institutions and Human Rights, 2007), pp. 172–173.

[47]*Beauregard v Canada* [1986] 2 SCR 56, p. 70. See also Renwick (2007) and White (2007).

[48]*Reference re Remuneration of Judges of the Provincial Court of Prince Edward Island* [1997] 3 SCR 3, para 84; and *Ell v Alberta* [2003] 1 SCR 857, para 18.

[49]*Re BC Motor Vehicle Act* (n 40) p. 503.

[50]*Beauregard v Canada* (n 47) pp. 72–73.

[51]*Mackin v New Brunswick (Minister of Finance)* [2002] 1 SCR 405.

perception that judges are able to act independently of either of the other branches of government.[52] Commenting on this issue, the Privy Council stated in *Boilermakers*:[53]

> [I]n a federal system the absolute independence of the judiciary is the bulwark of the constitution against encroachment whether by the legislature or by the executive. To vest in the same body executive and judicial power is to remove a vital constitutional safeguard.

In this respect, and relying on earlier formulations of the applicable test, the Supreme Court in *Re Application under section 83.28* concluded that it had to consider "whether a reasonable and informed person would conclude that the court [when acting under section 83.28] is independent".[54] In this regard, Paccioco has criticised section 83.28 for co-opting the judiciary into performing executive, investigatory, functions in place of the judiciary's normal adjudicative role.[55] The Supreme Court took this to be an assertion that judges acting under section 83.28 lack institutional independence and impartiality. The Supreme Court rejected this assertion and held that judicial investigative hearings did not violate the principles of judicial independence and impartiality guaranteed by section 11(d) of the Charter:[56]

> We find that the substance of such a criticism is not made out in the context of the s. 83.28 judicial investigative hearing. Judges routinely play a role in criminal investigation by way of measures such as the authorization of wire taps (s. 184.2 of the *Code*), search warrants (s. 487 of the *Code*), and in applications for DNA warrants (s. 487.05 of the *Code*). The thrust of these proceedings is their investigatory purpose, and the common underlying thread is the role of the judge in ensuring that such information is gathered in a proper manner. The place of the judiciary in such investigative contexts is to act as a check against state excess.

The Court stated that this conclusion was not affected by the ability of judicial investigative hearings to be held *in camera*.[57] Dissenting, Justice LeBel disagreed and took the view that, due to the manner in which section 83.28 structures relations between the judiciary, the investigative arm of the police and the Crown, it will inevitably lead to abuses and irregularities.[58] On the possibility of abuses and irregularities, LeBel and Binnie JJ concluded that the particular order in the case before it was granted on inappropriate terms and amounted to an abuse of process

---

[52]*Thomas v Mowbray* [2007] HCA 33, para 68. See also *Wilson v Minister for Aboriginal and Torres Strait Islander Affairs* (1996) 189 CLR 1, p. 11.

[53]*Attorney-General of the Commonwealth of Australia v The Queen* (1957) 95 CLR 529, pp. 540–541. See also *R v Quinn; Ex parte Consolidated Foods Corporation* (1977) 138 CLR 1, p. 11.

[54]*Re Application under section 83.28* (n 36) para 83. See also *Valente v The Queen* [1985] 2 SCR 673, p. 689; and *Ell v Alberta* (n 48), para 32.

[55]Paccioco (2002, p. 232).

[56]*Re Application under section 83.28* (n 36) para 86.

[57]*Re Application under section 83.28* (n 36) para 91.

[58]*Re Application under section 83.28* (n 36) para 169.

by the Crown.[59] Questioning the timing of the order, which was obtained by the Crown while the trial against Malik and Bagri was proceeding, and concluding that the Crown does not have the right to compel a reluctant witness to answer questions under oath before being called to give evidence in open court, Justice Binnie stated:[60]

> While the s. 83.28 hearing judge was persuaded that the "predominant purpose" of the Crown in seeking a s. 83.28 order was the ongoing Air India *investigation* rather than the ongoing Air India *trial*, it is clear that the *timing* of the Crown's attempt to obtain the appellant's s. 83.28 evidence was driven by trial tactics. By that I mean the Crown's desire to obtain a mid-trial examination for discovery of the appellant before a different judge to determine in advance precisely what the appellant will say or not say in the witness box. This is an abuse of the extraordinary powers granted under the *Anti-terrorism Act*, S.C. 2001, c. 41. In my view the s. 83.28 hearing should have been stayed until after the appellant testified at the Air India trial or the Crown declared that the appellant would not be called as a prosecution witness.

The constitutionality of the involvement of judicial officers in closed hearings is a matter which has also been considered by the High Court of Australia, in the context of closed hearings for the issuing, variation or revocation of control orders under Division 104 of the Criminal Code Act 1995 (Australia). While the majority of the Court concluded that Division 104 was constitutional in this respect, Justice Kirby (dissenting) took the view that it was at odds with the features of independence, impartiality and integrity. Requiring courts, as of ordinary course, to issue orders ex parte that deprive an individual of basic civil rights, on the application of officers of the executive branch of government and upon proof to the civil standard alone that the measures are reasonably necessary to protect the public from a future terrorist act, "departs from the manner in which, for more than a century, the judicial power of the Commonwealth has been exercised under the Constitution" he said.[61]

16.3.3 Open Administration of Justice

As discussed in Chap. 17 (Sect. 17.2.1), the open administration of justice is viewed as one of the central pillars of a fair hearing, albeit that the International Covenant on Civil and Political Rights and the European Convention on Human Rights both recognise that the press and public may be excluded for reasons of national security. This must, however, occur only "to the extent strictly necessary in the opinion of the court in special circumstances where publicity would prejudice the interests of

---

[59]*Re Application under section 83.28* (n 36) paras 111 and 169.

[60]*Re Application under section 83.28* (n 36) para 112.

[61]*Thomas v Mowbray* (n 52) para 366.

justice". In order to guarantee the fairness of a closed hearing, it will be important that this be accompanied by adequate mechanisms for observation or review.[62]

The starting point for the Supreme Court of Canada in *Re Vancouver Sun* was to seek to achieve an interpretation of section 83.28 of the Criminal Code which was consistently with the preamble to the Anti-terrorism Act and the fundamental characteristics of a judicial process, including the open court principle. This principle, said the Supreme Court, is "a hallmark of democracy and a cornerstone of the common law", guaranteeing the integrity of the judiciary and inextricably linked to the freedom of expression guaranteed by section 2(b) of the Canadian Charter of Rights and Freedoms.

A distinction between stages in section 83.28 proceedings should be made. The first stage, involving the judicial consideration of an *application* for an investigative hearing order is necessarily held *in camera* because such applications are *ex parte* (section 83.28(2)). The issues before the Supreme Court were whether the making of an investigative hearing order could be subject to non-disclosure to the public; and whether the second stage of proceedings (the investigative hearing itself) could be held *in camera*. On the latter point, section 83.28 of the Criminal Code does not expressly provide for any part of the investigative hearing to be held *in camera*. Restricting the openness of an investigative hearing can be achieved, however, through the discretion granted to judges to impose terms and conditions on the conduct of a hearing (section 83.28(5)(e)). The majority of the Supreme Court held that, in exercising that discretion, judges should reject the presumption of secret hearings.[63] The presumption of openness should only be displaced, said the majority, after consideration of the competing interests at every stage of the process, under the balancing exercise of the '*Dagenais/Mentuck* test'.

The *Dagenais/Mentuck* test was developed by the Supreme Court of Canada to adapt the essence of the *Oakes* test for the application of section 1 of the Canadian Charter to the situation of a conflict between the freedom of expression and other important rights and interests (on section 1 of the Charter, and the *Oakes* test, see Chap. 11, Sect. 11.5). The Court has said that a publication ban should only be ordered when:[64]

(a) Such an order is necessary in order to prevent a serious risk to the proper administration of justice because reasonably alternative measures will not prevent the risk; and

---

[62]Special Rapporteur's report on fair hearing (n 15) paras 30 and 44(c). See also the report of the Sub-Commission Rapporteur on terrorism and human rights, Specific Human Rights Issues: New Priorities, in Particular Terrorism and Counter-Terrorism: An updated framework draft of principles and guidelines concerning human rights and terrorism, UN Doc A/HRC/Sub.1/58/30 (2006) para 45.

[63]*Re Vancouver Sun* (n 37) p. 336.

[64]*R v Mentuck* [2001] 3 SCR 442, para 22; and *Dagenais v Canadian Broadcasting Corporation* [1994] 3 SCR 835.

(b) The salutary effects of the publication ban outweigh the deleterious effects on the rights and interests of the parties and the public, including the effects on the right to free expression, the right of the accused to a fair and public trial, and the efficacy of the administration of justice.

In applying this test, the judge is required to consider not only whether reasonable alternatives are available, but also to restrict the order as far as possible without sacrificing the prevention of the risk.[65] The Court in *Re Vancouver Sun* took the view that although the test was developed in the context of publication bans, it was equally applicable to all discretionary actions by a trial judge which would impact upon the freedom of expression by the press during judicial proceedings.[66] Applying the test to the case before it, the Supreme Court held that the level of secrecy was unnecessary. While the application was properly heard *ex parte* and *in camera*, it found no reason to keep secret the existence of the order or its subject-matter. It also determined that because the subject of the investigative hearing order was a potential Crown witness in the Air India trial, third party interests ought to have been considered and notice should have been given to counsel for the accused in the Air India trial. Without jeopardizing the investigation, as much information about the constitutional challenge in *Re Application under section 83.28 of the Criminal Code* should have been made public, subject, if need be, to a total or partial publication ban. The constitutional challenge should not have been conducted *in camera* since much of it could have been properly argued without the details of the information submitted to the application judge being revealed.[67]

Dissenting in part, Justices Bastarache and Deschamps drew their decisions from the notion that, although openness of judicial proceedings should be the norm, a court may sit *in camera* where the rights of third parties would be unduly harmed and the administration of justice rendered unworkable by the presence of the public. They took the view that this will normally be the case for investigative proceedings under section 83.28 because there is a legitimate law enforcement interest in maintaining the confidentiality of a witness's identity and testimony, since the premature disclosure of information about a terrorism offence would compromise and impede the investigation of the information gathered at the hearing. To do otherwise, they said, would normally render hearings under section 83.28 ineffective as an investigative tool.[68]

---

[65]*R v Mentuck* (ibid) para 36.

[66]*Re Vancouver Sun* (n 37) para 31.

[67]*Re Vancouver Sun* (n 37) p. 337.

[68]*Re Vancouver Sun* (n 37) p. 338. For comparable comments concerning the use of court orders to prevent or restrict reporting on terrorism cases in the United Kingdom, see The New York Times, 'Openness South in British Terror Trials', 25 May 2007, online: http://query.nytimes.com/gst/fullpage.html?res=9B0CE1D91630F936A15756C0A9619C8B63&sec=&spon=&pagewanted=all.

16.4   Conclusions

The investigative detention of persons without charge for the purpose of questioning suspects in the pre-charge process of police investigations is well developed in both the United Kingdom and Australia. Special powers of arrest to deal with terrorism were first introduced in the United Kingdom under the Prevention of Terrorism (Emergency Powers) Acts 1974–2001 relating to the troubles in Northern Ireland. The Police and Criminal Evidence Act 1984 allows for the detention without charge for up to 4 days of persons suspected of committing indictable offences, which includes various terrorism-related offences. The Terrorism Act 2000, as amended by the Criminal Justice Act 2003 and the Terrorism Act 2006, permits a series of police- and judge-authorised extensions of investigative detention up to a total period of 28 days. The 2000 Terrorism Act authorises police in the United Kingdom to arrest, without warrant, a person reasonably suspected of being a terrorist, linked both to the suspected commission of specific offences under that Act, as well as a much more broad and vague notion of being "*concerned* in the commission, preparation or instigation of acts of terrorism". This departs from the normal notion that police must have a particular offence in mind when arresting without warrant. It may also open the door for the arrest of persons based not on credible evidence but on more dubious intelligence information, then allowing police to conduct 'fishing' expeditions for evidence during prolonged periods of detention without charge. Investigative detention is also a tool used in Australia, both under the Crimes Act 1914 and the Australian Security Intelligence Organisation Act 1974.

Extended periods of police detention, without bringing a person before a judge, has been a long-standing issue of concern within both common law and civil law countries. Although the European Court of Human Rights has declined to say what the maximum period of detention might be before a person will be considered to have been brought 'promptly' before a judicial authority, it has ruled that a period of 4 days and 6 hours is too long. Although untested, it appears that the ability in the United Kingdom to detain persons for up to 4 days without judicial intervention in the case of suspected indictable offences should not run afoul of the right under articles 9(3) and 5(3) of the ICCPR and ECHR. This will always be a matter to be determined in the particular circumstances of the case, having particular regard to the seriousness of the alleged offence, the strength of evidence against the suspect, and the availability of alternative courses of action which would not prejudice investigations. An all facts considered approach is particularly relevant in the case of the special powers of detention under Australia's Crimes Act 1914 where, although detention may only be up to 24 hours, the application of 'dead time' resulted, in the case of Dr Haneef, in an overall period of detention without charge of 12 days.

In the case of the United Kingdom's Terrorism Act 2000, and the potential for investigative detention to continue to 28 days, the question of necessity and proportionality arises. Although the Act provides for judicial warrants for extended detention beyond 36 hours, much of the justification for extending periods of pre-charge detention has been premised on the inadmissibility of evidence, particularly intercept evidence, which must be shored up through interrogations conducted during periods of investigative detention. Bringing into question the necessity of prolonged investigative detention, however, many advocate lifting the ban on admitting intercept evidence, as is done in many common law jurisdictions, including Australia, Canada and New Zealand. Furthermore, the proportionality of such measures are not assured, since the Terrorism Act does not expressly require that a detainee be charged as soon as sufficient evidence has been obtained to provide a realistic prospect of conviction. Finally, the Act may also engage the right of a detainee to consult with legal counsel. The right to consult with counsel may, by a decision of the police, be postponed for 48 hours after arrest. While the grounds upon which postponement can be made appear sound to the author, the Human Rights Committee has taken the view that this should never occur even in the context of those arrested or detained on terrorism charges. Consultations between counsel and the detainee may also be monitored. While the Act protects against the deliberate passing on and use of information subject to legal professional privilege, it does not guard against the inadvertent or bad faith passing on or use of such information. Monitoring should therefore be rare and, as suggested by the UN Special Rapporteur, should not occur within hearing of police authorities.

Compelling a person to attend a judicial hearing on the investigation of terrorist acts is provided for in section 83.28 of Canada's Criminal Code 1985, as a result of its amendment under the Anti-terrorism Act 2001. The constitutional challenges posed by this were considered by the Supreme Court of Canada in late 2004. On the question of the privilege against self-incrimination, the Court accepted that the right not to incriminate oneself is a principle of fundamental justice protected by section 7 of the Canadian Charter of Rights and Freedoms. While this right is engaged, however, the Court concluded that it is not infringed since section 83.28(10) of the Criminal Code guarantees absolute use immunity and derivative use immunity, such that any answer given or thing produced during such hearings cannot be used in criminal proceedings against the person, even if the Crown was to establish that the evidence would have been discovered by alternative means. The Court at the same time noted that section 83.28(10) did not prevent the use of compelled testimony in extradition or deportation hearings. It warned that the issuing of investigative hearing orders should therefore include conditions extending use immunity to extradition or deportation proceedings against the person in respect of whom the order is made.

Investigative hearings also being into question the right to a fair hearing, first in the context of judicial independence and impartiality and, secondly, concerning the compatibility of the process with the open administration of justice. The twin aspects of judicial independence and impartiality require that the judiciary function independently from the executive and legislative branches of government, thereby protecting judges against conflicts of interest and maintaining public confidence in the administration of justice. While the minority of the Supreme Court took the view that the mechanism under section 83.28 involved relations between the judiciary, police and prosecution which will inevitably lead to abuses and irregularities, and that the matter before it did in fact amount to an abuse of process, the majority disagreed. Drawing from the routine role played by judges in criminal investigations, including the authorisation of wire taps and search warrants, the majority of seven-to-two concluded that a reasonable and informed person would conclude that a court, when acting under section 83.28, is independent. Concerning the open administration of justice, the Supreme Court of Canada has spoken of needing to balance a conflict between the freedom of expression and other important rights and interests. Restricting the openness of an investigative hearing, through conditions imposed on the conduct of such hearings, is permissible but should begin with a presumption against secret hearings. Consideration should be given to available alternatives, restricting the investigative hearing order only as much as is required to prevent serious risks to the proper administration of justice and the conduct of investigations.

References

Cameron, Iain. 2009. Fair Trial in Terrorism Cases and Problems and Potential in Evaluation States' Laws and Practices Relating to Fair Trial (paper presented at the Round Table *Fight against Terrorism: Challenges for the Judiciary*, 18–19 September 2009, Fiesole, Italy).

Carne, Greg. 2004. Detaining Questions or Compromising Constitutionality? The *ASIO Legislation Amendment (Terrorism) Act 2003*. 27(2) *The University of New South Wales Law Journal* 524.

Conte, Alex. 2007. *Counter-Terrorism and Human Rights in New Zealand*. Wellington: New Zealand Law Foundation.

Fenwick, Helen, and Phillipson, Gavin. 2005. Legislative over-breadth, democratic failure and the judicial response: fundamental rights and the UK's anti-terrorist legal policy. In Ramraj, Victor, Hor, Michael, and Roach, Kent (Eds). *Global Anti-Terrorism Law and Policy*. Cambridge: Cambridge University Press.

Millard, Jeremy. 2002. Investigative Hearings under the Anti-Terrorism Act. 60(1) *University of Toronto Faculty of Law Review* 79.

Joseph, Sarah. 2004. Australian Counter-terrorism Legislation and the International Human Rights Framework. 27(2) *The University of New South Wales Law Journal* 428.

Kennison, Peter, and Loumansky, Amanda. 2007. Shoot to Kill. Understanding police use of force in combating suicide terrorism. 47(3) *Crime, Law and Social Change* 151.

Paccioco, David. 2002. Constitutional Casualties of September 11: Limiting the Legacy of the *Anti-terrorism Act*. 16 *Supreme Court Law Review* (2d) 185.

Palmer, Andrew. 2004 Investigating and Prosecuting Terrorism: The Counter-Terrorism Legislation and the Law of Evidence. 27(2) *The University of New South Wales Law Journal* 373.

Renwick, James. 2007. The Constitutional Validity of Prevention Detention. In Lynch, Andrew, MacDonald, Edwina, and Williams, George (Eds). *Law and Liberty in the War on Terror*. Sydney: The Federation Press.

Stone, Richard. 2008. *Textbook on Civil Liberties and Human Rights*. Oxford: 7th edition, Oxford University Press.

Walker, Clive. 2009. *Blackstone's Guide to The Anti-Terrorism Legislation*. Oxford: 2nd Edition, Oxford University Press.

White, Margaret. 2007. A Judicial Perspective – The Making of Preventative Detention Orders. In Lynch, Andrew, MacDonald, Edwina, and Williams, George (Eds). *Law and Liberty in the War on Terror*. Sydney: The Federation Press.

Chapter 17
Derogations from the Right to Liberty

Chapter 10 of this title gave consideration to the question of limiting human rights under international law, recognising that the nature of international human rights law is such that, other than in the case of a limited number of absolute rights, the guarantee of rights and freedoms incorporates a level of flexibility. This allows States to give effect to rights and freedoms, while at the same time pursuing important democratic objectives designed to protect society and to maintain a balance between conflicting rights. In the context of the International Covenant on Civil and Political Rights (ICCPR),[1] and the European Convention on Human Rights (ECHR) to which the United Kingdom is also party,[2] this accommodation is effected through two means. Limitations are permitted by virtue of the particular expression of the right or freedom within the ICCPR and ECHR. There is also the capacity, under article 4 of the ICCPR or article 15 of the ECHR, to temporarily suspend the application of certain rights during a state of emergency which threatens the life of a nation. Acts of terrorism, or imminent threats thereof, may create circumstances which pose a threat to the life of the nation. The derogation mechanism is thus an important one to consider in the context of counter-terrorism. However, as recognised by Boyle, although conditions of violence and terrorism may justify resort to derogation, these are also conditions where rights and freedoms are most at risk.[3]

Chapter 10 gave some brief consideration to the second of these mechanisms, looking at the differences in text between the ICCPR and ECHR, and explaining the procedural conditions applicable to derogations under both instruments. It also

---

[1] International Covenant on Civil and Political Rights, opened for signature 16 December 1966, 999 UNTS 171 (entered into force 23 March 1976).

[2] Convention for the Protection of Human Rights and Fundamental Freedoms, opened for signature 4 November 1950, 213 UNTS 222 (entered into force 3 September 1953).

[3] Boyle (2004, p. 101).

A. Conte, *Human Rights in the Prevention and Punishment of Terrorism*,
DOI 10.1007/978-3-642-11608-7_17, © Springer-Verlag Berlin Heidelberg 2010

identified the substantive conditions under articles 4 and 15 of the ICCPR and ECHR. The current chapter examines the derogations by the United Kingdom from the right to liberty. Although the UK has given notice of derogation from liberty rights on several occasions, attention is paid to two case studies, first in the context of executive detention powers under the Prevention of Terrorism (Temporary Provisions) Acts, and then to the derogation made in 2001 in conjunction with the establishment of the UK's indefinite detention regime. The chapter begins with an overview and analysis of the procedural and substantive requirements of derogations under the ICCPR and ECHR and then, in light of these, considers and reflects upon the two UK derogations mentioned.

17.1   Procedure, Substance, and the Margin of Appreciation

For a State party to the ICCPR or ECHR to derogate from one of the rights enumerated in those instruments, it must first be established that the right in question is capable of derogation. Both instruments explain that there are certain rights which may not be derogated from, even during a state of emergency threatening the life of the nation (see Chap. 10, Sect. 10.4.1.1). The right to liberty may be subject to temporary derogation in such circumstances, a feature taken advantage of by the United Kingdom in the case of two legislative measures to combat terrorism.

17.1.1   Derogating from the ECHR in the United Kingdom

Common to the ICCPR and ECHR is the requirement that any derogation from those instruments must be officially proclaimed and notified to the Secretary-General of the United Nations (in the case of the ICCPR) or the Secretary-General of the Council of Europe (in the case of the ECHR), and through this to other States parties (see Chap. 10, Sect. 10.4.1.2). Added to this requirement, section 1(2) of the Human Rights Act 1998 (UK) qualifies the definition of "Convention rights" (those rights which have been incorporated into UK law) under the Act by providing that those rights "are to have effect for the purposes of this Act subject to any designated derogation or reservation". Section 14 of the Human Rights Act allows the Secretary of State to make an order by which the United Kingdom derogates from one of the rights under the ECHR (as permitted by article 15 of the Convention). A derogation order can be made in anticipation of the lodging of a notice of derogation from the European Convention. Designated derogations may only last for five years and, if they are to continue, they must be renewed by the government (section 16). There is no similar procedure provided for in the case of derogations from the ICCPR.

17.1.2 Margin of Appreciation in Declaring a State of Emergency and Implementing Derogating Measures

As alluded to in Chap. 10, there is a marked difference in approach to the issue of derogations by the European Court of Human Rights (in adjudicating on derogations under the ECHR) and the Human Rights Committee (concerning derogations under the ICCPR) – on the margin of appreciation generally, see Chap. 10, Sect. 10.2.1. The use of derogations from the European Convention first arose concerning derogating measures adopted by the United Kingdom over Cyprus while Cyprus was still under British rule. Greece brought two applications against the UK, which were considered by the Commission on Human Rights and, as a result of a political solution reached between the parties, was never considered by the European Court of Human Rights itself. In determining its competence to consider the matter, the Commission regarded itself as competent to both determine whether recourse to article 15 of the ECHR was possible and whether the measures taken were required by the exigencies of the situation.[4] The European Court, however, has taken a much less robust approach. Taking the view that a wide margin of appreciation must be afforded to States in determining whether a state of emergency exists, and that it should do no more than proclaim whether a government's decision is 'on the margin' of the powers conferred by a derogating provision, the European Court has said:[5]

> By reason of their direct and continuous contact with the pressing needs of the moment, the national authorities are in principle in a better position than the international judge to decide both on the presence of such an emergency and on the nature and scope of derogations necessary to avert it.

In contrast, the Human Rights Committee has taken the view that compliance with all aspects of article 4 of the ICCPR, including the determination of whether a state of emergency exists, is a matter in respect of which it has final say. Observing that "[n]ot every disturbance or catastrophe qualifies as a public emergency which threatens the life of the nation",[6] the Committee has on a number of occasions expressed its concern over States parties that appear to have derogated from rights protected under the ICCPR in situations not covered by article 4.[7] This has included

---

[4] *Greece v United Kingdom*, App 176/57 (1958–1959) 2 Yearbook *of the European Court of Human Rights* 174 and 182; *Greece v United Kingdom*, App 299/57 (1958–1959) 2 Yearbook *of the European Court of Human Rights* 178 and 186. See also *The Greek Case* (1969) 12 *Yearbook of the European Court of Human Rights* 1 at 32.

[5] *Ireland v United Kingdom* [1978] ECHR 1, para 207. See Marks (1995) and a similar judgment of the European Court of Human Rights in *Aksoy v Turkey* [1996] ECHR 68, para 68.

[6] General Comment 29: States of Emergency (Article 4), UN Doc CCPR/C/21/Rev.1/Add.11 (2001), para 3.

[7] See, for example, the Concluding Observations of the Committee concerning: Bolivia, UN Doc CCPR/C/79/Add.74 (1997), para 14; Colombia, UN Doc CCPR/C/79/Add.76 (1997), para 25; the Dominican Republic, UN Doc CCPR/C/79/Add.18 (1993), para 4; Israel, UN Doc CCPR/C/79/

reference to the first of the derogations by the United Kingdom from the right to liberty considered in this chapter. In its Concluding Observations in 1995, the Committee recommended that:[8]

> [g]iven the significant diminution in terrorist violence in the United Kingdom since the cease-fire came into effect in Northern Ireland and the peace process was initiated, the Committee urges the Government to keep under the closest review whether a situation of 'public emergency' within the terms of Article 4, paragraph 1, of the Covenant still exists and whether it would be appropriate for the United Kingdom to withdraw the notice of derogation, in accordance with Article 4 of the Covenant, which it issued on 17 May 1976.

As will be seen in the discussions that follow, it should be noted that the margin of appreciation has been applied by the European Court of Human Rights not only to the question of whether a state of emergency exists, but also to whether particular derogating measures are necessary. The degree of deference applied has been mixed. In *Ireland v United Kingdom*, the Court asked simply whether there was *some* basis, at the time of declaring the state of emergency, for the government to believe that the derogating measures were necessary.[9] The European Court noted in *Lawless v Ireland*, however, that this issue must be exercised carefully, in a manner which prevents abuse, or excessive use, of the derogating power.[10] Critics have nevertheless noted that the Court applied a very wide margin of appreciation to this issue in its 1993 decision concerning the United Kingdom's derogation from liberty rights under article 5 of the European Convention (this again relates to the UK's derogation from the right to liberty in Northern Ireland).[11] In stark contrast, the approach of the Human Rights Committee has been to require States to justify in full that each derogating measure is necessary.[12] The *Siracusa Principles on the Limitation and Derogation Provisions in the International Covenant on Civil and Political Rights* further state that "[i]n determining whether derogation measures are strictly required by the exigencies of the situation the judgment of the national authorities cannot be accepted as conclusive".[13]

Add.93 (1998), para 11; Lebanon, UN Doc CCPR/C/79/Add.78 (1997), para 10; Peru, UN Doc CCPR/C/79/Add.67 (1996), para 11; the United Kingdom of Great Britain and Northern Ireland, UN Doc CCPR/C/79/Add.55 (1995), para 23; the United Republic of Tanzania, UN Doc CCPR/C/79/Add.12 (1992), para 7; and Uruguay, UN Doc CCPR/C/79/Add.90 (1998), para 8.

[8] Concluding Observations of the Human Rights Committee: United Kingdom of Great Britain and Northern Ireland, UN Doc CCPR/C/79/Add.55 (1995), para 23.

[9] *Ireland v United Kingdom* (n 5) para 214. See also Bonner (1978).

[10] *Lawless v Ireland (No 3)* [1961] ECHR 2, para 37.

[11] *Brannigan and McBride v United Kingdom* [1993] ECHR 21, commented upon by Marks (1995).

[12] See General Comment 29 (n 6) para 5.

[13] Siracusa Principles on the Limitation and Derogation Provisions in the International Covenant on Civil and Political Rights, UN Doc E/CN.4/1985/4 (1985), Annex, para 57.

That contrasting approaches are taken by the European Court and the Human Rights Committee is clear. More contentious are the arguments for and against the existence of the margin of appreciation. While this is a reasonably academic debate, in light of the somewhat entrenched positions of each body, it is important to note. Marks explains the main reasons advanced for and against the application of a margin of appreciation:[14]

- First, while a government must react to an emergency on an urgent basis, it is argued that it would be inappropriate for a judicial organ to decide on issues with the benefit of hindsight. Taking this approach in *Ireland v United Kingdom*, the European Court stated that: "the Court must arrive at its decision in the light, not of a purely retrospective examination of the efficacy of those measures, but of the conditions and circumstances reigning when they were originally taken and subsequently applied".[15] This is far too generous an approach. While it is true that a government must react speedily to an emergency situation, it is also correct that it can take steps to review and refine its assessment afterwards. To restrict itself to the circumstances present when derogating measures were taken means that the Court blinds itself to subsequent events. The declaration of a long-term or semi-permanent 'emergency' can and should be regularly reviewed to ascertain its continued existence.[16] Caution must therefore be taken when relying on this argumentation.
- Secondly, one can argue that it is inappropriate for a judicial officer to make a proper assessment of derogating measures, since this involves political judgment. Related to this is the view that, where political judgments are involved, the Court should do not more than ensure that the government's conduct is at least 'on the margins' of the authority to derogate under article 15 of the ECHR. There is always a fine line to tread when speaking of judicial deference of this kind. It is not uncommon to see such positions, although it is notable that the House of Lords has been prepared to take a robust approach in recent years, even in matters concerning national security and counter-terrorism.[17]
- Marks then points to the more far-fetched view that, without applying a margin of appreciation, the European Court would face the risk of States perceiving that their vital interests are being compromised, which would in turn result in denunciations from the Convention or withdrawing recognition of the Court's competence.[18]

---

[14]Marks (1995, pp. 74–76).

[15]See, for example, *Ireland v United Kingdom* (n 5), para 214.

[16]Although not claimed by the applicants, this was in fact the contention of a group of non-governmental organisations joined tot he case of *Brannigan and McBride v United Kingdom* (n 11). See Marks (1995, p. 77).

[17]*A and Ors v Secretary of State for the Home Department* [2004] UKHL 56 (discussed below).

[18]O'Boyle (1977, p. 705).

17.1.3   Substantive Conditions Under the ICCPR and ECHR

Article 4(1) of the ICCPR sets out four substantive requirements applicable to the adoption by a State party of measures which derogate from the ICCPR:[19]

- The measures must be ones that are adopted during a "time of public emergency which threatens the life of the nation";
- The derogating measures must be limited to those "strictly required by the exigencies of the situation";
- The measures must not be "inconsistent with [the State's] other obligations under international law"; and
- Such measures must not "involve discrimination solely on the ground of race, colour, sex, language, religion or social origin".

The first three of these conditions are reflected in almost identical terms within article 15(1) of the ECHR, which provides:

> In time of war or other public emergency threatening the life of the nation any High Contracting Party may take measures derogating from its obligations under this Convention to the extent strictly required by the exigencies of the situation, provided that such measures are not inconsistent with its other obligations under international law.

Although not expressly mentioned in article 15 of the ECHR, the condition of non-discrimination is also applicable to derogations under the European Convention (as explained below).

17.1.3.1   War or Public Emergency

The ability under article 4 of the ICCPR to derogate from certain rights is triggered only "in a time of public emergency which threatens the life of the nation". The Human Rights Committee has characterised such an emergency as being of an exceptional nature.[20] Not every disturbance or catastrophe qualifies as such, and the Committee has commented that even during an armed conflict, measures derogating from the ICCPR are allowed only if and to the extent that the situation constitutes a threat to the life of the nation.[21] Interpreting the comparable derogation provision in article 15 of the European Convention on Human Rights, which refers to times of "war or other public emergency threatening the life of the nation",

---

[19] Article 4(1) of the ICCPR reads, in full: "In time of public emergency which threatens the life of the nation and the existence of which is officially proclaimed, the States Parties to the present Covenant may take measures derogating from their obligations under the present Covenant to the extent strictly required by the exigencies of the situation, provided that such measures are not inconsistent with their other obligations under international law and do not involve discrimination solely on the ground of race, colour, sex, language, religion or social origin".

[20] General Comment 29 (n 6) para 2.

[21] General Comment 29 (n 6) para 3.

the European Court of Human Rights has identified four criteria to determine whether such a situation exists. This list mirrors various aspects of the Human Rights Committee's General Comment 29 on article 4 of the ICCPR, and the *Siracusa Principles*, although the European Court's itemisation of these features is useful. The Court identified, in *Lawless v Ireland*, the following criteria:[22]

- The situation in question should be a crisis or emergency that is actual or imminent;[23]
- It must be exceptional, such that 'normal' measures are plainly inadequate;[24]
- It must threaten the continuance of the organised life of the community; and[25]
- It must affect the entire population of the State which is taking the derogating measures.[26]

On the latter point, early decisions of the European Court spoke of an emergency needing to affect the whole population, although it now appears to have been accepted that an emergency threatening the life of a nation might only materially affect one part of the nation at the time of the emergency.[27] This is consistent with the view expressed in the *Siracusa Principles* that the geographic scope of any derogating measure must be such as strictly necessary to deal with the threat to the life of the nation.[28] This is particularly relevant to the UK's derogation from the right to liberty in Northern Ireland, discussed below.

As to the question of an emergency constituting a threat to the continued existence of the community, the *Siracusa Principles* explain that this involves a threat to the physical integrity of the population, the political independence or territorial integrity of the State, or the existence or basic functioning of institutions indispensable to ensure and protect the rights recognised in the Covenant.[29] They also explain that internal conflict or unrest that do not constitute a "grave and imminent threat to the life of the nation" cannot justify derogations under article 4, and that economic difficulties cannot *per se* justify derogating measures.[30]

---

[22]*Lawless v Ireland* (n 10) para 28 (followed in *The Greek Case* (n 4) para 153). Note that, in *Lawless*, the European Court found that the Irish Government was entitled to deduce that a state of emergency of this kind did exist.

[23]Compare with: General Comment 29 (n 6) para 3; and Siracusa Principles (n 13) paras 40 and 54. See also Hartman (1985, especially pp. 91–92).

[24]Compare with General Comment 29 (n 6) paras 2 and 4.

[25]Compare with the Siracusa Principles (n 13) para 39(b).

[26]Compare with: General Comment 29 (n 6) para 4; and Siracusa Principles (n 13) para 39(a).

[27]*Ireland v United Kingdom* (n 5). See also *Sakik and others v Turkey* (1978) 2 EHRR 25, para 39, where the European Court of Human Rights considered a geographically restricted derogation by Turkey and held Turkey bound by the geographical restriction when it attempted to rely on the derogation to respond to acts occurring outside that area.

[28]Siracusa Principles (n 13) para 51.

[29]Siracusa Principles (n 13) para 39(b).

[30]Siracusa Principles (n 13) paras 40–41.

In light of the Committee's repeated emphasis upon the exceptional and temporary nature of derogating measures, which may continue only as long as the life of the nation concerned is *actually* threatened, it is important for a derogating State to continually review the situation faced by it to ensure that the derogation lasts only as long as the state of emergency exists.[31] The *Siracusa Principles* calls for such review to be independent and undertaken by the legislature of the State party concerned.[32] The European Court of Human Rights has also interpreted article 15 (3) of the ECHR as implying an obligation to keep derogating measures under permanent review so as to ensure that there continues to be a need for emergency measures.[33] While review might assist to ensure a more objective assessment of the necessity of derogating measures, as opposed to one undertaken by the government which declares the state of emergency, it must be recognised that the extent to which this is possible may be hindered by the classified status of any information concerning the continuing or imminent nature of a threat to the life of the nation. This point is dealt with later in this chapter (Sect. 17.4.1.2).

Notwithstanding this, it is important to recall that General Comment 29 declares that the restoration of a state of normalcy, where full respect for the provisions of the ICCPR can again be secured, must be the predominant objective of a State party derogating from the Covenant.[34] While internal review is very important, it should be further recalled that the ultimate task of monitoring derogating measures and assessing their compliance with article 4 belongs to the Committee and, to facilitate this role, the General Comment has called on States parties to include in their periodic reports "sufficient and precise information about their law and practice in the field of emergency powers".[35]

17.1.3.2 Exigencies of the Situation

Once it is established that a State can rely on article 4 of the ICCPR, or article 15 of the ECHR, i.e. that there is a war or public emergency within the meaning of those provisions, it must be shown that the derogation is limited "to the extent strictly required by the exigencies of the situation" (as expressed in both the ICCPR and ECHR). As reaffirmed by General Comment 29 and the *Siracusa Principles*, any derogating measure must therefore be both necessary and proportionate, principles which have been considered in more detail in Chap. 10 (see Sects. 10.2.3 and 10.2.4).[36] In practice, these requirements will act to ensure that no provision of the ICCPR or ECHR, however validly derogated from, will be *entirely* inapplicable

---

[31]General Comment 29 (n 6) para 2. See also the Siracusa Principles (n 13) paras 48–50.

[32]Siracusa Principles (n 13) para 55.

[33]*Brannigan and McBride v United Kingdom* (n 11) para 54.

[34]General Comment 29 (n 6) paras 1 and 2; Siracusa Principles (n 13) para 48.

[35]General Comment 29 (n 6) para 2.

[36]General Comment 29 (n 6) paras 3–5; Siracusa Principles (n 13) para 51.

to the behaviour of a State party.[37] Considering States parties' periodic reports, the Committee has nevertheless expressed concern over insufficient attention being paid to these principles.[38]

Again, there is a distinction to be made between the approaches of the Human Rights Committee and the European Court. In its General Comment 29, the Committee explained that States must provide careful justification not only for their decision to proclaim a state of emergency but also for any specific measures based on such a proclamation, based on an objective assessment of the situation. If States purport to invoke the right to derogate from the Covenant during, for instance, a natural catastrophe, a mass demonstration including instances of violence, or a major industrial accident, they must be able to justify not only that such a situation constitutes a threat to the life of the nation, but also that all their measures derogating from the Covenant are strictly required by the exigencies of the situation.[39] The European Commission on Human Rights has, when dealing with such issues, taken a similar position.[40] The European Court, however, has again applied a margin of appreciation, although it has explained that it must be the ultimate arbiter of whether this second substantive condition has been met. Reaffirming its position in *Brannigan and McBride v United Kingdom*, the Court stated in *Aksoy v Turkey*:[41]

> It is for the Court to rule whether, *inter alia*, the States have gone beyond the 'extent strictly required by the exigencies' of the crisis. The domestic margin of appreciation is thus accompanied by a European supervision. In exercising this supervision, the Court must give appropriate weight to such relevant factors as the nature of the rights affected by the derogation and the circumstances leading up to, and the duration of, the emergency situation.

Fundamental to understanding the derogations procedure, whether under the ICCPR or the ECHR, one must distinguish between measures capable of dealing with a crisis as might be permitted under the rights-specific limitation provisions of each instrument on the one hand, as opposed to the exceptional measure of derogating from rights under article 4 and "to the extent strictly required by the exigencies of the situation" (on rights-specific limitations, see Chap. 10, Sect. 10.3). Where a situation of crisis can be adequately addressed, or even partly addressed, by recourse to a rights-specific limitations provision, such recourse must be had and any action to derogate from the right(s) in question will be deemed to fall outside the exigencies of

---

[37]General Comment 29 (n 6) para 4.

[38]See, for example, Concluding Observations of the Human Rights Committee: Israel, UN Doc CCPR/C/79/Add.93 (1998), para 11.

[39]General Comment 29 (n 6) para 5.

[40]See the *Greek Case* (n 4), where the Commission considered that the burden of proving the existence of an emergency within the terms of article 15 of the ECHR lay with the respondent government.

[41]*Aksoy v Turkey* (n 5) para 68; *Brannigan and McBride v United Kingdom* (n 11) para 43.

the situation and thus in violation of article 4 or 15.[42] In referring to the 1998 Conclusions and Recommendations of the Committee on Israel, for example, the Special Rapporteur on the promotion and protection of human rights and fundamental freedoms while countering terrorism stated in his 2007 mission report to Israel that:[43]

> ...recourse to derogations under article 4 must be temporary and exceptional in nature, and that the enunciation of certain rights within the International Covenant on Civil and Political Rights already provide for the proportionate limitation of rights as prescribed by law and necessary for the protection of national security or public order, including articles 12(3), 19(3) and 21, relating to the freedoms of movement and residence, opinion and expression, and peaceful assembly.

Reference to the European Court decision in *Lawless v Ireland* can provide a practical flavour to this otherwise potentially academic discussion. The Court was in that case faced with the detention without trial of Lawless, who admitted being a member of the Irish Republican Army (IRA), in a military detention camp in Ireland. The Court accepted that the IRA had been formed for the avowed purpose of carrying out acts of violence to put an end to British sovereignty in Northern Ireland and that "at times the activities of these groups [the IRA] have been such that effective repression by the ordinary process of law was not possible".[44] In order to meet the situation created by the activities of the IRA, the Irish Parliament passed the Offences against the State Act 1939. Section 3(2) of the Act, as amended in 1940, conferred on Ministers of State special powers of detention without trial, "if and whenever and so often as the Government makes and publishes a proclamation declaring that the powers conferred by this Part of this Act are necessary to secure the preservation of public peace and order". By letter of 20 July 1957 the Irish Minister for External Affairs informed the Secretary-General of the Council of Europe that this part of the Act had come into force, thus activating the powers of detention without trial and derogating from the right to liberty. The European Court held that detention without trial was in the circumstances justified under article 15 of the ECHR. It had particular regard to the existence of a secret army (the IRA); the fact that the IRA was also operating outside the territory of Ireland; the steady and alarming increase in terrorist activities in the period before the emergency was declared; and also to the existence of a number of safeguards designed to prevent abuses in the operation of the system of administrative detention.[45]

Reviewing *Lawless* and other jurisprudence of the European Court of Human Rights, Ovey and White provide a useful summary of the factors commonly

---

[42]Siracusa Principles (n 13) para 53. See also General Comment 29 (n 6) para 4.

[43]Report of the Special Rapporteur on the promotion and protection of human rights and fundamental freedoms while countering terrorism, Martin Scheinin, Mission to Israel, including visit to occupied Palestinian Territory, UN Doc A/HRC/6/17/Add.4 (2007), para 10.

[44]*Lawless v Ireland* (n 10) para 6 of the facts.

[45]Ibid, paras 31–38 of the judgment.

considered by the Court in determining whether derogating measures are strictly required by the exigencies of the situation, i.e.:[46]

- The measures must be *necessary* to cope with the threat to the life of the nation. This might appear to be a reasonably obvious point to make, given that articles 4 and 15 of the ICCPR and ECHR refer to measures 'strictly required' by the situation. Necessity reinforces the point made earlier, however, that a distinction must be made between measures that can be adopted through use of rights-specific limitation provisions, as opposed to the exceptional measure of derogating from rights.
- They must go no further than required to deal with the emergency (i.e. they must be *proportional* and not so severe or so broad in their application so as to destroy the very essence of the right(s) being derogated from). Here, Ovey and White explain that examination of the safeguards provided where there is a derogation has taken on great significance in cases where the Court has been called on to determine the justifiability of derogating measures.[47]
- Although the duration of derogating measures has never been crucial to the outcome of the Court's decisions, the length of time of the general or specific application of derogating measures will be considered. This is both a reflection of the principle of proportionality (e.g. the length of detention must be no longer than required to deal with the emergency) and of the fact that a state of emergency must be in existence (referring back to the first substantive condition of derogations).

17.1.3.3 Other International Obligations

The third substantive condition applicable to derogations under the ICCPR and ECHR is that any measure derogating from those instruments must not be inconsistent with the State party's other obligations under international law, whether based on treaty law, or customary international law. This principle is reflected in article 5(2) of the Covenant, according to which there may be no restriction upon or derogation from any fundamental rights recognised in other instruments on the pretext that the Covenant does not recognise such rights, or that it recognises them to a lesser extent. It is also reflected in article 53 of the European Convention, which provides that:

> Nothing in this Convention shall be construed as limiting or derogating from any of the human rights and fundamental freedoms which may be ensured under the laws of any High Contracting Party or under any other agreement to which it is a Party.

Although this criterion is rarely referred to in the views or comments of the Human Rights Committee, or in the decisions of the European Court, it is a feature which

---

[46]Ovey and White (2002, pp. 374–375).

[47]See, for example, *Aksoy v Turkey* (n 5) paras 78 and 84, and *Brannigan and McBride v United Kingdom* (n 11).

has been important to the enumeration of the full list of non-derogable rights, as discussed in Chap. 10 (Sect. 10.1.2). The Human Rights Committee has emphasised that it is a requirement particularly relevant to the compliance of States with the rules of international humanitarian law during a state of emergency.[48]

17.1.3.4   Non-discrimination

The final substantive condition is that any derogating measure must not involve discrimination. In contrast to article 4 of the ICCPR, article 15 of the ECHR does not make specific mention of the need for derogating measures to be non-discriminatory. It must be remembered, however, that States derogating from the ECHR: (1) are bound by the general prohibition against discrimination in article 14 of the Convention; (2) they may not derogate from human rights in a manner which is inconsistent with other international treaties, as made clear by article 53 of the ECHR (discussed above); (3) nor may they derogate from the customary international law principles of non-discrimination (as a consequence of the third substantive condition of derogations). As will be seen from the discussion of the UK's indefinite detention regime, the principle of non-discrimination was particularly important to the House of Lords in considering the legality of that regime (see Sect. 17.3.2.2 below).

17.2   Executive Detention Powers Under the Prevention of Terrorism (Temporary Provisions) Acts

In 1974 the United Kingdom enacted the first of a series of Prevention of Terrorism (Temporary Provisions) Acts, which were renewed on an annual basis and continued until 2001 following the consolidation of the UK's counter-terrorism laws into a single Terrorism Act 2000 (see Chap. 8). Common sections 12 of the Acts gave police the power to arrest and detain without charge for up to 48 hours any person suspected of involvement in acts of terrorism (as defined by common sections 1, 9 and 10 of the Acts). Common sections 12 gave the Secretary of State the authority to extend detention for a further 5 days. Suspects could thereby be held without charge for a total of 7 days without the need for them to be brought before a judge. The powers in question were only applied in Northern Ireland and the UK's subsequent derogation from the right to liberty was limited to that territory.[49]

---

[48]General Comment 29 (n 6) para 9.

[49]This is confirmed by the fact the position adopted by the United Kingdom in *McVeigh, O'Neil and Evans v United Kingdom* Apps 8022/77, 8025/77 and 8027/77 (report of the Commission on Human Rights, 18 March 1981). The three applicants in the case arrived in Liverpool on a ferry from Ireland and were detained for 45 hours without charge. Despite the fact that the derogations from the right to liberty were in effect at that time, the UK government did not seek to invoke them

Until 1988, this format of 'seven-day executive detention' was enacted and renewed without the United Kingdom seeking to derogate from the right to liberty. Article 9(3) of the ICCPR and article 5(3) of the ECHR require that all persons who are detained must be brought 'promptly' before a judge or other judicial officer (see Chap. 16, Sect. 16.1.1). In *Brogan and others v United Kingdom*, the European Court was called on to determine whether the detention of four men under section 12 of the Prevention of Terrorism (Temporary Provisions) Act violated the right to be brought promptly before a judge. The four men had been detained for periods ranging from 4 days and 6 hours to 6 days and 16 and a half hours. The Court did not state what the maximum period could be for a person to be held without charge before article 5(3) was violated.[50] It did, however, rule that the least of the periods of detention in that case (4 days and 6 hours) was too long.[51]

The Parliamentary debates that followed this decision were focussed on two alternatives: to make the legislation consistent with the right to be brought promptly before a judge by introducing a judicial element into the procedure; or continue with the 7-day executive detention power and derogate from article 9(3) of the ICCPR and article 5(3) of the ECHR.[52] Reserving the possibility for 'further reflection' on the amendment of the mechanism, the Government took the latter option "against the background of the terrorist campaign, and the over-riding need to bring terrorists to justice".[53] The UK Permanent Representative to the Council of Europe presented a notice of derogation to the Secretary-General of the Council in December 1988, stating:[54]

> There have been in the United Kingdom in recent years campaigns of organised terrorism connected with the affairs of Northern Ireland which have manifested themselves in activities which have included repeated murder, attempted murder, maiming, intimidation and violent civil disturbance and in bombing and fire raising which have resulted in death, injury and widespread destruction of property. As a result, a public emergency within the meaning of Article 15(1) of the Convention exists in the United Kingdom.

---

in respect of the situation in Great Britain as opposed to that in Northern Ireland. See also Fenwick and Phillipson (2005).

[50]The European Court similarly avoided this question in *Koster v Netherlands* [1991] ECHR 53, where a period of 5 days was held to be too long.

[51]*Brogan and others v United Kingdom* [1988] ECHR 24, para 62. On the application of article 9(3) of the ICCPR see, for example: *Kennedy v Trinidad and Tobago*, Human Rights Committee Communication 845/1998, UN Doc CCPR/C/74/D/845/1998 (2002), para 7.6; *Borisenko v Hungary*, Communication 852/1999, UN Doc CCPR/C/76/D/852/1999 (2002), para 7.4; and *Kurbanov v Tajikistan*, Communication 1096/2002, UN Doc CCPR/C/79/D/1096/2002 (2003), para 7.2. See also: Conte and Burchill (2009, pp. 121–122); and General Comment 8: Right to liberty and security of persons (Art 9), UN Doc CCPR General Comment 8 (1982), para 2.

[52]Marks (1995, p. 71). See also Finnie (1989).

[53]See the Notice of Derogation to the Secretary-General of the Council of Europe, as reproduced in Schedule 3, Part I, of the Human Rights Act 1998, un-numbered para 7. The United Kingdom simultaneously notified the Secretary-General of the United Nations of its derogations from article 9(3) of the ICCPR.

[54]Notice of Derogation (ibid) un-numbered para 2.

One of a series of challenges to this derogation was the case of *Brannigan and McBride v United Kingdom*. The applicants challenged their detention for periods of 6 days 14 and a half hours, and 4 days 6 and a half hours. The United Kingdom conceded that the periods of detention were inconsistent with article 5(3) of the ECHR, but relied on the derogation from that provision. While they conceded that an emergency existed enabling the UK to derogate, in principle, from the Convention, Brannigan and McBride challenged the validity of the derogation on the basis that the measures under the Act were not required by the exigencies of the situation. It should be noted that, although the United Kingdom had also derogated from article 9(3) of the ICCPR, a challenge could not be brought before the Human Rights Committee because the UK had not (and still has not) ratified the ICCPR's Optional Protocol allowing for individual communications to the Committee.[55]

Three main arguments were put to the European Court in seeking to persuade it that the measures under section 12 of the Prevention of Terrorism (Temporary Provisions) Act 1988 were not required by the exigencies of the situation, i.e. that they were neither necessary nor proportionate. First, it was claimed that the derogation was not in response to the emergency situation, but was instead meant to circumvent the Court's earlier decision in *Brogan and others v United Kingdom*. The Government's response to this was that it had believed, prior to the decision in *Brogan*, that the measures were compatible with the right to be brought promptly before a judge. Only in light of that decision, said the Government, was it understood that the continuance of the measures required the United Kingdom to derogate from article 5(3) of the Convention. The Court confirmed that derogation was a viable alternative to compliance. Another argument proffered was that the derogation disproportionately impacted upon the right to *habeas corpus* which, although technically unaffected, was in practice impacted upon due to the ability of the executive to postpone any judicial hearing on the validity of a person's detention under section 12. This position met with little favour from the Court.

The Court's attention instead focused on the applicant's further argument that the exclusion of some element of judicial control in the 7-day detention mechanism was not necessary, i.e. that the mechanism could have functioned even with the introduction of judicial control. Here, the Government contended that the decision to extend a person's detention beyond 48 hours could only be made on the basis of highly sensitive information and that it was, as such, beyond the mandate of a judicial officer to assess the matter and could impact on the impartiality of a judicial officer by involving them in aspects of the investigation and prosecution process. In what is described by Marks as an "almost ostentatious deference paid to government discretion", the European Court of Human Rights accepted the Government's position as being within the margin of appreciation to be afforded to respondent governments.

---

[55]Optional Protocol to the International Covenant on Civil and Political Rights, opened for signature 16 December 1966, 999 UNTS 302 (entered into force 23 March 1976). On the complaints procedure under the Optional Protocol, see Conte and Burchill (2009, Chap. 2).

17.3 Indefinite Detention Regime Under the Anti-terrorism, Crime and Security Act 2001

As a consequence of enacting Part 4 of the Anti-terrorism, Crime and Security Act 2001 (ATCS Act), the United Kingdom made a designated derogation order under section 14 of the Human Rights Act 1998. The Human Rights Act 1998 (Designated Derogation) Order 2001 identified that the United Kingdom faced a threat from international terrorism requiring it to derogate from article 5(1)(f) of the ECHR.

17.3.1 Establishment of the Indefinite Detention Regime

Before explaining the operation of the indefinite detention regime, and the challenges to it, it is necessary to account for the reasons behind introduction of the regime. The Government's aim was to enable it to detain non-nationals who were suspected of being terrorists or who were deemed to pose a threat to the United Kingdom as potential terrorists. The UK's notices of derogation from the ICCPR and ECHR began by pointing to the terrorist attacks in the United States on September 11, describing the threat from international terrorism as a "continuing one" and thus concluding that:[56]

> There exists a terrorist threat to the United Kingdom from persons suspected of involvement in international terrorism. In particular, there are foreign nationals present in the United Kingdom who are suspected of being concerned in the commission, preparation or instigation of acts of international terrorism, of being members of organisations or groups which are so concerned or of having links with members of such organisations or groups, and who are a threat to the national security of the United Kingdom.

Despite this declared threat, the Government found itself unable to remove or detain the individuals alluded to for several reasons. The first of these was that there was a lack of admissible evidence allowing criminal charges to be brought against them, which could thereby have resulted in their incarceration through the imposition of sentences of imprisonment. Secondly, even though these individuals were identified by the Home Secretary as posing a threat to the security of the United Kingdom, the government was unable to use existing immigration laws to indefinitely detain the individuals concerned. Article 5(1)(f) of the ECHR only allows the detention of a non-national with a view to the person's deportation or extradition:

> 5(1). Everyone has the right to liberty and security of person. No one shall be deprived of his liberty save in the following cases and in accordance with a procedure prescribed by law:
> (f) the lawful arrest or detention of a person to prevent his effecting an unauthorised entry into the country or of a person against whom action is being taken with a view to deportation or extradition.

---

[56]United Kingdom Declaration of Derogation under Article 4 ICCPR, 18 December 2001, un-numbered para 4.

Under Schedule 3 of the Immigration Act 1971, the Secretary of State is permitted to detain foreign nationals pending the making of a deportation order, or pending actual deportation or removal (see paragraph 2). However, as held in *R v Governor of Durham Prison, Ex p Hardial Singh*, and later confirmed by the Privy Council in *Tan Te Lam v Superintendent of Tai A Chau Detention Centre*, such detention is permissible only for such time as is reasonably necessary for the process of deportation to be carried out.[57] This was something also confirmed by the European Court of Human Rights in *Chahal v United Kingdom*, where it explained that "any deprivation of liberty under article 5(1)(f) will be justified only for as long as deportation proceedings are in progress".[58] The Immigration Act could thus not be used for the long-term or indefinite detention of a non-UK national whom the Home Secretary wished to remove.

To further complicate matters, deportation or extradition action against a non-national is not always possible. This, and the limits of detention pending removal, was considered in detail by the European Court in *Chahal*. Chahal was an Indian citizen who, after entering the United Kingdom illegally, had been granted indefinite leave to remain in the United Kingdom. Chahal's activities as a Sikh separatist brought him to the notice of the authorities both in India and the UK. The Home Secretary decided that Chahal should be deported from Britain because his continued presence there was not conducive to the public good for reasons of a political nature, namely the international fight against terrorism. He was detained for deportation purposes pursuant to Schedule 3 of the Immigration Act. Chahal subsequently claimed political asylum, but the Home Secretary did not accept that, if returned to India, Chahal faced a real risk of death, or of torture in custody. He relied, instead, on an assurance from the Indian Government if Chahal were to be deported to India, "he would enjoy the same legal protection as any other Indian citizen, and that he would have no reason to expect to suffer mistreatment of any kind at the hands of the Indian authorities".[59] By the time Chahal's case came before the European Court of Human Rights, he had been detained for more than six years. The Court held that a foreign national who faces the prospect of torture or inhuman treatment if returned to his own country, and who cannot be deported to any third country and is not charged with any crime, may not be indefinitely detained even if judged to be a threat to national security.

As a result of these factors, and the declared emergency in the United Kingdom, provision was made in Part 4 of the Anti-terrorism, Crime and Security Act for an extended power to arrest and detain a foreign national "where it is intended to remove or deport the person from the United Kingdom but where removal or

---

[57]*R v Governor of Durham Prison, Ex p Hardial Singh* [1984] 1 WLR 704; *Tan Te Lam v Superintendent of Tai A Chau Detention Centre* [1997] AC 97.

[58]*Chahal v United Kingdom* (1996) 23 EHRR 413, para 113. On the application of the comparative provision of the ICCPR, see *JRC v Costa Rica*, Human Rights Committee Communication 296/1988, UN Doc Supp 40 (A/44/40) p. 293 (1989).

[59]*Chahal v United Kingdom* (ibid) para 37 of the facts.

deportation is not for the time being possible".[60] Section 23 of the ATCS Act allowed the detention of a "suspected international terrorist" (as designated under section 21 of the Act) despite the fact that deportation or extradition action against the person might not be possible. Section 23(1) provided:

> A suspected international terrorist may be detained under a provision specified in [the Immigration Act] despite the fact that his removal or departure from the United Kingdom is prevented (whether temporarily or indefinitely) by–
>
> (a) a point of law which wholly or partly relates to an international agreement, or
> (b) a practical consideration.

As provided for in section 21 of the Act, the Home Secretary was able to issue, and did issue, certificates indicating his belief that the presence in the UK of specified persons was a risk to national security and that he suspected the persons to be an international terrorist, i.e. a person who belongs to or has links with an international terrorist group or "is or has been concerned in the commission, preparation or instigation of acts of international terrorism".[61] Since this allowed for the indefinite detention of such persons, contrary to article 5(1)(f) of the ECHR (as confirmed in *Chahal*) and article 9(1) of the ICCPR, the United Kingdom derogated from both provisions just after enactment of the ATCS Act.

17.3.2 Evaluation of the Indefinite Detention Regime

The indefinite detention regime was subject to much criticism and debate in the lead up to its establishment under the Anti-terrorism, Crime and Security Act, and subsequently.[62] Criticisms have focussed on three aspects: (1) that no state of emergency, within the meaning of the derogating provisions in articles 4 and 15 of the ICCPR and ECHR, existed; (2) that, even if the derogations from the right to liberty were valid, they nevertheless involved unlawful discrimination contrary to articles 2(1) and 26 of the ICCPR and article 14 of the ECHR by virtue of the fact

---

[60]United Kingdom 2001 Declaration of Derogation (n 56) un-numbered para 6.

[61]On the designation of a person as a suspected international terrorist, the main parts of section 21 of the Anti-terrorism, Crime and Security Act 2001 read as follows:(1) The Secretary of State may issue a certificate under this section in respect of a person if the Secretary of State reasonably–(a) believes that the person's presence in the United Kingdom is a risk to national security, and(b) suspects that the person is a terrorist.(2) In subsection (1)(b) "terrorist" means a person who–(a) is or has been concerned in the commission, preparation or instigation of acts of international terrorism,(b) is a member of or belongs to an international terrorist group, or(c) has links with an international terrorist group.(3) A group is an international terrorist group for the purposes of subsection (2)(b) and (c) if–(a) it is subject to the control or influence of persons outside the United Kingdom, and(b) the Secretary of State suspects that it is concerned in the commission, preparation or instigation of acts of international terrorism.

[62]Part 4 of the ATCS Act was also the subject of consideration in the Concluding Observations of the Human Rights Committee following the fifth periodic report of the United to the Committee, UN Doc CCPR/CO/73/UK, para 6.

that section 23 of the ACTS Act applied only to foreign nationals; and (3) that the power of detention under section 23 of the Act was more like a power of indefinite detention and less like a power to detain pending removal,[63] thus making it disproportionate.

Soon after the entry into force of the ATCS Act, the legality of the regime under Part 4 of the Act was challenged by foreign nationals who had been detained under section 23 in what came to be known as the 'Belmarsh detainees case'. None had been charged with any offence. The detainees challenged the lawfulness of their detention, claiming that the powers of detention under section 23 were contrary to the obligations of the United Kingdom under the ECHR and that the UK's derogation from those obligations was not valid. The litigation went to the House of Lords who, in December 2004, issued a declaration under section 4 of the Human Rights Act 1998 that section 23 of the Anti-terrorism, Crime and Security Act was incompatible with articles 5 and 14 of the ECHR (on declarations of incompatibility under the Human Rights Act see Chap. 11, Sect. 11.2.3.1).[64]

Responding to the House of Lords decision, the detention provisions in the Act were repealed under section 16(2)(a) of the Prevention of Terrorism Act 2005. The derogations from the right to liberty were withdrawn in March 2005 and Schedule 3 of the Human Rights Act was amended to remove the designated derogation.[65] The UK Government stated that it would seek to deport the foreign nationals concerned where assurances against ill-treatment could be obtained from the destination country (on the subject of diplomatic assurances see Chap. 21, Sect. 21.3.3).[66] Those that could not be removed from the United Kingdom would be made subject to control orders under the Prevention of Terrorism Act (on control orders see Chap. 18, Sect. 18.1). The discussion that follows traces the principle arguments presented and findings made concerning the validity of the indefinite detention regime.

17.3.2.1   Existence of a Public Emergency Threatening the Life of the Nation

As seen from the text of Schedule 3 of the Human Rights Act quoted earlier, the derogation from article 5(1)(f) was said by the UK government to flow from the threat posed by international terrorism and the terrorist attacks of 9/11. Whether this amounts to a "war or public emergency" justifying derogation from the right to liberty is debatable.[67] No other party to the European Convention felt itself in a position where it was necessary to take measures to combat terrorism which required a derogation from rights and freedoms.

---

[63] As conceded by the Joint Committee on Human Rights: see Joint Committee on Human Rights – Fifth Report, Session 2002–2003, para 19.

[64] *A and Ors v Secretary of State for the Home Department* (n 17).

[65] See Human Rights Act 1998 (Amendment) Order 2005.

[66] Bates (2005, p. 275).

[67] See Bates (2005).

Nevertheless, in evidence before the Joint Committee on Human Rights, the Secretary of State asserted the existence of such an emergency, and indicated that his view was based on intelligence assessments and events such as the Bali bombing. In November 2001, the Committee concluded that it did not have sufficient evidence to satisfy itself of the existence of a public emergency threatening the life of the nation.[68] The matter was subsequently considered by the Special Immigration Appeals Commission (SIAC), which concluded that there was such an emergency. This view was endorsed by the Court of Appeal in 2002.[69] While the Joint Committee had not itself seen the evidence on which the Home Secretary's assessment or that of SIAC was based, it took the view that SIAC was "well placed to form an independent and reliable judgment".[70]

Despite that conclusion, the appellants in *A and Others* pointed to ministerial statements in October 2001 and March 2002 that: "There is no immediate intelligence pointing to a specific threat to the United Kingdom, but we remain alert, domestically as well as internationally"; and that "it would be wrong to say that we have evidence of a particular threat".[71] In the House of Lords, Lord Bingham did not agree that this lead to a conclusion that there was an absence of a public emergency within the terms of article 5 of the ECHR. For three main reasons, Lord Bingham concluded that a public emergency did exist in the United Kingdom: (1) he took the view that SIAC and the Court of Appeal had properly considered the matter; (2) he assessed that the situation faced by the United Kingdom as comparable to those in respect to which the European Court of Human Rights had accepted the existence of a public emergency;[72] and (3) he considered that weight should be given to the political judgment of the Homes Secretary.[73]

17.3.2.2   Discriminatory Effect of Part 4 of the ATCS Act

Sections 21–23 of the ATCS Act operate through immigration law and procedures by extending the power to detain under Schedules 2 and 3 of the Immigration Act 1971. They therefore apply only to people who are not nationals of the United Kingdom and engage the prohibition against discrimination since nationality is a prohibited ground of discrimination. On this point, the United Kingdom had not

---

[68]Joint Committee on Human Rights – Second Report, Session 2001–2002, para 30.

[69]*A, X and Y, and others v Secretary of State for the Home Department* [2002] EWCA Civ 1502, paras 33–34, 82–85, and 140–143.

[70]Fifth Report of the Joint Committee on Human Rights (n 63) para 27.

[71]*A and Others*, House of Lords, 2004 (n 17) para 21. See also Amnesty International report, Creating a shadow criminal justice system in the name of "fighting international terrorism", 16 November 2001, AI Index EUR 45/020/2001, p. 3; and Duffy (2005, pp. 345346).

[72]Lord Bingham referred to: *Ireland v United Kingdom* (n 5); *Brannigan and McBride v United Kingdom* (n 11); *Aksoy v Turkey* (n 5); and *Marshall v United Kingdom*, App 41571/98 (10 July 2001).

[73]*A and Others*, House of Lords, 2004 (n 17) paras 26–29.

sought to derogate from the non-discrimination provisions of the ICCPR or the ECHR. Indeed, as identified earlier, this is not possible because non-discrimination is itself a substantive condition of any derogation from those instruments (see Sect. 17.1.3.4). The Government instead argued that the different treatment accorded to nationals and non-nationals was objectively and rationally justified and was proportionate to a legitimate aim, thus not amounting to unlawful discrimination and compatible with the anti-discrimination provisions.[74] The Government's position, as summarised by the Joint Committee on Human Rights, was that:[75]

> Foreign suspected international terrorists are objectively and rationally in a different situation from United Kingdom nationals who are suspected international terrorists, because the United Kingdom owes a higher duty of protection towards its own nationals than towards foreign nationals. It is therefore rational to allow foreign nationals (but not United Kingdom nationals) to be removed if they threaten national security. If they cannot be removed without violating their human rights, it is rational, and proportionate to the threat that they pose, to allow them to be detained until a safe country can be found to accept them.

This argument was rejected by the Special Immigration Appeals Authority, which concluded that a power to detain indefinitely *all* suspected international terrorists, regardless of their nationalities, would have satisfied article 14 of the ECHR, and that there was not a reasonable relationship between the means employed (detention of foreign nationals only) and the aims sought to be pursued (furthering national security).[76] As summarised by Lord Justice Laws in *R (Carson) v Secretary of State*, the issue came down to the question of whether suspected international terrorists who were UK nationals were in a position so similar to the Belmarsh detainees so as to call (in the mind of a rational and fair-minded person) for a positive justification for the less favourable treatment of the Belmarsh detainees.[77] The Court of Appeal thought not because, according to Lord Woolf, "[UK] nationals have a right of abode in this jurisdiction but the aliens only have a right not to be removed".[78] The House of Lords disagreed, concluding that British terrorists and foreign terrorists could both be involved in international terrorism and that there was no way that the differential treatment could be objectively justified. As stated by Lord Bingham:[79]

> Article 15 requires any derogating measures to go no further than is strictly required by the exigencies of the situation and the prohibition of discrimination on grounds of nationality or immigration status has not been the subject of derogation. Article 14 remains in full force. Any discriminatory measure inevitably affects a smaller rather than a larger group, but cannot be justified on the ground that more people would be adversely affected if the measure were applied generally. What has to be justified is not the measure in issue but the

---

[74] As reflected in the Fifth Report of the Joint Committee on Human Rights (n 63) para 21.

[75] Fifth Report of the Joint Committee on Human Rights (n 63) para 36.

[76] *A & Ors v Secretary of State for the Home Department* [2002] UKSIAC (30 July 2002).

[77] *R (Carson) v Secretary of State for Work and Pensions* [2003] 3 All ER 577, para 61.

[78] *A & Ors* (Court of Appeal, 2002) (n 69), para 56.

[79] *A & Ors* (House of Lords, 2004) (n 17), para 68.

difference in treatment between one person or group and another. What cannot be justified here is the decision to detain one group of suspected international terrorists, defined by nationality or immigration status, and not another. To do so was a violation of article 14. It was also a violation of article 26 of the ICCPR and so inconsistent with the United Kingdom's other obligations under international law within the meaning of article 15 of the European Convention.

It is notable in this regard that, in a report of the Home Office in 2009 on terrorism arrests and outcomes in Great Britain for the period 11 September 2001 to 31 March 2008, it has been documented that 62% of terrorist prisoners in England and Wales were recorded as UK nationals, 21% of African nationality, 9% of Middle Eastern nationality and 4% of Asian nationality.[80]

17.4   Terrorism and the Derogation from Human Rights

Additional to the two case studies just considered, it is notable that a number of States have invoked the capacity to derogate from rights under the ICCPR and ECHR when responding to terrorist incidents.[81] The aim of the current section is to draw some general principles and observations about terrorism and the use of derogating measures from the above discussions, and make reference to further materials where appropriate.

17.4.1   The Threat of Terrorism as a State of Emergency

The first point to deduct is that terrorism, or the threat of terrorism, can trigger the ability of States parties to the ICCPR and ECHR to derogate from those instruments (provided that the derogation is declared and that it derogates only from those rights capable of derogation).

---

[80]Home Office Statistical Bulletin, Statistics on Terrorism Arrests and Outcomes in Great Britain (Home Office, London, May 2009), para 25.

[81]In October 1994, Azerbaijan proclaimed two 60-day states of emergency in the cities of Baku and Gyania following the wounding of two politicians by terrorist groups and the commission of acts of violence against the civilian population. On 16 September 1986, Chile notified the United Nations Secretary-General of a derogation from articles 9 (liberty), 12 (movement) and 13 (removal) based on "a wave of terrorist aggression", including an attack on the President of the Republic of Chile. Columbia has declared public emergencies twice in 1992, once in 1995 and twice in 1996 based on violent acts "attributed to criminal and terrorist organizations". El Salvador declared a 30-day suspension from articles 12, 17, 19, 21 and 21 of the ICCPR following "the use of terror and violence by the Frente Farabundo Marti". Since its establishment in May 1948, the State of Israel has maintained a state of emergency to derogate from various rights, including the right to liberty under article 9 of the ICCPR. Numerous declarations were made by Peru between 1984 and 1995. Acts of terrorism and violence were declared to be the basis of derogations by the Russian Federation in 1993 and 1994.

17.4.1.1 Derogating From the Right to Liberty

As seen from the case studies, the right to liberty has been accepted by the European Court as a right in respect of which derogating measures may be taken in a state of emergency caused by terrorist acts or threats.[82] However, in considering the deprivation of liberty in the context of counter-terrorism measures, the Human Rights Council has urged all States:[83]

> ...to take all necessary steps to ensure that persons deprived of liberty, regardless of the place of arrest or of detention, benefit from the guarantees to which they are entitled to under international law, including, inter alia, protection against torture, cruel, inhuman or degrading treatment or punishment, protection against refoulement, the review of their detention and, if subjected to trial, fundamental judicial guarantees.

While this decision was made against the background of discussions concerning rendition to places of secret detention, and in part goes to the question of necessity and proportionality, it also attaches to whether the right to liberty can be derogated from in all circumstances. Although liberty rights are not included in the express list of non-derogable rights under articles 4(2) of the ICCPR and 15(2) of the ECHR, the full complement of non-derogable rights is not reflected in those provisions. Derogating measures must comply with other obligations under international law, including customary international law (see Chap. 10, Sect. 10.1.2). The Human Rights Committee has observed that this includes the right of all persons deprived of their liberty to be treated with humanity and with respect for the inherent dignity of the human person.[84]

What is perhaps surprising, in the case of the United Kingdom, is that derogating measures were only taken by the UK after being found by the European Court of Human Rights to be in violation of article 5 of the ECHR. In the context of the 7-day executive detention provision in the Prevention of Terrorism (Temporary Provisions) Acts, its seems almost inconceivable that the detention of a person for up to 7 days before being brought before a judge could be considered to satisfy the requirement that persons be brought 'promptly' before a judge or other judicial officer. The six-year and continued detention of Mr Chahal under the Immigration Act 1971 is similarly astonishing, particularly in light of the 1984 decision in *ex parte Singh* that detention pending removal under the Immigration Act is permissible only for such time as is 'reasonably necessary' for the process of deportation.[85]

---

[82]*Brannigan and McBride v United Kingdom* (n 11).

[83]Human Rights Council Decision 1/122, Persons deprived of liberty in the context of counter-terrorism measures, 32nd Mtg, 26 November 2006, para 5.

[84]General Comment 29 (n 6) para 10.

[85]*Ex parte Singh* (n 57).

17.4.1.2 Terrorism as a Threat to the Life of the Nation

The first substantive condition for a valid derogation from the ICCPR or ECHR is that the derogating State is in a time of war or other public emergency which threatens the life of the nation. Four criteria apply in determining whether or not such an emergency exists which (see Sect. 17.1.3.1 above), when applied to the counter-terrorism context, results in the following observations:[86]

1. To be valid, a derogation need not be in respect of the entire territory of the State. It has been accepted that terrorism can trigger the adoption of derogating measures applying to distinct areas, for example Northern Ireland,[87] or south-east Turkey.[88]
2. The circumstances must amount to a crisis or emergency that is actual or imminent. In the terrorism context, this may arise in response to a particular terrorist act and for the purpose of dealing with that act alone. More probable, however, is reliance on a culmination of factors leading a State to claim that it faces the threat of terrorist acts being perpetrated within its borders or against its nationals. This is the key issue to be dealt with. The problem here is that derogating States will, as the United Kingdom has done, claim that it is not appropriate to disclose all of the information leading to a conclusion that a real and imminent threat of terrorism exists. While much information might be publicly available, the precise nature or source of threats of terrorism might come from intelligence assessments and information which cannot be openly disclosed without damaging counter-terrorist operations or exposing intelligence sources. Also problematic is the approach of the European Court of Human Rights, distinct to that of the Human Rights Committee, that governments should be afforded a wide margin of appreciation in the exercise of their political judgment to determine the existence and extent of a public emergency (see Sects. 17.1.2 and 17.1.3.1 above).

   While there are some merits in the application of a margin of appreciation in the terrorism context, and to the fact that sensitive information may be involved, there are valid counter-arguments and means through which a more objective assessment could be achieved. From a principled perspective, it is unfortunate to have seen the European Court defer to such a large extent to the political judgment of the UK government in *Brannigan and McBride*. While it is true that a terrorist threat may require a government to respond urgently to that threat, this should not be treated as excluding the competence of a human rights body to review and assess the reaction ex post facto. One should instead take an approach of aiming to achieve human rights compliance when countering terrorism by way of a collaborative enterprise between the government and the European Court and/or the Human Rights Committee.

---

[86]*Lawless v Ireland* (n 10).

[87]*Ireland v United Kingdom* (n 5), and *Brannigan and McBride v United Kingdom* (n 11).

[88]*Sakik and others v Turkey* (n 27).

There are two distinct questions that a reviewing body should consider in this regard. First, was the government acting within the margins of its powers to declare a state of emergency based on the information available to it at that time? This was, in fact, the approach taken by the European Court of Human Rights in *Brannigan and McBride*.[89] The Court did not, however, go on to ask the second question posed by this author, i.e. with the benefit of hindsight, and the information available at the time of review by the human rights body, is it still objectively reasonable to conclude that an imminent threat of terrorism exists? This is not the same as asking whether the derogating government was wrong in declaring a state of emergency. It is instead an opportunity to ensure that appropriate reflections are made and that, consistent with the terms of article 4 (1) of the ICCPR and article 15(1) of the ECHR, the declared emergency continues to exist to the extent that derogating measures are necessary.

A policy argument against such an approach can be anticipated, i.e. that asking the further question posited by this author would lead to an automatic series of challenges before the European Court or Human Rights Committee whenever a State declares a state of emergency. Counter-arguments also exist. First, this need not be a bad thing in principle, since recourse to derogating measures should be, and has been, reasonably limited. In any event, recourse to the derogation mechanisms in the ICCPR and ECHR have the effect of suspending the application of human rights during the life of the derogation. Strict controls on such a power are therefore justified. Furthermore, States can avoid such litigation by instituting independent domestic mechanisms for the regular review of a declared state of emergency.

On the question of access to information, this can again be linked to the establishment of internal review mechanisms. Mechanisms already exist for dealing with the judicial scrutiny of classified information including, for example, the establishment of special security-cleared panels which can access sensitive information, such as the UK's Special Immigration Appeals Commission (see further Chap. 18, Sect. 18.2.3).

3. The third criterion applicable to determining whether a public emergency exists is that the situation must threaten the continuance of the organised life of the community. This might involve a threat to the physical safety of the population of the declaring State, such as a bomb threat or the possibility of other forms of terrorist violence against nationals and other residents in the country, as was the case in the application of derogating measures in response to the IRA's avowed purpose of carrying out acts of violence to put an end to British sovereignty in Northern Ireland.[90] It may involve a threat to the political independence or territorial independence of a State.[91] Continuance of the organised life of the

---

[89] *Brannigan and McBride v United Kingdom* (n 11).

[90] *Lawless v Ireland* (n 10).

[91] On a related decision, although not involving a derogation from the ICCPR or ECHR, see *Zana v Turkey* [1997] ECHR 94 (considered in Chap. 10, Sect. 10.3.2.3).

community might also be threatened where a terrorist threat is aimed at undermining the existence or basic functioning of institutions indispensible to ensure and protect the full range of human rights, such as threats directed to medical services. However, internal conflict or unrest cannot by itself justify a derogation from rights. This will only be the case if it constitutes a grave or imminent threat to the life of the nation.[92]

4. The fourth and final requirement is that the situation in question must be exceptional, i.e. one that cannot be dealt with under normal measures. 'Normal' measures would involve those already provided for by law in the country and which have not required a derogation from rights. They may also involve the implementation of new measures which, although they might limit rights and freedoms, are compatible with the expression of rights within the ICCPR and ECHR. This final condition is closely linked to the requirement that derogating measures must be necessary.

17.4.2 A Necessary and Proportionate Response

Where, as a result of the latter analysis, where it is determined that there is an actual or imminent threat of terrorism which threatens the life of the nation, this will allow a State to adopt derogating measures if, and only if, such measures are strictly required by the exigencies of the situation. Although the European Court has applied a margin of appreciation here too, there is a greater degree of concurrence between the approaches of the Court and the Human Rights Committee. While the European Court will allow States to determine what measures are best suited to countering a threat of terrorism giving rise to a public emergency, the Court nevertheless regards itself as the ultimate judge of whether derogating measures limit the right in question to the extent necessary.[93] An adverse finding would be made, for example, if it could be shown that the measures could have been adopted through the imposition of limitations consistent with a rights-specific limitations provision under the ICCPR or ECHR, rather than through a derogation from one of those instruments.[94]

To be proportionate, the derogating measures must go no further than required and must not be so severe or so broad in their application so as to destroy the very essence of the right being derogated from.[95] It will be highly relevant, in this regard, if safeguards are provided against the potential for derogating measures to be abused. The duration of derogating measures may also be germane.

---

[92]Siracusa Principles (n 13), para 40.

[93]*Brannigan and McBride v United Kingdom* (n 11) para 43, and *Aksoy v Turkey* (n 5) para 68.

[94]General Comment 29 (n 6) para 4, and Siracusa Principles (n 13) para 53.

[95]General Comment 29 (n 6) para 4, and Ovey and White (2002, p. 375).

17.4.3   Consistency with International Obligations and the Principle of Non-discrimination

The third and fourth substantive conditions for a valid derogation under articles 4 and 15 of the ICCPR and ECHR are that the derogating measures must be consistent with the State's other international obligations, including treaty and customary law on human rights, and with the principle of non-discrimination. The former of these conditions has not played a direct or significant role in the review of derogating measures. As seen in the case study concerning the indefinite detention regime in the United Kingdom, however, the prohibition against discrimination can be particularly relevant to the application of derogating measures in the context of countering terrorism. This will be especially so where measures target foreign nationals, or disproportionately apply to persons on the basis of their nationality, ethnicity or religious beliefs (on profiling at border controls, see Chap. 21, Sect. 21.1.3). If any distinction between terrorist suspects is made on those grounds, the difference in treatment must be objectively and rationally justified, and proportionate.[96] One must be able to deduce (in the mind of a rational and fair-minded person) a positive justification for less favourable treatment than that applicable to all other terrorist suspects.[97] In making a declaration of incompatibility under section 4 of the Human Rights Act 1998, for example, the House of Lords concluded in *A and Others v Home Secretary* that such a conclusion could not be drawn between the indefinite detention of the Belmarsh detainees (who were foreign nationals) and terrorist suspects who were UK nationals.[98]

17.5   Conclusions

This chapter has considered the substantive conditions applicable to derogations under the International Covenant on Civil and Political Rights and the European Convention on Human Rights. It has undertaken two case studies concerning derogations by the United Kingdom from the right to liberty. Both case studies in the first instance involved breaches of the right to liberty and then, consequent to adverse findings by the European Court of Human Rights, the declaration of derogations from the right to liberty so as to enable the United Kingdom to continue with their detention mechanisms. In the context of the indefinite detention regime under the Anti-terrorism, Crime and Security Act, this went further due to the ability of the House of Lords to issue a declaration of incompatibility under section 4 of the Human Rights Act 1998. But for that facility, the indefinite detention regime might still be operating in the United Kingdom.

---

[96]*A and Ors*, House of Lords, 2004 (n 17).

[97]Ibid. See also *R (Carson) v Secretary of State* (n 77) para 61.

[98]*A and Ors*, House of Lords, 2004 (n 17).

For a State to derogate from rights and freedoms under the ICCPR or the ECHR, two procedural conditions, and four substantive conditions, apply:

- A State may only derogate from those rights which are capable of derogation. Certain rights are expressly or impliedly non-derogable, or not capable of limitation due to their absolute nature.
- The second procedural condition is that the State must proclaim a state of emergency and give notice of the derogation to the Secretary-General of the United Nations (or of the Council of Europe in the case of the ECHR) in terms that are at the very least sufficient to understand the nature and reasons for the derogation.
- Of the four substantive conditions: (1) it must be shown that the derogating measures are adopted during a "time of public emergency which threatens the life of the nation"; (2) the derogating measures must be limited to those "strictly required by the exigencies of the situation"; (3) the measures must not be "inconsistent with [the State's] other obligations under international law"; and (4) they must not "involve discrimination solely on the ground of race, colour, sex, language, religion or social origin".

Terrorism, and the threat of terrorism, can trigger the ability of States to derogate from certain provisions of the ICCPR and ECHR. This will be the case where a State faces an actual or imminent threat of terrorism, deduced from a culmination of factors and available information. The challenge in determining whether or not this is the case can be alleviated by adopting a two-stage approach. First, by considering whether the government in question was acting within the margins of its powers to declare a state of emergency based on the information available to it at the time. This will likely involve a degree of deference to the political judgment made at that time. The second stage would be to examine whether, with the benefit of hindsight and the information available at the time of subsequent review, it is still objectively reasonable to conclude that an actual or imminent threat of terrorism exists which threatens the life of the nation. While the European Court and the Human Rights Committee should act as ultimate arbiters, States can pre-empt this and likely avoid adverse findings by implementing independent domestic review mechanisms which have the ability of accessing and reviewing sensitive information.

In terms of other factors relevant to the question of whether a state of emergency exists which threatens the life of the nations, regard must also be had to whether the situation threatens the continuance of organised life of the community. Threats of terrorism will likely do so, since they more often than not involve threats to the physical safety of the population, or the critical infrastructure of the State, and may even involve threats to the political independence or territorial integrity of a State. Closely linked to the second substantive condition for a valid derogation from rights, the situation faced by the derogating State must be one that cannot be dealt with by existing law, or by new measures which would be otherwise compatible with rights and freedoms.

As just indicated, a valid derogation from rights and freedoms must also be necessary and proportional, i.e. it must be limited to the extent strictly required by the exigencies of the situation. In this regard, it will be relevant to consider: (1) whether the measures could have been adopted through the imposition of limitations consistent with a rights-specific limitations provision; (2) whether safeguards are provided to guard against abuse of the derogating measures; and (3) the duration of the derogating measures. Finally, derogating measures must be consistent with a State's other international obligations and with the principle of non-discrimination. In the litigation surrounding the indefinite detention of the 'Belmarsh detainees' in the United Kingdom, compliance with the prohibition against non-discrimination was particularly relevant and resulted in the House of Lords declaring that the indefinite detention regime under the Anti-terrorism, Crime and Security Act was incompatible with the right to liberty and the freedom from discrimination. As concluded by the House of Lords, British terrorists and foreign terrorists could both be involved in international terrorism and that there was no way that the differential treatment could be objectively justified.

References

Bates, Edward. 2005. A 'Public Emergency Threatening the Life of the Nation'? The United Kingdom's Derogation from the European Convention on Human Rights of 18 December 2001 and the 'A' Case. *The British Yearbook of International Law* 245.

Bonner, David. 1978. Ireland v United Kingdom. 27(4) *The International and Comparative Law Quarterly* 897.

Boyle, Kevin. 2004. Terrorism, States of Emergency and Human Rights. In Benedek, Wolfgang, and Yotopoulos-Marangopoulos (Eds). *Anti-Terrorism Measures and Human Rights*. Leiden: Martinus Nijhoff Publishers.

Conte, Alex, and Burchill, Richard. 2009. *Defining Civil and Political Rights: The Jurisprudence of the United Nations Human Rights* Committee. Aldershot: 2nd ed, Ashgate Publishing Ltd.

Duffy, Helen. 2005. *The 'War on Terror' and the Framework of International Law*. Cambridge: Cambridge University Press.

Fenwick, Helen, and Phillipson, Gavin. 2005. Legislative over-breadth, democratic failure and the judicial response: fundamental rights and the UK's anti-terrorist legal policy. In Ramraj, Victor, Hor, Michael, and Roach, Kent (Eds). *Global Anti-Terrorism Law and Policy*. Cambridge: Cambridge University Press.

Finnie, Wilson. 1989. The Prevention of Terrorism Act and the European Convention on Human Rights. 52(5) *The Modern Law Review* 703.

Hartman, Joan. 1985. Working paper for the Committee of Experts on the Article 4 Derogation Provision. 7(1) *Human Rights Quarterly* 89.

Marks, Susan. 1995. Civil Liberties at the Margin: The UK Derogation and the European Court of Human Rights. 15(1) *Oxford Journal of Legal Studies* 69.

O'Boyle, Michael. 1977. Torture and Emergency Powers under the European Convention on Human Rights: Ireland v United Kingdom. 71 *American Journal of International Law* 674.

Ovey, Clare, and White, Robin. 2002. *The European Convention on Human Rights*. Oxford: 3rd ed, Oxford University Press.

Chapter 18
Control Orders and Preventative Detention

The use of control orders is a tool adopted under counter-terrorism legislation in
the United Kingdom and Australia which has the potential to engage a number of
rights, the rights to liberty and fair hearing in particular. As discussed in the preceding chapter, the indefinite detention regime under Part 4 of the Anti-terrorism,
Crime and Security Act 2001 (UK) was declared by the House of Lords to be
incompatible with the rights to liberty and non-discrimination in 2004. Responding
to that declaration, the indefinite detention provisions in the Act were repealed
under section 16(2)(a) of the Prevention of Terrorism Act 2005 (PTA). The PTA at
the same time established a regime for the making of control orders imposing
obligations on persons for "purposes connected with protecting members of the
public from a risk of terrorism". By the end of the same year in which control orders
were introduced in the United Kingdom, Australia established the same mechanism
under Division 104 of the Criminal Code Act 1995.

Control orders have been criticised in both Australia and the United Kingdom,
and have been the subject of litigation in both countries. The regime in Australia has
been negatively commented upon by the UN Special Rapporteur on the promotion
and protection of human rights and fundamental freedoms while countering terrorism.[1] Control orders in the UK have also drawn criticism from the UN Human
Rights Committee.[2]

Additional to the ability of Australia to make control orders, amendment of
Australia's Criminal Code in 2005 saw the introduction of preventative detention
orders under Division 105 of the Code. This is a matter also examined in this
chapter.

---

[1]Special Rapporteur on the promotion and protection of human rights and fundamental freedoms
while countering terrorism, Australia: Study on Human Rights Compliance While Countering
Terrorism, UN Doc A/HRC/4/26/Add.3, chapter V, part C.

[2]Concluding Observations of the Human Rights Committee: United Kingdom, UN Doc CCPR/C/
GBR/CO/6 (2008), para 17.

A. Conte, *Human Rights in the Prevention and Punishment of Terrorism*,
DOI 10.1007/978-3-642-11608-7_18, © Springer-Verlag Berlin Heidelberg 2010

18.1   The Control Order Mechanisms in the United Kingdom and Australia

Controls orders in the United Kingdom and Australia are much the same in the overall nature of the making and review of such orders, and the type of obligations that may be imposed under them. Some differences exist in the tests to be applied (discussed at Sect. 18.4.1). The most important difference is that the conditions imposed under a control order in Australia must always be compliant with the right to liberty (within the bounds of necessary and proportional limitations consistent with the law and the International Covenant on Civil and Political Rights), whereas the UK legislation provides for the possibility of making control orders which would be accompanied by a derogation from the right to liberty. On the question of derogating from the right to liberty, and derogations more generally, see Chap. 16.[3]

18.1.1   Prevention of Terrorism Act 2005 (UK)

Section 1(1) of the Prevention of Terrorism Act defines control orders as "an order against an individual that imposes obligations on him for purposes connected with protecting members of the public from a risk of terrorism". Two types of control orders are permissible: (1) non-derogating control orders (which represents the class of control orders issued so far under the legislation); and (2) derogating control orders (which would be ones that are deemed to interfere with liberty rights to such an extent that a derogation from article 5 of the European Convention on Human Rights would be required – see section 4).

The Home Secretary may make a control order where he or she has reasonable grounds for suspecting that the individual is or has been involved in terrorism-related activity (section 2(1)(a)) and he or she considers that it is necessary, for the protection of the public from a risk of terrorism, to make a control order imposing obligations on that individual (section 2(1)(b)). For the purposes of the Act, "involvement in terrorism-related activity" is any one or more of the following:

- The commission, preparation or instigation of acts of terrorism (as defined by section 1 of the Terrorism Act 2000 (UK) – considered in Chap. 8, Sect. 8.1.5.1 – see section 15(1) of the PTA);
- Conduct which facilitates the commission, preparation or instigation of such acts, or which is intended to do so;
- Conduct which gives encouragement to the commission, preparation or instigation of such acts, or which is intended to do so (thus linked to the offence of the incitement to terrorism – see Chap. 8, Sect. 8.1.8.1); and/or
- Conduct which gives support or assistance to individuals who are known or believed to be involved in terrorism-related activity.

---

[3]On the question of derogations impacting on the right to a fair trial, see also Stavros (1992).

In the normal course of events, the Home Secretary will apply to the court for permission to make a non-derogating control order (section 3(1)(a)). Two exceptions exist to this requirement for judicial approval of a control order: (1) where the order contains a statement by the Secretary of State that, in his or her opinion, the urgency of the case required the order to be made without such permission (section 3(1)(b)); or (2) in respect of persons who were, under section 21(1) of the Anti-terrorism, Crime and Security Act 2001, designated as "suspected international terrorists" (section 3(1)(c)). In those situations, however, the control order must be referred to the court within 7 days after the making of the order (section 3(3)–(6)). The supervising court may only refuse to give its permission to the Home Secretary if it considers that the Secretary's decision is obviously flawed, within the meaning of the principles applicable in judicial review proceedings (section 3(2) and (11)). This includes the question of whether each of the obligations imposed by the order are "necessary for purposes connected with protecting members of the public from a risk of terrorism" (sections 2(1)(b) and 3(10)(b)).

If permission is granted, the court must give directions for a hearing in relation to the order as soon as reasonably practicable after it is made (section 3(2)(c)). The subject of the control order will be notified of the hearing under section 3(10) of the Act. The Schedule to the Act sets out certain matters concerning the conduct of control order proceedings. Paragraph 4(1) enables the court to make rules of procedure, including those concerning the mode of proof and evidence and the possibility of enabling or requiring proceedings to be determined without a hearing. In doing so, paragraph 4(3) of the Schedule requires that such rules must enable the Home Secretary to apply for the non-disclosure, or the provision of redacted summaries, of information or other material "the disclosure of which would be contrary to the public interest" (paragraph 4(3)(f)). The Schedule also provides for the use of a special advocate (paragraph 7). Part 76 of the Civil Procedure Rules gives effect to the procedural scheme authorised by the Schedule to the 2005 Act.[4]

A derogating control order has effect for six months, unless revoked or renewed (section 4(8)), provided that the accompanying derogation remains in force and that the designation order under the Human Rights Act was not made more than 12 months earlier (section 6(1)), and may be revoked or modified by the court (section 7(5)–(7)). A non-derogating control order has effect for a period of 12 months, and may be renewed on an annual basis, without a limit on the number of maximum renewals (section 2(4) and (6)). The obligations that may be imposed by a control order are any obligations that the Home Secretary or a court considers necessary for purposes connected with preventing or restricting the involvement of that individual in terrorism-related activity (section 1(3)). Section 1(4) of the PTA sets out a non-exhaustive list of the type of obligations that may be included in a control order, as follows:

---

[4]Civil Procedure Rules (UK), Part 76, Proceedings under the Prevention of Terrorism Act 2005, available online: http://www.justice.gov.uk/civil/procrules_fin/pdf/parts/part76.pdf.

- A prohibition or restriction on his or her possession or use of specified articles or substances;
- A prohibition or restriction on his or her use of specified services or specified facilities, or on his or her carrying on specified activities;
- A restriction in respect of his or her work or other occupation, or in respect of his or her business;
- A restriction on his or her association or communications with specified persons or with other persons generally;
- A restriction in respect of his or her place of residence or on the persons to whom he or she gives access to his or her place of residence;
- A prohibition on his or her being at specified places or within a specified area at specified times or on specified days;
- A prohibition or restriction on his or her movements to, from or within the United Kingdom, a specified part of the United Kingdom or a specified place or area within the United Kingdom;
- A requirement on him or her to comply with such other prohibitions or restrictions on his or her movements as may be imposed (for a period not exceeding 24 hours, by directions given to him or her in manner specified by the Act and by a specified person) for the purpose of securing compliance with other obligations imposed by or under the order;
- A requirement on him or her to surrender his or her passport, or anything in his or her possession to which a prohibition or restriction imposed by the order relates for a period not exceeding the period for which the order remains in force;
- A requirement on him or her to give access to specified persons to his or her place of residence or to other premises to which he or she has power to grant access;
- A requirement on him or her to allow specified persons to search that place or any such premises for the purpose of ascertaining whether obligations imposed by or under the order have been, are being or are about to be contravened;
- A requirement on him or her to allow specified persons, either for that purpose or for the purpose of securing that the order is complied with, to remove anything found in that place or on any such premises and to subject it to tests or to retain it for a period not exceeding the period for which the order remains in force;
- A requirement on him or her to allow him or herself to be photographed;
- A requirement on him or her to cooperate with specified arrangements for enabling his or her movements, communications or other activities to be monitored by electronic or other means;
- A requirement on him or her to comply with a demand made in the specified manner to provide information to a specified person in accordance with the demand; and/or
- A requirement on him or her to report to a specified person at specified times and places.

A person subject to a control order (the 'controlled person') is bound by a control order (or its renewal or modification) only if a notice setting out the terms of the order, renewal, or modification has been delivered to the controlled person (section 7(8)).

Failure to comply with obligations imposed under a control order amount to an offence under section 9(1) of the Prevention of Terrorism Act, punishable by up to 5 years imprisonment if convicted on indictment. It is an offence under section 9(3) of the Act to intentionally obstruct the service of a control order (as governed by section 7(9)). A complex offence is also established by section 9(2) of the Act concerning the exit from and re-entry into the United Kingdom. If a control order does not prohibit a person from leaving the United Kingdom, it will be likely that a condition of the order will require the person, whenever he or she re-enters the United Kingdom, to report to a specified person that he or she is or has been the subject of a control order. Where this is the case, and if the control order has expired since the person left the United Kingdom, it will be an offence for the person to fail to report to the specified person notwithstanding the expiry of the control order. In sentencing a person of an offence under section 9(1) or (2), the court may not conditionally discharge the person, or make a probation order against them (section 9(6)).

If, during the life of a non-derogating control order, the controlled person considers that there has been a change of circumstances affecting the order, he or she can make an application to the Secretary of State for revocation of the order, or modification of an obligation imposed by the order (section 7(1)). Where such an application is refused, or where a control order is renewed or modified without the consent of the controlled person, the controlled person may seek judicial review of the refusal, renewal, or modification (section 10).

18.1.2 Division 104 of the Criminal Code 1995 (Australia)

Division 104 of the Criminal Code 1995 (Australia) sets out the mechanisms for the issuing, variation and lapse of control orders. As indicated, there is no facility for 'derogating' control orders in Australia. The mechanism is otherwise very similar to that provided for in the United Kingdom. Having said that, the language used in Australia's control orders regime tends to be more precise than that in the UK. The purpose of control orders, for example, is described to be to allow obligations, prohibitions and restrictions to be imposed on a person by a control order "for the purpose of protecting the public from a terrorist act" (section 104.1) rather than the UK's more broad imposition of obligations "for purposes *connected* with protecting members of the public from a *risk* of terrorism" (section 1(1) of the PTA (UK), emphasis added).

The pre-conditions for an application for control order are also more stringent in Australia. The UK Home Secretary only requires suspicion that a person is or has been involved in "terrorism-*related* activity" (emphasis added) and that a control order is necessary for "purposes *connected* with protecting members of the public from a *risk* of terrorism" (emphasis added). For the Australian Federal Police to obtain the Attorney General's consent to apply for a control order, however, a senior member of the Police must establish that a control order "would *substantially* assist in *preventing a terrorist act*" (emphasis added) and that the officer suspects on reasonable grounds "that the person has provided training to, or received training from, a listed terrorist organisation" (rather than just being "involved in terrorism-related activity") – see section 104.2 of the Criminal Code. This is reflected in the tests to be applied by the courts in the granting of control orders (section 104.4(1)(c)).

Control orders are made by a two-step process, as is the case in the United Kingdom. An interim control order is made ex parte (sections 104.3–104.5), including the possibility for an urgent control order to be applied for in person or by telephone, fax, email or other electronic means (sections 104.6–104.11). Within 48 hours of the making of the interim control order, the controlled person must be provided with notice of the order and will be entitled to appear at a confirmation hearing to contest the order (sections 104.12–104.15). During a confirmation hearing, and for the purpose of protecting information likely to prejudice national security, persons made subject to a control order will only be entitled to a summary of the grounds upon which the order was made by the Court (section 104.5(2A)). This restriction applies to an appeal against, or review of, a decision made at a confirmation hearing. This is similar to the procedure prescribed by the Schedule to the UK's Prevention of Terrorism Act, and is a feature considered in more detail below (see Sect. 18.2).[5]

As in the case of non-derogating control orders in the United Kingdom, control orders under Division 104 of Australia's Criminal Code have effect for a period of up to 12 months (section 104.16(1)(d)). There is no restriction on the number of times a control order may be confirmed. At any time after a confirmed control order is served on the controlled person, or the Australian Federal Police, can apply to an issuing court for the court to revoke or vary the order (sections 104.18 and 104.19).

The range of obligations that may be imposed under an Australia control order (section 104.5(3)) are much the same as in the United Kingdom.[6] Section 104.5(3)(f)

---

[5]See also the National Security Information (Criminal and Civil Proceedings) Act 2004 (Australia).

[6]Section 104.5(3) of the Criminal Code Act 1995 lists the following obligations, prohibitions and restrictions that a court may impose on a controlled person:

(a) a prohibition or restriction on the person being at specified areas or places;
(b) a prohibition or restriction on the person leaving Australia;
(c) a requirement that the person remain at specified premises between specified times each day, or on specified days;
(d) a requirement that the person wear a tracking device;
(e) a prohibition or restriction on the person communicating or associating with specified individuals;
(f) a prohibition or restriction on the person accessing or using specified forms of telecommunication or other technology (including the Internet);
(g) a prohibition or restriction on the person possessing or using specified articles or substances;
(h) a prohibition or restriction on the person carrying out specified activities (including in respect of his or her work or occupation);
(i) a requirement that the person report to specified persons at specified times and places;
(j) a requirement that the person allow himself or herself to be photographed;
(k) a requirement that the person allow impressions of his or her fingerprints to be taken;
(l) a requirement that the person participate in specified counselling or education.

is perhaps a little more specific on the issue of restrictions on communications, expressly allowing a prohibition or restriction on the access or use by a controlled person of forms of telecommunication or other technology, including the internet (compare with section 1(4)(d) of the PTA, which simply allows "a restriction on his or her association or communications with specified persons or with other persons generally"). Unique to the control orders regime in Australia, a controlled person may be required to "participate in specified counselling or education" (section 104.5(3) (l)). Section 104.27 of the Criminal Code makes it an offence, imprisonable by up to 5 years, for a person subject to a control order to contravene the order.

18.2 The Making of Control Orders and the Right to a Fair Hearing

The sensitive nature of information upon which control orders may be based, and the provisions in the UK and Australia for the protection of such information, expose a common tension between procedural aspects of counter-terrorism law and the right to a fair hearing: a tension between the protection of information which might be prejudicial to national security versus the right of all persons to a fair hearing. As observed by the House of Lords in 2004:[7]

> The problem of reconciling an individual defendant's right to a fair trial with such secrecy as is necessary in a democratic society in the interests of national security or the prevention or investigation of crime is inevitably difficult to resolve in a liberal society governed by the rule of law.

It might be noted, at this point, that the non-disclosure of classified information is not unique to Australia and the United Kingdom.[8] New Zealand provides for the 'protection' of such information in its law on the designation of terrorist entities (see Chap. 19, Sect. 19.3.2). In Canada, Part 3 of the Anti-terrorism Act 2001 amended the Canada Evidence Act 1985 to protect the disclosure of information in legal proceedings which would encroach upon a public interest or be injurious to international relations or national defence or security (section 38.13 of the Canada Evidence Act).[9]

Two aspects of the right to a fair hearing are engaged and examined in this part of the chapter: (1) the open administration of justice; and (2) the right to disclosure

---

[7]*R v H* [2004] UKHL 3, para 23. See also Palmer (2004, pp. 390–396), and Starmer (2007, p. 126).

[8]Concerning Australia's National Security Information Act 2004, see Donaghue (2007).

[9]See, in this regard, *Doe v Canada* [2003] FC 1014, and *Canada (Attorney General) v Khawaja* [2008] FC 560; and Human Rights Committee, Concluding Observations: Canada, UN Doc CCPR/C/CAN/CO/5 (2006), para 13. On the operation of section 38.13 of the Canada Evidence Act 1985, see Fifth Report of the Government of Canada on the implementation of Security Council resolution 1373 (2001), UN Doc S/2006/185 (2006), pp. 8–10.

of information. The right to a fair hearing also involves the right to be heard by and independent and impartial tribunal. The constitutionality of the involvement of judicial officers in closed control order hearings is a matter which has been considered by the High Court of Australia and is also relevant to the question of investigative hearings (see Chap. 16, Sect. 16.3.2).

18.2.1   Open Administration of Justice

One of the central pillars of a fair trial under article 14 of the International Covenant on Civil and Political Rights (ICCPR) is the open administration of justice, important to ensure the transparency of proceedings and thus providing an important safeguard for the interest of the individual and of society at large.[10] The same guarantee is provided under article 6(1) of the European Convention on Human Rights (ECHR).[11] While article 14(1) of the ICCPR (and article 6(1) of the ECHR) permits exclusion of the press and public for reasons of national security, this must occur only "to the extent strictly necessary in the opinion of the court in special circumstances where publicity would prejudice the interests of justice".[12]

Should the public and press be excluded from hearings concerning the making, revision or revocation of control orders, it is conceivable that the latter condition will justify a closed or restricted hearing of the matter. As confirmed by the UN Special Rapporteur on the promotion and protection of human rights and fundamental freedoms while counter-terrorism terrorism, it will be important that this is limited to the extent strictly necessary and should be accompanied by adequate mechanisms for observation or review to guarantee the fairness of the hearing.[13] Compliance with these aspects will partly depend upon the particular circumstances of each case, although it can at least be said that appeals on questions of law are

---

[10]International Covenant on Civil and Political Rights, opened for signature 16 December 1966, 999 UNTS 171 (entered into force 23 March 1976). See General Comment 32: Article 14: Right to equality before courts and tribunals and to a fair trial, UN Doc CCPR/C/GC/32 (2007), para 67.

[11]Convention for the Protection of Human Rights and Fundamental Freedoms, opened for signature 4 November 1950, 213 UNTS 222 (entered into force 3 September 1953).

[12]See further Office of the High Commissioner for Human Rights, Human Rights in the Administration of Justice: A Manual on Human Rights for Judges, Prosecutors and Lawyers (New York and Geneva, 2003), pp. 262–265.

[13]Report of the Special Rapporteur on the promotion and protection of human rights and fundamental freedoms while countering terrorism, Protection of human rights and fundamental freedoms while countering terrorism, UN Doc A/63/223 (2008), paras 30 and 44(c). See also the report of the Sub-Commission Rapporteur on terrorism and human rights, Specific Human Rights Issues: New Priorities, in Particular Terrorism and Counter-Terrorism: An updated framework draft of principles and guidelines concerning human rights and terrorism, UN Doc A/HRC/Sub.1/58/30 (2006) para 45.

permissible in the case of control orders under both Australian and UK law. Closed investigative hearings can also take place in Canada, under section 82.28 of the Criminal Code, a subject considered in Chap. 16 (Sect. 16.3.3).

18.2.2 Right to Disclosure of Information

In general terms, the right to disclosure of information (upon which a case by the State is brought against an individual) arises from two provisions in the ICCPR and ECHR. The first set of provisions is not directly applicable to control orders, since they involve criminal rather than civil proceedings, i.e. the right, in the determination of any criminal charge against a person, to have adequate time and facilities for the preparation of one's defence (article 14(3)(b) of the ICCPR and article 6(3)(b) of the ECHR). The general right to a 'fair hearing' in article 14(1) of the ICCPR and article 6(1) of the ECHR is, however, applicable to both criminal proceedings and the determination of "civil rights and obligations" (in the words of the ECHR – referred to in the ICCPR as "rights and obligations in a suit at law").

The UK Home Secretary has accepted that hearings under section 3(10) of the PTA for the confirmation of control orders fall within this civil limb of the right to a fair hearing.[14] Although it has been argued that control orders involve proceedings which are criminal in nature,[15] an argument ultimately rejected by the House of Lords,[16] the distinction may not be important to the question of disclosure of information in those proceedings. Jurisprudence of the European Court has recognised the difficulty in some contexts of distinguishing between disciplinary and criminal proceedings and even between civil and criminal proceedings.[17] In the United Kingdom, however, judges have regarded the classification of proceedings as criminal or civil as less important than the question of what protections are required for a 'fair' hearing and have held that the gravity and complexity of the case will impact on what fairness requires.[18]

---

[14]*Secretary of State for the Home Department v MB and AF* [2007] UKHL 46, para 15.

[15]*Secretary of State v MB and AF* (ibid) para 15.

[16]*Secretary of State v MB and AF* (ibid) para 48.

[17]*Engel v The Netherlands (No 1)* (1976) 1 EHRR 647, para 82; *Campbell and Fell v United Kingdom* (1984) 7 EHRR 165, paras 70–71; *Albert and Le Compte v Belgium* (1983) 5 EHRR 533, para 30. See Conte and Burchill (2009, pp. 158–160), regarding the same difficulty in the jurisprudence of the Human Rights Committee.

[18]*International Transport Roth GmbH v Secretary of State for the Home Department* [2002] EWCA Civ 158, [2003] QB 728, paras 33, 148; *R v Securities and Futures Authority Ltd, Ex p Fleurose* [2001] EWCA Civ 2015, [2002] IRLR 297, para 14; and *Secretary of State for the Home Department v AF and another* [2009] UKHL 28, para 57.

This more general right to a 'fair hearing' includes the principle of 'equality of arms',[19] requiring the enjoyment of the same procedural rights by all the parties to civil and criminal proceedings unless distinctions are based on law and can be justified on objective and reasonable grounds, not entailing actual disadvantage or other unfairness to the defendant.[20] The latter qualification is particularly important to note. As recognised by the UN Special Rapporteur, this principle is fundamental to safeguarding a fair trial and may engage various particular aspects, including access to evidence.[21] The right to disclosure of information and the consequent ability of a person to respond to the case made against him or her is also a feature of the common law principle of natural justice.[22] Members of the Human Rights Committee have expressed that the principle of *audi alteram partem* (literally meaning "hear the other side") forms part of the right to a fair hearing under the ICCPR.[23] The House of Lords has accepted that both civil and criminal proceedings entail a right to disclosure of relevant evidence.[24] The same position has been taken by the Supreme Court of Canada and the US Supreme Court.[25]

This feature of the right to a fair hearing, and its application to the making of control orders, has been the subject of consideration by the House of Lords.[26] The first of these cases, *Secretary of State for the Home Department v MB and AF*, concerned the making of non-derogating control orders against MB, who was suspected of intending to return to Iraq to fight coalition forces, and AF, who was thought to be linked with Islamic extremists.[27] The control order against MB had been challenged in the High Court, which declared section 3 of the Prevention of Terrorism Act incompatible with MB's right to a fair hearing under article 6(1) of

---

[19]This is a term used by both the United Nations Human Rights Committee and the European Court of Human Rights to represent the idea of the procedural equality of parties. See, for example, Wasek-Wiaderek (2000).

[20]See General Comment 32 (n 10) para 13. See also: report of the Special Rapporteur on fair hearing (n 13) para 35; Cameron (2009, pp. 6–8); *Jansen-Gielen v The Netherlands*, Human Rights Committee Communication 846/1999, para 8.2; and Conte and Burchill (2009, pp. 163–164).

[21]Report of the Special Rapporteur on fair hearing (n 13) para 35.

[22]See, for example: *Kanda v Government of the Federation of Malaya* [1962] AC 322, p. 337 (Lord Denning, in the Privy Council); and *Ridge v Baldwin* [1964] AC 40, pp. 113–114. See also Harlow (2006, pp. 204–207); and Parliament of Australia Department of Library Services, Research Paper: Anti-terrorism control orders in Australia and the United Kingdom: a comparison (2008), p. 23.

[23]*Hermoza v Peru*, Human Rights Committee Communication 203/1986, para 4.

[24]See, for example, *R (Roberts) v Parole Board* [2005] 2 AC 738, para 17.

[25]*Charkaoui v Minister of Citizenship and Immigration* [2007] 1 SCR 350, para 53; *Hamdi v Rumsfeld* 542 US 507 (2004), p. 533. See also Salgado (1988) for an analysis of the Classified Information Procedures Act 1980 (US).

[26]For an overview of the judicial review proceedings in the United Kingdom up to, but not including, the House of Lords, see Walker (2007, pp. 1447–1454).

[27]*Secretary of State v MB and AF* (n 14).

the ECHR.[28] Because a declaration of incompatibility cannot invalidate the effect of legislation, however, the control order was maintained (on the making and effect of declarations of incompatibility, see Chap. 11 at Sect. 11.2.3.1). The Court of Appeal set aside the declaration on appeal.[29] In the case of AF, the court quashed the control order following a full hearing under section 3(10) of the PTA. The court did so based on the right to liberty (see Sect. 18.3.1 below), but determined that the procedures provided for by section 3 of the PTA and the Part 76 of the Civil Procedure Rules were compatible with the right to a fair hearing, even in circumstances where they resulted in the case made against AF being in its essence entirely undisclosed to him and with no specific allegation of terrorism-related activity being contained in open material.[30] Since MB also complained that the control order made against him relied heavily on undisclosed material, both MB and AF appealed to the House of Lords.

While accepting that the right to a fair hearing is applicable to control order proceedings, and that the disclosure of information is a constituent element of that right, the position of the Home Secretary in *MB and AF* was that this was not absolute. As recognised by the European Court of Human Rights:[31]

...the entitlement to disclosure of relevant evidence is not an absolute right. In any criminal proceedings, there may be competing interests, such as national security or the need to protect witnesses at risk of reprisals or keep secret police methods of investigation of crime, which must be weighed against the rights of the accused. In some cases it may be necessary to withhold certain evidence from the defence so as to preserve the fundamental rights of another individual or to safeguard an important public interest.

The European Court has nevertheless held that measures restricting the right to disclosure must be strictly necessary and sufficiently counterbalanced by judicial procedures so that, overall, the person still receives a fair hearing.[32] In the case of the control order confirmation hearing for MB, the High Court noted that the basis for the Security Service's confidence that MB would return to Iraq to fight coalition forces was wholly contained within closed material. Without access to that material, Justice Sullivan concluded that "it is difficult to see how, in reality [MB] could make any effective challenge to what is, on the open case before him, no more than a bare assertion".[33] His conclusion is in line with the position of the UN Special Rapporteur, the Council of Europe Commissioner for Human Rights, and the UK

---

[28]*Re MB* [2006] EWHC 1000.

[29]*Secretary of State for the Home Department v MB* [2006] EWCA Civ 1140.

[30]*Secretary of State for the Home Department v AF* [2007] EWHC 651 (Admin).

[31]*Jasper v United Kingdom* (2000) 30 EHRR 441, para 52, and *Fitt v United Kingdom* (2000) 30 EHRR 480, para 45.

[32]Ibid. See also: *Chahal v United Kingdom* (1996) 23 EHRR 413, para 131; and *Al-Nashif v Bulgaria* (2002) 36 EHRR 655, para 97.

[33]*Re MB* (n 28) para 67.

Joint Committee on Human Rights.[34] The Court of Appeal disagreed on this point, however, stating:

> If one accepts, as we do, that reliance on closed material is permissible, this can only be on terms that appropriate safeguards against the prejudice that this may cause to the controlled person are in place. We consider that the provisions of the [2005 Act] for the use of a special advocate, and of the rules of court made pursuant to paragraph 4 of the Schedule to the [Act], constitute appropriate safeguards...

On appeal to the House of Lords, the Court of Appeal's decision was overturned. Lord Bingham distinguished MB's position from that of the controlled person in *Secretary of State v E*, in which the order could be justified on the strength of the open material.[35] Nor was MB in a position, he concluded, where the thrust of the case was effectively conveyed to MB by way of summary, redacted documents or anonymised statements. It was instead a case in which MB was confronted by an unsubstantiated assertion by the Security Services which he could do no more than deny. Lord Bingham thus concluded that he could not accept that MB had enjoyed "a substantial measure of procedural justice, or that the very essence of the right to a fair hearing has not been impaired".[36]

The same conclusion had been drawn by Justice Ouseley in quashing the control order against AF. The judge had accepted that no clear or significant allegations of involvement in terrorist-related activity were disclosed by the open material in the control order proceedings against AF, that no such allegations had been gisted, and that the case made by the Home Secretary was in its essence entirely undisclosed to AF.[37] In the House of Lords, Lord Bingham agreed and found that AF's right to a fair hearing had also been violated.[38] Dissenting, Lord Hoffmann took a different view. He considered that the use of closed material, coupled with the protection afforded by special advocates, achieved a sufficient safeguard for the purpose of guaranteeing a fair hearing (on special advocates, see below).[39] The remaining three members of the House of Lords Committee reached conclusions which fell between those of Lord Bingham and Lord Hoffmann. They expressed the view that in some cases it would be possible for the controlled person, with the assistance of the special advocate, to have a fair trial notwithstanding the admission of closed material, and that in others it would not. They took the issue of fair hearing to be fact specific and concluded that the trial judge was best placed to resolve it. Both cases were therefore remitted to the Administrative Court for reconsideration.

---

[34]Report of the Special Rapporteur on Australia (n 1) para 39; Report by Mr Alvaro Gil-Robles, Commissioner for Human Rights, On his Visit to the United Kingdom 4th – 12th November 2004, COE Doc CommDH(2005)6, para 21; and Joint Committee on Human Rights – Twelfth Report of Session 2005–2006, HL Paper 122, HC 915, para 76.

[35]*Secretary of State for the Home Department v E* [2007] UKHL 47.

[36]*Secretary of State v MB and AF* (n 14) para 41.

[37]*Secretary of State v AF* (n 30) para 146.

[38]*Secretary of State v MB and AF* (n 14) para 43.

[39]*Secretary of State v MB and AF* (n 14) para 55.

At the conclusion of the House of Lords hearings, the Home Secretary stated that the Government would vigorously contest each control order. The Home Secretary subsequently decided to seek revocation of the control order against AF, stating that he did not want to release evidence which would put the Government's secret intelligence sources at risk.[40] This may signal that the remaining 20 or so control orders in the United Kingdom may also be revoked. The implications of this for the future of control orders will need to be seen, although the Home Secretary announced in September 2009 that the continuance of control orders was intended.[41]

18.2.3   The Use of Special Advocates

On a further appeal by AF and two other controlled persons, the House of Lords reflected on the issue once more in 2009, having particular regard to the use of special advocates.[42] A little over a week before the House of Lords hearing, the Grand Chamber of the European Court of Human Rights addressed the extent to which the admission of closed evidence is compatible with the right to a fair hearing in the context of proceedings to determine the lawfulness of one's arrest or detention (article 5(4) of the ECHR).[43] The European Court established that a minimum requirement of procedural fairness was that a person had to be given the opportunity effectively to challenge the allegations against him or her. This didn't avoid the conclusion of the House of Lords in *MB and AF* that the issue of a fair hearing is fact specific, but the Grand Chamber's decision was relied upon by the appellants in the 2009 appeal before the House. The appellants contended that, even with the assistance of special advocates, there could be no fair hearing because special advocates are prevented from taking instructions once they have been provided with access to the Crown's closed material. Where there was a closed hearing, they said, the special advocate could not effectively challenge the allegations unless sufficient information was provided to the client to enable him or her to give proper instructions to the advocate.

---

[40]Control Orders Quarterly Update: Written ministerial statement by Alan Johnson (Home Secretary), 10 September 2009, p. 1. See also: BBC News, 'Minister frees control order man', 7 September 2009, online: http://news.bbc.co.uk/2/hi/uk_news/8240997.stm; and BBC News, 'Control order suspect is released', 24 September 2009, online: http://news.bbc.co.uk/2/hi/uk_news/8272621.stm.

[41]Control Orders Quarterly Update (ibid), p. 2. It appears that the United Kingdom Independent Reviewer of terrorism laws, Lord Carlile, will give consideration to this issue: see BBC News, 'Review of control orders sought', 16 September 2009 online: http://newsvote.bbc.co.uk/mpapps/pagetools/print/news.bbc.co.uk/2/hi/uk_news/8258644.stm?ad=1.

[42]*Secretary of State v AF and another* (n 18).

[43]*A and others v United Kingdom* [2008] ECHR 113.

Use by the United Kingdom of special advocates in proceedings before the Special Immigration Appeals Commission (SIAC) in counter-terrorism legislation was first made in respect of the indefinite detention regime under Part 4 of the Anti-terrorism, Crime and Security Act 2001 (on that subject, see Chap. 16, Sect. 16.3). Section 21 of that Act had allowed the Home Secretary to certify a foreign national as a 'suspected international terrorist'. An appeal against certification as a suspected international terrorist lay to the SIAC, which continues to exists and is able to receive material in closed hearings at which the subject of the proceedings is represented by a 'special advocate'. Special advocates are legal counsel who have received sufficient clearance in order to allow them to view sensitive information which would otherwise be closed or redacted. As already indicated, while special advocates are able to consult freely with the person who is the subject of the proceedings prior to gaining access to closed material, no further consultations can occur once the advocate has viewed the material.

This model was adapted by the United Kingdom from the similar mechanism used by Canada's Special Intelligence Review Committee (SIRC). Under that process, a Federal Court judge holds an in-camera hearing of all the evidence, at which the non-State party is provided with a statement summarising, as far as possible, the case against him or her and has the right to be represented and to call evidence. The confidentiality of security material is maintained by requiring such evidence to be examined in the absence of both the party and his or her representative. Where a closed hearing of this kind occurs, the place of the party and legal counsel is taken by a security-cleared counsel instructed by the court, who cross-examines the witnesses and generally assists the court to test the strength of the State's case. A summary of the evidence obtained by this procedure, with necessary deletions, is then given to the party. The Supreme Court of Canada has taken the view, which it has subsequently confirmed in a number of decisions, that the SIRC procedures meet the requirements of fundamental justice under the Canadian Charter of Rights and Freedoms (on the requirements of fundamental justice under the Charter see Chap. 11 at Sect. 11.5.3).[44] The SIRC procedures were also favourably referred to in the 1996 decision of the European Court of Human Rights in *Chahal v United Kingdom*.[45]

The use of special advocates has been recognised in England as capable of helping enhance the measure of procedural justice available in cases involving the use of classified and sensitive information, although English courts have also noted their limitations.[46] As observed by Lord Woolf in *R (Roberts) v Parole Board*, a special advocate can never be "a panacea for the grave disadvantages of a person affected not being aware of the case against him".[47] The same reservation has been

---

[44]*Canada (Minister of Employment and Immigration) v Chiarelli* [1992] 1 SCR 711.

[45]*Chahal v United Kingdom* (n 32) para 131.

[46]See, for example: *M v Secretary of State for the Home Department* [2004] EWCA Civ 324, para 34; and *Secretary of State v MB and AF* (n 14) para 35.

[47]*R (Roberts) v Parole Board* (n 24) para 60.

expressed by the UN Special Rapportuer.[48] Some observations about the functioning of special advocates in the United Kingdom had also been made in the 2007 decision of the House of Lords in *MB and AF*. Lord Brown took the view that although the special advocate procedure is highly likely to sufficiently safeguard a person against significant injustice, the procedure cannot invariably be guaranteed to do so. Despite the best efforts of all concerned by way of redaction, anonymisation, and gisting, he feared that there could still be rare cases where it would be impossible to indicate sufficient aspects of the Home Secretary's case to enable the suspect to advance any effective challenge to it. Albeit rare, Lord Brown observed that the making or confirmation of a control order in such circumstances "would indeed involve significant injustice to the suspect".[49]

In *A v United Kingdom*, the European Court of Human Rights concluded:[50]

> ...the special advocate could perform an important role in counterbalancing the lack of full disclosure and the lack of a full, open, adversarial hearing by testing the evidence and putting arguments on behalf of the detainee during the closed hearings. However, the special advocate could not perform this function in any useful way unless the detainee was provided with sufficient information about the allegations against him to enable him to give effective instructions to the special advocate.

The court distinguished between three situations. In the first, it took an approach consistent with that of Lord Bingham in *MB and AF* that where the evidence is to a large extent disclosed and this open material played the predominant role in the determination, the opportunity effectively to challenge the reasonableness of the Home Secretary's belief will be available. It also accepted that there will be cases where, notwithstanding that most or all of the underlying evidence remains undisclosed, it will be possible for the person to provide his or her representatives and the special advocate with sufficient instructions if the allegations contained in the open material are sufficiently specific, i.e. even without knowing the detail or sources of the evidence which formed the basis of the allegations, the thrust of the case is effectively conveyed through the open information which is made available. Where, however, the open material consists purely of general assertions and the determination is based solely or to a decisive degree on closed material, the procedural requirements of a fair hearing will not be satisfied, even with the use of special advocates.

The decision of the court at Strasbourg on the latter point makes sense from a policy perspective, but may not always be accurate from a practical one. It is conceivable that, even where a person is faced with general assertions, the instructions taken by the special advocate prior to seeing the closed material are sufficient for the advocate to then respond to the essence of the allegations in the closed hearing. The difficulty is that one can never be sure this is the case. Despite all best efforts, can the special advocate ever be sure he or she has all the relevant

---

[48]Special Rapporteur report on fair hearing (n 13) para 41.

[49]*Secretary of State v MB and AF* (n 14) para 90.

[50]*A v United Kingdom* (n 43) para 220.

information from the person capable of fully responding to the allegation? Answering this is impossible, since the person will be instructing the special advocate 'blind'. The conclusion of the court at Strasbourg was accepted as correct by the majority of the House of Lords in *Secretary of State for the Home Department v AF and another*.[51] The majority therefore concluded that each case before it fell within the third situation described by the European Court and remitted them for further consideration in accordance with the decision of the House of Lords.

While accepting this, Trechel asks whether the use of special counsel could be improved, perhaps even to the extent of rendering fair an otherwise unfair trial. He posits that this might be the case if there is an increased level of involvement of the defence in the appointment of special counsel, and/or if there is an extended level of interaction between special counsel and defence counsel following the disclosure of closed material to special counsel.[52] Waldam doubts that this would be sufficient, and observes that legislative amendments to this effect would be unlikely and strongly contested by security services who would fear that special counsel might either deliberately or unknowingly disclose prejudicial information.[53]

18.2.4 Resulting Principles on the Right to a Fair Hearing

A number of general principles may be drawn from the discussions above concerning control order proceedings and the right to a fair hearing:

- Although one of the central pillars of the right to a fair hearing is the open administration of justice, the press and public may be excluded from a hearing for reasons of national security, although this must be limited to the extent strictly necessary in the opinion of the court in special circumstances where publicity would prejudice the interests of justice. This should be accompanied by adequate mechanisms for observation or review to guarantee the fairness of the hearing.
- While it has been argued that control orders involve proceedings which are criminal in nature, rather than civil, this distinction is not important to the question of disclosure of information in control order proceedings, or similar 'administrative' proceedings used in the context of combating terrorism. More important is the question of what protections are required to guarantee that a person receives a 'fair' hearing. The gravity and complexity of the case will impact on what fairness requires.
- It has been accepted that the right to a fair hearing is applicable to control order proceedings, and that the disclosure of information is a constituent element

---

[51] *Secretary of State v AF and another* (n 18) para 59 (Lord Hoffman dissenting).

[52] Treschel (2009).

[53] Treschel (2009) – intervention by Waldam, Lorne, Barrister and Solicitor, Lorne Waldam & Associates, Canada.

of that right in such proceedings. While it may be necessary in some cases to withhold information from a defendant or respondent so as to preserve an important public interest such a national security, measures restricting the right to disclosure must be strictly necessary and sufficiently counterbalanced by judicial procedures so that, overall, the person still receives a fair hearing. Whether a person has enjoyed a fair hearing will always be fact specific. One must here distinguish between three situations. The first, which will be unproblematic, is where a control order is sought largely or completely on the basis of open material so that the controlled person may answer the case against him or her. The second, which will require a careful approach to ensure that the essence of the right to a fair hearing is guaranteed, is where much of the material is closed but where the open material (or a redacted summary of the closed material) effectively conveys the thrust of the case against the person. The third and final situation, which will result in a violation of the right to a fair hearing, is where reliance on closed material is so great that the person is confronted by an unsubstantiated assertion which he or she can do no more than deny.

- Concerning the use of special advocates, the question is whether their use can transform a case which falls within the third category just described into one which is nevertheless compatible with the right to a fair hearing. Can a case which relies on closed evidence, to the extent that the respondent is confronted with a bare assertion which can only be denied, be compatible with the minimum requirement of procedural fairness (to be given the opportunity effectively to challenge the allegations) by allowing a closed hearing in which the interests of the respondent are represented by a special advocate? In particular, is this possible in light of the restrictions placed on special advocates preventing them from taking instructions once they have been provided with access to closed material? The European Court of Human Rights and the House of Lords have concluded that the use of special advocates does not render an otherwise unfair hearing compatible with the ECHR. The respondent in control order proceedings must be provided with sufficient information about the allegations to guarantee that he or she is able to give effective instructions to the special advocate.

This conclusion does not make the role of the special advocate redundant. The special advocate will play an important role during the closed hearing where the open material effectively conveys the thrust of the case against the person. His or her role will be particularly important in testing the evidence and its confidential sources. This will be relevant to whether the information should be treated as prejudicial to national security, i.e. whether the information should be closed or made openly available, and to the question of whether the information may be relied upon as admissible evidence. On the latter question, the UN Special Rapporteur has observed that methods of interrogation violating the prohibition on torture or other forms of cruel or inhuman treatment (reflected within articles 7 and 10 of the ICCPR, article 3 of the ECHR, and the Convention against Torture, and the *jus cogens* norm of customary international law to that effect which is binding on State *erga omnes*) are often used.[54] He has expressed great concern over the growing tendency to resort to such methods in the investigation of terrorist incidents, or during counter-terrorism intelligence operations more generally.[55]

When dealing with classified information, which may originate from various sources within or outside the country, the need to test the sources of evidence is therefore heightened. Especially relevant in this regard is the obligation of States, under article 15 of the Convention against Torture, to ensure that any statement which is established to have been made as a result of torture must not be used as evidence in any proceedings, except against a person accused of torture as evidence that the statement was made.[56] In *A (No 2) v Secretary of State for the Home Department*, Lord Bingham concluded that the exclusionary rule under article 15 assumed effect within the United Kingdom, in relation to proceedings before national courts.[57] As this applies to proceedings before the Special Immigration Appeals Authority, he stated that SIAC "should throughout be guided by recognition of the important obligation laid down in articles 3 and 5(4) of the European Convention and, through them, article 15 of the Torture Convention".

18.3 The Terms of Control Orders and Their Impact on the Enjoyment of Human Rights

Given the context in which the tool of control orders arose (following the declaration by the House of Lords that indefinite detention is incompatible with the ECHR), it is not surprising that control orders have implications for the enjoyment of liberty rights. The wide range of obligations and restrictions that may be imposed under control orders may also impact on other rights and freedoms.

---

[54]Special Rapporteur report on fair hearing (n 13) para 31. See also Convention against Torture and other Cruel, Inhuman or Degrading Treatment or Punishment, opened for signature 10 December 1984, 1465 UNTS 112 (entered into force 26 June 1987); and, in the context of the prohibition under the ICCPR, see General Comment 32 (n 10) para 41. On the application of the *jus cogens* prohibition under customary international law, see *Mohamed v Secretary of State for Foreign and Commonwealth Affairs* [2008] EWHC 2048 (Admin), para 162. See also CIA Office of Inspector General's May 2004 Counterterrorism Detention and Interrogation Activities Report and Supporting Documents – Documents Responsive to 2004 Torture FOIA (8/24/2009), available online from the American Civil Liberties Union: http://www.aclu.org/safefree/torture/40832res20090824.html.

[55]Special Rapporteur report on fair hearing (n 13) para 31. See also Report of the Special Rapporteur on the promotion and protection of human rights and fundamental freedoms while countering terrorism, Mission to the United States of America, UN Doc A/HRCA/6/17/Add.3 (2007), chapter IV.

[56]See also the Special Rapporteur report on fair hearing (n 13) para 32.

[57]*A (No 2) v Secretary of State for the Home Department* [2005] UKHL 71, para 56. Compare with Lord Hope (para 112) and Lord Carswell (para 151).

18.3.1   The Right to Liberty

In the normal manner of speaking, a person is taken to be deprived of his or her liberty when locked up in a prison cell or its equivalent. It has come to be accepted, however, that deprivation of liberty may take numerous forms other than classic detention in prison or strict arrest.[58] In a study of Australia's counter-terrorism legislation by the UN Special Rapporteur on the promotion of human rights and fundamental freedoms while countering terrorism, the Special Rapportuer stated that the imposition of obligations upon a person subject to a control order must not cumulate so as to be tantamount to detention.[59] He urged Australia to ensure that control orders impose obligations that are necessary and proportionate, and expressed the view that continuous house arrest (a 24-hour restriction to be in certain premises), which constitutes a form of detention, will only permissible during the course of a criminal investigation, while awaiting trial, during trial, or as an alternative to a custodial sentence.[60] The UK's independent reviewer of counter-terrorism laws, Lord Carlile, has himself acknowledged that 24-hour house arrest would require a derogation from the right to liberty.[61] In three decisions made in October 2007 concerning control orders made under the Prevention of Terrorism Act (UK), the House of Lords took a similar approach, although it was not faced with house arrest, but instead with curfews imposed on the controlled persons.[62]

In the first of these cases, *Secretary of State for the Home Department v JJ and others*, it was held by the High Court, and upheld by the Court of Appeal, that the obligations imposed on the respondents in the control orders made against them deprived the respondents of their liberty in breach of article 5 of the European Convention on Human Rights, and that the control orders should therefore be

---

[58]See, for example, *Guzzardi v Italy* (1980) 3 EHRR 533, para 95.

[59]Special Rapporteur report on Australia (n 1) para 37.

[60]Special Rapporteur report on Australia (n 1) para 71. For jurisprudence of the Human Rights Committee, see, for example: See: *Jaona v Madagascar*, Communication 132/1982, UN Doc CCPR/C/24/132/1982 (1985), paras 13–14; *Gorji-Dinka v Cameroon*, Communication 1134/2002, UN Doc CCPR/C/83/D/1134/2002 (2005), para 5.4; *Abbassi v Algeria*, Communication 1172/2003, UN Doc CCPR/C/89/D/1172/2003 (2007), para 8.3. For jurisprudence of the European Court of Human Rights, see, for example: *Mancini v Italy* (App 44955/98, 12 December 2001), para 17; *Vachev v Bulgaria* (App 42987/98, 8 October 2004), para 64; *NC v Italy* (App 24952/94, 11 January 2001), para 33; *Nikolova v Bulgaria (No 2)* (App 40896/98, 30 December 2004), para 60.

[61]First Report of the Independent Reviewer pursuant to section 14(3) of the Prevention of Terrorism Act 2005, February 2006, para 31.

[62]*Secretary of State v MB and AF* (n 14); *Secretary of State for the Home Department v JJ and others* [2007] UKHL 45; and *Secretary of State for the Home Department v E and another* [2007] UKHL 47.

quashed.[63] Accepting that deprivation of liberty may take numerous forms other than classic detention in prison or strict arrest, Lord Bingham in the House of Lords spoke of the need to consider the concrete situation of the particular individual so as to assess the impact of the measures under the control orders in the situation of each person subject to them.[64] Following the approach of the court at Strasbourg, account should be taken of a whole range of factors such as the nature, duration, effects and manner of execution or implementation of the measures in question.[65]

The general effect of the obligations imposed upon the controlled persons was described by the Court of Appeal as essentially identical, and summarised by that Court as follows:

> Each respondent is required to remain within his 'residence' at all times, save for a period of six hours between 10 am and 4 pm. In the case of GG the specified residence is a one-bedroom flat provided by the local authority in which he lived before his detention. In the case of the other five respondents the specified residences are one-bedroom flats provided by the National Asylum Support Service. During the curfew period the respondents are confined in their small flats and are not even allowed into the common parts of the buildings in which these flats are situated. Visitors must be authorised by the Home Office, to which name, address, date of birth and photographic identity must be supplied. The residences are subject to spot searches by the police. During the six hours when they are permitted to leave their residences, the respondents are confined to restricted urban areas, the largest of which is 72 square kilometres. These deliberately do not extend, save in the case of GG, to any area in which they lived before. Each area contains a mosque, a hospital, primary health care facilities, shops and entertainment and sporting facilities. The respondents are prohibited from meeting anyone by pre-arrangement who has not been given the same Home Office clearance as a visitor to the residence.

The controlled persons were also required to wear an electronic tag and to report to a monitoring company on first leaving their flat after a curfew period and on returning to it before a curfew period. They were forbidden to use or possess any communications equipment of any kind, apart from one fixed telephone line in their flat maintained by the monitoring company. They could attend a mosque of their choice if it was within their permitted area and approved in advance by the Home Office. In the High Court, Justice Sullivan took as his starting point the confinement of the controlled persons for 18 hours of each day of the week in a small flat. He noted that the controlled persons were all single men and accepted that the requirements incumbent on persons wishing to obtain Home Office approval to visit the men "deterred all but the most determined and courageous of visitors".[66]

---

[63] *Secretary of State for the Home Department v JJ, KK, GG, HH, NN, and LL* [2006] EWHC 1623 (Admin); and *Secretary of State for the Home Department v JJ, KK, GG, HH, NN, and LL* [2006] EWCA Civ 1141.

[64] *Secretary of State v JJ and others* (n 62) para 15 (compare this with the approach of Lord Hoffman at para 36). The House of Lords followed the approach, in this regard, of the European Court of Human Rights in *Engel v The Netherlands (No 1)* (1976) 1 EHRR 647, para 59; *Guzzardi v Italy* (n 58) para 92; and *HL v United Kingdom* (2004) 40 EHRR 761, para 89.

[65] *Engel v The Netherlands* (ibid) para 59; and *Guzzardi v Italy* (n 58) paras 92 and 94.

[66] *Secretary of State v JJ and others*, High Court (n 63) paras 60–62 and 66.

He concluded that the cumulative effect of the obligations had been to deprive the respondents of their liberty in breach of article 5 of the Convention.[67]

On appeal to the Court of Appeal and the House of Lords, the Home Secretary contended that Justice Sullivan had erred in law, including by identifying liberty too broadly. Lord Bingham concluded, as had the Court of Appeal, that there had been no legal error in the reasoning of the trial judge. The majority of the House of Lords upheld the decision that the conditions imposed under the control orders accumulated to a deprivation of liberty, Lord Bingham stating:[68]

> The effect of the 18-hour curfew, coupled with the effective exclusion of social visitors, meant that the controlled persons were in practice in solitary confinement for this lengthy period every day for an indefinite duration, with very little opportunity for contact with the outside world, with means insufficient to permit provision of significant facilities for self-entertainment and with knowledge that their flats were liable to be entered and searched at any time.

What is clear from this first of the three decisions on the impact of control orders on the right to liberty is that: (1) deprivation of liberty may take various forms other than detention in prison or strict arrest, including measures imposed under a control order; (2) in determining whether any given situation amounts to a deprivation of liberty, one must assess the cumulative impact upon the controlled person of the measures imposed, taking into account the full range of factors, including the nature, duration, effects and manner of execution or implementation of the measures; and (3) an 18-hour curfew, coupled with other factors, can (and in *JJ and others* did) amount to a breach of the right to liberty.

The first two points were reiterated by the House of Lords in *Secretary of State v E and another* and *Secretary of State v MB and AF*. The question remaining is whether there is a threshold over which the length of a curfew which would give rise to a presumption against compliance with the right to liberty. While any determination would have to be based on an assessment of the full range of applicable factors, is there a generally acceptable limit for the length of a curfew under a control order? In his first report reviewing the Prevention of Terrorism Act, Lord Carlile hinted that a curfew of 18 hours went too far, and this was borne out in *JJ and others*.[69] In that case, Lord Brown expressed the obiter view that a 16-hour curfew would be acceptable.[70]

In *Secretary of State v E and another*, the control order made against E was challenged on two grounds. First, that the conditions of the order amounted to a violation of his right to liberty.[71] And, second, that a control order should not have

---

[67]Ibid, para 73.

[68]*Secretary of State v JJ and others*, House of Lords (n 62) para 24.

[69]Report of Lord Carlile (n 61) para 43.

[70]*Secretary of State v JJ and others*, House of Lords (n 62) para 105.

[71]The obligations imposed on E by the control order contained obligations similar to those noted in *JJ and others*. E was required to wear an electronic tag; to reside at a specified address; to report to a monitoring company each day on first leaving his residence and on his last return to it;

been made against E, since the Crown could have instead brought a prosecution against E and should have done so (this second issue is considered below, at Sect. 18.4.2). These contentions succeeded in the first instance (a confirmation hearing under section 3(10) of the Prevention of Terrorism Act) and the control order was quashed.[72] The Court of Appeal reversed that decision.[73] Although the conditions imposed by the control order made against E were similar to those noted in JJ and others, E was subject to a curfew of 12 hours (from 7:00 p.m. to 7:00 a.m.), rather than 18 hours, and was able to enjoy some measure of a family and social life.[74] In the High Court, Beatson J had been influenced by the fact that there was the same level of control over visitors to the home and meetings outside the home, and the same liability to spot checks and searches by the police at any time. It was these features which, in his view, made the obligations particularly intense, as if E were accommodated in prison.[75] The judge recognised that E's position was more finely balanced than in the *JJ* cases, but concluded that the cumulative effect of the restrictions was to deprive E of his liberty.[76]

In contrast, the Court of Appeal treated physical liberty as the starting point and the central issue, and judged that the degree of physical restraint on E's liberty was far from a deprivation of liberty within the meaning of article 5 of the ECHR.[77] The House of Lords agreed. While Lord Bingham conceded that the matters which weighed with the judge in the High Court were not irrelevant, they "could not of themselves effect a deprivation of liberty if the core element of confinement [an overnight curfew of 12 hours]... is insufficiently stringent".[78]

In the third case of *Secretary of State v MB and AF*, the House of Lords had regard to the position taken by Ouseley J in the control order confirmation hearing

---

the permission of the Home Office was required in advance (with name, address, date of birth and photographic evidence of identity supplied) for most visitors to the residence; he had to obtain the agreement of the Home Office in advance to attend most prearranged meetings outside his residence; his residence was liable to be searched by the police at any time; and he was permitted to have no communications equipment of any kind except for one fixed telephone line and one or more computers, provided that any computer was disabled from connecting to the internet.

[72]*Secretary of State v E* (n 35).

[73]*Secretary of State v E and S* [2007] EWCA Civ 459.

[74]The residence specified in the order was his own home, where he had lived for some years, in a part of London with which he is familiar. By a variation of the order his residence was defined to include his garden, to which he thus had access at any time. He lived at his home with his wife and family, and Home Office permission was not required in advance to receive visitors under the age of ten. Five members of his wider family lived in the area, and had been approved as visitors. He was subject to no geographical restriction during non-curfew hours, was free to attend a mosque of his choice, and was not prohibited from associating with named individuals.

[75]*Secretary of State v E* (n 35) para 240.

[76]Ibid, para 242.

[77]*Secretary of State v E and S* (n 73) paras 62–63.

[78]*Secretary of State v E and another* (n 62) para 11. See also Lord Hoffman (para 23) Baroness Hale (para 25) Lord Carswell (para 31) and Lord Brown (para 36).

in *Secretary of State v AF*, i.e. that once a curfew reaches 12 hours a day, any additional restrictions on what can be done during those hours of curfew will likely result in the situation amounting a deprivation of liberty.[79] AF was himself subject to a 14-hour curfew.[80] However, while Justice Ouseley found the cumulative effect of the obligations on AF 'finely balanced' so as to amount to a deprivation of liberty, the House of Lords disagreed and held that the effect of the control order was not to deprive AF of his liberty in breach of article 5 of the ECHR.[81]

In summary, then, a 12-hour curfew (as in the case of AF) has been treated as within the bounds of compliance with the right to liberty. A curfew of 18 hours was, when combined with other factors, treated as going too far by the majority of the House of Lords in *JJ and others*, Lord Brown there suggesting that 16 hours would be an acceptable threshold. Finally, an overnight curfew of 14 hours (in the case of E) was treated as compliant, although the controlled person was there faced with conditions that allowed him to enjoy a family life and some degree of social interaction. While this suggests that Lord Brown might be correct in proposing a

---

[79]*Secretary of State v AF* (n 30) para 78.

[80]Among other obligations, AF was required to remain in the flat where he was already living (not including any communal area) at all times except for a period of 10 hours between 8 a.m. and 6 p.m. He was thus subject to a 14-hour curfew. He was required to wear electronic tag at all times. He was restricted during non-curfew hours to an area of about 9 square miles. He was to report to a monitoring company on first leaving his flat after a curfew period had ended and on his last return before the next curfew period began. His flat was liable to be searched by the police at any time. During curfew hours he was not allowed to permit any person to enter his flat except his father, official or professional visitors, children aged 10 or under or persons agreed by the Home Office in advance on supplying the visitor's name, address, date of birth and photographic identification. He was not to communicate directly or indirectly at any time with a certain specified individual (and, later, several specified individuals). He was only permitted to attend one specified mosque. He was not permitted to have any communications equipment of any kind. He was to surrender his passport. He was prohibited from visiting airports, sea ports or certain railway stations, and was subject to additional obligations pertaining to his financial arrangements.In his judgment on the hearing under section 3(10) of the PTA, Justice Ouseley summarised the evidence given by AF concerning the impact of the order upon him (paras 24–29). He had three times been refused permission to visit his mother. His sister and her family were unwilling to visit because of the traumatic experience of one child when AF was first arrested. Friends were unwilling to visit. He only had one Libyan or Arabic-speaking friend in the area he was allowed to frequent, which was not the area to which he had gravitated before. He was not permitted to attend the mosque he had attended before, and was confined to an Urdu-speaking mosque despite the fact that he could not speak Urdu. He could not visit his Arabic-speaking general practitioner. He could not continue his English studies, since there were no places at the college in his permitted area. He was cut off from the outside world, although, he had television access to Al Jazeera. The judge concluded that the effects of the control order as described were the effects which the restrictions were intended to have (para 54).

[81]*Secretary of State v MB and AF* (n 14) paras 11 (Lord Bingham), 47 (Lord Hoffman), and 78 (Lord Carswell). The House of Lords took the view that, had the trial judge had the benefit of viewing the decision of the Court of Appeal in *Secretary of State v E and S* (n 73), he would have arrived at a different conclusion.

threshold of 16 hours, *E and another* may well have been decided differently if E's curfew was combined with more restrictive conditions on his social interaction. While again recognising that each situation must consider the cumulative impact upon the controlled person of the measures imposed by the control order, it is therefore suggested that a generally acceptable threshold would be one of between 14 and 16 hours (which should include the normal hours of sleep).

18.3.2   The Exercise of Other Human Rights

Evident from the nature of the conditions imposed under the control orders described is the fact that control orders may impact not only on the right to liberty, but also on the exercise of other rights including, for example, the rights to family life, employment and education.[82] Although this was not raised in the appeals before the House of Lords, the UN Special Rapporteur has spoken of the need to ensure that control orders do not "unduly interfere" with such rights.[83] Determining whether or not this is the case will be facts-specific, relying on an application of the principles of necessity and proportionality (see Chap. 10, Sects. 10.2.3 and 10.2.4).

As discussed earlier, one of the unique features of the control orders regime in Australia is that a controlled person may be required to "participate in specified counselling or education" (section 104.5(3)(l) of the Criminal Code Act). While there is no right *not* to participate in counselling or education, it may be observed that such requirements are normally restricted to the sentencing of a convicted person, or a person committed under mental health legislation. The imposition of this condition may therefore sway a court to conclude that, cumulatively with other conditions, the control order amounts to a violation of the right to liberty.

18.4   Control Orders, Standards of Proof, and Criminal Proceedings

The principal focus of this chapter has been on the implications of control orders on the enjoyment of fair trial and liberty rights. Some further features of the control order regimes in the UK and Australia should be noted.

---

[82]As accepted by Lord Hoffman in *Secretary of State v JJ and others*, House of Lords (n 62) para 34. See also a letter of 18 October 2005 from the Australian National University Regulatory Institutions Network to the Chief Minister and Attorney General (on file with author), p. 7.

[83]Special Rapporteur report on Australia (n 1) para 37.

18.4.1 Standards and Burden of Proof

Given the nature of terrorism-related proceedings which fall short of criminal proceedings, and despite the serious consequences that may follow, the Special Rapporteur has also urged States to carefully consider the applicable standards of proof and whether a hybrid of the standards applicable to criminal and civil proceedings should be used. He has expressed concern, for example, that control orders may be imposed on a simple balance of probabilities but may nevertheless impose significant burden on a controlled person.[84]

A matter repeatedly observed in the House of Lords decisions considered above is that one of the two preconditions for the making of a non-derogating control order involves a low threshold, i.e. the Home Secretary must have "reasonable grounds" for suspecting that the individual is or has been involved in terrorism-related activity (section 2(1)(a) of the PTA).[85] This is in contrast to the applicable requirement for a control order which would require derogation from the right to liberty. Section 4(7)(a) requires the court, in confirming a derogating control order, to be satisfied, on the balance of probabilities, that the controlled person *is* an individual who is or has been involved in terrorism-related activity.

The making of a control order under Division 104 of Australia's Criminal Code Act 1995 instead requires that, in the making of any control order, the court be satisfied on the balance of probabilities that: (1) that making the order would substantially assist in preventing a terrorist act; or that the person has provided training to, or received training from, a listed terrorist organisation; and (2) that each of the obligations under the control order "is reasonably necessary, and reasonably appropriate and adapted, for the purpose of protecting the public from a terrorist act" (section 104.4(1)(c) and (d)). Although this is a higher threshold than applicable in the United Kingdom, the Law Council of Australia, amongst others, has criticised the control orders regime as being extremely broad since control orders are based on what the controlled person *might* do in the future, rather than what he or she has done, or is doing.[86] The Law Council thus concluded that control order undermine the right to be presumed innocent until proven guilty according to law.[87]

Combined with the observations made earlier about the preconditions for the making of control orders under section 2(1) of the PTA versus those in section 104.2

---

[84]Special Rapporteur report on fair hearing (n 13) para 42. See also ANU letter to the Attorney General (n 82) p. 9.

[85]See, for example, *Secretary of State v E and another* (n 62) para 5, *Secretary of State v JJ and others* (n 62) para 105, and *Secretary of State v MB and AF* (n 14) para 21.

[86]Law Council of Australia, Anti-Terrorism Reform Project: A consolidation of the Law Council of Australia's advocacy in relation to Australia's anti-terrorism measures, November 2008, online: http://www.lawcouncil.asn.au/initiatives/anti-terrorism_reform.cfm, p. 67. Contrast McDonald (2007).

[87]Ibid, p. 68.

of the Criminal Code (see Sect. 18.1.2 above), the different approaches taken point to a vastly greater authority in the hands of the UK Home Secretary compared to that for Australia's Attorney General. The Home Secretary need only have *reasonable grounds* for *suspecting* that a person is or has been involved in terrorism-*related* activity, together with the belief that a control order is necessary for purposes *connected* with protecting members of the public from a *risk* of terrorism. Australia's Attorney General must instead satisfy a court that, on the *balance of probabilities*, the making of the control order would either *substantially assist* in *preventing* a terrorist act or that the person *has* provided training to, or received training from, a listed terrorist organisation. This already points to much lower thresholds applicable in the United Kingdom. Additionally, however, the Attorney General in Australia must satisfy a court, again on the balance of probabilities, that the control order conditions are *reasonably necessary*, and *reasonably appropriate and adapted*, for the purpose of protecting the public *from a terrorist act*.

This is not simply a question of semantics. In his report on Australia's counter-terrorism law, the UN Special Rapporteur urged Australia to ensure that the imposition of obligations upon the subject of a control order are proportionate, and are only imposed for as long as strictly necessary, particularly having regard to the fact that control orders are issued based upon the non-criminal standard of proof on the balance of probabilities.[88] Guaranteeing that non-derogating control orders in the UK are necessary will be all the more difficult.[89]

One respect in which the control orders regime in the United Kingdom appears better than that in Australia is the fact that, in the UK, the burden of establishing the need for a control order lies with the Home Secretary. In Australia, however, the controlled person bears the onus of proving that the control order should be revoked or modified. Section 104.11 of the Criminal Code requires the person to give notice of the grounds on which revocation is sought. Given the inequality of arms arising from a lack of access to classified information, Byrnes, Charlesworth and McKinnon argue that the onus should not be on the controlled person.[90]

18.4.2 Criminal Proceedings as an Alternative to Control Orders

Section 8 of the Prevention of Terrorism Act 2005 focuses on the reasons that lead the Home Secretary to believe that a person has been involved in terrorism-related activity and effectively asks the Secretary to consider whether the information upon which a control order is based should give rise to a police investigation (section 8 (1)). Three obligations arise in this respect. First, before making or applying for a control order, the Home Secretary must consult with the Chief of Police about

---

[88]Special Rapporteur report on Australia (n 1) para 37. See also Chong et al. (2005, pp. 14–15).
[89]Metcalfe (2005, pp. 14–16).
[90]ANU letter to the Attorney General (n 82) p. 9.

whether there is evidence available that could realistically be used for the purposes of a prosecution of the individual for an offence relating to terrorism (section 8(2)). The Home Secretary must also notify the police whenever a control order is made (section 8(3)) and there is then a corresponding duty on the police to keep under review, throughout the period during which a control order has effect, the investigation of the controlled person's conduct with a view to that person's prosecution for a terrorism-related offence (section 8(4)).

It was accepted in *Secretary of State v E and another* that the fundamental premise of the PTA in general, and section 8 in particular, was that where there are realistic prospects of prosecuting an individual against whom it is proposed to make a control order, he will indeed be prosecuted, thus potentially avoiding the need for a control order to be made (since the individual might be remanded in custody pending trial and, if convicted, following conviction); and avoiding the possibility of a life-long series of extended control orders (by replacing the control order proceedings with criminal ones). In his report on the operation in 2007 of the Terrorism Act 2000 and Part I of the Terrorism Act 2006, Lord Carlile noted that there had been a reduction in the number of control orders in operation, observing that this may be due, at least in part, to the establishment of the offence of preparation of terrorist acts under section 5 of the Terrorism Act 2006. All are agreed, he said, that "it is better that state sanctions should follow conviction of crime, rather than being the result of administrative decisions".[91]

The Court of Appeal in *Secretary of State v MB* took a similar view, as it did in the appeal before it concerning E, describing it as implicit in the scheme of the Act that if there is evidence that justifies the bringing of a criminal charge, a suspect will be prosecuted rather than made the subject of a control order.[92] There had, in fact, been strong ministerial assurances to this effect when the Prevention of Terrorism Bill was debated in Parliament and, before the House of Lords in *E and another*, the Home Secretary accepted that: "The scheme of the [Act] is that control orders should only be made where an individual cannot realistically be prosecuted for a terrorism-related offence".[93] Going further than this, it was argued for E that the absence of a realistic prospect of prosecution is a condition *precedent* to the making by the Secretary of State of a non-derogating control order. It was contended that, unless the Home Secretary first came to believe that it was not feasible to prosecute the proposed controlled person with a reasonable prospect of success, it could not be "necessary" to impose obligations under a control order, since it would not be shown that the public could not be protected by arresting, charging and prosecuting the individual. This argument was rejected by the House of Lords. Construing the Act, it was clear to the House that the conditions precedent to the making of a

---

[91]Report by the Independent Reviewer Lord Carlile of Berriew QC, Report on the Operation in 2007 of the Terrorism Act 2000 and of Part I of the Terrorism Act 2006 (Presented to Parliament pursuant to section 26 of the Terrorism Act 2006, June 2008), para 36.

[92]*Secretary of State v MB* (n 29) para 53; *Secretary of State v E and S* (n 73) para 73.

[93]*Secretary of State v E and another* (n 62) para 14. See also Lord Carlile's report (n 61) para 54.

control order are set out in section 2(1) of the PTA, which do not include consideration of the matters raised by section 8(2).[94] The House also took this to be for good practical reasons. To make a control order, the Home Secretary must believe that there are reasonable grounds for suspecting that the individual concerned is or has been involved in terrorism-related activity (section 2(1)(a)). He must consider that it is necessary, for purposes connected with protecting members of the public from a risk of terrorism, to make a control order imposing obligations on that individual (section 2(1)(b)). As recognised by Lord Bingham, the risk may be very great, and there may be a need to act with urgency:[95]

> It is one thing to require the Secretary of State to consult, as section 8(2) does in cases falling within section 8(1), which is the great majority of cases. But it is quite another to require him to obtain a clear answer: this is something the chief officer of police is unlikely to be in a position to give, he himself being subject to a duty (section 8(5)) to consult the relevant prosecuting authority which will in turn require time to consider the matter, and very probably to seek the advice of counsel. The condition precedent contended for would have the potential to emasculate what is clearly intended to be an effective procedure, and cannot be taken to represent the intention of Parliament.

This is not to say, however, that the question of criminal proceedings as an alternative to control orders is redundant. One must here distinguish between the issue as one *precedent* to the making of a control order, versus a *continued* condition to the maintenance of the order. In its judgment in *MB*,[96] approved by the House of Lords in *E and another*,[97] the Court of Appeal held that the Home Secretary is under two duties. First, to keep the decision to impose a control order under review, so that the restrictions that it imposes, whether on civil rights or Convention rights, are no greater than necessary.[98] Second, implicit from the first duty, to provide the police with material in his possession which is or might be relevant to any reconsideration of prosecution.

The latter is a sensible approach, but one which may not necessarily result in achieving the objective of section 8 of the PTA. As warned by Lord Carlile in his first review of the Act, it remains feasible that the police or prosecution services may determine that there should be no investigation or prosecution on public interest grounds, even if provided with material by the Home Secretary in the way just described.[99] Although Lord Carlile was unaware of any cases where

---

[94]*Secretary of State v E and another* (n 62) para 15.

[95]*Secretary of State v E and another* (n 62) para 16. See also Baroness Hale (para 26) and Lord Carswell (para 32).

[96]*Secretary of State v MB* (n 29) para 44.

[97]*Secretary of State v E and another* (n 62) para 18.

[98]The UN Special Rapporteur on the promotion and protection of human rights and fundamental freedoms made the same point in his consideration of control orders in Australia (n 1) para 38.

[99]Report of Lord Carlile (n 61) para 55.

such a determination had been made, he noted that information from the police was "woefully thin" (as described by Walker) on reasons preventing prosecution.[100] It is just as well, then, that the United Kingdom has the benefit of regular oversight by an Independent Reviewer.

18.4.3 Double Jeopardy

A further issue of concern relating to control orders is the potential for their use contrary to the *ne bis in idem* principle (that a person should not be tried or punished twice for the same offence). It is an offence under section 101.2 of Australia's Criminal Code, for example, for a person to receive or provide training connected with a terrorist act. As observed by the UN Special Rapporteur, it is thus conceivable that, upon completion of a sentence following conviction for that offence, the person convicted may (because of the conviction) thereafter be made the subject of a control order, including conditions of house arrest. The Special Rapporteur therefore urged Australia to ensure that control orders are not imposed in a manner that would offend the *ne bis in idem* principle, and the same would be applicable to the United Kingdom.[101]

In late August 2006, Joseph Thomas became the first person in Australia to be subjected to a control order. A constitutional challenge to the control order regime, claiming that it involved judicial officers acting in an executive capacity, was rejected by the High Court of Australia, a matter discussed further in Chap. 16 (see Sect. 16.3.2).[102] On the question of double jeopardy, the Special Rapporteur noted that the control order against Thomas included curfew and reporting conditions. While he accepted that those conditions did not, by themselves, appear to unduly restrict Thomas's freedom of movement or liberty rights, the Special Rapporteur expressed concern that there appeared to be limited evidence upon which the control order was made and that the order came just days after a State Court of Appeal quashed a terrorist financing conviction against Thomas. He nevertheless observed that, where criminal proceedings cannot be brought, or a conviction maintained, a control order might (depending on the facts and the conditions of that order) be justifiable where new information or the urgency of a situation call for action to prevent the commission of a terrorist act.[103]

---

[100]Report of Lord Carlile (n 61) para 58. See Walker (2007, p. 1446).

[101]Special Rapporteur report on Australia (n 1) paras 40 and 71. See also the Parliament of Australia Department of Library Services research paper (n 22), pp. 21–22.

[102]See *Thomas v Mowbray* [2007] HCA 33.

[103]Special Rapporteur report on Australia (n 1) para 38.

18.5   Preventative Detention Orders in Australia

The Anti-Terrorism Act (No 2) 2005 established "preventative-detention orders" under a new Division 105 to the Criminal Code Act 1995. Preventative-detention orders may be issued in two situations. The first, as provided for under section 105.4(4) and (5), is where:

- There are reasonable grounds to suspect that a person will commit an imminent terrorist act (or is in possession of materials for that purpose, or has done something in pursuit of that purpose); and
- The person's detention would substantially assist in preventing a terrorist act from occurring; and
- Detaining the person is reasonably necessary for the latter purpose (sect. 105.4 (4) and (5)).

A person may also be made subject to a preventative-detention order if (see section 105.5(6)):

- A terrorist act has occurred within the last 28 days; and
- The person's detention is necessary to preserve relevant evidence; and
- Detaining the person is reasonably necessary for the latter purpose.

The normal period that a person may be detained under such orders is no more than 24 hours, and only one order can be issued against any person relating to any one event (sections 105.8(5), 105.6 and 105.10(5)). In limited circumstances, a "continued preventative-detention order" can see a person detained for up to 48 hours, upon extension by a judicial officer (section 105.12). A preventative-detention order can be accompanied by a "prohibited contact order", on terms issued by the court, although the right to contact one's lawyer is specifically preserved (see sections 105.15–105.17, and 105.34). As discussed in Chap. 5, Division 105 is accompanied by offences under section 105.41 prohibiting the disclosure of certain information by a person subject to preventive detention, as well as others involved in the process (Sect. 5.1.1.4 – see also Appendix 3, Table 2(A)).

Criticism of orders under Division 105 of the Criminal Code Act have concerned the potential for such orders to violate the freedom from arbitrary detention; and the potential use, in the making of preventive-detention orders, of secret information (see sections 105.7(2A), 105.8(6A), 105.11(3A) and 105.12(6A)).[104] The use of closed material has already been discussed above (Sect. 18.2.2). On the question of arbitrary detention, the issue is not with orders under section 105.4, where there are reasonable grounds to suspect that the person will commit an imminent terrorist. The concern is more with preventative detention under section 105.5, which may not be based on grounds related to imminent offending by the detained person, but instead on the fact that a terrorist act has occurred and that the person's detention is

---

[104]See, for example: Special Rapporteur report on Australia (n 1) para 45; ANU letter to the Attorney General (n 82) pp. 2–7; and Chong et al. (2005, pp. 16–17).

reasonably necessary to preserve relevant evidence. In commenting on the Bill to introduce this regime, Byrnes, Charlesworth and McKinnon expressed that the detention of persons who have not committed, or are not suspected of being about to commit, an offence was a serious encroachment on the right to liberty and the presumption of innocence.[105] While this is certainly true, earlier discussions in this text (above at Sect. 18.3.1, and Chap. 16 at Sect. 16.1.2) would tend to suggest that this scheme will not fall foul of human rights law, so long as it is implemented only when necessary and by proportional means.

18.6 Conclusions

Controls orders in the United Kingdom and Australia aim to deal with persons suspected of involvement in terrorism, against whom there is insufficient admissible evidence to bring criminal proceedings, but in respect of whom there is a perceived risk of harm to the public if left to live in society without restrictions upon them. The mechanisms in both countries are much the same, although the Home Secretary in the UK is vested with much broader authority to make control orders. Furthermore, while the conditions imposed under a control order in Australia must always be compliant with the right to liberty, within the bounds of necessary and proportional limitations, the UK legislation provides for the possibility of making control orders which would be accompanied by derogation from the right to liberty.

Given the context in which the tool of control orders arose (following the declaration by the House of Lords that indefinite detention is incompatible with the ECHR), it is not surprising that control orders have implications for the enjoyment of liberty rights. The wide range of obligations and restrictions that may be imposed under control orders may also impact on other rights and freedoms. On the question of the impact of control orders on the right to liberty, it must be recognised that the deprivation of a person's liberty may take numerous forms other than classic detention in prison or strict arrest. Continuous house arrest will only permissible during the course of a criminal investigation, while awaiting trial, during trial, or as an alternative to a custodial sentence. The imposition of such a condition under a control order would therefore require a derogation from the right to liberty if imposed as a condition under a control order.

A common condition of control orders imposed in Australia and the United Kingdom is a curfew to remain within particular premises for specified periods. Whether this constitutes a deprivation of liberty requires consideration of the concrete situation of the particular individual so as to assess the cumulative impact of all measures under the control order in the situation of the person subject to those conditions. Account should be taken of a whole range of factors such as the nature, duration, effects and manner of execution or implementation of the measures.

---

[105] ANU letter to the Attorney General (n 82) para 9.

While recognising that each situation must consider the cumulative impact upon the controlled person of the measures imposed, it appears that a generally acceptable threshold for a curfew would be one of between 14 and 16 hours (which should include the normal hours of sleep).

The making of control orders also engages the right to a fair hearing, due to the frequent use in control order proceedings of classified and sensitive information which is either redacted or summarised, or not shown to the respondent. It has been accepted that the right to disclosure of information is a constituent element of the right to a fair hearing in control order proceedings. However, for the purpose of preserving an important public interest such as national security, information may be withheld if necessary and if this is sufficiently counterbalanced by judicial procedures to ensure that, overall, the respondent is able to answer the case against him or her.

Whether a person has enjoyed a fair hearing will always be fact specific, and will fall into one of three situations. The first, which will be unproblematic, is where a control order is sought largely or completely on the basis of open material so that the controlled person may answer the case against him or her. The second, which will require a careful approach to ensure that the essence of the right to a fair hearing is guaranteed, is where much of the material is closed but where the open material (or a redacted summary of the closed material) effectively conveys the thrust of the case against the person. The third and final situation, which will result in a violation of the right to a fair hearing, is where reliance on closed material is so great that the person is confronted by an unsubstantiated assertion which he or she can do no more than deny.

The use of special advocates, who are able to view closed material after seeking instructions from a respondent, will not change the outcome of the third situation described. The respondent in control order proceedings must always be provided with sufficient information about the allegations to guarantee that he or she is able to give effective instructions to the special advocate. This does not, however, make the role of the special advocate redundant. The special advocate will play an important role during a closed hearing where the open material effectively conveys the thrust of the case against the person. His or her role will be particularly important in testing the evidence and its confidential sources, especially where the information may have been obtained through the use of torture.

It is implicit in the control order regime that if there is a reasonable prospect of bringing a criminal charge against a person, that person will be prosecuted rather than made the subject of a control order. In the United Kingdom, an evaluation of this question has not been treated as a condition precedent to the making of a control order, but it has been held that the implicit basis for the regime requires the decision to impose a control to be kept under regular review to ensure that its restrictions are no greater than necessary. Arising from this, the Home Secretary has also been seen as having a continuing duty to provide the police with material in his possession which is or might be relevant to any reconsideration of prosecution. Care must also be taken to ensure that control orders are not imposed contrary to the *ne bis in idem* principle.

In view of the recent revocation of the control order against AF, based on the UK Home Secretary's unwillingness to release evidence which he states would put the Government's secret intelligence sources at risk, the continuance of the control orders regime is uncertain.

References

Cameron, Iain. 2009. Fair Trial in Terrorism Cases and Problems and Potential in Evaluation States' Laws and Practices Relating to Fair Trial (paper presented at the Round Table *Fight against Terrorism: Challenges for the Judiciary*, 18–19 September 2009, Fiesole, Italy).

Chong, Agnes, Emerton, Patrick, Kadous, Waleed, Pettit, Annie, Sempill, Stephen, Sentas, Vicki, Stratton, Jane, and Tham, Joo-Cheong. 2005. *Laws for Insecurity? A Report on the Federal Government's Proposed Counter-Terrorism Measures* (online: http://www.piac.asn.au/publications/pubs/Laws%20for%20Insecurity%20Report.pdf).

Conte, Alex, and Burchill, Richard. 2009. *Defining Civil and Political Rights: The Jurisprudence of the United Nations Human Rights* Committee. Aldershot: 2nd ed, Ashgate Publishing Ltd.

Harlow, Carol. 2006. Global Administrative Law: The Quest for Principles and Values. 17(1) *The European Journal of International Law* 187.

McDonald, Geoff. 2007. Control Orders and Preventative Detention – Why Alarm is Misguided. In Lynch, Andrew, MacDonald, Edwina, and Williams, George (Eds). *Law and Liberty in the War on Terror*. Sydney: The Federation Press.

Metcalfe, Eric. 2005. Protecting a Free Society? Control orders and the Prevention of Terrorism Bill. *JUSTICE Journal* 8.

Palmer, Andrew. 2004 Investigating and Prosecuting Terrorism: The Counter-Terrorism Legislation and the Law of Evidence. 27(2) *The University of New South Wales Law Journal* 373.

Donaghue, Stephen. 2007. Reconciling Security and the Right to a Fair Trial: The National Security Information Act in Practice. In Lynch, Andrew, MacDonald, Edwina, and Williams, George (Eds). *Law and Liberty in the War on Terror*. Sydney: The Federation Press.

Salgado, Richard. 1988. Government Secrets, Fair Trials, and the Classified Information Procedures Act. 98(2) *The Yale Law Journal* 427.

Starmer, Keir. 2007. Setting the Record Straight: Human Rights in an Era of International Terrorism. *European Human Rights Law Review* 123.

Stavros, Stephanos. 1992. The Right to a Fair Trial in Emergency Situations. 41(2) *The International and Comparative Law Quarterly* 343.

Treschel, Stefan. 2009. Secret Evidence. Special Counsel – A Panacea? (oral presentation at the Round Table *Fight against Terrorism: Challenges for the Judiciary*, 18–19 September 2009, Fiesole, Italy).

Walker, Clive. 2007. Keeping Control of Terrorists without Losing Control of Constitutionalism. 59(5) *Stanford Law Review* 1395.

Wasek-Wiaderek, Malgorzata. 2000. *Principle of 'Equality of Arms' in Criminal Procedure Under Article 6 of the European Convention on Human Rights & its Function in Criminal Justice of Selected European Countries*. Leuven, Belgium: Leuven University Press.

Chapter 19
The Designation of Individuals and Groups as Terrorist Entities

In the absence of an internationally agreed definition of terrorism (discussed in Chap. 2), the designation and listing of particular individuals and entities associated with Al-Qa'ida and the Taliban has been a key to the targeting of sanctions against such persons, including the freezing of their assets and the implementation of travel bans against them.[1] An overview of this regime is presented in this chapter, together with a summary of implementing measures by Australia, Canada and the United Kingdom. The measures adopted by New Zealand, under its Terrorism Suppression Act 2002, is the focus of a case study on the subject. Consideration is given to the human rights implications of those measures, having particular regard to the right to peaceful assembly, the freedom of association, and the right to a fair hearing and associated principles of natural justice.

An observation should be made here about the interaction of the Charter of the United Nations, national measures to implement Security Council resolutions, and the international human rights obligations of UN member States. As discussed in Chap. 3, UN member States are bound by decisions of the Security Council by virtue of article 25 of the Charter of the United Nations (see Sect. 3.2.3). This includes decisions concerning sanctions imposed on individuals and groups on the UN Consolidated List, maintained by the Al-Qa'ida and Taliban Sanctions Committee (see Sect. 19.1.1 below). States are at the same time bound by human rights treaty obligations and customary international law on human rights (see Chap. 9). The Security Council, and the UN Global Counter-Terrorism Strategy, require that measures taken by States to combat terrorism comply with international law, including human rights, the Global Strategy adding that human rights violations amount to conditions conducive to the spread of terrorism.[2] This means that

---

[1] See First report of the Analytical Support and Sanctions Monitoring Team appointed pursuant to resolution 1526 (2004) concerning Al-Qaida and the Taliban and associated individuals and entities, UN Doc S/2004/679, para 5.

[2] SC Res 1624 (2005), UN SCOR, 5261st Mtg, UN Doc A/Res/1624 (2005), para 4; United Nations Global Counter-Terrorism Strategy, GA Res 60/288, UN GAOR, 60th Sess, 99th Plen Mtg, UN Doc A/Res/60/288 (8 September 2006), Pillar I, preambular para, and Pillar IV.

A. Conte, *Human Rights in the Prevention and Punishment of Terrorism*,
DOI 10.1007/978-3-642-11608-7_19, © Springer-Verlag Berlin Heidelberg 2010

national measures taken to implement sanctions on terrorist entities, as a result of their inclusion on the UN Consolidated List, must comply with human rights, a matter expressly affirmed by the Human Rights Committee in *Sayadi and Vinck v Belgium.*[3]

19.1 An Overview of the Designation of Individuals and Entities

In 1999, the Al-Qa'ida and Taliban Sanctions Committee was established under Security Council resolution 1267 (1999) for the purpose of listing and de-listing certain individuals and groups (see also Chap. 3, Sect. 3.2.4.2).[4] The Committee's work initially focussed on the imposition of sanctions on what was then Taliban-controlled Afghanistan, in response to the Taliban's support of Usama bin Laden and Al-Qa'ida. Since the events of 9/11, the work of the Committee is no longer limited to the territory of Afghanistan but now applies to any individuals or entities designated on the Committee's Consolidated List, wherever they may be. The designation of persons and groups as terrorist entities or terrorist organisations is provided for in each of the four case study jurisdictions and is linked to the work of the Al-Qa'ida and Taliban Sanctions Committee.

19.1.1 UN Listings

The Al-Qa'ida and Taliban Sanctions Committee has described itself as "a key instrument in the fight against terrorism".[5] The Sanctions Committee now maintains a list of individuals and entities that are part of, or associated with, the Taliban, Al-Qa'ida and Usama bin Laden. The Sanctions Committee operates under the mandate of several Security Council resolutions.[6] UN member States have an obligation to designate as terrorist entities those that are listed by the UN Sanctions Committee, that obligation arising from a combination of documents, including the following:

---

[3]*Sayadi and Vinck v Belgium*, Human Rights Committee Communication 1472/2006, UN Doc CCPR/C/94/D/1472/2006 (2008), paras 10.3 and 10.6.

[4]SC Res 1267, UN SCOR, 4051st Mtg, UN Doc S/Res/1267 (1999).

[5]Security Council Committee Established Pursuant to Resolution 1267 (1999), Guidance for Reports Required of all States pursuant to paragraphs 6 and 12 of Resolution 1455 (2003), online: http://www.un.org/Docs/sc/committees/1267/guidanc_en.pdf, un-numbered para 1.

[6]See: SC Res 1267 (n 4); SC Res 1333, UN SCOR, 4251st Mtg, UN Doc S/Res/1333 (2000); SC Res 1363, UN SCOR, 4352nd Mtg, UN Doc S/Res/1363 (2001); SC Res 1388, UN SCOR, 4449th Mtg, UN Doc S/Res/1388 (2002); SC Res 1390, UN SCOR, 4452nd Mtg, UN Doc S/Res/1390 (2002); SC Res 1452, UN SCOR, 4678th Mtg, UN Doc S/Res/1452 (2002); SC Res 1455, UN SCOR, 4686th Mtg, UN Doc S/Res/1455 (2003); SC Res 1456, UN SCOR, 4688th Mtg, UN Doc S/Res/1456 (2003); SC Res 1526, UN SCOR, 4908th Mtg, UN Doc S/Res/1526 (2004); and SC Res 1617, UN SCOR, 5244th Mtg, UN Doc S/Res/1617 (2005).

- Article 25 of the Charter of the United Nations, which requires UN members "to accept and carry out the decisions of the Security Council in accordance with the present Charter".
- Paragraph 4(b) of Security Council resolution 1267 (1999), requiring States to freeze assets of Taliban entities designated by the Sanctions Committee. Paragraph 4(b) provides that States shall:[7]

> Freeze funds and other financial resources, including funds derived or generated from property owned or controlled directly or indirectly by the Taliban, or by any undertaking owned or controlled by the Taliban, as designated by the Committee established by paragraph 6 below, and ensure that neither they nor any other funds or financial resources so designated are made available, by their nationals or by any other persons within their territory, to or for the benefit of the Taliban or any undertaking owned or controlled, directly or indirectly, by the Taliban, except as may be authorized by the Committee on a case-by-case basis on the grounds of humanitarian need.

- Paragraph 8(c) of Security Council resolution 1333 (2000), which then requests the Sanctions Committee to maintain a list of individuals and entities associated with Usama bin Laden and Al-Qa'ida (not just the Taliban) and requires UN member States to similarly freeze the assets of those individuals and entities.[8]
- Security Council resolution 1390 (2001), which modifies the sanctions initially imposed under resolution 1267 (1999).[9] As far as it affects the operation of the Terrorism Suppression Act 2002 (NZ) and its designation process, discussed below, the resolution does nothing more than reiterate the role of the Sanctions Committee and the obligations mentioned.
- Paragraph 1 of Security Council resolution 1617 (2005), which again reiterates the resolution obligations mentioned.[10] Paragraphs 2 and 3 go on to direct how it is to be determined that an individual or entity is "associated with" Usama bin Laden, Al-Qa'ida and the Taliban.

These obligations are complementary to and consistent with those under Security Council resolution 1373 (2001), and the International Convention for the Suppression of the Financing of Terrorism.[11] With regard to the Financing Convention, article 8(2) is notable on the subject of the forfeiture of funds, as it obliges States parties to "take appropriate measures ... for the forfeiture of funds used or allocated for the purpose of committing [terrorist offences] and the proceeds derived from such offences". States may request the Committee to add names to this list. The Committee also considers submissions by States to delete names from the

---

[7]SC Res 1267 (n 4).

[8]SC Res 1333 (n 6).

[9]SC Res 1390 (n 6).

[10]SC Res 1617 (n 6). See also SC Res 1735, UN SCOR, 5609th Mtg, UN Doc S/Res/1735 (2006), paras 1–4.

[11]SC Res 1373, UN SCOR, 4385th Mtg, UN Doc S/Res/1373 (2001); and International Convention for the Suppression of the Financing of Terrorism, opened for signature 10 January 2000, 2179 UNTS 232 (entered into force 10 April 1992).

Consolidated List, as well as submissions concerning exemptions to the freezing of assets under resolution 1452 (2002) and for the travel ban under paragraph 1 (b) of resolution 1617 (2005). The Consolidated List consists of four sections, relating to: (1) individuals belonging to or associated with the Taliban (142 individuals); (2) entities and other groups and undertakings associated with the Taliban (currently none, although this had included the Afghanistan Momtaz Bank); (3) individuals associated with Al-Qa'ida (256 individuals); and (4) entities and other groups and undertakings associated with Al-Qa'ida (111 entities).[12] The European Union has followed suit with its own regulations, adopting EU regulations to freeze the funds and other economic resources of persons and entities whose names appear on the UN's Consolidated List (under what is known as the EU/UN regime for the listing of terrorists).[13] The EU maintains two further lists: one for the purpose of enhancing sanctions called for under Security Council resolution 1373 (2001); and its own autonomous regime of restrictive measures against persons and entities within Europe who are involved in terrorism.[14]

There has been much criticism over the way in which the UN Committee undertakes its listing and de-listing functions, as well as concerns about potential conflicts between that process and the human rights and rule of law obligations of UN member States. During the early years of the Committee's operation, only general guidelines existed on the mandate and operation of the Committee,[15] with little guidance on the procedures by which the Committee was to designate individuals or entities, particularly not regarding the rights of those designated or proposed for designation.[16] An Analytical Support and Sanctions Monitoring Team was established in 2004 to assist the Committee in its work.[17] The Monitoring Team was tasked with reviewing the listing and delisting process and make recommendations

---

[12]See The Consolidated List established and maintained by the 1267 Committee with respect to Al-Qaida, Usama bin Laden, and the Taliban and other individuals, groups, undertakings and entities associated with them, online: http://www.un.org/sc/committees/1267/pdf/consolidatedlist. pdf (last updated 1 September 2009).

[13]See Council of Europe Common Position concerning additional restrictive measures against the Taliban and amending Common Position 96/746/CFSP, COE Doc 2001/154/CFSP (2001) – updated in 2002 under COE Doc 2002/402/CFSP. See also Tappeiner (2005, pp. 102–110).

[14]Council of Europe Common Position on the application of specific measures to combat terrorism, COE Doc 2001/931/CFSP (2001); and Council of Europe Regulations on specific restrictive measures directed against certain persons and entities with a view to combating terrorism, COE Doc EC 2580/2001 (2001).

[15]See Security Council Committee Established Pursuant to Resolution 1267 (1999), Guidelines of the Committee for the Conduct of its Work, adopted on 7 November 2002 and amended on 10 April 2003, online: http://www.un.org/Docs/sc/committees/1267Template.htm (last accessed 9 August 2005).

[16]Some broad roles of the Committee were expressed within para 5 of SC Res 1390 (n 6): and, more generally, SC Res 1455 (n 6) and SC Res 1526 (n 6).

[17]The Monitoring Team was established under SC Res 1526 (n 6) para 6. To that end, the Monitoring Team has produced nine reports between 2004 and 2009: see http://www.un.org/sc/ committees/1267/monitoringteam.shtml.

to the Committee on how UN member States could be assisted in the implementation of measures.[18] In December 2008, the Committee updated its guidelines to include reasonably detailed procedures for the listing and delisting of individuals and entities to implement the requirements imposed on the Committee under Security Council resolution 1822 (2008).[19] The Committee is now also required to maintain a narrative summary of the reasons for the inclusion of individuals and entities in the Consolidated List.[20] The latter steps are said, by the Monitoring Team, to have "added significantly to the fairness and transparency of the procedures followed by the Security Council Committee established pursuant to resolution 1267 (1999) to oversee the Al-Qa'ida and Taliban sanctions regime".[21]

19.1.2 The Domestic Designation of Terrorist Entities

Under Security Council resolution 1455 (2003), UN members States were required to report on steps taken to implement measures required by the sanctions regime.[22] The practical means by which States have sought to comply with these obligations is through the establishment of offences prohibiting the provision of financial or related assistance to designated entities, offences prohibiting the dealing with financial resources of designated entities (thus freezing these resources), and mechanisms allowing for the forfeiture of such resources.[23] The approach of each country is broadly similar. A summary of the national implementing measures in Australia, Canada and the United Kingdom is set out next. The measures adopted

---

[18]See SC Res 1735 (n 10), Annex II(g). See also the resulting paper, Experiences of Member States in the Implementation of the Al-Qaida/Taliban Sanctions Measures, 28 June 2007, online: http://www.un.org/sc/committees/1267/ExperiencesofMemberStates.pdf.

[19]SC Res 1822 (2008), UN SCOR, 5928th Mtg, UN Doc S/Res/1822 (2008). See: Security Council Committee established pursuant to Resolution 1267 (1999) Concerning Al-Qaida and the Taliban and Associated Individuals and Entities, Guidelines Of The Committee For The Conduct Of Its Work, 9 December 2008, online: http://www.un.org/sc/committees/1267/pdf/1267_guidelines.pdf, paras 6 and 7.

[20]As required by SC Res 1822 (ibid) para 13. The narrative summaries can be found on the Committee's website at http://www.un.org/sc/committees/1267/narrative.shtml.

[21]Ninth report of the Analytical Support and Sanctions Monitoring Team, submitted pursuant to resolution 1822 (2008) concerning Al-Qaida and the Taliban and associated individuals and entities, UN Doc S/2009/245 (2009), para 1.

[22]SC Res 1455 (n 6) para 6.

[23]In the case of each case study country, see: Report of Australia pursuant to Security Council resolution 1455 (2003) to the Security Council Committee established under Security Council resolution 1267 (1999), UN Doc S/AC.37/2003/(1455)/13 (2003); Report of Canada to the Security Council Committee established under Security Council resolution 1267 (1999), UN Doc S/AC.37/2003/(1455)/20 (2003); Response of New Zealand to the Security Council Committee under Security Council resolution 1455 (2003), UN Doc S/AC.37/2003/(1455)21 (2003); and Report of the United Kingdom pursuant to paragraphs 6 and 12 of resolution 1455 (2003), UN Doc S/AC.37/2003/(1455)/19 (2003).

by New Zealand, under its Terrorism Suppression Act 2002, is the focus of discussion at Sect. 19.2 below.

19.1.2.1 Designations in Australia

Australia has implemented its obligations to freeze the assets of entities listed by the Security Council's Al-Qa'ida and Taliban Sanctions Committee under Part 4 of the Charter of the United Nations Act 1945 and the Charter of the United Nations (Terrorism and Dealings with Assets) Regulations 2008.[24] Section 18 of the Act operates so that where the Sanctions Committee lists a person or entity under its procedures, that person or entity is automatically proscribed under Australian law and added to Australia's own Consolidated List, maintained by the Department of Foreign Affairs and Trade (DFAT).

The listing of an individual or entity does not itself establish a criminal offence (i.e. it is not an offence to be on the list). Certain acts done in relation to such entities are criminalised however. Once an individual or entity is listed on the DFAT Consolidated List, it becomes a criminal offence under the Charter of the United Nations Act 1945 to either deal with their assets (section 20) or to make available assets, directly or indirectly, to them (section 21). Conviction for either offence renders a person liable to a maximum term of 10 years' imprisonment. This has the effect of freezing property belonging to listed entities. Safeguards exist so that holders of assets are not liable for actions done in good faith and without negligence (section 24 – see also Chapter 5 of the 2008 Regulations), and that compensation is available for persons wrongly affected (section 25). The responsible Minister has the authority, under section 22 of the Act, to allow a person to use or deal with a terrorist asset in a specified way (see also Part 4 of the 2008 Regulations). Once listed, a person or entity can apply to the responsible Minister to have the listing revoked, although he or she is not required to consider the application if the application is made within 12 months of the listing (section 17). The Minister can remove a person or entity from the DFAT Consolidated List if satisfied that the listing is no longer necessary to give effect to a Security Council decision (section 16).

Additional to this process, Australia has taken steps to allow it to deal with "terrorist organisations". Although separate from the Sanctions Committee process, all 19 organisations listed in Australian law as a "terrorist organisation" are also listed by the Committee. A "terrorist organisation" is defined by section 102.1(1) of the Criminal Code Act as:

- An organisation that is directly or indirectly engaged in, preparing, planning, assisting in or fostering the doing of a terrorist act (whether or not a terrorist act occurs)

---

[24]The Charter of the United Nations (Terrorism and Dealings with Assets) Regulations 2008 repealed and replaced the Charter of the United Nations (Terrorism and Dealings with Assets) Regulations 2002 (see regulation 3 of the 2008 Regulations).

- An organisation that is specified to be so by the terrorist organisation regulations (i.e. listed under the Criminal Code Regulations 2002)

The listing of a "terrorist organisation" may therefore occur as a result of a judicial finding to that effect consequent to a prosecution of a person or entity for a terrorist offence. However, all currently listed terrorist organisations, have been listed under the authority of section 102.1(2) of the Criminal Code Act, which allows the Attorney-General to list an organisation if satisfied on reasonable grounds that the organisation (1) is directly or indirectly engaged in, preparing, planning, assisting in or fostering the doing of a terrorist act, or (2) advocates the doing of a terrorist act. This test is one of an ordinary, rather than criminal, standard of proof. This listing process is subject to various political safeguards, including giving notice to the Leader of the Opposition, the ability for a listed organisation to seek de-listing, and review of listings by a Parliamentary Joint Committee (section 102.1A). A listed organisation can apply in writing to be delisted (section 102.1(17)).

The effect of a listing under this process is more significant than a designation based upon a Sanctions Committee listing. Whereas the listing of a person or entity under the Charter of the United Nations (Terrorism and Dealings with Assets) Regulations 2008 is not itself an offence (see Sect. 5.2.2 below), it is an offence to be a member of, or associate with, a "terrorist organisation" listed under Division 102 of the Criminal Code Act 1995 (see sections 102.3 and 102.8). It is also an offence to direct the activities of, recruit persons into, receive training from or provide training to, receive funds from or make funds available to, or provide support or resources to a terrorist organisation (see sections 102.2, 102.4, 102.5, 102.6 and 102.7 respectively). Penalties for these offences can be up to 25 years' imprisonment. In his report on Australia's counter-terrorism laws, the UN Special Rapporteur expressed concern with the fact that an organisation can be listed based upon an ordinary, rather than criminal, standard of proof, with severe criminal penalties flowing from such a listing.[25]

19.1.2.2 Designations in Canada

Canada's Anti-terrorism Act 2001 introduced the concept of a "terrorist group", which is defined by section 83.01(1) as including an entity listed under section 83.05 of the Criminal Code 1985.[26] On the recommendation of the Minister of Public Safety and Emergency Preparedness, the Governor in Council is able to establish (and add to) a list of entities if the Governor is satisfied that there are reasonable

---

[25]Special Rapporteur on the promotion and protection of human rights and fundamental freedoms while countering terrorism, Australia: Study on Human Rights Compliance While Countering Terrorism, UN Doc A/HRC/4/26/Add.3, para 23. See also Ricketts (2002), Joseph (2004, pp. 436–440), Tham (2004), and Hogg (2008).

[26]See Dosman (2004). For a review of Canada's designation process, as compared with the United Kingdom and the United States, see Jenkins (2003).

grounds to believe that: (1) the entity has knowingly carried out, attempted to carry out, participated in or facilitated a "terrorist activity" (as defined above); or (2) the entity is knowingly acting on behalf of, at the direction of or in association with such an entity (section 83.05(1)). The Governor in Council has, as a result, established and updated the 2002 Regulations Establishing a List of Entities which, under regulation 1, includes Al Qa'ida. These are supplemented by the United Nations Al-Qaida and Taliban Regulations 1999, which were made to implement Security Council resolution 1267 (1999), and later amended following Security Council resolution 1373 (2001).

The Regulations Establishing a List of Entities comprise two regulations only. The first is the list of entities, under regulation 1. Regulation 2 provides for the entry into force of the Regulations. The procedural aspects pertaining to the making and maintenance of the List of Entities are exclusively dealt with under section 83.05–83.07 of the Criminal Code. Once an individual or entity is listed, it may be de-listed as a result of the following courses of action:

- Every two years, the Minister of Public Safety and Emergency Preparedness is required to review the List of Entities to determine whether there are still reasonable grounds for an entity to be a listed entity, i.e. reasonable grounds to believe that the entity has knowingly carried out, attempted to carry out, participated in or facilitated a terrorist activity, or is knowingly acting on behalf of, at the direction of, or in association with such an entity. Based on that review, the Minister must make a recommendation to the Governor in Council as to whether the listed entities should remain a listed (section 83.05(9)). Two reviews of the List of Entities have taken place so far.[27]
- The individual or entity concerned can apply in writing to the Minister, who will determine whether there are reasonable grounds to recommend to the Governor in Council that the applicant no longer be a listed entity (section 83.05(2)). If such a recommendation is not made within 60 days after the application is received, the Minister will be deemed to have recommended that the applicant remain a listed entity (section 83.05(3)). The Minister is required to give notice without delay to the applicant of any decision taken or deemed to have been taken (section 83.04(4)). Within 60 days after the receipt of the notice, the applicant can apply for judicial review of the Minister's decision (section 83.05(5)). The applicant cannot make a further application to the Minister unless there has been a material change in its circumstances since the time of the last application (section 83.05(8)). A fresh application can also be made following a review of the List of Entities under section 83.05(9) by the Minister of Public Safety and Emergency Preparedness (section 83.05(8)).
- Where an individual or entity claims to be the victim of mistaken identity, section 83.07 provides for a fast-track application to the Minister. In such

---

[27]Correct as at 1 April 2008: see Department of Justice. Human Rights Safeguards in the Anti-terrorism Act, online: http://www.justice.gc.ca/eng/antiter/sheet-fiche/SAFE-SUR.HTML.

cases, the Minister must, within 15 days after receiving the application, issue a certificate if he or she is satisfied that the applicant is not in fact a listed entity (section 83.07(2)).

Any property that is owned or controlled by or on behalf of a terrorist group is frozen by virtue of the prohibition under section 83.04, 83.08 and 83.12 against dealing with such property. As in other jurisdictions, the freezing of property in Canada is subject to certain exceptions. The Minister of Public Safety and Emergency Preparedness, or his or her delegate, can authorise a specific activity or transaction that would otherwise be prohibited under section 83.09, and can make this authorisation subject to any terms and conditions (section 83.09 (2) and (3)). Section 83.09(4) provides for any secured and unsecured rights and interests in the property to be maintained. Following the seizure and restraint of terrorist property under section 83.13, the Attorney General can apply to the Federal Court for an order of forfeiture to the Crown in respect of property owned or controlled by or on behalf of a terrorist group; or property that has been or will be used, in whole or in part, to facilitate or carry out a terrorist activity (section 83.14). Any proceeds from the disposal of such property can be used to compensate victims of terrorist activities, and to fund anti-terrorist initiatives (section 83.14(5.1)).

19.1.2.3 Designations in the United Kingdom

The United Kingdom has taken steps to allow it to deal with persons and organisations in the UN Consolidated List by two means. The first is through its ability, under the Terrorism Act 2000, to list organisations as "proscribed organisations" (see further Chap. 8, Sect. 8.1.5.2). The Act defines such organisations as those which are listed in Schedule 2 of the Act by the Secretary of State (section 3(1)). Listing will occur where the Secretary of State believes that the organisation is "concerned in terrorism" (section 3(4)). This expression is said to apply if the organisation commits or participates in acts of terrorism; prepares for terrorism; or promotes or encourages terrorism (section 3(5)(a)(c)); or if it "is otherwise concerned in terrorism" (section 3 (5)(d)). The latter 'catch-all' is not defined further and thus provides the Secretary of State with a wide authority to list proscribed organisations.

From a practical perspective, this feature of the Terrorism Act 2000 had not originally been used as the vehicle through which the United Kingdom proscribed individuals or entities listed by the Security Council resolution 1267 (1999) Sanctions Committee (on the Sanctions Committee, see Chap. 3, Sect. 3.2.4.2). It was instead used to proscribe organisations such as The Irish Republican Army, the Ulster Freedom Fighters, the Loyalist Volunteer Force and the Orange Volunteers. Since 2001, however, the organisations listed in Schedule 2 of the Act include organisations within the Consolidated List maintained by the United Nations including, for example, Jemaah Islamiyah and the Islamic Jihad Union. The proscription of organisations is linked to two features of the Terrorism Act 2000. First, a number of offences are linked to "proscribed organisations" including, for example, membership in a proscribed organisation (section 11 – see below). In addition, "action taken for the benefit of a proscribed organisation" falls within the definition of "terrorism" under section 1 of the Act without the need to establish that the action was designed to influence the British government or to intimidate the public (see section 1(3)) – see Chap. 8, Sect. 8.1.5.3.[28]

The second element for compliance with the UN Consolidated List, and with other related resolutions of the Security Council, is the Al-Qa'ida and Taliban (United Nations Measures) Order 2002. The Order defines "listed persons" as including Usama bin Laden and any person designated by the Sanctions Committee and listed in the Consolidated List (article 2). It establishes the several offences concerning dealings with listed persons (see Appendix 3, Table 5(N)).

19.2   The Designation of Terrorist Entities Under New Zealand Law

New Zealand's Terrorism Suppression Act 2002 (TSA) sets out a detailed process by which individuals or entities may be designated as terrorist or associated entities, either as a domestically initiated designation, or as a result of the listing of such entities by the UN's Al-Qa'ida and Taliban Sanctions Committee. This process had posed certain difficulties with respect to UN-listed entities and, due to those problems, the Terrorism Suppression Amendment Act 2007 removed reference to UN-listed entities leaving room for such entities to be automatically listed, rather than requiring executive action.[29]

19.2.1   The Making of Designations

Designations under the Terrorism Suppression Act, whether interim or final, have the same consequences in terms of their linkage with offences and with reporting obligations (impacting upon third parties directly, and upon designated entities as a result of the fact that dealings with them are prohibited). The designations can also impact upon designated entities by virtue of the fact that property owned or controlled by a person or group that is the subject of a final designation can be forfeited to the Crown if that property is in New Zealand.[30]

---

[28]See also the report of the Independent Reviewer Lord Carlile of Berriew QC, Report on the Operation in 2007 of the Terrorism Act 2000 and of Part I of the Terrorism Act 2006 (Presented to Parliament pursuant to section 26 of the Terrorism Act 2006, June 2008), paras 37–68.

[29]New Zealand Parliamentary Library, Bills Digest. Terrorism Suppression Amendment Bill 2007 (Bills Digest 1498, 21 March 2007), p. 5.

[30]Terrorism Suppression Act 2002, section 55. Forfeiture can only occur on application to the High Court by the Attorney-General and if the designation is one that has been extended beyond the

The primary differences between the two types of designation concerns the standard of belief required to be had before the making of a designation, and the life of each type of designation. An interim designation can be made where the Prime Minister has "good cause to suspect" that an entity has done certain things, while a final designation requires a belief "on reasonable grounds" to be held by the Prime Minister.[31] There is no requirement that an entity be first designated on an interim basis before designation on a final basis. A final designation can be made in respect of a group or person that has never been the subject of an interim designation, or is at that time the subject of an interim designation, or was the subject of an interim designation that subsequently expired or was revoked (section 23 (a)). If, however, a final designation is made in respect of an entity that is already the subject of an interim designation, the latter becomes revoked as a result of the making of the final designation (section 23(b)). In the case of an entity that has already been the subject of a final designation, and where that designation was revoked, a further final designation is permitted, but only if this is based on information that has become available since the revocation of the earlier designation (section 23(c)).

Other than granting a special status to information provided by the UN Security Council (section 31, which has since been repealed), the Terrorism Suppression Act 2002 did not, until 2007, distinguish between domestic designations (designations initiated by the New Zealand Government under the Act) and UN designations (the designation of individuals and entities that have been listed by the Al-Qa'ida and Taliban Sanctions Committee). On the basis of the obligations mentioned to designate UN-listed individuals and entities (see Sect. 19.1.1 above), and the consequences of not designating those individuals and entities, the Terrorism Suppression Amendment Act 2007 provided for the automatic designation by NZ of those persons or groups listed by the UN Sanctions Committee.

19.2.1.1 Terrorist and Associated Entities

A further distinction to be made, applicable to both interim and final designations, concerns the 'class' of designations that can be made. A person or group can be designated as either a "terrorist entity" or an "associated entity", the distinction essentially depending upon that person's or group's past conduct. Where there is good cause to suspect (interim designation) or a belief on reasonable grounds (final designation) that an entity "has knowingly carried out, or has knowingly

---

normal 3-year period (under section 35 of the Act) and the Court is satisfied that it would be appropriate to forfeit the property rather than simply continue with the prohibition against dealing with it (section 9). The property of a designated entity is thus "frozen", in that others are prohibited from dealing with it, but cannot be forfeited unless the designation is extended beyond three years and the prohibition against dealing with the property is not sufficient.

[31]Compare Terrorism Suppression Act 2002, section 22(1) and (3) (final designations) with section 20(1) and (3) (interim designations).

participated in the carrying out of, 1 or more terrorist acts", then that entity can be designated as a terrorist entity (section 20(1) and 22(1)). Associated entities can be designated where there is suspicion or belief that an entity is facilitating or participating in the execution of a terrorist act, or is acting on behalf of or at the direction of a terrorist entity, or is wholly owned or effectively controlled by a terrorist entity (section 20(3) and 22(3)). In the case of final designations, the Prime Minister can later change the description of the designation from "terrorist entity" to "associated entity" (or vice versa) by signing a written notice to that effect (section 29A).

19.2.1.2 Political Consultation

Before making *interim* designations of either terrorist or associated entities, the Prime Minister must consult with the Minister of Foreign Affairs and Trade (section 20(4)). The Prime Minister and Attorney-General must also advise the Leader of the Opposition of the making of an interim designation and, if requested, brief the Leader on the factual basis for the making of the designation (section 20 (5)). If practicable, this must be done before the designation is publicly notified, or as soon as possible after the notification.

In the case of *final* designations, the Prime Minister must first consult with the Attorney-General about any proposed final designation, rather than the Minister of Foreign Affairs and Trade (section 22(4)).[32] Advice to the Leader of the Opposition is not required.[33] Finally, the Prime Minister is bound to consult with the Attorney-General before deciding on whether to continue or revoke a designation (in a situation where the Prime Minister is requested under section 34(1) of the Act to reconsider the designation).

19.2.1.3 Material Upon Which Designations may be Based

In making either an interim or final designation, the Prime Minister can rely on "any relevant information" (section 30). Information provided by the United Nations Security Council had, prior to the 2007 amendment of the Act, been deemed by section 31(1) to be sufficient evidence of the matters to which it related, in the absence of any evidence to the contrary. With the provision for the automatic designation of UN-listed individuals or entities, however, section 31 was repealed.[34] A special category of information remains, being information held by the New Zealand police or an intelligence and security agency, where the head of the agency has certified that the information cannot be disclosed (section 4(1) and 32(1)). To be

---

[32]Compare this with interim designations, which require the Prime Minister to consult with the Minister of Foreign Affairs and Trade: section 20(4) of the Act.

[33]Compare with the need to advise and brief in the case of interim designations: section 20(5).

[34]See section 19 of the Terrorism Suppression Amendment Act 2007.

able to give such a certificate, the head of the agency must be of the opinion that the information is of a certain nature (as specified in section 32(2)), the disclosure of which would have certain prejudicial effects (as listed in section 32(3)). The protection of classified information, and the natural justice implications of this, are considered below at Sect. 19.3.2.

19.2.1.4 Notice of Designations

The designation itself must be made in writing and signed by the Prime Minister, then publicly notified in the Gazette as soon as practicable, and by any other means directed by the Prime Minister (by internet, for example).[35] Where a designated entity, or any representative of it, is in New Zealand, and if practicable, notice of the designation must also be given to the entity or representative with all reasonable speed (sections 21(d)(i) and 23(1)(f)). The content of any notice of interim or final designation is prescribed by section 26:

> A notice under section 21(d)(i) or section 23(f)(i) (to notify the designated entity of the making of the designation under section 20 or section 22)–
>
> (a) must state the section under which the designation is made, and whether the entity concerned is designated as a terrorist entity or as an associated entity:
> (b) may describe the entity concerned by reference to any name or names or associates or other details by which the entity may be identified:
> (ba) must state that any person who deals with the entity's property may be liable to prosecution for an offence under section 9;
> (c) must state the maximum period for which the designation may have effect or, if it is made under section 22, the maximum period for which it may have effect without being renewed under section 35:
> (d) must include general information about how it may be reviewed and revoked:
> (e) must include any other information specified for the purposes of this paragraph by regulations made under this Act

A notable omission from this prescription of what must be included within a notice is the need to provide reasons for the designation. This is a point that is further reflected upon later, at Sect. 19.3.2 below. The Prime Minister can direct that notice be given to any person that may be in possession of property owned or controlled by the entity, or who may be in a position to provide property or services to the entity.[36] This will normally involve notice being given to registered banks or other financial institutions so that they are in a position to comply with their reporting obligations under the Act (section 43–47). Just as designations must be

---

[35]See sections 21(b) and (c), 22(d) and (e), and 28(1). The example of notification by internet was given by the Foreign Affairs, Defence and Trade Committee in its interim report on the Terrorism Suppression Bill, Interim Report on the Terrorism (Bombings and Financing) Bill, 8 November 2001, un-numbered page 9. The content of such notices is prescribed by section 27 of the Act.

[36]See sections 9(1), 10(1), 21(d)(ii), 23(f)(ii) and 28(2). The content of such notices is prescribed by section 27 of the Act.

notified under the Act, so must the revocation, expiry or invalidity of designations (section 42).

19.2.2   The Expiry and Review of Designations

A direct reflection of the differing standards required for interim versus final designations is found in the length of time that each type of designation can remain in force. In the case of interim designations, requiring the lower standard of proof of "good cause to suspect", the designation can last only up to 30 days (section 21(e)), unless earlier revoked (section 34) or replaced by a final designation (section 22). Importantly, a person or organisation cannot be made the subject of repeated interim designations in an attempt to extend a designation under this lower threshold (section 21(a)). The only exception to this rule is that an interim designation will continue if it becomes the subject of judicial review or other proceedings before a court (and is not otherwise revoked) until those proceedings are withdrawn or finally determined (section 21(f)). Once a *final* designation is made, there are three means by which the designation may be reviewed or renewed.

19.2.2.1   Renewal of Final Designations

Final designations last for three years from the date they are made, unless earlier revoked (section 34).[37] As in the case of interim designations, if the final designation becomes the subject of judicial proceedings, that designation continues to operate, even beyond the 3-year period (section 23(h)). Prior to the 2007 amendment of the TSA, all final designations were required to be extended by an order of the High Court, including those relating to individuals or entities listed by the United Nations (sections 23(g)(ii) and 35(2)). To do so, the Attorney-General was required to satisfy the Court, on the balance of probabilities, that: (1) the entity was the subject of criminal proceedings for terrorist acts (whether in NZ or overseas: see section 37(a)); or (2) it had been convicted of terrorist acts in an overseas tribunal (on a final basis);[38] or (3) it was a terrorist or associated entity (section 35(c) and (d)). This could be done on a repeated basis (section 35(2) to (5)). A decision of the

---

[37]The Terrorism (Bombings and Financing) Bill 2001 had provided that designations remain active for five years: see clause 17V of the Bill, as contained within the select committee's interim report – Foreign Affairs, Defence and Trade Select Committee, Interim Report on the Terrorism (Bombings and Financing) Bill, 8 November 2001. In its final report on the Bill, the Committee recommended that this be reduced to three years, stating that "it is important that the designation of a person or group as a terrorist or associated entity expire, so designations do not continue after the reasons for making them cease to exist": see Foreign Affairs, Defence and Trade Committee, Final Report on the Terrorism <(Bombings and Financing)> Suppression Bill, 22 March 2002.

[38]That is, convicted in criminal proceedings that are not subject to any appeal and that are finally determined: see Terrorism Suppression Act 2002, section 23(b).

High Court on an application for the extension of a designation could be appealed to the Court of Appeal by any party to that application (section 41).

In the context of UN-listings, which number in the hundreds, this presented New Zealand with a significant administrative and judicial burden. This initially prompted the passing of the Terrorism Suppression Amendment Act (No 2) 2005, stretching extant final designations to five years instead of three.[39] The Terrorism Suppression Amendment Act 2007 removed this problem, as it applies to UN-listed entities, by making all such entities automatically designated under New Zealand law. This linkage also means that, if an individual or entity is removed from the UN's Consolidated List, the person or group is not designated under NZ law.

The 2007 Amendment Act went further than this, however, by placing the renewal of *domestically*-designated entities in the hands of the Prime Minster, instead of the High Court. Section 20 of the 2007 Act replaces earlier sections 35–37 of the 2002 Act. In brief, the earlier sections had provided that: final designations (those made under section 22 of the Act) expire after three years, unless extended by order of the High Court upon application of the Attorney-General (section 35); preservation of any final designation pending judicial review proceedings initiated by the designated entity, and associated matters (section 36); and a detailed list of grounds upon which the High Court is authorised to extend a final designation for a further period (section 37). These provisions were repealed and replaced by a new section 35 which reads as follows:

35 Designations under section 22 to expire after 3 years unless renewed by Prime Minister

(1) A designation made under section 22 expires 3 years after the date on which it takes effect, unless it is earlier–

(a) revoked under section 34; or

(b) renewed by an order under subsection (2) or (3).

(2) The Prime Minister may order that a designation made under section 22 remain in force for a further 3 years after the making of the order if the Prime Minister is satisfied that there are still reasonable grounds as set out in section 22 for an entity to be designated under that section.

(3) Before expiry of an order under subsection (2), the Prime Minister may make another order renewing the designation concerned for a further 3 years.

(4) After making an order under subsection (2) or (3), the Prime Minister must report to the Intelligence and Security Committee on the renewal of the designation.

(5) The Prime Minister may make any number of orders under subsection (3) in respect of the same designation.

The first rather obvious observation to make is that these amendments are significantly more simple that the earlier provisions on the renewal of designations. Furthermore, the grounds upon which an extension may be made are less than under the earlier regime, restricting the Prime Minister to the test under section 22

---

[39]New Zealand Ministry of Justice, Terrorism Suppression Amendment Bill (No 2) 2004, Government Bill, 242-1, Explanatory Note, presented to the House 14 December 2004, 2. See also Press Release, 'Amendments to Tighten Terrorism Suppression Act', online: http://www. beehive.govt.nz/ViewDocument.cfm?DocumentID=21825 at 8 January 2005.

for determining whether the person or group is a terrorist or associated entity. The Prime Minister need only have a belief on "reasonable grounds" of the matters in section 22 (sections 22 and new section 35(2)). These matters are not, however, of substantial concern, since any extension under section 35 remains subject to judicial review under section 33 of the Act (considered below at Sect. 19.3.2.4).

19.2.2.2 Internal, Government-Initiated, Reviews

The ability to revoke a designation under section 34 of the TSA can be initiated at the Prime Minister's own volition (section 34(1)). This is the only mechanism, however, by which an 'internal' review of designations can be initiated. In the form presented within the select committee's interim report on the Bill, the Terrorism Suppression Act was also to include a mandatory review of designations by the Inspector-General of Intelligence and Security. This proposal did not eventuate.

19.2.2.3 Judicial Review Initiated by a Designated Individual or Entity

Section 33 of the Terrorism Suppression Act is unrestricted in its terms, allowing "a person" (presumably *any* person) to bring any judicial review or other proceedings before a court arising out of, or related to, the making of a designation under the Act. A designated person, or a third party with "an interest in the designation",[40] may also apply in writing to the Prime Minister to revoke a designation (section 34 (1)). In doing so, the application must be based on one of two grounds: either (1) that the designation should be revoked because the entity concerned does not satisfy the prescribed requirements for designation; or (2) that the entity is no longer involved in any conduct that would otherwise legitimate a designation under the Act (section 34(3)). In determining such an application, the Prime Minister is required to consult with the Attorney-General (section 34(5)).

19.3 Human Rights Implications of the Designation of Individuals and Entities

Just as with many other measures designed towards the prevention of terrorism, the designation of persons and groups as terrorist entities, its consequences, as well as the process leading up to this, impacts upon the unlimited enjoyment of rights and freedoms. Considered next are the rights to peaceful assembly and freedom of association, as well as the rights to natural justice and a fair hearing. While these are the predominant rights engaged by the designation of individuals and groups as

---

[40]As defined by section 34(2) of the Act.

terrorist entities, other rights may be affected as a result of listing including, for example, the right to dispose of one's property and the right to privacy.[41]

19.3.1 Association and Peaceful Assembly

The freedom of association is a right protected by both the International Covenant on Civil and Political Rights (ICCPR)[42] and the New Zealand Bill of Rights Act 1990 (NZBORA). Section 17 of the Bill of Rights expresses the freedom in very simple terms, describing it as "the right to freedom of association". Article 22(1) of the ICCPR is not much more helpful:

> Everyone shall have the right to freedom of association with others, including the right to form and join trade unions for the protection of his interests.

Regrettably, the jurisprudence of the Human Rights Committee does not help define this right within the context of the current examination, since complaints before the Committee have concerned the membership of individuals in political parties or trade unions, and strike actions.[43] In the context of the Bill of Rights, there has likewise been little academic or judicial scrutiny of the freedom of association. The same can be said of the freedom of peaceful assembly, guaranteed by article 21 of the ICCPR (and section 16 of the NZBORA).[44] It has been recognised, however, that the right of peaceful assembly and the freedom of association are integral to human dignity, important to the exercise of electoral rights and democratic participation, and act as a platform for the exercise of other rights, including the freedom of expression and the work of human rights defenders.[45]

---

[41]In this regard, see *Möllendorf and Möllendorf-Niehuus v Germany*, judgment of the European Court of Justice of 11 October 2007 in case C-117/06. See also: Bowring (2007, pp. 90–92); Cameron (2006, pp. 10–12); the report of the Special Rapporteur on the promotion and protection of human rights and fundamental freedoms while countering terrorism, Protection of human rights and fundamental freedoms while countering terrorism, UN Doc A/61/267 (2006), para 31; and the report of the United Nations High Commissioner for Human Rights on the protection of human rights and fundamental freedoms while countering terrorism, UN Doc A/HRC/12/22 (2009), para 41. On the right to privacy, see *Sayadi and Vinck v Belgium* (n 3), paras 10.12–10.13.

[42]International Covenant on Civil and Political Rights, opened for signature 16 December 1966, 999 UNTS 171 (entered into force 23 March 1976).

[43]See Conte and Burchill (2009, pp. 92–95).

[44]Article 21 of the ICCPR states that "The right of peaceful assembly shall be recognized"; section 16 of the NZBORA provides that "Everyone has the right to freedom of peaceful assembly".

[45]Human Rights Committee, General Comment 25: The right to participate in public affairs, voting rights and the right of equal access to public service (Art. 25), UN Doc CCPR/C/21/Rev.1/Add.7 (1996), para 26; report of the United Nations High Commissioner for Human Rights (n 41) para 36; Special Rapporteur report on the listing of individuals and entities (n 41) para 9; and Rishworth et al. (2003, p. 354).

19.3.1.1 Peaceful Assembly, Association with Terrorist Entities, and the ICCPR

Freedom of association is not an absolute right, instead qualified by paragraph 2 of article 22 of the ICCPR:

> No restrictions may be placed on the exercise of this right other than those which are prescribed by law and which are necessary in a democratic society in the interests of national security or public safety, public order (ordre public), the protection of public health or morals or the protection of the rights and freedoms of others. This article shall not prevent the imposition of lawful restrictions on members of the armed forces and of the police in their exercise of this right.

The right to peaceful assembly is similarly qualified, allowing restrictions to be placed if in conformity with the law and "necessary in a democratic society in the interests of national security or public safety, public order (ordre public), the protection of public health or morals or the protection of the rights and freedoms of others". Considering articles 21 and 22 step by step, the first point is that restrictions imposed as a result of the designation of terrorist entities including, for example, offences of associating with designated entities (as is the case under section 102.8 of Australia's Criminal Code Act 1995), must be prescribed by law (on the meaning of this term, see Chap. 10, Sect. 10.2.2).[46] The second requirement is that the restrictions must be necessary in a democratic society for the furtherance of certain interests.[47] In the case at hand, it seems easily arguable that the consequences of designation are in pursuit of almost all of those interests identified in articles 21 and 22(2) of the Covenant by contributing to the international suppression of terrorism and by putting into place means by which terrorist threats or acts within can be suppressed and responded to: national security; public safety; the protection of public health; and the protection of rights and freedoms of others (including, for example, the right to life). As stated by the Special Rapporteur on the promotion and protection of human rights and fundamental freedoms while countering terrorism:[48]

> Proscribing associations which have as their aim the destruction of the State through terrorist means, or banning public demonstrations which call for the use of terrorist means to destroy the State may be covered by the limitation clauses of ICCPR. The Special Rapporteur underlines, however, that Governments must not use these aims/purposes as smokescreens for hiding the true purpose of the limitations. The systematic violation of human rights undermines true national security and may jeopardize international peace and

---

[46]Special Rapporteur report on the listing of individuals and entities (n 41) paras 16–18.

[47]The Special Rapporteur has reiterated that the prinicples of necessity and proportionality are applicable to measures implementing sanctions imposed by the Security Council: see Special Rapporteur report on the listing of individuals and entities (n 41) para 33. See also *Lee v Republic of Korea*, Human Rights Committee Communication 1119/2002, UN Doc CCPR/C/84/D/1119/2002 (2005), para 7.3; and *Belyatsky et al v Belarus*, Human Rights Committee Communication 1296/2004, UN Doc CCPR/C/90/D/1296/2004 (2007), para 7.3

[48]Special Rapporteur report on the listing of individuals and entities (n 41) para 20.

> security; therefore, a State shall not invoke national security as a justification for measures aimed at suppressing opposition or to justify repressive practices against its population. The onus is on the Government to prove that a threat to one of the grounds for limitation exists and that the measures are taken to deal with the threat.

One can therefore conclude that the non-association implications of designations are, in and of themselves, consistent with the ICCPR. This conclusion is dependent, however, on the proper and just designation of individuals and entities. An abuse of that process might, for example, be used to prevent membership in all Islamic organisations rather than properly proscribing membership of organisations that fall within the proper terms of the designation processes adopted for the purpose of preventing terrorism. As concluded by the Special Rapporteur, clear safeguards must be put in place by the law to prevent abuses.[49]

It should be mentioned that membership of proscribed organisations is not something new. In considering regulations made by the relevant Minister in Ireland for the "preservation of the peace and the maintenance of public order", the House of Lords had to determine in *McEldowney v Forde* whether it was proper for the Minister to have proscribed membership in a "republican club".[50] By three judges to two, the House of Lords held that Forde's conviction for being a member of such a club was proper. While the division in opinion might seem problematic, the dissenting judgments were on the question of whether there was sufficient evidence that "republican clubs" caused any prejudice to peace or good order.[51] There was no dispute as to whether membership *can* be proscribed for the purposes of preserving the peace and maintaining public order. Earlier still, the Nuremberg Tribunal held that proscribing membership of a criminal organisation was proper.[52]

19.3.1.2 Peaceful Assembly, Association with Terrorist Entities, and the NZBORA

Since the current case study has looked at the designation of individuals and entities under New Zealand law, consideration should be had to the implications of this for the NZ Bill of Rights Act. By reason of the plain expression of the right to peaceful assembly and the freedom of association under the NZBORA, it can be said that the provisions of the Terrorism Suppression Act (NZ) do impact upon the freedom. The expression of the right does not qualify itself in any way that could render those provisions consistent with its definition. The issue of consistency must therefore be determined by reference to the section 5 justified limitations provision (on the

---

[49]Special Rapporteur report on the listing of individuals and entities (n 41) paras 11, 27 and 29.

[50]*McEldowney v Forde* [1971] AC 632.

[51]Ibid, Lord Pearce (651–654) and Lord Diplock (658–665). See also Fellman (1961) and Cole (1999).

[52]International Military Tribunal, Nuremberg, judgment of 30 September 1946. For a discussion of this, see Keith (2003, pp. 32–33).

general application of the Bill of Rights, and section 5 in particular, see Chap. 11, Sects. 11.1.3.2 and 11.4).

As in the case of the ICCPR, the provisions at hand present a clear case of justified limitations upon rights and freedoms. The objectives of the various provisions are all directed, and rationally connected to, the suppression of the financing of terrorism, the participation in terrorist groups and the bringing to justice of the perpetrators of terrorist acts. Bearing in mind the consequences of terrorism, these prohibitions are manifestly proportional to the limitations upon the freedom of association. The provisions are 'consistent' with the Bill of Rights Act, within the meaning of Rishworth's second step in the application of the NZBORA (see Chap. 11, Sect. 11.1.3.2). No breach of the NZBORA occurs.

Again, however, this conclusion is arrived at on the proviso that there is a proper and just administration of the process by which a person or group may be designated a terrorist or associated entity. To some extent, this concern had been alleviated through the express qualifications within sections 8(2) and 10(2) of the TSA, which made it clear that those provisions did not make it an offence to provide or collect funds with the intention that they be used, or knowing that they are to be used, for the purposes of advocating democratic government or the protection of human rights, so long as such an organisation is not involved in carrying out terrorist acts. This safeguard was repealed, however, under the Terrorism Suppression Amendment Act 2007.

19.3.2 Natural Justice and the Right to a Fair Hearing

The right to a fair hearing, aimed at ensuring the proper administration of justice, encompasses a series of individual rights such as equality before the courts and tribunals, and the right to a fair and public hearing by a competent, independent and impartial tribunal established by law (see further Chap. 18, Sect. 18.2). The common law right to natural justice, reflected in section 27 of the NZ Bill of Rights Act, includes parallel features.

19.3.2.1 Due Process in Listings and De-listings by the United Nations

Several States have expressed concern that the UN listing and de-listing procedures of the Sanctions Committee (see Sect. 19.1.1 above) do not live up to the principles of due process.[53] Some have even taken the position that they will not actively assist the Committee by providing it with names of persons or entities that might become

---

[53]See, for example, the statement of Ellen Margrethe Løj (Danish Ambassador to the United Nations, and current Chair of the Security Council Counter-Terrorism Committee), UN Press Release, 'Security Council Reaffirms Terrorism One of Most Serious Threats to Peace', UN SCOR, 59th Sess, 5229th Mtg, UN Doc SC/8454 (2005).

listed until these concerns have been addressed.[54] Evidenced within statements of the Chair of the Security Council Counter-Terrorism Committee, there appears to be general acceptance that the Sanctions Committee guidelines need improvement.[55] In 2005, the World Summit Outcome called on the Security Council, with the support of the Secretary-General, "to ensure that fair and clear procedures exist for placing individuals and entities on sanctions lists and for removing them, as well as for granting humanitarian exemptions".[56] New Zealand's Permanent Representative to the United Nations expressed, in the same year, New Zealand's view that basic standards of due process must be met within the Committee's listing process and, in doing so, urged the Security Council to consider amendments to the Committee's regime to meet these concerns.[57]

A few months prior to the adoption by the Al-Qa'ida and Taliban Sanctions Committee of new guidelines on listing and de-listing, the UN Special Rapporteur repeated his concerns about the listing and de-listing individuals and groups as terrorist or associated entities, whether by the Security Council, the European Union, or by national procedures.[58] The Rapporteur stated that, so long as there is no independent review of listings at the United Nations level (which continues to be the case), there must be access to domestic judicial review of any implementing measure:[59]

---

[54]Ibid.

[55]Ibid, operative para 18 of SC Res 1617 (n 6) is said to further reflect a desire on the part of a number of Security Council member States to secure improvements in the Sanctions Committee's process. See also: EU Network of Independent Experts in Fundamental Rights, The Balance Between Freedom and Security in the Response by the European Union and its Member States to the Threat of Terrorism (EU Network of Independent Experts in Fundamental Rights, 2003); Ben Hayes, Terrorising the Rule of Law: The Policy and Practice of Proscription (Statewatch, 2005); and Yusuf and Al Barakaat International Foundation v Council and Commission (unreported judgment of the European Court of Justice of first instance, 21 September 2005), online: http://www.curia.eu.int/jurisp/cgi-bin/form.pl?lang=en&Submit=Submit&docj=docj&numaff=&datefs=&datefe=&nomusuel=&domaine=&mots=terror&resmax=100 (last accessed 3 November 2005).

[56]2005 World Summit Outcome, GA Res 60/1, UN GAOR, 69th Sess, 8th Plen Mtg, UN Doc A/Res/60/1 (2005), para 109. This was recalled by the UN Secretary-General in his report, Uniting Against Terrorism: Recommendations for a Global Counter-terrorism Strategy, UN Doc A/60/825 (27 April 2006), para 117.

[57]Rosemary Banks (New Zealand Permanent Representative to the United Nations), Statement on Counter-Terrorism to the President of the United Nations Security Council, 20 July 2005, online: http://nzmissionny.org/securitycouncil.htm (last accessed 17 August 2005). See also; Bowring (2007, pp. 102–112); and Cameron (2006, pp. 1–9).

[58]Report of the Special Rapporteur on the promotion and protection of human rights and fundamental freedoms while counter-terrorism terrorism, Protection of human rights and fundamental freedoms while countering terrorism, UN Doc A/63/223 (2008), para 16. See the Special Rapporteur's earlier report on the listing of individuals and entities (n 41) paras 26–41.

[59]Report of the Special Rapporteur on the right to a fair hearing (ibid), para 16. See also the Special Rapporteur's earlier report on the listing of individuals and entities (n 41) para 26; and the Opinion of the European Advocate General of 16 January 2008 in *Kadi v Council of the European Union and Commission of the European Communities*, Case C-402/05, para 54.

Even where listing does not result in the indefinite freezing of assets, but holds other consequences which might fall short of a criminal punishment, it should be noted that access to courts and a fair trial may also arise from the general provisions of article 14(1), as applicable to a suit at law. At a minimum, the standards required to ensure a fair hearing must include the right of an individual to be informed of the measures taken and to know the case against him or her as soon as possible, and to the extent possible, without thwarting the purpose of the sanctions regimes; the right to be heard within a reasonable time by the relevant decision-making body; the right to effective review by a competent and independent review mechanism; the right to counsel with respect to all proceedings; and the right to an effective remedy.

In 2009, and thus subsequent to the adoption of changes brought about by Security Council resolution 1822 (2008), the High Commissioner for Human Rights has commented that these changes are encouraging, but that they do not go far enough to ensure full enjoyment of all human rights.[60] There have been no less than 30 legal challenges involving individuals and entities on the UN's Consolidated List.[61] These have concerned three principal issues: (1) the hearing of persons during the making of designations, and the associated giving of notice to the designated person; (2) the rights of review and appeal; and (3) the treatment of classified security information.

19.3.2.2 The Making of Domestic Designations

Two features of New Zealand's Terrorism Suppression Act 2002 are relevant to the making of designations, and the rights to natural justice and a fair hearing. First, the making of a designation does not contain any procedure by which the alleged terrorist individual or entity can make its case prior to being designated under sections 20 or 22. Secondly, once a designation is made, any notice given to an entity which is within New Zealand's territorial jurisdiction (or its representative in NZ) does not need to give reasons for the designation, whether made on an interim or final basis.

The first issue identified is not overly problematic. As emphasised by the UN Special Rapportuer, the key is that there be access to an independent judicial review of designating measures.[62] Furthermore, Joseph summarises the point that natural justice does not include a right to be heard before an administrative decision-maker, but merely right to tender written submissions.[63] As to the second issue, however, it has already been noted that section 26 of the TSA does not require notices of interim or final designations to include reasons for the designation (see Sect. 19.2.1.4 above). Indeed, section 29(a) of the Act specifically expresses that a designation cannot

---

[60]Report of the United Nations High Commissioner for Human Rights (n 41) para 39. See also Fromuth (2009).

[61]Monitoring Team Ninth Report (n 21) Annex I, para 1.

[62]Report of the Special Rapporteur on the right to a fair hearing (n 58), para 16.

[63]Joseph (2001, p. 864).

be invalidated "just because. . . the entity concerned was not . . . given notice . . . or a chance to comment". This is out of step with the procedures of the Al-Qa'ida and Taliban Sanctions Committee which, as identified earlier and as required by Security Council resolution 1822 (2008), demands that the Committee maintain a narrative summary of the reasons for inclusion of individuals and entities in the Consolidated List.[64] It is also inconsistent with the desirability that administrative decision-makers should give reasons for their decisions, a feature which coincides with "public expectations of transparency and accountability in decision-making", as stated by Joseph.[65] Although there is no obligation at law to do so, at least not under New Zealand law, the giving of reasons for administrative decisions has been described as a public responsibility. As stated by Chief Justice Davison, in *Potter v New Zealand Milk Board*:[66]

> The giving of reasons helps to concentrate the mind of the tribunal upon the issues for determination: it enables litigants to see that their cases have been carefully considered and the arguments understood and appreciated; it enables a litigant dissatisfied with a decision to more readily consider whether there are grounds of appeal; and it enables an appellate Court or tribunal to ascertain the determinations of the tribunal on questions of fact, to which the appellate Courts pay deference on the hearing of an appeal and [it] also enables the appellate Court ... to know what principles of law have been applied and to consider whether such were correct.

As indicated by Davison CJ, one of the important reasons for giving reasons is to allow a person to determine whether or not there are grounds for appeal or judicial review. In the context of international listings, the European Court of Justice has gone further and held that a failure to communicate the reasons justifying restrictive measures imposed on a listed person infringes the right of such persons to effective judicial protection, since it precludes a right to defend against such measures.[67] The UK Court of Appeal has followed this lead, holding that the United Kingdom must provide a merits-based review of the reasons for listing an individual on the Consolidated List.[68]

In the New Zealand context, the need for the Prime Minister to include reasons for designation in any notice under section 26 of the Terrorism Suppression Act is strengthened by the application of section 6 of the NZ Bill of Rights Act. In attempting to identify the different interpretations of section 26, it should be noted that this provision does not *exclude* the inclusion of reasons for designation in the notice of designation. Interpretation of section 26 therefore includes, as one possibility, that notices must inform the individual or entity of the information upon

---

[64]SC Res 1822 (n 19) para 13.

[65]Joseph (2001, p. 871). See also the Special Rapporteur report on the listing of individuals and entities (n 41) para 38.

[66]*Potter v New Zealand Milk Board* [1983] NZLR 620, 624.

[67]*Kadi and Al Barakaat International Foundation v Council and Commission*, judgment of the European Court of Justice (Grand Chamber) of 3 September 2008 in joined cases C-402/05 and C-415/05.

[68]*A and others v HM Treasury* [2008] EWCA Civ 1187.

which the designation was based. This would have the effect of 'reading in' a requirement into the plain words of section 26 to make the provision consistent with the right to natural justice, which is protected under section 27(3) of the NZBORA. While this is an attractive proposition, and one which may well find favour in Canada (on 'reading in' under the Canadian Charter of Rights and Freedoms, see Chap. 11 at Sect. 11.1.2.2), New Zealand courts may be reluctant to do so. The right to natural justice does not, despite the comments of Davison CJ referred to above, include the requirement that administrative decision-makers give reasons for their decisions and it might therefore be concluded that to read in such a requirement would result in a strained interpretation of section 26 of the TSA. Such a result would be unfortunate, however, especially in light of the European and English decisions mentioned earlier.

If an obligation to give reasons was to be read into notices under section 26, a further observation should be made. Namely, it would be rational that such reasons need not disclose information that would be prejudicial to public interests such as national security. This is a restriction which would be justifiable under section 5 of the NZBORA. Such restrictions are discussed below.

19.3.2.3 Executive Review of Domestic Designations

As identified at Sect. 19.2.2 above, there are two means by which a domestically-designated person or group could challenge a designation in New Zealand: by asking the Prime Minister to reconsider the designation (section 34 of the Terrorism Suppression Act); or by seeking judicial review of a designation (section 33 of the Act). The latter option is discussed below. Concerning requests for reconsideration by the Prime Minister, section 34(1) of the Act provides:

> The Prime Minister may at any time revoke a designation made under section 20 or section 22, either on the Prime Minister's own initiative or on an application in writing for the purpose–
>
> (a) by the entity who is the subject of the designation; or
> (b) by a third party with an interest in the designation that, in the Prime Minister's opinion, is an interest apart from any interest in common with the public.

Section 34(1) does not expressly exclude an accompanying right to be heard by the Prime Minister, or to receive, in advance, information about the basis upon which the designation was made. Exclusion of the right to be heard in person is implied, however, by the fact that the provision applies to "an application in writing". It might be noted, however, that when reviewing the first draft of the Terrorism (Bombings and Financing) Bill (as it was then called) the Solicitor-General advised the Attorney-General that, in his view, the process of designation was consistent with the NZ Bill of Rights Act, including the right to natural justice.[69] Although the

---

[69]Letter from the Solicitor-General to the Attorney-General, "re Terrorism Suppression Bill: Slip Amendments – PCO 3814B/11 Our Ref: ATT114/1048 (15)", 9 November 2001, para 20.

Solicitor-General gave no reasons for arriving at this conclusion, it should further be noted that this version of the Bill provided for the Inspector-General of Security and Intelligence to be involved in the designation and review process. Rather than asking the Head of State to undertake a review under section 34, the involvement of the Inspector-General could have seen a more independent and impartial review process.

In an earlier assessment of the designation process in New Zealand, this author recommended the reinstatement of a modified form of the review of domestic designations by the Inspector-General of Security and Intelligence (IGSI),[70] involving three tasks for the IGSI:[71]

1. The first proposed role of the Inspector-General would be to exercise the function envisaged within the first redraft of the Terrorism Suppression Bill: to undertake a mandatory review of all designations and consider, in that review, whether the tests for designation were properly applied and satisfied, when weighed against the information received by the Prime Minister. In doing so, the IGSI would act as an internal check upon the exercise of the significant decision-making power of designation. Not only is this important to the integrity of the designation process itself, but also to the criminal responsibility implications of such designations. By introducing an immediate and mandatory checking mechanism, this also addresses the lack of notice and hearing prior to the making of a designation.

   Naturally, the power of review should come with the ability on the part of the Inspector-General to act upon his or her findings. Under the proposed regime in the Terrorism (Bombings and Financing) Bill, the Inspector-General was to have the power to revoke designations upon review and it is proposed that any reinstatement of the Inspector-General's role under the TSA include the same authority to revoke.[72] In essence, as summarised by the Solicitor-General in his review of the Bill when giving advice to the Attorney-General, the Inspector-General's review would amount to a *de novo* determination.[73] The decision of the Inspector-General should be accompanied with notice of the decision being given to the designated entity. By doing so, the entity will be in a better position to assess whether to seek judicial review of the decision.

   As was also provided for in the Bill, the Inspector-General's review function should be able to be triggered by the designated individual or entity. The Bill had

---

[70]As had been contained within the Terrorism (Bombings and Financing) Bill (see the Select Committee's interim report, Foreign Affairs, Defence and Trade report, Interim Report on the Terrorism (Bombings and Financing) Bill, 8 November 2001), but then removed in the later Terrorism Suppression <Bombings and Financing> Bill (see the Committee's final report, Foreign Affairs, Defence and Trade Committee, Final Report on the Terrorism <(Bombings and Financing)> Suppression Bill, 22 March 2002, 11).

[71]Conte (2007, pp. 348–351).

[72]Terrorism (Bombings and Financing) Bill [first redraft], clause 17T(1).

[73]Terrorism (Bombings and Financing) Bill [first redraft], clause 17P(1): see letter from the Solicitor-General to the Attorney-General (n 69) para 16.

provided, in that regard, that if a designated entity had unsuccessfully applied to the Prime Minister to have a designation revoked (current section 34(1) of the Act), then it could apply for review by the Inspector-General.[74]

2. The second role for the IGSI would be additional to that originally proposed by the Foreign Affairs, Defence and Trade Committee in its interim report on the Bill, and would involve a review of notification. This would require the Inspector-General to determine two things. First, whether the summary of information provided under the notice was a proper and fair reflection of the information upon which the designation was based. Next, it would require him or her to determine whether any exclusion of classified security information was necessary to the extent required to protect the public interests. This power of review should again be accompanied with the ability on the part of the IGSI to take any necessary action, including the ability to direct that the notice be amended to include any additional information s/he deems necessary, i.e. information upon which the designation was based, except classified security information (to the extent that this might prejudice the interests referred to in section 32(3)).

3. The final proposed role for the Inspector-General addresses the specific concern of the manner in which requests to the Prime Minister to reconsider a designation are dealt with under section 34. The point has been made that there is currently no express right, in such circumstances, to be heard or to receive information about the basis upon which the designation was made. The latter aspect has been addressed, it is suggested, by recommending amendment of section 26 to require the provision of information in the notice of designation and the associated power of review of the notice by the Inspector-General.

What is further recommended here is that the IGSI be empowered to receive submissions from an entity that requests review of their designation by the Prime Minister. A careful balancing act must be achieved here, however. The Inspector-General should not be expected to hear any frivolous evidence or submissions. Thus the following process is recommended:

- Where an entity, or a third party with an interest in the designation, requests reconsideration of a designation by the Prime Minister under section 34(1) of the Act, the written notice requesting reconsideration should first be referred to the Inspector-General of Security and Intelligence.
- If the written notice does not disclose any information which, in the view of the Inspector-General, challenges the basis upon which the designation was made, then the Inspector-General should consider whether the information upon which the designation was based satisfies the tests for designation under the Act, and advise the Prime Minister accordingly. He or she should not, however, be required to hear from the applicant if the application does nothing to challenge the basis of the designation. To do so would be pointless. Notwithstanding this, the Inspector-General should inform the applicant that the applicant's written notice does not disclose any information which

---

[74]Terrorism (Bombings and Financing) Bill [first redraft], clause 17N(2).

challenges the basis upon which the designation was made and that, in the absence of such further information, s/he has reached the conclusion that the designation should stand (or be revoked) and has made a recommendation to the Prime Minister accordingly. By doing so, the applicant is thereby advised of the Inspector-General's recommendation and the reasons for it.

- If, in contrast, the written notice *does* disclose information which challenges the basis upon which the designation was made, then the Inspector-General should be required to advise the applicant that they can: (1) file with the Inspector-General written submissions; and/or (2) attend at a specified time and place to be heard in person. After hearing from the applicant in this way, the Inspector-General should consider whether the information upon which the designation was based, together with any further information received, satisfies the tests for designation under the Act, and advise the Prime Minister accordingly. Again, it is recommended that the Inspector-General should advise the applicant that s/he has reached the conclusion that the designation should stand (or be revoked) and has made a recommendation to the Prime Minister accordingly.

Such a process would both guarantee the right to be heard (where there is something to be heard about) and at the same time limit the Prime Minister's involvement in that process and restrict frivolous applications from taking the time of both the Prime Minister and Inspector-General.

19.3.2.4   Judicial Review of Domestic Designations

Moving from executive review to judicial review, an important observation must first be made. Following the reform of the Terrorism Suppression Act in 2007, the designation process in New Zealand is limited to *domestic* designations, while the application of the Act to individuals and entities listed in the UN Consolidated List is automatic and continues until those entities are removed from the Consolidated List.[75] The practical implication of this is that, although section 33 of the TSA allows for judicial review of designations made under the Act, the right to judicial review does not apply in respect of UN-listed individuals and entities. This is in stark contrast to the recommendation of the UN Special Rapporteur that, so long as there is no independent review of listings at the UN level (which continues to be the case), there must be access to domestic judicial review of any implementing measure.[76]

---

[75]See Letter from the Solicitor-General to the Attorney-General, "LEGAL ADVICE. CONSISTENCY WITH THE NEW ZEALAND BILL OF RIGHTS ACT 1990: Terrorism Suppression Amendment Bill". Our Ref: ATT395/24, 4 December 2006, paras 2.1–2.3.

[76]Report of the Special Rapporteur on the right to a fair hearing (n 58), para 16. See also his report on the listing of individuals and entities (n 41) para 39.

Noting this as an inconsistency between New Zealand's designation process and the Rapporteur's view, the balance of this discussion focuses on the right to judicial review of domestic designations. The issue, here, is the protection from disclosure of "classified security information", which is information certified as being of this nature by the head of the agency providing the information.[77] Information might be categorised as classified security information where, for example, the information is provided by a security service of another country on a confidential basis (section 32 (2)(c)), the disclosure of which would thereby prejudice the confidential basis upon which the information was provided (section 32(3)(b)). Section 38 of the Act 'protects' such information, the operative parts of which read as follows:

(1) This section applies to any proceedings in a court arising out of, or relating to, the making of a designation under this Act.
(2) The Court must determine the proceedings on the basis of information available to it (whether or not that information has been disclosed to or responded to by all parties to the proceedings).
(3) If information presented, or proposed to be presented, by the Crown includes classified security information,–

---

[77]Section 32 of the Terrorism Suppression Act 2002 sets out, in reasonably detailed terms, the definition of classified security information, requiring the head of the agency concerned to certify in writing that he or she is of the opinion that (see section 31(1)(c)):

- the information is of a kind specified in section 32(2), being information that:
  (a) might lead to the identification of, or provide details of, the source of the information, the nature, content, or scope of the information, or the nature or type of the assistance or operational methods available to the specified agency; or
  (b) is about particular operations that have been undertaken, or are being or are proposed to be undertaken, in pursuance of any of the functions of the specified agency; or
  (c) has been provided to the specified agency by the government of another country or by an agency of a government of another country or by an international organisation, and is information that cannot be disclosed by the specified agency because the government or agency or organisation by which the information has been provided will not consent to the disclosure.

- and that disclosure of the information would be likely to do any of the following things, as listed in section 32(3):
  (a) to prejudice the security or defence of New Zealand or the international relations of the Government of New Zealand; or
  (b) to prejudice the entrusting of information to the Government of New Zealand on a basis of confidence by the government of another country or any agency of such a government, or by any international organisation; or
  (c) to prejudice the maintenance of the law, including the prevention, investigation, and detection of offences, and the right to a fair trial; or
  (d) to endanger the safety of any person.

    (a) except where the proceedings are before the Court of Appeal, the proceedings must be heard and determined by the Chief High Court Judge, or by 1 or more Judges nominated by the Chief High Court Judge, or both; and

    (b) the Court must, on a request for the purpose by the Attorney-General and if satisfied that it is desirable to do so for the protection of (either all or part of) the classified security information, receive or hear (the relevant part of) the classified security information in the absence of–

      (i) the designated entity concerned; and

      (ii) all barristers or solicitors (if any) representing that entity; and

      (iii) members of the public.

(4) Without limiting subsection (3), if the designated entity concerned participates in proceedings–

    (a) the Court must approve a summary of the information of the kind referred to in section 32(2) that is presented by the Attorney-General except to the extent that a summary of any particular part of the information would itself involve disclosure that would be likely to prejudice the interests referred to in section 32(3); and

    (b) on being approved by the Court, a copy of the statement must be given to the entity concerned.

The question of the right to disclosure of information for the purpose of answering a case has been discussed in detail in Chap. 18 concerning the non-disclosure of information and use of redacted summaries (see Sects. 18.2.2 and 18.2.4). It was concluded there that the right to a fair hearing requires disclosure of information to enable a person to answer the case against him or her, and will result in one of three situations. Adapting those conclusions to the question of judicial review of designations, the first situation, which will be unproblematic, is where a designation has been made largely or completely on the basis of open material so that the applicant in the judicial review proceedings may respond to the reasons for the making of the designation. The second, which will require a careful approach to ensure that the essence of the right to a fair hearing is guaranteed, is where much of the material is closed but where the open material (or a redacted summary of the closed material) effectively conveys the thrust of the reasons for the making of the designation. The third and final situation, which will result in a violation of the right to a fair hearing, is where reliance on closed material is so great that the person is confronted by an unsubstantiated assertion which he or she can do no more than deny.

Despite these conclusions, New Zealand courts will be limited in the extent to which they can apply section 38 of the TSA in a manner consistent with the right to a fair hearing, which is reliant, in the NZ context, on the natural justice principle of *audi alteram partem* (hear the other side) under section 27 of the Bill of Rights Act. This is the case because of a 'trump card' within section 38, i.e. the fact that subsection 38(6) provides that the protective measures under section 38 are to "apply despite any enactment or rule of law to the contrary". The effect of this provision is that, notwithstanding any finding that section 38 is inconsistent with the right to natural justice under the NZBORA, section 38 is nevertheless to be applied by virtue of section 4 of the Bill of Rights (see Chap. 11, Sect. 11.1.3.2). This is similar in effect to the 'notwithstanding' clause in section 33(1) of the Canadian Charter of Rights and Freedoms, except that the latter has effect for only five years, unless renewed (see Chap. 11, Sect. 11.3.1.2).

A somewhat peculiar result is exposed. Although section 38 may be applied in a manner which violates the right to a fair hearing under article 14(1) of the ICCPR, the combination of section 38(6) of the Terrorism Suppression Act and section 4 of New Zealand's Bill of Rights means that NZ courts will, in such situations, be powerless to act in a human rights-compatible way. The most they will be able to do is to make a declaration of incompatibility, although this has never before occurred in New Zealand (on declarations of incompatibility, see Chap. 11, Sect. 11.2.3.2). New Zealand will therefore need to give consideration to reform of section 38, including the possibility of using special advocates, although there are limitations upon which their use can render non-disclosure of information compatible with the right to a fair hearing (see Chap. 18, Sect. 18.2.3).

19.3.2.5   Third Parties

One of the consequences of designations under the Terrorism Suppression Act is to prohibit certain dealings with designated individuals or entities. The Act includes four such offences: dealing with property, knowing that the property is owned or controlled by a designated entity or derived from such property (section 9); making property, or financial or related services, to an entity, knowing that the entity is designated under the Act (section 10); recruiting a person as a member of a group, knowing that the group is a designated entity (section 12); and participating in a group, knowing that the group is a designated entity, with the aim of enhancing its ability to carry out, or participate in, a terrorist act (section 13). In the context of the last-mentioned offence, no problem occurs since the offence is not only linked with designation but also with an intention to facilitate terrorist acts. With the other three offences, however, the key to the offending is that the conduct is otherwise lawful (dealing with property, providing financial services, and recruiting group members) except that it is in respect of an entity that is known by the actor to be designated under the Act.[78] The problem that arises is where a defendant might seek to challenge the validity of the designation. To give an example:

> A (a New Zealand citizen) makes a donation to B (a Muslim organisation in Auckland). B has been made the subject of a final designation as an associated terrorist entity (the Prime Minister concluding under section 22(3)(b)(i) of the TSA, on receiving classified security information, that B [the associated entity] is acting on behalf of C to denounce the action of the United States military in Afghanistan). C is an organisation in Afghanistan, listed in the UN Consolidated List and designated under the Terrorism Suppression Act. B is not listed by the United Nations. A [the donor] knows that B [the associated entity] has been designated as an associated terrorist entity, but claims that he and B had no knowledge that C [the terrorist entity] had carried out, or was participating in, any terrorist act. A [the donor] is charged, under section 10(1) of the TSA, with making money available to B [the associated entity], knowing that B was designated under the Act.

---

[78]Concerning other aspects of fears associated with listing, i.e. the possibility of designation and the subsequent criminalisation of conduct, see *Mohiuddin v Canada* [2006] FC 664.

In that situation, A [the donor] would no doubt want to complain that B [the associated entity] had been improperly designated under the Act – i.e. that the Prime Minister was wrong in concluding that B was an associated entity, since B knew nothing of C's involvement in any terrorist conduct, and since peaceful protest about the military conduct of the United States in Afghanistan is not unlawful. It is not difficult to imagine such a situation arising. Indeed, fear of such an outcome was the basis of a number of submissions made by the public to the select committee's hearings on the Terrorism (Bombings and Financing) Bill.[79]

The first point to make is that A would be unable to make direct use of such an argument as a defence to criminal proceedings. The prosecution will only be required to satisfy a court of the elements of the offence and would, as such, argue that the only relevant issue before the court is whether A [the donor] knew that B [the associated entity] was designated under the Act. A prosecutor would furthermore properly argue that any challenge to the validity of the designation was not an issue for the court exercising its criminal jurisdiction in that matter, but was instead a civil matter. Notwithstanding the fact that a challenge to the validity of a designation could not act as a defence to a criminal charge, such a challenge could act to suspend the criminal proceedings.[80] Taking the same example: A [the donor], as a person with an interest in ascertaining the validity of the designation of B [the associated entity], could initiate proceedings under section 33 of the Terrorism Suppression Act.

In doing so, A [the donor] would seek to have the Prime Minister's decision concerning B [the associated entity] reviewed. Specifically, section 22(3)(b)(i) (which is the basis of B's designation in this scenario) provides that the Prime Minister can designate as an associated entity a group that s/he believes on reasonable grounds:

> (b) is acting on behalf of, or at the direction of,–
> > (i) the terrorist entity, *knowing that the terrorist entity has done what is referred to in sub-section (1)* [emphasis added]

In that regard, sub-section (1) of section 23 refers to the designation of an entity as a terrorist one if it has knowingly carried out or participated in a terrorist act. In the example given, A [the donor] would seek to argue (on judicial review of the Prime Minister's decision) that although B [the associated entity] was denouncing the US military role in Afghanistan at the direction of C [the terrorist entity], B did not

---

[79]See, for example, submissions by the New Zealand Council for Civil Liberties (submission number 22), the Democratic Peoples Republic of Korea Society (submission number 28), the Indonesia Human Rights Committee (submission number 36), the Canterbury Council for Civil Liberties (submission number 45), the Latina America Committee of New Zealand (submission number 88), and the Auckland Council for Civil Liberties (submission number 95). See also Smith (2003, 61).

[80]Where a defendant is proceeded against summarily, for example, the Court has an unfettered power to adjourn the hearing of any charge: Summary Proceedings Act 1957, section 45(1).

know that C had carried out or participated in a terrorist act, and that the test under section 22(3)(b)(i) was therefore not satisfied. A would argue that the Prime Minister had improperly concluded that B was an entity within the definition of section 22.

The issue of natural justice and the right to a fair hearing again comes into play with regard to those civil proceedings, since section 38 of the TSA could require the High Court to hear the classified security information in the absence of A [the donor] or B [the associated entity]. If the classified security information was the only basis on which the designation of B was made, the hearing would violate article 14 of the ICCPR, but the High Court would be bound to proceed in this manner.

19.4   Conclusions

The designation and listing of individuals and groups as terrorist entities is an important feature of implementing targeted sanctions against such entities, particularly in the absence of a universal, concise and comprehensive definition of terrorism. Most national measures of this kind are limited to the implementation of sanctions against entities listed in the UN Consolidated List, maintained by the Al-Qa'ida and Taliban Sanctions Committee. Australia, Canada, New Zealand and the United Kingdom have the capacity to designate individuals or groups outside the UN Consolidated List. In the case of Australia and the United Kingdom, special categories of "terrorist organisations" and "proscribed organisations" have also been established (the former overlapping somewhat with the UN Consolidated List, and the latter being limited to organisations associated with the troubles arising from Northern Ireland).

Through undertaking a case study of New Zealand's measures for the designation of terrorist entities under the Terrorism Suppression Act 2002, the principal human rights implications of designating individuals and groups as terrorist entities have been explored. Concerning the impact of designations on the right of peaceful assembly and the freedom of association, the designation of terrorist entities can justifiably limit those rights, provided that the designation process is pursuant to statutory provisions and is itself proper and just. Clear safeguards must be put in place to prevent abuses of designation processes, such as the possibility of their use to prevent membership in organisations simply because they are Islamic. While proscribing membership in organisations is permissible, and not unprecedented, this must (in the context of the designation of individuals and groups as terrorist entities) be limited to the prevention of terrorism, as properly defined, or as a consequence of their inclusion in the UN Consolidated List. In the New Zealand context, this concern had been partly alleviated through the express qualifications within sections 8(2) and 10(2) of the Terrorism Suppression Act, which made it clear that it is not an offence to provide or collect funds with the intention that they be used, or knowing that they are to be used, for the purposes of advocating democratic government or the protection of human rights, so long as such an organisation is not involved in carrying out terrorist acts. It is therefore regrettable that this safeguard was repealed under the Terrorism Suppression Amendment Act 2007.

On the subject of natural justice and the right to a fair hearing, there has been much criticism over the way in which the Al-Qa'ida and Taliban Sanctions Committee undertakes its listing and de-listing functions. Despite the fact that the Committee's guidelines have vastly improved since the end of 2008, there remains no independent review of listings at the United Nations level. The UN Special Rapporteur has therefore called for access to domestic judicial review of any implementing measures at the national level. Following the reform of the TSA in 2007, the designation process in New Zealand is limited to *domestic* designations, while the application of the Act to individuals and entities listed in the UN Consolidated List is automatic and continues until those entities are removed from the Consolidated List. The practical implication of this is that, although section 33 of the Terrorism Suppression Act allows for judicial review of designations made under the Act, the right to judicial review does not apply in respect of UN-listed individuals and entities. This is in stark contrast to the recommendation of the UN Special Rapporteur. Problems arise even where judicial review *is* available, i.e. in the case of a challenge to the designation of an entity not included in the UN Consolidated List. Here, the protection afforded to classified security information, through rules under section 38 of the Act providing for non-disclosure or redacted summaries of such information, have the potential to violate the right to a fair hearing in the same way as does the use of closed material in control order proceedings.

Despite this conclusion, New Zealand courts will be limited in the extent to which they can apply section 38 of the Terrorism Suppression Act in a manner consistent with the right to a fair hearing, which is reliant, in the NZ context, on the natural justice principle of *audi alteram partem* under section 27 of the Bill of Rights Act. Section 38(6) of the TSA provides that the protective measures under section 38 are to "apply despite any enactment or rule of law to the contrary" meaning that, notwithstanding any finding that section 38 is inconsistent with the right to natural justice under the NZBORA, section 38 is nevertheless to be applied by virtue of section 4 of the Bill of Rights. Although section 38 need *not* be applied in a manner which violates the right to a fair hearing under article 14(1) of the ICCPR (depending on the nature of the information upon which the designation is based), the combination of section 38(6) of the TSA and section 4 of New Zealand's Bill of Rights means that NZ courts will, in such situations, be powerless to act in a human rights-compatible way. The case study thus exposes the vulnerability of human rights in New Zealand to being overridden by ordinary statutes, in this case one which has been enacted for the suppression of terrorism. In the particular context, New Zealand will need to give consideration to reform of section 38.

New Zealand's designation process also raises natural justice issues in the context of inadequate notice to designated persons, or those affected by designations, of the reasons for designation. Specific reform has been advocated in this regard, as has reform for executive review of designations.

References

Bowring, Bill. 2007. The Human Rights Implications of International Listing Mechanisms for 'Terrorist' Organisations, in *Expert Workshop on Human Rights and International Co-operation in Counter-Terrorism. FINAL REPORT*, online: http://www.osce.org/documents/odihr/2007/02/23424_en.pdf, 75.

Cameron, Iain. 2006. The European Convention on Human Rights, Due Process and United Nations Security Council Counter-Terrorism Sanctions. Strasbourg: Council of Europe

Cole, David. 1999. Hanging with the Wrong Crowd: Of Gangs, Terrorists, and the Right of Association. *The Supreme Court Review* 203.

Conte, Alex. 2007. *Counter-Terrorism and Human Rights in New Zealand*. Christchurch: New Zealand Law Foundation (available online: http://www.alexconte.com/docs/CT%20and%20HR%20in%20New%20Zealand.pdf).

Conte, Alex, and Burchill, Richard. 2009. *Defining Civil and Political Rights: The Jurisprudence of the United Nations Human Rights* Committee. Aldershot: 2nd ed, Ashgate Publishing Ltd.

Dosman, E. Alexandra. 2004. For the Record: Designating 'Listed Entities' for the Purposes of Terrorist Financing Offences at Canadian Law. 62(1) *University of Toronto Faculty of Law Review* 1.

Fellman, David. 1961. Constitutional Rights of Association. *The Supreme Court Review*74.

Fromuth, Peter (2009). The European Court of Justice *Kadi* Decision and the Future of UN Counterterrorism Sanctions. 13(20) *American Society of International Law Insight*.

Hogg, Russell. 2008. Executive Proscription of Terrorist Organisations in Australia: Exploring the Shifting Border between Crime and Politics. In Gani, Miriam, and Mathew, Penelope. *Fresh Perspectives on the 'War on Terror'*. Canberra: Australian National University E-Press.

Jenkins, David. 2003. In Support of Canada's Anti-Terrorism Act: A Comparison of Canadian, British and American Anti-Terrorism Law. 66 *Saskatchewan Law Review* 419.

Joseph, Philip. 2001. *Constitutional and Administrative Law in New Zealand*. Wellington: 2nd edition, Brookers.

Joseph, Sarah. 2004. Australian Counter-terrorism Legislation and the International Human Rights Framework. 27(2) *The University of New South Wales Law Journal* 428.

Keith, Kenneth. 2003. Terrorism, Civil Liberties and Human Rights, a paper presented at the 13th Commonwealth Law Conference 2003, (CR4) Terrorism: Meeting the Challenges / Finding the Balances, 13–17 April 2003.

Ricketts, Aidan. 2002. Freedom of Association or Guilt by Association: Australia's New Anti-Terrorism Laws and the Retreat of Political Liberty. 6 *Southern Cross University Law Review* 133.

Rishworth, Paul, Huscroft, Grant, Optican, Scott, and Mahoney, Richard. 2003. *The New Zealand Bill of Rights*. Oxford: Oxford University Press.

Smith, John. 2003. *New Zealand's Anti-Terrorism Campaign: Balancing Civil Liberties, National Security, and International Responsibilities*. Ian Axford New Zealand Fellowship in Public Policy.

Tappeiner, Imelda. 2005. The Fight Against Terrorism. The lists and the gaps. 1(1) *Utrecht Law Review* 97.

Tham, Joo-Cheong. 2004. Possible Constitutional Objections to the Powers to Ban 'Terrorist' Origanistions. 27(2) *The University of New South Wales Law Journal* 482.

Chapter 20
Speech, the Media, and Incitement to Terrorism

The freedom of expression and of the media have been subject to limitations under counter-terrorism laws, even prior to the events of September 11. The United Kingdom had, as a continuation and extension of public order laws dating back to the early 1900s, created offences of inciting terrorism under the Terrorism Act 2000 and Terrorism Act 2006. New Zealand had established mechanisms in 1987 for the control of media broadcasts and publications relating to terrorist emergencies. The focus upon the media, and individual and group rights to the freedom of expression, has intensified in recent years. While not all issues in this subject area can be examined within the scope of a single chapter,[1] the focus of this chapter is on two case studies: media control under New Zealand's International Terrorism (Emergency Powers) Act 1987; and incitement to terrorism offences under the UK's Terrorism Act 2006.

20.1 Media Control

The 'War on Terror', and the legislative and executive action that followed 11 September 2001, have been cited as the cause of a decline in the freedom of the press.[2] Interestingly, in the case of New Zealand, there have been no legislative

---

[1]Consider, for example, the ban in Australia of two radical Islamic books in 2006: see Abjorensen (2006) and Saul (2006). Nor does this chapter examine the sedition offences under section 80.2(7) and (8) of Australia's Criminal Code Act 1995 (see Chap. 5, Sect. 5.2.1); or the question of attacks directed against, and killings of, journalists and media workers – see Human Rights Council resolution 12/67, UN Doc A/HRC/Res/12/16 (2009), preambular para 4 and 3(c); and the report of the Special Rapporteur on the promotion and protection of the right to freedom of opinion and expression, UN Doc A/HRC/11/4 (2009), paras 43–50.

[2]See, for example, the accounts of the organisation Reporters Without Borders, pointing to the physical violence and enforced disappearance suffered by journalists, the arrest and detention of media workers, censorship, and the surveillance of the internet: '2003 Round-Up', Reporters Without Borders, 6 January 2004, online: http://www.charter97.org/eng/news/2004/01/06/

A. Conte, *Human Rights in the Prevention and Punishment of Terrorism*, 619
DOI 10.1007/978-3-642-11608-7_20, © Springer-Verlag Berlin Heidelberg 2010

changes since September 11 impacting upon media control. Media control was, however, something legislated for under the International Terrorism (Emergency Powers) Act 1987 (NZ) following the Rainbow Warrior bombing in 1985 (on the Rainbow Warrior bombing, see Chap. 4 at Sect. 4.1.2.2). New Zealand stands out as the only one of the four case study countries to adopt such measures. These measures are not directed towards criticisms about sensationalised journalism in terrorism cases, or 'responsible journalism' in the area of national security.[3] They instead involve powers allowing the Prime Minister of New Zealand to impose media gags concerning matters relevant to an international terrorist emergency.

20.1.1   The International Terrorism (Emergency Powers) Act 1987

Under New Zealand's International Terrorism (Emergency Powers) Act 1987 (ITEPA), the Prime Minister of New Zealand is able to prohibit the publication or broadcasting of certain matters relevant to an "international terrorist emergency" (as defined in the Act – see Chap. 7, Sect. 7.3.2). Although an international terrorist emergency has never been invoked, Assistant Commissioner of Police responsible for counter-terrorism, Jon White, has reported that this was contemplated in 2003 when cyanide was mailed in threatening letters to the embassies of the United States and United Kingdom.[4] Section 14 of the ITEPA provides the Prime Minister with certain rights to control the media where an international terrorist emergency has been declared:[5]

> 14. Prime Minister may prohibit publication or broadcasting of certain matters relating to international terrorist emergency–
>
> (1) Where, in respect of any emergency in respect of which authority to exercise emergency powers has been given under this Act, the Prime Minister believes, on reasonable grounds, that the publication or broadcasting of–
> (a) The identity of any person involved in dealing with that emergency; or

---

borders; and 'United States', Reporters Without Borders, 22 June 2004, online: http://www.rsf.org/article.php3?id_article=10612 (as accessed on 11 March 2005 – copy on file with author). See also United Nations Foundation, 'Report Shows Decline of Press Freedom with War on Terror', UN Wire, 8 January 2004, online: http://www.unwire.org/UNWire (as accessed on 12 January 2004 – copy on file with author).

[3]Concerning this issue see, for example, Bassiouni (1981, pp. 14–19), and Dreher (2007). See also Council of Europe Parliamentary Assembly Recommendation on media and terrorism, Recommendation 1706 (2005), in which reference is made to the Committee of Ministers, Declaration on freedom of expression and information in the media in the context of the fight against terrorism of 2 March 2005 (available online: https://wcd.coe.int/ViewDoc.jsp?id=830679&Site=CM).

[4]Smith (2003, p. 11, note 57).

[5]Note that subsections (4) and (5) of section 14 (concerning the publication of section 14 notices in the Gazette and proceedings of the House of Representatives) have not been reproduced.

    (b) Any other information or material (including a photograph) which would be likely to identify any person as a person involved in dealing with that emergency – would be likely to endanger the safety of any person involved in dealing with that emergency, or of any other person, the Prime Minister may, by notice in writing, prohibit or restrict –

    (c) The publication, in any newspaper or other document; and

    (d) The broadcasting, by radio or television or otherwise, – of the identity of any person involved in dealing with that emergency, and any other information or material (including a photograph) which would be likely to identify any person as a person involved in dealing with that emergency.

(2) Where, in respect of any emergency in respect of which authority to exercise emergency powers has been given under this Act, the Prime Minister believes, on reasonable grounds, that the publication or broadcasting of any information or material (including a photograph) relating to any equipment or technique lawfully used to deal with that emergency would be likely to prejudice measures designed to deal with international terrorist emergencies, the Prime Minister may, by notice in writing, prohibit or restrict–

    (a) The publication, in any newspaper or other document; and

    (b) The broadcasting, by radio or television or otherwise, – of any information or material (including a photograph) of any such equipment or technique.

(3) The Prime Minister may issue a notice under subsection (1) or subsection (2) of this section notwithstanding that the emergency in respect of which the notice is issued has ended.

Section 15 of the Act then deals with the expiry, revocation and renewal of section 14 notices. Subsection (3) provides that, unless earlier revoked or extended (or unless the notice specifies the life of the notice), a section 14 notice will expire 12 months after the date on which it was issued. This provision is unaffected by whether the terrorist emergency continues to exist. Section 15(4) allows further extensions for periods of 5 years at a time, if renewal of the notice is necessary either to protect the safety of any person, or to avoid prejudice to measures designed to deal with international terrorist emergencies.

20.1.1.1 The Availability of Judicial Review

A potential problem with the Prime Minister's powers under sections 14 and 15 of the ITEPA is that the establishment and continuance of media gags might not be capable of being challenged. If this is correct, there is no guarantee that notices under sections 14 and 15 will indeed be connected with the stated objectives within those provisions. In the absence of a review mechanism, the effect of the provisions is to create the potential for an unfettered abuse of media control under the ITEPA. The issue thus arising is whether notices under sections 14 and 15 are reviewable.

    The starting point is to recognise that the ITEPA does not prohibit judicial review and, as such, the media may be able to challenge the continuance of media gags through judicial review proceedings. This will depend on whether decisions of the Prime Minister under sections 14 or 15 of the ITEPA are justiciable. The most recent word on the justiciability of ministerial decisions in New Zealand is the case of *Curtis v Minister of Defence*.[6] Citing its earlier decision in

---

[6]*Curtis v Minister of Defence* [2002] 2 NZLR 744.

CREEDNZ v Governor General,[7] and decisions of the Supreme Court of Canada and House of Lords, the New Zealand Court of Appeal concluded that:[8]

> A non-justiciable issue is one in respect of which there is no satisfactory legal yardstick by which the issue can be resolved. That situation will often arise in cases into which it is also constitutionally inappropriate for the Courts to embark.

Applying the test identified by the NZ Court of Appeal, decisions under sections 14 and 15 appear to be justiciable. Rephrasing the Court's test in the context of the ITEPA provisions, there are two questions to ask. First, are decisions under sections 14 and 15 ones in respect of which it would be constitutionally acceptable for the courts to embark? Second, is there a satisfactory legal yardstick by which to determine whether the Prime Minister's decisions under sections 14 and 15 have been properly made? The answer to both questions is in the affirmative.

Considering the first question, the determinations at hand are not ones of a constitutionally sensitive nature calling for judicial deference. The decisions concern the safety of persons and the potential prejudice of information to future counter-terrorist operations. Unlike *Curtis*, they are not decisions concerning the disposition of armed forces or other policy-based matters. Such a conclusion is consistent with the Court of Appeal's approach in the *Zaoui* case, where the decision to issue a security certificate was held to be subject to judicial review in the absence of an express exclusion of judicial review.[9] This also goes to answer the second question. In exercising judicial review of decisions under sections 14 and 15, the courts would be considering the application of facts to the statutory tests under those provisions to determine whether the establishment or continuance of notices is proper. The question to be considered or, in the words of the Court of Appeal, the legal yardstick to be applied by the courts would be this: Would the publication or broadcasting of the identity of any person involved in the emergency (or of other information or material that would lead to the identity of such a person) be likely to either (1) endanger the safety of that or any other person (sections 14(1) and 15(4)(a)), or (2) prejudice measures designed to deal with international terrorist emergencies (section 14(2) and 15(4)(b))?

The question is a justiciable one, capable of determination upon the application of facts, and judicial review is thus available as a safeguard against the improper use of sections 14 and 15 of the ITEPA. The consequence of this is significant to the question of the provisions' compatibility with the New Zealand Bill of Rights Act, which is considered below.

---

[7] *CREEDNZ v Governor General* [1981] 1 NZLR 359.

[8] *Curtis v Minister of Defence* (n 6) 752 (para 27).

[9] *Attorney-General v Zaoui (No 2)* [2005] 1 NZLR 690.

20.1.1.2   The Unique Nature of the Prime Minister's Powers

An observation to be made at this early stage is that the powers being considered under the ITEPA stand as a rare example of media control in counter-terrorism law and practice. Comparable powers are not known to exist in other Western democracies. Notwithstanding the uncommon nature of these powers, however, the position of this author is that they are justifiable within their particular statutory framework and having regard to the availability of judicial review.

If media control is indeed justifiable within those confines, one might therefore ask why New Zealand stands as an exception to general practice. There is no clear answer to this question and one can only speculate. Two alternative and potentially overlapping considerations may have dissuaded other jurisdictions from taking similar steps. First is the unpopularity of such legislative action being taken. Media control is something that is generally strongly opposed, although it may be that the pre-bill of rights mood in New Zealand existing at the time of the enactment of the ITEPA rendered such opposition ineffective. The other factor is that media control in this area may be perceived as unnecessary or, at least, that its absence does not pose a sufficiently high risk to warrant the potential political fall-out of taking legislative action. The type of information capable of protection under the ITEPA is, after all, unlikely to fall into the hands of the media, since such information will normally relate to covert operations, or operations that are conducted out of the sight or knowledge of the media.

20.1.2   *Freedom of the Press*

Freedom of expression is a matter dealt with under article 19(2) and (3) of the International Covenant on Civil and Political Rights (ICCPR).[10] Paragraph (3) sets out the permissible limitations upon the freedom (to be discussed), while paragraph (2) expresses the substantive right:

> 2. Everyone shall have the right to freedom of expression; this right shall include freedom to seek, receive and impart information and ideas of all kinds, regardless of frontiers, either orally, in writing or in print, in the form of art, or through any other media of his choice.

In very similar terms, section 14 of the New Zealand Bill of Rights Act 1990 (NZBORA) guarantees "the right to freedom of expression, including the freedom to seek, receive, and impart information and opinions of any kind in any form".

---

[10]International Covenant on Civil and Political Rights, opened for signature 16 December 1966, 999 UNTS 171 (entered into force 23 March 1976).

20.1.2.1 Freedom of Expression and Freedom of the Press

A question to briefly consider is whether article 19 of the ICCPR and section 14 of the NZBORA afford protection to the media. In contrast to section 2(b) of the Canadian Charter of Rights and Freedoms, neither the ICCPR nor the NZBORA expresses a 'freedom of the press'.[11] In the case of section 14 of the NZBORA, the approach of New Zealand courts has been to treat freedom of the press as an integral feature of the right of all members of the public to seek, receive and impart information and opinions. Gelber speaks of the freedom of expression as important to the creation and maintenance of an informed and critical public, capable of engaging in the deliberation necessary for democratic legitimacy.[12] The press plays a vital role in that process.[13] The High Court of New Zealand, in *Solicitor-General v Radio New Zealand Ltd*, stated that "the right of freedom of the press is no more and no less than the right of all and any member of the public to make comment".[14] Likewise, in *Television New Zealand Ltd v Attorney-General*, President Cooke stated for the Court of Appeal:[15]

> The freedom of the press is not separately specified in the New Zealand Bill of Rights, our Bill differing in that respect from s 2 of the Canadian Charter of Rights and Freedoms and the First Amendment in the United States, but it is an important adjunct of the rights concerning freedom of expression affirmed in s 14 of the New Zealand Bill of Rights Act. They include 'the freedom to seek, receive, and impart information ... Decisions of this Court have reflected the importance of media freedom, quite apart from the Bill of Rights'. *Attorney-General for the United Kingdom v Wellington Newspapers Ltd* [1988] 1 NZLR 129, 176 and *Auckland Area Health Board v Television New Zealand Ltd* [1992] 3 NZLR 406 are two of the numerous examples which could be cited.

The situation under the International Covenant is slightly more complicated. The words of the Covenant do not expressly include the freedom of the press, although the argument adopted by New Zealand courts is again applicable. This must be correct, since article 19(2) speaks of the right to *impart* information of any kind and in any way. The only difficulty lies in the fact that there is no jurisprudence in this area since complaints to the Human Rights Committee under the First Optional Protocol to the ICCPR are limited to communications by individuals.[16] It was on that basis that communications 360/1989 and 361/1989 were dismissed by the Committee

---

[11]Section 2(b) of the Canadian Charter of Rights and Freedoms 1982 guarantees, as a fundamental freedom, the: "Freedom of thought, belief, opinion and expression, including freedom of the press and other media of communication".

[12]Gelber (2007, p. 144). See also Countering Terrorism, Protecting Human Rights. A Manual (Warsaw: Organisation for Security and Cooperation in Europe Office for Democratic Institutions and Human Rights, 2007), pp. 219–226. See also HRC Res 12/16 (n 1) paras 9–11.

[13]See, for example, HRC Res 12/16 (n 1) preambular para 7.

[14]*Solicitor-General v Radio New Zealand Ltd* [1994] 1 NZLR 48, 61.

[15]*Television New Zealand Ltd v Attorney-General* [1995] 2 NZLR 641, 646.

[16]Conte and Burchill (2009, pp. 20–24).

as being inadmissible under the Optional Protocol.[17] The communications involved claims by printing companies, whose main purpose was to purchase and supply material to a publication company for the production, printing and publishing of weekly newspapers. Both communications were submitted on behalf of companies incorporated under the laws of Trinidad and Tobago. Under article 1 of the Optional Protocol, only individuals are able to submit a communication to the Human Rights Committee. As such, the particular communications were found to be inadmissible.

Importantly, however, this does not invalidate the application of article 19 to the freedom of the press. The effect of what has just been discussed simply means that only individuals, as opposed to media groups or corporations, may complain to the Human Rights Committee about interference with their freedom of expression. The freedom is still a right guaranteed under the Covenant and an obligation in respect of which New Zealand must, as a State party, comply. The non-justiciability of group rights under the optional complaints procedure established by the First Protocol must not be taken to exclude the application of rights to groups or other entities.

20.1.2.2 Limiting the Freedom of the Press when Responding to Terrorism

Control upon the media and its ability to publish or broadcast any matter clearly impacts upon the freedom of the press. In the language of the steps advocated by Rishworth for application of sections 4, 5 and 6 of the NZBORA, the right being invoked (the freedom of expression) applies to the circumstances being complained of (the Prime Minister's authority under sections 14 and 15 of the ITEPA) – see further Chap. 11, Sect. 11.1.3.2.[18] Because these provisions effect limitations upon the freedom of expression, the issue to then consider is whether the limitations are consistent with section 5 of the New Zealand Bill of Rights Act and the rights-specific limitations expressed within article 19(3) of the ICCPR.

In its 1991 report on emergencies, the New Zealand Law Commission spoke of the generally accepted notion that only in the most exceptional circumstances is it desirable or necessary to control the media in its coverage of events.[19] The report pointed to the siege of the Iranian Embassy in London in 1980 as a situation in which this almost arose. The police and SAS assault on the Embassy was filmed, although this was not broadcast live. In noting such occurrences, the report identified various factors that might call for media control, from the perspective of both

---

[17]*A Newspaper Publishing Company v Trinidad and Tobago*, Human Rights Committee Communication 360/1989, UN Doc CCPR/C/36/D/360/1989 (1989); and *A Publication and a Printing Company v Trinidad and Tobago*, Human Rights Committee Communication 361/1989, UN Doc CCPR/C/36/D/361/1989 (1989), para 12.2.

[18]Rishworth et al. (2003, pp. 135–157).

[19]New Zealand Law Commission Final Report on Emergencies, Report 22 (1991), para 7.140.

dealing with an instant terrorist emergency and the longer-term implications of broadcasting and publication. On the subject of dealing with an actual terrorist incident, the report noted:[20]

> Media coverage of terrorist events can compromise the efforts of the authorities to resolve those events and may also prejudice further responses to terrorist action. The primary concern is that the terrorist, by following the coverage of the incident, may be alerted to counteractive measures taken by the police and by the armed forces where they are involved. This forewarning may result in the failure of the operation and could place lives, of both anti-terrorist personnel and hostages (if any) at risk.

Other factors were also identified as having a potential impact upon the ability of authorities to deal with particular instances of terrorist activity.[21] First was the obstruction of authorities by the physical presence of the media, although this is a matter that could apply to the physical presence of any person and is, in any event, dealt with under section 10 of the ITEPA (see Chap. 7, Sect. 7.3.3). The Commissioner also identified that media representatives may become participants in an international terrorist event by communicating directly with the terrorists and thereby potentially undermining the conduct of authorities. Again, however, this is a matter that appears capable of being dealt with under the police powers to restrict entry and require evacuation of emergency areas under section 10 of the Act. The report also makes the point that media coverage may have an impact outside the operation of a particular terrorist emergency. This might occur through terrorist organisations gaining tactical information and technical knowledge from the media coverage of counter-terrorist operations. Such coverage might also expose the identity of members of counter-terrorist forces and thereby expose them to the risk of attack by terrorists. These are clearly undesirable consequences and, as discussed next, go to the heart of the justifiability of sections 14 and 15 of the ITEPA.

20.1.3   Media Control as a Justifiable Limit to the Freedom of the Press

Having established the scope of the powers under sections 14 and 15 of the International Terrorism (Emergency Powers) Act 1987, their susceptibility to judicial review, and that they impact upon the freedom of expression, this part of the chapter examines whether the ITEPA provisions are consistent with section 5 of the New Zealand Bill of Rights Act and the rights-specific limitations expressed within article 19(3) of the ICCPR.

---

[20]Ibid, para 7.142–7.143.

[21]Ibid, para 7.144.

20.1.3.1   Media Control and the ICCPR

Article 19(3) of the International Covenant on Civil and Political Rights sets out
a number of rights-specific limitations as follows:

> The exercise of the rights provided for in paragraph 2 of this article carries with it special
> duties and responsibilities. It may therefore be subject to certain restrictions, but these shall
> only be such as are provided by law and are necessary:
>
> (a) For respect of the rights or reputations of others;
> (b) For the protection of national security or of public order (*ordre public*), or of public
>   health or morals.

A number of preliminary observations can be made. First, as recognised within the
first sentence of paragraph (3), the exercise of freedom of expression carries with it
special duties and responsibilities. This permits the imposition of restrictions upon
the freedom, which may relate either to the interests of other persons (paragraph (3)
(a)) or to those of the community as a whole (paragraph (3)(b)). Any restriction
must be provided for by law, it must address one of the aims enumerated in
paragraph (3)(a) and (b), and it must be necessary to achieve those legitimate
purposes (as explained in the second sentence of article 19(3)). The cumulative
nature of these requirements was emphasised by the Human Rights Committee in
Mukong v Cameroon.[22] Any limitation must also be proportional and not implemented in a manner that nullifies the substance of the right to expression, as
explained by the Committee in its General Comment on article 19.[23] Where a
State seeks to justify a limitation as falling within the ambit of paragraph (3), the
Human Rights Committee will require the State party to specify the precise nature
of the threat allegedly posed by a person's exercise of freedom of expression and
how the limitation achieves dissipation of that threat.[24]

The question of limiting the freedom of expression on the basis of national
security was considered in *Park v Republic of Korea*. Korea stated, in that communication, that the restrictions in question (prohibiting the "praising, encouraging, or
siding with or through other means the activities of an anti-State organization")
were justified in order to protect national security, and that they were provided for
by law under article 7(1) of the National Security Law 1980 (Korea). Despite the
potentially sensitive nature of security issues, the Committee took the view that it
was nevertheless required to determine whether any measures taken were in fact
necessary for the purpose stated. On the facts of the communication, the State party
invoked national security by reference to the general situation in the country and the

---

[22]*Mukong v Cameroon*, Human Rights Committee Communication 458/1991, UN Doc CCPR/C/
51/D/458/1991 (1994), para 9.7.

[23]General Comment 10: Article 19, UN Doc HRI/GEN/1/Rev.6 at 132 (2003), para 4.

[24]See, for example, *Kim v Republic of Korea*, Human Rights Committee Communication 574/
1994, UN Doc CCPR/C/64/D/574/1994 (1999), para 12.5; *Laptsevic v Belarus*, Human Rights
Committee Communication 780/1997, UN Doc CCPR/C/68/D/780/1997 (2000), para 8.5; and
Pietrataroia v Uruguay, Human Rights Committee Communication r10.44/1979, para 17.

threat posed by "North Korean communists". The Committee considered that the State had failed to specify the precise nature of the threat posed by the author's exercise of freedom of expression and therefore found that there was no basis upon which the restriction could be considered compatible with article 19(3).[25]

In contrast to the adverse aspects of this communication, the ITEPA deals with specific emergencies (declared by no fewer than three Ministers upon advice from the Commissioner of Police, on the particular facts, to constitute an "international terrorist emergency"). Applying the various requirements of paragraph (3) identified above, the first requirement is clearly met, since sections 14 and 15 set out restrictions imposed by law. Next, to satisfy paragraph (3), the provisions must be in pursuit of the aims expressed in subparagraphs (3)(a) and (b). Sections 14 and 15 appear to fit well within the aim of protecting national security and, equally, protecting public order or public health. The Prime Minister's authority to restrict the media only arises where the information in question:

- "Would be likely to endanger the safety of any person involved in dealing with that emergency, or of any other person" (section 14(1)); or
- "Would be likely to prejudice measures designed to deal with international terrorist emergencies" (section 14(2)).

Likewise, extension of such notices can only occur where:

- "Renewal of the notice is necessary. . . to protect the safety of any person" (section 15(4)(a)); or
- "Renewal of the notice is necessary. . . to avoid prejudice to measures designed to deal with international terrorist emergencies" (section 15(4)(b)).

The final requirement of paragraph (3) is that any limitation upon the freedom of expression be proportional and in response to specific identifiable threats caused by a continuance of the freedom. In the main, proportionality appears to be met, and it is clear that these measures can only apply to identified, and expressly declared, states of international terrorist emergencies. The only matter of concern relates to section 14(3) of the ITEPA, which permits the continuance of restrictions or prohibitions notwithstanding that the emergency has ended. A notice under section 14 automatically lasts for one year, unless earlier revoked by the Prime Minister (section 15(2) and (3)). The restrictions can then be extended for 5 year periods under section 15(4) if renewal of the notice is necessary for the protection of any person or to avoid prejudice to measures designed to deal with terrorism. As identified earlier, the continued suppression of information may be necessary for the purpose of preventing the identification of counter-terrorist agents or to prevent terrorist organisations from gaining tactical or technical information on counter-terrorist operations and, to that extent, the ability for

---

[25]*Park v Republic of Korea*, Human Rights Committee Communication 628/1995, UN Doc CCPR/ C/64/D/628/1995 (1998). See also *Kim v Republic of Korea* (ibid) para 10.3.

restrictions to apply after a state of emergency seems reasonable. At face value, then, this seems appropriate.

The only question that remains is whether the Prime Minister's authority is subject to sufficient checks and balances. As concluded earlier, sections 14 and 15 are subject to judicial review. This might not give the media much comfort in the short-term, given the immediate effect of section 14 notices and the reality that judicial review will take time. One might observe, however, that the powers of the Prime Minister will only be activated during an "international terrorist emergency", declared on the basis of consensus on the part of at least three Ministers of the Crown based upon advice from the Commissioner of Police. The New Zealand Law Commission identified that the gravity of the circumstances giving rise to such an emergency will vary, as will the threat posed by the publication or broadcasting of information.[26]

As noted by the Law Commission, the Human Rights Committee has levelled criticism at the media provisions of the ITEPA in its consideration of New Zealand's reports under the ICCPR.[27] In its observations on New Zealand's second periodic report, the Committee noted that concerns raised by it during the examination of New Zealand's report concerning the scope of the ITEPA had not been alleviated.[28] The Committee expressed particular concern about the 'closure provisions' of the ITEPA media gags referring, it seems, to the means by which media gags may be discontinued. The ability to judicially review the continuance of notices and thereby allow such notices to be tested against the article 19(3) grounds for limiting freedom of expression should, however, satisfy the Committee.

20.1.3.2   Media Control and Section 5 of the NZBORA

Turning now to the question of whether sections 14 and 15 of the ITEPA impose justifiable limits in accordance with section 5 of the NZBORA, the first consideration (the existence of an important objective) seems easy to answer. To the extent that media gags are issued for the purposes identified under sections 14(1) and (2) and 15(4) of the ITEPA, those objectives are clearly pressing and substantial. They not only deal with instant emergencies, but are also aimed at preserving the integrity of counter-terrorist operations, and the safety of persons. Such objectives clearly satisfy the first limb of the *Oakes* and *Radio New Zealand* limitations test (see further Chap. 11, Sect. 11.5.2.1).[29]

In applying the second, proportionality, limb of the section 5 test one must first be satisfied that the legislative provision is rationally connected to the achievement

---

[26]New Zealand Law Commission Report 22 (n 19), para 7.151.

[27]Ibid, para 7.152.

[28]Human Rights Committee, Concluding Observations: New Zealand, UN Doc CCPR/A/44/40 (1989), paras 393 and 402.

[29]*R v Oakes* (1986) 26 DLR (4th) 200; and *Solicitor-General v Radio New Zealand Ltd* (n 14).

of the objective. Again, this seems easy to answer in the affirmative. The structure of sections 14 and 15 is such as to restrict or prohibit the publication or broadcasting of information likely to prejudice the safety of a person or the integrity of future counter-terrorist operations. The second proportionality factor requires the legislative provision to impair the right as little as reasonably possible. This goes to the question of whether sections 14 and 15 are the least intrusive means by which their objectives might be achieved. So long as safeguards exist against the improper use of these provisions, the minimal impairment test is also satisfied. The current statutory framework does not exclude judicial review of section 14 and 15 decisions and, as concluded above, these decisions are justiciable so that adequate safeguards against abuse are present. This conclusion goes to the final factor of the proportionality test also, rendering the effect of the provisions upon the freedom of the press proportional to the objectives of protecting the safety of persons and the ability to deal with future counter-terrorist operations. As such, sections 14 and 15 are 'consistent' with the New Zealand Bill of Rights Act 1990 and no further enquiry under Rishworth's steps is required.

20.1.3.3 Conclusions

Sections 14 and 15 of the International Terrorism (Emergency Powers) Act 1987 (NZ) stand as a rare example of media control by a State in counter-terrorism law and practice. Notwithstanding this, having regard to the susceptibility of ITEPA notices to judicial review and the purposes in respect of which notices may be made and extended, these provisions are compliant with both the ICCPR and the NZBORA. In a disappointingly brief and cursory examination of the ICCPR and NZBORA, the Law Commission's 1991 report on emergencies concluded that media control under the ITEPA was ineffective. The Commission gave no reasons for this conclusion, other than that the Act was 'cumbersome' in determining whether a terrorist emergency exists.[30] This does not, however, go to the question of whether the media control provisions are themselves effective.

The Commission also concluded that the encroachment of sections 14 and 15 upon the ICCPR and NZBORA was not justified, again without analysis as to how that conclusion was reached.[31] The Final Report on Emergencies therefore recommended the repeal of sections 14 and 15, preferring a model by which voluntary guidelines be adopted by the media. This author disagrees. Certainly, the provisions do limit freedom of the press, a freedom guaranteed by article 19 of the ICCPR and section 14 of the NZBORA. However, the restricted purposes in respect of which media gags may be issued, combined with the availability of judicial review as a safeguard against abuse of the powers under the provisions, mean that the ITEPA

---

[30]New Zealand Law Commission Report 22 (n 19), paras 7.160 and 7.161.
[31]Ibid, para 7.162.

provisions comply with the limitations provisions of article 19(3) of the ICCPR and section 5 of the NZBORA.

20.2 Incitement to Terrorism

The incitement to terrorism is becoming a common tool of terrorist organisations (see Chap. 14, Sect. 14.3.1). All UN member States are under an obligation to prevent the commission of terrorist acts, and have been urged and called upon by both the General Assembly and Security Council to prohibit the incitement to terrorism (see Chap. 14, Sect. 14.3.2.1). In respect of the incitement of conduct that is both terrorist in nature and also amounts to genocide, the prohibition of such incitement is required of States parties to the Rome Statute of the International Criminal Court. Furthermore, States parties to the International Covenant on Civil and Political Rights are obliged to criminalise the advocacy of national, racial or religious hatred that constitutes incitement to discrimination, hostility or violence (see Sect. 20.2.1 above). Those European States that become party to the Council of Europe Convention on the Prevention of Terrorism will be required to prohibit the unlawful and intentional public provocation to commit a terrorist offence, as defined within the Convention.[32] It should be noted that the incitement offence under article 5 of the Convention has been identified as a best practice in the area, as one combining the element of intent and the risk of the commission of a terrorist act (see Sect. 20.2.2.3 below):[33]

Article 5 – Public provocation to commit a terrorist offence

1. For the purposes of this Convention, "public provocation to commit a terrorist offence" means the distribution, or otherwise making available, of a message to the public, with the intent to incite the commission of a terrorist offence, where such conduct, whether or not directly advocating terrorist offences, causes a danger that one or more such offences may be committed.
2. Each Party shall adopt such measures as may be necessary to establish public provocation to commit a terrorist offence, as defined in paragraph 1, when committed unlawfully and intentionally, as a criminal offence under its domestic law.

Common to the prohibitions under the Rome Statute, the ICCPR, and the European Convention on the Prevention of Terrorism is the proactive nature of the prohibitions, not requiring the act incited to have been committed for an offence to occur. Of general application, sanctions imposed for those convicted of the incitement to terrorism should be particularly dissuasive and in conformity with the principle of

---

[32]Council of Europe Convention on the Prevention of Terrorism, opened for signature 16 May 2005, CETS 196 (entered into force 1 July 2007). The Convention was signed by the United Kingdom on 16 May 2005.

[33]Special Rapporteur on the promotion and protection of human rights and fundamental freedoms while countering terrorism, Protection of human rights and fundamental freedoms while countering terrorism, UN Doc A/61/267 (2006), para 28.

proportionality between the gravity of the sanction and the gravity of the act. In responding to the problem of the incitement to terrorism, the first option available to States is to implement a general proscription of incitement to discrimination, hostility or violence through the advocacy of national, racial or religious hatred, in compliance with the obligation under article 20(2) of the ICCPR (see Sect. 20.2.1 below). Such a proscription would capture conduct amounting to the incitement to terrorism. Reflecting the more general nature of such a proscription, however, the maximum penalties for such offending would need to be limited. This may not impose a sufficiently appropriate level of sanction, given the calls for terrorist offending to be punished by heavy sentences (see Chap. 14, Sect. 14.2.4). The better approach is for States to criminalise the particular conduct of incitement to terrorism, with an appropriately corresponding criminal sanction.

Considered within this part of the chapter is the freedom of expression and the permissible limits upon expression by individuals and groups in the context of proscribing the incitement to terrorism. Safeguards are identified, and then tested on a case study basis to the incitement offences in the United Kingdom under the Terrorism Act 2006.

20.2.1   The Freedom of Expression and Its Corollaries in the Context of Incitement Offences

Article 18(1) of the International Covenant on Civil and Political Rights guarantees the freedom of thought, mirrored in article 19(1) of the Covenant as the right to hold opinions without interference. The freedom of expression (including the freedom to seek, receive and impart information and ideas of all kinds, regardless of frontiers) is subsequently guaranteed under article 19(2). Recognised within paragraph (3) of article 19 is the fact that the exercise of the right to freedom of expression carries with it special duties and responsibilities permitting the imposition of restrictions upon the right, which may relate either to the interests of other persons or to those of the community as a whole:

> Article 19
>
> 3. The exercise of the rights provided for in paragraph 2 of this article carries with it special duties and responsibilities. It may therefore be subject to certain restrictions, but these shall only be such as are provided by law and are necessary:
>   (a) For respect of the rights or reputations of others;
>   (b) For the protection of national security or of public order (*ordre public*), or of public health or morals.

Within the terms of paragraph (3), any restriction must cumulatively meet the following conditions: it must be provided for by law, it must address one of the aims enumerated in paragraph (3)(a) and (b) of article 19, and it must be necessary to achieve those legitimate purposes. The cumulative nature of these requirements was emphasised by the Human Rights Committee in *Mukong v Cameroon*.[34] Any limitation must also be proportional and not implemented in a manner that nullifies the substance of the right to expression, as explained by the Committee in its General Comment on article 19.[35] Where a State seeks to justify a limitation as falling within the ambit of paragraph (3), the Human Rights Committee will require the State party to specify the precise nature of the threat allegedly posed by a person's exercise of freedom of expression and how the limitation achieves dissipation of that threat.[36] In 2009, the Human Rights Council stressed the need to ensure that the invocation of national security is not used unjustifiably or arbitrarily to restrict the right to freedom of expression, and called on States to refrain from using counter-terrorism as a pretext to restrict the freedom of opinion and expression in ways that are contrary to their obligations under international law.[37]

Added to the permissible limitations upon the freedom of expression within article 19(3), and of even greater relevance to suppressing the incitement to terrorism, article 20 of the ICCPR demands a further 'restriction' by way of a prohibition against certain forms of expression:

Article 20
1. Any propaganda for war shall be prohibited by law.
2. Any advocacy of national, racial or religious hatred that constitutes incitement to discrimination, hostility or violence shall be prohibited by law.

This is something that builds upon an early statement of the idea in the Universal Declaration of Human Rights.[38] Article 7 of the Declaration provides that: "All are equal before the law and are entitled without any discrimination to equal protection of the law. All are entitled to equal protection against any discrimination in violation of this Declaration and against any incitement to such discrimination". Article 20(2) of the ICCPR stands as a reflection of the context in which the document was negotiated (as a post-World War II human rights instrument),[39] and of the importance attached to the principle of non-discrimination. It is noteworthy in the latter regard that article 4 of the ICCPR provides that any derogation of rights in times of emergency may not involve discrimination solely on the ground

---

[34]*Mukong v Cameroon* (n 22) para 9.7.

[35]General Comment 10. Article 19, CCPR General Comment 10 of 1983, reprinted UN Doc HRI \GEN\1\Rev.1 at 11 (1994), para 4. See also Chap. 10 herein, at Sect. 10.2.4.

[36]See, for example, *Kim v Republic of Korea* (n 24) para 12.5; *Laptsevic v Belarus*, Human Rights Committee Communication 780/1997, para 8.5; and *Pietrataroia v Uruguay*, Human Rights Committee Communication r10.44/1979, para 17.

[37]HRC Res 12/16 (n 1), preambular para 6, and para 5(o).

[38]Universal Declaration of Human Rights, as adopted by the United Nations General Assembly in its resolution GA Res 217(III)A, UN GAOR, 3rd Sess, 183rd Plen Mtg, UN Doc A/Res/217(III)A.

[39]Consider the parallel in German and Austrian law (required of both States under the post-WWII Peace Treaties) prohibiting membership in, or glorification of, the National Socialist Party.

of race, colour, sex, language, religion or social origin.[40] In the context of terrorism and counter-terrorism, the Committee on the Elimination of Racial Discrimination has declared that the prohibition against racial discrimination is a peremptory norm of international law from which no derogation is permitted.[41] This gives further weight to the prohibition in article 20(2) of the ICCPR.

Significantly, article 20(2) not only impacts upon an individual's exercise of the freedom of expression, but also places a positive duty upon States parties to adopt the necessary legislative measures prohibiting the actions referred to in its provisions. Each of the paragraphs state that these forms of expression "shall be prohibited by law". In this respect, the Human Rights Committee has expressed disappointment that many State party periodic reports show that in some States such actions are not prohibited by law and that there do not appear to be appropriate efforts to do so.[42] For article 20 to become fully effective, the Committee articulated a need for legislative proscriptions making it clear that propaganda and prohibited advocacy are contrary to public policy, and providing for an appropriate sanction in the case of violation.[43] Lack of State action in this area is, interestingly, reflected in a lack of proper proscription of the incitement to terrorism by a number of States. This is the case in Canada, for example, and also in New Zealand (as discussed in Chap. 14, Sects. 14.3.3 and 14.3.4.1).

20.2.1.1 Human Rights Committee General Comment 11

As part of its practice under article 40(4) of the ICCPR, the Human Rights Committee issued a General Comment on article 20 of the Covenant for the guidance of States parties.[44] Three points were made of particular relevance to the current evaluation. The first is that article 20 contains a positive duty to prohibit incitement and propaganda, as already identified. This is particularly relevant to the proactive approach to criminalising incitement advocated by the UNODC, and the General Assembly and Security Council calls for action in this area (see Chap. 14, Sect. 14.3.2.1). The second aspect of the General Comment concerns the Committee's view on the compatibility of article 20 with the freedom of expression (as guaranteed under article 19 of the ICCPR). In describing the two provisions as fully compatible, the Committee emphasised that the exercise of the freedom of

---

[40]Emphasised in Human Rights Committee, General Comment 29: States of Emergency (Article 4), reprinted UN Doc HRI/GEN/1/Rev.6 at 186 (2003), paras 8 and 16.

[41]Committee on the Elimination of Racial Discrimination, "Statement on Racial Discrimination and Measures to Combat Terrorism", in Report of the Committee on the Elimination of Racial Discrimination, UN GAOR, 57th Sess of the UNGA, Supplement 18, 61st Sess of the CERD, UN Doc A/57/18, 107.

[42]Human Rights Committee, General Comment 11. Article 20, CCPR General Comment 11 of 1983, reprinted UN Doc HRI\GEN\1\Rev.1 at 12 (1994), para 1.

[43]Ibid, para 2. See also OSCE Manual (n 12) pp. 226–228.

[44]General Comment 11 (n 42). See also HRC Res 12/16 (n 1) para 6.

expression "carries with it special duties and responsibilities".[45] The final point, particularly pertinent to the transnational nature of terrorism and its incitement, was the Committee's clarification that the prohibition in article 20 applies "whether such propaganda or advocacy has aims which are internal or external to the State concerned". This reinforces a similar point made in the Declaration on Measures to Eliminate International Terrorism.[46]

For the sake of completeness, it is worth mentioning that the Committee made specific reference to the right of self-determination, recognising that article 20 does not prohibit advocacy of the sovereign right of self-defence or the right of peoples to self-determination and independence in accordance with the Charter of the United Nations.[47] It is clear, however, that acts of terrorism are not justified as the means of achieving self-determination or any other objective. Early resolutions of the UN General Assembly addressing the issue of terrorism contained express affirmations of the principle of self-determination.[48] Since the 1994 Declaration on Measures to Eliminate International Terrorism, however, the United Nations has been very clear that this does not legitimate the use of terrorism by those seeking to achieve self-determination (see Chap. 2, Sect. 2.1.4.1). As such, this part of General Comment 11 should not be misunderstood as legitimating the advocacy of terrorism within the context of self-defence or self-determination.

20.2.1.2 Parallel Human Rights Provisions

In similar terms to the ICCPR, article 10 of the European Convention on Human Rights guarantees the freedom of expression, subject to limitations prescribed by law and necessary in a democratic society.[49] The European Court of Human Rights has taken this to include not only ideas and information that are favourably received or regarded as inoffensive, but also those that "offend, shock or disturb", unless they may be proscribed within the terms of article 10(2).[50] In *Sener v Turkey*, the European Court reiterated that there is little scope under article 10(2) of the

---

[45]General Comment 11 (n 42), para 2. See also HRC Res 12/16 (n 1) preambular para 8.

[46]Declaration on Measures to Eliminate International Terrorism, adopted under GA Res 49/60, UN GAOR, 49th Sess, 84th Plen Mtg, UN Doc A/Res/49/60 (1994), para 5(a). See further Chap. 14, Sect. 14.3.2.1.

[47]General Comment 11 (n 42), para 2.

[48]See, for example, GA Res 3034(XXVII), UN GAOR, 27th Sess, 2114th Plen Mtg, UN Doc A/Res/3034(XXVII) (1972), para 3, which urged States to solve the problem of terrorism by addressing the underlying issues leading to terrorist conduct and then reaffirmed: "...the inalienable right to self-determination and independence of all peoples under colonial and racist regimes and other forms of alien domination and upholds the legitimacy of their struggle, in particular the struggle of national liberation movements, in accordance with the purposes and principles of the Charter and the relevant resolutions of the organs of the United Nations".

[49]Convention for the Protection of Human Rights and Fundamental Freedoms, opened for signature 4 November 1950, 213 UNTS 222 (entered into force 3 September 1953).

[50]See, for example, *Lingens v Austria* [1986] ECHR 7, para 41.

Convention for restrictions on political speech or on debate on questions of public interest, but continued:[51]

> Nevertheless, it certainly remains open to the competent State authorities to adopt, in their capacity as guarantors of public order, measures, even of a criminal-law nature, intended to react appropriately and without excess to such remarks... Finally, where such remarks incite people to violence, the State authorities enjoy a wider margin of appreciation when examining the need for an interference with freedom of expression.

The Inter-American Convention on Human Rights also proscribes the incitement to violence or racial hatred, article 13(5) providing:

> Any propaganda for war and any advocacy of national, racial, or religious hatred that constitute incitements to lawless violence or to any other similar action against any person or group of persons on any grounds including those of race, color, religion, language, or national origin shall be considered as offenses punishable by law.

These general limitations provisions are further reflected within article 29(2) of the Universal Declaration of Human Rights, with paragraph (3) of that article of particular relevance to the incitement to terrorism:

> 2. In the exercise of his rights and freedoms, everyone shall be subject only to such limitations as are determined by law solely for the purpose of securing due recognition and respect for the rights and freedoms of others and of meeting the just requirements of morality, public order and the general welfare in a democratic society.
> 3. These rights and freedoms may in no case be exercised contrary to the purposes and principles of the United Nations.

20.2.2 Safeguards in the Proscription of the Incitement to Terrorism

The most important question concerning the criminalisation of the incitement to terrorism is the description of the proscribed conduct, i.e. its constituent elements and the breadth of their potential application. Reference to various provisions of the ICCPR, together with elements drawn from the Handbook on Human Rights Compliance While Countering Terrorism (Appendix 4 herein, as discussed in Chap. 13), leads to the identification of three safeguards applicable to the proper proscription of the incitement to terrorism:

1. An offence of incitement to terrorism which prohibits the incitement of conduct falling outside the scope of article 20(2) of the ICCPR (incitement to discrimination, hostility or violence through the advocacy of national, racial or religious hatred) must limit the freedom of expression in a manner which is consistent with article 19(3)(b) of the ICCPR and (in the case of the United Kingdom) also consistent with article 10(2) of the ECHR, i.e.

---

[51]*Sener v Turkey* [2000] ECHR 377, para 40.

necessary for the protection of national security, or of public order and safety, or of public health or morals.

2. To conform with the requirement that any human rights limitation be prescribed by law (see article 19(3) of the ICCPR in the context of the freedom of expression and, more generally, Chap. 10 at Sect. 10.2.2), incitement to terrorism offences must be precise so as to ensure that the proscription is not so broad as to capture legitimate expressions or peaceful meetings. The principles of legality also demand that the proscription be non-discriminatory and non-retroactive.

3. As elements of best practice, incitement to terrorism offences should involve the unlawful and intentional incitement to terrorism. It is desirable that incitement to terrorism offences be restricted to 'unlawful' incitement to terrorism, i.e. leaving any conduct undertaken pursuant to lawful government authority unaffected, and preserving the application of any legal defences or principles leading to the exclusion of criminal liability. *Mens rea* should form an element of any proscription of the incitement to terrorism so that: (1) the act of communication is intentional; and (2) the communication is intended to incite the commission of a terrorist offence.

20.2.2.1 Necessity

Any proscription of the incitement to terrorism is likely to fall within the requirement under article 20(2) of the ICCPR to prohibit the incitement to discrimination, hostility or violence through the advocacy of national, racial or religious hatred (Sect. 20.2.1 above). It is conceivable, however, that a proscription against the incitement to terrorism could go further than this. A proscription might include, for example, a prohibition against inciting the unlawful and intentional miscommunication of information aimed at endangering the safety of an aircraft in flight for the purpose of compelling a government to do or abstain from doing something. While the conducted incited falls within the definition of terrorism (see Chap. 2, Sect. 2.3.6), and involves the incitement of a terrorist offence under article 1(1)(e) of the Montreal Convention,[52] the act of incitement does not itself instigate the matters captured under article 20(2) of the ICCPR. An offence of incitement might also fall outside the scope of article 20(2) by prohibiting the incitement to hostility or violence which is *not* through "the advocacy of national, racial or religious hatred".

Where a criminal law proscription goes beyond the scope of conduct which States must prohibit under article 20(2), States will need to ensure that the formulation of the proscription is in compliance with the provisions of article 19(3). This means that a formulation going beyond the bounds of article 20(2) will need to be

---

[52]Convention for the Suppression of Unlawful Acts Against the Safety of Civil Aviation, opened for signature 23 September 1971, 974 UNTS 177 (entered into force 26 January 1973).

"for the protection of national security or of public order (ordre public), or of public health or morals" (article 19(3)(b)).[53] Relevant also to the United Kingdom, as a party to the European Convention on Human Rights, is article 10(2) of the ECHR, requiring any limitation on the freedom of expression to be necessary in a democratic society, in the interests of national security, territorial integrity or public safety, for the prevention of disorder or crime, for the protection of health or morals. On the application and meaning of the latter objectives, see Sect. 20.1.3.1 above, and Chap. 10, Sect. 10.3.2.

20.2.2.2   Legality and Precision

Of relevance to the formulation of any criminal offence provision is article 15(1) of the ICCPR, which sets out various standards pertaining to the legality of criminal law proscriptions. The first of its requirements means that any prohibition against the incitement to terrorism must be undertaken by national or international prescriptions of law. In the context of limitations on the freedom of expression, this is reflected within the chapeau to article 19(3) of the ICCPR. To be 'prescribed by law' the prohibition must be framed in such a way that the law is adequately accessible (so that the individual has a proper indication of how the law limits his or her conduct) and is formulated with sufficient precision (so that the individual can regulate his or her conduct). This is considered in further detail in Chap. 10 (Sect. 10.2.2).[54]

On a more general note, the Sub-Commission Special Rapporteur on terrorism and human rights has commented that: "States must ensure that the expression of alternative political views, as well as peaceful meetings, are permitted...".[55] This is particularly relevant to the framing of any proscription against incitement to terrorism, to ensure that the wording of the proscription is not so broad as to capture legitimate expressions or peaceful meetings. There are, in this regard, five points to be made concerning the permissible bounds of the prohibition against the incitement to terrorism, and matters impacting upon its legality:

- In order to avoid use of the fight against terrorism as an excuse to unnecessarily extend the reach of criminal law, it is essential that any offence directed to the

---

[53]Special Rapporteur report on the listing of terrorist entities (n 33), para 28. See also Organisation for Security and Cooperation in Europe (OSCE) Office for Democratic Institutions and Human Rights, Background Paper on Human Rights Considerations in Combating Incitement to Terrorism and Related Offences (OSCE/Council of Europe Expert Workshop *Preventing Terrorism: Fighting Incitement and Related Terrorist Activities*, 19–20 October 2006, Vienna, Austria), pp. 13–15.

[54]See also OSCE Background Paper on Human Rights Considerations in Combating Incitement to Terrorism and Related Offences (ibid) pp. 4 and 8–9.

[55]Sub-Commission Special Rapporteur on terrorism and human rights, Specific Human Rights Issues: New Priorities, in Particular Terrorism and Counter-Terrorism. A Preliminary Framework Draft of Principles and Guidelines Concerning Human Rights and Terrorism, UN Doc E/CN.4/Sub.2/2005/39 (2005), para 55 comment.

incitement of terrorism (as opposed to a general incitement offence) be limited to countering terrorism, and the incitement of conduct which is truly 'terrorist' in nature.[56] This is a matter that has been identified and discussed in Chap. 13 (Sect. 13.3.3), and is contained in Condition 3.4 of the Handbook on Human Rights Compliance While Countering Terrorism (Appendix 4 herein). The absence of an agreed definition of terrorism has been identified as problematic in the context of the current discussion, a matter which is said to leave a broad margin of discretionary power to States in prohibiting and preventing incitement to terrorism.[57]

In the absence of a comprehensive and universal definition of terrorism, the incitement to terrorism should be limited in its application to the incitement of (1) acts committed with the intention of causing death or serious bodily injury, or the taking of hostages; (2) for the purpose of provoking a state of terror, intimidating a population, or compelling a government or international organisation to do or abstain from doing any act; and (3) constituting offences within the scope of and as defined in the international conventions and protocols relating to terrorism (on the definition of terrorism, and the distillation of the latter elements, see Chap. 2 at Sect. 2.3.6).

- A concerning trend has been the proscription of the glorification (*apologie*) of terrorism, involving statements which may not go so far as to incite or promote the commission of terrorist acts, but might nevertheless applaud past acts.[58] While such statements might offend the sensibilities of persons and society, particularly the victims of terrorist acts, it is important that vague terms such as "glorifying" or "promoting" terrorism are not used when restricting expression. A joint declaration of experts on the freedom of expression explains that "[i]ncitement should be understood as a direct call to engage in terrorism, with the intention that this should promote terrorism, and in a context in which the call is directly causally responsible for increasing the actual likelihood of a terrorist act occurring".[59]

- A further matter raised by the Special Rapporteur on the promotion and protection of human rights and fundamental freedoms while countering terrorism, and drawn from the structure of article 5(1) of the European Convention on the Prevention of Terrorism, is that the offence of incitement must include an actual

---

[56]Special Rapporteur on the promotion and protection of human rights and fundamental freedoms while countering terrorism, Promotion and Protection of Human Rights, UN Doc E/CN.4/2006/98 (2006), para 47. See also two reports of the Sub-Commission Special Rapporteur on terrorism and human rights: Final Report of the Special Rapporteur on Terrorism and Human Rights, E/CN.4/Sub.2/2004/40 (2004), para 33(c); and A Preliminary Framework Draft of Principles and Guidelines Concerning Human Rights and Terrorism (ibid) para 33.

[57]OSCE Background Paper on Human Rights Considerations in Combating Incitement to Terrorism and Related Offences (n 53) p. 4.

[58]See, for example, Ribbelink (2006, pp. 40–42 and 47–48).

[59]See the joint declaration of the UN Special Rapporteur on Freedom of Opinion and Expression, the OSCE Representative on Freedom of the Media, and the OAS Special Rapporteur on Freedom of Expression, 21 December 2005.

risk that the act incited will be committed.[60] This is consistent with Principle 6 (c) of the Johannesburg Principles on National Security, Freedom of Expression and Access to Information, which states that expression may be punished as a threat to national security only if a government can demonstrate that there is a direct and immediate connection between the expression and the likelihood or occurrence of such violence.[61]

- A matter required by article 26 of the ICCPR, and by the rule of law, is the need for any legal proscription to respect the principle of non-discrimination and equality before the law. This is also a matter discussed in Chap. 13 (at Sect. 13.3.3) and the Handbook on Human Rights Compliance While Countering Terrorism (Condition 3.2).[62]
- A further element of article 15 of ICCPR concerns non-retroactivity. Any provision defining a crime must not criminalise conduct that occurred prior to its entry into force as applicable law. Likewise, any penalties are to be limited to those applicable at the time that any offence was committed and, if the law has subsequently provided for the imposition of a lighter penalty, the offender must be given the benefit of the lighter penalty. In the context of counter-terrorism, these are again matters reiterated by the Special Rapporteur.[63]

20.2.2.3 Unlawful and Intentional Incitement

Resolutions of the General Assembly and the Security Council do not address the question of whether intention should form an express element of any proscription of the incitement to terrorism. Intention is an element of the Council of Europe Convention on the Prevention of Terrorism, but not expressed to be so within the ICCPR or Rome Statute of the International Criminal Court.

The Council of Europe Convention, in article 5(1), defines the public provocation to commit a terrorist offence as "the distribution, or otherwise making available, of a message to the public, with the *intent* to incite the commission of a terrorist offence..." (emphasis added). Article 5(2) in turn requires any public act of provocation to be intentional. This means that the act of communication must

---

[60]Special Rapporteur report on the listing of terrorist entities (n 33), para 28. See also report of the Counter-Terrorism Committee to the Security Council on the implementation of resolution 1624 (2005), UN Doc S/2006/737 (2006), para 7; Barendt 2007, pp. 9–10, and OSCE Background Paper on Human Rights Considerations in Combating Incitement to Terrorism and Related Offences (n 53) p. 9.

[61]Johannesburg Principles on National Security, Freedom of Expression and Access to Information, UN Doc E/CN.4/1996/39 (1996). See also OSCE Background Paper on Human Rights Considerations in Combating Incitement to Terrorism and Related Offences (n 53) pp. 12–13.

[62]See also: article 12(2) of the Council of Europe Convention on the Prevention of Terrorism (n 32); Principle 4 of the Johannesburg Principles (ibid); and OSCE Background Paper on Human Rights Considerations in Combating Incitement to Terrorism and Related Offences (n 53) pp. 15–16.

[63]Ibid, para 49.

also be intentional.[64] In contrast, article 20(2) of the ICCPR simply requires States parties to prohibit "any advocacy of national, racial or religious hatred that constitutes incitement to discrimination, hostility or violence..." (thus importing a purely objective assessment of whether the advocacy constitutes incitement). Similarly, the Rome Statute, in article 25(3)(e), requires a person to be made criminally responsible if he or she "directly and publicly incites others to commit genocide" (leaving out any mention of intention in this list of participation offences, many of which do expressly require intention as an element of the offence). Notwithstanding the neutral language of the ICCPR and the Rome Statute, three matters point to the desirability of intention forming an element of the offence of incitement to terrorism.

- The first concerns the nature of criminal law and the general presumption against strict liability offences, being offences where the intent of the perpetrator is not relevant to the issue of guilt. Strict liability offences are an exception to the general rule that criminal offending requires both an *actus reus* (an act or omission constituting the physical element(s) of the offence) and a *mens rea* (an intention on the part of the actor to certain ends). This presumption is borne out in the rule of many common law jurisdictions, including the four case study countries, that when a statute does not employ terms expressly importing the need for *mens rea*, the element of *mens rea* is nevertheless to be implied as an ingredient of the offence, unless there is sufficient reason to the contrary. The New Zealand Court of Appeal, for example, has accepted that it is "a universal principle that if a penal provision is reasonably capable of two interpretations, that interpretation which is most favourable to the accused must be adopted".[65] A need for the prosecution to establish *mens rea* is particularly likely when the offence is 'serious' or 'truly criminal', rather than being a 'public welfare' or 'regulatory' offence.[66] This approach can also be seen in the international context. Article 5 of the Statute of the International Criminal Tribunal for former Yugoslavia, for example, sets out the Tribunal's jurisdiction over crimes against humanity without any mention of intent.[67] The Tribunal has nevertheless ruled that intent is an element of the offence to be proved by the prosecutor.[68]
- The second matter calling for the inclusion of intention as an element of any offence relates to the text of the Council of Europe Convention. The Convention is the only treaty proscribing the incitement to terrorism and it is therefore not insignificant that the negotiating parties agreed upon a double requirement of intent to incite, with an objective danger that a terrorist offence might result.

---

[64]See also the Special Rapporteur's view to this effect (ibid) para 30.

[65]*Civil Aviation Department v MacKenzie* [1983] NZLR 78, p. 81.

[66]Consider, for example, the position to this effect in New Zealand: *Millar v MOT* [1986] 1 NZLR 660, p. 666.

[67]Statute of the International Criminal Tribunal for former Yugoslavia, adopted on 23 May 1993 by SC Res 827, UN SCOR, 3217th Mtg, UN Doc S/Res/827 (1993).

[68]See, for example, *Prosecutor v Kupreskic* Trial Chamber Case IT-95-16-T (14 January 2000), para 556.

- A final matter for consideration is the issue of certainty. Although this is a question to be answered upon consideration of the particular words of any offence provision, the absence of intent may mean that such a provision is applicable to so broad a range of conduct that certainty is not achieved.

Given the general presumption in favour of requiring intent for non-regulatory offences, the need for certainty, the presence of intent within the only agreed-upon treaty definition of the incitement to terrorism, and the identification of that definition as being a best practice, intent should form an element of any proscription of the incitement to terrorism.[69]

On the question of unlawfulness, the Council of Europe Convention on the Prevention of Terrorism requires States to proscribe the unlawful and intentional public provocation to commit a terrorist offence. The explanatory report to the Convention clarifies that the term 'unlawful' is used in order to leave any conduct undertaken pursuant to lawful government authority unaffected, and to also preserve the application of any legal defences or principles leading to the exclusion of criminal liability.[70] This would preserve the ability, for example, to claim a defence of duress where an individual is compelled to make an inciting public statement upon a threat of harm to the person or his or her family.

While desirable, the inclusion of this element is not *required* of any universal anti-terrorism or human rights instrument, nor advocated by any resolution of the General Assembly or Security Council. The Special Rapporteur has, however, identified the Council of Europe Convention proscription against the incitement to terrorism as an instance of best practice, and proscription of 'unlawful' incitement is therefore to be preferred.[71]

20.2.3 UK Incitement Offences Under the Terrorism Act 2006

In contrast to New Zealand's lack of legislative action on the subject of the incitement to terrorism, and the insufficiency of its current law to address the issue (see Chap. 14, Sect. 14.3), the United Kingdom has a number of provisions concerning the incitement to terrorism. Sections 59–61 of the Terrorism Act 2000 contains offences of inciting acts of terrorism, within or outside the United

---

[69]See the report of the Special Rapporteur on the listing of terrorist entities (n 33), para 28. See also the analysis by Barendt (2007, p. 8), concerning the implication by the US Supreme Court that incitement should be intentional (in *Brandenburg v Ohio* (1969) 395 US 444).

[70]Council of Europe, Explanatory Report to the Council of Europe Convention on the Prevention of Terrorism, online: http://www.conventions.coe.int/Treaty/EN/Reports/Html/196.htm, paras 81–83.

[71]Special Rapporteur on the promotion and protection of human rights and fundamental freedoms while countering terrorism, Australia: Study on Human Rights Compliance While Countering Terrorism, UN Doc A/HRC/4/26/Add.3, paras 26–27.

Kingdom, Each section deals with the incitement of acts which would constitute offences within the different territories of the United Kingdom, and are concerned with the incitement of murder, wounding with intent, poisoning, explosions, or endangering life by damaging property (see Chap. 8, Sect. 8.1.5.3).[72] More recently, two proactive incitement to terrorism offences were introduced under the Terrorism Act 2006 (the encouragement of terrorism, and the dissemination of terrorist publications). The relevant provisions of the Act have changed since their original articulation within the Terrorism Bill 2005 (as presented to the House of Commons). The original version of the Bill proposed a third offence of "glorification of terrorism", but this was removed before the Bill was brought for action by the House of Lords in November 2005. Subsequent debate saw further fine-tuning of the offence provisions. Sections 1 and 2 of the Terrorism Act 2006 set out the substantive offences of the encouragement to terrorism and the dissemination of terrorist publications, with sections 3 and 4 expanding upon the application of the offence provisions.

20.2.3.1   The Offence of the Encouragement of Terrorism

The offence of the encouragement of terrorism, under section 1 of the Terrorism Act 2006, comprises three elements. First, there must be an act of publishing a "statement" (or causing another to do so on the person's behalf) – section 1(2)(a). A statement includes a communication of any description, including one without words consisting of sounds or images or both (section 20(6)). "Publishing" a statement can occur in any manner, including provision of a statement by electronic means (section 20(2) and (4)).

Next, the published statement must be likely to be understood by members of the public to whom it is published (the public anywhere in the world – section 20(2) and (3)) as a direct or indirect encouragement or other inducement to them to the commission, preparation or instigation of acts of terrorism (section 1(1)). It is irrelevant, though, whether the statement directly relates to the commission, preparation or instigation of one or more particular acts of terrorism or Convention offences (section 1(5)(a)). The offence is a proactive one, since it is immaterial whether any person is in fact encouraged or induced by the statement (section 1(5) (b)). Statements that are likely to be understood by members of the public as indirectly encouraging the commission or preparation of acts of terrorism are deemed to include every statement which, according to section 1(3):

(a) Glorifies the commission or preparation (whether in the past, in the future or generally) of such acts or offences; and
(b) Is a statement from which those members of the public could reasonably be expected to infer that what is being glorified is being glorified as conduct that should be emulated by them in existing circumstances.

---

[72]See further Fenwick (2002, pp. 521–522).

This is to be determined having regard to both the contents of the statement as a whole and the circumstances and manner of its publication (section 1(4)). For the purpose of section 1(3)(b), glorification includes any form of praise or celebration (section 20(2)). The final element of the offence requires that the person publishing such a statement must intend (at the time of publication) that the statement be understood in the way just described, or be reckless as to whether or not it is likely to be so understood (section 1(2)(b)). In the case of recklessness (where it is not proved that a person *intended* to directly or indirectly incite terrorism), it is a defence for a person to show that the statement "neither expressed his views nor had his endorsement"; and that it was clear, in all the circumstances, that "it did not express his views and... did not have his endorsement" (section 1(6)).

20.2.3.2   The Offence of the Dissemination of Terrorist Publications

Section 2 of the Terrorism Act 2006 establishes an offence of the dissemination of terrorist publications. Dissemination includes various forms of distribution or transmission (see section 2(2)). For the purpose of section 2, a "publication" includes any article capable of storing data, or any record (permanent or otherwise) containing matter to be read, looked at, or listened to (sections 2(13) and 20(2)). A publication is a terrorist one in either of the following situations:

- Firstly, where the information in the publication is likely to be understood by members of the public to whom it is published as a direct or indirect encouragement or other inducement to them to the commission, preparation or instigation of acts of terrorism (this expression is accorded the same meaning as under the encouragement of terrorism offence) – section 2(3)(a), (4) and (5); or
- Secondly, where the information in the publication is likely to be useful in the commission or preparation of terrorist acts and to be understood, by some or all recipients, as having been made available wholly or mainly for the purpose of being useful in this way (section 2(3)(b)).

Similar to the encouragement of terrorism offence, it is irrelevant whether dissemination results in the likely effects described, or whether the information is actually used for the commission or preparation of a terrorism act (section 2(8)). As brought before the House of Lords in 2005, this offence was not to expressly include any element of *mens rea*. The inclusion of a new subsection (1) now requires that, at the time of the dissemination, the person intends to encourage or assist in the commission or preparation of terrorism acts, or is reckless as to whether this will be an effect of the dissemination. Where a person is reckless as to the likelihood of dissemination resulting in the encouragement to terrorism, it is a defence for the person to show that the information "neither expressed his views nor had his endorsement" and "that it was clear, in all the circumstances, that it did not express his views and ... did not have his endorsement" (section 2(9)).

20.2.4 Assessing the Offences Under the Terrorism Act 2006

Identified earlier were three human rights safeguards in the prohibition of the incitement to terrorism, each of which are now measured against the incitement provisions of the UK Terrorism Act 2006.

20.2.4.1 Do the Offences Involve Necessary Interferences with the Freedom of Expression?

Sections 1 and 2 of the Terrorism Act 2006 both contribute to the positive duty of the United Kingdom to prohibit the advocacy of hatred that constitutes incitement to hostility or violence (an obligation under article 20(2) of the ICCPR). The offences clearly also go further than this, however, and must therefore be shown to be in compliance with article 19(3) of the International Covenant (as necessary for the protection of national security, public order, or of public health of morals) and article 10(2) of the European Convention (as necessary in a democratic society, in the interests of national security, territorial integrity or public safety, for the prevention of disorder or crime, for the protection of health or morals).

The position of the United Kingdom is that these provisions do just what the latter provisions speak of. The Home Office Explanatory Notes to the Bill described the aim of the provisions to be to ensure that law enforcement agencies are given the necessary powers to counter the threat to the United Kingdom posed by terrorism.[73] The enactment of these provisions was also a response to the terrorist incidents in London in July 2005.[74] The aims of sections 1 and 2 therefore appear to fit within the permissible objectives of the ICCPR and ECHR. However, central to the determination of whether these provisions are justifiable is the question of their proportionality. Based upon the analysis that follows, this chapter takes the view that, although the offences may be necessary, they are not proportionate and thus fail to comply with other human rights standards.

20.2.4.2 Are the Offences Established Through Precise Prescriptions by Law?

The second identified safeguard is that any proscription must be adequately accessible and expressed in a precise manner so that the public is clear on what conduct is being prohibited. The requirements of article 15 of the ICCPR appear to be satisfied in the expression of the offences under sections 1 and 2. Although extensive, the provisions clearly define the proscribed conduct and elements of each offence. They

---

[73]Home Office, 'Terrorism Bill. Explanatory Notes', online: http://www.publications.parliament. uk/pa/ld200506/ldbills/038/en/06038x–.htm, para 3.

[74]Ibid, para 4.

are not retroactive in their application, a principle which, in its application to sentencing, is specifically expressed within sections 1(8) and 2(12) of the Act. The offence of encouragement to terrorism includes an element of actual risk that the incited conduct will be committed, since section 1(1) demands that the statement must be likely to be understood by members of the public to whom it is published as a direct or indirect encouragement or other inducement to them to the commission, preparation or instigation of acts of terrorism. Notwithstanding these positive aspects, three problems arise:

- Although the offences under sections 1 and 2 are linked to existing statutory definitions of terrorist acts or Convention offences, the definition of terrorism under section 1 of the Terrorism Act 2000 includes features which go beyond the proper characterisation of terrorism (see Chap. 14 at Sect. 14.1). The connection of the section 1 and 2 offences with "terrorism" and "Convention offences" is thus problematic and not confined to the countering of international terrorism. Furthermore, in the context of notices under section 3 of the Terrorism Act 2006 (discussed next), the lack of appropriate checks and balances render the provisions capable of improper application to the censorship of materials that are not "terrorist publications".
- Outside the expression of the offences themselves, a matter of concern is the content of notice provisions under section 3 of the Act. Section 3 relates to the publication of a statement in the course of providing, or using, an electronic service (relevant to the encouragement of terrorism under section 1) or to the dissemination of a publication in the course of providing, or using, an electronic service (relevant to the dissemination of terrorist publications under section 2) – section 3(1). The effect of the notice provisions is that, where they apply, a person will be deemed to have endorsed the statement or publication (section 3(2)). This means that if a prosecution relies on an accused's reckless intent (section 1(2)(b)(ii), or section 2(1)(c)), and where a section 3 notice applies, the defences of lack of endorsement (section 1(6), or section 2(9)) become unavailable. The integrity of the section 3 notice provisions is therefore important.

   Section 3(3) defines a notice as one which, inter alia, declares that (in the opinion of the constable giving the notice) a statement or article or record is unlawfully terrorism-related, and warns the person to whom the notice is given that failure to comply with the notice will result in the statement, or article or record, being regarded as having that person's endorsement. This places an enormous authority in the hands of the police. A notice may be given wherever a police constable is of the opinion that "the statement or the article or record is unlawfully terrorism-related" (section 3(3)(a)). Although the legal consequence of this power is limited, since it impacts only upon the availability of the 'lack of endorsement' defences, it is nevertheless troubling that the opinion of an ordinary police constable may have the effect of excluding a legal defence, without any apparent requirement for that opinion to be reasonably held or based upon external, reviewable, factors.

The practical result of this power is also worth noting. Outside the context of the application of the 'lack of endorsement' provisions, an innocent (or even intentional) misuse of the notice provisions has no legal effect. It does, however, result in the issuing of a notice expressing that a statement or article is "unlawfully terrorism-related" and that the notice is made under the Terrorism Act 2006 (section 3(2)). This may result in a considerable chilling effect, and the lack of internal checking mechanisms is troubling. While judicial review is available in such cases, the breadth of the power under section 3 is arguably disproportionate to the objectives of the offence under section 2 of the Act, and/or violates articles 15 and 19(3) of the ICCPR for lack of sufficient precision and certainty.

- Any proscription must also be expressed in a manner that respects the principle of non-discrimination which, on the face of the proscription clauses, appears to be met. Problematic, here, is the broad discretion of police to issue notices under section 3, which is at least open to application in a discriminatory manner.

20.2.4.3   Do the Offences Involve Unlawful and Intentional Incitement?

Although sections 1 and 2 of the Terrorism Act 2006 do not qualify the prohibited conduct in question as 'unlawful', the Act does not exclude the application of any defences normally available under the criminal law of the United Kingdom. The Act also sets out two defences applicable to these particular offence provisions.

As to *mens rea*, the offence of the encouragement of terrorism requires that an accused must have intended (at the time of publication) that the statement made be understood as encouraging terrorism, or be reckless as to whether or not it is likely to be so understood (section 1(2)(b)). The offence of dissemination of terrorist publications, demands that, at the time of the dissemination, the person intends to encourage or assist in the commission or preparation of terrorism acts, or is reckless as to whether this will be an effect of the dissemination. Intending a statement or publication to be understood in a certain manner incorporates the full extent of *mens rea* and is similar in its terms to article 5 of the Council of Europe Convention on the Prevention of Terrorism.

Recklessness as to whether a statement is likely to be understood in a certain manner involves a lower threshold.[75] This was a matter of considerable criticism during discussions concerning the formulation of the section 1 and 2 offences under the Terrorism Bill 2005. The effect of clause 1(2)(b) was understood to mean that it would be possible for a person to be guilty of encouraging terrorism even if he or she had not intention of doing so, e.g. where publication of a statement occurs with innocent intent but with knowledge that the statement *might* be misunderstood or

---

[75]See report of the Counter-Terrorism Committee (n 60), para 8.

misinterpreted by *unreasonable* people.[76] This understanding is reflected in the adverse comments of the Human Rights Committee in its 2008 Concluding Observations on the UK's sixth periodic report:[77]

> The Committee notes with concern that the offence of "encouragement of terrorism" has been defined in section 1 of the Terrorism Act 2006 in broad and vague terms. In particular, a person can commit the offence even when he or she did not intend members of the public to be directly or indirectly encouraged by his or her statement to commit acts of terrorism, but where his or her statement was understood by some members of the public as encouragement to commit such acts.

It is unclear whether the Committee's observation was arrived at with due consideration to the safeguards under sections 1(6) and 2(9) of the Terrorism Act 2006, which were added *after* the introduction of the Bill, and in apparent response to the criticisms noted above. As has been discussed, it will be a defence if the statement or publication neither expressed the views nor had the endorsement of the accused, and it was clear in all the circumstances that this was the case (sections 1(6) and 2 (9)). It should also be noted that the concept of recklessness has undergone intense judicial scrutiny in England, particularly in the context of the law of manslaughter, and there is consequently an extensive body of common law on the subject. In simple terms, recklessness requires proof of foresight of dangerous consequences that could well happen, together with an intention to continue the course of conduct regardless of that risk.[78] Although the element of recklessness appears problematic at first blush, the offences therefore include safeguards so as to involve adequate levels of unlawful and intentional behaviour.

20.3   Conclusions

The freedom of expression is a cornerstone of democratic societies, linked to the enjoyment of other rights and freedoms, including the freedom of thought, conscience and religion, and their manifestation through association and assembly rights. Individual and group rights to the freedom of expression, including the freedom of the press, carry special duties and responsibilities and may be limited for the purpose of protecting other important objectives, including national security, public order, or the rights or reputation of others. States parties to the ICCPR have an obligation under article 20(2) to prohibit the incitement to hostility or violence based on national, racial or religious hatred. UN member States also have a duty

---

[76]See, for example: submissions of JUSTICE on the Terrorism Bill 2005 to the House of Lords, January 2006, para 3; and submissions of Professor Clive Walker to the Joint Committee on Human Rights, October 2005, para 4.2.3.

[77]Human Rights Committee, Concluding Observations: United Kingdom of Great Britain and Northern Ireland, UN Doc CCPR/C/GBR/CO/6 (2008), para 26.

[78]See, for example, *R v Caldwell* [1981] 1 All ER 961.

to prevent the commission of terrorist acts, and have been called on to prohibit the incitement to terrorism. States which have become parties to the Council of Europe Convention on the Prevention of Terrorism are under a specific obligation, under article 5 of the Convention, to establish the public provocation to commit terrorist acts as an offence, a provision which has been identified as best practice in the area.

Given the call for dissuasive penalties to be applied in the sentencing of terrorist offenders, it appears to be prudent for States to criminalise the particular conduct of incitement to terrorism, with an appropriately corresponding range of criminal sanctions, rather than leaving this to a more general prohibition against incitement. Although the formulation of any particular proscription of the incitement to terrorism is a matter for each State to determine, three safeguards or minimum requirements have been identified. First, any proscription must be necessary, such that it either falls within the parameters of the obligation under article 20(2) of the ICCPR, or within the scope of permissible limits on the freedom of expression set out in article 19(3) of the Covenant and article 10(2) of the ECHR. The second safeguard for the guarantee of the proper proscription of the incitement to terrorism demands that the offence must be precise and not be so broad as to capture legitimate expressions or peaceful meetings. Legality and precision demand that: (1) the offence be limited to the incitement of conduct which is truly terrorist in nature; (2) the elements of the offence be precise and avoid using vague terms such as "glorifying" or "promoting" terrorism; (3) the offence include an element requiring proof that the act of incitement includes an actual risk that the conduct incited will be committed; (4) the offence, and its application, respect the principle of non-discrimination; and (5) the offence not be retroactive. The final safeguard involves, as elements of best practice, the restriction of the offence of incitement to terrorism to unlawful and intentional incitement, thus preserving any applicable legal defences and expressly incorporating *mens rea* as an element of the offence to require an intention on the part of the person to communicate his or her statement and thereby incite the commission of a terrorist offence.

The United Kingdom's Terrorism Act 2006 includes the offences of the encouragement of terrorism and the dissemination of terrorist publications. The offences fall within the scope of article 20(2) of the ICCPR and the permissible objectives of article 19(3) of the ICCPR and article 10(2) of the ECHR. On the positive side of things, the current prescriptions are non-retroactive and legal defences are not excluded. Furthermore, although the offences contain (as alternative elements of *mens rea*) precise intent and reckless intent, the combination of common law on the subject, together with accompanying defences, render a satisfactory outcome to the issue of intent. Overall, however, the incitement offences cannot be said to be formulated in proportionate terms. Sections 1 and 2 of the Act fail to meet the requirements of legality and precision since: (1) they lack precision (concerning notices under section 3); (2) they are not properly confined to the countering of terrorism (by virtue of their linkage to overly-broad definition of terrorism under section 1 of the Terrorism Act 2000); and (3) their lack of precision makes them vulnerable to use in a discriminatory manner.

On the subject of the freedom of the press, which is an integral feature of the right of all members of the public, under the freedom of expression, to seek, receive and impart information and opinions, New Zealand's International Terrorism (Emergency Powers) Act 1987 presents a rare example of powers of media control in counter-terrorism law. However, these powers are limited to the pursuit of objectives which fall within the scope of article 19(3) of the ICCPR and the more general notion, under section 5 of the NZ Bill of Rights, of limits demonstrably justifiable in a free and democratic society. The Prime Minister's authority to restrict the media only arises where the information in question would be likely to prejudice the safety of any person involved in dealing with an international terrorist emergency, or measures designed to deal with such emergencies. This authority is also subject to judicial review, thus incorporating a checking mechanism against abuse or over-extension of the powers under section 14 of the Act. It might be observed that judicial review of the exercise of statutory powers only requires reconsideration of the decision made and might not, therefore, achieve practice which is in fact consistent with the principles of necessity and proportionality. The statutory framework, however, appears sufficient.

References

Abjorensen, Norman. 2006. Strike up the ban: Censor joins the war on terrorism. Discussion Paper 26/06 in the Australian National Universty *Democratic Audit of Australia*, online: http://democratic.audit.anu.edu.au.

Barendt, Eric. 2007. Incitement to and Glorification of Terrorism (paper presented at the conference *Extreme Speech and Democracy*, 21–22 April 2007, Cambridge, United Kingdom).

Bassiouni, Cherif. 1981. Terrorism, Law Enforcement, and the Mass Media: Perspectives, Problems, Proposals. 72(1) *The Journal of Criminal Law and Criminology* 1.

Conte, Alex, and Burchill, Richard. 2009. *Defining Civil and Political Rights: The Jurisprudence of the United Nations Human Rights* Committee. Aldershot: 2nd ed, Ashgate Publishing Ltd.

Dreher, Tanja. 2007. News Media Responsibilities in Reporting on Terrorism. In Lynch, Andrew, MacDonald, Edwina, and Williams, George (Eds). *Law and Liberty in the War on Terror*. Sydney: The Federation Press.

Fenwick, Helen. 2002. *Civil Liberties and Human Rights*. London: 3rd edition, Cavendish Publishing Limited.

Gelber, Katharine. 2007. When are Restrictions on Speech Justified in the War on Terror? In Lynch, Andrew, MacDonald, Edwina, and Williams, George (Eds). *Law and Liberty in the War on Terror*. Sydney: The Federation Press.

Ribbelink, Olivier. 2006. Analytical Report. In Council of Europe. *"Apologie du terrorisme"* and "incitement to terrorism". Strasbourg: Council of Europe Publishing.

Rishworth, Paul, Huscroft, Grant, Optican, Scott, and Mahoney, Richard. 2003. *The New Zealand Bill of Rights*. Oxford: Oxford University Press.

Saul, Ben. 2006. Censorship of Religious Texts: The Limits of Pluralism. 8 *University of Technology, Sydney Law Journal* 49.

Smith, John. 2003. *New Zealand's Anti-Terrorism Campaign: Balancing Civil Liberties, National Security, and International Responsibilities*. Wellington: Ian Axford New Zealand Fellowship in Public Policy.

Chapter 21
Measures to Prevent the Transboundary Movement of Terrorists

The requirement to implement measures to prevent the transboundary movement of terrorists is seen throughout various documents making up the international counter-terrorism framework (see Chap. 3), particularly in Security Council resolutions 1373 (2001) and 1624 (2005).[1] Due to the transnational nature of modern terrorism (which can involve preparation, training, support and incitement in territories other than the territory in which a terrorist act is to occur), the question of preventing the transboundary movement of terrorists has been described by the UN Counter-Terrorism Committee and the Security Council Working Group established pursuant to resolution 1566 (2004) as essential in the fight against terrorism, requiring careful implementation.[2] As well as contributing to these preventive aspects, the movement of terrorist suspects from one territory to another is also an issue relevant to the punishment of terrorism, namely the extradition and/or prosecution of those who have committed acts of terrorism. The most relevant decisions and recommendations of the Security Council are to be found in the following extracts from resolutions 1373 (2001) and 1624 (2005):

Security Council resolution 1373 (2001)

2. *Decides also* that all States shall:
  (b) Take the necessary steps to prevent the commission of terrorist acts, including by provision of early warning to other States by exchange of information;
  (c) Deny safe haven to those who finance, plan, support, or commit terrorist acts, or provide safe havens;
  (d) Prevent those who finance, plan, facilitate or commit terrorist acts from using their respective territories for those purposes against other States or their citizens;
  (g) Prevent the movement of terrorists or terrorist groups by effective border controls and controls on issuance of identity papers and travel documents, and through

---

[1] SC Res 1373, UN SCOR, 4385th Mtg, UN Doc S/Res/1373 (2001); and SC Res 1624, UN SCOR, 5261st Mtg, UN Doc S/Res/1624 (2005).

[2] Report of the Counter-Terrorism Committee, Survey of the implementation of Security Council resolution 1373 (2001), UN Doc S/2008/379 (2008), para 148; and Report of the Security Council Working Group established pursuant to resolution 1566 (2004), UN Doc S/2005/789 (2005), para 21.

A. Conte, *Human Rights in the Prevention and Punishment of Terrorism*, 651
DOI 10.1007/978-3-642-11608-7_21, © Springer-Verlag Berlin Heidelberg 2010

measures for preventing counterfeiting, forgery or fraudulent use of identity papers and travel documents;

3. *Calls* upon all States to:

   (f) Take appropriate measures in conformity with the relevant provisions of national and international law, including international standards of human rights, before granting refugee status, for the purpose of ensuring that the asylum-seeker has not planned, facilitated or participated in the commission of terrorist acts;

   (g) Ensure, in conformity with international law, that refugee status is not abused by the perpetrators, organizers or facilitators of terrorist acts, and that claims of political motivation are not recognized as grounds for refusing requests for the extradition of alleged terrorists;

Security Council resolution 1624 (2005)

1. *Calls upon* all States to adopt such measures as may be necessary and appropriate and in accordance with their obligations under international law to:

   (c) Deny safe haven to any persons with respect to whom there is credible and relevant information giving serious reasons for considering that they have been guilty of such conduct;

2. *Calls upon* all States to cooperate, inter alia, to strengthen the security of their international borders, including by combating fraudulent travel documents and, to the extent attainable, by enhancing terrorist screening and passenger security procedures with a view to preventing those guilty of the conduct in paragraph 1(a) [incitement to terrorism] from entering their territory;

A proper evaluation of the human rights repercussions of the implementation of these decisions and recommendations is not possible within the scope of a single chapter. Nor does this chapter purport to be one which comprehensively addresses immigration and refugee law, since this is beyond the objective of this title, although attention is paid to some of the human rights issues which overlap with that body of law. Numerous issues are raised, and these may be categorised as falling within one of three phases: (1) measures to prevent the transboundary movement of terrorists at international borders; (2) measures within the territory of a State including, for example, the detention of non-nationals considered to be a risk to the security of a country; and (3) measures adopted by States concerning the return and/or transfer of terrorists and terrorist suspects. Particular attention is paid in this chapter to border security, the treatment of refugees and asylum-seekers in Australia, and the use by the United Kingdom of 'diplomatic assurances' when seeking to remove a terrorist suspect, or person deemed to be a threat to national security, to a country where that person is at a risk of being ill-treated.

21.1 Border Security

Effective border security is an important aspect in an effective counter-terrorism strategy, and the ability of States to prevent the transboundary movement of terrorists.[3] It is also a condition of Security Council resolution 1373 (2001),

---

[3]Ibid. See also the report of the Special Rapporteur on the promotion and protection of human rights and fundamental freedoms while countering terrorism, Protection of human rights and fundamental freedoms while countering terrorism, UN Doc A/62/263 (2007), para 36.

paragraph 2(g) of which requires States to have effective border controls, as well as measures preventing the use of fraudulent identity papers and travel documents. Supplementing this general demand for effective border security, which is reiterated in paragraph 2 of resolution 1624 (2005), States are required to provide early warning to other States through the exchange of information in order to prevent the commission of terrorist acts (resolution 1373 (2001), paragraph 2(b)). Border security, early warning systems, and the exchange of information relating to the movement of persons over international borders will also include and be relevant to the identification of terrorists and terrorist suspects. Three practices and groups of technology are relevant to these obligations: passenger screening in advance of travel to a country; the collection, storage and sharing of information about passenger movement, as well as other forms of technologies used at international borders; and the use of profiling techniques to identify suspected terrorists.

Before considering each of these features of border security in more detail, an observation affecting all features should be noted. In his thematic report to the UN General Assembly on challenges to refugee protection posed by counter-terrorism measures, the Special Rapporteur on the promotion and protection of human rights and fundamental freedoms while countering terrorism observed:[4]

> While the Special Rapporteur recognizes the need for increased border security as part of an effective counter-terrorism strategy, he is concerned that few concrete measures are taken to compensate for the increasing difficulties that persons encounter and must overcome in order to access protection. For persons seeking international protection, their only means of leaving their home country and accessing another State to seek protection is often the use of fraudulent travel documents and resorting to the assistance of smugglers. The principle of not penalizing the asylum-seeker for illegal entry is also recognized in article 31 of the 1951 Refugee Convention. Increasing border control and pre-screening measures without adequately addressing the difficulties encountered by persons seeking protection will undermine the global regime of refugee protection and human rights, inter alia the protection against refoulement.

21.1.1   Advance Passenger Screening

A tool first adopted by the United States in 1990 and now being widely used, including within the four case study countries, is the sharing of information between countries of departure and arrival to enable the 'screening' of passenger lists prior to travel commencing.[5] In Australia for example, which became the second country in the world to use this scheme, authorities have implemented the Advance Passenger Processing (APP) system, obliging all international flights into Australia to provide a list, in advance, of passengers and crew for inbound flights.

---

[4]Special Rapporteur report on challenges to refugee protection (ibid) para 38.

[5]See, generally, International Air Transport Association / Control Authorities Working Group Statement of Principles for Advance Passenger Information Systems, FAL/12-WP/60 (2004).

As acknowledged by the UN Special Rapporteur, the advantage of this type of system is that it allows the country of destination to verify the authority of passengers and crew to arrive before boarding a flight or international cruise ship.[6] In the case of Australia's APP system, it allows the Department of Immigration and Multicultural Affairs to issue boarding directives to airlines and cruise companies, thereby preventing the boarding of passengers and crew who do not have permission to travel to Australia.

According to Australian authorities, this system is very effective if used as part of a layered approach intended to prevent the transboundary movement of terrorists, and of others involved in criminal activity.[7] Notwithstanding this, the Special Rapporteur expressed concern about the APP system. He noted that the Convention relating to the Status of Refugees (the Refugees Convention), as well as article 12(2) of the International Covenant on Civil and Political Rights (ICCPR), guarantees to every person the right to leave any country, including one's own country.[8] States should be cautious, he said, of implementing measures that may effectively prevent persons from exercising this right, particularly in the context of those fleeing persecution in their own country with an intention to seek refugee status elsewhere.[9] As indicated in his thematic report on the subject of refugee protection, the ability to leave is essential to the operation of the framework safeguarding the rights of refugees.[10]

21.1.2   The Use of Databases and Other Technologies

Some of the measures used to implement border and immigration controls include technologies such as whole-body imaging, and Machine Readable Travel Documents. The use of these technologies is said to increase the efficiency and speed of passenger screening, as well as limiting more intrusive physical searches of passengers in the case of scanning technology.

---

[6]Special Rapporteur on the promotion and protection of human rights and fundamental freedoms while countering terrorism, Australia: Study on Human Rights Compliance While Countering Terrorism, UN Doc A/HRC/4/26/Add.3 (2006), para 50.

[7]Special Rapporteur on Australia (ibid) para 51.

[8]Convention relating to the Status of Refugees, opened for signature 28 July 1951, 189 UNTS 150 (entered into force 21 April 1954); and International Covenant on Civil and Political Rights, opened for signature 16 December 1966, 999 UNTS 171 (entered into force 23 March 1976).

[9]Special Rapporteur on Australia (n 6) para 51.

[10]Special Rapporteur on challenges to refugee protection (n 3) para 38. See also Office of the United Nations High Commissioner for Refugees, Executive Committee Conclusion on International Protection Nos. 6 (XXVIII), 85 (XLIX) and 99 (LV).

21.1.2.1 Machine Readable Travel Documents

Machine Readable Travel Documents (MRTDs), such as biometric passports and visas, and some forms of national identity cards, have embedded integrated circuits which can process and store data. The International Civil Aviation Organization (ICAO) advocates the use of MRTDs as tools capable of minimising handling time during check-in and arrival, and achieving more secure forms of travel documentation.[11] ICAO has warned, however, that this form of technology must be secure and not susceptible to 'skimming' or 'eavesdropping' whereby data might be read from the chip by non-authorised equipment within the vicinity.[12] Despite early claims by developers of radio-frequency identification chips (RFID chips), which allow the contact-less reading of the biometric and biographical data of individuals stored on Machine Readable Travel Documents, research has shown that RFID chips can be read from a distance of 69 feet and, with specialised eavesdropping equipment, at significantly longer ranges.[13] ICAO guidelines therefore recommend that "a technology supplier's claims alone are not sufficient to provide confidence in this respect, and trials should be undertaken in order to ascertain such susceptibility under field conditions".[14] This approach is consistent with article 17(2) of the ICCPR, which obliges States to protect individuals from arbitrary or unlawful interference with their privacy. ICAO Guidelines add:

> ...there is the much broader issue of what happens to the data after it has been read, who might have access to it and for what purpose. There has been an increasing trend to blur immigration control with law enforcement in many countries. This is a potentially serious issue as, on the one hand we are dealing with the legitimate person seeking rights to cross a border, while on the other we are dealing with criminal activity. If this distinction is not properly understood and catered for, there is a risk of citizens becoming disenchanted with the process and losing confidence in the government agencies and control authorities involved. There are perhaps two areas where reassurances might usefully be created. Firstly, by making it easy for document holders to see exactly what is encoded within the chip of their e-MRTD (as recommended by ICAO) and, secondly, the provision of clear statements as to exactly how that data is used, with whom it is shared and for what purpose. Furthermore, such a statement should cover factors such as data retention, access control and associated factors.

21.1.2.2 Body Scanning Technologies

Whole-body imaging technologies enable operators to see through clothing to reveal metallic and non-metallic objects, including weapons or plastic explosives.

---

[11]International Civil Aviation Organization Doc 9303 on Machine Readable Travel Documents, Annex 9, chapter 3, para 3.47.

[12]International Civil Aviation Organization, Guidelines on Machine Readable Travel Documents & Passenger Facilitation, 17 April 2008, p. 18.

[13]Scheiner (2005).

[14]ICAO Guidelines on Machine Readable Travel Documents & Passenger Facilitation (n 12) p. 18.

They also reveal a person's silhouette and the outlines of underwear, rendering what the Electronic Privacy Information Center describes as "naked" chalk line images of the person being scanned.[15] The full implications of body imaging scanning, relating to privacy as well as other matters including the medical and health implications of repeated exposure to whole body imaging technology, is not yet fully known. There has therefore been much debate on whether and when such technology can and should be used.[16] Because of the privacy concerns associated with the technology, it has become the practice of some transportation security authorities to make body scans optional for passengers. The United States, which is the greatest user of body scanning technology, has established rules concerning its use, and corresponding privacy safeguards.[17] The case study countries have not yet utilised this form of technology for border security purposes, although the United Kingdom has used the technology in its 2009 National Sizing Survey.

21.1.2.3 The Recording, Collection, Storage and Sharing of Information by Customs Authorities

It is becoming increasingly common for passengers arriving at international ports and airports to be required to provide fingerprints, or to have photographs or retinal scans taken. Customs and transport security authorities obtain other forms of information from incoming passengers, including travel dates and undertake travel pattern analyses through data obtained under advance passenger screening programmes, the contact-less reading of MRTDs, and more traditional forms of questioning at immigration counters and the like. Consistent with the obligation under article 17(2) of the ICCPR mentioned earlier, the World Customs Organization has stated, in its SAFE Framework of Standards, that "... national legislation must contain provisions that specify that any data collected and or transmitted by Customs must be treated confidentially and securely and be sufficiently protected, and it must grant certain rights to natural or legal persons to whom the information pertains".[18]

---

[15]See letter from the Electronic Privacy Information Center to the United States Secretary of Homeland Security dated 31 May 2009, online: http://epic.org/privacy/airtravel/backscatter/ Napolitano_ltr-wbi-6-09.pdf. For a video demonstration of the operation and use of body scanning technology, see: CNN.com, 'Airport security bares all, or does it?', online: http://edition.cnn.com/ 2009/TRAVEL/05/18/airport.security.body.scans/index.html#cnnSTCVideo.

[16]See generally, for example, Electronic Privacy Information Center, 'Whole Body Imaging Technology ("Backscatter" X-Ray and Millimeter Wave Screening)', online: http://epic.org/ privacy/airtravel/backscatter/.

[17]Aircraft Passenger Whole-Body Imaging Limitations Act 2009 (US).

[18]World Customs Organization SAFE Framework of Standards (2007), p. 22. See also: Human Rights Committee, General Comment 16: The right to respect of privacy, family, home and correspondence, and protection of honour and reputation (Art 17), UN Doc CCPR General Comment 16 (1988), para 10; Special Rapporteur report on Australia (n 6) para 52; and Council of Europe Convention for the Protection of Individuals with regard to Automatic Processing of

The effective protection of privacy rights includes measures to ensure that personal information does not reach the hands of unauthorised persons, including through the unauthorised interception of data on MRTD radio-frequency identification chips (discussed above); to ensure that personal information may never be used for purposes incompatible with human rights or incompatible with the specific purpose for which the information was obtained; and to limit the storage of such data only for as long as is necessary.[19] ICAO and World Customs Organization guidelines on advance passenger information note, for example:[20]

> Data privacy and data protection legislation typically requires that personal data undergoing automated (computer) processing:
>
> – should be obtained and processed fairly and lawfully;
> – should be stored for legitimate purposes and not used in any way incompatible with those purposes;
> – should be adequate, relevant and not excessive in relation to the purposes for which they are stored;
> – should be accurate and, where necessary, kept up to date;
> – should be preserved in a form which permits identification of the data subjects for no longer than is required for the purposes for which that data is stored.

21.1.3 Profiling

Pre-entry interception and detection measures include reliance by customs and transport security authorities on 'terrorist profiles'. The selection of persons for screening at international boundaries, as well as at other forms of security checkpoints, is either random or based on profiling, defined as the association of sets of physical, behavioural or psychological characteristics with particular offences of threats and their use as a basis for making law-enforcement decisions.[21]

21.1.3.1 The Permissible Limits of Profiling

In principle, profiling is a permissible activity, since detailed profiles based on factors that are statistically proven to correlate with certain criminal conduct may

---

Personal Data, CETS 108, and its Additional Protocol regarding supervisory authorities and transborder data flows, CETS 181.

[19]General Comment 16 (ibid) para 10. See also the Council of Europe Convention for the Protection of Individuals with regard to Automatic Processing of Personal Data, ibid, and its Additional Protocol regarding supervisory authorities and transborder data flows, ibid.

[20]World Customs Organization (WCO), International Air Transport Association (IATA) and the International Civil Aviation Organization (ICAO), Guidelines on Advance Passenger Information (2003), para 9.3.

[21]Report of the Special Rapporteur on the promotion and protection of human rights and fundamental freedoms while countering terrorism, Protection of human rights and fundamental freedoms while countering terrorism, UN Doc A/HRC/4/26 (2006), para 33.

be effective tools to better target limited law-enforcement resources.[22] However, profiling may violate the right to equality and non-discrimination when intelligence and law-enforcement agents use profiles that reflect unexamined generalisations. The principles of equality and non-discrimination are central to human rights law and are recognised as norms of *jus cogens*.[23] Equality refers to the equality of men and women, and to the equal treatment of all persons before the law. As well as a principle in its own right, non-discrimination (which prohibits discrimination on grounds such as race, colour, sex, language, religion, political or other opinion, national or social origin, property, birth or other status),[24] is also a specific condition upon the ability to derogate from certain rights (see Chap. 10, Sect. 10.2.5.1).[25] Compliance with the principle of non-discrimination is recognised as crucial for effectively countering terrorism and has been identified in the UN Global Counter-Terrorism Strategy as an essential measure in addressing conditions conducive to the spread of terrorism.[26] This means that the design and use of security infrastructure, including security at international borders, must always fully respect the principles of equality and non-discrimination. The UN General Assembly's Code of Conduct for Law Enforcement Officials, for example, provides that officials must maintain and uphold the human rights of all persons, including the right to non-discrimination.[27]

Profiling will be likely to violate the right to equality and non-discrimination if it is based on ethnic or national origin (racial profiling) or religion (religious

---

[22]Report of the Special Rapporteur on profiling (ibid) para 33. See also Report of the Special Rapporteur on Australia (n 6) para 52.

[23]See, for example: Committee on the Elimination of Racial Discrimination, Statement on Racial Discrimination and Measures to Combat Terrorism, in the Report of the Committee on the Elimination of Racial Discrimination, UN Doc A/57/18 (2002), p. 107, paras 4–6; report of the Special Rapporteur on profiling (n 21) para 41; report of the Special Rapporteur on the promotion and protection of human rights and fundamental freedoms while countering terrorism, Mission to the United States of America, UN Doc A/HRCA/6/17/Add.3 (2007), para 28; and report of the Independent Expert on the protection of human rights and fundamental freedoms while countering terrorism, UN Doc E/CN.4/2005/103, paras 71–76, especially para 72.

[24]ICCPR, article 26; and Convention on the Elimination of All Forms of Racial Discrimination, opened for signature 7 March 1966, 9464 UNTS 211 (entered into force 4 January 1969), article 5.

[25]See article 4(1) of the ICCPR; and Human Rights Committee, General Comment 29: States of Emergency (Article 4), UN Doc CCPR/C/21/Rev.1/Add.11 (2001), para 8.

[26]United Nations Global Counter-Terrorism Strategy, adopted under General Assembly resolution 60/288, UN Doc A/Res/60/288 (2006), Pillar I, preambular paragraph.

[27]United Nations Code of Conduct for Law Enforcement Officials, adopted under GA Res 34/169 (1979), article 2 and its Commentary (a). See also: GA Res 59/191, UN Doc A/Res/59/159 (2004), preambular para 12; GA Res 61/171, UN Doc A/Res/61/171 (2006) preambular para 13; GA Res 62/159, UN Doc A/Res/62/159 (2007), preambular para 11; Commission on Human Rights resolution 2005/80, UN Doc E/CN.4/Res/2005/80 (2005), preambular para 15; and report of the United Nations High Commissioner for Human Rights and Follow-up to the World Conference on Human Rights, Human Rights: A Uniting Framework, UN ESCOR, 58th Sess, UN Doc E/CN.4/2002/18 (2002), Annex entitled Proposals for "further guidance" for the submission of reports pursuant to paragraph 6 of Security Council resolution 1373 (2001), para 4(i).

profiling), and/or if profiling solely or disproportionately affects a specific part of the population.[28] Profiling may also be prohibited where it is based on a person's country of origin if this is used as a proxy for racial or religious profiling.[29] A difference in treatment based on criteria such as race, ethnicity, national origin or religion will only be compatible with the principle of non-discrimination if it is supported by objective and reasonable grounds. As stated by the Human Rights Committee in its General Comment on non-discrimination, "not every differentiation of treatment will constitute discrimination, if the criteria for such differentiation are reasonable and objective and if the aim is to achieve a purpose which is legitimate under the Covenant".[30] The general position, however, is that racial and religious profiling cannot be justified on objective and reasonable grounds because profiling practices based on ethnicity, national origin and religion have proved to be inaccurate and largely unsuccessful in preventing terrorist activity or in identifying terrorists.[31] Such practices affect thousands of innocent people, without producing concrete results, and entail considerable negative effects, thus making them disproportionate.[32] As noted by the UN Special Rapporteur in his thematic report on profiling:[33]

In some cases, police forces have relied on profiles based on a person's ethnic and/or religious appearance when conducting stops, document checks or searches for counter-terrorism purposes. In the United Kingdom of Great Britain and Northern Ireland, government officials have openly acknowledged that law-enforcement efforts in the counter-terrorism context focus on particular ethnic or religious groups. Accordingly, stops and searches under section 44 of the Terrorism Act 2000, which authorizes the police in designated areas to stop and search people without having to show reasonable suspicion, have affected ethnic minorities. Between 2001–2002 and 2002–2003, for example, the number of persons of Asian ethnicity subjected to section 44 searches rose by 302 per cent as compared to a rise of 118 per cent for white people. By 2003–2004, Asian people were about 3.6 times more likely, and black people about 4.3 times more likely, to be stopped and searched under counter-terrorism legislation than white people. Similarly, police forces in the Russian Federation have subjected ethnic minorities to stops and document checks,

---

[28]Human Rights Committee, General Comment 27: Freedom of movement (Article 12), UN Doc CCPR/C/21/Rev.1/Add.9 (1999), para 18; Report of the World Conference against Racism, Racial Discrimination, Xenophobia and Related Intolerance, UN Doc A/CONF.189/12, Programme of Action, para 72; Committee on the Elimination of Racial Discrimination, General Recommendation 30 on discrimination against non-citizens, UN Doc HRI/GEN/1/Rev.8 (2004), para 10; Special Rapporteur report on profiling (n 21) paras 36 and 40–42; Special Rapporteur report on Australia (n 6) paras 53–55; and Special Rapporteur report on the United States of America (n 23) para 45.

[29]Special Rapporteur report on profiling (n 21) para 36.

[30]Human Rights Committee, General Comment 18, Non-discrimination, UN Doc HRI/GEN/1/ Rev.1 at 26 (1994), para 13. See also *Brooks v The Netherlands,* Human Rights Committee Communication 172/1984, UN Doc CCPR/C/OP/2 (1990), para 13.

[31]Special Rapporteur report on profiling (n 21) paras 45–54.

[32]Special Rapporteur report on profiling (n 21) paras 55–58.

[33]Special Rapporteur report on profiling (n 21) para 37.

which are often carried out in response to terrorist threats. A study of police practices on the Moscow metro system in 2005 found that persons of non-Slavic appearance were, on average, 21.8 times more likely to be stopped than Slavs.

It would therefore be in violation of the principle of non-discrimination, for example, if police were to rely on a person's ethnic and/or religious appearance when conducting routine stops, document checks, or searches. The same would apply if male immigrants, who are not suspected of any criminal activity, were to be selected for questioning solely because they are of a certain age and originate from certain countries.[34] The exception to this position is where a terrorist crime has been committed, or is in preparation, and there is clear and specific information raising reasonable grounds to assume that the suspect fits a certain descriptive profile. In these circumstances, reliance on characteristics such as ethnic appearance, national origin or religion is justified.[35]

It should be noted that profiling based on behavioural indicators appears to be significantly more efficient than relying on ethnic, national and religious characteristics. As noted by the Special Rapporteur:[36]

> The importance of focusing on behaviour is highlighted, for example, by the experiences of the United States Customs Service. In the late 1990s, the Customs Service stopped using a profile that was based, among other factors, on ethnicity and gender in deciding whom to search for drugs. Instead, the customs agents were instructed to rely on observational techniques, behavioural analysis and intelligence. This policy change resulted in a rise in the proportion of searches leading to the discovery of drugs of more than 300 per cent. The Special Rapporteur believes that behaviour is an equally significant indicator in the terrorism context. He therefore urges States to ensure that law-enforcement authorities, when engaging in preventive counter-terrorism efforts, use profiles that are based on behavioural, rather than ethnic or religious, characteristics. . ..

Equally important to note is that reliance on behavioural indicators must be in a neutral manner and must not be used as mere proxies for ethnicity, national origin or religion. Where law-enforcement agencies are unable to rely on specific intelligence or useful behavioural indicators, the use of security infrastructure should affect everyone equally, i.e. it should used be on a genuinely random basis.[37]

21.1.3.2   Profiling Under the Terrorism Act 2000 (UK)

The limits of profiling in the context of countering terrorism in the United Kingdom was considered by the House of Lords in 2006 in *Gillan v Commissioner of Police for the Metropolis*.[38] Although the case did not concern profiling at international

---

[34]See the example in the Special Rapporteur report on profiling (n 21) para 36.

[35]Special Rapporteur report on profiling (n 21) para 59.

[36]Special Rapporteur report on profiling (n 21) para 60.

[37]Special Rapporteur report on profiling (n 21) paras 60–61.

[38]*Gillan and Another v Commissioner of Police for the Metropolis and Another* [2006] UKHL 12.

borders, the principles raised in it are relevant to the current discussion. The case concerned sections 44 and 45 of the Terrorism Act 2000 (UK), which authorise police to search members of the public without having to have any grounds to suspect wrongdoing on the part of the person. It involved the search of a student and freelance journalist in London, in respect of whom nothing incrimination was found. Both were told that they had been searched under the Terrorism Act 2000 for "articles concerned in terrorism". While the powers of arrest without warrant under sections 41–43 of the Act (see Chap. 16, Sect. 16.1) must be based on a reasonable suspicion that the person being arrested is a terrorist, sections 44–47 are not subject to that requirement. The authority to stop is instead triggered by an authorisation under section 44 of the Terrorism Act, subject to confirmation by the Secretary of State under section 46, and pertaining to a specified area. The actual authority for stop and search is contained in section 45 and "may be exercised whether or not the constable has grounds for suspecting the presence of articles of that kind [articles of a kind which could be used in connection with terrorism]" (section 45(1)). Section 47 makes it an offence punishable by imprisonment or fine or both to fail to stop when required to do so by a constable, or wilfully to obstruct a constable in the exercise of the power conferred by an authorisation under section 44.

One of the issues considered in *Gillan* by Lord Brown was that of safeguards to avoid the risk of the power under section 45 being abused or exercised arbitrarily. Lord Brown observed that: "It seems to me inevitable ... that so long as the principal terrorist risk against which use of the section 44 power has been authorised is that from al Qaeda, a disproportionate number of those stopped and searched will be of Asian appearance (particularly if they happen to be carrying rucksacks or wearing apparently bulky clothing capable of containing terrorist-related items)".[39] Adopting the same approach described above, i.e. that profiling may be justified if based on objective and reasonable grounds, Lord Brown concluded that the power of stop and search will not be inconsistent with the principle of non-discrimination if police officers exercising the power pay proper heed to paragraph 2.25 of Code A to the Police and Criminal Evidence Act 1985, which provides as follows:[40]

> The selection of persons stopped under section 44 of Terrorism Act 2000 should reflect an objective assessment of the threat posed by the various terrorist groups active in Great Britain. The powers must not be used to stop and search for reasons unconnected with terrorism. Officers must take particular care not to discriminate against members of minority ethnic groups in the exercise of these powers. There may be circumstances, however, where it is appropriate for officers to take account of a person's ethnic origin in selecting persons to be stopped in response to a specific terrorist threat (for example, some international terrorist groups are associated with particular ethnic identities).

---

[39] *Gillan v Commissioner of Police for the Metropolis* (ibid) para 80.
[40] *Gillan v Commissioner of Police for the Metropolis* (ibid) para 81.

21.2   The Treatment of Refugees and Asylum-Seekers

Having considered some of the features of border controls relevant to countering terrorism and enhancing security, this part of the chapter considers measures within the territory of a State, including the detention of persons considered to be a risk to the security of the State. By way of a case study, particular attention is paid to the treatment of refugees and asylum-seekers in Australia.

Duffy describes some of the most potentially serious consequences of counter-terrorism laws, particularly for those labelled as terrorists or suspected terrorists, as relating to asylum-seekers and refugees.[41] In paragraph 3(f) of its resolution 1373 (2001), the Security Council calls upon States members of the United Nations to take measures to ensure that refugee status is not granted to asylum-seekers who have planned, facilitated or participated in the commission of terrorist acts. Paragraph 3(g) calls on States members to ensure that refugee status is not abused by perpetrators, organizers or facilitators of terrorist acts. Both provisions require such measures must be in conformity with international standards of human rights and other relevant provisions of international law. Resolutions 1624 also calls on States to deny safe have to persons with respect to whom there is credible and relevant information for considering that they have been guilty of terrorist conduct.[42] Similarly, the UN Global Counter-Terrorism Strategy resolves that States will not grant safe haven to terrorism and will take appropriate measures to ensure that asylum is not granted to terrorist.[43]

Before considering the law and practice in Australia concerning the treatment of refugees and asylum-seekers, one further matter should be briefly addressed. Where a person who arrives at a border seeks asylum, that person must not be rejected entry at the border without a fair and efficient refugee status determination procedure. Any summary rejection of asylum-seekers, including at borders or points of entry, may amount to *refoulement*, which is prohibited by international refugee and human rights law (see Sect. 21.3.1 below) since all persons have the right to seek asylum.[44] International standards require that admission into asylum procedures may be denied only if: (1) the individual concerned has already found protection in another country, and such protection is both available and effective; or (2) if the applicant can be returned to a country through which he or she has passed en route to the country where asylum is requested, provided he or she will be re-admitted, will be able to access fair asylum procedures and, if recognised, will be able to

---

[41]Duffy (2005, pp. 357–358). See also the report of the Special Rapporteur concerning challenges to refugee protection (n 3) para 32; Harvey (2005); Larking (2004); Mathew (2005); and Taylor (2002).

[42]SC Res 1624 (n 1) para 1(c).

[43]United Nations Global Counter-Terrorism Strategy, GA Res 60/288, UN GAOR, 60th Sess, 99th Plen Mtg, UN Doc A/Res/60/288 (2006), Pillar II, paras 2 and 3.

[44]See the Universal Declaration of Human Rights, adopted under General Assembly Resolution 217(III), UN GAOR, 3rd Session, 183rd Plenary Meeting (1948), article 14.

enjoy effective protection there.[45] Furthermore, as a general rule, no information regarding an asylum application, or an individual's refugee status, should be shared with the country of nationality or, in the case of stateless persons, the country of former habitual residence.[46]

21.2.1 Detention Pending Removal

As in many other countries, Australia undertakes character and security checks as part of the application process for refugee status. Non-citizens of Australia who arrive in Australia without a valid visa, other than New Zealanders, are interviewed by Department of Immigration and Multicultural Affairs (DIMA) staff to determine whether to allow or refuse entry into Australia. Where such a person applies for protection, the record of entry interview is forwarded to a senior DIMA official for an assessment of whether the person prima facie engages Australia's obligations under the Convention Relating to the Status of Refugees. Where that is not the case, the person will be refused immigration clearance and detained until he or she can be reasonably removed from Australia (on the question of removal, see Sect. 21.3 below). The Special Rapporteur on counter-terrorism has noted that detention provisions of this kind are becoming increasingly common in many countries, raising issues related to the necessity and proportionality of such measures, the right to speedy and effective judicial review of any form of detention, the rights of detained persons (including their right to the best attainable health), and possible violations of the prohibition against discrimination.[47] Linked to these concerns is the increasing reliance by countries on intelligence information and the use of 'closed material' by tribunals and courts (on the use of such material in control order proceedings, and the impact of this upon the rights to a fair hearing and to natural justice, see Chap. 18, Sect. 18.2).[48]

---

[45]See, for example, Office of the United Nations High Commissioner for Refugees, Global Consultations on International Protection, 2nd Mtg, Asylum Processes (Fair and Efficient Asylum Procedures), UN Doc EC/GC/01/12 (2001), para 8.

[46]UNHCR Global Consultations (ibid), Preserving the Institution of Asylum and Refugee Protection in the context of Counter-Terrorism: the Problem of Terrorist Mobility, para 20(iv).

[47]Special Rapporteur report on challenges to refugee protection (n 3) para 41.

[48]Report of the Eminent Jurists Panel on Terrorism, Counter-terrorism and Human Rights, Assessing Damage, Urging Action (Geneva: International Commission of Jurists, 2009), p. 93. In New Zealand see, for example: *Zaoui v Attorney-General* [2004] 2 NZLR 339; *Attorney-General v Zaoui (No 2)* [2005] 1 NZLR 690; Human Rights Committee, Concluding Observations: New Zealand, UN Doc CCPR/CO/75/NZL (2002), para 11; and Evatt (2005). In Canada see, for example: *Charkaoui v Canada (Citizenship and Immigration)* [2007] 1 SCR 350; *Charkaoui v Canada (Citizenship and Immigration)* [2008] 2 SCR 326; *Re Charkaoui* [2009] CF 1030; Forcese (2007, Chap. 10); and Roach (2005, pp. 521–528). On the case of Adil Charkaoui and his treatment in Canada, see also Assessing Damage, Urging Action, pp. 98–100.

In his study on Australia's counter-terrorism laws, the Special Rapporteur urged Australia to ensure that detention pending removal complies with articles 9 and 10 of the ICCPR.[49] He noted the views of the Human Rights Committee in *A v Australia* that, in order to avoid a characterisation of arbitrariness, detention should not continue beyond the period for which there is appropriate justification.[50] In that case, the author's detention as a non-citizen without an entry permit continued, in mandatory terms, until he was removed or granted a permit. The Committee was critical that Australia had failed to demonstrate that alternative and less intrusive measures were available. In *C v Australia*, the Committee took the view that a double violation of article 9, paragraphs (1) and (4), had taken place.[51] The Human Rights Committee has noted its concern over Australia's mandatory detention regime and, in its concluding observations on Australia's reports under article 40 of the Covenant, has urged Australia to reconsider the regime with a view to instituting alternative mechanisms of maintaining an orderly immigration process.[52]

Notwithstanding this, the regime continues to operate, and it drew heavy criticism from the UN Special Rapporteur. It was of particular concern to the Special Rapporteur that a person could be *indefinitely* detained under the Migration Act 1958, and that the High Court of Australia has ruled that the mandatory and indefinite detention of unlawful non-citizens under the Act is valid, provided that this occurs for the purpose of removing or deporting the non-citizen from Australia.[53] He noted that a Kuwaiti refugee applicant was detained for two years between 1997 and 1999 based upon an incorrect assessment by the Australian Security Intelligence Organisation that he was a national security risk.[54] The applicant was subsequently awarded compensation for wrongful imprisonment. Notwithstanding this, and the fact that ASIO security certificates are subject to judicial review under paragraph 75(v) of the Constitution of Australia and section 39B of the

---

[49]Special Rapporteur report on Australia (n 6) para 58.

[50]*A v Australia*, Human Rights Committee Communication 560/1993, UN Doc CCPR/C/59/D/560/1993 (1997), para 9.4.

[51]*C v Australia*, Human Rights Committee Communication 900/1999, UN Doc CCPR/C/76/D/900/1999 (2002).

[52]Human Rights Committee, Concluding Observations of the Human Rights Committee: Australia, UN Doc A/55/40, paras. 526 and 527. Despite this, DIMA notes on its website that, as at 2 June 2006, 811 people were in immigration detention, including 75 in "residence determination arrangements" in the community: Government of Australia, Department of Immigration and Multicultural Affairs, "Immigration detention facilities", online at http://immi.gov.au/detention/facilities.htm. The Refugee Council of Australia reports, as at 31 December 2004, that of those in immigration detention more than 200 persons had been held in detention for longer than 24 months: Refugee Council of Australia, "Australia's refugee programme", online at http://www.refugeecouncil.org.au/arp/stats-02.html.

[53]See *Al-Kateb v Godwin* [2004], High Court of Australia 37; *Minister for Immigration and Multicultural and Indigenous Affairs v Al Khafaji* [2004] HCA 38; and *Behrooz v Secretary of the Department of Immigration and Multicultural and Indigenous Affairs* [2004] HCA 36.

[54]See Michael Head, "Refugee detained for two years on false ASIO intelligence" (2005), Alternative Law Journal vol. 30 No. 1, p. 34.

Judiciary Act, the Special Rapporteur expressed grave concern that Australian law allows a person to be held in detention for such a long period of time, potentially indefinitely.[55]

21.2.2 Application of Exclusion Clauses Under the Refugees Convention

Reflecting article 1F of the Refugees Convention, an application for a protection visa may be refused in Australia under section 501 of the Migration Act 1958 where an applicant declares an involvement in the commission of war crimes, crimes against humanity, crimes against the peace, or serious non-political crimes (or where there are reasons for believing that this is the case). Similarly, article 33(2) of the Convention provides an exception to the application of the *non-refoulement* principle within the framework of the Convention (but not in respect of general human rights treaties such as article 7 of the ICCPR) in the case of refugees that are a danger to the security of the State, or who have been convicted of a particularly serious crime and who are a danger to the community. This is reflected in Australian law under section 501(6)(d)(v) of the Migration Act.

In its communications with the Special Rapporteur, Australia reported that all offences established by the counter-terrorism instruments to which it is a party are considered by Australia to be serious non-political offences.[56] This implies that an adverse character assessment would be made under section 501(6) of the Migration Act 1958. The Special Rapporteur cautioned, however, that not all offences under the terrorism-related conventions are serious offences. The Convention on Offences and Certain Other Acts Committed on Board Aircraft, for example, calls on States to establish jurisdiction over acts that may or do jeopardise the safety of a civil aircraft, or of persons or property therein, or which jeopardise good order and discipline on board. While this is capable of capturing conduct of a terrorist nature, the description of acts over which States must establish jurisdiction is very broad and likely also to include conduct with no bearing at all on terrorism. The Special Rapporteur therefore reminded Australia that the cumulative characterisation of acts to be suppressed when countering terrorism is important to this issue (see Chap. 2, Sect. 2.3.2, and Chap. 14, Sect. 14.1).[57] The Rapporteur has noted that vague or broad definitions of terrorism are extremely problematic in this area and

---

[55]Special Rapporteur report on Australia (n 6) para 59. See also the report of the Special Rapporteur concerning challenges to refugee protection (n 3) para 44; and Human Rights Committee, Concluding Observations: Australia, UN Doc CCPR/C/AUS/CO/5 (2009), para 23.

[56]Special Rapporteur report on Australia (n 6) para 60.

[57]See also the Special Rapporteur report on Australia (n 6) paras 12–14.

create a real risk of the application, in practice, of overly broad interpretations of the exclusion clauses in the Refugees Convention.[58]

The Special Rapporteur also recalled that the Office of the UN High Commissioner for Refugees has issued guidelines in which it has emphasised that article 1F of the Refugee Convention is only triggered in extreme circumstances by activity which attacks the very basis of the international community's coexistence.[59] Such activity, state the Guidelines, must have an international dimension. In the view of the Special Rapporteur, this reinforces the need to ensure that only acts possessing the characteristics identified in Security Council resolution 1566 (2004) should result in an adverse character assessment for the purpose of the Migration Act 1958.[60]

Where an application for refugee status is refused in Australia, the applicant may seek a merits review of that decision by either the Refugee Review Tribunal or the Administrative Appeals Tribunal, depending on the basis for refusal. Under section 501(3) of the Migration Act 1958, the Minister for Immigration and Multicultural Affairs may personally decide to refuse a protection visa, with such decisions capable of judicial review under section 476(1)(c) of the Migration Act and section 75(v) of the Constitution. This will be the case where the Minister reasonably suspects that the person does not pass the character test under the Act and that the refusal or cancellation is in the national interest. The term "national interest" is not defined within the Act. In this regard, the Special Rapporteur again reiterated his comments concerning the characterisation of terrorist acts.[61]

21.3 The Return or Transfer of Terrorist Suspects

The transfer of persons in the fight against terrorism may take place in several contexts, including extradition, deportation and the "rendition" of persons outside the latter established procedures. The trans-national transfer of persons is not a new phenomenon, nor one that is isolated to countering terrorism. Nevertheless, issues concerning the legitimacy of such action (including the suspected covert transfer of persons to places of secret detention by the United States of America) have been raised in recent years in the context of the fight against terrorism. The Council of Europe Committee on Legal Affairs and Human Rights was in 2006 provided with a report by Rapporteur Dick Marty in which it was concluded that more than a

---

[58]Special Rapporteur report on challenges to refugee protection (n 3) paras 66–67.

[59]Office of the United Nations High Commissioner for Refugees, Guidelines on International Protection: Application of the Exclusion Clauses: Article 1F of the Convention relating to the Status of Refugees (HCR/GIP/03/05), para 17.

[60]Special Rapporteur report on Australia (n 6) para 60.

[61]Special Rapporteur report on Australia (n 6) para 61.

hundred persons had been subject to 'extraordinary rendition', many to places of secret detention.[62]

The forcible movement of a person from one jurisdiction to another (one that is without the consent of the person) necessarily involves an interference with that person's liberty and security. Amongst other international and regional instruments, liberty and the security of the person are legal rights guaranteed under the ICCPR and the European Convention on the Protection of Human Rights and Fundamental Freedoms (ECHR).[63] Relevant to the way in which detained persons might be treated is the prohibition against torture, reflected within the two treaties just mentioned, the Convention against Torture and other Cruel, Inhuman and Degrading Treatment or Punishment (CAT),[64] and customary international law. Of further relevance is the International Convention for the Protection of All Persons from Enforced Disappearance, which was adopted and made open for signature by members of the United Nations on 23 September 2005.

21.3.1   The Principle of Non-refoulement

Article 33(1) of the Refugees Convention provides that: "No Contracting State shall expel or return ("refouler") a refugee in any manner whatsoever to the frontiers of territories where his life or freedom would be threatened on account of his race, religion, nationality, membership of a particular social group or political opinion". While this principle, that of *non-refoulement*, is used at a specialised level in refugee law, it is also to be found in other international instruments, including article 3 of the Convention against Torture, and has been enlarged by modern international law to apply to broader categories of individuals, not only to refugees or asylum-seekers.[65]

---

[62]Council of Europe Parliamentary Assembly Committee on Legal Affairs and Human Rights, Alleged secret detentions in Council of Europe member states, Information Memorandum II of Rapporteur Mr Dick Marty of Switzerland, COE Doc AS/Jur (2006) 03 of 22 January 2006, para 66. See also European Group of National Institutions for the Protection and Promotion of Human Rights, Position Paper on the use of diplomatic assurances in the context of expulsion procedures and the appropriateness of drafting a legal instrument relating to such use (for consideration by the DH-S-TER during its first meeting, 7–9 December 2005).

[63](European) Convention for the Protection of Human Rights and Fundamental Freedoms, opened for signature 4 November 1950, 213 UNTS 222 (entered into force 3 September 1953).

[64]Convention against Torture and other Cruel, Inhuman or Degrading Treatment or Punishment, opened for signature 10 December 1984, 1465 UNTS 112 (entered into force 26 June 1987).

[65]As was acknowledged by the European Court of Human Rights in *Chahal v United Kingdom* (1996) 23 EHRR 413. See also Schabas (2006, p. 4); and the report of the Special Rapporteur concerning challenges to refugee protection (n 3) para 49.

The High Commissioner for Human Rights and the Special Rapporteur on the question of torture have emphasised the importance of remaining vigilant against practices that erode the absolute prohibition against torture in the context of counter-terrorism measures.[66] A background paper to a workshop of the Organisation for Security and Cooperation in Europe (OSCE) Office for Democratic Institutions and Human Rights, on legal cooperation in criminal matters related to terrorism, identified and discussed case law of the European Court of Human Rights establishing and confirming the principles that a State would be in violation of its obligations under the ECHR if it extradited[67] or deported[68] an individual to a State where that person was likely to suffer inhuman or degrading treatment or torture contrary to Article 3 of the ECHR.[69] The Human Rights Committee and the Committee against Torture have adopted similar positions.[70] In the context of *refoulement*, it is relevant to note that article 3(1) of the CAT refers to "substantial grounds for believing that [the person] would be in danger of being subjected to torture". The Committee against Torture has commented that this assessment must be made on grounds that go beyond mere theory or suspicion, although the risk does not have to meet a test of high probability.[71]

Despite this, the UN Special Rapporteur on Torture has received a large number of allegations involving persons in circumstances where the principle of *non-refoulement* has not been respected. He has noted that, in the fight against terrorism, several governments have transferred or proposed to return alleged terrorist suspects to countries where they may be at risk of torture or ill-treatment.[72]

---

[66]See, for example: High Commissioner for Human Rights, Statement on Human Rights Day (Council of Europe Group of Specialists on Human Rights and the Fight against Terrorism, Strasbourg, DS-S-TER(2006)003, 17 March 2006); and Report of the Special Rapporteur on Torture and other Cruel, Inhuman or Degrading Treatment or Punishment, UN Doc A/60/316 (2005), para 51.

[67]*Soering v The United Kingdom* (1989) 11 EHRR 439.

[68]*Chahal v United Kingdom* (n 65).

[69]OSCE Office for Democratic Institutions and Human Rights, *Background Paper on Extradition and Human Rights in the Context of Counter-terrorism* (Workshop on Legal Co-operation in Criminal Matters Related to Terrorism, held at Belgrade, 14–16 December 2005). See also the background paper of the same title prepared for the OSCE Experts Workshop on Enhancing Legal Co-operation in Criminal Matters Related to Terrorism, held at Warsaw, April 2005.

[70]See, for example, *C v Australia*, Human Rights Committee Communication 832/1998, UN Doc CCPR/C/72/D/832/1998; *Ahani v Canada*, Human Rights Committee Communication 1051/2002, UN Doc CCPR/C/80/D/1051/2002; and *Mutombo v Switzerland*, Committee against Torture Communication 13/1993, UN Doc A/49/44 at 45 (1994). Concerning *Ahani v Canada*, see Harrington (2003).

[71]Committee Against Torture, General Comment (Article 3), UN Doc A/53/44, Anne IX, para 6. See also Mole (2007, pp. 32–48); and Sitaropoulos (2007, pp. 90–93).

[72]Report of the Special Rapporteur on Torture (n 66) para 29.

21.3.2 The Return of Non-nationals Under Australia's Migration Act 1958

Although not restricted to counter-terrorism, Australia's Migration Act 1958 does not prohibit the return of an alien to a place where they would be at risk of torture or ill-treatment, thus running the risk of a breach by Australia of the principle of *non-refoulement*. The Minister for Immigration and Multicultural Affairs may, if he or she considers it to be in the public interest, intervene and substitute a more favourable decision than the Refugee Review Tribunal concerning the return of a non-national to his or her country of origin (section 417). Furthermore, the Minister has published guidelines identifying Australia's obligations under the ICCPR and the Convention against Torture as relevant to the exercise of the latter discretion. Notwithstanding this, the Special Rapporteur on counter-terrorism expressed concern that these guidelines are not binding and the Minister's discretion under section 417 of the Migration Act is non-compellable and non-reviewable. As emphasised by the Rapporteur, the principle of *non-refoulement* is an absolute one and must be adhered to in order to avoid the extradition, expulsion, deportation, or other forms of transfer of persons to territories or secret locations in which they may face a risk of torture or ill-treatment.[73]

21.3.3 Diplomatic Assurances

Discussed in Chap. 17 were derogations from the right to liberty made by the United Kingdom in the context of emergencies declared to have arisen from threats of terrorism. The most recent of those involved a derogation from article 5(1)(f) of the European Convention on Human Rights to allow the UK to introduce a regime under Part 4 of the Anti-terrorism, Crime and Security Act 2001 (ATCS) for the indefinite detention of foreign nationals suspected to be international terrorists (Chap. 17, Sect. 17.3). Following a decision of the House of Lords in *A and Ors v Secretary of State*, the detention provisions in the ATCS were repealed under section 16(2)(a) of the Prevention of Terrorism Act 2005.[74] The UK Government stated that it would seek to deport the foreign nationals concerned where assurances against ill-treatment could be obtained from the destination country.[75] Those that could not be removed from the United Kingdom would be made subject to control orders under the Prevention of Terrorism Act (on control orders see Chap. 18,

---

[73]Special Rapporteur report on Australia (n 6) paras 62 and 72. See also the statement of the High Commissioner for Human Rights, Address at Chatham House and the British Institute of International and Comparative Law (Council of Europe Group of Specialists on Human Rights and the Fight against Terrorism, Strasbourg, 17 March 2006).

[74]*A and Ors v Secretary of State for the Home Department* [2004] UKHL 56.

[75]Bates (2005, p. 275); and Bonner and Cholewinski (2007, p. 161).

Sect. 18.1). Similar steps to transfer persons on the basis of diplomatic assurances have been taken by Canada.[76]

In its 2004 Concluding Observations on the United Kingdom's periodic report under the CAT, the Committee against Torture expressed its concern at the UK's reported use of diplomatic assurances.[77] Since that time, the British Government has made it its policy to develop a system for the use of diplomatic assurances against torture in cases involving national security considerations. The system is based on "Memoranda of Understanding" with a number of countries to which people are to be deported. The Government has accepted that, because of the widespread use of torture and ill-treatment in these countries, it would be precluded by article 3 of the ECHR and articles 3 and 7 of the CAT and ICCPR from deporting people to them in the absence of diplomatic assurances.[78] On 11 July 2006, for example, the United Kingdom and Algeria signed four conventions on extradition, judicial co-operation in civil and commercial matters, the readmission of persons, and mutual legal assistance in criminal matters. President Bouteflika of Algeria acknowledged and approved a letter from the Prime Minister which included the statement that "this exchange of letters underscores the absolute commitment of our two governments to human rights and fundamental freedoms ...". By longstanding diplomatic convention this statement amounted to a commitment on the part of the Algerian government to respect those rights.[79] Further to this, the United Kingdom sought specific assurances concerning the treatment of three individuals if they were to be deported to Algeria on the ground that each was a danger to the national security of the United Kingdom. One of these assurances read as follows:[80]

Should the above named person (RB) be arrested in order that his status may be assessed, he will enjoy the following rights, assurances and guarantees as provided by the Constitution and the national laws currently in force concerning human rights:

a. the right to appear before a court so that the court may decide on the legality of this arrest or detention and the right to be informed of the charges against him and to be assisted by a lawyer of his choice and to have immediate contact with that lawyer;

b. he may receive free legal aid;

c. he may only be placed in custody by the competent judicial authorities;

---

[76]See *Suresh v Minister of Citizenship and Immigration* [2002] 1 SCR 3. On the latter case, see the Committee on Torture, Concluding Observations: Canada, UN Doc CAT/C/CR/34/CAN (2005), paras 4(a) and (b) and 5. See also the report of the Special Rapporteur on Torture (n 66) para 33. See also *Ahani v Canada*, Human Rights Committee Communication 1051/2002, UN Doc CCPR/C/80/D/1051/2002 (2004) para 10.8.

[77]Committee against Torture, Concluding Observations: United Kingdom of Great Britain and Northern Ireland, UN Doc CAT/C/CR/33/3 (2004), para 4. See also Human Rights Committee, Concluding Observations: United Kingdom of Great Britain and Northern Ireland, UN Doc CCPR/C/GBR/CO/6 (2008), para 12.

[78]House of Lords and House of Commons Joint Committee on Human Rights, Nineteenth Report, Session 2005–2006, para 98.

[79]*RB and another v Secretary of State for the Home Department* [2009] UKHL 10, para 24.

[80]As quoted in *RB and another v Secretary of State* (ibid) para 25.

d. if he is the subject of criminal proceedings, he will be presumed to be innocent until his guilt has been legally established;

e. the right to notify a relative of his arrest or detention;

f. the right to be examined by a doctor;

g. the right to appear before a court so that the court may decide on the legality of his arrest or detention;

h. his human dignity will be respected under all circumstances.

The Special Immigration Appeals Commission found that there was a residual risk that RB would be at risk of treatment at the hands of Algerian security services in a way that would infringe article 3 of the European Convention on Human Rights (which provides that no one shall be subjected to torture or to inhuman or degrading treatment or punishment) were it not for the assurances given by the Algerian authorities.[81] The Secretary of State had also accepted that Algeria was a country to which RB could not safely have been returned had the United Kingdom not received assurances as to the way in which he would be treated.[82] In dealing with the issue of the safety of the appellants if returned to Algeria, Mitting J turned to the test set out in *Chahal v United Kingdom*, namely that:[83]

> ...whenever substantial grounds have been shown for believing that an individual would face a real risk of being subjected to treatment contrary to article 3 if removed to another state, the responsibility of the contracting state to safeguard him or her against such treatment is engaged in the event of expulsion.

Justice Mitting commented that the assessment of risk was fact-specific and had to be related to the individual applicant. He then set out four conditions that had to be satisfied if the assurances were to carry the credibility necessary to permit RB's return to Algeria:[84]

1. The terms of the assurances had to be such that, if they were fulfilled, the person returned would not be subjected to treatment contrary to article 3 of the European Convention.

2. The assurances had to be given in good faith.

3. There had to be a sound objective basis for believing that the assurances would be fulfilled.

4. Fulfilment of the assurances had to be capable of being verified.

Considering the assurances given, and the situation in Algeria and relations between that country and the United Kingdom, the SIAC concluded that the first three conditions were satisfied.[85] On the last point of verification, Mitting J concluded that this could be achieved by a number of means, both formal and informal,

---

[81] Ibid.

[82] *RB and another v Secretary of State* (n 79) para 107.

[83] *Chahal v United Kingdom* (n 65) para 80. See *RB and another v Secretary of State* (n 79) para 22.

[84] *RB and another v Secretary of State* (n 79) para 23.

[85] *RB and another v Secretary of State* (n 79) paras 25–28.

of which monitoring was only one. He acknowledged, however, that effective verification was an essential requirement since an assurance the fulfilment of which was incapable of being verified would be of little worth. In this regard, the United Kingdom government had sought to persuade the Algerian Government to agree to monitoring, but had not succeeded. SIAC concluded that there was nothing sinister in this and pointed to other ways in which the performance of the Algerian assurances could be verified. British Embassy officials would be permitted to maintain contact with RB, if not in detention, and prolonged detention would itself be indicative of a breach of the assurances. Amnesty International and other non-governmental agencies could be relied upon, said SIAC, to find out if the assurances were breached and to publicise the fact. SIAC thus concluded that the fourth condition was satisfied.

In the House of Lords, it was argued that it was irrational and unlawful for SIAC to have relied on Algeria's assurances for two reasons. First, because Algeria had not been prepared to agree to independent monitoring of the manner in which RB would be treated. Secondly, because, on their true construction, the assurances did not promise that RB would not be subjected to inhuman treatment. Counsel relied on *Saadi v Italy,* where the European Court of Human Rights spoke of the requirement of the deporting Government to "dispel any doubts" about the safety of the deportee.[86] In considering this, Lord Phillips in the House of Lords took the view that this and other decisions did not establish a principle that assurances must eliminate *all* risk of inhuman treatment before they can be relied upon.[87] He instead formulated the applicable test as follows, while at the same time noting that assurances should be treated with scepticism if they are given by a country where inhuman treatment by State agents is endemic:[88]

> If ... after consideration of all the relevant circumstances of which assurances form part, there are no substantial grounds for believing that a deportee will be at real risk of inhuman treatment, there will be no basis for holding that deportation will violate article 3.

Non-governmental organisations, including Amnesty International, Human Rights Watch and the International Commission of Jurists, have taken the position that diplomatic assurances are not an effective safeguard against torture.[89] In his 2005 report to the General Assembly, the UN Special Rapporteur on Torture made a special point to note the difficulties of enforcing assurances of this kind. He referred

---

[86] *Saadi v Italy* [2008] ECHR 179, para 129. Counsel also referred to two recent cases where the court spoke of the need for diplomatic assurances to "ensure adequate protection against the risk of ill-treatment where reliable sources had reported practices resorted to or tolerated by the authorities which were manifestly contrary to the principles of the Convention": *Ismoilov and others v Russia* [2008] ECHR 348, para 127; and *Ryabikin v Russia* [2008] ECHR 533, para 119.

[87] *RB and another v Secretary of State* (n 79) para 114.

[88] *RB and another v Secretary of State* (n 79) paras 114–115.

[89] See, for example, Amnesty International's Campaign Fact Sheet. 'Diplomatic assurances' – No protection against torture or ill-treatment, online: http://www.amnesty.org/en/library/asset/ACT40/021/2005/en/c9223617-d474-11dd-8743-d305bea2b2c7/act400212005en.pdf. See also Assessing Damage, Urging Action (n 48) pp. 104–106; and Goodwin-Gill (2005).

to the Committee's decision in *Agiza v Sweden*, where the Committee against Torture found Sweden to have violated article 3 of the CAT in circumstances where the Committee noted that the assurances obtained by Sweden provided no mechanism for their enforcement and did not suffice to protect Agiza from the manifest risk of his ill-treatment in Egypt.[90] The Special Rapporteur concluded that:[91]

> ...diplomatic assurances are unreliable and ineffective in the protection against torture and ill-treatment: such assurances are sought usually from States where the practice of torture is systematic; post-return monitoring mechanisms have proven to be no guarantee against torture; diplomatic assurances are not legally binding, therefore they carry no legal effect and no accountability if breached; and the person whom the assurances aim to protect has no recourse if the assurances are violated. The Special Rapporteur is therefore of the opinion that States cannot resort to diplomatic assurances as a safeguard against torture and ill-treatment where there are substantial grounds for believing that a person would be in danger of being subjected to torture or ill-treatment upon return.

The Special Rapporteur on counter-terrorism and the UN High Commissioner on Human Rights have taken similar positions, noting that a weakness inherent in the practice of diplomatic assurances lies in the fact that they are sought where there is a need for such assurances, i.e. in circumstances where there is clearly an acknowledged risk of torture or ill-treatment.[92]

In its Nineteenth Report of 2006, the UK Joint Committee on Human Rights also considered the question of the practice by the United Kingdom of seeking diplomatic assurances to allow the rendition of persons. The Joint Committee heard submissions on the efficacy of monitoring mechanisms for diplomatic assurances, including the position by Human Rights Watch that: "torture and ill-treatment are practised in secret and occur within a highly sophisticated system specifically

---

[90]*Agiza v Sweden*, Committee against Torture Communication 233/2003, UN Doc CAT/C/34/D/233/2003 (2005). See also Committee Against Torture, General Comment (Article 3), UN Doc A/53/44, Annex IX, para 6, where the Committee commented that the risk of torture must go beyond mere theory or suspicion, but need not meet a test of high probability.

[91]Report of the Special Rapporteur on Torture (n 66) para 51.

[92]Report of the Special Rapporteur on the promotion and protection of human rights and fundamental freedoms while countering terrorism, UN Doc A/62/263 (2007), paras 52–53; Report of the Special Rapporteur on the promotion and protection of human rights and fundamental freedoms while countering terrorism, Mission to Spain, UN Doc A/HRC/10/3/Add.2 (2008), paras 39–40; and Office of the High Commissioner for Human Rights presentation, Human rights concerns related to the treatment and screening of individuals at the border (presentation at the fifth special meeting of the Counter-Terrorism Committee with international, regional and sub-regional organisations, Prevention of Terrorist Movement and Effective Border Security, 29–31 October 2007, Nairobi, Kenya), un-numbered para 17. See also: Independent Expert on the protection of human rights and fundamental freedoms while countering terrorism, Protection of Human Rights and Fundamental Freedoms While Countering Terrorism, UN Doc E/CN.4/2005/103, paras 56–61; United Nations High Commissioner for Refugees, Note on Diplomatic Assurances and International Refugee Protection, 2006, online: http://www.unhcr.org/refworld/docid/44dc81164.html, pp. 16–17; and Report of the Council of Europe Commissioner for Human Rights, COE Doc CommDH(2004)13, para 9.

designed to keep abuses from being detected. As a result, even if a sending government sought to engage in serious post-return monitoring, it would come up against the reality that those who use torture are adept at hiding it".[93] Furthermore, as noted by the House of Lords in *RB v Secretary of State*, verification of assurances is particularly difficult given that a person in detention may be understandably reluctant to complain to a monitor of torture or inhuman treatment.[94] The Committee itself concluded:

> We therefore agree with the UN Special Rapporteur on Torture, the European Commissioner for Human Rights and others that the Government's policy of reliance on diplomatic assurances against torture could well undermine well-established international obligations not to deport anybody if there is a serious risk of torture or ill-treatment in the receiving country. We further consider that, if relied on in practice, diplomatic assurances such as those to be agreed under the Memoranda of Understanding with Jordan, Libya and Lebanon present a substantial risk of individuals actually being tortured, leaving the UK in breach of its obligations under Article 3 UNCAT, as well as Article 3 ECHR. We are also concerned that Memoranda of Understanding lack enforceable remedies in an event of a breach of the terms of the Memoranda.

21.4 Conclusions

Due to the transnational nature of modern terrorism (which can involve preparation, training, support and incitement in territories other than the territory in which a terrorist act is to occur), the question of preventing the transboundary movement of terrorists has been described by the UN Counter-Terrorism Committee and the Security Council's resolution 1566 (2004) Working Group as essential in the fight against terrorism, requiring careful implementation. As well as contributing to these preventive aspects, the movement of terrorist suspects from one territory to another is also an issue relevant to the punishment of terrorism, namely the extradition and/ or prosecution of those who have committed acts of terrorism. Numerous issues are raised by this, not all of which have been canvassed in this chapter. The issues raised can be categorised as falling within one of three phases: (1) measures to prevent the transboundary movement of terrorists at international borders; (2) measures within the territory of a State including, for example, the detention of non-nationals considered to be a risk to the security of a country; and (3) measures adopted by States concerning the return and/or transfer of terrorists and terrorist suspects.

Effective border security is an important aspect in an effective counter-terrorism strategy, and the ability of States to prevent the transboundary movement of terrorists. It is also a condition of Security Council resolution 1373 (2001),

---

[93]House of Lords and House of Commons Joint Committee on Human Rights, Nineteenth Report, Session 2005–2006, para 116.

[94]*RB and another v Secretary of State* (n 79) para 116.

paragraph 2(g), and is impacted upon by paragraph 2(b) of the same resolution and paragraph 2 of resolution 1624 (2005). A tool first adopted by the United States in 1990 and now being widely used, including within the four case study countries, is the sharing of information between countries of departure and arrival to enable the advance 'screening' of passenger lists prior to travel commencing. In Australia for example, the Advance Passenger Processing system allows the Department of Immigration and Multicultural Affairs to issue boarding directives to airlines and cruise companies, thereby preventing the boarding of passengers and crew who do not have permission to travel to Australia. While apparently effective as part of a layered approach to prevent the transboundary movement of terrorists, the Special Rapporteur on counter-terrorism has warned that States should be cautious of implementing measures that may effectively prevent persons from exercising the right of every person to leave any country, including one's own country, particularly in the context of those fleeing persecution with an intention to seek refugee status elsewhere.

Also relevant to border security is the use of technologies such as whole-body imaging, and Machine Readable Travel Documents (MRTDs) such as biometric passports and visas. The use of these technologies is said to increase the efficiency and speed of passenger screening, as well as limiting more intrusive physical searches of passengers in the case of scanning technology. Despite early claims by developers of radio-frequency identification chips, which allow the contact-less reading of the biometric and biographical data of individuals stored on MRTDs, research has shown that these chips can be read from a distance. In pursuit of the obligation upon States to protect individuals from arbitrary or unlawful interference with their privacy, care must therefore be taken by States to ensure that such technologies are not susceptible to unauthorised interception. The right to privacy also demands that personal information collected and analysed by border authorities does not reach the hands of unauthorised persons, and that personal information may never be used for purposes incompatible with human rights or incompatible with the specific purpose for which the information was obtained.

The selection of persons for screening at international boundaries will either be random or based on profiling, defined as the association of sets of physical, behavioural or psychological characteristics with particular offences of threats and their use as a basis for making law-enforcement decisions. In principle, profiling is a permissible activity, since detailed profiles based on factors that are statistically proven to correlate with certain criminal conduct may be effective tools to better target limited law-enforcement resources. However, profiling can never violate the right to equality and non-discrimination, which will likely occur if profiling is based on ethnic or national origin (racial profiling) or religion (religious profiling), and/or if profiling solely or disproportionately affects a specific part of the population. Profiling may also be prohibited where it is based on a person's country of origin if this is used as a proxy for racial or religious profiling. A difference in treatment based on criteria such as race, ethnicity, national origin or religion will only be compatible with the principle of non-discrimination if it is supported by objective and reasonable grounds. The general position, however, is that racial and religious profiling cannot be justified on objective and reasonable grounds because profiling practices based on ethnicity, national origin and religion have proved to be inaccurate and largely unsuccessful in preventing terrorist activity or in identifying terrorists. The exception to this position is where a terrorist crime has been committed, or is in preparation, and there is clear and specific information raising reasonable grounds to assume that the suspect fits a certain descriptive profile. In these circumstances, reliance on characteristics such as ethnic appearance, national origin or religion is justified.

Some of the most potentially serious consequences of counter-terrorism laws, particularly for those labelled as terrorists or suspected terrorists, relate to refugees and asylum-seekers. As in many other countries, Australia undertakes character and security checks of those applying for asylum. Where applications for asylum are refused, and in some cases where they are pending, the applicant will be detained until either he or she can be removed from Australia or until the application process has been finally determined. The Special Rapporteur on counter-terrorism has noted that detention provisions of this kind are becoming increasingly common in many countries, raising issues related to the necessity and proportionality of such measures, the right to speedy and effective judicial review of any form of detention, the rights of detained persons (including their right to the best attainable health), and possible violations of the prohibition against discrimination. Linked to these concerns is the increasing reliance by countries on intelligence information and the use of 'closed material' by tribunals and courts, a matter considered earlier in this text. In the case of Australia, both the Special Rapporteur and the Human Rights Committee have expressed serious concern over Australia's mandatory detention regime, which can result in the indefinite detention of persons.

Reflecting the 'exclusion clauses' in articles 1F and 33 of the Convention on the Status of Refugees, Australia's Migration Act 1958 allows applications for a protection visa to be refused if the applicant is considered to have been involved in terrorism. In this regard, Australia has taken the position that all offences established by the counter-terrorism instruments to which it is a party are considered by it to be serious non-political offences. The Special Rapporteur has cautioned, however, that not all offences under the terrorism-related conventions are serious offences including, for example, some of the offences under the Convention on Offences and certain Other Acts Committed on Board Aircraft. He has reminded Australia that the cumulative characterisation of acts to be suppressed when countering terrorism is important to this issue, noting that vague or broad definitions of terrorism are extremely problematic in this area and create a real risk of the application, in practice, of overly broad interpretations of the exclusion clauses in the Refugees Convention.

Wherever substantial grounds are shown for believing that an individual would face a real risk of torture or ill-treatment if removed to another country, the State seeking the person's removal is under a responsibility to safeguard him or her against such treatment if removal occurs. Some countries, including Canada and the United Kingdom, have sought to discharge this responsibility by seeking what have come to be known as 'diplomatic assurances' from receiving countries that the person would not be subject to ill-treatment. This is a controversial approach, made inherently weak by the fact that such assurances will be sought in circumstances where there is a clearly acknowledged risk of torture or ill-treatment. Recognising that any assessment of risk will be fact-specific (or, more accurately, country-specific), an approach implicitly accepted by the House of Lords is to measure each situation against four conditions, namely that: (1) the terms of the assurances must be such that, if they are fulfilled, the person returned will not be subjected to torture or ill-treatment; (2) the assurances are given in good faith; (3) there is a sound objective basis for believing that the assurances will be fulfilled; and (4) fulfilment of the assurances is capable of being verified. The House of Lords has taken the view that assurances need not eliminate *all* risk of ill-treatment before they can be relied upon. While noting that assurances should be treated with some scepticism if they are given by a country where inhuman treatment by State agents is endemic, Lord Philipps has instead concluded that if, after consideration of all the relevant circumstances (of which the four conditions just mentioned will be key), there are "no substantial grounds for believing that a deportee will be at real risk of inhuman treatment", there will be no basis for holding that the removal is in violation of the prohibition against torture and ill-treatment.

The UN Special Rapporteur on Torture has instead concluded that diplomatic assurances are unreliable and ineffective in the protection against torture and ill-treatment and that post-return monitoring mechanisms have proven to be no guarantee against ill-treatment. Non-governmental organisations have noted that torture and ill-treatment are practices in secret and occur within a highly sophisticated system specifically designed to avoid detection of abuses. Effective verification of assurances is made more difficult given that a person in detention may be understandably reluctant to complain to a monitor of torture or inhuman treatment. Notwithstanding the decision of the House of Lords, or of application of the four conditions it is therefore concluded that diplomatic assurances present a substantial risk of individuals actually being tortured.

References

Bates, Edward. 2005. A 'Public Emergency Threatening the Life of the Nation'? The United Kingdom's Derogation from the European Convention on Human Rights of 18 December 2001 and the 'A' Case. *The British Yearbook of International Law* 245.

Bonner, David, and Cholewinski, Ryszard. 2007. The Response of the United Kingdom's Legal and Constitutional Orders to the 1991 Gulf War and the Post-9/11 'War' on Terrorism. In Guild, Elspeth, and Baldaccini, Anneliese (Eds). *Terrorism and the Foreigner: A Decade of Tension around the Rule of Law in Europe*. Leiden: Martinus Nijhoff Publishers.

Duffy, Helen. 2005. *The 'War on Terror' and the Framework of International Law*. Cambridge: Cambridge University Press.

Evatt, Elizabeth. 2005. Human Rights in New Zealand: the Zaoui case. *Human Rights Defender* 9.

Forcese, Craig. 2007. *National Security Law: Canadian Practice in International Perspective*. Toronto: Irwin Law.

Goodwin-Gill, Guy. 2005. Diplomatic Assurances and Deportation (paper presented at the *JUSTICE/Sweet & Maxwell Conference on Counter-terrorism and Human Rights*, 28 June 2005).

Harrington, Joanna. 2003. Punting Terrorists, Assassins and Other Undesirables: Canada, the Human Rights Committee and Requests for Interim Measures of Protection. 48 *McGill Law Journal* 55.

Harvey, Colin. 2005. And fairness for all? Asylum, national security and the rule of law. In Ramraj, Victor, Hor, Michael, and Roach, Kent (Eds). *Global Anti-Terrorism Law and Policy*. Cambridge: Cambridge University Press.

Larking, Emma. 2004. Human rights and the principle of sovereignty: a dangerous conflict at the heart of the nation state? *Australian Journal of Human Rights* 15.

Mathew, Penelope. 2005. Anti-terrorist = rights-resistant? The Work of the Counter-Terrorism Committee (paper presented at the 13th Annual Conference of the Australian and New Zealand Society of International Law, Canberra, Australia, 16–18 June 2005).

Mole, Nuala. 2007. *Asylum and the European Convention on Human Rights*. Strasbourg: Council of Europe Publishing.

Roach, Kent. 2005. Canada's response to terrorism. In Ramraj, Victor, Hor, Michael, and Roach, Kent (Eds). *Global Anti-Terrorism Law and Policy*. Cambridge: Cambridge University Press.

Schabas, William. 2006. Non-Refoulement (paper presented at the *Expert Workshop on Human Rights and International Co-operation in Counter-Terrorism*, 15–17 November 2006, Triesenberg, Liechtenstein).

Scheiner, Bruce. 2005. Fatal Flaw Weakens RFID Passports. Online publication: http://www.schneier.com/essay-093.html.

Sitaropoulos, Nicholas. 2007. The Role and Limits of the European Court of Human Rights in Supervising State Security and Anti-terrorism Measures Affecting Aliens' Rights. In Guild, Elspeth, and Baldaccini, Anneliese (Eds). *Terrorism and the Foreigner: A Decade of Tension around the Rule of Law in Europe*. Leiden: Martinus Nijhoff Publishers.

Taylor, Savitri. 2002. Guarding the Enemy from Oppression: Asylum-Seeker Rights Post-September 11. 26 *Melbourne University Law Review* 396.

Chapter 22
Conclusion

The focus of this title has been upon the legislative approaches of the four case study countries, Australia, Canada, New Zealand and the United Kingdom, to counter-terrorism and human rights. The methodology adopted has been to examine each subject of counter-terrorism and human rights in isolation first (Part I has examined terrorism and counter-terrorism, and Part II has looked at human rights law) and then, through Part III, to undertake an evaluation of the way counter-terrorism has interacted with human rights in the legislative approaches of each country. While not every aspect of law and practice involving the overlap between these two areas has been possible, the aim of this title has been to identify and explore those of most significance.

22.1 Terrorism and Counter-Terrorism

The focus of the first part of this title can also be characterised as being divided into different parts. Chapters 2 and 3 consider the subject of terrorism and counter-terrorism in the general context, while Chaps. 5–8 provide an overview, and general evaluation, of the counter-terrorism laws of each case study country. Chapter 4 acts as a bridge between the two sets of chapters, looking at the means by which the countries have implemented their international counter-terrorism obligations, including the constitutional reasons for these approaches, and the emerging trends in the countries examined.

22.1.1 Defining Terrorism

The nature and definition of terrorism is considered in Chap. 2, where it is noted that a range of conduct may fall within the ambit of a 'terrorist act', depending on how that term is defined and perhaps even upon the entity using the term. Terrorism

A. Conte, *Human Rights in the Prevention and Punishment of Terrorism*,
DOI 10.1007/978-3-642-11608-7_22, © Springer-Verlag Berlin Heidelberg 2010

will almost invariably involve criminal acts and may also be perpetrated during armed conflict. Chapter 2 distinguished terrorism from 'normal' criminal conduct on the basis of various factors. The focus of terrorist acts tends to be continuous, developing and escalating, rather than based upon the quite precise and short-term goals of non-organised criminal conduct. Terrorist organisations operate in a prepared and secure way, while at the same time relying upon wide dissemination of their conduct and ideology, and upon the recruitment of as many followers as possible. While criminal acts are targeted, terrorist ones are often indiscriminate. Relating also to targets, terrorism employs differential targeting whereby the physical targets of an act (people or infrastructure) are often used as tools to manipulate and put pressure upon an entity against whom the action is ultimately being taken (a government or international organisation). Inherent to the term 'terrorism', such acts are usually undertaken with the aim of intimidation or creating a situation of fear. Finally, terrorist acts are motivated by certain ideological, political or religious ideals.

The ideological motivations of terrorism are seen by most as the primary distinguishing feature of terrorist conduct from ordinary criminal offending. This affects the views of the perpetrator of terrorist acts as to the value of and culpability for such acts. On a more precise level, terrorist conduct tends to be motivated by secession, insurgency, regional retribution, and/or the 'global jihad'. Notably, while the particular individual terrorist may be driven by more personal goals, the motivations described are those of the person or entity by whom the individual actor is recruited or directed to act. Furthermore, the vast majority of the international community has been clear in stating that terrorist acts are unjustifiable in all circumstances, no matter what its motivations are.

It was concluded in Chap. 2 that these various features support a distinct approach to the criminalisation of terrorist conduct. The political interests of most States tend to favour a distinctive approach too. Despite this, there remains no concise, comprehensive and universal legal definition of the term terrorism. Notwithstanding this gap, Chap. 2 presented a definitional approach which is not impossible, nor overly difficult, for States to employ and which is restricted to acts of a truly terrorist nature. Not only is such an approach compatible with the human rights obligations of States, but it also lends considerably greater credibility to special counter-terrorist measures adopted by States if it can be shown that these are restricted to terrorism and are not being used as an excuse to abuse or unjustifiably expand upon executive powers. The approach set out in Chap. 2, which has been drawn from the views of the UN Special Rapporteur on counter-terrorism, existing international and regional terrorism-related conventions, the report of the UN High-Level Panel on Threats, Challenges and Change, and resolutions of the Security Council, can be summarised as follows:

1. Terrorist acts should be restricted to the three cumulative characteristics identified by the Security Council in its resolution 1566 (2004), namely:

    • the taking of hostages, or acts committed with the intention of causing death or serious bodily injury;

- where such conduct is undertaken for the purpose of either (i) provoking a state of terror, or (ii) compelling a government or international organisation to do or abstain from doing something;
- and where the conduct falls within the scope of the 'trigger offences' defined in the international terrorism-related conventions.

2. Conduct falling outside the scope of the trigger offences might still be classified as terrorist if such conduct possesses the first two characteristics identified in resolution 1566 (2004) and corresponds to all elements of a serious crime as defined by domestic law.
3. The approaches identified in items 1 and 2 above should apply also to the treatment of conduct in support of terrorist offences.
4. Finally, the definition of terrorist conduct (i) must not be retroactive, and (ii) must be adequately accessible and written with precision so as to amount to a prescription of law.

22.1.2 The International Framework for Combating Terrorism

Having considered in Chap. 2 the nature of terrorism and the way in which it can be defined, Chap. 3 provides an overview of the international framework on counter-terrorism. International law on counter-terrorism is principally based upon treaty law and the action of various agencies of the United Nations. Thirteen specific conventions relating to terrorism aim to either protect potential targets of terrorist conduct (civil aviation, operations at sea, and individual persons), or to suppress access to the means by which terrorist acts are perpetrated or funded (radioactive and nuclear materials, plastic explosives, bombings, and the financing of terrorism). These conventions do not, however, have general application and are limited in their binding nature to those States which have ratified or acceded to them. Having said this, the Suppression of Financing Convention does have potentially wider application in its description of conduct that may not be financed. The case study countries have signed all thirteen conventions, although the United Kingdom is currently the only one of those countries to have ratified the most recent treaty on countering terrorism, the International Convention for the Suppression of Acts of Nuclear Terrorism. All four countries are party to the remaining 12 terrorism-related conventions.

Additional to the terrorism-related conventions, the General Assembly and Security Council have issued numerous resolutions on the topic of counter-terrorism, culminating in the adoption by the General Assembly in September 2006 of the UN Global Counter-Terrorism Strategy. Although resolutions of the General Assembly are not binding, the Assembly has built on various guiding principles and expectations in its declarations on measures to eliminate international terrorism. The Security Council has adopted both binding and recommendatory decisions and has established a number of subsidiary bodies to deal with particular aspects of the fight against international terrorism, including creation of the Counter-Terrorism Committee very soon after the terrorist attacks of 11 September 2001. Three principal resolutions govern the action required by, or recommended to, members of the United Nations:

- Security Council resolution 1267 (1999), which requires members of the United Nations to impose a travel ban and an arms embargo on the Taliban and Al-Qa'ida, and to freeze funds and other financial resources controlled by or on behalf of the Taliban or any other individuals or entities designated by the Committee.
- Security Council resolution 1373 (2001), which imposes various obligations upon States (mainly focussed upon suppressing the financing of terrorism) and recommends further action.
- Security Council resolution 1624 (2005), which calls on States to adopt measures to prohibit the incitement to commit terrorist acts, and to prevent such conduct.

The challenges faced by the international framework for countering terrorism are many, and are not limited to the inherently difficult nature of defining terrorism. The application and enforceability of international treaties, as opposed to the more general application (but limited scope) of customary international law and obligations under Security Council resolutions, combine to create a complex web of intersecting laws and principles. The magnitude of organisations involved in various aspect of the fight against terrorism, coupled with the vast amount of legal instruments that States are required to implement and report upon, result in the need to take careful, coordinated action which takes capacity-building and technical assistance into account. This has been recognised by the United Nations and other regional organisations, and work is continuing to improve upon this important element of the fight to combat international terrorism.

22.1.3   Domestic Approaches to Counter-Terrorism

Bearing the latter observations in mind, Chaps. 5–8 provide an overview of counter-terrorism laws in Australia, Canada, New Zealand and the United Kingdom. Each chapter traces the legislative development of counter-terrorism laws in each country and concludes with a summary of compliance by them with the international framework on counter-terrorism, as this relates to the establishment of terrorism-related offences, treaty action and implementation, and implementation of the binding decisions of the Security Council. Linking this set of chapters with the overview of international counter-terrorism obligations in Chap. 3, Chap. 4 provides an overview and explanation of the mechanisms for implementation of international obligations in the case study countries, which are all common law jurisdictions and members of the Commonwealth and the United Nations.

Recognising that the geographical distribution of the case study countries, as well as their political histories, has resulted in a difference in the terrorist threats faced by each country, Chap. 4 also examined the question of whether counter-terrorism is relevant for all States. Despite differing levels of actual and potential threats faced, as well as diverging experiences of each country in dealing with terrorism, the countering of terrorism is indeed relevant to all four countries, whether as a result of their international legal obligations or their commitments to and support for an international framework on counter-terrorism. Measures to counter international terrorism are also capable of contributing to national interests, such as border security, international transport and external trade.

The final part of Chap. 4 provides a summary of the implementation of international counter-terrorism obligations by the case study countries, taking into account the Counter-Terrorism Committee's survey on the implementation of Security Council resolution 1373 (2001), and the report on practical aspects of implementing counter-terrorism obligations by the resolution 1566 Working Group of the Security Council. Chapter 4 concludes that there is a generally high level of implementation by the four countries, but also identifies some issues, such as preventing public provocation, which require further attention. The incitement to terrorism is a matter considered in Chaps. 14 (concerning its criminalisation) and 20 (concerning the compatibility of this with the freedom of expression).

Also noted within this discussion are a number of trends in the legislative responses to terrorism by the four case study countries which, in combination, show cause for concern. Legislative packages on counter-terrorism have, more often than not, involved lengthy texts which have received an expedited passage through Parliament, thus reducing the ability of legislators to give careful consideration and debate to provisions which might represent a shift from customary legal restraint. The speedy passage of such laws has also been to the detriment of allowing adequate public consultation. Of relevance here, the appearance of counter-terrorism legislation being drawn up in emergency circumstances is misleading. Taking the example of the UK's Prevention of Terrorism (Temporary Provisions) Act 1974, introduced following the Birmingham bombing and passed in just three days, the Home Office has subsequently admitted that the Act was drawn from a Bill drafted in 1973 but not introduced until after the bombing. These factors combined increase the risk of the enactment of anti-terrorism laws which run counter to the establishment under those laws of human rights limitations which are strictly necessary and proportionate. This is particularly problematic for jurisdictions such as Australia, which has no national bill of rights, and New Zealand and the United Kingdom, which can at best declare provisions incompatible with human rights and then leave the matter for consideration by the executive and parliament.

It has also been noted that counter-terrorism laws are in some cases not enacted as items of stand-alone legislation, instead establishing special and unusual powers within ordinary Acts, and thereby contributing to the risk of the normalisation of such powers and/or their eventual 'creepage' for use in traditional law enforcement. Of even greater concern is the practice of establishing special powers in terms such that they are not restricted to the countering of terrorism, but are instead applicable to the investigation of ordinary crimes. Cause for concern is in theory alleviated through the inclusion in counter-terrorism legislation of mechanisms such as sunset clauses, parliamentary review mechanisms, or the provision for independent review of legislation. Once laws are in place, however, practice shows that sunset clauses rarely result in a repeal or amendment of legislation, such laws instead often sliding into a state of de facto permanence. Parliamentary review can be an effective tool, but may be thwarted by timetabling issues, or an indifferent treatment of the subject at select committee level. The utility of independent reviews depends upon the terms of appointment of, and resources available to, the independent reviewer, not to mention whether reports of an independent reviewer are linked to a parliamentary select committee which is capable of then triggering debate in parliament.

22.2 Human Rights Law

22.2.1 International and Regional Human Rights Law

All four case study countries are parties to the International Covenant on Civil and Political Rights (ICCPR) and thus have a common reference point on the question of international human rights obligations. The United Kingdom is also a party to the European Convention on Human Rights (ECHR) and, recognising this, Chap. 9 provides an overview of the nature of international and regional human rights law under the ICCPR and the ECHR. This body of law obliges States to respect, protect and fulfil human rights, which involves not interfering with the enjoyment of rights and also taking steps to ensure that others do not interfere with their enjoyment. To ensure the fulfilment of human rights, States must adopt appropriate measures, including legislative, judicial, administrative or educative measures, in order to fulfil their legal obligations. States may be found responsible for attacks by private persons or entities upon the enjoyment of human rights. Human rights law also places a responsibility upon States to provide effective remedies in the event of violations. It is important to recall that human rights have extraterritorial effect, requiring States to ensure the enjoyment of rights and freedoms by anyone within their power or effective control, even if not situated within their own territory. International human rights law continues to apply in armed conflict.

Without diminishing the importance and application of States' obligations under international human rights law, Chap. 10 shifted its focus to the special question of limiting rights. The ICCPR and ECHR are both capable of accommodating rights limitations which pursue democratic objectives or a balancing between individual interests. It must be recognised at the outset, however, that certain rights are not capable of limitation in any circumstance, including a state of emergency, whether expressed in unqualified terms or as a result of their absolute status as norms of *jus cogens* under customary international law. Other than in the case of these absolute and non-derogable rights and freedoms, interference with the unrestricted enjoyment of rights is permitted through two principal means under the ICCPR and the ECHR. The application of certain rights and freedoms may be temporarily suspended during a state of emergency which threatens the life of a nation. Application of this mechanism in the terrorism context is a matter considered later in this concluding chapter.

Most other rights and freedoms are capable of limitation as a result of the means by which they are expressed in the substantive provisions of the International Covenant and the European Convention. Limitations can arise as a result of the interpretation of terms such as 'fair', 'reasonable' or 'arbitrary', or by application of express limitations provided for within the text of the Covenant or Convention. Express limitations can be either very specific (setting out the precise and limited extent to which a right or freedom may be restricted, resulting in a 'limited right') or more general (explaining that the pursuit of certain objectives can justify interference, thereby creating a 'qualified right'). Chapter 10 considered the meaning and general application of the objectives listed in the ICCPR and ECHR which are capable of justifying the limitation of qualified rights.

Any measure seeking to limit rights and freedoms, by whatever mechanism, must conform to three requirements. Limiting measures must be prescribed by national law, requiring the prescription to be accessible and precise. They must be necessary and proportionate and, although inter-linked, distinctive features are attached to each of these terms. Necessity requires any temporary derogation to be limited "to the extent strictly required by the exigencies of the situation". In the context of qualified rights, necessity demands the existence of a rational link between the limitation and the pursuit of one of the permissible objectives allowing for limitation of the right, and often also requires that the limitation is "necessary in a democratic society". Proportionality lies at the heart of any limitation upon rights and freedoms, such that the limiting measure may be no more restrictive than required to achieve the purpose of the limitation. Although proportionality requires a full evaluation of all relevant issues, regard will at least be had to the negative impact of the limiting measure upon the enjoyment of the right and the ameliorating effects of the limiting measure. Finally, any measure impacting upon the unrestricted enjoyment of rights and freedoms must be non-discriminatory in nature.

When considering recourse to the derogations regimes under article 4 of the ICCPR or article 15 of the ECHR, regard must first be had to whether the right or freedom is capable of temporary suspension. Certain rights are expressly or impliedly non-derogable, or not capable of limitation due to their absolute nature. On the other hand, some non-derogable rights are capable of limitation at any time due to the manner in which they are expressed. In the case of rights that are both derogable and capable of limitation (by interpretation of the substantive provision or by application of an express limitations clause), the State must pursue such limitation before making recourse to the derogations regime. Where recourse to the temporary suspension of a right is available, notice of the derogation must be given to the Secretary-General of the United Nations (or of the Council of Europe in the case of the ECHR) in terms that are at the very least sufficient for the Secretary-General to understand the nature and reasons for the derogation.

Any derogation must then satisfy four substantive conditions: (1) it must be shown that the derogating measures are adopted during a "time of public emergency which threatens the life of the nation"; (2) the derogating measures must be limited to those "strictly required by the exigencies of the situation" (reflecting the principles of necessity and porportionality); (3) the measures must not be "inconsistent with [the State's] other obligations under international law"; and (4) they must not "involve discrimination solely on the ground of race, colour, sex, language, religion or social origin". As indicated, the application of these substantive conditions in the context of threats posed by terrorism is explained later in this concluding chapter.

22.2.2 Domestic Approaches to Human Rights

The final chapter in this second part of the title, Chap. 11, provides an overview of the approaches by each case study country to the domestic protection of human rights. The chapter illustrates diverse approaches to human rights protection, which present interesting points for comparison. Although Australia's Capital Territory and State of Victoria have enacted human rights legislation, there is no national human rights instrument in Australia. The protection of civil liberties is dependent largely upon the common law, as well as a limited range of expressly recognised rights under the Commonwealth Constitution, and those implied from it. There are no federal mechanisms in Australia dealing specifically with the role of human rights in the enactment of laws, nor is there a generally-applicable right to remedies for violation of human rights. This, combined with a generally legalistic approach to the reception of international human rights law by the judiciary, leaves human rights in a vulnerable position in Australia

In contrast to Australia, Canada has a supreme and entrenched bill of rights under the Canadian Charter of Rights and Freedoms 1982. Canada's Supreme Court is able to invalidate inconsistent legislation, and has developed mechanisms to allow for the interpretation of ordinary law consistent with Charter rights. Federal and provincial mechanisms call for the scrutiny of new legislation to determine their compatibility with the Charter of Rights. While the federal parliament retains its sovereign ability to enact statutes that restrict rights and freedoms, it must do so by express reference to the notwithstanding clause in the Charter and can only effect such restrictions by 5-year, renewable, periods. The Charter provides for a broad remedial power and guarantees that the rights and freedoms set out within it may be subject only to reasonable limits prescribed by law as can be demonstrably justified in a free and democratic society.

New Zealand's Bill of Rights Act 1990 is modelled on the Canadian Charter but is weaker in three main respects. The Bill of Rights is not entrenched, nor does it include a remedies clause. It is also an ordinary statute and, by virtue of the 'parliamentary sovereignty clause' in section 4 of the Act, the rights contained in it are capable of limitation or exclusion when in an irreconcilable conflict with another enactment. The judiciary has nevertheless taken a rights-based approach to the application of the Act, developing remedies for the violation of rights, identifying the possibility of making declarations of incompatibility, and requiring provisions which allow for the making of subordinate legislation to be interpreted in a manner consistent with the Bill of Rights where possible. Although deficient in some respects, section 7 of the Act calls for the Attorney General to scrutinise proposed legislation for consistency with the Bill of Rights. Like Canada's Charter, the Bill of Rights includes a mechanism for the limitation of human rights where demonstrably justified in a free and democratic society.

The Human Rights Act 1998 in the United Kingdom is a non-autonomous instrument, incorporating the rights in the European Convention on Human Rights by reference rather than setting out them out within the Act. As in New Zealand, the judiciary is unable to invalidate legislation where there is an irreconcilable conflict between it and the Human Rights Act. The judiciary has the express power, however, to make declarations of incompatibility. Remedial orders allow for the subsequent modification of an offending provision to bring it into compliance with Convention rights. The executive government has a role in the scrutiny of, and reporting to parliament on, proposed legislation in a manner similar to Canada and New Zealand. The provision of remedies for the violation of human rights is again linked to the European Convention, as is any question of justifying limitations upon the unrestricted enjoyment of rights in the United Kingdom.

22.3   The Impact upon Human Rights of Terrorism and Its Prevention and Criminalisation

Part III of the title undertakes a comparative analysis of the interface between counter-terrorism and human rights. The first two chapters look at the relationship between terrorism, counter-terrorism and human rights. Chapter 12 considers the interface between *terrorism* and relevant aspects of international law pertaining to human rights law, the law of armed conflict, international criminal law, and refugee law. Chapter 13 examines the question of what is required to achieve human rights compliance when *countering* terrorism, and sets out a framework for achieving compliance, as well as addressing the issue of terrorism and the derogation from human rights. Chapters 14–21 evaluate subject-specific issues using thematic and case study based analyses.

22.3.1   The Dynamic Impact of Terrorism

Properly defined, a terrorist act will correspond to proscribed conduct under one of the universal terrorism-related conventions, or a serious crime under national law. Depending on the particular circumstances surrounding any given terrorist act, terrorism also impacts upon human rights and the rule of law and may in addition amount to: an act of aggression or use of force within the meaning of article 39 of the UN Charter; an act committed during the course of an armed conflict, and thus impacted upon by international humanitarian law; an international criminal law offence, whether under the universal terrorism-related conventions or the Statute of the International Criminal Court; and/or an act which has the result of precluding the actor's protection under international refugee law. There is therefore a dynamic interaction between terrorism and different, and sometimes overlapping, sets of international law norms. What is clear is that terrorism attacks the values that lie at the heart of the Charter of the United Nations: respect for human rights; the rule of law; rules of war that protect civilians; tolerance among people and nations; and the peaceful resolution of conflicts. The Security Council has itself pronounced that terrorism is (or at least may be) a threat to international peace and security and must therefore be suppressed for the maintenance of international peace and security.

Also clear is that terrorism does not create an additional justification for the use of force between States, but can instead be dealt with under the existing international law framework concerning *jus ad bellum*. While States are bound by the *jus cogens* prohibition against the use of force, the UN Charter allows for two exceptions. The first involves military action authorised by the Security Council where it determines that a particular act of terrorism amounts to a threat to the peace, breach of the peace, or act of aggression. The second is where a victim State, or group of States asked by the victim State for assistance, act under the right of individual or collective self-defence, provided that the act of terrorism (which will most likely be perpetrated by a non-State actor) can be attributed to the State against whom the self-defence action is taken. Less clear is the ability of States to take anticipatory self-defence action in the face of a suspicion that terrorist conduct is intended, at the very least not unless there is a necessity of self-defence, which is instant and overwhelming, leaving no choice of means, and no moment for deliberation.

Terrorist acts might amount to a crime against humanity or a war crime under the Rome Statute, depending upon the particular facts and circumstances involved. An act of terrorism might also involve the application of international humanitarian law, if committed during an armed conflict, since that body of law prohibits conduct which may include acts of terrorism. If that is the case, it is now a well-established principle that, regardless of issues of classification, international human rights law continues to apply in armed conflict, subject only to certain permissible limitations in accordance with the strict requirements contained in international human rights treaties.

22.3.2   Human Rights Compliance While Countering Terrorism

Given the deleterious impact of terrorism upon human rights, and society more generally, it is clear and undisputed that States have an obligation to protect those within their jurisdiction from acts of terrorism. Regrettably, however, it has been repeatedly noted that some States have engaged in various acts, said to be aimed at combating terrorism, which violate human rights and fundamental freedoms. Some have even argued that this is a necessary evil in the fight against terrorism. Rather than being opposed to each other, however, the aims of countering terrorism and maintaining human rights are complementary and mutually reinforcing. This is the case if one is pursuing a long-term, or even medium-term, goal of countering terrorism. The UN Global Counter-Terrorism Strategy reflects this approach and identifies respect for human rights and the rule of law as the fundamental basis of the fight against terrorism. It dedicates its attention to that subject in one of its four pillars, and it expressly recognises that a lack of the rule of law, and violations of human rights, amount to conditions conducive to the spread of terrorism. Human rights compliance also has practical law-enforcement implications, and avoids a descent into a moral vacuum where checks and balances against government agencies become ineffective such that those agencies threaten the very society they were designed to protect.

Politics and strategies aside, States have international human rights obligations under customary international law, applicable to all States, and international treaties to which they are parties. Human rights compliance is also mandated by the universal terrorism-related conventions. States are directed, in both mandatory and recommendatory terms, to comply with human rights while countering terrorism by the Security Council, the General Assembly, the Human Rights Council (HRC), and the HRC's predecessor (the Commission on Human Rights). At an institutional level, the General Assembly's reaffirmation in 2008 of the Global Counter-Terrorism Strategy confirms that UN agencies involved in supporting counter-terrorism should continue to facilitate the promotion and protection of human rights while countering terrorism. The Secretary-General has confirmed that this should be the basis of the technical assistance work of the UN Office on Drugs and Crime Terrorism Prevention Branch. The Security Council Counter-Terrorism Committee (CTC) has also made it clear that any measure taken to combat terrorism must comply with human rights, an approach which is now reflected in the CTC's reporting dialogue with UN member States.

22.3.2.1 Handbook on Human Rights Compliance While Countering Terrorism

Notwithstanding the clear position that measures to combat terrorism must comply with human rights, legislators, policy-makers, and judges are faced with difficult choices in determining the proper boundary between the unlimited enjoyment of human rights and the adoption and implementation of effective counter-terrorism strategies and action. Numerous guidelines, reports and recommendations on the relationship between human rights and counter-terrorism have been adopted since the proliferation of counter-terrorism legislation that followed the shocking events of September 11. Drawing from those documents, and more specific guidance and decisions on particular aspects of international human rights law, this author has produced a Handbook on Human Rights Compliance while Countering Terrorism (see Appendix 4 in this title). The Handbook advocates a step-by-step process aimed at guiding decision-makers through all relevant considerations on the subject, enabling him or her to progressively examine the validity of existing or proposed counter-terrorism law and practice. It identifies five cumulative conditions applicable to human rights compliance while countering terrorism:

- Condition 1 begins with the established notion that counter-terrorism law and practice must comply with applicable human rights law.
- Condition 2 draws from the flexibility of international human rights law to explain that, in determining the availability of any measure to combat terrorism which would limit a right or freedom, it must be determined whether the right in question in capable of limitation. Drawing from the discussion in Chap. 10, Condition 2 explains the nature of rights, including absolute and non-derogable rights, and the permissible framework for their limitation.
- Condition 3 focuses on the due process and rule of law aspects of permissible rights limitations, namely the requirement that any limitation be prescribed by law; that it respects the principles of non-discrimination and equality before the law; that discretionary powers be subject to appropriate checks and balances; and that counter-terrorism measures be confined to the countering of terrorism.
- Condition 4 concentrates on the principle of necessity, explaining that limitations imposed by measures to combat terrorism must be necessary to pursue a pressing and permissible objective, and that there must be a rational connection between that objective and the limitation imposed.
- The final condition, Condition 5, explains the important principle of proportionality, formulating the test that "having regard to the importance of the right or freedom..., is the effect of the measure or provision upon the right... proportional to the importance of the objective and the effectiveness of the legislative provision or measure?".

22.3.2.2   Terrorism and the Derogation from Human Rights

Reference is made in Condition 2 of the Handbook to the ability to derogate from certain rights during a state of emergency, a matter which is considered in Chap. 17 in the context of UK derogations from the right to liberty. As discussed earlier, there are four substantive conditions applicable to any derogation from the ICCPR or ECHR, the first of which is that derogating measures may only be adopted during a time of public emergency which threatens the life of the nation. Terrorism, and the threat of terrorism, can trigger the ability of States to derogate from certain provisions of the ICCPR and ECHR. This will be the case where a State faces an actual or imminent threat of terrorism, deduced from a culmination of factors and available information. The challenge in determining whether or not a State has properly invoked a state of emergency can be alleviated by adopting a two-stage approach. First, by considering whether the State was acting within the margins of its powers when deciding to declare a state of emergency based on the information available to it at the time. This will likely involve a degree of deference to the political judgment made at that time. The second stage would be to examine whether, with the benefit of hindsight and the information available at the time of subsequent review, it is still objectively reasonable to conclude that an actual or imminent threat of terrorism exists which threatens the life of the nation. While the European Court of Human Rights and the Human Rights Committee should act as ultimate arbiters, States can pre-empt this and likely avoid adverse findings by implementing independent domestic review mechanisms which have the ability of accessing and reviewing sensitive information.

On the question of whether a state of emergency exists which threatens the life of the nation, regard must also be had to whether the situation threatens the continuance of the organised life of the community. Threats of terrorism will likely do so, since they more often than not involve threats to the physical safety of the population, or critical infrastructure, and may even involve threats to the political independence or territorial integrity of a State. Forming part of this second substantive condition for a valid derogation from rights, the situation faced by the derogating State must be one that cannot be dealt with by existing law, or by new measures which would be otherwise compatible with rights and freedoms (including through the use of implied or express limitations on rights).

Next as just indicated, a valid derogation from rights and freedoms must be necessary and proportional, i.e. it must be limited to the extent strictly required by the exigencies of the situation. In this regard, it will be relevant to consider whether the measures could have been adopted through the imposition of limitations consistent with a rights-specific limitations provision; whether safeguards are provided to guard against abuse of derogating measures; as well as the duration of the derogating measures. Finally, derogating measures must be consistent with a State's other international obligations and with the principle of non-discrimination. In the litigation surrounding the indefinite detention of the 'Belmarsh detainees' in the United Kingdom, compliance with the prohibition against non-discrimination was particularly relevant and resulted in the House of Lords declaring that the indefinite detention regime under the Anti-terrorism, Crime and Security Act 2001 was incompatible with the right to liberty and the freedom from discrimination. As concluded by the House of Lords, British terrorists and foreign terrorists could both be involved in international terrorism and there was no way that the differential treatment could be objectively justified.

22.3.2.3 Human Rights in the Prevention and Punishment of Terrorism in Context

Chapters 14–21 evaluate subject-specific issues using thematic and case study based analyses. From this can be drawn a series of contextual conclusions from the interaction of human rights with the prevention and punishment of terrorism.

22.3.3   The Criminalisation of Terrorism

Chapter 14 takes a comparative approach to the question of the criminalisation of terrorism, paying attention to all four countries examined in this title. It considers the extent to which the criminalisation of terrorism goes beyond the requirements of international law on counter-terrorism, as well as the compatibility of the domestic terrorism-related offences with the human rights compatible approach to the definition of terrorism explained in Chap. 2.

22.3.3.1   Domestic Definitions of Terrorism

A large portion of the terrorism-related offences in the four case study countries relate to one of two features. Many are linked to domestic definitions of "terrorism" (as in the United Kingdom), a "terrorist act" (as in Australia and New Zealand) or "terrorist activity" (as in Canada). It is an offence in Canada, for example, to provide or collect property intending (or knowing) that this is to be used to carry out a "terrorist activity". Publishing a statement intended indirectly to encourage acts of "terrorism" is an offence under section 1 of the UK's Terrorism Act 2006. Other offences are linked to proscribed organisations, the description of which is likewise linked to definitions of terrorism. In Australia, for example, an organisation engaged in a "terrorist act" can be listed by the Attorney General as a terrorist organisation, with a range of offences linked to such organisations.

As well as having these important associations with criminal offences, the definitions of terrorism in Australia, Canada, New Zealand and the United Kingdom are also linked to special investigative powers, the cordoning of areas, and powers of detention and of stop and search. The domestic definitions adopted therefore have wide implications for criminal law offences and investigative powers in those countries. One of the problems in this area, as considered in Chap. 2, is that there is no overwhelming consensus within the international community on a definition of terrorism. This means that individual States have been required to formulate their own definitions of the term.

However, as also discussed in Chap. 2, a comprehensive, concise and human rights-compliant approach to defining terrorism is achievable. This relies on the Security Council's identification of three cumulative characteristics of conduct to be suppressed in the fight against terrorism, namely: (1) an intention to hijack, or to cause death or serious bodily injury; (2) an intention to provoke a state of terror, or to influence a government or international organisation; and (3) a correlation between the definition and the offences described in the universal terrorism-related conventions. As already indicated, the Special Rapporteur has expressed the view that, as an alternative to the latter 'trigger offence' characteristic, conduct may also be properly described as terrorist in nature if it bears the first two characteristics just mentioned *and* corresponds to the elements of a serious crime under national law.

Two principal approaches to the definition of terrorism emerge in the four case study countries. The first is to equate conduct prohibited under the universal terrorism-related conventions as amounting to terrorism, in and of itself, without any further element of intention (such as an intention to provoke terror or to influence a government or international organisation). This approach is taken by New Zealand and Canada in their definitions of a "terrorist act" and "terrorist activity". While this might seem logical, the problem with this definitional approach is that it is able to capture conduct which does not pass a certain threshold of seriousness, in terms of either intention or effect. This was a criticism of early definitions of terrorism in the United Kingdom. Nor is there a link in these definitions to one of the most commonly understood attributes of terrorist conduct: that it be perpetrated for the purpose of provoking a state of terror, or compelling a government or international organisation to do or abstain from doing something. When compared to Australia and the United Kingdom, New Zealand and Canada are therefore out of step in this approach, not to mention that this fails to correspond to the cumulative characteristics in Security Council resolution 1566 (2004).

The second definitional approach, which is common to all four countries, is to use definitions which comprise the following three elements:

- The first is that the conduct be undertaken for political, religious or ideological purposes. The definition in the United Kingdom also includes conduct undertaken to advance a racial cause. This first element is not included in the Security Council's characterisation of conduct to be suppressed in the fight against terrorism, although it is a commonly understood feature of terrorism. Inclusion of this element is not problematic, since it constitutes a restrictive feature of the definition of terrorism, thus narrowing its potential scope of application.
- The second element common to definitions in Australia, Canada, NZ and the UK is that the conduct must have a coercive or intimidatory character, i.e. undertaken for the purpose of either (1) provoking a state of terror, or (2) compelling a government or international organisation to do or abstain from doing something. This directly corresponds to the characteristic of terrorism identified in paragraph 3(b) of Security Council resolution 1566 (2004).
- The final common element is the one most problematic for consistency of the definitions with paragraph 3(a) of Security Council resolution 1566 (2004) and with the meaning of terrorism advocated by the Special Rapporteur on the promotion and protection of human rights and fundamental freedoms while countering terrorism. The definitions adopted by the case study countries require that the conduct must fall within one of a list of acts, including action which causes, or is intended to cause, death or serious bodily injury. While the example just given corresponds to paragraph 3(a) of resolution 1566 (2004), the list of acts included in the domestic definitions of terrorism goes beyond this.

On the latter point, Chap. 14 has pointed to the list of qualifying acts as including conduct which causes a serious risk to the health or safety of the public. As currently expressed, this is overly broad and may capture effects of conduct which, while appropriate to be suppressed and criminalised, is not truly 'terrorist' in nature, i.e. is not intended to cause death or serious bodily injury. This could be easily rectified by linking such conduct to that which is also likely to cause death or serious bodily injury. This would then capture acts, or threats, of biological, chemical, or radiological warfare which are likely to cause death or injury and which are intended to coerce or intimidate. It would retain the objective of protecting the public from acts of terrorism which target the health or safety of the public, while at the same time complying with the recommendation that offences falling outside the scope of the 'trigger offences' in the universal terrorism-related conventions (identified in paragraph 3(c) of resolution 1566) might still be classified as terrorist in nature if they coincide with the first two characteristics in resolution 1566 and if they correspond to elements of a serious crime under national law. Chapter 14 makes similar observations about the inclusion of conduct which constitutes a serious interference, disruption, or destruction of infrastructure or electronic systems; and conduct which causes substantial property damage. It is noted that, unique to New Zealand, the list of conduct which would constitute a terrorist act (if accompanied by ideological motives and coercive or intimidatory intent) includes conduct intended to cause economic and environmental damage and the prospect of the release of disease-bearing organisms. While this is perhaps not surprising for a country like New Zealand, which relies so heavily on agricultural exports, these are matters which can, and should, be dealt with as separate offences.

Regrettably, therefore, it has been concluded that the domestic definitions of terrorism adopted by all four case study countries go beyond the characteristics of terrorism identified by the Security Council and the definition of terrorism advocated by the UN Special Rapportuer on counter-terrorism. In saying this, it is important to once again clarify a point also made in Chap. 2. That an act is criminal does not, by itself, make it a terrorist act. Nor does a concise human-rights based approach to defining terrorism preclude criminal culpability. The important point, apparently missed by all four countries, is that States must clearly distinguish terrorist conduct from other forms of criminal conduct.

22.3.3.2 Terrorism Offences in the Case Study Countries

The implementation by the case study countries of their international counter-terrorism obligations entails, in part, the criminalisation of certain terrorist and terrorism-related conduct. Criminalisation is not only a legal obligation for States parties to the various terrorism-related treaties, and a response to Security Council decisions, but it is also a prerequisite for effective international cooperation in the form of extradition and mutual legal assistance. One of the common features of the universal terrorism-related conventions is that they not only call for a principal offender to be prosecuted and severely punished, but they also require States parties to criminalise the conduct of those who assist principal offenders, and those who attempt to commit the principal offence. Although this is not problematic by itself, it has been noted that counter-terrorism offences have begun to include 'precursor' offences, such as offences of possession of materials useful to terrorism, or possession of information useful to terrorism. In this regard, the UN Office on Drugs and Crime and the Special Rapporteur on counter-terrorism have acknowledged that preparatory offences constitute a necessary preventive element to a successful counter-terrorism strategy. The Special Rapporteur and others have warned, however, that the definition of terrorism and corresponding offences (including offences relating to preparatory conduct or conduct in support of terrorism), must be precise and must correspond to the cumulative requirements of Security Council resolution 1566 (2004).

Many, but not all, of the terrorism-related offences in the case study countries are directly linked to the universal terrorism-related conventions (e.g. hostage-taking, aircraft hijacking, or the financing of terrorism). Additional offences can be categorised as falling within one of the following categories: (1) those which are not expressly required by terrorism treaties or Security Council resolutions, but are in furtherance of them (such as trafficking in plastic explosives, for example); (2) offences that act as mechanisms for the enforcement of preventive measures, such as control orders; (3) some offences which are preventive in nature in their own right (such as the prohibition against communicating safeguarded information to a terrorist group); (4) a small category of offences that react to emergencies caused by a terrorist act and seek to ensure the effective operation of measures implemented in such emergencies; and (5) offences that do not fall within one of the former categories, but were introduced under counter-terrorism legislation, and go beyond the cumulative characterises of terrorism identified in Security Council resolution 1566 (2004). Falling within the latter category are the offences in Australia and New Zealand of committing a terrorist act, problematic because they are directly linked to the overly-broad definitions of terrorism in those countries. While important, bioterrorism offences introduced under New Zealand's Counter-Terrorism Bill 2003 also fail to correspond to the characteristics of terrorism. Some offences in the UK's Terrorism Act 2000 lack any direct link to terrorism, but are instead applicable in many other contexts. It is an offence under section 54 of that Act to provide weapons training, for example, although the offence is not limited to weapons training to terrorist groups or for terrorist purposes.

22.3.3.3   Incitement to Terrorism

Public provocation to commit acts of terrorism is described by the Security Council Working Group established pursuant to resolution 1566 (2004) as an insidious activity contributing to the spread of the scourge of terrorism. The Security Council has declared that knowingly inciting terrorist acts is contrary to the purposes and principles of the United Nations, and has called on States, under paragraph 1(a) of its resolution 1624 (2005), to prohibit by law incitement to commit a terrorist act or acts. There are two general means by which the incitement to terrorism may be criminalised. The first is by reactive means, whereby a person who has incited or glorified terrorism may be prosecuted as a party to a principal terrorist act. Many jurisdictions provide for the criminal responsibility of parties, through which the conduct of anyone who incites, counsels, or procures any person to commit an offence is also guilty of the offence. This is the case in all four case study countries. The second, proactive, means of criminalisation is one that seeks to create liability without needing to wait for a terrorist act to occur. A 'proactive' offence of this kind criminalises the act of incitement itself as a primary, rather than secondary, offence.

The UN Terrorism Prevention Branch has taken the view that the general obligation of States to abstain from tolerating terrorist activities implies that they must adopt active measures in order to prevent those acts. This is also encouraged within resolutions of the General Assembly and Security Council. Furthermore, article 20(2) of the International Covenant on Civil and Political Rights requires States to prohibit the advocacy of national, racial or religious hatred that constitutes incitement to discrimination, hostility or violence. Despite this, the United Kingdom is the only one of the four case study countries which has a specific offence of incitement to terrorism. The other countries instead rely on general provisions of law. In New Zealand's case, it has been concluded that these provisions are deficient in a number of ways. The incitement offence under the Human Rights Act 1993 (NZ) is limited in its application, by the fact that it does not expressly apply to the incitement of violence, and applies a low level of maximum penalty upon conviction. Party offences under section 66(1)(d) of the Crimes Act 1961 (NZ) are reactive, requiring an actual act of hostility, violence or terrorism to occur before proceedings can commence. Procuring offences under section 311 of the Crimes Act limit the maximum penalty upon conviction to not more than half of the relevant principal offence. Sedition offences under sections 81 and 82 of the Crimes Act have a maximum penalty of 2 years' imprisonment upon conviction and do not capture a person acting alone to incite terrorism. The 'threat of harm' offence under section 307A of the Crimes Act 1961 is limited in its application, by the reactive approach of the offence, and the fact that it only criminalises acts of incitement that themselves contain threats falling within the scope of section 307A. Furthermore, despite New Zealand's reasonably robust jurisdictional framework, none of the offences described are able to deal with the situation where a person incites others to commit terrorist acts abroad.

22.3.3.4 Special Investigative Techniques and the Role of Intelligence Agencies

The criminalisation of terrorism has been accompanied by special investigative techniques and rules of criminal procedure, a subject examined in Chap. 15. This is most often justified by what are described as the special nature and difficulties in combating terrorist conduct. Notwithstanding this, experiences (including those in Northern Ireland) have shown that special powers may be used in an oppressive manner which impacts upon innocent persons. The implementation of proper checks and balances, compatible with operational needs, is thus essential. This is all the more important due to the tendency of States to introduce special powers, under the guise of counter-terrorism legislation, which are in fact applicable beyond the framework of combating terrorism. The need for checks and balances is further accentuated by the frequent involvement of security intelligence services in the conduct and instigation of criminal investigations. Intelligence services play a vital contributing role to the prevention and investigation of terrorism, but the nature of information from intelligence sources calls for care to be taken.

There should always be a comprehensive legislative framework defining the mandate of intelligence services and the special powers afforded to them. Without such a framework, States are likely *not* to meet their obligation under human rights treaties to respect and ensure the effective enjoyment of human rights. It is crucial, in this regard, that legislation clarifies the threshold criteria which might trigger intrusive actions by intelligence services. Concerning the use of information gathered or analysed by intelligence services, it has been noted that the line between 'strategic intelligence' (information obtained by intelligence agencies for the purposes of policymaking) and probative evidence in criminal proceedings has become blurred in the fight against terrorism. This demands that care be taken by investigation, prosecution and judicial authorities when seeking to rely on information obtained from intelligence agencies, paying particular regard to the sources and nature of such information. It also calls for the prior judicial approval for the use of special investigative techniques in order to make permissible the fruits of such techniques as evidence in court.

Finally, the ex-ante and ex-post-facto oversight and accountability of intelligence services is crucial to ensure that the activities of intelligence agencies in the prevention and criminalisation of terrorism is conducted in a manner which is compatible with States' duty to comply with human rights. A lack of oversight and political and legal accountability has been noted as contributing, and even facilitating, illegal activities by the intelligence community. Several States have devised independent permanent offices, such as inspectors-general, judicial commissioners or auditors, through statutes or administrative arrangements which review whether intelligence agencies comply with their duties. A specific oversight role also falls upon parliament, which in the sphere of intelligence should play its traditional function of holding the executive branch and its agencies accountable to the general public. Parliamentary committees exercising this role should be independent. In the United Kingdom, for example, although the Intelligence Security Committee is composed of sitting parliamentarians, it is appointed by and answerable to the Prime Minister. Ex post facto accountability is equally important. States should create mechanisms through which independent investigations can be conducted into alleged human rights violations by intelligence services.

22.3.3.5   Sentencing for Terrorism Offences

The universal instruments related to terrorism specify that the penalties for terrorism offences must be serious, and in conformity with the principle of proportionality as between the gravity of the sanction and the gravity of the act. The UN Office on Drugs and Crime therefore advocates that the system of penalties for terrorism offence must be especially dissuasive and that heavy sentences need to be imposed for perpetrators of such acts. This is reflected in the range of maximum sanctions applicable to terrorism offences in Australia, Canada, New Zealand and the United Kingdom. The latter three countries have also taken the legislative step of directing judges to treat offences involving terrorism as an aggravating feature in the determination of the length of sentence to be imposed. Such directions are not problematic in principle, except that the directions use terms ("terrorist activity", "terrorist act" and "terrorist connection") which have been identified in this title as being overly broad and not restricted to the characteristics identified in Security Council resolution 1566 (2004).

22.3.4 The Right to Liberty

The right of every person to be free from restraints on their liberty is fundamental to democratic societies. The right to liberty is not absolute, however, a matter reflected in the ICCPR, the ECHR and the domestic laws of the four case study countries. A number of measures designed to prevent, or to investigate and prosecute, acts of terrorism impact on liberty rights.

22.3.4.1 Investigative Detention

Considered in Chap. 16 is the question of investigative detention, being the detention without charge of a person for the purpose of questioning him or her in the pre-charge process of police investigations. The matter of the arrest and pre-charge detention of persons is well developed in both the United Kingdom and Australia. Special powers of arrest to deal with terrorism were first introduced in the United Kingdom under the Prevention of Terrorism (Emergency Powers) Acts 1974–2001 relating to the troubles in Northern Ireland. The Police and Criminal Evidence Act 1984 (UK) allows for the detention without charge for up to 4 days of persons suspected of committing indictable offences, which includes various terrorism-related offences. The Terrorism Act 2000 (UK), as amended by the Criminal Justice Act 2003 and the Terrorism Act 2006, now permits a series of police- and judge-authorised extensions of investigative detention up to a total period of 28 days.

The 2000 Terrorism Act authorises police in the United Kingdom to arrest, without warrant, a person reasonably suspected of being a terrorist, linked both to the suspected commission of specific offences under that Act, as well as a much more broad and vague notion of being "*concerned* in the commission, preparation or instigation of acts of terrorism". This departs from the normal constraint that police must have a particular offence in mind when arresting without warrant. It may also open the door for the arrest of persons based not on credible evidence but on more dubious intelligence information, then allowing police to conduct 'fishing' expeditions for evidence during prolonged periods of detention without charge. Investigative detention is also a tool used in Australia, both under the Crimes Act 1914 and the Australian Security Intelligence Organisation Act 1974.

Extended periods of police detention, without bringing a person before a judge, has been a long-standing issue of concern within both common law and civil law countries. Although the European Court of Human Rights has declined to say what the maximum period of detention might be before a person will be considered to have been brought 'promptly' before a judicial authority, it has ruled that a period of 4 days and 6 hours is too long. Although untested, it appears that the ability in the United Kingdom to detain persons for up to 4 days without judicial intervention in the case of suspected indictable offences would not run afoul of the right under articles 9(3) and 5(3) of the ICCPR and ECHR. This will always be a matter to be determined in the particular circumstances of the case, having particular regard to the seriousness of the alleged offence, the strength of evidence against the suspect, and the availability of alternative courses of action which would not prejudice investigations. An all facts considered approach is particularly relevant in the case of the special powers of detention under Australia's Crimes Act 1914 where, although detention may only be up to 24 hours, the application of 'dead time' resulted, in the case of Dr Haneef in 2007, in an overall period of detention without charge of 12 days.

In the case of the United Kingdom's Terrorism Act 2000, and the potential for investigative detention to continue to 28 days, the question of necessity and proportionality arises. Although the Act provides for judicial warrants for extended detention beyond 36 hours, much of the justification for extending periods of pre-charge detention has been premised on the inadmissibility of evidence, particularly intercept evidence, which must be shored up through interrogations conducted during periods of investigative detention. Bringing into question the necessity of prolonged investigative detention, however, many have advocated lifting the ban on admitting intercept evidence, as is done in many common law jurisdictions, including Australia, Canada and New Zealand. Furthermore, the proportionality of such measures are not assured, since the Terrorism Act does not expressly require that a detainee be charged as soon as sufficient evidence has been obtained to provide a realistic prospect of conviction.

Finally, the Terrorism Act 2000 may also engage the right of a detainee to consult with legal counsel. The right to consult with counsel may, by a decision of the police, be postponed for 48 hours after arrest. While the grounds upon which postponement can be made appear sound to the author, the Human Rights Committee has taken the view that this should never occur even in the context of those arrested or detained on terrorism charges. Consultations between counsel and the detainee may also be monitored. Although the Act protects against the deliberate passing on and use of information subject to legal professional privilege, it does not guard against the inadvertent or bad faith passing on or use of such information. Monitoring should therefore be rare, and it has suggested that monitoring should not occur within hearing of police authorities.

22.3.4.2 United Kingdom Derogations from the Right to Liberty

Examined in Chap. 17 are two derogations by the United Kingdom from the right to liberty, first in the context of executive detention powers applying to Northern Ireland, and then to the 2001 derogation made in conjunction with the establishment of the UK's indefinite detention regime under the Anti-terrorism, Crime and Security Act 2001 (ACTS Act). What is perhaps surprising is that derogating measures were only taken by the United Kingdom after being found to be in violation of article 5 of the ECHR. In the context of the 7-day executive detention provision in the Prevention of Terrorism (Temporary Provisions) Acts, its seems almost inconceivable that the detention of a person for up to 7 days before being brought before a judge could have been considered to satisfy the requirement that persons be brought 'promptly' before a judge or other judicial officer. The 6-year and continued detention of Mr Chahal under the Immigration Act 1971 is similarly astonishing, particularly in light of earlier domestic decisions that detention pending removal under the Immigration Act is permissible only for such time as is 'reasonably necessary' for the process of deportation.

In the context of the indefinite detention regime under Part 4 of the Anti-terrorism, Crime and Security Act, the validity of that regime was challenged by the 'Belmarsh detainees' with the result that, in December 2004, the House of Lords issued a declaration (under section 4 of the Human Rights Act 1998) that section 23 of the ACTS Act was incompatible with the right to liberty and the requirement that any derogation must be non-discriminatory in its effect. Responding to that declaration, Part 4 of the Act was repealed and replaced by a dual approach to dealing with persons suspected of involvement in terrorism: their removal to their country of origin where assurances against ill-treatment can be obtained (discussed below); and control orders (discussed next).

22.3.4.3 Control Orders and Their Impact on Liberty Rights

Controls orders in the United Kingdom and Australia (examined in Chap. 18) aim to deal with persons suspected of involvement in terrorism, against whom there is insufficient admissible evidence to bring criminal proceedings, but in respect of whom there is a perceived risk of harm to the public if left to live in society without restrictions upon them. The mechanisms in both countries are much the same, although the Home Secretary in the UK is vested with much broader authority to make control orders. Furthermore, while the conditions imposed under a control order in Australia must always be compliant with the right to liberty, within the bounds of necessary and proportional limitations, the UK legislation provides for the possibility of making control orders which would be accompanied by derogation from the right to liberty. Also relevant to control orders is their impact on the right to a fair hearing (discussed later).

Subject to reservations about the means by which control orders are made, and the cumulative effect of conditions imposed under them, the general concept of control orders as a mechanism to prevent terrorism which falls short of actual detention has been viewed positively. It is implicit in the control order regime that if there is a reasonable prospect of bringing a criminal charge against a person, that person will be prosecuted rather than made the subject of a control order. In the United Kingdom, an evaluation of this question has not been treated as a condition precedent to the making of a control order, but it has been held that the implicit basis for the regime requires the decision to impose a control order to be kept under regular review to ensure that its restrictions are no greater than necessary. Arising from this, the Home Secretary has also been seen as having a continuing duty to provide the police with material in his possession which is or might be relevant to any reconsideration of prosecution. Care must also be taken to ensure that control orders are not imposed contrary to the *ne bis in idem* principle.

Given the context in which the tool of control orders arose (following the declaration by the House of Lords that indefinite detention was incompatible with the European Convention), it is not surprising that control orders have implications for the enjoyment of liberty rights. The wide range of obligations and restrictions that may be imposed under control orders may also impact on other rights and freedoms. On the question of the impact of control orders on the right to liberty, it must be recognised that the deprivation of a person's liberty may take numerous forms other than classic detention in prison or strict arrest. Continuous house arrest will only permissible during the course of a criminal investigation, while awaiting trial, during trial, or as an alternative to a custodial sentence. The imposition of such a condition under a control order would therefore require derogation from the right to liberty if imposed as a condition of the order.

A common condition of control orders imposed in Australia and the United Kingdom is a curfew to remain within particular premises for specified periods. Whether this constitutes a deprivation of liberty requires consideration of the concrete situation of the particular individual so as to assess the cumulative impact of all measures under the control order in the situation of the person subject to those conditions. Account should be taken of a whole range of factors such as the nature, duration, effects and manner of execution or implementation of the measures. While recognising that each situation must consider the cumulative impact upon the controlled person of the measures imposed, it appears that a generally acceptable threshold for a curfew would be one of between 14 and 16 hours (which should include the normal hours of sleep).

In view of the recent revocation of the control order against AF, based on the UK Home Secretary's unwillingness to release evidence which he stated would put the Government's secret intelligence sources at risk, the continuance of the control orders regime is uncertain.

22.3.5 *Natural Justice and the Right to a Fair Hearing*

The right to a fair hearing, aimed at ensuring the proper administration of justice, encompasses a series of individual rights such as equality before the courts and tribunals, and the right to a fair and public hearing by a competent, independent and impartial tribunal established by law.

22.3.5.1   Open Administration of Justice

One of the central pillars of a fair hearing is the open administration of justice, important to ensure the transparency of proceedings and thus providing an important safeguard for the interest of the individual and of society at large. While the ICCPR and ECHR permit exclusion of the press and public for reasons of national security, this must occur only to the extent strictly necessary in the opinion of the court in special circumstances where publicity would prejudice the interests of justice.

This is an issue which may arise, for example, in control order proceedings where those proceedings involve closed hearings. Should the public and press be excluded from hearings concerning the making, revision or revocation of control orders, it is likely that the condition upon which the public or press may be excluded will be met. It will be important that this is limited to the extent strictly necessary. Mechanisms such as the control orders regime which allow for closed hearings should be accompanied by adequate mechanisms for observation or review to guarantee the fairness of the hearing. Compliance with these aspects will partly depend upon the particular circumstances of each case, although it should be observed that appeals on questions of law are permissible in the case of control orders under both Australian and UK law.

The question of the open administration of justice is also brought to bear in the framework of judicial investigative hearings under Canada's Criminal Code 1985. In the context of excluding the media from investigative hearings, the Supreme Court of Canada has spoken of needing to balance a conflict between the freedom of expression and other important rights and interests. Restricting the openness of an investigative hearing, through conditions imposed on the conduct of such hearings, is permissible but should begin with a presumption against secret hearings. Consideration should be given to available alternatives, and to restricting the investigative hearing order only as much as is required to prevent serious risks to the proper administration of justice and the conduct of investigations.

22.3.5.2   Disclosure of Information

Examined also in Chap. 18 is the sensitive nature upon which control orders may be based, exposing a common tension between procedural aspects of counter-terrorism laws and the right to a fair hearing: a tension between the protection of information which might be prejudicial to national security, versus the right of all persons to a fair hearing. As well as being relevant to control order proceedings, this tension arises in the course of challenges to security certificates issued in respect of refugees and asylum-seekers, and others in respect of whom deportation might be sought on the basis that they pose a threat to the national security of the host State. To meet that challenge, the control orders regimes in the UK and Australia allow for the non-disclosure of such information. Non-disclosure of classified information is not unique to Australia and the United Kingdom. New Zealand provides for the protection of such information in its law on the designation of terrorist entities (considered in Chap. 19). In Canada, the Canada Evidence Act 1985 was amended under counter-terrorism legislation to protect against the disclosure of information which would encroach upon a public interest or be injurious to international relations or national defence or security.

While it has been argued that control orders involve proceedings which are criminal in nature, rather than civil, this distinction is not so important to the question of disclosure of information in control order proceedings, or similar administrative proceedings used in the context of combating terrorism. More important is the question of what protections are required to guarantee that a person receives a 'fair' hearing. The gravity and complexity of the case will impact on what fairness requires. It has been accepted that the right to disclosure of information is a constituent element of the right to a fair hearing in control order proceedings. However, for the purpose of preserving an important public interest such as national security, information may be withheld if necessary and if this is sufficiently counterbalanced by judicial procedures to ensure that, overall, the respondent is able to answer the case against him or her.

Whether a person has enjoyed a fair hearing will always be fact-specific, and will fall into one of three situations. The first, which will be unproblematic, is where a control order is sought largely or completely on the basis of open material so that the controlled person may answer the case against him or her. The second, which will require a careful approach to ensure that the essence of the right to a fair hearing is guaranteed, is where much of the material is closed but where the open material (or a redacted summary of the closed material) effectively conveys the thrust of the case against the person. The third and final situation, which will result in a violation of the right to a fair hearing, is where reliance on closed material is so great that the person is confronted by an unsubstantiated assertion which he or she can do no more than deny. The difficulty lies in delineating between the second and third scenarios and, in the context of the second scenario, achieving an objective assessment of whether the open or redacted material 'effectively' conveys the thrust of the case.

The use of special advocates, who receive special security clearance and are able to view closed material after seeking instructions from a respondent, will not change the outcome of the third situation described. The respondent in control order proceedings must always be provided with sufficient information about the allegations to guarantee that he or she is able to give effective instructions to the special advocate. This does not, however, make the role of the special advocate redundant. The special advocate will play an important role during a closed hearing where the open material effectively conveys the thrust of the case against the person. His or her role will be important in testing the evidence and its confidential sources. This will be relevant to whether the information should be treated as prejudicial to national security, i.e. whether the information should be closed or made openly available, and to the question of whether the information may be relied upon as admissible evidence. The latter question will be particularly important where the information may have been obtained through the use of torture.

22.3.5.3 The Role of Judges in Investigative Hearings

As mentioned, Canada's Criminal Code allows for orders to be made compelling a person to attend a judicial hearing on the investigation of terrorist acts. The twin aspects of judicial independence and impartiality require that the judiciary function independently from the executive and legislative branches of government, thereby protecting judges against conflicts of interest and maintaining public confidence in the administration of justice. While the minority of the Supreme Court has taken the view that the mechanism under section 83.28 of the Criminal Code involves relations between the judiciary, police and prosecution which will inevitably lead to abuses and irregularities, and that the matter before it did in fact amount to an abuse of process, the majority has disagreed. Drawing from the routine role played by judges in criminal investigations, including the authorisation of wire taps and search warrants, the majority of seven-to-two concluded that a reasonable and informed person would conclude that a court, when acting under section 83.28, is independent.

22.3.5.4 The Designation of Individuals and Groups as Terrorist Entities

The focus of Chap. 19 is upon the designation and listing of individuals and groups as terrorist entities. This is an important feature of implementing targeted sanctions against such entities, particularly in the absence of a universal, concise and comprehensive definition of terrorism. Most national measures of this kind are limited to the implementation of sanctions against entities listed in the UN Consolidated List, maintained by the Al-Qa'ida and Taliban Sanctions Committee. Australia, Canada, New Zealand and the United Kingdom have the capacity to designate individuals or groups outside the UN Consolidated List. In the case of Australia and the United Kingdom, special categories of "terrorist organisations" and "proscribed organisations" have also been established.

Through undertaking a case study of New Zealand's measures for the designation of terrorist entities under the Terrorism Suppression Act 2002, the principal human rights implications of designating individuals and groups as terrorist entities have been explored. On the subject of natural justice and the right to a fair hearing, there has been much criticism over the way in which the Al-Qa'ida and Taliban Sanctions Committee undertakes its listing and de-listing functions. Despite the fact that the Committee's guidelines have vastly improved since the end of 2008, there remains no independent review of listings at the United Nations level. The UN Special Rapporteur on counter-terrorism has therefore called for access to domestic judicial review of any implementing measures at the national level. Following the reform of the Terrorism Suppression Act in 2007, the designation process in New Zealand is limited to *domestic* designations, while the application of the Act to individuals and entities listed in the UN Consolidated List is automatic and continues until those entities are removed from the Consolidated List. The practical implication of this is that, although section 33 of the Act allows for judicial review of designations made under it, the right to judicial review does not apply in respect of UN-listed individuals and entities. This is in stark contrast to the recommendation for access to domestic judicial review of measures to implement the Consolidated List. Problems arise even where judicial review *is* available, i.e. in the case of a challenge to the designation of an entity not included in the UN Consolidated List. Here, the protection afforded to classified security information, through rules under section 38 of the Act providing for non-disclosure or redacted summaries of such information, have the potential to violate the right to a fair hearing in the same way as does the use of closed material in control order proceedings.

Despite this conclusion, New Zealand courts will be limited in the extent to which they can apply section 38 of the Terrorism Suppression Act in a manner consistent with the right to a fair hearing, which is reliant, in the NZ context, on the natural justice principle of *audi alteram partem* under section 27 of the Bill of Rights Act. Section 38(6) of the Terrorism Suppression Act provides that the protective measures under it are to apply "despite any enactment or rule of law to the contrary" meaning that, notwithstanding any finding that section 38 is inconsistent with the right to natural justice under the NZBORA, section 38 is nevertheless to be applied by virtue of section 4 of the Bill of Rights. Although section 38 need *not* be applied in a manner which violates the right to a fair hearing under article 14(1) of the ICCPR (depending on the nature of the information upon which the designation is based), the combination of section 38(6) of the Terrorism Suppression Act and section 4 of New Zealand's Bill of Rights means that NZ courts will, in such situations, be powerless to act in a human rights-compatible way. The case study thus exposes the vulnerability of human rights in New Zealand to being overridden by ordinary statutes, in this case one which has been enacted for the suppression of terrorism.

22.3.6   The Presumption of Innocence and Privacy Rights

The right to be presumed innocent until proven guilty is exercised through the burden upon the Crown throughout all stages of the criminal process, from investigation to conviction, and is guaranteed under human rights instruments, as well as the common law. Associated with this is the right to silence. An accused person has no obligation to give evidence at trial, nor to disprove any allegation against him or her. This is so even where the only person in possession of information relevant to the elements of an offence is the accused. Considered in Chaps. 15 and 16 are investigative hearings and special powers of police questioning, both of which impact upon the right not to incriminate oneself, as well as the onus for the granting of bail in terrorism cases.

Privacy is a deeply rooted value in human culture comprising the right of the individual to be left alone, the right of the individual to have control over the dissemination of information about him or her and the access to his or her person and home, and the right to be protected against the unwanted access of the public to the individual. The right to privacy is a matter addressed within the ICCPR, obliging States to both desist from interfering with privacy as well as to legislate in order to protect the privacy rights of those within their jurisdiction.

22.3.6.1 Privilege Against Self-Incrimination

Intimately linked with the presumption of innocence is the right not to incriminate oneself, a right principally protected by the common law but also, in Canada, by section 7 of the Charter of Rights and Freedoms and, in New Zealand, to a more limited extent by section 23(4) of the Bill of Rights. It is also generally recognised by international standards which lie at the heart of the right to a fair hearing.

Of the case studies examined in Chap. 16, the first concerned the inclusion of a new section 198B of the Summary Proceedings Act 1957 (NZ) to introduce special powers of questioning by the police, compelling a person to provide assistance to access computer data, or any other information required to access computer data. Section 198B does not limit itself to the investigation of terrorism, but is instead applicable to the investigation of any offence under NZ law which carries a maximum penalty greater than 3 months imprisonment. The provision does not preserve the right, under either the common law or the NZ Bill of Rights Act, not to incriminate oneself. Nor does it limit the interference with this right by providing for use immunity.

Compelling a person to attend a judicial hearing on the investigation of terrorist acts is provided for in section 83.28 of Canada's Criminal Code 1985, as a result of its amendment under the Anti-terrorism Act 2001. The constitutional challenges posed by this were considered by the Supreme Court of Canada in late 2004. On the question of the privilege against self-incrimination, the Court accepted that the right not to incriminate oneself is a principle of fundamental justice protected by section 7 of the Canadian Charter of Rights and Freedoms. While this right is engaged, however, the Court concluded that it is not infringed by the Criminal Code since section 83.28(10) of the Code guarantees absolute use immunity and derivative use immunity, such that any answer given or thing produced during such hearings cannot be used in criminal proceedings against the person, even if the Crown was to establish that the evidence would have been discovered by alternative means. The Court at the same time noted that section 83.28(10) did not prevent the use of compelled testimony in extradition or deportation hearings. It warned that the issuing of investigative hearing orders should therefore include conditions extending use immunity to extradition or deportation proceedings against the person in respect of whom such an order is made.

22.3.6.2   Reversal of Onus for the Granting of Bail

An issue touched on briefly in Chap. 15 is that of the onus for the granting of bail. In Australia, up to the end of April 2006, 26 persons were charged with various terrorism offences (three had pleaded guilty or been convicted, four had been committed for trial, and 19 were awaiting committal for trial). Of those persons, only four had been granted bail, a reflection of the operation of a new section 15AA of the Crimes Act 1914 (Australia), which prevents a bail authority from granting bail to a person charged with, or convicted of, certain terrorism and other offences unless the bail authority is satisfied that exceptional circumstances exist to justify bail. This not only reverses the burden of establishing the need for detention, but places a very high threshold upon an accused or convicted person to establish exceptional circumstances. The burden should instead be upon the State to establish the need for the detention of an accused person to continue. Where there are essential reasons, such as the suppression of evidence or the commission of further offences, bail may be refused and a person remanded in custody. The classification of an act as a terrorist offence in domestic law should not result in automatic denial of bail, nor in the reversal of onus. Each case must be assessed on its merits, with the burden upon the State for establishing reasons for detention.

22.3.6.3   The Engagement of Privacy Rights

Privacy rights will be occupied by a host of modern technologies allowing information to be recorded through satellite, aerial, or video surveillance, including by closed-circuit television (CCTV); the interception and recording of communications, whether by telephone or otherwise; and other monitoring tools including electro-optical and radar sensors and facial recognition software. At security checkpoints or border controls, authorities might require a person to provide fingerprints, or to have photographs or retinal scans taken. Machine Readable Travel Documents, such as biometric passports and some forms of national identity cards, have embedded integrated circuits which can process and store data. Widely used commercial technology, such as 'cookies', 'web bugs', and other advertising-supported software that monitor computer and online activities, are also now being used in security strategies. These various examples of security infrastructure technologies involve the recording, collection, and storing of information, all of which must be consistent with the right to privacy, within the scope of permissible limitations.

Particularly relevant to border security is the use of technologies such as whole-body imaging, and Machine Readable Travel Documents (MRTDs) such as biometric passports and visas. The use of these technologies is said to increase the efficiency and speed of passenger screening, as well as limiting more intrusive physical searches of passengers in the case of scanning technology. Despite early claims by developers of radio-frequency identification chips, which allow the contact-less reading of the biometric and biographical data of individuals stored on MRTDs, research has shown that these chips can be read from a distance. In pursuit of the obligation upon States to protect individuals from arbitrary or unlawful interference with their privacy, care must therefore be taken by States to ensure that such technologies are not susceptible to unauthorised interception. The right to privacy also demands that personal information collected and analysed by border authorities does not reach the hands of unauthorised persons, and that personal information may never be used for purposes incompatible with human rights or incompatible with the specific purpose for which the information was obtained.

Although the right to privacy may be subject to temporary derogation during genuine emergency situations threatening the life of a nation, surveillance, interception of communications, wire-tapping, and recording of conversations should normally be prohibited. It might be permissible to intercept communications if this has been authorised by an independent, preferably judicial, authority for specific and lawful purposes, with safeguards in place for the safe storage and limited use of the information. This should be limited to circumstances where there are reasonable grounds to believe that a serious crime has been committed or prepared, or is being prepared, and where other less intrusive means of investigation are inadequate. Secret surveillance can, in very exceptional circumstances, be justifiable, although this should be specifically authorised by legislation, and the authorising legislation should be accessible and precise.

22.3.6.4 Tracking Devices

Also introduced in New Zealand under the Counter-Terrorism Bill 2003 were provisions now included in the Crimes Act 1961 for attaching tracking devices to people or property. As with special powers of police questioning (discussed earlier), the provisions on tracking devices are applicable to all offences, not just those related to terrorism. Due to the subordinate protection given to privacy rights in New Zealand, they also suffer from a lack of adequate safeguards to sufficiently protect individuals from arbitrary or disproportionate interference with their privacy. Other than in the case of the exclusion of evidence which is obtained through tracking devices outside the directed terms of a warrant, courts have little power to grant a remedy where there are no subsequent proceedings relying on such evidence. Action is limited, for example, where a tracking device is obtained for one purpose, and then subsequently used for a completely different purpose which does not lead to criminal proceedings but nevertheless involves an undue interference with privacy. The civil and criminal liability of police will only follow if the use of a tracking device has been undertaken in bath faith or without reasonable care.

22.3.7 Speech and Association

The freedom of expression is a cornerstone of democratic societies, linked to the enjoyment of other rights and freedoms, including the freedom of thought, conscience and religion, and their manifestation through association and assembly rights. The rights of peaceful assembly and association have been considered in the context of the listing and designation of individuals and groups as terrorist entities. Freedom of expression, and of the press, has involved an evaluation of two subjects: media control in counter-terrorism operations; and the offence of the incitement to terrorism.

22.3.7.1 The Designation of Individuals and Groups as Terrorist Entities

The case study in Chap. 19 of New Zealand's measures for the designation of terrorist entities under the Terrorism Suppression Act 2002 concerned the right to a fair hearing, as well as the impact of designations on the right of peaceful assembly and the freedom of association. The designation of terrorist entities can justifiably limit those rights, provided that the designation process is pursuant to statutory provisions and is itself proper and just. Clear safeguards must be put in place to prevent abuses of designation processes, such as the possibility of their use to prevent membership in organisations simply because they are Islamic. While proscribing membership in organisations is permissible, and not unprecedented, this must (in the context of the designation of individuals and groups as terrorist entities) be limited to the prevention of terrorism, as properly defined, or as a consequence of their inclusion in the UN Consolidated List. In the New Zealand context, this concern had been partly alleviated through the express qualifications within sections 8(2) and 10(2) of the Terrorism Suppression Act, which had made it clear that it is not an offence to provide or collect funds with the intention that they be used, or knowing that they are to be used, for the purposes of advocating democratic government or the protection of human rights, so long as such an organisation is not involved in carrying out terrorist acts. It is therefore regrettable that this safeguard was removed under the Terrorism Suppression Amendment Act 2007.

22.3.7.2 Incitement to Terrorism

Individual and group rights to the freedom of expression, including the freedom of the press, carry special duties and responsibilities and may be limited for the purpose of protecting other important objectives, including national security, public order, or the rights or reputation of others. States parties to the ICCPR have an obligation under article 20(2) to prohibit the incitement to hostility or violence based on national, racial or religious hatred. UN member States also have a duty to prevent the commission of terrorist acts, and have been called on to prohibit the incitement to terrorism. States which have become parties to the Council of Europe Convention on the Prevention of Terrorism are under a specific obligation, under article 5 of the Convention, to establish as an offence the public provocation to commit terrorist acts, a provision which has been identified as best practice in the area.

Given the call for dissuasive penalties to be applied in the sentencing of terrorist offenders, it appears to be prudent for States to criminalise the particular conduct of incitement to terrorism, with an appropriately corresponding range of criminal sanctions, rather than leaving this to a more general prohibition against incitement. Although the formulation of any particular proscription of the incitement to terrorism is a matter for each State to determine, three safeguards or minimum requirements have been identified. First, any proscription must be necessary, such that it either falls within the parameters of the obligation under article 20(2) of the ICCPR, or within the scope of permissible limits on the freedom of expression set out in article 19(3) of the Covenant and article 10(2) of the ECHR. The second safeguard for the guarantee of the proper proscription of the incitement to terrorism demands that the offence must be precise and not be so broad as to capture legitimate expressions or peaceful meetings. Legality and precision demand that: (1) the offence be limited to the incitement of conduct which is truly terrorist in nature; (2) the elements of the offence be precise and avoid using vague terms such as "glorifying" or "promoting" terrorism; (3) the offence include an element requiring proof that the act of incitement includes an actual risk that the conduct incited will be committed; (4) the offence, and its application, respect the principle of non-discrimination; and (5) the offence not be retroactive. The final safeguard involves, as an element of best practice, the restriction of the offence of incitement to terrorism to unlawful and intentional incitement, thus preserving any applicable legal defences and expressly incorporating *mens rea* as an element of the offence to require an intention on the part of the person to communicate his or her statement and thereby incite the commission of a terrorist offence.

The United Kingdom's Terrorism Act 2006 includes the offences of the encouragement of terrorism and the dissemination of terrorist publications. The offences fall within the scope of article 20(2) of the ICCPR and the permissible objectives of article 19(3) of the ICCPR and article 10(2) of the ECHR. The offences in the UK are non-retroactive and legal defences are not excluded. Furthermore, although the offences contain (as alternative elements of *mens rea*) precise intent and reckless intent, the combination of common law on the subject, together with accompanying defences, render a satisfactory outcome to the issue of intent. Overall, however, the incitement offences cannot be said to be formulated in proportionate terms. Sections 1 and 2 of the Act fail to meet the requirements of legality and precision since: (1) they lack precision (concerning notices under section 3); (2) they are not properly confined to the countering of terrorism (by virtue of their linkage to the overly-broad definition of terrorism under section 1 of the Terrorism Act 2000); and (3) their lack of precision makes them vulnerable to use in a discriminatory manner.

22.3.7.3 Media Control

On the subject of the freedom of the press, which is an integral feature of the right of all members of the public under the freedom of expression, to seek, receive and impart information and opinions, New Zealand's International Terrorism (Emergency Powers) Act 1987 presents a rare example of powers of media control in counter-terrorism law. However, these powers are limited to the pursuit of objectives which fall within the scope of article 19(3) of the ICCPR and the more general notion, under section 5 of the NZ Bill of Rights, of limits demonstrably justifiable in a free and democratic society. The Prime Minister's authority to restrict the media only arises where the information in question would be likely to prejudice the safety of any person involved in dealing with an international terrorist emergency, or measures designed to deal with such emergencies. This authority is also subject to judicial review, thus incorporating a checking mechanism against abuse or over-extension of the powers under the Act. It might be observed that judicial review of the exercise of statutory powers only requires reconsideration of the decision made and might not, therefore, achieve practice which is in fact consistent with the principles of necessity and proportionality. The statutory framework, however, appears sufficient.

22.3.8   Measures to Prevent the Transboundary Movement of Terrorists

The final thematic chapter, Chap. 21, concerns the question of measures to prevent the transboundary movement of terrorists, a matter which has been described by the UN Counter-Terrorism Committee and the Security Council's resolution 1566 (2004) Working Group as essential in the fight against terrorism, requiring careful implementation. Numerous issues are raised by this, not all of which could be examined in this title. The issues raised can be categorised as falling within one of three phases: (1) measures to prevent the transboundary movement of terrorists at international borders; (2) measures within the territory of a State including, for example, the detention of non-nationals considered to be a risk to the security of a country; and (3) measures adopted by States concerning the return and/or transfer of terrorists and terrorist suspects. Particular attention is paid in Chap. 21 to border security, the treatment of refugees and asylum-seekers in Australia, and the use by the United Kingdom of 'diplomatic assurances' when seeking to remove a terrorist suspect, or person deemed to be a threat to national security, to a country where that person is at a risk of being ill-treated.

22.3.8.1   Border Security

Effective border security is an important aspect in an effective counter-terrorism strategy, and the ability of States to prevent the transboundary movement of terrorists. It is also a condition of Security Council resolution 1373 (2001), paragraph 2(g), and is impacted upon by paragraph 2(b) of the same resolution and paragraph 2 of resolution 1624 (2005). A tool first adopted by the United States in 1990 and now being widely used, including within the four case study countries, is the sharing of information between countries of departure and arrival to enable the advance screening of passenger lists prior to travel commencing. In Australia for example, the Advance Passenger Processing system allows the Department of Immigration and Multicultural Affairs to issue boarding directives to airlines and cruise companies, thereby preventing the boarding of passengers and crew who do not have permission to travel to Australia. While apparently effective as part of a layered approach to prevent the transboundary movement of terrorists, States have been warned that they should be cautious of implementing measures that may effectively prevent persons from exercising the right of every person to leave any country, including one's own country, particularly in the context of those fleeing persecution with an intention to seek refugee status elsewhere.

The selection of persons for screening at international borders will either be random or based on profiling, defined as the association of sets of physical, behavioural or psychological characteristics with particular offences of threats and their use as a basis for making law-enforcement decisions. In principle, profiling is a permissible activity, since detailed profiles based on factors that are statistically proven to correlate with certain criminal conduct may be effective tools to better target limited law-enforcement resources. However, profiling can never violate the right to equality and non-discrimination, which will likely occur if profiling is based on ethnic or national origin (racial profiling) or religion (religious profiling), and/or if profiling solely or disproportionately affects a specific part of the population. Profiling may also be prohibited where it is based on a person's country of origin if this is used as a proxy for racial or religious profiling. A difference in treatment based on criteria such as race, ethnicity, national origin or religion will only be compatible with the principle of non-discrimination if it is supported by objective and reasonable grounds. The general position, however, is that racial and religious profiling cannot be justified on objective and reasonable grounds because profiling practices based on ethnicity, national origin and religion have proved to be inaccurate and largely unsuccessful in preventing terrorist activity or in identifying terrorists. The exception to this position is where a terrorist crime has been committed, or is in preparation, and there is clear and specific information raising reasonable grounds to assume that the suspect fits a certain descriptive profile. In these circumstances, reliance on characteristics such as ethnic appearance, national origin or religion is justified.

Also relevant to border security is the use of technologies such as whole-body imaging, and Machine Readable Travel Documents such as biometric passports and visas, considered earlier in this concluding chapter within the context of privacy rights.

22.3.8.2 The Treatment of Refugees and Asylum-Seekers

Some of the most potentially serious consequences of counter-terrorism laws, particularly for those labelled as terrorists or suspected terrorists, relate to refugees and asylum-seekers. As in many other countries, Australia undertakes character and security checks of those applying for asylum. Where applications for asylum are refused, and in some cases where they are pending, the applicant will be detained until either he or she can be removed from Australia or until the application process has been finally determined. Detention provisions of this kind are becoming increasingly common in many countries, raising issues related to the necessity and proportionality of such measures, the right to speedy and effective judicial review of any form of detention, the rights of detained persons (including their right to the best attainable health), and possible violations of the prohibition against discrimination. Linked to these concerns is the increasing reliance by countries on intelligence information and the use of 'closed material' by tribunals and courts, a matter considered in Chap. 18 of this text. In the case of Australia, both the Special Rapporteur and the Human Rights Committee have expressed serious concern over Australia's mandatory detention regime, which can result in the indefinite detention of persons.

Reflecting the 'exclusion clauses' in articles 1F and 33 of the Convention on the Status of Refugees, Australia's Migration Act 1958 allows applications for a protection visa to be refused if the applicant is considered to have been involved in terrorism. In this regard, Australia has taken the position that all offences established by the counter-terrorism instruments to which it is a party are considered by it to be serious non-political offences. However, not all offences under the terrorism-related conventions are serious offences including, for example, some of the offences under the Convention on Offences and certain Other Acts Committed on Board Aircraft. The Special Rapporteur has reminded Australia that the cumulative characterisation of acts to be suppressed when countering terrorism is important to this issue, and has noted that vague or broad definitions of terrorism are extremely problematic in this area and create a real risk of the application, in practice, of overly broad interpretations of the exclusion clauses in the Refugees Convention.

22.3.8.3   Diplomatic Assurances

Wherever substantial grounds are shown for believing that an individual would face a real risk of torture or ill-treatment if removed to another country, the State seeking the person's removal is under a responsibility to safeguard him or her against such treatment if removal occurs. Some countries, including Canada and the United Kingdom, have sought to discharge this responsibility by seeking what have come to be known as 'diplomatic assurances' from receiving countries that the person would not be subject to ill-treatment. This is a controversial approach, made inherently problematic by the fact that such assurances will be sought in circumstances where there is a clearly acknowledged risk of torture or ill-treatment. Recognising that any assessment of risk will be fact-specific (or, more accurately, country-specific), an approach implicitly accepted by the House of Lords is to measure each situation against four conditions, namely that: (1) the terms of the assurances must be such that, if they are fulfilled, the person returned will not be subjected to torture or ill-treatment; (2) the assurances are given in good faith;

(3) there is a sound objective basis for believing that the assurances will be fulfilled; and (4) fulfilment of the assurances is capable of being verified. The House of Lords has taken the view that assurances need not eliminate *all* risk of ill-treatment before they can be relied upon. While noting that assurances should be treated with some scepticism if they are given by a country where inhuman treatment by State agents is endemic, Lord Philipps has instead concluded that if, after consideration of all the relevant circumstances (of which the four conditions just mentioned will be key), there are "no substantial grounds for believing that a deportee will be at real risk of inhuman treatment", there will be no basis for holding that the removal is in violation of the prohibition against torture and ill-treatment.

The UN Special Rapporteur on Torture has instead concluded that diplomatic assurances are unreliable and ineffective in the protection against torture and ill-treatment and that post-return monitoring mechanisms have proven to be no guarantee against ill-treatment. Non-governmental organisations have noted that torture and ill-treatment are practices in secret and occur within a highly sophisti-cated system specifically designed to avoid detection of abuses. Effective verifica-tion of assurances is made more difficult given that a person in detention may be understandably reluctant to complain to a person tasked with monitoring the assurances given. Notwithstanding the decision of the House of Lords, or of application of the four conditions mentioned, it has therefore been concluded that diplomatic assurances present a substantial risk of individuals actually being tortured.

Appendices

Appendix 1
United Nations Global Counter-Terrorism Strategy

The General Assembly,

Guided by the purposes and principles of the Charter of the United Nations, and reaffirming its role under the Charter, including on questions related to international peace and security,

Reiterating its strong condemnation of terrorism in all its forms and manifestations, committed by whomever, wherever and for whatever purposes, as it constitutes one of the most serious threats to international peace and security,

Reaffirming the Declaration on Measures to Eliminate International Terrorism, contained in the annex to General Assembly resolution 49/60 of 9 December 1994, the Declaration to Supplement the 1994 Declaration on Measures to Eliminate International Terrorism, contained in the annex to General Assembly resolution 51/210 of 17 December 1996, and the 2005 World Summit Outcome, in particular its section on terrorism,

Recalling all General Assembly resolutions on measures to eliminate international terrorism, including resolution 46/51 of 9 December 1991, and Security Council resolutions on threats to international peace and security caused by terrorist acts, as well as relevant resolutions of the General Assembly on the protection of human rights and fundamental freedoms while countering terrorism,

Recalling also that, in the 2005 World Summit Outcome, world leaders rededicated themselves to support all efforts to uphold the sovereign equality of all States, respect their territorial integrity and political independence, to refrain in their international relations from the threat or use of force in any manner inconsistent with the purposes and principles of the United Nations, to uphold the resolution of disputes by peaceful means and in conformity with the principles of justice and international law, the right to self-determination of peoples which remain under colonial domination or foreign occupation, non-interference in the internal affairs of States, respect for human rights and fundamental freedoms, respect for the equal

---

This chapter reproduces the text of GA Res 60/288, UN GAOR, 60th Sess, 99th Plen Mtg, UN Doc A/Res/60/288 (2006).

rights of all without distinction as to race, sex, language or religion, international cooperation in solving international problems of an economic, social, cultural or humanitarian character, and the fulfilment in good faith of the obligations assumed in accordance with the Charter,

Recalling further the mandate contained in the 2005 World Summit Outcome that the General Assembly should develop without delay the elements identified by the Secretary-General for a counter-terrorism strategy, with a view to adopting and implementing a strategy to promote comprehensive, coordinated and consistent responses, at the national, regional and international levels, to counter terrorism, which also takes into account the conditions conducive to the spread of terrorism,

Reaffirming that acts, methods and practices of terrorism in all its forms and manifestations are activities aimed at the destruction of human rights, fundamental freedoms and democracy, threatening territorial integrity, security of States and destabilizing legitimately constituted Governments, and that the international community should take the necessary steps to enhance cooperation to prevent and combat terrorism,

Reaffirming also that terrorism cannot and should not be associated with any religion, nationality, civilization or ethnic group,

Reaffirming further Member States' determination to make every effort to reach an agreement on and conclude a comprehensive convention on international terrorism, including by resolving the outstanding issues related to the legal definition and scope of the acts covered by the convention, so that it can serve as an effective instrument to counter terrorism,

Continuing to acknowledge that the question of convening a high-level conference under the auspices of the United Nations to formulate an international response to terrorism in all its forms and manifestations could be considered,

Recognizing that development, peace and security, and human rights are interlinked and mutually reinforcing,

Bearing in mind the need to address the conditions conducive to the spread of terrorism,

Affirming Member States' determination to continue to do all they can to resolve conflict, end foreign occupation, confront oppression, eradicate poverty, promote sustained economic growth, sustainable development, global prosperity, good governance, human rights for all and rule of law, improve intercultural understanding and ensure respect for all religions, religious values, beliefs or cultures,

1. *Expresses its appreciation* for the report entitled "Uniting against terrorism: recommendations for a global counter-terrorism strategy" submitted by the Secretary-General to the General Assembly;
2. *Adopts* the present resolution and its annex as the United Nations Global Counter-Terrorism Strategy ("the Strategy");
3. *Decides*, without prejudice to the continuation of the discussion in its relevant committees of all their agenda items related to terrorism and counterterrorism, to undertake the following steps for the effective follow-up of the Strategy:

(a) To launch the Strategy at a high-level segment of its sixty-first session;
(b) To examine in two years progress made in the implementation of the Strategy, and to consider updating it to respond to changes, recognizing that many of the measures contained in the Strategy can be achieved immediately, some will require sustained work through the coming few years and some should be treated as long-term objectives;
(c) To invite the Secretary-General to contribute to the future deliberations of the General Assembly on the review of the implementation and updating of the Strategy;
(d) To encourage Member States, the United Nations and other appropriate international, regional and subregional organizations to support the implementation of the Strategy, including through mobilizing resources and expertise;
(e) To further encourage non-governmental organizations and civil society to engage, as appropriate, on how to enhance efforts to implement the Strategy;

4. *Decides* to include in the provisional agenda of its sixty-second session an item entitled "The United Nations Global Counter-Terrorism Strategy".

99th plenary meeting
8 September 2006

Annex
Plan of action

We, the States Members of the United Nations, resolve:

1. To consistently, unequivocally and strongly condemn terrorism in all its forms and manifestations, committed by whomever, wherever and for whatever purposes, as it constitutes one of the most serious threats to international peace and security;
2. To take urgent action to prevent and combat terrorism in all its forms and manifestations and, in particular:

(a) To consider becoming parties without delay to the existing international conventions and protocols against terrorism, and implementing them, and to make every effort to reach an agreement on and conclude a comprehensive convention on international terrorism;
(b) To implement all General Assembly resolutions on measures to eliminate international terrorism and relevant General Assembly resolutions on the protection of human rights and fundamental freedoms while countering terrorism;
(c) To implement all Security Council resolutions related to international terrorism and to cooperate fully with the counter-terrorism subsidiary bodies of the Security Council in the fulfilment of their tasks, recognizing that many States continue to require assistance in implementing these resolutions;

3. To recognize that international cooperation and any measures that we undertake to prevent and combat terrorism must comply with our obligations under international law, including the Charter of the United Nations and relevant

international conventions and protocols, in particular human rights law, refugee law and international humanitarian law.

I. Measures to address the conditions conducive to the spread of terrorism

We resolve to undertake the following measures aimed at addressing the conditions conducive to the spread of terrorism, including but not limited to prolonged unresolved conflicts, dehumanization of victims of terrorism in all its forms and manifestations, lack of the rule of law and violations of human rights, ethnic, national and religious discrimination, political exclusion, socio-economic marginalization and lack of good governance, while recognizing that none of these conditions can excuse or justify acts of terrorism:

1. To continue to strengthen and make best possible use of the capacities of the United Nations in areas such as conflict prevention, negotiation, mediation, conciliation, judicial settlement, rule of law, peacekeeping and peacebuilding, in order to contribute to the successful prevention and peaceful resolution of prolonged unresolved conflicts. We recognize that the peaceful resolution of such conflicts would contribute to strengthening the global fight against terrorism;

2. To continue to arrange under the auspices of the United Nations initiatives and programmes to promote dialogue, tolerance and understanding among civilizations, cultures, peoples and religions, and to promote mutual respect for and prevent the defamation of religions, religious values, beliefs and cultures. In this regard, we welcome the launching by the Secretary-General of the initiative on the Alliance of Civilizations. We also welcome similar initiatives that have been taken in other parts of the world;

3. To promote a culture of peace, justice and human development, ethnic, national and religious tolerance and respect for all religions, religious values, beliefs or cultures by establishing and encouraging, as appropriate, education and public awareness programmes involving all sectors of society. In this regard, we encourage the United Nations Educational, Scientific and Cultural Organization to play a key role, including through inter-faith and intra-faith dialogue and dialogue among civilizations;

4. To continue to work to adopt such measures as may be necessary and appropriate and in accordance with our respective obligations under international law to prohibit by law incitement to commit a terrorist act or acts and prevent such conduct;

5. To reiterate our determination to ensure the timely and full realization of the development goals and objectives agreed at the major United Nations conferences and summits, including the Millennium Development Goals. We reaffirm our commitment to eradicate poverty and promote sustained economic growth, sustainable development and global prosperity for all;

6. To pursue and reinforce development and social inclusion agendas at every level as goals in themselves, recognizing that success in this area, especially on youth unemployment, could reduce marginalization and the subsequent sense of victimization that propels extremism and the recruitment of terrorists;

7. To encourage the United Nations system as a whole to scale up the cooperation and assistance it is already conducting in the fields of rule of law, human rights and good governance to support sustained economic and social development;

8. To consider putting in place, on a voluntary basis, national systems of assistance that would promote the needs of victims of terrorism and their families and facilitate the normalization of their lives. In this regard, we encourage States to request the relevant United Nations entities to help them to develop such national systems. We will also strive to promote international solidarity in support of victims and foster the involvement of civil society in a global campaign against terrorism and for its condemnation. This could include exploring at the General Assembly the possibility of developing practical mechanisms to provide assistance to victims.

II. Measures to prevent and combat terrorism

We resolve to undertake the following measures to prevent and combat terrorism, in particular by denying terrorists access to the means to carry out their attacks, to their targets and to the desired impact of their attacks:

1. To refrain from organizing, instigating, facilitating, participating in, financing, encouraging or tolerating terrorist activities and to take appropriate practical measures to ensure that our respective territories are not used for terrorist installations or training camps, or for the preparation or organization of terrorist acts intended to be committed against other States or their citizens;

2. To cooperate fully in the fight against terrorism, in accordance with our obligations under international law, in order to find, deny safe haven and bring to justice, on the basis of the principle of extradite or prosecute, any person who supports, facilitates, participates or attempts to participate in the financing, planning, preparation or perpetration of terrorist acts or provides safe havens;

3. To ensure the apprehension and prosecution or extradition of perpetrators of terrorist acts, in accordance with the relevant provisions of national and international law, in particular human rights law, refugee law and international humanitarian law. We will endeavour to conclude and implement to that effect mutual judicial assistance and extradition agreements and to strengthen cooperation between law enforcement agencies;

4. To intensify cooperation, as appropriate, in exchanging timely and accurate information concerning the prevention and combating of terrorism;

5. To strengthen coordination and cooperation among States in combating crimes that might be connected with terrorism, including drug trafficking in all its aspects, illicit arms trade, in particular of small arms and light weapons, including man-portable air defence systems, money-laundering and smuggling of nuclear, chemical, biological, radiological and other potentially deadly materials;

6. To consider becoming parties without delay to the United Nations Convention against Transnational Organized Crime and to the three protocols supplementing it, and implementing them;

7. To take appropriate measures, before granting asylum, for the purpose of ensuring that the asylum-seeker has not engaged in terrorist activities and, after granting asylum, for the purpose of ensuring that the refugee status is not used in a manner contrary to the provisions set out in section II, paragraph 1, above;

8. To encourage relevant regional and subregional organizations to create or strengthen counter-terrorism mechanisms or centres. Should they require co-operation and assistance to this end, we encourage the Counter-Terrorism Committee and its Executive Directorate and, where consistent with their existing mandates, the United Nations Office on Drugs and Crime and the International Criminal Police Organization, to facilitate its provision;

9. To acknowledge that the question of creating an international centre to fight terrorism could be considered, as part of international efforts to enhance the fight against terrorism;

10. To encourage States to implement the comprehensive international standards embodied in the Forty Recommendations on Money-Laundering and Nine Special Recommendations on Terrorist Financing of the Financial Action Task Force, recognizing that States may require assistance in implementing them;

11. To invite the United Nations system to develop, together with Member States, a single comprehensive database on biological incidents, ensuring that it is complementary to the biocrimes database contemplated by the International Criminal Police Organization. We also encourage the Secretary-General to update the roster of experts and laboratories, as well as the technical guidelines and procedures, available to him for the timely and efficient investigation of alleged use. In addition, we note the importance of the proposal of the Secretary-General to bring together, within the framework of the United Nations, the major biotechnology stakeholders, including industry, the scientific community, civil society and Governments, into a common programme aimed at ensuring that biotechnology advances are not used for terrorist or other criminal purposes but for the public good, with due respect for the basic international norms on intellectual property rights;

12. To work with the United Nations with due regard to confidentiality, respecting human rights and in compliance with other obligations under international law, to explore ways and means to:

    (a) Coordinate efforts at the international and regional levels to counter terrorism in all its forms and manifestations on the Internet;

    (b) Use the Internet as a tool for countering the spread of terrorism, while recognizing that States may require assistance in this regard;

13. To step up national efforts and bilateral, subregional, regional and international cooperation, as appropriate, to improve border and customs controls in order to prevent and detect the movement of terrorists and prevent and detect the illicit traffic in, inter alia, small arms and light weapons, conventional ammunition and explosives, and nuclear, chemical, biological or radiological

weapons and materials, while recognizing that States may require assistance to that effect;

14. To encourage the Counter-Terrorism Committee and its Executive Directorate to continue to work with States, at their request, to facilitate the adoption of legislation and administrative measures to implement the terrorist travel-related obligations and to identify best practices in this area, drawing whenever possible on those developed by technical international organizations, such as the International Civil Aviation Organization, the World Customs Organization and the International Criminal Police Organization;

15. To encourage the Committee established pursuant to Security Council resolution 1267 (1999) to continue to work to strengthen the effectiveness of the travel ban under the United Nations sanctions regime against Al-Qa'ida and the Taliban and associated individuals and entities, as well as to ensure, as a matter of priority, that fair and transparent procedures exist for placing individuals and entities on its lists, for removing them and for granting humanitarian exceptions. In this regard, we encourage States to share information, including by widely distributing the International Criminal Police Organization/United Nations special notices concerning people subject to this sanctions regime;

16. To step up efforts and cooperation at every level, as appropriate, to improve the security of manufacturing and issuing identity and travel documents and to prevent and detect their alteration or fraudulent use, while recognizing that States may require assistance in doing so. In this regard, we invite the International Criminal Police Organization to enhance its database on stolen and lost travel documents, and we will endeavour to make full use of this tool, as appropriate, in particular by sharing relevant information;

17. To invite the United Nations to improve coordination in planning a response to a terrorist attack using nuclear, chemical, biological or radiological weapons or materials, in particular by reviewing and improving the effectiveness of the existing inter-agency coordination mechanisms for assistance delivery, relief operations and victim support, so that all States can receive adequate assistance. In this regard, we invite the General Assembly and the Security Council to develop guidelines for the necessary cooperation and assistance in the event of a terrorist attack using weapons of mass destruction;

18. To step up all efforts to improve the security and protection of particularly vulnerable targets, such as infrastructure and public places, as well as the response to terrorist attacks and other disasters, in particular in the area of civil protection, while recognizing that States may require assistance to this effect.

III. Measures to build States' capacity to prevent and combat terrorism and to strengthen the role of the United Nations system in this regard

We recognize that capacity-building in all States is a core element of the global counter-terrorism effort, and resolve to undertake the following measures to develop State capacity to prevent and combat terrorism and enhance coordination and coherence within the United Nations system in promoting international cooperation in countering terrorism:

1. To encourage Member States to consider making voluntary contributions to United Nations counter-terrorism cooperation and technical assistance projects, and to explore additional sources of funding in this regard. We also encourage the United Nations to consider reaching out to the private sector for contributions to capacity-building programmes, in particular in the areas of port, maritime and civil aviation security;

2. To take advantage of the framework provided by relevant international, regional and subregional organizations to share best practices in counter-terrorism capacity-building, and to facilitate their contributions to the international community's efforts in this area;

3. To consider establishing appropriate mechanisms to rationalize States' reporting requirements in the field of counter-terrorism and eliminate duplication of reporting requests, taking into account and respecting the different mandates of the General Assembly, the Security Council and its subsidiary bodies that deal with counter-terrorism;

4. To encourage measures, including regular informal meetings, to enhance, as appropriate, more frequent exchanges of information on cooperation and technical assistance among Member States, United Nations bodies dealing with counter-terrorism, relevant specialized agencies, relevant international, regional and subregional organizations and the donor community, to develop States' capacities to implement relevant United Nations resolutions;

5. To welcome the intention of the Secretary-General to institutionalize, within existing resources, the Counter-Terrorism Implementation Task Force within the Secretariat in order to ensure overall coordination and coherence in the counterterrorism efforts of the United Nations system;

6. To encourage the Counter-Terrorism Committee and its Executive Directorate to continue to improve the coherence and efficiency of technical assistance delivery in the field of counter-terrorism, in particular by strengthening its dialogue with States and relevant international, regional and subregional organizations and working closely, including by sharing information, with all bilateral and multilateral technical assistance providers;

7. To encourage the United Nations Office on Drugs and Crime, including its Terrorism Prevention Branch, to enhance, in close consultation with the Counter- Terrorism Committee and its Executive Directorate, its provision of technical assistance to States, upon request, to facilitate the implementation of the international conventions and protocols related to the prevention and suppression of terrorism and relevant United Nations resolutions;

8. To encourage the International Monetary Fund, the World Bank, the United Nations Office on Drugs and Crime and the International Criminal Police Organization to enhance cooperation with States to help them to comply fully with international norms and obligations to combat money-laundering and the financing of terrorism;

9. To encourage the International Atomic Energy Agency and the Organization for the Prohibition of Chemical Weapons to continue their efforts, within their respective mandates, in helping States to build capacity to prevent terrorists from accessing nuclear, chemical or radiological materials, to ensure security at related facilities and to respond effectively in the event of an attack using such materials;

10. To encourage the World Health Organization to step up its technical assistance to help States to improve their public health systems to prevent and prepare for biological attacks by terrorists;

11. To continue to work within the United Nations system to support the reform and modernization of border management systems, facilities and institutions at the national, regional and international levels;

12. To encourage the International Maritime Organization, the World Customs Organization and the International Civil Aviation Organization to strengthen their cooperation, work with States to identify any national shortfalls in areas of transport security and provide assistance, upon request, to address them;

13. To encourage the United Nations to work with Member States and relevant international, regional and subregional organizations to identify and share best practices to prevent terrorist attacks on particularly vulnerable targets. We invite the International Criminal Police Organization to work with the Secretary- General so that he can submit proposals to this effect. We also recognize the importance of developing public–private partnerships in this area.

IV. Measures to ensure respect for human rights for all and the rule of law as the fundamental basis of the fight against terrorism

We resolve to undertake the following measures, reaffirming that the promotion and protection of human rights for all and the rule of law is essential to all components of the Strategy, recognizing that effective counter-terrorism measures and the protection of human rights are not conflicting goals, but complementary and mutually reinforcing, and stressing the need to promote and protect the rights of victims of terrorism:

1. To reaffirm that General Assembly resolution 60/158 of 16 December 2005 provides the fundamental framework for the "Protection of human rights and fundamental freedoms while countering terrorism";

2. To reaffirm that States must ensure that any measures taken to combat terrorism comply with their obligations under international law, in particular human rights law, refugee law and international humanitarian law;

3. To consider becoming parties without delay to the core international instruments on human rights law, refugee law and international humanitarian law, and implementing them, as well as to consider accepting the competence of international and relevant regional human rights monitoring bodies;

4. To make every effort to develop and maintain an effective and rule of law-based national criminal justice system that can ensure, in accordance with our obligations under international law, that any person who participates in the financing,

planning, preparation or perpetration of terrorist acts or in support of terrorist acts is brought to justice, on the basis of the principle to extradite or prosecute, with due respect for human rights and fundamental freedoms, and that such terrorist acts are established as serious criminal offences in domestic laws and regulations. We recognize that States may require assistance in developing and maintaining such effective and rule of law-based criminal justice systems, and we encourage them to resort to the technical assistance delivered, inter alia, by the United Nations Office on Drugs and Crime;

5. To reaffirm the important role of the United Nations system in strengthening the international legal architecture by promoting the rule of law, respect for human rights and effective criminal justice systems, which constitute the fundamental basis of our common fight against terrorism;

6. To support the Human Rights Council and to contribute, as it takes shape, to its work on the question of the promotion and protection of human rights for all in the fight against terrorism;

7. To support the strengthening of the operational capacity of the Office of the United Nations High Commissioner for Human Rights, with a particular emphasis on increasing field operations and presences. The Office should continue to play a lead role in examining the question of protecting human rights while countering terrorism, by making general recommendations on the human rights obligations of States and providing them with assistance and advice, in particular in the area of raising awareness of international human rights law among national law enforcement agencies, at the request of States;

8. To support the role of the Special Rapporteur on the promotion and protection of human rights and fundamental freedoms while countering terrorism. The Special Rapporteur should continue to support the efforts of States and offer concrete advice by corresponding with Governments, making country visits, liaising with the United Nations and regional organizations and reporting on these issues.

Appendix 2
Party Status of Case Study Countries to Conventions Related to Terrorism, Human Rights, Refugee Law and Humanitarian Law

Tables:

1 Party status to universal terrorism-related treaties
2 Party status to human rights treaties
3 Party status to refugee treaties
4 Party status to international humanitarian and criminal law treaties

Table 1 Party status to universal terrorism-related treaties (listed by date on which each treaty was opened for signature)

Convention on Offences and Certain Other Acts Committed on Board Aircraft, 704 UNTS 219 (opened for signature 14 September 1963, entered into force 4 December 1969)

Australia	–	Acceded 22 June 1970
Canada	Signed 4 November 1964	Ratified 7 November 1969
New Zealand	–	Acceded 12 February 1974
United Kingdom	Signed 14 September 1963	Ratified 29 November 1968

Convention for the Suppression of Unlawful Seizure of Aircraft, 860 UNTS 105 (opened for signature 16 December 1970, entered into force 14 October 1971)

Australia	–	Acceded 15 June 1971
Canada	Signed 16 December 1970	Ratified 20 June 1972
New Zealand	Signed 15 September 1971	Ratified 12 February 1974
United Kingdom	Signed 16 December 1970	Ratified 22 December 1971

Convention for the Suppression of Unlawful Acts Against the Safety of Civil Aviation, 974 UNTS 177 (opened for signature 23 September 1971, entered into force 26 January 1973)

Australia	Signed 12 October 1972	Ratified 12 July 1973
Canada	Signed 23 September 1971	Ratified 19 June 1972
New Zealand	Signed 26 September 1972	Ratified 12 February 1974
United Kingdom	Signed 23 September 1971	Ratified 25 October 1973

(continued)

Table 1 (continued)

Convention on the Prevention and Punishment of Crimes against International Protected Persons, including Diplomatic Agents, 1035 UNTS 167 (opened for signature 14 December 1973, entered into force 20 February 1977)

Australia	Signed 30 December 1974	Ratified 20 June 1977
Canada	Signed 26 June 1974	Ratified 4 August 1976
New Zealand	–	Acceded 12 October 1985
United Kingdom	Signed 13 December 1974	Ratified 2 May 1979

International Convention against the Taking of Hostages, 1316 UNTS 205 (opened for signature 18 December 1979, entered into force 3 June 1983)

Australia	–	Acceded 21 May 1990
Canada	Signed 18 February 1980	Ratified 4 December 1985
New Zealand	Signed 24 December 1980	Ratified 12 November 1985
United Kingdom	Signed 18 December 1979	Ratified 22 December 1982

Convention on the Physical Protection of Nuclear Material, 1456 UNTS 124 (opened for signature 3 March 1980, entered into force 8 February 1987)

Australia	Signed 22 February 1984	Ratified 22 September 1987
Canada	Signed 23 September 1980	Ratified 21 March 1986
New Zealand	–	Acceded 19 December 2003
United Kingdom	Signed 13 June 1980	Ratified 6 September 1991

Protocol on the Suppression of Unlawful Acts of Violence at Airports Serving International Civil Aviation, ICAO Doc 9518 (opened for signature 24 February 1988, entered into force 6 August 1989)

Australia	–	Acceded 23 October 1990
Canada	Signed 24 February 1988	Ratified 2 August 1993
New Zealand	Signed 11 April 1989	Ratified 2 August 1999
United Kingdom	Signed 26 October 1988	Ratified 15 November 1990

Convention for the Suppression of Unlawful Acts against the Safety of Maritime Navigation, 1678 UNTS 221 (opened for signature 10 March 1988, entered into force 1 March 1992)

Australia	–	Acceded 19 February 1993
Canada	Signed 10 March 1988	Ratified 18 June 1993
New Zealand	Signed 10 March 1988	Ratified 10 June 1999
United Kingdom	Signed 10 March 1988	Ratified 3 May 1991

Protocol for the Suppression of Unlawful Acts against the Safety of Fixed Platforms Located on the Continental Shelf, 1678 UNTS 304 (opened for signature 10 March 1988, entered into force 1 March 1992)

Australia	–	Acceded 19 February 1993
Canada	Signed 10 March 1988	Ratified 18 June 1993
New Zealand	Signed 10 March 1988	Ratified 10 June 1999
United Kingdom	Signed 10 March 1988	Ratified 3 May 1991

Convention on Marking of Plastic Explosives for the Purpose of Detection, ICAO Doc 9571 (opened for signature 1 March 1991, entered into force 21 June 1998)

Australia	–	Acceded 26 June 2007
Canada	Signed 1 March 1991	Ratified 29 November 1996
New Zealand	–	Acceded 19 December 2003
United Kingdom	Signed 1 March 1991	Ratified 28 April 1997

(*continued*)

Table 1 (continued)

International Convention for the Suppression of Terrorist Bombing, 2149 UNTS 286 (opened for signature 12 January 1998, entered into force 23 May 2001)		
Australia	–	Acceded 9 August 2002
Canada	Signed 12 January 1998	Ratified 3 April 2002
New Zealand	–	Acceded 4 November 2002
United Kingdom	Signed 12 January 1998	Ratified 7 March 2001
International Convention for the Suppression of the Financing of Terrorism, 2179 UNTS 232 (opened for signature 10 January 2000, entered into force 10 April 1992)		
Australia	Signed 15 October 2001	Ratified 26 September 2002
Canada	Signed 10 February 2000	Ratified 19 February 2002
New Zealand	Signed 7 September 2000	Ratified 4 November 2002
United Kingdom	Signed 10 January 2000	Ratified 7 March 2001
International Convention for the Suppression of Acts of Nuclear Terrorism, GA Res 59/290 (2005) (opened for signature 14 September 2005, entered into force 7 July 2007)		
Australia	Signed 14 September 2005	Not yet ratified (as at 01/10/09)
Canada	Signed 14 September 2005	Not yet ratified (as at 01/10/09)
New Zealand	Signed 14 September 2005	Not yet ratified (as at 01/10/09)
United Kingdom	Signed 14 September 2005	Ratified 24 September 2009

Table 2 **Party status to human rights treaties (listed by date on which each treaty was opened for signature)**

Convention for the Protection of Human Rights and Fundamental Freedoms, 213 UNTS 222 (opened for signature 4 November 1950, entered into force 3 September 1953)		
United Kingdom	Signed 4 November 1950	Ratified 8 March 1951
Convention on the Elimination of All Forms of Racial Discrimination, 9464 UNTS 211 (opened for signature 7 March 1966, entered into force 4 January 1969)		
Australia	Signed 13 October 1966	Ratified 30 September 1975
Canada	Signed 24 August 1966	Ratified 14 October 1970
New Zealand	Signed 22 October 1966	Ratified 22 November 1972
United Kingdom	Signed 11 October 1966	Ratified 7 Match 1969
International Covenant on Civil and Political Rights, 999 UNTS 171 (opened for signature 16 December 1966, entered into force 23 March 1976)		
Australia	Signed 18 December 1972	Ratified 13 August 1980
Canada	–	Acceded 19 May 1976
New Zealand	Signed 12 November 1968	Ratified 28 December 1978
United Kingdom	Signed 16 September 1968	Ratified 20 May 1976
Optional Protocol to the International Covenant on Civil and Political Rights, 999 UNTS 302 (opened for signature 16 December 1966, entered into force 23 March 1976)		
Australia	–	Acceded 25 September 1991
Canada	–	Acceded 19 May 1976
New Zealand	–	Acceded 26 May 1989
United Kingdom	Not signed	–

(*continued*)

Table 2 (continued)

International Covenant on Economic, Social and Cultural Rights, 993 UNTS 3 (opened for signature 16 December 1966, entered into force 3 January 1976)

Australia	Signed 18 December 1972	Ratified 10 December 1975
Canada	–	Acceded 19 May 1976
New Zealand	Signed 12 November 1968	Ratified 28 December 1978
United Kingdom	Signed 16 September 1968	Ratified 20 May 1976

Convention on the Elimination of All Forms of Discrimination Against Women, 1249 UNTS 13 (opened for signature 18 December 1979, entered into force 3 September 1981)

Australia	Signed 17 July 1980	Ratified 28 July 1983
Canada	Signed 17 July 1980	Ratified 10 December 1981
New Zealand	Signed 17 July 1980	Ratified 10 January 1985
United Kingdom	Signed 2 July 1981	Ratified 7 April 1986

Convention Against Torture and other Cruel, Inhuman or Degrading Treatment or Punishment, 1465 UNTS 112 (opened for signature 10 December 1984, entered into force 26 June 1987)

Australia	Signed 10 December 1985	Ratified 8 August 1989
Canada	Signed 23 August 1985	Ratified 24 June 1987
New Zealand	Signed 14 January 1986	Ratified 10 December 1989
United Kingdom	Signed 15 March 1985	Ratified 8 December 1988

Convention on the Rights of the Child, 1577 UNTS 43 (opened for signature 20 November 1989, entered into force 2 September 1990)

Australia	Signed 22 August 1990	Ratified 17 December 1990
Canada	Signed 28 May 1990	Ratified 13 December 1991
New Zealand	Signed 1 October 1990	Ratified 6 April 1993
United Kingdom	Signed 19 April 1990	Ratified 16 December 1991

Second Optional Protocol to the International Covenant on Civil and Political Rights, 1642 UNTS 414 (opened for signature 15 December 1989, entered into force 11 July 1991)

Australia	–	Acceded 2 October 1990
Canada	Not signed	–
New Zealand	Signed 22 February 1990	Ratified 22 February 1990
United Kingdom	Signed 31 March 1999	Ratified 10 December 1999

Table 3　Party status to refugee treaties (listed by date on which each treaty was opened for signature)

Convention relating to the Status of Refugees, 189 UNTS 150 (opened for signature 28 July 1952, entered into force 22 April 1954)

Australia	–	Acceded 13 January 1054
Canada	–	Acceded 4 June 1969
New Zealand	Signed 28 July 1951	Ratified 3 May 1956
United Kingdom	Signed 28 December 1951	Ratified 11 March 1951

Protocol Relating to the Status of Refugees, 606 UNTS 267 (opened for signature 18 November 1966, entered into force 4 October 1967)

Australia	–	Acceded 13 December 1973
Canada	–	Acceded 4 June 1969
New Zealand	–	Acceded 6 August 1973
United Kingdom	–	Acceded 4 September 1968

Table 4 Party status to international humanitarian and criminal law treaties (listed by date on which each treaty was opened for signature)

Convention on the Prevention and Punishment of the Crime of Genocide, 78 UNTS 277 (opened for signature 8 December 1948, entered into force 12 January 1951)

Australia	Signed 11 December 1948	Ratified 8 July 1949
Canada	Signed 20 November 1949	Ratified 3 September 1952
New Zealand	Signed 25 November 1949	Ratified 28 December 1978
United Kingdom	–	Acceded 30 January 1970

Geneva Convention for the Amelioration of the Condition of the Wounded and Sick in Armed Forces in the Field, 75 UNTS 31 (opened for signature 12 August 1949, entered into force 21 October 1950)

Australia	Signed 4 January 1950	Ratified 14 October 1958
Canada	Signed 8 December 1949	Ratified 14 May 1965
New Zealand	Signed 11 February 1950	Ratified 2 May 1959
United Kingdom	Signed 8 December 1949	Ratified 23 September 1957

Geneva Convention for the Amelioration of the Condition of Wounded, Sick and Shipwrecked Members of Armed Forces at Sea, 75 UNTS 85 (opened for signature 12 August 1949, entered into force 21 October 1950)

Australia	Signed 4 January 1950	Ratified 14 October 1958
Canada	Signed 8 December 1949	Ratified 14 May 1965
New Zealand	Signed 11 February 1950	Ratified 2 May 1959
United Kingdom	Signed 8 December 1949	Ratified 23 September 1957

Geneva Convention relative to the Treatment of Prisoners of War, 75 UNTS 135 (opened for signature 12 August 1949, entered into force 21 October 1950)

Australia	Signed 4 January 1950	Ratified 14 October 1958
Canada	Signed 8 December 1949	Ratified 14 May 1965
New Zealand	Signed 11 February 1950	Ratified 2 May 1959
United Kingdom	Signed 8 December 1949	Ratified 23 September 1957

Geneva Convention relative to the Protection of Civilian Persons in Time of War, 75 UNTS 287 (opened for signature 12 August 1949, entered into force 21 October 1950)

Australia	Signed 4 January 1950	Ratified 14 October 1958
Canada	Signed 8 December 1949	Ratified 14 May 1965
New Zealand	Signed 11 February 1950	Ratified 2 May 1959
United Kingdom	Signed 8 December 1949	Ratified 23 September 1957

Convention on the Non-Applicability of Statutory Limitations to War Crimes and Crimes Against Humanity, UN Doc A/7218 (1968) (opened for signature 25 November 1968, entered into force 11 November 1970)

Australia	Not signed	–
Canada	Not signed	–
New Zealand	Not signed	–
United Kingdom	Not signed	–

Protocol Additional to the Geneva Conventions of 12 August 1949, and Relating to the Protection of Victims of International Armed Conflicts (Protocol I), 1125 UNTS 3 (opened for signature 8 June 1977, entered into force 7 December 1978)

Australia	Signed 7 December 1978	Ratified 21 June 1991
Canada	Signed 12 December 1977	Ratified 20 November 1990
New Zealand	Signed 27 November 1978	Ratified 8 February 1988
United Kingdom	Signed 12 December 1977	Ratified 28 January 1998

(*continued*)

Table 4 (continued)

Protocol Additional to the Geneva Conventions of 12 August 1949 and Relating to the Protection of Victims of Non-International Armed Conflicts (Protocol II), 1125 UNTS 610 (opened for signature 8 June 1977, entered into force 7 December 1978)

Australia	Signed 7 December 1978	Ratified 21 June 1991
Canada	Signed 12 December 1977	Ratified 20 November 1990
New Zealand	Signed 27 November 1978	Ratified 8 February 1988
United Kingdom	Signed 12 December 1977	Ratified 28 January 1998

Statute of the International Criminal Court, 2187 UNTS 90 (opened for signature 17 July 1998, entered into force 1 July 2002)

Australia	Signed 9 December 1998	Ratified 1 July 2002
Canada	Signed 18 December 1988	Ratified 7 July 2000
New Zealand	Signed 7 October 1998	Ratified 7 September 2000
United Kingdom	Signed 30 November 1998	Ratified 4 October 2001

Appendix 3
Terrorism-Related Offences

The following tables set out the terrorism-related offences provided for under the 13 universal terrorism-related conventions (see Chap. 3, at Sect. 3.1.1), as well as conduct to be proscribed under Security Council resolutions on terrorism (see Chap. 3, at Sect. 3.2.2). The text of domestic law provisions incorporating these obligations in each of the case study countries is set out in Tables 2–5 (for an overview of these domestic laws, see Chaps. 5–8 inclusive).

Contents:

Table 1 Offences under the universal terrorism-related conventions and Security Council resolutions[1]

A. Offences relating to civil aviation (13 offences)

Convention	Offence
Tokyo Convention,[2] article 1(1)(a) and 1(2) [offences on an aircraft]	1. Offences against the penal law of a State party committed on board and aircraft, while that aircraft is "in flight" (as defined in article 1(3) of the Convention) or on the surface of the high seas or of any other area outside the territory of any State party
Tokyo Convention, article 1(1)(b) [aircraft safety and order]	2. Acts which may or do jeopardise the safety of the aircraft or of persons or property therein, or which jeopardise good order and discipline on board
Hague Convention,[3] article 1(a) [hijacking of aircraft]	3. Unlawful seizure or exercise of control of an aircraft "in flight" (as defined in article 3(1) of the Convention) by force or threat of force, or by any other form of intimidation, or attempts to perform any such act
Hague Convention, article 1(b) [party offences]	4. Participation as an accomplice of a person who performs or attempts to perform an act described in article 1(a) of the Convention
Montreal Convention,[4] article 1(1)(a) [violence on an aircraft]	5. Unlawful and intentional act of violence against a person on board an aircraft "in flight" (as defined in article 2 (a) of the Convention) if that act is likely to endanger the safety of that aircraft
Montreal Convention, article 1(1)(b) [aircraft destruction or damage]	6. Unlawfully and intentionally destroying or causing damage to an aircraft "in service" (as defined in article 2(b) of the Convention) which renders it incapable of flight or which is likely to endanger its safety in flight
Montreal Convention, article 1(1)(c) [devices for aircraft destruction or damage]	7. Unlawfully and intentionally places or causes to be placed on an aircraft in service, by any means whatsoever, a device or substance which is likely to destroy that aircraft, or to cause damage to it which renders it incapable of flight, or to cause damage to it which is likely to endanger its safety in flight
Montreal Convention, article 1(1)(d) [air navigation facilities]	8. Unlawfully and intentionally destroying or damaging air navigation facilities or interfering with their operation, if any such act is likely to endanger the safety of an aircraft in flight
Montreal Convention, article 1(1)(e) [false communications]	9. Unlawfully and intentionally communication information which the person knows to be false, thereby endangering the safety of an aircraft in flight

(continued)

[1]See Chap. 3, Sects. 3.1.1 and 3.2.2.

[2]Convention on Offences and Certain Other Acts Committed on Board Aircraft, opened for signature 14 September 1963, 704 UNTS 219 (entered into force 4 December 1969).

[3]Convention for the Suppression of Unlawful Seizure of Aircraft, opened for signature 16 December 1970, 860 UNTS 105 (entered into force 14 October 1971).

[4]Convention for the Suppression of Unlawful Acts Against the Safety of Civil Aviation, opened for signature 23 September 1971, 974 UNTS 177 (entered into force 26 January 1973).

Table 1 (continued)

Montreal Convention, article 1(1*bis*) (a) (as added by the Montreal Protocol,[5] article 2(1)(a)) [airport violence]	10. Unlawfully and internationally using any device, substance or weapon to perform an act of violence against a person at an airport serving international civil aviation which causes or is likely to cause serious injury or death, if such an act endangers or is likely to endanger safety at that airport
Montreal Convention, article 1(1*bis*) (b) (as added by the Montreal Protocol, article 2(1)(b)) [airport facilities destruction or damage]	11. Unlawfully and internationally using any device, substance or weapon to destroy or seriously damage the facilities of an airport serving international civil aviation or aircraft not in service located thereon or disrupts the services of the airport, if such an act endangers or is likely to endanger safety at that airport
Montreal Convention, article 1(2)(a) (as supplemented by the Montreal Protocol, article 2(2)) [attempts]	12. Attempt to commit any offence under article 1(1) or 1 (1*bis*) of the Convention
Montreal Convention, article 1(2)(b) [party offences]	13. Participation as an accomplice of a person who commits or attempts to commit any offence under article 1 (1) of the Convention

B. Offences relating to operations at sea (20 offences)

Convention	*Offence*
Rome Convention,[6] article 3(1)(a) [hijacking of ship]	1. Unlawful and intentional seizure or exercise of control over a "ship" (as defined in article 1 of the Convention) by force or threat of force, of by any other form of intimidation
Rome Convention, article 3(1)(b) [violence on ship]	2. Unlawful and intentional act of violence against a person on board a ship if that act is likely to endanger the safe navigation of that ship
Rome Convention, article 3(1)(c) [ship destruction or damage]	3. Unlawfully and intentionally destroying or causing damage to a ship or its cargo which is likely to endanger the safe navigation of that ship
Rome Convention, article 3(1)(d) [devices for destruction or damage]	4. Unlawfully and intentionally places or causes to be placed on a ship, by any means whatsoever, a device or substance which is likely to destroy that ship, or to cause damage to it or its cargo which endangers or is likely to endanger the safe navigation of that ship
Rome Convention, article 3(1)(e) [maritime navigation facilities]	5. Unlawfully and intentionally destroys or seriously damages maritime navigational facilities or seriously interferes with their operation, if any such act is likely to endanger the safe navigation of a ship
Rome Convention, article 3(1)(f) [false communications]	6. Unlawfully and intentionally communicates information known to be false, thereby endangering the safe navigation of a ship

(continued)

---

[5]Protocol on the Suppression of Unlawful Acts of Violence at Airports Serving International Civil Aviation, opened for signature 24 February 1988, ICAO Doc 9518 (entered into force 6 August 1989).

[6]Convention for the Suppression of Unlawful Acts against the Safety of Maritime Navigation, opened for signature 10 March 1988, 1678 UNTS 221 (entered into force 1 March 1992).

Table 1 (continued)

Rome Convention, article 3(1)(g) [causing injury or death]	7. Unlawfully and intentionally injures or kills any person, in connection with the commission or attempted commission of any of the offences under article 3(1)(a) to (f) of the Convention
Rome Convention, article 3(2)(a) [attempts]	8. Attempt to commit any offence under article 3(1) of the Convention
Rome Convention, article 3(2)(b) [party offences]	9. Abetting the commission of any offence under article 3 (1) of the Convention by any person
Rome Convention, article 3(2)(b) [party offences]	10. Participation as an accomplice of a person who commits any offence under article 3(1) of the Convention
Rome Convention, article 3(2)(c) [threat of offences]	11. Threaten (as is provided under national law), with or without condition, to commit any offence under article 3 (1)(b), (c) or (e) which is aimed at compelling a physical or juridical person to do or refrain from doing any act, if that threat is likely to endanger the safe navigation of the ship in question
Rome Protocol,[7] article 2(1)(a) [hijacking of fixed platform]	12. Unlawful and intentional seizure or exercise of control over a "fixed platform" (as defined in article 1(3) of the Rome Protocol) by force or threat of force, of by any other form of intimidation
Rome Protocol, article 2(1)(b) [violence on fixed platform]	13. Unlawful and intentional act of violence against a person on board a fixed platform if that act is likely to endanger its safety
Rome Protocol, article 2(1)(c) [fixed platform destruction or damage]	14. Unlawfully and intentionally destroying or causing damage to a fixed platform which is likely to endanger its safety
Rome Protocol, article 2(1)(d) [devices for destruction or damage]	15. Unlawfully and intentionally places or causes to be placed on a fixed platform, by any means whatsoever, a device or substance which is likely to destroy that fixed platform or to endanger its safety
Rome Protocol, article 2(1)(e) [causing injury or death]	16. Unlawfully and intentionally injures or kills any person, in connection with the commission or attempted commission of any of the offences under article 2(1)(a) to (d) of the Rome Protocol
Rome Protocol, article 2(2)(a) [attempts]	17. Attempt to commit any offence under article 2(1) of the Rome Protocol
Rome Protocol, article 2(2)(b) [party offences]	18. Abetting the commission of any offence under article 2 (1) of the Rome Protocol by any person
Rome Protocol, article 2(2)(b) [party offences]	19. Participation as an accomplice of a person who commits any offence under article 2(1) of the Rome Protocol
Rome Protocol, article 2(2)(c) [threat of offences]	20. Threaten (as is provided under national law), with or without condition, to commit any offence under article 2 (1)(b) or (c) which is aimed at compelling a physical or juridical person to do or refrain from doing any act, if that threat is likely to endanger the safety of the fixed platform

(continued)

---

[7]Protocol for the Suppression of Unlawful Acts against the Safety of Fixed Platforms Located on the Continental Shelf, opened for signature 10 March 1988, 1678 UNTS 304 (entered into force 1 March 1992).

Table 1 (continued)

C. Offences relating to the safety of persons (8 offences)	
Convention	*Offence*
Hostages Convention,[8] article 1(1) [hostage-taking]	1. "Hostage-taking", being the seizure or detention of a person (a "hostage") accompanied by a threat to kill, to injure or to continue to detain the hostage, in order to compel a third party (a State, an international intergovernmental organisation, a natural or juridical person, or a group of persons) to do or abstain from doing any act as an explicit or implicit condition for the release of the hostage
Hostages Convention, article 1(2)(a) [attempted hostage-taking]	2. Attempt to commit an act of hostage-taking under article 1(1) of the Convention
Hostages Convention, article 1(2)(b) [party offences]	3. Participation as an accomplice of a person who commits or attempts to commit an act of hostage-taking under article 1(1) of the Convention
Protected Persons Convention,[9] article 2(1)(a) [attack against PP]	4. Intentional murder, kidnapping or other attack upon the person or liberty of an "internationally protected person" (as defined in article 1(1) of the Convention)
Protected Persons Convention, article 2(1)(b) [attack against PP's premises, etc.]	5. Intentional violent act upon the official premises, the private accommodation or the means of transport of an internationally protected person which is likely to endanger his person or liberty
Protected Persons Convention, article 2(1)(c) [threats to attack]	6. Intentional threat to commit any act under article 2(1)(a) or (b) of the Convention
Protected Persons Convention, article 2(1)(d) [attempts]	7. Intentional attempt to commit any act under article 2(1) (a) or (b) of the Convention
Protected Persons Convention, article 2(1)(e) [party offences]	8. Intentional act constituting participation as an accomplice in any act under article 2(1)(a) or (b) of the Convention

D. Offences relating to the suppression of the means by which terrorist acts might be perpetrated or facilitated (28 offences)	
Convention	*Offence*
Plastic Explosives Convention[10]	No offences[11]
Bombing Convention,[12] article 2(1)(a)	1. Unlawfully and intentionally delivering, placing, discharging or detonating an "explosive or other lethal device" (as defined in article 1(3) of the Convention) in,

(continued)

---

[8]International Convention against the Taking of Hostages, opened for signature 18 December 1979, 1316 UNTS 205 (entered into force 3 June 1983).

[9]Convention on the Prevention and Punishment of Crimes against International Protected Persons, including Diplomatic Agents, opened for signature 14 December 1973, 1035 UNTS 167 (entered into force 20 February 1977).

[10]Convention on the Marking of Plastic Explosives for the Purpose of Detection, opened for signature 1 March 1991, ICAO Doc 9571 (entered into force 21 June 1998).

[11]The Plastic Explosives Convention does not require States parties to proscribe any conduct, but instead places obligations upon States relating to the marking of explosives: see articles 2 and 3(1).

[12]International Convention for the Suppression of Terrorist Bombing, opened for signature 12 January 1998, 2149 UNTS 286 (entered into force 23 May 2001).

Table 1 (continued)

[bombing with intent to cause injury or death]	into or against a "place of public use" (as defined in article 1(5)), a "State or government facility" (as defined in article 1(1)), a "public transportation system" (as defined in article 1(6)) or an "infrastructure facility" (as defined in article 1(2)) with the intent to cause death or serious bodily injury
Bombing Convention, article 2(1)(b) [bombing with intent to cause destruction]	2. Unlawfully and intentionally delivering, placing, discharging or detonating an explosive or other lethal device in, into or against a place of public use, a State or government facility, a public transportation system or an infrastructure facility with the intent to cause extensive destruction of such a place, facility of system, where such destruction results in or is likely to result in major economic loss
Bombing Convention, article 2(2) [attempts]	3. Attempt to commit an offence under article 2(1) of the Convention
Bombing Convention, article 2(3)(a) [party offences]	4. Participation as an accomplice in an offence under article 2(1) or 2(2) of the Convention
Bombing Convention, article 2(3)(b) [party offences]	5. Organising or directing others to commit an offence under article 2(1) or 2(2) of the Convention
Bombing Convention, article 2(3)(c) [party offences]	6. Intentionally contributing to the commission of an offence under article 2(1) or 2(2) of the Convention by a group of persons acting with a common purpose made either: (i) with the aim of furthering the general criminal activity or purpose of the group; or (ii) in the knowledge of the intention of the group to commit such an offence
Financing Convention,[13] article 2(1)(a) [financing terrorism-related convention offences]	7. By any means, directly or indirectly, unlawfully and wilfully, provides or collects funds (as defined in article 1(1) of the Convention) with the intention that should be used (or in the knowledge that they are to be used)[14] in full or in part to carry out an act which constitutes an offence within the scope of and as defined in one of the treaties listed in the Annex to the Convention (listed in this table as offences A(3)–(13), B (all), C(all), D(1)–(6) and D(13)–(20))[15] [see related action required by Security Council resolutions listed in this table as E(2) and (3)]

(continued)

---

[13]International Convention for the Suppression of the Financing of Terrorism, opened for signature 10 January 2000, 2179 UNTS 232 (entered into force 10 April 1992).

[14]According to article 2(3) of the Financing Convention, it is not necessary that the funds are actually used to carry out an offence under article 2(1) for an act to constitute an offence.

[15]The Annex lists the following nine Conventions: Hague Convention; Montreal Convention; Montreal Protocol; Rome Convention; Rome Protocol; Hostages Convention; Protected Persons Convention; Nuclear Materials Convention; and Bombing Convention. The Annex does not list: the Tokyo Convention on Offences and Certain Other Acts Committed on Board Aircraft (presumably due to the broad nature of the offences therein); the Convention on the Marking of Plastic Explosives for the Purpose of Detection (which does not require States parties to proscribe any conduct – see n 10 above); and the International Convention for the Suppression of Acts of Nuclear Terrorism (which was adopted after the entry into force of the Financing Convention itself).

Table 1 (continued)

Financing Convention, article 2(1)(b) [financing of terrorist act]	8. By any means, directly or indirectly, unlawfully and wilfully, provides or collects funds with the intention that should be used (or in the knowledge that they are to be used) in full or in part to carry out an act intended to cause death or serious bodily injury to a civilian, or to any other person not taking an active part in the hostilities in a situation of armed conflict, when the purpose of such act, by its nature or context, is to intimidate a population, or to compel a government or an international organization to do or to abstain from doing any act [see related action required by Security Council resolutions listed in this table as E(2) and (3)]
Financing Convention, article 2(4) [attempts]	9. Attempt to commit an offence under article 2(1) of the Convention
Financing Convention, article 2(5)(a) [party offences]	10. Participation as an accomplice in an offence under article 2(1) or (4) of the Convention
Financing Convention, article 2(5)(b) [party offences]	11. Organising or directing others to commit an offence under article 2(1) or (4) of the Convention
Financing Convention, article 2(5)(c) [party offences]	12. Intentionally contributing to the commission of an offence under article 2(1) or (4) of the Convention by a group of persons acting with a common purpose made either: (i) with the aim of furthering the general criminal activity or purpose of the group where such activity of purpose involves the commission of an offence under article 2(1) of the Convention; or (ii) in the knowledge of the intention of the group to commit an offence under article 2(1) of the Convention
Nuclear Materials Convention,[16] article 7(1)(a) [possession, etc., of nuclear material]	13. Intentional commission of an act without lawful authority which constitutes the receipt, possession, use, transfer, alteration, disposal or dispersal of nuclear material (as defined by article 1(a) of the Convention) and which causes or is likely to cause death or serious injury to any person or substantial damage to property
Nuclear Materials Convention, article 7(1)(b) [theft of nuclear material]	14. Intentional theft or robbery of nuclear material
Nuclear Materials Convention, article 7(1)(c) [obtaining nuclear material]	15. Intentional embezzlement or fraudulent obtaining of nuclear material
Nuclear Materials Convention, article 7(1)(d) [demanding nuclear material by threat]	16. Intentional commission of an act constituting a demand for nuclear material by threat or use of force or by any other form of intimidation

(continued)

---

[16]Convention on the Physical Protection of Nuclear Material, opened for signature 3 March 1980, 1456 UNTS 124 (entered into force 8 February 1987).

Table 1 (continued)

Nuclear Materials Convention, article 7(1)(e)(i) [threat to use nuclear material]	17. Intentional threat to use nuclear material to cause death or serious injury to any person or substantial property damage
Nuclear Materials Convention, article 7(1)(e)(ii) [threat to commit offences]	18. Intentional threat to commit an offence under art 7(1)(b) of the Convention in order to compel a natural or legal person, international organisation, or State to do or refrain from doing any act
Nuclear Materials Convention, article 7(1)(f) [attempts]	19. Attempt to commit an offence under article 7(1)(a), (b) or (c) of the Convention
Nuclear Materials Convention, article 7(1)(g) [party offences]	20. Participation in any offence under article 7(1)(a) to (f) of the Convention
Nuclear Terrorism Convention,[17] article 2(1)(a) [possession, etc., of radioactive material]	21. Unlawfully and intentionally possesses radioactive material (as defined by article 1(1) of the Convention), or makes or possesses a device (as defined by article 1(4) of the Convention), with the intent to cause: (i) death or serious bodily injury; or (ii) substantial damage to property or to the environment
Nuclear Terrorism Convention, article 2(1)(b) [use of radioactive material]	22. Unlawfully and intentionally uses in any way radioactive material or a device, or uses or damages a nuclear facility (as defined by article 1(3) of the Convention) in a manner which releases or risks the release of radioactive material with the intent to: (i) cause death or serious bodily injury; or (ii) substantial damage to property or to the environment; or (iii) compel a natural or legal person, an international organisation or a State to do or refrain from doing any act
Nuclear Terrorism Convention, article 2(2)(a) [threats]	23. Threatens, under circumstances which indicate the credibility of the threat, to commit an offence under article 2(1)(b) of the Convention
Nuclear Terrorism Convention, article 2(2)(b) [demanding radioactive material]	24. Demands unlawfully and intentionally radioactive material, a device or a nuclear facility by threat, under circumstances which indicate the credibility of the threat, or by use of force
Nuclear Terrorism Convention, article 2(3) [attempts]	25. Attempts to commit an offence under article 2(1) of the Convention
Nuclear Terrorism Convention, article 2(4)(a) [party offences]	26. Participates as an accomplice in an offence under article 2(1), (2) or (3) of the Convention
Nuclear Terrorism Convention, article 2(4)(b) [party offences]	27. Organises or directs others to commit an offence under article 2(1), (2) or (3) of the Convention

(continued)

---

[17]International Convention for the Suppression of Acts of Nuclear Terrorism, adopted by the General Assembly and opened for signature on 15 April 2005 under GA Res 59/290, UN GAOR, 59th Sess, 91st Plen Mtg, UN Doc A/Res/59/290 (2005) and entered into force 7 July 2007.

Table 1 (continued)

| Nuclear Terrorism Convention, article 2(4)(c) [party offences] | 28. Intentionally contributes to the commission of an offence under article 2(1), (2) or (3) of the Convention by a group of persons acting with a common purpose made either: (i) with the aim of furthering the general criminal activity or purpose of the group; or (ii) in the knowledge of the intention of the group to commit such an offence |

E. Security Council resolutions requiring, or calling upon,[18] criminalisation of conduct by persons within a State's territory (7 offences and associated requirements)

Convention	*Offence*
1267 (1999), para 8	1. Violation of measures under para 4 of the Resolution, namely:
[Taliban travel ban]	*4(a)* Requirement for States to deny permission for any aircraft to take off from or land in their territory if it is owned, leased or operated by or on behalf of the Taliban (as designated by the 1267 Committee), unless the particular flight has been approved in advance by the Committee on the grounds of humanitarian need, including religious obligation such as the performance of the Hajj; and
[Taliban freezing of funds]	*4(b)* Requirement for States to freeze funds and other financial resources, including funds derived or generated from property owned or controlled directly or indirectly by the Taliban, or by any undertaking owned or controlled by the Taliban (as designated by the 1267 Committee), and ensure that neither they nor any other funds or financial resources so designated are made available, by their nationals or by any persons within their territory, to or for the benefit of the Taliban or any undertaking owned or controlled, directly or indirectly, by the Taliban, except as may be authorized by the Committee on a case-by-case basis on the grounds of humanitarian need
1373 (2001), para 1(b) [financing of terrorist act]	2. Wilful provision or collection, by any means, directly or indirectly, of funds by their nationals or in their territories with the intention that the funds should be used, or in the knowledge that they are to be used, in order to carry out terrorist acts [see offences listed in this table as D(7) and (8)]
1373 (2001), para 1(c) [freezing of terrorists' assets]	*This is an obligation upon States which does not expressly call for criminalisation, but which has been responded to by criminalising dealings with terrorist property:* 3. Freeze without delay funds and other financial assets or economic resources of persons who commit, or attempt to commit, terrorist acts or participate in or facilitate the commission of terrorist acts; of entities owned or

(*continued*)

---

[18]States are called upon to prohibit the offence identified in SC Res 1624 (2005), para 1(a) [listed in the table as E(4)]. States are bound, under article 25 of the Charter of the United Nations, to criminalise all other offences. For a discussion on the distinction between binding and recommendatory features of Security Council resolutions see Chap. 3 herein, Sect. 3.2.3.

Table 1 (continued)

	controlled directly or indirectly by such persons; and of persons and entities acting on behalf of, or at the direction of such persons and entities, including funds derived or generated from property owned or controlled directly or indirectly by such persons and associated persons and entities
1373 (2001), para 1(d) [making assets or services available to terrorists]	4. Making any funds, financial assets or economic resources or financial or other related services available, directly or indirectly, for the benefit of persons who commit or attempt to commit or facilitate or participate in the commission of terrorist acts, of entities owned or controlled, directly or indirectly, by such persons and of persons and entities acting on behalf of or at the direction of such persons [see offences listed in this table as D(7) and (8)]
1373 (2001), para 2(a) [recruitment]	*This is an obligation upon States which does not expressly call for criminalisation, but which has been responded to by criminalising the recruitment of members of terrorist groups, and/or participation in terrorist groups:* 5. Suppressing recruitment of members of terrorist groups
1373 (2001), para 2(d) [prevention]	*This is an obligation upon States which does not expressly call for criminalisation, but which has been responded to by criminalising the harbouring or concealing of terrorists, as well as activities within a State's territory, such as weapons and other training:* 6. Prevent those who finance, plan, facilitate or commit terrorist acts from using their territory for those purposes
1624 (2005), para 1(a) [incitement]	7. Incitement to commit a terrorist act or acts

Table 2 **Terrorism-related offences in Australia**

A. Offences under the Criminal Code Act 1995 (see Chap. 5, at Sect. 5.1.1.4)

Offence	*Related Convention and/or SC resolution*
Terrorist bombing (section 72.3): (1) A person commits an offence if: (a) the person intentionally delivers, places, discharges or detonates a device; and (b) the device is an explosive or other lethal device and the person is reckless as to that fact; and (c) the device is delivered, placed, discharged, or detonated, to, in, into or against: (i) a place of public use; or (ii) a government facility; or (iii) public transportation system; or (iv) an infrastructure facility; and (d) the person intends to cause death or serious harm	Bombing Convention, article 2(1)(a)
(2) A person commits an offence if: (a) the person intentionally delivers, places, discharges or detonates a device; and (b) the device is an explosive or other lethal device and the person is reckless as to that fact; and (c) the device is delivered, placed, discharged, or detonated, to, in, into or against: (i) a place of public use; or (ii) a government facility; or (iii) a public transportation system; or (iv) an infrastructure facility; and (d) the person intends to cause extensive destruction to the place, facility or system; and (e) the person is reckless as to whether that intended destruction results or is likely to result in major economic loss	Bombing Convention, article 2(1)(b)
Trafficking in unmarked plastic explosives (section 72.12(1)): A person commits an offence if: (a) the person traffics in a substance; and (b) the substance is a plastic explosive; and (c) the plastic explosive breaches a marking requirement; and (d) the trafficking is not authorised under section 72.18, 72.19, 72.20, 72.21, 72.22 or 72.23	This offence is not required of the Plastic Explosives Convention, but is in furtherance to it – see Chap. 14 at Sect. 14.2.3
Importing or exporting unmarked plastic explosives (section 72.13): (1) A person commits an offence if: (a) the person imports or exports a substance; and (b) the substance is a plastic explosive; and (c) the plastic explosive breaches a marking requirement; and (d) the import or export is not authorised under section 72.18, 72.19, 72.20, 72.22 or 72.23	This offence is not required of the Plastic Explosives Convention, but is in furtherance to it – see Chap. 14 at Sect. 14.2.3

(continued)

Table 2 (continued)

Manufacturing unmarked plastic explosives (section 72.14): (1) A person commits an offence if: (a) the person: (i) engages in the manufacture of a substance; or (ii) exercises control or direction over the manufacture of a substance; and (b) the substance is a plastic explosive; and (c) the plastic explosive breaches the first marking requirement; and (d) the manufacture is not authorised under section 72.18 or 72.21	This offence is not required of the Plastic Explosives Convention, but is in furtherance to it – see Chap. 14 at Sect. 14.2.3
Possessing unmarked plastic explosives (section 72.15): (1) A person commits an offence if: (a) the person possesses a substance; and (b) the substance is a plastic explosive; and (c) the plastic explosive breaches a marking requirement; and (d) the possession is not authorised under section 72.18, 72.19, 72.20, 72.21, 72.22 or 72.23	This offence is not required of the Plastic Explosives Convention, but is in furtherance to it – see Chap. 14 at Sect. 14.2.3
Packaging requirements for plastic explosives (section 72.17): (1) A person commits an offence if: (a) the person manufactures a substance; and (b) the substance is a plastic explosive; and (c) within 24 hours after the manufacture of the plastic explosive, the person does not cause the plastic explosive to be contained, enclosed or packaged in a wrapper with: (i) the expression "PLASTIC EXPLOSIVE" (in upper-case lettering); and (ii) the date of manufacture of the plastic explosive; and (iii) if the plastic explosive is of a prescribed type – that type; and (iv) if the plastic explosive contains a detection agent for the purpose of meeting the first marking requirement – the name of the detection agent; and (v) if the plastic explosive contains a detection agent for the purpose of meeting the first marking requirement – the concentration of the detection agent in the plastic explosive at the time of manufacture, expressed as a percentage by mass; legibly displayed on the outer surface of the wrapper	This offence is not required of the Plastic Explosives Convention, but is in furtherance to it – see Chap. 14 at Sect. 14.2.3
Incitement (section 80.2(5)): A person commits an offence if: (a) the person urges a group or groups (whether distinguished by race, religion, nationality or political opinion) to use force or violence against another group or other groups (as so distinguished); and (b) the use of the force or violence would threaten the peace, order and good government of the Commonwealth	SC Res 1624 (2005), para 1(a)

(continued)

Table 2 (continued)

Urging a person to assist the enemy (section 80.2(7)): A person commits an offence if: (a) the person urges another person to engage in conduct; and (b) the first-mentioned person intends the conduct to assist an organisation or country; and (c) the organisation or country is: (i) at war with the Commonwealth, whether or not the existence of a state of war has been declared; and (ii) specified by Proclamation made for the purpose of paragraph 80.1(1)(e) to be an enemy at war with the Commonwealth	See Chap. 14 at Sect. 14.2.3
Urging a person to assist those engaged in armed hostilities (section 80.2(8)): A person commits an offence if: (a) the person urges another person to engage in conduct; and (b) the first-mentioned person intends the conduct to assist an organisation or country; and (c) the organisation or country is engaged in armed hostilities against the Australian Defence Force	See Chap. 14 at Sect. 14.2.3
Engaging in a terrorist act (section 101.1(1)): A person commits an offence if the person engages in a terrorist act	SC Res 1373 (2001), para 2(d), but see Chap. 14 and Sect. 14.2.3
Providing or receiving training connected with terrorist acts (section 101.2): (1) A person commits an offence if: (a) the person provides or receives training; and (b) the training is connected with preparation for, the engagement of a person in, or assistance in a terrorist act; and (c) the person mentioned in paragraph (a) knows of the connection described in paragraph (b). (2) A person commits an offence if: (a) the person provides or receives training; and (b) the training is connected with preparation for, the engagement of a person in, or assistance in a terrorist act; and (c) the person mentioned in paragraph (a) is reckless as to the existence of the connection described in paragraph (b)	SC Res 1373 (2001), paras 2(a) and (d)
Possessing things connected with terrorist acts (section 101.4): (1) A person commits an offence if: (a) the person possesses a thing; and (b) the thing is connected with preparation for, the engagement of a person in, or assistance in a terrorist act; and (c) the person mentioned in paragraph (a) knows of the connection described in paragraph (b).	SC Res 1373 (2001), para 2(d)

(continued)

Table 2 (continued)

(2) A person commits an offence if: (a) the person possesses a thing; and (b) the thing is connected with preparation for, the engagement of a person in, or assistance in a terrorist act; and (c) the person mentioned in paragraph (a) is reckless as to the existence of the connection described in paragraph (b)	
Collecting or making documents likely to facilitate terrorist acts (section 101.5): (1) A person commits an offence if: (a) the person collects or makes a document; and (b) the document is connected with preparation for, the engagement of a person in, or assistance in a terrorist act; and (c) the person mentioned in paragraph (a) knows of the connection described in paragraph (b). (2) A person commits an offence if: (a) the person collects or makes a document; and (b) the document is connected with preparation for, the engagement of a person in, or assistance in a terrorist act; and (c) the person mentioned in paragraph (a) is reckless as to the existence of the connection described in paragraph (b)	SC Res 1373 (2001), para 2(d)
Other acts done in preparation for, or planning, terrorist acts (section 101.6(1)): A person commits an offence if the person does any act in preparation for, or planning, a terrorist act	SC Res 1373 (2001), para 2(d)
Directing the activities of a terrorist organisation (section 102.2): (1) A person commits an offence if: (a) the person intentionally directs the activities of an organisation; and (b) the organisation is a terrorist organisation; and (c) the person knows the organisation is a terrorist organisation. (2) A person commits an offence if: (a) the person intentionally directs the activities of an organisation; and (b) the organisation is a terrorist organisation; and (c) the person is reckless as to whether the organisation is a terrorist organisation	SC Res 1373 (2001), para 2(d)
Membership in a terrorist organisation (section 102.3(1)): A person commits an offence if: (a) the person intentionally is a member of an organisation; and (b) the organisation is a terrorist organisation; and (c) the person knows the organisation is a terrorist organisation	SC Res 1373 (2001), para 2(a)

(continued)

Table 2 (continued)

Recruiting for a terrorist organisation (section 102.4): (1) A person commits an offence if: (a) the person intentionally recruits a person to join, or participate in the activities of, an organisation; and (b) the organisation is a terrorist organisation; and (c) the first-mentioned person knows the organisation is a terrorist organisation. (2) A person commits an offence if: (a) the person intentionally recruits a person to join, or participate in the activities of, an organisation; and (b) the organisation is a terrorist organisation; and (c) the first-mentioned person is reckless as to whether the organisation is a terrorist organisation	SC Res 1373 (2001), para 2(a)
Training a terrorist organisation, or receiving training from a terrorist organisation (section 102.5): (1) A person commits an offence if: (a) the person intentionally provides training to, or intentionally receives training from, an organisation; and (b) the organisation is a terrorist organisation; and (c) the person is reckless as to whether the organisation is a terrorist organisation. (2) A person commits an offence if: (a) the person intentionally provides training to, or intentionally receives training from, an organisation; and (b) the organisation is a terrorist organisation that is covered by paragraph (b) of the definition of terrorist organisation in subsection 102.1(1)	SC Res 1373 (2001), para 2(a) and (d)
Getting funds to, from, or for a terrorist organisation (section 102.6): (1) A person commits an offence if: (a) the person intentionally: (i) receives funds from, or makes funds available to, an organisation (whether directly or indirectly); or (ii) collects funds for, or on behalf of, an organisation (whether directly or indirectly); and (b) the organisation is a terrorist organisation; and (c) the person knows the organisation is a terrorist organisation. (2) A person commits an offence if: (a) the person intentionally: (i) receives funds from, or makes funds available to, an organisation (whether directly or indirectly); or (ii) collects funds for, or on behalf of, an organisation (whether directly or indirectly); and (b) the organisation is a terrorist organisation; and (c) the person is reckless as to whether the organisation is a terrorist organisation	SC Res 1373 (2001), para 1(b)
Providing support to a terrorist organisation (section 102.7): (1) A person commits an offence if: (a) the person intentionally provides to an organisation support or resources that would help the organisation	SC Res 1373 (2001), paras 1(d) and 2(d)

(continued)

Table 2 (continued)

engage in an activity described in paragraph (a) of the
definition of terrorist organisation in this Division; and
(b) the organisation is a terrorist organisation; and
(c) the person knows the organisation is a terrorist
organisation.
(2) A person commits an offence if:
(a) the person intentionally provides to an organisation
support or resources that would help the organisation
engage in an activity described in paragraph (a) of the
definition of terrorist organisation in this Division; and
(b) the organisation is a terrorist organisation; and
(c) the person is reckless as to whether the organisation
is a terrorist organisation

Associating with terrorist organisations (section 102.8):	SC Res 1373 (2001), para 2(d)

(1) A person commits an offence if:
(a) on 2 or more occasions:
(i) the person intentionally associates with another
person who is a member of, or a person who promotes or
directs the activities of, an organisation; and
(ii) the person knows that the organisation is a terrorist
organisation; and
(iii) the association provides support to the
organisation; and
(iv) the person intends that the support assist the
organisation to expand or to continue to exist; and
(v) the person knows that the other person is a member
of, or a person who promotes or directs the activities of,
the organisation; and
(b) the organisation is a terrorist organisation because of
paragraph (b) of the definition of terrorist organisation in
this Division (whether or not the organisation is a
terrorist organisation because of paragraph (a) of that
definition also).
(2) A person commits an offence if:
(a) the person has previously been convicted of an
offence against subsection (1); and
(b) the person intentionally associates with another
person who is a member of, or a person who promotes or
directs the activities of, an organisation; and
(c) the person knows that the organisation is a terrorist
organisation; and
(d) the association provides support to the organisation;
and
(e) the person intends that the support assist the
organisation to expand or to continue to exist; and
(f) the person knows that the other person is a member
of, or a person who promotes or directs the activities of,
the organisation; and
(g) the organisation is a terrorist organisation because of
paragraph (b) of the definition of terrorist organisation in
this Division (whether or not the organisation is a
terrorist organisation because of paragraph (a) of that
definition also)

(continued)

Table 2 (continued)

Financing terrorism (section 103.1): (1) A person commits an offence if: (a) the person provides or collects funds; and (b) the person is reckless as to whether the funds will be used to facilitate or engage in a terrorist act. (2) A person commits an offence under subsection (1) even if: (a) a terrorist act does not occur; or (b) the funds will not be used to facilitate or engage in a specific terrorist act; or (c) the funds will be used to facilitate or engage in more than one terrorist act	Financing Convention, article 2(1) SC Res 1373 (2001), para 1(b)
Financing a terrorist (section 103.2): (1) A person commits an offence if: (a) the person intentionally: (i) makes funds available to another person (whether directly or indirectly); or (ii) collects funds for, or on behalf of, another person (whether directly or indirectly); and (b) the first-mentioned person is reckless as to whether the other person will use the funds to facilitate or engage in a terrorist act. (2) A person commits an offence under subsection (1) even if: (a) a terrorist act does not occur; or (b) the funds will not be used to facilitate or engage in a specific terrorist act; or (c) the funds will be used to facilitate or engage in more than one terrorist act	Financing Convention, article 2(1) SC Res 1373 (2001), para 1(b)
Contravening a control order (section 104.27): A person commits an offence if: (a) a control order is in force in relation to the person; and (b) the person contravenes the order	Enforcement of preventive measures – see Chap. 14 at Sect. 14.2.3
Disclosure offences related to preventative detention (section 105.41): (1) A person (the subject) commits an offence if: (a) the subject is being detained under a preventative detention order; and (b) the subject discloses to another person: (i) the fact that a preventative detention order has been made in relation to the subject; or (ii) the fact that the subject is being detained; or (iii) the period for which the subject is being detained; and (c) the disclosure occurs while the subject is being detained under the order; and (d) the disclosure is not one that the subject is entitled to make under section 105.36, 105.37 or 105.39.	Enforcement of preventive measures – see Chap. 14 at Sect. 14.2.3

(continued)

Table 2 (continued)

(2) A person (the lawyer) commits an offence if:

(a) a person being detained under a preventative detention order (the detainee) contacts the lawyer under section 105.37; and

(b) the lawyer discloses to another person:

(i) the fact that a preventative detention order has been made in relation to the detainee; or

(ii) the fact that the detainee is being detained; or

(iii) the period for which the detainee is being detained; or

(iv) any information that the detainee gives the lawyer in the course of the contact; and

(c) the disclosure occurs while the detainee is being detained under the order; and

(d) the disclosure is not made for the purposes of:

(i) proceedings in a federal court for a remedy relating to the preventative detention order or the treatment of the detainee in connection with the detainee's detention under the order; or

(ii) a complaint to the Commonwealth Ombudsman under the Ombudsman Act 1976 in relation to the application for, or making of, the preventative detention order or the treatment of the detainee by an AFP member in connection with the detainee's detention under the order; or

(iia) the giving of information under section 40SA of the Australian Federal Police Act 1979 in relation to the application for, or making of, the preventative detention order or the treatment of the detainee by an AFP member in connection with the detainee's detention under the order; or

(iii) a complaint to an officer or authority of a State or Territory about the treatment of the detainee by a member of the police force of that State or Territory in connection with the detainee's detention under the order; or

(iv) making representations to the senior AFP member nominated under subsection 105.19(5) in relation to the order, or another police officer involved in the detainee's detention, about the exercise of powers under the order, the performance of obligations in relation to the order or the treatment of the detainee in connection with the detainee's detention under the order.

(3) A person (the parent/guardian) commits an offence if:

(a) a person being detained under a preventative detention order (the detainee) has contact with the parent/guardian under section 105.39; and

(b) the parent/guardian discloses to another person:

(i) the fact that a preventative detention order has been made in relation to the detainee; or

(ii) the fact that the detainee is being detained; or

(*continued*)

Table 2 (continued)

(iii) the period for which the detainee is being detained; or

(iv) any information that the detainee gives the parent/guardian in the course of the contact; and

(c) the other person is not a person the detainee is entitled to have contact with under section 105.39; and

(d) the disclosure occurs while the detainee is being detained under the order; and

(e) the disclosure is not made for the purposes of:

(i) a complaint to the Commonwealth Ombudsman under the Ombudsman Act 1976 in relation to the application for, or the making of, the preventative detention order or the treatment of the detainee by an AFP member in connection with the detainee's detention under the order; or

(ia) the giving of information under section 40SA of the Australian Federal Police Act 1979 in relation to the application for, or the making of, the preventative detention order or the treatment of the detainee by an AFP member in connection with the detainee's detention under the order; or

(ii) a complaint to an officer or authority of a State or Territory about the treatment of the detainee by a member of the police force of that State or Territory in connection with the detainee's detention under the order; or

(iii) making representations to the senior AFP member nominated under subsection 105.19(5) in relation to the order, or another police officer involved in the detainee's detention, about the exercise of powers under the order, the performance of obligations in relation to the order or the treatment of the detainee in connection with the detainee's detention under the order.

(4A) A person (the parent/guardian) commits an offence if:

(a) the parent/guardian is a parent or guardian of a person who is being detained under a preventative detention order (the detainee); and

(b) the detainee has contact with the parent/guardian under section 105.39; and

(c) while the detainee is being detained under the order, the parent/guardian discloses information of the kind referred to in paragraph (3)(b) to another parent or guardian of the detainee (the other parent/guardian); and

(d) when the disclosure is made, the detainee has not had contact with the other parent/guardian under section 105.39 while being detained under the order; and

(e) the parent/guardian does not, before making the disclosure, inform the senior AFP member nominated under subsection 105.19(5) in relation to the order that the parent/guardian is proposing to disclose information of that kind to the other parent/guardian.

(*continued*)

Table 2 (continued)

(5) A person (the interpreter) commits an offence if:
(a) the interpreter is an interpreter who assists in monitoring the contact that a person being detained under a preventative detention order (the detainee) has with someone while the detainee is being detained under the order; and
(b) the interpreter discloses to another person:
(i)   the fact that a preventative detention order has been made in relation to the detainee; or
(ii) the fact that the detainee is being detained; or
(iii) the period for which the detainee is being detained; or
(iv) any information that interpreter obtains in the course of assisting in the monitoring of that contact; and
(c) the disclosure occurs while the detainee is being detained under the order.
(6) A person (the disclosure recipient) commits an offence if:
(a) a person (the earlier discloser) discloses to the disclosure recipient:
(i) the fact that a preventative detention order has been made in relation to a person; or
(ii) the fact that a person is being detained under a preventative detention order; or
(iii) the period for which a person is being detained under a preventative detention order; or
(iv) any information that a person who is being detained under a preventative detention order communicates to a person while the person is being detained under the order; and
(b) the disclosure by the earlier discloser to the disclosure recipient contravenes:
(i) subsection (1), (2), (3) or (5); or
(ii) this subsection; and
(c) the disclosure recipient discloses that information to another person; and
(d) the disclosure by the disclosure recipient occurs while the person referred to in subparagraph (a)(i), (ii), (iii) or (iv) is being detained under the order.
(7) A person (the monitor) commits an offence if:
(a) the monitor is:
(i) a police officer who monitors; or
(ii) an interpreter who assists in monitoring; contact that a person being detained under a preventative detention order (the detainee) has with a lawyer under section 105.37 while the detainee is being detained under the order; and
(b) information is communicated in the course of that contact; and
(c) the information is communicated for one of the purposes referred to in subsection 105.37(1); and
(d) the monitor discloses that information to another person

(*continued*)

Table 2 (continued)

B. Offences under the Crimes (Aviation) Act 1991 (see Chap. 5, at Sect. 5.1.2)	
Offence	*Related Convention and/or SC resolution*
Aircraft hijacking (section 13): (1) A person who hijacks an aircraft [section 9 of the Act provides that "a person hijacks an aircraft if, while on board the aircraft, the person seizes, or exercises control of, the aircraft by force or threat of force, or by any other form of intimidation"] is guilty of an indictable offence if any of the following applies when the hijacking is committed: (a) the aircraft is in flight, within the meaning of the Hague Convention, and the Hague Convention requires Australia to make the hijacking punishable; (b) the aircraft is engaged in a prescribed flight; (c) the aircraft is a Commonwealth aircraft; (d) the aircraft is a visiting government aircraft. (2) A person who hijacks an aircraft is guilty of an indictable offence if: (a) the hijacking is committed outside Australia; and (b) the person who commits the hijacking is an Australian citizen; and (c) the aircraft would, if the Hague Convention applied, be considered to be in flight	Hague Convention, article 1(a)
Other acts of violence on an aircraft in flight (section 14): (1) Where: (a) a person on board an aircraft commits an act of violence against all or any of the passengers or crew; and (b) the act would, if committed in the Jervis Bay Territory, be an offence against a law in force in that Territory (other than this Act); the person is guilty of an offence if any of the following applies when the act is committed: (c) Article 4 of the Hague Convention requires Australia to establish its jurisdiction over the act; (d) the aircraft is engaged in a prescribed flight; (e) the aircraft is a Commonwealth aircraft; (f) the aircraft is a visiting government aircraft; (g) the aircraft is outside Australia but the person who does the act is an Australian citizen	Montreal Convention, article 1(1)(a); and Hague Convention, article 4
Taking control of an aircraft (section 16): (1) A person who takes or exercises control of a Division 3 aircraft is guilty of an offence punishable on conviction by imprisonment for 7 years. (2) A person who takes or exercises control of a Division 3 aircraft and who does so while anyone else, other than an accomplice of the person, is on board the aircraft, is guilty of an offence punishable on conviction by imprisonment for 14 years.	Hague Convention, article 1(a)

(continued)

Table 2 (continued)

(3) A person who takes or exercises control of a Division 3 aircraft and who does so: (a) by force or threat of force, or by any trick or false pretence; and (b) while anyone else, other than an accomplice of the person, is on board the aircraft;	
Destruction of an aircraft (section 17(1)): A person must not intentionally destroy a Division 3 aircraft	Montreal Convention, article 1(1)(b)
Destructions on an aircraft with intent to kill (section 18(1)): A person who destroys a Division 3 aircraft with the intention of causing anyone's death, or reckless as to the safety of anyone's life, is guilty of an indictable offence punishable on conviction by imprisonment for life	Montreal Convention, article 1(1)(b)
Prejudicing the safe operation of an aircraft (section 19(1)): A person must not do anything capable of prejudicing the safe operation of a Division 3 aircraft with the intention of prejudicing the safe operation of the aircraft	Tokyo Convention, article 1(1)(b)
Prejudicing the safe operation of an aircraft with intent to kill (section 20(1)): A person who does anything capable of prejudicing the safe operation of a Division 3 aircraft: (a) with the intention of prejudicing the safe operation of the aircraft; and (b) with the intention of causing anyone's death, or reckless as to the safety of anyone's life; is guilty of an indictable offence punishable on conviction by imprisonment for life	Tokyo Convention, article 1(1)(b)
Assaulting crew (section 21(1)): A person must not, while on board a Division 3 aircraft, assault, threaten with violence, or otherwise intimidate, a member of the crew of the aircraft in a manner that results in: (a) an interference with the member's performance of functions or duties connected with the operation of the aircraft; or (b) a lessening of the member's ability to perform those functions or duties	Tokyo Convention, article 1(1)(a)
Endangering safety of aircraft (section 22(1)): A person who, while on board a Division 3 aircraft, does an act, reckless as to whether the act will endanger the safety of the aircraft, is guilty of an offence	Tokyo Convention, article 1(1)(b); and Montreal Convention, article 1(1)(b) and (c)
Dangerous goods (section 23(1)): A person must not: (a) carry or place dangerous goods on board a Division 3 aircraft; or	Montreal Convention, article 1(1)(c)

(*continued*)

Table 2 (continued)

(b) deliver dangerous goods to anyone else with the intention of placing the goods on board such an aircraft; or (c) have dangerous goods in his or her possession on board such an aircraft	
Threats and false statements (section 24): (1) A person must not threaten to destroy, damage or endanger the safety of a Division 3 aircraft, or to kill or injure anyone on board such an aircraft (2) A person must not make a statement or communicate information, being a statement or information that he or she knows to be false, to the effect, or from which it can reasonably be inferred, that there has been, is or is to be, a plan, proposal, attempt, conspiracy or threat: (a) to take or exercise control, by force, of a Division 3 aircraft; or (b) to destroy, damage or endanger the safety of such an aircraft; or (c) to kill or injure anyone on board such an aircraft	– Montreal Convention, article 1(1)(e)
Endangering the safety of aircraft in flight (sections 10 and 25): 10(1) For the purposes of Division 4 of Part 2, a person commits an unlawful act if he or she: (a) commits an act of violence against anyone on board an aircraft in flight, being an act likely to endanger the safety of the aircraft; or (b) destroys an aircraft in service, or causes damage to such an aircraft which renders it incapable of flight or which is likely to endanger its safety in flight. 10(2) For the purposes of Division 4 of Part 2, a person commits an unlawful act if he or she does any of the following: (a) places, or causes to be placed, on an aircraft in service a substance or thing that is likely to destroy the aircraft; (b) places, or causes to be placed, on an aircraft in service a substance or thing that is likely to cause damage to the aircraft which renders it incapable of flight or which is likely to endanger its safety in flight; (c) destroys or damages any navigation facilities or interferes with their operation, being destruction, damage or interference that is likely to endanger the safety of an aircraft in flight; (d) communicates information which he or she knows to be false, thereby endangering the safety of an aircraft in flight. 25(1) A person who commits an unlawful act of the kind mentioned in subsection 10(1) is guilty of an offence if any of the following applies: (a) the Montreal Convention requires Australia to make the act punishable; (b) the aircraft concerned is:	Montreal Convention, article 1(1)

(*continued*)

Table 2 (continued)

(i) an aircraft in service in the course of, or in connection with, a prescribed flight; or (ii) a Commonwealth aircraft; or (iii) a defence aircraft; or (iv) a visiting government aircraft; (c) the person is an Australian citizen who commits the act outside Australia. 25(2) A person who commits an unlawful act of the kind mentioned in subsection 10(2) is guilty of an offence if any of the following applies: (a) the Montreal Convention requires Australia to make the act punishable; (b) except where paragraph (c) applies, the aircraft concerned is: (i) an aircraft in service in the course of, or in connection with, a prescribed flight; or (ii) a Commonwealth aircraft; or (iii) a defence aircraft; or (iv) a visiting government aircraft; (c) in the case of an act relating to air navigation facilities – the facilities are used in connection with: (i) prescribed flights; or (ii) flights of Commonwealth aircraft; or (iii) flights of defence aircraft; or (iv) flights of visiting government aircraft; (d) the person is an Australian citizen who commits the act outside Australia	
Acts of violence at airports (section 26): (1) A person is guilty of an offence if: (a) the person uses a substance or thing to commit an act of violence against anyone at a prescribed airport; and (b) that act: (i) causes or is likely to cause serious injury or death; and (ii) endangers, or is likely to endanger, the safe operation of the airport or the safety of anyone at the airport; and (c) the Montreal Convention, when read together with the Protocol, requires Australia to make the act punishable; and (d) Article 5 of that Convention, when so read, requires Australia to establish its jurisdiction over the offence.	Montreal Convention, article 1 (1bis)(a)
(2) A person is guilty of an offence if: (a) the person does any of the following things: (i) destroys or seriously damages the facilities of a prescribed airport; (ii) destroys or seriously damages any aircraft not in service that is at a prescribed airport; (iii) disrupts the services of a prescribed airport; and (b) doing so endangers, or is likely to endanger, the safe operation of the airport or the safety of anyone at the airport; and (c) either of the following applies: (i) the Montreal Convention, when read together with the	Montreal Convention, article 1 (1bis)(b)

(*continued*)

Table 2 (continued)

Protocol, requires Australia to make the act concerned punishable; (ii) if the act concerned relates to an aircraft – the aircraft is in Australia, or is a Commonwealth aircraft or a defence aircraft, or the act is committed by an Australian citizen, whether in Australia or not	

C. Offences under the Aviation Transport Security Act 2004 (see Chap. 5, at Sect. 5.1.2)

Offence	*Related Convention and/or SC resolution*
Weapons in airside areas, landside security zones and landside event zones (section 46): A person commits an offence if: (a) the person is in an airside area, a landside security zone or a landside event zone; and (b) the person has a weapon in his or her possession; and (c) the person is not: (i) a law enforcement officer; or (ii) a member of the Australian Defence Force who is on duty; or (iii) authorised by the regulations, or permitted in writing by the Secretary, to have the weapon in his or her possession in the airside area, landside security zone or landside event zone	This offence is not required of the Montreal Convention or Protocol, but can be described as being in furtherance to them – see Chap. 14 at Sect. 14.2.3
Carrying weapons through a screening point (section 47): A person commits an offence if: (a) the person passes through a screening point; and (b) the person has a weapon in his or her possession when he or she passes through the screening point; and (c) the person is not: (i) a law enforcement officer; or (ii) authorised by the regulations, or permitted in writing by the Secretary, to pass through the screening point with the weapon in his or her possession	This offence is not required of the Montreal Convention or Protocol, but can be described as being in furtherance to them – see Chap. 14 at Sect. 14.2.3
Possession of a weapon on an aircraft (sections 48 and 49): A person commits an offence if: (a) the person is on board a prescribed aircraft; and (b) the person: (i) carries a weapon; or (ii) otherwise has in his or her possession a weapon that is located at a place that is accessible to the person; and (c) the person is not a law enforcement officer; and (d) the carriage or possession of the weapon is not authorised by the regulations or permitted in writing by the Secretary; and (e) neither of the following apply: (i) the weapon is under the control of the pilot in command of the aircraft because the weapon forms part of the equipment of the aircraft in accordance with the operations manual for the aircraft;	This offence is not required of the Montreal Convention or Protocol, but can be described as being in furtherance to them – see Chap. 14 at Sect. 14.2.3

(*continued*)

Table 2 (continued)

(ii) the weapon is under the control of the pilot in command of the aircraft because an animal that could endanger the safety of the aircraft, or the safety of people on board the aircraft, is being carried on board the aircraft	

D. Offences under the Crimes (Ships and Fixed Platforms) Act 1992 (see Chap. 5, at Sect. 5.1.3)

Offence	*Related Convention and/or SC resolution*
Seizing a ship (section 8): A person must not take possession of, or take or exercise control over, a private ship [as defined by section 3] by the threat or use of force or by any other kind of intimidation	Rome Convention, article 3(1)(a)
Violence on a ship (section 9): A person must not perform an act of violence against a person on board a private ship knowing that the act is likely to endanger the safe navigation of the ship	Rome Convention, article 3(1)(b)
Destroying or damaging a ship (section 10): (1) A person must not engage in conduct that causes the destruction of a private ship. (2) A person must not engage in conduct that causes damage to a private ship or its cargo, knowing that such damage is likely to endanger the safe navigation of the ship	Rome Convention, article 3(1)(c)
Placing destructive devices on a ship (section 11): (1) A person must not place or cause to be placed on a private ship, by any means, a device or substance that is likely to destroy the ship. (2) A person must not place or cause to be placed on a private ship, by any means, a device or substance that is likely to cause damage to the ship or its cargo knowing that it is likely to endanger the safe navigation of the ship	Rome Convention, article 3(1)(d)
Destroying or damaging navigational facilities (section 12): A person must not engage in conduct that causes: (a) the destruction of maritime navigational facilities; or (b) serious damage to such facilities; or (c) serious interference with the operation of such facilities; if the destruction, damage or interference is likely to endanger the safe navigation of a private ship	Rome Convention, article 3(1)(e)
Communicating false information (section 13): A person must not communicate false information knowing that the communication will endanger the safe navigation of a private ship	Rome Convention, article 3(1)(f)
Causing death (section 14): A person who engages in conduct that causes the death of another person in connection with the commission or	Rome Convention, article 3(1)(g)

(*continued*)

Table 2 (continued)

attempted commission of an offence against any of sections 8 to 13 is guilty of an offence	
Causing grievous bodily harm (section 15): A person who engages in conduct that causes grievous bodily harm to another person in connection with the commission or attempted commission of an offence against any of sections 8 to 13 is guilty of an offence	Rome Convention, article 3(1)(g)
Causing injury (section 16): A person who engages in conduct that causes injury to another person in connection with the commission or attempted commission of an offence against any of sections 8 to 13 is guilty of an offence	Rome Convention, article 3(1)(g)
Threats to commit offences under the Convention (section 17): (1) A person must not threaten to do an act that would constitute an offence against section 9, 10 or 12 with intent to compel an individual, a body corporate or a body politic to do or refrain from doing an act, if that threat is likely to endanger the safe navigation of the ship concerned. (2) For the purposes of this section, a person is taken to threaten to do an act if the person makes any statement or does anything else indicating, or from which it could reasonably be inferred, that it is his or her intention to do that act	Rome Convention, article 3(2)(c)
Seizing control of a fixed platform (section 21): A person must not take possession of, or take or exercise control over, a fixed platform by the threat or use of force or by any other kind of intimidation	Rome Protocol, article 2(1)(a)
Violence on a fixed platform (section 22): A person must not perform an act of violence against a person on board a fixed platform knowing that the act is likely to endanger the safety of the platform	Rome Protocol, article 2(1)(b)
Destroying or damaging a fixed platform (section 23): A person must not engage in conduct that causes the destruction of, or damage to, a fixed platform knowing that the destruction or damage is likely to endanger its safety	Rome Protocol, article 2(1)(c)
Placing destructive devices on a fixed platform (section 24): A person must not place or cause to be placed on a fixed platform, by any means, a device or substance knowing that it is likely to destroy the fixed platform or endanger its safety	Rome Protocol, article 2(1)(d)
Causing death (section 25): A person who engages in conduct that causes the death of another person in connection with the commission or attempted commission of an offence against any of sections 21 to 24 is guilty of an offence	Rome Protocol, article 2(1)(e)

(continued)

Table 2 (continued)

Causing grievous bodily injury (section 26): A person who engages in conduct that causes grievous bodily harm to another person in connection with the commission or attempted commission of an offence against any of sections 21 to 24 is guilty of an offence	Rome Protocol, article 2(1)(e)
Causing injury (section 27): A person who engages in conduct that causes injury to another person in connection with the commission or attempted commission of an offence against any of sections 21 to 24 is guilty of an offence	Rome Protocol, article 2(1)(e)
Threatening to endanger a fixed platform (section 28): (1) A person must not threaten to do an act that would constitute an offence against section 22 or 23 with intent to compel an individual, a body corporate or a body politic to do or refrain from doing an act, if that threat is likely to endanger the safety of a fixed platform. (2) For the purposes of this section, a person is taken to threaten to do an act if the person makes any statement or does anything else indicating, or from which it could reasonably be inferred, that it is his or her intention to do that act	Rome Protocol, article 2(2)(c)

E. Offences under the Crimes (Hostages) Act 1989 (see Chap. 5, at Sect. 5.1.4)

Offence	*Related Convention and/or SC resolution*
Meaning of hostage-taking (section 7): For the purposes of this Act, a person commits an act of hostage-taking if the person: (a) seizes or detains another person (in this section called the hostage); and (b) threatens to kill, to injure, or to continue to detain, the hostage; with the intention of compelling: (c) a legislative, executive or judicial institution in Australia or in a foreign country; (d) an international intergovernmental organisation; or (e) any other person (whether an individual or a body corporate) or group of persons; to do, or abstain from doing, any act as an explicit or implicit condition for the release of the hostage.	Hostages Convention, article 1(1)
When hostage-taking an offence (section 8): (1) A person who, at any time after the Convention enters into force for Australia, commits an act of hostage-taking is guilty of an offence against this subsection. (2) The punishment for an offence against subsection (1) is imprisonment for life or for any lesser term. (3) Subject to section 9, a person shall not be charged with an offence against this Act unless: (a) the act alleged to constitute the offence was committed:	

(continued)

Table 2 (continued)

(i) in Australia; or
(ii) on an Australian ship or an Australian aircraft,
whether in or outside Australia; or
(b) where the act alleged to constitute the offence was
committed outside Australia (otherwise than on an
Australian ship or an Australian aircraft):
(i) the person was, at the time the act was committed, an
Australian citizen;
(ii) the person is present in Australia; or
(iii) the act was committed in order to compel a
legislative, executive or judicial institution in Australia
to do, or abstain from doing, any act

F. Offences under the Crimes (Internationally Protected Persons) Act 1976 (see Chap. 5, at
Sect. 5.1.4)

Offence	*Related Convention and/or SC resolution*
Attacks against the person or liberty of an internationally protected person (section 8(1) and (2)): (1) A person who murders or kidnaps an internationally protected person is guilty of an offence against this Act and is punishable on conviction by imprisonment for life. (2) A person who commits any other attack upon the person or liberty of an internationally protected person is guilty of an offence against this Act and is punishable on conviction: (a) where the attack causes death – by imprisonment for life; (b) where the attack causes grievous bodily harm – by imprisonment for a period not exceeding 20 years; or (c) in any other case – by imprisonment for a period not exceeding 10 years	Protected Persons Convention, article 2(1)(a)
Attacks against the premises of an internationally protected person (section 8(3)): A person who intentionally destroys or damages (otherwise than by means of fire or explosive): (a) any official premises, private accommodation or means of transport, of an internationally protected person; or (b) any other premises or property in or upon which an internationally protected person is present, or is likely to be present; is guilty of an offence against this Act and is punishable upon conviction by imprisonment for a period not exceeding 10 years. (3A) A person who intentionally destroys or damages (otherwise than by means of fire or explosive): (a) any official premises, private accommodation or means of transport, of an internationally protected person; or	Protected Persons Convention, article 2(1)(b)

(*continued*)

Table 2 (continued)

(b) any other premises or property in or upon which an internationally protected person is present, or is likely to be present; with intent to endanger the life of that internationally protected person by that destruction or damage is guilty of an offence against this Act and is punishable upon conviction by imprisonment for a period not exceeding 20 years. (3B) A person who intentionally destroys or damages by means of fire or explosive: (a) any official premises, private accommodation or means of transport, of an internationally protected person; or (b) any other premises or property in or upon which an internationally protected person is present, or is likely to be present; is guilty of an offence against this Act and is punishable upon conviction by imprisonment for a period not exceeding 15 years. (3C) A person who intentionally destroys or damages by means of fire or explosive: (a) any official premises, private accommodation or means of transport, of an internationally protected person; or (b) any other premises or property in or upon which an internationally protected person is present, or is likely to be present; with intent to endanger the life of that internationally protected person by that destruction or damage is guilty of an offence against this Act and is punishable upon conviction by imprisonment for a period not exceeding 25 years	
Threats to commit offences (section 8(4)): A person who threatens to do anything that would constitute an offence against subsection (1), (2), (3), (3A), (3B) or (3C) is guilty of an offence against this Act and is punishable on conviction by imprisonment for a period not exceeding 7 years	Protected Persons Convention, article 2(1)(c)

G. Offences under the Nuclear Non-Proliferation (Safeguards) Act 1987 (see Chap. 5, at Sect. 5.1.5)

Offence	*Related Convention and/or SC resolution*
Stealing nuclear material (section 33): A person shall not: (a) steal; (b) fraudulently misappropriate; (c) fraudulently convert to that person's own use; or (d) obtain by false pretences; any nuclear material	Nuclear Material Convention, article 7(1)(b) and (c)
Demanding nuclear material by threats (section 34): A person shall not demand that another person give nuclear material to the first-mentioned person or some	Nuclear Material Convention, article 7(1)(d)

(*continued*)

Table 2 (continued)

other person by force or threat of force or by any form of intimidation	
Carrying, sending or moving nuclear material (section 34A(1)): A person commits an offence if the person carries, sends or moves nuclear material into or out of Australia or a foreign country	Nuclear Material Convention, article 7(1)(d)
Use of nuclear material causing death or injury to persons or damage to property or the environment (section 35): A person shall not use nuclear material to cause: (a) the death of, or serious injury to, any person; or (b) substantial damage to property or to the environment	Nuclear Material Convention, article 7(1)(a)
Acts against nuclear facilities (section 35A): A person commits an offence if: (a) the person does an act that is directed against a nuclear facility or that interferes with the operation of a nuclear facility; and (b) the person does so intending that the act will cause, or knowing that the act is likely to cause: (i) the death of, or serious injury to, any person; or (ii) substantial damage to property or to the environment; by exposure to radiation or by the release of radioactive substances	Nuclear Terrorism Convention, article 2(1)(b)
Threat to use nuclear material (section 36): A person shall not: (a) threaten; (b) state that it is his or her intention; or (c) make a statement from which it could reasonably be inferred that it is his or her intention; to use nuclear material: (d) to cause the death of, or injury to, any person; or (e) to cause damage to property or to the environment; or (f) to commit an offence against section 35A	Nuclear Material Convention, article 7(1)(e)(i); and Nuclear Terrorism Convention, article 2(2)(a)
Threat to commit certain offences (section 37): A person shall not: (a) threaten; (b) state that it is his or her intention; or (c) make a statement from which it could reasonably be inferred that it is his or her intention; to do any act that would be a contravention of section 33, or section 35A, in order to compel a person (including an international organisation or the Government of Australia or of a foreign country) to do or refrain from doing any act or thing	Nuclear Material Convention, article 7(1)(e)(ii); and Nuclear Terrorism Convention, article 2(2)(a)

(*continued*)

Table 2 (continued)

H. Offences under the Charter of the United Nations Act 1945 (see Chap. 5, at Sects. 5.2.2 and 5.2.3)

Offence	*Related Convention and/or SC resolution*
Dealing with freezable assets (section 20): An individual commits an offence if: (a) the individual holds an asset [as defined by section 2]; and (b) the individual: (i) uses or deals with the asset; or (ii) allows the asset to be used or dealt with; or (iii) facilitates the use of the asset or dealing with the asset; and (c) the asset is a freezable asset [as defined by section 14]; and (d) the use or dealing is not in accordance with a notice under section 22	Financing Convention, article 2(1); SC Res 1267 (1999), para 4(b); and SC Res 1373 (2001), para 1(c)
Giving an asset to a proscribed person or entity (section 21): An individual commits an offence if: (a) the individual, directly or indirectly, makes an asset available to a person or entity; and (b) the person or entity to whom the asset is made available is a proscribed person or entity; and (c) the making available of the asset is not in accordance with a notice under section 22	Financing Convention, article 2(1); and SC Res 1373 (2001), para 1(b)
Contravening a UN Sanction enforcement law (section 27): (1) An individual commits an offence if: (a) the individual engages in conduct; and (b) the conduct contravenes a UN sanction enforcement law. (2) An individual commits an offence if: (a) the individual engages in conduct; and (b) the conduct contravenes a condition of a licence, permission, consent, authorisation or approval (however described) under a UN sanction enforcement law. (5) A body corporate commits an offence if: (a) the body corporate engages in conduct; and (b) the conduct contravenes a UN sanction enforcement law. (6) A body corporate commits an offence if: (a) the body corporate engages in conduct; and (b) the conduct contravenes a condition of a licence, permission, consent, authorisation or approval (however described) under a UN sanction enforcement law	
Regulatory prohibitions to which section 27 of the Act applies: 1. Supply of arms (regulation 8(3)): Using the services of an Australian ship or an Australian	SC Res 1267 (1999), paras 4 and 8

(*continued*)

Table 2 (continued)

aircraft to transport export sanctioned goods [arms and related materials, as defined in regulations 4 and 5] in the course of, or for the purpose of, making a sanctioned supply	
2. Providing technical advice, assistance or training related to military activities (regulation 9(3)): Using the services of an Australian ship or an Australian aircraft in the course of, or for the purpose of, providing a sanctioned service [technical advice, assistance or training related to military activities to the Taliban or Al-Qaida, as defined in regulations 4 and 7]	SC Res 1373 (2001), para 2(d)

Table 3 **Terrorism-related offences in Canada**

A. Offences under the Aeronautics Act 1985 (see Chap. 6, at Sect. 6.1.1)

Offence	Related Convention and/or SC resolution
Endangering the safety or security of an aircraft in flight (section 7.41): No person shall engage in any behaviour that endangers the safety or security of an aircraft in flight or of persons on board an aircraft in flight by intentionally (a) interfering with the performance of the duties of any crew member; (b) lessening the ability of any crew member to perform that crew member's duties; or (c) interfering with any person who is following the instructions of a crew member	Tokyo Convention, articles 1 (1)(a), 1(1)(b) and 1(2)

B. Offences under the Criminal Code 1985 (see Chap. 6, at Sects. 6.1.2 and 6.1.4.3)

Offence	Related Convention and/or SC resolution
Possession, use, transfer, etc., of nuclear material (section 7 (3.2)(a)): Possession, use, transfer the possession of, send or deliver to any person, transport, alter, dispose of, disperse or abandon nuclear material and thereby (i) cause or likely cause the death of, or serious bodily harm to, any person, or (ii) cause or likely cause serious damage to, or destruction of, property	Nuclear Material Convention, article 7(1)(a)
Theft, demand, threat to use, etc., of nuclear material (section 7(3.4)): Notwithstanding anything in this Act or any other Act, every one who, outside Canada, commits an act or omission that if committed in Canada would constitute an offence against, a conspiracy or an attempt to commit or being an accessory after the fact in relation to an offence against, or any counselling in relation to an offence against, (a) section 334, 341, 344 or 380 or paragraph 362(1)(*a*) in relation to nuclear material, (b) section 346 in respect of a threat to commit an offence against section 334 or 344 in relation to nuclear material, (c) section 423 in relation to a demand for nuclear material, or (d) paragraph 264.1(1)(*a*) or (*b*) in respect of a threat to use nuclear material shall be deemed to commit that act or omission in Canada if paragraph (3.5)(a), (b) or (c) applies in respect of the act or omission. [note: section 7(3.4) thereby links various other offences under the Criminal Code to nuclear material, i.e. its theft or robbery (sections 334 and 344), fraudulent obtaining (sections 341, 362(1)(a), and 380), demand by threat or use of force (section 423), or threat to use (section 264.1(1)(a) and (b))]	Nuclear Material Convention, article 7(1)(b) to (g)

(*continued*)

Table 3 (continued)

Hijacking (section 76): Unlawfully, by force or threat thereof, or by any other form of intimidation, seizing or exercising control of an aircraft with intent (a) to cause any person on board the aircraft to be confined or imprisoned against his will, (b) to cause any person on board the aircraft to be transported against his will to any place other than the next scheduled place of landing of the aircraft, (c) to hold any person on board the aircraft for ransom or to service against his will, or (d) to cause the aircraft to deviate in a material respect from its flight plan	Hague Convention, article 1(a)
Endangering the safety of an aircraft or airport (section 77): Every one who (a) on board an aircraft in flight (as defined by section 7(8)), commits an act of violence against a person that is likely to endanger the safety of the aircraft, (b) using a weapon, commits an act of violence against a person at an airport serving international civil aviation that causes or is likely to cause serious injury or death and that endangers or is likely to endanger safety at the airport, (c) causes damage to an aircraft in service that renders the aircraft incapable of flight or that is likely to endanger the safety of the aircraft in flight, (d) places or causes to be placed on board an aircraft in service anything that is likely to cause damage to the aircraft, that will render it incapable of flight or that is likely to endanger the safety of the aircraft in flight, (e) causes damage to or interferes with the operation of any air navigation facility where the damage or interference is likely to endanger the safety of an aircraft in flight, (f) using a weapon, substance or device, destroys or causes serious damage to the facilities of an airport serving international civil aviation or to any aircraft not in service located there, or causes disruption of services of the airport, that endangers or is likely to endanger safety at the airport, or (g) endangers the safety of an aircraft in flight by communicating to any other person any information that the person knows to be false, is guilty of an indictable offence and liable to imprisonment for life	Montreal Convention, articles 1(1) and 1(1*bis*)
Possession of offensive weapons and explosive substances (section 78): Taking on board a civil aircraft an offensive weapon or any explosive substance (a) without the consent of the owner or operator of the aircraft or of a person duly authorized by either of them to consent thereto, or (b) with the consent referred to in paragraph (a) but without complying with all terms and conditions on which the consent was given	This offence is not required of the Plastic Explosives Convention, but is in furtherance to it – see Chap. 14 at Sect. 14.2.3

(*continued*)

Table 3 (continued)

Seizing control of a ship or fixed platform (section 78.1(1)): Seizing or exercising control over a ship or fixed platform (as defined by section 78.1(5)) by force or threat of force or by any other form of intimidation	Rome Convention, article 3(1)(a); and Rome Protocol, article 2(1)(a)
Endangering safety of ship or fixed platform (section 78.1(2)): Every one who (a) commits an act of violence against a person on board a ship or fixed platform, (b) destroys or causes damage to a ship or its cargo or to a fixed platform, (c) destroys or causes serious damage to or interferes with the operation of any maritime navigational facility, or (d) places or causes to be placed on board a ship or fixed platform anything that is likely to cause damage to the ship or its cargo or to the fixed platform, where that act is likely to endanger the safe navigation of a ship or the safety of a fixed platform, is guilty of an indictable offence and liable to imprisonment for life	Rome Convention, article 3(1)(b)–(f); and Rome Protocol, article 2(1)(b)–(e)
False communication (section 78.1(3)): Communicating information that endangers the safe navigation of a ship, knowing the information to be false	Rome Convention, article 3(1)(f)
Threats to cause death or injury (section 78.1(4)): Threat to commit an offence under [section 78.1] paragraph (2)(a), (b) or (c) in order to compel a person to do or refrain from doing any act, where the threat is likely to endanger the safe navigation of a ship or the safety of a fixed platform	Rome Convention, article 3(2)(c); and Rome Protocol, article 2(2)(c)
Providing or collecting property for certain activities (section 83.02): Every one who, directly or indirectly, wilfully and without lawful justification or excuse, provides or collects property [as defined by section 2] intending that it be used or knowing that it will be used, in whole or in part, in order to carry out (*a*) an act or omission that constitutes an offence referred to in subparagraphs (*a*)(i) to (ix) of the definition of "terrorist activity" in subsection 83.01(1), or (*b*) any other act or omission intended to cause death or serious bodily harm to a civilian or to any other person not taking an active part in the hostilities in a situation of armed conflict, if the purpose of that act or omission, by its nature or context, is to intimidate the public, or to compel a government or an international organization to do or refrain from doing any act,	Financing Convention, article 2(1); and SC Res 1373 (2001), para 1(b)
Providing or making available property or services for terrorist purposes (section 83.03): Every one who, directly or indirectly, collects property, provides or invites a person to provide, or makes available property or financial or other related services (a) intending that they be used, or knowing that they will be used, in whole or in part, for the purpose of facilitating or carrying out any terrorist activity [as defined by	Financing Convention, articles 2(1) and 2(5)(c); and SC Res 1373 (2001), para 1(b) and (d)

(*continued*)

Table 3 (continued)

section 83.01(1)], or for the purpose of benefiting any person who is facilitating or carrying out such an activity, or (b) knowing that, in whole or part, they will be used by or will benefit a terrorist group [as defined by section 83.01(1)]	
Using or possessing property for terrorist purposes (section 83.04): (a) using property, directly or indirectly, in whole or in part, for the purpose of facilitating or carrying out a terrorist activity [as defined], or (b) possessing property intending that it be used or knowing that it will be used, directly or indirectly, in whole or in part, for the purpose of facilitating or carrying out a terrorist activity [as defined]	Financing Convention, art 2(1); and SC Res 1373 (2001) 1(c) and (d)
Dealing with terrorist property (sections 83.08 and 83.12 (1)): Knowingly: (a) deal directly or indirectly in any property that is owned or controlled by or on behalf of a terrorist group; (b) enter into or facilitate, directly or indirectly, any transaction in respect of property referred to in paragraph (a); or (c) provide any financial or other related services in respect of property referred to in paragraph (a) to, for the benefit of or at the direction of a terrorist group	SC Res 1373 (2001), para 1(c)
Participating in activities of a terrorist group (section 83.18 (1)): Knowingly participating in or contributing to, directly or indirectly, any activity of a terrorist group (as defined) for the purpose of enhancing the ability of any terrorist group to facilitate or carry out a terrorist activity (as defined)	SC Res 1373 (2001), para 2(d)
Facilitating terrorist activity (section 83.19): Knowingly facilitating a terrorist activity (as defined)	SC Res 1373 (2001), para 2(d)
Commission of an offence for a terrorist group (section 83.2): Commission of any indictable offence under the Criminal Code 1985, or any other Act of Parliament, for the benefit of, at the direction of, or in association with a terrorist group (as defined)	SC Res 1373 (2001), para 2(d)
Instructing to carry out activities for a terrorist group (section 83.21): Knowingly instructing, directly or indirectly, any person to carry out any activity for the benefit of, at the direction of or in association with a terrorist group (as defined), for the purpose of enhancing the ability of any terrorist group to facilitate or carry out a terrorist activity (as defined)	SC Res 1373 (2001), para 2(a)
Instructing to carry out a terrorist activity (section 83.22): Knowingly instructing, directly or indirectly, any person to carry out a terrorist activity (as defined)	SC Res 1373 (2001), para 2(a)

(continued)

Table 3 (continued)

Harbouring or concealing terrorists (section 83.23): Knowingly harbouring or concealing any person whom he or she knows to be a person who has carried out or is likely to carry out a terrorist activity (as defined), for the purpose of enabling the person to facilitate or carry out any terrorist activity	SC Res 1373 (2001), para 2(c)
Hostage-taking (section 279.1): Everyone takes a person hostage who – with intent to induce any person, other than the hostage, or any group of persons or any state or international or intergovernmental organization to commit or cause to be committed any act or omission as a condition, whether express or implied, of the release of the hostage– (a) confines, imprisons, forcibly seizes or detains that person; and (b) in any manner utters, conveys or causes any person to receive a threat that the death of, or bodily harm to, the hostage will be caused or that the confinement, imprisonment or detention of the hostage will be continued	Hostages Convention, article 1 (1)
Public incitement of hatred (section 319): (1) Every one who, by communicating statements in any public place, incites hatred against any identifiable group where such incitement is likely to lead to a breach of the peace is guilty of (a) an indictable offence and is liable to imprisonment for a term not exceeding 2 years; or (b) an offence punishable on summary conviction. (2) Every one who, by communicating statements, other than in private conversation, wilfully promotes hatred against any identifiable group is guilty of (a) an indictable offence and is liable to imprisonment for a term not exceeding 2 years; or (b) an offence punishable on summary conviction. (3) No person shall be convicted of an offence under subsection (2) (a) if he establishes that the statements communicated were true; (b) if, in good faith, the person expressed or attempted to establish by an argument an opinion on a religious subject or an opinion based on a belief in a religious text; (c) if the statements were relevant to any subject of public interest, the discussion of which was for the public benefit, and if on reasonable grounds he believed them to be true; or (d) if, in good faith, he intended to point out, for the purpose of removal, matters producing or tending to produce feelings of hatred toward an identifiable group in Canada	SC Res 1624 (2005), para 1(a)
Threats against an internationally protected person (section 424): Every one who threatens to commit an offence under section 235, 236, 266, 267, 268, 269, 269.1, 271, 272, 273,	Protected Persons Convention, article 2(1)(c)

(*continued*)

Table 3 (continued)

279 or 279.1 against an internationally protected person or who threatens to commit an offence under section 431 is guilty of an indictable offence and liable to imprisonment for a term of not more than 5 years	
Attack on premises, residence or transport of an internationally protected person (section 431): Violent attack on the official premises, private accommodation or means of transport of an internationally protected person that is likely to endanger the life or liberty of such a person	Protected Persons Convention, article 2(1)(b)
Use of explosive or other lethal device (section 431.2(2)): Every one who delivers, places, discharges or detonates an explosive or other lethal device to, into, in or against a place of public use, a government or public facility, a public transportation system or an infrastructure facility [as defined by subsection (1)], either with intent to cause death or serious bodily injury or with intent to cause extensive destruction of such a place, system or facility that results in or is likely to result in major economic loss, is guilty of an indictable offence and liable to imprisonment for life	Bombings Convention, article 2(1)

C. Offence under the Explosives Act 1985 (see Chap. 6, at Sect. 6.1.3)

Offence	*Related Convention and/or SC resolution*
Possession, etc., of explosives or restricted components (section 21): Except as authorized by or under this Act, every person who, personally or by an agent or a mandatary, acquires, is in possession of, sells, offers for sale, stores, uses, makes, manufactures, transports, imports, exports or delivers any explosive, or acquires, is in possession of, sells or offers for sale any restricted component, is guilty of an offence	This offence is not required of the Plastic Explosives Convention, but is in furtherance to it – see Chap. 14 at Sect. 14.2.3

D. Offences under the Security of Information Act 1985 (see Chap. 6, at Sect. 6.1.4.3)

Offence	*Related Convention and/or SC resolution*
Approaching and entering a prohibited place (section 6): Every person commits an offence who, for any purpose prejudicial to the safety or interests of the State (as defined under section 2(1)), approaches, inspects, passes over, is in the neighbourhood of or enters a prohibited place (as defined by section 2(1)) at the direction of, for the benefit of or in association with a foreign entity or a terrorist group (as defined by the Criminal Code)	Preventive measures – see Chap. 14 at Sect. 14.2.3
Communicating safeguarded information (section 16(1)): Every person commits an offence who, without lawful authority, communicates to a foreign entity or to a terrorist group (as defined by the Criminal Code) information that the	Preventive measures – see Chap. 14 at Sect. 14.2.3

(continued)

Table 3 (continued)

Government of Canada or of a province is taking measures
to safeguard if
(a) the person believes, or is reckless as to whether, the
information is information that the Government of Canada
or of a province is taking measures to safeguard; and
(b) the person intends, by communicating the information,
to increase the capacity of a foreign entity or a terrorist
group to harm Canadian interests (as defined in section 3(1))
or is reckless as to whether the communication of the
information is likely to increase the capacity of a foreign
entity or a terrorist group to harm Canadian interests

Communicating safeguarded information (section 16(2)): Every person commits an offence who, intentionally and without lawful authority, communicates to a foreign entity or to a terrorist group (as defined by the Criminal Code) information that the Government of Canada or of a province is taking measures to safeguard if (a) the person believes, or is reckless as to whether, the information is information that the Government of Canada or of a province is taking measures to safeguard; and (b) harm to Canadian interests (as defined in section 3(1)) results	Preventive measures – see Chap. 14 at Sect. 14.2.3
Communicating special operational information (section 17): Every person commits an offence who, intentionally and without lawful authority, communicates special operational information (as defined by section 8(1)) to a foreign entity or to a terrorist group (as defined by the Criminal Code) if the person believes, or is reckless as to whether, the information is special operational information	Preventive measures – see Chap. 14 at Sect. 14.2.3
Breach of trust in respect of safeguarded information (section 18): Every person with a security clearance given by the Government of Canada commits an offence who, intentionally and without lawful authority, communicates, or agrees to communicate, to a foreign entity or to a terrorist group any information that is of a type that the Government of Canada is taking measures to safeguard	Preventive measures – see Chap. 14 at Sect. 14.2.3
Terrorist-influenced threats or violence (section 20): Every person commits an offence who, at the direction of, for the benefit of or in association with a foreign entity or a terrorist group, induces or attempts to induce, by threat, accusation, menace or violence, any person to do anything or to cause anything to be done (a) that is for the purpose of increasing the capacity of a foreign entity or a terrorist group to harm Canadian interests; or (b) that is reasonably likely to harm Canadian interests	Preventive measures – see Chap. 14 at Sect. 14.2.3

(continued)

Table 3 (continued)

E. Offences created under the authority of the United Nations Act 1985 (see Chap. 6, at Sect. 6.2.1)

Offence	*Related Convention and/or SC resolution*
Compliance with UN travel ban and arms embargo against Al-Qa'ida and the Taliban, operating as a result of: 1. United Nations Act 1985 (section 3(1)): Any person who contravenes an order or regulation made under this Act is guilty of an offence 2. United Nations Al-Qaida and Taliban Regulations 1999 (regulation 4.2): No person in Canada and no Canadian outside Canada shall knowingly, directly or indirectly, export, sell, supply or ship arms and related material, wherever situated, to the Taliban or a person associated with the Taliban or Usama bin Laden or his associates 3. United Nations Al-Qaida and Taliban Regulations 1999 (regulation 4.3): No owner or master of a Canadian ship and no operator of an aircraft registered in Canada shall knowingly, directly or indirectly, carry, cause to be carried or permit to be carried arms and related material, wherever situated, destined for the Taliban or a person associated with the Taliban or Usama bin Laden or his associates 4. United Nations Al-Qaida and Taliban Regulations 1999 (regulation 4.4): No person in Canada and no Canadian outside Canada shall knowingly provide, directly or indirectly, to the Taliban or a person associated with the Taliban or Usama bin Laden or his associates technical assistance related to military activities	SC Res 1267 (1999), paras 4(a) and 8

Table 4 Terrorism-related offences in New Zealand

A. Offences under the Aviation Crimes Act 1972 (see Chap. 7, at Sect. 7.1.1)

Offence	Related Convention and/or SC resolution
Hijacking (section 3): Everyone commits the crime of hijacking and is liable on conviction on indictment to imprisonment for life, who, while on board an aircraft in flight, whether in or outside New Zealand, unlawfully, by force or by threat of force or by any form of intimidation, seizes or exercises control, or attempts to seize or exercise control, of that aircraft	Hague Convention, article 1(a)
Crimes in connection with hijacking (section 4): (1) Everyone who, while on board an aircraft in flight outside New Zealand, does or omits anything which, if done or omitted by that person in New Zealand, would be a crime, commits that crime if the act or omission occurred in connection with the crime of hijacking. (2) Without limiting the generality of subsection (1) of this section, an act or omission by any person shall be deemed to occur in connection with the crime of hijacking if it was done or omitted with intent– (a) To commit or facilitate the commission of the crime of hijacking; or (b) To avoid the detection of himself or of any other person in the commission of the crime of hijacking; or (c) To avoid the arrest or facilitate the flight of himself or of any other person upon the commission of the crime of hijacking	Hague Convention, article 1(b)
Crimes relating to aircraft (section 5): Everyone commits a crime, and is liable on conviction on indictment to imprisonment for a term not exceeding 14 years, who, whether in or outside New Zealand,– (a) On board an aircraft in flight, commits an act of violence which is likely to endanger the safety of the aircraft; or (b) Destroys an aircraft in service; or (c) Causes damage to an aircraft in service which renders the aircraft incapable of flight or which is likely to endanger the safety of the aircraft in flight; or (d) Places or causes to be placed on an aircraft in service anything which is likely to destroy the aircraft, or to cause damage to the aircraft which will render it incapable of flight, or which is likely to endanger the safety of the aircraft in flight; or (e) Destroys, damages, or interferes with the operation of any air navigation facility used in international air navigation, where the destruction, damage, or interference is likely to endanger the safety of an aircraft in flight; or (f) Endangers the safety of an aircraft in flight by communicating to any other person any information which the person supplying the information knows to be false	Tokyo Convention, articles 1 (1)(a), 1(1)(b) and 1(2); and Montreal Convention, articles 1 (1)(a), 1(1)(b), 1(1)(c), 1(1)(d), and 1(1)(e)
Crimes relating to international airports (section 5A): (1) A person commits a crime who, whether in or outside New Zealand, using any device, substance, or weapon, intentionally	Montreal Convention, articles 1 (1*bis*)(a) and 1(1*bis*)(b)

(*continued*)

Table 4 (continued)

does any of the following acts that endangers or is likely to endanger the safety of an international airport:
(a) At the international airport, commits an act of violence that causes or is likely to cause serious injury or death; or
(b) Destroys or seriously damages the facilities of the international airport; or
(c) Destroys or seriously damages an aircraft that is not in service and is located at the international airport; or
(d) Disrupts the services of the international airport

B. Offences under the Crimes (Internationally Protected Persons, United Nations and Associated Personnel, and Hostages) Act 1980 (see Chap. 7, at Sect. 7.1.2)

Offence	*Related Convention and/or SC resolution*
Crimes against protected persons (section 3): (1) Without limiting anything in the Crimes Act 1961, every one commits a crime who does an act or omits to do an act, if– (a) He or she does the act, or omits to do the act, in New Zealand or outside New Zealand; and (b) He or she does the act, or omits to do the act, to or in relation to a person whom he or she knows to be a person protected by a convention; and (c) The act or omission is one that constitutes, or would, if done or made in New Zealand, constitute,– (i) A crime referred to or described in a provision of the Crimes Act 1961 specified in Schedule 1; or (ii) An attempt to commit such a crime, if the crime is not itself constituted by a mere attempt	Protected Persons Convention, article 2(1)(a)
Crimes against premises or vehicles of protected persons (section 4): (1) Without limiting anything in the Crimes Act 1961, every one commits a crime who does an act or omits to do an act, if– (a) He or she does the act, or omits to do the act, in New Zealand or outside New Zealand; and (b) He or she does the act, or omits to do the act, to or in relation to– (i) Premises that he or she knows to be the official premises or private residence of a person protected by a convention; or (ii) A vehicle that he or she knows is used by a person protected by a convention; and (c) He or she does the act, or omits to do the act, while such a person is present in those premises or that residence or vehicle; and (d) The act or omission is one that constitutes, or would, if done or made in New Zealand, constitute,– (i) A crime referred to or described in a provision of the Crimes Act 1961 specified in Schedule 2; or (ii) An attempt to commit such a crime, if the crime is not itself constituted by a mere attempt	Protected Persons Convention, article 2(1)(b)
Threats against protected persons (section 5): (1) Every one commits a crime who threatens to do an act, if– (a) The act constitutes a crime against section 3; and	Protected Persons Convention, article 2(1)(c)

(*continued*)

Table 4 (continued)

(b) He or she makes the threat in New Zealand or outside New Zealand; and (c) He or she makes the threat to or in relation to a person whom he or she knows to be an internationally protected person. (1A) Every one commits a crime who threatens to do an act, if– (a) The act constitutes a crime against section 3; and (b) He or she makes the threat in New Zealand or outside New Zealand; and (c) He or she makes the threat to or in relation to a person whom he or she knows to be a United Nations person or an associated person; and (d) He or she makes the threat with the intention of compelling the person, or any other person, to do or refrain from doing an act	
Threats against premises or vehicles of protected persons (section 6): (1) Every one commits a crime who threatens to do an act, if– (a) The act constitutes a crime against section 4; and (b) He or she makes the threat in New Zealand or outside New Zealand; and (c) He or she makes the threat to or in relation to– (i) Premises that he or she knows to be the official premises or private residence of an internationally protected person; or (ii) A vehicle that he or she knows is used by an internationally protected person. (1A) Every one commits a crime who threatens to do an act, if– (a) The act constitutes a crime against section 4; and (b) He or she makes the threat in New Zealand or outside New Zealand; and (c) He or she makes the threat to or in relation to– (i) Premises that he or she knows to be the official premises or private residence of a United Nations person or an associated person; or (ii) A vehicle that he or she knows is used by a United Nations person or an associated person; and (d) He or she makes the threat with the intention of compelling the person, or any other person, to do or refrain from doing an act	Protected Persons Convention, article 2(1)(c)
Hostage-taking (section 8): (1) Subject to subsection (2) of this section, every one commits the crime of hostage-taking who, whether in or outside New Zealand, unlawfully seizes or detains any person (in this section called the hostage) without his consent, or with his consent obtained by fraud or duress, with intent to compel the Government of any country or any international intergovernmental organization or any other person to do or abstain from doing any act as a condition, whether express or implied, for the release of the hostage	Hostages Convention, article 1(1)

(*continued*)

Table 4 (continued)

C. Offences under the International Terrorism (Emergency Powers) Act 1987 (see Chap. 7, at Sect. 7.3)

Offence	*Related Convention and/or SC resolution*
Failure to comply with emergency powers (section 21): (1) Subject to subsection (4) of this section, every person commits an offence who,– (a) Without lawful excuse, fails or refuses to comply with any direction, requirement, prohibition, or restriction given to or imposed upon that person pursuant to section 10 of this Act– (i) By any member of the Police; or (ii) By any member of the Armed Forces acting under section 12 of this Act: (b) Contrary to any notice issued by the Prime Minister under section 14 of this Act, publishes or causes or allows to be published in a newspaper or other document, or broadcasts or causes or allows to be broadcast by radio or television or otherwise,– (i) The identity of any person involved in dealing with an emergency in respect of which authority to exercise emergency powers has been given under this Act, or any other information or material (including a photograph) which would be likely to identify any person as a person involved in dealing with any such emergency; or (ii) Any information or material (including a photograph) of any equipment or technique lawfully used to deal with any such emergency	Emergency measures – see Chap. 14 at Sect. 14.2.3
Disclosure of private communications (section 21): (3) Every person commits an offence and is liable on summary conviction to a fine not exceeding $1,000 who acts in contravention of section 18 of this Act	Emergency measures – see Chap. 14 at Sect. 14.2.3

D. Offences under the Maritime Crimes Act 1999 (see Chap. 7, at Sect. 7.1.3)

Offence	*Related Convention and/or SC resolution*
Crimes relating to ships (section 4): (1) A person commits a crime who intentionally– (a) By force or by threat of force or by any other form of intimidation seizes or exercises control over a ship; or (b) On board a ship, commits an act of violence that is likely to endanger the safe navigation of the ship; or (c) Destroys a ship; or (d) Causes damage to a ship or the ship's cargo and that damage is likely to endanger the safe navigation of the ship; or (e) Places or causes to be placed on a ship anything that is likely to destroy the ship; or (f) Places or causes to be placed on a ship anything that is likely to cause damage to the ship or the ship's cargo and that damage endangers or is likely to endanger the safe navigation of the ship; or	Rome Convention, article 3(1)

(*continued*)

Table 4 (continued)

(g) Destroys, seriously damages, or seriously interferes with the operation of any maritime navigational facilities, if the destruction, damage, or interference is likely to endanger the safe navigation of a ship; or (h) Endangers the safe navigation of a ship by communicating to another person information which the person communicating the information knows to be false. (2) A person commits a crime who intentionally– (a) Causes the death of any person in connection with the commission or attempted commission of any of the crimes against subsection (1) in circumstances where the conduct concerned is the same as conduct described as murder or manslaughter under sections 158, 160, 167, 168, and 171 of the Crimes Act 1961; or (b) Injures any person in connection with the commission or attempted commission of any of the crimes against subsection (1) or paragraph (a) of this subsection	
Threats to commit crimes relating to ships (section 4): (3) A person commits a crime who threatens to do, in relation to a ship, any act that is a crime against any of paragraphs (b) to (d) or paragraph (g) of subsection (1) if the threat– (a) Is in order to compel any other person to do or abstain from doing any act; and (b) Is likely to endanger the safe navigation of the ship	Rome Convention, article 3(2)(c)
Crimes relating to fixed platforms (section 5): (1) A person commits a crime who intentionally– (a) By force or by threat of force or by any other form of intimidation seizes or exercises control over a fixed platform; or (b) On board a fixed platform, commits an act of violence that is likely to endanger the safety of the platform; or (c) Destroys a fixed platform; or (d) Causes damage to a fixed platform and that damage is likely to endanger the safety of the platform; or (e) Places or causes to be placed on a fixed platform anything that is likely to destroy the platform or to endanger the safety of the platform. (2) A person commits a crime who intentionally– (a) Causes the death of any person in connection with the commission or attempted commission of any of the crimes against subsection (1) in circumstances where the conduct concerned is the same as conduct described as murder or manslaughter under sections 158, 160, 167, 168, and 171 of the Crimes Act 1961; or (b) Injures any person in connection with the commission or attempted commission of any of the crimes against subsection (1) or paragraph (a) of this subsection	Rome Protocol, article 2(1)
Threats to commit crimes relating to fixed platforms (section 5): (3) A person commits a crime who threatens to do, in relation to a fixed platform, any act that is a crime against any of paragraphs (b) to (d) of subsection (1) if the threat–	Rome Protocol, article 2(2)(c)

(*continued*)

Table 4 (continued)

(a) Is in order to compel any other person to do or abstain from doing any act; and
(b) Is likely to endanger the safety of the platform

E. Offences under the Terrorism Suppression Act 2002 (see Chap. 7, at Sect. 7.1.4.)

Offence	*Related Convention and/or SC resolution*
Terrorist act (section 6A): A person commits an offence who engages in a terrorist act	SC Res 1373 (2001), para 2(d), but see Chap. 14 and Sect. 14.2.3
Terrorist bombing (section 7): (1) A person commits an offence who, intentionally and without lawful justification or excuse, delivers, places, discharges, or detonates an explosive or other lethal device in, into, or against a relevant place, facility, or system, with the intent to cause– (a) death or serious bodily injury; or (b) extensive destruction– (i) of the relevant place, facility, or system; and (ii) that results, or is likely to result, in major economic loss	Bombing Convention, article 2 (1)
Financing of terrorism for terrorist purposes (section 8): (1) A person commits an offence who, directly or indirectly, wilfully and without lawful justification or reasonable excuse, provides or collects funds intending that they be used, or knowing that they are to be used, in full or in part, in order to carry out 1 or more acts of a kind that, if they were carried out, would be 1 or more terrorist acts	Financing Convention, article 2 (1); and SC Res 1373 (2001), para 1(b) and (c)
Financing of terrorism for the benefit of persons engaged in terrorism (section 8): (2A) A person commits an offence who, directly or indirectly, willfully and without lawful justification or reasonable excuse, provides or collects funds intending that they benefit, or knowing that they will benefit, an entity that the person knows is an entity that carries out, or participates in the carrying out of, 1 or more terrorist acts	Financing Convention, article 2 (5)(c); and SC Res 1373 (2001), para 1(b) and (c)
Dealing with terrorist property (section 9): (1) A person commits an offence who, without lawful justification or reasonable excuse, deals with any property knowing that the property is– (a) property owned or controlled, directly or indirectly, by an entity for the time being designated under this Act as a terrorist entity or as an associated entity; or (b) property derived or generated from any property of the kind specified in paragraph (a)	SC Res 1267 (1999), para 8; and SC Res 1373 (2001), para 1(c)
Prohibition on making property, or financial or related services, available to a designated terrorist (section 10): A person commits an offence who makes available, or causes to be made available, directly or indirectly, without lawful justification or reasonable excuse, any property, or any financial or related services, either to, or for the benefit of, an entity,	SC Res 1373 (2001), para 1(d)

(*continued*)

Table 4 (continued)

knowing that the entity is an entity for the time being designated under this Act as a terrorist entity or as an associated entity	
Recruiting members of terrorist groups (section 12): (1) A person commits an offence who recruits another person as a member of a group or organisation, knowing that the group or organisation is– (a) a designated terrorist entity; or (b) an entity that carries out, or participates in the carrying out of, 1 or more terrorist acts	SC Res 1373 (2001), para 2(a)
Participating in terrorist groups (section 13): (1) A person commits an offence who participates in a group or organisation for the purpose stated in subsection (2) [to enhance the ability of any entity (being an entity of the kind referred to in subsection (1)(a) or (b)) to carry out, or to participate in the carrying out of, 1 or more terrorist acts], knowing that or being reckless as to whether the group or organisation is– (a) a designated terrorist entity; or (b) an entity that carries out, or participates in the carrying out of, 1 or more terrorist acts	SC Res 1373 (2001), para 2(a)
Harbouring or concealing terrorists (section 13A): (1) A person commits an offence who, with the intention of assisting another person to avoid arrest, escape lawful custody, or avoid conviction, harbours or conceals that person,– (a) knowing, or being reckless as to whether, that person intends to carry out a terrorist act; or (b) knowing, or being reckless as to whether, that person has carried out a terrorist act	SC Res 1373 (2001), para 2(d)
Using or moving unmarked plastic explosives (section 13B): (1) A person commits an offence and is liable on conviction on indictment to a term of imprisonment not exceeding 10 years or a fine not exceeding $500,000, or both, who– (a) possesses, uses, or manufactures unmarked plastic explosives, knowing they are unmarked; or (b) imports or exports unmarked plastic explosives to or from New Zealand, knowing they are unmarked	This offence is not required of the Plastic Explosives Convention, but is in furtherance to it – see Chap. 14 at Sect. 14.2.3
Offences involving physical protection of nuclear material (section 13C): A person commits an offence who,– (a) without lawful authority, receives, possesses, uses, transfers, alters, disposes of, or disperses nuclear material, knowing it is nuclear material, and– (i) that causes death, injury, or disease to any person or substantial damage to property; or (ii) with intent to cause, or being reckless as to whether it causes death, injury, or disease to any person or substantial damage to property; or (iii) that causes, or is likely to cause, substantial damage to the environment; or	Nuclear Materials Convention, article 7(1)(a)–(e)

(continued)

Table 4 (continued)

(b) commits theft, as defined in section 219 of the Crimes Act 1961, of nuclear material knowing that it was nuclear material; or (c) fraudulently obtains nuclear material, knowing that it was nuclear material; or (d) makes a demand for nuclear material by threat, or by use of force, or by any other form of intimidation with intent to steal it; or (e) with intent to intimidate, threatens to use nuclear material to cause– (i) death, injury, or disease to any person; or (ii) substantial damage to any property or the environment; or (f) with intent to compel any person, international organisation, or State to do, or refrain from doing, any act, threatens to steal nuclear material; or (g) without lawful authority, commits an act, or threatens to commit an act against a nuclear facility, or interferes with the operation of a nuclear facility with intent to cause, or being reckless as to whether it causes, death or serious injury to any person or substantial damage to property or to the environment by exposure to radiation or release of radioactive substances	
Importation, acquisition, etc., of radioactive material (section 13D): A person commits an offence and is liable on conviction on indictment to a term of imprisonment not exceeding 10 years who imports, acquires, possesses, or has control over any radioactive material with intent to use it to commit an offence involving bodily injury, or the threat of violence, to any person	Nuclear Materials Convention, article 2(1)(a)
Offences involving radioactive material and radioactive devices (section 13E): (1) A person commits an offence who– (a) makes or possesses a radioactive device or possesses radioactive material with intent to cause death or serious injury to any person or substantial damage to property or to the environment; or (b) uses radioactive material or a radioactive device or uses or damages a nuclear facility in a manner that releases or risks the release of radioactive material– (i) with intent to cause death or serious injury to any person or substantial damage to property or to the environment; or (ii) with intent to compel any person, international organisation, or State to do, or refrain from doing an act; or (c) threatens to commit an offence set out in paragraph (b); or (d) unlawfully and intentionally demands radioactive material by threat, in circumstances that indicate the credibility of the threat; or (e) by use of force,– (i) uses or threatens to use radioactive material or a radioactive device; or (ii) uses or damages or threatens to use or damage a nuclear facility	Nuclear Materials Convention, articles 2(1)(b) and 2(2)

(*continued*)

Table 4 (continued)

F. Offences created under the Counter-Terrorism Bill 2003 (see Chap. 7, at Sect. 7.1.5.3)

Offence	*Related Convention and/or SC resolution*
Causing disease or sickness in animals (Crimes Act 1961, section 298A): (1) Every one is liable to imprisonment for a term not exceeding 10 years who, without lawful justification or reasonable excuse, directly or indirectly causes or produces in an animal a disease or sickness that causes a situation of a kind described in subsection (2) to occur, either– (a) intending a situation of that kind to occur; or (b) being reckless as to whether a situation of that kind occurs. (2) A situation of a kind referred to in subsection (1) is a situation that– (a) constitutes a serious risk to the health or safety of an animal population; and (b) is likely, directly or indirectly, to cause major damage to the national economy of New Zealand	This offence has no link with the characteristics of conduct to be suppressed in the fight against terrorism, as identified in para 3 of SC Res 1566 (2004) – see Chap. 14, at Sect. 14.2.3
Contaminating food, crops, water, or other products (Crimes Act 1961, section 298B): Every one is liable to imprisonment for a term not exceeding 10 years who contaminates food, crops, water, or any other products, without lawful justification or reasonable excuse, and either knowing or being reckless as to whether the food, crops, water, or products are intended for human consumption, and– (a) intending to harm a person or reckless as to whether any person is harmed; or (b) intending to cause major economic loss to a person or reckless as to whether major economic loss is caused to any person; or (c) intending to cause major damage to the national economy of New Zealand or reckless as to whether major damage is caused to the national economy of New Zealand	This offence has no link with the characteristics of conduct to be suppressed in the fight against terrorism, as identified in para 3 of SC Res 1566 (2004) – see Chap. 14, at Sect. 14.2.3
Threats of harm to people or property (Crimes Act 1961, section 307A): (1) Everyone is liable to imprisonment for a term not exceeding 7 years if, without lawful justification or reasonable excuse, and intending to achieve the effect stated in subsection (2), he or she– (a) threatens to do an act likely to have one or more of the results described in subsection (3); or (b) communicates information– (i) that purports to be about an act likely to have one or more of the results described in subsection (3); and (ii) that he or she believes to be false. (2) The effect is causing a significant disruption of one or more of the following things: (a) the activities of the civilian population of New Zealand: (b) something that is or forms part of an infrastructure facility in New Zealand:	This offence has no link with the characteristics of conduct to be suppressed in the fight against terrorism, as identified in para 3 of SC Res 1566 (2004) – see Chap. 14, at Sect. 14.1

(*continued*)

Table 4 (continued)

(c) civil administration in New Zealand (whether administration
undertaken by the Government of New Zealand or by
institutions such as local authorities, District Health Boards, or
boards of trustees of schools):
(d) commercial activity in New Zealand (whether commercial
activity in general or commercial activity of a particular kind).
(3) The results are–
(a) creating a risk to the health of one or more people:
(b) causing major property damage:
(c) causing major economic loss to one or more persons:
(d) causing major damage to the national economy of New
Zealand

G. Offences created under the authority of the United Nations Act 1946 (see Chap. 7, at
Sect. 7.2.1) offence

Offence	*Related Convention and/or SC resolution*
Compliance with UN travel ban and arms embargo against Al-Qa'ida and the Taliban, resulting from the operation of: 1. United Nations Act 1946 (section 3): (1) Every person who commits, or attempts to commit, or does any act with intent to commit, or counsels, procures, aids, abets, or incites any other person to commit, or conspires with any other person (whether in New Zealand or elsewhere) to commit any offence against any regulations made under this Act shall be liable on summary conviction, in the case of an individual, to imprisonment for a term not exceeding 12 months or to a fine not exceeding \$10,000, or, in the case of a company or other corporation, to a fine not exceeding \$100,000. 2. United Nations Sanctions (Al-Qaida and Taliban) Regulations 2007 (regulation 14): Every person commits an offence against these regulations, and is liable accordingly under section 3 of the United Nations Act 1946, who acts in contravention of or fails to comply in any respect with any of the provisions of these regulations	SC Res 1267 (1999), paras 4(a) and 8

Table 5 Terrorism-related offences in the United Kingdom

A. Offences under the Explosive Substances Act 1883 (see Chap. 8, at Sect. 8.1.1.1)

Offence	*Related Convention and/or SC resolution*
Causing an explosion likely to endanger life or property (section 2): A person who in the United Kingdom or (being a citizen of the United Kingdom and Colonies) in the Republic of Ireland unlawfully and maliciously causes by any explosive substance an explosion of a nature likely to endanger life or to cause serious injury to property shall, whether any injury to person or property has been actually caused or not, be guilty of an offence and on conviction on indictment shall be liable to imprisonment for life	Bombing Convention, article 2(1)
Attempt to cause explosion, or making or keeping explosive with intent to endanger life or property (section 3(1)): (1) A person who in the United Kingdom or a dependency or (being a citizen of the United Kingdom and Colonies) elsewhere unlawfully and maliciously– (a) does any act with intent to cause, or conspires to cause, by an explosive substance an explosion of a nature likely to endanger life, or cause serious injury to property, whether in the United Kingdom or the Republic of Ireland, or (b) makes or has in his possession or under his control an explosive substance with intent by means thereof to endanger life, or cause serious injury to property, whether in the United Kingdom or the Republic of Ireland, or to enable any other person so to do, shall, whether any explosion does or does not take place, and whether any injury to person or property is actually caused or not, be guilty of an offence and on conviction on indictment shall be liable to imprisonment for life, and the explosive substance shall be forfeited	Bombing Convention, article 2(2)
Accessories (section 5): Any person who within or (being a subject of Her Majesty) without Her Majesty's dominions by the supply of or solicitation for money, the providing of premises, the supply of materials, or in any manner whatsoever, procures, counsels, aids, abets, or is accessory to, the commission of any crime under this Act, shall be guilty of felony, and shall be liable to be tried and punished for that crime, as if he had been guilty as a principal	Bombing Convention, article 2(3)

B. Offences under the Biological Weapons Act 1974 (see Chap. 8, at Sect. 8.1.1.2)

Offence	*Related Convention and/or SC resolution*
Development of biological agents, toxins and weapons (section 1): (1) No person shall develop, produce, stockpile, acquire or retain–	Bombing Convention, article 2(3)

(*continued*)

Table 5 (continued)

(a) any biological agent or toxin of a type and in a quantity
that has no justification for prophylactic, protective or other
peaceful purposes; or
(b) any weapon, equipment or means of delivery designed to
use biological agents or toxins for hostile purposes or in
armed conflict.
(1A) A person shall not–
(a) transfer any biological agent or toxin to another person
or enter into an agreement to do so, or
(b) make arrangements under which another person
transfers any biological agent or toxin or enters into an
agreement with a third person to do so,
if the biological agent or toxin is likely to be kept or used
(whether by the transferee or any other person) otherwise
than for prophylactic, protective or other peaceful purposes
and he knows or has reason to believe that that is the case

C. Offences under the Chemical Weapons Act 1996 (see Chap. 8, at Sect. 8.1.1.3)

Offence	*Related Convention and/or SC resolution*
Use, etc., of chemical weapons (section 2(1)): No person shall– (a) use a chemical weapon; (b) develop or produce a chemical weapon; (c) have a chemical weapon in his possession; (d) participate in the transfer of a chemical weapon; (e) engage in military preparations, or in preparations of a military nature, intending to use a chemical weapon	Bombing Convention, article 2(3)

D. Offences under the Civil Aviation Act 1982 (see Chap. 8, at Sect. 8.1.2.1)

Offence	*Related Convention and/or SC resolution*
Offences on an aircraft (section 92): (1) Any act or omission taking place on board a British-controlled aircraft or (subject to subsection (1A) below) a foreign aircraft while in flight elsewhere than in or over the United Kingdom which, if taking place in, or in a part of, the United Kingdom, would constitute an offence under the law in force in, or in that part of, the United Kingdom shall constitute that offence; but this subsection shall not apply to any act or omission which is expressly or impliedly authorised by or under that law when taking place outside the United Kingdom. (1A) Subsection (1) above shall only apply to an act or omission which takes place on board a foreign aircraft where– (a) the next landing of the aircraft is in the United Kingdom, and (b) in the case of an aircraft registered in a country other than the United Kingdom, the act or omission would, if taking place there, also constitute an offence under the law in force in that country	Tokyo Convention, article 1

(*continued*)

Table 5 (continued)

E. Offences under the Aviation Security Act 1982 (see Chap. 8, at Sect. 8.1.2.2)

Offence	*Related Convention and/or SC resolution*
Hijacking (section 1): (1) A person on board an aircraft in flight who unlawfully, by the use of force or by threats of any kind, seizes the aircraft or exercises control of it commits the offence of hijacking, whatever his nationality, whatever the State in which the aircraft is registered and whether the aircraft is in the United Kingdom or elsewhere, but subject to subsection (2) below. (2) If– (a) the aircraft is used in military, customs or police service, or (b) both the place of take-off and the place of landing are in the territory of the State in which the aircraft is registered, subsection (1) above shall not apply unless– (i) the person seizing or exercising control of the aircraft is a United Kingdom national; or (ii) his act is committed in the United Kingdom; or (iii) the aircraft is registered in the United Kingdom or is used in the military or customs service of the United Kingdom or in the service of any police force in the United Kingdom	Hague Convention, article 1(a)
Destroying, damaging or endangering safety of aircraft (section 2): (1) It shall, subject to subsection (4) below, be an offence for any person unlawfully and intentionally– (a) to destroy an aircraft in service or so to damage such an aircraft as to render it incapable of flight or as to be likely to endanger its safety in flight; or (b) to commit on board an aircraft in flight any act of violence which is likely to endanger the safety of the aircraft. (2) It shall also, subject to subsection (4) below, be an offence for any person unlawfully and intentionally to place, or cause to be placed, on an aircraft in service any device or substance which is likely to destroy the aircraft, or is likely so to damage it as to render it incapable of flight or as to be likely to endanger its safety in flight; but nothing in this subsection shall be construed as limiting the circumstances in which the commission of any act– (a) may constitute an offence under subsection (1) above, or (b) may constitute attempting or conspiring to commit, or aiding, abetting, counselling or procuring, or being art and part in, the commission of such an offence. (4) Subsections (1) and (2) above shall not apply to any act committed in relation to an aircraft used in military, customs or police service unless– (a) the act is committed in the United Kingdom, or (b) where the act is committed outside the United Kingdom, the person committing it is a United Kingdom national	Montreal Convention, article 1 (1)(a), (b) and (c)

(*continued*)

Table 5 (continued)

Other acts endangering or likely to endanger safety of aircraft (section 3):	Montreal Convention, article 1 (d) and (e)

Other acts endangering or likely to endanger safety of aircraft (section 3):

(1) It shall, subject to subsections (5) and (6) below, be an offence for any person unlawfully and intentionally to destroy or damage any property to which this subsection applies, or to interfere with the operation of any such property, where the destruction, damage or interference is likely to endanger the safety of aircraft in flight.

(2) Subsection (1) above applies to any property used for the provision of air navigation facilities, including any land, building or ship so used, and including any apparatus or equipment so used, whether it is on board an aircraft or elsewhere.

(3) It shall also, subject to subsections (4) and (5) below, be an offence for any person intentionally to communicate any information which is false, misleading or deceptive in a material particular, where the communication of the information endangers the safety of an aircraft in flight or is likely to endanger the safety of aircraft in flight.

(4) It shall be a defence for a person charged with an offence under subsection (3) above to prove–

(a) that he believed, and had reasonable grounds for believing, that the information was true; or

(b) that, when he communicated the information, he was lawfully employed to perform duties which consisted of or included the communication of information and that he communicated the information in good faith in the performance of those duties.

(5) Subsections (1) and (3) above shall not apply to the commission of any act unless either the act is committed in the United Kingdom, or, where it is committed outside the United Kingdom–

(a) the person committing it is a United Kingdom national; or

(b) the commission of the act endangers or is likely to endanger the safety in flight of a civil aircraft registered in the United Kingdom or chartered by demise to a lessee whose principal place of business, or (if he has no place of business) whose permanent residence, is in the United Kingdom; or

(c) the act is committed on board a civil aircraft which is so registered or so chartered; or

(d) the act is committed on board a civil aircraft which lands in the United Kingdom with the person who committed the act still on board.

(6) Subsection (1) above shall also not apply to any act committed outside the United Kingdom and so committed in relation to property which is situated outside the United Kingdom and is not used for the provision of air navigation facilities in connection with international air navigation, unless the person committing the act is a United Kingdom national

(*continued*)

Table 5 (continued)

F. Offences under the Aviation and Maritime Security Act 1990 (see Chap. 8, at Sect. 8.1.2.3)

Offence	*Related Convention and/or SC resolution*
Endangering safety at aerodromes (section 1):	Montreal Convention, article 1
(1) It is an offence for any person by means of any device,	(1*bis*)
substance or weapon intentionally to commit at an	
aerodrome serving international civil aviation any act of	
violence which–	
(a) causes or is likely to cause death or serious personal	
injury, and	
(b) endangers or is likely to endanger the safe operation of	
the aerodrome or the safety of persons at the aerodrome.	
(2) It is also, subject to subsection (4) below, an offence for	
any person by means of any device, substance or weapon	
unlawfully and intentionally–	
(a) to destroy or seriously to damage–	
(i) property used for the provision of any facilities at an	
aerodrome serving international civil aviation (including	
any apparatus or equipment so used), or	
(ii) any aircraft which is at such an aerodrome but is not in	
service, or	
(b) to disrupt the services of such an aerodrome,	
in such a way as to endanger or be likely to endanger the safe	
operation of the aerodrome or the safety of persons at the	
aerodrome.	
(4) Subsection (2)(a)(ii) above does not apply to any act	
committed in relation to an aircraft used in military, customs	
or police service unless–	
(a) the act is committed in the United Kingdom, or	
(b) where the act is committed outside the United Kingdom,	
the person committing it is a United Kingdom national	
Hijacking of ships (section 9):	Rome Convention,
(1) A person who unlawfully, by the use of force or by	article 3(1)(a)
threats of any kind, seizes a ship or exercises control of it,	
commits the offence of hijacking a ship, whatever his	
nationality and whether the ship is in the United Kingdom or	
elsewhere, but subject to subsection (2) below.	
(2) Subsection (1) above does not apply in relation to a	
warship or any other ship used as a naval auxiliary or in	
customs or police service unless–	
(a) the person seizing or exercising control of the ship is a	
United Kingdom national, or	
(b) his act is committed in the United Kingdom, or	
(c) the ship is used in the naval or customs service of the	
United Kingdom or in the service of any police force in the	
United Kingdom	
Seizing or exercising control of fixed platforms (section 10	Rome Protocol, article 2(1)(a)
(1)):	
A person who unlawfully, by the use of force or by threats of	
any kind, seizes a fixed platform or exercises control of it,	

(*continued*)

Table 5 (continued)

commits an offence, whatever his nationality and whether
the fixed platform is in the United Kingdom or elsewhere

Destroying ships or fixed platforms or endangering their safety (section 11): (1) Subject to subsection (5) below, a person commits an offence if he unlawfully and intentionally– (a) destroys a ship or a fixed platform, (b) damages a ship, its cargo or a fixed platform so as to endanger, or to be likely to endanger, the safe navigation of the ship, or as the case may be, the safety of the platform, or (c) commits on board a ship or on a fixed platform an act of violence which is likely to endanger the safe navigation of the ship, or as the case may be, the safety of the platform. (2) Subject to subsection (5) below, a person commits an offence if he unlawfully and intentionally places, or causes to be placed, on a ship or fixed platform any device or substance which– (a) in the case of a ship, is likely to destroy the ship or is likely so to damage it or its cargo as to endanger its safe navigation, or (b) in the case of a fixed platform, is likely to destroy the fixed platform or so to damage it as to endanger its safety. (5) Subsections (1) and (2) above do not apply in relation to any act committed in relation to a warship or any other ship used as a naval auxiliary or in customs or police service unless– (a) the person committing the act is a United Kingdom national, or (b) his act is committed in the United Kingdom, or (c) the ship is used in the naval or customs service of the United Kingdom or in the service of any police force in the United Kingdom	Rome Convention, article 3(1)(b), (c) and (d); and Rome Protocol, article 2(1)(b), (c) and (d)
Other acts endangering or likely to endanger safe navigation (section 12): (1) Subject to subsection (6) below, it is an offence for any person unlawfully and intentionally– (a) to destroy or damage any property to which this subsection applies, or (b) seriously to interfere with the operation of any such property, where the destruction, damage or interference is likely to endanger the safe navigation of any ship. (2) Subsection (1) above applies to any property used for the provision of maritime navigation facilities, including any land, building or ship so used, and including any apparatus or equipment so used, whether it is on board a ship or elsewhere. (3) Subject to subsection (6) below, it is also an offence for any person intentionally to communicate any information which he knows to be false in a material particular, where the communication of the information endangers the safe navigation of any ship.	Rome Convention, article 3(1) (e) and (f)

(*continued*)

Table 5 (continued)

(6) For the purposes of subsections (1) and (3) above any danger, or likelihood of danger, to the safe navigation of a warship or any other ship used as a naval auxiliary or in customs or police service is to be disregarded unless– (a) the person committing the act is a United Kingdom national, or (b) his act is committed in the United Kingdom, or (c) the ship is used in the naval or customs service of the United Kingdom or in the service of any police force in the United Kingdom	
Offences involving threats (section 13(1)): A person commits an offence if– (a) in order to compel any other person to do or abstain from doing any act, he threatens that he or some other person will do in relation to any ship or fixed platform an act which is an offence by virtue of section 11(1) of this Act, and (b) the making of that threat is likely to endanger the safe navigation of the ship or, as the case may be, the safety of the fixed platform	Rome Convention, article 3(2)(c); and Rome Protocol, article 2(2)(c)
Offences involving injury or death (section 14): (1) Where a person (of whatever nationality) does outside the United Kingdom any act which, if done in the United Kingdom, would constitute an offence falling within subsection (2) below, his act shall constitute that offence if it is done in connection with an offence under section 9, 10, 11 or 12 of this Act committed or attempted by him. (2) The offences falling within this subsection are murder, attempted murder, manslaughter, culpable homicide and assault and offences under sections 18, 20, 21, 22, 23, 28 and 29 of the Offences against the Person Act 1861 and section 2 of the Explosive Substances Act 1883	Rome Convention, article 3(1)(g); and Rome Protocol, article 2(1)(e)

G. Offences under the Internationally Protected Persons Act 1978 (see Chap. 8, at Sect. 8.1.3.1)

Offence	*Related Convention and/or SC resolution*
Attacks and threats of attacks on protected persons (section 1): (1) If a person, whether a citizen of the United Kingdom and Colonies or not, does outside the United Kingdom– (a) any act to or in relation to a protected person which, if he had done it in any part of the United Kingdom, would have made him guilty of the offence of murder, manslaughter, culpable homicide, rape, assault occasioning actual bodily harm or causing injury, kidnapping, abduction, false imprisonment or plagium or an offence under section 18, 20, 21, 22, 23, 24, 28, 29, 30 or 56 of the Offences against the Person Act 1861 or section 2 of the Explosive Substances Act 1883; or (b) in connection with an attack on any relevant premises or on any vehicle ordinarily used by a protected person which is made when a protected person is on or in the premises or	Protected Persons Convention, article 2(1)(a) and (b)

(*continued*)

Table 5 (continued)

vehicle, any act which, if he had done it in any part of the United Kingdom, would have made him guilty of an offence under section 2 of the Explosive Substances Act 1883, section 1 of the Criminal Damage Act 1971 or article 3 of the Criminal Damage (Northern Ireland) Order 1977 or the offence of wilful fire-raising, he shall in any part of the United Kingdom be guilty of the offences aforesaid of which the act would have made him guilty if he had done it there.	
(2) If a person in the United Kingdom or elsewhere, whether a citizen of the United Kingdom and Colonies or not– (a) attempts to commit an offence which, by virtue of the preceding subsection or otherwise, is an offence mentioned in paragraph (a) of that subsection against a protected person or an offence mentioned in paragraph (b) of that subsection in connection with an attack so mentioned; or (b) aids, abets, counsels or procures, or is art and part in, the commission of such an offence or of an attempt to commit such an offence, he shall in any part of the United Kingdom be guilty of attempting to commit the offence in question or, as the case may be, of aiding, abetting, counselling or procuring, or being art and part in, the commission of the offence or attempt in question.	Protected Persons Convention, article 2(1)(d) and (e)
(3) If a person in the United Kingdom or elsewhere, whether a citizen of the United Kingdom and Colonies or not– (a) makes to another person a threat that any person will do an act which is an offence mentioned in paragraph (a) of the preceding subsection; or (b) attempts to make or aids, abets, counsels or procures or is art and part in the making of such a threat to another person, with the intention that the other person shall fear that the threat will be carried out, the person who makes the threat or, as the case may be, who attempts to make it or aids, abets, counsels or procures or is art and part in the making of it, shall in any part of the United Kingdom be guilty of an offence and liable on conviction on indictment to imprisonment for a term not exceeding 10 years and not exceeding the term of imprisonment to which a person would be liable for the offence constituted by doing the act threatened at the place where the conviction occurs and at the time of the offence to which the conviction relates	Protected Persons Convention, article 2(1)(c)

H. Offences under the Taking of Hostages Act 1982 (see Chap. 8, at Sect. 8.1.3.2)

Offence	*Related Convention and/or SC resolution*
Hostage-taking (section 1(1)): A person, whatever his nationality, who, in the United Kingdom or elsewhere,– (a) detains any other person ("the hostage"), and (b) in order to compel a State, international governmental organisation or person to do or abstain from doing any act,	Hostages Convention, article 1(1)

(*continued*)

Table 5 (continued)

threatens to kill, injure or continue to detain the hostage,
commits an offence.

I. Offences under the Nuclear Material (Offences) Act 1983 (see Chap. 8, at Sect. 8.1.4)

Offence	*Related Convention and/or SC resolution*
Extended application of existing offences (section 1): If a person, whatever his nationality, does outside the United Kingdom, in relation to or by means of nuclear material, any act which, had he done it in any part of the United Kingdom, would have made him guilty of– (a) the offence of murder, manslaughter, culpable homicide, assault to injury, malicious mischief or causing injury, or endangering the life of the lieges, by reckless conduct, or (b) an offence under section 18 or 20 of the Offences against the Person Act 1861 or section 1 of the Criminal Damage Act 1971 or Article 3 of the Criminal Damage (Northern Ireland) Order 1977 or section 78 of the Criminal Justice (Scotland) Act 1980, or (c) the offence of theft, embezzlement, robbery, assault with intent to rob, burglary or aggravated burglary, or (d) the offence of fraud or extortion or an offence under section 15 or 21 of the Theft Act 1968 or section 15 or 20 of the Theft Act (Northern Ireland) 1969, he shall in any part of the United Kingdom be guilty of such of the offences mentioned in paragraphs (a) to (d) above as are offences of which the act would have made him guilty had he done it in that part of the United Kingdom	Nuclear Material Convention, article 7(1)(b), (c) and (d)
Offences involving preparatory acts and threats (section 2): (2) A person contravenes this subsection if he receives, holds or deals with nuclear material– (a) intending, or for the purpose of enabling another, to do by means of that material an act which is an offence mentioned in paragraph (a) or (b) of subsection (1) of section 1 above; or (b) being reckless as to whether another would so do such an act. (3) A person contravenes this subsection if he– (a) makes to another person a threat that he or any other person will do by means of nuclear material such an act as is mentioned in paragraph (a) of subsection (2) above; and (b) intends that the person to whom the threat is made shall fear that it will be carried out. (4) A person contravenes this subsection if, in order to compel a State, international governmental organisation or person to do, or abstain from doing, any act, he threatens that he or any other person will obtain nuclear material by an act which is an offence mentioned in paragraph (c) of subsection (1) of section 1 above	Nuclear Material Convention, article 7(1)(a) and (e)

(continued)

Table 5 (continued)

J. Offences under the Terrorism Act 2000 (see Chap. 8, at Sect. 8.1.5.3)

Offence	*Related Convention and/or SC resolution*
Membership in a proscribed organisation (section 11(1)): A person commits an offence if he belongs or professes to belong to a proscribed organisation	SC Res 1373 (2001), para 2(a) and (d)
Support for a proscribed organisation (section 12): (1) A person commits an offence if– (a) he invites support for a proscribed organisation, and (b) the support is not, or is not restricted to, the provision of money or other property (within the meaning of section 15). (2) A person commits an offence if he arranges, manages or assists in arranging or managing a meeting which he knows is– (a) to support a proscribed organisation, (b) to further the activities of a proscribed organisation, or (c) to be addressed by a person who belongs or professes to belong to a proscribed organisation. (3) A person commits an offence if he addresses a meeting and the purpose of his address is to encourage support for a proscribed organisation or to further its activities	SC Res 1373 (2001), para 2(a) and (d)
Wearing a uniform or emblem of a proscribed organisation (section 13(1)): A person in a public place commits an offence if he– (a) wears an item of clothing, or (b) wears, carries or displays an article, in such a way or in such circumstances as to arouse reasonable suspicion that he is a member or supporter of a proscribed organisation	SC Res 1373 (2001), para 2(a) and (d)
Fund-raising for terrorist purposes (section 15): (1) A person commits an offence if he– (a) invites another to provide money or other property, and (b) intends that it should be used, or has reasonable cause to suspect that it may be used, for the purposes of terrorism. (2) A person commits an offence if he– (a) receives money or other property, and (b) intends that it should be used, or has reasonable cause to suspect that it may be used, for the purposes of terrorism. (3) A person commits an offence if he– (a) provides money or other property, and (b) knows or has reasonable cause to suspect that it will or may be used for the purposes of terrorism	Financing Convention, article 2 (1); and SC Res 1373 (2001), para 1(b) and (d)
Use or possession of money for terrorist purposes (section 16): (1) A person commits an offence if he uses money or other property for the purposes of terrorism. (2) A person commits an offence if he– (a) possesses money or other property, and (b) intends that it should be used, or has reasonable cause to suspect that it may be used, for the purposes of terrorism	Financing Convention, article 2 (1); and SC Res 1373 (2001), para 1(b) and (d)

(*continued*)

Table 5 (continued)

Funding terrorism (section 17): A person commits an offence if– (a) he enters into or becomes concerned in an arrangement as a result of which money or other property is made available or is to be made available to another, and (b) he knows or has reasonable cause to suspect that it will or may be used for the purposes of terrorism	Financing Convention, article 2 (1); and SC Res 1373 (2001), para 1(b) and (d)
Money laundering for terrorist purposes (section 18(1)): A person commits an offence if he enters into or becomes concerned in an arrangement which facilitates the retention or control by or on behalf of another person of terrorist property– (a) by concealment, (b) by removal from the jurisdiction, (c) by transfer to nominees, or (d) in any other way	Financing Convention, article 2 (1); and SC Res 1373 (2001), para 1(b) and (d)
Weapons training (section 54): (1) A person commits an offence if he provides instruction or training in the making or use of– (a) firearms, (b) explosives, or (c) chemical, biological or nuclear weapons. (2) A person commits an offence if he receives instruction or training in the making or use of– (a) firearms, (b) explosives, or (c) chemical, biological or nuclear weapons. (3) A person commits an offence if he invites another to receive instruction or training and the receipt– (a) would constitute an offence under subsection (2), or (b) would constitute an offence under subsection (2) but for the fact that it is to take place outside the United Kingdom	SC Res 1373 (2001), para 2(d), but not restricted to the countering of terrorism – see Chap. 14 at Sect. 14.2.3
Directing a terrorist organisation (section 56(1)): A person commits an offence if he directs, at any level, the activities of an organisation which is concerned in the commission of acts of terrorism	SC Res 1373 (2001), para 2(a) and (d)
Possessing an article for terrorist purposes (section 57(1)): A person commits an offence if he possesses an article in circumstances which give rise to a reasonable suspicion that his possession is for a purpose connected with the commission, preparation or instigation of an act of terrorism	SC Res 1373 (2001), para 2(a) and (d)
Collection of information for terrorist purposes (section 58(1)): A person commits an offence if– (a) he collects or makes a record of information of a kind likely to be useful to a person committing or preparing an act of terrorism, or (b) he possesses a document or record containing information of that kind	SC Res 1373 (2001), para 2(a) and (d)

(*continued*)

Table 5 (continued)

Eliciting, publishing or communicating information about members of armed forces (section 58A): A person commits an offence who– (a) elicits or attempts to elicit information about an individual who is or has been– (i) a member of Her Majesty's forces, (ii) a member of any of the intelligence services, or (iii) a constable, which is of a kind likely to be useful to a person committing or preparing an act of terrorism, or (b) publishes or communicates any such information	Not restricted to the countering of terrorism – see Chap. 14 at Sect. 14.2.3
Inciting terrorism in England and Wales (section 59): (1) A person commits an offence if– (a) he incites another person to commit an act of terrorism wholly or partly outside the United Kingdom, and (b) the act would, if committed in England and Wales, constitute one of the offences listed in subsection (2). (2) Those offences are– (a) murder, (b) an offence under section 18 of the Offences against the [1861 c. 100.] Person Act 1861 (wounding with intent), (c) an offence under section 23 or 24 of that Act (poison), (d) an offence under section 28 or 29 of that Act (explosions), and (e) an offence under section 1(2) of the [1971 c. 48.] Criminal Damage Act 1971 (endangering life by damaging property)	SC Res 1624 (2005), para 1(a)
Inciting terrorism in Northern Ireland (section 60): (1) A person commits an offence if– (a) he incites another person to commit an act of terrorism wholly or partly outside the United Kingdom, and (b) the act would, if committed in Northern Ireland, constitute one of the offences listed in subsection (2). (2) Those offences are– (a) murder, (b) an offence under section 18 of the Offences against the [1861 c. 100.] Person Act 1861 (wounding with intent), (c) an offence under section 23 or 24 of that Act (poison), (d) an offence under section 28 or 29 of that Act (explosions), and (e) an offence under Article 3(2) of the [S.I. 1977/426 (N.I. 4).] Criminal Damage (Northern Ireland) Order 1977 (endangering life by damaging property)	SC Res 1624 (2005), para 1(a)
Inciting terrorism in Scotland (section 61): (1) A person commits an offence if– (a) he incites another person to commit an act of terrorism wholly or partly outside the United Kingdom, and (b) the act would, if committed in Scotland, constitute one of the offences listed in subsection (2). (2) Those offences are– (a) murder, (b) assault to severe injury, and (c) reckless conduct which causes actual injury	SC Res 1624 (2005), para 1(a)

(*continued*)

Table 5 (continued)

Terrorist bombings (section 62): (1) If– (a) a person does anything outside the United Kingdom as an act of terrorism or for the purposes of terrorism, and (b) his action would have constituted the commission of one of the offences listed in subsection (2) if it had been done in the United Kingdom, he shall be guilty of the offence. (2) The offences referred to in subsection (1)(b) are [see Tables 5(A), (B) and (C) above]– (a) an offence under section 2, 3 or 5 of the Explosive Substances Act 1883 (causing explosions, & c.), (b) an offence under section 1 of the Biological Weapons Act 1974 (biological weapons), and (c) an offence under section 2 of the Chemical Weapons Act 1996 (chemical weapons)	Bombing Convention, article 2(1)
Terrorist financing (section 63(1)): If– (a) a person does anything outside the United Kingdom, and (b) his action would have constituted the commission of an offence under any of sections 15 to 18 if it had been done in the United Kingdom, he shall be guilty of the offence	Financing Convention, article 2 (1); and SC Res 1373 (2001), para 1(b) and (d)

K. Offences under the Anti-terrorism, Crime and Security Act 2001 (see Chap. 8, at Sect. 8.1.6.3)

Offence	*Related Convention and/or SC resolution*
Use of nuclear weapons (section 47(1)): A person who– (a) knowingly causes a nuclear weapon explosion; (b) develops or produces, or participates in the development or production of, a nuclear weapon; (c) has a nuclear weapon in his possession; (d) participates in the transfer of a nuclear weapon; or (e) engages in military preparations, or in preparations of a military nature, intending to use, or threaten to use, a nuclear weapon, is guilty of an offence	Not restricted to the countering of terrorism – see Chap. 14 at Sect. 14.2.3
Assisting or inducing weapons-related acts overseas (section 50): (1) A person who aids, abets, counsels or procures, or incites, a person who is not a United Kingdom person to do a relevant act outside the United Kingdom is guilty of an offence. (2) For this purpose a relevant act is an act that, if done by a United Kingdom person, would contravene any of the following provisions– (a) section 1 of the Biological Weapons Act 1974 (offences relating to biological agents and toxins); (b) section 2 of the Chemical Weapons Act 1996 (offences relating to chemical weapons); or (c) section 47 above (offences relating to nuclear weapons)	Not restricted to the countering of terrorism – see Chap. 14 at Sect. 14.2.3

(continued)

Table 5 (continued)

L. Offences under the Prevention of Terrorism Act 2005 (see Chap. 8, at Sect. 8.1.7)	
Offence	*Related Convention and/or SC resolution*
Contravention of a control order (section 9(1)): A person who, without reasonable excuse, contravenes an obligation imposed on him by a control order is guilty of an offence	Enforcement of preventive measures – see Chap. 14 at Sect. 14.2.3
Leaving and re-entering the United Kingdom without notification (section 9(2)): A person is guilty of an offence if– (a) a control order by which he is bound at a time when he leaves the United Kingdom requires him, whenever he enters the United Kingdom, to report to a specified person that he is or has been the subject of such an order; (b) he re-enters the United Kingdom after the order has ceased to have effect; (c) the occasion on which he re-enters the United Kingdom is the first occasion on which he does so after leaving while the order was in force; and (d) on that occasion he fails, without reasonable excuse, to report to the specified person in the manner that was required by the order	Enforcement of preventive measures – see Chap. 14 at Sect. 14.2.3
Obstructing the service of a control order (section 9(3)): A person is guilty of an offence if he intentionally obstructs the exercise by any person of a power conferred by section 7(9)	Enforcement of preventive measures – see Chap. 14 at Sect. 14.2.3
M. Offences under the Terrorism Act 2006 (see Chap. 8, at Sect. 8.1.8.1)	
Offence	*Related Convention and/or SC resolution*
Encouragement of terrorism (section 1): (1) This section applies to a statement that is likely to be understood by some or all of the members of the public to whom it is published as a direct or indirect encouragement or other inducement to them to the commission, preparation or instigation of acts of terrorism or Convention offences. (2) A person commits an offence if– (a) he publishes a statement to which this section applies or causes another to publish such a statement; and (b) at the time he publishes it or causes it to be published, he– (i) intends members of the public to be directly or indirectly encouraged or otherwise induced by the statement to commit, prepare or instigate acts of terrorism or Convention offences; or (ii) is reckless as to whether members of the public will be directly or indirectly encouraged or otherwise induced by the statement to commit, prepare or instigate such acts or offences.	SC Res 1624 (2005), para 1(a)

(*continued*)

Table 5 (continued)

(3) For the purposes of this section, the statements that are
likely to be understood by members of the public as
indirectly encouraging the commission or preparation of
acts of terrorism or Convention offences include every
statement which–
(a) glorifies the commission or preparation (whether in the
past, in the future or generally) of such acts or offences; and
(b) is a statement from which those members of the public
could reasonably be expected to infer that what is being
glorified is being glorified as conduct that should be
emulated by them in existing circumstances

Dissemination of terrorist publications (section 2): (1) A person commits an offence if he engages in conduct falling within subsection (2) and, at the time he does so– (a) he intends an effect of his conduct to be a direct or indirect encouragement or other inducement to the commission, preparation or instigation of acts of terrorism; (b) he intends an effect of his conduct to be the provision of assistance in the commission or preparation of such acts; or (c) he is reckless as to whether his conduct has an effect mentioned in paragraph (a) or (b). (2) For the purposes of this section a person engages in conduct falling within this subsection if he– (a) distributes or circulates a terrorist publication; (b) gives, sells or lends such a publication; (c) offers such a publication for sale or loan; (d) provides a service to others that enables them to obtain, read, listen to or look at such a publication, or to acquire it by means of a gift, sale or loan; (e) transmits the contents of such a publication electronically; or (f) has such a publication in his possession with a view to its becoming the subject of conduct falling within any of paragraphs (a) to (e). (3) For the purposes of this section a publication is a terrorist publication, in relation to conduct falling within subsection (2), if matter contained in it is likely– (a) to be understood, by some or all of the persons to whom it is or may become available as a consequence of that conduct, as a direct or indirect encouragement or other inducement to them to the commission, preparation or instigation of acts of terrorism; or (b) to be useful in the commission or preparation of such acts and to be understood, by some or all of those persons, as contained in the publication, or made available to them, wholly or mainly for the purpose of being so useful to them. (4) For the purposes of this section matter that is likely to be understood by a person as indirectly encouraging the commission or preparation of acts of terrorism includes any matter which–	This offence is not required of SC Res 1624 (2005), para 1(a), but is in furtherance to it – see Chap. 14 at Sect. 14.2.3

(*continued*)

Table 5 (continued)

(a) glorifies the commission or preparation (whether in the past, in the future or generally) of such acts; and (b) is matter from which that person could reasonably be expected to infer that what is being glorified is being glorified as conduct that should be emulated by him in existing circumstances. (5) For the purposes of this section the question whether a publication is a terrorist publication in relation to particular conduct must be determined– (a) as at the time of that conduct; and (b) having regard both to the contents of the publication as a whole and to the circumstances in which that conduct occurs	
Preparation of terrorist acts (section 5(1)): A person commits an offence if, with the intention of– (a) committing acts of terrorism, or (b) assisting another to commit such acts, he engages in any conduct in preparation for giving effect to his intention	SC Res 1373 (2001), para 2(d)
Training for terrorism (section 6): (1) A person commits an offence if– (a) he provides instruction or training in any of the skills mentioned in subsection (3); and (b) at the time he provides the instruction or training, he knows that a person receiving it intends to use the skills in which he is being instructed or trained– (i) for or in connection with the commission or preparation of acts of terrorism or Convention offences; or (ii) for assisting the commission or preparation by others of such acts or offences. (2) A person commits an offence if– (a) he receives instruction or training in any of the skills mentioned in subsection (3); and (b) at the time of the instruction or training, he intends to use the skills in which he is being instructed or trained– (i) for or in connection with the commission or preparation of acts of terrorism or Convention offences; or (ii) for assisting the commission or preparation by others of such acts or offences. (3) The skills are– (a) the making, handling or use of a noxious substance, or of substances of a description of such substances; (b) the use of any method or technique for doing anything else that is capable of being done for the purposes of terrorism, in connection with the commission or preparation of an act of terrorism or Convention offence or in connection with assisting the commission or preparation by another of such an act or offence; and (c) the design or adaptation for the purposes of terrorism, or in connection with the commission or preparation of an act of terrorism or Convention offence, of any method or technique for doing anything	SC Res 1373 (2001), para 2(d)

(*continued*)

Table 5 (continued)

Attendance at a place used for terrorist training (section 8): (1) A person commits an offence if– (a) he attends at any place, whether in the United Kingdom or elsewhere; (b) while he is at that place, instruction or training of the type mentioned in section 6(1) of this Act or section 54(1) of the Terrorism Act 2000 (weapons training) is provided there; (c) that instruction or training is provided there wholly or partly for purposes connected with the commission or preparation of acts of terrorism or Convention offences; and (d) the requirements of subsection (2) are satisfied in relation to that person. (2) The requirements of this subsection are satisfied in relation to a person if– (a) he knows or believes that instruction or training is being provided there wholly or partly for purposes connected with the commission or preparation of acts of terrorism or Convention offences; or (b) a person attending at that place throughout the period of that person's attendance could not reasonably have failed to understand that instruction or training was being provided there wholly or partly for such purposes. (3) It is immaterial for the purposes of this section– (a) whether the person concerned receives the instruction or training himself; and (b) whether the instruction or training is provided for purposes connected with one or more particular acts of terrorism or Convention offences, acts of terrorism or Convention offences of a particular description or acts of terrorism or Convention offences generally	SC Res 1373 (2001), para 2(d)
Making and possession of devices or materials (section 9(1)): A person commits an offence if– (a) he makes or has in his possession a radioactive device, or (b) he has in his possession radioactive material, with the intention of using the device or material in the course of or in connection with the commission or preparation of an act of terrorism or for the purposes of terrorism, or of making it available to be so used	Nuclear Terrorism Convention, article 2(1)(a)
Misuse of devices or material and misuse and damage of facilities (section 10): (1) A person commits an offence if he uses– (a) a radioactive device, or (b) radioactive material, in the course of or in connection with the commission of an act of terrorism or for the purposes of terrorism. (2) A person commits an offence if, in the course of or in connection with the commission of an act of terrorism or for the purposes of terrorism, he uses or damages a nuclear facility in a manner which–	Nuclear Terrorism Convention, article 2(1)(b)

(*continued*)

Table 5 (continued)

(a) causes a release of radioactive material; or (b) creates or increases a risk that such material will be released	
Terrorist threats relating to devices, materials or facilities (section 11): (1) A person commits an offence if, in the course of or in connection with the commission of an act of terrorism or for the purposes of terrorism– (a) he makes a demand– (i) for the supply to himself or to another of a radioactive device or of radioactive material; (ii) for a nuclear facility to be made available to himself or to another; or (iii) for access to such a facility to be given to himself or to another; (b) he supports the demand with a threat that he or another will take action if the demand is not met; and (c) the circumstances and manner of the threat are such that it is reasonable for the person to whom it is made to assume that there is real risk that the threat will be carried out if the demand is not met.	Nuclear Terrorism Convention, article 2(2)(b)
(2) A person also commits an offence if– (a) he makes a threat falling within subsection (3) in the course of or in connection with the commission of an act of terrorism or for the purposes of terrorism; and (b) the circumstances and manner of the threat are such that it is reasonable for the person to whom it is made to assume that there is real risk that the threat will be carried out, or would be carried out if demands made in association with the threat are not met. (3) A threat falls within this subsection if it is– (a) a threat to use radioactive material; (b) a threat to use a radioactive device; or (c) a threat to use or damage a nuclear facility in a manner that releases radioactive material or creates or increases a risk that such material will be released	Nuclear Terrorism Convention, article 2(2)(b)

N. Offences under the Al-Qa'ida and Taliban (United Nations Measures) Order 2002 (see Chap. 8, at Sect. 8.2.2)

Offence	*Related Convention and/or SC resolution*
Supply of restricted goods (article 3(1)): Any person who– (a) supplies or delivers, (b) agrees to supply or deliver, or (c) does any act calculated to promote the supply or delivery of, restricted goods from the United Kingdom to a listed person shall be guilty of an offence under this Order unless he proves that he did not know and had no reason to suppose that the goods in question were to be supplied or delivered to a listed person	SC Res 1267 (1999), paras 4 and 8

(continued)

Table 5 (continued)

Provision of certain technical assistance or training (article 5(1)): Any person who directly or indirectly provides to a listed person any technical assistance or training related to– (a) the supply, delivery, manufacture, maintenance or use of any restricted goods, or (b) military activities, shall be guilty of an offence under this Order unless he proves that he did not know and had no reason to suppose that the technical assistance or training in question was to be provided to a listed person	SC Res 1373 (2001), para 2(d)
Use of ships, aircraft and vehicles: restricted goods, technical assistance and training (article 6): (1) Without prejudice to the generality of article 3, no ship or aircraft to which this article applies, and no vehicle within the United Kingdom, shall be used for the carriage of restricted goods if the carriage is, or forms part of, carriage of those goods to a listed person. (2) This article applies to ships registered in the United Kingdom, to aircraft so registered and to any other ship or aircraft that is for the time being chartered to any person who is– (a) a British citizen, a British Dependent Territories citizen, a British Overseas citizen, a British subject, a British National (Overseas), or a British protected person; or (b) a body incorporated or constituted under the law of the United Kingdom. (3) If any ship, aircraft or vehicle is used in contravention of paragraph (1) of this article then– (a) in the case of a ship registered in the United Kingdom or any aircraft so registered, the owner and the master of the ship or, as the case may be, the operator and the commander of the aircraft; or (b) in the case of any other ship or aircraft, the person to whom the ship or aircraft is for the time being chartered and, if he is such a person as is referred to in sub-paragraph (a) or sub-paragraph (b) of paragraph (2) of this article, the master of the ship or, as the case may be, the operator and the commander of the aircraft; or (c) in the case of a vehicle, the operator of the vehicle, shall be guilty of an offence under this Order, unless he proves that he did not know and had no reason to suppose that the carriage of the goods in question was, or formed part of, carriage to a listed person	SC Res 1267 (1999), paras 4(a) and 8
Making funds available to Usama bin Laden and associates (article 7): Any person who, except under the authority of a licence granted by the Treasury under this article, makes any funds available to or for the benefit of a listed person or any person acting on behalf of a listed person is guilty of an offence under this Order	SC Res 1373 (2001), para 1(b)

(continued)

Table 5 (continued)

Contravention of a freezing order (article 8(9)): (1) Where the Treasury have reasonable grounds for suspecting that the person by, for or on behalf of whom any funds are held is or may be a listed person or a person acting on behalf of a listed person, the Treasury may by notice direct that those funds are not to be made available to that person, except under the authority of a licence granted by the Treasury under article 7. (9) Any person who contravenes a direction under paragraph (1) is guilty of an offence under this Order	SC Res 1267 (1999), paras 4(b) and 8; and SC Res 1373 (2001), para 1(c)
Facilitation of activities prohibited under article 7 or 8(9) (article 9): Any person who knowingly and intentionally engages in any activities the object or effect of which is to enable or facilitate the commission (by that person or another) of an offence under article 7 or 8(9) is guilty of an offence under this Order	SC Res 1267 (1999), paras 4(b) and 8; and SC Res 1373 (2001), para 1(b) and (c)
Failure to disclose knowledge or suspicion of measures offences (article 10): A relevant institution is guilty of an offence if– (a) it knows or suspects that a person who is, or has been at any time since the coming into force of this Order, a customer of the institution, or is a person with whom the institution has had dealings in the course of its business since that time– (i) is a listed person; or (ii) is a person acting on behalf of a listed person; or (iii) has committed an offence under article 7, 8(9) or 12(2); and (b) it does not disclose to the Treasury the information or other matter on which the knowledge or suspicion is based as soon as is reasonably practicable after that information or other matters comes to its attention	SC Res 1267 (1999), paras 4(b) and 8; and SC Res 1373 (2001), para 1(b) and (c)

O. Offences under the Terrorism (United Nations Measures) Order 2001 (see Chap. 8, at Sect. 8.2.3)

Offence	*Related Convention and/or SC resolution*
Making funds available (article 3): Any person who, except under the authority of a licence granted by the Treasury under this article, makes any funds or financial (or related) services available directly or indirectly to or for the benefit of– (a) a person who commits, attempts to commit, facilitates or participates in the commission of acts of terrorism, (b) a person controlled or owned directly or indirectly by a person in (a), or (c) a person acting on behalf, or at the direction, of a person in (a), is guilty of an offence under this Order	SC Res 1373 (2001), para 1(d)

(continued)

Table 5 (continued)

Contravention of a freezing order (article 4(9)):	SC Res 1267 (1999), paras 4(b)
(1) Where the Treasury have reasonable grounds for suspecting that the person by, for or on behalf of whom any funds are held is or may be–	and 8; and SC Res 1373 (2001), para 1(c)
(a) a person who commits, attempts to commit, facilitates or participates in the commission of acts of terrorism,	
(b) a person controlled or owned directly or indirectly by a person in (a), or	
(c) a person acting on behalf, or at the direction, of a person in (a), the Treasury may by notice direct that those funds are not to be made available to any person, except under the authority of a licence granted by the Treasury under this article.	
(9) Any person who contravenes a direction given under paragraph (1) is guilty of an offence under this Order	

Appendix 4
Handbook on Human Rights Compliance While Countering Terrorism

Executive Summary

In September 2006, the Center on Global Counterterrorism Cooperation published the *Report on Standards and Best Practices for Improving States' Implementation of UN Security Council Counter-Terrorism Mandates.*[1] The report provided an assessment of core standards and best practices for implementing relevant Security Council counterterrorism resolutions. For the purpose of assisting policymakers and practitioners in understanding and implementing the multiple requirements of Security Council Resolution 1373, the report identified three broad areas of counterterrorism implementation: combating terrorist financing, improving legal practice and law enforcement, and enhancing territorial control. It also identified three cross-cutting categories that apply to all implementation requirements: international cooperation, the provision of technical assistance, and compliance with human rights standards.

This *Handbook on Human Rights Compliance While Countering Terrorism* provides practical guidance on one of the three cross-cutting topics applicable to all aspects of implementation: human rights compliance while countering terrorism. This topic is particularly relevant given the adoption of the *United Nations Global Counter-Terrorism Strategy* by the UN General Assembly in September 2006, which underlines the mutually reinforcing relationship between the promotion

---

This chapter is reproduced with the kind permission of the Center on Global Counterterrorism Cooperation from its publication *Handbook on Human Rights Compliance While Countering Terrorism* (January 2008, available online at http://www.globalct.org/images/content/pdf/reports/human_rights_handbook.pdf), a project supported by the Ford Foundation and written by the author of this book. The Center on Global Counterterrorism Cooperation is a non-partisan research and policy institute that works to improve internationally coordinated non-military responses to the continually evolving threat of terrorism by providing governments and international organisations with timely, policy-relevant research and analysis (see http://www.globalct.org).

[1]Available online at http://www.globalct.org/pdf/060831_CT_report_1.pdf (last accessed 12 December 2007).

and protection of human rights and counterterrorism measures. Through the Strategy, all UN member States have committed to adopting measures to ensure respect for human rights and the rule of law as the fundamental basis of the fight against terrorism. They further resolve to take measures aimed at addressing conditions conducive to the spread of terrorism, including violations of human rights and lack of rule of law, and ensure that any measures taken to counter terrorism comply with their obligations under international law, in particular human rights law, refugee law, and international humanitarian law.[2]

Although sometimes portrayed as an obstacle to an effective response to the threat of terrorism, human rights are a key component of any successful counterterrorism strategy. International human rights instruments are structured to respond to conflict and to provide mechanisms to ensure peace and stability. In fact, a commitment to comply with international human rights standards ensures that measures taken to combat terrorism are sustainable, effective, and proportionate. Counterterrorism measures that violate human rights standards may instead give rise to adverse effects. Perceived as unjust and discriminatory, they may increase support for militant parts of society and thus diminish rather than enhance security in the long run.

The objectives of this Handbook are twofold: first, to provide practical and functional assistance to decision-makers on the subject; and second, to do so in a manner that is able to give proper account to a State's international human rights obligations, while recognizing the duty of States to protect their societies from terrorism and to contribute to the maintenance of international peace and security. To that end, this Handbook identifies five conditions applicable to human rights compliance while countering terrorism. These conditions are cumulative in nature and are presented in a chronological manner, enabling the decision-maker to progressively examine the validity of existing or proposed counterterrorism law and practice.

1. Counterterrorism law and practice must comply with human rights law.
2. The right or freedom to be restricted by counterterrorism measure must allow for limitation.
3. Counterterrorism law and practice must be established by due process.
4. Counterterrorist measures seeking to limit rights must be necessary.
5. Counterterrorist measures seeking to limit rights must be proportional.

In setting out and explaining these conditions, reference is made to international human rights treaties, norms of customary international law, and to various guidelines and documents that have been adopted or issued concerning or relevant to the subject of counterterrorism and human rights. Key documents include:[3]

---

[2]UN General Assembly, *The United Nations Global Counter-Terrorism Strategy*, UN Doc A/RES/60/288 (2006).

[3]Although not legally binding, these documents and guidelines provide useful references for a generally recognized interpretation of international human rights norms and obligations.

- The *Siracusa* Principles *on the Limitation and Derogation Provisions in the International Covenant on Civil and Political Rights*[4]
- Human Rights Committee's General Comment 29, States of Emergency[5]
- Guidelines of the UN Commissioner for Human Rights in Criteria for the Balancing of Human Rights Protection and the Combating of Terrorism[6]
- The Council of Europe's Guidelines on Human Rights and the Fight Against Terrorism[7]
- The Inter-American Commission on Human Rights' *Report on Terrorism and Human Rights*[8]

Condition 1: Counterterrorist Law and Practice Must Comply with Human Rights Law

1.1 The Duty to Comply with Human Rights

States must ensure that any measures taken to counter terrorism comply with all of their obligations under international law, in particular international human rights law, refugee law, and humanitarian law.

The UN Global Counter-Terrorism Strategy recognizes the protection and promotion of human rights as an essential component of a sustainable and effective response to the threat of terrorism. In addition to this imperative of public policy, States must comply with their international human rights obligations when countering terrorism. These legal obligations stem from customary international law

---

[4]UN Commission on Human Rights, *Siracusa Principles on the Limitation and Derogation Provisions in the International Covenant on Civil and Political Rights*, UN Doc E/CN.4/1985/4, Annex (1985).

[5]UN Human Rights Committee, *General Comment 29, States of Emergency (Article 4)*, UN Doc CCPR/C/21/Rev.1/Add.11 (2001), reprinted in *Compilation of General Comments and General Recommendations Adopted by Human Rights Treaty Bodies*, UN Doc HRI/GEN/1/Rev.6 (2003) at 186.

[6]UN Commission on Human Rights, *Report of the United Nations High Commissioner for Human Rights and Follow-up to the World Conference on Human Rights*, UN Doc E/CN.4/2002/18 Annex (2002) ("Proposals for 'further guidance' for the submission of reports pursuant to paragraph 6 of Security Council resolution 1373 (2001): Compliance with international human rights standards") [hereinafter Commissioner's Guidelines].

[7]Council of Europe, *Guidelines on Human Rights and the Fight Against Terrorism* (Council of Europe Publishing, 2002) [hereinafter Council of Europe's Guidelines].

[8]Inter-American Commission on Human Rights, *Report on Terrorism and Human Rights*, OEA/Ser.L/V/II.116 (22 October 2002).

(applicable to all States)[9] as well as from international treaties (applicable to States parties to such treaties).[10] As confirmed by world leaders during the 2005 World Summit:[11]

> ... international cooperation to fight terrorism must be conducted in conformity with international law, including the [UN] Charter and relevant international conventions and protocols. States must ensure that any measures taken to combat terrorism comply with their obligations under international law, in particular human rights law, refugee law and international humanitarian law.

This position is reflected within resolutions of the UN Security Council, General Assembly, the Commission on Human Rights and its successor the Human Rights Council, as well as in reports of the UN Security Council's Counter-Terrorism Committee (CTC).

Resolutions of the UN Security Council

Security Council resolutions concerning terrorism have confined their attention to the threat of terrorism to international peace and security, reflecting the role of the Security Council as the organ of the United Nations charged with the primary responsibility for the maintenance of international peace and security.[12] That role is reflected in the language and scope of Security Council resolutions on terrorism, which, compared with General Assembly and Commission on Human Rights resolutions on the subject, are much narrower in focus. The Security Council's resolutions generally address the adverse impacts of terrorism on the security of States and the maintenance of peaceful relations only, while the General Assembly and Commission on Human Rights take a much broader approach to the subject given their plenary roles.

Apart from two notable exceptions, the main inference that can be taken from Security Council resolutions about counterterrorism measures and their need to comply with human rights law arises from general statements that counterterrorism is an aim that should be achieved in accordance with the UN Charter and international law.[13] This means that such measures must be compliant with the principles

---

[9]*Military and Paramilitary Activities in and against Nicaragua (Nicaragua v United States of America)* (Merits) [1986] ICJ Reports, 76 ILR 349, paras. 172-201 [hereinafter *Nicaragua v. United States of America*].

[10]See *Vienna Convention on the Law of Treaties*, 1155 UNTS 331, article 34.

[11]UN General Assembly, *2005 World Summit Outcome*, UN Doc A/RES/60/1 (2005), para 85.

[12]Under article 24 of the UN Charter, the Security Council is charged with the maintenance of international peace and security, paragraph 1 providing that: "[i]n order to ensure prompt and effective action by the United Nations, its members confer on the Security Council primary responsibility for the maintenance of international peace and security, and agree that in carrying out its duties under this responsibility the Security Council acts on their behalf".

[13]See, for example, Security Council Resolution (SC Res) 1373 (2001), preambular para 5; SC Res 1438 (2002), preambular para 2; SC Res 1440 (2002), preambular para 2; SC Res 1450 (2002), preambular para 4; SC Res 1455 (2003), preambular para 3; SC Res 1456 (2003), preambular para 8;

of the Charter (which include the promotion and maintenance of human rights) and human rights law as a specialized subset of international law. Notable is the fact that members of the United Nations have undertaken, under article 55(c) of and through the preamble to the UN Charter, to observe human rights and fundamental freedoms for all without distinction as to race, language, or religion.

The first, more express, exception mentioned is the 2003 Declaration of the Security Council meeting with Ministers of Foreign Affairs, adopted under Resolution 1456. The Declaration directs its attention to the question of compliance with human rights, paragraph 6 providing that:

> States must ensure that any measure [sic] taken to combat terrorism comply with all their obligations under international law, and should adopt such measures in accordance with international law, in particular international human rights, refugee, and humanitarian law.

Although persuasive in its wording, the status of the Declaration should be noted. The contents of Security Council resolutions, when couched in mandatory language, are binding upon members of the United Nations.[14] In the context of the Declaration adopted under Resolution 1456, the text of the Declaration is preceded by the sentence, "The Security Council therefore *calls for* the following steps to be taken" (emphasis added). Such an expression, although influential, is exhortatory and therefore not a binding "decision" within the meaning of article 25 of the UN Charter.[15]

The second resolution to be considered is Security Council Resolution 1624, adopted in 2005. It is largely focused on the steps States are to take to prevent the incitement to terrorism. Included in the resolution, however, is a provision that repeats the language in Resolution 1456, providing that:[16]

> States must ensure that any measures taken to implement paragraphs 1, 2 and 3 of this resolution comply with all of their obligations under international law, in particular international human rights law, refugee law, and humanitarian law.

UN Counter-Terrorism Committee

In its comprehensive review report of December 2005, which was endorsed by the Security Council, the CTC reiterated that States must ensure that any measure taken to combat terrorism should comply with all their obligations under international law

---

SC Res 1535 (2004), preambular para 4; SC Res 1540 (2004), preambular para 14; SC Res 1566 (2004), preambular paras 3 and 6; SC Res 1611 (2005), preambular para 2; SC Res 1618 (2005), preambular para 4; SC Res 1624 (2005), preambular para 2 and operative paras 1 and 4.

[14]UN member States have agreed to be bound by "decisions" of the Security Council. See UN Charter, article 25.

[15]In the Namibia Advisory Opinion, the International Court of Justice (ICJ) took the position that a resolution couched in nonmandatory language should not be taken as imposing a legal duty upon a member State. *Legal Consequences for States of the Continued Presence of South Africa in Namibia (South-West Africa) Notwithstanding Security Council Resolution 276 (1990)* (Advisory Opinion) [1971] ICJ Reports 53.

[16]SC Res 1624 (2005), para 4.

and that they should adopt such measures in accordance with international law, in particular human rights law, refugee law, and humanitarian law.[17] It also stressed that the CTC's Executive Directorate should take this into account in the course of its activities.

Resolutions of the UN General Assembly

The General Assembly has adopted a series of resolutions concerning terrorism since 1972, initially taking the form of resolutions concerning measures to eliminate international terrorism, then addressing more directly the topic of terrorism and human rights, as well as counterterrorism and human rights. The latter series of General Assembly resolutions began in late December 1993, with the adoption of Resolution 48/122, entitled *Terrorism and Human Rights*.[18] Both series of resolutions contain various statements about the need to comply with international human rights standards when implementing counterterrorist measures. A common formulation of this principle is contained in General Assembly Resolution 50/186 (1995):[19]

> Mindful of the need to protect human rights of and guarantees for the individual in accordance with the relevant international human rights principles and instruments, particularly the right to life,
>   Reaffirming that all measures to counter terrorism must be in strict conformity with international human rights standards . . .
>   Calls upon States to take all necessary and effective measures in accordance with international standards of human rights to prevent, combat and eliminate all acts of terrorism wherever and by whomever committed.

A slightly less robust expression of these ideas was seen in Resolution 56/88 (2001) following the events of September 11, although still requiring measures to be taken consistent with human rights standards.[20] Its language should not be taken as a

---

[17]UN Counter-Terrorism Committee, *Report of the Counter-Terrorism Committee to the Security Council for Its Consideration as Part of Its Comprehensive Review of the Counter-Terrorism Committee Executive Directorate*, UN Doc S/2005/800 (2005).

[18]General Assembly Resolution (GA Res) 48/122 (1993).

[19]See GA Res 50/186 (1995), preambular paras 13 and 14 and operative para 3; GA Res 52/133 (1997), preambular paras 12 and 13 and operative para 4; GA Res 54/164 (1999), preambular paras 15 and 16 and operative para 4; GA Res 56/160 (2001), preambular paras 22 and 23 and operative paras 5 and 6; GA Res 58/174 (2003), preambular paras 20 and 21 and operative para 7.

[20]GA Res 56/88 (2001), preambular para 9 and operative para 3. The preambular paragraph returned to the language of combating terrorism "in accordance with the principles of the Charter" and operative paragraph 4 talked of combating terrorism in accordance with international law, "including international standards of human rights". For similar statements, see GA Res 57/27 (2002), preambular para 8 and operative para 6; GA Res 58/81 (2003), preambular para 9 and operative para 6; GA Res 58/136 (2003), preambular para 10 and operative para 5; GA Res 59/46 (2004), preambular para 10 and operative para 3.

signal that the General Assembly was minded to turn a blind eye to the adverse impacts of counterterrorism upon human rights. To the contrary, the issue became the subject of annual resolutions on that subject alone, entitled *Protection of Human Rights and Fundamental Freedoms While Countering Terrorism.*[21] The first operative paragraphs of these resolutions affirm that:

> States must ensure that any measure taken to combat terrorism complies with their obligations under international law, in particular international human rights, refugee and humanitarian law.

These directions on the part of the General Assembly are reasonably strong in their language. It must be recalled, however, that resolutions of the General Assembly do not hold the same weight as international conventions or binding resolutions of the Security Council. Indeed, article 10 of the UN Charter specifically provides that resolutions and declarations of the General Assembly are recommendatory only.[22] This principle is equally applicable to resolutions of the Commission on Human Rights, as a subsidiary organ of the Economic and Social Council,[23] and those of the new Human Rights Council, a subsidiary organ of the General Assembly.[24] Thus, the resolutions just discussed, and those of the Human Rights Commission to be discussed, represent guiding principles and non-binding recommendations (what might be termed "soft law") rather than binding resolutions, treaty provisions, or norms of customary international law ("hard law"). Nonetheless, these resolutions are influential and, importantly, representative of international comity. They may also constitute evidence of customary international law, if supported by State conduct that is consistent with the content of the resolutions and with the accompanying *opinio juris* required to prove the existence of customary law.[25]

---

[21]GA Res 57/219 (2002); GA Res 58/187 (2003); GA Res 59/191 (2004). See also GA Res 59/46 (2004), preambular para 10 and operative para 3; GA Res 59/153 (2004), preambular paras 11 and 12; GA Res 59/195 (2004), preambular paras 5, 23, and 24 and operative paras 8 and 10; GA Res 60/158 (2005), preambular paras 2, 3, and 7 and operative para 1.

[22]Article 10 of the UN Charter provides that the "General Assembly may discuss any questions or any matters within the scope of the present Charter or relating to the powers and functions of any organs provided for in the present Charter, and, except as provided in article 12, may make recommendations to the members of the United Nations or to the Security Council or to both on any such questions or matters".

[23]UN Charter, article 62(2).

[24]The UN Human Rights Council was established by the General Assembly in 2006 under Resolution 60/251 as a subsidiary body of the General Assembly.

[25]For an example of the use of General Assembly resolutions to determine the content of customary rules, see *Nicaragua v United States of America*, above n 9 (where the ICJ gave consideration to two General Assembly resolutions as evidence of the content of the principle of nonintervention: the *Declaration on the Inadmissibility of Intervention in the Domestic Affairs of States*, GA Res 213 [XX] [1965]; and the *Declaration on Principles of International Law Concerning Friendly Relations and Co-Operation Among States*, GA Res 2625(XXV) (1970)).

Resolutions of the UN Commission on Human Rights

The Commission on Human Rights paid considerable attention to the issue of the adverse consequences that counterterrorism can have upon the maintenance and promotion of human rights. It did so even before the flurry of antiterrorism legislation that followed Security Council Resolution 1373 (2001). Pre-9/11 resolutions of the Commission and its Sub-Commission on the Protection and Promotion of Human Rights affirmed that all States have an obligation to promote and protect human rights and fundamental freedoms and that all measures to counter terrorism must be in strict conformity with international law, "including international human rights standards".[26] Post-9/11 resolutions of the Commission became more strongly worded. Two such resolutions were adopted in 2004 alone. The issue was first addressed within the Commission's annual resolution on human rights and terrorism.[27] In a resolution later that month, the Commission again reaffirmed that States must comply with international human rights obligations when countering terrorism.[28] The Commission's Resolution 2005/80, pursuant to which it appointed a Special Rapporteur on the promotion and protection of human rights and fundamental freedoms while countering terrorism, stated at paragraphs 1 and 6 that it:

> [r]eaffirms that States must ensure that any measure taken to combat terrorism complies with their obligations under international law, in particular international human rights, refugee and humanitarian law...
>
> [r]eaffirms that it is imperative that all States work to uphold and protect the dignity of individuals and their fundamental freedoms, as well as democratic practices and the rule of law, while countering terrorism.

The 2005 report of the Sub-Commission's Special Rapporteur on terrorism and human rights also addressed the matter.[29] Although the original mandate of this Special Rapporteur was to consider the impact of terrorism on human rights,[30] she commented in her 2004 report that a State's overreaction to terrorism can itself also impact upon human rights. The Sub-Commission Special Rapporteur's mandate was therefore extended to develop a set of draft principles and guidelines concerning human rights and terrorism. Of note, the first-stated principle under the heading "Duties of States Regarding Terrorist Acts and Human Rights" reads:[31]

---

[26]UN Commission on Human Rights Resolution (CHR Res) 2001/37, preambular paras 18 and 19 and operative paras 7 and 8. Preambular para 19 was later reflected in preambular para 13 of UN Sub-Commission on Human Rights Resolution 2001/18.

[27]CHR Res 2004/44, preambular para 24 and operative paras 10–12.

[28]CHR Res 2004/87, paras 1 and 2.

[29]Kalliopi Koufa, *Specific Human Rights Issues: New Priorities, in Particular Terrorism and Counter-Terrorism*, UN Doc E/CN.4/Sub.2/2005/39 (2005) (working paper).

[30]This mandate was consequent to the request of the General Assembly for the Commission to do so and through the Commission's own decision to consider the issue. See GA Res 49/185 (1994), para 6; and CHR Res 1994/4 286.

[31]Koufa, above n 29, para 25.

All States have a duty to promote and protect human rights of all persons under their political or military control in accordance with all human rights and humanitarian law norms.

Also of relevance, in September 2003 the UN Office of the High Commissioner for Human Rights produced a digest of jurisprudence on the protection of human rights while countering terrorism.[32] Its declared aim was to assist policymakers and other concerned parties to develop counterterrorist strategies that respect human rights, stating that:[33]

[n]o one doubts that States have legitimate and urgent reasons to take all due measures to eliminate terrorism. Acts and strategies of terrorism aim at the destruction of human rights, democracy, and the rule of law. They destabilize [sic] governments and undermine civil society. Governments therefore have not only the right, but also the duty, to protect their nationals and others against terrorist attacks and to bring the perpetrators of such acts to justice. The manner in which counter-terrorism efforts are conducted, however, can have a far-reaching effect on overall respect for human rights.

The Human Rights Digest considers decisions of UN treaty-monitoring bodies, such as the Human Rights Committee, and those of regional bodies, including the European Court of Human Rights and the Inter-American Court of Human Rights. It looks at general considerations, states of emergency, and specific rights. On the subject of general considerations, two types of jurisprudence are relevant here. The first emphasizes the duty of States to protect those within their territories from terrorism.[34] The second emphasizes the jurisprudence observing that the lawfulness of counterterrorism measures depends upon their conformity with international human rights law.[35]

1.2   Applicable Human Rights Law

States are bound by international human rights treaties to which they are party, as well as by human rights norms reflected within customary international law. These obligations have extraterritorial application and continue to apply during armed conflict.

It has been mentioned in the preceding section that States have international human rights obligations under customary international law (applicable to all States) and international treaties (applicable to States parties to such treaties). This pertains

---

[32]UN Office of the High Commissioner for Human Rights (OHCHR), *Digest of Jurisprudence of the UN and Regional Organizations on the Protection of Human Rights While Countering Terrorism*, September 2003 [hereinafter *Human Rights Digest*]. The OHCHR is currently working on an updated edition of the Digest.

[33]Ibid, p. 3.

[34]Ibid, pp. 11–12. See, for example, UN Human Rights Committee, *Delgado Paez v Colombia*, Communication 195/1985 (1990), para 5.5.

[35]OHCHR, *Human Rights Digest*, pp. 13–15.

to the enjoyment of rights and freedoms by all within the territory of the State, not only nationals of the State. Two aspects concerning the application of human rights law should be clarified at this point, since these are matters that may be of particular importance to counterterrorism.

The Extraterritorial Application of Human Rights Law

Particularly important to transnational counterterrorist operations, whether involving military action or the transfer of persons from one jurisdiction to another, is the fact that human rights are legally binding upon a State when it acts outside its internationally recognized territory. At a minimum, a State is responsible for acts of foreign officials exercising acts of sovereign authority on its territory, if such acts are performed with the consent or acquiescence of the State.[36] A State is also obliged to respect and ensure the rights and freedoms of persons within its power or effective control, even if not acting within its own territory.[37]

The Interaction Between International Humanitarian Law and International Human Rights Law

It is also a well-established principle that regardless of issues of classification, international human rights law continues to apply in armed conflict. This is a point made clear, for example, by the Human Rights Committee in its *General Comment 31* and confirmed by the International Court of Justice (ICJ).[38] As explained in its Advisory Opinion *Legal Consequences of the Construction of a Wall in the Occupied Palestinian Territories*, the ICJ stated that "the protection offered by human rights conventions does not cease in case of armed conflict, save through the effect of provisions for derogation of the kind to be found in article 4" of the International Covenant on Civil and Political Rights (ICCPR).[39] The conduct of

---

[36]See *Agiza v Sweden*, UN Doc CAT/C/233/2003 (2005); *Alzery v Sweden*, UN Doc CCPR/C/88/D/1416/2005 (2006).

[37]See UN Human Rights Committee, *General Comment 31, Nature of the General Legal Obligation on States Parties to the Covenant*, UN Doc CCPR/C/21/Rev.1/Add.13 (2004), reprinted in *Compilation of General Comments and General Recommendations Adopted by Human Rights Treaty Bodies*, UN Doc HRI/GEN/1/Rev.8 (2006) at 235, para 10; *Legal Consequences of the Construction of a Wall in the Occupied Palestinian Territories, Advisory Opinion* (2004) ICJ Reports 136, at 179, para 109.

[38]See *General Comment 31*, ibid, para 11; *Legality of the Threat or Use of Nuclear Weapons, Advisory Opinion* (1996) ICJ Reports 226, at 240, para 25.

[39]*Legal Consequences of the Construction of a Wall in the Occupied Palestinian Territories*, above n 37, at 178, para 106. The ICJ more recently applied both human rights law and international humanitarian law to the armed conflict between the Congo and Uganda. See *Armed Activities on the Territory of the Congo (Democratic Republic of the Congo v Uganda)*, (Merits) [2005] ICJ Reports, paras 216–220 and 345(3).

States involved in armed conflicts must therefore comply not only with international humanitarian law, but also with applicable international human rights law.

Condition 2: The Right or Freedom to Be Restricted by a Counterterrorism Measure Must Allow for Limitation

In determining the availability of any measure taken to counter terrorism that seeks to limit a right or freedom, it must be determined whether the right in question is capable of limitation.

Most counterterrorism measures are adopted on the basis of ordinary legislation. In a limited set of exceptional circumstances, some restrictions upon the enjoyment of certain human rights may be permissible. Ensuring both the promotion and protection of human rights and effective counterterrorism measures can raise serious practical challenges for States, including, for example, the protection of intelligence sources. These challenges are not insurmountable. States can meet their obligations under international law through the use of the accommodations built into the international human rights law framework. Human rights law allows for the possibility of recourse to limitations in relation to certain rights and, in a very limited set of exceptional circumstances, to derogate from certain human rights provisions.

Where it is understood that certain measures to counter terrorism must go beyond ordinary legislation that permits the full enjoyment of rights, the first matter to consider is whether the right being impacted is capable of limitation. If it is not, then the counter-terrorist measure is impermissible. This question depends on the nature of the right being affected. Although all rights and freedoms are universal and indivisible, they can be classified into four categories:

1. The right is a peremptory norm of customary international law.
2. The right is nonderogable under applicable human rights treaties.
3. The right is only derogable during a state of emergency threatening the life of the nation.
4. The right falls outside one of the three latter categories.

2.1 Peremptory Rights at Customary International Law (Jus Cogens *Rights)*

Counterterrorist measures may not impose any limitations upon rights or freedoms that are peremptory norms of customary international law.

Rights or freedoms that fall into the category of peremptory norms of customary international law (*jus cogens* rights) cannot be restricted or limited in any circumstances. The question of whether or not a specific right qualifies as a peremptory norm can be controversial and will not be examined in greater detail in this Handbook.[40] It is generally accepted, however, that certain rights hold this absolute status. Least controversial is the status of the prohibition against torture (the commission of which is also an international crime).[41] The prohibition against torture falls within the category of peremptory norms of international law that may not be subject to any form of limitation (*jus cogens*).[42] The Committee on the Elimination of Racial Discrimination has also identified the principle of nondiscrimination on the grounds of race as a norm of this character.[43]

2.2   Nonderogable Rights Under Human Rights Treaties

Where a counterterrorist measure seeks to limit a right that is nonderogable under an applicable human rights treaty, this will normally mean that the measure cannot be adopted, although this will depend upon the particular expression of the right.

The distinction between peremptory rights at customary international law and nonderogable rights under applicable human rights treaties is a fine but important one.[44] Peremptory rights may not be limited at all. Nonderogable rights, on the other hand, may in certain circumstances be capable of limitation, depending on the particular expression of the right.

---

[40]For efforts to identify fundamental rights applicable in all circumstances, however, see Richard Lillich, "The Paris Minimum Standards of Human Rights Norms in a State of Emergency" (1985) 79 *American Journal of International Law* 1072; UN Commission on Human Rights, *Siracusa Principles*, above n 4. For identification by the Human Rights Committee of rights within the International Covenant on Civil and Political Rights (ICCPR) that reflect norms of general (customary) international law, see *General Comment 29*, above n 5, para 13.

[41]See generally *R v Bow Street Metropolitan Stipendiary Magistrate, ex p Pinochet Ugarte (No 3)* [1999] 2 WLR 827.

[42]The International Law Commission has identified this, together with the prohibition against slavery, as a norm of *jus cogens*. International Law Commission, "Commentary on the Vienna Convention on the Law of Treaties" (1966) 2 *Yearbook of the International Law Commission* 248. See also Matthew Lippman, "The Protection of Universal Human Rights: The Problem of Torture" (1979) 1(4) *Universal Human Rights* 25; Bruce Barenblat, "Torture as a Violation of the Law of Nations: An Analysis of 28 U.S.C. 1350 Filartiga v. Pena-Irala" (1981) 16 *Texas International Law Journal* 117; Eyal Benvenisti, "The Role of National Courts in Preventing Torture of Suspected Terrorists" (1997) 8 *European Journal of International Law* 596; Richard Clayton and Hugh Tomlinson, *The Law of Human Rights* (Oxford University Press, 2000), pp. 381–382; Erika de Wet, "The Prohibition of Torture as an International Norm of *Jus Cogens* and Its Implications for National and Customary Law" (2004) 15(1) *European Journal of International Law* 97.

[43]Committee on the Elimination of Racial Discrimination, "Statement on Racial Discrimination and Measures to Combat Terrorism" in *Report of the Committee on the Elimination of Racial Discrimination*, UN Doc A/57/18 (2002), 107.

[44]See *General Comment 29*, above n 5, para 11.

Article 4(2) of the ICCPR sets out a list of rights from which no State may derogate, even when a public emergency is declared by a State party to the Covenant. Similar provisions exist within regional human rights treaties, including article 15 of the (European) Convention for the Protection of Human Rights and Fundamental Freedoms and article 27 of the American Convention on Human Rights.

The List of Nonderogable Rights

The ICCPR identifies several nonderogable rights and freedoms, including the:

- Right to life
- Freedom from torture or cruel, inhuman, or degrading treatment or punishment
- Prohibition against slavery and servitude
- Freedom from imprisonment for failure to fulfill a contract
- Freedom from retrospective penalties
- Right to be recognized as a person before the law
- Freedom of thought, conscience, and religion[45]

This list is not exhaustive. The Human Rights Committee has made the point that provisions of the ICCPR relating to procedural safeguards can never be made subject to measures that would circumvent the protection of the nonderogable rights just identified.[46] Thus, for example, any trial leading to the imposition of the death penalty must conform to all the procedural requirements of articles 14 and 15 of the ICCPR.

Referring to article 4(1) of the ICCPR, which provides that any derogating measures must not be inconsistent with a State's other international law obligations and must not involve discrimination solely on the ground of race, color, sex, language, religion, or social origin, the Human Rights Committee has also pointed out that the full complement of "nonderogable rights" includes rights applicable as part of obligations under international human rights law, international humanitarian law, and international criminal law.[47] Expanding upon this position, the Committee identified certain rights under customary international law (applicable to all States) as being nonderogable. These include the:

- Right of all persons deprived of their liberty to be treated with humanity and with respect for the inherent dignity of the human person
- Prohibition against taking of hostages, abductions, or unacknowledged detention
- International protection of the rights of persons belonging to minorities

---

[45]ICCPR, 999 UNTS 171, articles 6, 7, 8(1), 8(2), 11, 15, 16, and 18 (opened for signature 16 December 1966; entered into force 23 March 1976).

[46]*General Comment 29*, above n 5, para 15.

[47]Ibid, paras 9 and 10.

- Deportation or forcible transfer of population without grounds permitted under international law
- Prohibition against propaganda for war or in advocacy of national, racial, or religious hatred that would constitute incitement to discrimination, hostility, or violence[48]

The Limitation of Nonderogable Rights

In its *General Comment 29*, the Human Rights Committee explains that the status of a substantive right as nonderogable does not mean that limitations or restrictions upon such a right cannot be justified. The Committee gives the example of the freedom to manifest one's religion or beliefs (article 18 of the ICCPR).[49] Article 18 is listed within article 4(2) and cannot therefore be derogated from under the article 4 procedure. This listing does not, however, remove the permissible limitations upon the right expressed within article 18(3) (limitations as are prescribed by law that are necessary to protect public safety, order, health, or morals or the fundamental rights and freedoms of others). Thus, whereas a peremptory right may not be the subject of any limitation at all, a nonderogable treaty right may be capable of limitation depending upon its particular expression. Such a limitation must be both necessary and proportional to the exigencies of the situation (see Conditions 4 and 5 herein).[50]

2.3   Rights Derogable Only in States of Emergency

Where a counter-terrorist measure seeks to limit a right that is only derogable during a state of emergency threatening the life of the nation, the State must determine whether such an emergency exists and invoke the applicable derogation mechanisms.

The third category of rights are those that are only derogable in times of emergency threatening the life of the nation. By way of illustration, article 4 of the ICCPR provides that:

[i]n time of public emergency which threatens the life of the nation and the existence of which is officially proclaimed, the States Parties to the present Covenant may take measures derogating from their obligations under the present Covenant to the extent strictly required by the exigencies of the situation, provided that such measures are not inconsistent with their other obligations under international law and do not involve discrimination solely on the ground of race, colour, sex, language, religion or social origin.

---

[48]Ibid, para 13.

[49]Ibid, paras 7 and 11.

[50]See the international guidelines discussed earlier; and *General Comment 29*, above n 5, paras 4 and 5.

Assuming that the right in question is one from which a State can derogate (see Condition 2.2), four requirements must be noted, each dealt with next.

Determining the Existence of a Public Emergency

The ability to derogate under article 4(1) of the ICCPR is triggered only "in a time of public emergency which threatens the life of the nation". The Human Rights Committee has characterized such an emergency as being of an exceptional nature.[51] Not every disturbance or catastrophe qualifies as such. The Committee has commented that even during an armed conflict, measures derogating from the ICCPR are allowed only if and to the extent that the situation constitutes a threat to the life of the nation.[52] Whether terrorist acts or threats establish such a state of emergency must therefore be assessed on a case-by-case basis.

Interpreting the comparable derogation provision in article 15 of the European Convention on Human Rights, the European Court of Human Rights has identified four criteria to determine whether any given situation amounts to "a time of public emergency which threatens the life of the nation":

- It should be a crisis or emergency that is actual or imminent.
- It must be exceptional, such that "normal" measures are inadequate.
- It must threaten the continuance of the organized life of the community.
- It must affect the entire population of the State taking measures.[53]

On the latter point, early decisions of the European Court spoke of an emergency needing to affect the whole population. The Court appears to have subsequently accepted that an emergency threatening the life of a nation might only materially affect one part of the nation at the time of the emergency.[54]

Outside the immediate aftermath of a terrorist attack or in the situation where clear intelligence exists of an imminent threat of a terrorist act, it is doubtful that a continual state of emergency caused by the threat of terrorism can exist for the purpose of these derogating provisions.[55]

---

[51]*General Comment 29*, above n 5, para 2.

[52]Ibid, para 3.

[53]See *Lawless v Ireland (No 3)* (1961) ECHR Series A, para 28; *The Greek Case* (1969) 12 *Yearbook of the European Court of Human Rights* 1, para 153.

[54]*Brannigan and McBride v United Kingdom* (1993) ECHR Series A. For contrast, see ibid (dissenting opinion of Judge Walsh, para 2).

[55]See generally UN Commission on Human Rights, *Siracusa Principles*, above n 4, paras 39–41. See also Alex Conte, "A Clash of Wills: Counter-Terrorism and Human Rights" (2003) 20 *New Zealand Universities Law Review* 338, 350–354; James Oraa, *Human Rights in States of Emergency in International Law* (Clarendon Press, 1992); UN Human Rights Committee, *Concluding Observations of the Human Rights Committee: Israel*, UN Doc CCPR/C/79/Add.93 (1998), para 11.

Proclamation and Notice of a State of Emergency

Upon establishment that an emergency exists, a proclamation of derogation must be lodged in accordance with the requirements of the particular treaty.[56] In the case of the ICCPR, before it can implement any derogating measure(s), a State party must officially proclaim the existence within its territory of a public emergency that threatens the life of the nation.[57] Through the intermediary of the UN Secretary-General, a derogating State must also immediately inform other States parties to the ICCPR of the provisions from which it has derogated and the reasons for which it has done so.[58] The Human Rights Committee has emphasized that notification should include full information about the measures taken and a clear explanation of the reasons for them, with full documentation attached concerning the relevant law.[59] A further communication is required on the date on which a State terminates such derogation.[60]

Review

In the context of the ICCPR derogations provisions, the Human Rights Committee has repeatedly stated that measures under article 4 must be of an exceptional and temporary nature and may continue only as long as the life of the nation concerned is actually threatened. Thus, it will be important for the derogating State to continually review the situation faced by it to ensure that the derogation lasts only as long as the state of emergency exists.[61] The Committee has added that the restoration of a state of normalcy where full respect for the provisions of the ICCPR can again be secured must be the predominant objective of a State party derogating from the Covenant.[62] This position was reflected in the 1995 concluding observations of the Committee concerning the derogation of the United Kingdom under the ICCPR, where it recommended that:[63]

> [g]iven the significant decline in terrorist violence in the United Kingdom since the cease-fire came into effect in Northern Ireland and the peace process was initiated, the Committee urges the Government to keep under the closest review whether a situation of "public

---

[56]For an example, see ICCPR, article 4(3); *General Comment 29*, above n 5, paras 2 and 17. See also UN Commission on Human Rights, *Siracusa Principles*, above n 4, paras 42–47.

[57]ICCPR, article 4(1).

[58]Ibid, article 4(3).

[59]*General Comment 29*, above n 5, paras 5, 16, and 17.

[60]ICCPR, article 4(3).

[61]*General Comment 29*, above n 5, para 2; and the *Siracusa Principles*, above n 4, paras 48–50.

[62]*General Comment 29*, above n 5, paras 1 and 2.

[63]UN Human Rights Committee, *Concluding Observations of the Human Rights Committee: United Kingdom of Great Britain and Northern Ireland*, UN Doc CCPR/C/79/Add.55 (1995), para 23.

emergency" within the terms of Article 4, paragraph 1, of the Covenant still exists and whether it would be appropriate for the United Kingdom to withdraw the notice of derogation which it issued on 17 May 1976, in accordance with Article 4 of the Covenant.

Permissible Extent of Derogating Measures

The extent to which a State derogates from any right must be limited "to the extent strictly required by the exigencies of the situation". Any derogating measure must therefore be both necessary and proportionate, thus calling into consideration Conditions 4 and 5 in this Handbook.[64] The General Assembly has reaffirmed that any derogating measures are to be of an exceptional and temporary nature.[65] Considering States-parties' reports, the Human Rights Committee has expressed concern over insufficient attention being paid to the principle of proportionality.[66]

2.4 Other Rights

Where a counter-terrorist measure seeks to limit a right that is not a peremptory norm of international law, the limitation upon the right must be within the permissible range of limits provided within the applicable treaty or customary definition of the right.

The final category of rights are those that are neither peremptory, nonderogable, nor subject to limitation only in states of emergency. The Human Rights Committee has acknowledged in this regard that the limitation of rights is allowed even in "normal times" under various provisions of the ICCPR.[67] The permissible scope of the limitation of such rights will primarily depend upon their expression within the human rights treaty. This will give rise to two possible means of limitation, by a definitional mechanism[68] and/or by a rights-specific limitations clause.[69] Where it

---

[64]*General Comment 29*, above n 5, paras 4 and 5; and the *Siracusa Principles*, above n 4, para 51.

[65]GA Res 59/191 (2005), para 2; GA Res 60/158 (2006), para 3. See CHR Res 2005/80, para 3.

[66]See, for example, *Concluding Observations of the Human Rights Committee: Israel*, above n 55, para 11.

[67]*General Comment 29*, above n 5.

[68]Definitional limitations are ones that fall within the meaning of the words contained in the expression of the right itself. For example, the right to a fair and open hearing does not provide a person with the right to a hearing that favors the person in all respects. Rather, it guarantees that a person be afforded a "fair" and open hearing. A counter-terrorist measure imposing limitations on the disclosure of information, based upon the need to protect classified security information, might for example be "fair" if the person's counsel (with appropriate security clearance and restrictions on the sharing of that information) is permitted access to the information.

[69]Rights-specific limitations are those that are authorized by a subsequent provision concerning the circumstances in which the right in question may be limited. In the context of the ICCPR and again using the example of the right to a fair and open hearing, the first two sentences of article 14(1)

is determined that a specific right allows for limitation or restriction, legislators and decision-makers must examine four key questions in order to comply with international human rights law:

- Is the limitation set out within a "prescription by law" (see Condition 3.1 herein)?
- Does the measure pursue one of the objectives permitted within the expression of the right or freedom (see Conditions 4.1 and 4.2)?
- Is the interference necessary and proportionate (see Conditions 4 and 5)?
- Is the interference nondiscriminatory (see Condition 3.2)?

Condition 3: Counterterrorism Law and Practice Must Be Established by Due Process

A number of procedural requirements are applicable to ensure that counter-terrorist measures are established and undertaken by proper means.

Consideration of Conditions 1 and 2 of this Handbook will lead to the following conclusions: (1) counterterrorism law and practice must comply with human rights law; and (2) "compliance" with human rights law, by virtue of the flexibility incorporated within that body of law, can permit the limitation of certain rights in limited circumstances. Where it is determined that a counterterrorist measure must limit the enjoyment of a right or freedom to achieve its objective(s) and that the right in question is capable of limitation, it is next necessary to determine compatibility of the measure with the procedural requirements of due process. That is, the counter-terrorist measure must:

- Be prescribed by law
- Respect the principles of nondiscrimination and equality before the law
- Impose appropriate restrictions upon discretionary powers
- Be confined to the objective of countering terrorism

---

express the substance of the right, as just discussed. The next sentence then sets out the circumstances in which it is permissible to limit the right to an "open" hearing, allowing the exclusion of the press for reasons of morals, public order, or national security. The third sentence of article 14 (1) provides that: [t]he press and the public may be excluded from all or part of a trial for reasons of morals, public order (*ordre public*) or national security in a democratic society, or when the interest of the private lives of the parties so requires, or to the extent strictly necessary in the opinion of the court in special circumstances where publicity would prejudice the interests of justice; but any judgement [sic] rendered in a criminal case or in a suit at law shall be made public except where the interest of juvenile persons otherwise requires or the proceedings concern matrimonial disputes or the guardianship of children.

3.1 Establishing Counterterrorism Measures Through Legal Prescriptions

Counter-terrorist measures seeking to impose limitations upon rights and freedoms must be prescribed by law, requiring such prescriptions to be adequately accessible and formulated with sufficient precision so that citizens may regulate their conduct.

Common to all instruments authorizing the limitation of rights, any measure seeking to limit a right or freedom must be prescribed by law. The expression "prescribed by law" has been subject to examination both by domestic and international courts and tribunals with clear pronouncements on its meaning. The term was considered, for example, by the European Court of Human Rights in the *Sunday Times* case of 1978, where the Court concluded that two requirements flow from it:

- The law must be adequately accessible so that the citizen has an adequate indication of how the law limits his or her rights.
- The law must be formulated with sufficient precision so that the citizen can regulate his or her conduct.[70]

The same language is found in the Commissioner's Guidelines, the guidelines of the Council of Europe, and the report of the Inter-American Commission on Human Rights.[71] It is likewise reflected in the Human Rights Committee's *General Comment 29* and the *Siracusa Principles*.[72]

3.2 Respect for the Principles of Nondiscrimination and Equality Before the Law

Counterterrorist measures must respect the principles of nondiscrimination and equality before the law.

To comply with the rule of law, any legal prescription must respect the principles of nondiscrimination and equality before the law.[73] As a general principle,

---

[70]*Sunday Times v United Kingdom* (1978) 58 ILR 491, 524–527. This test was later reaffirmed by the European Court. See *Silver v UK* [1983] 5 EHRR 347.

[71]See Commissioner's Guidelines, above n 6, paras 3(a) and 4(a); Council of Europe's Guidelines, above n 7, Guideline III; Inter-American Commission on Human Rights report, above n 8, para 53.

[72]*General Comment 29*, above n 5, para 16; and the *Siracusa Principles*, above n 4, paras 15 and 17.

[73]Consider Albert Venn Dicey's notion of the rule of law, requiring (1) the regulation of government action so that the government can only act as authorized by the law, having the consequence that one can only be punished or interfered with pursuant to the law; (2) the equality of all persons before the law, which is the context in which this document refers to the rule of law; and (3) the requirement of procedural and formal justice. See Albert Venn Dicey, *Introduction to the Study of the Law of the Constitution* (London: MacMillan, 1885), pp. 175–184.

a distinction will be considered discriminatory if it has no objective and reasonable justification; it does not have a very good reason for it; or it is disproportionate. In the counterterrorism context, particular attention has to be given to ensure that measures are not adopted or applied that discriminate on grounds of race, religion, nationality, or ethnicity.[74] Recent resolutions of the General Assembly and Commission on Human Rights have also stressed that the enjoyment of rights must be without distinction upon such grounds.[75]

3.3   Discretionary Powers Must Not Be Unfettered

Counter-terrorist law must not confer an unfettered discretion, it must not be arbitrarily applied, and it must be implemented by means that establish adequate checks and balances against the potential misuse or arbitrary application of counterterrorist powers.

Counterterrorism measures prescribed by law may involve a conferral of a discretion. This brings two matters into consideration:

- Any law authorizing a restriction of rights and freedoms must not confer an unfettered discretion on those charged with its execution.
- Any discretion must not be arbitrarily applied.

Both requirements call for the imposition of adequate safeguards to ensure that the discretion is capable of being checked, with appropriate mechanisms to deal with any abuse or arbitrary application of the discretion. These restrictions on the conferral of discretions are reflected within the Commissioner's Guidelines and the guidelines of the Council of Europe, as well as within the *Siracusa Principles*.[76]

3.4   Confining Measures to the Objective of Countering Terrorism

Counter-terrorist measures must be confined to the countering of terrorism.

A final matter relevant to the establishment or review of counterterrorism measures concerns the potential scope of application of any counterterrorist prescription or authorizing provision. The objective of countering terrorism must not

---

[74]See ICCPR, articles 4(1) and 26.

[75]The Committee on the Elimination of Racial Discrimination has declared that the prohibition against racial discrimination is a peremptory norm of international law from which no derogation is permitted. See GA Res 59/191 (2005), preambular para 12; CHR Res 2005/80, preambular para 15; "Statement on Racial Discrimination and Measures to Combat Terrorism", above n 43, 107.

[76]See the Commissioner's Guidelines, above n 6, paras 3(b) and 3(j); Council of Europe's Guidelines, above n 7, Guideline II; and the *Siracusa Principles*, above n 4, paras 16 and 18.

be used as an excuse by the State to broaden its powers in such a way that those powers are applicable to other matters. This is an important issue expressly dealt with by the Commission and Sub-Commission Special Rapporteurs on counterterrorism.[77] It is also reflected within the guidelines adopted by the Committee of Ministers to the Council of Europe and the Inter-American Commission on Human Rights. These guidelines require that those measures seeking to limit or restrict rights or freedoms for the purposes of counterterrorism must be defined as precisely as possible and be confined to the sole objective of countering terrorism.[78] This principle is relevant to the creation and application of counterterrorism measures.

Although seemingly unproblematic in theory, this issue may pose considerable difficulties in practice due to the lack of a universally agreed-upon definition of "terrorism". The first substantive report of the UN special rapporteur on the promotion and protection of human rights and fundamental freedoms while countering terrorism, however, provides a useful starting point to address these practical challenges.[79]

Links to Existing Operational Definitions ("Trigger Offenses")

None of the 13 universal terrorism-related conventions and protocols contain a comprehensive definition of "terrorism". Rather, the conventions are operational in nature and confined to specific subjects, whether air safety, maritime navigation and platforms, the protection of persons, or the suppression of the means by which terrorist acts may be perpetrated or supported. Neither do resolutions of the various UN bodies expressly adopt a definition.

Nonetheless, several recent instruments utilize a useful trigger in determining what conduct, in the absence of a comprehensive definition, should be characterized as "terrorist" by linking the term to existing conventions related to terrorism. The first is the Council of Europe Convention on the Prevention of Terrorism, which defines a "terrorist offence" as any of the offenses within 10 of the 12 antiterrorism conventions in force at the time of adoption, excluding the Tokyo Convention on Offences and Certain Other Acts Committed on Board Aircraft and the Convention on the Marking of Plastic Explosives for the Purpose of Detection.[80] All of the

---

[77]See Martin Scheinin, *Protection of Human Rights and Fundamental Freedoms While Countering Terrorism*, UN Doc A/60/370 (2005), para 47; Koufa, *Specific Human Rights Issues*, above n 29, para 33.

[78]See Council of Europe's Guidelines, above n 7, Guideline III(2); Inter-American Commission on Human Rights report, above n 8, paras 51 and 55; and the *Siracusa Principles*, above n 4, para 17.

[79]Martin Scheinin, *Promotion and Protection of Human Rights*, UN Doc E/CN.4/2006/98 (2005), chapter III.

[80]Council of Europe Convention on the Prevention of Terrorism 16 *Council of Europe Treaty Series* 196 (adopted 16 May 2005, not entered into force as of July 2006). The list of conventions mirrors the list contained within the International Convention for the Suppression of the Financing of Terrorism, but also includes the latter convention.

offenses within the Council of Europe Convention are thus linked to offenses created by and definitions within the universal conventions on countering terrorism that are currently in force. A similar approach is taken in article 2(1)(a) of the International Convention for the Suppression of the Financing of Terrorism.

The UN Special Rapporteur on the promotion and protection of human rights and fundamental freedoms while countering terrorism has confirmed that this approach is a proper starting point.[81] Although subject specific, the conventions are universal in nature, so that use of offenses described in them can be treated as broadly representative of international consensus.[82] By itself, however, this approach is not sufficient to determine what conduct is truly terrorist in nature. The point can be illustrated with reference to the Tokyo Convention on Offences and Certain Other Acts Committed on Board Aircraft. The Convention calls on States to establish jurisdiction over acts that jeopardize the safety of a civil aircraft or of persons or property therein or that jeopardize good order and discipline on board.[83] Although this certainly would capture conduct of a terrorist nature, the description of acts over which States must establish jurisdiction is very broad and likely also to include conduct with no bearing at all to terrorism.

Cumulative Characteristics of Conduct to Be Suppressed

The solution to the problem just identified can be drawn from Security Council Resolution 1566 (2004). Although the resolution did not purport to define "terrorism", it called on all States to cooperate fully in the fight against terrorism and, in doing so, to prevent and punish acts that have the following three cumulative characteristics:

- Acts, including against civilians, committed with the intention of causing death or serious bodily injury, or the taking of hostages
- Irrespective of whether motivated by considerations of a political, philosophical, ideological, racial, ethnic, religious or other similar nature, also committed for the purpose of provoking a state of terror in the general public or in a group of persons or particular persons, intimidating a population, or compelling a government or an international organization to do or to abstain from doing any act

---

[81]Scheinin, above n 79, para 33.

[82]This approach must be qualified in one respect, to note that this linkage is not applicable in the case of the Convention on the Marking of Plastic Explosives for the Purpose of Detection. Because the convention does not actually proscribe any conduct but instead places obligations upon states relating to the marking of explosives, it cannot be used as a "trigger offence" treaty. Convention on the Marking of Plastic Explosives for the Purpose of Detection, ICAO Doc 9571, articles 2 and 3(1) (opened for signature 1 March 1991; entered into force 21 June 1998).

[83]Convention on Offences and Certain Other Acts Committed on Board Aircraft, 704 UNTS 219, articles 1(1), 1(4), and 3(2) (opened for signature 14 September 1963; entered into force 4 December 1969).

- Such acts constituting offences within the scope of and as defined in the international conventions and protocols relating to terrorism[84]

The third criterion represents the "trigger offense" approach discussed above. The important feature of the resolution is the cumulative nature of its characterization of terrorism, requiring the trigger offense to be accompanied with the intention of causing death or serious bodily injury or the taking of hostages, for the purpose of provoking terror, intimidating a population, or compelling a government or an international organization to do or to abstain from doing any act. This cumulative approach acts as a safety threshold to ensure that it is only conduct of a truly terrorist nature that is identified as terrorist conduct.[85] Not all acts that are crimes under national or even international law are acts of terrorism, nor should be defined as such.[86]

By way of further example, there are clear parallels between acts of terrorism and other international crimes, including crimes against humanity, whether in the terms set out in the Statute of the International Criminal Court or in the proscription of such crimes under general international law. As already identified, the Security Council, General Assembly, and Commission on Human Rights have also identified terrorism as something that:

- Endangers or takes innocent lives
- Has links with transnational organized crime, drug trafficking, money laundering, and trafficking in arms as well as illegal transfers of nuclear, chemical, and biological materials
- Is also linked to the consequent commission of serious crimes such as murder, extortion, kidnapping, assault, the taking of hostages, and robbery[87]

Notwithstanding such linkages, counterterrorism must be limited to the countering of offenses within the scope of and as defined in the international conventions and protocols relating to terrorism or to the countering of associated conduct called

---

[84]SC Res 1566 (2004), para 3.

[85]A cumulative approach is, in fact, the one taken in defining prohibited conduct under the International Convention Against the Taking of Hostages. Hostage-taking is defined as the seizure or detention of a person (a hostage) accompanied by a threat to kill, injure, or continue to detain the hostage in order to compel a third party to do or to abstain from doing any act. To that extent, hostage-taking, as described, encapsulates all three characteristics identified within SC Res 1566.

[86]Scheinin, above n 79, para 38.

[87]See SC Res 1269 (1999), preambular para 1; SC Res 1373 (2001), para 4; SC Res 1377 (2001), para 6; SC Res 1456 (2003), preambular paras 3 and 6; SC Res 1540 (2004), preambular para 8; GA Res 3034 (XXVII) (1972), para 1; GA Res 31/102 (1976), para 1; GA Res 32/147 (1977), para 1; GA Res 34/145 (1979), para 1; GA Res 36/109 (1981), para 1; GA Res 48/122 (1993), preambular para 7; GA Res 49/185 (1994), preambular para 9; GA Res 50/186 (1995), preambular para 12; GA Res 52/133 (1997), preambular para 11; GA Res 54/164 (1999), preambular para 13; GA Res 56/160 (2001), preambular para 18; GA Res 58/136 (2004), preambular para 8; GA Res 58/174 (2003), preambular para 12; CHR Res 2001/37, preambular para 16 and operative para 2; CHR Res 2004/44, preambular para 7.

for in Security Council resolutions, including the requirements as set out in Resolution 1566.[88]

Condition 4: Counterterrorist Measures Seeking to Limit Rights Must Be Necessary

Where a counter-terrorist measure seeks to limit a right, this limitation must be necessary to pursue a pressing objective and rationally connected to the achievement of that objective.

The final two steps in determining whether rights limitations imposed through counter-terrorist measures are in compliance with international human rights law involves consideration of the necessity (Condition 4) and proportionality (Condition 5) of such measures. Necessity involves three requirements:

- The pursuit of an objective permitted by the expression of the right concerned
- The need for that objective to be pressing and substantial in a free and democratic society
- The existence of a rational connection between the objective and the measure in question

4.1   The Pursuit of Permissible Objectives

Where a counterterrorist measure seeks to limit a right, this limitation must be in furtherance of the permissible objectives identified in the expression of the right.

A matter considered earlier in this Handbook (see Condition 2.4) was that the permissible scope of any limitation of rights will ultimately depend upon their particular expression. A number of human rights and fundamental freedoms codified by international instruments, such as the ICCPR, contain specific references to

---

[88]The recently adopted International Convention for the Suppression of Acts of Nuclear Terrorism is at odds with this cumulative approach. The Convention requires states parties to prohibit the possession or use of nuclear material or devices with the intent (1) to cause death or serious bodily injury, (2) to cause serious property damage or damage to the environment, or (3) to compel a person, organization or State to do or abstain from doing any act. The wording of article 2(1) does not fit with Security Council Resolution 1566, treating the resolution's first two characteristics (intent to cause death or injury or the taking of hostages; for the purpose of influencing conduct) as alternative rather than cumulative requirements. The UN Special Rapporteur on the promotion and protection of human rights and fundamental freedoms while countering terrorism has expressed concern that, just as in the case of the Tokyo Convention already discussed, this may capture conduct that does not meet the general criteria for defining what acts are terrorist in nature. See Scheinin, above n 79, para 41.

objectives that may justify limitation or restriction. Those of relevance to counter-terrorism might include the protection of national security, territorial integrity, public order and safety, or the rights and freedoms of others.[89] Reference to the particular expression of the right or freedom will be necessary in each case.

4.2   Pressing and Substantial Concerns in a Free and Democratic Society

In principle, the objective of countering terrorism is one that is pressing and substantial in a free and democratic society and one that may therefore justify the limitation of human rights falling outside the category of peremptory norms. Notwithstanding the importance of counterterrorism per se, however, it is the objective of the particular legislative provision or counterterrorist policy/measure that must be assessed.

A common feature of rights-limitation provisions, particularly within domestic human rights instruments, is the requirement that any limitation be necessary in a free and democratic society. In this regard, the State has an undeniable duty to protect its nationals; and it cannot be doubted that counterterrorism is a sufficiently important objective in a free and democratic society to warrant, in principle, measures to be taken that might place limits upon rights and freedoms. The fear-inducing nature of terrorist acts has far-reaching consequences. Likewise, the means through which terrorist activities are facilitated have links to other negative conduct and impacts upon individuals, societies, and international security. This is clearly recognized within the international guidelines mentioned and within a multitude of resolutions of the Security Council, General Assembly, and Commission on Human Rights.

There is clear recognition, then, that terrorism impacts both individuals and society as a whole so that the countering of those adverse effects must constitute an important objective in and of itself. Care should be taken not to oversimplify this position. Regard must be had to the objectives of the particular counter-terrorist measure being examined. Paragraph 4 of the Commissioner's Guidelines advocates that limits must be necessary for public safety and public order (limiting this to the protection of public health or morals and for the protection of the rights and freedoms of others); must serve a legitimate purpose; and must be necessary in a democratic society. It will be instructive in this regard to consider the following objectives of counterterrorism law and practice.

---

[89]See, for example, ICCPR, article 19(3) (Freedom of Expression, providing that "[i]t may therefore be subject to certain restrictions, but these shall only be such as are provided by law and are necessary: (a) For respect of the rights or reputations of others; (b) For the protection of national security or of public order, or of public health or morals").

The Countering of an *Actual* Threat of Terrorism Against the State

Due to the manner in which terrorist organizations operate, it is a very difficult thing to assess the existence and level of the threat of terrorism, whether actual or potential. Determining the actual threat of terrorist acts against the State is a natural starting point for determining the threat of terrorism to the State and the importance of the objective of a counterterrorist measure directed to assuaging such a threat. Although the obvious place to begin, evidence of actual threats is not so palpable. Establishing the existence of actual threats relies upon intelligence that, although very important, has its own set of complications.[90] Intelligence is not always available,[91] reliable,[92] or properly assessed.[93] Further complicating matters, the absence of intelligence does not mean an absence of a threat.

The Countering of a *Potential* Threat of Terrorism Against the State

Assessing the threat of terrorist acts against the State, which is to be measured both against the probability of that potential being actualized and the probable consequences of such acts, also relies upon intelligence, but to a lesser extent.[94] Potential threats can also be assessed by analyzing the motivation and operational capacity of terrorist networks. In this regard, "operational capacity" refers to the ability of

---

[90]John Lewis, deputy director of the FBI Counterterrorism Division, acknowledged that "[i]ntelligence is an imperfect business at best". John Lewis, paper presented at ICT's Fifth International Conference on "Terrorism's Global Impact", Interdisciplinary Center Herzliya, Israel, 13 September 2005.

[91]This is said to be the case leading up to the Bali bombings of October 2002 and 2005 and the London bombings in July 2005. Concerning the 2002 Bali bombings, see Mark Forbes, "No Warning of Bali Bombing", *Age*, 11 December 2002, http://www.theage.com.au/articles/2002/12/10/1039379835160.html. For assertions that intelligence agencies did indeed have information pointing to such an event, see, for example, Laura Tiernan, "Australian Intelligence Inquiry Into Bali Warnings 'a Whitewash'", World Socialist Web Site, 7 January 2003, http://www.wsws.org/articles/2003/jan2003/igis-j07.shtml. For the London bombings on 7 July 2005, compare Wikipedia, "7 July 2005 London Bombings", http://en.wikipedia.org/wiki/7_July_2005_London_bombings; and Wikinews, "Coordinated Terrorist Attack Hits London", 7 July 2005, http://en.wikinews.org/wiki/Explosions,_'serious_incidents'_occuring_across_London.

[92]This was the case with the intelligence failures concerning the presence of weapons of mass destruction in Iraq in the lead-up to the 2003 invasion of Iraq. See, for example, "Report: Iraq Intelligence 'Dead Wrong'", *CNN.com*, 1 April 2005, http://www.cnn.com/2005/POLITICS/03/31/intel.report.

[93]This is said to be the case prior to the 11 September 2001, attacks in the United States of America. Subcommittee on Terrorism and Homeland Security, House Permanent Select Committee on Intelligence, *Counterterrorism Intelligence Capabilities and Performance Prior to 9-11*, July 2002, http://www.fas.org/irp/congress/2002_rpt/hpsci_ths0702.html.

[94]On the issue of assessing potential threats of terrorism, see, for example, Artificial Intelligence Lab, Eller College of Management, University of Arizona, *Terrorism Knowledge Discovery Project: A Knowledge Discovery Approach to Addressing the Threats of Terrorism* (September 2004).

terrorist networks to gain access to the territory or to facilities of the State and perpetrate terrorist acts therein. Although States have paid increased attention to border security in the new millennium, transboundary activity and the inexpensive means of perpetrating terrorist acts means that the operational capacity of most terrorist entities should be viewed as being reasonably high.[95] Concerning the second factor in assessing the potential threat of terrorism, "motivation" refers (in simple terms) to the question of whether the State is a likely or possible target of terrorist networks.[96]

The Contribution of the Measure to the International Antiterrorist Framework

This next consideration is one that will be common to all States: the question of the State's contribution to the international framework on antiterrorism and how the measure being examined furthers this objective. US Ambassador to the United Nations John Danforth made this point in an address to the CTC in 2004:[97]

> [The Committee] must never forget that so long as a few States are not acting quickly enough to raise their capacity to fight terrorism or are not meeting their international counter-terrorism obligations, all of us remain vulnerable.

Rational Connection

For a counterterrorism measure to "necessarily" limit a right or freedom, it must be rationally connected to the achievement of the objective being pursued by the measure in question.

The final component of necessity requires limiting measures to be rationally connected to the achievement of the objective being pursued. This component is relatively simple in its application and is drawn from the international guidelines on counterterrorism and human rights and the jurisprudence of the Supreme Court of Canada. Rational connection will require that the counter-terrorist measure being scrutinized logically further the objective of countering terrorism. The Supreme Court of Canada in *Lavigne v. Ontario Public Service Employees Union*, for

---

[95]See, for example, Marc E. Nicholson, "An Essay on Terrorism", AmericanDiplomacy.org, 19 August 2003, http://www.unc.edu/depts/diplomat/archives_roll/2003_07-09/nicholson_terr/nicholson_terr.html.

[96]See Alex Conte, *Counter-Terrorism and Human Rights in New Zealand* (Wellington: New Zealand Law Foundation, 2007), pp. 8–16, http://www.lawfoundation.org.nz/awards/irf/conte/index.html.

[97]UN Foundation, "Counterterrorism Cooperation Improving, Security Council Told", *UN Wire*, 20 July 2004, http://www.unwire.org/UNWire (last accessed 20 November 2007).

instance, explained that the inquiry into "rational connection" between objectives and means "requires nothing more than a showing that the legitimate and important goals of the legislature are logically furthered by the means the government has chosen to adopt".[98] Evidence of this connection might be necessary, however, where such a link is not plainly evident.[99] This first requirement links with the Commissioner's Guidelines and the guidelines of the Council of Europe and the Inter-American Commission on Human Rights.[100]

Condition 5: Counterterrorist Measures Seeking to Limit Rights Must Be Proportional

As well as being necessary, any limitation upon the enjoyment of rights imposed by a counterterrorist measure must be proportional.

The principle of proportionality is not explicitly mentioned in the text of human rights treaties, but it is a major theme in the application of human rights law. Proportionality requires a reasonable relationship between the means employed and the aims to be achieved. Useful questions to ask when determining whether a measure limiting a right meets the requirements of proportionality include but are not limited to the following:

---

[98]*Lavigne v Ontario Public Service Employees Union* [1991] SCR 211, 219. The Supreme Court Directions on the Charter of Rights notes that the court has seldom found that legislation fails this part of the test, although there are instances where this has occurred. See David Stratas et al., *The Charter of Rights in Litigation: Direction From the Supreme Court of Canada* (Aurora, Ontario: Canada Law Book Inc, 1990), 6:06. In *R v Oakes*, for example, section 8 of the Narcotic Control Act of 1970 was found to lack rational connection. Section 8, which had certain criminal process implications and thereby impacted upon criminal process rights, contained a statutory presumption that possession of even small amounts of narcotics meant that the offender was deemed to be trafficking in narcotics. There was no rational connection, said the court, between the possession of small amounts of narcotics and the countering of trafficking: *R v Oakes* [1986] 1 SCR 103.

[99]*Figueroa v Canada (Attorney General)* [2003] 1 SCR 912. The Supreme Court of Canada was critical here of aspects of the Canada Elections Act 1985 concerning the registration of political parties and the tax benefits that flow from such registration. The Act required that a political party nominate candidates in at least 50 electoral districts to qualify for registration. Although the Court held that it was a pressing objective to ensure that the tax credit scheme was cost efficient, it found no rational connection between that objective and the 50-candidate threshold requirement. Iacobucci J. for the majority was particularly critical of the fact that the government had provided no evidence that the threshold actually improved the cost efficiency of the tax credit scheme.

[100]See Commissioner's Guidelines, above n 6, paras 4(b) and 4(d) (requiring limitations to be necessary for public safety and public order and necessary in a democratic society). See also Council of Europe's Guidelines, above n 7, Guideline III(2); Inter-American Commission on Human Rights report, above n 8, paras 51 and 55.

- Is the restriction or limitation in question carefully designed to meet the objectives in question?
- Is the restriction or limitation in question arbitrary, unfair, or based on irrational considerations?
- Is a less restrictive measure possible?
- Has there been some measure of procedural fairness in the decision-making process?
- Does the restriction or limitation in question destroy the "very essence" of the right in question?
- Does the restriction or limitation impair the right in question as little as possible?
- Do safeguards against abuse exist?

A number of aspects and nuances of these questions will be subject to closer examination and explanation in the following paragraphs.

5.1   Limitation, Rather than Exclusion, of Rights

To achieve proportionality, the counterterrorism measure or legislative provision must effect a "limitation" upon rights, rather than an exclusion of them or such a severe limitation that would impair the "very essence" of the right or freedom being affected.

The starting point in determining proportionality is that limitations imposed by counterterrorist measures must not impair the essence of the right being limited.[101] This is a matter that will be achieved through the proper application of Condition 2 herein (determining the permissible scope of limitations upon the right or freedom).

---

[101]Commissioner's Guidelines, above n 6, para 4(c). Although decided only once by the Supreme Court of Canada and controversially so, a similar position was arrived at under the Canadian Charter of Rights and Freedoms. In *Quebec Protestant School Boards*, the Court had to consider the validity of the "Quebec clause" of the Charter of the French Language (Quebec Bill 101), which limited admission to English-language schools to children of persons who themselves had been educated in English in Quebec. In accepting that the Quebec clause was inconsistent with section 23(1)(b) of the Charter, the Court held that it amounted to a denial of the Charter right and therefore refused to be drawn into the question of any justification under the general limitations provision. *Attorney General for Quebec v Quebec Protestant School Boards*, [1984] 2 SCR 66. Professor Peter Hogg criticizes the distinction between "limits" and "denials" due to the fact that there is no legal standard by which Charter infringements can be sorted into the two categories. See Peter Hogg, *Constitutional Law of Canada*, (Thomson Carswell, student ed, 2005), p. 799. In a later Canadian case, the court described the *Quebec Protestant School Boards* case as a "rare case of a truly complete denial of a guaranteed right or freedom" and, in doing so, recognized that most if not all legislative qualifications of a right or freedom will amount to a denial of the right or freedom to that limited extent. On the other hand, it observed, a limit that permits no exercise of a guaranteed right or freedom in a limited area of its potential exercise is not justifiable: *Ford v Quebec (Attorney General)*, [1988] 2 SCR 712, 773–734.

5.2 Assessing the Human Rights Impact of the Counterterrorist Measure

Assessing the human rights impact of the counterterrorist measure requires identification of the importance of or the degree of protection provided by the right or freedom affected and the effects (impact) of the limiting provision or practice upon the right or freedom.

Assessing the impact of a counterterrorist provision or measure upon human rights requires consideration not just of the level to which the measure limits a right but also the level of importance the right itself holds. Guidance here is again drawn from helpful decisions of the Supreme Court of Canada on the question of the limitation of rights. Although the Court has properly taken the approach of assessing each case individually, it has provided some assistance as to how one can undertake this task. In the well-known decision of *R v. Oakes*, the Court spoke of the need to ensure that the law that restricts the right is not so severe or so broad in its application as to outweigh the objective. In the case of *R v. Lucas*, the Court added that this requires consideration of the importance and degree of protection offered by the human right being limited.[102] This distinction between the importance of the right versus the impact upon the right recognizes that a minor impairment of an important right, for example, might be more significant than a major impairment of a less important right. Privacy, for example, could be treated as a right less important than the right to life. Even a minor interference with the right to life will need to be treated as a serious matter.

5.3 Assessing the Value of the Counterterrorist Measure

Assessing the "value" of the counterterrorist measure requires identification of the importance of the objective being pursued by the counterterrorist provision or measure and the effectiveness of that provision or measure in achieving its objective (its ameliorating effect).

The value or importance of the counterterrorist objective being pursued must also be assessed, as well as the efficacy of it, recognizing that different counterterrorist measures will not just impact upon rights in a different way but will have different levels of effectiveness. The importance of the counterterrorist measure will have already been assessed when determining whether the measure is necessary (Condition 4 herein). Equally crucial, an analysis must be undertaken whether the measure limiting or restricting the right in question will be effective.[103] It is

---

[102]*R v Oakes* at 106; *R v Lucas* [1998] 1 SCR 439, para 118.

[103]See, for example, Commissioner's Guidelines, above n 6, paras 4(b) and 4(e)–(g).

beyond question that it can be notoriously difficult to make fair estimates on the effectiveness of counterterrorism measures. Yet, the difficulty of the task cannot be an excuse for the lack of thorough analysis and sound decision-making. An in-depth analysis may include an examination of the experiences from previous terrorism crises and comparable campaigns, such as the so-called war on drugs.

5.4 Assessing the Proportionality of the Counterterrorist Measure

A further proportionality requirement of international and national human rights law is that measures of limitation or restriction must impair rights and freedoms as little as reasonably possible.[104] If the particular human rights limitation is trivial, then the availability of alternatives that might lessen that impact have tended to be seen as falling within the appropriate exercise of legislative choice, rather than one demanding intervention by the judiciary.[105] Other than this understandable and reasonably minor degree of deference, this requirement fits with paragraph 4(g) of the Commissioner's Guidelines (being the least intrusive means of achieving the protective function of the limitation). In doing so, this also appears to fit with the reasonably broad requirement in paragraph 4(h) that any limitation must be compatible with the objects and purposes of human rights treaties. Arising from the latter requirements but expressly stated within paragraph 4(d) of the Commissioner's Guidelines is the important point that any counter-terrorist provisions be interpreted and applied in favor of rights.

With these points in mind, one must undertake the final task of "balancing" the human rights and counterterrorist scales with the aim of producing the least reasonably intrusive means of achieving the counterterrorist objective. To that end, this final Condition formulates the following substantive question for determination by the decision-maker:

Having regard to the importance of the right or freedom [Condition 5.2], is the effect of the measure or provision upon the right [Condition 5.2] proportional to the importance of the objective and the effectiveness of the legislative provision or measure [Condition 5.3]?

---

[104]See *R v Oakes* at 106; *R v Edwards Books and Art Ltd* [1986] 2 SCR 713, 772–773.

[105]In *R v Schwartz*, for example, it was suggested that the statutory provision, which provided for a presumption that a person did not have a firearms license if he or she failed to produce one upon request, unnecessarily infringed the presumption of innocence. Counsel for Schwartz argued that police could simply check their computerized records to ascertain whether a license had indeed been obtained. McIntyre J stated that "[e]ven if there is merit in the suggestion... Parliament has made a reasonable choice in the matter and, in my view, it is not for the Court, in circumstances where the impugned provision clearly involves, at most, minimal – or even trivial – interference with the right guaranteed in the Charter, to postulate some alternative which in its view would offer a better solution to the problem": *R v Schwartz* [1988] 2 SCR 443, 492–493.

The issues raised by the question formulated will not normally be black and white, and its consideration is likely to require debate and the complex interaction of value judgments. Dispute remains over the peremptory versus qualified status of some human rights. Cultural ideals and political persuasions will likewise result in different values being attached to certain rights, a matter that is inherently recognized in the margin of appreciation jurisprudence of the European Court of Human Rights.[106] What this Handbook seeks to ensure, however, is that such debate reflects upon all relevant factors germane to both countering terrorism and complying with international human rights obligations.

---

[106]The margin of appreciation doctrine involves the idea that each society is entitled to certain latitude in resolving the inherent conflicts between individual rights and national interests or among different moral convictions. See Eyal Benvenisti, "Margin of Appreciation, Consensus, and Universal Standards" (1999) 31 *International Law and Politics* 843, 843–844. For a comprehensive discussion of the doctrine, see Yutaka Arai-Takahashi, *The Margin of Appreciation Doctrine and the Principle of Proportionality in the Jurisprudence of the ECHR* (Antwerp: Intersentia, 2002).

Index

Printed by Printforce, the Netherlands